OLD TESTAMENT

VOLUME 3 THEOLOGY

Israel's Life

John Goldingay

IVP Academic

An imprint of InterVarsity Press
Downers Grove, Illinois

InterVarsity Press
P.O. Box 1400, Downers Grove, IL 60515-1426
ivpress.com
email@ivpress.com

InterVarsity Press® is the book-publishing division of InterVarsity Christian Fellowship/USA®, a student movement active on campus at hundreds of universities, colleges and schools of nursing in the United States of America, and a member movement of the International Fellowship of Evangelical Students. For information about local and regional activities, visit intervarsity.org.

All Scripture quotations, unless otherwise indicated, are the author's own translation.

Design: Cindy Kiple
Cover image: Crossing the Red Sea, Galambos, Tamas, Private Collection, Bridgeman Images

ISBN 978-0-8308-2496-0 (paperback)
ISBN 978-0-8308-2563-9 (hardcover)
ISBN 978-0-8308-7923-6 (digital)

Printed in the United States of America ∞

Library of Congress Cataloging-in-Publication Data

Goldingay, John.
  Israel's Gospel/John Goldingay.
     p. cm.—(Old Testament theology)
Includes bibliographical references and index.
  ISBN 0-8308-2561-4 (cloth: alk. paper)
   1. Bible. O.T.—Criticism, Narrative. 2. Narration in the bible.
   I.
Title.
  BS1182.3.G65 2003

                                                                    2003013828

P   20   19   18   17   16   15   14   13   12   11   10   9   8   7   6   5   4   3   2   1

Y   33   32   31   30   29   28   27   26   25   24   23   22   21   20   19   18   17   16

Theology as a whole and in all its disciplines

is a threatened and dangerous undertaking, since it is menaced

by every kind of human pride. . . .

Its only purpose is to make itself superfluous.

KARL BARTH, *Church Dogmatics*

There is always an underground Bible awaiting discovery.

KATHLEEN D. BILLMAN AND DANIEL L. MIGLIORE, *Rachel's Cry*

Biblical scholars . . . have hardly begun to rid

themselves of the cloak of the theologian for whom historiography

is essentially subordinate to theology.

KAREL VAN DER TOORN, *Family Religion in Babylonia, Syria and Israel*
[I wear this cloak with pride.]

CONTENTS

ABBREVIATIONS

AB	Anchor Bible
ANET	*Ancient Near Eastern Texts Relating to the Old Testament.* Edited by James B. Pritchard. 3rd ed. Princeton: Princeton University Press, 1969.
ASTI	*Annual of the Swedish Theological Institute*
BDB	Brown, Francis, S. R. Driver, and Charles A. Briggs. *A Hebrew and English Lexicon of the Old Testament.* Corrected ed. Oxford/New York: Oxford University Press, 1962.
BHS	*Biblia hebraica stuttgartensia.* Edited by R. Kittel et al. Stuttgart: Deutsche Bibelstiftung, 1977.
Bib	*Biblica*
BibInt	*Biblical Interpretation*
BSac	*Bibliotheca sacra*
BZAW	Beihefte zur Zeitschrift für die alttestamentliche Wissenschaft
CBQ	*Catholic Biblical Quarterly*
DCH	*The Dictionary of Classical Hebrew.* Edited by D. J. A. Clines. 8 vols. Sheffield, U.K.: Sheffield Academic Press, 1993-
DDD	*Dictionary of Deities and Demons in the Bible.* 2nd ed. Edited by Karel van der Toorn et al. Leiden: Brill; Grand Rapids: Eerdmans, 1999.
EVV	English versions (chiefly NRSV, TNIV, JPSV)
f.	feminine
FCB	A Feminist Companion to the Bible
GKC	*Gesenius' Hebrew Grammar.* 2nd ed. Edited and enlarged by E. Kautzsch. English translation by A. E. Cowley. 1910. Reprint, Oxford/New York: Oxford University Press, 1966.
HALOT	Koehler, Ludwig, Walter Baumgartner et al. *The Hebrew and Aramaic Lexicon of the Old Testament.* 2 vols. Leiden/Boston: Brill, 2001.
HUCA	*Hebrew Union College Annual*
Int	*Interpretation*
JBL	*Journal of Biblical Literature*
JPSV	*JPS Hebrew-English Tanakh.* 2nd ed. Philadelphia: Jewish Publication Society, 1999
JSOT	*Journal for the Study of the Old Testament*

JSOTSup	Journal for the Study of the Old Testament: Supplement Series
K	Kethib, the written text of MT
KJV	King James [Authorized] Version.
LHBOTS	Library of Hebrew Bible/Old Testament Studies
LXX	Septuagint
m.	masculine
MT	Masoretic Text
NIDOTTE	*New International Dictionary of Old Testament Theology and Exegesis*. Edited by Willem A. VanGemeren. 5 vols. Grand Rapids: Zondervan, 1996; Carlisle, U.K.: Paternoster, 1997
NRSV	New Revised Standard Version.
OTS	*Oudtestamentische Studiën*
OTT 1	Goldingay, John. *Old Testament Theology*. Vol. 1, *Israel's Gospel*. Downers Grove, Ill.: InterVarsity Press, 2003; Carlisle, U.K.: Paternoster, 2006.
OTT 2	Goldingay, John. *Old Testament Theology*. Vol. 2, *Israel's Faith*. Downers Grove, Ill.: InterVarsity Press, 2006; Carlisle, U.K.: Paternoster, 2006.
1Q etc	Qumran manuscripts from Cave 1, Cave 2, etc.
Q	Qere, the text of MT as read out
RevExp	*Review and Expositor*
SBLDS	Society of Biblical Literature Dissertation Series
SBLSP	Society of Biblical Literature Seminar Papers
Sym	Symmachus's Greek translation
Syr	Syriac text
TDOT	*Theological Dictionary of the Old Testament*. Edited by G. Johannes Botterweck et al. Translated by J. T. Willis, G. W. Bromiley and D. E. Green. 16 vols. Grand Rapids: Eerdmans, 1974-
TLOT	*Theological Lexicon of the Old Testament*. Edited by Ernst Jenni and Claus Westermann. Peabody, Mass.: Hendrickson, 1997
Tg(s)	Targums; Targumic
TNIV	Today's New International Version
Vg	Vulgate
VT	*Vetus Testamentum*
VTSup	Vetus Testamentum Supplement
WBC	Word Biblical Commentary
ZAW	*Zeitschrift für die alttestamentliche Wissenschaft*

PREFACE

The page proofs for this volume arrived on the day of a memorial service for my wife, Ann, who died on June 28, 2009. In April 1966 as a medical student she walked into the emergency room at her hospital and told them that she had diagnosed herself as having multiple sclerosis. Subsequently for forty-three years she served God and served other people as she lived by faith with this illness. I noted in the preface to volume two of this project that I would be embarrassed if I died before finishing volume three, and in the present preface I planned to comment that I was glad to report I did not do so. Now I am prompted to reflect on someone's comment a day or two ago, that Ann's dying at this point made him wonder if she had committed herself to staying with me to the completion of the project, but now felt able to say her *Nunc Dimittis:* "Now, Lord, you let your servant go in peace." Another friend observed at the memorial service that she is on the page of everything I write, and I am grateful to her for sitting with me in her silent disability through the production of the three volumes; I apologize for the shortcomings that she will detail to me over the first decade in heaven.

I am also grateful to Steven and Mark, Sue and Sarah, and Daniel and Emma for being great delights to us, even at 6,000 miles distance; to Fuller Theological Seminary for hoisting me across the Atlantic to a place where the sun shines in the winter and where every band comes to play, and for encouraging faculty to write; to Chris Duryee for finding the apartment we have lived in, with the marvelous patio on which I have written much of the three volumes; to my agent Pieter Kwant, to InterVarsity Press and Paternoster, especially my editor Dan Reid, for their wise and open-minded support and advice; to Francis Bridger, Philip Jenson, Richard Hicks, and InterVarsity Press's anonymous referee for their comments on the volume in draft; to Richard for his work on the indexes; and to God for persevering with me.

In referring to the Psalms, Isaiah, Jeremiah and Daniel, I have often presupposed positions for which I have argued in commentaries on those books (listed in the bibliography), and have sometimes adapted material from there. Commonly the treatment in the commentaries will be found to expand on the points made here, though I recognize that the length of this work is unlikely to leave any normal person asking for more.

1

INTRODUCTION

Gospel, Faith, Life

The first volume of this study of the theology of the First Testament sought to describe Israel's gospel: not its history as we might reconstruct it on the basis of sources within the First Testament and without, but its history as the First Testament wanted people to remember it and learn of it. Volume two sought to describe Israel's faith: not what Israelites actually believed as we might infer it from within the First Testament (which records much critique of what Israelites actually believed) and from archaeological discoveries (which also indicate that their religious practice was not what the First Testament says it should have been), but Israel's faith as the First Testament reckons it should have been and should be. Analogously, volume three studies Israel's life: not the life Israel actually lived (which is also often critiqued) but the life the First Testament reckons Israel should/could live or should/could have lived.[1] Over a period of centuries during the Persian and Greek periods (and perhaps earlier, and perhaps later), the Judean community allowed or arranged for a set of Scriptures to accumulate. The compilation expressed a collection of perspectives on that life, with the implication that they should guide the community in the present and in the future. This volume seeks to encapsulate that vision in the implausible conviction that it implies a vision for the Jewish and Christian community and the world in the twenty-first century.

One might reckon that in the study of Scripture the vision and its implementation is ultimately what counts; what matters is not merely what story we tell or what we think, but what life we are living.[2] The First Testament implies something of that sort in expounding Yhwh's expectations at such length in the teaching that dominates the Torah. In keeping with this, Juda-

---

[1] Cf. John Barton's comments on the ambiguity of expressions such as "Israelite ethics," *Understanding Old Testament Ethics* (Louisville/London: Westminster John Knox, 2003), pp. 16-17.

[2] Cf. Dan R. Stiver, "Theological Method," in *The Cambridge Companion to Postmodern Theology*, ed. Kevin J. Vanhoozer (Cambridge/New York: Cambridge University Press, 2003), pp. 170-85; see p. 185.

ism is often said to be interested in orthopraxy not orthodoxy.[3] "Our dogmas are allusions, intimations, our wisdom is an allegory, but our actions are definitions."[4] Yet even for Judaism praxis rests on some theological convictions.[5] It is often said that within the First Testament, commandment depends on narrative, though this is an oversimplification.[6] But the Torah frequently points to rationales lying behind God's commands, rationales that might inspire us to obey them.[7]

"The test of each story is the sort of person it shapes,"[8] and (as the authors of that comment would grant) the sort of community it shapes. "The practice of community establishment and maintenance was at the center of the social ethic of earliest Christianity"[9] as it had been of the First Testament's social ethic. This encourages reflection on what happens if we look at the First Testament through spectacles prescribed by thinkers such as Alasdair MacIntyre and James W. McClendon. Israel (we will then find ourselves noting) has a shared story; a destiny, to reveal God to the world; a way of life, which is to be the means of that, as it is characterized by virtues such as faithfulness, decisiveness, compassion, discernment, visionary realism and an openness about failure and wrongdoing, along with means of dealing with these; forms of worship, festivals, disciplines and rites that give expression to the way of life and the virtues, and encourage their cultivation; and forms of leadership that also encourage their cultivation.

McClendon, whose threefold organization of his *Systematic Theology* overlaps with mine,[10] thus dedicated his *first* volume to ethics. This empha-

---

[3]See, e.g., David de Sola Pool, "Judaism and the Synagogue," in *The American Jew,* ed. Oscar I. Janowsky (New York: Harper, 1942), pp. 28-55; see p. 35.

[4]Abraham Joshua Heschel, *Moral Grandeur and Spiritual Audacity* (New York: Farrar, Straus, Giroux, 1996), p. 5.

[5]Cf. Judith Plaskow, *The Coming of Lilith* (Boston: Beacon, 2005), p. 65; compare the preceding paper in this collection (pp. 56-65), "The Right Question Is Theological." Heschel himself was of course a theologian; he emphasizes theology's importance in *Moral Grandeur and Spiritual Audacity*, pp. 154-63.

[6]See Jon D. Levenson, "The Theologies of Commandment in Biblical Israel," *Harvard Theological Review* 73 (1980): 17-33.

[7]For the New Testament, Richard A. Burridge's study of its ethics, *Imitating Jesus* (Grand Rapids: Eerdmans, 2007), illustrates the point by the amount of attention it gives to Christology.

[8]Stanley Hauerwas and David Burrell, "From System to Story," in *Why Narrative?* ed. Stanley Hauerwas and L. Gregory Jones (Grand Rapids: Eerdmans, 1989), pp. 158-90; see p. 185; reprinted from Stanley Hauerwas, *Truthfulness and Tragedy* (Notre Dame, Ind.: University of Notre Dame Press, 1977), pp. 15-39; see p. 35.

[9]James W. McClendon, "The Practice of Community Formation," in *Virtues and Practices in the Christian Tradition: Christian Ethics after MacIntyre,* ed. Nancey Murphy et al. (Harrisburg, Penn.: Trinity, 1997), pp. 86-110, see p. 102.

[10]James W. McClendon, *Systematic Theology,* 2nd ed. (Nashville: Abingdon, 1986 [2002], 1994, 2000).

sis fits with the focus on ethics implicit in liberation theology[11] and with the fact that "the central issue of postmodernity is the possibility of ethics, that is, right action."[12] "Postmodernity implies that . . . we should be *doing* theology rather than talking about *how* to do it";[13] that is all the more true about worship, ethics and spirituality. At a Society of Biblical Literature panel discussion of my first volume, Jon D. Levenson perceived in its focus on "gospel" the usual Christian underestimate of the "law."[14] I am still struck by the fact that the First Testament begins with "gospel" and sets "law" in its context, and I do not expect necessarily to satisfy a Jewish interpreter that I get the law "right," but I recognize that considering Israel's gospel and its faith is not complete until we have considered the worship, prayer, practices, attitudes and life that issue from them and dominate the Torah itself.

Admittedly, part of the background to that point about postmodernity is its doubt whether anything can be said about God; all you therefore have left is ethics.[15] The problem then is that ethics does depend on theology as well as vice versa.[16] "Dogmatics . . . has the problem of ethics in view from the very first," but conversely "the ethical question . . . cannot rightly be asked and answered except within the framework, or at least the material context, of dogmatics," which thus "guards ethics against arbitrary assertions."[17] To put it more strongly, it is questionable whether "something called 'ethics' exists prior to or independent from 'doctrine.' "[18] Likewise, *lex credendi lex orandi*, the way you believe is the way you pray, or the way you pray is the way you believe. The way you pray, the hymns you sing, indicates (frighteningly) what

---

[11]See, e.g., German Gutiérrez, "Ethic of Life and Option for the Poor," in *Latin American Liberation Theology*, ed. Ivan Petrella (Maryknoll, N.Y.: Orbis, 2005), pp. 75-94; see p. 90.

[12]Kevin J. Vanhoozer, summarizing Jean-François Lyotard, in "Theology and the Condition of Postmodernity," in *The Cambridge Companion to Postmodern Theology*, ed. Kevin J. Vanhoozer (Cambridge/New York: Cambridge University Press, 2003), pp. 3-25; see p. 10.

[13]Stiver, "Theological Method," p. 171, summarizing the work of William C. Placher in *Unapologetic Theology* (Louisville: Westminster John Knox, 1989); and cf. Stanley Hauerwas, *Against the Nations* (Minneapolis: Winston, 1985), pp. 1-9.

[14]Cf. Jon D. Levenson, *Sinai and Zion* (Minneapolis: Winston, 1985), pp. 2, 42-45.

[15]Cf. Stanley Hauerwas's paper "Only Theology Overcomes Ethics," *A Better Hope* (Grand Rapids: Brazos, 2000), pp. 117-28; see p. 118.

[16]This is one weakness in Gershom M. H. Ratheiser's proposal to *replace* Old Testament Theology by *"Mitzvoth* Ethics" (Mitzvoth *Ethics and the Jewish Bible*, LHBOTS 460 [New York/London: T & T Clark, 2007]).

[17]Karl Barth, *Church Dogmatics* (Edinburgh: T & T Clark, 1969), III/4:3. On this conviction underlying the *Dogmatics*, see John Webster, *Barth's Ethics of Reconciliation* (Cambridge/New York: Cambridge University Press, 1995); and further, Karl Barth, *The Christian Life* (Grand Rapids: Eerdmans, 1981), pp. 3-4.

[18]Stanley Hauerwas, "On Doctrine and Ethics," in *The Cambridge Companion to Christian Doctrine*, ed. Colin E. Gunton (Cambridge/New York: Cambridge University Press, 1997), pp. 21-40; see p. 22.

you believe and shapes what you believe. Doctrine needs to be singable; songs need to be believable.

Karl Barth titles one of his chapters "The Life of the Children of God," and tells us that he owes the title to Adolf von Harnack, who said that if he were to write a dogmatics, that would be his title for the entire work. For Harnack, Barth comments, that meant replacing dogmatics by personal confession, so that the "proper object of faith is not God in His revelation, but man himself in believing in the divine."[19] The same is true for a rigorous postmodernity. But if we know that there is a metanarrative, a gospel, and that there is truth, a faith (even if we also know that we have only glimpses of either), then these come first. But our life can also feature—as volume three.

1.1 God, Community, Self

McClendon also suggests a three-strand analysis of Christian ethics, involving "our embodied existence, . . . our communal structures, . . . and the ongoing engagement of God in our individual and social lives."[20] He notes that the interweaving of these is important; the realization of God's goal for the community's life depends on the spirituality of the individual and vice versa. Analogously, Bruce C. Birch sees the Torah as relating to community, moral identity and divine will.[21] I have taken a framework such as this for my broader analysis of the life Israel was invited to live. It was a life in relation to God, a life in community and a life as a self; it involved living with God, with other people and with oneself. Broadly, it involved worship and prayer, ethics and spirituality.

This section does not seek to outline the contents of this threefold life but to consider the interrelationship of its different aspects: of a focus on God, community and self, of the relationship of community and individual, of ethics and worship, of worship and spirituality, of prayer and ethics, of ethics and spirituality.

A Significant Order

In understanding what it means to be human, whereas the modern world starts with the autonomous individual, and the postmodern world (at least in theory) starts with the community, the premodern world could be reckoned to start with God. This might seem naive, given that our human understanding has to start with us. But in the order of being, God comes first. God's reality undergirds the reality and significance of humanity, and the community's

---

[19]Barth, *Church Dogmatics* (Edinburgh: T & T Clark, 1970), I/2:367.
[20]McClendon, "The Practice of Community Formation," pp. 85-110.
[21]Bruce C. Birch, *Let Justice Roll Down* (Louisville: Westminster John Knox, 1991), pp. 164-68.

reality undergirds the reality and significance of the individual.

It is either no coincidence or a nice coincidence that the Decalogue moves from questions about God in its first four statements, to questions about the community and about behavior in its next five,[22] to a question about the inner dynamic of the individual in its tenth; succeeding pages of the Torah expand on these. Right attitudes to Yhwh link with right relationships in the community and right attitudes in oneself. Right attitudes in oneself link with right attitudes to Yhwh and to other people. None of these stands on its own. They form a whole.

Genesis has already pointed to a similar awareness. It starts with God. Neither the human individual nor the human community comes first; the reason for creating human beings relates to God's purpose. They are created to subdue the earth, to serve the garden. Then, "rather than beginning with the possibilities of individuality and autonomy—two concepts at the heart of Western values—the family etiology of Genesis begins with the human community."[23] One might even argue that the attitude to the significance of the individual when the narrative eventually comes to it (see Gen 3-4) is rather gloomy.

Job's culture, too, "did not take the average individual as its basic building block. . . . In its place stood the value of the family." Thus Job "has meaning and significance in his world as the embodiment of his family, as its patriarch, its male head who ruled it within and represented it in its dealings with outsiders. . . . He was not a free agent, but the servant of that larger and ongoing unit which he embodied." If he exists for its sake, that is even more true of his wife and their children.[24] Then, while a devastating aspect of his life's collapse is its effect on his relationship with his family and community, one major significance of Yhwh's speech to him is to question the assumption that he is the center of the universe and therefore has a right to understand his place in it.

In light of some loss of confidence in modernity the study of ethics, of the Scriptures and of their interrelationship has seen a "turn to the community."[25] "The text is a product of community. . . . The biblical text is directed to the formation of community. . . . The biblical text is made available for its task of community formation by the canon."[26] The First Testament's sharing the per-

---

[22]Further, the sabbath command integrates these two; it "ties together our obligations to God, to other humans, to our own well-being, and to nature" (Dennis T. Olson, "Sacred Time," in *Touching the Altar*, ed. Carol M. Bechtel [Grand Rapids/Cambridge: Eerdmans, 2008], pp. 1-34; see p. 5).

[23]J. Andrew Dearman, "Family in the Old Testament," *Int* 52 (1998): 117-29; see p. 119.

[24]L. William Countryman, *Dirt, Greed, and Sex* (Philadelphia: Fortress, 1988), pp. 150, 151.

[25]Lisa Sowle Cahill, "The New Testament and Ethics," *Int* 44 (1990): 383-95; see p. 386.

[26]Bruce C. Birch, "Moral Agency, Community, and the Character of God in the Hebrew

spective of premodernity is now easier to perceive as a strength rather than a limitation. We no longer see the story of our culture as tracing the emancipation of the individual from the group but as recounting our loss of community and our bondage to the individual. Admittedly this is only a theoretical perspective, a matter on which scholars mostly work alone writing articles and books with our individual name at the head and on the spine. We are not ready to abandon our individualism. Like the Israelites in Egypt, we find our bondage more comfortable (it is the bondage we know) than some journey into the wilderness with a mixed multitude from whom we cannot get away. At best, as a kind of unself-conscious compromise, we like to *talk about* relationship and being relational, as if this solved the problem; but in such talk, the individual "I" remains the starting point. In a traditional society such as that presupposed by the First Testament, the opposite is the case. When community is the starting point, people look at the world in a similar way and have a sense of group identity and group solidarity. There are downsides to this, but there are significant upsides.

Community and Individual

Awareness of being a community does not imply that people have no individual awareness or that individuals do not matter. From Genesis 2 onward, they do have that awareness, and the stories in Genesis 12–50 concern not just families but individuals interacting with each other and with their families. The Sinai narrative assumes that both the people as a whole and individuals need to commit themselves to Yhwh. While "the entire people answered as one" and "with one voice" (Ex 19:8; 24:3), the Decalogue and the other regulations in between these two statements mostly use the second or third person singular and thus imply the responsibility of individuals for their actions. It is one indication that this teaching is not law, since law does not issue exhortations to the individual. Yhwh's exhortation to the people as a whole to bring gifts for the wilderness sanctuary is expressed in the plural but then applied to "every person whose heart moves him" (Ex 25:2). The actual word "people" (*'am*) can take either a singular or a plural verb. After the making of the gold calf, it would be logical to infer that the clan of Levi, who subsequently declare themselves "for Yhwh" (Ex 32:26), had not been involved in the making of the calf and in the celebration that followed, but the narrative has not said so; the act is undertaken by "the people." The covenant is made between Yhwh and the people, corporately and individually. In postscriptural usage, in connection with covenants the stress came to be on covenants that people make with

---

Bible," *Semeia* 66 (1994): 23-41; see pp. 25, 26, 27; the sentences are italicized as section headings.

one another or that individuals make with the corporate body; such ideas are at most inferences from the ways of thinking in Exodus 19–34.[27]

The requirements in Leviticus are meant for "all Israelites" and are not addressed only to people such as priests. Abraham Maimonides observes that whereas among Christians and Hindus there are some pious people, while the rest of the community is given to licentiousness, the entire Israelite community is called to holiness.[28] There is no double standard in Israel. The same expectations bind the whole people. Neither are they merely addressed to "all Israel," the corporate entity, but to "all Israelites." Everyone has individual responsibility for their obedience and their holiness. "Speak to Aaron and his sons and all the Israelites" (Lev 17:2). "Speak to the Israelites" (Lev 18:2). "Speak to the whole community of the Israelites" (Lev 19:2). "Any individual" (Lev 17:3; 18:6; 19:3). Deuteronomy, in turn, moves somewhat systematically between singular and plural address. Analogously, Jeremiah urges, "turn [plural] each person from his wicked way and make good your ways and your deeds [all plural]" (Jer 18:11; cf. 25:5; 26:3; 35:15). The plural suggests corporate responsibility and regulation while the singular encourages individual acceptance of responsibility.[29] In connection with praise, prayer and thanksgiving, the Psalms keep moving between "we" and "I," and the Prophets and the Psalms expect the individual to be prepared to stand over against the community when uprightness or divine vocation requires that. If there is any sense in which "in Israelite society the individual conformed unthinkingly to the norms and values that derive from the communities in which he or she lived,"[30] that is likely no more so than it is in Western society with its stress on the individual. Israel has a strong sense of solidarity and community combined with a living individuality, an awareness of personal responsibility for one's own life.[31]

It is the balance between these that distinguishes it from Western awareness. In Israel, it is more obviously the case that the group experience shapes people as individuals, and God relates to groups at least as much as to indi-

---

[27]See the comments in Michael Walzer, *Exodus and Revolution* (New York: Basic, 1985), pp. 83-84.

[28]See Jacob Milgrom, *Leviticus 17–22*, AB (New York: Doubleday, 2000), p. 1604.

[29]Baruch Halpern associates this especially with Deuteronomy, but it seems a broader phenomenon. See "Jerusalem and the Lineages in the Seventh Century BCE," in *Law and Ideology in Monarchic Israel*, ed. Baruch Halpern and Deborah W. Hobson, JSOTSup 124 (Sheffield, U.K.: Sheffield Academic Press, 1991), pp. 11-107; see p. 75.

[30]Cyril S. Rodd's summary (*Glimpses of a Strange Land* [London: T & T Clark, 2001], p. 273) of comments by Gerhard von Rad (*Wisdom in Israel* [Nashville: Abingdon/London: SCM Press, 1972], p. 75); Rodd here omits von Rad's important qualifier "as a rule," which he later quotes (see p. 274).

[31]Walther Eichrodt, *Theology of the Old Testament* (London: SCM Press/Philadelphia: Westminster, 1967), 2:232.

viduals. God is concerned for the building up of a community at least as much as for the building up of individuals. In a modern context, the traditional set of assumptions was reversed.[32] Modern thinking saw our human existence as the one sure starting point for understanding anything. We know we exist; the question is whether God does. God's existence is dependent on ours. God exists for our sake. God is made in our image. Further, these plural pronouns are misleading; rather "I" know that "I" exist. The existence of God and community is secondary to my existence. The individual is the default state of human life. And U.S. society

> is on the verge of violent fragmentation, owing to the breakdown of community at all levels, from nation to church and family. Such emerging conflict reflects tectonic shifts in cultural values. Divisive confrontation, complaint, and blame have come to characterize much of our public discourse. . . . Sports and entertainment seem to constitute the only sense of common ground left in the public arena.[33]

The First Testament came into being in contexts that often involved fragmentation and conflict. But it did not anticipate this abandonment of the community or the notion that I am who I am as an independent, bounded individual who may contract into a relationship with a family or a group—but that is what I do; I do not inherently belong, and have no inbuilt commitments except to myself. In the First Testament I am who I am as a member of my family, and my experience, work, decisions, and fate are interwoven with, indeed dependent on, those of my family. Given that goodness leads to blessing and wrongdoing to trouble, and given that our lives are lived in relationship, not in isolation, "goodness is a matter of living in such a way that it brings blessing on the community."[34] In terms of worship, in the context of modernity it is the individual's relationship with God that counts. In the Torah the sanctuary is at the center of the community.

Life as One Whole

In the First Testament, life is one whole. Leviticus and Deuteronomy, for instance, intermingle what we would call the ethical and the ritual without giving any sign that these belong in different categories; they also intermingle ethics, honor and shame.[35] Indeed, Leviticus not only "recognizes no dis-

---

[32]For what follows, see Stanley J. Grenz, "Ecclesiology," in *The Cambridge Companion to Postmodern Theology*, ed. Kevin J. Vanhoozer (Cambridge/New York: Cambridge University Press, 2003), pp. 252-68; see pp.253-56, and his references.

[33]William P. Brown, *The Ethos of the Cosmos: The Genesis of Moral Imagination in the Bible* (Grand Rapids/Cambridge: Eerdmans, 1999), p. 25.

[34]Rodd, *Glimpses of a Strange Land*, p. 275, following von Rad, *Wisdom in Israel*.

[35]Rodd, *Glimpses of a Strange Land*, pp. 5-27, with particular reference to Lev 19; Deut 25:5-10.

tinction between these two forms of command but presents them jointly while ignoring many ethical categories that we usually regard as essential" (such as those individualistic notions of guilt and responsibility); to put it positively, Leviticus has "an integrated cultic and ethical perspective."[36] The interweaving of purity concerns and ethical concerns (as we distinguish them) then makes it harder to reduce the latter to a "self-propelled human crusade."[37]

Stanley Hauerwas and Samuel Wells generated a whole book that is called a "companion to Christian ethics," yet whose starting point is a regret that Christian ethics ever had to be invented and a conviction that the discipline of Christian ethics urgently needs to be reframed through the lens of Christian worship.[38] In Israel, our life in relation to God, other people and ourselves is indeed set in the context of worship, where the story is told, the Torah is read, the vision is shared and the character is stamped. Liturgy is concerned with the forming of a holy people, and Christian ethics (or Israelite ethics) is distinctive to the people who belong to the God of Israel, who became incarnate in Christ (or brought Israel out of Egypt).[39] Life is one whole. Eventually this raises the question whether there can be any ethics that is not theological, and how far Jews or Christians can make common cause with the secular world about issues such as justice or marriage or contraception or abortion.

Isaiah surveys every kind of worship the people offer—their sacramental rites, their gathering in Yhwh's presence, their offerings, their celebrations, their prayer meetings. All of this they do with enthusiasm. But Yhwh hates it all (Is 1:10-15). That applies not merely to outward acts, such as sacrifice, but to all forms of worship, including prayer. Isaiah does not attack worship that is outwardly correct but not sincerely meant; this is not the antithesis he works with. He assumes that the people mean every hallelujah. His critique is rather that their enthusiastic worship of Yhwh is not matched by an enthusiastic living before Yhwh in everyday life. There is a mismatch between their worship and their community life, not between their outward worship and their inner attitude. The people of Jerusalem might have had some justification for being rather pleased with themselves for the relative orthodoxy of their worship. While Isaiah will indeed go on to accuse them of leaving Yhwh and will indicate the need for them to come back, and will castigate them for

---

[36]Antony Cothey, "Ethics and Holiness in the Theology of Leviticus," *JSOT* 30 (2005): 131-51; see pp. 143, 144.

[37]Walter Brueggemann, *Theology of the Old Testament* (Minneapolis: Fortress, 1997), p. 194.

[38]Stanley Hauerwas and Samuel Wells, ed., *The Blackwell Companion to Christian Ethics* (Oxford/Malden, Mass.: Blackwell, 2004), p. 3.

[39]Hauerwas, *In Good Company*, pp. 153-68.

their religious practices (Is 1:27-29; cf. 2:8; 8:19), he talks in these terms much more rarely than Hosea, Jeremiah and Ezekiel. When he declares that Jerusalem "has become immoral," he does not go on to refer to worship of other deities; the immorality lies in the community wrongdoing that puts blood on its hands (Is 1:21-23). It has no basis for a pride in the faithfulness of its worship; when this is accompanied by faithlessness in the rest of life, it becomes just another kind of immorality. Judah has left Yhwh and needs to come back, even if it keeps worshiping Yhwh with enthusiasm.

Through Amos, too, Yhwh insists that attention be transferred from the committed, enthusiastic sacrificial worship that the worshipers much enjoy, to committed, sacrificial, enthusiastic and faithful ordering of society. Here too Yhwh disallows Israel's entire practice of worship, including the great festivals, the sacramental aspect to their liturgy and their songs of praise (Amos 5:21-25). Yhwh's feelings about these are expressed in the strongest possible terms, doubling up verbs to convey repudiation or hatred and rejection or contempt. Their praise is an unpleasant noise that Yhwh wishes to be rid of. With more apparent moderation, Yhwh says "I will not accept/pay attention," but that is a devastating threat regarding the people's offerings and thus their prayers. It means they will have no way of reaching out to Yhwh. Yhwh's nostrils, eyes and ears are all shut to them.[40] The object of this repudiation is that people may transfer their attention somewhere else. At the moment worship is rolling and streaming, and nothing interferes with its flow. But things do interfere with the flow of faithful decision-making in the community, things such as the human selfishness of Israel's rich and powerful.

Yhwh goes on to refer to the people's worship of Sakkut and Kaiwan, Assyrian planetary deities (Amos 5:26-27), suggesting a second way their enthusiastic worship of Yhwh fails to connect with their life outside worship. As well as not connecting with their life in society, it does not connect with their political life. It is just—worship. For that, they will end up in exile.

There is an irony about the fact that those festivals at Gilgal and Bethel, with their offerings and songs of praise, celebrate a stage in Israel's life when the very forms of worship that involve them were not operating. Amos hardly implies there was no worship during the forty years in the wilderness, but rather that (by the very nature of the case) it was not the kind of great pilgrim festival worship that Israel now enjoys. That in itself, Amos infers, hints that the main thing about Israel's relationship with Yhwh was not the offering of such worship. A relationship with Yhwh that does not involve the enthusiastic and committed worship characterized by the festivals would be odd, but

---

[40]Cf. Hans Walter Wolff, *Joel and Amos* (Philadelphia: Fortress, 1977), p. 264.

it is not unimaginable. A relationship with Yhwh that involves this enthusiastic and committed worship but does not insist on faithful decision-making in society cannot be imagined.

Ethics and Worship

The critique in Isaiah and Amos reappears in Jeremiah:

> Is there stealing, murder, adultery, false swearing, making offerings to the Master *[habbaʿal]*,[41] and going after other gods that you had not acknowledged, and then you come and stand before me in this house which is called by my name and say "We have been rescued"—to do all these abominations?

It is as if the temple were a "gangsters' cave," a den for people who live by violence and theft (Jer 7:9-11). Jeremiah, too, does not fault Israel for proper outward religious observance that lack proper "inner attitudes and dispositions"[42] but for failing to accompany proper outward religious acts with proper outward behavior toward other people (e.g., Jer 6:6). He challenges Israel to a life of goodness, and defines it positively and negatively and with increasing concreteness as requiring that we make proper decisions, do *mišpāṭ*, to one another; to do *mišpāṭ* is not to be involved in defrauding the powerless, or to cause the death of the innocent, or to go after other gods (Jer 7:5-7). In the absence of obedience to Yhwh in the rest of life, heartfelt worship counts for nothing. "Add your burnt offerings to your sacrifices and eat the meat" (Jer 7:21). "Burnt offerings" (*ʿōlâ*) are ones of which the offerers do not partake; they do partake of "sacrifices" (*zebaḥ*), which express a two-sided relationship with Yhwh. Yhwh dismisses both by declaring that the offerers might as well eat the whole of each of them. Like Amos, he notes that in bringing the people out of Egypt, Yhwh had not spoken about burnt offerings and sacrifices: "This is what I commanded them: Listen to my voice, and I will be God for you and you will be a people for me. And walk by every word that I command you" (Jer 7:23). That was indeed what Yhwh said to them on their arrival at Sinai (see Ex 19:1-8).

It is idle to ask whether these prophets dismiss the people's worship only in the context of the disorder of the rest of the community's life, and to argue that they would be able to affirm their worship if the rest of their life were in

---

[41]The article on *baʿal* indicates it is not a name but a common noun meaning lord, owner, master and thus husband (e.g., Ex 21:3, 22, 28-29). It has similar meaning to *ʾādōn*, and both words are used for human masters, but in connection with deity the First Testament generally keeps *ʾādōn* for Yhwh and *baʿal* for gods other than Yhwh. I thus translate *baʿal* "Master" and *ʾādōn* "Lord," while transliterating the actual name *yhwh*. The plural *bĕʿālîm* may reflect the way the Master was worshiped under a different name in different places, or that *bĕʿālîm* was a generic term for the traditional gods of the land.

[42]So J. A. Thompson, *The Book of Jeremiah* (Grand Rapids: Eerdmans, 1980), p. 262.

order. That involves seeking to divert them into answering what they would see as a theoretical question and abandoning the point that needs making in the context. It is when we set them in the context of the rest of the First Testament that we can answer the question concerning the significance of festivals, offerings and songs of praise. The Torah does make the system of worship a very important part of the story of Israel's journey from Egypt to Canaan (see Ex 25–40).

In contexts such as those of antisacramental Christianity or the post-Christian West or a church that is focused on justice ministries, one can thus imagine Yhwh turning the argument in Amos on its head. It is not enough to be socially involved or to have a close private relationship with God. People are wholes, and life with God is a whole. Yhwh expects this to receive sacramental expression as well as social and private expression. So communities that are not inclined to pay attention to God need to be urged to do so and offer their worship, whereas communities that are good at worship need to be asked to examine the rest of their lives. Communities that offer extravagant worship need to be invited to reflect on what it implies about who they think God is and what is the basis of a relationship with God, whereas communities that offer rather small-scale and low-key worship need to be asked whether something more extravagant might be appropriate.

After the exile once more people are experiencing poor harvests and cannot raise the resources to set worship in Jerusalem on its right footing again, but Haggai is not sympathetic. He does not suggest that the toughness of their circumstances is the result of worshiping other gods or tolerating other forms of faithlessness in community life; they are faithful to one another and in a sense faithful to Yhwh. But their commitment to Yhwh does not extend to rebuilding the temple. They have rebuilt their own houses, but not Yhwh's. That is why things are going badly.

Worship and Spirituality

"Offer true sacrifices and trust in Yhwh," Psalm 4:5 [MT 6] urges. It thus qualifies the significance of "sacrifices" in two ways. True sacrifices (sacrifices of ṣedeq) will be ones offered in the proper liturgical fashion. But there is more to the idea than that. The psalm begins by addressing Yhwh as "my true God" (the God of my ṣedeq), my faithful God. These sacrifices will be expressions of truth and faithfulness that appropriately mirror Yhwh's truth and faithfulness. And one of the indicators will be that they are accompanied by trust in Yhwh. So sacrifices are to be accompanied by a right inner attitude to Yhwh and a right reflecting of Yhwh's character and also by the right attitude in politics.

The command to love God *and* our neighbor points to two distinct spheres of activity, but spheres in which we live with one consistent attitude.[43] Loving God without loving one's neighbor is impossible; loving one's neighbor without loving God is incomplete and perhaps also impossible. "The emergence of original Calvinism represented a fundamental alteration in Christian sensibility, from the vision and practice of turning away from the social world in order to seek closer union with God to the vision and practice of working to reform the social world in obedience to God."[44] Life with and for God means "more than inwardness." It does involve the heart, but it involves more than the heart. "Spirituality is not the way." On the other hand, "no religious act is properly fulfilled unless it is done with a willing heart and a craving soul." Deed and devotion are both vital.[45]

The Torah's interweaving of teaching about worship with teaching about the rest of life thus has further implications for what we call spirituality, though this is a category that compares with doctrine and ethics in being foreign to the First Testament, which offers us so much opportunity for reworking our categories for thinking about our lives.

The people's worship provides them with a context in which to demonstrate that they pay no attention to Yhwh's teaching. Ephraim faithfully and enthusiastically celebrates those festivals at the great sanctuaries at Bethel and Gilgal, commemorating Yhwh's appearance to their ancestors and their arrival in Canaan. It does that with all the right forms of worship, such as the bringing of offerings and tithes, and with generosity and the proper public testimony to what Yhwh has done for it as a people and has done for individuals. It loves to be involved thus in worship of Yhwh and thus to respond to Yhwh's invitation to worship. And Amos speaks like a priest inviting people to worship in Yhwh's name (see, e.g., Ps 100) or teaching them about the nature of worship, but he adds barbs to the invitations: "Come to Bethel—and rebel, come to Gilgal—add to rebellion" (Amos 4:4-5). He goes on to speak of the offerings in sarcastically exaggerated terms. People might be expected to offer sacrifices every year at a festival and to bring tithes every three years (e.g., 1 Sam 1; Deut 26:12). But these people are so enthusiastic in their relationship with Yhwh, they sacrifice every day and bring tithes every three days![46] Yet all this, Amos says, is actually an expression of rebellion, not of worship.

Here, there is no explicit mention of their worship being objectionable be-

---

[43]Cf. Barth, *Church Dogmatics*, III/4:48-49.

[44]Nicholas Wolterstorff, *Until Justice and Peace Embrace* (Grand Rapids: Eerdmans, 1983), p. 11.

[45]Abraham Joshua Heschel, *God in Search of Man* (New York: Farrar, Straus and Giroux, 1976), pp. 293, 296, 306.

[46]Cf. J. Alberto Soggin, *The Prophet Amos* (London: SCM Press, 1987), p. 71. Thus TNIV incredulously translates "every three years."

cause it is unaccompanied by right living outside of worship or mixed with
adherence to other deities or compromised by their use of divine images.
Amos refers only to the fact that they love worship, and thus raises the question whether this is what is wrong with it. They are not coming to worship
Yhwh (who is tellingly unmentioned as the object of their devotion) but coming to express their enthusiasm (they are "your sacrifices," "your tithes," not
Yhwh's). It is thus that "the pilgrimage becomes a rebellion."[47]

Likewise, Hosea comments on the fact that on one hand, Ephraim has built
lots of altars, and on the other, Yhwh has given Ephraim lots of teaching. But
Ephraim has treated the teaching as something alien and foreign, and consequently the altars have become means of making sin worse. When they offer
sacrifices, Yhwh does not accept them but keeps thinking about the people's
wrongdoing and guilt, and plans to attend to their sins (Hos 8:11-13). Hosea
speaks of Yhwh's putting into writing the many teachings to which he refers
and implicitly contrasts that with the situation regarding the details of how to
offer sacrifices. That corresponds with traditional scholarly theories about the
origin of the teachings in Exodus-Deuteronomy, which see the detail about
matters such as how to offer sacrifice as relatively late. It also corresponds to
an aspect of the Torah itself, where Yhwh's original set of instructions concerning Israel's covenant obligations (Ex 20–24) majored on life outside worship. The people are ignoring these and giving their attention to their worship, which is not so much Yhwh's priority. Thus "they have transgressed my
covenant and rebelled against my teaching" (Hos 8:1).

Both worship and spirituality can be me-focused. The First Testament's
vision is for them to be God-focused.

Prayer and Ethics

One of the contributors to *The Blackwell Companion to Christian Ethics* even asserts that "no issue is more central to Christian ethics than worship." Human
gathering, such as gathering for worship, decisively shapes the moral imagination. Notwithstanding our theoretical convictions about it being the individual that counts, we do not generate our understanding of the world by
individual reflection. Because we are social creatures, our gathering together
presupposes and reinforces our understanding of the world and of life, of
what deserves to have worth ascribed to it. It is here that the community declares who Yhwh is and what Yhwh has done, and thus finds an identity for
itself and submits to a reforming of its attitude to itself and to the world.[48]

---

[47]Wolff, *Joel and Amos*, p. 219.
[48]Philip Kenneson, "Gathering," in *The Blackwell Companion to Christian Ethics*, ed. Stanley
Hauerwas and Samuel Wells (Hoboken, N.J.: Wiley-Blackwell, 2004), pp. 53-67; see pp. 53,
55, 65.

The interwovenness of ethics, worship and prayer in the Psalms has similar implications. The Psalter begins by declaring God's blessing on people who are always talking to themselves and to other people about Yhwh's Torah, and who embody it in their lives rather than walking in the way of the faithless. Psalm 1 does not identify this Torah, and it might be referring to the Psalter itself as a book of Torah, a book of teaching on praise and prayer, but here too the teaching interweaves this with comments about the nature of the faithful life. The two belong together. The Psalter requires a commitment to a certain way of living in the world in association with the praise and prayer it commissions; it also suggests that the praise and prayer it embodies are a resource for people committed to living this way.

It further implies the need to commit oneself to a certain picture of the world (Ps 2). It presents the nations as under Yhwh's authority, Israel and its king as the means of Yhwh's exercising that authority, and the nations as inclined to resist this. It urges the nations to submit to Yhwh and to Yhwh's anointed; they can then prove with Israel that blessings come to people who take refuge with Yhwh. This understanding of the relationship between Yhwh, Israel and the nations again has implications for the way one sees politics and political ethics, and the way Israel relates to other nations.

The Psalter goes on to protest about how things are in the world (Ps 3; 4; 5). Here a link between politics and ethics on one hand and prayer on the other becomes more overt. The world's not being as it should be may be a reason for human initiative; it is certainly a reason for prayer. Ethical commitment without calling on God appropriates too much responsibility to us as human beings. The Psalms will later declare that "Yhwh reigns" or "Yhwh is king" or "Yhwh has become king" (e.g., Ps 96:10). Generally speaking, it does not look as if this is the case. Israel's world often looked like one in which Pharaoh or Sennacherib reigned, not Yhwh, as our world does not look like one in which Jesus is Lord. Like us, then, when Israel entered worship and declared that Yhwh reigned, it was often making statements that went against the evidence. It was creating a world.[49] Admittedly, talk of "creating a world" could be misleading. The Psalms' conviction is that in the real world (as opposed to the world that we see) Yhwh indeed reigns. In worship we are making that already-real reality a reality in our ears and before our eyes. We may then be inspired to go and live out our ethical and political commitment in the world outside worship in the knowledge that the world in which Yhwh reigns is indeed the real world. But we would be unwise to make that a covert way of reckoning that it is our task to bring about Yhwh's reign, which would be laughable if it were not a Christian heresy that is alive and well.

---

[49]Cf. Walter Brueggemann, *Israel's Praise* (Philadelphia: Fortress, 1988).

A related point regarding our lives as individuals emerges from Psalm 119, which assumes that our relationship with Yhwh is founded on Yhwh's grace, commitment and compassion, yet that it also depends on our obedience. I am responsible for walking in Yhwh's way, yet I depend on Yhwh's help in doing so. My wholehearted commitment is a necessary but not a sufficient prerequisite to my living by Yhwh's declarations. Indeed, I need Yhwh's help if I am even to understand these declarations. One might have thought that Yhwh had done all that was needed in giving us the corpus of teaching in the Torah, but this is not so. We also need Yhwh to work in us to open our eyes to its wonders, to make us enthuse over it and therefore commit ourselves to it. It is when we see things Yhwh's way that we may be able to live in light of that understanding.

Ethics and Spirituality

Without referring to the Torah, Proverbs makes some similar assumptions. From the beginning it presupposes that its practical advice links on one hand with questions of "faithfulness, judgment and uprightness" and on the other with "reverence for Yhwh" (Prov 1:2-7). Pragmatics, religion and ethics belong together (cf. Prov 8:1-14). It has been suggested that wisdom was originally secular in its orientation and was only later set in a religious framework.[50] In principle it seems more likely that a traditional society such as Israel would always have operated with an implicitly religious framework, even if individual sayings do not make that overt. Either way, in the First Testament itself the material stands in that framework.

This conviction about the interrelationship between pragmatics, religion and ethics stands as a framework around the teaching that follows. Proverbs then commonly works by the conviction that we can learn from life itself how to live life. Its epistemology is radically empirical. Yet the outworking of that epistemology differs from its outworking in a modern context, precisely because it assumes that God and ethics are part of the picture, part of the framework with which it looks at human experience. Modern empiricism works within the framework of a set of assumptions about matters such as the reality of the world that we see and the consistency of the way it works. First Testament wisdom works with a broader set of assumptions, about this empirical world as one where God is active and one into which faithfulness, judgment and uprightness are written. Knowledge, instruction, discernment and insight go along with faithfulness, judgment and uprightness; there is no tension between them. Indeed, wisdom that is not related to reverence for God and faithfulness to other people does not count as wisdom, because it

---

[50]See, e.g., the discussion in von Rad, *Wisdom in Israel*, pp. 57-65.

does not recognize the true nature of reality as it reflects God's own being and thus recognize the true nature of human experience in God's world. Paradoxically, people involved in deceiving their neighbors and seeking to deceive Yhwh are in the end deceiving themselves and making fools of themselves. Folly is a further element in the nature of faithlessness or sin.

Life with God, life with other people and life as a self is an expression of wisdom. Thus "the Israelite wisdom literature, especially the book of Proverbs," provides "an exegetical base for renewing a biblically informed virtue tradition."[51] After all, according to Thomas Aquinas, prudence is the bedrock of all moral behavior, as it is key to identifying the right course of action.[52]

Talk in terms of providing an exegetical base for renewing a biblically informed virtue tradition reveals that the notion of a virtue tradition comes from outside the Scriptures; its expositors simply seek to utilize the Scriptures (or rather one small element within them) in order to resource it, as "isms" do (feminism, pacifism, evangelicalism, teetotalism, fundamentalism, Calvinism, vegetarianism). If we ask what is more intrinsic to the wisdom writings, then we may begin from the observation that "the wisdom writings have often been castigated as being 'conservative.' " Rodd denies the charge,[53] though his further comments (for instance, "the wise men accepted the *status quo*") point rather to the response "And what is so wrong about being conservative?" What Proverbs seeks is primarily "a *satisfactory* style of life which contributes to the well-being and stability of that society"; conversely, what the aphorisms worry about is people who threaten the community's stability and well-being.[54] Rebellious (adult) children do that; people who commit adultery do that; dishonesty does that. Concern for oneself, for other people and for God need to cohere.

1.2 The First Testament as a Source

In what way are we to expect the First Testament to offer us guidance on this threefold life? Coincidentally, I think, in the arrangement in which they appear in the synagogue, the books in the First Testament comprise three divisions. The first, the Torah, issued from a gradual process whereby Yhwh guided Israel in the way over the centuries, but we know very little about the nature of that process and cannot rely on convictions as to its nature in seeking to understand the Torah. And something similar is true about the rest of the material, though we can imagine what were the general community needs

---

[51]Ellen F. Davis, "Preserving Virtues," in *Character and Scripture,* ed. William P. Brown (Grand Rapids/Cambridge: Eerdmans, 2002), pp. 183-201; see p. 186.
[52]Davis, "Preserving Virtues," p. 189, referring to *Summa theologiae* 2a2ae.55.2.
[53]Rodd, *Glimpses of a Strange Land,* p. 273.
[54]Ibid., pp. 277, 278.

that led to its development. One of those is the need for God to shape the whole community's thinking, attitudes and life. Viewing the First Testament, and particularly the Torah, as "law," is inclined to make us think of the Torah as a kind of manual for courts to use, one whose main point was literal implementation. But its nature shows that it is more like the Sermon on the Mount, a collection of illustrations of how life with God, with other people and with oneself is supposed to work out. And its narratives offer not merely examples to follow or avoid, but stories that shape our thinking about God, about the community and about ourselves.

Torah, Prophets, Writings

Within the First Testament, the first great repository of direct instruction is the account of Israel's stay at Sinai, which occupies more than half of Exodus, the whole of Leviticus and the beginning of Numbers; the second is the account of Israel's stay in the Jordan Valley some years later, occupying the end of Numbers and the whole of Deuteronomy. At the same time the Torah as a whole suggests a broader narrative and theological framework for understanding God, community and self. Jewish thinking recognizes the significance of the opening chapters of Genesis, especially for Gentiles, and can see in the stories of Israel's ancestors in Genesis 12–50 "the genesis of ethics."[55] While the Torah thus has a "forensic face," this is not its only face.[56]

In Jewish thinking the Torah is the supremely authoritative material in the First Testament. The Former and Latter Prophets (Joshua to Kings less Ruth, and Isaiah to Malachi less Lamentations and Daniel) come second, the Writings third. The synagogue reads the whole of the Torah in its weekly worship, but reads the Prophets only selectively, while the Writings do not feature in the sabbath lectionary at all.[57] In contrast, Christian faith has put more emphasis on the Latter Prophets such as Isaiah, though the Psalms have had the most prominent place in lectionaries.

I am not clear that the First Testament in itself implies any priority between its different parts. It would be as plausible to reckon that they simply sit there in conversation and make complementary contributions to the shaping of the community's life.

A consideration of the material itself points in this direction. The Torah often works with the down-to-earth and gloomy practicalities of how to cope when things go wrong in the community, and often starts from the fact that the community is "stiff-necked." The Latter Prophets are less accepting of this

---

[55]Burton L. Visotzky, *The Genesis of Ethics* (New York: Crown, 1996).
[56]See Mary E. Mills, *Biblical Morality* (Aldershot, U.K./Burlington, Vt.: Ashgate, 2001), p. 3.
[57]The Five Scrolls (Song of Songs, Ruth, Lamentations, Ecclesiastes and Esther) are read on five special annual occasions; the Psalms of course also feature in worship.

fact about the community; they lambaste the community for it, and they lay before it Yhwh's ultimate standards. The Torah, too, lays down Yhwh's ultimate standards and lambastes, but it is more characterized by concrete prescription that often takes the people's waywardness for granted and seeks to work with it. So Torah and Prophets stand in fruitful juxtaposition.

Starting from the other end, one could say that the prophets deal with high-flown abstractions and criticize what has gone wrong, whereas the Torah is more practical and down-to-earth, never so heavenly minded that it fails to be of earthly use, turning abstractions into reformatory proposals that might get something done.

Both stand in fruitful conversation with the Writings. What the Torah has to say about relationships between men and women is not very romantic; the Song of Songs adds that other perspective. The Writings have much to say about coping with suffering and disappointment, and about everyday relationships in the community, complementing the Torah and the Prophets. What the Torah has to say about sacramental worship is complemented by what the Psalms have to say about words and music in worship. And whereas Torah and Prophets work within the framework of Yhwh's distinctive relationship with Israel and talk about exodus and covenant, exile and Yhwh's day, the Wisdom books refer to none of those distinctives and focus on life as it actually is for any people living in God's world. They also offer the nearest thing to philosophical thinking in the First Testament, so that James M. Gustafson's analysis of moral discourse as taking prophetic, narrative, ethical and policy form[58] might be correlated with the Latter Prophets, the narratives, the Wisdom books and the regulations in the Torah (praise and prayer then being the major omission from Gustafson's typology).[59]

A consideration of the life Israel is invited and exhorted to live will thus gain from reflecting the implicit conversation in the First Testament between Torah, Prophets and Writings. There is no particular regular order in which this conversation needs to happen.

The Collections of Material in the Torah

By no means, then, does a consideration of Israel's life confine itself to the Torah. But the Torah does comprise Israel's rule for life. Properly attending to it raises some tricky questions.

Some of these issue from its being not so much a single rule for life as a

---

[58]James M. Gustafson, "Varieties of Moral Discourse," in *Seeking Understanding: The Stob Lectures, 1986–1998* (Grand Rapids/Cambridge: Eerdmans, 2001), pp. 43-76.

[59]Richard Nysse adds "theological," which might make up for that ("Moral Discourse on Economic Justice: Considerations from the Old Testament," *Word and World* 12 [1992]: 337-44).

compilation of rules for life, a number of collections of regulations and exhortations. They do not relate very much to the lives of the people the narrative describes, people at Sinai, in the wilderness or in the Plains of Moab. They concern the practicalities of the lives of farmers and town dwellers, and people who live in houses rather than tents. They assume situations such as bad harvests that make people sell themselves into indentured labor. They start from a situation when people want to appoint kings and when they need to discern between prophets who truly speak Yhwh's word and prophets who do not. They give detailed accounts of which creatures in the land can be eaten and which cannot, and of how to clean a house affected by phenomena that resemble skin disease. They offer instructions on the needs of Levites who leave their home to come to serve at the sanctuary. It is centuries after the time of Moses when many of these issues arise. Now Yhwh could anticipate the need for instruction for these situations and give such instruction, but they nevertheless make a surprising collection of issues for Yhwh to focus on at Sinai, in the wilderness, or even at the point when Israel is about to enter the land. Further, many of them are handled several times in different ways, and that before any version of their teaching is to be implemented.

For they are not a systematic set of instructions. The same topics keep recurring. Sometimes Moses repeats a command word-for-word: for instance, he three times tells people not to cook a baby goat in its mother's milk (Ex 23:19; 34:26; Deut 14:21). Sometimes he gives several different sets of instructions for the same need: for instance, he gives three different sets of instructions about handling indentured service (Ex 21:1-11; Lev 25; Deut 15:1-18) and three times tells people in different terms about celebrating the annual pilgrimage festivals (Ex 23:14-17; Lev 23; Deut 16:1-17). All this comes before the teaching will have been implemented even once. These features of Exodus-Deuteronomy raise the question whether the teaching all actually derives from the context of Israel's life between Egypt and its arrival in the land.

We know that much later, Jews did speak of teaching that belonged to subsequent centuries as if it came from Moses' time. *Jubilees*, for instance, a second-century work focusing on events related in Genesis, describes itself as an account of a revelation of God to Moses on Sinai.[60] The Qumran *Temple Scroll* is a restatement of the contents of teaching in the Torah expressed as words from God in Moses' time.[61] Rabbinic Judaism attributes to Moses at Sinai the oral teaching that accumulated over later centuries and is put in writing in

---

[60]See, e.g., James H. Charlesworth, ed., *The Old Testament Pseudepigrapha* (Garden City, N.Y.: Doubleday/London: Darton, Longman & Todd, 1985), 2:35-142.

[61]See, e.g., Florentino García Martínez and Eibert J. C. Tigchelaar, ed., *The Dead Sea Scrolls Study Edition* (Leiden and Boston: Brill/Grand Rapids and Cambridge: Eerdmans, 1998), 2:1228-307.

the Mishnah.[62] Analogously, the Christian church gave the name "The Apostles' Creed" to a creed of the church in Rome that comes from much later than the apostles. The conviction expressed in such practices is that these later expressions of faith and life are a proper restatement of what Moses or the apostles said.

The nature of the material in Exodus-Deuteronomy suggests it came into being by a similar process.[63] These books bring together a series of collections of teaching that God inspired Israel to formulate in different social and historical contexts over the centuries, beginning in Moses' day but extending over many centuries. They came into being in different geographical contexts, such as Sinai, Canaan, Judah, Ephraim and Babylon. They came into being in different historical and social contexts, such as those of the people without a central government or other regular authority structure in the Judges period, of the monarchy in Israel and then in the separate kingdoms of Judah and Ephraim, of people under Babylonian government in the land and forced exile from their land, and of people living in voluntary dispersion from their land and of existence as a city-state and province of the Persian empire. The content of the regulations reflects these different contexts; it represents an ongoing process whereby Yhwh guided the community in its life in these different contexts.

Understanding the Torah in Its Context

It would seem to aid interpretation considerably if we could link the different sets of regulations and exhortations to their particular contexts, and for well over a century scholars have been seeking to do so but have reached virtually no consensus on the matter; or rather, for a century they reached a consensus (specifically, that associated with the letters JEDP) but then let the consensus fall apart, so that the questions that seemed to have been answered all became open questions again. Thus Frank Crüsemann, writing as someone who puts central emphasis on attempting to understand the material in the Torah against its social and historical context, describes the demand in Deuteronomy 12 that people take their offerings to a single sanctuary as "one of the most significant turning points in Israelite cultural history," but then observes that "we do not know what happened to bring about this earthshaking idea, and its application remains veiled."[64] Leading critics date the origin of the material in Leviticus in the premonarchic period, the time of Solomon,

---

[62]See *m. Abot* 1.1-18.

[63]Jesus of course refers to the Torah as Moses'; I assume this does not imply a declaration about authorship ("this is Moses' work not that of JEDP") but a declaration about authority (this is authoritative torah).

[64]Frank Crüsemann, *The Torah* (Minneapolis: Fortress/Edinburgh: T & T Clark, 1996), p. 222.

the divided monarchy, the exile and the Second Temple period.[65]

The future will see further change in scholarly theories about the contexts in which the material emerged, but it will see no resolution of the questions because the evidence does not make resolution possible. Discovering what the Torah can tell us about Israel's life cannot base itself on theories about the nature of this process. We have to accept that we do not know the material's origin.

Might scholarly uncertainty about the development of the Torah suggest that the logical move is to go back to the assumption that Moses wrote the Pentateuch? This is no solution, because the nature of the Torah makes the idea that Moses wrote it less convincing than any other theory. There is indeed a sense in which it is "Moses' Torah." All these regulations and exhortations issue from Yhwh's guiding the community over the centuries in working out what Moses would say if he were still present, in working out what are now the implications of Yhwh's involvement with Israel from the exodus onward. The story of Israel's rules for life is the story of its exercise of discernment with the guidance of the Holy Spirit over the centuries. The Torah makes clear that Yhwh kept guiding Israel into new understandings of its rule for life. But it conceals the history of that process.

Yet the fact that such a process went on is significant. John H. Yoder has suggested that in Acts "the basic work of the Holy Spirit . . . is to guide in discernment," to enable the church to see how to respond to new circumstances (see, e.g., Acts 13; 15).[66] It is in this way that the church gets to know what is right. And God affirms that whatever the community then affirms *is* the right thing: what disciples bind on earth is bound in heaven (Mt 16:19). This dynamic in the New Testament (not surprisingly) corresponds to the one that brought into being the collection of rules for life in the Torah. As centuries passed, new questions would continually arise in Israel's life, such as what attitude to take to monarchy or to prophecy, and Israelites had to seek to discern before God what attitude to take to these questions. Old questions would arise in new form, such as to the way poverty led to people having to sell their freedom. The community's crediting its own acts of discernment to Moses suggests that their understanding of that process indeed involved their seeking to discern the contemporary implications of Mosaic faith. And the evidence that what they bound on earth is bound in heaven is the fact that these human acts of discernment appear in God's book.

---

[65]See, e.g., the survey in J. G. McConville, "Fellow Citizens," in *Reading the Law,* J. G. Wenham Festschrift, ed. J. G. McConville and Karl Möller, LHBOTS 461 (London/New York: Continuum, 2007), pp. 10-32; see pp. 11-13.

[66]See John H. Yoder, "Practicing the Rule of Christ," in *Virtues and Practices in the Christian Tradition,* ed. Murphy et al. (Harrisburg, Penn.: Trinity, 1997), pp. 132-60; see p. 138.

In the chapters that follow, I make the basic assumption that Exodus-Deuteronomy developed over nearly a millennium, from the time of Moses at least to the time of Ezra. I take as a working hypothesis that most of Exodus 20–24 and 32–34 is older than the rest, and that Leviticus and Deuteronomy represent subsequent reworkings of that earlier material and rethinkings of the issues it covers, in different contexts or by different groups (though they themselves will have their own history of development). Compared with Exodus, for instance, Deuteronomy reflects a more urbanized context, covering questions raised by the monarchy and by the development of prophecy. It also gives less attention to matters such as property questions, injury and homicide, and more to underlying attitudes, to worship and festivals (whose regulations it significantly reworks), marriage and sex, institutions of leadership, and the support of the weak, and it shows more indication of theological reflection.[67] If Deuteronomy intended to replace Exodus, the community that put the Torah into its final form (which I presume happened in the Persian period) put both there as deposits of God's guiding the community in its reflection.

Understanding Prophets and Poetry in Their Context

Similar considerations apply to the origin of the Prophets and Wisdom books. The Latter Prophets characteristically begin by challenging readers to treat what they read as "the word of Yhwh" or as a "vision" that came to the prophet. Yet they also suggest that their work needs to be understood against its personal, historical and social context, and they indicate this more overtly than the Torah does. The vision is Isaiah's vision or Obadiah's vision; it comes in the time of particular kings, and it relates to particular people, such as Judah or Samaria or Jerusalem. The messages in the books often refer to particular situations and people that the prophet addresses. Yet the preserving of their words reflects the conviction that they have significance beyond that context, and sometimes they lack concrete references to people and situations in a way that invites their hearers to treat them as of general significance; Isaiah 40:12-31 is an example. Sometimes they explicitly indicate an origin in a specific context other than the one the book's opening refers to. The clear example is Isaiah 40–55 as a whole; here the prophecy speaks of exile coming to an end, of Babylon falling and of Cyrus the Persian, not as future certainties but as present realities. Sometimes the Prophets point to a concrete later period without making specific allusion to events or people; Isaiah 56–66 suggests the period after the exile in this way. Sometimes they leave us with-

---

[67]See Bernard M. Levinson, *Deuteronomy and the Hermeneutics of Legal Innovation* (New York/ Oxford: Oxford University Press, 1997).

out clear pointers to a context. Joel, for instance, has therefore been dated in most centuries from the ninth to the second. Fortunately, this makes surprisingly little difference to the book's interpretation, since Joel makes quite clear what *kind* of situation it addresses. The implications for Israel's life can be clear even though we cannot date the material in a prophetic book.

The material in Proverbs developed over many centuries, like that in the Torah and in parallel with it. Like it, the aphorisms in Proverbs sometimes suggest the life and teaching of the family, sometimes the life of the city. In parallel to the Torah's also reflecting the needs of priests for guidance in their work, Proverbs reflects the agenda of the court college and that of the theological school. A tradition of scholarship is inclined to see the city and the court college as key in interpreting Proverbs' background and to interpret the book in light of the kind of views one might expect to be held by a ruling group in the community.[68] But like theories about the origin of the Torah, this requires considerable connecting of dots. Sociological studies may be heuristically useful, but the possibilities they generate need to stand or fall on their own merits,[69] and it is easy for sociological studies of the First Testament to behave in ways that look somewhat circular, positivist, reductionist, relativist and determinist, as if they have the one objective answer that is actually bound up with their presuppositions and systematically rules out moral or theological values.[70]

The material in the Psalter again developed over centuries. The First Testament pictures Israelites composing psalms from the beginning of their history and again indicates that from the beginning such composing can reflect concrete historical events (see Ex 15:1-18), yet the vast majority of psalms are so sparing in their reference to concrete historical events that one can only infer that this reserve is deliberate. Whereas readers have often wanted to link them with specific events (for instance, in the life of David), attempts to do so are exercises in imagination. They too may be heuristically useful in enabling us to imagine the psalm being prayed in a particular context, but they risk compromising the psalms' own nature as prayers that avoid concrete reference to make them usable in any context.

The Torah, Prophets and Writings as we have them issued from the community bringing together the fruits of processes of development in a way that

---

[68]See, e.g., J. David Pleins, "Poverty in the Social World of the Wise," *JSOT* 37 (1987): 61-78; *The Social Visions of the Hebrew Bible* (Louisville: Westminster John Knox, 2001), pp. 452-83.

[69]Cf. Cyril S. Rodd, "On Applying a Sociological Theory to Biblical Studies," *JSOT* 19 (1981): 95-106.

[70]Cf. Gary Herion, "The Impact of Modern and Social Science Assumptions on the Reconstruction of Israelite History," *JSOT* 34 (1986): 3-33 = Charles E. Carter and Carol L. Meyers, ed., *Community, Identity, and Ideology* (Winona Lake, Ind.: Eisenbrauns, 1996), pp. 230-57.

makes clear that the material issued from specific contexts yet omits much information on these contexts. It apparently reckoned that they could fulfill the function of shaping its life without providing that information, and we have no alternative but to assume that it was right. The force of the declaration "it is written" does not depend on our having this information. When we are confronted then with several sets of regulations and exhortations regarding a matter such as the treatment of servants or the celebration of pilgrimage festivals, or the differences between the theology of different Wisdom books, or the differences in spirituality in different psalms, we have to ask about their significance and mutual interrelation without basing our understanding on knowledge of their specific historical, geographical or social context (though theories about possible contexts may indeed function heuristically in enabling us to reach understanding). The presence in the First Testament of this material collected into a whole is Israel's and God's promise that this is inspired, authoritative, instructive and intelligible teaching, whatever the history of its origin.

The Need for Instruction

Why did the material come into being? The story of God's speaking to Israel at Sinai is preceded by an instructive preamble in which Moses receives advice from his father-in-law. Exodus 18 in fact comprises a two-part story. In the synagogue lectionary, it forms the beginning of the Sinai narrative, but commentators see it as the end of the exodus story and begin the Sinai story with Exodus 19.[71] Jethro's visit bridges these two. He has come to see Moses, bringing the wife and sons that Moses had sent to stay with him during the exodus period, and in light of what he hears he comes to acknowledge Yhwh. This forms the great conclusion to the story of Israel's deliverance. Jethro then finds Moses preoccupied by sorting out disputes between individuals in the community, sees the danger of this overwhelming him, and suggests two (rather obvious) actions. Moses should teach the people how to live their lives together so they can avoid getting into disputes, and should appoint arbitrators to decide disputes that do arise, referring only major cases to him.

This event leads into God's speaking at Sinai. The teaching there constitutes what the people and their arbitrators need. The Decalogue comprises a religious and moral framework for the community's life, while the detailed instructions that follow indicate how to handle some specific problems. Historically, many of the instructions may be the result of the arbitration process. Moses and the arbitrators, and their equivalents in the promised land, will

---

[71]See, e.g., Brevard S. Childs, *Exodus* (London: SCM Press, 1974) = *The Book of Exodus* (Philadelphia: Westminster, 1974), pp. 318-36.

have had to help people work out what to do when tricky questions arise. What should happen when (say) two men fight and one seriously injures the other (Ex 21:18-19) or when someone borrows an animal and it dies while in his possession (Ex 22:14-15 [MT 13-14])? To judge from similarities between declarations in the Torah and declarations that appear in other, older Middle-Eastern documents such as Hammurabi's so-called law code, the Israelites did not start from scratch in working out the answers to such questions. There was no need to reinvent the wheel. On the other hand, there was need to relate the customary practices of the Middle East to what they knew of God through their being the exodus people, and one can sometimes see the regulations in the Torah doing that. In the conviction that God helped them to work out the right answers, such case law will have come to be incorporated in covenant teaching. So the chapters form a manual for the teaching of the people and for use by arbitrators.

Yet we have virtually no information on whether the teaching was ever used in this way or in any other way. When we compare the contents of the teaching with accounts in books such as Samuel-Kings that describe how life actually worked out, we do not get the impression that Israel handled issues in light of the Torah in this way. For instance, the books record many occasions when people committed acts for which the Torah prescribes the death penalty (such as worshiping other gods, murder, adultery and rebellion against one's parents), but never record that the death penalty was imposed.[72] The narrative of course indicates or implies that these acts were wrong, but it does not suggest that Israel behaved wrongly in not implementing the Torah's sanctions. People did not assume the Torah was designed for literal implementing, and the narrative assumes they were not wrong to see things that way.

The idea that the regulations in the Torah were not designed simply to be implemented in Israel's life might seem counterintuitive. This reaction reflects the longstanding assumption that this teaching is "law"; and we know what "law" is. But that is simply an assumption, certainly not supported by the description of the teaching as *tôrâ*,[73] since *tôrâ* does not mean "law." There are other words used in the Torah, such as *ḥôq*, that might be so translated (EVV often render *ḥôq* "statute"), but *tôrâ* also applies to the teaching of a prophet, a sage or a parent. It means something more like "teaching" or "instruction."

It might similarly seem obvious that the regulations in a document such as Hammurabi's "Laws" were designed to be implemented in his realm. But this

---

[72]See, e.g., Henry McKeating, "Sanctions Against Adultery in Ancient Israelite Society," JSOT 11 (1979): 57-72.

[73]See, e.g., the survey of possible approaches in Bernard S. Jackson, "The Ceremonial and the Judicial," *JSOT* 30 (1984): 25-50; see pp. 33-40.

does not seem to have been regularly so in the case of such Middle-Eastern "law" collections. Hammurabi is no guide to the way Babylonian law worked, as the Torah is no guide to the way Israelite law worked. Hammurabi's "laws" provide the king with a way of declaring what *kind* of laws and practices he was committed to.[74] The Torah indicates what *kind* of laws Israel was to be committed to.[75]

The Role of the Teaching

One should not assume that none of the regulations were designed for literal implementing.[76] But the purpose of the Torah as a whole is "to educate the people of God in the will of God for the whole of their life as his people, to create and develop the conscience of the community."[77] In this connection its teaching can be illustrative or didactic or visionary in intent, and the regulations that resemble laws are often interwoven with moral exhortations and instructions about matters such as worship. Further, the regulations by no means cover all the areas that would need to be covered by a "law code."

Indeed, "the belief that adjudication should be governed by laws and not by people" is a culturally contingent Western concept.[78] It is people such as the elders in the community who do this adjudication; the regulations show them the kind of priorities and principles to bear in mind when they are doing so. Further, Jethro implies that these regulations will also function like material in Proverbs; they are for the edification of ordinary people, to help them see how to handle disputes in the community without their reaching a court. They start off, at least, as "self-executing laws" or "self-help mechanisms."[79] They

---

[74]Cf. A. Leo Oppenheim, *Ancient Mesopotamia,* rev. ed. (Chicago/London: University of Chicago Press, 1977), p. 158; also Gerda Lerner, *The Creation of Patriarchy* (New York/Oxford: Oxford University Press, 1986), p. 103.

[75]Cf., e.g., Bernard S. Jackson, *Essays in Jewish and Comparative Legal History* (Leiden: Brill, 1975), pp. 26-29.

[76]Victor H. Matthews defends the view that, for example, Ex 21:1-11 reflects the bringing together of case law for the guidance of future decision-making ("The Anthropology of Slavery in the Covenant Code," in *Theory and Method in Biblical and Cuneiform Law,* ed. Bernard M. Levinson, JSOTSup 181 [Sheffield, U.K.: Sheffield Academic Press, 1994], pp. 119-35; see p. 120).

[77]Richard Bauckham, *The Bible in Politics* (London: SPCK/Louisville: Westminster John Knox, 1989), p. 26; cf. Joseph Blenkinsopp, *Sage, Priest, Prophet* (Louisville: Westminster John Knox, 1995), p. 38.

[78]Jonathan P. Burnside, *The Signs of Sin,* JSOTSup 364 (London/New York: Sheffield Academic Press, 2003), p. 10 (and pp. 11-15 for the continuation in this paragraph), following Bernard S. Jackson, "Ideas of Law and Legal Administration," in *The World of Ancient Israel,* ed. Ronald E. Clements (Cambridge/New York: Cambridge University Press, 1989), pp. 185-202.

[79]Bernard S. Jackson, *Wisdom-Laws* (Oxford/New York: Oxford University Press, 2006), p. 389.

might then become adapted and developed in connection with the work of state-established courts when these come into being, though even when Deuteronomy 16:18-20 and 17:8-13 lay down instructions for the work of courts, they make no reference to the courts following the laws that appear in Deuteronomy or anywhere else (similarly 2 Chron 19:6-7). The Torah is for the teaching of the whole people (cf. 2 Chron 17:9; Neh 8–10).[80] It is a vision rather than a law code or even a program for reform, though this does not mean it is just a piece of daydreaming not designed to affect the life of the community.[81]

Something similar may be true about the regulations concerning worship. Perhaps no one ever pretended that all Israelite males were going to make pilgrimage to appear before Yhwh three times a year. Whether or not instructions about sacrifice were intended to be implemented, they also embody and teach an understanding of God, the world, the social order and morality. This is reflected in the way they continued to be studied assiduously by Jews at Qumran who had separated themselves from Jerusalem and by Jews scattered by the destruction of Jerusalem by the Romans, and by the Jewish community ever since. Their exposition of rules for sacrifice did not come into being to prescribe what should happen in the temple several centuries later. In Leviticus real practices are gathered with other material in order to create a system that expresses philosophical or religious principles.[82] In Deuteronomy the instruction material is there to be the exposition of a theology.[83] "Ritual functions as a kind of rhetoric, as a way to persuade participants through ritual language and action of the truth of a social group's worldview and moral system,"[84] and simply to bring home the nature of that worldview and moral system. Torah "does not so much tell us what to do as it teaches us how to think about what to do."[85]

Theory and Practice

Much of the Torah is thus similar in intent to much of Jesus' teaching, as the church has usually understood it. Christians have not generally assumed that they were supposed simply to implement his instructions about how to han-

---

[80]Cf. §1.1 "Community and Individual."

[81]See Walter J. Houston, *Contending for Justice*, LHBOTS 428 (New York/London: T & T Clark, 2006), e.g., pp. 173-202 on utopia and ideology in Deuteronomy and Lev 25.

[82]So Philip R. Davies, "Leviticus as a Cultic System in the Second Temple Period," in *Reading Leviticus*, ed. John F. A. Sawyer, JSOTSup 227 (Sheffield, U.K.: Sheffield Academic Press, 1996), pp. 230-37; see p. 233.

[83]Cf. J. G. McConville, *Law and Theology in Deuteronomy*, JSOTSup 33 (Sheffield, U.K.: JSOT, 1984).

[84]David Janzen, *The Social Meanings of Sacrifice in the Hebrew Bible*, BZAW 344 (Berlin/New York: de Gruyter, 2004), p. 27.

[85]Peter J. Haas, "The Quest for Hebrew Bible Ethics," *Semeia* 66 (1994): 151-59; see p. 153.

dle anger or abuse, about eyes or hands that lead us into sin, or about divorce, oaths, secret prayer, or saving (Mt 5:21–6:21). While some of our not doing so indicates failure to do what Jesus literally meant us to do, some of it rightly perceives that Jesus did not intend us simply to do what he said. He was not laying down laws but laying out a vision or providing illustrations or offering teaching. He was following the nature of the Torah, which was also not simply laying down laws but offering an exposition of theological ethics in the form of law. Its sanctions draw attention to areas people need to take really seriously. Its prescriptions give concrete embodiment to a vision. Thus, for instance, the instructions for returning land to its original owners every fifty years (Lev 25) may have been designed to express a dream rather than to give instructions for straightforward implementation. This would explain the fact that there seem to be logistical difficulties about implementing them, as well as linking with the fact that there is no record of Israel ever doing so.

This awareness does not remove the bite from the teaching in the Torah. It does the opposite, and that for three reasons. First, if the teaching is simply rules for implementing, we can go ahead, implement the rules and then sit back, relax and congratulate ourselves. If the teaching expresses a vision or provides illustrations of how principles may be embodied in life or teaches us about the way God wants us to look at different areas of life, it places greater demands on us. We have to ask how we could redream and implement this vision, how we could embody it, how we need to change our thinking in the light of it. It is not open to being treated legalistically.

Second, if the teaching is simply rules for implementing, it belongs in the life of Israel, which is distant from us. Many readers of the Torah now live in urbanized, industrial or postindustrial societies to which the Torah's instructions do not directly speak. Our living in the period when the Torah has reached its *telos* (its purpose or termination; Rom 10:4) gives us further grounds for reckoning we can ignore it. But if the teaching was designed to be visionary or illustrative or didactic, we have to ask how its vision, its concrete examples and its teaching reaches beyond traditional societies and beyond the point where as "law" it ceases to hold. Inner values develop outward action and character issues in actions, but outward action develops inner values and character, and illustrations of appropriate outward action can also function thus.

Third, if the teaching is simply rules for implementing, we might feel free to dismiss it because it works with lower standards than the ones Christ places on us. As well as being visionary, illustrative and didactic, it is often lenient. While its teaching often lays before us issues we need to consider, it works with the tension between standards that go back to creation and are reaffirmed in God's deliverance of Israel, and the practical need to apply these standards to the lives of people who resist them.[86] When it does that, it is still being visionary, illustrative and didactic. In seeking to be lenient without losing touch with God's ideals, and to keep hold of God's ideals without losing touch with the practicalities of where people are, it is modeling a path of discipleship for us to follow. The New Testament again follows its example (e.g., in its attitude to slavery).

Commands, Principles and Rationales

It might also seem natural to assume that regulations in the Torah have principles or rationales behind them. They are not random commands, given simply to require Israel to express obedience to Yhwh (though some might be that). And some regulations make explicit the principles they embody or the rationales they presuppose. Israel is to observe the sabbath because God did so in creating the world, and because God at the exodus had mercy on people in servitude (Ex 20:8-11; Deut 5:12-15). Israel is not to wrong a resident alien because that was its position in Egypt (Ex 22:21 [MT 20]; 23:9). Israel is not to make images of Yhwh because these belie the way Yhwh appeared to Israel (Deut 4).

But such statements of principle or rationale are the exception rather than the rule. (The ones just noted from Exodus 20–23 include the clearest examples in those chapters.) Admittedly it will often seem that the principle or rationale is quite obvious. Who needs to be told why murder, adultery, theft or false testimony is wrong? Yet one could also ask who needs to be given a reason why oppressing a resident alien is wrong. Further, the Torah is also sparing in offering rationales for declarations where these seem less obvious to us but might have seemed obvious to an Israelite (famously, that repeated prohibition on cooking a kid goat in its mother's milk). This also reminds us that rationales that seem obvious to us may emerge from our culture rather than Israel's. The identification of principles and rationales is hazardous, and the history of the interpretation of the Torah suggests that our inferences often reflect the convictions of the interpreter more than those of the text.[87] Some Christians believe the sixth command does not apply to war or capital punishment, others take it to exclude both, others take it to exclude war but not capital punishment, yet others take it to exclude capital punishment but not war.

What shall we do with this allusiveness? Anthropological approaches to the Torah that compare its regulations with phenomena from other Middle-Eastern societies or from other traditional cultures have the potential to of-

---

[86]See further §4.1.

[87]Cf. Jackson, *Essays in Jewish and Comparative Legal History*, pp. 25-63. His starting point is a critique of Moshe Greenberg, "Some Postulates of Biblical Criminal Law," reprinted in *A Song of Power and the Power of Song*, ed. Duane L. Christiansen (Winona Lake, Ind.: Eisenbrauns, 1993), pp. 283-300.

fer illumination. The Torah itself points to the possibility of letting one part of the Torah elucidate another. Its arrangement in Exodus and in Deuteronomy points to our reading the Decalogue and the regulations that follow in light of each other. The Decalogue is in fact oddly located in Exodus. At the end of Exodus 19 both Israel and Moses are at the bottom of the mountain, and they are also there in Exodus 20:18-21 [MT 15-18], until Moses returns to approach Yhwh's presence. Thus from a narrative angle, Yhwh's making the statement in Exodus 20:1-17 [MT 1-14] comes at a puzzling point. It does not appear in the narrative at the moment when God actually uttered it; at this point Moses is not on the top of the mountain with God. Whenever God uttered it, it has been brought back to a position of prominence early in the account of God's appearing at Sinai. In relation to what precedes, this suggests that the Decalogue offers a first outline exposition of what is involved in being Yhwh's covenant people (see Ex 19:3-8). In addition, it offers an anticipatory summary of key requirements that will appear in what follows: the arrangement makes the Decalogue an introduction to the regulations in Exodus 20:22 [MT 19]–23:33.

Deuteronomy 5:22 [MT 19] emphasizes its significance in a parallel way by commenting on the fact that Yhwh spoke these words "and did not add"; there is a sense in which they say all that needs to be said. The arrangement in Exodus whereby the Decalogue introduces what follows then reappears in more overt form in Deuteronomy. It is part of an exposition of Yhwh's fundamental expectations of Israel in Deuteronomy 4–11, while Deuteronomy 12–26 spells out these expectations. All but the tenth command are in fact paralleled elsewhere in the Torah.[88] There are several different ways of making the commands count up to ten; the instinct to reckon that there are ten corresponds to the conviction that they comprise a succinct account of some basic priorities and an account that is somewhat complete and rounded.

Given that many of the individual instructions in the Torah offer no indication of their rationale, relating them to the Decalogue (as well as to material from elsewhere in the First Testament) may give us clues as to principles lying behind them. Conversely, many of the ten commands themselves are so succinct as to be hard to interpret, and the subsequent detailed commands (as well as material from elsewhere in the First Testament) may help us understand them and see how they work themselves out in life situations.

---

[88]Cf. Moshe Weinfeld, "The Decalogue," in *Religion and Law,* ed. Edwin B. Firmage et al. (Winona Lake, Ind.: Eisenbrauns, 1990), pp. 3-47; see pp. 4-9; Moshe Weinfeld, "The Uniqueness of the Decalogue and its Place in Jewish Tradition," in *The Ten Commandments in History and Tradition,* ed. Ben-Zion Segal (Jerusalem: Magnes, 1990), pp. 1-44; see pp. 1-2; William P. Brown, "Introduction," in *The Ten Commandments,* ed. William P. Brown (Louisville/London: Westminster John Knox, 2004), pp. 1-11; see p. 4.

The Ten Statements

"The initial and primary category for thinking about the Decalogue is divine command," though this command belongs in the context of covenantal relationship and aims at godliness, not merely rote obedience.[89] The Decalogue is an expression of divine authority. Yet Exodus and Deuteronomy do not describe its provisions as "commands." In Exodus 20:1-17 [MT 14] they are simply *kol-haddĕbārîm hā'ēlleh*, "all these words/sentences/statements"; in Exodus 34:28 (cf. Deut 4:13; 10:4) they become "the ten statements"[90]—*deka logoi*, in fact. The Septuagint and the Vulgate preserve that phraseology; as far as I have been able to discover, the Geneva Bible of 1560 first uses the expression "Ten Commandments." Perhaps the scriptural description anticipates the need not to treat them legalistically. It fits with the fact that they mostly take the form of statements or declarations ("you will not . . .") rather than exhortations ("you are not to . . .").[91] These declarations are prescriptive, and strongly so; the exceptions, the positive imperative pronouncements relating to parents and the sabbath, make this explicit. But their form is descriptive, like that of a New Testament statement such as "the person who is born of God does not commit sin" (1 Jn 3:9). That defines or describes what Christians are; the Ten Statements define or describe what Israel is.

One should not exaggerate the relationship of mutual interpretation between the Decalogue and the rest of the Torah. Following his exposition of the Decalogue, Philo outlines how the rest of the teaching in the Torah could all be subsumed under one or other of the Ten Statements, and then expounds the detailed laws in light of this.[92] John Calvin takes this approach in his commentary on Exodus-Deuteronomy,[93] and it has been applied to Deuteronomy in particular by recent scholars.[94] But some of the material in the Torah fits under the Ten Statements more readily than other material, and some areas of

---

[89]Patrick D. Miller, "Divine Command and Beyond," in *The Ten Commandments*, ed. William P. Brown (Louisville/London: Westminster John Knox, 2004), pp. 12-29; see p. 12.

[90]If Ex 34:28 refers back to Ex 20:1-17 [14] and not to Ex 34 itself: see J. Philip Hyatt, *Commentary on Exodus* (London: Oliphants, 1971) = *Exodus* (Grand Rapids: Eerdmans, 1980), pp. 319-22; and on other decalogues, Walter Harrelson, *The Ten Commandments and Human Rights* (Philadelphia: Fortress, 1980), pp. 33-40.

[91]That is, they use the negative *lō'* not *'al*. The same is true of the declarations in Ex 20:22 [19]–23:33.

[92]See Philo's *The Decalogue* 29-32 [154-74] and *The Special Laws*.

[93]John Calvin, *Commentaries on the Four Last Books of Moses* (Grand Rapids: Eerdmans, 1950). Cf. Rousas John Rushdoony, *The Institutes of Biblical Law* (Nutley, N.J.: Presbyterian & Reformed, 1973).

[94]See, e.g., Georg Braulik, "The Sequence of the Laws in Deuteronomy 12–26," in *A Song of Power and the Power of Song*, ed. Duane L. Christensen (Winona Lake, Ind.: Eisenbrauns, 1993), pp. 313-35; Mark E. Biddle, *Deuteronomy* (Macon, Ga.: Smith & Helwys, 2003), p. 201; Dennis T. Olson, *Deuteronomy and the Death of Moses* (Minneapolis: Fortress, 1994), pp. 62-65, and his references.

life treated elsewhere in the Torah are missing from the Decalogue. It does not cover concern for the needy (except in its reference to the sabbath), whereas we know from elsewhere in the Torah, and from the Prophets and the Writings, that this is one of God's major priorities. The beginning of the Torah also suggests that managing creation was God's very first priority (see Gen 1–2), and this may give us a clue to the wider significance of some material in Exodus-Deuteronomy, but the Decalogue hardly refers to it, unless it does so in the preamble to the sabbath command with its talk of six days of serving (*ʿābad*) and doing all your work (*mĕlāʾkâ*), two key words in Genesis 1–2.[95]

So there is a broad reciprocal relationship between the Decalogue and what follows, but we cannot link each of the Ten Statements with something that follows, or see each of these detailed regulations as an exposition of some aspect of the Decalogue. The Decalogue is not a comprehensive statement of the principles underlying the Torah or a summary of it.[96] Nor is it a timeless, comprehensive statement of God's priorities. Perhaps there are some things it omits because they can be taken for granted, and others that it omits because they were not pressing needs when it came into being. Further, while there is substantial (but not complete) identity between the two forms of the Decalogue, there are substantial differences in the detailed regulations that follow in Exodus and Deuteronomy and spell out their implications in different social and cultural contexts. The basic principles do not change; the detailed outworking changes.[97] Yet the Decalogue's position indicates that it is presented as a telling-enough list of things God thinks are important.

The Significance of Narrative

The regulations in the Torah, the pronouncements of the prophets, the Wisdom books, and the praises and prayers of the Psalms are set in the context of narrative. They are set in the context of a literary macronarrative of creation, rebellion, covenant promise, divine rule, human rule, political collapse, prophetic hope and partial restoration in Genesis-Kings and Chronicles-Ezra-Nehemiah. They are set in a theological macronarrative or metanarrative extending forward into a more complete realization of Yhwh's purpose for Israel and for the world that goes back to creation. The way we construe either of these macronarratives makes significant differences to the way we construe

---

[95]Judith Plaskow notes that there is no declaration in the Torah that says "Thou shalt not lessen the humanity of women": see *The Coming of Lilith*, ed. Donna Berman (Boston: Beacon, 2005), p. 57; she refers to Cynthia Ozick, "Notes Toward Finding the Right Question," *Lilith* 6 (1979): 19-29; see pp. 27, 29.

[96]Cf. Eckhart Otto, *Theologische Ethik des Alten Testaments* (Stuttgart: Kohlhammer, 1994), pp. 208-19.

[97]Cf. Patrick D. Miller, *Deuteronomy* (Louisville: John Knox, 1990), p. 69.

our life with God, our life with one another, and our life as selves. In Western Christian culture, for instance, our construal of our individual selves has most of the attention; it is my identity and God's purpose for me that counts. This is not a new preoccupation; it is from this that Yhwh was concerned to wean Job, who may be pardoned for having become preoccupied with himself. But it is a distinctive preoccupation within contemporary Western Christian culture, and (among other things) it ends up making people unhappy at the fact that their lives contain small-scale Job-like experiences.

Individual narratives within this macronarrative offer concrete representations of what it means to be human, corporately or individually, within God's people or outside it. They portray what humanity is or what it should be, what Israel is or what Israel should be, who I am or what I should be. They thus portray before their readers both vision and reality.

In the Greek and Hebrew traditions, telling stories has been a chief way of undertaking reflection in relation to ethics. That is so in Homer, who portrays people living in a heroic society with its set social roles. It is so in the tragedians, who portray people living with the ambiguities and dilemmas that people face when virtues and obligations come into conflict with one another. It is so in Genesis and Joshua, Exodus and Numbers, Judges, Samuel, and Kings, Jonah, Ruth and Esther. "We build our characters story by story."[98]

For much of the twentieth century the study of ethics focused mainly or exclusively on direct moral statements. It would be foolish to replace that by paying attention only to narrative. The discursive genres are complemented by narrative; narrative is complemented by the discursive genres.[99] Although narrative is the vital framework of the First Testament, in connection with the way the Scriptures are designed to shape the community's life "the 'story' is only half the story." The fact that narrative mingles with prophecy, psalm and wisdom "is sign enough that *sola scriptura* need not now be replaced with 'story alone.' "[100] We toggle precepts and stories.[101] But story is indeed a vital way of conveying what is involved in living with God, with other people and with ourselves.

As well as generally not showing Israel applying to its life the requirements of the Torah, First Testament narratives do not very often show Israel getting into trouble for failing to do so. The questions this raises become both more and less complex in connection with the stories in Genesis, which have been a traditional focus of devotional and ethical reflection. Issues covered by

---

[98]Deirdre N. McCloskey, *The Bourgeois Virtues* (Chicago/London: University of Chicago Press, 2006), p. 273.
[99]Brian Brock, *Singing the Ethos of God* (Grand Rapids/Cambridge: Eerdmans, 2007), p. 33.
[100]Pleins, *Social Visions of the Hebrew Bible*, p. 520.
[101]McCloskey, *Bourgeois Virtues*, p. 272.

the regulations in the Torah arise there more often than they do in subsequent narratives, over matters such as marriage and family life, and the ancestors are commonly described without comment as not living by those regulations. This might simply indicate an awareness that the ancestors could not be expected to live by the rules that issued from Sinai. Indeed, it has been argued that some regulations in Leviticus and Deuteronomy are drafted to make sure that incidents and practices from the time of the ancestors do not recur.[102] On the other hand, some of these incidents and practices (such as ignoring the rule of primogeniture) recur without comment in the narrative after Sinai.[103] Law can undercut narrative; narrative can undercut law.[104]

Stories That Reveal God

Further, the narratives in Genesis relate without comment a number of incidents that it is hard to see the narrator expecting readers not to see as unsavory or wayward, such as Abraham and Isaac's imperiling of their wives or Lot's offering his daughters to the men of Sodom, neither of which is directly covered by any subsequent regulation. Genesis surely expects its readers to be able to make the appropriate moral judgment on such acts without their needing a special revelation, even if it also has some sympathy with people placed in such troublesome situations as Abraham, Lot and Isaac, or Lot's daughters. They share such an assumption with Amos and Paul, who write on the basis that human beings are well aware of God's fundamental moral expectations (see Amos 1–2; Rom 1–2). You need a special revelation to tell you to circumcise baby boys, or for that matter to sacrifice your son. You do not need a special revelation to tell you that those other actions of Abraham, Lot and Isaac were wrong, even if the three men had managed to rationalize their way into their action ("Well, I must protect these strangers"; "Well, she *is* my sister").

"There is no ethically neutral narrative."[105] Implicitly or explicitly a narrative expresses a vision of human life and of right and wrong. Thus "the strategy of persuasion undertaken by the narrator is aimed at imposing on the

---

[102]See the work of Calum M. Carmichael, e.g., *The Laws of Deuteronomy* (Ithaca, N.Y.: Cornell University Press, 1974); *The Spirit of Biblical Law* (Athens/London: University of Georgia Press, 1996).

[103]Cf. Robert M. Cover, "*Nomos* and Narrative," *Harvard Law Review* 97, no. 4 (1983): 4-68; see pp. 19-24.

[104]Cf. Nanette Stahl, *Law and Liminality in the Bible,* JSOTSup 202 (Sheffield, U.K.: Sheffield Academic Press, 1995), p. 17.

[105]Paul Ricoeur, *Oneself as Another* (Chicago/London: University of Chicago Press, 1992), p. 115; cf. pp. 163-64; also Athena Gorospe, *Narrative and Identity* (Leiden/Boston: Brill, 2007), p. 47.

reader a vision of the world that is never ethically neutral."[106] Wayne C. Booth titles his book on ethical criticism of literature *The Company We Keep;*[107] he sees the implied authors of works that we read as like friends. Our friends influence us. The practice of ethical criticism involves looking for the understanding of life expressed in a work as a whole, not simply fastening on particular sentences or particular characters removed from their context.[108]

Genesis's failure to make explicit moral judgments in its stories links with the fact that it is a story about how God acted and acts, not one about how we ought to act. The most important way its stories shape our moral lives is by its vision of God and of God's relationship with the world and with us, which can revolutionize our understanding of ourselves in relation to God, the world and other people. We discover who we are and who we might be through the stories of people such as Cain and Abel, Sarah and Hagar, Joseph and his brothers, Egypt and Israel, Israel's life in the Judges period, Ruth and Naomi, Samuel and Saul, David and Bathsheba. In narratives we see experiences of life concretely represented and we thus gain insight on what living life is.

More fundamentally, we also discover who God is, with the behavioral implications of that. As primarily God's story, not Israel's story, the First Testament is an account of what it means for Yhwh to be compassionate, gracious, long-tempered, committed, truthful, carrying waywardness, not acquitting, and attending to waywardness in the way family life works out. It is this story that then plays a key role in enabling people to see the nature of compassion, grace and those other qualities as they receive varied expression in different contexts, and letting this portrayal shape their own characters. Narrative resources ethics by mediating between the domain of actual life, the events that lie behind the narrative, and the domain of the life to be lived by readers, the events that could lie ahead of it. It is related closely enough to actual life to make sense to people living actual life, but it is distanced enough from it through the use of faith, creativity and imagination (e.g., by the way it has turned actual events into a story with a beginning, a middle and an end) to take such people on from where they are.[109]

Stories in Which We Find Ourselves

Many of these narratives are very nasty. They are certainly not escapist litera-

---

[106]Paul Ricoeur, *Time and Narrative,* 3 vols. (Chicago: University of Chicago Press, 1984, 1985, 1988), 3:249.

[107]Wayne C. Booth, *The Company We Keep* (Berkeley/London: University of California Press, 1988), see esp. pp. 169-224.

[108]Cf. Martha Nussbaum, who develops the image of friendship in *Love's Knowledge* (New York/Oxford: Oxford University Press, 1990), pp. 237-40.

[109]See Gorospe, *Narrative and Identity,* pp. 21-30, with her references to Ricoeur, *Time and Narrative.*

ture. They do not offer models for behavior, even negative models ("this is what not to do"). Christians thus feel some discomfort with them because we are inclined to assume they should offer moral example. Actually what they offer is illumination and inspiration. It is in this way that they contribute to the formation of the character that expresses itself in what we do.

Their declining to comment on the unsavory nature of the stories they tell or to offer an overt moral evaluation of the characters' acts in a story such as that in Judges 19 provokes the question, How can the Bible be both horrifying *and* Scripture? Yet subtly and deftly, "everyone in the story, except the women, . . . is in some way censured by the narrative."[110] "The story has no heroes; nor does it allow the reader to differentiate clearly between offenders and victims."[111] The Samson story likewise does not endorse its violence; indeed, it makes clear that this violence does not generate an integrated, peaceful society, and it suggests a critique of the use of violence to establish or renew authority.[112] The stories in Judges portray violence against women in such a way as to drive communities who acknowledge these Scriptures to face equivalent events in their own world.[113] Genesis, too, a book full of unsavory stories about dysfunctional families, "mirrors our lives and our desires," and in the process of studying its stories, moral transformation can take place; that can and does come about through reading novels and watching movies, but the fact that these stories come in Scripture gives them distinctive purchase—they demand that we take them seriously.[114]

The stories do not offer accounts of people wrestling with moral issues or personal dilemmas. Only occasionally are there "little cameos in the Old Testament of characters who would not be at all out of place in a Greek tragedy," such as Jephthah and his daughter or Paltiel son of Laish (Judg 11; 2 Sam 3:14-16).[115] In a postmodern context "morality is incurably *aporetic*. Few choices . . .

---

[110]Jacqueline E. Lapsley, *Whispering the Word* (Louisville: Westminster John Knox, 2005), pp. 35, 36.

[111]Ilse Müllner, "Lethal Differences," in *Judges,* ed. Athalya Brenner, FCB 2/4 (Sheffield, U.K.: Sheffield Academic Press, 1999), pp. 126-42; see p. 139.

[112]Cf. Richard C. Bowman and Richard W. Swanson, "Samson and the Son of God," *Semeia* 77 (1996): 59-73.

[113]See, e.g., Yani Yoo, "*Han*-Laden Women," *Semeia* 78 (1997): 37-46.

[114]Visotzky, *Genesis of Ethics,* pp. 11, 209.

[115]John Barton, "Reading for Life," in *The Bible in Ethics,* ed. John W. Rogerson et al., JSOTSup 207 (Sheffield, U.K.: Sheffield Academic Press, 1995), pp. 66-76; see p. 72. Barton goes on (p. 73) to suggest that most of 1–2 Samuel can be read with an eye to the complexity of human ethical dilemmas, while Visotzky says Genesis is "rich in moral dilemmas" (*Genesis of Ethics,* p. 15; the sentence is italicized), but I cannot see this is so; usually the moral issue is clear. It is the absence of such ambiguity that makes Genesis a little like a soap opera (p. 9). But it is indeed true that the stories in 1–2 Samuel would not be out of place in a Greek tragedy in the sense that they unfold as a series of terrifying portrayals of fragile people who are the victims of circumstances and life and themselves and God. Barton

are unambiguously good. . . . The moral self moves, feels, and acts in the context of ambivalence and is shot through with uncertainty."[116] In the First Testament it is more Israel's successive collections of commands than its narratives that recognize this, as they change in the requirements they issue; these collections thus come closer to reflecting the problem of coping with ambiguity. But whereas a Greek tragedy shows its characters "searching for the morally salient; and it forces us, as interpreters, to be similarly active,"[117] in general First Testament narrative is not so interested in how we cope with ambiguity as in the more common and arguably more pressing human problem of our failure to do the unambiguously good and our inclination to do the unambiguously wayward. "Before the commandment of God man does not permanently stand like Hercules at the crossroads. He is not everlastingly striving for the right decision." But "before the commandment of God man may at last move forward along the road."[118] In First Testament narratives we do look at characters such as Abraham, Jacob or David and find ourselves in our ambiguity, but it is not the ambiguity of situations and questions that they portray but the ambiguity of people who can be alternately heroic or cowardly, or whose hearts can be impossible to discern.

---

notes J. Cheryl Exum's *Tragedy and Biblical Narrative* (Cambridge/New York: Cambridge University Press, 1992).

[116]Zygmunt Bauman, *Postmodern Ethics* (Oxford/Cambridge, Mass.: Blackwell, 1993), p. 11.

[117]Martha Nussbaum, *The Fragility of Goodness* (Cambridge/New York: Cambridge University Press, 1986), p. 14; cf. McCloskey, *Bourgeois Virtues*, p. 270.

[118]Dietrich Bonhoeffer, *Ethics* (New York: Simon & Schuster, 1995), p. 279.

PART ONE

LIVING WITH GOD

Living with God involves responsibility and privilege. Both issue from being put into the position of servants in relation to a master. Broadly, in chapter two we are concerned with the responsibility, in chapter three with the privilege.

2

SUBMISSION AND CELEBRATION

As Yhwh's servants, Israel is to live a life of obedience to what Yhwh says and is to manifest the attitudes proper to a servant, such as respect and trust. As well as acknowledging Yhwh in substantial ways, Israel recognizes Yhwh in symbolic forms in its worship, in its sacrifices and offerings, its festivals, and its praise. Christians sometimes assume that Israel's relationship with God focused on outward obedience whereas Jesus cares about the heart.[1] This is not the picture either Testament gives. Both expect outward expressions of commitment in worship and in life in the world; both also care about the heart or mind. The Torah emphasizes that there is little value in an outward symbol of submission, such as circumcision, unless it is a symbol of actual submission, inward as well as outward: "Cut off the foreskin from your mind and do not stiffen your neck any more" (Deut 10:16). God asks for the life, but also for the heart. Neither outward obedience nor inner attitude is enough on its own; we are whole people and the relationship involves the whole person.

2.1 Obeying Yhwh

It has been said that in Christian faith "the term or ultimate goal of human existence" is "a personal union of the believer with God."[2] And in some Western cultures, *relational* is the ultimate adjective and *intimacy* is the ultimate noun, largely because the collapse of family and community means that many people do not know how to be relational, and they both love and fear intimacy. My students are therefore inclined to find in Genesis 1–3 a God who is supremely relational and who desires intimacy. (It is possible to find most things in Genesis 1–3.) They find this in Exodus too. (When they read Leviticus, they can also find it there.)

Yhwh is indeed relational and desires intimacy (though those are warm and fuzzy words rather than well-defined notions), but this is by no means the central feature of Genesis 1–3 or Exodus. Much more prominent is the

---

[1]See, e.g., Thomas Aquinas, *Summa theologica* IIa, Q. 107. Aquinas goes on to acknowledge that some Israelites had an inner grace while some New Testament Christians lack that.
[2]Romanus Cessario, *The Moral Virtues and Theological Ethics* (Notre Dame, Ind./London: University of Notre Dame, 1991), p. 45.

awareness that Yhwh is the supreme and lordly God who lays down the law for humanity and needs to be taken seriously in this connection. Whereas "the idea of mystic union with God is alien to biblical thought,"[3] Yhwh is "a God who commands . . . and Israel's crucial mode of engagement with Yahweh is by obedience."[4] "To the modern mind, religion is a state of the soul, inwardness; feeling rather than obedience. . . . To Judaism, religion is not a feeling for something that is, but *an answer* to Him who is asking us to live in a certain way. . . . 'God asks for the heart,' " but also for the life.[5]

Deferring to Yhwh

Life is to be lived in accordance with what God says. The Torah starts with that assumption in portraying God laying the law down for the first human beings, in Genesis 1 and Genesis 2. At the Beginning, humanity was to serve Yhwh by serving creation.[6] In the garden that people were to serve, one fruit tree was forbidden to them, a sacramental tree that could convey wisdom, the capacity to discern the difference between good and bad. The First Testament subsequently makes clear that Yhwh intends humanity to have such wisdom and capacity, and given that such gifts are especially important for rulers and that humanity is to rule the world on God's behalf, it is weird that Yhwh imposes this prohibition. As the serpent says, the sacramental tree conveys its gifts as people eat its fruit, even when Yhwh forbids them to do so (Gen 3:5, 22); the very act of eating is their deciding on what is good and what is bad. But the fruit goes rotten in their mouths. Paradoxically, it is also and more truly the case that the tree conveys its gifts through people *not* eating its fruit. Obedient deference to Yhwh is the stance that opens up the way to real wisdom and discernment. Submission involves deference, doing what the master says even when it does not make sense and the master is just testing you.

Adam and Eve's failure does not mean henceforth people no longer face the choice between submission and rebellion, or are not responsible for making that choice. Yhwh tells Cain that it is up to him to "do what is good" (the verb related to "good" in Gen 3) and to "rule over" the moral and religious failure that is at his door, where it lies in repose (but waiting to pounce?) rather in the manner of the serpent in the orchard (Gen 4:7). Yet Genesis also implies that there is a certain inevitability about how people make their choices. Humanity's behavior speedily and comprehensively deteriorates as

---

[3]Yehezkel Kaufmann, *The Religion of Israel* (Chicago: University of Chicago Press, 1960/London: George Allen, 1961), p. 77 ("biblical" refers to the Jewish Scriptures).
[4]Walter Brueggemann, *Theology of the Old Testament* (Minneapolis: Fortress, 1997), p. 181.
[5]Abraham Joshua Heschel, *God in Search of Man* (New York: Farrar, Strauss & Giroux, 1976), p. 293, quoting *b. Sanhedrin* 106b, which itself refers to 1 Sam 16:7.
[6]See §6.3 "Serving God's World."

the story unfolds. Even the people who best submit to Yhwh, such as Abraham, Moses and David, are flawed, men who fall short of Yhwh's standards (women such as Ruth and Esther do rather better).

When Adam and Eve have become people who refuse submission to Yhwh, it is important that they not be allowed to eat of the other sacramental tree and live forever in their wayward state. They are thus barred from the orchard and have to accept their mortality. We cannot force our way back into the orchard. We serve the ground outside it.

When starting again, in Genesis 12, Yhwh bids "Go," and Abraham goes, "as Yhwh told him" (Gen 12:4). This means leaving his family (though not Lot and his very substantial household and his resources) and leaving his homeland, though it is not clear how this is significant. Perhaps for him it is also a test of obedience. But he also keeps his distance from his neighbors in his new land. He will accept no goods from them; "you shall not say, 'I am the one who made Abram rich' " (Gen 14:23). Abraham's story is framed by accounts of obedience. If Genesis 12 is one extraordinary such act, raising questions about how Abraham knew this was Yhwh's bidding, then the twin story in Genesis 22 is exponentially extraordinary and hugely magnifies those questions. Here the divine bidding is explicitly a test. It establishes that Abraham really does revere God (Gen 22:12).

Notwithstanding the way these acts of obedience frame his story, Abraham is indeed no paragon of virtue. The occurrence of a famine is another test; Abraham leaves the land for Egypt where there is food, but there he lies about Sarah's status to save his skin, with the result that the Pharaoh takes her into his harem, and Yhwh afflicts him for her sake; though everything turns out all right (and Abram does not decline to be made rich by the Pharaoh). It is hard to say exactly when Abraham went wrong; he found himself making a series of decisions that seemed all right at first but ended up all wrong. Something similar follows in Genesis 16 and Genesis 20, and there is even some ambiguity within the coda to the main part of his story in Genesis 23–25. Has Abraham any business buying land in the country Yhwh has promised to give?

Yhwh's servant "takes warning" from Yhwh's teaching, declarations, charges, command, instruction about reverence, and decisions (Ps 19:11 [MT 12]), the way people take warning from a lookout (cf. Ezek 33:1-6). In other words, among other things Yhwh's teaching warns of the consequences of a life lived other than Yhwh's way, and the wise person therefore heeds it. To put it positively (Ps 19:7-9 [MT 8-10]), this teaching is characterized by integrity, reliability, uprightness, cleanness, purity and truthfulness. Heeding it therefore turns us into people with those qualities. To these people it restores life, gives insight, joys the heart and lights up the eyes; it is altogether faithful and it stands forever.

Acknowledging Yhwh

Such heeding involves acknowledging Yhwh; faithlessness involves declining to do that. The verb *yāda'* covers the meaning of the English verb *know*, referring to knowing facts and knowing people in a personal way. But it also covers the verbs *acknowledge* or *recognize*.[7] Domestic animals acknowledge their master, Yhwh observes, but "Israel does not acknowledge, my people does not pay attention" (Is 1:3). Israel is a gang of adulterers, betrayers and liars who "have advanced from evil to evil and do not acknowledge me" (Jer 9:2-3 [MT 1-2]). Without commenting on the nature of the link, Jeremiah moves seamlessly from unfaithfulness to Yhwh to unfaithfulness within the community, only to revert to the former in saying "they do not acknowledge me." He then repeats this move, spelling out the implications of the unfaithfulness to one another as meaning no one can afford to trust anyone else, and after this reverting once more to "they refuse to acknowledge me" (Jer 9:4-6 [MT 3-5]).

Hosea speaks in similar terms. The commitment to Yhwh *(ḥesed)* that Israel made at the beginning of their relationship, which was so short-lived, can also be spoken of as acknowledgment of Yhwh, something that would express itself in living by Yhwh's standards (Hos 6:4, 6). In the absence of this acknowledgment, worship is pointless. And the people are ruined because of a lack of this acknowledgment (Hos 4:6). Hosea's words point to a personal involvement by Yhwh, who speaks not just of "the people" or "this people" but of "my people," those of whom Yhwh has said "Not-my-people" (Hos 1:9-10 [MT 1:9–2:1]) but intends again to say "My-people" (Hos 2:1, 23 [MT 3, 25]). At the moment, Yhwh has to say "my people are ruined," and there is a sense of grief about the *my*. It is a kind of lament. But there is also a sense of affront. It is a kind of protest. This people that belonged to Yhwh and was designed to serve and glorify Yhwh is just a useless ruin. And that has come about because of a lack of acknowledgment. Traditionally EVV have "lack of knowledge," but the problem is not that no one has told the people that Yhwh is the real God or told them that Yhwh requires faithfulness and compassion to characterize their life. The problem is that they do not acknowledge that this is so by making it so in their lives (JPSV renders "because of disobedience"). The context suggests a reference to acknowledgment of God (Hos 4:1), and *da'at* is regularly used absolutely, as here, without our being told the object of this acknowledgment (cf. Is 5:13; 53:11), in the way we can use the word *obedience* and with similar meaning.

---

[7]It is also used of sexual intercourse, without implying that it then refers to a deep personal way of knowing someone, since it is used of quite casual sexual encounters; it is simply a euphemism.

"I am Yhwh, your God since the land of Egypt: you could acknowledge no God apart from me; there was no deliverer but me." That would be a response to Yhwh's attitude: "I myself acknowledged you in the wilderness." Yhwh's acknowledgment, too, received practical expression; Yhwh looked after them. But in a green land where the people did not have the same needs, "they put me out of mind" (Hos 13:4-6). Acknowledging Yhwh alone in Egypt and in the wilderness was one thing; it was clear enough that they had no other deliverer. Doing that in Canaan was a different matter. At some level they likely still acknowledge those facts (they may still be emotionally moved by them and still worship Yhwh in these terms), but they do not acknowledge them in their lives. Either they have recourse to other gods to get their needs met, or they follow the human inclination to congratulate oneself when things go well and assume that one has the capacity to make sure that they continue to do so. One can thus put God out of mind rather than reckon that one needs to keep God in mind. "They did not acknowledge that I healed them" (Hos 11:3). Deuteronomy 8:11-20 offers a longer version of a critique like this.

The scholarly, after all, can exult in their insight, the strong in their strength, and the rich in their wealth, but if they are to be realistic, "people who exult (*hālal* hitpael) must exult in this, in having the insight to acknowledge me, that I am Yhwh, one who acts with commitment, with decisive faithfulness (*mišpāṭ ûṣĕdāqâ*) in the world, because in these things I delight" (Jer 9:23-24 [MT 22-23]). Insight, strength and riches are good gifts of Yhwh until they become diversions from or alternatives to the acknowledgment of Yhwh. The first three forms of exulting have forgotten that these things are gifts from Yhwh, so that they beguile us into exulting in the gift and putting the giver out of mind. Exulting has Yhwh alone as its proper basis. When we exult in things such as insight, strength or riches, these become good things in their own right and they sideline moral issues such as questions of commitment and decisive faithfulness. Acknowledging Yhwh involves recognizing Yhwh's inherently moral character and thus shaping one's own life by commitment and decisive faithfulness. Thus when Jeremiah comments on Josiah's acting with *mišpāṭ ûṣĕdāqâ* and exercising authority on behalf of the lowly and needy, he adds that this is what constitutes acknowledging Yhwh (Jer 22:15-16).[8] When John Calvin's Geneva Catechism declares that the chief end of human life is to know God, it goes on to make clear that this knowing consists in acknowledging, by obeying God's will.[9]

---

[8]Cf. Gustavo Gutiérrez, *A Theology of Liberation* (Maryknoll, N.Y.: Orbis, 1973/London: SCM Press, 1974), pp. 194-96.

[9]Nicholas Wolterstorff, *Until Justice and Peace Embrace* (Grand Rapids: Eerdmans, 1983), pp. 13-14.

Walking Yhwh's Way

Acknowledging Yhwh's decisive faithfulness implies imitating it; in other words, it implies keeping Yhwh's way (Gen 18:19). Keeping Yhwh's way can have at least two different implications.

One is that Yhwh has the right or authority or power to lay a way before humanity, and in particular to lay down requirements of Israel, simply because of being God. Moses' job was to "enjoin upon them the laws and the teachings and make known to them the way they are to walk in and the deeds they are to do" (Ex 18:20; cf. Deut 5:32-33 [MT 29-30]). Joshua and Samuel do the same (Josh 22:5; 1 Sam 12:23). Yhwh's way or the way of the faithful person is set over against the way of the wicked person (Ps 1), and the people need to stick (dābaq) to Yhwh's way and avoid temptations to leave it (Deut 13:4 [MT 5]). Sticking to Yhwh is the center of obedience to Yhwh's requirements (Deut 4:1-4), and following Yhwh's way implies following Yhwh as opposed to following other deities (e.g., Judg 2:22). The wisdom and the faithfulness or rightness of Yhwh's requirements then expresses itself in their mediating a relationship with a God who is always near to Israel (Deut 4:5-8). The trouble is, the people soon turn aside from this way (Ex 32:8; Deut 9:12, 16; Judg 2:17) and instead travel a stubborn way (Judg 2:19). "This is the way; walk in it," says the voice behind us (Is 30:21). "I am Yhwh your God, one who teaches you to succeed, directs you in the way you should go. If only you had attended to my commands. Then your well-being would have been like a river" (Is 48:17-18).

"I am Yhwh" is the declaration attached to many requirements in the Torah (e.g., Lev 19:12, 14, 16, 18, 28, 30, 32, 37). To nuance this, "I am Yhwh your God" or "I Yhwh am your God" (e.g., Lev 19:4, 10, 25, 31, 34). To nuance it further, "I am Yhwh your God who brought you out of the land of Egypt" (Lev 19:36); "to be your God" (Lev 22:33 adds). The Decalogue nuances it yet further: "I am Yhwh your God who brought you out of the land of Egypt, out of the household of servants" (Ex 20:2). All these formulations explain why Yhwh has authority over Israel. Yhwh's way is the way Israel is obliged to walk because Yhwh says so. Your obedience to Yhwh is an expression of reverence for your God (Lev 19:14, 32). "You shall observe all my laws and all my decisions, and do them; I am Yhwh" (Lev 19:37).

So Leviticus 19 closes. But its list of commands opens with "you shall be holy, because I, Yhwh your God, am holy" (Lev 19:2). Yhwh's moral imperatives are not merely demands written into human awareness at creation or laws imposed on Israel, and walking in Yhwh's way is not only a matter of walking in the way Yhwh points to. It is a matter of walking in the way Yhwh walks. The context of Genesis 18:19 points to that idea, as Abraham's subsequent pressing of Yhwh over the destruction of Sodom keeps coming back to questions about faithful people (*ṣaddîqîm*) and about Yhwh's decision-making (*mišpāṭ*). The *ṣĕdāqâ ûmišpāṭ* to which Abraham calls Yhwh is the *ṣĕdāqâ ûmišpāṭ* to which Yhwh calls Abraham. Israel's life is to imitate Yhwh's.[10] Indeed, Abraham J. Heschel declares, "the Torah is primarily *divine ways* rather than *divine laws*."[11] It reveals God's ways so that we may walk in them. It is because Yhwh spent six days creating the world and then rested that Israel is to shape its life in that way (Ex 20:8-11). "Yahweh, who comes to his people, wishes to have his nature reflected in theirs."[12] This will also mean that Israel manifests the distinctiveness suggested by the idea of holiness.

From Leviticus 19:2 one might therefore look back over Genesis 1 through Leviticus 18, ask how Yhwh's deity spells itself out, and ask how that comes to be replicated in Israel's life. A theme that continues to be embodied in Israel's story is that Yhwh is one who keeps carrying Israel's wrongdoing and continues to keep Israel in being, yet who disciplines Israel for that wrongdoing. Yhwh's holiness is embodied in the exercise of a decisive faithfulness that can work against Israel (Is 5:16), but also in an inability to cast Israel off (Hos 11:8-9). Israel's calling to be Godlike will then involve confronting and disciplining people when they are in the wrong, but in such a way that they can find cleansing and restoration to their place in the community.

Following Yhwh

In the First Testament and in twenty-first-century Western spirituality, the image of life as a journey is prominent, but the image has quite different significance in the two contexts. Western spirituality emphasizes that each of us is on our individual journey. Further, the journey is largely one we are undertaking inside our heads (our hearts or spirits, we may prefer to say). The emphasis of First Testament spirituality (taken up by the New Testament) is that Yhwh has laid out a moral path or track before Israel within whose parameters we are all to walk. This walk does involve the mind or heart or spirit, but it more obviously involves the feet (and hands and mouth), because a walk is something visible and outward. Letting our thinking develop in ways that are authentic to us is not enough, though it is also not enough to be outwardly walking Yhwh's way but inwardly or privately worshiping other gods or plotting trouble for people. The question is whether we are letting our lives de-

---

[10]See Eryl W. Davies, "Walking in God's Ways," in *In Search of True Wisdom*, R. E. Clements Festschrift, JSOTSup 300, ed. Edward Ball (Sheffield, U.K.: Sheffield Academic Press, 1999), pp. 99-115. Cyril S. Rodd may be right that Davies exaggerates the significance of this motif, though not to the extent that Rodd suggests (*Glimpses of a Strange Land* [London: T & T Clark, 2001], pp. 65-76).

[11]Abraham J. Heschel, *God in Search of Man* (New York: Farrar, 1986), p. 288.

[12]Walther Zimmerli, *Old Testament Theology in Outline* (Atlanta: Knox/Edinburgh: T & T Clark, 1978), p. 142. See further §6.1.

velop in ways that correspond to where Yhwh points. What counts is not the distinctive journey that I make as an individual, finding out who I am and making my distinctive personal contribution to the achievement of Yhwh's purpose; indeed, looking for my own way is likely to mean finding it is the way to death rather than the way to life (Prov 14:12; 16:2, 9, 25; 21:2; Is 66:3; Jer 21:8). What counts is whether I am walking in Yhwh's way with other people who are also committed to that way. We walk after or follow Yhwh like an army following its king as it advances to battle or follows the standards with the divine symbols that symbolize the divine presence.[13]

The "way" can as easily be referred to as plural "ways" (e.g., Deut 8:6; 10:12; 11:22; 26:17; 28:9; 30:16). There is a unity and coherence about this way; it is not merely a collection of disparate individual commands. But it also has concreteness and specificity; it does not stop at "love God and do what you like." I walk in the way (singular) of good people and keep to the paths (plural) of faithful people (Prov 2:20). Both the unity and coherence of the one way and the specificity of its detailed requirements help to keep me on the straight and narrow. So I need to pay attention to it. Yhwh's way has integrity (Ps 18:30 [MT 31]); it involves taking action in faithfulness, mišpāṭ ûṣĕdāqâ. All Yhwh's deeds and ways involve making decisions that have integrity (Deut 32:4); all Yhwh's paths are commitment and steadfastness (Ps 25:10).

The image of the way recurs in Psalm 119. It starts by commenting on "the good fortune of people of integrity in their way of life, who walk in Yhwh's teaching" and thus "in his ways." They want their ways to be "firm in keeping your laws." They have "rejoiced in the way of your declarations as over all wealth." Walking in Yhwh's way is not a grin-and-bear-it kind of obedience but a walk characterized by enthusiasm, a walk we enjoy more than accumulating all the wealth in the world. Enthusiasm will take us further down this road than mere duty does. But one reason this is possible is that Yhwh's ways or the ways of Ms. Wisdom are lovely or delightful and full of *shalom*, whereas the way of the faithless is total darkness and makes people fall over (Prov 3:17; 4:19; cf. 8:32; 9:6; 10:29; 12:28). " 'Follow me,' . . . is a phenomenon which is absolutely terrifying in its impossibility. It provokes the question of the disciples: 'Who then can be saved?' " But " 'he that followeth me shall not walk in darkness, but shall have the light of life' (Jn. 8[12])."[14]

"I have kept your orders and your declarations, because all my ways are before you" (Ps 119:168). All our ways being before Yhwh might be bad news, but it might be good news because it means Yhwh watches over us and knows

---

[13]Cf. Deryck Sheriffs, *The Friendship of the Lord* (Carlisle, U.K.: Paternoster, 1996), pp. 100-102.

[14]Karl Barth, *Church Dogmatics* (Edinburgh: T & T Clark, 1967), IV/2:535, 537.

all that happens to us. In speaking of walking Yhwh's way, Psalm 119 emphasizes that our life is lived in light of Yhwh's commands and Yhwh's promises. The psalm has a range of words by which to refer to Yhwh's word, such as teaching, word and declaration, and most are capable of referring both to commands and to promises. That itself may be theologically suggestive. It corresponds to the fact that there is a built-in link between commands and promises, though a covenantal and intrinsic one, not a legal, contractual one. Behavior has promises attached to it that correspond to the links between exercise and good health, or love and having good friends, or openness and the deepening of relationship. Both the commands and the promises reflect who Yhwh is, what Yhwh wants and the way Yhwh has made the world.

Living in Light of God's Act of Deliverance

As well as linking God's expectations of Israel with Yhwh's authority as God, the Decalogue links these with God's act of deliverance. "I brought you out of Egypt; here are some key implications in connection with how you must now live" is the implication of Exodus 20:2 as its introduction.

Yhwh's first expectation in this connection is that there should be no other gods for Israel before Yhwh or besides Yhwh or over against Yhwh (Ex 20:3). The expression ʿal-pānāy (besides my face? against my face?) is allusive, but clearly enough the command expects Israel not to allow Yhwh's position to be rivaled by that of any other deity, because Yhwh took Israel out of the situation of servitude to Pharaoh that it was in. Alongside the allusiveness of that expression, the use of the "colorless and neutral" verb hāyâ is also strange, as is the failure to prohibit or demand a specific act in the manner of the succeeding commands (contrast Ex 34:14). Yet the verse formulates the "ultimate distillation of a fundamental principle."[15] The command is not concerned with mere monotheism; its aim is not merely to limit the number of entities the people regard as God. It is concerned with the identity of the one they regard as God. Being delivered by Yhwh from servitude should make them keen to acknowledge Yhwh alone.

Indeed, Yhwh had acted to remove them forcibly from the service of Pharaoh precisely so that they could enter the service of Yhwh, and acknowledging Yhwh alone is the first way they will do that. Exodus as a whole is arguably "the story of the first commandment"; it expounds the meaning and the rationale for the first commandment in telling how Israel was taken from the service of Pharaoh to the service of Yhwh.[16] The motif of servitude or service recurs in the Decalogue. One implication of Yhwh's act is that Israel must not

---

[15]Zimmerli, *Old Testament Theology in Outline*, p. 116.
[16]Patrick D. Miller, *The Way of the Lord* (Grand Rapids/Cambridge: Eerdmans, 2007), pp. 68-79. Miller sees the meaning and the story continued in Joshua (pp. 80-90).

enter into the servitude of other gods or images (Ex 20:5).[17] To enter any other form of servitude is to deny the nature of what Yhwh did. Its liberation from servitude in Egypt does not mean it is free to do as it likes. It is not free to serve other gods. It is free and bound now to bind itself to Yhwh. In leaving the service of Egypt it entered not its own service but the service of Yhwh. The demand for exclusive allegiance is "Yahweh's primal command."[18] Our relationship with God is not just one of privilege but one of bondage.[19]

The point is taken further in the Deuteronomic version of the sabbath command, which underlines the need to make sure that servants rest on the sabbath. If their masters are inclined to forget this, they should recall the fact that *they* were servants and that Yhwh rescued them from their servitude. That shows the nature of Yhwh's priorities. Nor are they free to look after themselves rather than their parents, or to love whom they like, or to take what they like, or even to feel what they like. The requirements that follow up the Decalogue in Exodus 20–23 only rarely articulate their underlying principle or rationale, but the clearest way they do so is by appealing to Israel's experience of being aliens in Egypt (Ex 22:21 [MT 20]; 23:9).

One basis for the nature of Israel's life, then, lies in the specifics of its story. The account of the deeds whereby Yhwh delivered Israel reaches its goal when it pushes Israel into obedience to Yhwh.[20] The gold calf story (Ex 32:1-6) illustrates the first three expectations in the Decalogue, and perhaps the fourth. Israel determines to have gods to lead it on, manufactures an image and makes offerings to it, holds this celebration on a special day, and calls it a festival in honor of Yhwh.[21] The festivals and other rites that the Torah commissions indicate the proper relation of worship to that story and keep bringing it home to people. Its family life reminds people of it. Sharing in this story is what binds it as a community; it is, indeed, what constitutes it as a community.

Other Middle-Eastern "law codes" may open and close by referring to a god, but the First Testament is distinctive for the systematic way it sees the Torah as an expression of God's will, so that any breach of it is an offense against God. Connected with this is the fact that its distinctiveness often lies not so much in its content (most societies disapprove of murder, adultery and

---

[17]The relationship of vv. 5-6 to vv. 3-4 is one of the factors in deciding how the sentences add up to ten. I take vv. 5-6 to underline the implications of both the command in v. 3 and that in v. 4.

[18]Brueggemann, *Theology of the Old Testament*, p. 183.

[19]Walter Harrelson, *The Ten Commandments and Human Rights* (Philadelphia: Fortress, 1980), pp. 173-81.

[20]Cf. Jon D. Levenson, *Sinai and Zion* (Minneapolis: Winston, 1985), p. 45.

[21]See Calum M. Carmichael, *The Spirit of Biblical Law* (Athens/London: University of Georgia, 1996), pp. 86-92. Carmichael argues that the first four commands in the Decalogue were crafted in light of this story.

theft) but in the way it links moral precepts with religious commands.[22] It is not possible to focus on religious observance and avoid moral commitment, or focus on social justice and avoid worship. "Israel's work of obedience is to bring every aspect of its life under the direct rule of Yahweh."[23]

When the New Testament expects an implausibly demanding lifestyle of the Christian community on the basis of the fact that in Jesus God has come to reign,[24] it is taking up the First Testament's stance. Israel knows that God has come to reign in the story of the exodus and the Red Sea deliverance. The First Testament already expects an implausibly demanding lifestyle of the Israelite community. Neither the First Testament nor the New Testament sees its expectations realized, but both know that there is a power in the events their story tells that makes it possible to be sure they will be realized, and both thus continue to issue their challenge to their communities to make them reality.

Responding in Covenant

The same understanding may be expressed by portraying the framework for Israel's life as its covenant relationship with Yhwh. That relationship starts from Yhwh's making promises and keeping them, but it reaches fulfillment only when Israel lives in covenant with Yhwh.

The priority of Yhwh's promises and Yhwh's acts is emphasized by the story of the covenant. Its prehistory is the covenant with Noah. (There is no covenant with Adam, perhaps because a covenant becomes necessary only to link parties that do not have a natural relationship; before disobedience entered in, there was a "natural" relationship.) The story of Yhwh's covenant with a particular people begins with Yhwh making promises to Abraham concerning his coming into possession of a land and becoming a great family.

In these promises there is some ambiguity about the relationship between divine initiative and human commitment. The Noah covenant (Gen 9:8-17) is an unearned gift to humanity, but it is prefaced by some declarations about what humanity is to do (Gen 9:1-7). God does not say that the covenant will hold only if the commands are fulfilled, but God does rule out the idea that the human response to God counts for nothing. The first Abraham covenant (Gen 15:1-6), as Paul points out (Rom 4), is pure gift; there are no prior conditions and no subsequent demands. The second

---

[22]Walther Eichrodt, *Theology of the Old Testament* (London: SCM Press/Philadelphia: Westminster, 1961), 1:74-77.

[23]Brueggemann, *Theology of the Old Testament*, p. 183.

[24]Robin Scroggs notes how a series of scholars emphasize the link of eschatology and ethics in the New Testament ("The New Testament and Ethics," *Perspectives in Religious Studies* 11 [1984]: 77-93).

Abraham covenant also comes into being purely because of a divine initiative (Gen 17:1-22), but like the Noah covenant it is preceded by a challenge to Abraham to walk before Yhwh and be wholly committed. Further, like the Noah covenant, it has a sign attached to it, but this time it is a sign that the recipients of the covenant have to implement, and if they fail to do this, they will lose their place in the covenant people.

The ambiguous relationship between divine act and human commitment finds new expression as Israel arrives at Sinai. Yhwh has brought Israel out of Egypt and thus gone half way to fulfilling the covenant undertaking reiterated to Moses (Ex 6:2-8). It is quite clear that Israel has been treated as "Yhwh's people." Yhwh took the initiative in bringing Israel out of Egypt. The initiative of action is then followed up by an initiative of speech: Yhwh says, "You have seen what I did to the Egyptians. . . . Now if you will really listen to my voice and keep my covenant . . ." And Israel responds, "All that Yhwh has spoken we will do" (Ex 19:4-8), and makes this commitment before knowing what Yhwh's expectations are. The Talmud reports a Sadducee pointing out that this was rash; they should surely have listened to the commands first.[25] Israel does know the sort of person Yhwh is, and that carries implications for the kind of expectations Yhwh is likely to make. Yet Israel does not actually know what they are, and in this sense the narrative points to a *"precedence of faith over knowledge"*; as in marriage, we do not explore first and decide afterward, but accept in order to be able to explore.[26]

Yhwh does not here tell Israel it must respond, like the head of a superpower dictating the terms of a treaty relationship with an underling.[27] But nor does Yhwh invite Israel to make a choice about whom it will serve, implying that there are several possibilities, as Joshua will (Josh 24). Nor does Yhwh suggest that Israel has to decide whether or not to obey Yhwh. Such obedience is the morally and theologically necessary and inevitable response to what Yhwh has done, but Israel has to make this response (compare the argument of Rom 6).

There are other covenants where the relationship between divine and human initiative is reversed. In bringing about a coup to dethrone Athaliah, the priest Jehoiada sealed a covenant between himself, the people and the new king that they would be a people of Yhwh (2 Chron 23:16).[28] In the Chronicles

---

[25]*B. Shabbat* 88a.

[26]Heschel, *God in Search of Man*, pp. 81, 82.

[27]Cf. John I. Durham, *Exodus*, WBC (Waco, Tex.: Word, 1987), p. 262; though he goes on to compare Ex 19 with Josh 24, whereas I go on to contrast them.

[28]Literally in this standard expression for making a covenant, he "cut" it: the image likely comes from the nature of a rite like that described in Gen 15:8-21, which could be involved in making a covenant.

version of the story, this is a very rare instance of a covenant that is primarily made between people; only in the version in 2 Kings 11:17 is Yhwh one of the parties to the covenant. But a commitment to Yhwh is the point about the covenant. Likewise Josiah leads his people in sealing a covenant before Yhwh and in standing by the covenant, though that is a response to discovering the contents of the covenant scroll (2 Kings 23:1-3). On Ezra's arrival in Jerusalem, when the matter of intermarriage is brought up, Shecaniah ben Jehiel proposes the sealing of a covenant with Yhwh to eject the foreign women and their children (Ezra 10:1-3). In Nehemiah 9:38–10:39 [MT 10:1-40] the people seal a broader pledge (*'ămānâ*). In each case the people are reaching out to Yhwh with a commitment in the hope that Yhwh will accept it and will respond, but only in the act of making the commitment will they discover whether this is so.

Keeping Commitment

The ambiguity of the relation between divine act and human obedience continues through the First Testament and into the New Testament. This does not reflect unclear thinking on the part of the biblical authors; rather the opposite. It reflects the fact that the relationship is a covenant, not a contract. In a contract the nature and the limits of a mutual commitment are precisely clear. Each party performs in specified ways on condition that the other party performs in its specified ways. Contracts are designed to eliminate ambiguity, trust and risk, and their usefulness lies in their success in doing so. But contracts are no basis for person-to-person relationships such as marriage. There, two people commit themselves unreservedly to one another, and do this on the assumption that both of them are doing so, yet it would be misleading to picture one person as thinking, "I make this commitment only on condition that you reciprocate it." Both make their commitment as an act of trust and risk. The other person's commitment is absolutely necessary to this covenant working, but it is not exactly a condition of its working.[29] Analogously, Israel's living by Yhwh's instructions is essential to the covenant working, without exactly being a condition of its working.

It is easy for Christian faith to be legalistic, and in this connection talk of obedience is dangerous. Alternatively, it is easy for Christian faith to assimilate to the culture and in a Western context to reckon that our vocation is to "be ourselves," to live out the potential of what God made us to be, and to reckon that it would be inauthentic and legalistic to submit ourselves to rules. Either stance loses the dynamic of covenant in which submission to God is

---

[29]On the notion of commitment, see Lewis B. Smedes, "The Making and Keeping of Commitments," in *Seeking Understanding: The Stob Lectures, 1986–1998* (Grand Rapids/Cambridge: Eerdmans, 2001), pp. 43-76.

our personal response to God's personal reaching out to us.[30] God's relationship with us is neither conditional nor unconditional. It involves willing mutual commitment, like that of two friends or bride and groom or teacher and student or pastor and congregation.

The word *commitment* is a common feature of Christian parlance; it is odd that the word does not come in English translations of the Bible. It is in fact the equivalent English word to the Hebrew word *ḥesed*, commonly translated "steadfast love" or "constant love"; the New Testament's equivalent is *agapē* when that is used in its full theological sense. Yet significantly, *ḥesed* is only rarely used of our commitment to God, and even then it carries some irony. I do look for this kind of commitment from you, says Yhwh, but actually your commitment is like the marine layer that burns off without depositing any rain (Hos 6:4, 6). Only centuries ago was your commitment a reality (Jer 2:2).

On the other hand, the statistics for *ḥāsîd* are the reverse. It is rarely used to denote Yhwh as committed to us, but often used to describe us as people committed to Yhwh. It is the ultimate courtesy title, a First Testament equivalent to "saints" when used to describe the position of all who believe in Christ. "Sing to Yhwh, people committed to him" (Ps 30:4 [MT 5]). "The people committed to you resound" (Ps. 132:9). "Love Yhwh, people committed to him" (Ps 31:23 [MT 24]): the psalm is inviting people to become what they are or to give expression to who they are. In later times the Hasidim are the people within Israel who seek to be especially committed to God and Torah, and are enthusiastic in their attitude in this commitment; but the word denotes the vocation of all Israel.

Loving Yhwh

Hosea, indeed, emphasizes the marriage-like nature of the relationship of Yhwh and Israel. Deuteronomy, too, talks much about love, though it does not refer to the relationship between Yhwh and Israel in marriage terms. Whereas "if God were a theory, the study of theology would be the way to understand Him," love is the way you get to know a person.[31] "Listen, Israel: Yhwh our God Yhwh one,[32] and you are to love Yhwh your God with all your heart and with all your spirit and with all your might" (Deut 6:5). The Jewish people take this as Yhwh's most fundamental expectation, and Jesus sees it as the first of the two commands on which the rest of the Torah hangs (Mk 12:29-31).

---

[30]See, e.g., Walter Brueggemann, *The Covenanted Self* (Minneapolis: Fortress, 1999), pp. 35-38; *Theology of the Old Testament*, pp. 198-201.

[31]Heschel, *God in Search of Man*, p. 281.

[32]We do not know where to put the "is" (maybe more than one) in this noun clause; see NRSV and its mg for four guesses.

What kind of love does Moses commission? The verb *ʾāhēb* is the First Testament's all-purpose word for affection, liking, friendliness, passion, ardor, infatuation, enthusiasm, devotion, caring and dedication. Lovers are personal friends, sexual partners and religious devotees. Isaac loves Rebekah, Esau and stew (Gen 24:67; 25:28; 27:4). The Psalms speak of loving violence, faithfulness, the temple, Yhwh's deliverance, cursing and words that consume (Ps 11:5, 7; 26:8; 40:16 [MT 17]; 52:4 [MT 6]; 109:17). But they speak especially of loving Yhwh's commands, teaching, declarations and precepts (Ps 119:47, 48, 97, 113, 119, 159).

The broad and narrow context suggests that Deuteronomy's "love" expresses itself at least as much in doing what the Torah says as in feeling fervent about it. The commission to love is set in the context of exhortation to keep Yhwh's instructions, laws and commands (Deut 6:1-3, 16-25; cf. 10:12-13; 11:1, 13, 22). The qualifiers "with heart, spirit, and might" tally with that. All the people's energy is to go into their obedience. Jesus' observation, "If you love me, you will keep my commands" (Jn 14:15) coheres with the Torah. Loving Yhwh's commands and precepts means dedicating oneself to them and doing what they say.

Deuteronomy thus assumes that love can be commanded, and it sees love as expressed in service and obedience. Its love recalls Hiram's love for David as much as Hosea's for Gomer (1 Kings 5:1 [MT 15]). Love is the language of diplomacy in the Middle East, suggesting the commitment of kings to one another.[33] Nations entering into treaty alliances spoke in terms of a relationship of love. Such covenant relationships imply mutual commitment and loyalty; so does the relationship between Israel and Yhwh. Yhwh *is* like the head of a superpower dictating the terms of a relationship with an underling, and Israel is the underling who sees it would be wise to accept them. The relationship of covenant commitment between Yhwh and Israel is thus mutual but hierarchical. One party is the beneficent giver who then lays down expectations that relate to this giving, and the other party is first the recipient of this beneficence, but then the one who keeps the terms of the covenant (e.g., Jer 11:1-5). Keeping Yhwh's covenant means doing what Yhwh laid down as the covenant terms (e.g., Gen 17:9; Ex 19:5) as opposed to breaking it.

Neither Testament invites us into a relationship with God in which we are buddies or lovers. Western Christian piety is fond of telling God "We love you," but the First Testament never makes quite such a statement, at least using the regular word for love, *ʾāhēb*. The NRSV and TNIV begin Psalm 18 "I love you, O LORD." But the verb is *rāḥam*, which elsewhere always comes in the piel

---

[33]Cf. William L. Moran, "The Ancient Near Eastern Background of the Love of God in Deuteronomy," *CBQ* 25 (1963): 77-87.

and means "have compassion," though in Aramaic it has similar meaning to
ʾāhēb and it seems likely to be an Aramaism here and to suggest commitment
more than affection or intimacy.[34] EVV begin Psalm 116 "I love the LORD"; here
the verb is ʾāhēb, but the translation involves some paraphrase. More literally
the psalm begins, "I love, because Yhwh hears my voice." Yhwh must be the
object of this love (though the phraseology could hint at love that extends to
other people as well), but the psalm does not actually say "I love Yhwh."

While Hosea speaks of Yhwh's love for Israel as like that of a husband for
a wife or a father or mother for a child, and speaks of the people's love for
other deities, he does not speak of Israel's relationship with Yhwh as one of
love. The relationship is one in which God is master and we are servants, or
God is (old-school) husband and we are submissive wife, or God is father and
we are obedient children, or God is king and we are subjects.[35] This does not
mean the relationship is oppressive. None of those relationships need be
domineering or tyrannical. They can be relationships in which the master,
husband, father or king cares for the servant, wife, child or subjects. But they
are not egalitarian relationships.[36] Our response to God as master, husband,
father and king is to recognize that this is who God is, and to live by it.

Delighting in Yhwh

Proper regard for Yhwh's teaching is thus expressed in the practice of obedience, but it also has an affective aspect. This is conveyed by describing it as
more desirable than vast quantities of fine gold and as sweeter than honey—
not regular date honey but the greater delicacy of bee honey (Ps 19:10 [MT 11]).
The trees in God's garden were "desirable," and in the end were more so than
Yhwh's instructions (Gen 2–3); Adam and Eve did not take the view of Yhwh's
teaching expressed in Psalm 19. But living with God means your "pleasure"
lies in Yhwh's teaching; you talk about it all the time (Ps 1:2). The "teaching"
(tôrâ) comprises Genesis-Deuteronomy; applied to these five books as a whole,
"teaching" might have a broad sense, denoting the story the books tell as well
as the instructions built into and onto that story. Living with God then means
taking pleasure in that story, which would not be difficult, given the way it
tells of Yhwh's work as creator, promise-giver, promise-keeper and deliverer,
the person behind the acts that made the people's life what it was. But it also
means taking pleasure in the instructions built into and onto that story. Plea-

---

[34]See HALOT.

[35]Cf. Karl Barth, Church Dogmatics (Edinburgh: T & T Clark, 1970), I/2:272.

[36]Contrast Samuel Balentine, who suggests that the covenant between God and Israel is an
egalitarian relationship. In a Western understanding, the marriage covenant is egalitarian, but covenants are not inherently so (Prayer in the Hebrew Bible [Minneapolis: Fortress,
1993], pp. 41-47).

sure is a more surprising word in this connection, yet one can see it is possible to suggest more than one reason why it is an appropriate feeling. Insofar as Yhwh's instructions are built onto that story, they provide the framework for a delighted response to what Yhwh has done for us. Insofar as they contain built-in promises of the blessing that follows from obedience (as Ps 119 also does), they encourage a delighted response. Insofar as both story and instructions embody the real truth about the world and humanity, and the way to live in the world, an entire alternative worldview that we would never have dreamed up, they encourage a delighted response.

So people take pleasure in Yhwh's deeds and therefore investigate them and study them and seek to learn from them; they delight in Yhwh's commands. This is an expression of their reverence for Yhwh—no revering without delighting, no delighting without revering (Ps 111:2; 112:1; 119:35). Life with God is a life of delight. Of course it is possible to fool oneself about our "pleasure" or "delight" (Is 58:2), and "the churches are tempted to think that they will serve the world well by drafting more and more radical statements. Yet the church's social ethic . . . is first and foremost found in its ability to sustain a people who are not at home in the liberal presumptions of our civilization and society."[37] And this sustaining involves the affective.

To put it Proverbs' way, all the things in the world that you could take pleasure in do not compare with Ms. Wisdom's teaching (Prov 3:15; 8:11); contrast the nondelight of the stupid person (Prov 18:2). "Teaching" is again *tôrâ*, and while much of the content of Ms. Wisdom's *tôrâ* would be the same as that of Genesis-Deuteronomy, they are not coterminous. Likewise the teaching in which Psalm 1 takes its pleasure might not be confined to Genesis-Deuteronomy. Wisdom's teaching, Yhwh's teaching in the Prophets, the five books of teaching in the Psalter itself, all deserve delight. Presenting the Psalter as five books of teaching presupposes that our relationship with God expressed in our praise and prayer is not one in which we simply do what comes naturally. We learn from the Psalms how to praise and pray; and we are of course delighted so to be instructed, because we know we are learning from teaching that will make that relationship work. Again, in our worship we create a world.[38] We declare, for instance, in singing Psalm 95, that Yhwh is the great God and the great King. Against all appearances we affirm that this is the real truth, and re-create for ourselves the reality of that world, then leave worship to live in light of its being the real world. This makes the teaching of the psalm about Yhwh's deserving reverent submission something to delight in.

---

[37]Stanley Hauerwas, *Against the Nations* (Minneapolis: Winston, 1985), pp. 11-12.
[38]Cf. §1.1 "Prayer and Ethics."

A person who takes pleasure in Yhwh's teaching talks about it or recites it or reads it out day and night, all the time (Ps 1:2). The verb, *hāgâ*, is traditionally translated "meditate," which appropriately renders one aspect of the activity involved. It entails letting Yhwh's teaching occupy the mind so that we reflect on it and let it have its way with our own thinking. But the distinctive significance of the verb is that it refers to something that people do out loud. The mouth or tongue is involved in the action denoted by this verb (Ps 35:28; 37:30; 71:24). In other connections it refers to the mourning of doves (Is 38:14; 59:11). Applied to Yhwh's teaching, it suggests taking it on one's lips as one reads, reading it aloud. Thus Yhwh bids Joshua, "This book of teaching must not depart from your *mouth*, but you are to talk about it/recite it/read it out day and night, so that you may take care to act in accordance with everything that is written in it" (Josh 1:8). It thereby comes to occupy not merely the mind but the body. The whole person is committed to the study of Yhwh's teaching, as the whole person is committed to living by it. It is not mere spiritual meditation.

As is the case with delight, the topic of this talk is Yhwh's actions as well as Yhwh's commands (Ps 35:28; 71:24; 77:12-13 [MT 13-14]; 143:5). It is thus the kind of talk that builds up trust and the assurance that Yhwh will answer prayer. Having Yhwh means one wants or takes pleasure in no one or nothing else (Ps 73:25).

Heeding Torah

So Israel's response to Yhwh is expressed in heeding Yhwh's teaching. But, Yhwh laments, "they have not given heed to my words, and my teaching—they have spurned it"; hence disaster will come (Jer 6:19; cf. 26:4-5). Both "Yhwh's teaching" (*tôrâ*) and "Yhwh's words" can refer to the words and teaching of prophets or to those of the Torah or to both, but often the "word" is the business of prophets while the "teaching" is the business of priests (Jer 18:18), and that makes sense in this context. The people are ignoring both their main means of knowing Yhwh's will.

The trouble is that the people who "handle the teaching," perhaps the theologians and interpreters rather than the priests in general, "did not acknowledge me" (Jer 2:8; cf. 8:8). In Jeremiah the "teaching" is usually "my teaching." It is an expression of the relationship between Yhwh and the people, not a cold, objective entity like a law code, though that heightens the enormity of the people's abandoning it instead of walking by it (e.g., Jer 9:13 [MT 12]); in light of this, as usual translating *tôrâ* "law" is misleading. In general the context often indicates that the way the people failed to walk by Yhwh's teaching was not so much by omitting to observe individual requirements of a detailed code but by ignoring the central thrust of this teaching, its concern that people should acknowledge Yhwh and not acknowledge other deities (e.g., Jer 9:13-14 [MT 12-13]; 16:11; 44:8-10). Yhwh's teaching did not make what Christians would call legalistic, or even quasi-legal, demands of people, any more than the words of the prophets did. It looked for a commitment to Yhwh to the exclusion of other deities, and it is this that people declined to give. It is for this reason that a prophet such as Jeremiah can presuppose an identity of concern between Yhwh's teaching and Yhwh's words through a prophet.

To think of ancient Israel as reading Scripture is generally anachronistic, yet the First Testament emphasizes or presupposes something that would be Israel's equivalent to such reading as the means whereby people became acquainted with Torah in such a way as to be able to heed it. Through teaching in the home or in the sanctuary, people got to know the stories of what Yhwh had been doing with Israel over the centuries and the expectations written into the Torah. It is a plausible theory that the setting in which the Decalogue would be declaimed is that of worship, as used to be the case in Christian worship.[39]

Something more like the reading of Scripture begins after the exile. Ezra comes from Babylon bringing the Torah; one has the impression that they do not have a copy in Jerusalem, presumably because only now does it exist in its complete form. In the seventh month, the time of year for the septennial reading prescribed in Deuteronomy 31:10-13, Ezra brings out the Torah scroll and reads from it to the community assembled in Jerusalem (Neh 8). Certain other people and "the Levites" also read from it and explain it to the people, perhaps in groups. The people were inclined to respond with mourning to the reading, apparently because they knew they were not doing what it said. One example concerned the proper observance of Sukkot, the festival of the seventh month, in which they should have been involved. Interestingly, the Levites tell the people they have no business mourning, because this is, after all a holy day! They are to eat and drink and make sure other people can do so, and to rejoice in Yhwh because that is a source of strength. They make their shelters and celebrate the festival for a week, listening to readings from the Torah each day. A further gathering follows (Neh 9) when fasting and solemnity is evidently allowed as people read from the scroll further, confess their shortcomings and the waywardness of their ancestors, but also join in praise for Yhwh's relationship with them over the centuries and draw Yhwh's attention to their current servitude to the Persian imperial power. They commit themselves to walking by Yhwh's teaching in the future (Neh 10) and make specific undertakings that pre-

---

[39]See, e.g., the Holy Communion service in the Church of England *Book of Common Prayer.*

sumably reflect current issues in the community, such as refraining from intermarriage with other communities, keeping the sabbath, observing the sabbath year and providing the practical provisions required by the worship of the temple.

The story perhaps opens a window on the nature of worship in Judah during the Second Temple period, with its stress on listening to the Torah, committing oneself to doing what it says and perceiving where lay its present concrete demands.

Heeding Prophecy

Like Jeremiah, Isaiah declares that Israel was no more inclined to heed prophecy than to heed teaching. "You have rejected the teaching of Yhwh Armies,[40] spurned the word of Israel's holy one" (Is 5:24). Here the parallelism may suggest that *tôrâ* refers to prophetic teaching (that is, Isaiah's own). Isaiah has critiqued the people for the self-indulgence of their lives, made possible by their depriving other people of their rights and their land, and has warned them of the trouble Yhwh therefore intends to bring them (Is 5:8-23). They have ignored everything Yhwh has said through Isaiah. In effect they tell seers not to see and to speak nice things to them even though these are illusory, and they bid them to get out of the way (Is 30:9-11). Isaiah is putting words on people's lips; they do not see themselves as wishing to live by illusions or directly tell prophets to prophesy illusions, but that is the implication of their rejecting Isaiah's message because it is too uncomfortable. Further, there is perhaps more than one level of meaning in the words Isaiah attributes to them. In some sense they acknowledge a prophet such as Isaiah as someone who is leading them along the way set before them as a nation, but in declining to heed his message and asking for a more encouraging one, they are asking him to lead them off the right road onto the wrong one. Wanting to carry on along the road they have identified, they find themselves confronted by Isaiah and the God he allegedly speaks for, declaring that they are treading the wrong road, and they want to get Isaiah and his God out of the way so that they can proceed on the road that they are convinced is right. Yet in bidding Isaiah to get out of their way they are also bidding him to get out of *the* way, out of the right way, out of Yhwh's way.

When Micah speaks of people swindling others out of their land and speaks of the people as a whole being thrown out of their land, understandably there are those who want to silence him and whose attitude has similar implications (Mic 2:6-11). " 'Don't preach,' they preach; 'people should not

---

[40]The more literal meaning of the phrase usually translated "the LORD of Hosts" or "the LORD Almighty."

preach about these things.' " Yhwh is not the kind of God who is short-tempered, as you portray Yhwh. Micah's response is to observe sardonically that the kind of preacher this people needs is "someone with a lying spirit, deceiving" who will preach to them about wine and liquor. One test of prophecy is whether it fits what we know already. People apply that test to Micah and point out that he fails it. Yhwh's classic self-description includes being slow to get angry and abounding in commitment (Ex 34:6). In effect, people say, Micah claims that Yhwh is quick to get angry and attributes to Yhwh the kind of deeds that Yhwh does not do. The trouble is they ignore the second half of that self-description and ignore the moral side to the relationship between Yhwh and Israel. Micah is as concerned about things being good for the people as Moses was (e.g., Ex 33:19; Deut 6:24; 12:28). But that only works for people who live uprightly (e.g., Ex 15:26; Deut 6:17-19; 12:28).

There are no knockdown proofs concerning the truth of a prophecy; people can slant the theological implications of Yhwh's self-revelation in the way that suits them. Micah makes the point by a more pointed moral comment. The reason people want a different preacher from Micah is not their theological acumen. They want a theology that colludes with their dishonesty, and thus they want prophets who are themselves deceived and will deceive the people by encouraging their self-indulgence. A great harvest of grapes and barley and thus a plentiful supply of wine and other drinks was one of God's promises to the people, part of the "good" that a prophet like Micah himself would want to promise (cf. Amos 9:13; Joel 3:18 [MT 4:18]). There is only a hairsbreadth between promising God's blessings in God's way and turning them into self-indulgence.

Perhaps Hosea speaks more literally when he accuses people of saying, "The prophet is a fool, the man of the spirit is crazy" (Hos 9:7). Both "prophet" and "man of the spirit" may be implicitly insulting terms. "Prophesying" involved strange behavior; it could be read as a sign of being under supernatural influence or simply as strange behavior. "Man of the spirit" recalls the expression "man of God,"[41] which has similar implications. Hosea and his ilk are people who behave in odd ways, and the Ephraimites are inclined to see them as just strange people, not people under divine influence. That gets them off the hook of paying attention to the content of their message.

Heeding Warnings

After the fall of Jerusalem, one of Nebuchadnezzar's staff is credited with the realization that "Yhwh your God spoke of this disaster for this place and has brought it about. Yhwh has done as he said, because you failed Yhwh and did

---

[41]Cf. Hans Walter Wolff, *Hosea* (Philadelphia: Fortress, 1974), p. 157.

not listen to his voice. So this thing has happened to you" (Jer 40:2-3). Nebuchadnezzar's Judean appointee over affairs in Judah then urges people to submit to Babylonian authority. Well, he would, wouldn't he? But it is no coincidence that he is telling people to do what Jeremiah had long been telling them. It would be a sign of accepting that Babylonian occupation is a consequence of the people's own resistance to Yhwh's word, and thus of owning their disobedience to Yhwh.

Gedaliah's assassination is conversely a sign of their continuing resistance and disobedience. The point becomes explicit when the Judeans identified with the assassination realize they may have made a mistake and come to Jeremiah to ask him to pray for them and ask what they should do now.

> May Yhwh be a true and trustworthy witness against us if we do not act in accordance with every word that Yhwh your God sends you for us. Whether good or bad, we will listen to the voice of Yhwh our God to whom we are sending you, so that it may go well with us when we listen to the voice of Yhwh our God. (Jer 42:5-6)

If only.

Jeremiah delivers the same old message. Settle down here. Do not be afraid of the Babylonians. Yhwh is with you to protect you. Do not take up the idea of going to Egypt; the sword and famine that you could escape here will follow you there. But the community "did not listen to Yhwh's voice" and set off for Egypt (Jer 43:4-7). They carry on behaving in the manner of the Jerusalem community before the city's fall. They do this in their religious life, too, as they themselves make explicit. Life went well when they served those other gods; it was after Josiah's reform that everything fell apart (Jer 44). This consistency of theirs will mean they experience Yhwh's consistency—and Nebuchadnezzar's. He will continue to be Yhwh's servant and will repeat his action against Jerusalem. Jeremiah makes the point vividly by taking up some words formulated in connection with Jerusalem and reapplying them to Tahpanhes (Jer 43:11). Once again Yhwh is intent on doing ill to the community rather than good (Jer 44:27).

In Yhwh's sequence of declarations in Leviticus 19 the unstated implication of "I am Yhwh" is "and I will take action if you ignore this command." The First Testament is not afraid of threats in case of disobedience and of positive incentives to obedience. Indeed, "the possibility of good conduct unmotivated by the expectation of future benefit is in fact very rare in Old Testament texts. . . . To say that we should be moral, but not for the sake of gaining anything, would have struck [ancient Israelites] as an unrealistic refinement of piety."[42] Thus Leviticus 26:3-13 promises that obedience will mean well-being, Yhwh's face shining on the people, Yhwh walking among the people; "I will be God for you and you—you will be a people for me." And Leviticus 26:14-33 warns that disobedience will mean Yhwh attending to them, Yhwh's face set against them, Yhwh's discipline and destruction imposed on them, Yhwh walking with them in wrath and loathing. The warnings go into greater detail: Rashi comments, "The emptyheaded who remarked (in puzzlement) that the curses are more numerous than the blessings, have not told the truth. The blessings are stated as generalizations whereas the curses are stated in detail in order to frighten the hearers."[43] The combination of promise and warning reappears in the Sermon on the Mount, and there too (at least in Mt 5) more space is given to warnings than to promises.[44] Even if we emphasize the solemn side to the fact that our ways are before Yhwh (Ps 119:168), in a strange way this is still good news, because being watched is an incentive to obedience: Who does not slow down when a police car appears? (cf. Heb 4:13).

The Wisdom books major on incentives, in a distinctive way. Proverbs never tires of assuring its readers that one way the behavior it encourages represents wisdom is that it will issue in blessing. Right living pays. Its assurances should not be absolutized; it implicitly recognizes that its rules work most of the time, not all the time. (If what it says about hard work issuing in having enough to eat were invariably true, it would not need so many exhortations regarding generosity to the poor.) In reckoning that right living generally pays, it is one with the Torah; its distinctive emphasis lies in the conviction that this is so because such linkages are built into the way the world works. A tree naturally produces fruit; right living naturally produces blessing. God made the world in such a way that right living produces blessing as naturally as an apple tree produces apples.

2.2 Revering Yhwh

Obedience is an expression of the way we revere Yhwh as well as an expression of love for Yhwh. While there is an unnecessary form of fear of Yhwh,

---

[42]John Barton, *Ethics and the Old Testament* (London: SCM Press/Harrisburg, Penn.: Trinity, 1998), pp. 88, 90. Barton's only examples of disinterested piety are Job, Dan 3 and perhaps Hab 3:17-18.

[43]Rashi, quoted in Jacob Milgrom, *Leviticus* (Minneapolis: Fortress, 2004), p. 317.

[44]Some Middle-Eastern law collections also close with blessings and (longer) curses, but they are more concerned with people emending the laws than with people obeying them: see, e.g., *ANET*, pp. 161 (Lipit-Ishtar), 178-80 (Hammurabi). Contrast the treaty of Esarhaddon in *ANET*, pp. 534-41 (long curses and no blessings) and the other Middle-Eastern treaties in *ANET*, pp. 201, 205, 206, where the blessings and curses are more equal and briefer and the curses come first.

there is also an appropriate form of that fear, which we might rather call awe. It involves a wonder at what Yhwh does, an openness to Yhwh's knowledge of us, an honor and respect for Yhwh, and a certain diffidence, yet also an enthusiastic, passionate joy and a relaxed trust.

Fear

The Scriptures first mention fear as a consequence of disobeying Yhwh (Gen 3:10), and the New Testament declares that "perfect love excludes fear" (1 Jn 4:18). Yet a few pages previously it urges Christians to fear God (e.g., 1 Pet 2:17), and Paul affirms his fear of the Lord (2 Cor 5:11). When we give thanks for what God has done and will do, "we worship God acceptably, with reverence and awe, yes because our God is a consuming fire" (Heb 12:28-29, quoting passages such as Deut 4:24).

The First Testament speaks in similar apparently contradictory ways. Loving Yhwh, the first great command, is an expression of fear (Deut 6:5; cf. 10:12; 10:20–11:1). In Hebrew as in Greek the most common word for a debilitating or paralyzing fear or dread is also a common word for a positive respect, a reverence issuing in willing deference to someone's authority. Indeed, in the First Testament *yārē'* is often translated "worship" (e.g., 1 Kings 18:12; 2 Kings 17:32-41). A person of great piety and commitment is someone who "fears" God (e.g., Job 1:1, 8-9; 2:3; cf. Acts 10:2, 22, 35). Precisely because we *may* love God (because that awesome possibility is opened to us), we *must* fear God.[45] "The fear of YHWH stands . . . for religion, and quite simply for piety."[46] "It is doubtless true that the 'fear of Yahweh' repeatedly recalls the distance that separates creatures from their creator and Lord," but "in all its talk of the fear of Yahweh, the faith of the Old Testament never was diverted into mere trepidation before God."[47] "As 'slavery' was reconstrued by the Priestly tradents to denote the liberating integrity of 'servanthood,' the 'fear of Yahweh' marks for the sages an exodus of the will, from fear of the world to reverence of and obedience to Yahweh, a 'fear' that banishes all fear ([Prov] 3:25)."[48] Thus to speak of "fearing Yhwh" is to speak of being a true believer, of worshiping Yhwh in the proper way, of recognizing Yhwh as the real God (1 Kings 8:43). "The fear of God is the soul of godliness."[49] In the First Testament it is "the

---

[45]Karl Barth, *Church Dogmatics* (Edinburgh: T & T Clark, 1964), II/1:33-36. Barth assumes that the fear of 1 Jn 4:18 is fear of people and things other than God, but this seems difficult in the context.

[46]Horst Dietrich Preuss, *Old Testament Theology,* 2 vols. (Louisville: Westminster John Knox/ Edinburgh: T & T Clark, 1995, 1996) 2:159.

[47]Zimmerli, *Old Testament Theology in Outline,* p. 146.

[48]William P. Brown, *The Ethos of the Cosmos: The Genesis of Moral Imagination in the Bible* (Grand Rapids/Cambridge: Eerdmans, 1999), p. 310.

[49]John Murray, *Principles of Conduct* (Grand Rapids: Eerdmans/London: Tyndale, 1957), p. 229.

principle religious virtue."[50] "Fear of Yahweh" or "service of Yahweh" is the First Testament equivalent to "spirituality."[51]

Like love, "fear" naturally results in deferring to what someone says—in other words, in obedience (Deut 5:29 [MT 26]; 6:2, 24; 8:6; 17:19; 28:58; 31:12-13; Ps 119:63; Eccles 12:13; Jer 44:10). References to fear again indicate that integrity and maturity do not involve coming to one's own thought-through adult decisions about what to do. They involve doing what Yhwh says. The person who "fears Yhwh" is the one who "delights greatly in his commands" (Ps 112:1). Both expressions combine the feelings and the will, like love. Fearing implies a respect and deference that issues in submission and obedience; delight implies an enthusiasm that expresses itself in the same way. Yhwh's servants are people who delight to fear Yhwh (Neh 1:11). Their wanting then corresponds to Yhwh's wanting (Ps 40:6, 8 [MT 7, 9]). Fear or enthusiasm without obedience, or obedience that does not relate to fear and enthusiasm, would both be odd. Psalm 119:119-20 similarly affirms, "I love your declarations. My flesh tingles through awe for you; I fear your decisions." The collocation of love for Yhwh's declarations and awe or fear for Yhwh's decisions makes clear that there is no tension between love and awe or fear (cf. Deut 10:12), partly because both express themselves in obedience. The word *tingle* (*sāmar*) suggests that we should not lose the affective implication of the word for "awe" (*pahad*), a strong synonym for "fear." Again, in Psalm 96:4 Yhwh is both to be "praised" (*hālal* pual), which suggests wordless enthusiasm,[52] and to be "feared" (*yārē'* niphal), which suggests respectful submission.

Such "fear" holds people back from unfaithfulness (Jer 3:8). There is a fear of God that makes people do the right thing even when they could be inhibited by fear of human beings (Ex 1:15-21); it makes them disobey human authorities and lie over their action.[53] It also makes people do the right thing when they could get away with the wrong thing, such as belittling the deaf, tripping the blind, disrespecting the old, taking advantage of the needy, ill-treating servants or making promises that will be impossible to keep (Lev 19:14, 32; 25:17, 36, 43; Eccles 5:1-7 [MT 4:17–5:6]). It involves both heart and spirit (Deut 10:12-13); it is neither mere outward deference nor mere servile fright. It goes along with serving Yhwh, sticking to Yhwh and swearing by Yhwh's name (Deut 10:20; cf. 6:13; 13:4 [MT 5]). It thus has a prominent place among the basic attitudes Moses looks for in people when he is preaching his final ser-

---

[50]Heschel, *God in Search of Man*, p. 76.
[51]David Sperling, "Israel's Religion in the Ancient East," in *Jewish Spirituality,* 2 vols., ed. Arthur Green (New York: Crossroad, 1986-1987/London: Routledge, 1986-1988), 1:5-31; see p. 7.
[52]On this verb, see §2.7 "Sound and Movement."
[53]See further §6.6 "Painful Words, True Words."

mon to them; the same applies to Joshua (Josh 24:14) and Samuel (1 Sam 12:24).

Awe

So *yir'â* is a complicated matter. There is a right fear of/reverence for/awe before God and a negative fear of God that is an appropriate response when we are in the wrong (e.g., Gen 18:15). It is usually easy to tell which a text refers to, though occasionally it is hard, or Hebrew plays with the double meaning of its words. "All the earth should revere Yhwh, all the world's inhabitants be in awe of him" as their creator and one who deserves their worship and submission (Ps 33:8-9). But the psalm goes on to comment on the way Yhwh has frustrated the nations' plans and foiled their intentions; so is it "all the earth should fear Yhwh, all the world's inhabitants be in dread of him"? Perhaps they choose which reaction is appropriate.

Possibly in the context of political intrigue in Judah (a plot to remove Ahaz?), Yhwh says to Isaiah and his company,

> Do not call conspiracy
>   everything that this people call conspiracy.
> What they fear/revere, do not fear/revere,
>   or be in dread/awe of it.
> Yhwh Armies, he is the one you should regard as holy;
>   he the one to fear/revere, he the one to be in dread/awe of. (Is 8:12-13)

Isaiah's first uses of *yārē'* and *'āraṣ* suggest fear and dread in relation to the intrigue. It would be natural to fear this harbinger of further political instability. But Yhwh urges them to get things in perspective. The proper function of those verbs is to refer to an attitude of reverence and awe for Yhwh. That is actually what constitutes a proper recognition of and response to Yhwh's holiness.

Exodus 20:18-21 [MT 15-18] brings out some of the complexity of the relationship between fear and awe. Witnessing thunder, lightning and Mount Sinai smoking, the Israelites fall back in fear. They do not wish to hear Yhwh speak with them; that would be too much like seeing God. It could mean their death. In the order of the narrative, moreover, Yhwh has just proclaimed the Decalogue, so that the narrative hints that they also find the content of Yhwh's words fearful and do not wish to hear any more; the same ambiguity about the two possible reasons for fear appears in Deuteronomy 5:5.[54] Yet they also declare that they are willing to obey what

---

[54]On the understanding of the Exodus verses in this context, see, e.g., Brevard S. Childs, *Exodus* (London: SCM Press, 1974) = *The Book of Exodus* (Philadelphia: Westminster, 1974), pp. 371-73.

Moses passes on to them on Yhwh's behalf. With some contradiction Moses bids them not be fearful but tells them Yhwh has come to test them so that they will always revere God and not go astray. Yhwh's aim is exactly the one they have just indicated will be fulfilled; they have said they will obey, not go astray.

Wherein lies the testing? Presumably it lies partly in the audio-visual phenomena. Paradoxically, these are not a sign that people should be fearful in relation to God. They are designed to reveal what attitude people really take to Yhwh. Will they revere God in such a way as to do what God says (cf. Deut 4:10)? Will they let their fear in the realm of the emotions transmogrify into a revering in the realm of the will? That links with the incorporation of the Decalogue into the story, "interrupting" the more straightforward narrative movement from Exodus 19. Yhwh wants to discover not only whether they will respond to the phenomena with the appropriate fear, but whether they will respond to the declaration of Yhwh's expectations with the appropriate revering. These two can be related, as Yhwh's later recollection of the Sinai event implies. People were overwhelmed by the voice coming out of the darkness above the mountain blazing with fire; how is it possible to hear the living God's voice and live? Yhwh comments, "they have done well in everything they have spoken. Oh that they may have this mind so as to revere me and keep my commands always" (Deut 5:28-29 [MT 25-26]). The sense of being overwhelmed does not in itself count as revering, because revering is a matter of action as well as feeling (cf. Deut 6:1-2). But the feeling can issue in a revering that expresses itself in obedience.

The complex meaning of fear/awe reappears in connection with Samuel's farewell address. He challenges Israel to "revere Yhwh, serve him, and heed his voice." In response to his prayer, Yhwh sends thunder and rain to drive Israel to see the wrong it did in asking for a king, "and all the people greatly feared Yhwh and Samuel." They ask Samuel to pray for their forgiveness. Samuel bids them, "Do not fear. You yourselves have done all this wrong, yet do not turn from following Yhwh. Serve Yhwh with all your heart" (1 Sam 12:14, 18, 20).

Heschel suggests that fear is the antithesis of awe. Awe is compatible with love and joy; it is the root of faith; it makes us draw near, not shrink.[55] There is a right fear that makes people apprehensive about too close contact with Yhwh (Gen 28:17; Ex 3:6; 2 Sam 6:9), though Yhwh may then reassure them that they need not be apprehensive (Judg 6:23). There are advantages about distinguishing "fearing" and "revering," but there are also advantages in having just the one word; it points to links between the two ideas.

---

[55]Heschel, *God in Search of Man*, p. 77.

Wonder

In turn, awe is closely related to wonder. The Red Sea event, when Yhwh acted in majestic and powerful fashion to put down people who thought they could pursue and overtake and kill and plunder, means Yhwh is someone to be held in awe (*nôrāʾ*, the niphal participle from *yārēʾ*; Ex 15:11). The event is an act of deliverance for Israel, but Israel cannot help being aware of its frightening nature. Israel is right there when something powerful and overwhelming happens. It makes people bow in awe before Yhwh. Yet if Yhwh is on your side, the awareness of being overwhelmed goes along with a sense of relief and a desire to sing and exult. The event is awesome, marvelous and wonderful. It even deepens your trust in Yhwh, so that fearing the Pharaoh yields to fearing Yhwh (Ex 14:10-14, 31). The deed Yhwh will do in displacing the Canaanites will likewise be *nôrāʾ* (Ex 34:10).

Whereas there is every reason to be in awe of Yhwh, because Yhwh is mighty in power, there is no need to be in awe of the images the nations make, because they cannot do anything—anything bad (to other people) or anything good (for you) (Jer 10:5, 7). The problem with the Judeans after the exile is that they are misdirecting their awe (Is 57:11). Here, the appropriate antithesis is not between fear or wonder and trust or love, but between fear or wonder in relation to other so-called gods and fear or wonder in relation to Yhwh.

"I know that everything that Yhwh brings about will be forever (to it nothing is to be added and from it nothing is to be taken away), and God has brought about that people are in awe of him" (Eccles 3:14). The context suggests that *yārēʾ* does not here denote the reverence that issues in obedience nor the respect that issues in worship, but it again talks about joy and about God's giving; it hardly implies being afraid of God, and neither does the rest of Ecclesiastes point in that direction.[56] The recognition of a divine sovereignty that places constraints on us and also limits our understanding of the mystery of what God is doing in the world parallels the recognition expected in light of Yhwh's words in Job 38–39 and requires here as there a response of awed wonder or enhanced respect.[57] It is the kind of awareness that leads to a natural acceptance of the fact that it is impossible to see God or see God's glory and to the posting of the Levites to make sure that ordinary people do not come too near to Yhwh, "so that wrath may not come on the Israelite community" (Num 1:53).

Jeremiah 5:22-24 also speaks of awe in connection with Yhwh's being the creator, though in a different connection. Surely people should revere and

---

[56]Against, e.g., James L. Crenshaw, *Ecclesiastes* (London: SCM Press, 1988), p. 100.
[57]Cf. Roland E. Murphy. *Ecclesiastes,* WBC (Dallas: Word, 1992), p. 35.

tremble *(ḥûl)* before Yhwh as the one who set limits to the sea and gives the gift of rain. The use of the second verb, the word for twisting or writhing in pain or anguish, suggests that the revering must be more than mere recognition and obedience. Yet the appeal to Yhwh's activity as creator relates not to its frightening or incomprehensible aspects but to the beneficent deeds whereby dangerous forces are restrained and forces of blessing are released. The fact that Yhwh's creative power is applied to our protection and blessing is reason for wonder.

"How mighty is your name in all the earth." Back at the Beginning you "put your majesty above the heavens" and "founded a barricade" to restrain resistance to your ordering the world. You stand in authority *above* the whole creation and therefore the earth itself testifies to your might; and worship acknowledges that this is so (Ps 8:1-2 [MT 2-3]). The statement is made by faith or declares what deserves to be so. It is not obvious that Yhwh's name is mighty in all the earth. But the psalm's argument is that the wonder of Yhwh's restraining disorder in the cosmos, through exercising authority back at the Beginning, makes us acknowledge Yhwh's mightiness in the world in the present. In light of that, how extraordinary that Yhwh should take any notice of feeble humanity—indeed, put it in charge of the earthly world (Ps 8:3-8 [MT 4-9]).[58]

Openness

Wonder, awe and fear could be appropriate responses to Yhwh's knowledge of us.

> Yhwh, you have examined me and got to know me,
> You yourself have got to know my sitting and my rising,
>> you have gained insight into my intention, from afar;
> My journeying and my reclining you have measured,
>> with all my ways you have become familiar,
> For there is not a word on my tongue:
>> there, Yhwh, you have got to know all of it. (Ps 139:1-4)

Is this good or bad news? The psalm expresses a "terrifying and comforting awareness" of being bound up with God.[59] "Behind and in front you have bound me; you have put your hand on me." Is Yhwh the cosmic policeman? "Your knowledge is too extraordinary for me; it has gone high, I cannot prevail over it." I recognize that I cannot get beyond it.

---

[58]And how risky: see Keith Carley, "Psalm 8," in *Readings from the Perspective of Earth*, ed. Norman C. Habel (Sheffield, U.K.: Sheffield Academic Press/Cleveland: Pilgrim, 2000), pp. 111-24.

[59]Erhard S. Gerstenberger, *Theologies in the Old Testament* (Edinburgh: T & T Clark/Minneapolis: Fortress, 2002), p. 80.

The psalm's second paragraph (Ps 139:7-12) at best extends the ambiguity as it goes on to speak of Yhwh's capacity to reach me wherever I am.

> Where could I go from your spirit,
>> where could I flee from your face?
> If I were to climb up to the heavens, you would be there,
>> and if I were to make Sheol my bed, there you would be.
> Were I to take the wings of the dawn,
>> settle on the far side of the sea,
> Even there your hand would be leading me,
>> your right hand would be taking hold of me.

I might want to evade Yhwh to do things Yhwh did not observe, such as worship other deities or plan deceit against my neighbor. Or I might want to flee the consequences of having already done something of that kind; this is the connection in which Amos 9:1-4 speaks in these terms. But even if I tried to hide in the dark, I would find that dark and light are all the same to Yhwh. There is no hiding.

Another consideration undergirds that fact. Yhwh has been involved with and aware of every detail of my life since before I was born (Ps 139:13-18). From the very beginning I have had a destiny within Yhwh's purpose. If the psalm's opening two sections were a little worrying, this third section is less so, though it leaves us at this point in the psalm uncertain what we are saying to God, or uncertain why we are saying it. Christian spirituality takes these affirmations as good news. If Yhwh knows all about me wherever I am and whatever I do, can reach me and protect me anywhere, and has been involved with every detail of my life since before I was born, this gives me great security. That is so, if I am a person of commitment.

The last paragraph (Ps 139:19-24) resolves any ambiguity. At last it becomes explicit why I am making these affirmations.

> If only you would kill the faithless, God;
>> murderous people, leave me,
> People who speak of you in order to deceive,
>> who have lifted you in connection with emptiness, as your foes.

Some psalms that talk about enemies ask that my enemies should become Yhwh's enemies. This psalm affirms rather that I am prepared to make Yhwh's enemies my enemies.

> Do I not oppose the people who oppose you, Yhwh,
>> and do I not repudiate the people who rise up against you?
> I totally oppose them;
>> they have become enemies for me.

It is tempting to join such people. They are the people who are looking after their own interests. They often seem to be the successful people in the community. Yes, it is tempting to join them. But rather, I totally repudiate them. (The psalm has no time for hating the sin but loving the sinner. Loving means being committed to them and their actions, and the suppliant is determined to loathe, not love.)

Is this determination real? Those first three paragraphs seek to affirm its reality. If I acknowledge that Yhwh knows all about me, can reach me anywhere and has been involved with every detail of my life from the beginning, I would be foolish even to think of joining the faithless. As is often the case, the psalm speaks both to the self and to God, directly saying to Yhwh, "I'm not stupid, you know," and saying to the self, "Don't be stupid."

Do I really mean it? Do I even know myself? The closing lines follow from that. "Examine me, God, and know my mind, test me and know my concerns, see if there is an idolatrous way in me and lead me in the ancient way." I open myself to Yhwh's scrutiny.

Honor

Reverence, awe and wonder are also closely related to honoring (*kābēd* piel). Powerful peoples will come to honor and revere Yhwh because Yhwh has turned cities into ruins to rescue people from tyrants, and/but has been a refuge to the poor and needy (Is 25:2-5). We are to love Yhwh's name (Ps 5:11 [MT 12]), to be dedicated to it or committed to it, to be people who care about Yhwh's reputation and give themselves to its enhancing rather than its shaming. "Yhwh's name be worshiped," declared Job after his first series of calamities (Job 1:21). Applied to God, I take *bārak* (here pual) to mean "bow the knee" and thus "worship" or "praise" (TNIV) rather than "bless"; there is no indication in the use of the verb that it denotes the idea that one somehow adds something to God, as is the case when God blesses human beings.[60] Literally and symbolically Job is someone who bows the knee to God.

Job has already expressed concern lest his grown-up children might have "worshiped" God (Job 1:5). The verb there apparently has the opposite to its usual significance, and has the meaning of a verb such as *qālal* (piel), belittle or despise or treat with contempt or blaspheme (so JPSV).[61] Its use is then designed to avoid explicitly uttering the terrible expression "revile God," as

---

[60]But Christopher Wright Mitchell in his monograph *The Meaning of* brk *"to Bless" in the Old Testament*, SBLDS 95 (Atlanta: Scholars, 1987), while accepting that point, dismisses the explanation in terms of a link with kneeling and notes other ways by which the verb might have come to mean "praise."

[61]The usual EVV translation "curse" is misleading, both for the euphemistic *bārak* and for *qālal* itself (contrast Job 3:8, where *ʾārar* and *qābab* "curse" do come).

when we say in English "bless him" when we mean the opposite. It was the sin Eli's sons were guilty of, and their father did nothing about (1 Sam 3:13). Job would not make that mistake. The Adversary is convinced that Job himself will soon revile rather than revere God if the fruits of his revering disappear (Job 1:11), but Job continues to use the verb with the meaning "worship" (Job 1:21). "Worship God and die," Job's wife urges him when further calamity falls (Job 2:9). Stop praising God the way you have been doing and start denying that God is God, despising God, turning from worship to contempt. Surely such an attitude will call down God's punishment, as is implied by the apodictic prohibition of Exodus 22:28 [MT 27] (cf. also Lev 24:10-23).

Job does not sin with his lips, yet; but in light of what follows, we may suspect that during his week of silence the dynamics of Psalm 39 are present.[62] Subsequently, "though Job never does 'curse' God, strictly speaking, his railing, taunting, protesting, and summoning of his divine assailant is nothing like 'blessing' God either. Though he does not follow his wife's advice to the letter, he is from this point entirely infused by its spirit."[63] Is the Adversary right that he will revile God, and is his wife wrong that this will lead to death, or is his reviling something other than that of which they spoke? "Alleging that God has given the earth into the hands of the wicked and even corrupt judges (9:24) is blasphemy. So is Job's description of God as one who acts destructively in apparent random fashion against whole peoples (12:13-25)." Yet "Job's blasphemous words are not a farewell to God but a searing truth-telling to the God he will not leave."[64] His declarations about God do not count as the reviling of which the Adversary and Job's wife spoke—he does not repudiate God.

When Calvin defines "the chief aim of human life" as "to know God," he more extensively defines "true and right knowledge of God" by affirming that it means, "He is so known that due honor is paid to him." So "What is the method, of honoring him duly?" "To place our whole confidence in him; to study to serve him during our whole life by obeying his will; to call upon him in all our necessities, seeking salvation and every good thing that can be desired in him; lastly, to acknowledge him both with heart and lips, as the sole Author of all blessings."[65]

---

[62]On Ps 39, see §3.1 "The Impossibility of Silence."

[63]David J. A. Clines, *Job 1–20*, WBC (Dallas: Word, 1989), p. 52.

[64]Carol A. Newsom, "The Book of Job," *The New Interpreter's Bible* (Nashville: Abingdon, 1996), 4:317-637; see p. 525.

[65]"Catechism of the Church of Geneva," Center for Reformed Theology and Apologetics <www.reformed.org/documents/index.html?mainframe=http://www.reformed.org/documents/calvin/geneva_catachism/geneva_catachism.html>. Cf. Karl Barth, *Church Dogmatics* (Edinburgh: T & T Clark, 1968), III/2:182-86. Cf. §2.1 "Deferring to Yhwh."

Respect

The difference between God and us is that God never thinks he is us. Because of our capacity for getting confused over this question, Yhwh lays down some arrangements to underline the point. From Sinai onward there are holy space (such as the sanctuary), time (such as the sabbath), acts (such as sacrifice) and people (such as priests), entities that belong distinctively to Yhwh and that humanity is to treat with huge deference and awe, not to say from which humanity is to keep off. There is little of these in Genesis; there is virtually no reference to holiness in Genesis. "Holiness" is the category that marks God's distinctiveness and thus comes to mark the distinctiveness of the entities that God claims, and a system to signify this comes into being at Sinai. It does so first against the background of Yhwh's warning Moses about the holiness of the mountain of God at Horeb (Ex 3:4-5). Then when Moses brings the people to the mountain, he warns them about touching it; they have to treat it as holy, and the priests have to keep themselves holy (Ex 19:22-23). Yet Moses also takes steps to keep the people holy, because they are to meet with God, by washing their clothes and abstaining from sex (Ex 19:14-15).[66] Similarly, when the Israelites are to cross the Jordan, they are bidden to stay close to the covenant chest—but not too close (Josh 3:1-6), and Joshua is warned about the holiness of the ground where he stands before the commander of Yhwh's army (Josh 5:15).

Thus another form of disrespect for Yhwh would be to profane (*hālal* piel) the things that are holy to Yhwh (Ezek 23:39; 44:7) or to profane Yhwh's name by acts such as swearing falsely or by Canaanite-style observances or by breaking a covenantal commitment (Lev 21:6; Jer 34:16; Ezek 20:39). And because the name stands for the person, profaning Yhwh's name implies profaning Yhwh's own person (Ezek 13:19; 22:26). "Lifting up the name of Yhwh your God to something empty" would surely count as dishonoring it or profaning it, and "Yhwh will not acquit someone who lifts up his name to something empty" (Ex 20:7). One way of doing that would be to "swear by my name for deceit" (Lev 19:12). False prophecy would also count (Ezek 13). "Emptiness" *(šāw')* suggests something that claims or is claimed to have content but actually has none. It characterizes gods who have no real existence or power, and human statements that are false, and people who make false statements; it is the word for "false" witness (Deut 5:20 [MT 17]) and a false report of something (Ex 23:1). So it might suggest swearing by Yhwh's name that something false is actually true. Or it might imply declaring that Yhwh's name is empty and powerless. (Concern to avoid this dishonoring likely led to the sense that it was wisest not to take it at all and was thus one of the fac-

---

[66]See §6.2, which takes further the issues in this subsection.

tors that led to replacing the name Yhwh by "the LORD".)

Profaneness is the opposite of holiness. That does not make it bad; it is fine for the nonholy, everyday, ordinary, regular to be everyday, ordinary, regular. The problem lies in treating the extraordinary, set apart, as if it were not extraordinary and set apart. There is a realm of the holy and a realm of the everyday, and people must observe that distinction. They are to keep off the holy because it is Yhwh's realm. If they invade it, they cause offense to Yhwh; it is like walking into someone's house uninvited, or encroaching on their personal space or their time, or raiding their refrigerator, declining to observe the boundaries of the relationship.

People have thus "violated" Yhwh's teaching in showing contempt for Yhwh's holy things (Ezek 22:26) as priests declined to maintain the distinction between the taboo and the clean, and between the holy and the ordinary, as well as that between the sabbath and other days. To judge from the Torah, this will have involved (for instance) treating sacrificial food as if it were ordinary food, and thus keeping leftovers for eating next day, or taking part in a sacrificial meal when one was in a taboo state (cf. Lev 7:15-21; 19:6-8).[67] In behaving in such ways, people have implied there was nothing special or extraordinary or supernatural about Yhwh, no reason why Yhwh should be acknowledged by anyone.

The terrifying story of Nadab and Abihu relates how they died because they offered "alien fire that Yhwh had not commanded" (Lev 10:1-2).[68] The fire was perhaps alien because it was ordinary fire rather than holy fire. Presumably the fire for the incense was supposed to come from the altar fire (cf. Lev 16:12; Num 17:11). Exodus 30 had warned about burning alien incense and went on to emphasize the distinction between holy oil and incense on one hand and ordinary oil and incense on the other (Ex 30:7, 31-37). People were not to use holy oil and incense for everyday purposes, on penalty of being cut off from the community; Leviticus 10 implies that the priests had done the opposite. Such a story expresses in narrative form how vital it is to keep right away from the illicit incense offerings that were a common feature of Israelite life and easily involve the worship of "strange" gods. It leads into a warning that priests should not drink alcohol when taking part in the worship because their role is "to distinguish between the holy and the ordinary and between the taboo and the pure," and to teach the Israelites all the regulations Yhwh has given through Moses (Lev 10:8-11).

---

[67]Cf. Moshe Greenberg, *Ezekiel 21–37*, AB (New York: Doubleday, 1997), p. 455.

[68]But they died "before Yhwh"; and through them, Yhwh says, "I show myself holy and show myself glorious" (Lev 10:2-3). Philo infers that "they die in order that they may live"; they die (in order to go to live) before Yhwh eternally (*On Flight and Finding* 59). Jesus thus picks up Yhwh's words in speaking of his own life and death (Mt 6:9; Jn 12:28); see Jacob Milgrom, *Leviticus 1–16*, AB (New York: Doubleday, 1991), pp. 603-4.

Exclusiveness

All this would cohere with the assumption that the commitment Israel owes Yhwh is an exclusive one. Having recourse to gods other than Yhwh might not involve abandoning worship of Yhwh but rather seeking help from other gods as well—hedging one's bets. Yet if people bow down and swear oaths to Yhwh, but also swear by "their King," the title of another god, that makes them people who have actually turned back from following Yhwh, because they do not seek help from Yhwh or turn to him for the meeting of their needs (Zeph 1:5-6). They have given up revering Yhwh. So people are not to make mention (*zākar* hiphil) of the names of other gods (Ex 23:13). The "mention" the command refers to is the naming of other gods in worship, giving praise to them and asking them for help. Not worshiping the gods of the people of the lands they occupy implies also that "you are not to act as they act but totally demolish them [that is, the gods] and totally smash their pillars" (Ex 23:23-25; we do not know what these pillars [*maṣṣēbōt*] signified). The reason Israel is to make no alliance with these people and with their gods is that this will lead them into serving these gods; that is a trap Israel must not fall into (Ex 23:32-33). Indeed, it is an offense that deserves death, no matter how close the offender to you (Num 25:1-9; Deut 13:1-18 [MT 2-19]). It imperils Israel's very being.

For a man or a woman there is something deeply offensive and sordid about one's spouse going with someone else. Turning to other gods is as offensive and sordid as that. It is not even as if Israel is like a man who has truly fallen in love with someone else. It is more like someone who falls in bed with a series of women (Jer 2:20). "The land is totally promiscuous in relation to Yhwh" (Hos 1:2). Translations often render *zĕnût* "prostitution" or "whoring," but this imperils the point (anyway, Jerusalem was as ready to pay for sex as to charge for it: see Ezek 16:31). The word refers to socially unacceptable sexual activity, which approximately equates with extramarital sex.[69]

An appropriate attitude to Yhwh involves passion for Yhwh to be honored, a passion that mirrors Yhwh's,[70] but is again allied to revering Yhwh. "My passion has destroyed me, because my foes have ignored your words" (Ps 119:139). The psalmist might have wished not to feel so strongly about people's ignoring Yhwh's word, but passion does not give options; it consumes like fire (Cant. 8:6; for *qinʾâ*, translations here and elsewhere sometimes have "jealousy," which is a subset of passion). Declaring this passion signals that the psalmist is definitely not someone who ignores Yhwh's words. Psalm 69:9 [MT 10] speaks similarly about the way passion for Yhwh's house has destroyed

---

[69]See further §7.6 "Experientially."
[70]Cf. Karl Barth, *The Christian Life* (Grand Rapids: Eerdmans, 1981), pp. 113-14.

the suppliant, who experiences the reviling of people who revile Yhwh.

An embodiment of such passion is Elijah, who kills the prophets who served the Master and then proclaims, "I have been truly passionate for Yhwh God Armies, because the Israelites have abandoned your covenant, torn down your altars and slain your prophets with the sword" (1 Kings 19:10). We may wonder whether Elijah gave too much scope to his passion; Hosea apparently takes this view of the passionate Jehu (Hos 1:4; cf. 2 Kings 10:16-17). We might feel the same about the passionate Phinehas, though Yhwh seems to have no such uneases, not least because Phinehas's action protected the people from Yhwh's own passion (Num 25:6-13).

Joy and Relaxedness

Reverence and joy also go together. Seeing and revering (as Yhwh puts down oppressors) issue in discussing what we have seen and proclaiming it in the hearing of others, and in rejoicing and taking refuge in Yhwh; such revering contrasts with the fearlessness of the oppressors themselves (Ps 64:4, 9-10 [MT 5, 10-11]). When someone is delivered from trouble by Yhwh and reappears in worship to speak of that experience, "many will see and revere, and trust in Yhwh" (Ps 40:3 [MT 4]). While psalms more commonly speak of hearing what Yhwh has done, they also like to put seeing and revering alongside each other; the verbs are very similar (*yir'û* and *yîrā'û*) and this suggests an inner link between what they refer to. Either seeing causes you to be afraid or it causes you to worship; in Psalm 40:3 [MT 4] the context makes clear that the second verb has the positive connotation. Having heard someone say, "That was a charming service," Abraham Heschel reports, "I felt like crying. . . . God is grave; He is never charming. . . . Prayer is joy and fear, trust and trembling together."[71]

Psalm 130:4 makes a parallel point: "Pardon is with you, so that you may be revered." There is something overawing about God's forgiveness. Indeed, when Yhwh forgives and restores Israel, this involves acts that inspire not just Israel but the world to revere Yhwh (Ps 102:15 [MT 16]). The whole world resounds at what Yhwh does for Israel (Ps 65:5, 8 [MT 6, 9]). Yhwh's blessing Israel means the world properly acknowledges, confesses, rejoices, resounds— and reveres (Ps 67).

"See and revere" recurs again in Psalm 52:6 [MT 8], where they then issue in laughing. The first time Sarah laughs (Gen 18:12-15), it is usually taken as a laugh of unfaith or mockery, though the story is ambiguous and there may be at least an element of wonder in her laugh. There is a link with the fact that

---

[71]Abraham Joshua Heschel, *The Insecurity of Freedom* (New York: Farrar, Straus & Giroux, 1967), p. 243.

her son's name, Isaac, will refer to laughter or play. In the psalm the laughter links with both mockery and faith as well as with seeing and revering. When Yhwh puts down people who trust in their wealth and on that basis oppress the godly (or who become wealthy through oppressing the godly), it will be possible to see and revere and laugh. Revering and laughing go together.

Related to this is the way revering expresses itself in a relaxedness that waits on Yhwh's action rather than taking responsibility ourselves (Ps 33:18). For the nations, too, it expresses itself in submission to Yhwh as lord in political events. Such waiting contrasts with the assumption that it is our responsibility to fix things. Psalm 131 notes how mistaken this assumption is. It means we make too much of ourselves. We are too impressed by our own impressiveness. We think we can "go about" with "great things" and "wonders." But "great things" and "wonders" are most often great acts of God. The psalmist has not merely avoided seeking to understand things that are too great but has avoided aspiring to go about (*hālak* piel, "walk with determination") and *do* great wonders, like God. Going about in faithfulness (the same verb; Prov 8:20) is enough. The psalmist speaks of fleeing "vain ambition"[72] and opposes the *hybris* of the Spirit.[73]

The theme of making too much of ourselves is expounded most systematically in Isaiah 2:5-22; it is Judah's great danger in Isaiah's day. Uzziah provides an individual example: when he became strong, his heart or mind became lofty and that led to his trespassing against Yhwh by undertaking priestly acts (2 Chron 26:16; cf. 32:25). Being lofty in heart or mind suggests having a high opinion of oneself. The high opinion may be justified; the problem is what it leads to. High eyes are a little different. They are the first thing Yhwh is against in Proverbs 6:16-19 (cf. 30:13; also Ps 18:27 [MT 28]). The context there implies not a self-assertiveness over against God but one over against other people, something more like ambition than pride. But both a lofty heart and high eyes lead to action that treats me as the only person that counts. "There is no passage in the Bible in which power as such, whether physical, mental or political, is praised as good or even desirable."[74] Rather its significance is severely downplayed (e.g., Ps 33:16-17; Zech 4:6). Job, in particular, is about "knowing our limits."[75]

Diffidence

Micah has a distinctive way of making the point about reverent relaxedness

---

[72]H. Stephen Shoemaker, "Psalm 131," *RevExp* 85 (1988): 89-94; see p. 93.

[73]Cf. Walter Beyerlin, *Wider die Hybris des Geistes* (Stuttgart: KBH, 1982).

[74]Karl Barth, *Church Dogmatics* (Edinburgh: T & T Clark, 1969), III/4:391.

[75]Carol M. Bechtel, "Knowing Our Limits," in Bechtel, *Touching the Altar* (Grand Rapids/ Cambridge: Eerdmans, 2008), pp. 179-211.

when he speaks of "walking diffidently [ṣānaʿ] with your God" (Mic 6:8). His verb comes only here in the First Testament, but Proverbs 11:2 indicates the nature of people who are ṣānûaʿ. It is the opposite of being arrogant; in later Hebrew it suggests restraint and carefulness, reserve or modesty, a hesitation about reckoning that you always know what to do, a humble submissiveness to God that is the human correlative to God's holiness. To serve Yhwh "is to exist in an ultimate and profound irresponsibility." We participate in Yhwh's work as mere human beings, and further as disobedient human beings, "and therefore quite unsuitable for the work." We participate on the basis of God's grace, so that "it is not a participation which involves anxiety and worry whether we can really do what we are required to do."[76]

Psalm 127 notes that it is possible to attach final significance to the energy we put into things and not realize how mistaken we are. We can put huge effort into building a house, but if Yhwh is not involved in the building, the whole effort may issue in collapse; the house may be demolished by flood or fire or enemy attack. We can put huge effort into guarding the city from that enemy attack, but if Yhwh is not involved in guarding it, that may be a complete failure; we may discover that enemies are attacking and be unable to withstand them. It is possible to get up early every day to get to work, be hesitant even to take off time for lunch, and refuse to come home for dinner until it gets dark, so that you "eat the bread of great toil," and to forget that Yhwh "gives sleep to his beloved one" and also that the whole effort may again be pointless because drought may mean the harvest fails anyway.

So sometimes we can do everything we can and things may not work out; disasters happen that are (sometimes) no one's fault if Yhwh does not stop them. The implication is not that we do not go in for house building or watchfulness or work; that will certainly mean no houses or security or food. It is that we do not attach sole significance to our efforts, as if everything depends on us. It depends on Yhwh. There is a First Testament polemic against laziness, but there is also a polemic against workaholism. It urges us to reckon we can afford to relax and enjoy that sleep that Yhwh gives—gives to us as people whom Yhwh loves, not people who are simply on our own, all responsibility and no resources.

Psalm 127 goes on to make a point that could be totally unrelated, yet its collocation with the earlier point invites reflection. Sons, it points out, are a blessing from Yhwh. The psalmist would grant that daughters are just as indispensable as sons to the work of the house and farm. But the sons are the fighters, and that is the point Psalm 127 is concerned with. In a time of con-

---

[76]Barth, *Church Dogmatics*, I/2:274, 275.

flict they are the arrows in the quiver belonging to the head of the family. They do not actually need to fight; they only have to look imposing when the family is threatened by a theft or a scam or a false accusation. They mean the family is home and dry. Perhaps the collocation invites the reflection that even from a practical viewpoint, the head of the householder should see how important the family is and not put all the emphasis on working all hours of the day and night.

A fruit of God's liberation is our "deliverance from the ocean of apparently unlimited possibilities" by our "transference to the rock of the one necessity." We have "awakened from the dream or nightmare of a freedom of choice" in which we "might always in all respects do different things, loving, choosing, grasping and executing now one thing and now another." We are instead called simply "to be a witness of Jesus Christ," one who "finds a Lord and becomes His servant."[77] We are thus creatures who are placed under limitation. We do not decide what it means to be human; God decides. We begin and end, and we do not decide when we come to being and when we die; God does.[78]

Yet there is a strange feature of the people's journey from Sinai to the promised land. The cloud that symbolized but concealed Yhwh's presence would stay over Yhwh's dwelling. When it moved, Israel would move; when it stopped again, Israel would camp again. If it stayed still for two days or a month or a year, Israel would also do so (Num 9:15-23; 10:33-36). But this does not stop Moses urging his Midianite father-in-law to come with Israel because he knows where they should camp in the wilderness: "you will be eyes for us" (Num 10:31).

The Mystery of Disobedience

If Yhwh's teaching and instruction are so desirable because they restore life and light up the eyes, "Who can understand wanderings?" (Ps 19:12 [MT 13]).[79] The EVV have the psalm asking who can understand their own wanderings, but no pronoun is expressed, and this question does not follow very logically on what proceeds, whereas there is logic about the more general question. Given the positive significance of Yhwh's teaching, how can one understand our human inclination to wander from it? But wander we do. So the psalm goes on, "free me from secret acts." In the context, the "cleansing" (EVV) for which the psalm asks is not forgiveness but the removal of the inclination to

---

[77] Karl Barth, *Church Dogmatics* (Edinburgh: T & T Clark, 1962), IV/3, ii:665.
[78] Ibid., III/4:565-71.
[79] I link the hapax noun *šĕgî'ōt* with the verb *šāgâ*, which suggests deliberate going astray more often than inadvertent error, rather than with *šāgag*, which does refer to inadvertent error.

go our own way.[80] The mystery of this deliberate wandering makes it necessary for us to cast ourselves on Yhwh to do the work on our personalities that gives us the instinct to obey rather than disobey, and to do so over things no one knows about as well as public acts, such as the plots that may lead to deception and wrongdoing, and the worship of other deities in the privacy of one's home.

The mystery is increased or in part explained by the way we can be led astray by other people. The psalm goes on, "yes, withhold your servant from the willful people. May they not rule over me, then I shall be a person of integrity, and free of great rebellion" (Ps 19:13 [MT 14]). In some ways this plea resolves the mystery. While we would like to think that we are individual autonomous agents who make free decisions of our own, in reality our attitudes and decisions are substantially shaped by the culture we live in.[81] So as Christians in the West we "wander" in our attitudes to family, sex and wealth because that is the nature of the culture we belong to. It is very hard to separate oneself from the attitudes of one's culture. As Israelites might assume that their culture was basically biblical and that they could identify with it, Christians in the West may do the same.

The suppliant is aware of the need to take a different stance from the "willful," the people who make up their own minds what to do, and is also aware of the nature of that cultural pressure. Fortunate is the person who manages not to follow the plans or take the same stance or even join in the deliberations of the faithless, the people who fall short of Yhwh's targets or even do not aim at them, indeed who mock them (Ps 1:1). Hence the plea to be held back from the willful, so that I am not ruled by them in the sense of letting them determine who I am and how I live. I need to avoid being swallowed up by them if I am to be a person of integrity as opposed to a person guilty of "great rebellion." The phrase recalls the expression "great sin," which denotes unfaithfulness to one's spouse and then unfaithfulness to God. "Willful" people may remain nominally committed to Yhwh, but they have become practical atheists, people whose lives are lived as if God did not exist. The psalmist is aware of the ease with which that can happen and of needing supernatural help if one is to be held back from it.

To put it positively, "May the words of my mouth be acceptable and the talk of my heart come before you, Yhwh, my crag, my restorer" (Ps 19:14 [MT 15]). The words of the mouth and the talk of the heart are two key expressions of who we are. The mouth and the heart are loci of willfulness and rebellion.

---

[80]Indeed, the verb is never used in this connection, except negatively: acquitting people of wrongs they have done is itself wrong.

[81]See §1.1 "A Significant Order" and "Community and Individual."

They are key to the question whether we do ill to other people or seek help from other deities (the noun *talk* is related to the verb *talk* in Ps 1:2).[82] The suppliant knows we need God's help if our words and our thinking are to be the kind Yhwh can find acceptable, if we are to be the kind of people who can come before Yhwh as people who speak and think. I bring my sacrifices before Yhwh and make sure that there is nothing wrong with them, and that they are thus the kind that find acceptance, the suppliant implies, but I know this does not work unless the words of my mouth and the secret speech that comes from my heart is also the kind that can find acceptance.

Fear of Human Beings and Fear of God

Immediately after their miraculous escape from Egypt the Israelites fill with fear as Pharaoh follows them, and they wish they had been left to serve the Egyptians (Ex 14:10-14). Moses bids them not be afraid but to stand firm in the confidence that they will see the deliverance that Yhwh will bring about. Yhwh will fight for them; they only have to stand still. It is not clear what their response is to all that, but the deliverance happens, and then "the people revered Yhwh and trusted in Yhwh and in Moses' his servant" (Ex 14:31). Fear recurs when they are nearing the land as their spies report on the strength of the people they have to dispossess; Yhwh asks, "how long will this people despise me? How long will they not trust in me, for all the signs I have performed in their midst?" (Num 14:9, 11; cf. Deut 1:32; 9:23).

The twin ideas of trust in Yhwh and revering Yhwh naturally go together. They are suggestively interwoven in Psalm 34:7-10 [MT 8-11].

> Yhwh's aide camps
>> around people who revere him and delivers them.
> Sense and see how good Yhwh is;
>> the good fortune of the man who relies on him.
> Revere Yhwh, his holy ones,
>> because there is no lack for people who revere him.
> Apostates[83] have been in want and starved,
>> but people who seek help from Yhwh lack no good thing.

To trust Yhwh is to live by the awareness that Yhwh is Lord and does care for us, and thus it implies revering Yhwh. To rely on ourselves or on our weaponry or on other deities is to live as if Yhwh is not Lord or does not care for us, and thus it implies declining to revere Yhwh. Naturally this proves itself in experience. People who revere and thus rely on Yhwh find protection

---

[82]See §2.1 "Delighting in Yhwh."
[83]Elsewhere in the First Testament *kĕpîrîm* means "lions," but the root's meaning in later Hebrew suggests "apostates," which makes sense here.

and provision; people who turn from Yhwh do not. So when I am surrounded by assailants, people who think their wealth makes it possible for them to buy themselves long life and my speedy death (and wealth does give power), "why should I be afraid?" (Ps 49:5 [MT 6]). I know Yhwh is more powerful than them and can reverse those expectations, giving them a quicker journey to Sheol than they expect and rescuing me from there.

And people who revere/fear Yhwh do not fear bad news. Perhaps that is because they know bad news will not come, or perhaps it is because their heart is established and they know they can face whatever news does come. Their heart is held firm; they will not be afraid, until they look on their foes (Ps 112:1, 7, 8; "be afraid" is *yirā*', "look" is *yir'eh*); until they look down on them, we might say in English. They know they will do that. "Fear him, ye saints, and you will then have nothing else to fear."[84]

There is something to be said for fear, as there is for anger and hatred. It can hold one back from stupidity and wrongdoing (Deut 13:11 [MT 12]; 17:13; 19:20; 21:21). Analogous to the kind of fear of God that denotes reverence issuing in obedience, there is a fear of human beings that may be wise and proper (Num 12:8; Josh 4:14). There is a natural fear associated with age or position (Judg 6:27; 8:20; 1 Sam 3:15; 31:4; 2 Sam 1:14). But there is also a possibly justi-fied, but possibly unjustified, fear of human beings (Gen 26:6-11; 31:31). There is a fear of human beings that ignores Yhwh (Num 14:9; 21:34). Conversely, Yhwh's reassurance can make fear unnecessary in even the most fearful of situations, when Yhwh bids people, "Do not fear, because I am with you" (Gen 26:24; cf. 21:17; 46:3; Ex 14:10-14). (Midwives tell Rachel and Phinehas's wife not to be afraid when they are dying in childbirth [Gen 35:17; 1 Sam 4:20]; perhaps giving birth gives them an aspect of their ultimate human fulfill-ment even at this moment.)

Fear and Confidence

When Moses recalls the people's fear about entering the land, he makes ex-plicit that fear (at least the paralyzing fear that issues in a refusal to take ac-tion) and confidence in Yhwh are mutually exclusive, and that confidence has bases: Yhwh has acted on the people's behalf in the past and can therefore be trusted for the future (Deut 1:29-33). Fear and trust do not go together; the second replaces the first. "When I am afraid, I trust in you"; indeed, "in God, whose word I praise—in God I have trusted. I am not afraid; what can flesh do to me?" (Ps 56:3-4 [MT 4-5]; cf. 118:6). There is some paradox here. At one level, fear and confidence do coexist. The psalm speaks of being hounded all day; fear is a rational response to the fact that this hounding continues. Yet

---

[84]Cf. Leslie C. Allen, *Psalms 101–150*, WBC, rev. ed. (Nashville: Nelson, 2002), p. 131.

the suppliant knows that "God is mine" or "God is for me" and that this hounding will not have the last word. Confidence is therefore possible. And at another level, then, "I am not afraid." There is a sense in which flesh can do terrible things to me. There is another sense in which it cannot do anything; God protects me. In between these double statements about fear and trust comes the factor that makes the difference, the word from God that promises protection (Ps 56:4 [MT 5]). There is no need to be afraid of the frightening enemy attack or the devastating epidemic that can catch you by night or by day, because you have a refuge to rely on (Ps 91:4-6).

In all sorts of situations, people have good reason to fear. The Judeans' position in Babylon in the 540s is an example. A Persian king is storming through the Middle East and causing justified panic in Babylon. A prophet imagines distant parts of Israel's world reacting with fear as they watch the progress of this conqueror and anxiously setting about the construction of a new divine image (Is 41:1-5). In that crisis the reassurance given to individuals such as Isaac is applied to the people as a whole: "Do not be afraid, because I am with you; do not be alarmed, because I am your God. I am strengthening you, and supporting you, and upholding you with my faithful right hand" (Is 41:10). The fact that Israel is Yhwh's servant, chosen and not spurned, gives basis for confidence rather than fear. Yhwh twice repeats the bidding, adding the promise of divine help (Is 41:13-14). Yhwh thereby signals that this is the heart of the divine word at this point, as well as indicating where lies the heart of the people's need. "Do not be afraid" is not a mere exhortation. On the way toward the operating room, it is one thing for a friend to say, "Don't worry." It is another thing for the surgeon to say, "Don't worry." Yhwh's "Don't be afraid" has built-in grounds for taking it seriously. As Yhwh puts it, "I am the one who says to you, 'Do not be afraid'" (Is 41:13). "I am with you" is the assurance that backs up the exhortation "Do not be afraid" addressed to individuals such as Isaac and Joshua, and to the people as a whole (Gen 26:24; Deut 7:21; Josh 1:9).

Yhwh also backs up this exhortation or invitation or reassurance with qatal verbs: "Do not be afraid, because I have restored you" (Is 43:1). The EVV render these verbs as future, "I will help you," and the act of restoration indeed lies in the future. But the act is more certain than a future tense verb implies. The qatal verb suggests that in Yhwh's purpose this act has already happened or is already happening, as when we say "It's as good as done" or say "I'm coming" when we have not yet put on our shoes. (Of course, such statements on Yhwh's lips are more reliable than on ours.)

The exhortation not to be afraid recurs in Isaiah 51:7, in the form of a bidding not to be afraid of human reproach and taunting. One trouble with reproaches and taunts is that they often voice our own inner suspicions. If Babylonians or Edomites thought about it, they might well reckon that Israel was finished, but there was little reason for them to think about it. Their taunting is the externalizing of the Judeans' own sense of their feebleness and shame. They and their God are surely finished. Talk of a future is illusory.

The exhortation recurs again addressed to Ms. Zion (Is 54:4). Talk of her future too looks illusory, like that of a woman who is unable to have children, or who has been divorced or widowed (such experiences may be even harder in a traditional culture than in a modern one). She has no place in the community. That is how Jerusalem is in the world of the nations. No, you will have a future, says Yhwh. Do not be afraid.

Fear and Comfort

Although reproaches and taunts externalize our inner worries, they are not necessarily unreal. People are "fearful continually, every day, in the face of the fury of the distresser as one setting to destroy" (Is 51:13). This fury is not just imagination. In a time of crisis both government and ordinary people in a place such as Babylon are inclined to fall into suspicion or hostility in relation to a minority ethnic group such as the Judeans, who might be suspected of sympathy with anyone who was going to put the empire in its place.

In that context Yhwh reminds the Judeans, "I, I am the one who comforts you" (Is 51:12). The verb is used with two meanings; the parallelism or the context usually clarifies which meaning is dominant. When Yhwh first commissions the comforting of Jerusalem (Is 40:1), it suggests reference to a verbal consoling and encouraging of the city and the people (cf. Is 49:13; 51:19; 61:2; 66:13; Jer 31:13). But the basis for this verbal consoling is the fact that Yhwh is also engaged in a comforting that involves action (cf. Is 51:3; 52:9). Setting comfort over against fear likely indicates that Yhwh refers to comfort in the form of encouragement, but Yhwh goes on to refer to putting the distresser to flight, which implies that comfort as consolation does have its basis in the promise of comfort as restoration. In both senses Yhwh's declaration is a response to a reasonable lament that people have been uttering since the fall of Jerusalem, when the city began to cry out, "I have no comforter" (Lam 1:2, 9, 16, 17, 21).

In both senses the fact of comfort confronts the fact of fear and offers to replace it by confidence. The fact of fear indicates that people do not believe they are going to be comforted (by events) and do not feel comforted (in their spirits). In Isaiah 51:12-15 Yhwh confronts fear with two facts.

One is the mortality of those whom the people fear. It is easy for both the powerful and the powerless to assume that the present arrangement between them will last forever and to forget that power arrangements never do last forever. Powers wax and wane. Empires always fall. Emperors are not immortal. And the moment when the pressure is greatest is also when the empire is most vulnerable. Palestinian people had a much easier time in the 1970s than in the 1990s, but the former context was never going to lead to their having a state of their own. The moment of fear can be the moment when there is most hope. So it is for the Judeans in Babylon. There really is reason for hope and reason to stand firm when it is tempting to be terrified. The imperial authorities and the neighbors who are themselves fearful are mortal.

The other fact is the nature of Yhwh. Fear means forgetting, putting out of mind or discounting that Yhwh is "your maker, spreader of the heavens, founder of the earth." The people have accused Yhwh of putting them out of mind (Is 49:14); Yhwh reverses the accusation. As is often the case, statements about creation and about bringing Israel into being are not merely statements about something Yhwh did millennia or centuries ago but statements about Yhwh's relationship of sovereignty in the contemporary world. The participles maker/spreader/founder help to make the point. Making, spreading and founding are not just past acts but aspects of Yhwh's ongoing relationship with the world and with Israel. To put it another way, Yhwh is the "stiller of Sea when its waves roar."[85] The waves of imperial power threaten to drown the Judean community, but Yhwh says "Stop!" and they do so.

Those facts make it possible to live in the present in light of the future. "Where is the fury of the distresser?" Very present, actually—a reality in people's everyday lives and likely to get more of a reality. But in another reality, a reality so certain that it can be spoken of as if already present, that fury has gone, and the eye of faith can see a person bent down in submission straightening up into liberation and racing for the gates of the metaphorical prison. Whereas it looks as if the empire is immortal and its prisoners liable to death, actually the empire is about to die and its prisoners will not die and go to the Pit (Sheol). They will do so eventually, but not before they have seen Jerusalem. When it looks as if the powerful have all the resources and the powerless may not have enough to eat and keep them alive, the powerful will be gone and the powerless will eat.

Acceptance of Yhwh's Vision

The trouble is we usually prefer our way of looking at the future to the one Yhwh offers (Is 55:6-9). There before the people of God is Yhwh, "making himself available to them," standing like a servant, wondering if anyone wants to ask for anything. This is not a point about people's everyday religious life but about their relationship to Yhwh's intentions for them and for

---

[85]The EVV have Yhwh stirring up the sea, but that is usually what powers that assert themselves against Yhwh do; stilling the sea is Yhwh's act. I thus take the verb here as *rāgaʿ* II "be at rest" not *rāgaʿ* I "disturb."

the world. Yhwh has intentions for their destiny, purposes to restore Jerusalem and carry the exiles back there, and is thus available to take them to that destiny. The prophet urges them to open themselves to this, to seek Yhwh in the sense of laying hold on the resources that there are in Yhwh, to call on Yhwh to do the thing that Yhwh intends, to implement the purpose to restore them.

But their understanding of the way the future needs to work out and thus of the kind of thing Yhwh ought to be doing is very different from Yhwh's. They have a way of life they are quite happy with, perhaps a settled life in Babylon. They do not want this to be disturbed by talk of packing up in order to go "back" to an obscure and uncivilized far-off corner of the empire that most of them have never seen. They have ideas of their own about how the future ought to work out. They might even reckon they can be good witnesses to Yhwh in Babylon in a way they cannot be in a Judean ghetto. But in fact, they are going to have to abandon their settled way of life in Babylon, the houses they have built and the gardens they have planted with the encouragement of an earlier prophet, and the businesses they built up. Jeremiah himself had made that clear. While bidding them to settle down, he had also declared that this was not forever, and that Yhwh's "plans" included their having a future back in Judah. A time would come when they would "seek help from Yhwh" as Yhwh would be "available to them" (Jer 29:11-14). Isaiah 40–55 declares that this moment has arrived, but they are as resistant to Jeremiah's ideas about leaving as they had once been to Jeremiah's ideas about settling down.

They will have to abandon their plans. Being in Babylon is a sign of being cast off by Yhwh, and they have still not faced up to the implications of that. This moment when Yhwh intends to act is when they must turn to Yhwh. They can do so knowing that Yhwh does not sit in the heavens feeling judgmental toward them, but longs to have compassion on them and pardon them for the wrongdoings that led to exile and that still stand between them and Yhwh, or the wrongdoings of exile (the attraction to Babylonian gods?). So the prophet's message overlaps with that of earlier prophets. The people need to turn to Yhwh (šûb, the verb often translated "repent"). Their plans, the ways they would go about shaping their future, are radically different from God's. The prophet redefines "faithlessness" and "wrongdoing" as an insistence on one's own understanding of the way Yhwh must act in the world. The prophet has spent sixteen chapters trying to get them to look at things God's way, and this is the final shot at that. Brothers and sisters, says the prophet, isn't it obvious? (Things tend to be obvious to this prophet, who struggles through the sixteen chapters to get them to see the obvious.) The sky is high above the earth, is it not? Yhwh's ways are thus higher than ours, are they not? It would be surprising, would it not, if Yhwh's plans for taking us to our destiny corresponded to ours? We should surely expect them to be different?

People sometimes complain that they look to Yhwh and do not meet with a response. Yhwh can feel the shoe is on the other foot. The people think the situation is hopeless and that Yhwh has abandoned them. But Yhwh responds by claiming once more, "I was available to people who did not ask me, I was accessible to people who did not have recourse to me" (Is 65:1). The prophecy thus opens in a similar way to Isaiah 55:6-9. In due course it speaks again about the people's looking to other deities rather than to Yhwh, but it speaks first about the scandal of what they did not do. There was Yhwh humiliatingly available to them, saying "Here I am" just like a servant summoned by a master (e.g., 1 Sam 22:12). Yhwh stands with hands outstretched, another way of reversing the posture of suppliant and lord, since it is supposed to be Israel that spreads its hands toward Yhwh, humbly appealing for provision and help (cf. Ps 44:20 [MT 21]). Not only is the lord spreading out his hands to the suppliants but the suppliants are ignoring him and not asking for anything, not having recourse to Yhwh for what they need. They do not call on Yhwh by name to that end (Is 65:1 LXX), so that they are not like people who are called by Yhwh's name (Is 65:1 MT). They are turning away from Yhwh and turning in other directions, to resources that in their view seem more sensible. The description recalls the lament that whereas they are supposed to be Yhwh's servant, they are treating Yhwh as their servant, making Yhwh carry the burden of their wrongdoing (Is 43:22-24).

2.3 Trusting Yhwh

Fear is thus designed to give way to trust. Trust has special emphasis in the First Testament. One could argue that this goes back to the Beginning, when the question is whether Eve and Adam will trust the goodness of Yhwh's bidding or rather believe the serpent's questioning of it. While Abraham is initially remarkable for his obedience to Yhwh, so that when Yhwh says "Go," he goes (Gen 12:1-6), subsequently a key issue in Abraham's life is whether he will trust Yhwh. His story thus announces a key issue in Israel's own relationship with Yhwh.[86] It is not clear that Abraham trusts Yhwh in subsequent stories in Genesis 12 or Genesis 16 or Genesis 20, though he does so in Genesis 13 and explicitly in Genesis 15. The verb *he ʾĕmîn* first comes here. The EVV often translate it "believe," but "the notion of mere 'holding an opinion,' which is one of the senses of the English word 'believe,' is totally absent from the Hebrew."[87] The verb rather denotes an active self-commitment on the basis of an aware-

---

[86]On its significance for politics, see §5.2.
[87]Zimmerli, *Old Testament Theology in Outline*, p. 147.

ness that there is something there that can be trusted, a self-commitment involved in Abraham's original going when bidden. Martin Buber sees a difference between "faith" in Israel, where it meant trusting someone, and in the early church, where it meant acknowledging something to be true. Each naturally leads to the other, but in both cases one is primary.[88]

Trust for the Harvest

In what connections does trust operate, and what is the opposite of trusting Yhwh? Life depends on the harvest. If the crops do not grow, people have nothing to eat. When that happens, they ask, "Who shows us good?" (Ps 4:6 [MT 7]). In theory Yhwh shows us good, but this is not how things are turning out. The light of Yhwh's face is not lifted over us. Many people have therefore turned to other deities. Trust in Yhwh has failed.

Hosea speaks in similar terms in a context where there is no crisis. The reason Israel said "I will go after my lovers" was the conviction that they "give me my bread and my water, my wool and my linen, my oil and my drink," not acknowledging that it was Yhwh who gave all that and, through their prosperity, gave the silver and gold that they then used in worship of the Master. I will take back these gifts, then, says Yhwh (Hos 2:2-13 [MT 4-15]). Given that there is no implication of a crisis in Hosea, why have people turned to the Master for the gift of rain and the fertility of the ground? Hosea does not say. Why do people have affairs? There is some mystery about such questions. Perhaps Israelites associated Yhwh more with bringing serfs out of bondage than with making crops grow. Perhaps they were influenced by living among the longstanding inhabitants of the land who knew about getting crops to grow, and it seemed wise to follow their methods. Perhaps they themselves were by background the adherents of that kind of religion. They are then like Christians who usually think as much in light of their culture as in light of the gospel. Whatever the reason, look to the Master was what Israel did.

Perhaps it was the images that drew them. It is easier to trust a god whose representation you can see rather than one who is totally invisible. Yet Psalm 115 contrasts Yhwh's power as the God who lives in the heavens ("everything that he wishes, he has done") with the powerlessness of the images to which other peoples bowed down, images that had all the outward symbols of a capacity to act (mouths, eyes, ears, nose, hands, feet) but nothing of what these symbols represented. "Their makers become like them," it comments, "everyone who relies on them." Through relying on these images that cannot do anything, they end up just as unable to achieve anything as the images

---

[88]Martin Buber, *Two Types of Faith* (London: Routledge, 1951), pp. 7-8.

themselves are. Yet Israelites often relied on such images for the success of their harvest, like other peoples. The psalm therefore goes on to urge, "Israel, rely on Yhwh; he is their help and their shield" and to promise, "Yhwh, who has been mindful of us: he will bless us."

It concludes with two further statements that cohere with that. On one hand, "The heavens are heavens that belong to Yhwh, but the earth he gave to human beings." On the other, "The dead do not praise Yah, not any who go down to silence." Religions regularly attempt to storm the heavens so as to be able to understand more of what goes on there and to gain access to the realm of the dead and thus allay our fears about death and our sadness over the family and friends that we have lost. The psalm looks these two possibilities in the eye and acknowledges that Yhwh has confined us to the world and to the realm of the living. The rest we must leave to Yhwh. Another aspect of the attractiveness of the traditional religion of the land may lie here; it encouraged contact with the dead. But it is in the here and now, the psalm adds, that we are blessed, and in the here and now that we may worship. Its opening has already affirmed a concern that honor should be given to Yhwh, "not to us," in a context where people around are asking with mockery, "So where is their God?" It is Yhwh's honor that counts.

Trust for the Future

Worshiping the god of love and marriage reflects the vital importance to a community that its women bear children. Hosea's description of Israelites as "children of promiscuity" (Hos 2:4 [MT 6]) perhaps implies that these children were born after their mothers had been asking the Master to make them conceive, but that is more explicit in a subsequent declaration that Israel's daughters are promiscuous, their brides adulterous, while the men "go off with loose women, sacrifice with holy women" (Hos 4:13-14). Hosea's linking of sexual activity and people's relationship with God suggests he refers not merely to ordinary promiscuity but to sexual unions designed to be acted prayers for human fertility. The First Testament is not explicit about the nature of such practices, nor about what is wrong with them except insofar as they are overtly undertaken in connection with calling on other deities, but they indicate how religious practices can imply we think we can make things happen in a way semi-independent of God's personal action. They can reflect the toughness of simply relying on God for human fertility as well as for the fertility of nature. Trust is hard to live by when it involves accepting we are not in control of whether we have food to eat or children to care for us and to carry on our line. These practices also reflect the deep importance of sex to people and the way sex and religion get interwoven. It might be tempting to sit in judgment on the women involved in these rites, but Yhwh does not do so. In some way they were victims of a culture, and their men were at least as guilty.

It may be hard for us to understand a religion that worked as this religion did, and Hosea himself has a hard time understanding it. There is again something fiendishly mysterious about it. It is as if drink, or simply the longing that there should be a good grape harvest that will eventually generate lots of wine, has taken away people's understanding and made them act in a stupid way (Hos 4:11; cf. 7:14). It is as if a promiscuous spirit possesses them. Talk in terms of a spirit suggests simultaneously something deeply ingrained in people, deeply possessive of them, and also something strange and inexplicable. It is so hard to believe people are behaving as they are that one starts thinking they must be subject to some power from outside them. Once again the First Testament is puzzled by the mystery of disobedience. Its usage does not suggest we should reify this spirit or power, as if there are objectively existent supernatural entities that represent a distillation of a particular quality or inclination and can influence or take over a person, possibly against their will. But when someone acts in bewildering ways, it is *as if* some force external to them possesses them.

The people themselves do not see involvement in these rites as an abandoning of Yhwh. They still swear their oaths by Yhwh and attend the great festivals at Bethel and Gilgal. But Hosea will not let them have it both ways. Having recourse to other gods and indulging in these rites whereby they look to the gods to transmit life-giving power means they have actually abandoned Yhwh, because Yhwh insists on being the sole life-giving power. They cannot both take part in these rites and name the name of Yhwh.

Subsequently, it may have been Assyrian domination in Israel and Judah that led to increased emphasis on the worship of sun, moon, planets and stars, "to which they dedicated themselves, which they served and followed, from which they sought guidance, and to which they bowed down" (Jer 8:2). The sequence of verbs underlines the enormity of the turning to these so-called deities; all these verbs are appropriate only with Yhwh as object. As human beings we are naturally concerned about how the future will work out. Christian faith often responds by assuring people that God has a plan for each individual's life and encouraging them to seek to discover that plan, despite the fact that the Bible does not say this. Israelites similarly sought ways of satisfying that concern.

Trust for Our Destiny

Isaiah 57:3-4 addresses people as "children of a sorceress," which might mean people inclined to sorcery or might designate the people of Jerusalem, *the* sorceress; the reference to sorcery does suggest seeking guidance about the future and seeking to influence the future in order to prevent bad things happening or to make good things happen. The prophet's polemic is initially based not (for instance) on the conviction that this does not work but on the fact that it involves disloyalty to Yhwh. It again makes Israel like people who are sexually unfaithful, an image that as usual presupposes that they have not abandoned their allegiance to Yhwh but combine their Israelite faith with other observances, in the conviction that one does not have to choose between the two. They thus resemble (for instance) people keeping Christian commitment but also practicing voodoo. People do not see that they are playing about with Yhwh and mocking Yhwh. Yhwh is in charge of what happens in the world and is the one from whom people must seek their guidance, to whom they must bring their prayers and to whose will they must submit, rather than thinking they can influence events in a way that bypasses Yhwh.

Far from having recourse to Yhwh, they are telling Yhwh to keep away from them (Is 65:5). They have a different form of consecration in relation to Yhwh, a consecration in another direction.[89] Like other prophetic indictments (e.g., Is 28:15), this accusation will not be telling us what people actually said. They did not literally tell Yhwh to keep away because they were now holy to another deity. They will have been involved in the worship of Yhwh but also in these other observances or will have seen these observances as part of their worship of Yhwh. But the implication of their practices is that actually they have turned their backs on Yhwh. They have scorned Yhwh, treated Yhwh as someone who can be ignored. Yhwh's help is not something that can be any use to them. They need to have recourse to other means if their needs are to be met. Indeed, they are neither people who call on Yhwh's name nor people called by Yhwh's name.[90] They "lay a table for Fortune, fill a goblet for Destiny," which grievously means "I summoned but you did not answer, I spoke but you did not listen" (Is 65:11-13). Even if they also still worship Yhwh, they are abandoning Yhwh when they cease to treat seeking help at Yhwh's holy mountain as the key to their facing their personal future, and have recourse to other deities that allegedly influence the future. Yhwh is reaching out to them, but they do not respond because Yhwh's concerns do not correspond to theirs.

So the Torah forbids practicing divination or looking for omens (Lev 19:26). People are not to try to discover what the future is nor to seek to change it

---

[89] qĕdaštīkā means "I am holy you," which is odd in Hebrew as in English, but occasionally such an intransitive verb can have a suffix with quasi-dative significance (GK 117x; JM 125ba). "I am too holy for you" (NRSV, cf. TNIV) or "I would render you consecrated" (JPSV) are grammatically harder to justify and harder to make sense of in the context.

[90] In Rom 10:20-21 Paul uses vv. 1-2 to illustrate the way Gentiles had responded to God's gospel message when Jews had not done so—which is all very well for a fellow Jew, though dangerous when Gentiles read it.

when they think they have done so (Lev 19:26-28 then all concern attitudes to death). They are not to turn to ghosts or seek help from mediums and thus be defiled (Lev 19:31; "ghosts" [*ōbōt*] is likely a derogatory spelling of *ʾābōt* and thus suggests consulting one's ancestors).[91]

In a world that always urges people to be active, the scriptural community "dares to gather and wait upon God" with "a kind of disciplined inactivity." It knows it "has not been given the task of engineering a future of its own devising, but instead one of recognizing, announcing, welcoming, and 'mid-wifing' a future that God is bringing."[92]

Trust in Ourselves and Our Creations

Like Hosea, Jeremiah is bewildered at the way people abandon Yhwh when Yhwh has provided all their needs, and swear their oaths by no-gods (Jer 5:7). What you use to guarantee your oaths shows what you take really seriously or what you want people to believe you take really seriously (even if you then break your oaths). Paradoxically, the human flourishing that is a gift of God gives people the means to turn away from Yhwh and put their trust in re-sources they have acquired or devised for themselves. This flourishing is thus one factor that leads to making images, the work of people's own hands and fingers. They bow down to these (and in a sense to themselves) rather than before the real awesomeness and loftiness of Yhwh (Is 2:6-21). Isaiah thus finally comments, "Get yourselves away from human beings, who have breath in their nostrils, because how are they to be esteemed?" (Is 2:22).

Turning to deities they had made is where the book of Jeremiah starts in analyzing the people's faithlessness: "I will tell them my decisions because of all their wrongdoing, in that they have abandoned me and made offerings to other gods, bowed down to things their hands made" (Jer 1:16). They are only following their ancestors' example, for they already "went far away from me and went after emptiness" (*hebel*, a mere breath; Jer 2:5). The gods they went after looked as if they had substance (you could see them), but they actually had none, so that they contrasted with the God whom you could not see but who did have substance. Those earlier generations had already failed to ask, "Where is Yhwh?" (Jer 2:6). It is a question often asked scathingly (e.g., Ps 42:3, 10 [MT 4, 11]), but it is a proper question when people want to get God to act, especially if God seems to have turned the other way (2 Kings 2:14; Job 35:10).

But "the priests did not say 'Where is Yhwh?' the experts in the Teaching

---

[91]Gordon J. Wenham, *The Book of Leviticus,* NICOT (Grand Rapids: Eerdmans, 1979), p. 273.
[92]Philip Kenneson, "Gathering," in *The Blackwell Companion to Christian Ethics,* ed Stanley Hauerwas and Samuel Wells (Oxford/Malden, Mass.: Blackwell, 2004), pp. 53-67; see pp. 64, 65.

did not acknowledge me, the shepherds rebelled against me, the prophets prophesied by the Master, and they went after things that would not bene-fit" (Jer 2:8). It was the priests' job to lead in prayers in the temple, which were accompanied by the sacrifices they offered; Jeremiah perhaps then re-fers to the Levites in general in speaking of a teaching role. "Shepherds" is a more general term for leaders. Here, at least, the context may suggest reli-gious leaders as much as political leaders; Jeremiah apparently describes himself as a shepherd (Jer 17:16). This fits with the fact that the last group he describes as having failed to trust are the prophets, who prophesied by the Master, bringing the people's needs to the Master or seeking his inspiration or speaking in his name.

The people have thus alienated themselves from Yhwh, turned themselves into strangers (*nāzōrû* from *zûr*, Ezek 14:5). Ezekiel goes on to reexpress the point by means of an inventive use of *nāzar*, the verb linked with the idea of the nazirite vow. Hosea used this verb to describe the people as dedicating themselves to the Master, and Ezekiel now comments that they have thus dedicated themselves away from Yhwh (Hos 9:10; Ezek 14:7). Jerusalem did not merely yield to the temptation to a one night stand with a man who flat-tered her. "You gained confidence because of your beauty, and became pro-miscuous on the basis of your fame and lavished your sexual favors on every passerby" (Ezek 16:15). Jerusalem did not think about the way Yhwh had ad-opted her when she was an abandoned child. Yhwh's gifts became the means of her indulging herself sexually, and she offered her children as sacrifices to these lovers (the literal shows through the parable).

A visionary scene had already confronted Ezekiel that comprised a com-posite of worship practices in Jerusalem over the centuries, as well as ones undertaken by people in their homes. All illustrate the instinct to put trust anywhere but in Yhwh. At the edge of the temple complex there is a statue that arouses Yhwh's fury, apparently a statue of Yhwh's alleged consort, a goddess of love and marriage (Ezek 8:3-6; cf. 2 Kings 21:7; Jer 44:17-30). In pri-vate, even the people's leaders are worshiping serpent and animal deities, who have their own shrines in their homes (Ezek 8:7-13). Near the main tem-ple building, women are taking part in mourning rites for a god who went down to the realm of death, a symbol of the death of the growing world in the long dry summer with the threat that it may never come back to life (Ezek 8:14-15). At the door of the temple itself, men are bowing down to the sun (Ezek 8:16).

Trust and Mindfulness

When Deuteronomy 5–11 lays out the key principles of a relationship with Yhwh, being mindful (*zākar*) and not putting out of mind or ignoring (*šākah*) is one of its features. The EVV often speak of "remembering" and "forgetting," but the First Testament puts more emphasis on intentionality than these English words commonly imply. When Hosea 13:4-6 parallels failing to "acknowledge Yhwh" with "putting Yhwh out of mind," it implies we are responsible for our remembering and forgetting. Isaiah 57:11-13 likewise parallels fear of or reverence for other deities with failing to keep Yhwh in mind, then adds that "the people who take refuge in me will hold the land, will possess my holy mountain." Being mindful links closely with trust.

Israel has "abandoned me, . . . betrayed me, . . . lied to Yhwh" (Jer 5:7, 11, 12); people's pretending to belong to Yhwh when they are not really committed again involves failing to keep in mind the way Yhwh acted on their behalf in the past. After all, Yhwh reminds them, I destroyed the hugely impressive and threatening Amorites before you, brought you out of Egypt, took you through the wilderness, and gave you prophets and nazirites, but you made the nazirites drink wine and ordered the prophets not to prophesy (Amos 2:9-12). This reminder follows on an indictment about the oppression of the poor (Amos 2:6-8). The lines about destroying the Amorites put all the emphasis on the power and thoroughness of Yhwh's act. The reminder is frightening, not reassuring. Ephraim is living a life that risks Yhwh's coming down on it, and is thus perilously ignoring Yhwh's capacity to act in devastating ways. This capacity that once worked for it will now work against it. Bringing Israel from Egypt through the wilderness to occupy the Amorites' land was also an act of power that Israel is unwise to put out of mind. There is again no allusion to the act's being undertaken for Israel's sake. Yhwh brought Israel from Egypt as an act of authority that demonstrated Yhwh's power equally over Egyptians, Israelites and Amorites. Yhwh is able to move the pieces around the chessboard and demonstrate such authority over peoples and land. By its acts of rebellion and oppression Israel is unwisely annoying a manifestly sovereign power.

Yhwh has demonstrated this power again in raising up prophets and nazirites. The verb (qûm hiphil) is one that can describe the raising up of nations that will attack Israel (Amos 6:14; Hab 1:6). It is a sovereign act. And so is the turning of young people into prophets and nazirites. Only Yhwh could bring that about. Will this sign of Yhwh's power not draw Israel to submit itself to Yhwh? Will they not accept the young people's challenge to a lifestyle that does not involve turning festivals into self-indulgent drinking bouts and reckoning that money is all that counts? Will they not heed the words of these messengers from the great King? But all it made Israel do is beguile these young nazirites into drinking and tell the young prophets to shut up. Yhwh raised them up; Israel shut them up. For their continuous rebellions Yhwh will not revoke the punishment.

"They put his deeds out of mind, the wonders that he showed them" (Ps 78:11). Psalm 78 is a gargantuan exposition of this theme, designed to encourage Israel to put its confidence in Yhwh. It seeks to achieve this by retelling the story of the wilderness period as one in which Israel failed to trust in Yhwh, and then painting the broader canvas of the period from Egypt to the monarchy. The story shows that Ephraim found itself rejected by Yhwh and that Yhwh chose Judah and David, but it does not thereby suggest that Judah and David can afford to relax their commitment and trust. On the contrary, it warns them about the danger they risk if they fail to maintain their trust. It is vital that Israel passes on this story so that every generation can be mindful of it; the psalm locates itself between the telling that the ancestors did, of which the present generation is the beneficiary, and the telling that the present generation must do for the sake of its descendants, "so that they might put their confidence in God, and not ignore God's deeds but observe his commands" (Ps 78:7). Only as Israel listens to the story of the past does it know who it is and how to live in relation to its God. And only as Israel passes on the story does the next generation know these things. This also heightens the importance of the way it passes on the story. The psalm does so in a different way from the narrative in Exodus–2 Samuel, and each time communities or teachers tell the biblical story, they do so in new ways. They had better do so in ways that foster true mindfulness.

Trust and Hopefulness

"They did not trust in God, they did not rely on his deliverance" (Ps 78:22). Whereas the main body of the Psalms is classically divided into hymns, protests and thanksgivings, many of the protests or prayer psalms are characterized more by trust and hopefulness than by lament and protest. These suppliants know Yhwh is watching (Ps 11; 14). They know Yhwh keeps us safe (Ps 23; 27). They know Yhwh puts the wicked down (Ps 62; 75). What is it that decides whether they trust in Yhwh? These psalms do not imply that it is whether or not we are people of faith, people with an inherent capacity for trust or people who lack any instinct to be worried or anxious or afraid. They imply that people trust because they have evidence, and they suggest various forms of evidence; perhaps when one form of evidence is under pressure, we turn to another. In one direction or another, mindfulness is key to hope.

In general, it is knowing what God has done that gives us a basis for trusting God in the future, and it is reflection on those acts of God that builds up hope. There are reasons for trust and hope that issue from our own experience. Many naturally relate to Yhwh's own actions. Psalm 16:7 refers to the way Yhwh has spoken to me, guiding me by night as my spirit instructs me. Psalm 36 and Psalm 84 speak of encountering Yhwh's presence in the temple.

Psalm 41 and Psalm 129 speak of the way Yhwh has kept me safe in the past. Psalm 67 speaks of Yhwh's provision of something to eat. I know from my own experience that Yhwh is "my strength . . . my cliff, my fastness, the one who enables me to escape . . . my crag on which I take refuge, my shield, my peak that delivers, my haven" (Ps 18:1-2 [MT 2-3]). Other psalms recollect my own actions, such as my commitment to Yhwh (Ps 101; 119) or my stand against wrongdoing (Ps 139).

There are also reasons for trust outside my own experience. There is the fact of Yhwh's power and love (Ps 62:11-12 [MT 12-13]); Yhwh is a help and a shield (Ps 115:9-11). There is Yhwh's creation of the world and sovereignty in it (e.g., Ps 93; 121). There is Yhwh's deliverance of the people at the Red Sea (Ps 77). There is Yhwh's commitment to Jerusalem (Ps 46; 76; 132). There is Yhwh's commitment to David (Ps 132). There are Yhwh's promises, general (Ps 119) and specific (Ps 108).

One side of sin is confidence in oneself, making oneself God, but its obverse is resignation or despair or hopelessness.[93] "Humanness is pervasively hope-filled, not in the sense of a buoyant, unreflective optimism, but in the conviction that individual human destiny is powerfully presided over by this One who wills good and who works that good." Thus "Israel does not hope for something, but hopes in God. That is, Yahweh is not *instrumental* to the hope of Israel, but Yahweh is the very substance of that hope."[94] "So now, what do I look to, my Lord? My hope is in you" (Ps 39:7 [MT 8]). There is a telling movement between these two parallel cola, a move from looking for *something* to hoping in *someone*. "You have been my hope, my Lord Yhwh, my trust from my youth" (Ps 71:5). "The good fortune of all who wait for him!" (Is 30:18). "Hope is encountered in the Psalter, not as a by-product of the relationship with God, but rather as the foundational structure of Yahwistic faith."[95]

Trust and Expectancy

Isaiah 51:1-8 speaks to people "who chase after faithfulness, who have recourse to Yhwh." The EVV have them chasing after justice or righteousness and seeking Yhwh, but these translations give a misleading impression. The word *ṣedeq* connotes something Yhwh brings about, Yhwh doing the right thing by Israel in restoring the people; they are longing for that to happen. In at least this sense they are people who "have recourse to [*biqqēš*] Yhwh," who are turning to Yhwh, not just seeking Yhwh in the sense of coming to worship; the verb implies seeking something from Yhwh, coming to Yhwh

---

[93]Jürgen Moltmann, *Theology of Hope* (London: SCM Press/New York: Harper, 1967), pp. 22-26.

[94]Brueggemann, *Theology of the Old Testament*, p. 479.

[95]Preuss, *Old Testament Theology*, 2:267.

as one who acts in the world and can be called on to act on their behalf. It implies an attitude of trust that issues in expectancy.

Oddly, these people who thus look to Yhwh are told to look somewhere else, to the rock from which they were cut. They themselves are mere left-overs and their future might seem not very promising. But the community has been here before. It once comprised one old man and his sterile post-menopausal wife. Just remind yourselves of that, says the prophet, and let your chasing and recoursing be encouraged. It is not hopeless. Expectant looking to the future involves looking to the past. It involves being mindful.

It also involves looking to the future, which requires the use of imagination. In the prophet's imagination, desolation is replaced by comfort, which here suggests action and not mere words; it is an expression for renewal or restoration. Wilderness and steppe are turned into something like the Garden of Eden. And mourning and grief at what Yhwh has done in bringing about destruction and exile are turned into joyful testimony to what Yhwh has done to reverse that. Be bold enough to imagine this in order to find encouragement now, the prophet urges. "People who wait for Yhwh find new strength, grow wings like eagles" (Is 40:31).

Isaiah 51:1-8 goes on to another exhortation about where people are to look, but now the direction is not back or forward, but up. When Psalm 8 looks at the heavens, it does so in amazement. Yhwh here invites a different look, another look of the imagination, and not an encouraging one. Imagine the heavens shredding (in Los Angeles we cannot see stars or planets, so that requires little imagination) and the earth wearing out (our devastation of the earth makes that easy to picture) and its population dying (and our awareness of famine, AIDS, conflict devastating some regions and birthrates plummeting in others makes that all too easy to picture). Before people's actual eyes in this prophet's day the world order is collapsing as the Persians rampage through the Middle East, but even this will look a triviality if the heavens and earth fall apart. At first that indeed looks discouraging, but the prophet's logic works in the opposite direction. Yes, the world is falling apart, but that makes for a contrast with the act of deliverance Yhwh is bringing about, the act of faithfulness whereby Yhwh does the right thing by Israel as Yhwh's people. Indeed, in that light it is not just Yhwh's people who have a right to do some waiting and hoping. The declaration that Yhwh is issuing, the revelation about what Yhwh intends to do with Israel and with the world, is either reason for the nations to start waiting and hoping, or is a response to their waiting and hoping. Either way, waiting and hoping is a proper stance for peoples and foreign shores too, because Yhwh activity in the world is good news for them.

The community the prophet addresses is a people who "acknowledge faithfulness" (Is 51:7) in the sense that they trust the reality of Yhwh's faithfulness to them and Yhwh's commitment to do the right thing by them. That is who they are by virtue of being Israel. They are a people who know Yhwh's teaching or *tôrâ*. They have it in their mind. Here, the "teaching" does not denote the instruction about behavior that appears in *the* Torah but the revelation about a purpose at work in history, focused on Israel, that is being implemented in current events, a purpose that expresses God's faithfulness. The prophet's listeners are (in theory, at least) a people who have that in their minds. In light of their theoretical commitment to that teaching, Yhwh can bid this people not to be afraid, not to be shattered, by the ridicule of their neighbors and masters in Babylon.

Sometimes people wait and hope not knowing whether their hopes will be empty. Yhwh invites the Judeans to wait and hope for something that they know will happen because Yhwh has taken them this way before, declaring intentions and then fulfilling them. They have a basis for trust.

Trust and Waiting

In the manner of Micah 6:8, Hosea 12:6 [MT 7] talks about exercising authority with commitment and then adds a further bidding, but where Micah has "walk diffidently with your God," Hosea has "wait for your God continually." Diffidence and trust are related; and one aspect of the fundamental stance toward God that can be described as trust is that it expresses itself in being prepared to wait.

Like English, Hebrew has a series of words for waiting, hoping and expecting; the two most frequent are *yāḥal* and *qāwâ*, both in the piel. The piel is perhaps resultative; it puts the emphasis on the results of hope or the object of hope. There is little difference in the meaning of the different verbs; I translate the former "hope" and the latter "wait." Each can signify both an ongoing attitude of hopeful waiting and a stance of expectant anticipation regarding a particular event.

After expressing its commitment to not making too much of ourselves, Psalm 131 closes with an exhortation to "hope in Yhwh" and offers as the model for our attitude a baby nursed with its mother, sated and content. Israel needs to hope in Yhwh and to go to sleep in its mother's arms; it cannot work out its destiny. And it needs to be prepared to hope in Yhwh like this "from now and forevermore." Maybe it will be a very long time before (for instance) Yhwh gives Judah independence from Persia. Judah has to be prepared to live in hope for as long as it takes, not to try to bring in the kingdom of God itself. Another fruit of God's liberation is that we no longer have "to desire and demand" but "may now receive." We do not have to make anything happen; we can wait for it expectantly.[96]

---

[96]Barth, *Church Dogmatics*, IV/3, ii:667, 668.

Proverbs and Job are the books that make most use of the nouns for "hope." Some occurrences refer to "ordinary" human hope, the kind whose deferral saddens (Prov 13:12), but many refer to God's involvement in our ordinary lives, even if Job spends much of his time questioning whether there is such hope (e.g., Job 14:19-20; 19:10).[97] Further, hope is a fundamental human possibility for the earth. God has looked in the eye the possibility of totally destroying the earth and held back from doing so, and has made a commitment never to do so (Gen 9:8-17). Hope is not only a positive attitude to the future as such but an attitude to God that issues in a positive attitude to the future.[98]

The conviction that God is not finished is an important feature of First Testament spirituality. Christians emphasize how Christ has fulfilled the First Testament's expectations, but after two thousand years that raises the question "Is that all there is?" Or do we have expectation for our own individual lives and our enjoyment of the resurrection, but no positive expectation for the world? Or do we have a commitment to seeking peace and justice, but no clarity about how or whether God will be involved in bringing about a reign of peace and justice? Or do we reckon that God has written off the world and it is on the way to hell in a hand basket? The First Testament invites us into an expectation that this is not all there is for the world.[99]

The herald in Isaiah 40:9 is bidden to have no fear in proclaiming that Yhwh is returning to Jerusalem. Another voice (Is 40:6-7) has been hesitant to issue any proclamation; the people look so much like withered grass with no life potential left. Hoping for Yhwh's word to be fulfilled, waiting for Yhwh's comfort, can seem to last forever and to use up the whole person so that there is nothing left (*kālâ*; Ps 119:81-82). This herald is bidden to resist such fear.

Knowing that Yhwh's promises will be fulfilled makes it possible to live as a sojourner until that comes about (Gen 26:1-5).

Trust and Risk

While Yhwh's bidding to Abraham "Don't be afraid" (Gen 15:1) comes against the background of mixed evidence in preceding chapters for Abraham's confidence or fearfulness, Abraham's response to Yhwh suggests that here Yhwh is anticipating a problem, not merely picking up an existent one. Abraham has no son and sees no future for his household—at least, no future that is-

---

[97]Cf. Walther Zimmerli, *Man and His Hope in the Old Testament* (London: SCM Press/Naperville, Ill.: Allenson, 1971), pp. 12-25.

[98]Cf. Zimmerli, *Man and His Hope,* in dialogue with Ernst Bloch, *The Principle of Hope,* 3 vols. (Oxford: Blackwell/Cambridge, Mass.: MIT Press, 1986).

[99]Cf. Kornelis H. Miskotte, *When the Gods Are Silent* (London: Collins/New York: Harper, 1967), pp. 283-88.

sues from him. What about Yhwh's promise that he will become a mighty nation? It will happen, says Yhwh. You will become as many as the stars. "And he trusted in Yhwh, and he counted it for him as faithfulness." Perhaps that is Yhwh counting Abraham's trust as faithfulness, though it is more natural to assume that Abraham continues to be the subject of the verbs;[100] the statement then spells out the implications of "trust." Abraham reckoned that Yhwh would indeed be faithful. He moved from fear about the future to confidence for the future. It might seem that he did this simply because Yhwh reaffirmed the promise, though more may be going on when Yhwh directs him to look at the stars in their multiplicity. By implication, the stars remind Abraham that Yhwh is their creator; multiplying Abraham's family is a smallish task for such a creator. As happened with Noah and the rainbow, divine power and commitment have come to be associated with the wonder of the created world. That wonder becomes the basis for confidence with regard to the particulars of Abraham's own destiny.

In Genesis 16, however, Abraham is agreeing with Sarah that they need to do something themselves to see that Yhwh's promise comes true. In Genesis 17, he is laughing at the idea that he and Sarah could have a son (why will Yhwh not settle for Ishmael?), and soon Sarah is following his example. Yet his hope in Yhwh finds mysterious expression in Genesis 22. "We will go over there and bow down and return to you": What does he mean? "God is the one who will provide for himself the sheep for a whole offering": What does he mean?

The First Testament does not cross-refer to Genesis 22 in the way Judaism and the New Testament do. Like the stories of Abraham's finding a wife for Isaac, or of Enoch walking with God and disappearing, or of the action and death of Nadab and Abihu, Genesis 22 stands as a testimony to events in another time that have no parallel in the experience of ordinary Israelites in ordinary time. Nor do Genesis 12 and Genesis 22 raise the question, How did Abraham know this was really God speaking? They perhaps imply that when that happens, things are clear. God did not leave any ambiguity about whether Abraham was to leave his homeland or sacrifice his son. They do not raise this question despite the fact that some Israelites did think God wanted them to sacrifice their sons. Perhaps one function of the story was to establish that this is something God never requires; God has thought about it and decided against it, while prepared to take Abraham's descendants close to annihilation at their enemies' hands though not at their own hands.

Perhaps the Abraham story likewise establishes that a move from Babylon to Canaan had a once-for-all nature. Abraham's son is not to leave the land, even to find a wife or because they have no food (Gen 24:5-6; 26:1-3), though

---

[100]Cf. OTT 1:266-67.

Rebekah and Isaac do encourage their son to go back to Haran to find a wife and to escape his brother's wrath (Gen 27:41–28:5) and subsequently the entire family leaves the land because of a famine. Once delivered from Egypt, Israel is never called to leave this land (compare Jeremiah's warning to Judeans in the 580s, Jer 42–44), even though God has also been prepared to remove them from it. But perhaps the story then sometimes reminds the descendants of people who have been scattered that they should seize the opportunity to "return" to the land. Perhaps that call does not come to all, but does come to some. And they know.

And from time to time an ordinary Israelite or a leader or the people as a whole know themselves placed under monumental demands by God that would test who they were and how much God and God's promise counted to them. The demand placed before Daniel's three friends (Dan 3) was like that.

Trust and Composure

The life of human communities is full of inequality; some people do better than others, maybe much better. One possible reaction is to be encouraged, reckoning that this suggests anyone can succeed. Another is to reckon this inequality is not fair, particularly when evil people are the ones who do well. Psalm 37 is a homily encouraging people not to fret at this, not to be vexed, be angry, get worked up. The First Testament often takes a positive view of anger, divine and human, as an aspect of divine and human nature that energizes commitment to right action, but it also recognizes that anger can energize commitment to wrong action. If you are a weak person, in no position to take action to put the faithless down, it may just be a waste of energy.

The opening section of Psalm 37 urges composure rather than vexation on the basis of the argument that Yhwh will take the action that you cannot. It comes to an end by urging silence, a stillness that implies a quietist attitude; we do not take matters into our own hands, but wait for Yhwh. Here the antonym of trust is vexation or fretting at evil people who may turn out to be a threat to us. And trust appears in parallelism with delight. Whereas trust suggests poise and equanimity, delight suggests fervor and enthusiasm. Trust is a profound stance to take; delight is a more affective one. Yhwh can be trusted to provide; that makes it possible to be enthusiastic about reliance on Yhwh. As an affective attitude, delight also constitutes a correlative attitude to fretting. A delighted trust in Yhwh that is confident in what Yhwh will do has the capacity to melt vexation. Looking with delight to Yhwh makes it possible to stop looking with vexation at other people. Or perhaps the abandoning of vexation makes it possible to begin delighting in Yhwh. Trust then also appears in parallelism with a vivid expression for "committing" our way to Yhwh. MT's verb is a form of *gālal,* suggesting that we "roll" our way onto

Yhwh. LXX and Tg imply a form of *gālâ*, suggesting we "reveal" our way to Yhwh.

"Yet a little while and there will be no faithless person, and you will look at his place and there will be no one; but the weak—they will take possession of the land and delight in abundance of well-being" (Ps 37:10-11; Jesus takes up the penultimate half-line in Mt 5:5). Trusting in Yhwh and living uprightly are the keys to seeing your hopes fulfilled. "Don't let your anger draw you into taking on the moral shortcomings of the people you are angry at. Better to settle for the little you have, because the abundance of the faithless will be short-lived."

Psalm 37 is one of a string of psalms strategically scattered through the Psalter, along with Psalms 1, 73, 91 and 119, all affirming that Yhwh is faithful to the upright even while explicitly or implicitly acknowledging how experience often belies this. The tension between affirmation and experience is underlined by the context of this string of psalms in the sequence of prayers characterized by pain and protest, particularly in the first half of the Psalter. The tension parallels that in Ecclesiastes between the affirming of truths concerning theological and moral order, and the owning of empirical facts that do not fit in with those truths. Like Ecclesiastes, Psalm 37 speaks for people who are not personally threatened by starvation or oppression, but who do see many other people doing well in life despite their lack of integrity. Both books insist on facing two sets of facts.[101] It is important to own the facts about empirical experience. But it is important not to be overwhelmed by them. And it is possible not to be overwhelmed by them partly because (Ps 37 declares) today is not the only day, and Yhwh promises there will be another day.[102] Yhwh has not actually reduced us to starvation, and it is actually better to have enough to get by with integrity and security than to have plenty with faithlessness and insecurity. The First Testament does not reckon that goodness is its own reward; it does reckon that faithfulness will see its reward.

Trust and Silence

While silence will usually not do in First Testament prayer,[103] Psalm 62 almost makes it do. It begins its expression of trust in Yhwh in a novel way: "toward God my spirit is silent." Here silence is an expression of trust, and the psalm keeps silence in relation to Yhwh until its very last verse. (Admittedly this may take its rhetoric too simply at face value. After all, the suppliant is declaiming this psalm before Yhwh, even though for the most part it does not

---

[101]Cf. §3.3 "Plea and Praise"; §3.4 "Protesting and Believing."

[102]See Walter Brueggemann, *The Psalms and the Life of Faith* (Minneapolis: Fortress, 1995), pp. 235-57.

[103]See §3.1 "The Impossibility of Silence."

address Yhwh. So it says before Yhwh that it is not saying anything to Yhwh.)

In the meantime it does address the suppliant's attackers, the suppliant's own self and the people in general, and this nonsilence is also an expression of trust. In other contexts the question "How long will you attack a person" would implicitly be an expression of anxiety, but here the protest is set in the context of a declaration that Yhwh is "my crag and deliverance." The confrontation is an expression of trust. Yet perhaps the lines also again imply that trust does not mean the suppliant's spirit is calm and restful. As courage can coexist with fear, so trust can coexist with anxiety, because trust, like courage, is a practical stance not a feeling. Trust implies the reality of some pressure or peril. Any fool can trust when there is no peril or pressure. And the suppliant needs to maintain an argument with the self to encourage it to keep reaffirming the psalm's opening stance: "Yes, be silent for God, my spirit." The encouragement reminds the self of those facts about Yhwh as crag and deliverance.

Any implication that the suppliant is wavering in trust is countered by the subsequent exhortation to the community as a whole, "Trust in him at all times, people." They could be tempted to reckon that the attackers' methods are the ones that pay. Rather, "Do not trust in extortion, do not become worthless through robbery; when resources blossom, do not give them your heart." Trust in Yhwh, not in Mammon with the implication that any way of acquiring wealth is all right. In situations of pressure and danger, "pour out your heart before him, God our refuge." One normally pours out anger, so this expression suggests pouring out the kind of negative feelings we have when under attack—the anger, resentment, grief and fear. That would be an expression of trust. People can trust that it will be proved that human beings (the kind who are attacking them) are mere breath, deceptive and self-deceived in their pretension to be able to bring the community down. Apparently powerful people can be here today but gone tomorrow. There is no substance to them.

Only after addressing the attackers, the self and the community does the suppliant break silence toward Yhwh, but arguably still maintains the silence that the psalm earlier spoke of, because even here there is no plea. The lack of a plea implies a continuing trust; there is no need to ask Yhwh for anything. The psalm's words are an explicit declaration of two convictions implied by the way it has addressed those other parties: "that God has strength and that you, my Lord, have commitment, for you recompense a person according to their deeds." The attackers look as if they have power, but Yhwh is really the one with power. Further, whereas the attackers are people who perhaps should be committed to us (but if so, they are not), Yhwh is one who is committed to us, and will exercise that power. Power and commitment are two key divine characteristics.

2.4 Serving Yhwh

We continue to be concerned not so much with the life before God that Israel actually lived but with the life before God that its later generations believed it could live and should have lived, the heritage they wished to pass on to future generations. We come in this section to a consideration of worship in the First Testament, but our consideration of Israel's worship is different from that proper to a volume on the history of Israelite religion. For instance, archaeological investigation suggests that Israelites practiced much more home-based religion than the First Testament tells us, and academic study of such aspects of Israel's actual religion can itself be a theologically focused enterprise, but that too is a different task from studying the theological implications of the Scriptures of the First Testament itself.

Worship is a way Israel serves Yhwh. That is symbolized by the forms of bodily expression that worship involves, forms that connote submission to Yhwh. Rejoicing is also involved, but so is listening to Yhwh. Sacramental action, too, has a prominent place, and this implies a place for worship and accoutrements for worship. The nature of these then needs to balance on one hand human instincts and aids to worship that worshipers will find helpful, and on the other the necessity not to give a misleading expression of who Yhwh is.

Worship

"Worship" is another word capable of many different understandings. Worship involves acknowledging God's "worth-ship," but this illuminating definition works only in English and only on the basis of the etymological fallacy, the idea that one discovers the meaning of words by considering their history rather than their usage, and if one asks how the First Testament speaks of acknowledging God's worth-ship, then this would involve the use of words such as "honor."[104] For many Christians, "worship" means the singing of praise songs that occupies the first part of their church service, before you get to the sermon, but this is an understanding that works only in a particular cultural context.[105]

In the KJV "worship" usually represent a word that more concretely means "bow down" (hištaḥăwâ, or in Aramaic sāgad). The parsing of the Hebrew word is a matter of scholarly debate,[106] but there is no doubt that it refers to

---

[104]Much of §2.2 is thus about worship in this sense.
[105]§2.7 is about worship in this sense.
[106]Contrast BDB with *HALOT*.

the physical act of prostration (e.g., Gen 22:5; Ex 4:31; Deut 26:10; also in the New Testament, e.g., Jn 4:23; Acts 8:27; 1 Cor 14:25).

In modern translations *worship* often represents the word for "serve" (ʿ*ābad*; e.g., Ex 3:12; 4:23; Deut 5:9; in the New Testament, e.g., Lk 2:37; Acts 7:7; Phil 3:3). This was the purpose for which Israel left Egypt to celebrate a festival in the desert. Indeed, it can be argued that "service" (ʿ*ăbōdâ*) is close to being a comprehensive term for "worship."[107] A church "service" is thus an occasion when we worship God. The First Testament also occasionally uses in this connection another verb for serve, *šārat*; whereas ʿ*ābad* can denote serving in both a more and a less menial sense, *šārat* only has the less menial sense of "minister to" (e.g., Ezek 20:32), suggesting the honor conveyed by serving.

All this suggests more than one irony in relation to the modern and ancient worlds. For many Western Christians the criterion for evaluating worship is how good it makes them feel: whether they enjoy it, whether it gives them a sense of being in God's presence, whether they feel encouraged and built up by it. The First Testament takes for granted that worship means being in God's presence and that it involves joy, but insofar as it evaluates worship, it does so on the basis of whether it is offered for Yhwh's sake. If worship is service, whether it makes us feel good is totally irrelevant to its evaluation. At the same time, etymology is once again a dubious guide to meaning. When a religion has images, by means of an image people can literally serve the deity, especially by feeding it. Israel often made images of Yhwh and could then "serve" the image, but the First Testament disallows this. In such a connection "serving" the deity has become a dead metaphor, as it is in English when we talk about church "services." Yet Israel does make offerings to Yhwh. Further, servants do bow down to their master as a sign of their subservience, their commitment to serving the master, and there is thus a substantial link between worship as bowing down and worship as service. Our bowing down in worship is an expression of our willingness to serve.

While Christian parlance does talk about church "services," we mostly think of "serving" God as something that takes place outside church in our everyday lives, in our work in the world. In First Testament parlance "serving" Yhwh is mostly a worship activity. Israelites are of course to serve Yhwh in that broader sense, but the First Testament rarely uses words such as ʿ*ābad* or ʿ*ăbōdâ* in this connection (though it does use ʿ*ebed*, "servant"). As Psalm 100 expresses it, the only "service" the First Testament affirms is shouting and resounding, or if we add the activities of its later lines, acknowledging, confessing, praising and worshiping. Yet the First Testament's use of *serve* and *servant* encourages us to see the link between worship and the rest of life,

---

[107]Cf. Preuss, *Old Testament Theology,* 2:211.

without identifying the two. Bowing down before the master and doing what the master wants done are related but not the same. Both are important.

Gesture and Ritual

Worship then has a series of facets, including honoring attitudes, symbolic actions and words of praise. We are gesturing creatures before we are speaking creatures, and in the order of things in the First Testament, the gestures come first. Cain and Abel make offerings to Yhwh, as does Noah; Abraham builds altars to Yhwh; Leviticus prescribes at great length how Israel should go about these tasks and others. Subsequently, Miriam and Moses lead Israel in singing Yhwh's praise in words at the Red Sea, and in due course the Psalter provides an anthology of words to sing and say to Yhwh that is even more gargantuan than the prescriptions of Leviticus.

It is not surprising that worship involves both acts and words. While acts without words are blind, words without acts are empty. Keeping us on our toes, however, the Pentateuch is spare in telling us how to link the acts with the words, and the Psalter is spare in telling us how to link the words with the acts. What is clear is that worship is not something that is essentially of the heart or the mind; it is also necessarily of the voice and the body, the hands and the feet. It involves the whole person. Likewise it is not the case that religious experience, personal and spontaneous piety, is primary, and outward expression is necessary but secondary.[108] The inner and personal and the outward and communal are equally intrinsic to worship, and neither has logical or experiential priority. Whereas modern thinking assumed that true religion lay in people's inner experiences and attitudes, though recognizing that these may then find outward expression in rituals, premodern and postmodern thinking makes the opposite assumption. Symbolic actions such as eucharist, baptism or fasting are part of what makes it possible to experience the realities they reflect.

Human life can hardly proceed without rituals such as birthday parties, weddings, funerals, commencements, inaugurations, thanksgivings and meetings of learned societies. These are recurring communal events involving acts that look ordinary but are undertaken in ways, times and places hallowed by tradition, are accompanied by set words, and have special meaning recognized by the participants. They express, reaffirm and strengthen the way the people involved look at life. They change, but they do so in gradual fashion because one of their functions is to declare and reassert the presence of order in the seemingly patternless nature of human life. They mark and facilitate significant transitions in people's lives. They express, reaffirm,

---

[108]As Eichrodt suggests, *Theology of the Old Testament*, 1:98-101.

strengthen, restore and modify the way the participants relate to each other or the position of an individual in their midst. They thus are typically "thick" with meaning, complex in their significance. Much is happening in a ritual.

The same is true of religious rituals such as circumcision, sacrifices, pilgrim festivals, washings, anointings, baptism, eucharist, foot washing and ordination. These also more explicitly have within their purview not merely the society itself but the whole of reality within which they are set, including God.[109] It has been said that Genesis 1 presupposes the idea that through the cult we are enabled to cope with evil, because the cult "builds and maintains order, transforms chaos into creation, ennobles humanity, and realizes the kingship of God. . . . It is through obedience to the directives of the divine master that his good world comes into existence."[110] The more obvious implication of Genesis 1 is that if other peoples believed this was so, Genesis 1 contrasts with their view in making this a story about something that God did. The world *is* in order; one function of our obedience in worship and in other aspects of life is to align ourselves with that order.[111]

It is important to get a ritual such as a wedding, a commencement or a thanksgiving meal right. That is an aspect of letting it be the means whereby we set ourselves in a wider context of meaning in life. The same is true about religious ritual. Whereas Deuteronomy emphasizes the joyfulness of worship,[112] Leviticus (while also assuming that worship will be exuberant: Lev 23:40), puts its emphasis on getting the formal details of liturgy right. Prescribing the detail of the worship reminds people of the dynamic relationship between worshiping in accordance with human instincts in a culture and worshiping in light of who God is and what God has revealed. Leviticus and Deuteronomy thus complement each other. The concern for the detail corresponds to an instinct expressed in different forms of Christian worship. More catholic worship leaders may be concerned for precision in the choreography of a liturgy. More evangelical worship leaders may spend hours practicing worship songs so as to lead them well. Doing the worship right will seem a proper gift to God and an upbuilding experience for the congregation.

---

[109]On the nature of ritual, see, e.g., Frank H. Gorman, *The Ideology of Ritual,* JSOTSup 91 (Sheffield, U.K.: Sheffield Academic Press, 1990), pp. 13-38, and his references.

[110]Jon D. Levenson, *Creation and the Persistence of Evil* (Princeton, N.J./Chichester, U.K.: Princeton University Press, 1994), p. 127. In common with a number of other scholars, for the First Testament Gorman too, in *The Ideology of Ritual,* puts considerable emphasis on the link between ritual and creation order, more emphasis (it seems to me) than is justified by theoretical considerations or by the textual evidence.

[111]Cf. Antony Cothey, "Ethics and Holiness in the Theology of Leviticus," *JSOT* 30 (2005): 131-51; see pp. 147-48.

[112]See §2.7 "Joy."

Symbol and Sacrament

A further consideration enters in. Worship needs both to reflect the culture outside church and to be distinguished from it. More catholic worship focuses more on the second of these, while more evangelical worship focuses more on the first. Catholic worship makes the worshipers aware of coming to take part in something that suggests another world, that takes people out of the ordinary world. Evangelical worship makes the worshipers aware of taking part in something that links with the world in which they live the rest of their lives. Israel's sacramental worship has both these features. Its forms of sacrifice parallel those of other Middle-Eastern peoples, as Christian forms of worship (singing, preaching, meals, baptism) compare with those of other religions. The difference lies in the God they honor, though that may have some affect on the practice itself. There is little difference in the way the Master's prophets make their offerings in 1 Kings 18 and the way Yhwh's prophet does so; "the distinctiveness of the Israelite cult is nothing other than the limitation of cultic activity to one particular patron deity."[113] In Israelite worship, Yhwh alone is to be honored and there are no images of Yhwh to help this worship.

Israel's worship involves material symbols such as the sanctuary, the altars, the candelabra, the table with the presence bread, the cherubim and the covenant chest. The names of these symbols may suggest aspects of their significance, as may the textual contexts in which they are mentioned, but sometimes this does not happen. The significance of the symbols is not limited or static. But in seeking to understand their contribution to the First Testament's understanding of life with God, it would be unwise to infer significance from them that contradicts what the First Testament says elsewhere. We have noted that the First Testament's ban on images works against the idea of offering food for God to eat. Its understanding of God excludes the idea that God eats, so it would also be inappropriate to infer from the presence in the sanctuary of a table with bread that the bread was for God to eat, or to think that God was reckoned to eat the sacrifice whose smell was so pleasing. Israel did not "serve" Yhwh in that sense. Word and symbol interpret and reinforce each other. The relationship between Yhwh and bread elsewhere in the First Testament is that Yhwh is one who gives bread and human beings are the people who receive it, rather than vice versa; the symbolism of the table with the presence bread will embody that.

There is indeed a quasi-magical element to some aspects of Israel's religion. It includes a rite whereby water and dust and a written curse are reck-

---

[113]Gary A. Anderson, *Sacrifices and Offerings in Ancient Israel* (Atlanta: Scholars, 1988), p. 3 (the sentence is italicized in the original).

oned to have a physiological effect on a woman accused of adultery (Num 5:11-31), and one whereby Israelites bitten by snakes look to a representation of a snake and thus get healed (Num 21:4-9). But the rites are *quasi*-magical. The first regulation emphasizes that the rite takes place "before Yhwh," the woman brings an offering to Yhwh that thus accompanies what is actually a prayer for Yhwh to act, and the priest explicitly prays for Yhwh to bring about the physiological consequences of the rite if she is guilty. The second rite comes about because Moses pleads with Yhwh, and Yhwh gives the instruction about making the bronze snake. (Moses' sin in Numbers 20:10-11 involved his behaving more like a magician.)[114] The First Testament accepts the assumption that there is a unity about reality and that there are links built into reality, the assumption underlying "sympathetic magic"[115] and homeopathy or alternative medicine. But it assumes that this is an aspect of Yhwh's world and that Yhwh is involved in varying ways in its working.

"Whatever is shown us today in the sacraments, the Jews of old received in their own—that is, Christ with his spiritual riches,"[116] and the book of Acts shows how the first Christians continued the ritual and ceremonial practices of Judaism. Christianity's subsequent abandonment of such practices perhaps issued from the gospel's move into Europe. "Had Christianity spread first to the eastern Asiatic regions, it would have developed specific ritual and ceremonial practices based on the Jewish law in order to become a genuine religion in that part of the world."[117] "The abrogation of the Jewish laws within the early centuries of the Church is connected with the fact that already at an early stage Christianity was turning into a religion of non-Jews," in particular (in the first instance) people who revered the God of Israel but had not taken on the obligation of full obedience to the Torah.[118] There is no theological reason why sacrifice and other practices should not continue in the church, though the Christ event would nuance their meaning.

The Altar

We have noted that a first striking feature of the First Testament's treatment of worship is that both narrative and regulation begin with worship in its sacramental form. In Genesis 4:3-4, Cain and Abel bring offerings to Yhwh, and in Genesis 8:20 Noah takes the initiative in altar-building and making

---

[114]So Jacob Milgrom, *Numbers*, JPS Torah Commentary (Philadelphia: Jewish Publication Society, 1989), pp. 448-56.

[115]Cf. Baruch A. Levine, *Numbers 21–36*, AB (New York: Doubleday, 2000), p. 89.

[116]John Calvin, *Institutes of the Christian Religion* (Philadelphia: Westminster/London: SCM Press, 1961) 4.14.23; see p. 1299.

[117]David Flusser, *Jesus*, 3rd ed. (Jerusalem: Magnes, 2001), p. 56.

[118]Ibid., p. 75.

offerings. Abraham's first altar-building is a response to Yhwh's appearing at Shechem (Gen 12:7; cf. 26:24-25; Ex 17:15; Judg 6:24), though his second and third are his own initiative, at Bethel and at Hebron (Gen 12:8; 13:18; cf. 33:20; Josh 22:10; Judg 21:4; 1 Sam 7:17), while his fourth responds to Yhwh's bidding him offer Isaac (Gen 22:9; cf. 35:1-7; Josh 8:30-32; Judg 6:25-26). It is on Yhwh's initiative that Sinai becomes the place where Yhwh meets with Israel and in Exodus 20:22-26 [MT 19-23], Yhwh gives a regulation concerning the altar where offerings are brought, specifying what form it may and may not take. Leviticus 1–7 starts from the same place as Genesis 4: "When one of you presents an offering to Yhwh . . ." It is David's initiative that brings the covenant chest to Jerusalem and makes plans for a sanctuary there, though that then becomes the only sanctuary that Yhwh really approves of.

The First Testament thus gives complementary accounts of who takes the initiative in connection with worship. The worshipers' taking the initiative corresponds to the way worship, and particularly sacramental, sacrificial worship, is a universal human instinct (except in modern Western society). Yhwh's initiatives then implicitly presuppose some human instincts and designate channels for them, specifying where worship can be offered or what form it needs to take while also implying some flexibility within a framework.

Altars are independent of sanctuaries and precede them; they can be known to nonsettled peoples.[119] But ritual and thus worship nevertheless usually happen at a set place. The regulation in Exodus 20:22-26 [MT 19-23] about making an altar follows a ban on making gods of gold and silver "with me" and implies a contrast (cf. NRSV). The thing for Israel to make is not an image of another deity nor an image of Yhwh but an altar where people can present offerings that are simply gifts to Yhwh, and offerings that are shared by themselves and Yhwh. It is these that express and build up a relationship with Yhwh. Yhwh draws near and blesses not by coming and indwelling an image and being revealed through this, but by having the name Yhwh declared in various places. The name is the replacement for an image because the name conveys more of the actual character of Yhwh than an image can. Declaring the name in connection with making offerings leads to the coming of Yhwh in person (a little like the way uttering the name Jesus may convey a sense of his presence), which is evidently distinguished from the declaring of the name, even though the name also implies the presence.

The prescription regarding the nature of the altar perhaps continues a stress on simplicity. Simple earth is fine; the command does not mention the common mud-brick altar, but that might be covered by "earth." If people want

---

[119]Cf. Menahem Haran, *Temples and Temple-Service in Ancient Israel* (Winona Lake, Ind.: Eisenbrauns, 1985), p. 17.

to build with rocks in their natural state, this is fine, but dressed stone is not allowed, and neither is a big altar that needs steps to get onto it. Perhaps cutting the stone would profane the altar. There might be a parallel with the requirement that a sacrificial animal's blood was to be kept separate from anything leavened (Ex 23:18), because the blood distinctively belonged to Yhwh whereas the leavening of bread takes it from its pure, natural state. Likewise, a sacrificial animal's fat parts were not to be kept overnight, again perhaps because they belonged distinctively to Yhwh and needed to be offered promptly rather than held onto. But the instructions about the altar may intend a contrast with the magnificent stone altars in Canaanite sanctuaries, as the closing comment about priests exposing themselves may make a polemical point over against Canaanite religion, if it was reckoned to bring sex into religion in a way that Israelite religion did not.

The Sanctuary

Whereas an altar is a structure where people can offer sacrifices, a sanctuary suggests a place where God does deign to dwell. While there is a presence of Yhwh in the whole world and in a palace in the heavens and in the company of Israel as it journeys from Egypt to Sinai, there is also such a presence in an earthly sanctuary. T. C. Vriezen distinguishes between four types of sanctuary: ones in homes, open air sanctuaries to which a village or a number of villages had access (the "high places"), traditional temple sanctuaries such as Shechem and Bethel that Israelites also came to use, and temple sanctuaries that were built especially for Yhwh; Vriezen instances Gilgal and Shiloh.[120] The Meeting Tent (Ex 33:7-11) and the wilderness sanctuary are perhaps variants on the third, the state temple sanctuary in Jerusalem a variant on the fourth. These sanctuaries thus have differing religious and theological significance.

Exodus and Leviticus emphasize Yhwh's detailed instructions for the wilderness sanctuary as the place of worship, and Deuteronomy emphasizes worship at the place Yhwh chooses.[121] While human beings can take the initiative in worshiping Yhwh and thus in building an altar, they cannot take the initiative in getting Yhwh to dwell in a particular place among them, or at least they are dependent on Yhwh's being willing to come to dwell there. You can build, but Yhwh may not come.

Once Israel is in the land, people are to bring sacrifices, tithes and offerings not wherever they like but only where Yhwh says (Deut 12:4-19). Although Exodus 23 and Exodus 34 do not specify that there is only one sanctu-

---

[120]T. C. Vriezen, *The Religion of Ancient Israel* (London: Lutterworth/Philadelphia: Westminster, 1967), pp. 175-77.
[121]See further *OTT* 1:392-401.

ary, they do speak in terms of pilgrimage festivals (*ḥag*), which implies at least that people were to go to a regional sanctuary; they were not to celebrate these agricultural occasions at a local sanctuary in their home or village. Exodus 34:24 is instructive as it presupposes that people would go some way from home and thus leave their land vulnerable to people who were not going to the festival—that is, their Canaanite neighbors. Exodus also refers to "every place [*māqôm*] where I cause my name to be mentioned" (Ex 20:24 [MT 21]). It goes on to refer to a "place" of asylum with its altar, which implies a sanctuary (Ex 21:13-14), and to the "place" Yhwh has made ready for Israel, which Yhwh's aide will bring them to; the form of expression again implies reference to a sanctuary. Yhwh goes on to speak of Israel destroying Canaanite images and columns (Ex 23:20-24).[122] Israel may not simply take over traditional sanctuaries and rededicate them to Yhwh.

Admittedly the First Testament then implies that Israel did something close to this without incurring regular divine disapproval; Israelite sanctuaries were located in the same places as Canaanite ones. But a prophet such as Ezekiel is implacably hostile to the use of the traditional places for making offerings. They are commonly termed *bāmôt*, traditionally "high places," and often they likely were on hilltops or on elevated platforms like the one at Dan (or they *were* the platforms or were like cairns).[123] Like churches built on hilltops, they pointed to heaven and drew their worshipers toward the divine abode, and also made appropriate places from which the savor of offerings could ascend to heaven. Ezekiel therefore indicts the mountains, which symbolize these elevated sanctuaries, warning of their destruction along with their altars, incense stands and pillars, where the lovely fragrances of their offerings had wafted (Ezek 6). None of these words suggests something that is inherently objectionable (unlike "image"). Worship that the First Testament approves utilizes altars, incense stands, lovely fragrances and sometimes pillars, while "green trees" and "leafy oaks" are part of God's good creation. But the words Ezekiel uses for incense stands and pillars (*ḥammānîm* and *gillûlîm*) are used only in connection with alien religious observance, and the latter is also vocalized so as to rhyme with *šiqqûṣîm* (abhorrent things).[124] Outwardly the observances of traditional ("Canaanite") religion were not so different from Israel's. Yet Ezekiel is devastating in his warnings about these religious

---

[122]Cf. Frank Crüsemann, *The Torah* (Minneapolis: Fortress/Edinburgh: T & T Clark, 1996), pp. 171-81.

[123]Cf. Haran, *Temples and Temple-Service in Ancient Israel*, pp. 18-25; and on the mystery of the word, W. Boyd Barrick, *BMH as Body Language*, LHBOTS 477 (New York/London: T & T Clark, 2008).

[124]EVV have "idols" for *gillûlîm*, which conveys the word's pejorative connotations; it may originally have denoted a rock but also a turd (cf. John F. Kutsko, *Between Heaven and Earth* [Winona Lake, Ind.: Eisenbrauns, 2000], pp. 32-34).

resources. They will be destroyed, smashed, demolished, and their worshipers killed or scattered.

One reason it is not surprising that Jerusalem worships in these traditional ways is suggested by Ezekiel's reminder of its Canaanite and Hittite origins (Ezek 16:3). It had been a Jebusite city that David captured. Its people were vanquished but not exterminated. Israel did not practice ethnic cleansing but absorbed the Jebusites, or was absorbed by them. The traditional religious ways of its people continue in its "Israelite" population, as the traditional religious ways of Latin American or African or European people continue under the surface of their Christian profession. We tailor worship to the culture rather than making it shape a different culture and character. In the West this means that in worship as outside it, we are amusing ourselves to death.[125]

The Worshipers

In contrast, the First Testament's vision is for worship to involve "resituating" the life of the community of faith in the presence of God.[126] Israel is "the people who come near him" or "the people he comes near" (Ps 148:14): either translation is possible, and both illumine the nature of worship (for the people coming near Yhwh, see Lev 9:5; Ps 73:28, while for Yhwh coming near the people, see Ps 145:18; Is 55:6). The sanctuary is the place where Yhwh is present in person, albeit invisibly, as is the case with Christian worship. People thus bring their offerings "before Yhwh," more literally "to the face/presence of Yhwh" (e.g., Lev 1:3, 5, 11). They themselves come near to and stand before Yhwh (Lev 9:5) in the sanctuary court, and at the altar they bring the offerings near to Yhwh (e.g., Lev 3:7, 12). They cause the offerings to cook there as a smell that Yhwh can savor (e.g., Lev 1:9, 13, 17). Ordinary people as much as well-to-do people can do so, because the regulations allow for less imposing offerings such as birds and grain as well as expensive ones.

Worship by its nature involves coming into God's presence. "Come before him with resounding. . . . Come into his gates with confession, into his courts with praise" Psalm 100 invites. "Come before him" implies standing in God's very presence. In worship people stand within the very gates of Yhwh's dwelling, in the very courtyards of the house, where a person receives visitors. The plural hints at the fact that Yhwh's dwelling is more a palace than an ordinary house and thus has multiple courtyards; indeed, Hebrew has no word for "temple," and the word most commonly so translated (*hêkāl*) is the word for a royal palace. The model for understanding this worship is that of the presence of a king in his court, before whom people can appear to pay homage

---

[125]Neil Postman, *Amusing Ourselves to Death* (New York: Viking Penguin, 1986); cf. Marva J. Dawn, *Reaching Out Without Dumbing Down* (Grand Rapids: Eerdmans, 1995), pp. 12-13.

[126]Walter Brueggemann, *Worship in Ancient Israel* (Nashville: Abingdon, 2005), p. 1.

and seek help. It really is possible to come into the presence of God.[127]

Yhwh bids Moses issue the instructions about offerings, sabbath and festivals to "the Israelites" in general (Lev 1:1-2; 23:1-2). It is not a secret revelation meant only for priests, as was sometimes the case among other peoples.[128] "The teaching that Moses commanded us" is "the property of the congregation of Jacob" (Deut 33:4). While it is the priests who make the daily offerings to Yhwh, with the community in general not present because they have other work to do, these offerings still count as made by the people as a whole. Other forms of worship involve not the leaders doing the acting and speaking with the congregation functioning as audience or spectators, as is often the case in Christian worship. The worshipers take an active part. Worship is the privilege and responsibility of the whole community.

In the Psalms the speaker may be an "I," but an "I" that speaks for the congregation and may seek to draw in the entire congregation, or an "I" that invites each individual to identify with the praise and prayer. The exhortation "worship Yhwh, my soul" seeks to draw each person into that worship; thus Psalm 103 moves from this exhortation to speaking in many lines about "us." Other psalms (e.g., Ps 115; 118) indicate by changes in the speaking voices and in the implied addressees that they form liturgies in which different parts are declaimed by different people, such as a minister, a lay individual such as a king, and a group such as a choir or congregation; often these are in dialogue with one another, which underlines both the diversity and distinctives of these different participants and their common membership of the worshiping community.

Psalm 147 addresses its hearers in intricate and subtle ways. The speaker addresses the worshipers in second-person plural verbs but interweaves these with first-person plural forms that suggest identifying with the congregation. The psalm also describes the recipients of Yhwh's gifts, speaking of them in the third person, even though both the leader and worshipers are among these recipients. In this way it draws them into looking at themselves from the outside, seeing themselves as built up, healed and restored even as they see the faithless being brought down. It also uses the third person in speaking of people who revere and hope, thus inviting the worshipers to imagine such people and ask whether they would belong to their company. Later it addresses the city of Jerusalem, which is again both identical with the people who are being addressed and distinct from them. A city is more than the sum total of its current inhabitants, and in this sense it can be distinguished from them, and they can be invited to think about it. Yet it is actually these wor-

---

[127]On the temple, see further *OTT* 1:562-72. Cf. the comments in §2.4 "Worship," above.
[128]Cf. Milgrom, *Leviticus 1–16*, pp. 143-44.

shipers who are its current inhabitants and are urged to offer the praise that is due from the city, precisely because they *are* its current inhabitants. Further, in the description of the city's experience, they see themselves. They *are* its children.

Images

The first principle of worship is to offer it to Yhwh alone; the second is to offer it without the use of images (Ex 20:3-6). The command refers to images representing Yhwh; otherwise it would add nothing to the first. The two principles are quite distinct. Yet the Decalogue goes on to comment that Yhwh is ʾēl qannāʾ. This has usually been understood to mean "jealous God" and might thus seem to confuse the two commands, though it can plausibly be reckoned to denote "impassioned God," which sidesteps the problem.[129] The Roman Catholic and Lutheran Churches solve the problem by treating the two commands as one (they then divide the tenth in order still to have ten), which makes it easier to refer the whole of Exodus 20:3-6 to worship of other deities. But the logic of the Decalogue and other instructions in the Torah make it likely rather that Yhwh issues two prohibitions. The second presupposes the near-universal practice of making images as aids in worship.

Given the emphasis on concrete acts of worship such as sacrifice, one might have expected Yhwh to affirm the appropriateness of images, or at least to allow them as a condescension to human need, as Yhwh allows the temple. The Decalogue gives no reason for banning them, but Deuteronomy 4 does so. As representations of Yhwh, images fall so short that they are worse than useless. Israel's experience at Sinai, when they heard a voice but saw no form, reflects the fact that Yhwh is not the kind of deity who can be so represented. Indeed, in effect worship offered to an image is not really worship offered to Yhwh at all, which encourages the close association or confusion of the first two commands; Deuteronomy also mingles reference to images with reference to bowing down to the planets or stars (Deut 4:19).

All this matters because worship is mind-forming and character-forming. It portrays God. Perhaps imagining God purely as male is an analogous form of idolatry "in that it identifies a finite image with the reality of God."[130] That too is character-forming.

The expansiveness of the prohibition on images in Exodus 20:4-6 hints at the extent to which it goes against the grain,[131] and the length of the rationale for it in Deuteronomy 4 points in the same direction. Indeed, this is the first injunction that Israel disobeys; Exodus 32:1-8 manifests a further tell-

---

[129]See §2.2 "Exclusiveness."
[130]So Judith Plaskow, *The Coming of Lilith* (Boston: Beacon, 2005), p. 75.
[131]Cf. Durham, *Exodus*, p. 286.

ing ambiguity over whether the gold calf is an image of Yhwh or of some other deity.

It would be illogical to infer a prohibition on the more general representation involved in art.[132] Beyond the stories about origins in Genesis 4, the First Testament has nothing directly to say about art or culture, about music or poetry or drama in their own right. Beauty in itself is thus not a topic for First Testament theology. But the First Testament has much indirectly to say about these, in that it uses form and beauty, especially in its poetry. The Bible itself is a work of literature.[133] It is hard to imagine that Israel's sacrifices or festivals (or its music) would appeal to Western aesthetics, but it seems that aesthetic considerations did enter into the design and building of the wilderness sanctuary and the temple, which were characterized by precious metal, precious stones, color, fabric and weaving, leather, wood and carving, spices, symmetry, and artistic design. They were designed to be "something beautiful for God."[134] It is then no coincidence that there may be a similarity between the sanctuary and the world itself described in its beauty in Genesis 1.[135]

But for worship purposes, there are to be no images of human beings or of other creatures (Deut 4:15-18). Nor may people set up an asherah or any kind of sacred column or stone pillar (Deut 16:21-22). Deuteronomy begins its comments on images by declaring that Israel is to live by rules Yhwh has issued, decisions Yhwh has laid down, and not to add to them or subtract from them (Deut 4:1-2; cf. vv. 5, 8). They are evidences of Israel's wisdom and discernment such as other peoples will marvel at. The context suggests this refers in particular to instructions about worship. The focus of the exhortation as a whole is the worship of Yhwh alone without making images; it is such an exclusive adherence to Yhwh that will be the focus through Deuteronomy 4–11 and will underlie much of the exhortation that follows. In Deuteronomy 4:25-28, making images is *the* potential cause of exile; and for Ezekiel, "idolatry is the quintessential cause of the Babylonian exile."[136] It was indeed the person of Yhwh and the content of Yhwh's instructions to Israel (not least on worshiping one God without making images) that commended the faith of Israel to peoples all around in the Second Temple period.[137]

---

[132]See Joseph Gutman, "The 'Second Commandment' and the Image in Judaism," *HUCA* 32 (1961): 161-74.

[133]In this connection, see Yochanan Muffs, *The Personhood of God* (Woodstock, Vt.: Jewish Lights, 2005), pp. 97-112.

[134]Teresa of Calcutta: see Malcolm Muggeridge, *Something Beautiful for God* (London: Collins/Fountain, 1977), p. 114

[135]See *OTT* 1:394-96.

[136]Kutsko, *Between Heaven and Earth*, p. 25.

[137]This development is thus more illuminating in considering Deut 4:6 than comparison of the Torah with law collections such as Hammurabi's.

Worship involves some self-abnegation. We cannot worship God as we are inclined (for instance, by means evaluated on the basis of whether we find them helpful). We worship in accordance with constraints Yhwh has laid down, not randomly, but because they correspond to aspects of Yhwh's nature.

Regard for Who Yhwh Is

Worship involves coming into Yhwh's presence, and the First Testament emphasizes the danger that can attach to drawing near Yhwh. In the twenty-first-century Western world, Christians like to think in egalitarian terms about our relationship with God, to talk in terms of intimacy, friendship and mutuality. Both Testaments offer some hints in this direction, but they more characteristically speak in hierarchical terms. God is father, we are children. God is shepherd, we are sheep. God is king, we are subjects. God makes the covenant; we agree to it. The father-child relationship makes most clear a point that is also implicit in the other models, that hierarchy does not have to exclude intimacy. The temple is not a place that distances people from God; rather the opposite.[138] But God is not our buddy. There is nothing egalitarian about our relationship with God. God is—well, God. Come on.

It is thus important (vitally important, rather literally) to safeguard the sanctuary from things that compromise the difference between God and us. Thus the warning narrative and the safeguards of Leviticus 10 and Leviticus 11–15 follow the building of the sanctuary and the ordination of its priests. The Levites look after the dwelling, and on the journey to the land ordinary people are to be wary of the wrong kind of contact with it (Num 1:47-53; 3–4; cf. 1 Sam 6; 2 Sam 6). The presence there of what is taboo imperils Israel (Lev 15:31; cf. Num 5:1-4) and threatens Yhwh's withdrawal, though fortunately its consequences can be dealt with (Lev 16).

Yet the relationship between Yhwh and the people is not authoritarian or oppressive, any more than that between parents and children need be. The wonder is that the holy one is one who cares and listens and invites us to speak without fear of causing offense. God's servants (worshipers) are not expected to be yes men and yes women, any more than a king's ministers are so expected, if the king is wise. The prayers and praises in the Psalms show the freedom with which Israelites could plead with their "king" even while bringing their "tribute" to him in the form of sacrifice.

A concern to avoid compromising Yhwh's distinctive deity underlies many regulations in the Torah. In Deuteronomy people can kill animals for food in their settlements, but they must drain the blood and then eat the animals in

---

[138]Against Balentine (*Prayer in the Hebrew Bible*, pp. 41-47), when he makes a point overlapping with the one I make here.

the manner of animals that cannot be sacrificed such as deer and gazelle, or deformed firstlings, because this killing does not count as sacrifice (Deut 12:15, 20-25; 15:19-23). It does not then matter whether the people who take part in the feast are ritually clean or not, because the concern with cleanness and taboo relates to polluting the sanctuary. The emphasis on coming to *the* place that Yhwh chooses is a spelling out of the first statement in the Decalogue.[139] Admittedly, confining sacrifices and offerings to one sanctuary could leave a "religious vacuum" in people's lives.[140] It secularizes this aspect of life, along with justice, asylum, warfare, and sin and punishment.[141] And actually neither Deuteronomy nor Leviticus explicitly declares that there is to be only one sanctuary; if they intend that, in each it is a byproduct of another concern. The emphasis lies on this being the place Yhwh chooses rather than on there being only a single such place.[142] But sticking to one place is a weapon against "poly-Yahwism," the idea that there could be a Yhwh of Dan (cf. Amos 8:14), a Yhwh of Teman, and a Yhwh of Samaria.[143] There is one Yhwh, and thus one sanctuary.[144]

When Israel denies having been unfaithful to Yhwh (Jer 2:23), the implication may be that in a formal sense people did not worship the Master.[145] The problem then is that while they still use the name Yhwh, they think of Yhwh in terms of the Master. People can change the inner meaning of their religion while keeping the outward form, and Israel is worshiping Yhwh, but doing so in the way people worshiped the Master. They would view the trees and stones that they used in worship as aids to worship of Yhwh, but the aids too easily became identified with the deity (Jer 2:27). Turning to Yhwh in the way people turned to the Master was, in effect, turning to the Master.

Displacement

While worship involves both liturgical words and ritual acts, both the Pentateuch and the Psalter make clear that both gestures and words need to link with another kind of act, another kind of use of hands and feet, and the

---

[139]Mark E. Biddle, *Deuteronomy* (Macon, Ga.: Smith & Helwys, 2003), p. 205.

[140]So Jeffrey H. Tigay, *Deuteronomy*, JPS Torah Commentary/Philadelphia: Jewish Publication Society, 1998), p. 119.

[141]So Moshe Weinfeld, *Deuteronomy and the Deuteronomic School* (Oxford/New York: Oxford University Press, 1972), pp. 233-43.

[142]See, e.g., J. G. McConville, *Law and Theology in Deuteronomy*, JSOTSup 33 (Sheffield, U.K.: JSOT, 1984), pp. 21-38.

[143]So the Kuntillet 'Ajrud inscriptions (see, e.g., J. A. Emerton, "New Light on Israelite Religion," *ZAW* 94 [1982]: 2-20).

[144]Cf. Crüsemann, *The Torah*, p. 222.

[145]Jeremiah uses the plural "Masters," as if the different objects that represented the Master in different sanctuaries were different gods. Thus he can declare that they have as many gods as they have towns (Jer 2:28).

prophets emphasize this (e.g., Is 1:10-20).[146] Coming into Yhwh's presence at the sanctuary involves being properly circumcised and properly purified (Christians might say people must be baptized or must speak in tongues), but this is not enough. To put it in modern Jewish terms, keeping kosher does not count if the way we treat people is not kosher. While one cannot appear before a human king without the proper clothing, equally one cannot spend time in the king's presence as a committed rebel or traitor. "The Temple is a place of electrifying holiness that cannot tolerate injustice," and the cultic and the ethical are "two sides of the same experience."[147] So one cannot spend time with Yhwh except as a person of integrity, faithfulness to one's neighbors and to justice, and a right attitude to wealth (Ps 15; cf. Ps 24). There are moral considerations that determine whether people can dwell on God's hill or join the circle of those who seek Yhwh's face. Joyful praise is appropriate to the faithful or upright because faithfulness and uprightness characterize the words and deeds of the one they praise (Ps 33:1-5).

When Israel ignores such considerations, there is trouble. By its nature, worship involves a dialogue, though to call it a conversation might imply something too egalitarian. In the Psalms sometimes Yhwh takes the initiative (Ps 50), sometimes Yhwh responds to Israel's (Ps 81; 95), but either way, Yhwh characteristically speaks somewhat confrontationally. "Our God comes and cannot be silent" (Ps 50:3). Yhwh comes to address Israel in worship in order to announce a decision, to exercise authority. It is a decision against Israel, a solemn indictment, an accusation. The people of God are sometimes inclined to think that what matters to God is that their worship is properly offered, with the right outward form or the right inner attitude or the right level of enthusiasm, and other psalms and books such as Leviticus make clear that these things matter. People can get preoccupied with such questions and can fret about whether there is something wrong with their offerings or with their attitude. Relax, says Psalm 50:7-15. The relationship between Yhwh and you is basically simple. You call on Yhwh; Yhwh rescues you; you bring an offering that demonstrates the way you honor Yhwh. It's not so complicated. When you start fretting about the nature of your worship it rather implies that you think Yhwh needs your enthusiasm. Yhwh does not.

So why would people fret about their worship? It looks to Yhwh like a massive case of displacement. When people focus on their worship and the question of its acceptability, they can be avoiding the question about what Yhwh is really concerned for, which is more their life outside worship. This is not to say that life outside worship is always more important than the life of wor-

---

[146]See further §1.1 "Life as One Whole" and "Ethics and Worship."
[147]Jon D. Levenson, *Sinai and Zion* (Minneapolis: Winston, 1985), pp. 170, 172.

ship. When people are concerned only for social justice and not for worship, there is something wrong there too. It is another form of displacement.[148] But Psalm 50 aims its barbs at a community that focuses on worship to avoid facing what is wrong with its community life: not merely the existence of theft, adultery, deceit and smear, but the high level of tolerance of such wrongs. Yhwh confronts the community in worship in order to declare that such tolerance means it has no right to be there. The areas about which Yhwh raises questions overlap with the areas covered by the Decalogue and may reflect the use of the Decalogue in worship, not least in connection with celebrating Yhwh's covenant relationship with Israel. The community gathers as the people that once made a covenant with Yhwh over sacrifice. If Yhwh refers to a rite such as that described in Genesis 15, the recollection is a solemn one. Israel, like Yhwh, had agreed that if it failed to keep the terms of the covenant, it should be treated like the animal that was sacrificed. Now it gathers to celebrate that covenant and to proclaim its terms, but this involves gross hypocrisy as well as great risk. How could Yhwh be silent and give the impression of the same displacement as the community goes in for (Ps 50:3, 16-21)?

Listening

In Psalm 81 Yhwh almost engages in external debate about these matters. Resounding, shouting, raising the music, sounding the tambourine and blowing the horn are "a law for Israel, a decision by Jacob's God, a declaration in Joseph." But Yhwh then reminds the people about the deliverance from servitude in Egypt and at the Red Sea, and about the expectation that they would therefore make Yhwh their God and would "listen" to Yhwh (the verb comes five times in the psalm). Their making that noise and music would be one way they indicated that Yhwh was indeed their God. But other aspects of their life and worship did not match it. The noise (especially the blowing of a horn) could signal the beginning of a festival such as Pesah or Sukkot, and such festivals were occasions when Yhwh's words and expectations were proclaimed. "But my people did not listen to my voice; Israel was unwilling to listen to me," and thus Yhwh sent them off to do as they wished. "If only my people were listening to me, if only Israel would walk on in my ways," Yhwh says, speaking "like a man weeping and lamenting," like a saddened father.[149] Then they would not experience defeat and they would find themselves filled with the finest wheat and with not merely water from the rock but honey from the rock.

Worship involves both noise and attentiveness. Both are appropriate re-

---

[148]See further §1.1 "Ethics and Worship."
[149]John Calvin, *Commentary on the Book of Psalms*, 5 vols. (Grand Rapids: Eerdmans, 1948-1949), 3:323.

sponses to what Yhwh has done. Listening without noise is not enough; noise without listening is not enough.

It is therefore wise to declare, "I shall listen for what Yhwh will speak" (Ps 85:8 [MT 9]). There is then some irony in the fact that Psalm 85 subsequently gives Yhwh no opportunity to speak. Indeed, the "I" (a prophet or priest?) goes on, "because he will speak of well-being to his people, to his committed ones." It is usually false prophets who assume that Yhwh speaks of well-being. It is dangerous to assume before listening that one knows what Yhwh says. Now the presence of the psalm in the Psalter indicates that the community recognized this particular declaration as correct. But it is risky. Someone who thinks they know what Yhwh will say still needs to listen. Sometimes the risk lies in assuming that Yhwh will *not* speak of well-being, the exiles' assumption as we learn it from Ezekiel and Isaiah 40–55. Sometimes being prepared to listen to a word bringing good news from Yhwh is the bold act to which the community is called.

Psalm 95 begins with enthusiastic praise and down-low prostration, and one might see its first two-thirds as a balanced expression of worship coming to a profound conclusion. But Yhwh has other ideas and inspires a snorting response that says, "This shouting and prostration is all very well, but I have heard and seen it all before, at Sinai, and in the long run it didn't mean anything because it just led into forty years' making me disgusted and angry by refusing truly to acknowledge me. So could you just shut up for a minute and listen?" Perhaps this exhortation led liturgically into an actual reading of the Decalogue. In reminding the people that they could end up sharing the fate of the Sinai generation, which did not enter the land, Yhwh speaks to the people almost as if they were not yet in the promised land. It is possible to be in the land in a physical sense, but not in some deeper sense, or it is possible to be in it and find yourself cast out. Hebrews 3–4 sees the church in a similar position, invited to enter a metaphorical sabbath rest in the land, but in danger of forgoing it.

Psalm 138 promises, "I will confess you with all my heart, before the gods I will make music for you; I will bow down to your holy palace, and I will confess your name for your commitment and for your truthfulness." If Psalm 82 challenges the gods in the heavenly cabinet about the way they fulfill their responsibilities (or rather do not), then Psalm 138 puts them in their place (or rather seeks to keep them there) by affirming before them what Yhwh has done. It goes on to affirm, "all the kings of the earth are to confess you, because they have heard the words of your mouth; they are to sing of Yhwh's ways, because Yhwh's honor is great, because Yhwh is on high, but he sees the lowly; lofty, he acknowledges from afar." The kings have two things in common with the gods. They too are responsible for seeing that their communities are characterized by faithfulness and compassion; they too are inclined to become too attached to their position of power and majesty and to want to do their own thing. The psalm affirms that they will find themselves listening to what Yhwh has done and joining in confession of Yhwh's honor and Yhwh's concern for the lowly.

2.5 Giving to Yhwh

The bodily and physical aspect of worship receives concrete expression in sacrifices and offerings. Prayer and praise are not merely feelings or words; a sacrifice is "a prayer which is acted"[150] or an act of praise that is acted. Sacrifices and offerings are gifts to Yhwh that express commitment, develop fellowship, dissolve taboo and make up for shortcomings.

Act and Interpretation

Understanding the significance of sacrifices and offerings is complex because the texts that describe or prescribe them (notably, Lev 1–7) are sparing in their explication. Thus they can have many meanings attributed to them; indeed, it can seem that rituals, "like sacred Rorschach tests, are incapable of resisting any interpretation whatsoever."[151] In effect, in focusing on the right way to offer sacrifices, texts leave it to offerers to let them signify what they wish to signify by them, like a New Testament writer finding significance in a First Testament text that does not emerge from the text's inherent meaning. Boundaries for such interpretation are then set by the Scriptures as a whole; as is the case with allegorical interpretation, it would be inappropriate to find significance in the text or the rite that clashed with the inherent meaning of other Scriptures.

If Leviticus 1–7 tells us little of the meaning of sacrifice, what do other Scriptures tell us? The classic Christian understanding issues from Hebrews, that the point of sacrificial worship is to deal with the problem of sin. At the same time the rest of the New Testament speaks of sacrifice in other connections (e.g., Rom 12:1; 15:16), and the First Testament does not make a close or dominant link between sacrifice and sin. That broader New Testament usage picks up the fact that sacrifice is a way of giving outward embodiment to all aspects of worship; in Leviticus 1–7 itself, sacrifice as a way of dealing with wrongdoing comes only at the end. Leviticus 1:4 does note that the whole offering of a bull makes expiation, and perhaps all offerings were made with an awareness of shortcomings and a need of expiation if any worship or offering

---

[150]Roland de Vaux, *Ancient Israel* (London: Darton, Longman & Todd,/New York: McGraw-Hill, 1961), p. 451; cf. Preuss, *Old Testament Theology,* 2:244.

[151]Nancy Jay, *Throughout Your Generations Forever* (Chicago/London: University of Chicago Press, 1992), p. 1.

is to find acceptance,[152] as all Christian worship involves recognizing that we come to God only on the basis of Christ's dying for us. But this is not the central point about sacrifice in general or this sacrifice in particular (and the observation is made only in connection with a bull offering), as it is not the only point about Christian worship.[153] Nor does expiation relate to sin in the broad sense but only to things that cause taboo. Nor do the texts bring the savor of the sacrifice into association with expiation, as if implying that savoring this smell means Yhwh is not angry; Leviticus never refers to Yhwh being angry. Nor does the regulation for the whole offering make any reference to pardon, which comes only (and frequently) with the purification offering and reparation offering.

A second classic Christian view is that sacrifice is a way people seek to redeem themselves, an act of self-help taken over from the heathen.[154] Once again, this is not the First Testament's own perspective. Sacrifice indeed began as a human initiative that was then regulated by divine instruction, but so did prayer (Gen 4:26), and Abel's sacrifice met with divine favor, not divine hesitation (Gen 4:3-4). In the First Testament "the cult is not something man does for God . . . nor is it performed in order to obtain something from God." Rather "the cult exists as a means to integrate the communion between God and man which God has instituted in His covenant."[155] While prophets critique sacrifice, they do not argue that sacrifice and other rituals are means of people seeking to redeem themselves. This is a problem that surfaces first in the New Testament, as an intra-Christian issue.

René Girard suggests that the subliminal significance of sacrifice is to protect the community from its own violence by diverting that violence onto the animal it offered. It breaks the vicious cycle of vengeance. When the sacrificial system breaks down, as the preexilic prophets see it as doing, this accompanies the flourishing of reciprocal violence.[156] Girard, too, thus implies that

---

[152]Cf. Hans-Joachim Kraus, *Worship in Israel* (Oxford: Blackwell/Richmond: Knox, 1966), p. 116. Vriezen declares that "the whole of the sacrificial cult is dominated by the idea of atonement," but glosses this to mean that it relates to "the renewal of the relation" between God and people (*Outline of Old Testament Theology,* pp. 286-87 [2nd ed., pp. 261-62]).

[153]See further §3.6 "Penitence and Sacrifice."

[154]So Ludwig Köhler, *Old Testament Theology* (Philadelphia: Westminster, 1957), p. 181. Contrast the comments in Preuss, *Old Testament Theology,* 2:210.

[155]So Vriezen, *Outline of Old Testament Theology,* p. 280 (2nd ed., p. 255); the second sentence is italicized.

[156]See René Girard, *Violence and the Sacred* (Baltimore/London: Johns Hopkins, 1989), pp. 8, 43. George Pattison interestingly applies this to the story of relationships between the Israelites clans and the resolution of internal conflicts in Israel ("Violence, Kingship and Cultus," *ExpT* 102 [1990-91]: 135-40), but this presupposes that the story of how Israel became Israel in the land involved conflict between various indigenous groups rather than

sacrifice has one meaning, whereas actually its meaning is like the meaning of a word; it changes with time and context.[157] More specifically, it is hard to establish a correlation between times when the sacrificial system flourished and the community was relatively peaceful, and the converse. But Girard's theory is suggestive for an understanding of what sacrifice might signify in some contexts.

Act and Word

Importance attaches to the simple act of making an offering; from Leviticus, one could reckon it was done in silence.[158] But the Psalms associate offering sacrifices with shouting, singing, making music and calling on Yhwh or confessing Yhwh's name (Ps 27:6; 54:6 [MT 8]; 107:22; 116:17).[159] The two aspects of worship, the correlation of acts and words, appear in Psalm 54:6 [MT 8]: "For your munificence[160] I will sacrifice to you; I will confess your name, Yhwh, for it is good." It involves both the symbolic action and the words testifying to what Yhwh has done. Genesis points in a similar direction as speechless offerings and calling on Yhwh alternate or come together (Gen 4:3-4, 26; 12:7-8).[161] Thanksgiving and praise accompany the daily whole offerings (1 Chron 23:30-31); the word *tôdâ* itself refers both to a prayer of thanksgiving and a thankoffering.[162] Deuteronomy emphasizes the words of prayer and thanksgiving,[163] and Leviticus 5:5 requires a confession of one's offense to accompany a purification offering. The fact that there was nothing very distinctively Israelite in most of the acts involved in offering would also make it

---

people coming from outside in the way the story works.

[157]See David Janzen, *The Social Meanings of Sacrifice in the Hebrew Bible,* BZAW 344 (Berlin/ New York: de Gruyter, 2004), pp. 1-8.

[158]See Kaufmann, *Religion of Israel,* pp. 303-4. But this seems to be an argument from silence . . .

[159]Cf. Kraus, *Worship in Israel,* p. 124. Israel Knohl sees the Levitical regulation as "an idealized approach," designed as a recognition of God's loftiness (*The Sanctuary of Silence* [Minneapolis: Fortress, 1995], p. 149; see also Knohl, *The Divine Symphony* (Philadelphia: Jewish Publication Society, 2003), pp. 71-74.

[160]The EVV have "A freewill offering"; but as the psalmist is making a promise to bring an offering when Yhwh has answered the prayer, it will not then be a freewill offering but the fulfillment of a promise. (See Lev 7:11-18 and the discussion of "fellowship offerings," which follows here.) More likely, then, the expression refers here to Yhwh's generosity, not the suppliant's.

[161]Samuel E. Balentine draws an interesting contrast between Noah's speechless worship (Gen 9:20) and Abraham and Sarah's use of words (Gen 15–17) (*The Torah's Vision of Worship* [Minneapolis: Fortress, 1999], p. 135).

[162]Janzen comments that the only thing that interests the Chronicler about sacrifice apart from that it should be done in front of the covenant chest is "the Levitical praise that constantly accompanies sacrifice in the Chronicler's eyes" (*Social Meaning of Sacrifice in the Hebrew Bible,* p. 238).

[163]See Weinfeld, *Deuteronomy and the Deuteronomic School,* p. 213.

natural to reckon that act and word went together.[164]

Psalm 65 does begin "To you silence is praise,[165] God in Zion," though the fact that it then goes on at some length to articulate outward praise would make it deconstruct and raises a question about its meaning; the clue likely lies in the similar beginning to Psalm 62, "Yes, toward God my spirit is silent," which continues, "from him is my deliverance." Silence is praise in the sense that a still, trusting reliance on God is an indication of recognizing that God is the one in whom we put our hope. Thus Psalm 65 also goes on, "And to you a promise is fulfilled, one who listens to prayer." Silence is the mark of resting in the God to whom we pray when we are under pressure, and to whom we look forward to bringing our grateful offerings when Yhwh has responded. And that expression of gratitude will need to be noisy in order to fulfill its object of bearing witness.[166] Perhaps that is the point of the declaration that, when Yhwh puts down my attackers and delivers me, praising and exalting Yhwh with a song of thanksgiving will please Yhwh more than an ox (Ps 69:30-31 [MT 31-32]). But this psalm may presuppose a situation when it is impossible to offer sacrifices, because the temple is not functioning (cf. Ps 51:16-19 [MT 18-21]) or because the suppliant cannot go there (cf. Ps 42); it would be this that prompts the comment that as symbols ideally need to accompany words, so words are vitally important in their own right. While offerings are unacceptable when not linked to a life of self-offering to Yhwh and to other people, a converse is also true. There is something perverted about love for one's neighbor without love for God, and something inadequate about offerings without words.

"Sing" and "proclaim," Psalm 96 begins, and then goes on, "bestow on Yhwh honor and might" (*bestow* repeats three times, as did *sing* earlier). English translations have "ascribe" honor, suggesting that Yhwh has the honor and people are to recognize it, which is of course true, but the verb (*yāhab*) means "give." So more likely the implication is that people have honor, and they are to give it over to Yhwh. The psalm goes on to indicate that it is by making an offering and bowing down before Yhwh, like subjects bringing tribute to a king, that they bestow honor on Yhwh. The offering and bowing thus complement the singing. Once more, worship involves not merely an attitude of heart but the sounding of a voice and the bringing of something solid that costs. And once again the psalm moves on from the outward gesture to the declaration that it embodies: "Say among the nations: 'Yhwh be-

---

[164]Cf. Brueggemann, *Worship in Ancient Israel*, p. 25.

[165]At least, it probably does, but LXX, Syr have "praise is fitting" (cf. EVV), a true and good though less striking point that requires considerable stretching of the meaning of the root with which they are linking the word *dāmâ* or *dūm*, "resemble."

[166]Cf. Barth, *Church Dogmatics*, IV/3, ii:866.

gan to reign.' " The bringing of tribute expresses recognition of this, in such a way as to proclaim it publicly; again, an honoring with the heart does not have that effect.

Gifts

All sacrifice involves the giving of a gift to the deity.[167] But gifts can have a variety of meanings. In human relationships, giving can be an expression of love or gratitude or regret, or a way of seeking to create or develop a relationship or an obligation or a commitment, or it can be a bribe. Analogous significances may attach to sacrifice as a gift. As gifts, sacrifices have been seen as inherently "rituals of defence."[168] They recognize that human beings are in a position of dependence, impotence and vulnerability in relation to deity as children are in relation to parents, under their care and control but subject to actions on their behalf that they experience as suffering, neglect and deprivation. Even sacrifices that express joy and gratitude then express this vulnerability rather than spontaneous love. It would be unduly cynical to reckon that this is the inherent underlying nature of relationships with parents or deity, but one can recognize that this can be an aspect of the relationship. A variant on this understanding starts from the way sacrifices also accompany movements or changes of status such as the move from being a layperson to being a priest. Sacrifices themselves involve something moving from the human to the divine realm; hence the need for this movement to be properly supervised by someone who is acceptable to both worlds. The design of a sanctuary symbolizes the existence of the two realms and the facilitating of movement between them.

All the various significances of giving presuppose something about a mutual relationship, one actual or desired or made the pretext for something the giver wants to achieve. Conversely, relationship presupposes giving; if there is no mutual giving, there is hardly relationship. So Yhwh gives to Israel, and Israel gives to Yhwh.

Its community sacrifices are thus part of its relationship with God; they are mostly offered according to a calendar. Numbers 28:3-8 prescribes whole offerings each morning and evening, a way of making a regular act of honoring Yhwh,[169] though there are indications elsewhere (e.g., Ezek 46:13-15) that this was not the pattern throughout Israel's history.[170] The Psalms too refer to

---

[167]Cf. George Buchanan Gray, *Sacrifice in the Old Testament* (Oxford: Clarendon Press, 1925).

[168]So Meyer Fortes, preface to *Sacrifice*, ed. M. F. C. Bourdillon and Meyer Fortes (London/ New York: Academic Press, 1980), pp. v-xix; see p. xiv.

[169]Cf. Philip P. Jenson, *Graded Holiness*, JSOTSup 106 (Sheffield, U.K.: Sheffield Academic Press, 1992), pp. 155-56.

[170]See Milgrom, *Numbers*, pp. 486-88.

worship in the morning and at night (Ps 92:2 [MT 3]) but more often to morning worship alone (Ps 5:3 [MT 4]; 59:16 [MT 17]; 88:13 [MT 14]). There are to be double offerings on the sabbath, larger-scale offerings for the new moon, for Massot, Weeks, Horns, and Expiation Day, and yet larger ones for Sukkot (Num 28:9–29:38). Numbers 7 relates how the leaders of the clans brought carts and oxen for the transport of the covenant chest, and for the altar's dedication brought offerings of silver bowls, silver basins, ladles, flour, oil, incense and sacrificial animals, all of which Yhwh told Moses to accept. These are called gifts (*qorbān*, from *qārab*, something brought near), essentially a synonym of the word for an offering *(minḥâ)*. The account compares with the people's bringing gifts for the making of the sanctuary, with the difference that there Yhwh tells Moses to bid the people bring gifts (Ex 25:1-2). Here the clan leaders take the initiative, and Yhwh tells Moses how to respond.

There are also individual offerings, part of the individual's relationship with God; these are mostly occasional. They can be a bull or sheep or goat, but for many of them the regulations allow poorer people to give something more manageable than that expected of people who are better off (Lev 1:14-17; 5:7-13; 12:8; 14:21-32; 27:2-8). There is no suggestion that the smaller offering is inferior. As with gifts between human beings, it is not the monetary value of the offering that counts.

Naturally, an animal to be offered must be a fine, complete example of its species, though a male is acceptable even though it is more expendable and thus less valuable. While the acknowledging of someone's worth-ship is not the living meaning of the English word *worship*, that etymology does point to the significance of a complaint in this connection in Malachi 1:6–2:3. People are offering as sacrifices animals that are blind, lame, sick or stolen. The earlier plaints in this list might make one wonder whether this is just a sign of people's hardship, though even then one suspects that Malachi, like Haggai, would still reckon that the best should go to Yhwh. But in any case, the addition of reference to animals that people have stolen takes the matter to another level. Such offerings are no way to "honor" God or "revere" God; the connotations of those verbs are not so far from those of "worship." Such sacrifices rather suggest contempt. Yhwh would rather the priests lock the temple doors and stop lighting fires on the altar than collude with such offerings.

Whole Offering and Grain Offering

In its systematic treatment of sacrifices, Leviticus 1–7 begins with the whole offering, *ʿolâ* or *kālîl*. The first word suggests it is something that "goes up" to Yhwh as it ascends in the form of smoke, a nice smell for Yhwh to savor. This expression occurs occasionally in connection with other offerings, but most often in connection with the whole offering and the grain offering (e.g., Lev 1:9, 13, 17; 2:2, 9, 12). Israel offers something nice to Yhwh, and Yhwh likes it. While whole offerings can be offered on their own (e.g., Gen 22:1-14; Judg 6:26; 13:16; Ezra 8:35), when people offer several sacrifices, the whole offering is often mentioned first (e.g., Ex 18:12; 24:5; 32:6; Lev 12:6; Deut 12:6, 11; 27:6-7), though on some occasions it is preceded by the purification offering (e.g., Lev 8). If the full order is purification offering, then whole offering, then fellowship offering (Lev 9),[171] then the Christian instinct that sees confession and absolution as needing to be the first element in worship corresponds to this.

The word *kālîl* underlines the fact that "all" of this offering goes to Yhwh. Its blood is splattered all around the altar, perhaps on all four horns at the four corners. Thus, whereas the worshiper shares in some other kinds of offering, a whole offering means what it says. Such offerings are indeed a means of giving something to God.[172] In the context of other religions, expressions such as "a relaxing smell" (e.g., Lev 1:9) or "their God's food" (e.g., Lev 21:6) would imply people feed God and God eats, but Leviticus and other books in the First Testament lack the framework of thinking that would fit that idea. The terms are "petrified linguistic survivals," which even ordinary people would likely not dream of taking literally, otherwise neither Leviticus nor the prophets would have used them.[173] Rather, talk of Yhwh liking the smell of a sacrifice is a vivid way of indicating that Yhwh accepts it. The fact that the offering is burned in its entirety in the sanctuary courtyard and nothing is taken into the holy place or the very holy place as happened with other religions, might safeguard against the idea that the offering is actually food for God.[174]

A whole offering can accompany prayer (e.g., 1 Sam 7:9-10; 13:8-12; 2 Sam 24:21-25): it "was a signal to God that His worshipers desired to bring their needs to His attention."[175] The nice barbecue smell attracts that attention. This is perhaps implicit in the first whole offerings in Genesis 8:20-21. Israel

---

[171]Cf. Anson F. Rainey, "The Order of Sacrifices in Old Testament Ritual Texts," *Biblica* 51 (1970): 485-98; Patrick D. Miller, *The Religion of Ancient Israel* (Louisville: Westminster John Knox/London: SPCK, 2000), pp. 123-24.

[172]The TNIV makes this point more concrete as it translates Lev 1:9 "it is a burnt offering, a food offering [*'iššeh*], an aroma pleasing to the LORD." In light of the existence of the word *'ēš* "fire," *'iššeh* has usually been translated "offering by fire," but this does not fit all occurrences, and Tg renders "presentation" while Akkadian and Ugaritic have similar words for "gift" or "offering" (cf. John E. Hartley, *Leviticus*, WBC [Dallas: Word, 1992], pp. 13-14).

[173]Cf. Kaufmann, *The Religion of Israel*, p. 111. Cf. the comments in §2.4 "Symbol and Sacrament."

[174]See Milgrom, *Leviticus 1–16*, p. 59.

[175]Baruch A. Levine, *Leviticus*, JPS Torah Commentary (Philadelphia: Jewish Publication Society, 1989), p. 5.

thus reaches out to Yhwh when it wants Yhwh to meet with the people, in keeping with Yhwh's own invitation to do so (e.g., Lev 9), as is the case with the regular whole offerings (Ex 29:38-43; cf. Num 23), or when it seeks something from Yhwh (for instance, in the rite in Num 5:11-31). But elsewhere the whole offering can fulfill a vow or be a voluntary offering, like the fellowship offering (e.g., Lev 22:17-19). Perhaps something of the history of sacrifice is reflected here.

The grain offering *(minḥâ),* of raw grain or grain baked into bread and enriched by olive oil and spices, could be made as an accompaniment to other offerings (e.g., Ex 29:40-41; 40:29), like bread to go with meat. But in Leviticus 2 it is simply an offering in its own right, as the word suggests: in itself, *minḥâ* simply means "offering" (or "tax"), and it can apply to an animal sacrifice (Gen 4:3-5; 1 Sam 2:17) and to ordinary gifts, especially from subordinates to people above them whose favor they wish to win or regain or retain. Like the whole offering, it can be a way of seeking expiation (Lev 14:20; 1 Sam 3:14), but as a gift it can have other significance, such as accompanying prayer. It is an even more "humble," everyday offering than a dove or pigeon, and an even more meaningful one for ordinary people (cf. Lev 5:11-13). In contrast to the whole offering, only a token portion (the *ʾazkārâ*) is offered directly to Yhwh by being burned, while the main part goes to the priests. The offerer thus still gives up the whole; it is something "very holy" (Lev 2:3).

Leviticus 1–7 does not include regulations for the wine offering, though it has been prescribed in Exodus 29:40-41 in association with the whole offering and grain offering (cf. Lev 23:13, 18, 37; Num 15:1-16; 28–29). It would be natural to accompany a meal with wine as well as bread.

The Fellowship Sacrifice

We are not sure how to translate the expression for the third form of offering (Lev 3), *zebaḥ šĕlāmîm.* A sacrifice *(zebaḥ)* is an act that involves killing something that is then shared by worshipers and Yhwh (see, e.g., Deut 27:7; 1 Sam 1:4-5). It is thus not "very holy," absolutely holy; ordinary people can join in eating it. But it is "holy," and all of it must be eaten on the day it is offered, or the next day; anything left until the third day must be burned, not eaten. The word *šĕlāmîm* could have various connotations, but it does recall *šālôm* and thus might suggest "well-being" (NRSV) or "fellowship" (TNIV). The latter is the more obvious implication as these sacrifices are occasions when families or the whole community eat together, and do so in fellowship with Yhwh. "If . . . the notion of sacrifice as food for the deity was not prominent in ancient Israel, the function of sacrifice as food for human beings in order to effect or generate solidarity and community is evident in the centrality of table fellowship as part of the ritual of sacrifice." Eating together before Yhwh brings into being or cements their relationship.[176]

Yhwh desires to be in the kind of fellowship with Israel that involves eating together, though people eat "before" Yhwh not "with" Yhwh, and once again Leviticus hardly implies that Yhwh ate the sacrifice. While the portions allocated to Yhwh are described as "food" (Lev 3:11, 16), these portions were not very edible. The animals offered at a fellowship sacrifice indeed constitute food, for the offerer (the whole offering and grain offering, from which the offerer did not eat, were not described as food). The priest offers the animal to Yhwh, and it thus belongs to Yhwh, so that what the offerers then eat is the food of God. The actual expression "food of God" can also be used more generally of the offerings, though there too the fellowship offerings may be especially in mind. (Leviticus 21:22 refers to the fact that the priests eat the food of God, which would not apply to the whole offering.)

All this may point to one of the rationales for sacrifice. Eating meat was not Yhwh's original intention for humanity, but it was subsequently allowed, apparently as a realistic concession to humanity's disobedient inclinations, on condition that people drain the blood before eating (Gen 1:29; 9:2-4). The blood symbolized the life of the animal, the life that humanity shares with animals and that comes from God and belongs to God. Not being distanced from animal slaughter by the supermarket, Israelites might be aware of the ongoing ambiguity of eating meat: it is nice and Yhwh allows it, but it is barbaric. Making the animal an offering to Yhwh (even if the worshipers then eat most of it) turns a barbecue into a worship event. Coming before Yhwh to kill and eat an animal perhaps helps people handle the inherent ambiguity of eating meat. Leviticus 17:10-12 thus not only prohibits the consuming of blood but also notes that this same blood is the means of expiation for the lives of the people eating. Its regulation would affect only the fellowship sacrifice, because this is the one sacrifice that the offerer chiefly eats, and it is thus the one when the question of consuming the blood might arise. When Leviticus 17:10-12 adds to the explicit regulation for the fellowship sacrifice that the offering of the blood on this occasion makes expiation for the offerers, perhaps the wrong for which it is making expiation is the wrong inherent in killing an animal with Yhwh's life in it.[177]

Leviticus 7:11-18 does make clear three reasons for making a fellowship sacrifice. It may be a freewill or voluntary offering, simply expressing self-giving to God. It may be a thanksgiving offering, expressing gratitude to God for something. Or it may be a votive offering, which also implies such gratitude, but with the implication that in praying for something the person had

---

[176]Miller, *Religion of Ancient Israel*, p. 128.
[177]See Milgrom, *Leviticus 1–16*, pp. 704-13.

promised to come back with an offering and is now doing so because God has granted the prayer. Psalm 66:13-20 has someone making whole offerings to fulfill a vow. These whole offerings accompany or are accompanied by testimony to what Yhwh has done, and thus they resemble fellowship sacrifices, but perhaps they are whole offerings (in which the offerer does not share) as a mark of how great is Yhwh's deliverance and how heart-felt the person's praise.

The Purification Offering

The *haṭṭāʾt* offering (Lev 4:1–5:13; 6:24-30 [MT 17-23]) presupposes that people have acted (or failed to undertake some action) in a way that fell short of Yhwh's standards. They have gone astray (*šāgag/šāgâ*; Lev 4:2, 13, 22, 27). The offenders may be a priest or ruler (whose offenses would affect the whole people), the people as a whole, or ordinary individuals. The traditional rendering "sin offering" is misleading. The *haṭṭāʾt* need not relate to "sin" in the sense of religious or moral wrongdoing; the "solution" to sin is repentance, which brings Yhwh's forgiveness as Yhwh personally carries the sin, pays the price for it.[178] The offenses to which a *haṭṭāʾt* relates are inadvertent ones, done by accident or without a realization that what one did was wrong, or perhaps done through fear or negligence; they might or might not have moral implications. Numbers 15:17-31 restates the instructions regarding inadvertent failure to keep Yhwh's regulations and then makes explicit that such offerings cannot make up for deliberate offenses. Deliberate offenders are "cut off from the midst of their people," which might mean they may not take part in worship or might mean they are liable to action by Yhwh that would cut them off from the community. They must "carry their wrongdoing," unless they repent and beseech Yhwh to carry it.

Elsewhere than in Leviticus 4, the purification offering often relates not to acts but to states of things, such as that of the altar when it has just been built (Ex 29:36) or of a woman who has just given birth (Lev 12) or of someone who has recovered from skin disease (Lev 14). The point is that the act or the state brings taboo on the person; it introduces an incompatibility between who they are and who Yhwh is.[179] If they come into the sanctuary, that would bring taboo on it (cf. Lev 15:31). Indeed, their very presence in the community centered on the sanctuary could have this effect (cf. Num 19). And the result of that would be an unwillingness on Yhwh's part to be present there among the people.

A person affected by such taboo can be purified by waiting and washing

---

[178]See *OTT* 2:123-29.
[179]See further §6.2-3.

(see, e.g., Lev 15) or can make expiation and be pardoned through making an offering (Lev 4:20, 26, 31, 35). It is to the sanctuary that the blood of the offering is then applied (Lev 4:7, 17-18, 25, 30, 34). The particular concern of the purification offering is thus with the offense's affect on the sanctuary itself, though it seems implausible to argue that the rite did not also effect purification for the person.[180] It is a means of "de-failing" or decontaminating: the verb *ḥāṭāʾ* can be used in the piel privative, suggesting removal of the shortcoming or taboo (e.g., Lev 6:26 [MT 19]).

Leviticus 5:1-4 goes on to give some concrete illustrations of actions that require a purification offering: failure to testify in a legal case (not realizing that one had germane evidence or being negligent in coming forward?), or unwitting contact with something taboo, or uttering an oath (presumably that one could not or did not keep). These seem rather different in kind from the acts presupposed by Leviticus 4, though all have implications for the sanctuary (this could include failure to offer testimony, since the sanctuary was also the place where people came to have conflicts resolved). People who have committed such acts must confess them (Lev 5:5), which puts things right in their personal relationship with God and with the community, and thus deals with the relational implications of the act. But its objective result still needs handling. In effect, confession is able "to convert deliberate sins into inadvertences, thereby qualifying them for sacrificial expiation."[181] Simply offering a sacrifice in connection with an offense would not be enough; one has to own what one has done. Simply confessing one's offense is not enough; one has to make the appropriate offering, to make expiation for the defiling consequences of the act.

The regulations for the purification offering put much more emphasis on acts with the animal's blood than is the case with other offerings. As is the case with many aspects of the regulations, they do not explain what the acts achieve or how they work. The offerer also presses his or her hand on the animal, which might in different contexts signify transference of something from one to another (in this context, transferring stain or guilt, which is then expunged through the animal's death, substituting for the death of the offender), or the identification of a person with something (indicating that it stands for and substitutes for this particular person), or the consecration or dedication of something by someone, or the ownership of something.[182]

---

[180]Cf. Jenson, *Graded Holiness*, pp. 157, 172-73; Lester L. Grabbe, *Leviticus* (Sheffield, U.K.: Sheffield Academic Press, 1993), p. 40; Roy Gane, *Cult and Character* (Winona Lake, Ind.: Eisenbrauns, 2005), pp. 106-43; also more broadly, N. Kiuchi, *The Purification Offering in the Priestly Literature*, JSOTSup 56 (Sheffield, U.K.: JSOT, 1987).

[181]Milgrom, *Leviticus 1–16*, pp. 301-2.

[182]Cf. Gorman, *Ideology of Ritual*, p. 96.

The Reparation Offering

Leviticus 5:14–6:7 [MT 5:14-26] continues to speak in terms of people falling short (*ḥāṭā*ʾ) and going astray (*šāgag*) with regard to Yhwh's sacred things, but adds that in doing so they have committed an offense or trespass (*maʿal*; Lev 5:15). They have encroached on something belonging to Yhwh; they have committed sacrilege. Achan did so at Ai in taking from what belongs to Yhwh; King Uzziah did so in offering incense in the temple (Josh 7:1; 2 Chron 26:16). The men of the Second Temple community did so in mixing holy seed with the local peoples (Ezra 9:1-2; cf. Ezra 10:19 for the reparation offering that follows). The action of Eli's sons (1 Sam 2:12-17) is not described as *maʿal*, but would count as a shocking example. So would any withholding of due offerings.

In such situations people need to bring a trespass offering (KJV) or reparation offering (*ʾāšām*; Lev 5:15); the common rendering "guilt offering" is too general. It involves making up for their shortcoming (*šallēm*) but also adding an extra fifth as reparation for the failure. This reparation is also required in connection with false oaths, when someone has committed theft or fraud and sworn that they have not done so (Lev 6:1-7 [MT 5:20-26]). An offering is then due to Yhwh in respect of (for instance) the false oath, as well as reparation being due to the defrauded human being (cf. Num 5:5-8). Perhaps the wrong done to someone else is seen as in itself also an offense against Yhwh, a profound theological point that fits other aspects of the way the First Testament talks. But in the context the regulations more likely assume that a wrong done to someone else is also an offense against Yhwh when a person misuses Yhwh's name in swearing that they are innocent when actually they are guilty. Such offense is not, of course, an unwitting or accidental one. The regulation again covers the situation when someone confesses their wrongdoing rather than simply being found out or living in denial or refusing to acknowledge that they did wrong. Then it is as if their intention has changed; the offense indeed happened, but it can now be treated as an inadvertent one.[183]

In connection with the reparation offering, the purification offering and others, I have translated the verb *kipper* as "make expiation"; it may be that the word's more literal meaning is either "wipe clean" or "cover" or "ransom," but we do not know.[184] The object of *kipper* is the offense that a person has committed, not the one they have offended. Thus sacrifices do not propitiate God, as if they presuppose that God was angry (we have noted that

---

[183]See Milgrom, *Leviticus 1–16*, pp. 365-78. I do not follow Milgrom in reckoning that in this context *ʾāšām* can mean "feel guilt" (cf. also Milgrom, *Cult and Conscience* [Leiden: Brill, 1976]). The notion of becoming aware of guilt is denoted by the use of the verb "know" (e.g., Lev 5:1-4) and it is the public confession (Lev 5:5) that evidences the change of intention.

[184]See, e.g., *TDOT; NIDOTT*.

there are no references to God's anger in Leviticus).[185] While there are certainly occasions when God feels wrath toward Israel, sacrifices cannot deal with that wrath because sacrifices do not deal with deliberate, "proper" sin. The only way to deal with that sin is to turn away from it for the future and cast yourself on God's mercy for the past. Insofar as sacrifices have a relationship with God's anger, the relationship is that by dealing with whatever has happened, by expiating it, they proactively make sure there is no reason for God to get angry.

One way or the other the verb *kipper* indicates that the offense no longer affects the offerer. "It does not greatly signify, in explaining it, whether we start from the idea of *covering over* or from that of *wiping out:* in either case, the idea which the metaphor is intended to convey is that of *rendering null* and *inoperative.*"[186] In itself this does not signify reconciliation or atonement; *expiation* is not a relational word, like the word atonement.[187] While the First Testament is indeed concerned about at-one-ment between people and God, expiation relates more directly to the need to deal with something that threatens whether Yhwh can possibly be present with people.

The Offering of the First

All human beings and animals belong to Yhwh because Yhwh is the source of their life. Yhwh shapes their bodies and breathes into them their breath. It is a common conviction that special significance attaches to the firstborn, the one who opens a woman's womb and gives first expression to a man's manly vigor (cf. Deut 21:17); the birth of the firstborn opens up the possibility of there being further offspring and a whole new generation to follow. Special responsibilities, hopes and privileges attach to the firstborn. The First Testament works both with and against this set of assumptions. In Genesis God keeps working against it, privileging Abel over Cain, Isaac over Ishmael, Jacob over Esau, Ephraim over Manasseh. But then Yhwh claims all that open the womb (Ex 13:1-2), and the Torah does not allow parents to ignore the position of the firstborn, as happened to Esau (Deut 21:15-17). The Torah's basis for this claim lies in Yhwh's deliverance of the people from Egypt (Ex 13:11-16), because Israel is (as it were) Yhwh's firstborn son, and if Israel is not given over to Yhwh voluntarily, Yhwh will take him by force and will take the firstborn of Egypt into the bargain. In commemoration of that event, Israel's firstborn animals and sons are owed to Yhwh; a "natural" observance comes to

---

[185]See, e.g., Hartley, *Leviticus,* pp. 64-65.
[186]S. R. Driver, "Propitiation," in *A Dictionary of the Bible,* ed. James Hastings (Edinburgh: T & T Clark/New York: Scribner's, 1947), 4:128-32; see p. 128; cf. Gane, *Cult and Character,* p. 194.
[187]Cf. Brueggemann, *Theology of the Old Testament,* p. 193.

have a link with Yhwh's special act toward Israel. In practice this means the firstborn of livestock are owed to Yhwh (Deut 15:19-23), while firstborn sons are redeemed (Ex 13:11-16; 34:19-20); the means of redemption is unstated, though Exodus may imply one offers a sheep. (Numbers 18:16 sets a redemption price of five shekels.) Subsequently Yhwh declares the intention to accept the clan of Levi with their livestock instead of the firstborn and theirs (Num 3:11-13, 40-51; 8:15-18).

People were expected similarly to dedicate the first of the harvest to Yhwh, and the best of it (Ex 23:16, 19; 34:22, 26; Lev 23:17, 20; Num 18:13). To make things practical, people can turn their tithe and firstlings into money in order to be able to take it to the sanctuary, then reconvert it to the wherewithal for a feast when they get there (Deut 14:22-26). And to bring things home within the family, from the first batch of dough people are to offer a loaf (Num 15:17-21). When people plant fruit trees, they must not eat their fruit at all for three years, when they are still on their way to maturity and full fruitfulness, in the fourth year their fruit is to be exultant holiness for Yhwh, then from the fifth year people can use it in the regular way (Lev 19:23-25). Like other observances, many of these practices were also harnessed to meeting the needs of people who did not have land: the priests and Levites' needs were met through the dedication of the first of the harvest, as offerings support the priests and tithes support the Levites (Num 18:8-32).

To come into Yhwh's presence, then, do you have to bring costly or copious offerings, even give Yhwh your own firstborn, in order to make up for the way you have rebelled against him and fallen short of him? Does Yhwh make demands of the people that wear them out? "My people, what have I done to you, how have I wearied you?" Yhwh asks (Mic 6:3-7). They behave as if Yhwh had let them down or exhausted them *(lā'â)*. Perhaps Yhwh had done so in bringing them out of serfdom in Egypt or in providing them with leaders for their subsequent journey or in rescuing them from the curses planned by Balak or in taking them from Shittim across the Jordan? I have not let you down *(hel'ētîkā)* but brought you up *(he'ēltîkā)*, says Yhwh. If they do think about that story, it will surely lead them to acknowledge Yhwh's faithfulness rather than implicitly finding fault with the way Yhwh has dealt with them.[188] No, Yhwh does not make demands that wear people out. First Testament offerings have a token, symbolic nature. They do not pretend to make up for wrongdoing in a quantitative way. They do not cause Yhwh to accept people; the instinct to do so comes from inside Yhwh. Further, more important than these offerings is a turning round of the life that replaces rebellion and failure with *mišpāṭ* and

---

[188]Cf. Leslie C. Allen, *The Books of Joel, Obadiah, Jonah and Micah* (London: Hodder/Grand Rapids: Eerdmans, 1976), p. 366.

ḥesed, commitment to other people expressed in decisive action toward them, and also a different stance in relation to God (Mic 6:8).[189]

The Offering of Human Beings

The sacrifice of one's child (not necessarily a small child) is an extreme act of dedication in which a person might indulge when feeling particular need to get a prayer answered; and it may work (see 2 Kings 3:27). Moses and the prophets reckon it self-evident that this is an abhorrent practice (e.g., Is 57:5-6). There is no need to justify condemning people when they build sanctuaries for incinerating Judah's sons and daughters (Jer 7:31). People will find their own destiny lies in these canyons: they will find themselves sucked into the fate of these children.

Isaiah 66:3-4 puts together slaughtering an ox, beating a person, sacrificing a sheep, strangling a dog, offering pigs' blood, offering incense and worshiping wickedness. In LXX and 1QIs[a] this description of wrongdoing makes a comparison: offering "proper" worship can be no better than offering false worship, if the rest of people's lives clashes with their worship. In MT people are trying to have things both ways, as they did before the exile. They offer proper worship of Yhwh, but they also sacrifice human beings, offer dogs and pigs, and worship idols. The prophecy does not describe these acts in literal, neutral terms. It does not assume we should be respectful of other people's religious practices. Sacrificing one's child would be a costly and grievous act, but Yhwh speaks of it as an act of assault, a mugging, a beating. Reference to observances involving pigs and dogs is designed to be especially disgusting. Worshiping another god or using an image in worship becomes worshiping wickedness. In such observances, people will have seen themselves as calling on Yhwh, but as Yhwh sees it, they do no such thing. Indeed, whereas Yhwh had called on them, presumably through prophets summoning them to reform, they did not respond. They made their choices in accordance with what they liked. Yhwh will do the same. Their worship, with its hedging of bets, is designed to maximize the possibility of guarding against calamities they dreaded, but it will have the opposite effect.

One could describe a child offered to Yhwh as *ḥērem*, which is "a process of consecration through destruction. . . . It is the ultimate in dedication."[190] Modern readers agree with the prophets that also no argument is required to demonstrate the abhorrent nature of this practice. Yet the offering of a beloved son is a central or foundational element in Judaism (following Gen 22) and in Christianity. A "barbaric ritual" is thus subjected to a "transfor-

---

[189]See §2.2 "Diffidence."

[190]Jacob Milgrom, *Leviticus 23–27*, AB (New York: Doubleday, 2001), pp. 2417, 2418, following Philip D. Stern, *The Biblical Ḥerem* (Atlanta: Scholars, 1991), p. 1.

mation . . . into a sublime paradigm of the religious life."[191]

It is not only living things that can be devoted; such devoting does not inherently imply their death. People can commit themselves to offering a piece of land or some other possession as *ḥērem* as well as a person or animal (Lev 27:28; Num 18:14). In connection with a person, the idea that this would involve killing him or her would be hard to fit with other attitudes expressed in the Torah. Rather, it means giving the person over to God irrevocably, so that he or she comes into the service of the temple and priesthood, like Samuel. But the term *ḥērem* first features in the Torah as a way of describing execution, specifically for sacrificing to a god other than Yhwh (Ex 22:20 [MT 19]; cf. Deut 13:12-18 [MT 13-19]; this could explain the postscript in Lev 27:29). Yhwh is claiming these people because of their faithlessness and waywardness, and Israel is handing them over to Yhwh in accordance with that claim. Such execution does not simply fulfill a function in connection with the framework of law or act as a deterrent or resolve issues within the community or give redress to people who have lost a family member.[192] In connection with the worship of other gods, the execution pays for an offense against Yhwh. But it is a form of sacrifice, a ritual expression of beliefs and values that definitively removes from the community a person thought to be depraved.[193] Such sacrifice links with the notion of devoting a whole people, which first appears in Numbers 21:1-3, where it is Israel's proposal, accepted by Yhwh. In the framework of Israelite thinking and instinct, war, death, sacrifice and *ḥērem* are integrally associated, and understanding *ḥērem* requires us to see it in connection with the realm of the sacred and with sacrifice.[194] In light of their wrongdoing, the Canaanites require to be given over to God. They become absolutely holy; they cannot be returned to everyday usage. They are not quite unique in this respect. Yhwh issues the same command about the Amalekites (1 Sam 15), and in due course acts in this way toward Israel (Is 43:28). The last, at least, indicates that we have to be careful about how literally we take references to *ḥērem*.[195]

Offerings and Death

The sacrifice of children is also a feature of the worship of Molek: "You are not to give any of your offspring for passing over to Molek; you are not to

---

[191]Jon D. Levenson, *The Death and Resurrection of the Beloved Son* (New Haven, Conn./London: Yale University Press, 1993), p. x.

[192]See the discussion of execution in §4.4.

[193]M. F. C. Bourdillon, introduction to *Sacrifice*, pp. 1-27; see pp. 13-14.

[194]Susan Niditch, *War in the Hebrew Bible* (New York/Oxford: Oxford University Press, 1993), p. 40, referring to Stern, *Biblical Ḥerem*.

[195]See §4.1 "Thinking Exegetically."

profane the name of your God; I am Yhwh" (Lev 18:21). Molek may not be a real name but a word comprising the consonants of the word for king, *melek*, or of the actual name of a deity, perhaps Malik, combined with the vowels of the word for shame, *bōšet*.[196] The pronouncing of the name thus passes a theological judgment on the practice it bans; Malik or the supposed king is an object of shame. Apparently people could offer a child to Molek as a sacrifice, killing the child and then burning it as they did with animal sacrifice, yet see themselves as serving Yhwh, Molek being Yhwh's underling; hence the declaration that actually they are profaning Yhwh's name, and polluting the sanctuary (Lev 20:1-6) as they come into it with blood on their hands (Ezek 23:37-39). Indeed, they profane the land (Ps 106:38), turning it into a land like any other, not a land that truly belongs to Yhwh.

This sacrifice of children is also linked with turning to ghosts and spirits, trying to make contact with dead members of one's family in order to get guidance (see Lev 20:1-6; Deut 18:10-11; 2 Kings 17:17; 21:6; 2 Chron 33:6; Is 8:19-20). The offerers are not worshiping their ancestors, but they are looking to them for something for which they should look only to Yhwh. The link may suggest that people saw Molek as (under Yhwh) the king of Sheol; Isaiah 57:9 refers to offerings to "the king," likely a reference to Molek where his title has not been bowdlerized, and makes a connection with journeys to Sheol. The indications of a link between Molek and Sheol fit with the indications from elsewhere that Malik was a god of the underworld.[197] Making offerings to Molek was a way of trying to ensure that one made contact with people there, and offering one's child would be an extreme way of seeking to ensure that.

It is a distinctive feature of First Testament faith to recognize the distinction between life and death, and recognize Yhwh as the God of life.[198] Yhwh being the only God, it would have been possible to make Yhwh the God of Sheol as well as the God of this earth, and certainly the First Testament knows that Yhwh is the Lord of Sheol in the sense that there is no other deity in charge there; Yhwh determines who goes there and who comes out of there. But Yhwh generally chooses not to be involved with Sheol, and no other deity is involved there (e.g., Ps 6:5 [MT 6]; 88:10-12 [MT 11-13]). This is a countercultural conviction, clashing with natural human instincts among the Canaanites and Israelites.[199] But the First Testament itself has turned its back on these natural human instincts. In having recourse to "the King," people have re-

---

[196]See George C. Heider, *The Cult of Molek,* JSOTSup 43 (Sheffield, U.K.: JSOT, 1985); John Day, *Molech* (Cambridge/New York: Cambridge University Press, 1989).

[197]Cf. *DDD* "Malik." On theories regarding Molek, see Hartley, *Leviticus,* pp. 333-37.

[198]See further §6.3.

[199]See, e.g., Karel van der Toorn, *Family Religion in Babylonia, Syria and Israel* (Leiden/New York: Brill, 1996), pp. 206-35.

course to a lie and are acting out a lie (cf. Is 28:15). Trusting in Yhwh continues to be the key to the future.

The ban on sacrificing children to Molek first appears in the context of regulations concerning sexual activity (Lev 18:21-23), and the development of this regulation (Lev 20:1-6) refers three times to the fact that the person in question is sacrificing "his offspring." There is thus a further objection to this practice. As well as dishonoring Yhwh by acting as if Molek really represented Yhwh, and seeking to treat the dead as a resource for guidance, it involves despising your offspring. Contact with the dead, with those who came before you, is more important to you than your concern for the living and for the future of your family and your people.

2.6 Sojourning with Yhwh

For most Western Christians, the dynamic of worship centers on a meeting with God and with other people that happens once a week and lasts an hour or two. In the First Testament more significance attaches to meetings that take place at different times in the year and last a week or so, especially Pesah/ Massot, Shavuot and Sukkot, and to the Expiation Day. Ideally, each year families will make pilgrimage to Yhwh's home on such occasions. There they will spend time celebrating what Yhwh has done for them in nature and in their story of deliverance, recalling the obligations that issue from this and ensuring that they do their part to remain a people among whom Yhwh can indeed dwell. The First Testament assumes both that there is something special about being in Yhwh's presence on the occasion of pilgrim festivals, but also that the same presence of Yhwh can be a reality in all of life.

The Worship Year

Leviticus 23 gives the most complete account of Israel's liturgical year. As an account of "set times" or "holy occasions," it begins with the sabbath. In describing the calendar it starts in March/April with Pesah (Passover), in keeping with the instruction to view this as the beginning of the year (Ex 12:2); Massot (Unleavened Bread) follows. Seven weeks later comes Shavuot (Pentecost), marking the grain harvest. In July/August, later practice added the observance of the Ninth of Av, an occasion for mourning over the destruction of the temple, using Lamentations. The first day of the seventh month (September/October) was a holy occasion marked by blasts on a horn; this may simply herald the importance of this month in the calendar or may mark the beginning of the agricultural year. As Exodus 23:16 notes, the agricultural year begins in the fall, as the arrival of the rains makes possible the beginning of the agricultural cycle for another year. The tenth day of this seventh month is Expiation Day (the Day of Atonement); Sukkot (Tabernacles), marking the fruit harvest, begins on the fifteenth. In December later observance added Hanukkah (Dedication), celebrating the rededication of the temple after its desecration by Antiochus Epiphanes in the 160s. The visions in Daniel 7–12 portray this desecration; the rededication is not mentioned in the First Testament but it is related in 1 Maccabees 4:52-59, which also records the festival celebrating it, on the twenty-fifth day of the ninth month (cf. Jn 10:22). Finally, in February/March comes Purim (Lots), commemorating an extraordinary deliverance of the Jewish people in Susa, celebrated on the fifteenth day of the twelfth month; the casting of lots plays a key role in the story (Esther 3:7; 9:18-28). The dynamic of Israel's calendar inspired the church's year running from Advent through Christmas, Epiphany, Lent, Good Friday, Easter and Pentecost, denying that the real year is the one marked by New Year, Valentine's Day, tax day, Labor Day, commencement, Independence Day, Memorial Day, Halloween and Thanksgiving.

While Leviticus 23 gives specific dates for each festival, as Exodus 12 does for Pesah, Exodus 23 and Exodus 34 locate Massot in the month Abib but set no dates for the other festivals, perhaps implying they were celebrated at the time the harvests actually came. Exodus 34:22 does refer to the grain festival as Shavuot, "Weeks"; Deuteronomy 16 explicitly dates it seven weeks after Massot, but sets no date for Sukkot.

Massot, Shavuot and Sukkot are the three annual occasions when Israel is to "hold a festival [ḥāgag] for me" (Ex 23:14). The verb first appears when Moses initially appears before the Pharaoh to declare that Yhwh requires Israel to do this at the place in the wilderness where Yhwh has appeared to Moses, at Sinai (Ex 5:1; 10:9). By definition a festival (ḥāg) involves a pilgrimage to such a place, and the three annual festivals involve pilgrimage to the sanctuary, though for much of Israel's history Pesah was celebrated at home; hence it is not mentioned in Exodus 23:14-17; 34:18-24; or Deuteronomy 16:16-17. It is not described as a pilgrimage festival, except in association with Massot in Exodus 12:14. Indeed, the story of Elkanah and Hannah in 1 Samuel 1 takes for granted that a family makes pilgrimage once a year, and to a sanctuary not too far away. It seems likely that people did not make pilgrimage to a far-off sanctuary three times annually, but this need not stop them celebrating nearer home.[200] Appearing before Yhwh necessarily involves offerings (Lev 23:5, 8, 12-14, 18-20, 25, 36, 37); one cannot come before Yhwh "empty"—that is (presumably) empty-handed (Ex 23:15; 34:20; Deut 16:16-17). The festivals are "for me" (Ex 23:14). They are "Yhwh's set occasions" or "set times" and "holy

---

[200]Admittedly the event in 1 Sam 1 is not referred to as a ḥāg, and Haran thinks it was rather a family or clan occasion like that in 1 Sam 20:6 (*Temples and Temple-Service in Ancient Israel*, pp. 304-7).

events" (Lev 23:2, 4, 7, 8, 21, 24, 35, 44). They involve giving up work, not to give the worshipers a break but to recognize the holiness of the occasion (Lev 23:8, 21, 24-25, 35-36, 39).

They are occasions when all males appear before the Lord Yhwh (Ex 23:17; 34:23). That is not to imply that women are absent from the festivals, as Deuteronomy makes explicit even while repeating the note about the males (Deut 16:1-17); women play as much part in offering sacrifices as men.[201] Deuteronomy portrays the festivals as inclusive occasions, emphasizing the involvement of the whole family, parents and children, free and servants, Israelites and aliens. Here there is neither Jew nor Greek, slave nor free, male nor female (cf. Gal 3:28). In a patriarchal society the reference to the men reminds them of their responsibility to make the pilgrimage happen and asserts Yhwh's lordship over them, as happens when the sign of the covenant is one that applies directly to them. In the whole Sinai story, only in connection with these festivals (in Ex 23:17 and the parallel Ex 34:23) is Yhwh described as "Lord," *ʾādōn*, the word otherwise used for the master of the household (Ex 21:2-11). The men appear before Yhwh as the real Lord, Master and Owner. (The reference to males might say something else to cultures where religion is seen as women's business.) That had to mean that male householders, for instance, took a different attitude outside the festival to foreigners, servants and women from the one they might otherwise have taken, and this is supported by the instructions for everyday life in the Torah. Thus "through worship God trains his people to take the right things for granted."[202]

A Day in Your Courts

Psalm 122 expresses a sense of wonder at the privilege of having been in Jerusalem for one of these festivals. "I rejoiced in the people who said to me, 'We are going to Yhwh's house.' " And then the pilgrim wonders at the fact that "Our feet have been standing within your gates, Jerusalem," the city that attracted "Yah's clans" for these great occasions when people come "to confess Yhwh's name," and the city where Davidic kings rule.

At a festival people come "to appear before God" (Ps 42:2 [MT 3]). The expression is an odd one[203] and the Targum has "to see the face of God"; perhaps MT has repointed the verb to avoid giving the impression that one could "really" see God. There is a sense in which that is possible, a sense in which it is impossible. To see someone's face is to come right into their presence; the expression applies particularly to the experience of being allowed to come into

---

[201]Miller, *Religion of Israel*, pp. 203-4

[202]Hauerwas and Wells, *Blackwell Companion to Christian Ethics*, p. 25.

[203]Normally "before" would be *lipnê*, lit., "to the face of"; here it is simply *pĕnê*, so the expression literally says "to appear the face of God."

the presence of a person such as a king. So in Esther 1:14 the expression can be paraphrased as meaning "have access to the king." In this sense it is certainly possible to see God's face (Ps 11:7; 17:15), and it makes little difference whether one speaks of "seeing God's face" or "appearing before God's face." Either way the psalm speaks of the reality of being in God's presence. But the power and splendor of the king can also make it dangerous to see the king's face, to come into his presence (e.g., Ex 10:28). In this sense it is impossible to see God's face and live. The First Testament does not argue that one cannot see God's face because God does not have a face; that would risk denying the reality of God and the reality of being in God's presence.

When Christian spirituality speaks of longing and thirsting for God, it often refers to an inner sense of God's reality and presence. When Israel speaks thus, it refers to a longing to get to the sanctuary, a longing that relates to the assurance that Yhwh is objectively present there. Yhwh is not elusive, and an assurance of being in Yhwh's presence is not dependent on a worshiper's inner feelings. Yhwh actually dwells in the sanctuary. It is Yhwh's "shelter" or "house" (Ps 42:4 [MT 5]). To be there is to be with Yhwh and thus (for instance) to know that Yhwh has heard one's prayers and praises. This is not to imply that people's inner beings are not involved. Psalm 42 makes clear that relating to God involves the whole person, body and spirit, and it involves the individual but in relation to community.

How much loved, then, is the Jerusalem sanctuary, Yhwh's dwelling (Ps 84:1 [MT 2]). The suppliant had looked forward with such enthusiasm to making the pilgrimage there, to getting to those courtyards, the place in a home where people meet and eat and talk.[204] "I am like a bird that has been able to find a secure place to nest with my young. So now that I am here, I resound to the living God." This is the place where Yhwh agreed to live. You can be sure of meeting God here. It is not surprising that the suppliant chooses to come here to hang about Yhwh's house, reckoning that just a day in these courtyards is a fabulous experience. The suppliant lives somewhere such as Beersheba or Lachish, several days' journey away, and thus can come to the sanctuary only for great festival occasions. How marvelous it would be actually to live here, to be able to come back day after day to praise God. But after these few days, the family has to go back to Lachish or Beersheba and get on with everyday work and life. So alongside the delight about being here is a certain poignancy about not being able actually to live here.

Christians may often properly feel ambivalent about having to live their lives from Monday to Saturday among people who do not share their relationship with and commitment to Christ, and may look forward to the day

---

[204]See further the comments on Ps 100 in §2.4 "The Worshipers."

when they can be in the company of people gathered in his name, where he is in the midst. Or they may properly feel ambivalent about having to live their lives fifty-one weeks of the year thus, and treasure the week in the year they spend on a Christian retreat.

A Thousand Elsewhere

Yet there is a paradox about the psalm's attitude as it comments on "the good fortune of the person who finds strength in you," when "the highways are in their mind," the highways that lead to Jerusalem. The way the psalm goes on to speak of passing through Balsam Vale implies a dynamic whereby the prospect of visiting the sanctuary transforms the life of worshipers even before they get there. The dynamic is similar to that in Isaiah 40:28-31, which promises that people who wait for Yhwh get new strength even now. "The good fortune of the person who trusts in you" is not confined to the time when they are there, when arguably trust is less necessary. It transforms the life that people live in Beersheba or Lachish over the weeks and months between pilgrimages as they look back on and savor the last visit and look forward to and plan the next one. Thus it transpires that the reality of Yhwh's presence in the sanctuary does not mean Yhwh is not present in Lachish or Beersheba. Rather it mysteriously promises Yhwh's presence there too. When Christians meet with God on Sunday or on a retreat, this deepens the awareness that God is also present with them in their place of work through the week and through the fifty-one weeks, rather than reinforcing the conviction that God is absent there. We live in faith and hope: faith in what God has done and hope in what God will do.

So whereas the confession that a day in Yhwh's presence is better than a thousand ordinary days living among people such as Philistines or Edomites (Ps 84:10 [MT 11]) might seem to presage the gloomy conclusion that only one week in the year is worth living, that is not where the confession leads. The reason for enthusing over Yhwh's sanctuary is that "Yhwh God is a sun and shield" who "gives favor and honor; he does not withhold good things for people who walk with integrity," and the psalm concludes with one more exclamation about good fortune, regarding "the person who trusts in you." None of those comments apply only to people who *live* in Jerusalem. The psalm deconstructs, in an encouraging way. The person who finds strength in Yhwh is the person who walks with integrity and trusts in Yhwh. It is possible to live in Jerusalem and not be that person; the prophets could give one the impression that most Jerusalemites were not like that, and such people forfeit the protection that being there should bring. And it is possible to live fifty miles away and experience all those realities. Yhwh is at home in Jerusalem, but not confined there. While pilgrimage is a wonderful week's experience of being at home with Yhwh, and families look forward to it all year, one of its functions is to encourage them with the reality of Yhwh as one present anywhere to people of integrity and trust.

Psalms 42–43 manifest more tension over having access to the sanctuary, apparently because something other than the calendar is preventing this. They grieve over being unable to get there. The difference is signaled by the difference in the tenses over against Psalm 84, not "my whole being craved, yes exhausted itself, for Yhwh's courtyards" but "my whole being strains . . . thirsts" as I ask when I shall be able to be there.[205] But the longing of Psalm 42 again does not imply that Yhwh is present and accessible only at the sanctuary. After all, the psalm addresses God, who is assumed to be capable of listening to someone who at this moment cannot get there. Indeed, here "God is omnipresent in a poem that complains of his absence," and "ironically, the pain of separation is a way of feeling the presence."[206] The suppliant's enemies also unwittingly testify to the recognition that God can be known elsewhere. "Where is your God," they ask (Ps 42:3, 10 [MT 4, 11]). Given that the psalm's premise is that the suppliant cannot get to the sanctuary, their question presupposes that a decent God is not confined to the sanctuary but is also involved in the everyday world, being present and active where people are. Yet none of this takes away from the significance of being able to get to the sanctuary for a festival, an occasion when one adds one's own testimony to the confessions offered there that affirm how Yhwh acts in the world, and when one celebrates the great acts of Yhwh for the people and thus has one's conviction deepened about Yhwh's capacity to act in the world.

Staying with God

Psalm 15:1 speaks of staying (gûr) in Yhwh's tent (an anachronistic way of designating a home) and of dwelling (šākan) on Yhwh's mountain. While the temple courts would provide space where a person could sleep, no one exactly lived there, though people such as priests and Levites might stay there overnight when they were on duty in the temple, and perhaps laypeople might also do so. The verb for "stay" links with the word gēr for a resident alien and suggests somewhere you stay as a guest, with some security though not with the same rights as a permanent citizen. The verb for "dwell" links with the word miškān for the wilderness dwelling; this verb, too, suggests be-

---

[205]The allusiveness of the Hebrew verbal system means the EVV can translate the qatal verbs in Ps 84 with present tense verbs, the same way as the yiqtol verbs in Ps 42, but this seems a little perverse; and anyway, the contents of Ps 84 as a whole indicate that the worshiper is free to go to the sanctuary (subject to the practicalities of geography) rather than prevented from doing so, as in Ps 42.

[206]Konrad Schaefer, *Psalms* (Collegeville, Minn.: Liturgical Press, 2001), p. 109.

ing somewhere for longer than one might have expected but not necessarily forever. Psalm 65:4 [MT 5] declares "the good fortune of the one you choose and bring near to dwell in your courtyards." We might initially wonder if this is a priest or king, but the verse continues, "We shall be filled with the goodness of your house, your holy palace." It rather implies that the previous line individualizes the experience of the whole people that Yhwh invites to the palace for a festival. In the immediate context the good things there will be the fine food and drink that people enjoy at a royal banquet. But these good things will be symbols of something broader. The festival celebrates the divine goodness that gave people the land and gives them this year's harvest. It is from God's presence there that good things flow out.

"I shall stay in your tent forever, I shall find refuge in the shelter of your wings" (Ps 61:4 [MT 5]). In other contexts the tent would again be an image for the temple, which can also be spoken of as a place of refuge and shelter (1 Kings 1:50). But the second colon makes it more likely that the whole line has more metaphorical reference. Not being able to find shelter in the temple does not mean being without shelter. The image of God's wings recalls the wings of the cherubim in the temple and thus appeals to that figure for protection, but it does not imply that God's protection is known only there. One can be in Yhwh's tent, finding refuge in the shelter of Yhwh's wings, when far away from the temple. People can know Yhwh's protective presence in the dangers of everyday life in the world (cf. Ps 17:8; 36:7 [MT 8]; 57:1 [MT 2]). The imagery of protection recurs in Psalm 11, which begins with a declaration about "relying" on Yhwh or "taking refuge" with Yhwh *(ḥāsâ)* and draws a contrast with a bird that seeks refuge on a mountain ridge (cf. Ps 7:1 [MT 2]; 16:1; 31:1 [MT 2]).

It is almost as if Yhwh's tent spreads its curtains over the whole land. One just needs to see them, as Elisha's servant needs to see the army surrounding him and Elisha (2 Kings 6:17). The temple is but a visible, localized concretion of that wider reality. Elisha has no power of his own over against that of the kings of Ephraim or Syria, but prayer makes it possible to refer the situation to one who has power, and the effect of Elisha's prayer is to enable his servant to see things differently, specifically to see the world as a place where God is ruling.[207]

"I am a sojourner *[gēr]* with you, a transient *[tôšāb]* like all my ancestors" (Ps 39:12 [MT 13]). Israel's ancestors were only ever sojourners, resident aliens, in Canaan; the psalm's double expression is one Abraham himself uses (Gen 23:4). The suppliant has that position in the world. In life we are sojourners and transients, but we are that "with you." (The expression comes at the cen-

---

[207]Cf. Walter Brueggemann, *Interpretation and Obedience* (Minneapolis: Fortress, 1991), pp. 35-36.

ter of the line and has some prominence, applying to both cola.) I am insecure, but I am secure. Even far away from the temple, Yhwh can lead someone to a high crag that provides safety. Indeed, Yhwh in person can be that: "for you have been a refuge to me, a strong tower before the enemy." Through Yhwh's providing a refuge, which functions like the fortified tower within a city where its inhabitants could hide when an enemy threatened to overwhelm the city itself, it becomes clear that Yhwh *is* a refuge.

A Refuge from Danger

Thus "if an army should encamp against me, my heart would not fear; if a war should arise against me, in this I trust" (Ps 27:3). Whereas many psalms referring to opposition and attack could be composed for ordinary people, this kind of statement suggests one composed for a leader such as a king, who functions as the army commander-in-chief on the battle field, not just in the war room in Jerusalem or Samaria. One of the enemy's priorities will then be to kill him (e.g., 1 Kings 22). So a leader has special reason to be apprehensive about war, and the psalm's twice-asked question, "Whom should I fear?" is not so rhetorical. The answer is: Anybody who attacks Israel. There is good reason to fear; except that there is not, because "Yhwh is my light, my deliverance" and "the stronghold of my life" (Ps 27:1). The leader has proved this, has seen adversaries fall even as they were trying to put him down.

His confidence in Yhwh relates to more than one way of being in Yhwh's presence. He recalls having asked from Yhwh (and having been granted, he implies) the privilege of living in Yhwh's house (Ps 27:4a). Living with Yhwh means enjoying safety and provision there, though here in a psalm that focuses on the pressures of life out in the world, "living in Yhwh's house" may denote living in Yhwh's household rather than living in the temple building. In this sense, too, I may aspire to live with Yhwh, but know I can do so out in the world, where Yhwh can be with me, so that "my body will dwell in confidence" (Ps 16:8-9).

Then, when battle threatens, the king knows what it is like to seek an audience at Yhwh's palace (Ps 27:4b). The temple is the palace where the divine king lives and exercises authority; the word can refer to Yhwh's palace in the heavens, of which the earthly palace is an earthly outpost where people can approach Yhwh. There is some irony or some appropriateness about the human king coming to the divine King's court to seek support when under pressure from other peoples. He is acting in the way his own subjects might act in relation to him, when they are under pressure from other people and they appeal to the king. When the human king responds to such a plea, one can imagine the subject's heartfelt gratitude. When the divine King responds to such a plea, the human king similarly returns to Yhwh's dwelling (which has now become a "tent," as it was in the early years of Yhwh's relationship with Israel) to express such gratitude (Ps 27:6).

The king also speaks of being hidden in Yhwh's "shelter" and lifted high on a crag in such a way as to be protected from death in battle (Ps 27:5). Here, once more, the shelter is not the Jerusalem temple but the reality of Yhwh's dwelling and presence out in the world. Perhaps one should think of it as another version of an earthly outpost of the heavenly temple, but now it is an invisible reality apart from the temple. Unlike the wilderness tent, it has the disadvantage of being invisible and incalculable, but like the wilderness tent, it has the advantage of being mobile. While "living in Yhwh's house all the days of my life" might then refer hyperbolically to a freedom to keep coming into Yhwh's presence in the temple, it might more plausibly suggest a continuing freedom to seek shelter in this invisible, mobile dwelling. The king appeared in the Jerusalem temple to ask for "one thing" that was a matter of life and death, to be able always to dwell in the protection of a presence of Yhwh that can accompany him wherever he has to go, specifically "on the day of evil," the day when trouble threatens (Ps 27:4-5). Living in Yhwh's house is a continual reality, while making request at Yhwh's palace is a recurrent one; the response to such requests is often to make it possible for the continual reality to provide hiding and escape. If Psalm 23:6 refers to "living in Yhwh's house for long years" (so LXX), this has the same implication; but MT implies "returning" rather than "living."[208]

Ordinary Life in the Context of the Festivals

The experiences that narratives and psalms describe and the prayers that psalms pray indicate that one does not need to be in the temple to pray. "It can be done at sea, in the wilderness, in prison, or from the sickbed"; and conversely, the worship of the temple depends for its life on people's experience of Yhwh's involvement in their everyday lives in response to such prayers.[209] "They are to confess to Yhwh his commitment, his wonders for human beings, to lift him up in the congregation of the people, to praise him in the session of the elders" (Ps 107:31-32).

While much First Testament prayer issues out of crises, Israelites did not live their whole lives in the midst of crises, and many First Testament prayers presuppose that people are not in a predicament today, though they know this might change tomorrow. It is this kind of regular, noncrisis prayer that is nearer to what "prayer" often means for Christians. And it is the festivals that frame the dynamic of Israel's regular, ongoing life with God.

---

[208]That is, MT has *wĕšabtî*; for LXX's understanding, one would expect *wĕšibtî*.
[209]Othmar Keel, *The Symbolism of the Biblical World* (New York: Seabury, 1978), pp. 322, 335.

Psalm 63 suggests a threefold pattern to this ongoing life. First, it involves longing: "I search for you; my whole person longs for you." Etymologically, "searching" (*šāḥar* piel) suggests getting up early in the morning to do something; that is how serious is the suppliant's desire to get to God's presence. The psalm goes on to speak of being in a land that is dry and faint, which might sometimes be literal reality (it might imply living far away from the temple, or a king might have to spend time far away, on a campaign) but it also suggests a metaphor (cf. Ps 42). For one reason or another, the suppliant cannot get to Yhwh's house at the moment.

Second, while waiting to be able do so, "when I have been mindful of you on my bed, in the night watches I talk about you." I think about you and meditate and murmur out loud about you, like someone separated from a loved one and longing for a reunion. I remember the way you have been my help in the past, and I thus resound with praise in the shade of your wings. In this way "my whole person has stuck to you," like a man sticking to a woman (Gen 2:24). I have adhered to Yhwh rather than seeking help from other deities. And "your right hand has upheld me."

This psalm thus again presupposes the recurrent paradox about the idea of being with Yhwh. Yhwh is not confined to the temple, and the suppliant knows Yhwh's presence and support in a location far from there. It is possible to shelter under Yhwh's wings anywhere. But the temple is Yhwh's personal abode, and the suppliant therefore keenly wants to get there. And from time to time that is possible. Campaigns come to an end; festival times arrive. Thus "I have seen you in the sanctuary, beholding your power and glory." The "seeing" perhaps suggests on one hand the festival processions and the proclamation of what Yhwh did in events such as the exodus, and on the other the inner awareness of Yhwh's real presence brought home by this drama. The suppliant had been with God in a different sense from the one that applied when far away from the temple.

The festival comes to an end, but it carries an aftertaste. I continue to savor it. Because it brings home the wonder of Yhwh's commitment, "my lips will glorify you. So I will worship you throughout my life; in your name I will lift my hands." This is the third element in the pattern of ongoing life that the psalm suggests. While First Testament faith manifests a dynamic whereby God's deliverance leads to immediate thanksgiving and testimony, and also to ongoing praise, in this psalm there is no crisis from which the suppliant needs delivering, but there is a similar dynamic whereby fulfilling the longing to return to God's presence issues in ongoing praise. I move from being thirsty, dry and faint, to feasting and being full. I know that when people seek my life, they will not succeed. Life with God thus comprises longing, presence and assurance.

Christian practice has manifested a similar ambiguity to Israel's. Whereas Jesus declared that place does not matter and Paul declared that the community is God's temple, the church soon located worship in dedicated buildings and called them "the house of God" or "the sanctuary." A pattern has recurred whereby new Christian movements initially abandon existent dedicated buildings but in due course build their own. Churches have commonly sat at the center of a village or town, like the wilderness sanctuary at the center of the Israelite encampment, holding the society together. The church is usually a building made in a style and of materials unlike any other building and thus separate from it, and there are gradations of separateness within it based on those of the wilderness sanctuary and the temple—an area where laypeople sit, a choir area and a fenced area designated the "sanctuary" in a narrow sense. The church links earth and heaven. It is at the center of the village but separate from it. In practice Christian faith affirms both that God's presence is independent of sanctuaries but also that it requires sanctuaries.

Pesah

Just before the end of the great struggle for Israel's body and soul between Moses and the king of Egypt, the story of Israel's deliverance from Egypt is dramatically put on hold while we are told of the way the coming event will be commemorated over the millennia in the festival of Pesah. We do not know the origin or meaning of the word *pesah;* the conventional translation "Passover" reflects the way the verb *pāsah* is used by paronomasia in Exodus 12:13, but there may be no implication that the noun *pesah* originally suggested "passing over." The LXX sometimes translates on this assumption but sometimes takes it to denote "protect."[210]

In inserting a set of ritual instructions into the narrative, like the regulations for sacrifice in Leviticus 1–7, Exodus 12:1 has Yhwh giving the original instructions for Pesah when the exodus has not yet happened. The festival is inaugurated when the people are still in Egypt. Christian annual commemorations such as Christmas and Easter were devised decades or centuries after the events they mark. In Exodus 12, Pesah is an anticipation, a statement of promise and a statement of faith, a kind of prophecy. The event that is coming is so certain that the arrangements for its future commemoration can be laid down. The more frequent Christian celebration of the Eucharist takes up this pattern, for this is also initiated when the conflict between light and darkness has not yet reached its head, and when only trust in God can be the basis of confidence that it will issue in the victory of freedom over bondage.

Consequently, when people celebrate Pesah they transport themselves

---

[210]Cf. Milgrom, *Leviticus,* p. 276. See further *TDOT.*

back to the moment before the conflict had come to its head. The festival is designed to ensure that the exodus is always "remembered" or kept in mind (Ex 12:14) as the beginning of the people's story, the event that defines who they are. Its celebration makes them the exodus people again; the Eucharist is similarly designed to take us back to the event it commemorates and thus to be a means of our being mindful ("do this in remembrance"). The remembering involved in the event is a conscious application of the mind that takes one into another reality. It accompanies this by activity of the body that ensures that the whole person is engaged. It entails drama in the way people dress up and the way they eat (Ex 12:11). Later it would involve a journey to the place Yhwh designates; 2 Chronicles 30 and 2 Chronicles 35 give vivid imaginative accounts of how such a central Pesah might have been (cf. also Ezra 6:19-22). As the event recurs it embraces the participants once again and takes them in their own experience from bondage to freedom. If they are actually living in some Egypt, its doing so is the more important, so that the real world in which service of the king gave way to service of Yhwh becomes again the world that shapes the lives of people who are tempted to live as if the world in which this does not take place is the truly real world. It is as if celebrating the Eucharist convinces people facing their own cross that carrying it will not be empty or futile.

The occasion when the people celebrate Pesah is to become for them the beginning of the year (Ex 12:2). As far as we know, Israel never took this as a literal instruction about the calendar. Whenever we can trace it, the year began as the Jewish year does now, not in March-April but in September-October, at the turn of the agricultural year. But the festival was designed to ensure that the exodus event was always kept in mind as the beginning of the people's story, the event that defines who they are.

A Family Celebration

Pesah involves a family meal. It is a real meal, not merely a fragment of bread and a mouthful of wine, still less of grape juice. It is a family affair, not something that works with individuals. Nor does it involve people gathering as nuclear families, or even necessarily as extended families if the group would not be big enough. In that case, people gather in groups of families as local communities (Ex 12:3-4); there is nothing sacrosanct or closed off about the family unit. The group needs to be big enough to eat a whole lamb without leaving any over (Ex 12:10), and this requirement brings about an underlining of the communal nature of the event. Even the groups of families are manifestly part of a wider entity. The whole people is killing its lambs at the same moment. Indeed, the requirement of Deuteronomy 16 is that the whole celebration happens with the entire people together at the one place Yhwh chooses. The celebration is exclusive in the sense that people who are present in the community but do not belong to it (merchants or diplomats) may not join in, but inclusive in the sense that people of any nationality may join if the males accept the covenant sign of circumcision and thus become part of the covenant people. "Resident aliens," underclass foreigners who have taken refuge here because their life in their own country had collapsed (or they might be Israelites from elsewhere who had had to leave their own land) and who wish to be adopted into Israel are treated the same way as native-born Israelites (Ex 12:43-49; cf. Num 9:14).

The celebration gives children a special place (Ex 12:26; 13:8, 14-16). It is a dramatic event involving individual and community, body, mind, and spirit, a powerful event that makes children wonder what it is all about. It thus becomes the means of their discovering the story of their people's deliverance and the importance of that story, the means of their becoming Israelites in their awareness and experience as well as their person. Through it they become part of the exodus people. This process is repeated generation after generation. It takes place in people's hearts through the stimulus of events involving the outer being—the meal itself, and the putting of signs on the forehead and the hand (Ex 13:9). Later Israel, at least, interpreted such signs quite literally, in keeping with the spirit of the instruction. After all, how could a figurative act serve as a sign?

In a strange way the event involves spilled blood. There is little background in the First Testament story for the spilling of animal blood suddenly becoming important, but it will now be very important in the people's life. In the Pesah commemoration the spilling of blood is a reminder of death and a safeguard against death (Ex 12:7, 12-13). This moment is one when Yhwh is declaring ownership of Israel as firstborn (Ex 4:22-23), but the king of Egypt is disputing Yhwh's claim. Yhwh is therefore asserting rights in relation to the firstborn of Egypt, and thereby showing that this claim is a serious one. All this means Israel is dangerously near the action and in danger of being consumed by friendly fire. But Yhwh will allow the spilled blood to protect the family from having its blood spilled. There has been a death in this house already; there is no need for another. The slain lambs provide protection for the people Yhwh might otherwise claim; this provision gave the early Christians a way of thinking through how Christ's death protects people. The Pesah celebration is thus a sign or a sacrament. It is a sign for the recipients, because they are affected by it, and also a sign that God sees and is affected by (Ex 12:13). It does something.

One might have thought that this made it essential to perform this celebration in exactly the right way, otherwise it will not "work." And the First Testament does believe that it is important to perform rites in the prescribed way;

to fail to do so is to slight God. But the First Testament is not legalistic about such matters. If there are people who cannot observe Pesah at the prescribed time because they have had to bury someone and are therefore in a state of taboo or because they have been away, let them celebrate it a month later (Num 9:1-13). Indeed, it might even be that there are people who take part in the celebration while in a state of taboo that they could have avoided or rectified: even then it may be possible to ask for God's expiation and healing (2 Chron 30:18-20). (In contrast, a nazirite who unintentionally breaks a vow has to make expiation and start the period of the vow again; Num 6:9-12.)

Nature and History

Like the church's calendar, Israel's calendar comprised both events associated with nature and events associated with God's acts of deliverance. These were related to each other in a number of different ways, and ways that likely changed over time and varied in different areas. This also happens with the church's observances. In Britain, for instance, there was a Sunday in the middle of Lent called Refreshment Sunday that provided people with a break from the rigor of the Lenten Fast. That became the occasion when girls who worked away from home as servants were allowed to go home to see their mothers; hence "Mothering Sunday." As "Mother's Day" it then lost its association with the religious calendar in everything but date, and became assimilated in significance (though not in date) to the U.S. "Mother's Day," which had never had an association with the church's calendar, though it was marked liturgically. Subsequently, "Father's Day" was imported into Britain from the United States and a process whereby this is marked liturgically is under way.

All of Israel's festivals took place at times of life-or-death significance in the agricultural year, when crops were beginning to be harvested or this process was coming to an end, and people were wondering about the rains that were needed to bring the crops to ripen or to soften the ground for the next year. Agricultural festivals that signified the gift of life and provision for the coming year could become also commemorations of the gift of life and freedom at the exodus.

Yet if this is so, it is below the surface of the Torah. There, Pesah and Massot are the nearest to being occasions that relate wholly to the story of Yhwh's deliverance of Israel.

It has been suggested that the practices involved in this double festival had a background in the ordinary life of pastoral and agricultural people, and were thus for the most part not innovations in people's lives. One can imagine how each year desert shepherds might roast a lamb, season it with wild herbs, eat unleavened bread and meet for a feast dressed ready for their departure for summer pasturage (cf. Ex 3:18?). The observance of Pesah would then sanctify such celebrations, for instance requiring the sacrifice to be eaten that night rather than being profaned. More significantly, it would give the celebration as a whole a new interpretation, often ascribing new significance to individual aspects of it: for instance, bitter wild herbs now suggest the bitterness of life in Egypt. All this would make Pesah like other Jewish and Christian observances that take an observance relating to the annual cycle of nature and seek to transform it by linking it to a story of God's once-and-for-all deliverance. In Christian faith this happened with the midwinter and spring festivals that became Christmas and Easter; we are now at the end of the opposite process whereby Christmas and Easter have reverted to being nature festivals.

But strong arguments have been adduced against this influential theory regarding the origin of the festival.[211] Indeed, even if the theory is right, it is striking that the Torah makes no mention of such links with pastoral and agricultural life but links the festival exclusively with the exodus. Shavuot is then its mirror image, the nearest to a self-standing nature festival that simply marks the grain harvest; the First Testament gives it no link with the story of Israel's deliverance.

Massot and Shavuot

In Exodus 12 and in the calendars in Leviticus 23 and Deuteronomy 16, Pesah is thus associated with Massot (cf. 2 Chron 30; 35:17; Ezra 6:19-22; Ezek 45:21). It comes at the time of the barley harvest (cf. Lev 23:4-14), the first of the harvests. Yet Exodus 12 actually links both Pesah and Massot with the deliverance from Egypt (cf. Ex 23:15; 34:18), while Joshua 5:10-12 links them with the people's arrival in the land.[212] Israel is to observe the festival of Massot by eating only flat bread, bread that had not been leavened, for seven days (Ex 23:15; see further Ex 12:14-20; 13:2-10); this would be the natural food of people on the move. But whereas Pesah is inherently a family event rather than a pilgrimage festival, Massot is a pilgrimage festival, and it appears separately in Exodus 13 and with the other pilgrimage festivals in Exodus 23:15; 34:18-24; 2 Chronicles 8:13.

While shepherds did celebrate a spring festival that involved roasting a lamb, there is no evidence for a farming festival like Massot, but the asso-

---

[211]See B. N. Wambacq, "Les origines de la *Pesah* israélite," *Biblica* 57 (1976): 206-24, 301-26; "Les Maṣṣôt," *Biblica* 61 (1980): 31-54; Jörn Halbe, "Passa-Massot im deuteronomischen Festkalender," *ZAW* 87 (1975): 147-68; "Erwägungen zu Ursprung und Wesen des Massotfestes," *ZAW* 87 (1975): 324-46 (cf. John Van Seters, *The Life of Moses* [Kampen: Kok, 1994], pp. 113-27).

[212]Cf. Hartley, *Leviticus*, pp. 378-79.

ciation of Massot with the barley harvest could still imply a connection with nature and thus suggest a link between nature and history. The bread will be the first made from the new year's barley harvest, and making it without leaven would mark the transition from the old to the new, as the existent leaven would necessarily have come from the previous year's produce. It may also have been reckoned to respect and draw attention to the raw material itself, as was the case with the avoidance of leaven in other offerings (Ex 23:18; 34:25). But if so, all this is unmentioned. If there was such a common observance, it is turned into a festival celebrating the people's leaving Egypt at this time of year. Like the lamb feast itself, the banning of "proper" bread for a week becomes a reenactment of an aspect of the exodus story (Ex 12:34). It again brings children into the celebration (Ex 13:8). As poor bread it becomes "affliction bread" (Deut 16:3), bread that reminds people of their affliction in Egypt.

A link between Massot and nature could be underscored by the chronological connection between Massot and Shavuot, which comes seven weeks after Massot in accordance with the fact that the grain harvest comes about seven weeks after the barley harvest. Shavuot is explicitly a festival when people rejoice in this harvest itself and present its firstfruits to Yhwh (Ex 23:16; 34:22; Lev 23:15-21; Deut 16:9-10). But in Deuteronomy 26:1-11, the offering of firstfruits in a more general sense is also explicitly linked with Yhwh's gift of the land of Canaan to Israel. The linking of Pesah/Massot and Shavuot also opens up the possibility of linking Shavuot with Sinai, because the people reach Sinai eight weeks after leaving Egypt. When Pentecost subsequently comes to be linked with Sinai, this is thus roughly in keeping with the Torah's own chronology.[213] Deuteronomy 16:9-12 makes another link with the exodus. The great rejoicing of the harvest is to be one in which everyone joins, including servants and vulnerable people such as resident aliens, orphans and widows; and in case families might neglect that aspect of the festival, they are to bear in mind during this festival that they were once serfs in Egypt. Without a reference to the exodus, Leviticus 23:22 similarly reminds people in connection with the prescription for Shavuot not to reap to the very edge of a field but to leave something for the needy and the resident alien.

Sukkot

In September/October comes the festival celebrating the harvest of summer fruits such as grapes and olives. Sukkot was apparently *the* feast of the year (1

---

[213]E.g., *b. Pesah* 68b. On this development, see Sejin Park, *Pentecost and Sinai*, LHBOTS 342 (New York/London: T & T Clark, 2008).

Kings 8:2); it involved more sacrifices than any other (Num 29), and it was an occasion of great rejoicing (Lev 23:40). The agricultural year is now over; there is a basis (hopefully) for great rejoicing and for prayer for the coming year. And pending the arrival of the rains, there is nothing pressing to do on the farm, whereas at Pesah/Massot and Shavuot there is much to do. (When Pesah became the great pilgrim festival centuries later, this was in the context of the Jewish people being less predominantly a farming community, and of the development of the Dispersion.)[214]

The distinctive practice of Sukkot, which gives it its name, is the building of bivouacs or shelters in which families live for the period of the festival (Lev 23:39-43). There would be a practical background to such a practice in connection with the harvest. Some people's land would be some distance from their village, and sleeping on the land during this busy time would make the job more practical or make it possible to guard the fruit. But the harvest is over by the time of the festival, and another practicality would be that for this most widely observed pilgrimage festival, makeshift shelters would be necessary near the sanctuary.[215]

While Sukkot thus has great significance in the context of everyday life, Leviticus 23:43 makes a link with the exodus, declaring that people then had to sleep in makeshift shelters. Israel's teachers thus take a practical, everyday event or necessity and turn it into a reminder of how Israel came to be Yhwh's people. Sukkot is the festival that most explicitly has links both with the agricultural year and with the story of Israel's deliverance.

Deuteronomy 31:9-13 makes a further link with the gift of Torah to Israel. Every seven years at Sukkot the entire community, men, women, children and resident aliens, are to read Moses' teaching in Deuteronomy and thus renew their covenant commitment to Yhwh. Perhaps such an event would be the context in which categorical commands of the kind that appear in the Decalogue were especially proclaimed.[216] Nehemiah 8:1-18 then gives an account of a celebration a little like that.[217]

Judges 21:16-25 relates an incident in Israel's disorderly days when there is no king in Israel and people do what is right in their own eyes, and the men of Benjamin take advantage of this celebration to abduct girls from Shiloh. Great festival events can be occasions where things go wrong and people use the celebration to pursue aims that may be oppressive rather than liberative. First Samuel 1 relates what is in the end a much more encouraging incident

---

[214]Cf. Milgrom, *Leviticus 23–27*, p. 2028.

[215]Cf. ibid., pp. 2048-50

[216]Cf. Albrecht Alt, "The Origins of Israelite Law," in *Essays on Old Testament History and Religion* (Oxford: Blackwell, 1966), pp. 79-132; see pp. 123-30.

[217]See §2.1 "Heeding Torah."

from those days; in the Hebrew Bible, 1 Samuel 1 immediately follows Judges 21. Here, Sukkot is again assumed to be a time when people may indulge themselves to excess, and it is also a time when leaders make mistakes. But in the midst of this, it is a time for individuals to bring their prayers and their griefs before Yhwh and have Yhwh reach out to them. And it is a time to keep promises one made on such occasions.

The inclusive aspect to Sukkot is radicalized in Zechariah 14:16-19, which envisions a time when all the people who did not lose their lives in warring against Jerusalem will make pilgrimage there to celebrate Sukkot. Sukkot is a time for foreigners, for Gentiles, even for people who had been Jerusalem's attackers. By its nature it is a time for seeking the blessing of rain for the coming year, and the nations join in that. The passage does warn that if people decline to join in, they will lose this blessing, and thoughtfully adds that there will need to be special treatment for Egypt, which is not dependent on rain. If people do not seek, they do not receive.

The End of the Year

At the beginning of the month in which Sukkot falls, there is a blast on horns (Lev 23:23-25; Num 29:1-6). As part of the subsequent observances the high priest is to follow a rite "to make expiation for the Israelites for all their shortcomings, once a year" (Lev 16:34). The instructions for this annual Expiation Day[218] appear in the midst of the narrative in the Torah, like the instructions for Pesah/Massah. While emphasizing adherence to Yhwh's biddings about worship, Leviticus recognizes that as the original creation was marred through events in the garden, so the sanctuary, the microcosm of creation, is marred through events there. Like the rebellion in the garden, this will not be a once-off problem; there will be other acts like those of Nadab and Abihu. Therefore Yhwh does not leave matters there. There is to be an annual purifying of the sanctuary and the people, "a ritual of restoration—it serves to restore the community to its prescribed and founded state. Thus, restoration will include in this context the idea of re-founding—a return to the founded order of creation."[219]

In Babylon the high point of the religious year was a festival at the New Year in the spring, a celebration of Marduk's kingship. In First Testament calendars the New Year comes in the autumn, and it has been hypothesized that Sukkot was in effect a parallel New Year festival, a celebration of Yhwh's

---

[218]On expiation/*kipper*, see §2.5 "The Reparation Offering," which notes that *kipper* does not really mean "atone for." The expression *yôm kippûr* does not come from the First Testament, though *yôm kippurîm* comes in Lev 23:27-28; 25:9; the plural is presumably abstract or intensive.

[219]Gorman, *Ideology of Ritual*, p. 61.

kingship,[220] or of Yhwh's choice of David and of Zion,[221] or of the covenant at Sinai.[222] In modern Judaism the "high holidays" in the fall incorporate the celebration of the New Year, and it would be natural for ancient Israel so to have viewed the transition from ingathering at the end of the summer to the anticipation of the rains that will make possible the beginning of the new agricultural year. It would be a month when Israel looked back over the year in relationship to Yhwh and thus over the viability of its religious life, as well as in relation to its harvest and thus over the viability of its physical life. The Expiation Day would then be a sacramental way of dealing with the short-comings and infringements that had accumulated over the year that is coming to an end.

Perhaps this was so; yet the fall events are never described in these terms.[223] Indeed, Leviticus 23:5 is explicit that the first month of the year is the month in which Pesah falls. There is no New Year celebration in the First Testament, nor is there explicit reference to a celebration of Yhwh's kingship or of Yhwh's choice of David and of Zion or of the covenant at Sinai. In Leviticus 16 the background of the Expiation Day is the offense of Nadab and Abihu; they had come close before Yhwh, and the preamble to the regulations then warns Aaron not to come "at any time" (any time he decides) into the innermost part of the sanctuary, behind its curtain (that is, the most holy place), and instructs him how to do so. According to Leviticus 10:1 Nadab and Abihu had offered before Yhwh alien fire such that Yhwh had not commanded. Moses had sub-sequently warned Aaron that he and his sons should not drink before enter-ing the Meeting Tent because they need to be able to distinguish between sacred and profane, taboo and clean.[224] More immediately, indeed, the Expia-tion Day regulations follow on the chapters that enable people to observe those distinctions (see Lev 11–15).

The Expiation Day's concern with Israel's shortcomings relates to the way these affect the sanctuary. There is no reference to the people's being par-doned, as there is in Leviticus 4; the people are not even there for the Expia-tion Day ritual, as they are for Massot, Shavuot and Sukkot.[225] Its point is that if Yhwh is to be present in the sanctuary on an ongoing basis, this has to be a place not spoiled by things that conflict with who Yhwh is. Many of

---

[220]See Paul Volz, *Das Neujahrsfest Jahwes* (Tübingen: Mohr, 1912); Sigmund Mowinckel, *Psal-menstudien,* 2 vols. (Amsterdam: Schippers, 1961), Buch 2; *The Psalms in Israel's Worship* (Oxford: Blackwell, 1962), 1:106-92.

[221]See Hans-Joachim Kraus, *Psalms 1–59* and *Psalms 60–150* (Minneapolis: Augsburg, 1988, 1989).

[222]See Artur Weiser, *The Psalms* (London: SCM Press/Philadelphia: Westminster, 1962).

[223]See, e.g., Kraus, *Worship in Israel,* pp. 66-68.

[224]See further §2.2 "Respect."

[225]Cf. Hartley, *Leviticus,* p. 226; Jenson, *Graded Holiness,* pp. 198-99.

the regulations in Leviticus are concerned to ensure this; notably, nothing that speaks of death is to come into the sanctuary. But inevitably such taboos would get broken from time to time through human carelessness or willfulness or ignorance, so that (for instance) the taint of death would come to affect the sanctuary.

The Expiation Day Rites

The Expiation Day dealt with this taint by its sacrifices and by ceremonially transferring the taint to a goat and driving the goat away. The blood of sacrifices has the capacity to absorb the taint and its effects that have come to attach to the sanctuary. By association the bodies of the animals whose blood has this effect also come to be affected by this process, so they must be taken outside the camp and burned.

Why are there two rites, the sacrifices and the expulsion of the goat? Perhaps they link with the two ways of describing the "problem" that the Expiation Day deals with, or the two ways of looking at that problem. One is the taint that people have brought on the sanctuary, much of it accidental. The other is the people's "waywardnesses" and "rebellions," which may also refer to infringement of the rules about purity, but here culpable ones, or may refer to moral and social sins, which also convey pollution. To judge from the way the sacrifices work, a willful or unrepented offense is more serious than an accidental or repented one, and a communal or high-priestly sin is more serious than an individual one.

As usual, there are two ways taint and rebellion might be related. Waywardness and rebellion bring taint onto people, so when people come into the sanctuary as wayward and rebellious, they bring taint there. Conversely, when people have become taboo without necessarily being at fault (for instance, through contact with death) but have then knowingly come into the sanctuary without observing the prescribed purification procedures, their action has become an expression of waywardness and rebellion. Either way, waywardness and taint interweave. The two rites perhaps deal with the two aspects of the problem. Possibly the sacrifice deals especially with the sanctuary's pollution while the goat ritual deals with the waywardnesses and rebellions in a way comparable to the talk of casting them into the depths of the sea. But the chapter does not divide up the language tidily, and it is hard to be sure that each rite deals with one of the aspects, perhaps precisely because they interweave and affect each other.

The Expiation Day is one when the people as a whole afflict or humble themselves (ʿānâ [piel] *nepeš*). The NRSV offers the alternative translation "fast." That is hardly the actual translation (the word for fast is *ṣûm*) but the affliction would be likely to involve fasting; "afflict yourselves" and "fast" come in parallelism in Isaiah 58:3-5. But the self-affliction might also involve other observances such as wearing sackcloth and adopting a posture of prostration (cf. Ps 35:13; also David's actions in 2 Sam 12:16-20). The people are to do no work; it is a "sabbath of sabbathness" (a total sabbath), "for them" (not "for Yhwh") (Lev 16:29-31; Lev 23:26-32 underlines the point). As is the case with offerings in general, the emphasis lies on actions rather than attitudes such as penitence. While inner penitence would be expected, it would effect nothing without the appropriate outward expression, and the concern of the Expiation Day is the objective pollution that has come upon the sanctuary.

Aaron is to make offerings for himself, and then to undertake the expiation rite for the people and the sanctuary. He places lots upon the two goats, one for Yhwh, one for Azazel. He then offers his own bull to make expiation for himself and his household, and sprinkles its blood over the cover of the covenant chest and offers the goat for Yhwh as a similar purification offering for the people. "Thus he is to make expiation for the sanctuary for the pollutions of the Israelites and their rebellions, for all their shortcomings; and so he is to do for the Meeting Tent, which stays with them in the midst of their taboos" (Lev 16:16).

Azazel

Aaron goes on also to make expiation for the altar. Then comes the most distinctive aspect of the rite. He lays his hands on the live goat and confesses over it all the waywardnesses, rebellions and shortcomings of the Israelites, and puts them on the head of the goat, which is then sent off into the wilderness, carrying on itself all the people's waywardnesses to an inaccessible land, where it is set free. The addition of waywardness to shortcoming, pollution and rebellion may further indicate a reference to moral and social wrongs, or may be another way of referring to willful or negligent infringement of the purity rules. Penitence on the priest's and people's part is no doubt again presupposed, but the chapter is concerned with the objective, outward, sacramental action that is needed if the problem of sin is to be dealt with.

Whereas the sacrificial goat is "for Yhwh," the second goat is "for Azazel." The word comes only in Leviticus 16, nowhere else in the First Testament nor elsewhere before the book of Enoch. There and in other Jewish literature Azazel is a demon, and that may be so here, though the reference is allusive. First Enoch 8–13 is part of an expanded version of Genesis 6:1-4 and other aspects of the early chapters of Genesis, and it gives Azazel an important role with other demons in the development of sin in the world. It thus reflects Jewish interest in demons, and we should be wary about reading this back into Leviticus 16. The interest in demons in other Middle-Eastern cultures would also provide background to Azazel, though again we need to work with the contrast whereby the First Testament is very reticent about speaking in terms of demons. The same insight emerges from the allusiveness of the First Testament's occasional references to goat demons in particular (cf. Lev 17:7). "Chapter 16 mirrors in official Israelite religion the ancient rites forbidden in the law of 17:7! Chapter 16 transforms the sacrificial worship of demons into a set of rites that coerce and subjugate the sinful and evil forces identified with the demon"; when the he-goat returned to the wilderness, it went back to its home.[226] Purgation on the live goat "returns the moral faults of the Israelites to their source: Azazel."[227]

If Azazel was a demon, in Leviticus 16 he has almost been demythologized, as happens when people who do not believe in demons speak of "evil forces being at work," and it is significant that the word ʿăzāʾzēl can also be plausibly interpreted as a name for the goat's function as what came to called a scapegoat (cf. LXX, Jerome) or for the rite or for the wilderness place where the goat was sent (cf. Targum Pseudo-Jonathan).[228] Like the notion of sacrifices as food for God, the notion of a sacrifice to Azazel as a demon would then be a linguistic fossil. "Instead of being an offering or a substitute, the goat is simply the vehicle to dispatch Israel's impurities and sins" in a way that effects "the banishment of evil to an inaccessible place."[229] This distinctive feature of the rite relates to its distinctive concern with the holiness of the sanctuary, and particularly the integrity of the most holy place: "Azazel represented the extreme opposite of God's holy presence in the Holy of Holies, . . . the mirror opposite to God's presence in his holy sanctuary."[230]

But there is little indication in the First Testament that wilderness is a place of chaos and disorder, any more than is the case with everyday use of the word *wilderness* in English.[231] It is simply country that has insufficient rainfall to support settled dwelling or farming, but country where sheep can be pastured (e.g., Ex 3:1). In Leviticus 16, it is simply the territory outside the camp.

2.7 Praising Yhwh

The relationship of servants to their master is a serious and solemn one. But a master is also someone who cares about his servants, looks after them, protects them and delivers them. So their attitude to him is also one of celebration, appreciation and enthusiasm. Before the servants of some other master, they cannot but sing his praises. The praise of this Master involves sound and

---

[226]Levine, *Leviticus*, p. 252.
[227]Gane, *Cult and Character*, p. 261.
[228]For discussion see, e.g., *DDD*.
[229]Milgrom, *Leviticus 1–16*, p. 1021.
[230]Jenson, *Graded Holiness*, p. 203.
[231]Again, e.g., Gorman, *Ideology of Ritual*, p. 98.

movement, music and singing, joy and self-abnegation. It involves the community and the individual, the weak and the strong, humanity and nature. It responds to Yhwh's acts in nature, in Israel's history and in the current experience of the community and of the individual.

Sound and Movement

As well as inner attitudes and sacramental acts, First Testament worship involves praise that in its multifaceted nature expresses itself in posture, sound, words and music. It involves the body (waving and prostration), the heart (joy and grief), and the mind and voice (declaring who Yhwh is and what Yhwh has done). Thus Psalm 34 begins by referring to "worship" physically expressed (*bārak* piel, implying bending the knee), to "praise" vocally expressed (*těhillâ* points to ululating) and to the "spirit" (*nepeš*) exulting, suggesting the involvement of the whole inner and outer person. Praise mediates between the worshiper and the one worshiped, whom we extol and exalt (enlarge and lift high) with body, voice and spirit. Psalm 92:1-4 [MT 2-5] has people confessing, proclaiming, and reciting, and also making music and resounding. Psalm 33 begins, "Resound . . . praise . . . confess Yhwh with the lyre, make music to him with the ten-stringed harp, sing him a new song, play well with a shout." The opening to this praise psalm makes only one reference to words (though it will go on to counterbalance that); sound is at the heart of praise, both noise and music, both singing and instruments.

Psalm 145 suggests that worship involves exalting, worshiping, praising, lauding, declaring, murmuring, talking, proclaiming, pouring forth (like water bubbling up, gushing and overflowing), commemorating, resounding, confessing, talking, speaking, making known, but not fathoming. That string of verbs suggests why praise cannot be offered in silence. By its nature it is exuberant; it cannot be quiet or tranquil. And by its nature it is designed to communicate to other people as well as to God. Psalm 105 likewise begins, "Confess Yhwh, call in his name, make known his deeds among the peoples, sing for him, make music for him, murmur about all his wonders, exult in his holy name; may the heart of people who seek help from Yhwh rejoice. Have recourse to Yhwh and his might, seek help from his face continually, be mindful of his wonders, the ones that he has done, his portents, the decisions of his mouth." The proclaiming of Yhwh's name is a performative act; it makes Yhwh's presence a reality, because where Yhwh's name is present, Yhwh is present.[232]

The onomatopoeic verb most commonly translated "praise," *hālal* (piel), which lies behind that noun *těhillâ*, suggests that praising means saying lala-

---

[232]Cf. John W. Kleinig, *The LORD's Song*, JSOTSup 156 (Sheffield, U.K.: JSOT, 1993), p. 146. Cf. the comments on the name in §2.4 "The Altar."

lala. The derived expression "hallelujah" (e.g., Ps 148; 150) is thus an ejaculation combining this verb with the short form of the name of Yhwh. Less frequent is another onomatopoeic word, *rānan* (also usually piel), which suggests resounding or making a nananana noise (e.g., Ps 81:1 [2]; 95:1). It is commonly translated "sing/shout for joy," but joy is not the only emotion it can imply (see Lam 2:19). Both these verbs indicate the important role of noise in offering praise. There is something elemental about praise; the praiseworthiness of an object arouses primal compulsions from within that we allow to escape from our conscious mental control. The point is underlined by the prevalence of words such as "shout" in connection with praise. Praise bursts the bounds of orderly restraint and decorum. In Psalm 98:4, the earth is to "break out" in praise (*pāṣaḥ*), and in this psalm as a whole praise is all about singing, shouting, breaking out, resounding, making music (with references to instruments), thundering and clapping.

Although the Psalter is dominated by prayer, it ends in Psalm 150 with praise, or rather with a psalm that comprises only an exhortation to praise; implicitly, everything that has preceded provides the reasons for this praise. Its systematic insistence on noisesome worship issues the Psalter's closing exhortation to intellectual and socially activist readers of the Psalms, reminding us that sharp thinking, heartfelt sincerity, moral integrity, joyful feelings, loving commitment, willing obedience and social involvement are not the only important things in the world. It closes with simple enthusiasm in self-abandonment and adoration.[233]

Music and Singing

Alongside the formlessness of shouting and ululating that expresses the untamed and undomesticated fervor of praise is the form and order of music that also enhances praise as it channels and thus enhances that fervor. "Clap hands, shout with resounding voice . . . make music . . . make music, make music . . . make music . . . make music," bids Psalm 47. The word conventionally translated "psalm" (*mizmôr*), which especially recurs in psalm headings, comes from this verb "make music" (*zāmar* piel); it indicates how the praise and prayer of the Psalms are intrinsically musical.

The key musical aspect to Israel's praise is rhythm. We have little evidence of melody or harmony in Israelite music; the musical aspect to worship would likely not strike a Western person as very musical at all. The stress does not lie on the aesthetically pleasing facets of the sound. Israel's musical instruments are mostly rhythmic, stringed instruments (such as harp and lyre) or

---

[233]Cf. Walter Brueggemann, *The Message of the Psalms* (Minneapolis: Augsburg, 1984), p. 167.

types of drums (such as tambourines). The singing itself will be something like chanting; it seems a fair guess that the line going back from Anglican chant to plainsong to synagogue chanting extends back into the temple's worship. The instruments thus function like the rhythm section in a jazz or rock band, without a front line. Even the horn to which the Psalms refer is a means of drawing people's attention to something rather than an instrument that plays a tune.

The function and nature of the sound would thus resemble those of the crowd at a football game or the work of a rapper more than those of regular Christian worship. In a First Testament context a comparison with the coronation of a king would be more appropriate, and would be theologically telling. The acclamation declares that Israel's real king is its heavenly one. At a football game the crowd's shouting, sounding horns, booing, jumping and non-rhythmic clapping expresses its instinctive, spontaneous, uncalculated and artless response to events. Its rhythmic clapping, stamping and chanting gives more calculated form to that response and enables it to be more systematically corporate.

Psalm 150 urges praise with the horn, harp, lyre, tambourine, dancing, strings, pipe and two sorts of cymbals. Some of these instruments belong more in temple worship, some belong more outside it; every means is summoned to magnify Yhwh. Some of the instruments would be played by priests (the horn, whose blast proclaimed the beginning of worship). Some would be played by Levites (harp and lyre, the regular stringed instruments mentioned in the Psalms, and cymbals). Some might be played by laypeople (strings, pipe and tambourine or hand drum, which goes with dancing because women played it as they danced; none of these are elsewhere associated with temple worship). Here too all the emphasis lies on noise.

In keeping with the traditional attitudes of some denominations, especially in the Calvinist tradition, Barth questions the organ accompaniment of singing in church, wondering whether the main point of this is "to conceal the feebleness with which the community discharges the ministry of the *vox humana* [the human voice] committed to it."[234] There is no danger that the accompaniment of Israel's praise had this intent (though Calvin himself reckoned that the use of instruments belonged only to the pre-Christian dispensation)[235] as it was primarily percussive and rhythmic rather than characterized by melody and harmony.

While it is misleading that translations are inclined to render *zāmar* "sing" (as is indicated by its commonly being accompanied by reference to instru-

---

[234]Barth, *Church Dogmatics*, IV/3, ii:867.
[235]Calvin, *Psalms*, 3:495.

ments), praise certainly involves singing *(šîr)*. "Sing for Yhwh a new song, sing . . . sing," Psalm 96 begins; *song* is another word that commonly appears in the headings to psalms. Given that singing would take the form of chanting, a form that emphasizes words at least as much as music, the exhortation in Psalm 96 naturally continues, "announce from day to day his deliverance, proclaim among the nations his honor." Music adds affect to the words; words add rational content to the music. "Singing the Psalter . . . combines the reading of Scripture and praying."[236] "In singing together it is possible . . . to speak and pray the same Word at the same time."[237] Thus making music for Yhwh is good, it is fine; it glorifies or beautifies Yhwh as the one who is our praise (Ps 147:1). One can see how "Unless we learn how to sing, unless we know how to love, we will never learn how to understand Him."[238]

Lifting Up and Bowing Down

Because all human beings are created in God's image, they stand on a level and look each other in the eye. When they set a king on a throne above them, they exalt him and thereby symbolize their honoring him; and when they bow the knee before him, they symbolize their submission to him. We have noted that in KJV *worship* commonly represent a word that more concretely means "bow down" *(hištaḥăwâ)*.[239] People "bow down" before a king (2 Sam 14:22, 33), and in worship we bow down in this way before Yhwh, who is to be praised because "Yours, Yhwh, is the greatness, the might, the splendor, the majesty, the glory, because everything in the heavens and on the earth is yours, Yhwh, the kingship, the eminence as head for all" (1 Chron 29:10-13).

In its distinctive use of repetition in making this point, Psalm 95 puts the expressions of worship into a suggestive sequence. It begins with praise that involves resounding, shouting, making music and meeting God face to face (EVV render "come into his presence"). These expressions of worship suggest a wild enthusiasm that has great confidence about being face to face with Yhwh. But the psalm goes on to speak of bowing down *(hištaḥăwâ)*, bowing low *(kāraʿ)* and bending the knee *(bārak* piel) before the great King, thus exalting him and making him on high in relation to us. Again all three verbs are body words, and English verbs such as *kneel* do not quite convey their significance. The psalm suggests a prostration of the whole person flat on the ground, in the manner of Muslim worship; worshipers have no kneelers and

---

[236]Brian Brock, *Singing the Ethos of God* (Grand Rapids/Cambridge: Eerdmans, 2007), p. 357.
[237]Dietrich Bonhoeffer, *Life Together/Prayerbook of the Bible* (Minneapolis: Fortress, 1996), p. 66; cf. Brock, *Singing the Ethos of God*, p. 358.
[238]Heschel, *God in Search of Man*, p. 281.
[239]See §2.4 "Worship."

get no helpful support from the pew in front. Yhwh *is* on high, *is* in supreme authority, *is* the holy one. Praise lifts Yhwh high, acknowledging this in words; bowing low makes the same point by enacting it (cf. Ps 99:2, 5, 9).

So praise involves resounding, shouting and music, and also bowing, kneeling and prostration. What it cannot involve is sitting, clasping hands and closing one's eyes. The two exhortations in Psalm 95 have a common focus on sound and body movement. English translations incorporate words such as *joy* in the invitations, and joy is no doubt presupposed, but beyond its one reference to confession *(tôdâ)*, the psalm simply talks about sound and posture. Once more inward feelings mean nothing if they are not accompanied by outward expression. Human beings are not essentially thoughts and feelings, and it would be unsatisfactory for other people not to *see* this confession. Psalm 134 likewise bids, "worship Yhwh . . . you who stand in Yhwh's house through the night, raise your hands to the sanctuary, worship Yhwh." Given that *worship* (again *bārak* piel) etymologically suggests "kneel," once more all these are body words. The ministers are to kneel (the posture of submission), stand (the posture of waiting upon one's master) and raise their hands (the posture of appeal).

The movement from noise to prostration in Psalm 95 is suggestive. So is the theo-logic of the bases for this worship. We shout with enthusiasm because Yhwh is the great King over all the gods and the one to whom the whole cosmos belongs, as its maker. We then bow in prostration because this God is our God, our maker, our shepherd. One might have expected the logic to be the reverse: we enthuse because God is our shepherd, we bow because God is creator. The psalm's logic suggests the more thought-provoking notion that the prostration of the worshipers is the deeper because of the realization that the sovereign God is the one committed to us.

All this might seem to take this worship to a profound conclusion, but Yhwh has other ideas (Ps 95:7b-11).[240] Like sacrifice, praise is valueless unless linked to the life people live outside worship (cf. Amos 5:23-24). It fits with this that the Psalms themselves are "saturated with justice";[241] they embody "the hope of the poor."[242]

Joy

First Chronicles 15 and Nehemiah 12 give vivid accounts of great praise occasions celebrating key moments in the life of the preexilic and postexilic communities. Like the Psalms, they illustrate how First Testament piety is charac-

[240]See §2.4 "Listening."
[241]Paul Westermeyer, *Let Justice Sing* (Collegeville, Minn.: Liturgical Press, 1998), p. 29.
[242]J. Clinton McCann, "The Hope of the Poor," in *Touching the Altar*, pp. 155-78.

terized by "exuberance."[243] "Joy, not mystic union, is the basic emotional content of the Israelite cult."[244]

"Rejoice in Yhwh and be joyful, you faithful; resound, all you upright in heart" (Ps 32:11). The suppliant had been trying to evade owning wrongdoing but had eventually given in to the pressure inside, acknowledged it and found forgiveness, and now wants everyone to shout out loud in exultation at the wonder of this aspect of the dynamic of life with Yhwh. "In him our heart will rejoice" (Ps 33:21): the statement comes at the end of a psalm that has covered the A to Z of praise (it has the same number of lines as there are letters in the alphabet), and provides part of the appropriate response to Yhwh's character and Yhwh's creation of the world, to Yhwh's involvement in international events and in delivering Israel.

Like love, worship or reverence, the joy of which the Torah speaks is not a mere attitude of heart but an aspect of the people's communal life that, like those other attitudes (love, worship or reverence), is outwardly expressed in festivity. It is this that makes it possible to *tell* people to be joyful as it makes it possible to tell people to love. Like love, joy is an action; being festive is not merely a matter of feeling but of doing. It involves celebration, a liturgical event, which in Israel is particularly embodied in sacrificing.[245] Chronicles especially emphasizes the complementarity of sacrifice and singing praise. Thus it inserts into the story of David's bringing the covenant chest to Jerusalem the singing of a long composite psalm of thanksgiving, emphasizing the importance of David's inauguration of choral music.[246]

Psalm 97 does not urge people to shout, clap or resound, like many psalms, but simply declares in its opening and closing lines that the world and the faithful are to rejoice; there are six references to joy in the psalm's twelve lines. This links interestingly with its emphasis on the dark and fiery nature of Yhwh's appearance and the shaming of people who worship images. But the latter are the accompaniments or consequences of the fact that Yhwh has begun to reign, asserting sovereignty in the world as one who exercises authority in faithfulness; *ṣedeq ûmišpāṭ* is the foundation of Yhwh's throne. Thus even the discrediting of the gods (who have the good sense to resign their positions and recognize Yhwh) and their images is, in its way, good news for a world that formerly had no alternative but to trust in them but can now

---

[243]Vriezen, *Outline of Old Testament Theology*, p. 302 (2nd ed., p. 276).

[244]Kaufmann, *Religion of Israel*, p. 112.

[245]Cf. Gary A. Anderson, *A Time to Mourn, a Time to Dance* (University Park, Penn.: Pennsylvania State University Press, 1991), pp. 19-20; "The Praise of God as a Cultic Event," in *Priesthood and Cult in Ancient Israel*, ed. Gary A. Anderson and Saul M. Olyan, JSOTSup 125 (Sheffield, U.K.: Sheffield Academic Press, 1991), pp. 15-33.

[246]Cf. Kleinig, *The LORD's Song*, esp. pp. 144-45.

honor Yhwh. Yhwh's reigning is a threat to people who think they reign, but for their subjects it is powerful reason for rejoicing. Their worship is a subversive activity that "involves a more or less open act of defiance against any claim of ultimacy by the current regime."[247]

In this context further significance attaches to the exhortation to "serve Yhwh with gladness" and "serve Yhwh with reverence and rejoice with trembling" (Ps 100:1-2; 2:11). Psalm 100 uses a particularly suggestive combination of verbs for worship. It involves shouting, serving and rejoicing, coming before Yhwh and resounding, acknowledging that Yhwh is God, coming into Yhwh's gates and confessing, praising, and worshiping Yhwh's name. Only in the Psalm 2 and Psalm 100 does *serve* come in the imperative, and it has political implications. But this service is one to which joy attaches.

Individual and Communal

"You are to eat there before Yhwh your God and rejoice in all the undertaking of your hand, you and your household, in which Yhwh has blessed you. . . . You are to rejoice before Yhwh your God, you and your sons and your daughters and your male and female servants and the Levite who is within your gates, because he has no allocation or possession with you" (Deut 12:7, 18; cf. 14:26; 16:11, 14; 26:11; 27:7; Lev 23:40). Joy is a dominant note in the way Deuteronomy thinks about worship, and the rejoicing it commends is an activity involving other people; Israelites rejoice with their family, with the needy and with their servants. Perhaps one can experience joy only if one brings others joy.[248] In its instructions about offerings, Deuteronomy puts a "constant emphasis" on sharing the sacrificial meal with other people; one could get the impression that the main point about the offerings was to feed the needy.[249] While Deuteronomy says little about the details of how to do liturgy, it "never tires of enumerating the participants in sacrifices or feasts": men and women, adults and children, independent people and servants, landed, family people and Levites, resident aliens, widows and orphans.[250] Joy is thus a great leveler; for the duration of the joy of the festival, such distinctions disappear.[251] This joy is an anticipation of the Day of Yhwh. Deuteronomy's insistence on

---

[247]Eugene Peterson, *Where Your Treasure Is* (Grand Rapids: Eerdmans, 1993), p. 65.

[248]So Barth, *Church Dogmatics*, III/4:379-80.

[249]Weinfeld, *Deuteronomy and the Deuteronomic School*, pp. 211-12. He thus calls Leviticus theocentric, Deuteronomy anthropocentric (p. 189). The same contrast emerges from a comparison of the sabbath regulation in Ex 20 and in Deut 5 (p. 222), and of the sabbath year in Leviticus, where the land has a sabbath for Yhwh, and in Deuteronomy, where debts are released (p. 223).

[250]Cf. Georg Braulik, *The Theology of Deuteronomy* (North Richmond Hills, Tex.: BIBAL, 1994), pp. 27-65; see p. 52.

[251]Cf. the comments in §2.6 "The Worship Year."

stopping celebrations at regional and local sanctuaries (Deut 12) might make it seem a killjoy; this emphasis counters that. It might also suggest a contrast with Canaanite worship, which sometimes focused on what happens to the deity (dying and then coming back to life); Israelite joy is an expression of gratitude that focuses on what Yhwh has done for the people, not on what has happened to the deity. It is a response to blessing.[252] But the contextual reason for its emphasis may not be so important. Communal joy is simply a natural part of worship.

Praise essentially combines the individual and the communal. "I will worship Yhwh at all times," Psalm 34 begins; it goes on, "extol Yhwh with me; let us exalt his name together" (v. 3). By its nature praise is extended in time and in fellowship, or is spread out in time yet concentrated in fellowship. "The community which does not sing is not the community"[253] and unison singing suggests we are all joining in the one voice of the one church; our joining in that praise affirms that praise is by its nature communal.[254] Enthusiasm begs to be shared; there is something incomplete about being excited and animated on one's own. We want other people to share our passion for our beloved or our baby or our team. That magnifies the honor due to it. Thus the praise of God can naturally be expressed as an invitation or exhortation to praise that is addressed to other people. It commonly takes the form, "Come on, let us resound to Yhwh" or "Sing for Yhwh a new song" or "Shout to Yhwh, all the earth" (Ps 95:1; 96:1; 98:1). The same features appear elsewhere with subtle variation. In Psalm 97:1, in effect they come in reverse order: "Yhwh began to reign: earth is to be glad." The order is less usual but more logical or direct as the content of the praise comes first and thus has prominence and the human response is relegated to the second place it deserves.

Unexpected Agents of Praise

Psalms 96, 97 and 98, among others, urge both Israel in particular and the world as a whole to rejoice in Yhwh. The shortest of the Psalms, Psalm 117, expresses a paradoxical aspect of this. "Praise Yhwh, all you nations," it urges, "because his commitment has been strong over us." As praise it indeed works with the same instinct as the one that causes a proud lover to want everyone to appreciate their beloved. Yet the nations do not actually hear the psalm's exhortation. Addressing them in this way involves Yhwh's actual worshipers affirming that Yhwh is not merely their little local God but one sovereign over the whole world. At the same time the psalm implies

---

[252]Cf. Braulik, *Theology of Deuteronomy*, p. 45.
[253]Barth, *Church Dogmatics*, IV/3, ii:867.
[254]Cf. Bonhoeffer, *Life Together*, pp. 67-68; cf. Brock, *Singing the Ethos of God*, p. 359.

some theo-logic, that Yhwh's commitment to Israel is good news for the nations as well as for Israel. Yhwh's commitment and truthfulness are not something they cannot know because of who they are, but something they can know because of who Israel is. Yhwh's commitment and truthfulness are inclusive, not exclusive. The nations do not merely grudgingly bow down to Yhwh; they praise Yhwh, worship Yhwh with ecstatic enthusiasm, like Israel. That carries several implications for Israel's understanding of itself and of the nations. In the context of a praise psalm it indirectly enhances Yhwh's significance, and thus enhances Yhwh's deserving of praise by the people who actually offer that praise.

Most of the exhortations in Psalm 98 are addressed to "all the earth" or "the world and its inhabitants"; the reason for the noise is the acts of deliverance that Yhwh has undertaken for Israel, which are again good news for the world. The putting down of a superpower such as Assyria, Babylon or Persia, effected for Israel's sake, is good news for all the nations that are subject to it along with Israel. Psalm 66 likewise has the world shouting, making music, speaking, bowing low, kneeling in worship, praising; they do so because they "come and see" what Yhwh has done (cf. Ps 46:8 [MT 9]). What would they see? We have no indication that they would see a dramatization of events such as the exodus. More likely by coming to Jerusalem they would see the evidence that Yhwh had acted to protect it and defeat its attackers; perhaps these are the events proclaimed in the testimony that comes as the last part of the psalm.

Israel's worship involves the public proclamation or confession of who Yhwh is and what Yhwh has done, so that "the praise of God makes plain upon earth who this God is."[255] Praising God, Karl Barth suggests, is the first ministry of the people of God. While such praise has worth even if done in secret, and while it incidentally brings uplift to the worshipers, it is more fundamentally an aspect of its witness to the world, the modeling of that praise in which all the world is destined to join as "every breath [thus, everything that breathes] is to praise Yhwh" (Ps 150:6, the last line in the Psalter).[256] Israel does not have the obligation to get the nations to praise, as if it had the responsibility to bring in the kingdom of God. That is God's responsibility. It just has the responsibility to praise Yhwh now, as the firstfruits of that worldwide praise, so that Yhwh at least has a rejoicing community to bring the nations into. "Only the praising church will endure. Thus the central act of the church is not a mode of living that those outside the church also do, such as moral deliberation or pedagogy, but it is a mode of resonating with the reality

---

[255]Zimmerli, *Old Testament Theology in Outline*, p. 148.
[256]Barth, *Church Dogmatics*, IV/3, ii:865.

of God's work."[257] This is one significance of the understanding of praise as prophecy in Chronicles.[258]

The nations are not the only unexpected agents of the praise of Yhwh. Praise is the particular vocation of weak people, because they are in a position to testify to Yhwh's assertive actions on their behalf, to the way Yhwh delivers them from the attacks that would bring them death (Ps 9:11-14 [MT 12-15]). Yet the nonweak are invited to join in their praise. The weak help the strong discern and affirm an aspect of their humanness; for praise is a key marker of humanness as it expresses the true relationship of human beings to their creator. "The being of man is a being in gratitude," so that "only as he thanks God does man fulfil his true being."[259] "Praise is a key marking of Israel's discernment of humanness."[260] Thus the praise of the nations would embrace both peoples rescued from the power of other nations, and those nations that had once been exercising the power but have been put down.

Nor is praise confined to the human world. When Psalm 96 talks about joy, it is the joy of inanimate objects (as we would call them), the heavens and the earth. The thundering of the sea and the resounding of the trees are expressions of it. The fact that they can (to our way of thinking) only manage the outward signs of joy such as noise highlights how much the outward really counts. "Through the Psalter God has given us entry into the universe's eternal song of praise, and to take up the Psalms is to join that congregation."[261] Psalm 98:7-9 likewise declares that "the sea and its fullness are to thunder, the world and the beings that live in it; the rivers—they are to clap hands altogether, the mountains—they are to resound before Yhwh" in an "ecology of praise."[262] "Earth is a subject capable of raising its voice in celebration and against injustice."[263]

Praise Has Its Reasons

The description of worship with its emphasis on shouting and ululating could imply it is intuitive and uncalculated. But people are expected to decide to praise Yhwh; it is something to which they make a commitment of the will.

---

[257]Brian Brock, *Singing the Ethos of God*, p. 150, summarizing implications of Augustine's comments on Ps 22.

[258]Cf. Kleinig, *LORD's Song*, pp. 148-57.

[259]Karl Barth, *Church Dogmatics* (Edinburgh: T & T Clark, 1968), III/2:167, 170.

[260]Brueggemann, *Theology of the Old Testament*, p. 478.

[261]Brock, *Singing the Ethos of God*, p. 357.

[262]So David F. Ford and Daniel W. Hardy, *Living in Praise* (Grand Rapids: Baker, 2005), p. 2.

[263]One of the Earth Bible Team's "Guiding Ecojustice Principles": see Habel, ed., *Readings from the Perspective of Earth*, p. 46 (italicized there). See further the studies of earth's praise in the Psalms in Norman C. Habel, ed., *The Earth Story in the Psalms and the Prophets* (Sheffield, U.K.: Sheffield Academic Press/Cleveland: Pilgrim, 2001), pp. 23-122.

And the provision of the reasons for or content of the praise also suggests there is a rational and calculated aspect to it. We have noted that psalms can begin with the content of their praise. Psalm 8 is another example: "Yhwh, our Lord, how mighty is your name in all the earth!" But much more commonly psalms begin with an exhortation to praise and express its content only indirectly, as the reason for the praise: "Sing for Yhwh a new song, because . . ." (Ps 98:1). One can imagine various statements that might have followed the "because": because it is fitting, because it makes us feel good, because it glorifies Yhwh. What actually follows is the content of the praise, which is also the reason for it: "because Yhwh is the great God," or "because Yhwh is great," or "because he has done wonders" (Ps 95:3; 96:4; 98:1). Praise is "an attempt to cope with the abundance of God's love,"[264] and also a recognition of God's power (cf. Lk 19:37). It responds to God as the one who acts in power and love (cf. Ps 62:11-12 [MT 12-13]).

The adoption of a conventional form such as that of exhortation to praise followed by reasons for or contents of praise is one aspect of the way praise is commonly expressed in the terms of a familiar tradition. Another is the reuse of familiar expressions, such as "a new song," "Yhwh began to reign," "faithfulness and authority." Using a shared tradition of expression gives praise extra power. Yet the talk of a "new song" suggests a new awareness of Yhwh's faithfulness and sovereignty. Old songs, mere tradition, are not enough.

Psalm 135 begins and closes with biddings to praise whose wording corresponds to that of other psalms. When it comes to the content or reasons for it, it parallels the language of Exodus and Deuteronomy in the way it speaks of Yhwh's deeds on Israel's behalf, but it again parallels other psalms in the way it speaks of who Yhwh is, and especially what images are. Many of these links will reflect the psalmist's familiarity with Israel's worship, the context in which the psalms are used and Israel's story is told, though some might issue from a scribe's reading scrolls of the Torah and taking phrases from written texts. Known through worship or known as written texts, then, these narratives and praises provide the raw material for the worship expressed by the psalm, shaping its understanding of Israel and of Yhwh. Yet the psalm also again works creatively with these raw materials. Individual words and phrases gain new meanings and enable new things to be said, and all become part of a fresh whole with a message of its own. To express the point anachronistically, the Scriptures are the community's resource for the shaping of its praise, while also making it possible for the Holy Spirit and the human spirit to express fresh insights with the stimulus of these words.

In Psalms 47, 98 and 100 the sequence of exhortation followed by the con-

---

[264]So Ford and Hardy, *Living in Praise*, p. 2.

tent or reasons comes twice, and in Psalms 97, 99 and 147 three times (such repetition also features in laments and thanksgivings). While this may involve some development in the "argument" (notably in Ps 95), as big a factor is the demand of theo-logic or rhetoric. For the psalmist and the people for whom the psalm is composed, urging praise and justifying it is not complete when it has been done once. There is more in the spirit of worshiper and congregation than can be adequately expressed in one sequence, because there is more in Yhwh than can be adequately expressed in one sequence. Even if the second or third sequence does little more than reexpress similar ideas in different words, it contributes to a more adequate expression of the worshiper's spirit and of Yhwh's deserve.

When praise involves exhortation followed by content or reasons for worship, or even the reverse order, this risks giving the worshipers too much prominence. It is therefore apposite that the praise of the Psalms can also leave out the worshipers altogether and focus exclusively on Yhwh. We have noted that Psalm 97 comes close to this;[265] Psalm 93 is more radical. It begins by talking about Yhwh rather than to Yhwh, implicitly addressing listeners who are challenged to be worshipers, but they are invisible; and when the latter part of the psalm addresses Yhwh, they disappear altogether.

Reigning in Creation and Nature

Psalm 145 begins, "I will exalt you, my God, the king," and goes on to exult in Yhwh's royal power, goodness and provision. It affirms that Yhwh, "my God," reigns over all, that Yhwh is to be exalted, worshiped and praised, that all peoples are to acknowledge the glory of Yhwh's reign, that as King Yhwh exercises power on behalf of the needy and fills all things with divine favor. It describes people looking to Yhwh for their needs, and has Yhwh giving generously to them. It knows that Yhwh is gracious, compassionate and long-tempered, but that it is possible not to call on Yhwh in truth. It pictures Yhwh upholding the falling, watching over the suppliants and destroying the faithless who oppress us. Its praise is thus taken up in the Lord's Prayer, which is a further embodiment of this kind of praise and works out its implications.[266] Because "my God" reigns over all, I can address God as "our Father who is in heaven." I urge that God's name be hallowed, that God's reign become a reality, that God's will be done. I ask for bread for each day, for the forgiveness of my wrongdoing, for protection from temptation and deliverance from evil. All this corresponds to Psalm 145. The liturgical addition to the Lord's Prayer,

---

[265]See §2.7 "Individual and Communal."

[266]Cf. Erich Zenger, " 'Dass alles Fleisch den Namen seiner Heiligung segne,' " *Biblische Zeitschrift* 41 (1997): 1-27; cf. Reinhold G. Kratz, "Die Gnade des tägliche Brots," *Zeitschrift für Theologie und Kirche* 89 (1992): 1-40; see pp. 25-28.

"Thine is the kingdom, the power, and the glory, for ever and ever," sums up the Psalms.

Four topics recur in the content of Israel's praise: Yhwh's original act of creation, nature as we know it, Yhwh's deliverance of Israel from Egypt and gift of the land to Israel, and Yhwh's ongoing sovereignty in history. Psalm 136 opens and closes with exhortations to confess Yhwh that enfold an account of Yhwh's acts in creation, in establishing Israel as a people and in generally caring for Israel and for all humanity. The account of these again corresponds to the number of letters in the alphabet, perhaps here suggesting that it covers all the bases of Yhwh's acts. The celebration expounds a conviction expressed in the second colon of each line: "his commitment is forever."

The Psalter's first great praise song begins its reasoning by explaining, "for Yhwh's word is upright, his every deed is characterized by truthfulness; he is dedicated to faithfulness in exercising authority [*ṣĕdāqâ ûmišpāṭ*], the earth is full of Yhwh's commitment" (Ps 33:4-5). How is that expressed? The psalm goes on to declare, "by Yhwh's word the heavens were made, all their army by the breath of his mouth, gathering the waters of the sea as in a dam, putting the deep in storerooms" (Ps 33:6-7). Yhwh's work as creator was the first expression of those opening characteristics, of the working of that word of Yhwh. In itself it might suggest two reasons why that work as creator would be reason for praise. One is Yhwh's extraordinary sovereign power, which would make it appropriate to bow down in submission. The other is the way this work as creator benefited people; the preceding affirmation of Yhwh's truthfulness, faithfulness in exercising authority and commitment, would suggest that the beneficent aspect to creation has the prominence. The references to Yhwh's word as the means of creation and to the way Yhwh's work benefited humanity parallel Genesis 1.

Whereas the waters of the sea, the tumultuous deep, would be a threat to humanity and to the rest of the animate world, Yhwh set bounds to the sea and turned a threat into a resource. According to the MT Yhwh turned the waters of the sea into a reservoir, bound by a dam. One might think of the little dams hand-built out of stones that stop desert rains simply flowing away and make them available for sheep or for irrigation. But the word is also used of the heaping up of the waters of the Red Sea and the Jordan, to enable Israel to cross. And then according to the ancient versions, Yhwh rather gathered them in the way one puts water into a skin so as to have it available for when one is thirsty.[267] Either reading underlines the ease with which Yhwh puts the mighty waters in their place, for the protection and blessing of the entire animate world.

---

[267]That is, LXX, Jerome, Tg, and Sym imply *nōd* (= *nōʾd*) for MT's *nēd*.

Psalm 104 lauds Yhwh as one who put on honor and majesty, wrapped on light like a coat, established a home in the heavens and means of transport around the cosmos, founded the earth itself in such a way that it was secure, with potentially overwhelming waters placed under firm constraint. The psalm then interweaves praise of Yhwh for the ongoing nature of the created world as well as for the mode of its origin. Not only did Yhwh once stretch out the heavens and put the waters under constraint. Yhwh makes the waters the means of providing what they need for animals, birds, and human beings, makes sun and moon means of structuring life for the animal and human world. "To you all of them look, to give them their food at its time. You give to them, they gather; you open your hand, they eat their fill of good things" (Ps 104:27-28).

Deliverance in Israel's History

After its praise of Yhwh as creator, Psalm 33 goes on to declare that the whole world should revere Yhwh "because he is the one who has spoken and it has come to be; he is the one who has commanded and it has stood up" (Ps 33:9). One might initially reckon that the psalm continues to speak of creation, but this language is also used of Yhwh's activity in history (Is 48:5, 13), and that is the focus of what follows in the psalm: "Yhwh has frustrated the plan of nations, foiled the intentions of peoples. . . . The good fortune of the nation that has Yhwh as its God!" (Ps 33:10, 12). The psalm goes on to develop the point as a generalization: "Yhwh's eye is on people who revere him, on people who wait for his commitment, to rescue them from death, to keep them alive when food is gone" (Ps 33:18-19). The effectiveness of Yhwh's care thus contrasts with the ineffectiveness of the efforts of kings and warriors to deliver themselves when battle rages.

Yhwh's involvement with Israel issues from grace, and the way it engages them as recipient's of God's covenant commitment is that it requires the response of gratitude. *Charis* evokes *eucharistia*.[268] One could see the Psalms as "a meditation on the first commandment."[269] Praise celebrates or commemorates what Yhwh has done, makes mention of it and causes people to be mindful of it (*zākar* hiphil; e.g., Ps 71:16; cf. the noun *zēker*, e.g., Ps 145:7). It confesses what Yhwh has done for the people (*yādâ* hiphil). In the narrow sense confession, testimony or thanksgiving refers to the particular acts of deliverance that Yhwh has done for this generation or for an individual, but the importance for every generation of Yhwh's great acts for Israel makes it natural also to use the word to refer to the deeds Yhwh has done for the community at the

---

[268]Karl Barth, *Church Dogmatics* (Edinburgh: T & T Clark, 1961), IV/1:43.
[269]Miller, *Way of the Lord*, pp. 91-122.

beginning and over the years (e.g., Ps 33:2; 111:1).

Psalm 105 recounts Israel's story from the time of the ancestors via Joseph to the oppression in Egypt, the people's deliverance from there, the provision through the wilderness and the occupation of the land (vv. 39-45b). It thus summarizes the familiar story in Genesis-Joshua, but makes no reference to Yhwh's revelation at Sinai or to the rebellions in the wilderness; the people go straight from Egypt to Canaan. The psalm thus focuses the agenda for praise on God's actual acts. It is these that are the decisive factor in Israel's story, not the need for human response. Further, in telling the story it uses terms that recall and recognize the community's difficult situation in the exile and afterward. The praise brings home the story's implications for the people, affirming that the God who was with Israel at the beginning is the same God for them. This praise too is praise, but it is also teaching, related to the worshipers' needs in their context.

Psalm 105 begins, "confess Yhwh, call in his name, make known his deeds among the peoples," and then recounts the story of Yhwh's activity in Israel's history. Psalm 106 and Psalm 107 begin similarly. Psalm 111 has "I confess Yhwh with all my soul in the council of the upright, the assembly." Here too the celebration of things Yhwh has done and regularly does has a strong didactic function, and its alphabetic form (22 cola beginning with the successive letters of the alphabet) may also link with this. It more explicitly covers the praise of Yhwh from A to Z, which both suggests comprehensiveness and facilitates memorizing. In its last two lines the psalm explicitly commends the "wisdom" or "insight" of what it expresses. It thus affirms that insight and worship belong together. Awareness of what Yhwh has done and does issues in worship for what Yhwh has done and does, and worship issues in awareness. Worship and reflection are not different preferences for different sorts of people. Both belong to the nature of humanity and of the true life of God's people.

Psalm 107 in turn recounts the people's experience with God in later times; the psalm's introduction suggests these are experiences that came to people in connection with the exile. There were people who had fled from Judah and found themselves wandering about in uninhabited country, but they cried out to Yhwh and Yhwh brought them to a city where there was food and water. There were people who failed to escape their conquerors and found themselves in captivity, but they cried out to Yhwh and Yhwh brought them out of their prisons. There were people who got sick and were near death, but they cried out to Yhwh and Yhwh healed them. There were people who crossed the Mediterranean to try to find a new life and almost drowned, but they cried out to Yhwh and Yhwh led them to a safe haven. There were people whose land was devastated by natural disaster, but Yhwh reversed it. It might be tempting for Judeans after the exile to reckon that the prophets' great promises of restoration had failed them. Psalm 107 says, "No, look at what Yhwh has done for us in all those ways, in fulfillment of those promises. Rejoice in what Yhwh has done, consider Yhwh's acts of commitment, testify to them." This praise, too, is praise, but also teaching: it closes with the question, "Who is the wise person who notes these things?—they consider Yhwh's acts of commitment."

Deliverance in Current Experience

Psalm 147 praises Yhwh as the God of Jerusalem, builder of the city, gatherer of its exiles, healer of the broken, restorer of the weak and putter-down of the faithless. In the midst of these descriptions is the fact that Yhwh is sovereign over the stars and makes nature work and provides for its needs. And closing it is the fact that Yhwh has revealed decrees and decisions to Israel about how events in history are to work out. Sing and confess Yhwh, it goes on, with a double surprise in the basis for this. It does not lie in what Yhwh has done for these people themselves, the usual topic of confession. It does not lie in what Yhwh has done for human beings at all. It lies in what Yhwh does for the animate world that is independent of humanity and exists in its own right. Yet the further basis for confession is that Yhwh does not delight in military resources, because Yhwh's own power is the key to the city's destiny.

Psalm 48 specifically celebrates the way Yhwh has protected Jerusalem and defeated its attackers. People have not merely heard from their ancestors about that, they have seen it for themselves. As those who come there for worship, "we think about your commitment, God, within your palace." The verb *dāmâ* (think) links with the word for an image, *děmût*: we form an image in our minds of the acts whereby Yhwh has expressed commitment to its people. The psalm goes on to imply something more concrete than a mere act of imagination. People can go round Zion and count its towers, ramparts, and citadels, and be impressed by what they see that stands as testimony to the God who lives there, who has made sure that the city of the great King stands firm.

Psalm 103 combines features of a testimony psalm and a praise psalm. It is a quite personal celebration of who Yhwh is, but it celebrates how Yhwh's way was made known to Moses long ago at the beginning, then how Yhwh has not dealt with us in accordance with our waywardness but has distanced our rebellions from us and shown compassion to us in recognition of the fact that we are just dirt. It begins with an exhortation to worship addressed to the self (proper to a confession) and closes with one addressed to the supernatural and natural world (proper to a praise psalm). The former illustrates how praise, like prayer, can involve a conversation with the self: "Worship Yhwh, my soul, all that is within me [worship] his holy name; worship Yhwh, my

soul, and do not ignore all his dealings" (Ps 103:1-2). Such a psalm assumes
that we can argue with ourselves and that we need to and should stir ourselves up to faith and worship. The last set of exhortations to the self imply a
bodily action, as "worship" (*bārak* piel again) implies kneeling before Yhwh,
but the parallelism of "everything within me" also make explicit that an exhortation to the *nepeš* addresses itself to the whole person; body, emotions,
mind and will are to respond to Yhwh in praise. The further parallelism of
"worship" and "do not ignore" also underlines this. Like its converse, being
mindful, ignoring involves mind and will, and worship is an act of the will,
something we decide to do.

As Yhwh's act of deliverance takes place in current experience, in everyday
life, that is where praise for deliverance starts, though not where it finishes.
People "are to praise his name with dancing, with tambourine and lyre they
are to make music for him" (Ps 149:3; cf. 150:4; Ex 15:20). The psalm adds that
"The committed are to exult in their honor, they are to resound on their beds."
Exulting is not especially a word that belongs in worship, and resounding on
one's bed does not sound like an activity in the temple. The First Testament
does not refer to people staying overnight in the sanctuary and worshiping
there "on their beds," but it does refer to one's bed as a place of fasting and
lamentation (1 Kings 21:27; Ps 6:6 [MT 7]), of the kind of mourning that gets
turned into dancing when Yhwh acts (Ps 30:11 [MT 12]). Most references to
dancing as an act of praise indicate that it occurs out in the world rather than
in the sanctuary (again, cf. Ex 15:20). So the psalm points to exulting and resounding that takes place in some context outside the temple, in the setting
where people actually experience Yhwh's act that turns their mourning into
dancing. That fits with the succeeding reference to "acclamations of God in
their mouth and a two-edged sword in their hand, to execute redress among
the nations, rebukes among the countries" (again, compare the worship of 2
Chron 20). In the context of modernity, the combination of "praise the Lord"
and "pass the ammunition" meets with the disapproval of Western commentators, both Christian and Jewish (not of Christian and Jewish commentators
in earlier times or outside the Western world). And it is not a psalm for Western powers, for whom it is a threat as it offers encouragement to weak peoples
oppressed by imperial powers. Instead of lying on their beds in dust and
ashes, people are to get up, praise God and wield their swords, as Nehemiah
urged (Neh 4:13, 18 [MT 7, 12]). The people's service of Yhwh includes being the
means of Yhwh's taking redress on wrongdoing, even when they are weak
and outnumbered.

Praise characteristically relates to Yhwh's great acts, but the First Testament occasionally refers to the little stories of people's lives that are set in the
context of Yhwh's big story. In Psalm 113 praise relates to ordinary people's

experience. Yhwh is "on high above all nations, his honor above the heavens," but this does not imply being remote and uninvolved. Yhwh is "the one who looks down low," taking an interest in what happens on earth. In particular, Yhwh is "one who lifts the poor from the dirt, raises the needy from the rubbish-heap, to set them with the nobles, with the nobles of his people." There are not many biblical texts that justify the notion that God exercises a "preferential option for the poor," but this psalm does so (cf. Ps 107:41; 109:31). Someone with no status in the community gains status. It is a further expression of the same attitude that God is "one who sets the woman who is childless in the household as the mother of children, rejoicing." The particular way Yhwh relates to the lives of ordinary people is by rescuing the poor and making it possible for someone to have a baby.

In Israel the praise of Yhwh was often under threat. The danger was not that Israelites might give up praise but that they might give their praise to another deity. In the everyday Western Christian world, we are more inclined to congratulate and praise one another than to praise the wrong deity.[270] In worship the congregation may be more inclined to applaud the choir than God. Theological study in turn commonly encourages a stance of suspicion or noncommitment or suspension of judgment.[271] All these idiosyncrasies mean we surrender the capacity of praise to make a world.[272] We no longer have the experience of affirming who God is and thereby seeing the world in a new way. The Psalms' repeated exhortations to praise speak to all such situations where praise is under threat.

---

[270]Cf. Rolf Jacobson, "The Costly Loss of Praise," *Theology Today* 57 (2000): 1-9.
[271]Cf. Ford and Hardy, *Living in Praise*, pp. 15-16.
[272]See §1.1 "Prayer and Ethics."

3

PRAYER AND THANKSGIVING

Prayer and thanksgiving parallel submission and celebration as expressions of the relationship between servants and their master. Submission and celebration constitute the servants' response to the master's rights; prayer and thanksgiving focus on the servants' needs. As well as being committed to acknowledging the master and doing the master's will, servanthood means having a claim on the master and being able to call on him. Whereas praise expresses "the full abandonment of the self to God," lament expresses "the full assertion of self over against God."[1] The Psalms illustrate this. They "are evidences of Israel's resolve to keep its life dialogical . . . (for which the biblical term may be *covenantal*)." They presuppose that God welcomes engagement from people, not mere silent submission.[2] In prayer, I cry out to "my God" and make appeal to "my Lord"; Yhwh's being "my Lord," my master, is my confidence in this connection (Ps 16:1-2; 30:2, 8 [MT 3, 9]). Our position as servants means our master is committed to us, under obligation to protect us as the other side of our commitment to serving him.

3.1 Communication

There are many understandings of prayer, and no single "right" definition. Prayer can denote silent reflection, meditation and contemplation that we undertake in God's presence. It can denote "conversation with God."[3] It can denote worship, with its focus on praise, such as we have considered in chapter two. "Prayer in the church has been understood to be a practice of piety" rather than an actual transaction with God.[4] This chapter is concerned with prayer that centrally involves pleading with God to do things, which is a very prominent activity in the First Testament. As it happens, this use of the word

---

[1]Walter Brueggemann, *The Covenanted Self* (Minneapolis: Fortress, 1999), p. 18.

[2]Walter Brueggemann, "Psalms as Subversive Practice of Dialogue," in *Diachronic and Synchronic*, ed. Joel S. Burnett et al., LHBOTS 488 (New York: London: T & T Clark, 2008), pp. 3-25; pp. 7, 24.

[3]Patrick D. Miller, *They Cried to the Lord* (Minneapolis: Fortress, 1994), p. 33; the words are italicized.

[4]Dale Patrick and Kenneth Diable, "Persuading the One and Only God to Intervene," in *My Words Are Lovely*, ed. Robert L. Foster and David M. Howard, LHBOTS 467 (New York/London: T & T Clark, 2008), pp. 19-32; see p. 32.

prayer fits its origin in Latin words that suggest entreaty.

Silent meditation does not feature in the First Testament. The two words often translated "meditate," *hāgâ* and *śiah*, and their related nouns, refer to reflection outwardly expressed in reading aloud or musing aloud or talking about something.[5] Likewise, in the First Testament prayer is not silent. "The art of praying is neither something ritual" in the sense of something that follows a set form and might be expected to work on that basis, "nor an individual meditation. Rather it is *communication*."[6] Prayer involves words; a common verb in connection with prayers is the simple verb *said*. It involves words addressed to someone else, not words that simply help me articulate something for myself; it is an exercise in person-to-person communication. It means I speak and God hears; it is relational. But it is communication of a certain kind, communication that aims to get the other person to act in a certain way. "The Old Testament is the story of a relationship . . . rooted in the crying out of God's people on the one hand and God's hearing of these cries on the other."[7] The Psalter's first prayer psalm makes that explicit by the way it speaks of prayer: literally, "[with] my voice to Yhwh I call" (Ps 3:4 [MT 5]). The nature of "calling" is to involve the voice, to be "out loud." And petition is "the constitutive element in what takes place in prayer. . . . While prayer is a matter of worship and penitence, . . . in the first it is an asking, a seeking and a knocking directed towards God," as the Lord's Prayer shows.[8] It means we come to God with empty hands.[9]

Conversation

Conversation is prominent in people's relationship with God in the First Testament. While there are occasions when God simply makes an announcement to someone or someone makes a pronouncement to God, there are other occasions when God initiates a conversation (Gen 3:9-19; 4:9-15; 16:7-13). There are yet others when the addressee chooses to respond to a declaration and turns the occasion into a conversation (Gen 15:1-21; 17:1-22; 20:3-7; Ex 6:10-12, resumed in Ex 6:28–7:5; 32:9-14; 34:1-10; Num 14:11-35; 2 Sam 7:4-29; 2 Kings 20:1-6). There are yet others when someone takes an initiative and asks Yhwh for something, and Yhwh responds positively (1 Kings 8–9; 2 Chron 6–7). There are yet others when someone takes an initiative and protests to Yhwh, per-

---

[5]See §2.1 "Delighting in Yhwh."
[6]Eep Talstra, "The Discourse of Praying: Reading Nehemiah 1," in *Psalms and Prayers*, ed. Bob Becking and Eric Peels, OTS 55 (Leiden/Boston: Brill, 2007), pp. 219-36; see p. 235.
[7]Richard Nelson Boyce, *The Cry to God in the Old Testament*, SBLDS 103 (Atlanta: Scholars, 1988), p. 1.
[8]Karl Barth, *Church Dogmatics* (Edinburgh: T & T Clark, 1961), III/3:267-68.
[9]Karl Barth, *Church Dogmatics* (Edinburgh: T & T Clark, 1969), III/4:97.

haps implicitly asking for something, and Yhwh responds positively (Ex 5:22–6:1; 17:4-6; Num 27:15-21; 2 Kings 19:15-35; 2 Chron 20:6-17) or negatively (Num 12:13-14; Deut 3:23-28; Josh 7:7-15; Jer 12:1-6). There are prayers where the interchange is quite complex (2 Sam 24:10-25; the book of Job; Jer 15:15-21; Habakkuk). There are prayers where someone takes an initiative and asks for something and there is no response in words but there is a response in acts (Gen 24:12-27; Judg 6:36-40; 13:8-9; 15:18-19; 16:28-30; 2 Sam 15:31; 1 Kings 17:20-22; 18:36-39; 2 Kings 6:17-20; 1 Chron 4:10; 2 Chron 14:10-11; Neh 1:4-11). There are prayers where it is not clear whether Yhwh responds (1 Chron 29:10-19; Neh 4:4-5; 6:14). Many psalms imply a response, while others imply the absence of a response. There are prayers of Jeremiah's where there seems to be no response (Jer 17:14-18; 18:19-23; 20:7-18), though "in the face of a silent God Jeremiah continues to pray. He does not retreat into silence. He does not abandon God for more responsive dialogue partners." Indeed "as despair increases so does the intensity, the urgency, the passion of prayer."[10]

Conversation covers a broader range of interaction than is involved in prayer in the sense of pleading with God for things. I shall not think of a conversation such as that in Genesis 3:9-19 as a prayer,[11] though the conversation in Genesis 18:22-33 is one, as are some of the two-and-fro conversations with God initiated by Moses, Jeremiah and Habukkuk. These examples may suggest that such conversations are prophetic experiences; perhaps all prayer presupposes being in the position of a prophet.[12] Psalm 12 illustrates similar dynamics; perhaps it is a prophetic psalm. It begins by urging Yhwh to act in deliverance because faithfulness is totally gone from the community and everything is deceit; divine action is needed. And Yhwh responds: "'Because of the groaning of the needy, now I will arise' Yhwh says. 'I will take my stand as deliverance,' he witnesses to him" (Ps 12:5 [MT 6]). The suppliant then has a triple reaction. There is a statement of faith in Yhwh's response, in the form of a generalization that applies to these words in particular: "Yhwh's words are pure words," as perfect and therefore reliable as precious metals that have been rigorously smelted. There is a restatement of the prayer, for Yhwh to do what the undertaking said. Then, more surprisingly, there is a restatement of the protest at the faithlessness and triviality that characterizes the community, as if to underline the plea to Yhwh to turn words into action. This prayer is conversation-like.

So prayer may be a subset of conversation, in which I speak and God responds, or God speaks and I respond. Or we may rather see it as an ongoing

---

[10]Samuel E. Balentine, *Prayer in the Hebrew Bible* (Minneapolis: Fortress, 1993), p. 162.
[11]Cf. ibid., p. 30; Balentine adds Gen 4:9-15, but I am not so sure about excluding that.
[12]See further §3.5.

conversation or a series of conversations, like the exchanges between parents and children, which involve asking questions, listening, talking about oneself, protesting and apologizing. But further, prayer presupposes that the other person can do something for me, and it incorporates words designed to get this person to act on my behalf. It is not an activity in which I tell God things but do not feel the need to ask for anything.[13] And in this sense, in its essential nature prayer is "direct address to God," not conversation.[14] Prayer is "speech in which a person or a group of people brings before God their fundamental or immediate situation."[15] It can thus also include vows, the seeking of guidance, blessings, thanksgivings and concerns for other people.

The Tradition of Prayer and the Individuality of Prayer

Christian prayers have traditional ways of beginning and ending, and often use forms of speech that belong especially to prayer. First Testament forms of speech such as pleas and thanksgivings also commonly follow familiar patterns. Elements that recur in prayer psalms are invocation of Yhwh, recollection of Yhwh's deeds in the past, protest at the contrast in how things are now, a declaration of how the suppliant nevertheless still trusts Yhwh, a plea for Yhwh to pay heed, to put down assailants and to deliver the suppliant, a promise to come back to give praise to Yhwh when this has happened, a declaration of the conviction that Yhwh has listened to the prayer and made a commitment to act, and an offering of praise for this.

Few prayer psalms come near to following this whole template; as much interest attaches to ways a prayer offers a distinctive take on a familiar pattern. Notably, after an opening invocation and plea for a hearing, Psalm 88 comprises only a protest, at the suppliant's suffering and at Yhwh's abandonment; and while most protest psalms work their way to closure, this one simply stops. It thereby reflects the nature of the suppliant's experience, which contains no closure. Some psalms can be difficult to relate to any recognizable pattern; Psalm 139 is an example. But most take a familiar way of praying as their point of departure. Form then facilitates prayer. Suppliants know that a prayer psalm usually includes (for instance) a statement of trust, so they are driven to offer one, which may change the way they see the situation (or be driven to make a point by not offering one). They know that the form encourages a pouring out of hurt and anger, which they might otherwise hesitate to do. Alphabetic form (Ps 9–10; 25; 34; 37; 111; 112; 145;

---

[13]Cf. Karl Barth, *Church Dogmatics* (Edinburgh: T & T Clark, 1969), III/4:96-97.

[14]Rodney A. Werline, "Defining Penitential Prayer," in *Seeking the Favor of God*, ed. Mark J. Boda et al. (Atlanta: Society of Biblical Literature, 2006) 1:xiii-xvii; see p. xv.

[15]Henning Graf Reventlow, *Gebet im Alten Testament* (Stuttgart: Kohlhammer, 1986), p. 89.

and most extravagantly, Ps 119) requires something to be said under each letter and thus covers its subject from A to Z; it also means the psalm both uses stereotyped expressions that make telling affirmations of the fundamentals of Israelite faith, and additionally makes striking innovative statements and expresses convictions that would not otherwise have emerged, and thereby generates food for thought.

Similarly, some psalms gain some of their effectiveness through their individual distinctive language, but many share common imagery and language. They talk in similar terms about the trouble out of which they pray and the way people are treating them (compare, for instance, Ps 70; 71). They talk in similar terms about what they need from Yhwh and what Yhwh is for them (e.g., crag, stronghold, cliff and fastness: e.g., Ps 18; 31). They talk in similar terms about their hurt, anger, questioning and desire for Yhwh to take redress (e.g., Ps 79 in relation to many psalms). In a crisis people do not try to pray in a new way. They pray in light of the way they have prayed before, and the way their people have prayed before, and have proved what is acceptable to Yhwh and what maybe gains a response from Yhwh.

There can be a dynamic relationship between faithfulness to ways of praying that come from the past and the necessity to say what needs to be said in another age. Psalm 144:1-11 takes up phrases from Psalm 18 and a number of other psalms but then strikes out on its own in verses 12-15 (unless these lines come from a psalm that is otherwise lost). Thus it begins by praising Yhwh as "my crag, the one who trains my hands for encounter, my fingers for war," in terms appropriate to the king and commander-in-chief. Yet the last part looks beyond that to speak of the blessing of flourishing families, full storehouses, and thriving flocks and herds. In other words, it yearns for a quiet life, for the chance not to "live in interesting times" or exciting ones.

Individual and Community

These prayers thus express themselves in deeply-felt personal ways yet in structures, images and words that they do not personally devise but that come from the way people have heard other people pray, as the church's liturgical prayers have taken up the phrases of Scripture and as individual Christians have prayed in cadences that recall the King James Bible. They take up a language that has developed depth and resonance and that places the individual in the fellowship of people who have long prayed this way. "Biblical prayer with its emphasis on common history . . . is *intertextual* by definition."[16] Its traditional language reflects familiarity with the right way to pray, the tradition of psalmody and the instinct to use the "natural" language of prayer

---

[16]Talstra, "Discourse of Praying," p. 236.

that is sanctified by usage. These are phrases suppliants have often uttered; they remind Yhwh of prayers that have been answered in the past. They also mean that "the singer was not as isolated as he felt",[17] or even that he knew he was not as isolated as his words could suggest. "We are not alone when we pray; we have more support than most of us realize. We are part of a great tradition."[18] The sets of links and distinctives set prayer within the established framework of the relationship between Yhwh and Israel while also reflecting the individuality of the situation and the person who is praying. We pray as people who belong to a community that has been praying this way over centuries. We know we are praying the kind of prayer God answers. Perhaps the use of expressions the community has long used makes it easier to express strong feelings of offense, loss, hurt, anguish, shame and desire for redress. Using the language of prayers that people know Yhwh has already accepted makes it possible to express feelings that might seem unacceptable. To see prayer as naturally a communal affair is not to imply that formal, liturgical prayer comes before artless, spontaneous prayer, but neither need the reverse be true. Individual, spontaneous prayer often also reflects liturgical and traditional ("scriptural") forms, and formal, liturgical prayer reflects the everyday speech of "free" prayer.

In prayer, then, individuals set themselves within the context of the praying Israelite community of the past. They also set themselves within the context of the praying Israelite community of the present. When "prayer" suggests a broad reference to relating to God, with considerable emphasis on personal reflection and meditation, it may be natural to think of it as primarily an activity undertaken on one's own; it then contrasts with public "worship." In the First Testament, prayer is not inherently private over against worship, which is corporate. Prayer in the sense of asking God for things for oneself or for other people, and thanking God for things, are more characteristically activities undertaken with other people.[19] It is regularly the community that prays, or the individual prays in a community context, at the festivals or in the context of the family or village. We pray together for ourselves in light of our needs. We pray together for other people and their needs. We pray together for individuals among us who are in need. "The prayer of the Psalms teaches us to pray as a community. . . . That lifts me above my personal concerns and allows me to pray selflessly." The parallelism of their structure, with its implication that they are prayed antiphonally, suggests

---

[17]Derek Kidner, *Psalms*, 2 vols. (London/Downers Grove, Ill.: InterVarsity Press, 1973-1975), 2:360.

[18]Johann Baptist Metz, in Johann Baptist Metz and Karl Rahner, *The Courage to Pray* (London: Burns & Oates, 1980), p. 5.

[19]Cf. Reventlow, *Gebet im Alten Testament*, p. 228.

this. There are always two voices; the one who prays never prays alone.[20] It is "we" who pray, as is the case when Jesus teaches his disciples to pray. Even when it is "I" who pray, the "I" still prays as one of this "we."

To judge from stories in the First Testament, "in ancient Israel anyone could pray and be heard. . . . The Israelite Everyman resorted freely to prayer whenever need, gratitude or admiration moved him."[21] "Yhwh is near to all who call him, to all who call him in truth" (Ps 145:18). But the story of Hannah suggests that even individual prayers may naturally take place at the sanctuary, though one may then pray them as an individual not in the context of the community's worship. Praying on your own is possible but is often a sign of things being wrong in some way. To have to pray on one's own is a sign of how needy one is, abandoned by or separated from other people. An aspect of the predicament out of which one then prays is the individual's isolation from the community. The prayers "take place not *in* the community but because there *is no* community."[22] The "we" of the Psalms is set over against any individualistic "I," though it is not an exclusive "we"; it represents and summons the world.[23] "Whoever cannot be alone should beware of community. . . . Whoever cannot stand being in community should beware of being alone."[24]

Human Initiative and Divine Response

For all the importance of tradition and form, like any conversation prayer cannot be programmed. Scholarly theory has hypothesized that the move from prayer to praise in a psalm such as Psalm 22 is explained by a divine word that gave the suppliant something to give thanks for. If this is so, the divine word is strikingly absent. Psalm 22 points to something like a conversation, but it gives us only one side to the conversation. Perhaps this indicates that whereas we can decide what we will say to God, we cannot decide what God will say in response.

Psalms do sometimes incorporate a divine word where we might not have expected one. Perhaps we should anticipate that Yhwh will speak when we do not expect it and not speak when we do expect it. In Psalm 32:8 the suppliant, who has been addressing Yhwh with a kind of testimony to divine forgiveness and protection, suddenly incorporates a line of response from Yhwh: "I will instruct you and teach you in the way that you should go; I will coun-

---

[20]Dietrich Bonhoeffer, *Life Together/Prayerbook of the Bible* (Minneapolis: Fortress, 1996), p. 57.

[21]Moshe Greenberg, *Biblical Prose Prayer* (Berkeley/London: University of California Press, 1983), p. 51.

[22]Patrick D. Miller, *The Way of the Lord* (Grand Rapids/Cambridge: Eerdmans, 2007), p. 203.

[23]Barth, *Church Dogmatics*, III/4:102-3.

[24]Bonhoeffer, *Life Together*, p. 82 (Bonhoeffer puts both sentences in italics, and the English translators insert one German word).

sel you—my eye will be upon you." The suppliant has spoken of the way Yhwh responded to confession with forgiveness; Yhwh now adds a comment that looks to the future and the path the suppliant needs to walk, a path that contrasts with the earlier waywardness. "My eye will be upon you" can be read both as a promise and a warning; indeed, that is true of the line as a whole. But the suppliant's subsequent exhortation to the congregation ("Do not be like a horse or a mule, without insight, whose advance must be curbed with bridle and bit"; the verbs are now plural) suggests that the suppliant hears the words in an admonitory way, which is not unwise given the recalcitrance the earlier part of the psalm has acknowledged.

This also fits the nature of the divine intervention in Psalm 95.[25] In the opening lines the congregation exhorts itself (or a leader exhorts it) to come and shout Yhwh's praise and then to prostrate itself before Yhwh. In verse 7c the speaker stands over against the congregation and urges it to listen rather than make a noise, and passes on Yhwh's challenge to responsiveness rather than stubbornness. While the move from shouting to bowing may prepare the way for this exhortation, nothing has prepared us for its confrontational tone. The congregation has an agenda it assumes Yhwh shares; this reaction shows that Yhwh's agenda lies somewhere else.

Psalm 132 exemplifies the conversational potential of prayer. The people's petition comprises a long recollection of David's initiative in bringing the covenant chest to Jerusalem, framed by an appeal to "be mindful for David" of all the effort and commitment that were involved in that initiative, and for David's sake not to "turn away the face of your anointed" (the current heir to David's throne, who might or might not actually be king, depending on the period). What David did in the past is the basis for leaning on Yhwh on behalf of David's successor. The earlier part of the psalm thus compares with other psalms that recall events from the past that ought to have implications for the present, though it contrasts with them in speaking of the people's past acts rather than Yhwh's. In turn Yhwh's response, occupying the second half of the psalm, initially does not bring a new word but itself looks back to the events that the first half spoke of. Yhwh's response to David's initiative was to make a commitment, and Yhwh's response to the people's prayer is to recall that commitment, then reaffirm it: "Yhwh swore to David in truthfulness; he will not turn from it." Yhwh will be faithful to the promise about David's successors and the promise about dwelling on Zion.

Another form of conversation comes in the further very brief psalm that shortly follows, Psalm 134. "Worship Yhwh, all you servants of Yhwh, who stand in Yhwh's house through the night," it begins. Presumably it is the

---

[25]See further §2.7 "Lifting Up and Bowing Down."

priests who so stand (though *"through* the night" is still puzzling), and it is perhaps the worshipers in general who give them their bidding, possibly as they leave the temple. Then in response to the bidding voice comes another: "Yhwh bless you from Zion," blessing each individual in the manner of Numbers 6:24-26. Verbally, a conversation takes place between a congregation and its ministers; substantially, it is a conversation between congregation, ministers and God. The congregation or leader encourages the service of God; the ministers encourage the responsive blessing of each worshiper, or the leader, by God.

Divine Initiative

David and Yhwh interact in another way in connection with building a house (2 Sam 7; 1 Chron 17). David thinks building a house for Yhwh is a good idea and goes through the motions of consulting Yhwh by consulting Nathan, who thinks the answer is obvious. Yhwh intervenes to point out a few reasons why the answer is not at all obvious and to take an initiative in wresting control of the conversation about this matter by changing the meaning of the word *house*. David's subsequent prayer is then a response to Yhwh's promise concerning a house(hold), a wise response that in its asking does little more than urge Yhwh to fulfill that promise. Solomon's prayer at the dedication of this house (1 Kings 8; 2 Chron 6) then notes how Yhwh's promises have been fulfilled and urges Yhwh to continue this pattern.

Petrified at the prospect of meeting Esau, whom he had swindled of his birthright, Jacob pleads with Yhwh for deliverance, in the way the Psalms will encourage (Gen 32:9-12). In contrast to most psalms, Jacob admits his unworthiness, though we may wonder whether he means this seriously enough. This would not be the only respect in which the story illustrates how it is quite possible to pray in the right fashion but not to be praying aright. The point is further hinted by the fact that Yhwh does not answer. (Though the Psalms again show that one cannot take the lack of an answer as proof that there is something wrong with a prayer.) Meanwhile "Jacob immediately resumes his own strategizing for his imminent encounter with Esau. . . . Both before and after his prayer he assumes the posture of one who is in control of his own destiny."[26] By not answering, Yhwh colludes, for the moment. But then, in God's own time, Jacob finds himself in a wrestling bout, not one he initiates but one initiated by a mysterious human-like figure (Gen 32:25-32). It eventually becomes clear that the mysterious wrestler is God, but the story is told from Jacob's perspective; for most of the night, he does not know who is

---

[26]Balentine, *Prayer in the Hebrew Bible*, p. 69. The account of his prayer thus becomes "a means of caricature" (p. 64), as it is also with Jonah.

wrestling with him. It is God, seeking to win his willing submission, but once again failing.

Prayers in which God takes the initiative further illustrate the conversational potential of prayer (e.g., Gen 18:22-33).[27] In 1 Kings 3:4-15, Solomon goes to Gibeon to sacrifice, but there Yhwh takes the initiative in appearing to Solomon, to say, "Ask, what shall I give you?" It is a devastating question. What follows indicates that it matters not just what you do ask for (wisdom to make decisions for this people) but what you do not ask for (long life, wealth, the life of your enemies).

In the preamble to his exposition of the Lord's Prayer in The Large Catechism, Martin Luther comments:

> The first matter is to know that it is our duty to pray because of God's commandment. For thus we heard in the Second Commandment: Thou shalt not take the name of the Lord, thy God, in vain, that we are there required to praise that holy name, and call upon it in every need, or to pray. For to call upon the name of God is nothing else than to pray. Prayer is therefore as strictly and earnestly commanded as all other commandments: to have no other God, not to kill, not to steal, etc. Let no one think that it is all the same whether he pray or not, as vulgar people do, who grope in such delusion and ask, Why should I pray? Who knows whether God heeds or will hear my prayer? . . .
>
> Praying, as the Second Commandment teaches, is to call upon God in every need. This He requires of us, and has not left it to our choice. . . .
>
> Now, from the fact that it is so solemnly commanded to pray, you are to conclude and think, that no one should by any means despise his prayer, but rather set great store by it. . . .
>
> Therefore you should say: My prayer is as precious, holy, and pleasing to God as that of St. Paul or of the most holy saints. This is the reason: For I will gladly grant that he is holier in his person, but not on account of the commandment; since God does not regard prayer on account of the person, but on account of His word and obedience thereto. . . .
>
> Let this be the first and most important point, that all our prayers must be based and rest upon obedience to God, irrespective of our person, whether we be sinners or saints, worthy or unworthy. . . . He will not suffer our prayers to be in vain or lost. For if He did not intend to answer your prayer, He would not bid you pray and add such a severe commandment to it.[28]

It can thus be argued that the one central command that God gives us is "invocation," "the frightened and joyful *invocation* of the gracious God in gratitude, praise and above all petition"; Calvin calls invocation of God the

---

[27]On this conversation, see §3.5 "A Divine Invitation."

[28]"The Large Catechism, The Book of Concord <www.bookofconcord.org/largecatechism/5_ourfather.html>.

"chief exercise of faith."[29] So "the invocation 'Father!' can itself be a prayer" (e.g., Jer 3:4, 19), a confession of creatureliness and dependence.[30] "The basis of prayer . . . is man's freedom before God. . . . A man prays because he is permitted to do so by God, because he may pray, and because this very permission has become a command," and not merely (for instance) because we feel the need.[31] It is a way of acknowledging that God is God and that we look to God and to no other help. At the same time (Barth notes), the more succinct comments on prayer in the Reformed Heidelberg Catechism begin with the important complementary explanation that prayer is necessary for Christians "because it is the chief part of thankfulness which God requires of us."[32] We pray because we are invited, because we are commanded, because we are grateful.

"It is the Hebrew intuition that God is capable of all speech-acts except that of monologue which has generated our arts of reply, of questioning and counter-creation."[33] One might question the "except," but in other respects the statement provides a foundation for prayer.

Human Asking

Calvin goes on, "it is . . . by the benefit of prayer that we reach those riches which are laid up for us with the Heavenly Father. . . . Nothing is promised to be expected from the Lord, which we are not bidden also to ask of him in prayers. . . . Words fail to explain how necessary prayer is."[34] In bidding "Ask, what shall I give you?" Yhwh uses the ordinary Hebrew verb for "ask"; Hebrew has a word meaning "pray," *ʿātar*, but it is inclined to use everyday words rather than special religious words. The First Testament narrative relates a number of brief pleas that suggest the place of such asking in ordinary people's lives. Abraham's servant goes off a crucial task in relation to the future of God's promise, though he is just a servant undertaking a task for his master (Gen 24). Near Nahor's city,

> He said, "Yhwh, God of my master Abraham, do make it happen before me to-

---

[29]Karl Barth, *The Christian Life* (Grand Rapids: Eerdmans, 1981), p. 43; cf. John Calvin, *Institutes of the Christian Religion* (Philadelphia: Westminster/London: SCM Press, 1961) 3.20; see p. 850.

[30]Sheldon H. Blank, "Some Observations Concerning Biblical Prayer," *HUCA* 32 (1961): 75-90; see p. 81. He notes that the New Testament picks up this invocation.

[31]Barth, *Church Dogmatics*, III/4:91.

[32]"The Heidelberg Catechism," Center for Reformed Theology and Apologetics <www.reformed.org/documents/heidelberg.html>.

[33]George Steiner, *Real Presences* (London: Faber/Chicago: University of Chicago Press, 1989), p. 225; cf. Walter Brueggemann, *Worship in Ancient Israel* (Nashville: Abingdon, 2005), epigraph.

[34]Calvin, *Institutes of the Christian Religion,* 3.20.1; see p. 851.

day, show commitment with my master Abraham. Now. I am standing at the spring. May it happen that the girl to whom I say, 'Do lower your jar so that I may drink,' and she says, 'Drink, and I will water your camels too,' that she is the one you have decided on for your servant, for Isaac."

The script duly unfolds. The man discovers whose family Rebekah belongs to, and bows before Yhwh: "Praised be Yhwh . . . who has not withheld his commitment and truthfulness from my master. As I was on the way, Yhwh has led me to the house of my master's kin."

That technical word for prayer is used in connection with Isaac's prayer for this same Rebekah when she could not conceive (Gen 25:21). The account goes on to report that "Yhwh let himself be prayed to" by Isaac. The same verb is thus used in the niphal, which is interestingly a relatively frequent aspect of its use. Ezra 8:21-23 twice has Ezra and his company "seeking" from Yhwh and then relates how Yhwh "let himself be prayed to by us"; in other words, Yhwh responded to their prayer. Yhwh similarly "let himself be prayed to" by the Israelites when they cried out in the midst of a battle (1 Chron 5:20), and will "let himself be prayed to" by the Egyptians when they need healing (Is 19:22). The verb thus points again to the dialogical nature of prayer,[35] which is not just a matter of entreating but of finding a response.

When Rebekah's unborn babies struggle inside her, she goes to "inquire of" Yhwh, and Yhwh tells her of her sons' destiny (Gen 25:22-23). Rebekah assumes one can ask questions of God and get an answer. The verb *dāraš*, like its synonym *bāqaš* (piel) can mean "seek," as when one looks for something lost (e.g., Ezek 34:6). But more characteristically God is the verbs' object. It is another word for prayer, used in connection with Ezra in the passage just noted.[36] Whereas "seeking the face of God, striving to live in His presence and to fashion the life of holiness appropriate to God's presence" have been defined as the core of the religion of Israel and of Judaism,[37] and a Christian could reckon they constitute the core of Christian religion, this is not what "seeking the face of God" means in the First Testament. The image points toward the significance of what we are doing. When someone seeks the face of a person such as a king, they do so not in order to live in that person's presence but in order to gain an audience and solicit their help. We seek God's face in order to gain God's help by acting on our behalf or giving us guidance. The two verbs for "seek" denote treating God as our resource for help and guidance.

Exodus 33:7-11 presupposes that all Israelites can "seek of Yhwh" in this

---

[35]Miller, *They Cried to the Lord*, p. 43.
[36]See also §2.3 "Trust and Expectancy."
[37]Arthur Green, introduction to *Jewish Spirituality*, 2 vols., ed. Arthur Green (New York: Crossroad, 1986-1987/London: Routledge, 1986-1988), 1:xiii-xxv; see p. xiii.

way at the Meeting Tent outside the camp. But the account of this provides background to Moses' request to "make known to me your way" (not "your ways," as translations have), which in the context suggest something like the way you intend to take. And Yhwh grants that (Ex 33:12-17). Moses further asks to see Yhwh's splendor, but Yhwh denies that request. As Yhwh leads the people, Moses will see Yhwh's back, but not Yhwh's glorious face (Ex 33:18-23).[38] Not all prayers are granted, even for the likes of Moses.

Subsequently, the Urim and Thummim in some way made it possible to seek God's guidance.[39] When Saul proposes to pursue the Philistines after winning a battle against them, the priest urges that they draw near to God, and Saul asks of God *(šāʾal)* regarding what they should do. They get no answer, so they then need to draw near to God to ask why that is, so they can deal with the issue (1 Sam 14:36-42); this second inquiry involves the Urim and Thummim. When David fears that Saul is about to capture him, he inquires of Yhwh by the same means (1 Sam 23:10-12). He does the same after a reverse at the hands of the Amalekites (1 Sam 30:7-9).

Servant and Master

"Toward you I have raised my eyes, you who sit in the heavens. Now: like the eyes of servants toward their masters' hand, like the eyes of a maid toward her mistress's hand, so are our eyes toward Yhwh our God, until he is gracious to us" (Ps 123:1-2). From their lowly position servants look to their master and expect assistance if they are belittled, ignored or attacked by the master of some other household. Yhwh's servants do the same. The master's exalted position does not make that impossible; rather, it makes it possible. The nature of a master's relationship to a servant places obligations on the master, like those of a covenant. Indeed, they *are* those of a covenant. The servant serves; the master provides and protects. As the people of God, we appeal to God on this basis.

Psalm 86 begins by urging Yhwh to listen "because I am weak and needy," but then moves on to a different form of argument: "look after my life, because I am committed; deliver your servant: you are my God. As the one who trusts in you, be gracious to me, my Lord, because I call to you all day long. Rejoice the soul of your servant, because it is to you, my Lord, I lift up my soul, because you are my Lord." After first arguing on the basis of the suppliant's need, it goes on to argue on the basis of the master's obligation. The ex-

---

[38]See further *OTT* 1:402-7.
[39]See §7.3 "A Ministry of Supervision and a Ministry of Music."

pression "my Lord" comes seven times in the psalm,[40] while the suppliant three times describes himself as "your servant." The convention whereby translations replace the name Yhwh by a word for "the Lord" makes this seem a routine designation for Yhwh, but actually it is not. Usually the Psalms address Yhwh by name. So this appeal by a servant to a master is very pointed. It recurs in Psalm 90, which opens and closes with an appeal to "my Lord" and before the end twice issues a plea on behalf of "your servants." The common address "my God/our God" may also imply the correlative "my servant[s]." These terms also presuppose that relationship.

"Lord and master" language sounds patriarchal. It is thus striking that the First Testament makes little use of it. When it does use it in such psalms, this is for the benefit of the servant(s); the psalms are reworking or subverting any patriarchal implications that the language carries. To be someone's lord means to be in a position of responsibility and obligation; to be someone's servant means to be able to claim the obligations that come with being a master. The story of Abraham and his servant in Genesis 24 illuminates the relationship of mutual trust and commitment that ideally obtains between a servant and a master. The relationship is not merely contractual, like that between an employer and an employee. A master may not treat a servant as if he were a mere employee. The relationship is more covenantal or familial. Being a servant takes away from a servant's freedom but provides security. A master has power, prestige and resources, and is under obligation to be prepared to use them for his servant's benefit; so being a master also takes away from a master's freedom. A servant is totally dependent on the master's care but is in a position to appeal to it as one who is weak (lacking power and independent position) and needy (lacking resources). That is an everyday reality. Its significance emerges further when such a person is in trouble—for instance, if accused of some wrongdoing. A servant then needs the master to give public indication of support, if the accusers are to be confuted (cf. Ps 86:17). In Psalm 86 other expressions underline the nature of the servant's claim on the master. The servant is someone committed to the master (ḥāsîd), someone charac-

---

[40]The expression ʾădōnāy, is an odd formation, different from the regular form denoting a human master, ʾădōnî. It is formed like a plural, like ʾĕlōhîm. Both words apparently use the plural to emphasize Yhwh's majesty. As ʾĕlōhay then means "my God," I take ʾădōnāy to mean "my Lord." Admittedly one would have expected the pointing ʾădōnay, analogous to that of ʾĕlōhay. This pointing does occur in connection with the apparently human figures in Gen 19:2; perhaps the form used for God is deliberately different. Further, Ugaritic had a similar ending to this -ay with an emphatic or intensifying sense, and this Hebrew ending might likewise function simply to reinforce the meaning of the word, as if to say "the Lord" (cf. EVV; and, e.g., IBHS 7.4.3ef). But "my Lord" makes sense in a passage such as Ps 86, though even if one understands the expression to mean simply "the Lord," the point about the servant-master relationship would hold. (The psalm also, of course, includes occurrences of the name Yhwh, which EVV render "the LORD").

terized by steadfast obedience and faithfulness. The servant is someone who has to look to the master and does so. It is to the master that the servant's soul is lifted up, to whom the servant looks for the meeting of needs. The servant is totally dependent on the master's support and provision. The servant is not just a recent acquisition but "the son of your maid," someone born in the household and thus a longstanding member of the family.

In Numbers 11:11 Moses protests, "Why have you done wrong to your servant, and why have I not found favor in your eyes in putting the burden of this people on me?" It is the question the Israelite foremen had put to the Pharaoh as their master (Ex 5:15), and it is the action Moses has attributed to the Pharaoh and to Yhwh on an occasion when Moses already asked "Why?" (Ex 5:22-23; cf. 32:11, 12).[41] The servant's objection is now that Yhwh does wrong to him, and that the master asks too much. Moses does not get into trouble for this protest; Yhwh agrees to do something about this burden.

The Impossibility of Silence

The First Testament is ambivalent about silence, in relation to human beings and to God, recognizing that there are times when silence would be a good idea but also that silence is hard to maintain. The dynamics of this difficulty differ from those in Western culture, where it is hard for us to escape the noise that comes from the world around and from inside ourselves. "Be still, and know that I am God" (Ps 46:10 [MT 11] NRSV) means something different in its context from the meaning it has acquired in Western devotion. There it suggests "Stop [fighting] and acknowledge that I am God," also an exhortation that Western piety could benefit from heeding.[42]

In worship silence may be beautiful, "but has it any spiritual meaning? Can it be established and justified theologically?"[43] Psalm 39 begins with a recollection: "I said, I will keep watch on my ways so as not to sin with my tongue. I will keep a muzzle on my mouth while the faithless is still before me." This determination may denote a resolution not to respond to the accusations or jibes of the faithless, or not to protest to Yhwh while in the presence of the faithless. Either way, it does not work; the silence is impossible to maintain. "I kept dumb, in silence; I kept quiet more than it was good. And my pain—it stirred." Trying to muzzle oneself is like putting a cap on a geyser. It can be effective for a while, but when the pressure builds up, eventually the geyser blows. The suppliant's silence means sitting on pain, which may not work in the long term. God did not make us that way.

If the suppliant wanted to avoid responding to the faithless, the implica-

---

[41]Cf. Balentine, *Prayer in the Hebrew Bible*, p. 129.
[42]See also §2.3 "Trust and Silence."
[43]Barth, *Church Dogmatics*, III/4:112.

tion is that though this silence is fine, we need some way of expressing what we feel. The Psalms express to God the anger and hostility the suppliants feel toward other human beings. They imply it is unnecessary to deny the reality of these reactions toward other people or to try to repress them. It is also useless; they will come out in other ways. Expressing them to friends or family (if they are not the enemies!) or to God avoids that negative dynamic. If the suppliant wanted to avoid protesting to Yhwh while in the presence of the faithless, then it is necessary to find a way of making such protests when the faithless are not present.

A Western context might again make one reckon that we do this on our own. But the psalm goes on to imply that the suppliant had tried that. "As I talked, fire burned." The talking is the kind of outwardly expressed but essentially personal musing that Psalm 1:2 refers to.[44] Talking under one's breath simply encouraged the fire to burn; it did not calm it down. Perhaps the suppliant needed to express those protests more openly with friends and family away from the public location of the sanctuary. Of course there is risk in that. Job managed to say silent for a week but then broke into cursing his birth, and his friends could not cope with knowing what he was saying to God.

Psalm 39 later refers back to this failed silence. "When I kept dumb, I would not open my mouth, because you were the one who acted." Again, the logic inverts that which normally obtains in the Psalms. They usually imply that Yhwh's being the one who acted is precisely the reason why we do open our mouths. If trouble came to us purely through other people's actions or as "just one of those things," there is less basis for calling on Yhwh to act than is the case if trouble came to us because Yhwh acted. But there stands in tension with this a natural human instinct to reckon that we should submit to whatever Yhwh does, and at some level Yhwh's speech to Job takes that stance, even though Yhwh goes on to declare that Job has spoken the truth about Yhwh in a way that his friends have not (Job 42:7). In Psalm 39 the suppliant gives up the attempt at silence in order to plead, "Turn away from me your affliction." In the end, silence will not do. And in such a psalm of protest "Israel has momentarily wrested from Yahweh the initiative for the relationship." It has not rejected Yhwh; and its way of speaking to God is accepted, to judge from the presence of these words in the Psalter. "Rather this positioning of Israel vis-à-vis Yahweh is regarded as a legitimate and proper way in which to relate to Yahweh." It is "a legitimate and appropriate form of covenantal faith."[45]

---

[44]See the introduction to §3.1; I take the noun *hāgîg* as related to a byform of *hāgâ*.

[45]Walter Brueggemann, *Theology of the Old Testament* (Minneapolis: Fortress, 1997), p. 380.

In contrast to the stance the suppliant of Psalm 39 attempted, a prayer such as that in Psalm 77 speaks of crying out, which implies a loud, urgent and pained noise, and of doing so with one's voice, which underlines the point; it is a way of seeking help from Yhwh and not from anyone else, and of complaining or seething or fuming. All this indicates that the suppliant makes plenty of outward noise in prayer, as in praise. The psalm also speaks of calling God to mind rather than giving in to the temptation to put God out of mind, and of murmuring or muttering or whispering as one's spirit faints. Something is going on inside the suppliant, though "murmuring" as usual indicates that the words were outwardly expressed.

Manner, Place and Time

Communication involves the whole person, body and spirit. The same is true of prayer, as it is true of worship. And again like worship, while prayer involves the heart and not just outward rites and actions, it does not just involve the heart, but also those outward rites and actions. In prayer I lift up my hands, my eyes and my spirit (Ps 25:1; 28:2; 86:4; 123:1; 143:8). Prayer is not a mental exercise. In pleading with a human king, one lifts up hands, eyes and spirit to one who is exalted on a throne in his palace. In pleading with the divine King, one does the same in relation to the God who is exalted in the heavens or in the temple; expressions such as these appear in parallelism with references to trust and to pleading for grace. As well as crying out, "my hand has reached out and does not grow numb" (Ps 77:2 [MT 3]). Reaching out one's hand (though the verb literally means "flow") is a common gesture of appeal; here the psalm indicates that the hand has been kept out and has not given in to tiredness.

Isaiah recalls Yhwh calling Jerusalem to weeping and lamenting, to tonsuring the hair and putting on sackcloth; but all that the people would do is celebrate the narrow escape they had had, ignoring the warnings that execution has only been delayed (Is 22:12-14). If all they do is fast and prostrate themselves, clothed in sackcloth and smeared with ash, while abusing their workers and letting needy fellow members of the community go hungry, the second form of body language will outshout the first (Is 58:1-7). But if they claim to grieve but do not show it outwardly, that will also constitute a contradiction. In Ezra 9:3-5, Ezra tears his clothes, hair and beard, and sits to mourn and grieve, then gets up to kneel in order to pray. He spreads out his hands to Yhwh, but cannot look Yhwh in the face because of his people's waywardness. Ezra 10:1 adds that he was weeping and falling down. Ezra 10:6 adds further that he ate no bread and drank no water; 1 Esdras 9:2 makes explicit that he maintained self-denial overnight, which is not usually required for fasting.

In Solomon's prayer in 1 Kings 8, the great significance of the temple is as a place of prayer.[46] It is a place where people would come (or toward which they would pray) to make confession of their wrongdoing in connection with matters such as military defeat, drought, famine, epidemic, invasion or individual sickness (1 Kings 8:30, 33-40). It is a place where foreigners would be welcome to come to pray about their needs, and where the people would pray before battle (1 Kings 8:41-45). In connection with confession, Solomon's prayer eventually makes explicit the significance of the temple for people after the destruction of Jerusalem and the exile (1 Kings 8:46-53). Daniel in exile prays toward the temple (Dan 6), and prays at the time of the evening offering (Dan 9:21), while Isaiah 56:1-8 presupposes that the temple has become especially a place of prayer for the postexilic community and also affirms how foreigners are to rejoice in Yhwh's prayer house and how their offerings are to be accepted on Yhwh's altar. The times of the temple offerings, dawn and dusk, are the classic times of prayer; prayer and sacrifice naturally go together (cf. Ezra 9:5).[47] Once again, the First Testament implies that if a man said he loved his wife but never gave her a gift, one would wonder what his words were worth, but if he gave expensive gifts but never said "I love you," she would likely be dissatisfied. Prayer without sacrifice would be odd; sacrifice without prayer would be odd.

In Psalm 141:2 the suppliant stands before the heavenly King as before the Supreme Court, lifting hands in a gesture of appeal and pressing for action: "May my plea stand firm before you with incense, the lifting of my hands with the evening offering." The metaphor of the court combines with the literal reference to incense and evening offering. Here too prayers and offerings accompany one another, and as usual worship of Yhwh is multifaceted; it involves words, music, gestures and offerings. The ascending incense "became the visible manifestation of prayer" ascending to God.[48] If incense links especially with expiation, then it constitutes an appeal to Yhwh to listen to prayer notwithstanding our shortcomings.

In that connection a suppliant declares (perhaps hyperbolically), "I have anticipated the twilight and cried for help as I waited for your word" (Ps 119:147). The natural time for prayer is the moment when the morning or evening sacrifice was due ("twilight" might suggest the transition from dark to light or from light to dark), though the urgency of a situation might make it impossible to wait for that. The middle of the day is the next classic time to pray that marks a person seriously committed to Yhwh (Dan 6; cf. Ps. 55:17 [MT

---

[46]Cf. Balentine, *Prayer in the Hebrew Bible*, pp. 80-88.
[47]See the introduction to §2.5, and §2.5 "Whole Offering and Grain Offering."
[48]Milgrom, *Leviticus 1–16*, p. 238.

18]?). Hyperbolically again, perhaps, someone might speak in terms of getting up in the middle of the night to pray or of praising Yhwh seven times a day (Ps 119:62, 164). Indeed, "my eyes have anticipated the watches, murmuring about your statement" (Ps 119:148). The night watches are the night's divisions as these govern the changes between lookouts. The suppliant resembles a sentry arriving for duty early, so keen to be on watch, or this might be another reference to someone itching for the last watch of the night to end, the dawn moment for the morning offering. The community waits and longs for Yhwh's promises to be fulfilled; metaphorically, at least, but maybe also literally, it yearns for Yhwh in the night, and gets up early for the morning worship time (*šāḥar*) to pray that Yhwh will implement those promises (Is 26:8-9).

3.2 Protest

Communication, conversation asking—these are temperate and calm notions. But much prayer in the First Testament is neither temperate nor calm. It involves confronting, calling out, summoning, crying out, asking questions, asking for grace and attention and encounter, challenging, and claiming.

Confronting

In the First Testament prayer commonly issues out of crises, and it protests before God at the trouble these have brought. Joshua says, "Oh, Lord Yhwh, why have you actually brought this people across the Jordan to give it into the hand of the Amorites," and goes on to point out the disrepute that this will bring on Yhwh (Josh 7:7-9). Israel together ask, "Why has this happened, Yhwh, God of Israel, so that today one clan is missing from Israel?" (Judg 21:3). Of course these two protests come unstuck.[49] But half the Psalms are such prayers arising out of crises, so that "the laments of scripture," as such psalms are conventionally called, "are the preeminent petitionary prayer of the Old Testament."[50] Such prayer means "disclosures of hurt and articulations of hope."[51]

"Protests" is a better description than laments. Laments suggest an acceptance of victim status. Protests do not accept. Laments need not be addressed to anyone in particular; they constitute the suffering person letting off steam. Protests are addressed to someone; they are designed to get a person with power to use their power to change a situation.[52] We respond to suffering,

---

[49]See §3.6 "Confession and Protest."

[50]Miller, *Way of the Lord*, p. 203.

[51]Walter Brueggemann, *Old Testament Theology: Essays on Structure, Theme, and Text* (Minneapolis: Fortress, 1992), p. 45.

[52]Cf. ibid., p. 29.

death and holocaust not by atheism or agnosticism but by "protest theism."[53] "Israel is incapable of resignation. Resignation would be to give up finally on Yahweh and on Yahweh's commitment to Israel. This Israel will not do, even if Yahweh gives hints of such abandonment."[54]

The protests in the Psalter are in fact the main way the First Testament handles the question of theodicy. This "is not a speculative question for armchair philosophy but a life-and-death question of marginalized people in the struggle to survive." Further, it is not merely a question for discussion between people but a question addressed to God—with some paradox, because the one thus addressed as if accessible is the one who has hidden. And it is a question that demands an active and not a theoretical response.[55] In the First Testament there are many people who pray and there are many model prayers, but the only people who talk about prayer are Job's friends, who never actually pray.[56]

"Israel is profoundly aware of the incongruity between the core claims of covenant faith and the lived experience of its life."[57] There is less tension than we might reckon between the obligation to covenant submission and the assumption that we are free to protest Yhwh's action. Submission to Yhwh means doing what Yhwh commands, and Yhwh does not command shutting up when we feel let down. Protest is a paradoxical form of submission. It means declining to turn away from Yhwh or turn to other deities or give in to false views of Yhwh. To protest does not (or need not) mean one "takes a posture of autonomy."[58] In human relationships, where a relationship has broken down or the other person has attacked you, it is possible to appeal to someone else to mediate between you or support you. In a polytheistic context, where you suspect that one god has abandoned you or attacked you, it is possible to do the same.[59] Christians do this when they think of the wrathful God being against them but of Jesus taking their side. Israelites know that Yhwh is the only God and that we have no such avenues open. We cannot split the wrathful God and the loving God. We have to confront the one God.[60]

---

[53]G. Tom Milazzo, *The Protest and the Silence* (Minneapolis: Fortress, 1992), p. 161.

[54]Brueggemann, *Theology of the Old Testament*, p. 436.

[55]Richard Bauckham, *The Bible in Politics* (London: SPCK/Louisville: Westminster John Knox, 1989), pp. 57-58.

[56]Cf. Dale Patrick, "Job's Address of God," *ZAW* 91 (1979): 268-82; see p. 269; Erhard S. Gerstenberger, *Der bittende Mensch* (Neukirchen: Neukirchener, 1980), p. 157; cf. Balentine, *Prayer in the Hebrew Bible*, p. 169.

[57]Brueggemann, *Theology of the Old Testament*, p. 378 (the sentence is italicized).

[58]Brueggemann, *Theology of the Old Testament*, p. 401.

[59]Paul Sanders notes how the possibility that one may have been treated capriciously by a god other than the one to whom one is praying is one of the few differences between the prayers of the Psalms and the prayers of Mursili ("*Argumenta ad Deum* in the Plague Prayers of Mursili II and in the Book of Psalms," in *Psalms and Prayers*, pp. 181-207).

[60]See Patrick and Diable, "Persuading the One and Only God to Intervene."

Calling Out

The Psalter's first two prayer psalms nuance the understanding of prayer as involving communication or conversation. Both understand prayer to involve our calling and Yhwh's answering (Ps 3:4 [MT 5]; 4:1 [MT 2]). The very first prayer psalm begins with the invocation "Yhwh" (Ps 3:1 [MT 2]): addressing God by name is a key feature of First Testament prayer, and it is no coincidence that the name Yhwh appears most frequently here in the First Testament. Further, it shows that in prayer we do not have to get to God via some intermediary or to get God in the right mood. While the First Testament can see Yhwh as behaving like a distant God, this implies not that God is being inaccessible but that God is not taking action. Even then, one can be in touch with God, and protesting about this noninvolvement. "Old Testament prayer is part of a lived, not merely striven after, community with God, a community that was graciously given and that even the worshiper who considered himself or herself abandoned by God (Ps. 22:2) could still call upon."[61] There is admittedly some paradox about addressing Yhwh as if Yhwh's face was turned away. That implies Yhwh is not looking or listening, so how can I address Yhwh? The assumption that I can do so presupposes an aspect of First Testament ways of thinking about such looking and listening. For God and for us, it relates directly to action. The verb *šāma‛* means "obey" as well as "listen," and God's face shining implies that God blesses. Talk of ignoring or hiding the face implies Yhwh has allowed to develop a disjunction or short-circuiting within Yhwh's seeing and hearing. In some sense Yhwh may see and know, and be aware of the suppliant's plea, but Yhwh is not behaving as if this is so.[62]

It is important that prayer is not just us talking to ourselves or just us talking to God because an integral aspect of prayer is our urgently calling on Yhwh for help; such a cry is no use unless it receives an answer. "Call" and "answer" summarize a key aspect to life with God in the First Testament and epitomize the dynamically personal nature of God's relationship with Israel. There is a call or summons from God to which the people or an individual are to respond; there is also a call or summons from the people or an individual to God, to which God is to respond. Sometimes God is disappointed (as the prophets show) and sometimes the people or the individual are disappointed (as the Psalms show), but this does not make either side finally lose faith in the dynamic of this relationship.

Calling out (*qārā᾽*) is different from talking inside our head, from merely

---

[61]Horst Dietrich Preuss, *Old Testament Theology*, 2 vols. (Louisville: Westminster John Knox, 1995/Edinburgh: T & T Clark, 1996), 2:247, 250.
[62]See further §3.4 "Protesting and Believing."

speaking and from much invocation as Christian worship practices it. Psalm 3 underlines that by nuancing the verb: literally, "[with] my voice to Yhwh I call out." There is urgency about this calling. When I really need to get someone to hear, I call out. Indeed, the prayer needs to be loud enough for Yhwh to hear, "from his holy mountain" (Ps 3:4 [MT 5]). The person praying knows that Yhwh is everywhere; Yhwh fills heaven and earth (Jer 23:24). Yet that was a bit too general to be totally satisfying, and Yhwh acceded to David and Solomon's requests to be especially present in the sanctuary. You could be sure to meet with Yhwh there. But while this was fine if you had access to it (cf. Ps 43:3-4), usually when you need Yhwh to rescue you from people's attacks, you are somewhere else, so you need to call out loud so that Yhwh can hear in the sanctuary. Both your inner need to call out with urgency because of the pressure of your situation, and your awareness that you have to get the attention of Yhwh in the sanctuary, make you call out loudly.

Further, in another sense Yhwh's regular location, the palace where the heavenly cabinet meets and considers pleas brought to it, is in the heavens; it is from there that Yhwh looks, listens and responds to people (e.g., Ps 33:13-19). So on one hand, "I can come to your house," the earthly sanctuary; on the other, in reverence for you "I bow low to your holy palace" in the heavens, to which I look as one who is on earth (Ps 5:7 [MT 8]). I call out to Yhwh in both locations. Yhwh is seated on Zion as the object of Israel's worship; Yhwh is seated in the heavens in the cabinet where decisions get taken for the nations (Ps 9:7, 11 [MT 8, 12]). That will give further reason for calling aloud. Not only is it a long way away; you have to get your item onto that meeting's agenda and given priority there.

Summoning

There is another aspect to the boldness of this calling. In Psalm 3 and Psalm 4 the suppliant "calls to Yhwh," a common expression. And one may call by day and by night: in other words, continually. The reason for doing so would be that one gets no answer (e.g., Ps 22:2 [MT 3]). Day and night calling goes along with day and night weeping (Ps 42:3 [MT 4]). Both reflect a day and night pressure of Yhwh's hand on a person (Ps 32:4).

But many psalms omit the "to." People simply "call Yhwh": "On the day when I am in trouble, I call you, because you answer me" (Ps 86:7; cf. 17:6). It is a blunt and peremptory invocation. Yhwh is often the subject of this verb, when summoning a servant to go off to another land (Is 41:8-9); Yhwh's call is no gentle inquiry about whether a certain vocation might suit him. It is a master's command to a servant. In the Psalms, Yhwh can be the object of this verb. A suppliant may call in this forthright fashion, because Yhwh invites it, like a professor inviting a student to call when they are in difficulty with their paper: "Call me on the day of trouble" (Ps 50:15). "He calls me and I answer him; I am with him in trouble" (Ps 91:15). "Yhwh is near to all who call him, to all who call him with truthfulness" (Ps 145:18). Such direct calling is a response to Yhwh. "This was a weak man who called, and Yhwh listened, and delivered him from his troubles"; therefore the weak should listen to this testimony, and rejoice (Ps 34:2, 6 [MT 3, 7]).

Psalm 12 expresses urgency and boldness in a different way by the starkness of its opening: "Deliver, Yhwh!" Only Psalm 69 parallels this direct beginning, though it is tempered in Psalm 12 by the use of the slightly polite form of the imperative.[63] "Here are the two best prayers I know: 'Help me, help me, help me,' and 'Thank you, thank you, thank you.'"[64] Psalm 79 begins with another form of abruptness: "God, the nations came into your possession."

Given that talking to an earthly king about things that concern us sometimes involves risk (e.g., Neh 2; Esther 4–5), it might seem that talking to the heavenly King requires much more observance of convention, but apparently this is not so. When people call out to God, they are acting in the same way as they do when urgent need makes them call out to their king with audacity. They let their urgent need compel them to overcome the deterrent of the vast difference in status and power between them and the king in order to interrupt him and press their urgent need on him (e.g., 1 Kings 20:35-43; 2 Kings 6:24-31).[65] And one may not only call out during the day, when the king expects to hear such appeals, but also by night (Ps 77:1-2 [MT 2-3]), given that one's need does not go away just because the sun has gone down.

Prayer does not have to express the niceties. It does not have to observe social or liturgical or theological proprieties. In Psalm 12 the point that is made clear by the psalm's opening recurs at its close. When Yhwh declares the intention to act, the suppliant responds with a declaration of trust in Yhwh's word; he does not just say "Thank you, thank you, thank you" but urges, "Come on then, because the situation is what it is, and nothing has changed yet."[66]

The Psalter often "echoes the people of the covenant trembling for its pres-

---

[63]As usual, that is, the form is *hôšīʿâ* with the sufformative rather than the bare *hôšaʿ* which occurs only in Ps 86:2 (though there the suppliant uses a sufformative form in the previous colon, and follows this verb by the self-description "your servant") and Jer 31:7 (where Yhwh commissions use of the straight short form).

[64]Anne Lamott, *Traveling Mercies* (New York: Pantheon, 1999), p. 82. Seeing these as elemental forms of human communication, John D. Witvliet adds "I love you" and "I'm sorry" (*The Biblical Psalms in Christian Worship* [Grand Rapids/Cambridge: Eerdmans, 2007], p. 11).

[65]Cf. Boyce, *Cry to God in the Old Testament*, p. 40.

[66]The EVV's understanding, which reads the penultimate line as a declaration of confidence that Yhwh *will* act, is less likely in the context, but even if that is right, the last line still makes the confrontational point.

ervation in final extremity before its all-powerful enemies. The Christian community always has good reason to see itself in this people and to take on its own lips the words of its helpless sighing, the cries which it utters from the depths of its need."[67]

Crying Out

The urgency in such a call, and its basis, can be suggested by means of verbs meaning "cry out." Among general words for prayer, one might distinguish between function words, process words and action words.[68] Function words such as *say, answer, declare* and *recount* (*'āmar, 'ānâ, nāgad* hiphil, *sāpar* piel) characteristically have an object, the content of the speaking. Process words such as *ask, seek from* and *have recourse to* (*šā'al, dāraš, bāqaš* piel) also have an object, but it is the person addressed or the thing sought. Action words such as *fall, prostrate oneself, kneel* and *pour out* (*nāpal, kāna'* niphal, *kāra',* *šāpak* hitpael) denote nonvocal activity that accompanies the verbal prayer. Words for "cry" are then rather different from any of these. They are more common than "ask" with reference to prayer, which usually refers to seeking direction or instruction.[69] Prayer is often too urgent to be mere "asking." The verbs *rānan* and *ānah* (niphal) suggest inarticulate exclamation and intense volume; *śiah* is a nearer equivalent to "lament"; *zā'aq/ṣā'aq* and *šāwa'* (piel) suggest brief articulation and emotional intensity; *qārā'* also suggests extended articulations.[70]

Whereas *call* is peremptory and may presuppose a position of power (so that Yhwh is its natural subject), *cry out* is an appeal issuing from a position of weakness and helplessness. Actually, it seems that "prayer has been ordained only for the helpless. It is the last resort of the helpless. Indeed, the very last way out. We try everything before we finally resort to prayer. . . . We offer many and beautiful prayers, both privately and publicly, without helplessness as the impelling power. But I am not at all positive that this is prayer."[71]

One verb meaning "cry out," *šāwa'* (piel), nicely resembles the verb "deliver," *yāša'.* It suggests a cry for help. Yhwh "implements his favor for the people who revere him, listens to their cry for help [*saw'ātām*] and delivers them [*yôšî'ēm*]" (Ps 145:19). Another, *ṣā'aq/zā'aq*, is the verb for the cry of the oppressed people in Sodom and the oppressed Israelites in Egypt; the related nouns come in Genesis 18:20-21; Exodus 3:7, 9. The story of the exodus begins with this cry; that is how fundamental is this cry to Israel's relationship with

---

[67]Karl Barth, *Church Dogmatics* (Edinburgh: T & T Clark, 1967), IV/2:671.
[68]So Boyce, *Cry to God in the Old Testament*, pp. 9-16.
[69]Miller, *They Cried to the Lord*, p. 35.
[70]Boyce, *Cry to God in the Old Testament*, pp. 20-21.
[71]Otto Hallesby, *Prayer* (London: Inter-Varsity Fellowship, 1959), p. 11.

God.[72] One reason "why the so-called Old Testament is in the one book of the Scriptures is that we may learn to confess and speak out our pain before the face of God."[73] Admittedly, a cry, like speech, may not amount to a prayer. When "the Israelites groaned because of their servitude and cried out, and their cry for help because of their servitude went up to God" (Ex 2:23) and God heard their cry, Exodus does not say that it was addressed to God; perhaps it was simply a cry of pain. But it reached God's ears.

First Testament prayers do not usually address God as Father, though this is more a formal than a substantial point. The First Testament is aware of this image for God, and when it does speak of God as Father, it is more inclined than is the New Testament to note the image's encouraging significance (e.g., Ps 103:13).[74] In the New Testament the Father is first the Father of our Lord Jesus Christ; for the First Testament, calling on God by name as Yhwh is equivalent to calling on God as Father, and the extraordinary freedom of the prayers in the Psalms shows that people prayed with the freedom and confidence of children talking to their father (as is reflected in the way these prayers often scandalize Christians). They illustrate how "to call upon him is to take up their position by him, to take him at his word that he is our Father and we are his children."[75] So prayer addresses Yhwh by name, "Yhwh," "Yhwh," "Yhwh" (Ps 9:19 [MT 20]–10:1). It is a grievous irony that Israel's first great leader asked to know God's name and was told it, and that Israelites were therefore consistently able to address Yhwh by name, but that the successors of First Testament Israel in the Jewish and Christian communities decline to do so.

Asking Questions

Psalm 13:1-2 [MT 2-3] introduces another form of urgency and directness in prayer, the asking of questions: "How long, Yhwh? Are you going to ignore me forever? How long are you going to hide your face from me? How long? . . . How long?" Both the particle and the verbs play a part. The question is rhetorical, though this is not to imply that it does not look for an answer. But an answer along the lines of (say) "two years" would not make the suppliant say, "Oh, fine, thanks for the clarification." "How long" means "Stop, and stop now" (cf. Ps 6:3 [MT 4]; 35:17; 79:5; 80:4 [MT 5]; 89:46 [MT 47]; 94:3), and the answer it looks for is "Okay." The verbs in Psalm 13:1-2 [MT 2-3] are confrontationally bold; it is quite something to accuse God of ignoring and turning the

---

[72]Boyce, *Cry to God in the Old Testament*, pp. 47-70.
[73]Kornelis H. Miskotte, *When the Gods Are Silent* (London: Collins/New York: Harper, 1967), p. 246.
[74]Cf. Barth, *Christian Life*, pp. 59-60.
[75]Barth, *Christian Life*, p. 85.

face. When bad things happen to good people, we would rather not think that this might be because Yhwh is deliberately looking the other way. The psalm not merely envisages but presupposes that this is so and rhetorically gives Yhwh no way of denying the fact. Yhwh can only reply to the question on the basis of acknowledging having ignored and turned away. If Yhwh has some other explanation of what is going on, the suppliant might reckon, this will be fine; but let us have it. The rhetoric is designed one way or another to sting Yhwh into speech and action.

"How long, Yhwh, have I been crying for help, and you do not listen?" Habakkuk asks, and then goes on, "Why do you make me see waywardness and look at wrongdoing?" (Hab 1:2-3; cf. 1:13). Jeremiah similarly asks, "How long will the land languish, the grass in all the countryside wither," and also "Why does the way of the faithless succeed, why do all the people who act perfidiously thrive?" (Jer 12:1-4). Job 21:7 asks the same question; "it is ostensibly a question about 'the wicked,' but clearly it is posed as a question about Yahweh."[76] It is open to a number of frightening possible answers. Because Yhwh does not care about the distinction between faithlessness and faithfulness? Because Yhwh cannot or does not exercise authority and take decisions in the world? These are the two questions raised by Abraham in Genesis 18:25. Psalm 62:11-12 [MT 12-13] says that power and commitment ($\dot{o}z$ and $\dot{h}esed$) belong to Yhwh. Is this true?

Psalm 74:10-11 likewise moves from "How long shall the foe scoff, God— shall the enemy revile your name permanently?" to "Why do you turn back your hand, yes, withholding your right hand from the midst of your garments?" This *why* is the Psalms' other recurrent rhetorical question. "Why do you stand far off, Yhwh, why do you hide?" (Ps 10:1). "Why have you abandoned me?" (Ps 22:1 [MT 2]; cf. 43:2; 44:23-24 [MT 24-25]; 74:1; 88:14 [MT 15]). Verbs such as *hide* and *abandon* appear with both these interrogative particles. The particle removes an ambiguity. *How long* allows for the possibility that the turning away was deserved, with the protest just implying that it is unjustifiably prolonged. *Why* sounds as if it allows for the possibility that the turning away was deserved, but actually it excludes it. The implication of the *why* is, "There is no justification for your abandoning me, and therefore I call on you to come back to me, and now." The question *why* might provoke an answer in terms not only of "for what cause?" but of "to what end?" But like *how long*, it is characteristically not merely or not at all a request for information but simply a protest.[77] If Job had been given the answer to his *why* along the lines of revealing what we know from Job 1–2, it is again not clear that he would have

---

[76]Brueggemann, *Theology of the Old Testament*, pp. 386-87.
[77]Cf. Milazzo, *Protest and the Silence*, p. 43.

said, "Oh, that's okay, then." And when Yhwh eventually does turn him round, this does not involve answering that question but explicitly declining to do so, even though the question has an answer. Job is "a failed attempt to call God to account."[78]

A third interrogative particle present in these protests is *where*.[79] "Where are your former acts of commitment, my Lord, which you promised David by your truthfulness?" (Ps 89:49 [MT 50]). How can Yhwh claim that recent events are in keeping with those commitments? More often, suppliants report the taunt, "Where is your God" (Ps 42:3; 79:10; 115:2); much of its force lies in the way it externalizes the question that occupies the suppliants' own spirit.

A further telling question simply involves an interrogative prefix and by its nature cannot be addressed to Yhwh: "Is Yhwh in our midst or not?" (Ex 17:7). "Is it forever that my Lord will spurn, will he never again delight? Has his commitment permanently ceased to exist, his word failed for all time? Has God put showing grace out of mind, or has he shut off his compassion in anger?" (Ps 77:7-9 [MT 8-10]). Formally, such words themselves do not address Yhwh; yet they are recalling *to Yhwh* the way the suppliant has been thinking and the question that needs a response.

Asking for Grace and Pleading

Psalms often appeal to Yhwh to be gracious (*ḥānan*; e.g., Ps 4:1 [MT 2]; 6:2 [MT 3]; 56:1 [MT 2]). It is the only thing that Psalm 123 appeals for; everything else will flow from that. Grace or favor is the attitude someone in power shows to someone in a lower position who has no grounds for making a claim on them, no basis for pleading on the basis of deserve or of existent commitments or relationships or for appealing to the person's own interests. In that circumstance all one can do is ask for undeserved favor or grace. As a foreigner Ruth has no claim on the people of Bethlehem or specifically on Boaz; she does not belong to the body of servants for whom he has responsibility. All she can hope for is that she will find grace or favor with someone, and subsequently all she can do is express amazement that she has found grace or favor with Boaz (Ruth 2:2, 10, 13), in keeping with the commendations of Proverbs (Prov 14:21, 31; 19:17; 28:8—the verb *ḥānan*).

While the Psalms use this verb, they do not use the noun *ḥēn* to refer to God's grace, but they do use the noun *tĕḥinnâ* or the intensive plural nouns *taḥănûnîm* and *taḥănûnôt* to describe their prayers, which constitute appeals to God's grace, appeals for God to be gracious (e.g., Ps 6:9 [MT 10]; 28:2, 6; 55:1 [MT 2]; 86:6). Translations often use words such as *supplication* or *plea*, and translate

---

[78]Jeremy Young, *The Violence of God and the War on Terror* (London: Darton, Longman & Todd, 2007/New York: Seabury, 2008), p. 77.

[79]Cf. Brueggemann, *Theology of the Old Testament*, pp. 321-23.

the verb *be merciful*, which point to the position of the person praying as like that of someone throwing themselves on someone else's mercy. Showing favor or grace and having mercy or pity or compassion are closely related (see Job 19:21; Lam 4:16). Grace is the attitude that lies at the back of mercy and commitment, the attitude that shows favor to someone when they have no deserve, when the one who shows favor has nothing to get out of it.

Perhaps these words implicitly appeal to an aspect of Yhwh's self-revelation, as one who is "compassionate and gracious" (Ex 34:6), the self-revelation to which First Testament prayers often appeal (e.g., Neh 9:17, 31; Ps 86:15; 103:8). The actual verb *be gracious* links more directly with the earlier declaration to Moses, "I will be gracious to whomever I will be gracious" (Ex 33:19). Moses has appealed four times to Yhwh's grace, and Yhwh has agreed that he is the object of Yhwh's grace (Ex 33:12-17). Prayer therefore follows Moses' example in appealing to this aspect of Yhwh's character. The "whomever" is not a way of limiting Yhwh's graciousness but of emphasizing the breadth of its reach. That encourages prayer. On the other hand, the suppliant would have to be aware that this *whomever* is followed by a *but*. On the basis of the gracious favor Yhwh has granted in the past, Moses looks for more gracious favor now, and in some sense Yhwh grants this, but in some other sense refuses it; "you cannot see my face." Appealing to grace has risk about it, because the nature of grace is that it lies in the discretion of the giver. It cannot actually be claimed. As a model for understanding our relationship with God, then, it complements the appeal to our status as servants, which implies that God does have obligations toward us.

Etymologically, at least, the word that more directly designates prayer as a "plea" is *těpillâ* (e.g., Ps 4:1 [MT 2]; 6:9 [MT 10]). The verb meaning "plead" (*pālal* hitpael), commonly translated "pray," has a background in legal procedures and thus suggests pleading with a court (cf. 1 Sam 2:25). The community court's business is to protect the weak and needy from people who could take advantage of them, and in prayer people are casting themselves in their weakness on Yhwh the judge who chairs the heavenly court. It is my king with whom I plead (Ps 5:2 [MT 3]).[80] Rarer than this but with related significance is *pāgaʿ*, which signifies meeting with someone to ask for something for oneself or for someone else, intervening or interceding for them (Gen 23:8; cf. the hiphil in Jer 15:11); this image can then be applied to interceding with God (Job 21:15; Jer 7:16; 27:18; cf. the hiphil in Is 53:12)

We make our plea "before Yhwh," more literally "to Yhwh's face." We ask Yhwh not to hide that face, not to turn the other way or to push "your ser-

---

[80]On *těpillâ* and *pālal*, see *HALOT*; contrast E. A. Speiser's view that their basic idea is assessment ("The Stem *pll* in Hebrew," *JBL* 82 [1963]: 301-6).

vant" aside, but rather to be prepared to take us in when everyone else (even our parents) have abandoned us (Ps 27:4, 8-10). The reference to Yhwh's face again suggests that prayer involves coming to the King's court and seeking a personal audience, especially in a situation where I am falsely accused and in danger of my life (Ps 27:11-12). We ask and inquire (*šāʾal, bāqaš* piel) of Yhwh's face. The verbs suggest asking *for* something, such as protection, and also asking *about* something, about how to go about seeking protection or seeking victory. We need to be instructed in Yhwh's way and led on a level path (Ps 27:11). It is easy to imagine that the king would have far more important priorities than listening to some ordinary person with their trivial problem. The psalm assumes that we can come with confidence to the heavenly King and reckon we will be given a hearing. "Unless I believed in seeing good from Yhwh in the land of the living . . ." (Ps 27:13). "There is something wistful, threatening, and defiantly faithful about this congery of statement and allusion."[81]

Asking to Be Heard and Seen and Thought About

My first need in prayer is to be listened to. Indeed, all Psalm 130 asks for is Yhwh's attention. It can be assumed that everything else will then follow.

The number of different words for this appeal links with that.[82] I pray, "Attend to my words, Yhwh, consider, . . . give ear" (Ps 5:1-2 [MT 2-3]). "Listen . . . attend . . . give ear," Psalm 17 begins. Whereas some psalms are direct and concrete regarding what they ultimately want from Yhwh, and confrontational in how they demand it, this one begins more deferentially, with three imperative verbs all ending in the polite suformative –*â*, followed by a deferential jussive, "May my decision come from your presence." On the other hand, when resuming the plea, the suppliant declares, "I myself call you" (not "call to you"), and proceeds with the regular pithy imperatives in urging, "extend your ear, listen" (Ps 17:6). "Do not be deaf toward me, lest you keep silence toward me" (Ps 28:1; cf. 109:1). If God declines to keep silence, this means God speaks in the court on the suppliant's behalf, or commissions someone to take action, or shouts in the course of taking action in person. The suppliant needs listening, but then speech.

"Give ear to my plea, God, do not hide from my prayer for grace; pay heed to me, answer me" (Ps 55:1-2 [MT 2-3]). Tellingly, the second verb usually refers to hiding from other people instead of taking action to help them (e.g., Is 58:7).

---

[81]David R. Blumenthal, *Facing the Abusing God* (Louisville: Westminster John Knox, 1993), p. 184.

[82]Cf. Anneli Aejmelaeus's comments in Aejmelaeus, *The Traditional Prayer in the Psalms*; Ludwig Schmidt, *Literarische Studien zur Josephgeschichte*, BZAW 167 (Berlin/New York: de Gruyter, 1986), pp. 26-29.

Psalm 12 brings the community's grim moral state to Yhwh's attention, but when Yhwh responds, it is "because of the devastation of the weak, because of the groaning of the needy" (Ps 12:5 [MT 6]). Yhwh has not merely listened to the suppliant's appeal but has listened to the moan of the needy themselves; maybe the suppliant is among them, but Yhwh has been listening to *them* (plural), and apparently it is their devastation that Yhwh has been looking at. There is no necessary implication that they have been looking to Yhwh or groaning in prayer; maybe they were just groaning, as in Exodus 2:24. But provoked by the suppliant, Yhwh listened. When Israel is hurt, it says so; it voices hurt in a bold act of self-assertion. To voice hurt is already in itself to imply hope, that things could be different ("It's not the despair I can't stand, it's the hope");[83] if one cannot envisage this, one buries the hurt. Israel voices hurt in the conviction that there is someone who listens. The community has "a bold voice for hurt"; Yhwh has "an attentive ear for hurt."[84]

Prayer appeals to Yhwh's eyes as well as Yhwh's ears. "Be gracious to me, Yhwh; look at my weakness" (Ps 9:13 [MT 14]). "Your eyes must see what is righteous" (Ps 17:2), what needs doing. After all, in the past "you looked"; it is in fact characteristic of Yhwh to "pay attention to troublemaking and aggression" (Ps 10:14). "Yhwh is faithful. . . . His face beholds the upright person" (Ps 11:7 [MT 8]). More broadly, "Yhwh in his holy palace, Yhwh whose throne is in the heavens—his eyes behold, his gaze examines, human beings"; the next line makes explicit that this includes both faithful and faithless (Ps 11:4-5 [MT 5-6]). The majestic position of Yhwh enthroned in the heavens puts Yhwh in a position of exaltedness. Does it make Yhwh remote, as the king can be in his palace at the height of the city exalted above ordinary people? No, Yhwh not only looks but beholds and examines, looking inside doors and hearts so as to know who really are the faithful and who the faithless. "Do give ear to my cry for help; do not be silent at my tears" (Ps 39:12 [MT 13]). "It is a Rabbinic saying that there are three kinds of supplication, each superior to the other; prayer, crying, and tears. Prayer is made in silence, crying with a loud voice, but tears surpass all. 'There is no door through which tears do not pass,' and, 'The gates of tears are never locked.' "[85]

Prayer appeals to Yhwh's mind or memory. "Be mindful for David; do not turn away the face of your anointed" (Ps 132:1, 10). The king comes before Yhwh in the way an ordinary person comes before the king. The suppliant wants the heavenly King not to turn him away, the plea unheeded, but to grant it, and appeals to Yhwh to take David's commitment into account as

---

[83]I paraphrase a line from the John Cleese movie *Clockwise*.
[84]Brueggemann, *Old Testament Theology: Essays on Structure, Theme, and Text*, pp. 47, 51.
[85]A. F. Kirkpatrick, *The Book of Psalms* (Cambridge: Cambridge University Press, 1910), pp. 206-7; cf. *t. Berakot* 32b.

motivation for doing so. If Yhwh is thus mindful, everything else will follow. In Psalm 137, the only plea is for Yhwh to be mindful of Edom.[86]

Psalm 142 tries four ways of winning Yhwh's attention and response. It begins, "With my voice I will cry out to Yhwh": that is, it talks about the way the suppliant intends to pray. It does not make clear who it is addressing (the self? other people in the sanctuary?), but it is certainly not addressing Yhwh. Yet Yhwh can overhear this statement, and when we overhear something not addressed to us, this can affect us more than hearing something directly addressed to us. It goes on, "When my spirit faints away within me, you yourself know my path." On that basis, the suppliant can draw Yhwh's attention to people's plotting and ask, "Look at my right hand and see: for me there is no one who recognizes me." The psalm talks directly to Yhwh about how things are. It assumes that Yhwh knows, but talking about these things brings them to Yhwh's attention and may make it possible to get them to the top of Yhwh's agenda. Third, the psalm urges Yhwh to "attend" on the basis of Yhwh's being the only "refuge" the suppliant has. Fourth, in urging Yhwh actually to act, to rescue and bring release, it points out how this will bring Yhwh glory.

Asking for Encounter with Yhwh

The repeated "How long" in Psalm 13:1-2 [MT 2-3] introduces the three directions of a prayer's protest. "How long are you to hide your face from me? How long am I to . . . lay up sorrow in my heart through the day? How long is my enemy to stand high over me?" The pain out of which prayer comes is a pain in relation to myself and how I feel, in relation to other people and their action, and in relation to Yhwh and Yhwh's abandonment.

Living in God's presence is like living in another human being's presence. I live many hours in my wife's presence, but sometimes I am focusing on her, sometimes I am rightly (or wrongly) focusing on something else, sometimes I am doing something for her, sometimes we are doing something together but focusing on that other thing, sometimes I am physically away from her and may then think of her and in a sense be with her (like Paul in 1 Cor 5:3). The notion of living in God's presence is similar. Sometimes I am focusing on God, sometimes rightly focusing on other things, but still in God's presence, sometimes I am asking God to do something for me, and God does, and God is present with me in a more dynamic sense. Sometimes God moves away from me in the sense of not protecting me or not acting on my behalf; sometimes I move away from God in the sense of failing to walk in God's way, to walk with God, to do the right thing. Living in relation to God's presence is a dynamic, multifaceted business.

---

[86]See further §3.5 "Claiming Yhwh's Promise."

Job wants to meet with God, to be in the presence of God, but he does not merely want a sense of being in God's presence so that this comforts him in his suffering. The Psalms too are not concerned with whether we feel God is there. They know God is there; what they are concerned about is not God's felt presence but God's actual activity. Job wants Yhwh to remove the hand that is bringing suffering for him and to summon him so that Job can respond, or to let Job speak in such a way that God can reply (Job 13:22-23). "Come on then," says Job, "let's have a list of the offenses that would justify what you are doing to me." The purpose of encounter is confrontation and cross-questioning. Job is desperate for such an encounter. He longs to know how to bring about such a meeting so as to lay out his case before Yhwh as he might before a member of the community who has done wrong to him, and to know how Yhwh will answer, even though he recognizes that it is a terrifying idea to be in the presence of the powerful, sovereign, life-giving but death-dealing El Shadday. He knows he has not done wrong. But wherever he looks, east or west, north or south, he cannot get the meeting with Yhwh that would enable him to argue this. Yhwh evades him (Job 23:1-17). If only he had someone to listen to his case! If only Shadday would respond to him and put into writing the case against him! He would then be able to give an account of his behavior (Job 31:35-37).

Sarah afflicts Hagar (the verb is ʿānâ piel, the verb used to describe Egypt's treatment of the Israelites in Ex 1:11-12), and Hagar flees from her (as the Israelite will flee from Egypt; Ex 14:5) (Gen 16). Yhwh's aide finds her and asks, "Where have you come from and where are you going?" Hagar is to stick with Abraham and Sarah, to be the mother of countless offspring, and she is to call her son Ishmael, "God listens," because Yhwh has listened to her affliction. "Yhwh decide between you and me," Sarah had said. Like a father, Yhwh perhaps declines to do so, but Yhwh has certainly not decided against Hagar. And in light of her experience, she herself says, "You are El-roi," the God of my seeing, the God I have seen, the God who saw me; it is an act of confession whereby Hagar becomes a theologian, a woman who names God.[87] Yhwh's actual listening becomes more explicit later (Gen 21:8-19). Once more it involves Yhwh mediating in what may seem an odd way between Sarah and Abraham and Ishmael, letting Abraham agree to Sarah's desire to throw Hagar out, though doing so for different reasons from Sarah's; Yhwh intends that Isaac be the son through whom the promise is fulfilled. Once more it involves Yhwh in looking for Hagar in the wilderness, or rather in listening to Ishmael's cry and providing the sustenance that will ensure the two of them survive to see their own promise fulfilled.

---

[87]Phyllis Trible, *Texts of Terror* (Philadelphia: Fortress, 1984), p. 18.

Disjointedness

Prayer can accommodate the widest range of attitudes on the part of people in need. Some psalms manifest a quiet trust in Yhwh in contexts of trouble and pressure. Some express the feelings of people in depths of distress and distraction, of desperation and wretchedness. In the most extreme example, Psalm 88 begins by describing Yhwh as (literally) "the God of my deliverance," that is, "my God who delivers," but this is also its last note of hope, and the psalm constitutes a vast questioning of whether this description of Yhwh is true or why experience does not correspond to its declaration. It goes on to ask that its plea may meet with Yhwh's sight and attention, but otherwise the entirety of its twenty lines is given to a pained and protesting howl of protest; it has already implied in its first line that the suppliant's day and night crying out has met with no response. In some sense the suppliant's plea has come before Yhwh, but all the evidence suggests that Yhwh has taken no notice of it, and in this sense it has not reached Yhwh at all. Yhwh is thinking about something else. Listen to the noise, listen to the pain, the psalm begs.

It is simply an exposition of the awfulness of the suppliant's experience, couched in the classic three directions, though in a distinctive way. "My whole person is full of trouble. . . . I have come to count with people who go down to the Pit; I have become like a man who is without strength. . . . I have been weak and dying since youth." "You have put me in the deepest Pit. . . . With all your breakers you have afflicted me. . . . Why, Yhwh, do you spurn me, hide your face from me?" But the third-person verbs that would have completed the sequence are overwhelmed by more second-person verbs: "You have put my friends at a distance from me; you have made me a great abomination to them. . . . You have put loved one and neighbor at a distance from me; my acquaintances darkness." The psalm thus ends with disjointedness and incoherence. Ancient or modern alternative forms of the text offer smoother endings, but MT suggests the disjointedness of the experience to which the psalm testifies and from which the suppliant has gained no relief, no order, no closure. It is fortunate that the music to which one prays protest psalms has the capacity to express the same disharmony and reflect the same lack of closure, though unfortunate that in practice the music to which we actually pray the protest psalms rarely does so.[88]

It is no coincidence that there is no psalm more dominated by death than Psalm 88. Initially the suppliant is simply near death. "My life has arrived at Sheol." I am at death's door, as we say. "I have come to count with people who go down to the Pit." People see me as someone who is on the way out. "I have

---

[88]Cf. the general argument of the feminist theology of music in Heidi Epstein, *Melting the Venusberg* (New York/London: Continuum, 2004).

become like a man who is without strength," the strength to keep going, "among the dead an outcast, like the slain, lying in the grave." Part of the reason for that assessment and that comparison is that these are people "of whom you have not been mindful anymore; they have been cut off from your hand." The realm of death is one that Yhwh chooses not to enter; except for one or two extraordinary instances (e.g., 1 Kings 17); once you are dead, Yhwh lets you stay dead. Yhwh does not think about the dead, in the sense of deciding to act on their behalf. They are not in the realm where Yhwh chooses to lift a hand to do something, and therefore there is never any basis for giving testimony in the realm of Sheol; there is nothing there to testify to. There is no pain or suffering there; but neither is there any experience of God acting. In that sense Yhwh is not thinking about the suppliant, nor lifting a hand on the suppliant's behalf; that is to be effectively in the realm of the dead. In effect, "you have put me in the deepest Pit, in great darkness, in the depths." If Yhwh is going to treat me as if I were dead (that is, ignore my predicament)— well, in effect I *am* dead.

Logic would make the suppliant stop praying from this realm to which Yhwh does not pay attention. But Psalm 88 works with the same logic or rhetoric as Psalm 22 with its invoking as "My God" the God who has abandoned. For children, anything goes in order to get the parents' attention, and in prayer, anything goes in order to get God's attention. That is all the psalm attempts to do. If it can do this, everything else will follow. Neither logic nor theo-logic nor grammar need be faultless, to judge from the fact that this psalm gained acceptance into the collection of things that can be said to God. It is an extraordinary indication of how far prayer can go and how bold and incoherent it is possible to be with God.

Holding Yhwh to Account

A "rhetorical preoccupation with God" appears in a number of First Testament prayers,[89] including David's (2 Sam 7:22-24; 1 Chron 29:11), Solomon's (1 Kings 8:23), Hezekiah's (2 Kings 19:15-19), Jeremiah's (Jer 32:17-23), Nehemiah's (Neh 1:5; 9:6, 32) and Daniel's (Dan 9:4). They focus on Yhwh's sovereignty and the consequent possibility of appealing for deliverance, and on Yhwh's mercy and the consequent possibility of appealing for forgiveness. Often they seek to hold Yhwh to account.

There are a number of reasons for seeking to do so. Jeremiah 11:18–12:4 begins from the prophet's awareness of people's attacks and opposition, then raises the question why faithless people are so successful. It is not merely because of the trouble the faithless cause to him that he is holding Yhwh to

---

[89]Balentine, *Prayer in the Hebrew Bible*, p. 90.

account. The lines conclude with a set of *how long?* questions that concern not his personal destiny but the destiny of the country. People's faithlessness has brought not only danger to Jeremiah but devastation to the land (compare the further description of a drought in Jer 14:1-6). That underlies his charges.

Yhwh has several responses. One is that Jeremiah is faltering because the going is tough. It is tough for him personally, but more to the point it is tough in the way the people are resisting Yhwh, and it is tough in the way Yhwh is responding to him. Unfortunately Jeremiah has to come to terms with the fact that things are going to get worse before they get better. It is no good trust operating only when the going is easy; trust is going to need to operate in country where it is much harder to run (Jer 12:5).[90] Specifically, although Jeremiah was not concerned about his own fate in particular, Yhwh is so concerned and wants him to be aware of one way things are going to get tougher before they get easier. His own family have been acting against him even though they speak in friendly fashion (Jer 12:6).

Only in third place does Yhwh come to a response that more directly addresses the issue Jeremiah raised, though typically it does not constitute a straight reply (Jer 12:7-13). Why is Yhwh doing nothing about the faithlessness of Judah and its consequences in the withering of nature and the suffering of the animal creation? In reply, Yhwh says, "How do you imagine I feel? Do you think I enjoy turning my own personal estate into a desolation?" It is not explicit how far Yhwh is talking about the land, the city or the people; all might be included. "I was caught," Yhwh implies. The country, the city, the people had become aggressive toward Yhwh, as aggressive as a lion(!), vigorously and forcefully resisting Yhwh's involvement in its life, insisting on maintaining control of its own territory. So Yhwh has been aggressive back, but that has involved causing foreign armies to devastate Yhwh's own delightful personal portion. So Yhwh loses, and the people lose; the best and most committed farming in the world cannot work if there is no rain.

Jeremiah's two challenges to Yhwh thus produce two contrasting responses (Jer 11:18–12:13). Twice Jeremiah challenges Yhwh about the faithlessness of the people of God. Yhwh responds to the first challenge with a declaration that Yhwh will attend to the matter and to the second by agreeing, "Yes, the situation is bad, isn't it, and it will get worse, and I don't like it either." Both are necessary aspects of a divine response to our faithlessness.[91]

---

[90]The NRSV translates *bôṭēaḥ* "fall down" rather than "trust," on the basis of a similar Arabic word, and if such a word was known in Hebrew, Jeremiah may have been working with the paronomasia, but it seems likely that his hearers would assume the familiar word (see William L. Holladay, *Jeremiah 1* [Philadelphia: Fortress 1986], pp. 379-80).

[91]On Jeremiah's prayers and protests, see further chap. 7.

Claiming Yhwh's Commitment

Psalm 44 begins with a fine praise-like recollection of Yhwh's giving the land to Israel and giving Israel victory over its enemies, and churches use these first eight verses as a praise psalm. But this recollection serves to provide the backing for a protest, which is the psalm's real focus. The huge "yet" with which verse 9 opens introduces almost as long a contrasting account of the way Yhwh has been acting more recently. As in Psalm 88, second-person verbs are prominent: "You have spurned and disgraced us; you do not go out among our armies. You turn us back from the foe, and the people who are against us have plundered at will. You make us like sheep for food; you have scattered us among the nations. You sell your people for no value; you have not set a high price for them. You make us a reproach for our neighbors, derision and scorn for the people around us. You make us a byword among the nations, a reason for shaking the head among the countries."

Although such action on Yhwh's part is often a response to Israel's faithlessness, in the background of this psalm is the conviction that this time, "All this has come upon us and we had not ignored you or been false to your covenant. Our heart had not turned aside or our feet deviated from your path."[92] The suppliants are well aware that if this were not so, Yhwh would know, "for he gets to know the secrets of the heart." No, "because of you we have been slain every day," simply because of being Yhwh's people. So the question is, what is Yhwh going to do about it? Yhwh needs to wake up and get up and act.

> It is far from a model prayer, according to approved taste. The worshiper says in effect that he has heard that old story of God's saving deeds until he is sick of it. No doubt it is true that once God helped his people, saw to their needs, delivered Moses and the slaves from Egypt, provided a rich and good land for their descendants. But look at us now. . . . Either he cannot any longer help or he will not. . . . The important point here is that the worshiper says so, and says so passionately. He is as deeply involved in the act of communion with God as is the worshiper who is praising and extolling God's virtues and excellencies. . . . The saving history is for him a bitter irony, and he is not slow to say just that.[93]

The psalm closes, "redeem us for the sake of your commitment." Its final appeal is not to the community's integrity but to Yhwh's. Commitment (ḥesed)

---

[92]The earlier part of this claim to faithfulness could be taken to refer to the people's behavior since Yhwh abandoned them, but by the time we get to the end, the psalm is at least implicitly claiming that the trouble came because of their commitment to Yhwh not because of the lack of it, and it makes more coherent sense to take the whole in this way.

[93]Walter Harrelson, *From Fertility Cult to Worship* (Garden City, N.Y.: Doubleday, 1970), pp. 90-91; cf. Brueggemann, *Worship in Ancient Israel*, p. 9.

is supposed to be one of Yhwh's defining qualities. So let it be shown. The psalm implicitly begins with Yhwh's love for Israel and explicitly closes with that love. Of course we believe in your loving faithfulness, in those characteristics that were expressed in the actions for which the opening part of the psalm gave praise. But *please* will you show them again? We know that nothing can separate us from the love of Yhwh. But *please* will you make that a reality?

Claiming God's Past Word

"In prayer the community keeps God to His Word." Like praise, prayer is an aspect of the community's witness to the world. It is an "unreserved confession that we can do nothing in our own strength but that all things are possible to Him."[94] But it means that we have to claim God's promises and challenge God about keeping that word.

Psalm 119 especially emphasizes the significance of Yhwh's promise (there is no Hebrew word for *promise*; a promise is simply something Yhwh has said): "Make me live, in accordance with your word. . . . Lift me up, in accordance with your word. . . . I have relied on your word. . . . Be mindful of the word to your servant, by which you have made me wait. . . . For your word I have waited" (Ps 119:25, 28, 42, 49, 107, 114, 147). One fact that makes it possible thus to wait is that such waiting has been vindicated in the past: "This is my comfort in my weakness, that your statement has made me live. . . . You have done what is good for your servant, Yhwh, in accordance with your word" (Ps 119:50, 65). Partly on that basis I reckon, "Your word stands in the heavens" (Ps 119:89). And thus I keep waiting for its fulfillment, and pray, "do not take right away from my mouth your truthful word, because I have waited for your decisions. . . . People who revere you—they will see me and rejoice, because I have waited for your word. . . . My spirit has come to an end for your deliverance; for your word I have waited; my eyes have come to an end for your statement in saying, 'When will you comfort me?' " (Ps 119:43, 74, 81-82).

Psalm 60 confronts Yhwh in a similar way to Psalm 44, accusing Yhwh of "spurning" the people. But instead of drawing a contrast between Yhwh's recent action in the people's experience and Yhwh's action long ago when the people gained possession of the land, it draws a contrast between Yhwh's recent action and a word Yhwh spoke in connection with Israel's gaining possession of the land. "God spoke by his holiness: I will exultantly allocate Shechem and measure out the valley of Sukkot; Gilead will be mine, Manasseh will be mine." The psalm's formulation is a kind of poetic restatement

---

[94]Karl Barth, *Church Dogmatics* (Edinburgh: T & T Clark, 1962), IV/3, ii:883.

of the declaration Yhwh implicitly made in connection with giving Israel the land, asserting sovereign rights over the whole land, west and east of the Jordan, north and south, and thus over peoples around, peoples that might attempt to take parts of the land for themselves ("Moab will be my washbasin, at Edom I will throw my shoe; raise a shout against me Philistia"—see where that will get you!).

But the psalm then goes on again to assert that Yhwh has spurned the people. Whereas that declaration had said that Ephraim and Judah were Yhwh's means of exercising authority in battle (my helmet, my scepter), now Yhwh has not even gone out among Israel's armies. Israel needs Yhwh once again to give it help against foes such as Edom, Moab and Philistia. But this word from the beginning gives it a basis for prayer and for urging Yhwh to act. After all, Yhwh then spoke "by his holiness," a very solemn declaration of intent, like an oath (cf. Amos 4:2). Alongside the solemnity is the impassioned enthusiasm indicated by Yhwh's exulting (only here in the First Testament does Yhwh "exult").

An appropriate response when God is not doing what an earlier promise implies is to protest at what God has been doing, to remind God of what that word said, to urge God to act in accordance with that word, and confidently to acknowledge our dependence on God's doing so and our commitment to acting in light of that confidence.

Psalm 108 takes up that same declaration of God's, making even more explicit the assumption that a word from God is not limited to being fulfilled once. Indeed, one fulfillment establishes that it really was a word from God, and provides the basis for looking for another. It can be appealed to in different psalms at different times.[95]

Protest or Complaint?

The Psalms imply that protest is a regular aspect of the life of the people of God. But Job gets rebuked for his protests, and so does Israel in the wilderness (Num 11–20). "Israel complains about Moses, Moses complains about Israel, God complains about Israel, Israel complains about God, God complains about Moses, and Moses complains about God. That such a narrative should have been preserved and elevated to the status of sacred scripture and national classic was an act of the most profound literary and moral originality."[96] Is it possible to distinguish between protests that will get us into trouble, and ones that will not?

It may not finally be possible. In human relationships we can never be sure

---

[95]Cf. Peter R. Ackroyd, "The Vitality of the Word of God in the Old Testament," *ASTI* 1 (1962): 7-23.
[96]Jack Miles, *God: A Biography* (New York/London: Simon & Schuster, 1995), p. 133.

what response a protest will receive when we utter it to a person we love. There is always some risk involved. This need not mean that the relationship is endangered when a protest or complaint provokes a negative response. It may simply mean that the two parties have to work through the issues. If they do so, they will often find that their relationship is strengthened.

But the stories in Numbers (and in Ex 14–17) and the book of Job do offer pointers. First, Numbers 11 opens with the people "whining." The verb (*'ānan*) comes only here and in Lamentations 3:29, where it explicitly denotes complaints for which there are no grounds; and Numbers 11:1 gives no specific grounds for the people's complaint. Literally, they "became like whiners" or "became real whiners."[97] Second, on most occasions in Numbers the people do not actually protest and complain to Yhwh. Sometimes they just talk to themselves, as children and adults often do, everyone standing at their tent door complaining about the boring manna (Num 11:4-10). They had begun well when their first reaction to danger and fear was to cry out to Yhwh, but they immediately segue into complaining to Moses (Ex 14:10-12), and complaining to Moses and Aaron dominates the stories (Ex 15:24; 16:2; 17:2-3; Num 14:2-3; 20:2-3; 21:4-5). Third, their complaints amount to a desire to get out of being Yhwh's people and to a longing for life back in Egypt (Num 11:4-6). "You have rejected Yhwh who is among you and wept before him, saying 'Why did we ever leave Egypt?' " (Num 11:20). They themselves declare, "If only we had died in the land of Egypt, or if only we had died in this wilderness," and they determine, "Let's return to Egypt" (Num 14:2-4; cf. 20:4-5; 21:5; Ex 14:11-12; 16:3; 17:3). Yet these stories also show that the instinct to show mercy means God may respond to the cry of people who whine to one another or whine about their leaders or try to go back on their vocation instead of protesting to God (cf. Ex 2:23-25; Is 40:27-31).

Why does Yhwh so rebuke Job if he can also say to his friends, "you have not spoken of me what is established/securely determined/substantiated [*nĕkônâ*], like my servant Job" (Job 42:7)?[98] In that rebuke Yhwh had directed Job to the wonder and complexity of a world that does not exist for humanity's sake, and to the forces of disorder that Job cannot reckon to control. Yhwh's implicit point was that Job assumes (as human beings do) that the world revolves around him and that he could do a better job of running the world. Yhwh's point is that it does not and he could not. When our suffering drives us to reckon the opposite, we may get rebuked, though not cast off.

---

[97]The preposition *k* can indicate identity, though BDB, p. 454b, excludes this instance.
[98]See §3.1 "The Impossibility of Silence."

3.3 Plea

When people call out to God, as well as being a protest expressing their distress and hurt, it is a cry for help whereby they reach out urgently to another and seek a change in the situation.[99] In other words, another reason why biblical prayer is noisy, not silent, is that the way to get trouble dealt with is to make a noise about it.

A commonly articulated Christian conviction sees prayer as not designed to change God but to change me, and many contemporary liturgical prayers seem rather like expressions of self-exhortation or resolve ("Lord, make us more concerned for the needy"). Christian faith has thus abandoned a key scriptural conviction about prayer. The Qumran scrolls offer an instructive contrast; petition remains a feature of Qumran prayer and worship even though the theology of the distinctive Qumran scrolls often seems deterministic and thus to undermine the presupposition of petition, that the future remains open.[100] The First Testament sees prayer as designed to change the way God is acting, to change circumstances and to change other people.

Whereas a more implicit Christian conviction sees prayer as designed to make me feel better, possibly by letting it all hang out even if that does not change the way God acts, the First Testament sees letting it all hang out as a means of leaning on God, even if it makes me feel worse. The purpose of prayer is not therapeutic. Prayer is designed to get God to listen and to get God to act. In her classic prayer, Hannah brings her misery and tears and sadness and wretchedness to Yhwh, but she does that in order to plead with Yhwh to do something about the situation that causes it (1 Sam 1:1-16).

"Prayer is more than a cry for the mercy of God," Abraham Heschel says. Really? But he goes on, "Perhaps all prayer may be summarized in one utterance: 'Do not forsake us, O Lord.' "[101]

Decision and Action

Psalms do usually give more space to describing the pain and trouble out of which a prayer comes than to telling Yhwh what to do about it, though Psalm 17 is one where plea is more prominent. Two lines at the beginning focus on getting Yhwh's attention. Four lines in the middle combine appealing for attention with appealing for action. Three lines at the end focus on getting ac-

---

[99]Cf. *TLOT,* p. 1089; Boyce, *Cry to God in the Old Testament,* p. 22.

[100]See Eileen Schuller, "Petitionary Prayer and the Religion of Qumran," in *Religion in the Dead Sea Scrolls,* ed. John J. Collins and Robert A. Kugler (Grand Rapids: Eerdmans, 2000), pp. 29-45.

[101]Abraham Joshua Heschel, *The Insecurity of Freedom* (New York: Farrar, Straus & Giroux, 1967), pp. 254, 257.

tion. While psalms can imply that listening, looking or remembering is really all that is needed, these are of no use if action does not follow, and prayers naturally also ask for both attention and action. A woman who had fled from Baghdad in 2007 where Christians were under attack relates how "We were saying to Jesus, 'See us and save us.' "[102]

It follows that Yhwh's "answering" prayer has two aspects. Stage one is listening, looking and being mindful, and thus making a commitment to do something. Stage two is actual action. Mediating between a plea for attention and a plea for action is a plea for Yhwh to "turn," the end of stage one (e.g., Ps 6:4 [MT 5]; 80:14 [MT 15]; 90:13), and to "awake" or "arise," the beginning of stage two (e.g., Ps 7:6 [MT 7]; 35:2, 23; 59:4-5 [MT 5-6]). Some prayer psalms are simply engaged in urging Yhwh to listen. Some eventually imply the conviction that Yhwh has listened, looked, thought and maybe even turned; they have not seen stage two, the second aspect of the answer, but by some means they know they have seen the first aspect, and they can begin to praise God even now for having answered their prayer (in that stage one sense). They do not stop praying (because they have not seen stage two, which is what really counts). But they do start praising (because they have seen stage one).

The two aspects to the answer are closely linked: the first implies the making of a decision, the second denotes its implementing. Psalm 7:6-8 [MT 7-9] presses at length the need to make a decision: "Rise, Yhwh in your anger; lift yourself up at the outbursts of my assailants. Awake, my God. . . . Decide for me, Yhwh." While Yhwh's anger against wrongdoing is bad news when I am the wrongdoer, when I am the victim it is good news. When hearing about the wrong that has been done, it is appropriate for the president of the heavenly court to be angry; there is something amiss if it is possible to hear of a person being wronged and not to get angry. The president is normally in the court chairing the proceedings, the position from which he exercises authority (cf. Ps 9:7-8 [MT 8-9]). The suppliant wants him to stand, as an indication of declaring the court's decision, or perhaps as a sign of a strongly felt reaction. The bidding to rise recurs in similar contexts in Psalm 9:19 [MT 20] and Psalm 10:12, where it adds "lift your hand."

There is more bite about the bidding to "awake," which in other contexts could imply that the president has dozed off and needs to be aroused. "Israel's experience of their own undeserved suffering . . . could lead them to believe that God is not dead, to be sure, but close to it; for example, dangerously, irresponsibly asleep" (see Ps 44:23-26 [MT 24-27]).[103] That is how it

---

[102]*New York Times*, June 27, 2007, p. A4.

[103]Jon D. Levenson, *Creation and the Persistence of Evil* (Princeton, N.J./Chichester: Princeton University Press, 1994), p. xxii.

looks when a decision needs to be taken in the course of justice and no decision is forthcoming. Or perhaps the court has simply not been in session
and Yhwh needs to return to it, to reconvene it and get a decision taken.
Psalm 9:4 [MT 5] likewise looks forward to when Yhwh will have "given decisive judgment for me," "sat on your throne as one who makes decisions
faithfully."

That decision then has to become effective on earth. It is no use Yhwh making decisions like a president who has lost authority and will not be able to
implement them. The faithless person declares that Yhwh "does not seek for
requital," does not act to implement justice. In effect this person is saying,
"There is no God. . . . Your decisions are on high, away from him." Yhwh
makes those decisions high in the heavens; they have no effect here on the
ground (Ps 10:4-5). They need to have that effect.

When Yhwh Asks Questions or Says No

As suppliants can ask Yhwh questions, such as "why," Yhwh or Yhwh's representative can ask questions.

> Who has measured the waters? . . . To whom can you liken God? . . . Have you
> not listened? . . . Why do you say, Jacob . . . ? (Is 40:12-27)

> What wrong did your ancestors find in me? . . . Has a nation changed gods?—
> and those are not gods. . . . Is Israel a servant? . . . Is it not this that you do for
> yourselves? . . . What is there for you in going to Egypt? . . . How can you say, "I
> am not defiled?" . . . Where are your gods that you made for yourself? . . . Why
> do you bring charges against me? . . . Have I been a wilderness to Israel? . . . Can
> a girl put her jewelry out of mind? (Jer 2:4-32)

> Who is this who obscures my purpose? . . . Where were you when I founded the
> earth? . . . Have you ever commanded the morning? . . . Have you been to the
> sources of the sea? . . . Have the gates of death shown themselves to you? . . .
> Have you got to know the laws of the heavens? . . . Who prepares its food for the
> raven? . . . Who let the wild donkey free? . . . Will the buffalo agree to serve you?
> . . . Do you give the horse its strength? . . . Do you criticize my decisions? . . . Do
> you have an arm like God's? . . . Can you draw Leviathan with a hook? (Job
> 38:1–41:1 [MT 38:1–40:25])

These are all aggressive questions, though they can have positive implications.[104]

Yhwh's response to a prayer can be simply negative, even angry, but this
need not mean that a suppliant simply shuts up. At a place that came to be
called Contention, Yhwh confronted Moses and Aaron for breaking down

---

[104]Cf. Miller, *They Cried to the Lord*, pp. 169-70.

in their trust and in their commitment to honor Yhwh's holiness, and declared that they will not be the people to lead Israel into Canaan but will die outside the land like the rest of their generation (Num 20:2-13). Moses subsequently asks Yhwh for grace (*ḥānan* hitpael) so that he may after all be able to cross the Jordan and see the land, but Yhwh will not listen (Deut 3:23-26). Yhwh declares peremptorily, "Enough! Do not ever speak to me about this matter again," which suggests that Moses' reference to Yhwh's wrath is not merely a recollection of Yhwh's wrath at Contention but an indication that Yhwh is still angry. Indeed, along with Deuteronomy 1:37, which I assume also refers to the incident at Contention (cf. also Deut 4:21), this is the first time Yhwh has been said to be angry with Moses since his original resistance to Yhwh's summons (Ex 4:14); on several occasions in between, Moses and Yhwh have got pretty angry, but never with each other. Yhwh is angry with Moses "on your [Israel's] account," because Israel put the pressure on him that pushed him into the action to which Yhwh responded with anger. (The context at Deuteronomy 1:37 might add that conversely he had ultimately failed to win them to trust in Yhwh.) But his dying outside the land also draws attention to the fact that ultimately leaders serve God for God's sake, not for what they get out of it.[105] Yet this anger no more causes an ongoing barrier or gulf between Yhwh and Moses than did the anger at the beginning of their story. It is possible to be angry but to stay in relationship. Here, Yhwh's straight answer with its refusal of grace is accompanied by a mitigating act of grace, that he may see the whole land from just outside, even though not from inside (Deut 3:27).

Christians sometimes speak of God answering a prayer by saying no. The First Testament would not regard that as an answer; or rather, it would not reckon that this settles the question, any more than a child does when a parent says no. Yhwh has made absolutely clear to Abraham that the son that matters is to be born of Abraham and Sarah themselves, but this does not stop Abraham (finding it hard to believe that they are going to have a child at their age) saying, "If only Ishmael might live before you!" (Gen 17:18). Typically, Yhwh says both yes and no, as Yhwh says no and yes to Moses. Ishmael will live with Yhwh's blessing, but Yhwh still intends that the covenant will come to fulfillment through Abraham and Sarah's son.

You do not have to wait until God tells you what to ask before asking, as if prayer is simply a way of your submitting yourself to God. This is a real relationship like that between a servant and a master or a child and a parent; you can always ask, as even Cain and Lot recognize (Gen 4:13-15; 19:17-21). Negotiation is always worth trying, and often works.

---

[105]Cf. Mark E. Biddle, *Deuteronomy* (Macon, Ga.: Smith & Helwys, 2003), p. 76.

Speed and Urgency

Christian spirituality encourages us to submit ourselves to God's timing.[106] The First Testament looks for Yhwh to listen *now*: "Yhwh, I call you, hurry to me, give ear to my voice when I call to you" (Ps 141:1). The implication will be that this listening leads to speedy action, as is explicit elsewhere: "God, to save me, Yhwh to my help, hurry. . . . God, hurry to me. . . . Yhwh, do not delay" (Ps 70:1, 5 [MT 2, 6]; cf. Ps 71:12). Like the disjointedness at the end of Psalm 88, the disjointedness of this psalm's syntax helps make the point. The prayer of the Psalms generally concerns matters that are urgent. When people are trying to kill you, urgency is of the essence. It is said that God may answer prayer with yes, no or wait. The Psalms do not suggest we are obliged to be content with the third response any more than the second. They feel free to urge that Yhwh's response should be yes, and that it should be yes *now*.

Psalm 59 opens in a quite civilized fashion, "Save me from my enemies, my God; will you set me on high above those who rise against me." But it grows in anxiety or urgency: "Get up to meet with me, look, yes, you, Yhwh, God, Armies, God of Israel. Wake up to attend to all the nations; do not show grace to any harmful betrayers." If the exhortation to God to wake up is bold, then so is the exhortation to God not to show grace, though of course God's showing grace to some people carries with it the implication that God does not show grace to others, and the psalm does not want grace to be shown in an immoral way. The background to the anxiety expressed in the psalm is the way nations are growling and bellowing, which harbingers devastating attack. The suppliant would rather have them defeated than killed, not for their own sake but so that they continue to be a reminder for the people (of what Yhwh did?). But with some incoherence the suppliant then urges Yhwh to put an end to them so that they are no more.

The psalm thus develops in intensity and incoherence as it goes on, gradually making clear that it prays out of grave danger and thus with extreme urgency. It again shows that prayer does not have to be measured, balanced or moderate. When our circumstances are extreme, our prayer can be extreme. This psalm too models a huge freedom in speaking to God, like the freedom of children talking to their parents, confident that they can say whatever they feel and ask for whatever they want. In a strange way the awareness that God

---

[106]I should perhaps make clear that when I speak about "Christian spirituality" I mean spirituality as conceived and practiced by Christians. I do not imply that everything that is Christian is true or right. Something equivalent is true when the adjective *Christian* qualifies some other word. On the other hand, if I speak of "First Testament spirituality" or "New Testament spirituality," or put those expressions before some other word, I do assume that I am talking about what is true and right.

will decide what to do with our prayers adds to that freedom.

In particular, people in dangerous situations can bring to God their terror and their yearning for their attackers to be put down. The problem when Christian piety assumes that we cannot express anger, despair or fear to God is that "we cannot have an intimate relationship with someone to whom we cannot speak honestly."[107] While it is obviously ideal to be confident that Yhwh will answer our prayers, the loss of such confidence is not a barrier to prayer or a barrier to God's answering. In New Testament terms the warning that the wavering person cannot expect to receive anything from the Lord (Jas 1:6-8) has to have set against it the plea, "Lord, I believe; help my unbelief" (Mk 9:24). "Counselees today would undoubtedly make greater use of the cry for vengeance if there were not such strong social sanctions against it, and if they had confidence that the pastor could genuinely accept these negative feelings."[108]

Challenge and Change

Prayer does not accept things as they are. Psalm 108 juxtaposes part of the praise of Psalm 60 and part of the plea of Psalm 57 to this end, thereby complementing the psalm that precedes it. Psalm 107 says, "Do not undervalue what Yhwh has done in fulfilling the glorious promises of the prophets." Psalm 108 says, "But do not overestimate it either; do not settle for unfulfilled promises." It begins by declaring the intention to confess among the nations Yhwh's commitment and truthfulness; the prayer that follows thus implies, "Given that confession, Yhwh, you must act in accordance with its declaration." Its second half then starts by recollecting Yhwh's own words about being sovereign in relation to Israel and the peoples around Israel, so that the further prayer that follows implies, "Given that claim, Yhwh, you must act in accordance with it."

Psalm 77 speaks once more about a rejection that threatens to last forever. The suppliant has been reaching out to Yhwh for a long time, and looks back over that time and refuses to be comforted, refuses to accept the situation and to stop urging Yhwh to do something about it. Christians often ask for themselves or for other people that they may have peace in the midst of troubles, but peace means giving up striving. Like the woman in Jesus' parable (Lk 18:1-8), the suppliant refuses to yield to that temptation. In the long run peace is not the important thing. The important thing is to keep pressing God for action.

Psalm 77 also looks behind recent experience to an earlier period that

---

[107]Ellen F. Davis, *Getting Involved with God* (Cambridge, Mass.: Cowley, 2001), p. 8.
[108]Donald Capps, *Biblical Approaches to Pastoral Counseling* (Philadelphia: Westminster, 1981), p. 67.

seems to have gone forever. What causes pain is "the years of the right hand of the Most High . . . the deeds of Yah . . . your wonders of old . . . your work . . . your deeds," Yhwh's victory at the Red Sea and leading Israel through the sea. It is painful to look back to what Yhwh did at the beginning of Israel's story, because Yhwh is not behaving that way now. One could reckon that God's commitment has permanently ceased to exist, that God's word has failed for all time. Both possibilities raise unthinkable thoughts. It is a cardinal principle that Yhwh's commitment lasts forever. How could it have ceased? It is a cardinal principle that Yhwh's word stands forever. How could it have failed? The psalm asks Yhwh questions that undermine fundamental principles of Israel's faith. They imperil the world in which Israel lives. Yet it does that because experience has done so. It goes on to ask whether God has abandoned grace and compassion, which also imperils the world in which Israel lives; these are the first two characteristics claimed by Yhwh's primal self-revelation in Exodus 34:6.

This psalm issues no explicit exhortation to Yhwh to take action on the people's behalf, nor even any actual description of the trouble the community is in except the phrase "a time of distress." It simply comprises recollection: pained recollection of the prayer the suppliant has been praying, and pained recollection of the way things once were for the people. Yet the presupposition of the recollection is that it may be hopeful as well as painful. It may induce hope in the suppliant, and it may induce action in Yhwh. The recollection of the Red Sea event functions as part of the internal argument that can go on in prayer as one side of the suppliant's awareness reasons with the other side, but the retelling is actually addressed to Yhwh and thus functions as an implicit plea to Yhwh to act in that way again. Twice the suppliant spends several lines talking about God and then moves to talking to God, pulling the self out of merely talking to itself and making sure it talks to God and eventually lets the conversation stop there.

Perceiving that the people of God is in a sorry state suggests that the appropriate response is not to avoid facing the fact, or to assume it is simply our fault or simply the result of social forces, or to try to fix things ourselves. It is rather to charge God with having abandoned us and ask whether this is to go on forever. It is to urge God to look at our sorry state, at the way this brings discredit on God's own name, at the obligations that God's covenant relationship with us imposes on God, and at the contradiction between the way God is acting now and the way God acted in creating the world and in redeeming us.

Mercy and Punishment

Late in the exile Yhwh admits to having been calm and mute and quiet for a long time (Is 42:14). There can be reason for that. Israel knew in its own experience, in keeping with the revelation at Sinai, that by nature Yhwh is long-tempered. Time gives opportunity even to superpowers such as Babylon to change their ways, as it gives opportunity to people like the Judeans to change their ways. For the Amorites' sake, Israel's ancestors had to wait for four generations or centuries to be given the land they were promised (Gen 15:16); if Yhwh were not committed to being long-tempered, the Israelites might never have seen serfdom in Egypt. But the moment comes for moving from silence to action, to shouting and roaring like a warrior (Is 42:13). Psalm 83 wants Yhwh to act in keeping with that undertaking: "God, you must not keep silence, you must not be mute, you must not be still." Yhwh's enemies are raging and planning to destroy Yhwh's people and take over Yhwh's pastures. The psalm puts the emphasis on the way this affects Yhwh rather than on the way its affects Israel: "against you they have sealed an agreement." And Yhwh is doing nothing about it.

When Yhwh declares that the time has come to bring calamity on people for their waywardness (whether this is Israel or foreigners), one proper response is to urge Yhwh not to do so (e.g., Gen 18:16-33; Ex 32:7-14; Num 14:13-19). But another proper response is to urge Yhwh to do so. These two responses correspond to the two sides to Yhwh's character. Yhwh is centrally a God of love and mercy who holds back from bringing on people the trouble they deserve. Yhwh is also, more peripherally, a God capable of being tough with wrongdoers and of reaching the point of being prepared to exercise that capacity. The New Testament has the same view of God, though it is more worrying because now that includes sending people to hell.

The two sides to Yhwh and the two sides to prayer, for forgiveness and for punishment, link with the paradoxical nature of the closing prayer in Psalm 83, "Fill their faces with humiliation so that they may seek help from your name, Yhwh; may they be shamed and terrified forever, may they be disgraced and perish, so that they may acknowledge that you, whose name is Yhwh alone, are the Most High over all the earth." It would simplify matters if the people who get humiliated and killed were different from the people who seek help from Yhwh and acknowledge Yhwh, but that involves some reading into the text and the surrender of some suggestive insights. These contradictory exhortations correspond to the conflicting needs of the situation and the complex nature of who Yhwh is. Yhwh is God, and that suggests a prayer for the humiliation of people who will not treat Yhwh as God and the death of people who bring death to others. Yet the object of killing them is that they may come to acknowledge Yhwh! And the fact that Yhwh is love suggests a prayer for them to make Yhwh their resource, the place where they look for help and deliverance as Israel does. Their humiliation is the way to bring about that positive result; they will turn to Yhwh when they have come to a truer view of themselves. Shame is the way to blessing. Often it may not be possible to achieve all the aims of which the psalm speaks (for instance, exposing the shame of aggressors and having mercy on them), and Yhwh may have to choose which to prioritize in different situations. This particular psalm leaves that to Yhwh.

Relief

All this might suggest a number of possible aims for prayer: (1) to see the faithless repent and turn to Yhwh, (2) to be rescued from their attacks, (3) to see them put down so that they can no longer oppress me in the future, (4) to see them punished for Yhwh's sake, (5) to see them punished for my sake, so that I am vindicated from their charges, and (6) to gain Yhwh's help in putting them down myself. In practice the prayers that pursue these aims arise out of crises, look for deliverance from the overwhelming pressure of the moment and seek vindication; they are less inclined to look for long-term solutions to long-term problems. They are concerned with Yhwh's doing the right thing in punishing wrongdoing and faithlessness more than with bringing about the repentance of the wicked. They mostly ask for Yhwh to act, though they sometimes assume that the suppliant acts (e.g., Ps 18; 20).

A feature of the petitions in First Testament prayer is how short they are, providing a basis for Jesus' exhortation not to go on and on in prayer (Mt 6:7-8). They do not repeat themselves. Psalms are typically only eight or ten or twelve lines long, and within them the actual petitions are remarkable for their brevity. Generally the Psalms focus on describing the toughness of the situation and are rather unspecific in their requests.[109] Prayers outside the Psalter can sometimes be quite specific: "do make folly of Ahithophel's planning, Yhwh" (2 Sam 15:31). There was a man called Jabez whose name resembles the word for "pain" and reminded his mother of the pain she bore in birthing him; he looked a "born loser."[110] But he called on Yhwh to reverse all this by blessing him, giving him more land, supporting him and protecting him from hurt and from the pain his name spoke of; and Yhwh did so (1 Chron 4:9-10).[111]

Perhaps the Psalms are less specific in order to make them easily applicable in different situations. They focus on asking quite briskly for rescue and

---

[109]This point emerges in Aejmelaeus's list of the imperative verbs in the Psalms (*Traditional Prayer in the Psalms*, pp. 15-53).

[110]Leslie C. Allen, "The First and Second Books of Chronicles," in *The New Interpreter's Bible* (Nashville: Abingdon, 1999) 3:297-659; see p. 331.

[111]In *The Prayer of Jabez* (Sisters, Ore.: Multnomah, 2000), Bruce Wilkinson encourages Christians to take Jabez's prayer as a model. While one might question much of the substantial detailed critique to which his book has been subjected, there is no basis for taking Jabez's rather unusual story as a key to prayer.

punishment. In prayer we "throw" onto Yhwh (or at Yhwh?) the things that have been given to us (Ps 55:22 [MT 23]). We were thrown onto Yhwh when we were born (the same expression in Ps 22:10 [MT 11]); in our maturity we are in a position to throw onto Yhwh ourselves and the things that come to us, and thus to have Yhwh "sustain" or "nourish" or "endure" us (*kûl*; cf. Jesus' words in Mt 17:17). "He will never allow the faithful person to fall down," Psalm 55:22 [MT 23] goes on to explain: it will be their attackers rather than they who end up in Sheol.

The rest of Psalm 55, a straightforward enough prayer psalm dominated by plea for Yhwh to listen and act in light of the suppliant's need and the friends' wrongdoing, suggests what it looks like to throw on Yhwh "the things that have been given us." The word translated by that phrase (*yĕhobkā*) comes to mean "burden," but it is suggestive that it comes from a verb meaning "give." There are things that life gives us, that people give us or that God gives us that are pleasant, and things that are unpleasant, which we therefore wish to pass on to someone else as quickly as possible. Prayer makes that possible. Less metaphorically and more analogically, we are passing on responsibility for them to Yhwh. We are saying, "people are treating me like this, and I cannot do anything about it, so you must." If Yhwh is the implicit agent of the word that refers to things that are "given" to us, then we are saying, "You gave these things to us; we are giving them back (throwing them back) to you."

Restoration

Psalm 55 throws onto God the inner turmoil of our hearts, the outer turmoil that causes this inner turmoil, and the longing to be able to escape the context where these turmoils assail us. It speaks much of fear, deathly terror, trembling and shuddering, apprehension concerning the terrible things people are planning to do to us. We throw onto God our desire that our attackers should be foiled ("divide their speech," set them against each other) and our expectation that God will ensure they suffer the fate they seek for us. We thus forgo to God any activity of our own that would seek to bring them down; we yield to God responsibility for that too. In a rather paradoxical way, violence (for instance, persecution, racism, abuse and rape)[112] can reduce people to silence, as if the attackers impose their own assessment of them on their victims so that they see themselves as worthless or guilty and deserving of what happened to them. Prayer gives the victim speech, speech toward a person who does not view them in this way and can do something about what hap-

---

[112]On Ps 55 as a prayer that might be prayed by a victim of rape or battering, see Ulrike Bail, " 'O God, Hear my Prayer,' " in *Wisdom and Psalms*, ed. Athalya Brenner and Carole R. Fontaine, FCB 2/2 (Sheffield, U.K.: Sheffield Academic Press, 1998), pp. 242-63.

pened, even if the action itself can never be undone.

Suffering can be an experience of constraint. In Psalm 4:1 [MT 2], the word for constraint *(ṣar)* is one that can refer more generally to distress, but etymologically it suggests being confined somewhere narrow with no room to move, and the psalm goes on to picture Yhwh's act of deliverance by means of a word with the opposite meaning; *rāḥab* means "be broad." Deliverance takes the form of giving us room. The line works with the sharper picture suggested by the two words' etymology, an image of restoration.

As occasions when the community gathered to pray, alongside enemy invasion were natural disasters such as drought, famine and epidemic. In his prayer at the temple dedication, Solomon envisages wrongdoing leading to the people's being routed by an enemy or to the rains failing or to an epidemic or to an individual being afflicted with illness or to the people being exiled. They might then turn to Yhwh, confess Yhwh's name (that might imply they had been denying it) and plead with Yhwh for grace, and turn from their wrongdoing; and Yhwh might pardon them and return them to the land or send down rain on it or take other appropriate action (1 Kings 8:33-53). Lamentations similarly starts from the fall of Jerusalem and its terrible consequences, and from acknowledgment that this was deserved, even if it implies that Yhwh has surely gone too far.[113] It represents the kind of prolonged lament and plea that occupied people in Jerusalem for decades (cf. Zech 7–8). It looks for restoration.

Joel likewise urges people to wail, mourn, lament, howl and cry out because an army of locusts has consumed everything in the land; there is nothing to eat and nothing to offer in the temple (Joel 1:8-14). The EVV give the impression that people therefore need to "return" to Yhwh (Joel 2:12), but the verb *šûb* just as easily means "turn" without any implication that people have turned away. There is nothing in Joel to imply that the epidemic is an act of judgment and that people need to repent, and no reference to Yhwh pardoning them. "Turn to me with your whole heart and with fasting, weeping and lamenting; rend your heart, not [merely] your clothes, turn to Yhwh your God," Joel urges, and supports the appeal with a reminder from Exodus 34:6 of Yhwh's grace, compassion, long-temperedness and commitment. He adds that Yhwh relents about bringing trouble and might well also turn, as the people turn (Joel 2:12-14). While all of this may presuppose a need for the people to repent, it does not require it.[114] (With some irony, Isaiah 19:22 speaks of the Egyptians also "turning" to Yhwh when Yhwh hits them, and finding

---

[113]See further §3.6.

[114]See the discussion in, e.g., John Barton, *Joel and Obadiah* (Louisville/London: Westminster John Knox, 2001).

that Yhwh heals them.) Either way the focus of the pleas lies on Yhwh's restoration of the land. As usual the prayer concentrates on describing the awfulness of the situation. But maybe Yhwh may relent and have the epidemic leave something over (the verb is the one linked to the word for the "remains" or "remnant"), enough to make an offering possible. Yhwh's response is to promise much more than that, compensation for what the epidemic has consumed (Joel 2:25).

Protection

Like Psalm 17, Psalm 83:9-18 [MT 10-19] is a partial exception to the rule that the petitions in psalms are very brief; perhaps there is a link with the unusual feature that it relates to an attack that is threatened rather than one that has actually happened. It first urges Yhwh to act in accordance with precedent, drawing attention to a story from the past that provides a model for the action needed now. Then it urges Yhwh to act in accordance with promises that recur in the Prophets and elsewhere (e.g., Is 17:12-14), treating the nations that threaten the community like stubble, storming after them. And third it urges some aims for Yhwh's action such as their shaming and their seeking help from Yhwh.[115] In the end this long plea thus tests the rule rather than disproving it. It does not so much make suggestions to Yhwh about what to do, as appeal to "scriptural" precedent, promise and logic in order to motivate Yhwh to act in a way that it does not quite specify concretely. Israel regularly lived its life vulnerable to pressure from the nations that represented their resistance to Yhwh's purpose in the world (cf. Ps 2). Psalm 83 thus complements Psalm 82, the one representing an earthly perspective, the other a heavenly one, but both urging Yhwh to take action in a way that affects the world.

So sometimes suppliants pray because trouble is imminently threatened, perhaps by someone's plotting, rather than because it has actually arrived. In the Psalms people are often surrounded by enemies and need to be led in their lives in a way that offers protection. It is often the words of their attackers that are the biggest threat, untruths designed to threaten their lives or plots that are the preliminaries to attack. They need Yhwh to "cover over them," like a mother bird covering her chicks with her wings (Ps 5:8-11 [MT 9-12]; cf. Ps 17:8; 91:4). They are like people threatened by a flash flood or a hostile army who therefore plead, "rescue me . . . save me . . . be a crag, a stronghold for me, a fastness, to deliver me. Because you are my cliff, my fastness . . . you lead me, guide me . . . you take me out of the net that people have hid for me, for you are my stronghold" (Ps 31:1-4 [MT 2-5]).

So people plead, "watch over me" or "keep me" (Ps 16:1; cf. Ps 17:8; 25:20;

---

[115]See further §3.3 "Mercy and Punishment."

86:2). The verb *(šāmar)* first occurs in this connection in a conversation between Yhwh and Jacob (Gen 28:13-22). Yhwh undertakes to watch over Jacob, to be with him and to bring him back to the land he is leaving in fear. Jacob responds by reformulating those undertakings and spelling out a further implication, that Yhwh will surely make sure he has food to eat and clothes to wear until he comes back to the land. When he does come back, he prays with great theological correctness for Yhwh to protect him from Esau (Gen 32:9-12 [MT 10-13]). There may be some irony about this prayer, as about his previous one,[116] yet in itself it is a model prayer, recalling Yhwh's promises, acknowledging Yhwh's faithfulness in keeping those earlier commitments, confessing unworthiness and pleading briefly for deliverance. Watching over the people is then Yhwh's promise to the Israelites for their journey to the land; Yhwh's aide will make sure they get there (Ex 23:20). Deuteronomy 32:10-14 is a vivid picture of this active protection in the wilderness.

The need for that protection applies for the people's ongoing journey in the midst of dangers. Yhwh thus watches over and protects your feet (1 Sam 2:9; cf. Prov 3:26). It is the first way Aaron's blessing spells out what blessing means (Num 6:24). The abandonment of this protection is the first way Job summarily spells out his regrets (Job 29:2); now Yhwh watches over him in a different way (Job 33:11). But in the regular course of things, Yhwh "will command his aides for you, to watch over you on all your ways" (Ps 91:11), always protecting you from perils and attacks on your journey (cf. Ps 121:3-8). The protective aides embody Yhwh's integrity and uprightness (Ps 25:20-21), Yhwh's truth and commitment (Ps 40:11 [MT 12]; 61:7 [MT 8]). Yhwh's watching over people who live with insight can also be expressed in terms of Insight herself watching over them (e.g., Prov 2:6-11; 4:5-6).

Thus when danger threatens, one can pray, "may God send his commitment and his truthfulness" to deliver me (Ps 57:3 [MT 4]). "Send your light and your truth; they will lead me, bring me to your holy mountain" (Ps 43:3). Perhaps I am hesitant to ask for God to come in person; God may have other things to do, and I may hesitate to ask for personal divine attention for my need, which is trivial on an eternal canvas even if huge on mine. I can then ask for God simply to send a representative who embodies the divine qualities I need applied to me.

Praying out of Weakness

Prayer emerges out of weakness. The weak *(ʿănîwîm/ʿănāyîm)* are prominent in Psalms 9–10 (one psalm divided into two), so they spell out the implications.

---

[116]See further §3.1 "Divine Initiative."

Out of weakness, I pray by faith, which gives substance to things hoped for (Heb 11:1). So I pray looking forward to the time when God will have answered my prayer, and imagining that this moment is already here (Ps 9:1-4 [MT 5-9]). I am not here making this declaration of faith to myself, seeking to build up my own faith, as is sometimes the case in the Psalms. The declaration implicitly addresses other people, which implies giving attention to keeping the weak together. Under attack, it might be easy for me to turn in on myself to make sure that I keep myself together. The psalm is concerned with people who may be weaker than me, and wants to draw them into faith and hope. But the declaration explicitly addresses Yhwh. In a situation of such pressure, the crucial need is neither to keep me going nor to keep other people going but that God should act and change the situation. So the psalm focuses on appealing to God's imagination, on getting God to look forward to the moment when I will give praise for my deliverance, and thus on motivating God to do the thing that God alone can do.

Out of weakness, I pray by remembrance, declaring once more the deeds Yhwh did back at the beginning of Israel's story (Ps 9:5-12 [MT 6-13]). This doubtless bolsters my own faith as a "broken" person for whom Yhwh is a haven, but the psalm overtly addresses other people and Yhwh. Following up a declaration of intent to praise God (in due course) for what God will have done is an exhortation to fellow members of the community to make music to Yhwh now in the hearing of the nations who are the powerful oppressors at the moment. The community's faith is built up by recalling how Yhwh defeated such people at the decisive moment when Israel came into being. It is challenged to declare its faith in Yhwh as one who reigns now. And once again the psalm reminds Yhwh of actions undertaken at that time and thus implicitly urges Yhwh to continue to be the same God, the one who "did not ignore the cry of the weak."

Out of weakness, I pray for grace, as a "needy" person (Ps 9:13-18 [MT 14-19]). Once more the prayer reminds Yhwh of the past actions that should surely provide a model for the present and seeks to motivate Yhwh by anticipating the praise of the future. It again moves between addressing Yhwh and addressing other people, though who these people are is less explicit. Perhaps the suppliant engages both in an internal conversation and in a conversation with other people in declaring, "the needy person is not ignored without end; the hope of the weak ones does not perish forever."

Out of weakness I confront Yhwh in all ways possible (Ps 9:19 [MT 20]– 10:2, 12-18). I speak to Yhwh in the imperative: "Arise," "Lift your hand," get up off the throne and make a pronouncement. I urge action: "Break the strength of the faithless." I speak to Yhwh in the prohibitive: "Do not ignore the weak." I speak in the jussive: "A mere human being must not prevail";

Yhwh must assert divine authority. I ask directly aggressive questions: "Why do you stand far off, Yhwh, why do you hide in times of trouble?" I describe the situation: "In his loftiness the faithless hounds the weak person." I ask indirect questions: "Why has the faithless disdained God?" (that is, why does God let them get away with it?). I again remind Yhwh of the deeds of the past that need to be repeated: "You looked," "You have been a helper," "You listened." I remind Yhwh that there is no one else to turn to: "The wretched leaves it to you."

Out of weakness I thus take control of the "social conversation."[117] This feature appears at length in a protest (Ps 10:3-11) that once again combines address to Yhwh with address to other worshipers. If "knowledge is power,"[118] then speech is also power, and speech and power are mutually reinforcing. Control of the social conversation means control of what happens to people. The faithless disdain Yhwh as not being involved in this-worldly affairs, and thus encourage the community to leave Yhwh out of account. They malign the faithful and thus imperil their position in the community. But in prayer the suppliant has already reasserted Yhwh's position as one who really does make decisions regarding what happens in the world, and the people who hear and acknowledge that confession are thereby caused to reframe their understanding of power in the community. The suppliant also directly recharacterizes the people who have been exercising this power: they are actually robbers, profane, fraudulent, oppressors and troublemakers. Again, the community hears that declaration, and has the opportunity to acknowledge it and reframe its understanding of another aspect of power in the community, and to refuse to collude with the propaganda of the faithless. Outside of worship, in the gathering of the elders at the city gate, the weak may have no power to control the conversation. In the context of worship, the weak may be able to do so. That will make a difference because of what it says to Yhwh and because of what it says to the rest of the community.

Putting Down the Powerful

In Psalm 69 the suppliant declares, "I have sunk in a deep flood, where is no foothold," and goes on to speak of weariness with calling on Yhwh; "my eyes have failed, waiting for my God." The plea that follows speaks of the need of rescue from a vast force of human attackers and of being on the way to the grave at their hands. The suppliant thus prays,

---

[117]Walter Brueggemann, *The Psalms and the Life of Faith* (Minneapolis: Fortress, 1995), p. 226.
[118]The aphorism goes back to Francis Bacon ("Meditationes sacrae: Of Heresies," in *The Works of Francis Bacon* [Philadelphia: Hart, 1852], 1:71), though it has taken on a life of its own.

> May their table become a trap before them,
>> and for their partners a snare.
> May their eyes grow dark so that they cannot see,
>> make their loins shudder continually.
> Pour out your wrath on them;
>> may your angry burning overtake them. (Ps 69:22-24 [MT 23-25])

Why does the psalm pray in this chilling fashion? It opens with "deliver me, God," and its plea closes with "when I am weak and suffering, may your deliverance, God, set me on high," safe from their reach (Ps 69:1, 29 [MT 2, 30]). The psalm itself closes with a promise of praise that declares how the weak will see and be glad and how those who seek help from God will find their spirit revive, "because Yhwh is one who listens to the needy and does not despise his captives." As the attackers did not appear in the first five lines, which focus on the suppliant's trouble, so they disappear at the end. The whole psalm's focus is on deliverance from trouble; the assumption behind the plea for trouble for the attackers is that this is the way deliverance needs to come. The suppliant is not seeking vengeance or even justice, but deliverance. So the meal (a festive meal such as Sukkot?) needs to have an effect that is the opposite to the one they intend. The eyes that watch for opportunity and the loins on which they strap their weapons need to be disabled. Instead of their being the agents of Yhwh's wrath as they believe, they need to be its victims. They need to be totally and finally disposed of so that they cannot act this way again.

Psalm 79 similarly laments the nations' intruding into Yhwh's possession (an event such as an Assyrian or Babylonian invasion), their defiling of Yhwh's sanctuary, their turning Jerusalem into ruins, their killing Yhwh's servants ("they poured out their blood like water") and leaving their bodies unburied for birds and animals to scavenge, their taunting the people as a whole for thinking that Yhwh could enable them to stand firm. Will Yhwh not pour out fury (like that blood) on these nations that have not acknowledged Yhwh? Will Yhwh not take redress for the blood the nations have shed, so that they acknowledge the wrong they have done? Will Yhwh not turn back on them the reviling they have heaped on Yhwh?

As Psalm 5:10 [MT 11] puts it, "Make them pay, God." The verb is *ʾāšam* (hiphil), linked to the noun *ʾāšām* for a restitution offering, so it suggests offering compensation for an offense. Wrongdoing is not just an attack on a human being or a contravention of moral standards but an offense against God, and people should make restitution for that. Such pleas are in keeping with what Yhwh declared the intention to do and did (e.g., Is 10:5-19; 37:21-38; Zech 1:10-17). While Jesus prays for his enemies' forgiveness (Lk 23:34), he also warns that this giving of restitution will happen again and warns about how God does not always forgive people (Mt 6:15; 23:34-35). Subsequently the Christian martyrs plead with God more forcefully for this redress, and God agrees to grant their prayer (Rev 6:9-11). Like those Christian martyrs, psalms such as this one encourage us to pray for our enemies' punishment.

Both prayer for their forgiveness and prayer for their punishment give expression to aspects of truth. But "how we read the statements about enemies in the psalms may depend more on whether our names appear in the files of the secret police than on Hebrew exegesis"; further, given the reality of spousal abuse, child abuse and racial violence, we should be wary about spiritualizing the enemies.[119] If we belong to the powerful not the weak—to powerful nations, powerful groups within nations—and want to become people of prayer, psalms such as this invite us to identify with weak people and pray with them and for them; we also need to find ways of evading the prayers that are properly prayed against people like us.[120]

Praise and Plea

It is on the basis of Yhwh's being the subject of the verbs in its praise and in the protest that follows that Psalm 44 can come to its eventual plea in the way that it does, urging Yhwh to get up and not sleep, to wake up, not to reject, not to hide the face, not to ignore our weakness and oppression, but to rise and help and redeem and manifest commitment (Ps 44:23-26 [MT 24-27]). *Plea* is not really the word; it is too subservient an expression. Elijah chides people who prayed to the unresponsive Master with the possibility (among others) that their god was asleep (1 Kings 18:27), and Psalm 121:4 declares that Yhwh is not the kind of God who takes a nap. Psalm 44 presupposes an experience that makes it sure look as if Yhwh does. The disciples experienced Jesus doing so (Mk 4:38), and the Jewish people found God doing so in the Second World War.[121] If it is not so, Yhwh needs to show it. The point about the psalm's outrageous challenge is to try any means of provoking Yhwh to action.[122]

Psalm 89 expounds the logic of Psalm 44 most spectacularly. For thirty-eight lines it behaves like a praise psalm; this part has been used thus in Christian worship like the opening verses of Psalm 44. But it transpires that all this is but the introduction to a confrontational challenge occupying the psalm's last fourteen lines: "But you—you spurned, rejected, raged at your anointed, you renounced your servant's covenant." It asks, "Where are your former acts of commitment, my Lord, which you promised to David by your truthfulness?" and urges Yhwh to be mindful of the scorning that has come

---

[119]Deryck Sheriffs, *The Friendship of the Lord* (Carlisle, U.K.: Paternoster, 1996), pp. 12-13.
[120]See further the comments on Ps 137 in §3.5 "Claiming Yhwh's Promise."
[121]Cf. Blumenthal, *Facing the Abusing God*, pp. 99-100.
[122]See further §3.2 "Claiming Yhwh's Commitment."

upon Yhwh's "anointed," scorning that reflects the questions in the suppliant's own spirit concerning the reliability of Yhwh's undertakings. How can Yhwh reconcile the events of recent experience with the truths the psalm has confessed? "What has preceded is deeply deconstructed by what follows."[123] The psalm does not question whether Yhwh really is the Lord of heaven and earth, and really made a commitment to David; it rather challenges Yhwh about whether this recent action is compatible with the person it knows Yhwh to be. It presupposes an analogous experience to that of Psalm 88, but instead of omitting all praise from its prayer because experience belies the confessions that praise makes, it emphasizes praise in its prayer and challenges Yhwh to handle the incongruity between the confession and the experience. It also has in common with Psalm 88 that as the latter's only actual prayer is for the suppliant's plea to reach Yhwh, so the only plea in Psalm 89 is for Yhwh to "be mindful" (Ps 89:47, 50 [MT 48, 51]). If that can be achieved, everything has been achieved.

Psalm 90 expounds the logic of Psalm 44 more poignantly.[124] For centuries Yhwh had been Israel's shelter. As one for whom a millennium counts as no longer than a day, Yhwh had swept away empires that thought the sun would never set on them and thought they could always reinvent themselves. But then Yhwh also swept away Israel itself. In a sense, Israel cannot complain; it needs to learn to acknowledge the reality and the significance of Yhwh's anger in order to learn to live a wiser (and thus more obedient) life. But Yhwh seems insistent on never forgetting its long ago waywardness. Decades pass without it being brought back to fullness of life; the time goes beyond the seventy years that passages such as Jeremiah 29 speak of. The psalm then indulges in a much fuller petition than Psalm 88 or Psalm 89. It does not ask Yhwh to listen. It wants Yhwh to act, to turn and relent; the bidding takes up that of Moses in Exodus 32:12. In asking "How long," it wants to get Yhwh to live by our time frame (where seventy or eighty years is a very long time) rather than by the divine time frame. It wants Yhwh to manifest commitment; human commitment withers (Is 40:6), but Psalm 90 implies that Israel's withering reflects the withering of divine commitment. It wants to see Yhwh act in majesty so that the enjoyment of a good harvest replaces the affliction the community has experienced, so that its hard work is fruitful rather than futile. It wants to be able to resound and rejoice in Yhwh, instead of lamenting and protesting.

---

[123]Walter Brueggemann, "A Fissure Always Uncontained," in *Strange Fire*, ed. Tod Linafelt (Sheffield, U.K.: Sheffield Academic Press/New York: New York University Press, 2000), pp. 62-75; see p. 72.

[124]Its use at funerals takes it as a reflection on the transitory nature of individual human life, but the actual petition suggests it is a community prayer, perhaps from after the exile.

Plea and Praise

Psalm 126 expresses the point more affectively. "When Yhwh brought about the restoration of Zion, we became like people dreaming"—or perhaps "like people healing"; there are two verbs spelled *ḥālam*. Either we were like people with God-given dreams of restoration that came true, or like people who had recovered against the odds from some injury or illness. As a consequence "our mouth filled with laughter, our tongue with resounding," and the resounding was heard miles away or among the neighbors who would rather Judah stayed unrestored. But things have slid back, in the way one reads in Nehemiah, Joel and Haggai. The psalm continues, "Yhwh, bring about our restoration, like channels in the Negeb," in the way winter rains can transform the wilderness landscape. Then when there is a good harvest again, instead of weeping and crying there can once more be resounding. (Doubtless after that, there will be weeping again; that is the alternation that characterizes individual and communal life.)

Psalm 74 suggests the same logic but reverses the order in which people speak to Yhwh. It begins in more confrontational fashion with the *why* and the declaration about rejecting forever that comes later in Psalm 44, and focuses more on what Yhwh has let happen to the sanctuary and on the discrediting of Yhwh's name than on what has happened to the people. After the protest it comes to affirm that Yhwh is "my king," the one who "of old" parted the Sea and shattered Leviathan, making one think both of Yhwh's victory at creation and of Yhwh's victory at the Red Sea. Then like Psalm 44 it raises a question about the covenant relationship between Yhwh and the people, though it does so with an interesting difference. Psalm 44 affirms that the people have kept their side of the covenant, and implies that Yhwh has not done so. Psalm 74 directly challenges Yhwh to have regard for the covenant; it is the only direct appeal to the covenant in the Psalms. It may imply both that Yhwh has not been doing so, and that the people have. But it does not say this, and it may be appealing to Yhwh's grace in a context like that of the exile when the people would have a hard time claiming innocence. Both psalms close by urging Yhwh not to ignore what is happening to the people but to rise up and take action.

Psalm 80 expresses even more vividly, even whimsically, the point about Yhwh's activity: "You set a vine on the move from Egypt, you drove out the nations and planted it; you cleared the way before it, and it took deep root and filled the land." It puts even more forcefully Yhwh's involvement in the calamity that has come upon the people: "Why have you broken its walls?" The people's reversal is Yhwh's direct activity. But that does make it logically possible to urge Yhwh to exercise the same sovereignty in restoring them, as it several times does: "Restore us, shine your face so that we may be delivered."

The psalms set alongside each other two sets of facts; they deal with "when truths collide."[125] They vary over whether praise or prayer, trust or questioning has the first or the last word. Psalm 22 is another that works the second way, starting with protest and resolving the debate in favor of hope. It thus contrasts with Psalm 89, which resolves the debate—or rather, gives the interim last word—in favor of questioning.[126] (Ironically, the subsequent declaration, "Yhwh be worshiped forever, yes, yes," the line designated Psalm 89:52 [MT 53] which is actually the coda to book three of the Psalter as a whole, then reverses this "resolution.") Psalms 42–43 testify to an unfinished debate going on within the suppliant, who tries to do justice to both and to live with both.

Self-defense

There were many occasions when reversal and abandonment had a logical explanation. Israel had turned its back on Yhwh. Any protest at Yhwh's abandonment has to forestall the snorting response "Yes I did abandon you, and you quite deserved it!" Psalm 44 thus incorporates a self-defense anticipating this response: we had not been false to your covenant and we do not deserve the way you have treated us. This claim offends Christians who believe in "worm theology."[127] But the First Testament reckons that Israel should be committed to Yhwh not to other deities, that this is not that complicated, and that Israel should therefore be able to claim such commitment. It knows that everyone is affected by sin but at the same time assumes that it is possible to be basically committed to Yhwh's way. When you pray, you need to be able to claim to be such people; otherwise your prayers will not be heard. When Hezekiah gets ill in midlife and seems in danger of death, all he does is point Yhwh to his steadfastness and integrity; there is no petition other than that Yhwh should be mindful of these, though there is some weeping. The reminder and the tears are all that is needed to persuade Yhwh to grant him healing (2 Kings 20:1-5).

The Psalter thus begins by encouraging people to see the world as divided into two camps. There are the faithful, people who keep studying Yhwh's teaching, and the faithless, people who know all they need to know already (Ps 1). There are people who want the freedom to be independent and make their own choices, and people prepared to serve Yhwh (Ps 2). While the distinction between the two camps may implicitly be a moral one, explicitly it is religious. The distinction concerns whether or not you walk Yhwh's way. People who pray do so as those who can say they have nothing to do with the

---

[125]Scott A. Ellington, *Risking Truth* (Eugene, Ore.: Pickwick, 2008), p. 12.
[126]See further §3.4 "Protesting and Believing."
[127]See §3.4 "Protesting and Believing."

attitudes or stance of the faithless and the mockers. In prayer I need to be able to claim I can pass the test set by Psalm 1.

The first actual prayers that follow in the Psalter carry the same implication; the suppliants belong to a camp affirming that "deliverance is Yhwh's; your blessing is on your people" and stand over against a camp that has exchanged the God it should honor for a god of which it should be ashamed (Ps 3:8 [MT 9]; 4:2 [MT 3]). They also indicate that these two groups are indeed like military camps, drawn up in mutual opposition. The faithless are people who attack those who trust in Yhwh. That becomes more explicit in the succeeding psalms. The faithless are people who speak falsehood, who seek bloodshed; they are aggressive assailants (Ps 5:6 [MT 7]; 6:7 [MT 8]).

The plea for deliverance in Psalm 26 gives most of its space to a claim to have lived faithfully. "Decide for me, Yhwh, because I—I have walked in my integrity, and I have trusted in Yhwh" (Ps 26:1). There are thus two aspects of its claim to faithfulness. There is a moral commitment to a life that means not associating with deceptive and faithless people in the sense of not colluding with or coming to share their attitudes and actions (Ps 26:3-5; the imagery compares with Psalm 1). There is also a religious commitment; trust in Yhwh implies not trusting in other deities or other resources, and being committed to proclaiming Yhwh's deeds before the people (Ps 26:6-8). An indication that the claim is serious is an openness to Yhwh's testing, not only with regard to the outward life but with regard to the heart and mind (Ps 26:2; cf. Ps 17:3-5). Psalm 44 implies the same assumption with its recognition that God gets to know the secrets of the heart and thus to know whether in the apparent privacy of their hearts or homes people have been turning their backs on Yhwh and looking to some other deity for their needs. No, it is "because of you" that we have defeated and decimated, not because of our faithlessness to you but because of our faithfulness to you (so Paul takes it in Rom 8:36) or because of your turning your back on us.

Pleading as a Sinner

Things may look very different from the other side. Often sincere groups of people confront each other, both convinced that God is with them. Using the Psalms involves being aware of the ease with which we can claim to be on the side of faithfulness but be wrong. The Psalter implicitly recognizes that all worshipers are inclined to see themselves as the faithful and others as the faithless, but that it is easy to fool ourselves. Hence it comes back from time to time to reminding us of the kind of questions we need to ask if we are to present ourselves as belonging to the former category (e.g., Ps 15; 19; 24). Further, while there is a mystery of disobedience,[128] there is also a mystery of obedi-

---

[128]§2.1 "The Mystery of Disobedience."

ence. Whereas Adam and Eve mysteriously disobey Yhwh, Abraham and Sarah mysteriously obey Yhwh when bidden to leave one land and go to another. Why do they do that? Somehow, Yhwh's bidding generates a positive response. The Israelites knew they were responsible to provide Yhwh with a response of obedience and in some sense wanted to do so; they also knew we do not always do the things that at one level we want to do (cf. Rom 7). So they make their own obedience something they pray about (see Ps 119).

While many psalms require of people who use them a declaration that we do manifest honesty and abjure deception, support the faithful and oppose the violent, and submit ourselves to Yhwh's testing in this connection, Psalm 80 offers a contrast in making no claim to faithfulness, to not having deserved calamity, though it makes a commitment for the future: "We will not turn aside from you . . . we will call on your name." If that is tantamount to an admission of guilt, like Moses on Sinai the psalm then appeals not to the people's deserve but to Yhwh's nature, person and activity. Yhwh is the one shepherding Israel, driving Joseph, sitting on the cherubim, the one who set that vine on the move and prepared soil for it and planted it. Surely Yhwh wishes to persist with this project? Judges supports this as it describes a recurrent pattern. Israel puts Yhwh out of mind and serves other deities, Yhwh gets angry and gives them into the power of a foreign king. Then they cry out to Yhwh as they had in Egypt (Judg 3:9, 15; 4:3; cf. Ex 2:23), and Yhwh causes a deliverer or leader to arise for them. He takes on their overlord and defeats him. Faithlessness does not make turning to Yhwh impossible.

In itself to pray out of weakness is not to imply anything about the causes of weakness. Psalm 25 draws attention twice to the suppliant's weakness (vv. 9, 16) and a number of times to the related prospect of being overwhelmed by enemies, and one might infer that the trouble is quite undeserved. But the suppliant also acknowledges shortcomings, rebellions and waywardness, and eventually prays, "Look at my weakness and my trouble and carry all my failings" (Ps 25:18). Trouble may not be undeserved, yet this does not make it impossible to appeal to Yhwh's compassion, commitment and goodness.

A suppliant may grant, "God, you are the one who knows of my stupidity; my guilty deeds are not hidden from you" (Ps 69:5 [MT 6]). But the acknowledgment of this looks somewhat notional. Its point is to underline the fact that other people do not know in what ways the suppliant has been behaving in a morally obtuse fashion; only God knows how that might have been so. Thus they have no basis for their attacks on the suppliant, attacks that actually respond to a "passion for your house" expressed in grief at the way affairs there are conducted (the psalm presumably refers to the form of worship offered there, such as is condemned in Ezekiel).

More Motivation: Vows and Promises, and the Honor of Yhwh's Name

"Petitionary prayer is fundamentally an act of persuasion, seeking to lure or coax God into responding to the cry for help."[129] One way of seeking to do that is to make a promise regarding what one will do when the prayer has been answered.

Vows have a prominent place in Israelite religious life;[130] as they do in the life of the early Christians (Acts 18:18; 21:23); one might also compare baptism, marriage, tithing and ordination vows.[131] When people need Yhwh to act on their behalf, they may well promise to come back to give glory to Yhwh when their prayer has been answered (Ps 7:17 [MT 18]; 9:1 [MT 2]; 35:18; 42:5, 11 [MT 6, 12]; 43:5). They may promise something more concrete and sacrificial (cf. Lev 7:16; Jon 2:9 [MT 10]). If Yhwh makes it possible for Hannah to have a baby, she will give him to Yhwh for all the days of his life, as a nazirite (1 Sam 1:11). Her husband also made a vow (1 Sam 1:21), but this seems to be a separate matter, perhaps a vow in connection with prayer for a successful harvest. Leviticus 27 instances the kind of gift someone might promise (a person such as oneself or a member of the family or a servant or an animal or a house or some land, but not anything that belongs to God anyway, such as firstlings or tithes or anything "devoted," *ḥērem*).

Hannah's vow would be costly to keep, but she keeps it. Vows obligate us. They must be fulfilled, and the First Testament warns about vows that may be difficult to fulfill (cf. Deut 23:21-23 [MT 22-24]; Prov 20:25; Eccles 5:4-6 [MT 3-5]). It urges, "make vows and fulfill them to Yhwh your God" (Ps 76:11 [MT 12]). Don't try to cheat on them (Lev 22:17-23; Mal 1:14). This is not the First Testament's only caveat about vows, which tend to get people into trouble (Judg 11). Some hesitation and irony attaches to many references to vows (Gen 28:20-22; 2 Sam 15:7-9); the first reference to "devoting" cities (*ḥāram* hiphil) comes in a vow (Num 21:2). But Yhwh provides ways of commuting vows (compare and contrast the stories about the vows of Jephthah, Hannah and Saul).[132] The reason for the discussion in Leviticus 27 is to explicate how to compute the value of something if you need to substitute a monetary gift for the thing itself. The evaluation of a human being varies with age and sex, being apparently based on their productivity; while such substitution would be the norm

---

[129]Patrick D. Miller, "Prayer and Divine Action," in *Israelite Religion and Biblical Theology*, JSOTSup 267 (Sheffield, U.K.: Sheffield Academic Press, 2000), pp. 445-69; see p. 449; cf. Miller, "Prayer as Persuasion," in *Israelite Religion and Biblical Theology*, pp. 337-44; *They Cried to the Lord*, pp. 114-26.

[130]Cf. Jacques Berlinerblau, *The Vow and the "Popular Religious Groups" of Ancient Israel*, JSOTSup 210 (Sheffield, U.K.: Sheffield Academic Press, 1996).

[131]Thomas B. Dozeman, "The Book of Numbers," in *The New Interpreter's Bible* (Nashville: Abingdon, 1998) 2:1-268; see p. 237.

[132]Cf. Wenham, *Book of Leviticus*, p. 337.

with a human being, with other vows a person may make an undertaking in
a crisis and subsequently realize it was unwise and need to commute it. The
sanctuary itself would often find monetary contributions more useful than
gifts in kind.[133] Where a woman makes a vow that may implicate her father or
husband, there are rules to enable him to get her to cancel it (Num 30).

Prayer involves going before the heavenly cabinet and persuading it to
take action. It has many items on its agenda; there are many tasks it might
undertake, many causes it might take up. Why should it take up yours? An
argument Christians use in prayer is that what they request is for God's glory
or that they are praying for God's name's sake, and this sums up a line of argument in the First Testament. There is nothing to be gained by letting me
die, the worshiper in Psalm 30:8-9 [MT 9-10] had argued: "Can dirt confess
you, proclaim your truthfulness?" Yhwh had apparently accepted the argument and not let this worshiper die: "You brought me up from Sheol" (Ps 30:3
[MT 4]). And that is why this psalm exists as a testimony to Yhwh's act of healing. If Yhwh had not so acted, there would have been no such testimony to
Yhwh's faithfulness. "Act for your glory's sake, for your name's sake," the
worshiper had argued. It is in your interest.

"Be on high over the heavens, God, over all the earth your honor" (Ps 57:5,
11 [MT 6, 12]). The psalm's desperate concern is that Yhwh should protect and
deliver, but the motivation it offers in this refrain appeals to Yhwh from another angle. Protecting and delivering will involve an assertion of Yhwh's
majesty in the sight of the world such as will demand that it be acknowledged. Psalm 67 asks[134] that God may bless Israel, graciously smiling on the
people; its reference to earth giving its produce indicates the characteristic
form that blessing takes. The psalm's language is very similar to that of the
Aaronic blessing (Num 6:24-26) but it has a distinctive motivation, that the
earth, the nations, the peoples, the countries, all the ends of the earth may
acknowledge, confess, rejoice, resound and revere Yhwh. They may rejoice
because Yhwh's dealings with Israel are a paradigm for Yhwh's dealings with
the world.

3.4 Confidence

Like protest and plea among the components of prayer, expressing confidence
that God is trustworthy and will act can be such a prominent feature that it
may come to dominate a prayer. When suppliants become convinced that
Yhwh has answered (stage one) but they have not yet seen the answer (stage

---

[133]Thus Baruch A. Levine calls this chapter "Funding the Sanctuary" (*Leviticus* [Philadel-
phia: Jewish Publication Society, 1989], p. 192).

[134]I assume that the translations are right in taking at least some of the yiqtol forms in the
psalm as having jussive significance.

two), they then relate to need, attack, danger and unbelief in new ways. It does not mean they stop praying; it means they are now praying for Yhwh to implement the intention Yhwh has declared. Urgent prayer and statements of trust and confidence can then coexist until Yhwh does so. Hope continues to base itself on what Yhwh has done in the past and on what Yhwh has done for the community as well as for the individual.

When Yhwh Says Yes

There are psalms where an extraordinary change comes over the suppliant. Psalm 6 speaks of anger, dismay, weariness, weeping, wasting away and feebleness, but then suddenly bids the people causing the dismay to get away, "because Yhwh has listened to the sound of my weeping, Yhwh has listened to my prayer for grace: Yhwh receives my plea." The suppliant is now convinced that these attackers will end up shamed (Ps 6:8-10 [MT 9-11]). We do not know what explains this transition (a message from God brought by someone else? a conviction God directly gives to the suppliant? a conviction that simply issues from having prayed?). But by some means the suppliant knows that Yhwh has "listened"—to the weeping, to the content of the prayer—and "receives" the prayer, accepts it. There is a form of listening and accepting that implies sympathy but no action on our part ("I hear you," "I can see that"). This was not that sort of listening and accepting, but one that implied recognizing an obligation to do something. The suppliant has been heard, though not yet delivered; stage one has come, though not yet stage two.[135] But the movement in the psalm has taken the suppliant from not knowing whether there will be action to certainty that there will be. Psalm 7 similarly moves from "deliver me from my persecutors, or one will tear me apart like a lion" and "awake, my God," to "God is my shield. . . . I will confess Yhwh for his faithfulness."

In Psalm 57 the suppliant is threatened by destruction, lying among metaphorical lions, aware that people "are setting a net for my feet." But alongside that can be put the fact that "my heart is set, God, my heart is set; I will sing and make music." The nets are set, but the heart is set (*kûn* hiphil and niphal). It is a strong statement; a throne (David's or God's) is something one describes as "set" or "established." The suppliant's heart is "set" on seeking help from Yhwh, not looking anywhere else, and thus set on treating Yhwh as God, not on so treating anyone else. And it is set even now on praising Yhwh as the one characterized by commitment and truthfulness.

In case it is not set enough, the suppliant continues with the exhortation, "awake, my soul," and then goes on to awake harp and lyre. Such praise does

---

[135]See §3.3 "Decision and Action."

not necessarily happen naturally, but neither are we helpless to affect what happens. We can stir up ourselves, our inner beings. We can engage in conversation with ourselves, even confrontational conversation (cf. Ps 42:5, 11 [MT 6, 12]; 43:5). We can wake ourselves up, like one person waking another. Waking the musical instruments stands appropriately alongside this: we wake up the inner person and the outward means of praise. Or perhaps waking the instruments is a means of waking the praise in the inner person. Indeed, the suppliant determines to "wake up the dawn." The suppliant is waiting urgently and enthusiastically for the dawn to arrive, for the moment when the morning sacrifices are offered, and waiting rather impatiently; dawn cannot come soon enough. Usually the dawn wakes us; here the usual rule will be reversed.[136] This psalm has no fears about the possibility that God is asleep (contrast Ps 44:23 [MT 24]) and can thus focus elsewhere its attempts at awakening. The suppliant is even prepared to begin praising Yhwh "among the peoples . . . among the countries." It is a bold testimony that will be given before they have actually been able to see the exaltation of Yhwh's majesty above the heavens; but the suppliant is sufficiently convinced of Yhwh's commitment and truthfulness.

Psalm 69:32-36 [MT 33-37] declares its confidence in a similar way, expressing a strong conviction of the certainty of Yhwh's deliverance, though it makes no actual declaration that Yhwh "has listened" or "has answered"; still less does it speak as if Yhwh's act of deliverance had already happened. Yet the suppliant knows that Yhwh's act is certain, though still lying in the future, because of the character of Yhwh as "one who listens to the needy." "If we would pray fruitfully, we ought . . . to grasp with both hands this assurance of obtaining what we ask, which the Lord enjoins with his own voice." Such proper prayer is "born . . . out of such presumption of faith" (e.g., Ps 33:22; 56:9); after all, the definition of God is as one "who listens to prayer."[137]

When Eli eventually recognizes that Hannah is pouring out her pain and grief before Yhwh, he declares, "Go in peace, and the God of Israel give the thing that you asked from him." Hannah understands this as more than a prayer. It is a performative act. So "she went her way, and ate and her face was no longer down" (1 Sam 1:17-18). Her situation is no different from when she came to the festival. She is no more pregnant than she was. But through Eli Yhwh has responded to her prayer. And therefore everything has changed.

The suppliant thus stands between two realities. There is the reality of present oppression, but there is also the reality of coming deliverance. It is so real, it can be spoken of and confessed as if already present (again, compare

---

[136]See *The Midrash on Psalms* (New Haven, Conn.: Yale University Press, 1959), 1: 501-2.
[137]Calvin, *Institutes of the Christian Religion* 3.20.12, 13, pp. 865, 867.

Heb 11:1). It is as if chronology collapses, because Yhwh has made a commitment to act in deliverance; that makes deliverance a more real reality than oppression. Over against the reality of present oppression is the reality of Yhwh's commitment and truthfulness.

When Need Troubles

The frame of Psalm 23 concerns things to eat and drink, and concerns not bare but generous provision and thus spectacular enjoyment. Metaphorically, I am a sheep and Yhwh is the shepherd to whom I look for grass and water; and Yhwh provides. Finding grass in the wilderness is a challenge, but the sheep knows that this shepherd does more than provide the bare minimum; "He makes me lie down in grassy pastures." Finding pools of water is also a challenge, but the shepherd finds pools expansive enough to rest by (or perhaps the background is the frightening torrents that winter storms may bring), guides by "completely restful waters," and thus "restores my life." A little less metaphorically, "you lay a table before me in the presence of my enemies. You bathe my head with oil; my cup amply satisfies." It could be tempting to look to some other shepherd; it is wiser to trust this one.

In referring to the presence of enemies, this second picture in the psalm gives more prominence to a feature of Yhwh's fine provision that was also present in the first. To get the sheep to the place where there is grass and water, the shepherd led the sheep through deep and dark canyons, but knew how to find the right paths. Wild animals could lurk there; but "your rod and your staff—they comfort me." I am secure because the shepherd has the weapons to beat off lions or leopards. It is fortunate that shepherds are tough guys who are prepared to be hardnosed killers, as David reminded Saul (1 Sam 17:34-36). So it is not wild animals that "chase" me, but "good and commitment" that do so—good and commitment that protect and provide. They make sure that I get to Yhwh's house, the place on which provision and protection depend.

The believer's life is lived between unhindered enjoyment of God's presence with the provision and protection it provides for body and soul, and the precariousness of whether we will have provision for our needs or be overwhelmed by people's attacks. Martin Luther links the way the psalm speaks with his idea of the *Anfechtungen* that assail us, the temptations, pains and afflictions.[138] We will enter God's kingdom through much tribulation (Acts 14:22). But the psalm draws us into a confidence in Yhwh that is brave yet also logical. While its middle lines address Yhwh, its opening and closing lines

---

[138]Martin Luther, *Selected Psalms*, 3 vols., Luther's Works 12-14 (St Louis: Concordia, 1955, 1958, 1958), 1:155.

speak of Yhwh in the third person, and one can imagine its statement of confidence implicitly addressing other members of the congregation and urging them to trust Yhwh, and implicitly addressing the enemies and urging them to give up their futile attacks, and implicitly urging the self to live by these declarations.

Psalm 91 comprises another implied invitation to trust in the context of trouble, as it offers a description of the trustworthy one. Yhwh is available to Israelites or their leaders as shelter and shade, refuge and stronghold, rescuer and protector. Concretely, this means not being caught in traps, destroyed by epidemics, hit by arrows, bitten by snakes, attacked by lions, tumbled by rocks. While the promises are concrete, it is impossible to know where the metaphorical ends and the literal starts, though perhaps that is the point; there are many ways of cashing them. The more puzzling question is how an Israelite lived with their disconfirmation, the disconfirmation that many psalms speak of. Perhaps that too is the point. There would be no need to talk about trust if Israelites or their leaders invariably found themselves so comprehensively protected. This would then be a different world from the one it is. The psalm invites people to believe that God will fulfill its promises even though anyone can see they do not always work out.

When Armies Attack

A suppliant can be surrounded by attackers who are convinced that God is on their side and will not act on the suppliant's behalf, and this can issue in the kind of urgent plea that often appears in psalms. Psalm 3 presupposes that experience and does eventually issue a brief appeal, but it is dominated by a confident declaration that Yhwh is a shield protecting me and is my honor (that is, one who maintains my honor rather than abandoning me and letting me be shamed), and one who lifts my head, makes it possible for me to keep my head high or lift it high again (a concrete way of saying the same thing). It is possible to make such a declaration because this is the way Yhwh has acted in relation to me in the past (there are qatal verbs here, though some translations render them as present). I have known what it is to call out to Yhwh, to have Yhwh answer with a promise of deliverance and then fulfill the promise by putting down the faithless, and therefore to be able to sleep and wake up and not need to fear a massive army of attackers. Perhaps the idea is sleeping soundly because I need not worry, or perhaps it is sleeping safely because I don't get killed. I know the attackers are wrong in reckoning God is with them and not with me, but I cannot prove that except by actually casting myself on God. The psalm closes with another statement of confidence in Yhwh as deliverer and as one whose "blessing is on your people," which suggests yet another basis for confidence. This lies not merely in Yhwh's commitment to me as an individual but in Yhwh's prior and more important relationship with the people as a whole. I might be dispensable, but if I can see my need as relating to the people's need, that would increase the pressure on Yhwh to take care for me.

Psalm 13 begins by presupposing that Yhwh has turned away, and asks confrontationally how long that situation is to obtain, but after a few lines it has made a transition to a declaration of confidence. Nothing has happened to turn questioning into confidence. These coexist. Perhaps questioning is itself an expression of trust. While trust can imply a relaxed confidence in God that makes it possible to be still and quiet under pressure, it can also imply a freedom to ask, "how long?" Its consistent nature is to exclude trying to fix things for ourselves. It recognizes that it takes God to fix things. Other gods cannot do so, political agencies cannot do so, and we cannot do so. Prayer lives in the space between trust and its vindication, and lives with the tension of what is and what will be.

Psalm 35 is a particularly sustained prayer issuing from being under attack by people, and it looks forward with conviction to giving testimony when Yhwh has acted in response to the prayer. It is thus a particularly sustained expression of confidence, with no hint of despair. Nor does the suppliant have any plans either for defense or for attacking the attackers, or for surrender or submission to them. Yet this confidence does not mean the suppliant is calm and cool. Confidence may not imply peacefulness. Perhaps the suppliant would plead with Yhwh less urgently and less effectively if that were so. Trust can mean praise despite the circumstances; it can also mean protest because of the circumstances.

When I am being hounded and oppressed, "on the day when I am afraid, I do trust in you. In God whose word I praise—in God I have trusted. I am not afraid; what can flesh do to me?" (Ps 56:3-4 [MT 4-5]). That seems like a definitive statement. Yet the psalm then goes back to the reality of harassment, before repeating a variant form of the same declaration of confidence. Fear and protest argue with trust and confidence until the psalm closes with a declaration that Yhwh has saved my life (that is, will have done so or has undertaken to do so). A suppliant has to be prepared to persist in an argument with the self as well as with God. Perhaps the self is harder to convince and change. There are two objective realities that need to be acknowledged, the reality of people's attacks and the reality of God's power and trustworthiness. There are also two subjective realities that need to be owned: "I am afraid, I trust, I praise, I am not afraid." Here too confidence does not bring an end to fear, but it does make it possible to live with fear without being paralyzed. The distinctive key in this psalm is God's word, God's word of promise. Only in this psalm is God's word the object of praise.

When Death Confronts or the Faithless Flourish

"You will not abandon me to Sheol; you will not let someone committed to you see the Abyss. You will make known to me the way to life; joyful abundance will be with your face, lovely things in your right hand always" (Ps 16:10-11). In his inspired reinterpretation of these lines, Peter gives them quite a different sense in commenting that David was of course abandoned to Sheol, but Jesus was not (Acts 2:27-31). In the psalm Yhwh can be relied on to protect us from being abandoned to Sheol; whereas that is where we will end up for a while at the end of our life when we go to be with our families, Yhwh will not let this happen before its time (David, indeed, had much experience of Yhwh not abandoning him to Sheol in this sense). Until then, Yhwh shows us the way to life, gives us joyful abundance in life, gives us lovely things to enjoy all through our lives.

People reckon that "good things" (Ps 16:2) such as the fertility of the flocks and the flourishing of the crops depends on adherence to the right gods. To refuse to join with people who reckon you are not turning to the right gods would seem to risk your life. No harvest, no food, no sustenance; being abandoned to Sheol will follow. The attitude contrasts with, yet in another sense strangely parallels, the modern assumption that we can and must exercise control of our environment and take whatever steps are necessary to make sure our crops grow and our supermarket shelves are stocked. On both assumptions Yhwh is not the God of this life. God may be involved in religious life and in granting us resurrection life, but not in matters concerning land and food. Yet in reality Yhwh watches over, provides and protects, and we need this because we do not live by bread alone but on the basis of decisions that proceed from Yhwh's mouth.

Thus in danger of death we can say, "Into your hand I entrust my spirit" (Ps 31:5 [MT 6]). We do this when we die. In Jesus' understanding, this presupposes that dying is not an end but a kind of hiatus (Lk 23:46). He is entrusting his spirit to the Father to look after for the next two days. So when we die, we entrust our spirits to the Father until resurrection day. But before that, in danger of death we entrust our spirits to God in the conviction that God also looks after them now and can return them to us, so that death does not claim us. "Into your hand I entrust my spirit" has similar implications to "my times are in your hand" (Ps 31:15 [MT 16]), these times when troubles assail me (Ps 9:9 [MT 10]; 10:1).

When the faithless thrive in the way grass and flowers flourish after it rains, it is easy to imagine they will continue to do well forever. That is the assumption stupid people make. But it is easy for the faithful then to be overcome by exhaustion and hopelessness as they face people's opposition and the apparent possibility that the situation will continue as it is forever. But that fails to make allowance for the breadth and depth of the perspective Yhwh brings to things. Yhwh has the capacity carefully and thoughtfully to make plans and implement them, so as to treat the flourishing of the faithless in just the way the sun treats the flourishing of growth in nature after the rainy season, and in contrast to make the faithful person flourish like a date palm or cedar even when they are very old (Ps 92). So the apparently worldly wise turn out to be stupid and the naively trusting turn out to be people of perception.

Psalm 94 confronts stupid people in a similar way. Eminent but faithless people are going about crushing widow, orphan and immigrant in the conviction that Yhwh ignores such action. But the psalm begins by describing Yhwh as by nature and activity "God of redress," and then urges Yhwh to live up to this name; one might infer that it has some uncertainties about whether Yhwh will do so. But the confrontation of the "stupid" and the exhortation to them to recognize Yhwh's nature undermines any such doubts on our part. It is ridiculous to suppose that the one who plants the ear does not listen to the cries of the oppressed or that the one who shapes the eye does not discern what people are doing to them or that the one who rebukes the nations for their behavior and demands their recognition does not issue rebukes to Israelites. It would be impossible to imagine that Yhwh is involved only in religious questions or questions of the spirit, though Yhwh certainly is so involved. As a statement of confidence, the psalm affirms that God is also involved in the rest of our lives. It would be impossible to imagine that Yhwh will act at the End with regard to wrongdoing but does not do so now, though Yhwh certainly will so act. As a statement of confidence, the psalm affirms that we can also look for that involvement now.

The last section of the psalm begins with the question who arises to support the suppliant when under attack, and that points to another misapprehension a modern reader might have, that it is our responsibility as human beings to bring about faithfulness in the world. We are indeed responsible to work for faithfulness in the human community, but that assumption can leave us with too much responsibility, as if everything depends on us, or with too much guilt and sense of failure. In other First Testament contexts the question might imply the charge that Yhwh is not acting thus. Here the rhetorical question leads into a different point. There are no human beings so arising, but this does not lead the suppliant into despair, because Yhwh is the suppliant's help, upholder, comforter, haven, crag—and the one who indeed terminates the people who gang together against the faithful. As a statement of confidence the psalm affirms that we can live in the certainty of God's achieving what we cannot.

When People Stop Believing in Yhwh

In Psalm 4 the basis for the clash between suppliant and attackers is different. These are not people who acknowledge Yhwh, reckon Yhwh is on their side and are threatening the suppliant's honor, and there is little indication that they are actively causing trouble. They are people who have given up honoring Yhwh, thinking they have found something more worthy of honor. The suppliant knows that actually this thing is emptiness, falsehood and also that being committed to Yhwh (being a *ḥāsîd*) means being someone Yhwh is committed to. Yhwh is "my faithful God" (ʾĕlōhê ṣidqî). It means being someone Yhwh "sets apart"; the verb is the one used of Yhwh making a distinction between the Israelites and the Egyptians, and thus protecting the Israelites from disasters that come on their oppressors (e.g., Ex 9:4; also Ex 33:16). Perhaps the basis of assurance is this very looking at oneself in light of the story that established Israel as Yhwh's people. If Yhwh looked after the people then, Yhwh will look after me now. That conviction gives the suppliant confidence to confront the skeptics whose trust has collapsed. They are people who once trusted Yhwh to provide them with blessings such as a successful harvest, but Yhwh's loving face turned away from them and they therefore looked elsewhere, and they have now proved that looking to the Master works. The suppliant knows this cannot be right. The entities they look to are empty and false. Yhwh is the only real God. In this conviction it is possible to stay joyful even when these other people have grain and wine, and the people who stay faithful to Yhwh do not. There will be *shalom*, well-being and prosperity.

"When the foundations are destroyed, the faithful—what could he have done?" (Ps 11:3 [MT 4]). The "foundations" seem to be the bases on which the society rests. The upright get attacked for no reason and no one can do anything about it. So when these foundations collapse, what is the faithful person to do? People bade the psalmist to flit like a bird flitting to the mountains. "How can you say that?" the psalm asks. Relying on Yhwh makes it possible to stand firm in the conviction that Yhwh is committed to acting.

"The scoundrel has said in his heart, 'God is not here,' " and behaves accordingly (Ps 14:1). The world's corruption, about which God does nothing, makes it tempting to reckon the scoundrel is right. For some reason, God leaves the world to its own devices. "There is no God" (EVV) gives a misleading impression. The Hebrew expression often refers to something that was there a while ago but has now vanished. Ironically, it is often used of human beings disappearing (e.g., Ps 39:13 [MT 14]; 103:15-16). God is supposed to be the one whose presence outlasts that of humanity, but actually (the scoundrel points out) the evidence is that God is just as evanescent. Or (also ironically) God is like Enoch, who was there and then was not there, because he had disappeared to heaven (Gen 5:24).

The psalmist cannot believe that God simply sits in the heavens taking no notice of what happens on earth. To begin with, "Yhwh has looked out from heaven at human beings to see if there is anyone showing insight, seeking help from God" (Ps 14:2). There is no one. But at least Yhwh has looked and knows this. Yhwh is not uninvolved. Indeed, it is not just a matter of looking but of being present. "Yhwh is among the faithful company" (Ps 14:5). That implies Yhwh is taking action; we have noted that the First Testament is not very fond of the idea that God is present with you sharing your suffering but not doing anything about it. These scoundrels will be seized by terror (Ps 14:5). Actually the psalm says they *have been* seized by terror. Before the psalmist's mind's eye it has already happened, though later the point is expressed as a wish and as an anticipation of the rejoicing that will follow when Yhwh does "bring about a restoration of his people" (Ps 14:7). That will come "from Zion," which implies another insight on the question where Yhwh is. In a sense Yhwh is in heaven, but looks out from there to see what is happening on earth. Yet Yhwh also has a residence on the earth, on Zion, and that will be the source of Israel's deliverance. No, Yhwh cannot be written off as someone uninvolved in the world.

Protesting and Believing

Psalm 22 illustrates how prayer can involve facing and honoring two sets of facts.[139]

> The first verse contains two remarkable sentences, which, although apparently contrary to each other, are yet ever entering into the minds of the godly together. When the Psalmist speaks of being forsaken and cast off by God, it seems to be the complaint of a man in despair.... And yet, in calling God twice his own God, and depositing his groanings into his bosom, he makes a very distinct confession of his faith.[140]

As the psalm unfolds, it develops this argument. On one hand, there is the fact that Yhwh has abandoned me (Ps 22:1-2 [MT 2-3]). As Jesus' taking up of this cry on the cross indicates, it is not merely that Yhwh seems to have abandoned me. While the Father is there watching the Son suffer, so that suffering also envelops the Father, the Father is declining to rescue him and in this sense has abandoned the Son. Likewise Job knows from what has happened to him that God has abandoned him, and he accuses God accordingly. So the psalm presupposes that when I am left to the mercy of my enemies, Yhwh actually has abandoned me and is "far from deliverance." Yhwh grants hav-

---

[139]Cf. §3.3 "Plea and Praise."

[140]John Calvin, *Commentary on the Book of Psalms,* 5 vols. (Grand Rapids: Eerdmans, 1948-1949), 1:357.

ing abandoned Israel in Isaiah 54:7, not merely having seemed to abandon Israel, but insists on having done so only for a time. This does help us to hold together with this psalm other declarations in the Psalms that Yhwh does not abandon: for example, Psalm 9:10 [MT 11]. Yhwh does not *finally* abandon. But God does abandon, and the suppliant wants to know why.

In reality, of course, the suppliant does not want to know why. The presupposition of the *why* is that there is no reason, no justification.[141] Asking for the reason is a way of pressing Yhwh to reverse the abandonment. If the abandonment is only apparent, I cannot urge Yhwh to come back to me and to deliver me. All I can ask for is that I may be kept steadfast. But the psalm is acknowledging one set of facts. Yhwh has abandoned me and does not respond to my bellows. Day and night I call and Yhwh does not answer. Yhwh behaves like a deaf person rather than as one who listens to prayers.

Against that has to be set another fact. You "sit" there in the heavens enthroned "as the holy one" who is "the great praise of Israel." There is good reason for your being thus the object of praise. Our ancestors trusted in you and cried out to you in trouble, and you rescued them. They escaped from their trouble. You did not shame them (Ps 22:3-5 [MT 4-6]). My present experience of abandonment stands in stark contrast to the experience of my ancestors.

The psalm reverts to the first set of facts. "I am a worm, not a human being." This is not an expression of the "worm theology" that expresses astonishment that Christ would die "for such a worm as I."[142] That Christian stance corresponds to one presupposed by Mesopotamian prayers, which emphasize the suppliants' sinfulness, but not to the way the Scriptures speak.[143] Here as in Isaiah 41:14, wormhood does not relate to sin, and it is not a regular self-perception; it is more an indication of other people's attitude as a result of Yhwh's abandonment, which makes the suppliant "the reproach of others, despised by people" and the object of mockery (Ps 22:6-8 [MT 7-9]). People's taunts come too close to home as they urge the suppliant to commit things to Yhwh: "he must rescue him, he must save him, since he likes him." Yhwh is not doing so.

Yet people's declaration that Yhwh is the one who has to deliver takes us back to the second set of facts. Let this be a declaration of fact and not just of scorn. After all, Yhwh has been the one who has given me life and preserved my life from its very beginning, even when I was learning to trust on my mother's breast. "On you I was thrown from birth" (Ps 22:9-10 [MT 10-11]).

The middle third of the psalm (Ps 22:11-22 [MT 12-23]) holds together the two sets of facts in a different way. It is dominated by a pained description of

---

[141]See §3.2 "Asking Questions."

[142]See Isaac Watts's hymn "Alas! and Did My Saviour Bleed!" (1707).

[143]See Patrick and Diable, "Persuading the One and Only God to Intervene," pp. 21-22.

the suppliant's predicament: I am surrounded by attackers as dangerous and threatening as steers or lions or dogs. They have reduced me to melting wax, my strength dried up, my voice silenced. (Presumably the reference is to the voice speaking to the attackers, as it can evidently speak to God.) Death stares me in the face and the attackers are already haggling over my effects. And you, Yhwh, are responsible for this: "You put me in deathly dirt." But this anti-testimony or anti-thanksgiving is bracketed by a double plea, "Do not be far away." I have no other helper or rescuer, so be my help, my rescue ('āzar is conventionally translated "help," but this underrepresents the significance of the word, which suggests action that makes something happen that I could not bring about myself). The suppliant prays thus despite having begun with an assertion that presupposes, "You abandoned me." Further, the psalm not only urges Yhwh to answer that prayer, but envisages the situation when Yhwh has done so: "I will tell of your name to my kindred, in the midst of the congregation I will praise you" (Ps 22:22 [MT 23]).

The last third of the psalm (Ps 22:23-31 [MT 24-32]) takes this even further in exhorting people to praise Yhwh now on the basis of Yhwh's act of deliverance not as something future but as something already brought about: "For he has not despised . . . the lament of the weak. He has not turned his face from him, but when he cried for help, listened to him." It goes on to declare the implications of this for "all the ends of the earth" that "must be mindful and turn to Yhwh." It is only stage one of the answer that has come, but the suppliant does know Yhwh has heard the prayer and answered it, in the sense of setting in motion the process of rescue. Perhaps a minister has brought reassurance that this is so; perhaps coming before Yhwh has engendered the assurance.

Remembering and Hoping

Psalm 30 similarly presupposes how in prayer we live between being put down and being restored to honor, crying for help and being healed, being at the door of Sheol and being brought back to fullness of life, experiencing momentary wrath and finding lifelong acceptance, weeping and resounding, Yhwh's face hiding and Yhwh being gracious, my experiencing terror and Yhwh's becoming my helper, calling and confessing, pleading for grace and proclaiming, mourning and dancing, sackcloth and joy, wailing and music-making. But it does so the other side of Yhwh's actual act of deliverance, after stage two. In a situation of trouble we remember and hope; when Yhwh has acted, we remember hoping and we give thanks.

The dynamic of remembering and hoping persists in different formulations through Israel's story.[144] In Egypt and at the Red Sea Israel failed to come

---

[144]On remembering, cf. Ellington, *Risking Truth*, pp. 83-93.

to an understanding of the significance of the wonders Yhwh had already done in their experience and to be mindful of them, and thus they panicked and accused Yhwh of abandoning them—which on this occasion Yhwh had not done. Yhwh then did a further wonder that led them to a position of trust. But they subsequently also failed to keep that wonder in mind and could not believe in Yhwh's plan to take them through the wilderness to their destination; nor could they see that trying to make an image of this God was really stupid (Ps 106:7, 12-13, 19-22). In Psalm 129 Israel remembers that people have been attacking it since its youth: "but they have not prevailed over me." Metaphorically, people such the Amalekites, Assyrians and Babylonians had often plowed over Israel's back or tied Israel up, but "Yhwh—he is faithful; he cut the rope of the faithless." So now Israel can affirm or pray (the verbs are ambiguous) that Yhwh will do so again.

By the rivers of Babylon, Judean exiles sat and wept and "were mindful of Zion." In Jerusalem that mindfulness would have meant singing songs about Zion such as Psalms 46, 48 and 76, but here they have hung their lyres on poplars growing by those watercourses. Lyres are especially associated with praise, and no praise can be offered in connection with Zion here. The people's very presence in Babylon reflects the disconfirmation of what the Zion psalms said (cf. Lam 2:15). The Judeans' captors underline the point (perhaps only in the captives' imagination) by snidely inviting them to sing one of those psalms. It is impossible to sing Yhwh's song in a foreign land. This is not because Yhwh is not there; there is no place from which Yhwh is absent, and Ezekiel has seen and heard from Yhwh in Babylon. It is because the exiles' presence there reflects that disconfirmation of those psalms' statements about Zion. Yhwh has not vindicated the vision they speak of. One might have expected the exiles to chide Yhwh for failing to keep a commitment to Zion (the kind Ps 132 celebrates), but if Psalm 137 thinks in those terms, it does so only very indirectly. In this protest psalm all the emphasis lies on "I/we" and "they."

It is impossible to praise, but it is not impossible to be mindful, though in the absence of praise, this is more difficult; hence the self-curse that follows. Initially, it is doubly incoherent: "If I put you out of mind, Jerusalem, may my right hand put out of mind." It is quite regular for a self-curse to lack a statement of the consequence of default; this one even lacks an object for its verb. The next line will suggest that it is something such as "its skill" in playing, as the psalmist goes on, "May my tongue stick to my palate, if I am not mindful of you, if I do not lift up Jerusalem above the pinnacle of my joyfulness." May I never be able to play or sing again if I do not stay mindful of Jerusalem, even though I cannot at this moment play or sing about it. What then is the point of the mindfulness? Rhetorically, the next line suggests, it is to challenge Yhwh also to be mindful.

"It is between the Scylla of simplistic faith and the Charybdis of stoic resignation that the lament runs its perilous course."[145]

Individual and Community

For someone who has been traumatized, healing may involve a three-stage
process comprising "the establishment of safety," "remembrance and mourning" in the hearing of someone else and "reconnection with ordinary life."[146]
The Psalms point to an analogous process, one of reasserting who God is in
power, love and trustworthiness, telling it like it is and like it has been, and
grieving and protesting about it, and telling the story of how it has now been
possible to resume a life in community.[147]

Psalm 9 begins by looking forward to the time when it will be possible to
make confession of the way Yhwh has acted decisively for the suppliant. Its
conviction that this time will come is based on the fact that Yhwh has acted
that way in the community's experience. This psalm also again indicates that
prayer and confidence involve remembering and hoping. The suppliant expects in the future (it had better be soon) to be in a position to confess Yhwh's
awesome deeds when Yhwh has given decisive judgment and put down the
attackers (Ps 9:1-4 [MT 2-5]). Yhwh's having done this in the past encourages a
confidence about Yhwh's having power and authority in the present and thus
being one whom a broken person can trust (Ps 9:5-12 [MT 6-13]). But the suppliant has to live between the reality of Yhwh's acts of deliverance in the past
and the need for deliverance to come now, and to live in trust and praise, to
live between memory and expectancy. The memory may relate to what Yhwh
has done for us personally, but in this psalm, as is often the case, it relates to
what Yhwh has done for the people to whom we belong. This provides more
reliable clues to reality than our own narrow experience. The expectancy also
implicitly relates to Yhwh's involvement with the people as a whole. Perhaps
Yhwh may not deliver me. If Naboth prays this prayer, Yhwh does not do that.
But this does not (or may not) mean that Yhwh has abandoned the people you
belong to.

Psalm 103 gives praise for the way we can experience as individuals the
way Yhwh pardons, heals, restores, garlands, satiates and renews. But it sets
this in the context of Yhwh's ways having been made known to Moses and
Israel in acts of faithfulness and in compassion, grace and commitment. Here
too, understanding the significance of our personal experiences of God's love

---

[145]Levenson, *Creation and the Persistence of Evil*, p. 25.

[146]So Judith L. Herman, *Trauma and Recovery* (New York: Basic, 1997), p. 155.

[147]So Serene Jones, " 'Soul Anatomy': Calvin's Commentary on the Psalms," in *Psalms in
Community*, ed. Harold W. Attridge and Margot E. Fassler (Atlanta: Society of Biblical
Literature, 2003), pp. 265-84.

is furthered as we look at them in light of the way Yhwh has related to the community. Yhwh does not relate primarily to individuals and then perhaps to the community as a collection of individuals. Our significance as individuals lies in our relationship with the community with which Yhwh has been at work over the generations. Conversely, Yhwh's involvement with the community over the generations undergirds Yhwh's involvement with us as individuals. The community's memory of the way Yhwh has acted in its life enables us as individuals to understand what Yhwh does with us, even as it is our own experience of Yhwh's involvement in our lives that enables us to understand our community's traditions concerning Yhwh's acts.[148]

"There is no private piety in the Psalms." People pray in the company of their family and friends, appeal to the way Yhwh is committed to the people corporately, and when their prayer has been answered, give thanks before the "great congregation" (Ps 22:25 [MT 26]).[149]

3.5 Intercession

In the Psalms almost invariably people pray for "me" or "us" rather than for "him" or "her" or "them." In the First Testament story the balance is the other way round; usually people pray for "her" or "him" or "them." Whereas a prayer for grace *(tĕhinnâ)* is usually a prayer prayed for oneself or on behalf of one's own people, a plea *(tĕpillâ)* is more easily a prayer prayed on someone else's behalf. Thus we plead *(pālal* hitpael) "on behalf of" someone *(baʿad;* e.g., Gen 20:7; Deut 9:20; Jer 7:16, discouragingly). Intercession involves standing before the court of heaven urging it to make a decision on behalf of the people we are concerned for, and then to implement that decision.

A Divine Invitation

The first account of intercession uses no such expressions. It is the first of a number of occasions when Yhwh announces the intention to bring calamity to a people (Gen 18:17-33), almost as if to invite disagreement or protest. Yhwh has shown up at Abraham's encampment along with two aides; all three appear looking like human beings. It eventually becomes clear that they are on their way to Sodom. Yhwh has decided to do something in response to the cries of hurt that arise from Sodom, but wishes first to check out how things really are there and to tell Abraham about all this. It will become clear that there is no one who deserves saving in Sodom itself, so perhaps the people Sodom oppresses are people who live in the surrounding area, or perhaps they are people who have died in Sodom whose blood cries out like Abel's.

---

[148]Cf. Gene Rice, "An Exposition of Psalm 103," *Journal of Religious Thought* 39 (1982-1983): 55-61; see p. 57.
[149]Hans-Joachim Kraus, *Worship in Israel* (Oxford: Blackwell/Richmond: Knox, 1966), p. 219.

The two aides proceed there, but Yhwh apparently hangs about, and "Abraham was still standing before Yhwh" in the posture of a suppliant. He draws near and asks whether Yhwh really intends to sweep away faithless with faithful. Would Yhwh do that if there are fifty faithful people there? Would Yhwh sweep away the city rather than "carry" it for the sake of the fifty faithful? That would be no way for the one who exercises authority over the entire world to exercise authority. (Abraham uses the participle from *šāpaṭ* and the noun *mišpāṭ*). So affirms the man whom the world is due to take as a model of blessing and whom Yhwh has designated as one to instruct his family in the faithful exercise of authority (Gen 18:19). Yhwh grants his point. Acknowledging that he speaks as a mere mortal ("I am dirt and ash"), Abraham asks how it would be if there were forty-five faithful, or forty or thirty or twenty or ten, twice asking Yhwh not to get angry with his question. Each time Yhwh says, "I will not destroy the city."

The story does not say in so many words that Abraham prayed or that Yhwh had a change of mind, but Abraham surely thinks he is seeking to get Yhwh to have a change of mind, otherwise the deference would make little sense. And one might wonder what is the point of Yhwh's announcement if it is not to invite disagreement or agreement; otherwise, why does Yhwh not simply act? Being told about Yhwh's intentions is tantamount to an invitation to comment on them; Yhwh was almost standing there waiting for Abraham to do so, as the other two visitors go off. Indeed, the story closes by telling us not that Abraham has been speaking with Yhwh, as we thought; Yhwh has been speaking with Abraham.

The aftermath is also instructive. In the event there are not ten faithful people in Sodom. Lot's behavior shows he does not belong in that category, and in light of subsequent events it is at least questionable whether anyone else in his family does. Yet the story closes with the comment that when destroying the cities of the plain, "God was mindful of Abraham and sent Lot from the midst of the upheaval." Is Yhwh mindful of and responsive to Abraham's prayer in a different way than he envisaged?

Moses' interaction with Yhwh in Exodus 32:7-14 has overlapping dynamics. When Yhwh declared the intention to destroy Israel and start again with Moses, he "sought Yhwh's favor." The expression is *ḥillâ pānîm*, which literally means "sweeten the face, make the face pleasant"; it suggests causing someone in a superior position to take a positive, friendly stance toward the suppliant and thus be prepared to grant the request that follows.[150] Here the request is that Yhwh not thus be angry toward the people. They are a people Yhwh delivered from Egypt; the Egyptians will say Yhwh did so with evil

---

[150]See *TDOT*.

intent. And they are the descendants of people Yhwh swore to give the land to. So the basis for not taking the action Yhwh had announced lies in Yhwh's reputation and in the need to be faithful to who Yhwh is. "And Yhwh relented over the calamity that he spoke of causing to his people."

Changing God's Mind

When a boss tells an assistant to do something, it is sometimes the assistant's role to ask whether that is really the appropriate action, and so it is with Yhwh's assistants. It is in this way that they fulfill the role of intercessors. For Moses as for Abraham, being told Yhwh's intentions was indeed tantamount to an invitation to comment on them. His intercession does not involve wresting mercy from an unwilling deity. As Yhwh's subsequent self-revelation will suggest (Ex 34:6-7), there is good reason for grace as well as for toughness from within Yhwh. Moses flees from God to God, appeals from God to God and thus shows himself truly to have understood God as he makes his demand from the very heart of God.[151] Yhwh's decisions about Sodom or about Israel have to deal with a tension within God between mercy and wrath. So "Moses was not so much arguing *against* God, . . . as participating in an argument *within* God."[152] Yhwh's undertaking to reinscribe the Decalogue is an indication of willingness to restore the covenant and of agreeing to Moses' argument. Moses utilizes similar arguments in Numbers 14:13-19: Yhwh risks surrounding nations inferring that Yhwh does not have the power to bring the people into the land, and needs to act in accordance with that self-revelation in Exodus 34:6-7 by pardoning the people.

> If ever there was a miserable anthropomorphism, it is the hallucination of a divine immutability which rules out the possibility that God can let Himself be conditioned in this or that way by His creature. God is certainly immutable. But He is immutable as the living God and in the mercy in which He espouses the cause of the creature. . . . He can give to this creature a place in His will.[153]

The Zohar notes Solomon's testimony that "not one word has failed of every good word that he spoke by means of his servant Moses" (1 Kings 8:56) and comments that if this read "of every word," it would have been better if the world had never been created. But fortunately (it goes on), an argument does go on within God.[154] So bad words often do not get fulfilled, because

---

[151]Karl Barth, *Church Dogmatics* (Edinburgh: T & T Clark, 1961), IV/1:426.

[152]Christopher Wright, *Deuteronomy* (Peabody, Mass.: Hendrickson/[Carlisle]: Paternoster, 1996), p. 140.

[153]Barth, *Church Dogmatics,* III/4:109.

[154]See the selections in *Zohar: The Book of Enlightenment* (New York: Paulist Press, 1983), p. 137; cf. Biddle, *Deuteronomy,* p. 160.

Yhwh's mercy overwhelms Yhwh's wrath. On the other hand, the primacy of grace in God's person means Yhwh's wrath can never overturn the intention to bless; it is in such a connection that Balaam declares that God does not have a change of mind (Num 23:19).

Mercy and wrath also meet within Moses. The Moses who pleads for mercy is soon taking wrathful action (Ex 32:19-29). He shares Yhwh's rage at Israel's behavior and smashes the stones inscribed with the Decalogue, thereby confirming that the covenant is annulled. Yet he also casts himself down before Yhwh and fasts for forty days and nights in an act of vicarious penitence,[155] and Yhwh listens to him, as Yhwh did when Moses appealed on behalf of Aaron as ringleader (Deut 9:19-20). The sequence then repeats (Ex 32:30–33:6). Israel's story from the day it left Egypt until the day it stood on the edge of the promised land is a story of provoking Yhwh to anger and destruction (Deut 9:7-14) and thus of driving Moses to intercession (see Num 11:2; 21:7). Moses cannot change Yhwh's mind about his own destiny, but he can change Yhwh's mind about Israel's destiny. Paul likewise cannot change God's mind about the thorn in his flesh, but this does not stop him praying fervently for other people.

Prayer is designed not to change us but to change God,[156] and it is designed not to change what happens to us but to change what happens to other people. This illumines the contrast between Genesis 18 and Genesis 22, where Abraham offers no objection to Yhwh's command to sacrifice Isaac. Whereas the announcement about other people in Genesis 18 almost invites Abraham to question it, the command to Abraham himself (only indirectly about Isaac) invites only obedience. "If Genesis 18 represents the (qualified) autonomy of humanity over against divine decrees, we may take Genesis 22... as the parade example of human heteronomy before the inscrutable command of God."[157]

A Prophetic Commission

In these stories it is significant who intercedes. Abraham does so because of Yhwh's vision for his position in relation to nations such as Sodom (Gen 18:17-18). Moses does so as one who has just met with Yhwh on the mountain. Intercession is especially the task of particular people, such as leaders and prophets who have special access to God,[158] and who are seeking to evoke a change in God's intent to judge a sinful people. Such intercession is expected

---

[155]Such a forty-day fast would require divine sustenance, in line with Deut 8:3; but Exodus may assume the convention that fasting applies to the daylight hours and that he was free to eat and drink after nightfall (cf. §3.1 "Manner, Place and Time").

[156]See the introduction to §3.3.

[157]Levenson, *Creation and the Persistence of Evil*, p. 151.

[158]Cf. Reventlow, *Gebet im Alten Testament*, pp. 228-64.

by God and incorporated into the divine activity.[159] Prophets intercede for people by virtue of their position. Their summons locates them between Yhwh and people, identified with both. It takes them into membership of Yhwh's cabinet. There they discover what Yhwh intends and how the members of the cabinet are to implement Yhwh's intentions, so that they can speak of them to their people. But this also means they are in a position to protest these plans and be involved in their finalizing.

Thus Samuel undertakes to plead with Yhwh for the people in a similar situation to that in Exodus 32, and the people subsequently ask, "Do not be deaf to us so as not to cry out to Yhwh our God so that he may deliver us"; subsequently Samuel promises, "far be it from me to fail Yhwh in refraining from pleading for you." In between there is another more ambiguous plea arising out of the people's request for a king (1 Sam 7:5, 8; 8:6; 12:19, 23). The task of pleading with Yhwh is one laid on Samuel by the people and also by Yhwh, so that Samuel would be coming short of his task as a prophet if he so failed. Hezekiah likewise assumes that Isaiah can plead with Yhwh for the people (2 Kings 19:4).

A woman's son gets ill and seems near death. It must have been a common experience in Israel's world. But this woman has had a close relationship with Elijah; he has cared for her, and she has cared for him. She therefore challenges him about what has happened, and he challenges Yhwh: "The woman that I am guest of: are you really bringing calamity on her by letting her son die?" Then he stretches out over the boy three times and calls to Yhwh again, "Yhwh my God, may this boy's life return within him." It does (1 Kings 17:20-22). Prayer and action combine, as do praise and action. In isolation from prayer, Elijah's lying on the boy might seem like an attempt at magic, while in isolation from ritual action, prayer might seem like uninvolved, docetic words.

Elisha similarly pleads with Yhwh for the dead son of the woman who gives him hospitality at Shunem (2 Kings 4:19-37). When the boy dies, she focuses resolutely on going to see Elisha, who is surprised that Yhwh has not revealed to him what is going on. Elisha is the cause of her trouble (she would have had no child if he had not promised one), and she insists that he come to the boy; merely sending the staff that it may touch the boy will not do. Elisha pleads with Yhwh, lies on the boy twice, and he comes back to life. On another occasion, Elisha can see things that Gehazi cannot, so Elisha pleads for his eyes to open so he can see the heavenly forces surrounding them and protecting them; and he successfully pleads for the earthly forces that are coming to arrest him to become blind for a while (2 Kings 6:17-18).

---

[159]Miller, "Prayer and Divine Action," p. 217.

Prophetic Confrontation

Yhwh commissions Jeremiah to warn the people to prepare for imminent attack, and yet implies that such preparation is futile. The people may as well put on mourning garb and lament: "The king's heart and the leaders' heart will fail, the priests will be appalled, the prophets will be aghast." Jeremiah's response is to comment, "Lord Yhwh, you really have totally deceived this people and Jerusalem, in saying 'There will be *shalom* for you' when a sword has reached their throat" (Jer 4:9-10). It is a vivid illustration of the free nature of his interaction with Yhwh as a prophet, on the people's behalf.

During the bulk of his ministry the entire political and religious leadership does not believe that calamity is coming, and it will thus be shattered when it does. People believe prophets and priests who keep saying "'It will be well, it will be well,' when it will not be well" [*shalom, shalom*, when there is no *shalom*] (Jer 6:14; 8:11; cf. Jer 8:15; 14:19). Such prophets mislead the people; Yhwh has not sent them nor spoken to them (Ezek 13:6-7, 10, 16). "The prophet who prophesies about things being well: when the prophet's word comes about, it will be acknowledged that Yhwh truly sent the prophet" (Jer 28:9).

But in Jeremiah 4 Jeremiah protests that Yhwh has totally deceived (*haššē᾽ haššē᾽ tā*) the people. Perhaps he reckons that in some sense Yhwh is responsible for everything that happens, or has to accept responsibility for what people say in Yhwh's name unless Yhwh intervenes, or is responsible for what these prophets say because sending them is an act of punishment (cf. 1 Kings 22; Ezek 14:7-9). Whatever lies behind his words, they are an audacious protest and accusation. Yhwh does not strike him dead for them. Being a prophet means standing with the people as well as with Yhwh. It involves saying outrageous things to the people on Yhwh's behalf, and outrageous things to Yhwh on the people's behalf. In both cases, the aim is to induce change: to get the people to change and to get Yhwh to change.

More than once during the siege of Jerusalem, King Zedekiah sends to Jeremiah to ask him to inquire of Yhwh on the city's behalf (Jer 21:2; cf. Jer 37:17) or to plead with Yhwh for the city (Jer 37:3). On the first occasion Zedekiah is hoping Yhwh might do a wonder for the people, like the wonders of the past, and make Nebuchadnezzar withdraw. In the event on each occasion Jeremiah promises the opposite to what Zedekiah hopes for. Zedekiah recognizes the two aspects to what a prophet is for. He is in a position to stand in Yhwh's presence, and he can tell Israel what Yhwh says (and press for a response) and tell Yhwh what Israel longs for (and press for a response).

When Ezekiel hears Yhwh commissioning Jerusalem's executioners, he falls on his face and cries out, "Oh, Lord Yhwh, are you destroying the entire remains of Israel?" (Ezek 9:8). On this occasion the prophet fails to change Yhwh's mind. Even though his question is odd, as Yhwh has already made clear that people who sigh and groan over the city's abominations are to be exempted, Yhwh's reply is not to point this out but to justify the magnitude of the slaughter. That is how wicked the city is. The exiles have to face facts about themselves. When one of the Jerusalem leaders drops dead, apparently an earnest of the fulfillment of his prophecy, Ezekiel tells us, "I fell on my face and cried out with a loud voice, 'Oh, Lord Yhwh, you are making an end of the remains of Israel!'" (Ezek 11:13); the protest does not have an interrogative, like the one in Ezekiel 9:8, but it is implicitly a question (cf. NRSV, TNIV). Yhwh's response consists in a promise about the future of Ezekiel's own community, which provides an oblique answer to the implied question and again does not suggest that his protest gets him anywhere. The prophet's freedom to pray is matched by Yhwh's freedom to refuse to listen.

Talking About Prayer

Among the Latter Prophets, Amos and Jeremiah are the great intercessors. They thus do not fall short as prophets. Amos has two visions of natural disaster in the land (Amos 7:1-6). In reaction to the first he exclaims, "Lord, Yhwh, do pardon! How will Jacob stand, because it is small!" Yhwh relents; "it will not happen." In reaction to the second Amos exclaims, "Lord Yhwh, do stop." The plea is thus different, though the succeeding argument about Jacob is the same, and Yhwh's response is the same. When Amos thus intervenes, "the effect is sensational."[160] It makes Amos a participant in the scene rather than a mere observer. In turn the reporting of the scene has a different affect on Amos's audience from that of ordinary words. They too are drawn into the drama of a scene where Yhwh declares an intention, then modifies it.

For prophet and audience there is then a telling and worrying contrast between the first two visions and the next two (Amos 7:7-9; 8:1-3). Here Yhwh preempts any intervention on Amos's part by personally seizing the initiative in the conversation, taking it toward a declaration that "I will not pass over them again." Amos takes the hint and does not issue any appeal. "At most, intercession buys time";[161] when Yhwh has a change of heart and mind, the question is whether Israel will also do so, in order that passing over can become pardon.

The significance of these second two scenes might be less immediately self-evident than that of the first two, and the visions are not as obviously threatening. We are not sure what Yhwh was holding when standing at or on a wall (Amos 7:7-9). The word (ʾănāk), traditionally translated "plumb line," is not the regular word for plumb line, and whatever it was, it is not self-evident

---

[160]Francis I. Andersen and David Noel Freedman, *Amos*, AB (New York: Doubleday, 1989), p. 621.
[161]Ibid., p. 639.

what Yhwh was doing with it. Perhaps the word was inherently ambiguous; the subsequent vision that pairs with it (Amos 8:1-3) depends on a paronomasia, so perhaps this one also does.[162] When Yhwh points Amos to a basket of figs, pardonably Amos seems at first not to see the point about it; perhaps he has a hunch that there is something significant here, but does not know what it is. It is again Yhwh who sets the agenda for and the pace in the conversation. Before Amos has chance to ask Yhwh not to demolish the nation or not to bring its life to an end, Yhwh has already affirmed the intention not to pass by them again, no longer to refrain from action. Paradoxically, Amos's being excluded from the conversation at this point has even greater impact on him and on his audience than his initiating the conversation earlier, precisely because Yhwh effectively preempts any possibility of his doing so. All Amos can do (he is almost manipulated into doing it) is articulate the message about calamity and thus both affirm it and let it loose.[163]

Amos's prayers thus adopt another, more somber angle for looking at the relationship between the demands of divine wrath and divine mercy as these relate to prayer. Amos's prayer moves from "pardon" to "stop" and then becomes silent. Yhwh's response moves from a double responsive relenting to a double anticipatory declaration that there is to be no more passing over. The story of what happened at Bethel, placed in the midst of the account of the visions, helps to explain why Amos no longer asks for Yhwh to pardon Israel or even to hold back from punishing for a while.[164] But is this Yhwh's last word? Amos is relating his experiences to someone; these sections of his book are part of his prophetic ministry. Perhaps the declaration that Yhwh will not pass by again, and Amos's ceasing to pray, is yet another attempt to break through to the people. In other words, praying is one thing; reporting one's prayers is another.

A Prophetic Decommission

So what response is called for from the audience of Amos (the man or the book)? Is it simply to recognize that there are moments when one can appeal to Yhwh and moments when one cannot? Or that it should take up where Amos left off and imitate the boldness of Abraham and Moses, who took Yhwh's announcements of intention as a challenge to prayer rather than a prohibition of prayer? Might this be what Yhwh is waiting for, as seems to be the case when Yhwh stands waiting before Abraham? Is the firmness of Yhwh's words a sign of Yhwh's awareness that if the prophet does intervene on the people's behalf in keeping with his position as someone admitted to

---

[162]Cf. ibid., p. 757.
[163]Cf. ibid., p. 615.
[164]Cf. Jörg Jeremias, *The Book of Amos* (Louisville: Westminster John Knox, 1998), p. 137.

the heavenly cabinet, Yhwh will have a hard time resisting him?[165] When Isaiah recalls the proverb "human beings bow, people drop down,"[166] what goes up comes down, he evidently recognizes that of course Yhwh could make Judah an exception to that generalization, but he does not urge this, unlike Abraham, Moses or Amos when they pray. On the contrary, he adds, "but do not carry it for them" (Is 2:9). Yet this too is the report of a prayer and the report is part of his ministry, perhaps designed to make the people turn and ensure that his prayer is not granted.

Jeremiah's reports of his prayers are also part of his ministry. He reports the people urging him to plead for them (Jer 37:3; 42:1-4), but the result is never good news. Yhwh's response may be negative (Jer 37:6-10) or the people may perceive it so (Jer 43:1-3). Strangely (or not strangely, in light of that), his first reference to prayer concerns his decommission. Rather in the manner of Amos's prayer account, Jeremiah 7 relates Yhwh's declaration that the temple is doomed, but then relates Yhwh's frightening bidding to Jeremiah: "And you, do not plead for this people, do not raise a pleading shout for them, do not intercede with me [*pāgaʿ*], because I am not listening to you" (Jer 7:16; cf. 11:14). Once again, this declaration looks from another, more somber angle at the relationship between the demands of divine wrath and divine mercy as these relate to prayer. "God expects to be affected by the intercession of Jeremiah and staves it off before it can come."[167] Yet if Yhwh is so affected, perhaps there is still hope? Or perhaps the prayer report constitutes yet another attempt to break through to the people.

Jeremiah 14–15 begins with a lament at a natural disaster, and follows that with the people's prayer for Yhwh not to abandon them, a prayer apparently voiced by Jeremiah as their prophet. Yhwh is chillingly unmoved and once more bids Jeremiah, "Do not plead for good for this people." I am not listening (Jer 14:11). Again Jeremiah voices their prayer, acknowledging their waywardness (Jer 14:19-22), with some theo-logic matching the prayer that Moses uses: Be mindful of the covenant, act for your name's sake. Once again Yhwh's response is a snort: "If Moses and Samuel stood before me, I would have no concern for this people" (Jer 15:1). "I am weary of relenting" (Jer 15:6).

Jeremiah's vocation to intercession is not confined to him; his comments conform to the place of intercession within a prophet's vocation. In bidding people to take no notice of the prophets who promise a speedy return from exile, he makes a paradoxical addition to his forthright critique of the other prophets. They are inclined to promise the people that things are going to

---

[165]Cf. Andersen and Freedman, *Amos*, p. 616.

[166]Cf. Hans Wildberger, *Isaiah 1–12* (Minneapolis: Fortress, 1991), p. 111.

[167]Miller, *They Cried to the Lord*, p. 276.

work out all right: for instance, that the people will soon see the return of the accoutrements from the temple that Nebuchadnezzar took in 597. That is a false promise, says Jeremiah; furthermore, "If they are prophets and Yhwh's word is with them, they should intercede with Yhwh Armies so that the vessels remaining in Yhwh's house, in the king of Judah's house, and in Jerusalem may not go to Babylon" (Jer 27:18). It is another indication that one reason why prophets are (allegedly) apprised of Yhwh's intentions is so that they may urge Yhwh not to implement them. There are two aspects of the ministry of these prophets, as of any prophet, and they fail in both. In contrast, by praying Jeremiah represents the people to God as well as God to the people, like Samuel, though with wholly negative results. Prophets who want to do their job properly and safely will focus on prayer as much as on prophecy.

Intercessors as Lookouts

Whether intercessors fulfill Yhwh's commission really makes a difference. Prophets were supposed to be people who climbed into the gaps in the city walls and repaired them (Ezek 13:4-5). Instead, the designated intercessors have been like jackals scrabbling about and foraging among these broken walls. Ezekiel 22:30 makes more explicit that it is intercession that constitutes repairing the walls, as it describes Yhwh looking for someone "building a wall or standing in the breach before me on behalf of the land so that I might not destroy it." But, Yhwh adds, "I did not find one," and therefore it is being destroyed. Apparently Ezekiel's intercession was not enough to win the argument in Yhwh's cabinet, even if it was enough to get the cabinet to resolve that preserving and renewing the exiles should ensure there would be a future (Ezek 11:13-21).

After the destruction another prophet takes up Ezekiel's ministry and appoints others to stand on the city's wall. "For Zion's sake I will not be silent, for Jerusalem's sake I will not keep quiet, until its faithfulness issues like brilliance, its deliverance like a burning torch" (Is 62:1). Once again the prophet's task is to speak to the city about Yhwh's intentions for it and thus bring it comfort and encouragement, and also to speak to Yhwh about the city, and to do so faithfully and persistently.[168] Yhwh made a commitment to act with ṣĕdāqâ in bringing about the city's spectacular restoration; that gives purchase to the prophet's prayers. Yhwh is a CEO who has affirmed certain policy intentions, and the prophet is a company employee who is a member of the

---

[168]In isolation a declaration of intent not to be silent or quiet could be Yhwh's words, responding to the bidding to Yhwh not to be so (e.g., Ps 28:1; 83:1 [MT 2]). But it was the prophet who was speaking in the previous chapter, and the present speaker refers to Yhwh in the third person, and the subsequent lines have lookouts commissioned not to be silent. All this suggests that the prophet speaks here

board with responsibility to press for these to be implemented, to make sure there is no slippage between declaration and event. The prophet is to be a real nuisance in the meetings of the board, refusing to shut up about what has to happen and having no need to be hesitant about doing this, as if it might be presumptuous; after all, it was the CEO who appointed this employee representative to the board. The prophet declares the intention to be faithful to the task of urging Yhwh to be faithful to the task of restoring the city.

The employee representative does not have to fulfill this demanding task alone. Rather the prophet appoints others to share in it. "On your walls, Jerusalem, I have appointed guards; all day and all night, continually, they are not to be silent. You who bring things to Yhwh's mind, there must be no rest for you, and give him no rest, until he establishes Jerusalem and makes it a reason for praise in all the earth" (Is 62:6-7). "Guards" is a surprising way to think of intercessors (the word here is *šōmēr* not *ṣōpeh*, "lookout," as in passages such as Is 56:10). Perhaps its point is that like lookouts they are people watching keenly for things to happen; in this case, they are watching for that act of *ṣĕdāqâ* that brings deliverance, watching for the city to be established and made a reason for people to praise Yhwh or to praise the city itself. They are to take no rest; lookouts or guards who drop off to sleep have totally failed in their task. In addition, as they watch for the coming of the events that everyone is looking for, they are also not to be silent, like the prophet. As well as taking no rest themselves, they are to allow Yhwh no rest. They too are to keep pressing questions on the chair of the board, to keep bringing things to Yhwh's attention, to keep insisting on action in fulfillment of those commitments that the CEO has long made.

This commission to the guards leads into an oath by Yhwh to make sure the city's enemies will never again appropriate the harvest for which it has labored, and a renewed commission by the prophet concerning a clearing of the way for Yhwh to come to the city with its people (Is 62:8-12). There is nothing new in the oath and the commission; they repeat promises and commissions that have recurred in Isaiah 40–55 and Isaiah 60–61. It would make sense to take them as implicitly responses to those urgings of the prophet and the guards. They thus parallel Ezekiel 11:14-21 as a reply to the cry of protest in Ezekiel 11:13. The intercessions of such figures do meet with a response, but it remains one that can be heard but not seen. It thus stimulates more bringing to Yhwh's attention, rather than removing the need for that.

Praying for the City

Psalm 102 begins like other individual protest psalms, as the prayer of someone who desperately needs Yhwh to listen and answer, who is consumed as by fire, crushed and withered, groaning and wakeful, taunted and distraught, lifted up and thrown away like chaff by God. It then goes on, "But you—you, Yhwh, will sit forever, your renown will endure generation after generation," and segues into a declaration that "You will arise, you will have compassion on Zion, because it is time to show grace to her." The individual prays as someone living in Jerusalem or representing the city, in the manner of the individual in Lamentations 3. The psalm is concerned for the suppliant's personal needs, but in praying about these it is praying for the city. Perhaps portraying the city's suffering in terms of an individual's helps reinforce the point, like a newspaper seeking to convey the implications of policies or problems by portraying their effect on an individual. The community's pain and loss is expressed vividly through its being portrayed as that of an individual, and this has the potential to move God to act to relieve it.

In themselves the declarations just quoted can be read either as descriptive or prescriptive. Yhwh has to decide whether the suppliant means "I know you have heard my prayer and you are going to do this" or means "You must hear my prayer and do this." Either way, it is in keeping with Yhwh's everlasting enthronement and renown: this either means Yhwh is acting or that Yhwh must act. The psalm adds the further backing, that "your servants have delighted in her stones and they show grace to her dirt," which rather suggests the declarations do continue the earlier prayer. The suppliant knows Yhwh delights in this people and this land and has intentions for this city's stones (Ps 44:3 [MT 4]; 85:1 [MT 2]; Is 54:11-12), but Yhwh is not behaving in light of that. Can the Judeans "revive the stones out of the heaps of dirt?" Sanballat asked (Neh 4:2 [MT 3:34]). This puts more pressure on Yhwh: we delight in, we care about these stones, indeed we show grace to this city's dirt. If we do, so should you! The suppliant knows Yhwh does so, and the result of Yhwh's having compassion on Zion will be to cause the nations to acknowledge Yhwh and cause future generations of Jerusalem's own people to recount Yhwh's praise. The psalm looks forward with confidence to the time when that will have happened.

Psalm 122 urges people to pray for Jerusalem. It is the exhortation of a pilgrim, someone who does not live there but rejoices in having been able to set foot within the gates of this city that is built with an impressive kind of strong compactness and is a center for the making of faithful decisions for its own destiny in relation to the peoples who live around and for the families who live in it and around it. The psalm thus speaks not of Zion, the religious entity, but of Jerusalem, the more political one. Perhaps it presupposes that the city often does not enjoy well-being or peace. Its rampart and citadels testify to its being less strong than it might look. It may relate to other nations and to the people who live there unfairly rather than with decisive faithfulness. It was often a place of conflict and of prosperity and flourishing for some people but not for others. Therefore, pray for its *shalom*, the psalm urges.

Nehemiah is no prophet but just a cupbearer for Artaxerxes (though this might make him a man of prayer, if his job involved tasting the emperor's drinks to make sure they were not poisoned). While being a leader might lay on someone a commitment to plead for people, perhaps a compulsion to plead for people can issue in becoming a leader. Certainly, when the cupbearer hears about the state of things in Jerusalem, he falls into weeping, mourning and fasting, and pleads to the God of heaven (Neh 1:4-11). He reminds Yhwh of the key divine characteristics of awesomeness and commitment, acknowledges the people's failures without inferring that these mean Yhwh can go back on that commitment, and urges Yhwh to be mindful of promises concerning a return from exile. Yet like a psalmist he is very unspecific about what exactly he wants Yhwh to do for the people; indeed, his nearest to a specific plea is for success in speaking with Artaxerxes (cf. Neh 2:4).

Daniel prays in the manner of Nehemiah but as what we might call a student of Scripture on the basis of what he reads in the words of a prophet (Dan 9); he too is rather unspecific. He too reminds Yhwh of key divine attributes, of the sad state of the people in Judah and in the dispersion, and pleads for the divine wrath to turn from the city and for Yhwh to show grace to the sanctuary, not because the people deserve it (he acknowledges their waywardness) but because of the divine mercy and for the sake of Yhwh's name.

Praying for Your Enemies

Abraham's questioning Yhwh about Sodom's destiny was not exactly a prayer for his enemies, but his prayer for Abimelech (Gen 20) is more unequivocally so. The story is quite humiliating. Abraham misleads a foreign king about his relationship with Sarah, as he did in Genesis 12, and Yhwh again intervenes to send some physical chastisement and warn the king of the danger he is in. Yhwh also tells Abimelech that Abraham is a prophet, so he can pray for the king's restoration. If he is a prophet, he is supposed to be delivering warning messages to a king, but in the circumstances, Yhwh in person has to do the prophesying. Yet in connection with the healing, Yhwh declines to act without the unnecessary middleman; Abraham, after all, is designed to be a blessing to other peoples, so he can still do the praying.

The effectiveness of his prayer is not dependent on his integrity. He is hopelessly defensive; he has reason to be. The king is the only person of faithfulness and integrity in the story. Contrary to Abraham's belief, he is someone who reveres God. The effectiveness of Abraham's prayer is dependent on the will of Yhwh, who has just made a commitment to listening when Abraham intercedes. While the prayer of a righteous man is very effective (Jas 5:16), the prayer of an unrighteous man turns out to be just as effective. As was the case in Genesis 18, prayer is Yhwh's own means of getting things done.

Moses likewise prays for the Pharaoh, his people's oppressor. Moses is the means of bringing about natural disasters to Egypt, the epidemics of frogs, insects and locusts, and the thunder and hail. Each time the Pharaoh asks him to plead with Yhwh to remove the scourge, Moses pleads with Yhwh or cries out to Yhwh in the manner that Israel had because of the Pharaoh's oppression or spreads his hands to Yhwh and prays for the Pharaoh in connection with the natural disasters he brings about. And each time Yhwh accedes (Ex 8:8-13, 28-31 [MT 4-9, 24-27]; 9:27-33; 10:16-19). If this had been Israel, one might have expected Yhwh to start saying no, but of course each scourge and each answering of prayer increases the demonstration of Yhwh's power and of Moses' significance over against the Pharaoh.

In light of the prophets' scathing denunciations of Babylon, Jeremiah's bidding to the exiles to pray for the *shalom* of Babylon, where they are in exile (Jer 29:7) also recalls Abraham's praying for Sodom. More individually, Moses cries out with five-word briskness for Miriam after she attacks him and Yhwh inflicts her: "God, please, heal her, please" (Num 12:13). A prayer would often comprise address to God, the actual petition, and some motivation, and here the last is missing. It is difficult to know whether this suggests disdain or urgency.[169] But the prayer is not, "Let her continue to suffer for the wrong she did."

And Yhwh bids Job's friends to seek Job's prayer as Yhwh had bidden Abimelech to seek Abraham's (Job 42:7-10). The difference is that Abimelech has suffered because of Abraham, whereas Job's friends have multiplied his anguish. But he prays for them, Yhwh accepts his prayer, and this leads Yhwh to restore Job's own fortunes. One cannot assume that Yhwh would have done so if he had not prayed; after all, Yhwh has been somewhat confrontational to Job over Job 38–41. Perhaps his intercession makes all the difference.

Claiming Yhwh's Promise

The Psalms assume that a proper stance in relation to wrongdoing is to want to see it punished. Thus Psalm 28:4-5 urges Yhwh to give recompense to the faithless in keeping with their deeds; the likelihood that the faithless are the suppliant's attackers is only implicit. Elsewhere it is explicit. Psalm 79 interweaves concern for Yhwh's name and the pain that enemy attack has brought to the people. It does not see why Yhwh should continue pouring out wrath on Jerusalem and thinks it is time for it to be poured out on Jerusalem's attackers, in return for their treatment of Israel and their treatment of Yhwh. It

---

[169]Cf. Greenberg, *Biblical Prose Prayer*, p. 15.

asks for compassion for Israel both in respect of its suffering and in respect of its wrongdoing, but not for its attackers.

"May I see your punishment on them, because I have passed my case to you," Jeremiah asks. Yhwh's response (to judge from the arrangement of the book of Jeremiah) is in the affirmative. Because his people are seeking his life, "Now: I am attending to them. The young men will die by the sword, their sons and daughters will die by famine, and there will be nothing left over for them, because I will bring disaster on the people of Anathoth, the year when attention is paid to them" (Jer 11:20, 22-23). Psalm 69:22-29 [MT 23-30] similarly prays that Yhwh may pour out wrath on the suppliant's attackers, so that they find their table becoming a trap, their eyes growing dark so that they cannot see, their encampment becoming desolate, their names erased from the scroll of the living. The psalm's description of the suppliant's experience is hyperbolic, and so perhaps is the prayer, but this does not remove all its sharpness. The background of the prayer and its content recalls those of Jeremiah and Nehemiah.

In the New Testament Peter and Paul indicate their appreciation of Psalm 69 (Acts 1:16, 20; Rom 11:9-10) as they use it to interpret events in their own experience. Readers are often inclined to reckon that both retribution and praying for retribution are alien to the New Testament, though it is then odd that the New Testament treats the psalm as an illuminating theological resource and quotes it as easily as other psalms, interpreting it in a different way but still working with the retribution element in it. Revelation 6:9-11 is a New Testament prayer that works like these psalms themselves, and it receives a positive response, even though one with a "Wait" attached. It is another indication that New Testament writers had no difficulty with prayers such as Psalm 69. Nor did subsequent premodern readers; commentators such as Augustine, Calvin and Spurgeon manifest no embarrassment about them. It was in the context of modernity that bourgeois Christians started being scandalized by them. Notwithstanding his exhortations regarding forgiving people, Jesus similarly promises that God will grant a woman's prayer for justice against her adversary (Lk 18:1-8), and warns the disciples that his Father does not forgive everybody (Mt 6:15).

The plea in Psalm 137 is more chilling than at first it sounds: "Yhwh, be mindful for the Edomites concerning Jerusalem's day, the people who were saying, 'Expose it, expose it, to the foundations of it.' " The first part of the psalm has made a moving commitment to mindfulness, but it has not addressed Yhwh, and it perhaps implies some denial of the feelings and desires in the suppliants' hearts. If so, coming to address Yhwh now leads to their articulation. Mindfulness might seem a mild request, but this is not so. Arguably it is the key to everything (compare Nehemiah's prayers in Neh 6:14).

When Yhwh is mindful, things follow. Implicitly the psalm is urging that Yhwh be mindful of certain undertakings concerning Edom; Jeremiah 49, Ezekiel 25 and Obadiah record terrifying promises about Yhwh's bringing retribution on Edom for its action against Judah. The psalm simply asks for Yhwh's action to conform to Yhwh's word.

The exclamation that follows in Psalm 137 takes a noticeably different stance toward Babylon from that in Jeremiah 29. It is in a different way more chilling than its form suggests: "Mademoiselle Babylon, to be destroyed, the good fortune of the person who recompenses you for the dealings you had with us, the good fortune of the person who seizes your babies and dashes them on the crag." Its words about Babylon involve no plea, even for mindfulness, nor a curse; it is more a statement of confidence. By implication, it is simply assuming that Yhwh will act in accordance with known declarations of intent that appear in Isaiah 13–14; 47; and Jeremiah 50–51.[170] The psalm develops no ideas of its own for the way Babylon might be punished. As prayer psalms often do, every word in this disturbing declaration takes up Yhwh's promises and envisages them being fulfilled. Then justice will have been done.

Praying Against the Faithless

Why might the Holy Spirit have allowed the presence of such prayers in the Scriptures?

First, being falsely accused is a most dangerous experience. It threatens the loss of one's means of livelihood, or of the security of one's marriage and home, or of one's place in the community, or of one's life (e.g., Ex 22:8 [MT 7]; Num 5:11-31; Deut 17:8-13; 19:15-21; 1 Kings 21:1-14). A person in this position desperately needs the false accusers to be put out of business. Psalm 109 prays most urgently for that. The suppliant is one who is weak and needy, agonizing, fading out like day as shadows lengthen, collapsing from hunger, scorned and cursed. The accusers' aim is to get the suppliant condemned, taken by death, his property confiscated, his children orphaned, his wife widowed. The suppliant brings their words to Yhwh like Hezekiah bringing Sennacherib's letter before Yhwh (2 Kings 19:14-19).[171] Modern readers who are of-

---

[170]It might be that Yhwh's promises concerning Edom and Babylon are actually later than the psalm, and are thus responses to it. This would require a reformulation of the point made here, though it would perhaps make it stronger, not weaker.

[171]I take Ps 109:6-19 as their wish for the suppliant not the suppliant's wish for them, without implying that this lets him off the hook of the violence of the prayer (since he then asks that what they seek may happen to them). On the latter assumption, a California pastor suggested that people should make the wish a model for people praying against the leaders of the organization Americans United for the Separation of Church and State (*Los Angeles Times*, August 16, 2007, p. B4).

fended by these psalms are people who live in comfortable middle-class Western contexts. People who are abused do not react to them in the same way. In order to understand the place of such prayers, we might seek to read them from the place of the kind of people for whom they were written, people surrounded by those who are planning to kill them.[172]

Second, for such people in peril, it is vital that the world is a moral place in which evil-doers find trouble recoiling onto their heads, and a place where sometimes Yhwh intervenes to make this happen. These psalms affirm that God does bring redress for wrongdoing. This fits with the emphasis on retribution in the New Testament (e.g., Mt 23:32-36; 2 Thess 1:6-10; 1 Tim 1:20).

Third, such prayers are an indication that we truly do dissociate ourselves from the action of the faithless. At the close of its long act of praise for the deeds of Yhwh as the one who originally created the world and continues to make it work, Psalm 104:35 prays, "May sinners come to an end from the earth; the faithless: may there be none of them any more." Here there is no suggestion that the faithless are causing the worshiper a problem. The psalm has just asked, "May my murmuring give delight to him," and perhaps this declaration is an indication of having meant this prayer. Such prayers against the faithless are indications that the worshiper really does not belong to them. In the New Testament, 1 Corinthians 16:22 and Galatians 1:8-9 might be examples of prayers for people's punishment that could have this implication.

Fourth, such prayers mean that one is leaving redress to God rather than seeking to take it oneself. Redress is God's business. Knowing Yhwh is a God of recompense as well as a God of love, we can bring to Yhwh our longing for recompense as we could not if Yhwh is just a forgiving God; we then have nowhere to go. But there we surrender to God our desire and need for recompense. In Psalm 137, both the plea and the declaration contain no indication that the suppliants expect or want to be among the baby-dashers. (Ezekiel 25 would open up this possibility, but Isaiah 13 sees the Medes in this role). If anything, what they do is surrender such desires to Yhwh in the conviction that it is to Yhwh that recompense belongs, as Deuteronomy 32:35 says and Paul reaffirms (Rom 12:19). Paul's own prayers for people to be "cursed" (NRSV, TNIV) are in line with that (Gal 1:8-9; 1 Cor 16:22); "cursed" is *anathema*, the Greek word for something devoted to God that the Septuagint uses to translate *ḥērem*.[173] And "it is an act of profound faith to entrust one's most precious

---

[172]David Tuesday Adamo illustrates this from the use of these psalms in Nigeria in "The Imprecatory Psalms in African Context," in *Biblical Interpretation in African Perspective*, ed. David Tuesday Adamo (Lanham, Md./Oxford: University Press of America, 2006), pp. 139-53.

[173]Cf. John N. Day, "The Imprecatory Psalms and Christian Ethics," *BSac* 159 (2002): 166-86; see p. 184.

hatreds to God, knowing they will be taken seriously."[174] Perhaps it is when we do this that we can sing Yhwh's song on foreign soil. The reality of the psalms' submission to Yhwh is reflected in the fact that Yhwh did not destroy Edom or Babylon in the way these prophecies said. Babylon did fall, but somewhat painlessly. After losing independence to Babylon, like Judah, Edom/Idumea gained in power through the Second Temple period, then fell under Judean control and accepted the Jewish religion, so that there were many Idumeans among the Jews who came to follow Jesus.

Fifth, the desire for redress is a reality of the human heart and declining to express it to God is to live in unreality. Psalm 120 illustrates the point well. "I am for peace," the last line claims. But the suppliant has earlier asked, "What will you be given, what more will you be given, tongue of deceit?" and answered, "A warrior's arrows, sharpened, with coals of broom-shrubs." These are not the words of a man of peace. The psalm is providing evidence of some tension in the heart and the words of the suppliant. As usual, that is not a reason for not praying or for praying in a way different from what one's heart says. If we need to be delivered from our own tongues as well as from those of other people, we start by speaking the truth from the heart about our desires and by bringing them to God, rather than denying their existence. That will be more likely to open up the possibility of giving them up.

Sixth, referring a situation to God's justice can thus be the first step toward loving and forgiving one's enemies. One can renounce personal vengeance and forgive if one has given this over to God, as Deuteronomy 32:35 and Proverbs 25:21-22, and then Paul (Rom 12:19), encourage people to do.[175]

Confronting the Gods

The bulk of Psalm 82 addresses the subordinate heavenly beings to whom Yhwh delegates some responsibility for running the world, and challenges them about the way they fulfill their responsibility—or rather, fail to do so. Interpreters usually assume it is Yhwh who issues this challenge, though there is no indication that Yhwh speaks, and it is more natural to reckon that a representative of the congregation speaks, as usually happens in psalms. Either way, more directly significant for prayer itself is the way the last line holds Yhwh to account: "Arise, God, exercise authority for the earth [šāpaṭ it is the psalm's key verb], because you yourself own all the nations." As a leader, Yhwh can delegate authority and delegate a task but cannot delegate responsibility for it. If a leader's aides fail, the leader has to take action. The gods are exercising authority, as they are supposed to, but they are exercising

---

[174]Walter Brueggemann, *The Message of the Psalms* (Minneapolis: Augsburg, 1984), p. 77.
[175]Bauckham, *Bible in Politics*, p. 67.

that authority in favor of the wicked, elevating the faithless. What they are supposed to do is exercise authority in faithful fashion, for the poor and orphan, the people who are weak and in want. God is the one who exercises authority in the world by virtue of being the president of the cabinet in heaven, and the challenge is that God should actually exercise it instead of continuing to leave these subordinates to do so in their faithless way.

"Do you really speak faithfully, gods? . . . With your hands you mete out violence." Psalm 58 confronts these heavenly beings in a similar way. Such a prayer again assumes the possibility of taking part in a meeting of this heavenly cabinet like a prophet, and presses it to make a decision on the community's behalf or on behalf of the people the suppliant is concerned for. Behind the wrongdoing in the world is not merely human initiative but supernatural initiative. The gods are supernatural beings subordinate to Yhwh who are supposed to be means of executing Yhwh's purpose in the world, but (events suggest) they are often doing the opposite. "Our struggle is not with flesh and blood but with the rulers, with the authorities, with the world powers of this darkness, with the wicked spiritual realities in the heavens" (Eph 6:12). In prayer we take part in that struggle as we insist on joining in the debates in the cabinet and confront these powers.

There is then a correlation between the way the gods are speaking (making decisions) and acting and the way people are acting in the world, which the psalm goes on to describe in terms of faithlessness and falsehood that can be lethal in their affect on other people, though it does not specify the nature of the correlation: are these deeds that issue from the gods' devising, or deeds they collude with instead of acting against? The psalm therefore goes on to appeal above the gods' heads to God as the president of the cabinet who must take responsibility for what happens in light of the failure of these aides. We thus engage in a persistent pleading "for all the saints" (Eph 6:18). The language the psalm uses in doing so is not for the squeamish; it is language that reflects a serious engagement with the horrible suffering that is imposed on people by supernatural and human oppressors like us, who hold power in the world.

Once more the suppliant does not expect to take action against wrongdoers; the psalm does reckon that God should do so. The world the suppliant is surrounded by is characterized by moral anarchy; God's action will make it possible to affirm that (contrary to present impressions) God has not simply delegated responsibility to a collection of morally incompetent subordinates and then left them to it. Once more, God can delegate power, but not delegate responsibility. God must and will take action. Jesus' promise that God will do so for the oppressed among God's chosen corresponds to the psalm's plea (Lk 18:8; cf. Is 24:21).

"The true motivation for prayer is not . . . the sense of being at home in the universe, but rather the sense of not being at home in the universe," given the evil, suffering and sin within it. "To pray means to bring God back into the world."[176]

Praying "As"

The First Testament thus incorporates many intercessory prayers, yet the Psalms pray more for "me" or "us" than for "him" or "her" or "them." But the first-person form of these psalms may give us a misleading impression. When Jeremiah prays for people, he does not pray for "them" but for "us" (Jer 14:7-9, 19-22). It is hard to know how many people would say amen to his prayers; perhaps no one would. He prays on people's behalf, but prays in the first person, not the third. He thus uses the same forms as a psalm, but he is actually interceding. His example suggests that as well as praying the psalms for themselves, people could use them in praying for other people.

In praying the way he does, Jeremiah may want to draw the people into his prayer. He is praying the way he wants them to pray. Likewise, in using prayers of protest, lament and trust with people, we might seek to draw them into addressing God, protesting, expressing trust, pleading, listening and looking forward to praise. The Psalms make the assumption that Yhwh is or should be committed to the powerless, the neglected and the falsely accused. It is an assumption with a basis in Israel's experience; it matches Yhwh's actions in delivering Israel from Egypt. It is an assumption that is further vindicated by the incarnation and the crucifixion. These events express in the most vivid way possible God's identifying with the powerless, the neglected and the falsely accused.[177] The exodus story and the prayers in the Psalms presuppose this identification. We seek to draw people into prayer that accepts this assumption.

So people could pray the psalms in "I" or "we" form when they were praying for other people. To protest on someone's behalf is a powerful sign of identification with the people for whom we pray. "Openness to suffering, embracing the pain of the other, and responding in protest and healing constitute the charge we are given from God."[178] Lament engages in advocacy for the victim.[179] The laments of mediators such as Moses and Jeremiah suggest

---

[176]Abraham Joshua Heschel, *The Insecurity of Freedom* (New York: Farrar, Straus & Giroux, 1967), p. 258.

[177]Cf. Jürgen Moltmann, *The Spirit of Life* (Minneapolis: Fortress, 1992), pp. 129-31.

[178]David R. Blumenthal, "Confronting the Character of God," in *God in the Fray,* ed. Tod Linafelt and Timothy K. Beal, Walter Brueggemann Festschrift (Minneapolis: Fortress, 1998), pp. 38-51; see p. 51.

[179]Balantine, *Prayer in the Hebrew Bible*, pp. 290-92.

that people who deal with human suffering "cannot help raising their own laments to God on the sufferer's behalf." The sufferer's agony, discouragement, opposition and protests become the mediator's.[180] We pray "as" them, as if we have become them.

One can imagine using psalms such as Psalm 35 in this way. Intercession involves identifying with people in their need, in this case in their fear and rage at the attacks on them. Sometimes we do find ourselves incensed at things that have happened to people—at bombings or rape or abuse or persecution. The psalm suggests that the identification expressed in such rage provides energy for intercession; it finds proper natural expression in the urgent crying out to Yhwh that characterizes the psalm. All the protest psalms are potentially intercessory psalms.

3.6 Penitence

As is the case with intercession, there is a marked difference between penitential prayer in the Psalms and elsewhere in the First Testament. Prayers in the Psalms make little confession of wrongdoing and more often affirm the suppliant's commitment to God, like Paul in Acts 23:1 or 2 Timothy 4:7. Only Psalm 38 and Psalm 51 focus on confession of wrongdoing in a way comparable to prayers such as Lamentations, Ezra 9, Nehemiah 9 and Daniel 9. Prayer in the First Testament as a whole thus incorporates both declarations of commitment and confessions of sin. Those long penitential prayers outside the Psalter come from the exile or afterward, which may indicate that Israel was more aware of its failures in that later period, though people such as prophets were well aware of them from the beginning of Israel's story. Moses, Samuel, Jeremiah and Hosea all express penitence on the community's behalf. Perhaps the historical setting of the confessions reflects the way Israel acknowledged the exile as deserved rather than undeserved suffering[181] and turned from protest to penitence in a movement that was reversed in study of the Psalms in the late twentieth century.[182] The relatively late setting of the penitential prayers would then link with a further characteristic; they commonly rework the words of already existent, recognized praises, prayers and stories, their quasi-Scripture.

The essential nature of penitence involves owning what we have done and turning from our waywardness. It is not incompatible with beseeching God to do something about the trouble that has come to us as a result of our wrongdoing. It focuses on "serious" wrongdoing more than general sinfulness or

---

[180]Capps, *Biblical Approaches to Pastoral Counseling*, p. 70.
[181]See, e.g., Mark J. Boda, *Praying the Tradition*, BZAW 277 (Berlin/New York: de Gruyter, 1999); "The Priceless Gain of Penitence," *Horizons in Biblical Theology* 25 (2003): 51-75.
[182]Cf. William S. Morrow, *Protest Against God* (Sheffield, U.K.: Sheffield Phoenix, 2006).

small offenses. It appeals for Yhwh to carry, cover, cancel, remove, put out of mind, pardon, cleanse and renew.

Coming to Your Senses, Owning, Turning

Penitential prayer characteristically involves declaring what we have done, acknowledging that Yhwh is in the right, pleading for forgiveness and pleading for remission of punishment.[183] Confession thus begins by owning that something is true (*yādâ* hitpael; e.g., Ezra 10:1); this being the meaning of the verb, it can be used of confessing the good things that Yhwh has done as well as the wayward things we have done. When someone admits to another human being that he or she has done wrong, it means saying "I have sinned" (*ḥāṭāṭî*; 1 Sam 26:21; 2 Kings 18:14) and following that up with a request; the same is true in relation to God.[184] Coming to Yhwh when they have been chastised for their wrongdoing, people again find that Yhwh is willing to be prayed to (*'ātar* niphal, the technical word for prayer),[185] and accepts their prayer (2 Sam 21:14; 24:25; 2 Chron 33:13, 19; Job 22:27; 33:26).

Protest psalms take experiences of trouble as indicating that Yhwh is angry, but express bewilderment regarding why that should be so. The Deuteronomic/Deuteronomistic perspective is different. Moses assumes that people will see such experiences as chastisement for wrongdoing and be driven to repentance (e.g., Deut 4:25-31). If people then have recourse to Yhwh with heart and soul, and thus "turn to Yhwh your God and listen to his voice," Yhwh will prove to be compassionate and mindful of the covenant with their ancestors. In Deuteronomy 30:1-6, penitence similarly starts from experiencing Yhwh's blessings and curses, and thinking about them. Then people may "turn" to Yhwh their God, and Yhwh will "turn" their fortunes, have compassion, and "turn," and gather them from all the places they have been scattered in order to take them back to the land; yet further, Yhwh will circumcise their minds so that they dedicate themselves to Yhwh with heart and soul, and live. The simple but broad meaning of the verb most often translated "repent," literally "turn" (*šûb*), makes it open to paradoxical usage in this connection, as the same verb means "turn away," "turn to someone else" and "turn back." Jeremiah especially plays on its range of meanings (e.g., Jer 3:1-14; 15:19). Turning to Yhwh means turning away from other resources or loyalties that we have turned to in order to seek Yhwh or seek Yhwh's face or have recourse to Yhwh (e.g., 2 Chron 7:14; Is 55:6-7; 65:1; Jer 29:13; Hos 5:15).

In 1 Kings 8:33-53, Solomon like Moses envisages penitence starting from experiences of trouble such as defeat or natural disaster, which are recog-

---

[183]Werline, "Defining Penitential Prayer," xvi-xvii.
[184]Cf. Greenberg, *Biblical Prose Prayer*, pp. 24-27.
[185]Cf. 3.1 "Human Asking."

nized as resulting from sin and the response of divine anger. That leads people to think about it (literally, "to make [it] turn to their mind"), to turn from their sins and turn to Yhwh with heart and soul and confess Yhwh's name. They own their waywardness ("we sinned, we wandered, we acted faithlessly"), spread their hands, plead and ask for grace. Yhwh then listens, considers whether the turning is genuine, and on the basis of their being the people whom Yhwh brought out of Egypt and made a personal possession, answers, pardons, points to the right way, acts, and restores, turning them [back] to their land, so that henceforth they may revere Yhwh. In contrast to the expectations of Moses and Solomon, prophets such as Isaiah express bewilderment that people refuse to see experiences of trouble as Yhwh's chastisement for their wrongdoing and to let them drive them to repentance (e.g., Is 1:5-9).

When trouble hits us, the First Testament thus recognizes that this *may* not issue from our wrongdoing, but also that it *may* do so (the New Testament also allows for both possibilities: see, e.g., Jn 9:3; Mk 2:1-12), so that we are wise to ask whether there is waywardness lying behind it. While the Psalms put much more emphasis on trouble that comes from other people's wrongdoing than on trouble that comes from our own, they also allow for the latter possibility. In lamenting the trouble that comes through other people's wrongdoing, the Psalms implicitly emphasize how easy it is for people to behave like Job's friends in applying that first theory to sufferers—that is, these psalms speak of the way people assume sufferers are sinners. But the Psalms also allow for the ease with which we avoid facing our own waywardness. "When I kept quiet, my limbs wasted through my anguish all day long, because day and night your hand was heavy on me" (Ps 32:3-4). Wasting, anguish and the heaviness of Yhwh's hand are common experiences reported in Israelite prayers. Given that silence is an unusual reaction to them, there is something suspicious about silence. What is it concealing?

Confession and Protest

In light of our modern instinct to understand things psychologically, we might reckon that it is the suppliant's silence that causes the wasting. Body and spirit interact; when the spirit is refusing to face things, tensions within the person exact a toll of the body. In other contexts such wasting and anguish issue from the attacks of other human beings or from a divine wrath that has no obvious reason (e.g., Ps 6). But the suppliant's inner being knew that on this occasion such an argument would not work. Eventually the suppliant gave up this odd silence. "I acknowledged my failure to you, I did not cover over my wrongdoing, I said, 'I will confess my rebellions to Yhwh' " (Ps 32:5). The silence involved an attempt at cover up, but eventually the suppliant comes clean. Whereas cover-up seemed a good idea, seemed the way to preserve oneself, actually it was a bad idea. It was a way to hold onto or deepen one's anguish, and even worse, to hold onto or deepen one's sin. "In this silence he withstood God, and God withstood him."[186]

After the defeat at Ai, Joshua tears his clothes, prostrates himself before the covenant chest, covers his head in dirt and confronts Yhwh in the manner of a protest psalm, or even more in the manner of Moses. But Yhwh gives him his comeuppance. This is no time for lament that presupposes that the defeat is inexplicable. There is a perfectly good reason for it. "Israel has sinned, yes, transgressed my covenant that I commanded them." The offender who took plunder at Jericho from things that were owed to Yhwh has committed an "outrage" (nĕbālâ; Josh 7:11, 15). The people are to stand up and deal with that, not prostrate themselves and complain.

Psalm 38 qualifies as a penitential psalm by virtue of its recognition of failure, waywardness and stupidity. The suppliant acknowledges having come short of Yhwh's expectations, chosen the wrong way and been morally or religiously astray in thinking. But like other expressions of contrition, it reframes our understanding of penitence. It is a psalm of deeply felt emotion, but none of this emotion relates to the accepting of responsibility for failure, waywardness, stupidity and wrongdoing; it relates to the trouble that has come as a result of the waywardness. While the psalm is explicit in its acceptance of responsibility, its focus lies not on the suppliant's deeds but on their consequences. The suppliant is the object of Yhwh's wrath, fury and rage. That has meant chastisement from Yhwh's heavy hand, wounds and weakness, pain and moaning. "My acts of waywardness have passed over my head; like a heavy burden, they are too heavy for me" (Ps 38:4 [MT 5]). The psalm refers not to being overwhelmed by the burden of sin itself but being overwhelmed by the trouble that has come as the result of sin; it is expressed like that in other prayers in terms of what "you" have done, what "they" have done and how "I" am experiencing all this. Its acknowledgment of sin is almost incidental to its expression of rejection, pain and abandonment. The anxiety that sin has brought to the suppliant concerns the trouble the sin has brought rather than the sin itself. The psalm contains no plea for forgiveness in light of its admission of sin, only a plea for God not to rebuke and chastise (as God has been doing), not to abandon and be far off but to hasten to deliver. The First Testament does not see confession and protest as alternatives, as if either you acknowledge your waywardness and recognize that you got all you deserved, or you know you were not wayward and therefore protest at being treated the way you have been.

---

[186]Cf. Barth, *Church Dogmatics*, IV/1:578.

Psalm 38 does go on to declare, "I affirm my wrongdoing" (Ps 38:18 [MT 19]). Affirming or declaring or announcing (*nāgad* hiphil) is usually something one does to good things. Whereas a Christian might put "Sorry, sorry, sorry" alongside "Help me, help me, help me" and "Thank you, thank you, thank you" as favorite prayers,[187] in Psalm 38 there is no "sorry."[188] It is the recognition and the acknowledgment that count, not the feelings about it. Confession of sin is about facts more than feelings. Praise, prayer and thanksgiving all focus as much on what Yhwh has done or not done, on what other people have done and on what has happened, as on my emotional response to it. Expressions of penitence do that with remarkable rigor. They can involve a sense of shame and disgrace, and grief like that of a mourner (Ezra 9:6; 10:6), but they are more characteristically an acknowledgement of wrongdoing and a turning from it. "I do acknowledge my rebellions," the suppliant says; indeed, "my failure is before me continually" (Ps 51:3 [MT 5]).

Guilt and Relative Innocence

Related to its combining penitence and protest is the way Psalm 38 incorporates some of the claims to relative innocence that appear in many psalms. The suppliant's attackers "who repay evil for good, attack me for pursuing good" (Ps 38:20 [MT 21]). The suppliant recognizes failure, waywardness and stupidity in relation to Yhwh but not in relation to these other people, and thus carries a double burden—trouble from Yhwh that is deserved, and trouble from other people that is not. (It is not explicit whether the second is the means of bringing about the first.)

The following psalms also combine acknowledgment of having come short of Yhwh's expectations with appeal for Yhwh to deliver us from trouble. Psalm 39:8-11 [MT 9-12] pleads, "turn away from me your affliction" and "rescue me from all my rebellions" that led to the affliction that constitutes "rebukes for waywardness." Psalm 40:12 [MT 13] acknowledges, "my wayward acts caught up with me and I could not see. They were more than the hairs of my head; my heart failed me." Psalm 41:4 [MT 5] illogically entreats, "heal me, because I have failed you." In addition, all these psalms also imply some claim to integrity. "I said, I will keep watch on my ways so as not to sin with my tongue" (Ps 39:1 [MT 2]). "The good fortune of the man who has made Yhwh his trust and has not attended to the defiant and people who turn to falsehood!" (Ps 40:4 [MT 5]). "In my integrity you upheld me and made me stand before you forever" (Ps 41:12 [MT 13]).

In its complex dynamics Psalm 38 overlaps with the prayers in Ezra 9 and

---

[187]See §3.2 "Summoning."

[188]The NRSV has one in v. 18b [19b] in translating *dāʾag*, but this verb suggests being anxious or troubled, not directly being regretful or repentant.

Nehemiah 9. These hold together awareness of waywardness that has characterized the community over the centuries, and of being under chastisement expressed via peoples whom the Judeans have not wronged; Ezra 9 adds an awareness of particular acts of waywardness in the present community. So it is possible to combine a general awareness of sinfulness in relation to God that means there is a sense in which we cannot complain at the trouble that has come to us, with a conviction that we have not wronged other people in any dramatic way. And it is possible thus to recognize that our trouble could be an appropriate chastisement for our general waywardness but still plead that Yhwh might nevertheless relieve our trouble. Job makes a similar assumption. It is key to the book's argument that he is a person of remarkable commitment to Yhwh. Yet he evidently recognizes that he is a sinner like everyone else and that this might provide a basis for Yhwh sending trouble to him, so he asks, "Why do you not carry my rebellion, remove my waywardness?" (Job 7:21).

In fact, Israel seems to have been more committed to Yhwh in the Second Temple period than before the exile. So perhaps its awareness of its sinfulness actually increases as its commitment to Yhwh deepens and thus the undeserve of its domination by the superpowers increases. This compares with the strange fact that when John the Baptist and Jesus proclaim that God's reign is near, they challenge the oppressed Judean people to repent. Perhaps they need to repent of what the oppressors have done to their soul, of the way they get shaped into the mirror image of their enemy.[189] Or perhaps everyone needs to come to a change of mind *(metanoia)* when confronted by the good news that God's reign is here (Lk 3:3). "Who is ready for this subordination? . . . For whom does it not go against the grain?"[190] Or perhaps everyone has to recognize that its demands go against those of any predictable piety or commitment (see Lk 3:11). Certainly they have to be prepared to acknowledge that God is in the right (Lk 7:29). Seeking forgiveness involves such acknowledgment.

Realism and/or Relaxedness

Confession is common in Christian faith, but it is mostly concerned with general sinfulness and with peccadilloes, whereas First Testament faith is more preoccupied with concrete big sins (worship of other deities, worship by means of images, swindling people, killing people). The psalms just noted provide some justification for the common Christian emphasis on our coming short of God's expectations in general terms; we are sinners. They may even suggest awareness of particular wrongdoings and see this as lying behind the troubles

---

[189]Cf. Miroslav Volf, *Exclusion and Embrace* (Nashville: Abingdon, 1996), pp. 111-19.
[190]Karl Barth, *Church Dogmatics* (Edinburgh: T & T Clark, 1969), IV/4:57.

they experience. Yet these psalmists can nevertheless claim to have their lives fundamentally oriented in the right way toward Yhwh or others. They are not like people who have served other deities or plotted against the life of others. There is nothing in their lives that would warrant the kind of experience of suffering they have experienced. There is a sense in which they cannot complain at what comes to them; they are sinners. There is another sense in which they can so complain; they are no more sinners than other people who are doing all right. Hence the fact that we can acknowledge that our general sinfulness and even particular sinful acts lie behind trouble that Yhwh has sent or allowed to come to us, but still appeal for Yhwh to deliver us.

The First Testament does not reckon that our sins separate us from Yhwh. Although wrongdoing has an affect on a relationship, it does not make God unwilling to have anything to do with us. But there are indeed occasions when our sins can do this (see Is 59:2), when we let them do so because we do not turn back to Yhwh, or when Yhwh decides that enough is enough and there will be no mercy on this occasion and that prayers will not be answered. In Psalm 143 the suppliant wants to make sure that this is one of those occasions. "Yhwh, listen to my plea, give ear to my prayer for grace, in your truthfulness, answer me, in your faithfulness," it begins, and continues, "do not contend with your servant, because no living person is faithful before you."

There is some ambiguity about that declaration. It is one of the Scripture verses that can introduce confession of sin in the Church of England's *Book of Common Prayer,* in the company of verses from Psalm 51, on the assumption that it acknowledges that no one is faithful by the standard of Yhwh's faithfulness; this fits the apparent allusion in Romans 3:20. Yhwh's faithfulness never fails; human faithfulness always does, at some point or other. As Job's friends emphasize, we all fall short of Yhwh's expectations of us, and if Yhwh takes that into account when we approach Yhwh's throne, there is no hope of a favorable hearing (cf. Job 4:17; 15:14; 25:4).

On the other hand, "no living person is faithful before you" could simply recognize realistically a fact about power and authority, which Job also recognizes (cf. Job 9:2). It is Yhwh who makes the decisions about that whether or not we are faithful. All we can do is cast ourselves on the mercy of the one who has that power.

On either understanding, the suppliant is not paralyzed by the point. As is the case in Psalm 130, the appeal to being Yhwh's servant reflects this. Once more, it is part of the suppliant's confidence. A master is expected to make allowance for a servant's shortcomings (within the context of a life that is basically committed to the master) or to exercise that power to complete job performance evaluations in a way that reflects a master's commitment to a servant.

Confession and Hope

Lamentations especially embodies the coexistence of confession and protest. It starts with grief and protest at the disaster that has overcome Jerusalem, which sits there like a widow with no one to comfort her (that phrase keeps recurring). The queen has become a slave. Her people have gone into exile, and there is no one to celebrate her festivals. Indeed, godless foreigners have invaded the sanctuary. She sits in sorrow and disgrace. And this has come about through Yhwh's action. The point is taken further in Lamentations 2, where Yhwh is the subject of many more of the sentences: Yhwh threw out, was not mindful, swallowed up, did not pity, tore down, brought low, dishonored. It is underlined by the multiple references to and terms for Yhwh's anger, the overflowing, burning, raging wrath and fury. It is further underlined by the theological comment put on the lips of people who pass by the city (but no one does pass by, because it is not on the way to or from anywhere; this is the city's own question): "Is this the city that they call 'perfect in beauty, a joy to all the earth'?" (Lam 2:15).[191] The psalms say that about it (Ps 48:2); events belie it. So the poem bids the city wall to become the wailing wall, the wall that weeps over its people, and as women eat the corpses of their babies it bids Yhwh, "Look, behold, to whom you have done this" (Lam 2:18-20). The two alphabetic poems expound the suffering of the city from A to Z. Lamentations 3 continues the expression of grief, now in the form of the lament of an individual man; Lamentations 4 reverts to speaking about the city, taking up the lament and protest again. Once more there is a frightening theological reflection about the uncovenanted fate of "Yhwh's anointed" (Lam 4:20).

The poems note that all this has happened "because Yhwh—he made her suffer because of the multitude of her rebellions." She was disgraced because "Jerusalem really sinned." She behaved in a way that made her taboo, without giving a thought to the future. Thus in fact "Yhwh is ṣaddīq [faithful and thus in the right], because I rebelled against his word" (Lam 1:5, 8, 9, 18). But there is less of this kind of acknowledgment in Lamentations 2–4, while Lamentations 5:7 might seem to go back even on those limited admissions: "Our ancestors [or parents] sinned and are no more, but we ourselves have carried their acts of waywardness."

It is easy to pay attention to just one of these two aspects of the chapters. Some writers on Lamentations attempt to "tone down, expunge or belittle the language of lament and anguish," perhaps as "a strategy for 'surviving Lamentations,' " for dealing with its pain and devastation. They hasten to get beyond Lamentations 1–2 into the more hopeful material in Lamentations 3,[192]

---

[191]Cf. §3.4 "Remembering and Hoping."
[192]Tod Linafelt, "Zion's Cause," in *Strange Fire*, pp. 269-79; see p. 269.

or within Lamentations 1, emphasize the deserved nature of this suffering, which means it fits into a meaningful universe. Other writers put all the emphasis on the grief and protest and ignore the admission of guilt. But the interwovenness of these two aspects is a significant feature.[193] Here too expressing pain and grief does not exclude accepting responsibility; accepting responsibility does not exclude protesting at the events that have brought pain and grief. Grief can involve being torn by conflicting emotions: depression and hope, anger and sadness.[194] Lamentations "suggests a people torn between self-recrimination and anger against God."[195]

The combining of lament and confession (one can hardly call it a tension; at least, Lamentations does not seem to see it thus) is paralleled by a combining of confession and hope at the center of the book (Lam 3:21-42). Having protested over his affliction, the man who speaks in Lamentations 3 make a sudden sideways move. "My spirit does call to mind, bows low within me. I turn my heart to this; therefore I hope. Yhwh's acts of commitment: because we have not come to an end, because his acts of compassion have not stopped. They are new every morning; great is your truthfulness" (Lam 3:20-23). The lines are jerky (the transition comes in the middle of the lines beginning with z), and thus match the jerkiness of the reality they testify to.

Wherein lies the basis for the poem's hope? The poem proceeds to a simple series of theological statements: "Yhwh is good to people who wait for him. . . . The Lord does not reject forever. . . . He has not afflicted from the heart" (Lam 3:25, 31, 33). It does not give a basis for believing this; it just knows it is true. It is in light of those facts about Yhwh that the suppliant can go on to invite people to turn to Yhwh, to lift up hearts and hands to God in the heavens, and to declare, "We—we rebelled, defied; you—you did not pardon" (Lam 3:40-42). The poem then reverts to protest about the consequences (you have slain without pity, screened yourself off so that no plea gets through to you; Lam 3:43-54) before making another transition such as often appears in a protest or lament, to expressing the knowledge that Yhwh has heard and responded and then asking Yhwh to move on to the action that needs to follow (Lam 3:55-66). That in itself is not so surprising, though much of the content is unexpected. The suppliant does not thank Yhwh for pardon but gives thanks because "you took up my cause, you restored my life." And the poem closes with an appeal for Yhwh to pursue and destroy the suppliant's enemies.

---

[193]Jill Middlemas offers a nuanced account of the role of confession of sin in Lamentations (see *The Troubles of Templeless Judah* [Oxford/New York: Oxford University Press, 2005], pp. 210-16).

[194]Paul Joyce, "Lamentations and the Grief Process," *BibInt* 1 (1993): 304-20.

[195]Morrow, *Protest Against God*, p. 119.

Corporate Confession and Public Confession

Psalm 105 is a confession of Yhwh's involvement with Israel in the story from Abraham to Joshua. Psalm 106 begins with the same exhortation to "confess Yhwh" and continues with a parallel recounting of Israel's story, but in its version this story is dominated by an acknowledgment of the people's waywardness over the centuries. It thus sees the significance of the story in quite a different way and makes a different kind of confession. Psalm 105 emphasizes Yhwh's mercy in delivering the people; Psalm 106 does the same, but sees the people's need of deliverance as resulting from their faithlessness, at the Red Sea, at Sinai, on the way to the land, in Canaan and in the exile. Gerhard von Rad called the books of Kings an implicit *Gerichtsdoxologie*, an act of praise at the justice of Yhwh's judgment.[196] Psalm 106 is more explicit in its acknowledgment of the justice of Yhwh's judgment, though also in its affirmation of Yhwh's mercy. It even begins with an affirmation of Yhwh's goodness and commitment. Passages such as Ezra 9 and Daniel 9 likewise involve an explicit *Gerichtsdoxologie*, "Yhwh, God of Israel, you are faithful" (Ezra 9:15), "to you belongs faithfulness" (Dan 9:7).[197] After Psalm 50:6 describes Yhwh as coming to announce and implement decisions about the community that were in accordance with faithfulness, Psalm 51:4 [MT 6] also grants that in confronting and chastising, Yhwh has been acting with faithfulness and justification. Indeed, "what is the confession of sin other than the discovery of the true situation, not of man alone, but of man in relation to God?"[198]

In contrast to Psalm 32's comment on silence, Psalm 65 begins affirmatively, "To you silence is praise, God in Zion." The paradox is heightened when the declaration continues, "and to you a promise is fulfilled, one who listens to prayer," because the promises associated with prayer require one to give audible testimony to what God has done.[199] The paradox is heightened further by the next two lines: "All flesh can come right to you with their wayward deeds; whereas our rebellions are too mighty for me, you are the one who expiates them." The alternation between *our* and *me* suggests the psalm is voiced by a leader speaking on behalf of the community, and this fits the psalm as a whole, prompting the reflection that a scene in which a leader stands up in public and willingly acknowledges wrongdoing "is nearly unthinkable in our public life."[200] A leader cannot admit mistakes and a people

---

[196]Gerhard von Rad, *Old Testament Theology*, 2 vols. (Edinburgh: Oliver & Boyd/New York: Harper, 1962; 1965) 1:357-58.

[197]Rodney A. Werline, *Penitential Prayer in Second Temple Judaism* (Atlanta: Scholars Press, 1998), p. 75.

[198]Barth, *Church Dogmatics*, IV/1:579.

[199]See further §2.5 "Act and Word."

[200]Brueggemann, *Message of the Psalms*, p. 135.

cannot acknowledge they have done wrong. An Israelite leader is expected to do so. If the leader is priest rather than king, it prompts the further reflection that it is the vocation of pastors to lead their people in acknowledging the sins of the nation and the church, not as if we were not party to them, but acknowledging them as *"our* acts of waywardness."* On the other hand, scenes in which leaders make public confession of their sexual or financial sin have become rather common, and this is a questionable development insofar it seems to imply that the main point about confession is that it is pretty likely to make it possible to make a comeback.[201]

Coming to God with our sins requires words of confession. Further, the freedom to confess our wrongdoings despite the fact that they are too big for us to do anything about and the discovery that God expiates them would surely require some further words of thanksgiving and praise. Perhaps the psalm implies the recognition that in some contexts there is nothing that can be said either by way of confession or by way of praise. Awed silence is the only appropriate recognition of the magnitude of what Yhwh has done or is an expression of trustful rest in Yhwh.[202]

The alternation between "I" and "we" also reminds us that it is integral to the notion of confessing sins that we do so publicly. This reflects the fact that nothing we do fails to affect other people. Our holiness contributes to the holiness of the community and builds it up before God. Our wrongdoing takes away from the holiness of the community and imperils its relationship with God. The Achan story provides a vivid illustration.

Innocence and Identification

The prayer in Ezra 9 arises from a particular "trespass" *(maʿal)* on the part of the community of returned exiles. Many of the men, including priests, Levites and other community leaders, have married women from the non-Judean peoples around, compromising the holy nature of Israel.[203] Apprised of what has been happening, Ezra tears his clothes, his hair and his beard, and sits desolate. When the time comes for the evening offering, the natural time for prayer, Ezra moves from his sitting position, the posture for mourning, to prostration, the posture for prayer. He sees recent events as in line with the waywardness of his people over the centuries; they have always had a hard time being committed to Yhwh alone. Ezra did not need to identify with his people over previous centuries or with his fellow Judeans in the present, but he does so. He assumes that vertically he cannot distance himself from his

---

[201]See Susan Wise Bauer, *The Art of the Public Grovel* (Princeton, N.J.: Princeton University Press, 2008).

[202]Cf. §2.5 "Act and Word."

[203]On the issue here, see §4.2 "Sex Demythologized."

forebears. They are all one people, he shares in blessings that come from them, and he shares in responsibilities that come from them and in troubles that issue from their actions. He also acknowledges that Yhwh has been merciful to the people over preceding decades. They are still imperial serfs, now of Persia, but they are back in a portion of the promised land and have been able to rebuild the temple. Yet "we" have responded to this mercy by marrying people from other communities.

Perhaps it is significant that people respond to this prayer in which Ezra identifies with them by identifying with him and joining in weeping, acknowledging their trespass, and sending the women and their children back to their homes. Yet when they do this Ezra becomes confrontational. Speaking to God, he says "We." Speaking to the people, he says "You." He bids them "make confession [tôdâ] to Yhwh your God and do what pleases him and separate yourselves from the peoples of the land, from the foreign women" (Ezra 10:1-11). There is responsibility he can share, but there is also responsibility he cannot take from them; there is responsibility they must accept.

The prayer in Nehemiah 1:5-11 similarly incorporates a confession that involves identifying with the failures of the past. Nehemiah supports his prayer with theology in the manner of Moses rather than Ezra. He begins with a reference to Yhwh's greatness and commitment, and after his confession appeals to Yhwh's promise to Moses about restoring the people and to their being "your servants and your people, whom you redeemed by your great power and your strong hand."

The Levites' prayer in Nehemiah 9[204] is even stiffer with theology. Three-quarters of it proclaims the story of Yhwh's acts, with recognition of the people's waywardness interwoven through the story. Slightly surprisingly, the prayer then appeals to Yhwh on the basis of the people's affliction since the time of the Assyrian kings. Once more the fact that the affliction was deserved (the Levites speak both of "they" and of "we") does not mean one cannot ask Yhwh to bring it to an end. What such a prayer does require is a commitment to obedience in the present and future with regard to the particular issues in their context that will constitute the sharp end of Yhwh's expectations (Neh 10).

Like the prayer in Nehemiah 1, the penitential prayer in Daniel 9 has no concrete reason for penitence, and like that prayer, it starts from the desolate state of Jerusalem. Its particular background lies in Jeremiah's having said this desolation would last seventy years. That time has passed; so when will there be restoration? Again like Nehemiah, Daniel opens with reference to Yhwh's greatness and commitment and goes on to review Israel's story in an

---

[204]So MT; the LXX makes it Ezra's prayer.

act of confession in which he identifies with his people over the centuries ("pleading and confessing my sin and my people Israel's sin"), almost on the scale of the Levites' prayer. He accumulates terms for the wrongdoing he acknowledges, as shortcoming, waywardness, faithlessness, rebellion, deviation and disobedience, in relation to the laws and the prophets. The people cannot complain at their circumstances: this prayer, too, acknowledges that Yhwh is the one who is in the right, that *ṣĕdāqâ* belongs to Yhwh. Yet it goes on to urge Yhwh to give up being angry with the city and its people, and does so on the basis of that same *ṣĕdāqâ* of Yhwh's. In other words, Daniel says, "not because of our acts of *ṣĕdāqâ* are we laying down our prayers for grace before you but because of your abundant compassion." It is "for the Lord's sake," because of who you are and because your name is attached to the city and the people, that they urge, "Lord, listen, Lord, pardon, Lord, attend and act, do not delay."

Penitence and Sacrifice

Confession means owning that something is true. One does that in connection with offering a sacrifice when there is wrong to be dealt with (Lev 5:5; 16:21; Num 5:7). The owning does not wholly solve the problem of the offense, but it makes it more like something one did accidentally.[205] The owning is also a disowning. It is as if I broke your favorite vase deliberately, then I recognized that I had done wrong. As well as doing something to make up for breaking the vase, as I would if I had broken it accidentally, I also make confession of the wrong I did and implicitly undertake not to act in that way again. In the penitential prayers the stress lies on a change of behavior that accompanies the confession (Ezra 10:1; Neh 1:6; 9:2-3; Dan 9:4, 20; cf. Lev 26:40).

Whereas Christians often reckon that offering sacrifices was the means whereby Israelites got right with God,[206] Psalm 51:16-17 [MT 18-19] declares, "You would not like a sacrifice, were I to give it; you would not accept a whole offering. The godly sacrifice is a broken spirit; a broken, crushed heart, God, you would not despise." The next lines make clear that the psalm is not rejecting sacrifice in principle, but Yhwh does not welcome sacrifice when people have acted rebelliously in the way the psalm has acknowledged. Sacrifice is a form of worship, and it thus presupposes that the relationship between Yhwh and Israel is fundamentally in order; sacrifice is then a means of expressing devotion or gratitude or of making recompense for some small shortcoming. But in connection with deliberate rebellion and waywardness, sacrifice will not do.

---

[205]See §2.5 "The Purification Offering" and "The Reparation Offering."
[206]See §2.5 "Act and Interpretation."

In Psalm 51 the suppliant's heart and spirit are broken and crushed, and that is the basis of its appeal as it throws itself on Yhwh's mercy. The EVV have the heart and spirit being "contrite," and the psalm shows that they were, but that is not the basis of its appeal. The words are niphal participles from words for "break" and "crush" (šābar, dākâ). Heart and spirit are simply broken and crushed by the chastisement Yhwh has imposed. The psalm is not arguing that the suppliant qualifies for Yhwh's forgiveness by being contrite. It really is appealing to Yhwh's mercy; describing this broken and crushed heart and spirit as a sacrifice underlines the point. The suppliant has nothing to offer Yhwh that could compensate for the rebellion and the waywardness. The only thing the suppliant has to offer is quite worthless, yet Yhwh will accept it, not because it has any value but because of those divine characteristics of grace, commitment and compassion.

The relative insignificance of sacrifice in connection with forgiveness is illustrated by material relating to the exile, when sacrifice is neither possible nor of use. It can never compensate for waywardness or win Yhwh's forgiveness. In any context the only way to gain that forgiveness is to turn from waywardness, turn to Yhwh and cast oneself on Yhwh's mercy. Israelites never appeal for forgiveness on the basis of offering sacrifice. What puts things right with God is the confession. It is a speech act. It makes atonement.[207] It thus functions in the same way as confession between human beings.

Appealing for Yhwh to Carry, to Cover, to Cancel

What does penitence seek? Yhwh sometimes punishes the wayward for their wrongdoing or abandons them to its consequences, but Yhwh sometimes carries it and carries them, bears responsibility for it instead of making them bear it; the verb most commonly translated "forgive," nāśā', literally means "carry." We do not have to keep carrying the burden of responsibility for our wrongdoing. Yhwh is quite willing to carry it and arguably is doing so all the time (otherwise the world would implode in wrath). Instead of our carrying responsibility for it and having to live with the consequences, Yhwh undertakes to accept that responsibility. Yhwh's carrying our sin is therefore the subject of many of the psalms' appeals and testimonies (e.g., Ps 25:18; 32:1, 5; 85:2 [MT 3]; 99:8).

The reason why our sins thus do not separate us from God (at least, on God's side) is that God declines to let them do so. In this sense forgiveness does not require the cooperation of the person in the wrong. But forgiveness does require the cooperation of the person in the wrong. Objectively I

---

[207]See Jay C. Hogewood, "The Speech Act of Confession," in *Seeking the Favor of God*, ed. Mark J. Boda et al. (Atlanta: Society of Biblical Literature, 2006), 1:69-82.

may not be carrying my wrongdoing (carrying responsibility for it) if Yhwh has decided to do so, but subjectively I may be doing this. Reconciliation too requires the cooperation of the person who is in the wrong. The attitude of the wronged person to the wrongdoer may be fine, but if the attitude of the wrongdoer to the wronged person remains the same, the relationship is not put right. In that sense Yhwh's carrying does not become a reality until the suppliant allows it to be so. If I do wrong, I carry responsibility for it until I let the other person do so. "I said, 'I will confess my rebellions to Yhwh,' and you yourself carried my sinful wrongdoing" (Ps 32:5).

Hence the suppliant can now proclaim, "The good fortune of the one whose rebellion is carried, whose sin is covered over!" (Ps 32:1). The opening of the psalm thus provides an alternative image for forgiveness to the image of Yhwh's carrying it. Yhwh covers it up. As there is only one person in a relationship who carries sin (either we avoid acknowledging that we carry responsibility and therefore have to do so, or we acknowledge that we carry responsibility and thereby make it possible for Yhwh to do so), so there is only one person who covers sin. The fact that (eventually) "I did not cover over my wrongdoing" means that I enjoy the good fortune of one "whose sin is covered over" (Ps 32:1, 5). The image of "covering" may suggest whiting out a charge in a legal record (cf. Neh 4:5 [MT 3:37]) or concealing something that would be shameful (cf. Prov 12:16) or hiding something that would cause an outcry (cf. Ezek 24:8). In personal relationships, covering something up for someone else can be an expression of love and faithfulness, and a way to win love (Prov 10:12; 11:13; 17:9). Admittedly it can be as unethical as covering up our own wrongdoing, but when the person doing the covering up is the person who was wronged, it is a different matter. When the prodigal son acts as he does or when a man is unfaithful to his wife, a parent or wife might choose to cover the son's or husband's unfaithfulness with love and thereby take away its power.

Thus Psalm 85:2-3 [MT 3-4] confesses, "You carried the waywardness of your people, you covered all their shortcoming (Selah), you withdrew all your fury, you turned from your angry burning." It would be quite appropriate for that wife or parent to be consumed with anger at the husband's or son's unfaithfulness, and the husband or son would have no basis for complaint if they stayed that way forever. But in due course they could let their anger die down. That is what God has done. When we come to God in penitence, we appeal to God as one who has done this in the past (Sinai provides the supreme example), as we do with other needs. We thus plead with God again to "cancel your vexation with us" rather than being angry with us forever (Ps 85:4-5 [MT 5-6]).

After referring to Yhwh's "carrying" rebellion and "covering" failure,

Psalm 32:1-2 goes on to speak of Yhwh's not "counting" waywardness. While the verb may suggest not thinking about it, putting it out of mind, forgetting it, it may again point to the image of a king keeping records of people's wrong-doings. Does Yhwh do that? Once again a paradox is involved. If we deny wrongdoing, the record stands. If we own it, the record gets cancelled.

In this psalm the suppliant has now found healing from wasting, comfort from anguish. Either the wasting and anguish resulted from the wrongdoing or they resulted from not facing up to the wrongdoing; whichever it is, giving up deceit (Ps 32:2) and owning things puts matters right. Fortunate indeed is the person who discovers that.

Appealing for Yhwh to Remove, Put Out of Mind, Expiate

To cancel sin is to make it go away. Job asks, "Why do you not carry my rebel-lion, remove ['ābar hiphil] my waywardness?" (Job 7:21). "In accordance with the distance of east from west he has distanced [rāḥaq hiphil] our rebellions from us" (Ps 103:12). "Who is a God like you, one who carries waywardness, passes over ['ābar 'al] rebellion. . . . He will subdue our wayward acts, throw [šālak hiphil] all their shortcomings in the depths of the sea" (Mic 7:18, 19). Our wayward acts and shortcomings are enemies Yhwh will overcome or treat the way the Egyptians were treated at the Red Sea.[208] They are enemies that can ravage the land and the people's lives; Yhwh promises that they will not be able to have this effect. "You have thrown all my shortcomings behind your back" (Is 38:17).

After the exile Zechariah has a vision of an adversary laying an accusation against Joshua, the high priest, who is tainted by exile (Zech 3). Being in a foreign land is not tainting in itself, but perhaps he had been involved in the worship of images there, or perhaps he is tainted by the fact that exile was the punishment for sin. Whatever its basis, Yhwh dismisses the charge. The im-plication is not that it was false. Rather, Yhwh declares "I have removed your waywardness from you"; Joshua does need to make sure that henceforth he walks Yhwh's way. Yhwh further promises to "take away [mûš] the wayward-ness of that land in one day." The verb appears only here in connection with taking away sin. Zechariah goes on to speak of people inviting each other to the shade of their vines and fig trees, so perhaps the verb indicates that Yhwh takes away the aftereffects of the community's wrongdoing and restores the land to what it was designed to be. "Removing" sin may not do that (see 2 Sam 12:13-14); but this taking away does so.

In Psalm 79:8-9 the community first pleads, "Do not bear in mind against us the wayward acts of an earlier generation" (one could imagine this as the

---

[208]Cf. Hans Walter Wolff, *Micah* (Minneapolis: Augsburg, 1990), pp. 230-31.

prayer of Jerusalem as the exilic period draws on). It supports that plea with an appeal to Yhwh's compassion, but then continues, "rescue us and expiate our shortcomings, for your name's sake." In that earlier line it might seem to be disclaiming responsibility for its life and its situation, on the grounds that it was not its own deeds that made its life and situation what they were. But here it implies the more usual assumption that we are one with previous generations and cannot dissociate ourselves from them. If Yhwh is not to hold those wayward acts against us as members of the same people, we have to cast ourselves on the mercy of the person we have wronged. The vivid way the psalm does that is by appealing to Yhwh to "expiate" them.[209] It is usually human beings who go about "expiating" shortcomings, and it is doubtful if we can "expiate" deliberate sins. With a boldness of metaphor, the psalm asks Yhwh to do the expiating (cf. Ps 65:3 [MT 4]; 78:38), and to do it with regard to "wayward acts." Yhwh's provision of the Expiation Day ritual is one way Yhwh does this; through its ritual Yhwh provides a means whereby sin can be pushed out into the realm where it belongs and can do no more harm.[210]

Prayer keeps the community in God and God in the community.[211] It keeps the community mindful of God and living in light of that mindfulness and keeps God mindful of the reasons for staying committed to Israel and the church despite their waywardness (e.g., Ex 32:11-14). But mindfulness is a two-edged sword. "Be mindful of your compassion, Yhwh, and your great commitment. . . . Do not be mindful of my youthful failures or my rebellions; in accordance with your commitment be mindful of me yourself, for the sake of your goodness" (Ps 25:6-7). The possibility of Yhwh's keeping in mind my shortcomings and rebellions is surrounded by an exhortation rather to keep in mind "your compassion," "your commitment" and simply "me" (also implicitly "your goodness"). If I look at my youth I see shortcomings; if I look at my adulthood, I see rebellion. Wherever I look in my life, I see waywardness, great waywardness, so all I can do is ask Yhwh not to look in that direction but to focus instead on "your compassion/commitment/goodness" and to pardon me "for the sake of your name," in light of who you have revealed yourself to be (Ps 25:11). Act in light of who you are, not in light of who I am.

The First Testament does not assume that punishments must simply be accepted. But you can never be sure what a confession or plea for mercy will yield. Achan needs to acknowledge what he did and thus "give honor to Yhwh, the God of Israel, and make confession to him." That involves Achan in saying, "It is true. I myself sinned against Yhwh the God of Israel. This is

---

[209]On the verb *kipper*, see §2.5 "The Reparation Offering."
[210]See §2.6 "Azazel."
[211]Balentine, *Prayer in the Hebrew Bible*, pp. 273, 284.

exactly what I did"; he goes on to make a simple statement of his action (Josh 7:19-21). But his story does not end happily. Achan and his family are tainted by a wrongdoing that has effects that confession cannot undo. When Cain is confronted by Yhwh (Gen 4:9-12), his response is not to acknowledge his wrongdoing but only to protest at the seriousness of his punishment, which falls short of immediate execution but will threaten him with death. Yhwh's response is to promise his protection, though he has to live with consequences of his sin. When David's child gets ill, David seeks the reversal of this punishment, but Yhwh does not accede (2 Sam 12:13-14). After numbering the people, "David's heart hit him," and he said to Yhwh, "I have sinned greatly in what I have done, but now, Yhwh, do remove the waywardness of your servant." Yhwh's response is to give David opportunity to choose his punishment (2 Sam 24:10-12). Jeremiah 29 bids the exiles settle down in Babylon; they can build houses, plant gardens, marry and have children and marry them off, and seek the welfare of their adoptive city. There is to be no quick return from exile. If the wandering in the wilderness lasted a generation, the exile will last much longer. People should settle down. Punishments need not simply be accepted, but you cannot predict what will be the result of protest.

Appealing for Yhwh to Pardon

To put it another way, penitence seeks that wrongdoing should be pardoned (sālaḥ). The basis for coming to Yhwh in penitence is the fact that "he is the one who pardons all your waywardness, who heals all your illnesses, who restores your life from the Abyss" (Ps 103:3-4; cf. Ps 10-12). Pardon suggests forgiveness by a person in a superior position (e.g., a king); the more regular word translated "forgive," the word meaning "carry," has a less circumscribed reference and can apply to the forgiveness of peers. Given that not everyone gets healed or pardoned, the psalm's statement may be hyperbolic or may affirm that all pardon and healing that ever happens comes from Yhwh; none comes from any other source.

Indeed, "pardon is with you" (Ps 130:4). It belongs to you or it stands next to you waiting to be sent to do your work. Psalm 130 begins by speaking as if relating to an individual's waywardness, but by the end it is relating to Israel's. The individual or the community have been calling Yhwh "from the depths," the depths of trouble. They need "grace" and they need "redeeming." In Christian parlance that would suggest deliverance from sin, but in the First Testament this is not so. The original act of redemption was Israel's deliverance from Egypt, and this did not involve deliverance from Israel's waywardness but from Egypt's. The First Testament recognizes that Israel needs deliverance from its sin, but it does not use "redemption" or "deliverance" language to describe this, and it uses "grace" language for all sorts of acts of Yhwh's love and generosity. The suppliant needs deliverance from the depths of trouble.

Psalm 130 is another of that small number of psalms presupposing that it is because of their own waywardness that the suppliant or the people are in these depths, while it also parallels a number of these in being at least as concerned with the suffering that has issued from this waywardness as with the waywardness itself. Indeed, the suppliant does not go in for explicit confession of sin or appeal for pardon, but only calls, looks and waits. Perhaps it implies individuals and the community caught up in the consequences of and in responsibility for the wrongdoing that led to the exile. They need redemption from their waywardness because their waywardness is the cause of their trouble. To that end, they need Yhwh to pardon this waywardness, like a king pardoning someone who has conspired against him, or an emperor pardoning a king who has entered into treaty relations with another nation. If the king "kept acts of waywardness," kept hold of them, preserved them and looked after them *(šāmar)* instead of throwing them into the sea, the offender would not be able to "stand," to survive. But the suppliant appeals to Yhwh as "my Lord," which implies the possibility of compassion because that is built into the master-servant relationship.

Thus "pardon is with you," the suppliant goes on, with the striking logic, "so that you may be revered." It might be easy for mercy to encourage an offender to continue to flout the authority of the king or the King, but the suppliant makes the bolder and deeper assumption that it might generate a relieved submission to that authority; the suppliant will not make the same mistake again. God's kindness is meant to lead Israel to repentance (Rom 2:4). As usual Yhwh risks disappointment. People can take the gracious master for granted and might even decide to sin so that grace might abound (Rom 6:1). But Paul's own logic corresponds to that of the First Testament, that God's pardon may arouse a gratitude that will lead to people forsaking waywardness and committing themselves to obedience. The extraordinary fact of Yhwh's pardon would cause Yhwh's teaching to be written into Israel's inner being as it had not been before (Jer 31:31-34).

In Psalm 130 the suppliant does not yet know whether pardon will be forthcoming. There is no way of knowing ahead of time. Yhwh has to decide whether this is a moment for mercy and compassion or for justice and punishment, a moment when Israel must carry the responsibility for its waywardness rather than Yhwh doing so. Thus "I have looked to Yhwh, my spirit has looked," and I am still doing so. "I have waited for his word," the word that brings joy and gladness because it says I am pardoned, and I am still doing so, waiting more keenly than guards waiting for morning to dawn with its indication that the demands and responsibility of their watch are over. The suppliant urges Israel to wait in the same way, but with expectation, "because with Yhwh the commitment, and the redemption with him, is great." While not yet knowing as a matter of experience that this will happen, in another sense the suppliant "knows" it will. Looking to Yhwh and waiting are not a form of hopefulness that is unsure whether it will be vindicated but one that knows this because it knows who Yhwh is. "Pardon is with Yhwh" because "with Yhwh" is commitment and redemption (or vice versa). All are aides who keep company with Yhwh and whom Yhwh regularly sends on their way to do Yhwh's own work, because they are part of Yhwh's character.

Appealing for Yhwh to Renew

Penitence seeks cleansing, joy, renewal and the opportunity to give testimony.

It seeks cleansing and purification (Ps 51:1-2, 7, 9 [MT 3-4, 9, 11]); the psalm adds another image to those of carrying, covering, canceling, removing, expiating and putting out of mind. We have noted the accusation that Joshua was tainted by exile. One of the effects of sin is to make us defiled and taboo. It is like the effect of contact with a corpse or of contact with false religion or of eating strange creatures. It means Yhwh can hardly have contact with us. Our merely being human does not make Yhwh's relating to us something problematic; as human beings we are made in God's image. But when we are affected by a taboo like that of death, we become something alien to the nature of the living God. Our defilement has to be removed. Paradoxically, God is the only one we can ask to effect that. When someone's tent was defiled by a death, their friend was to sprinkle them and their tent with hyssop to "decontaminate" them (Num 19:14-20). The psalm uses the same verb (ḥāṭāʾ piel) in asking Yhwh to behave like that friend. Jesus does so when he washes his friends' feet (Jn 13).

Penitence seeks a return of joy (Ps 51:8-9, 12 [MT 10-11, 14]). When we have done wrong by someone and we confess it, we wait anxiously to discover their reaction. Will the confession make them explode or will they say, "Oh; it's okay." The latter is the suppliant's hope: "Will you make me hear joy and gladness, may the bones you crushed rejoice." The plea again presupposes that the suppliant is physically affected by the consequences of the wrongdoing; Yhwh has acted in chastisement in bringing defeat or epidemic. But Yhwh's restoration will bring healing (reference to healing is surprisingly rare in the Psalms).

Penitence seeks to be changed as a person (Ps 51:10-11 [MT 12-13]). The suppliant needs not only cleansing but renewing: "Make a new, steadfast spirit within me. . . . Do not take your holy spirit from me. . . . Uphold me with a wholehearted spirit." Is the psalm referring to the human spirit within the suppliant or the divine spirit that comes to operate on the human? The question involves a false antithesis. "Spirit" is the great marker of deity, yet creating humanity meant putting spirit within it. Like the expression "in God's image," it points to the link between humanity and deity. The expression "holy spirit" underlines the point. But rebellion imperils that link. It will not be enough if Yhwh merely decontaminates the person and restores the relationship with them. The future needs safeguarding. Israel is so inclined to go and serve other gods; it needs to be given a spirit that is steadfast in its commitment to Yhwh. It needs to be upheld with a spirit that is wholehearted in self-giving to Yhwh (*nĕdābâ*, the term for a "freewill" offering).

Penitence seeks the opportunity to give testimony (Ps 51:13-15 [MT 15-17]). Like any answering of prayer, finding cleansing and renewal makes it possible to proclaim to other people what Yhwh has done. Thus "I will teach rebels your ways. . . . May my tongue resound your faithfulness; my Lord, will you open my lips, may my mouth tell your praise." A person who has confessed to being a rebel is in a strong position to testify to the way Yhwh deals with rebels who come to admit their rebellion. The prayer thus leaps from the beginning of what the suppliant needs to its total completion. There is no gradual process or painful climb out of the depths. Romans 8:30 agrees with this: whom God justified, God glorified. Forgiveness and a whole new possibility of living "naturally" go together.[212]

Psalm 51, the First Testament's most fervent and measured appeal for forgiveness, actually begins (astutely) with the basis for its appeal: "Be gracious to me, God, in accordance with your commitment, in accordance with the abundance of your compassion." It appeals to Yhwh's nature as constituted by unearned grace, inescapable commitment and motherly compassion. There is nothing else to appeal to. Christians take as the basis for such appeals that the penalty has been paid for our sins, at the cross. The psalm is in effect already asking Yhwh to pay the price for our sins, as Yhwh has been doing for Israel from the beginning.[213] It is not surprising that Christ should die for people when they were still ungodly, sinners and enemies (Rom 5:6-11); this is what Yhwh had been doing through the world's story and through Israel's story. The covenant relationship begins with Yhwh saying "I would rather die than break this covenant." But the main part of the story of that covenant involves Yhwh dying because Israel breaks the covenant.[214] If the cross is the logical end to the Jesus story, the Jesus story with that ending is the logical end to the Yhwh story. God's becoming incarnate in love leads to the cross. God's becoming involved in the world with Israel

---

[212]Barth *Church Dogmatics*, IV/1:580.
[213]See further *OTT* 2:108-29.
[214]I adapt formulations from Volf, *Exclusion and Embrace*, p. 155.

already led to the cross. It met mostly with resistance or indifference.

The implication of such prayer is that God cares about people who do wrong as well as people who are wronged. In the Prophets, this comes out in Yhwh's care for Egypt, Assyria, Philistia and Moab, as well as for the Israel whom they oppress.[215] The same applies to Israel when it is itself the agent of oppression. "He will redeem Israel from all its wayward acts" (Ps 130:8). In the context the immediate significance of that redemption is that Yhwh will deliver Israel from the consequences of its wrongdoing, from the depths of trouble it finds itself in. But the implication of that conviction is that Yhwh is prepared to look the other way with regard to the waywardness that has got Israel into trouble.

The appeal to Yhwh's grace, commitment and compassion is an appeal to the nature of Yhwh's self-revelation in Exodus 34:6-7. It is one of a number of indications that Psalm 51 is in origin a prayer expressing the penitence of the people as a whole (perhaps speaking as a corporate "I," perhaps functioning by having each individual identify with its stance). But the penitential psalms assume the same dynamics of grace apply to individual Israelites. Psalm 51 focuses on sin against Yhwh. But its heading adds reference to David's sin against a human being, a woman who had no opportunity to say no, and their story involves sin against a man who was a foreigner but whose name suggests he is committed to Yhwh[216] and who is a committed servant of David. The psalm can assume that Yhwh is not locked into punishing even such wickedness as David's but might be willing to forgive the wicked person.

3.7 Thanksgiving

Suppliants often promise to come back to give glory to Yhwh when their prayer has been answered; indeed, it is natural to do so whether or not they made a promise. "They cried out to Yhwh in the trouble that came to them; he would deliver them from their pressures": and therefore "they are to confess to Yhwh his commitment, his wonders for human beings, to offer thanksgiving sacrifices and recount his deeds with resounding" (Ps 107:19-22). "Praise perfects perfection" and "thanks complete what is completed." It makes the praiseworthy act "overflow into the present and the future."[217]

Answering

"I called to Yhwh and he answered me" (Ps 120:1). Prayer is indeed a dialogue, not a monologue, and thanksgiving "is a part of the continuing dialogue that

---

[215]See §5.2 "The Politics of Compassion."

[216]Uriah means "Yah is my light," though it may be a Hebraized version of a foreign name (see *HALOT*).

[217]David F. Ford and Daniel W. Hardy, *Living in Praise* (Grand Rapids: Baker, 2005), p. 10.

is prayer." Indeed, "there is some sense in which praise is the end of the conversation," unless Yhwh does not let it be that (e.g., Ps 50; 95); "praise intended to glorify God can also be sung to one's own damnation" (e.g., Amos 5:21-24).[218]

But we have noted that answering is a systematically ambiguous notion; there are two stages to answering, as there are two aspects to a plea, and thus there are two stages to thanksgiving.[219] Stage one of Yhwh's answering is that Yhwh listens, pays attention, considers, heeds, and thus stage one of thanksgiving relates to this. "Yhwh himself listens when I call to him" (Ps 4:3 [MT 4]). "He has bent his ear to me" (Ps 116:2). "You listened to the desires of the weak. . . . You bend your ear" (Ps 10:17). But stage two of Yhwh's answering must then follow. Psalm 28:6-9 begins, "Yhwh be worshiped, because he has listened to the sound of my prayer for grace," and goes on to declare, "So I will be helped," and prays, "Deliver your people, bless your possession, shepherd them and carry them forever." The suppliant's cry has been heard, and I can therefore give a stage one thanksgiving. But Yhwh has not yet acted; the suppliant stands between listening and granting on one hand, and action on the other. Yhwh's stage one answer involves saying "Yes, I have heard you, I am coming, I will act to deliver you," and when Yhwh has answered thus, I can relax and sleep the sleep of the secure even if I am still surrounded by people who might attack, because I know Yhwh will uphold me (Ps 3:4-6 [MT 5-7]). But stage two answering must follow. In Psalm 12, when divine action is needed, the suppliant reports: "'Because of the groaning of the needy, now I arise,' Yhwh says. 'I take my stand as deliverance,' he witnesses to him" (Ps 12:5 [MT 6]). Yhwh stands up in the cabinet meeting and solemnly avers that action will now follow. This deserves stage one thanksgiving. But stage two answering must follow.

Psalm 31 begins by praying for Yhwh to listen, protect and rescue, then thanks God for deliverance, then prays again and at greater length for rescue, then again thanks God for having heard the prayer for grace, and finally encourages the congregation as people who are waiting for Yhwh. It would make sense if the second prayer presupposes that the first has been answered in the sense that it has been heard, but not in the sense that the answer has yet been implemented; thus the second prayer focuses entirely on the need for action. Further, the second prayer incorporates a substantial lament and protest, emphasizing how long the trouble has been going on, which would fit with having gained the assurance that Yhwh has heard but not yet seen its fruit; the closing encouragement presupposes the experience of having re-

---

[218]Miller, *They Cried to the Lord*, pp. 135, 223, 225.
[219]Cf. §3.3 "Decision and Action."

ceived the assurance that Yhwh has accepted the plea but still being in the position of waiting for the answer to be implemented. Likewise, in Psalm 6:8-10 [MT 9-11], the suppliant has certainly heard Yhwh's answer, but has not yet seen this answer.

"The fundamental question of prayer is: Does anything happen?"[220] This might seem an overstatement, though in the context of the prayers in the First Testament (where "prayer" commonly emerges from desperate need), it might not seem so. "Answering" needs to involve action, not just words. And a stage two thanksgiving psalm relates to Yhwh's having done something, not just promised something. Such thanksgiving receives succinct expression in Psalm 118:5-6: "Out of constraint I called Yah—Yah answered me with roominess; Yhwh being for me, I will not be afraid: what can a human being do to me?" Characteristically, this thanksgiving recollects the troubles I was in, recollects the way I prayed, recollects Yhwh's answer, and declares my consequential confidence. The opening lines of this psalm have already proclaimed the significance of this for other people. "I cried for help to you and you healed me"; I thus moved from weeping to resounding, from mourning to dancing, from sackcloth to joy, from wailing to music (Ps 30).

Words and Music

In human relationships, expressing appreciation for something a person has done might have at least three components: words, enthusiasm and something concrete by way of a gift. All three feature in thanksgiving.

"Make music to Yhwh, . . . confess his holy remembrance" (Ps 30:4 [MT 5]). Thanksgiving involves the affective expression of relief and joy, in melody and rhythm. Weeping gives way to resounding, sackcloth to dancing, wailing to music (Ps 30:5, 11-12 [MT 6, 12-13]). "May all who rely on you rejoice, resound forever; . . . may they exult in you" (Ps 5:11 [MT 12]). While in English rejoicing might suggest an inner attitude and not so directly its outward expression, resounding emphasizes the outward expression in particular, and exulting suggests a wild and uninhibited reveling like that of a triumphant army (Jer 50:11).[221]

Thanksgiving also involves words describing the event that brought relief and joy, "remembrance" (zēker), the naming of Yhwh and the making mention of what Yhwh has done. Whereas praise can be wordless and still fulfill its function, thanksgiving necessarily emphasizes words because it is these that express why Yhwh is to be glorified. So dancing and music are accompanied by confession (Ps 30:12 [MT 13]). A parallel combination appears in the com-

---

[220]Miller, *They Cried to the Lord*, p. 135.
[221]See §2.7, "Sound and Movement" and "Deliverance in Current Experience."

mitment, "I will confess you with the harp. . . . I will make music for you with the lyre. My lips will resound when I make music for you, my whole being, which you have redeemed. Yes, my tongue will talk of your faithfulness all day" (Ps 71:22-24). Thanksgiving combines words and music, words and noise (resound), the voice and the whole being, the essentially public (confession) and the semiprivate (talk), the temporal and the continuous.

"You are my God and I will confess you; my God, I will exalt you"; so Psalm 118 almost ends (Ps 118:28), while Psalm 30 begins "I will exalt you, Yhwh." Like praise,[222] thanksgiving lifts Yhwh up (*rûm* polel). The notion is a paradoxical one. Either Yhwh is on high or Yhwh is not; if it is not the case, there is surely nothing that humanity can do to bring it about. Further, Yhwh is the one who exalts, who lifts up (e.g., Ps 18:48 [MT 49]; 27:5). Rudolf Bultmann argued that when Christians say "Jesus is Lord," they are not making a metaphysical statement but a commitment of the will; they are declaring the intention to make Jesus Lord of their lives. The statement actually has both significances. Jesus *is* Lord; therefore I make him my Lord.[223] That process is analogous to the one applying to Yhwh. Yhwh *is* on high, and in light of my experience of Yhwh's lifting me up, I exalt Yhwh. My exalting Yhwh also implies my declining to exalt myself. One indication of this is that the subject of the sentences in a thanksgiving psalm is often "Yhwh" or "you" rather than "I" or "we." "You did not let my enemies rejoice . . . you healed me . . . you brought me up . . . you restored me to life . . . you turned . . . you undid . . . you girded" (Ps 30).[224] Indeed, it implies my being prepared to humble myself (Ps 99:5, 9).

"I will exalt you because you put me down[225] but did not let my enemies rejoice over me," Psalm 30 begins. Like prayer, thanksgiving does not have to mince words. The assumption that Yhwh was responsible for the suppliant's trouble is reexpressed in terms of being the victim of Yhwh's anger and is later spelled out further (Ps 30:4-7 [MT 5-8]). There was a time when I was doing fine, at ease or prosperous (*běšalwî*). The expression might suggest complacency, but there is no particular pointer to that, and such an interpretation seems calculated to support our instinct to explain reversals as deserved and therefore intelligible, whereas the Psalms are inclined to see them as undeserved and unintelligible but therefore open to protest. There was no reason

---

[222]See §2.7 "Lifting Up and Bowing Down."

[223]See John Goldingay, *Models for Interpretation of Scripture* (Grand Rapids: Eerdmans/Carlisle: Paternoster, 1995), pp. 212-15.

[224]Cf. Claus Westermann, *The Living Psalms* (Grand Rapids: Eerdmans/Edinburgh: T & T Clark, 1989), pp. 168-69.

[225]The EVV have "because you lifted me up," which links neatly with "I exalt you," but this translation of *dillîtānî* is hard to justify.

for me to think I would experience catastrophe. I had been treated as someone who had Yhwh's acceptance. Yhwh had given me a strong position in life. Then all that collapsed. You put me down. You behaved as if you were angry with me. You hid your face. That meant disaster. Yhwh's face shining on us means blessing; Yhwh's face turned away means calamity. I therefore became terrified, and so I prayed. "Yhwh, my God, I cried for help to you. . . . On you, Yhwh, I called, to my Lord I pleaded for grace" (Ps 30:2, 8 [MT 3, 9]). The psalm uses three of the key verbs for prayer (cry for help, call, plead for grace) in recalling this. And now the supplicant is in a position to rejoice with words, sound and body.

Thankfulness and Thank-offering

So when Yhwh has done something for me, it is appropriate that I should express my thankfulness. The First Testament does not comment on the logic of this, but it corresponds to commonplaces of human experience. When someone has done something for me, expressing gratitude is appropriate for me and appropriate for the relationship. It means I understand and own what has happened, and own it in connection with the relationship. As the act strengthens the relationship, so the response strengthens it further; failing to respond with gratitude would weaken it.

The fact that *tôdâ* is also the word for a thank-offering draws attention to the fact that (like other forms of prayer) a thank-offering, as well as being vocal and not merely internal, is embodied in action as well as expressed in words. Sacrament and word again go together. "To you I will sacrifice a thank-offering and call out in Yhwh's name, I will fulfill my vows to Yhwh, yes, right before all his people" (Ps 116:17-18). Words without offerings would not cost anything.

So I declare, "my promises to you are binding on me, God, I will fulfill my thank-offerings to you, for you have saved my life from death, yes, my feet from being tripped, so as to walk before God in the light of life" (Ps 56:12-13 [MT 13-14]). I then "go around your altar, Yhwh, letting people hear the sound of thanksgiving and telling of all your awesome deeds" (Ps 26:6-7). Dancing round the altar accompanies the sacrifice. "I will confess Yhwh with all my heart in the council of the upright, the assembly" (Ps 111:1). The line nicely combines the assumption that this confession involves the whole person and energy, and thus the inner person, with the assumption that it needs to be outwardly expressed so that the worshiping community hears it. In Nehemiah 12:27-43 thanksgiving is acted out in a procession round the walls that the people are celebrating. "Sacrifice a thank-offering to God and fulfill your promises to the Most High; call me on the day of trouble; I will rescue you and you will honor me" (Ps 50:14-15). The second line summarizes the dynamic of a relationship with Yhwh. People call on Yhwh in a time of trouble, Yhwh rescues them, and they then honor Yhwh. The way they do so is by sacrificing a thank-offering in the company of people and thereby fulfilling the promise they made when they prayed, the promise to give glory to Yhwh if Yhwh answered their prayer (cf. Ps 107:22). "I am your servant, the son of your maid; you have loosed my bonds. To you I will sacrifice a thank-offering and call out in Yhwh's name. I will fulfill my vows to Yhwh, yes, right before all his people" (Ps 116:16-18).

The background of Psalm 116 is an overwhelming experience that had threatened to mean death, or had been death-like: "the ropes of death encompassed me" and turned me into someone overcome by death's sorrow. So I called out "in Yhwh's name" (not "on Yhwh's name"), pleading for action on the basis of Yhwh's commitment to me, action that would bring honor to Yhwh's name. And Yhwh's action proved once again what this name stands for, that "Yhwh is gracious and faithful, our God is one who shows compassion; Yhwh watches over simple people—I sank low, and he delivered me." "You have pulled away my life from death, my eye from tears, my foot from being pushed down," and therefore I can now have confidence for the future: my spirit can rest and I can "walk about before Yhwh in the lands of the living." My thanksgiving consists in my telling this story.

As often happens, the second half of the psalm restates the point. As the first half began "I love/give myself/dedicate myself,"[226] the second begins "I came to trust." The psalm might refer to a trust that took the worshiper through the experience of trouble or to a trust that has resulted from it. Either way, I articulate how weak and powerless was my position and how deceptive everyone was and how afraid I was—but Yhwh "loosed my bonds" and thus gave me even more basis for trust than I had before. Now I know even more certainly that Yhwh cares about the life of people who are committed, that the Master keeps faith with the servant. It is as if I have the status not merely of someone who *became* this master's servant (perhaps because I got into debt) but that of someone who was born in the master's house (Ps 116:16). I am a member of the family. And therefore I will come and make the thank-offering I promised, in Yhwh's courts, in the presence of the people, and will once again "call out in Yhwh's name" in their hearing, not now because of what I need but because of what I have received.

Love and trust are the twin bases of life with Yhwh (are they the twin bases of any relationship?).[227] The thank-offering expresses a love that re-

---

[226]See §2.1 "Loving Yhwh."
[227]Cf. Hermann Spiekermann, "Lieben und Glauben," in *Meilenstein*, ed. Manfred Weippert and Stefan Timm, H. Donner Festschrift (Wiesbaden: Harrassowitz, 1995), pp. 266-75.

sponds to God's mercy and acknowledges the way trust has been vindicated or built up.

Confession

Words are essential to a thanksgiving in order to make it also an act of confession. "Give thanks" is *yādâ* (hiphil); "thanksgiving" (in words or as an offering) is *tôdâ*. Both verb and noun can refer to acknowledging that one has done something wrong (e.g., Ps 32:5; Prov 28:13; Josh 7:19; Ezra 10:11), so the translation "thanksgiving" does not convey quite the right impression; "confession" is nearer because we can both confess our sins and confess the faith.[228] What these have in common is that they are narrative accounts of something. Confessing sins means saying "this is what I did." Confessing the faith means saying "this is what God did." "Thanksgiving" does come to be used in a broader sense to refer to confessing the great acts that made Israel Yhwh's people centuries ago (Ps 100:4), Yhwh's ongoing acts (Ps 67:3, 5 [MT 4, 6]) and even Yhwh's ongoing lordship over creation (Ps 147:7), or to refer to the simple confession of Yhwh's name (Ps 122:4) when there is nothing to give thanks for (1 Kings 8:33, 35); Psalms 105, 106, 107 and 136 are introduced by this verb. And translations render *yādâ* (hiphil) and *tôdâ* as "praise." But this misses the concrete nature of thanksgiving, which focuses on proclaiming things that Yhwh has done. Confession is concrete, narrative and personal. I tell my own story, or we tell our own story of things Yhwh has done just now, for the individual or the community. Arguably, the first great thanksgivings, and the classic ones, are the Songs of Moses and Miriam and of Deborah and Barak (Ex 15; Judg 5), even though they are not designated as thanksgivings. They illustrate vividly the concrete, narrative and personal nature of thanksgiving, as does Joseph's succinct declaration, "Whereas you planned harm for me, God planned it for good, to act today to keep alive a numerous people" (Gen 50:20).

Psalm 18 and Psalm 30 illustrate how the nature of the words in a thanksgiving is to tell a story. I exalt Yhwh by telling the story of Yhwh's exalting me. Yet again Psalm 30 does so by telling this story twice; one telling of our story may not be enough, as one plea or one expression of praise may not be enough. I get to the end and have to start again. The story relates the trouble I was in, the way I prayed, the way Yhwh answered, the way Yhwh acted and the praise I am now committed to and invite other people to share.

In Psalm 18 thanksgiving involves another fourfold remembering. First, I recall the trouble I was in. "Death's ropes encompassed me, Belial's torrents overwhelmed me, Sheol's ropes encircled me, death's snares confronted me"

---

[228]See §3.6 "Coming to your Senses, Owning, Turning."

(Ps 18:4-5 [MT 5-6]). The psalm does not give a literal description of what happened, though the context implies a battle and the attack of enemy forces. Rather it focuses on the implication of what was happening. Death stared the worshiper in the face. Recalling the seriousness of the trouble serves to enhance the glorifying of Yhwh that is the purpose of thanksgiving. Recalling the seriousness of the trouble in this particular way suggests it involved an assertion of one power over another power, Death or Belial or Sheol over against Yhwh.

Second, I recall the way I prayed. "In my trouble I called Yhwh, to my God I cried for help" (Ps 18:6a [MT 7a]). The psalm uses two of the Psalms' strong expressions for prayer. The worshiper did not merely call to Yhwh but summoned Yhwh, and urged the need to turn a cry for deliverance (*'ăšawwēa'*) into an act of deliverance (*'iwwāšēa'*, Ps 18:3 [MT 4]).

Third, I recall the way Yhwh responded. There were the usual two stages to that. "From his palace he heard my voice; my cry for help came to his ears" (Ps 18:6b [MT 7b]). Like the earthly king (hopefully) hearing the cry of the oppressed and needy from the city, below the palace, the heavenly King heard the cry of the oppressed and needy from the earth, below the palace. The cry was loud enough, the listening was sharp enough.

Thus fourth, I recall the way Yhwh responded with action. Initially, Psalm 18 gives a detailed but highly metaphorical account of this, corresponding to the metaphorical account of the predicament (both contrast with the more analogical account of Yhwh's "listening"). It was as if the earth shook and mountains quaked as Yhwh swooped down from the heavens to the earth. It was as if Yhwh reached down and scooped me up when waters were overwhelming me. But then it gives a more literal one.

A thanksgiving such as Psalm 18 thus spends most of its time recounting what has gone on. It looks at the experience from the three angles that can appear in a lament, speaking of what "you" have done (Ps 18:35-36a, 39-40a, 43a [MT 36-37a, 40-41a, 44a]), what "I" have experienced and done (Ps 18:36b-38a, 40b, 42 [MT 37b-39a, 41b, 43]), and of what "they" have experienced and done (Ps 18:38b, 41, 43b-45 [MT 39b, 42, 44b-46]). It juxtaposes what Yhwh has done with what the worshiper has done without exploring their interrelationship.

Testimony

The vocal thanksgiving would be appropriate if there were no one but Yhwh to hear me utter it, but I actually utter it in people's hearing. The thank-offering would be appropriate even if no words accompanied it, but without words it would not give testimony to other people. Thanksgiving or confession exalts Yhwh by lifting Yhwh up in the hearing and thus in the eyes of other people. This works only on the assumption that other people are present to hear the words of praise. The thanksgiving addressed to Yhwh, which is a confession, is also a testimony addressed to other people. Psalm 124 is purely testimony, addressing only an unidentified human audience and never addressing Yhwh. In Hannah's thanksgiving song (1 Sam 2:1-10), "personal joy is linked to public destiny";[229] Samuel is not merely a gift to Hannah but a gift to the whole people. Through his anointing of Saul, he will be a means whereby Israel can exult over its attackers and know Yhwh as one who enables people who are falling to get new strength and who lifts the needy from the trash heap.

The opening summary of the longest thanksgiving in the Psalter points to this feature of thanksgiving, as it is addressed not to Yhwh but to other people: "I called on Yhwh, and I was delivered from my enemies" (Ps 18:3 [MT 4]).[230] The psalm then keeps moving between addressing Yhwh and talking about Yhwh because the psalmist is talking to other people. Sometimes it is a thanksgiving addressed to Yhwh, sometimes a testimony addressed to other Israelite worshipers who are present, or to the nations for whom Yhwh's acts in relation to Israel are also significant. The implication is not that the psalmist consciously keeps moving between these; under the surface the whole psalm is addressed in both directions. Likewise Psalm 30, after three lines addressing Yhwh in thanksgiving, turns from Yhwh to the congregation: "Make music to Yhwh, people committed to him; confess his holy remembrance"—that is, confess what Yhwh has done in such a way as to make mention of Yhwh's name (Ps 30:4 [MT 5]). The confession is not limited in significance to the immediate recipient of Yhwh's act. Giving testimony means other people are invited to join in the "confession" even though they were not the beneficiaries of Yhwh's action.

Psalm 111 begins, "I confess Yhwh with all my soul in the council of the upright, the assembly." Worship involves the whole being, the inward and the outward; it has to be both individual and public. Here the words *council* and *assembly* (not *congregation*) suggest testimony in a regular, public context, not merely that of worship. Thanksgiving or testimony or confession is thus the way the people of God fulfills its vocation to be witnesses to what Yhwh has done. The word *witness* is used in a variety of ways, and in Western thinking can mean no more than declaring our deep conviction or something we know

---

[229]Balentine, *Prayer in the Hebrew Bible*, p. 219, summarizing Walter Brueggemann, *First and Second Samuel* (Louisville: John Knox, 1990), p. 17.

[230]The verbs are yiqtol, and the NRSV thus has "I call . . . so I shall be saved." But the psalm goes on to include many yiqtol verbs that must have past reference, as the NRSV recognizes (e.g., "in my distress I called upon the LORD," v. 6 [MT 7]), and more likely this sequence begins already in v. 3 [MT 4] (cf. TNIV, JPSV).

others will contradict or something we cannot prove or something on which we just give our angle. In the Scriptures, *witness* denotes something we have seen that is absolutely and objectively true. Witnesses testify to what they have seen and heard. God delivers them not merely so that they can be free but so that they can tell others what God has actually done for them, so that these others glorify God

Psalm 40:6-10 [MT 7-11] underlines the indispensability of this confession in a particularly strong way. You did not want me to make sacrifices and offerings in response to your act of deliverance, the suppliant avers. The psalm no doubt exaggerates to emphasize the point. If an incredulous family member had said, "Do you really mean you are not going to make an offering to the God who has delivered you?" I imagine the suppliant would respond by declaring that this interrogator was missing the point. The point is that it was not merely sacrifices that Yhwh wanted. While the sacrifice says something, it is not very eloquent. There was something else Yhwh wanted: the public confession that a thanksgiving psalm makes. And the suppliant has given that testimony. "I heralded your faithfulness in the great congregation; there—I did not close my lips. . . . I did not hide your faithful act within my heart; I told of your truthfulness in deliverance. I did not conceal your true commitment before the great congregation." While the thanksgiving without the thank-offering would be incomplete, the thank-offering without the thanksgiving or testimony would certainly be incomplete. Perhaps that is the point of the promise, "I will praise the name of God with a song, I will exalt him with thanksgiving, and it will please Yhwh more than an ox, a bull having horns and divided hoofs" (Ps 69:30-31 [MT 31-32]). Like a grateful attitude of heart that is not expressed in words people can hear, an offering (even a valuable one) without the words that proclaim what Yhwh did to deserve it does not fulfill its purpose.[231]

Thanksgiving thus has in common with penitence that publicly acknowledging something is integral to the notion. It is this that makes thanksgiving testimony. While thanksgiving can take place in the privacy of the heart (though only with difficulty, because thanksgiving implies enthusiasm), in its capacity as also testimony it cannot do so. And a reluctance to give public testimony to what Yhwh has done would cast doubts on the genuineness of the gratitude.[232]

---

[231]But here the implication might be that the worshiper could not make an offering because the temple had been destroyed or because the worshiper was in exile.

[232]Testimony in the Psalms thus has a different focus from the one that has been usual in Christian spirituality (and see Alan Jacobs, *Looking Before and After: Testimony and the Christian Life* [Grand Rapids/Cambridge: Eerdmans, 2008]).

Teaching

A concern to teach is inherent in testimony psalms. Psalm 34 follows the form of a testimony psalm in beginning with a declaration of intent to give praise to Yhwh and an invitation to other people to join in, and follows that with an account of what Yhwh has done for this worshiper, but it then has two distinctive features that stand in some mutual tension. At no point does it address Yhwh; in this sense it is pure testimony, wholly addressed to the congregation. It never expresses thanksgiving to Yhwh. And its actual account of what Yhwh did is rather brief. In general terms it says what one needs to say in a thanksgiving or testimony ("I sought help from Yhwh and he answered me, rescued me from all my terrors. . . . This was a weak man who called, and Yhwh listened, and delivered from all his troubles"). But there is no concrete account of what this involved; the formulation is formulaic. Instead, the psalm moves briskly to the ongoing implications of this testimony, the lessons people should draw from it. The energy in the psalm lies here. Alongside giving glory to Yhwh, by their nature testimonies exist in order to urge other people to note what Yhwh has done and draw the implications for their lives. Psalm 34 focuses on that, underlining a consistent aspect of the aim of testimony. The Psalms thus work with a significant understanding of teaching, one also assumed elsewhere in the First Testament. They combine substantial theological information with substantial explicit directives concerning the implications for people's lives. They neither comprise theological exposition without implications, nor exhortations without theology.

Psalm 92 is a further thanksgiving psalm that suggests a concern to teach, with its didactic tone ("It is good to confess Yhwh") and its subsequent reference to things that a stupid person would not acknowledge (that the flourishing of the faithless does not last). So this testimony psalm offers instruction regarding the way Yhwh acts in relation to the faithful and the faithless, with its implications for who Yhwh is, upright and reliable as a refuge. In a similar way Psalm 94, a psalm of trust, also directly confronts the "stupid" about recognizing the way Yhwh does know what is going on in the world and does intervene there, and offers similar instruction.

As we are used to distinguishing supplications and intercessions, pleas for ourselves and pleas for someone else, so we distinguish thanksgivings for what God has done for me and thanksgivings for what God has done for someone else, though we do not have terms for that. The Psalms subvert that distinction. In Psalm 118:1 the community as a whole is challenged to "confess" what Yhwh has done for its leader. This might seem natural enough, because an act of deliverance for its leader is an act of deliverance for the community itself. But in addition, the fact that Yhwh so acts for the leader is evidence for everyone that "he is good" and "his commitment lasts forever."

Thus the people go on to respond to the leader's testimony with "it is better to rely on Yhwh than to depend on a human being" or "on leaders" (perhaps implying that they realized they must not rely even on this human leader but on the God on whom the leader relied, or perhaps that they must not rely on allies). Related to that is an unexpected plea near the close of the psalm, "Oh now, Yhwh, do deliver, oh now, Yhwh, do give success." Perhaps this reflects how one great deliverance may not mean everything is resolved, or how resolution now does not preclude the need for deliverance again in the future, or the need for Yhwh to be involved with leader and community on an ongoing basis. The people have learned from the testimony. It has done its work.

In Psalm 21, too, the people rejoice in what Yhwh has done for the king. Again, this is not purely selfless; what God has done for the king benefits the people. The destiny of king and people are interwoven. So the people declare how Yhwh answered the king's prayer and gave him life (Ps 21:2-7 [MT 3-8]). But interwoven with these declarations are yiqtol comments on Yhwh's ongoing relationship with the king. Yhwh is one who sets a crown on him and gladdens him with joy. One might take these yiqtol forms as also referring to Yhwh's past act in answering prayer; but the psalm goes on to six more verses of yiqtol forms that do not refer to the king, and more likely these are indeed descriptions of Yhwh's ongoing acts that reflect the fact that Yhwh's actions on the king's behalf are significant for the people as a whole. This psalm with some logic has people in general giving the vicarious testimony that they know is significant for them. Thus they rejoice in what Yhwh has done (Ps 21:13 [MT 14]).

Inference

While a thanksgiving such as Psalm 18 spends most of its time recounting what Yhwh has done, it does not stop there, but goes on to the implications that are a large point of the testimony. We listen to people's testimonies (or read their stories or memoirs) because of the way they may help us reflect on our own lives. The Psalms spell out ways they do that. What Yhwh has done for the worshiper is assumed not to be significant only for that one person. It illustrates something that can be true for others. "My God is my crag on which I take refuge, my shield," the psalm began; but it goes on to "he is a shield for all who take refuge in him" (Ps 18:30 [MT 31]).

Thanksgivings or testimonies thus regularly make a move from speaking of Yhwh's concrete past act for a particular person to speaking of the implications of this for other people. After its initial testimony, Psalm 30:4-5 [MT 5-6] goes on to urge people in general to make music to Yhwh and confess Yhwh. This seems a little illogical. The worshiper has a basis for confession as the beneficiary of Yhwh's action, but the congregation in general has not been brought up from Sheol. Yet the form of these lines is that of a hymn of praise; the worshiper's individual "I" disappears. The lines presuppose that the worshiper's experience is not just a random, once-off event. As the basis for urging this confession the psalm offers a generalization: "for there is an instant in his anger, a life in his acceptance. In evening weeping takes up lodging, but at morning there is resounding." These are mostly noun clauses, but the invitation implies they are more than statements of something Yhwh did just once for this individual, and the sole verb "takes up lodging," a yiqtol, supports this. Yet the lines invite the congregation into confession, as if what Yhwh had done was done for them, which in a sense it was.

Correlative to the problem of suffering is the problem of blessing and the problem of mercy. In a sense it is a much bigger problem, because there is such a disparity between the amount of blessing Yhwh gives and the amount of trouble Yhwh sends. "There is an instant in his anger, a life in his acceptance." The worshiper knows we normally live our lives as people accepted and loved by Yhwh, welcomed into an ongoing relationship of delight and commitment. We can deal with a short time when that inexplicably gives way to wrath (that is, when trouble hits us) because we know this is not the normal situation; the norm will soon be restored. Suffering that can seem as if it has come to stay forever can turn out to be time-limited: "in evening weeping takes up lodging, but at morning there is resounding." The individual's experience of this can be the pattern in which the congregation trusts. And my thanksgiving extends not only to other people, as testimony; it extends to other times: "Yhwh my God, I will confess you forever" (Ps 30:12 [MT 13]).

Indeed, several of these psalms have implied, this is not limited to Israel. Because "I will confess you with all my heart, before the gods I will make music for you, I will bow down to your holy palace, and I will confess your name for your commitment and for your truthfulness," therefore "all the kings of the earth are to confess you, because they have heard the words of your mouth; they are to sing of Yhwh's ways, because Yhwh's honor is great" (Ps 138:1-5). "May peoples confess you, God, may peoples confess you, all of them, may countries rejoice and resound, because you decide for peoples with uprightness; the countries on the earth—you lead them" (Ps 67:3-4 [MT 4-5]). Why should they do that, and how do they know this is so? The opening of the psalm has indicated the answer: "May God be gracious to us and bless us, may he shine his face with us (Selah), so that your way is acknowledged on the earth, your deliverance among all nations." What Yhwh does for Israel is what leads to the nations acknowledging Yhwh; and one of the ways this works is by means of the testimony Israel is able to give to what Yhwh has done.

Thanksgiving-Prayer-Thanksgiving-Praise

Christian piety has suggested several ways of interrelating various ways of speaking to God. Liturgies may suggest adoration-thanksgiving-penitence-intercession-petition or penitence-adoration-intercession-supplication. A popular individual scheme suggests adoration-confession-thanksgiving-supplication (ACTS). Is there a pattern in the First Testament?

Psalm 44 and Psalm 89 begin with praise that turns out to be but the preamble to plea. The longer the praise goes on, the more powerful is the plea that presupposes Yhwh has not been behaving in accordance with the content of the praise. There can be a parallel dynamic about the relationship of thanksgiving and prayer. Thanksgiving looks back to prayer and deliverance and forward to ongoing praise. It can also be the background to renewed prayer. Looking back at what Yhwh has done encourages prayer concerning what we need Yhwh to do. So testifying to Yhwh's having taken thought for us stimulates us to urge Yhwh to take thought for us (Ps 40:5, 17 [MT 6, 18]). Testifying to Yhwh's deliverance stimulates us to pray as people who are dedicated to Yhwh's deliverance (Ps 40:10, 16 [MT 11, 17]). It encourages us to reckon that such a prayer is worth praying. Further, the psalm emphasizes that the suppliant has made the confession Yhwh looks for in testimony to what Yhwh did. That is one basis for pressing Yhwh to act again. More significantly and more overtly, the declaration of Yhwh's past act is a basis for pressing Yhwh to act in consistency with that previous action: "You did it before; therefore you can and should do it again." The dynamic of the psalm corresponds to that of Psalm 89. The longer the confession goes on, the more compelling is the plea to which it leads. Psalm 144 takes up expressions from a number of psalms but especially from Psalm 18, from which it then has the interesting difference that Psalm 18 is a testimony, Psalm 144 a prayer. The deliverance that testimony celebrates becomes a model for the deliverance this suppliant seeks; and the testimony thereby fulfills its purpose.

The community thanksgiving Psalm 124 closes with the declaration "Our help is the very name of Yhwh,[233] maker of the heavens and the earth," and thus with an affirmation that belongs in a praise psalm rather than a thanksgiving. The psalm has celebrated the way Yhwh was "for us, when human beings arose against us," so as to make it possible for us to escape from them rather than being swallowed alive, but it ends with this timeless descriptive statement. Such declarations have their natural home in praise psalms. They then appear in protest psalms as statements of trust in what Yhwh will surely turn out to be or as protests at what Yhwh is not being. They reappear in tes-

---

[233]Not "our help is in the name of Yhwh," which does not make much sense; the *b* is *b* of identity, *b essentiae* (see *IBHS* 11.2.5e).

timony psalms on the basis of the fact that what Yhwh has then done provides further evidence of their truth. They thus witness to the dialectical relationship between praise and testimony and the complex relationship between praise, prayer and testimony. Praise depends on testimony to keep it alive; testimony is designed to lead into praise.

Sigmund Mowinckel sees the heart of the Psalms as lying in the hymn of praise.[234] Claus Westermann sees it as lying in thanksgiving or declarative praise, praise that declares what Yhwh has done; thanksgiving mediates between the lament and the hymn of praise.[235] Walter Brueggemann sees it as lying in the lament itself, which mediates between the hymn of praise and the thanksgiving; orientation gives way to disorientation, disorientation to renewed orientation.[236] Rather, praise, protest, plea and thanksgiving (and penitence and a life of commitment) work in a dynamic interrelationship. This interrelationship is not linear but circular, or rather spiral. Prayer may begin with praise or protest or plea or thanksgiving according to the circumstances of the worshiper. It may simply undertake that form of address of God, or it may move on any distance round the circle, and it may then go round it again. Indeed, one's life with God involves repeatedly navigating this circle, though not in a repetitive manner, because each time I come to any staging point in the circle, I am a different person relating to God in different ways from what was true the last time. This is the nature of the ongoing life with God that the First Testament lays before its readers.[237]

---

[234]Sigmund Mowinckel, *The Psalms in Israel's Worship* (Oxford: Blackwell, 1962), 1:81-105.

[235]Claus Westermann, *The Praise of God in the Psalms* (Richmond: Knox, 1965); enlarged ed., *Praise and Lament in the Psalms* (Atlanta: Knox, 1981), p. 154.

[236]See, e.g., Walter Brueggemann, *The Psalms and the Life of Faith* (Minneapolis: Fortress, 1995), pp. 3-32.

[237]See John Goldingay, "The Dynamic Cycle of Praise and Prayer in the Psalms," *JSOT* 20 (1981): 85-90.

PART TWO

LIVING WITH ONE ANOTHER

The First Testament deals with a series of contexts in which people relate to one another. We will consider them approximately in the order in which they come into focus in its story, which is also the order in which they immediately impinge on ordinary people's lives. We thus first consider marriage, family and the local community or village where most people live, where key questions surface about the purpose of life, about the good life and about living the right kind of life. An Israelite might reckon that the family is prior to the married couple, but there is some logic in starting with the smallest unit, and Genesis tells the human story beginning with the first couple, then broadens the narrative to speak of the family, the community, the city and the nation.[1] We then look at city, nation and state, which were of less day-to-day significance for most people but had huge indirect importance even for village communities far from centers of power. But before considering these questions, section 4.1 takes a step back to ask about method in seeking to discover how the First Testament offers insight on such questions.

---

[1]Waldemar Janzen in his *Old Testament Ethics* (Louisville: Westminster John Knox, 1994) similarly starts from the family and sees it as the First Testament's "preeminent paradigm" (p. 3).

4

FAMILY AND COMMUNITY

Some distinctive difficulties attach to interpreting the First Testament in connection with marriage, family and local community. Interpreters can write as if the Torah's regulations describe how life actually was, or were designed to relate to life as it actually was, or are an appropriate starting point for understanding how the First Testament as a whole sees the issue they speak of.[1] And if "law is an index of a civilization which reflects the underlying value concepts inherent within that civilization,"[2] it would follow that these regulations are "the primary subject matter of an ethics of the Hebrew Bible."[3] But actually they give us "a very partial and to that extent misleading picture of the relevant social realities"[4] and a very partial and thus misleading picture of Israelite values.[5] A description of marriage and family in the United States that based itself on what state or federal law said would give us a very weird impression of them (though it would conceal other aspects of their weirdness). The main aim of law, after all, is to help a society cope with problems and stop conflicts getting out of hand. This is not the sole aim of the instructions in Exodus-Deuteronomy; telling people to love God is not a function of law, which illustrates the limitations of "law" as a paradigm for understand-

---

[1]See, e.g., L. William Countryman, *Dirt, Greed, and Sex* (Philadelphia: Fortress, 1988), pp. 151-67.

[2]Shalom M. Paul, *Studies in the Book of the Covenant in the Light of Cuneiform and Biblical Law,* VTSup 18 (Leiden: Brill, 1970), p. 1.

[3]Eckhart Otto, "Of Aims and Methods in Hebrew Bible Ethics," *Semeia* 66 (1994): 161-72: see p. 162; cf. his *Theologische Ethik des Alten Testaments* (Stuttgart: Kohlhammer, 1994).

[4]Joseph Blenkinsopp, "The Family in First Temple Israel," in Leo G. Perdue et al., *Families in Ancient Israel* (Louisville: Westminster John Knox, 1997), pp. 48-103; see p. 66; cf. Hilary Lipka, *Sexual Transgression in the Hebrew Bible* (Sheffield, U.K.: Sheffield Phoenix Press, 2006), pp. 12-13. I thus accept Cyril S. Rodd's critique (*Glimpses of a Strange Land* [London: T & T Clark, 2001], p. 316) of my discussion of "The Old Testament as a Way of Life" (*Approaches to Old Testament Interpretation* [revised ed., Leicester/Downers Grove, IL: 1990], pp. 38-65) as giving too much prominence to the laws, though oddly enough I think his own volume is vulnerable to the same critique.

[5]Cf. Gordon J. Wenham, *Story as Torah* (Edinburgh: T & T Clark, 2000/Grand Rapids: Baker, 2004), pp. 79-80; also David Pleins's *The Social Visions of the Hebrew Bible* (Louisville: Westminster John Knox, 2001), which gives only one chapter to law. Erhard S. Gerstenberger likewise comments on how misleading it is to start from "the legal dimension of the 'law texts,' " as if Israel was a state rather than a faith community (*Theologies in the Old Testament* [Edinburgh: T & T Clark/Minneapolis: Fortress, 2002], p. 262).

ing the Torah. But it is one of the aims, particularly when the Torah handles topics such as marriage and family.[6] I shall approach these questions by attending also to the Wisdom books, which are overtly designed to instruct, and to the narratives, which describe how family actually was or how it could be plausibly portrayed.[7] But that points us to another aspect of the topic's trickiness, the task of discerning in what way the working of family and community in Israel is designed to be instructive and in what way it is simply a cultural datum, the background to the material's real concern with what God is doing. At least it gives us another set of understandings and experiences to think against, and one through which we know God worked.

4.1 Thinking About Life with One Another

How do we discover what the life of First Testament Israel has to say to the life of the third millennium world?

Thinking Theologically

The topics we study in part two would count in a modern context as part of the study of ethics, though ethics is not a biblical category, and the presuppositions of the study of ethics are very different from First Testament assumptions about God and us, and about God's authority in relation to us. Torah and prophecy presuppose that God lays the law down. In other words, they presuppose theonomy, and "the essence of theonomy is the trust in God and his guidance," but "the essence of ethics is the questioning of all authority and individual responsibility for the setting of norms."[8] Ethics involves me as an individual being convinced that a certain norm of behavior should be followed. It is sometimes argued that the First Testament itself appeals to an ethical or theological principle outside Yhwh's word that is reckoned to sit in judgment on it. There would then be insight and truth that human beings can

---

[6]This is so even if Anne Fitzpatrick-McKinley is right in seeing the whole as moral and legal advice that has only moral authority (*The Transformation of Torah from Scribal Advice to Law*, JSOTSup 287 [Sheffield, U.K.: Sheffield Academic Press, 1999]). Gerstenberger calls the Torah a collection of catechisms (*Theologies in the Old Testament*, p. 263).

[7]Cf. David Biale, *Eros and the Jews* (New York: Basic, 1992), pp. 11-13, who comments on the non-monolithic nature of the First Testament's account of sexuality; he then begins his examination with Ruth and notes how "eroticism, procreation, and agricultural fertility are intertwined throughout the book" (p. 14).

[8]Ze'ev W. Falk, "Law and Ethics in the Hebrew Bible," in *Justice and Righteousness*, Benjamin Uffenheimer Festschrift, ed. Henning Graf Reventlow and Yair Hoffman, JSOTSup 137 (Sheffield, U.K.: Sheffield Academic Press, 1992), pp. 82-90; see p. 87. With Falk's use of the word *theonomy*, compare that in Roman Catholic thinking, as expressed in Pope John Paul's encyclical *Veritatis splendor* <www.vatican.va/edocs/ENG0222/_INDEX.HTM>. *Theonomy* is used in a different sense in United States Reformed writings (see §4.1 "Thinking Exegetically").

discover, and are responsible to discover, so that Israel's theonomy tolerates also ethical thought.[9] Yet passages such as Genesis 18:24-25 and Exodus 32:11-13, quoted in this connection, fail to prove the point. They appeal to Yhwh's nature, not to something outside Yhwh. "The Old Testament is not familiar with the concept of doing good for the sake of the good; rather, it is YHWH's will that lays claim to human lives."[10] "The good" is defined by who God is.[11]

Affirming such theonomy, Karl Barth declares that we misunderstand God's command in Scripture if we think we can and must abstract from it a collection of general moral rules that ethics can then expound and apply in particular. "The commands of God in the Bible are not general moral doctrines and instructions but absolutely specific directions which concern each time the behaviour, deeds and omissions" of particular people.[12] We must not systematize ethics so that it becomes under our control and ceases to be God's word to us.[13] It is not we who decide what is right in life situations. It is God, the God who commands. Yet Barth's own work makes clear that this does not imply there is nothing to learn from the many commands in both Testaments to particular people and also the many commands that look like generalizations. Dietrich Bonhoeffer similarly declares that "the only possible object of a 'Christian ethic' " is "an object which lies beyond the 'ethical,' namely, 'the commandment of God,' " definite and concrete;[14] the attempt to determine what is good once and for all issues either in vague generalization or in unmanageable casuistry.[15] But he also notes that we need to "discern" what God's will is (Rom 12:2; Phil 1:9-10). It is not a matter of pure intuition without reflection. "The voice of the heart is not to be confused with the will of God."[16]

While the Decalogue, for instance, and exhortations such as "be holy because I am holy," are addressed to Israel in the context of its particular life, they are designed to govern Israel's life from beginning to end, and they do that partly because they are not random commands but ones that link directly with who God is as creator and redeemer.[17] People such as prophets do seem to take such general commands and declare what is their current de-

---

[9]Falk, "Law and Ethics in the Hebrew Bible," p. 90.

[10]Horst Dietrich Preuss, *Old Testament Theology*, 2 vols. (Louisville: Westminster John Knox/ Edinburgh: T & T Clark, 1995; 1996) 2:191.

[11]Cf. Karl Barth, *Church Dogmatics* (Edinburgh: T & T Clark, 1969), III/4:4.

[12]Barth, *Church Dogmatics*, III/4:12.

[13]Cf. John Webster, *Barth's Ethics of Reconciliation* (Cambridge/New York: Cambridge University Press, 1995), p. 18.

[14]Dietrich Bonhoeffer, *Ethics* (New York: Simon & Schuster, 1995), p. 272.

[15]Ibid., p. 87.

[16]Ibid., p. 41.

[17]Cf. Nigel Biggar, "Barth's Trinitarian Ethic," in *The Cambridge Companion to Karl Barth*, ed. John Webster (Cambridge/New York: Cambridge University Press, 2000), pp. 212-27.

mand. And a framework of thinking that reflects things God has already declared in Scripture opens up the possibility of discerning what God is saying and of testing what we think God might be saying, even if we might nevertheless sometimes come to the conclusion that God is saying something outrageous to us, as God does in Genesis 22. In a twenty-first-century context our problem is the opposite of the one Barth seeks to guard against. Our problem is the danger of reckoning we have heard God's voice and received God's guidance on the basis of a feeling that "this must be right."

Thinking Attentively

"God said it, I believe it, that settles it." The bumper sticker's declaration should not be dismissed, but God's saying it does not always settle it because we may not be clear what the "it" is, or God may not have said an "it" in connection with the issue we need to resolve. And even if we have such an "it," God may not want us to be legalistic about the matter. What should happen if a layperson eats of holy things without realizing (Lev 22:14)? God had said that such a person's life becomes forfeit for the profanation. No, says God, not if was an accident, it's not a problem. Just have him or her make compensation to the priest.

In connection with Israel's journey from Sinai, Yhwh sometimes lives up to the bumper sticker and takes the initiative in guiding Israel. That is so in connection with the census (Num 1, and again Num 26), a risky undertaking if you do not have such divine permission (2 Sam 24). It is so in connection with other arrangements for the journey (Num 2–8). Yhwh guides on the journey itself by means of the cloud that both draws attention to and conceals the divine presence (Num 9:15-23). Yhwh speaks in connection with the deaths of Aaron and of Moses (Num 20:22-28; 27:12-14). But questions arise on this journey for which neither the revelation at Sinai nor Yhwh's initiative resources Israel. Some men have had to bury someone just before Pesah and they are therefore taboo because of the contact with death, so they cannot offer the Pesah sacrifice. What are they to do (Num 9:6-13)? There is a man collecting wood on the sabbath. What is the community to do (Num 15:32-36)? There are women whose father has died without having a surviving son, so there is no one to inherit his land: may they inherit it (Num 27:1-11)? In each situation Moses consults Yhwh, and Yhwh tells him the answer. And he is promised that his successor will always be able to consult the Urim for a decision about such questions (Num 27:21), though the questions may need careful formulating, since it often seems that the Urim and Thummim give only yes and no answers.[18]

---

[18]See further §7.3 "A Ministry of Supervision and a Ministry of Music."

On other occasions Moses simply decides what to do without consulting Yhwh, sometimes in circumstances that raise eyebrows. He asks Hobab to accompany the people to guide them through the wilderness, even though Yhwh has undertaken to do that (Num 10:29-32). He decides to avoid fighting Edom (Num 20:14-20). He offers to devote Arad (Num 21:1-3). He tries to avoid fighting Sihon (Num 21:21-25). His successor sends spies to reconnoiter Jericho (Josh 2) with mixed results and rather oddly since Israel is only going to need to blow trumpets to make the city's walls fall down.

When we think Yhwh takes the initiative and speaks or responds to our asking, how do we test what we think Yhwh says? Or how do we work out for ourselves what to do? How do we decide when a situation should be viewed as exceptional? How do we exercise that discernment to which the people of God is called? The Torah, the Prophets and the Writings are then our resource. How do we use them?

Thinking Exegetically

Although it can sometimes seem that life is dominated by controverted questions and that Scripture is full of material whose meaning is unclear, the commands in the Decalogue or the Sermon on the Mount are largely of clear enough meaning; most of the time it is not so hard to know whether something counts as murder, adultery, stealing or giving untrue testimony. A traditional Jewish and Christian approach to knowing what to do thus assumes it is possible to consider the statements in the Scriptures in a straightforward fashion and just ask what they mean, what they refer to, what they imply. Admittedly it may need care to see how they apply to us, and Judaism thus reckons it wise to "make a fence around the Torah."[19]

So what does it mean to observe the sabbath? The Torah makes explicit that it means lighting no fire. Does that mean not igniting the oven for a meal or not pressing an elevator button and thus producing an electrical spark? To be on the safe side, it would be wise to reckon that it indeed excludes these, so we will use the automatic timer on the oven and have the elevator stop automatically at all floors. How can we make sure we do not cook a kid goat in its mother's milk? We will keep meat products and milk products totally apart so that we can never risk infringing this command. Establishing what Scripture says about abortion or capital punishment or war may involve detailed exegetical discussion of passages such as Exodus 21:22-25 and Psalm 139:13-16, or Genesis 9:6 or Exodus 20:13.

A radical Christian application of an exegetical approach to the Torah also uses the term *theonomy*, and emphasizes that the Torah given to Israel was to

---

[19]See, e.g. *m. Abot* 1.1.

provide a pattern for all societies. Israel is designed to be God's exemplar or working model as it lives by the Torah.[20] Thus societies are in rebellion against God insofar as they do not implement the Torah in their life, and theonomy urges that the moral aspect to the Torah be implemented in the life of the nation. This is surely right in principle, even if theonomy cannot carry through its principle with consistency; it has to grant that some aspects of the Torah belonged only to its cultural context.[21] (Ironically, opponents of theonomy such as the contributors to the symposium *Toward a Just and Caring Society*[22] share the view that the Torah's prescriptions are like laws that the state should enforce; they just focus on different prescriptions, those relating to care for the poor.)

A further problem with theonomy lies in the legal and punitive aspect of the focus of its implementation of the Torah. "The binding force and authority of any particular commandment always lies in its penal threat. . . . A person is not *demanded* to act in a certain way unless his disobedience is followed by the application of a penal sanction."[23] Thus Christian Reconstruction argues for "the continuing validity of Old Testament civil laws, including especially the law's negative sanctions."[24] The First Testament itself suggests two difficulties about this thesis. One is that there is an odd aspect to the way it treats these penalties. It relates many occasions when Israelites commit wrongs to which the Torah attaches the death penalty, such as adultery and murder, but it is the rule rather than the exception for the community not to apply the Torah's penalty to these. It does not take the Torah's sanctions as directives for sentencing bodies. They are more like theological and ethical statements for households, kin groups and local communities.[25] The First Testament does not seem to reckon that the authority of commandments lies in their legal

---

[20]See, e.g., Greg L. Bahnsen, *Theonomy in Christian Ethics,* 2nd ed. (Phillipsburg, N.J.: Presbyterian & Reformed, 1984); *No Other Standard: Theonomy and its Critics* (Tyler, Tex.: Institute for Christian Economics, 1991); "The Theonomic Reformed Approach to Law and Gospel," in *Five Views on Law and Gospel,* ed. Wayne G. Strickland (Grand Rapids: Zondervan, 1996), pp. 93-143; Gary North, ed., *Theonomy: An Informed Response* (Tyler, Tex.: Institute for Christian Economics, 1991); cf. also Christopher J. H. Wright, *Old Testament Ethics for the People of God* (Downers Grove, Ill./Leicester, U.K.: Inter-Varsity Press, 2004), pp. 62-73, though he distances himself from theonomy, while speaking of Israel as God's paradigm; I have avoided this word here because I use it in a different sense under "Thinking Paradigmatically."

[21]Cf., e.g., Robert P. Lightner's critique "Theological Perspectives on Theonomy," *BSac* 143 (1986): 26-36, 134-45, 228-45; see pp. 231-32.

[22]David P. Gushee, ed., *Toward a Just and Caring Society* (Grand Rapids: Baker, 1999). For critique, see also William S. Barker and W. Robert Godfrey, ed., *Theonomy: A Reformed Critique* (Grand Rapids: Zondervan, 1990).

[23]Bahnsen, *Theonomy in Christian Ethics,* p. 435.

[24]Gary North, *Victim's Rights* (Tyler, Tex.: Institute for Christian Economics, 1990), p. 3.

[25]Cf. §1.2 "The Need for Instruction."

threat. The other difficulty is that theonomy's disciplinary system centers on magistrates and works top down,[26] whereas Israel's disciplinary system worked bottom up, with responsibility diffused among households, kin groups and local communities. The state is not responsible for people's obedience to the Torah. (Again ironically, people concerned for a just and caring society often seem especially concerned about top-down action rather than the local action the Torah envisages.)

Sometimes an exegetical approach can help us with questions that arise in our own context but did not arise in scriptural times. Israel had no reason to fret about ecology and conservation, but its substantial reflection on the theological significance of the earth is open to explication in connection with that question.[27] Admittedly, the ease with which we "turn the Old Testament writers into late twentieth-century environmentalists"[28] draws attention to the importance of continuing to bear in mind the differences between their agenda and ours. We can spot our agenda by noting the "isms" that preoccupy us (conservationism, evangelicalism, feminism, fundamentalism, vegetarianism, Calvinism, pacifism, Anglicanism). An "ism" will be a preoccupation of ours that may find more or less confirmation or disconfirmation or elaboration in Scripture, but by definition it constitutes our agenda rather than Scripture's.

Thinking Hermeneutically

That example provides a segue into thinking about the First Testament hermeneutically. By a hermeneutical approach I mean one that consciously aims to set up a dialogue between a contemporary situation and a text that did not have this situation in mind. Acts 15 provides a neat example as it relates how Christian leaders allowed what God had been doing in the church to interact with the First Testament Scriptures. "The interpretation of Scripture is guided by the testimony about the Spirit's work."[29] At the same time, the community

---

[26]See Bahnsen, *Theonomy in Christian Ethics*, pp. 317-472.

[27]See, e.g., Wright, *Old Testament Ethics for the People of God*, pp. 103-45, and his references; John Barton, *Ethics and the Old Testament* (London: SCM Press/Harrisburg, Penn.: Trinity, 1998), pp. 38-44; Ellen F. Davis's comments on the way the Song of Songs "evokes a healed relationship between humanity and the natural world" (*Getting Involved with God* [Cambridge, Mass.: Cowley, 2001], p. 83, also pp. 185-208); also now her *Scripture, Culture, and Agriculture* (Cambridge/New York: Cambridge University Press, 2008); and the discussion of Gen 1–2 in *OTT* 1:42-130 and of "The World" in *OTT* 2:647-731.

[28]Rodd, *Glimpses of a Strange Land*, p. 249; see further pp. 234-49.

[29]Stephen Fowl, "How the Spirit Reads and How to Read the Spirit," in *The Bible in Ethics*, ed. John Rogerson et al., JSOTSup 207 (Sheffield, U.K.: Sheffield Academic Press, 1995), pp. 348-63; see p. 357, summarizing Luke T. Johnson, *Decision Making in the Church* (Philadelphia: Fortress, 1983), p. 84; he also compares Richard B. Hays, *Echoes of Scripture in the Letters of Paul* (New Haven, Conn.: London: Yale University Press, 1989), p. 108.

looks to Scripture for guidance as it reflects on the Spirit's work and its impli-cations.[30]

The sabbath provides a broader instance of the Scriptures themselves us-ing this approach.[31] The First Testament always assumes Israel must observe the sabbath, but the significance of doing so keeps changing. In Exodus 20:8-11 it reflects the pattern of God's work as creator. In Deuteronomy 5:12-15 it reflects the pattern of God's deliverance of serfs from Egypt. In Amos's day it confronts the desire of merchants to make money (Amos 8:4-7). After the ex-ile, it provides people such as eunuchs and foreigners with an identity marker for commitment to the God of Israel (Is 56:1-8).[32] In the modern West, it con-fronts the 24/7 mentality of the culture.[33] There is no doubt we should ob-serve the sabbath, but the significance of doing so has radically changed.[34]

Tithing provides another example.[35] The First Testament always assumes that Israel must tithe, but the significance of tithing keeps changing. It can be an expression of gratitude (Gen 14:17-24), or a means of indulging our instinct to calculate (Gen 28:10-22), or a temptation to avoid fulfilling our obligations (Lev 27:30-33), or a way of supporting the ministry (Num 18:21-32), or a way of supporting the poor (Deut 14:22-29), or a way for leaders to oppress ordi-nary people (1 Sam 8:15-17), or a way of avoiding Yhwh's lordship (Amos 4:4). In the modern West it might not be a way to underwrite the cost of services that we require (keeping our churches ambient, financing new sound sys-tems and paying the pastor's salary), but a way to share our resources with churches and other communities in the Two-thirds World to enable them to have clean water, basic education and basic health care.

In each of these cases the hermeneutical process involves an act of imagi-nation whereby people perceive the significance of Scripture in the context of a new question. Interpretation always involves the imagination, but here the

---

[30]On differing approaches to this dialectic in connection with the debate on homosexuality, see Philip Groves, ed., *The Anglican Communion and Homosexuality* (London: SPCK, 2008), pp. 105-6.

[31]See Walter Brueggemann, *Finally Comes the Poet* (Minneapolis: Fortress, 1989), pp. 91-96.

[32]Hagith Sivan hints that the length of the sabbath commandment reflects it importance in the Second Temple context (*Between Woman, Man and God*, JSOTSup 401 [New York/London: T & T Clark, 2004], p. 87).

[33]Cf. Brueggemann, *Finally Comes the Poet*, pp. 97-99. Although the sabbath is thus "not, on the face of it, inflammatory or partisan" (p. 91), and might seem a safe example of hermeneutical reflection, in another sense it is a very dangerous one, since observing the sabbath would strike at the foundations of the U.S. economy.

[34]The song with which Jews welcome the sabbath combines the "remember" and "observe" of Ex 20:8 and Deut 5:12. At the beginning of Israel Knohl's study *The Divine Symphony: The Bible's Many Voices* (Philadelphia: Jewish Publication Society, 2003), p. xi, he notes the midrash on which the lines from the song are based, which itself quotes Ps 62:11 [12], and summarizes, "the divine speech is one, but it has within it many different voices."

[35] See §6.4 "Tithing as an Intuition" and "Reworking Tithing."

leap of imagination is easier to see. Exegesis by its nature cannot generate the insight to see what sabbath or tithing mean in a new context. The insight comes because a spark flashes between the interpreter's understanding of a present context and some scriptural motif that has nothing to do with it within Scripture, but could be brought into relationship with it. Put theologically, God enables us to see something.

The next challenge of any hermeneutical approach, any approach that gives scope to the imagination, any approach that stresses the guidance of the Holy Spirit, any right-brain approach is to establish whether its result does reflect the guidance of the Holy Spirit or rather that of some other spirit. In the end, that is a judgment call, an act of discernment, though here the different approaches we are considering complement each other; more analytical, exegetical, left-brain approaches make a contribution to this act of discernment.

Thinking Paradigmatically

A hermeneutical approach issues from the interpreter's context. If one is to be deliberate about it, it involves understanding the way First Testament passages address their context and also understanding the context in which we live; the act of imagination bridges the two.

A companion contextual approach puts more emphasis on analytical, left-brain thinking. To reckon that the concrete regulations in the Torah embody principles seems a better wager than to reckon that they are random imperatives with no rationale beyond the desire to get Israel to live in obedience to God. They then constitute a paradigmatic embodiment of such principles.[36] Abstract rules have little meaning. "No rule exists apart from its applications"; as a bare rule it is vacuous.[37] A mark of the First Testament's genius is that its teaching is concrete, ad hoc and occasional.[38] It illustrates principles applied to cases or contexts. The interpretive task includes identifying the principles underlying regulations, but then seeking to reembody those principles in equivalent regulations for our context.

Thomas Aquinas gave systematic formulation to a distinction between

---

[36]For the notion of paradigms, see also Janzen, *Old Testament Ethics*: he speaks of the familial, priestly, wisdom, royal and prophetic paradigms; and Gershom M. H. Ratheiser, *Mitzvoth Ethics and the Jewish Bible*, LHBOTS 460 (New York/London: T & T Clark, 2007), pp. 162-267: Joshua the exemplary warrior is then his instance of such a paradigm.

[37]Alasdair MacIntyre, "Does Applied Ethics Rest on a Mistake?" *The Monist* 67 (1984): 498-513; see p. 502, as quoted by Stanley Hauerwas, *In Good Company* (Notre Dame, Ind./London: University of Notre Dame, 1995), p. 171.

[38]Cf. Charles H. Cosgrove, *Appealing to Scripture in Moral Debate* (Grand Rapids/Cambridge: Eerdmans, 2002), p. 67.

moral, religious and social regulations,[39] but this does not work very well; for instance, there are moral principles involved in the civil and ceremonial laws.[40] I have rather asked whether a given regulation most centrally concerns people's relationship with God, or the life of the family or community or nation, or the life of the individual, though these also overlap.

There is a series of questions we might ask in this connection.[41] What was the regulation's function in the society, how did it relate to the social system and what was its objective? What kind of situation was it trying to promote or prevent? Whose interests was it aiming to protect? Who would have benefited from it and why? Whose power was it trying to restrict and how did it do so? What rights and responsibilities were embodied in it? What kind of behavior did it encourage or discourage? What vision of society motivated it? What moral principles, values or priorities did it embody or instantiate? What motivation did it appeal to? What sanction or penalty (if any) was attached to it, and what does that suggest regarding its relative seriousness or moral priority? We may never be able to answer all those questions, but we will usually be able to answer some. We can then ask an equivalent set of questions about our own context in order to think out how we can implement the regulation's objective there.[42] The Torah offers a model for the implementation of God's will in society in a particular cultural context. We learn from it not by lifting out particular principles or practices that look immediately applicable in ours but by gaining an understanding of its understanding of life in society as a whole.[43]

To say that understanding the First Testament's teaching involves seeing it in its cultural context is a dangerous observation. Evangelicals undertake this move when they do not like what the Scriptures say; reckoning that scriptural material relates to a cultural context can then be a basis for not heeding it. (Non-evangelicals are free simply to say that it is wrong.) In relation to this move several points may be made. First, every statement in every part of both Testaments needs to be understood against its cultural context. That includes statements that we like; ignoring their cultural context turns them into proof texts. Second, understanding against a cultural context is different from offering a negative evaluation on the basis of a cultural context. Indeed, the

---

[39]Thomas Aquinas *Summa theologica* II/1, questions 99-103.

[40]But for a defense of this distinction (and some account of its history), see Oliver O'Donovan, *Resurrection and Moral Order* (Leicester, U.K.: Inter-Varsity Press/Grand Rapids: Eerdmans, 1986), pp. 159-60.

[41]Cf. Wright, *Old Testament Ethics for the People of God*, pp. 321-23.

[42]Cf. the discussion of "the rule of purpose" in Cosgrove, *Appealing to Scripture in Moral Debate*, pp. 12-50.

[43]Michael Schluter and Roy Clements, *Reactivating the Extended Family* (Cambridge: Jubilee Centre, 1986), pp. ix-x.

more we understand against a cultural context, the less we will be inclined to offer a negative judgment, because we will see how a regulation makes sense in that context. Third, and most important, we ourselves belong in a cultural context. Frequently, the reason we think certain things are important or true and other things are unimportant or inconceivable is not because we understand God better than the scriptural writers but because we are limited by our cultural context. This is especially so for Christians in the West, where both our philosophical context (in modernity and the Enlightenment or its aftermath in postmodernity) and our social context (in an urbanized, sexualized and media-dominated society) put us at a distance from the context of life in a traditional society like Israel's. Thus the occasions when we find biblical material not fitting with what we think in our cultural context are the occasions when it very likely has the capacity to deliver us from the limitations of our cultural context.

Our understanding of Scripture is decisively shaped by the people we are. One aspect of this shaping is our relationship to power. Christian slave-traders and slave-owners often interpreted the scriptural material on slavery differently from people who were not slave-traders or slave-owners. Male church leaders often interpret scriptural material on the role of women in leadership differently from women who would like to be involved in leadership. Our interpretation needs to be resourced by self-suspicion.

Thinking Sociocritically

Actual regulations too can be aimed to protect interested parties. In describing "the family in First Temple Israel," Joseph Blenkinsopp notes that the biblical source material has the character of *"canonical* texts," from which he infers that their stance was "dictated by the agenda and ideology of those who put the collection together." He thus reads the material suspiciously and comments (for instance) concerning the regulation in Deuteronomy 22:23-29 about a woman who has been raped that "the law's indifference to her interests in general is too clearly in evidence to require comment." [44]

Whose interests do the regulations in the Torah serve? They are sometimes open to a variety of interpretations in this connection and thus to a variety of evaluations. The rules about stealing animals (Ex 22:1-4 [21:37–22:3]) might protect the rich and penalize the poor who "borrow" and then cannot pay back; "this regulation may have been an important source for slavery."[45] But they might protect the poor from having anyone (including the rich) appro-

---

[44]See Joseph Blenkinssop, "The Family in First Temple Israel," in Leo G. Perdue et al., *Families in Ancient Israel* (Louisville: Westminster John Knox, 1997), pp. 48-103, see pp. 49, 63.

[45]So Frank Crüsemann, *The Torah* (Minneapolis: Fortress/Edinburgh: T & T Clark, 1996), p. 164.

priating animals that are crucial to their livelihood. Something similar is true about the regulation concerning rape. The point that is "too clearly in evidence to require comment" is not at all clear to the commentators on Deuteronomy; according to one of the most rigorously historical-critical of them, the regulation "protects" the woman.[46] But it also protects her father's interests, and it is common for regulations in the Torah to balance interests in this way. If the Decalogue presupposes that the people who count in the community are men who are the heads of households and possess property,[47] nevertheless it goes on to try to keep them in order and to safeguard the community by restraining disorder. Statutes about servitude (Ex 21:1-11) involve compromise between the interests of the powerful and those of the weak; they offer some protection to the latter but also support the former.

The nature of law is to include protection for the political, social and economic interests of the people who propound the laws, and Deuteronomy (for instance) might be no exception even in what it has to say about widow, alien and orphan; hence the critique in a passage such as Isaiah 10:1-4.[48] Biblical interpretation therefore accepts "an obligation to encounter the Other when developing ethical principles from biblical texts"[49] in the sense of asking how they look to the person whom they view negatively. But it would be overly cynical to say that protecting the powerful is the only aim of law. Some people who frame laws are concerned for people other than themselves. It can be argued that the Torah's regulations work in light of a more exalted understanding of human dignity than that which prevailed in other Middle-Eastern cultures and was reflected in their declarations about social policy (their "law codes"), both in taking steps toward treating everyone the same (for instance, men and women, landholders and servants, Israelites and resident aliens) and treating everyone as responsible.[50]

---

[46]A. D. H. Mayes, *Deuteronomy* (London: Oliphants, 1979/Grand Rapids: Eerdmans, 1981), p. 313.

[47]See David J. A. Clines, "The Ten Commandments, Reading from Left to Right" in *Interested Parties*, JSOTSup 205 (Sheffield, U.K.: Sheffield Academic Press, 1995), pp. 26-45.

[48]So Crüsemann, *The Torah*, pp. 167-68; Harold V. Bennett, *Injustice Made Legal* (Grand Rapids/Cambridge: Eerdmans, 2002), esp. pp. 174-76. Cf. Robert B. Coote and Mary P. Coote, "Power, Politics, and the Making of the Bible," and Naomi Sternberg, "The Deuteronomic Law Code and the Politics of State Centralization," in *The Bible and Liberation*, ed. Norman K. Gottwald and Richard A. Horsley, rev. ed. (Maryknoll, N.Y.: Orbis/London: SPCK, 1993), pp. 343-64; 365-75.

[49]Cheryl B. Anderson, "Biblical Laws," in *Character Ethics and the Old Testament*, ed. M. Daniel Carroll R. and Jacqueline E. Lapsley (Louisville/London: Westminster John Knox, 2007), pp. 37-49; see p. 47.

[50]So Otto, *Theologische Ethik des Alten Testaments*, e.g., pp. 62-64, 75-81, 90-92; cf. John Barton, *Understanding Old Testament Ethics* (Louisville/London: Westminster John Knox, 2003), pp. 1-2.

The Torah is thus "both the agent of divine order and the locus of an underlying theological tension."[51] It is the nature of law to involve such compromise, and being divinely inspired does not change this. If a country has a private health care system, for instance, proposals to introduce universal health care may need to compromise between the health needs of its people and the desire of its current health care providers to stay in business and continue to make a profit. "In most societies what the law enforces is not the same as what upright members of that society feel is socially desirable let alone ideal. . . . Law tends to be a pragmatic compromise between the legislators' ideals and what can be enforced in practice."[52] Law is historically situated and constituted, and prone to partiality. Thus "law *(droit)* is essentially deconstructible" whereas "justice in itself . . . is not deconstructible." Indeed, "deconstruction takes place in the interval that separates the undeconstructability of justice from the deconstructability of *droit* (authority, legitimacy, and so on)."[53] But "one deconstructs in the name of a justice to come, justice beyond present human formulations."[54] Law needs justice; law can be unjust. Justice needs law; "it has . . . no teeth."[55] Law is about what is politically possible. The prophets are about the theo-poetics of the impossible.[56]

Thinking Critically

Like Isaiah, Jesus points us toward a critical approach to the regulations in the First Testament, though on a different basis from the one that sometimes attaches to the phrase "a critical approach." In a series of statements he says, "You have heard that it was said, . . . but I tell you" (Mt 5:21-48). He is not exactly taking a critical approach to the Scriptures themselves. He is not saying that whereas the Torah forbad murder, adultery, breaking oaths and excessive punishment, and required love of one's neighbor, he is now withdrawing those expectations. Rather, he is building on those expectations by pushing beyond them. That is so even when he withdraws the recognition of divorce; Deuteronomy 24:1-4 puts a constraint around divorce, and Jesus tightens it.

---

[51]Stahl, *Law and Liminality in the Bible*, p. 16.

[52]Wenham, *Story as Torah*, p. 80. Cf. Gordon J. Wenham, "The Gap Between Law and Ethics in the Bible," *Journal of Jewish Studies* 48 (1997): 17-29.

[53]Jacques Derrida, "Force of Law," in *Deconstruction and the Possibility of Justice*, ed. Drucilla Cornell et al. (New York: Routledge, 1992), pp. 3-67; see pp. 14, 15.

[54]Kevin J. Vanhoozer, summarizing Jacques Derrida, in "Theology and the Condition of Postmodernity," in *The Cambridge Companion to Postmodern Theology*, ed. Kevin J. Vanhoozer (Cambridge/New York: Cambridge University Press, 2003), pp. 3-25; see p. 17. On the tensions within Ex 20:22–23:33 see specifically Paul D. Hanson, "The Theological Significance of Contradiction within the Book of the Covenant," in *Canon and Authority*, ed. George W. Coats and Burke O. Long (Philadelphia: Fortress, 1977), pp. 110-31.

[55]John D. Caputo, *What Would Jesus Deconstruct?* (Grand Rapids: Baker, 2007), p. 63.

[56]Ibid., p. 87.

The more extensive treatment of divorce elsewhere from which Matthew 5:31-32 is an excerpt, in Matthew 19:1-12, puts us on the track of his critical principle in relationship to the Torah.[57] Asked about the propriety of divorce, he points people to the Torah's accounts of God making humanity male and female and of a man and woman leaving father and mother and becoming one flesh (Mk 10:1-12 puts it differently, but not so as to affect the point). The reason the Torah allows men to divorce their wives was the fact that they were hardhearted. It was not like that at the Beginning, as those verses from Genesis 1–2 make clear.[58]

Jesus thus points to a critical principle for approaching the Torah. It is not a critical principle from outside the Torah, even one from Jesus himself, but from within it. There are tensions within the Torah, and one explanation is that parts of the Torah express how things were at the Beginning (how God designed humanity to be) while parts make allowance for human sinfulness or "hardness of heart." That Greek word (*sklērokardia*) picks up the one the Septuagint uses to translate an expression the Torah itself uses in describing Israel (Deut 10:16; cf. also *sklērotrachēlos*, *sklērotēs* and *sklēros* in Deuteronomy 9:6, 13, 27; 31:27). (David F. Wright comments that John Calvin's "tireless emphasis on the willfulness, blindness, and sluggishness" of the people, in his commentaries on the Pentateuch, suggests "some reflection of his own experience as pastor.")[59] Even Deuteronomy implicitly points to a self-critical awareness. For readers appalled at the low standard of some regulations, the Torah itself suggests an explanation.

This critical principle does not suggest decanonizing the material reflecting human hardness of heart. It also has Moses' authority. Its presence indicates that Yhwh did not merely reveal to Israel the ultimate divine standards

---

[57]Ulrich W. Mauser declares that "the passages both in Mark and in Matthew cannot reflect a genuine origin in Jesus' life" ("Creation and Human Sexuality in the New Testament," in *Biblical Ethics and Homosexuality*, ed. Robert L. Brawley [Louisville: Westminster John Knox, 1996], pp. 3-15; see p. 4); I am not convinced by his argument, but I do not think this would make a difference to the significance of the passages as identifying this critical principle within the Torah itself, and neither, I think, does Mauser. See further John Goldingay, *Models for Interpretation of Scripture* (Grand Rapids: Eerdmans/Carlisle, U.K.: Paternoster, 1995), pp. 104-20.

[58]Thus the principle Jesus suggests provides a way of approaching what Judith Plaskow, from a Jewish feminist perspective, calls "the profound injustice of Torah itself" in the way it views women (*The Coming of Lilith* [Boston: Beacon, 2005], p. 63). In connection with the Bible's acceptance of patriarchy, Rosemary Radford Ruether conceptualizes the matter in another way by speaking of the Bible's "two religions," one providing a "sacred canopy" for the existing social order, the other denouncing the religion of the sacred canopy ("Feminism and Patriarchal Religion," *JSOT* 22 [1982]: 54-66; see pp. 55-56); cf. Jeffrey S. Siker, *Scripture and Ethics* (New York/Oxford: Oxford University Press, 1997), pp. 173-74.

[59]David F. Wright, "Calvin's Pentateuchal Criticism," *Calvin Theological Journal* 21 (1986): 33-50; see p. 47.

and then leave Israel on its own when it failed to live up to them, with the result (for instance) that women thrown out by their husbands were left with no evidence of their status.[60] Notwithstanding what was so from the Beginning, marriages break down, and in a patriarchal world women suffer. Yhwh therefore inspires a regulation to protect them from some of the consequences of their husbands' behavior. It is part of the Torah's pastoral strategy to start where people are.[61] Many of the regulations in the Book of the Covenant likewise "assume that interpersonal violence is a part of life and merely try to codify it, not forbid it."[62] In light of Jesus' comments, it is appropriate to utilize a suspicious hermeneutic in reading the First Testament and ask how it is allowing for human stubbornness, or (as Western thinking might put it) whose interests it serves. Jesus shows that acknowledging the authority of the Scriptures does not exclude a suspicious reading. But his principle for evaluation comes from within the Torah itself, not from himself or the thinking of his day.

Thinking Visionally

The tension between how things were at the Beginning and how things are when one makes allowance for human hardness of heart runs through the Torah, and in principle one can plot all its regulations on an axis between these two. Yhwh is always concerned to pull Israel toward realizing the vision of how things were at the beginning, but is always starting where people are.[63] The Torah's vision is not so much eschatological as restorative; the fulfillment of God's final purpose, the arrival of the reign of God, comes about through the realization of God's creation purpose. The Jewish notion of *tiqqun ha'olam*, the repair of the world, corresponds to this idea. Its aim is not to get forward but to get back, or to get forward by getting back.[64]

The way to give the First Testament's vision for society some purchase in

---

[60]The matter is one of continuing significance for the Jewish community: see Plaskow, *Coming of Lilith*, pp. 147-51.

[61]See John Goldingay, *Theological Diversity and the Authority of the Old Testament* (Grand Rapids: Eerdmans, 1987/Carlisle, U.K.: Paternoster, 1995), pp. 153-66, on Deuteronomy in particular.

[62]Jack Miles, *God: A Biography* (New York/London: Simon & Schuster, 1995), p. 120.

[63]William J. Webb calls this a "redemptive movement hermeneutic," though he does not stress the link with creation (*Slaves, Women & Homosexuals* [Downers Grove, Ill.: InterVarsity Press, 2001]).

[64]Cf. the comments in O'Donovan, *Resurrection and Moral Order*, p. 15. It thus raises questions that in *A Royal Priesthood? The Use of the Bible Ethically and Politically*, ed. Craig Bartholomew et al. (Grand Rapids: Zondervan/Carlisle, U.K.: Paternoster, 2002), pp. 91-146, whose further subtitle is "A Dialogue with Oliver O'Donovan," the relationship of creation and of eschatology to ethics in the First Testament are considered in separate contributions.

our society is then to look for ways in which the presuppositions or values underlying contemporary social policy differ from biblical norms, so that we can identify "goals, or limited objectives, for a programme of reform."[65] We do not lay out utopia but suggest steps in a direction. This task is both aided and complicated by the fact that the Torah is already involved in doing that. There, Yhwh guides people in expressing First Testament faith in the context of an existent set of assumptions deriving from the culture, many of which are unstated. This applies to many of its conventions about matters such as marriage, the family, children and economic life. The Torah is then not a comprehensive guide to community life, and the significance of its regulations may lie in the way they may adapt conventions or make them means of teaching a point.

Francis Bacon formulated the expression "intermediate axioms" or "middle axioms," [66] which has come to be applied to ethics in this connection, among others. When J. H. Oldham introduced the expression into twentieth-century debate, he defined it as signifying "the directions in which, in a particular state of society, Christian faith must express itself."[67] Middle axioms mediate between scriptural ideals and the practicalities of a given social situation, which means they can make allowance for the limitations of what can be achieved in a given situation and accept the need for compromise that this implies. Ethics has to stay in dialogue and in touch with the moral consensus of the society in which it operates, which will have its strengths and its weaknesses.[68] G. K. Chesterton observed that "the Christian ideal has not been tried and found wanting. It has been found difficult; and left untried."[69] Given human unwillingness to try the Torah's ideal or the Christian ideal, their al-

---

[65]Schluter and Clements, *Reactivating the Extended Family*, p. x.

[66]See Francis Bacon, *Novum Organum* (Chicago: Open Court, 1994), pp. 110-11.

[67]J. H. Oldham, "The Function of the Church in Society," in *The Church and its Function in Society*, ed. W. A. Visser't Hooft and J. H. Oldham (London: George Allen, 1937), p. 210. John C. Bennett took up and elaborated the notion in *Christian Ethics and Social Policy* (New York: Scribner's, 1946), pp. 76-85. Cf., e.g., Carl-Henric Grenholm, *Christian Social Ethics in a Revolutionary Age* (Uppsala: Verbum, 1973), pp. 117-18; more recently Lisa Sowle Cahill, *Theological Bioethics* (Washington, D.C.: Georgetown University Press, 2005), pp. 44-48.

[68]Cf. John W. Rogerson, *Theory and Practice in Old Testament Ethics*, JSOTSup 405 (New York/London: T & T Clark, 2004), e.g., p. 16, though he speaks of a moral consensus "common to sensitive and thoughtful people" and adds that he believes this moral consensus has become more sensitive over time, which is not clear to me. Following N. H. G. Robinson's *The Groundwork of Christian Ethics* (London: Collins, 1971), pp. 31-54, Rogerson also speaks of this "moral consensus" as "natural morality," though that phrase usually suggests something like "natural law" or "creation ethics," which is not what he means (but it is the case that Robinson is opposing the way Barth rejects "natural morality"—as he rejects "natural law").

[69]G. K. Chesterton, *What's Wrong with the World* (London: Cassell/New York: Dodd, Mead, 1910), p. 37.

lowances for humanity's continuing hardness of heart remain important.[70]

"Ethics has to do with prophecy. I learned that from Rabbi Abraham Heschel."[71] Yet it can also be said that whereas "most students of the Old Testament see the prophets as at the heart of Old Testament ethics," this is actually strange, because "ethics in our sense does not form a major part of their message."[72] They spoke little of concrete issues or ethical dilemmas. Rather, they were people who proclaimed their nightmares and their visions, grounded on what they knew of God and what they assumed the people knew about right and wrong. They thus witness to a vision of the world as God wishes it were and intends it to be, and to some assumptions about being human. Western values include the centrality of the individual, freedom of choice and freedom of thought, personal choice and personal realization, social and geographical mobility, individual initiative, achievement, success, and fame, self-expression and self-reliance, democracy and tolerance, and equality irrespective of race and gender. The prophets (and the First Testament as a whole) have a quite different profile of values, of assumptions and presuppositions, of norms and standards. Reading the First Testament means visiting a "strange land," in light of which we may be able to look at our own world with fresh eyes.[73]

Thinking Canon-Within-the-Canonically

The diversity of standards within the Torah is one aspect of the way the canon does not comprise one single view but brings together contrasting views. Is there any way of seeing it as one coherent whole? The principle Jesus suggests in connection with the divorce question suggests one form of canon within the canon that helps us approach the diversity within Scripture. His comment that the entire Torah and Prophets hang on the commands to love God and love one's neighbor (Mt 22:40) complements that. "Much (perhaps all) of the legal interpretation found in the Sermon on the Mount makes good sense if we view it as Jesus' way of interpreting the law by the double commandment."[74] Even in his comments on oaths "it was not his purpose either to slacken or to tighten the law, but to bring back to a true and genuine understanding what had been quite corrupted."[75] His formulation follows

---

[70]Cf. Hays' comments in *Echoes of Scripture in the Letters of Paul*, pp. 185-86.

[71]Reported by James M. Gustafson, "Varieties of Moral Discourse," in *Seeking Understanding: The Stob Lectures, 1986–1998* (Grand Rapids/Cambridge: Eerdmans, 2001), pp. 43-76; see p. 47.

[72]Rodd, *Glimpses of a Strange Land*, p. 292.

[73]Rodd, *Glimpses of a Strange Land*, p. 329.

[74]Cosgrove, *Appealing to Scripture in Moral Debate*, p. 158; see further pp. 154-80.

[75]John Calvin, *Institutes of the Christian Religion*, 2.8.26 (Philadelphia: Westminster/London: SCM Press, 1961), p. 392.

one expressed in earlier Jewish writings such as the *Testament of Issachar* 5:1:

> Keep the Law of God, my children;
> achieve integrity; live without malice,
> not tinkering with God's commands or your neighbor's affairs.
> Love the Lord and your neighbor;
> be compassionate toward poverty and sickness.[76]

Philo identifies in a similar way the two major principles from which flow innumerable truths: relating to God with piety and holiness, and to people with love and righteousness.[77]

This twofold principle can help us decide between conflicting interpretations of the Torah. Historical interpretation often leaves passages unclear or subject to rival understandings. The rule of love is then analogous to the rule of the faith in helping us to see the right way to take a passage. This does not mean overriding the text's meaning so as to make everything in Scripture fit with our cultural instinct to want everything neat or to reckon that God must be nice and we must be nice. But it can provide us with a clue to the meaning of the text (it functions hermeneutically) and provide us with somewhere to go when we reach certain interpretive impasses.

As regulations in the Torah can be read as encouraging patriarchy or as constraining it, "Psalm 37 can be read as a profound assertion of the status quo, a self-affirmation of the landed class. It can also be read, however, as an act of radical hope by the disenfranchised, who are confident that current unjust land distribution cannot endure, and that the land eventually will be reassigned to 'the righteous.' "[78] Qohelet can be read as reflecting the attitudes of the powerful and comfortable, or as a call to oppressed people "to resist the fascinations of the dominant culture."[79] Indeed, "is the Bible, taken as a whole and ignoring differences in detail, a witness to the God of justice who delivers the oppressed and saves the poor; or is it in the first place an expression of the attitudes and interests of the oppressors and the locus of the class struggles of ancient Israel and Judah? To some extent this is a matter of how one chooses to view the text." In late apartheid South Africa, Allan Boe-

---

[76]*Testament of Issachar* 5:1, quoted from James H. Charlesworth, ed., *The Old Testament Pseudepigrapha* (Garden City, N.Y.: Doubleday, 1983) 1:803. See further David Flusser, "The Ten Commandments and the New Testament," in *The Ten Commandments in History and Tradition*, ed. Ben-Zion Segal (Jerusalem: Magnes, 1990), pp. 219-46.

[77] Philo, *The Special Laws* 2.15 [2.63]; cf. Flusser, "The Ten Commandments and the NT," p. 244.

[78]Walter Brueggemann, *The Book that Breathes New Life* (Minneapolis: Fortress, 2005), 160; cf. *The Psalms and the Life of Faith* (Minneapolis: Fortress, 1995), pp. 235-57.

[79]Jorge Pixley, "Christian Biblical Theology and the Struggle Against Oppression," in *Jews, Christians, and the Theology of the Hebrew Scriptures*, ed. Allis Ogden Bellis and Joel S. Kaminsky (Atlanta: Society of Biblical Literature, 2000), 173-77; see p. 175.

sak and Desmond Tutu on one hand and Itumeleng Mosala on the other read the Bible differently because they had different such starting points.[80] It is quite possible to reckon that the people who exercise power and who see which books get preserved in a community could be driven to preserve books that express the interests of the people as a whole and not just their own interests, and thus open themselves to critique by their own standards.[81]

The rule of love helps us see the right way to read texts that can be read more than one way. This canon within the canon is not a basis for deciding which parts of the Scriptures really count (so that the canon within the canon becomes the actual canon). The canon within the canon is an aid to understanding the canon and a canon for evaluating interpretations of the canon.

Thinking Canonically

A principle for sidelining the First Testament's teaching as a whole is suggested by dispensationalism, a nineteenth-century theory developed in Britain but deported to the United States. Dispensationalism analyzes the way God relates to humanity differently in different theological epochs or dispensations, in Eden, from Adam and Eve to Noah, from Noah to Abraham, from Abraham to Moses, from Moses to Christ, from Christ to the millennium, and in the millennial age. An advantage of one version of the dispensationalist scheme is that it sees the Sermon on the Mount as destined for implementing only in the millennial age; we are therefore released from seeking to live by it now.[82] The First Testament indeed expressed God's expectations of people in earlier dispensations, but it does not do so now. The Torah has served its purpose; it is not binding on Christians.

Like theonomy, its mirror-image, dispensationalism is not as mistaken as its detractors can make it sound.[83] As law, the Torah is indeed not binding on the Christian community. It was binding on Israel; its authority does not carry over to that reconstituted version of Israel that we call the Jewish-Gentile church. Yet the declaration that all Scripture (that is, the First Testament) is useful for equipping the Christian community to do good work (2 Tim 3:16) becomes vacuous on dispensationalist presuppositions. As it is implausible to infer that no practical implications attach to Jesus' teaching in the Sermon on

---

[80]Walter J. Houston, *Contending for Justice,* LHBOTS 428 (New York/London: T & T Clark, 2006), p. 10. He refers to Itumeleng Mosala, *Biblical Hermeneutics and Black Theology in South Africa* (Grand Rapids: Eerdmans, 1989).

[81]Cf. Houston, *Contending for Justice,* pp. 12-15.

[82]Donald Grey Barnhouse, *His Own Received Him Not, But . . .* (New York/London: Revell, 1933), pp. 37-50.

[83]For the debate between these two (and other views on the significance of Exodus-Deuteronomy), see Strickland, ed., *Five Views on Law and Gospel;* also Daniel P. Fuller, *Gospel and Law* (Grand Rapids: Eerdmans, 1980).

the Mount, so it is implausible to infer that no practical implications attach to
the inclination of Jesus and the New Testament writers to submit to the Torah
and say "It is written" or "Scripture says" in such a way as to imply "that
settles it."

If the First Testament has no purchase on us, we need to be embarrassed
that the New Testament does not cover important topics such as sex, marriage, the family, the local community, the city and the nation (and worship
and prayer) in the extensive way the First Testament does. Further, we are less
embarrassed than we should be that its treatment of these topics is sometimes
more troubling than that in the First Testament. New Testament slavery, for
instance, is a much more oppressive, chattel-like institution than First Testament slavery or servitude, and the First Testament never tells slaves to obey
their masters or sends an escaped slave back to his master; it rather bids people welcome him. The First Testament likewise never tells women to obey
their husbands or be silent in worship, as the New Testament does, and although in many ways Jesus takes an egalitarian stance, he includes only men
in the twelve disciples.[84] "Except for *porneia*" and "not everyone can accept
this word" (Mt 19:9, 11) instance how Moses was not the only person who
needed to make allowance for human stubbornness, as does "sell your cloak
and buy a sword" (Lk 22:36), whether or not it is relevant to the question of
Christian participation in war. Christ's coming, dying, rising from the dead
and pouring out the Spirit of God did not stop his disciples from being prey
to hardness of heart. The distinction between what is said in light of how
things were from the Beginning and what is said in light of that hardness of
heart runs through the New Testament as it runs through the Torah. While a
negative reading of the First Testament can facilitate a reading that exalts the
New Testament,[85] that involves a selectivity in reading both Testaments.

In the context of modernity, Christians' implicit model for understanding
the relationship between the Testaments was an evolutionary one, which we
baptized and called progressive revelation. This understanding made it possible to reckon that God made allowance for human weakness in the earlier
stages of revelation but was able gradually to make things clearer until offering the ultimate revelation in Christ. In light of that, earlier misty understandings of a topic such as war or slavery can fall away like fossils; they were significant in their day but cease to be so as they have fulfilled their role in the
process that unfolded.

This is a neat theory but at multiple points it fails to account for the facts,

---

[84]Cf. Ruether's comments on patriarchy in the New Testament, "Feminism and Patriarchal
    Religion," pp. 57-58.
[85]See, e.g., Countryman, *Dirt, Greed, and Sex*, e.g., pp. 147-67.

as instances such as slavery illustrate (I leave aside whether that is true of the theory of evolution in nature).[86] There are also no pointers to it in Scripture.[87] Jesus' view of the process's dynamic reverses the theory; the deepest insight appears at the beginning of the story, and what follows involves regress more than progress. In the story of Israel, insights are lost as often as they are gained, and the development of insight into truth through First Testament times (insofar as we can trace it) is neither upward nor gradual; nor does the New Testament as a whole represent a more advanced ethical stance than the First Testament. If "neither Jew nor Greek, slave nor free, male or female" (Gal 3:28) offers a structure for New Testament social ethics in terms of the cultural, social and sexual mandates of the gospel,[88] what is then striking is that in none of these areas does the New Testament as a whole represent a "higher" view. In the subjects they cover and in the depth with which they cover them, the two Testaments offer complementary insights on life with God, life in community and life as a self, with both implying that distinction between how things were at the Beginning and how they are when God makes allowance for human hardness of heart. Working canonically involves taking the whole canon into account.

Thinking Self-critically

Whereas Christians faced with Scriptures they do not like often resort to noting that this particular Scripture is limited by its context, it is less common for us to observe that we are limited by our context.[89] "We never take up our ethical inquiries in a purely rational form"; our ethical questions and frameworks reflect our culture.[90] Joseph Blenkinsopp is sometimes explicit that his suspicious reading of canonical texts takes as its criterion the convictions of "most modern readers."[91] Eryl W. Davies begins his study of approaches to

---

[86]Nor is it clear to me that the story of slavery in the world in general is one of positive development (as Rogerson suggests in *Theory and Practice in Old Testament Ethics*, p. 18); on one hand, slavery got worse through biblical times in Israel's world, and despite its "abolition" in the nineteenth century it continues to prevail in the twenty-first-century world; in 2006 a Vatican official described human trafficking as now worse than two centuries ago (see, e.g., Jonathan Tran, "Sold into Slavery," *Christian Century*, November 27, 2007, pp. 22-26).

[87]Myron S. Augsburger refers to Gal 4:4 (but it is about God's sending his Son to redeem) and Heb 1:2 (but it is about the difference between a variegated revelation and a unified revelation) ("Christian Pacifism," in *War: Four Christian Views*, ed. Robert G. Clouse, rev. ed. [Downers Grove, Ill.: InterVarsity Press, 1991], pp. 81-97; see p. 86).

[88]Richard N. Longenecker, *New Testament Social Ethics for Today* (Grand Rapids: Eerdmans, 1984).

[89]See §4.1 "Thinking Paradigmatically."

[90]Thomas W. Ogletree, *The Use of the Bible in Christian Ethics* (Philadelphia: Fortress: 1983/ Oxford: Blackwell, 1984), p. 35.

[91]Blenkinsopp, "Family in First Temple Israel," p. 84.

"the morally dubious passages in the Hebrew Bible" by noting that it is "us" as "modern readers" who raise these questions, and when supporting a critical approach to the text, he does not suggest any criteria for critique beyond how things seem to readers' "own court of ethical judgment."[92] David J. A. Clines is particularly conscious and explicit about making judgments on the basis of "the way I and people like me think"; what else could one do?[93]

In some areas it may be the case that if our cultural contexts happens to be that of "modern" people, we can get nearer the creation ideal than is possible in cultural contexts that Scripture needs to address. Sometimes we may not be able to get very near; for instance, we are in a terrible mess about marriage, family and community, and cannot get very near some of the assumptions that either Testament makes. But in some related areas, such as the possibility of a more egalitarian relationship between the sexes, we may be able to get nearer the creation ideal than was possible in most biblical contexts. Yet we would surely be unwise to reckon that the views of most modern readers are usually the best canon for determining where wisdom lies. Indeed, Blenkinsopp's observation that these texts have canonical status points us in a complementary direction from the one he takes. We might choose to identify with the fact that the Jewish and Christian communities gave them that status.

"In biblical interpretation much depends on one's underlying assumptions about the nature of the text. To read the Bible as Scripture means operating out of a foundational assumption that the text is trying to shape us in life-affirming ways, and so we must listen most carefully when we suspect that the word is being whispered, not shouted"[94]—and when it seems to be working the opposite way to the way we would think. There is another sense in which the Scriptures are a source of moral problems rather than a place where we can discover the answers to problems. They make us aware of problems where we saw none before. Scripture is a trouble-maker as well as a trouble-shooter.[95] It is part of the way it is a resource before it is a canon, or it is a canon in the sense of a resource.

Scripture is not merely a canon in the sense of a rule. But it is a rule whereby we can measure ourselves. A willingness to measure ourselves by a canon such as Scripture's that is independent of us, rather than maintaining the as-

---

[92]Eryl W. Davies, "The Morally Dubious Passages in the Hebrew Bible," in *Currents in Biblical Research* 3 (2005): 197-228; see pp. 197, 199, 219.

[93]See esp. Clines, *Interested Parties*.

[94]Jacqueline E. Lapsley, *Whispering the Word* (Louisville: Westminster John Knox, 2005), p. 85.

[95]James F. Childress, "Scripture and Christian Ethics," *Int* 34 (1980): 371-80; see p. 380, referring to Ralph B. Potter, "The Logic of Moral Argument," in *Toward a Discipline of Social Ethics*, W. G. Muelder Festschrift, ed. Paul Deats (Boston: Boston University, 1972), pp. 93-114; see pp. 105-6.

sumption that we are our own canon, is more likely to further one of the stated aims of ideological interpretation, which is that interpretation should be ethical.[96] If we assume ahead of time that our perspective as modern people is right and evaluate the Scriptures in light of it, this inhibits us from changing or becoming more ethical. If we assume the Scriptures might have a positive ethical contribution to make to our understanding and lives, this opens us to change and ethical development. "None of us should lose the suspicion that our sophistication concerning the cultural and theological qualifications about 'biblical morality' often hides a profound unwillingness to have our lives guided by it."[97]

Questions about ideology that generate a suspicious interpretation can coexist with a consensual interpretation that assumes the community was right to accept these texts into its Scriptures, and in the end reckons it appropriate to prefer interpretations that fit with this assumption.

Thinking Communally

A Mennonite statement declares:

> Believing that the Scriptures of the Old Testament are likewise [i.e., like the New Testament] divine in origin and authoritative in character, Mennonites hold that these Scriptures are a record of the progressive revelation of the nature and will of God, leading to the full and final revelation found in the New Testament. Therefore, Old Testament Scriptures which are sometimes cited in support of Christian participation in war may not be used to contradict clear New Testament teaching, but must be interpreted in the light of the teaching of Christ and the Apostles, for in Christ we find the norm for the whole of Scripture. The national history of Israel as recorded in the Old Testament cannot have normative significance for us, for much in it contradicts Christ.[98]

We have already questioned the notion of progressive revelation. Another difficulty in this statement is the word *clear*. The notion that Christians may not participate in war is an inference from statements in the New Testament, not an aspect of its "clear teaching." That is (partly) why Christians disagree on the matter.

Further, the statement's position on the relationship between the authority of the Scriptures and the authority of Jesus does not seem self-consistent. It describes the First Testament as divine in origin and authoritative in character, yet reckons it can be used in a way that contradicts the New Testament,

---

[96]See. e.g., Elisabeth Schüssler Fiorenza, "The Ethics of Interpretation," *JBL* 107 (1988): 3-17.
[97]Stanley Hauerwas, "The Moral Authority of Scripture," *Int* 34 (1980): 356-70; see p. 369.
[98]In Donald F. Durnbaugh, ed, *On Earth Peace* (Elgin, Ill.: Brethren Press, 1978), p. 51; cf. Willard M. Swartley, *Slavery, Sabbath, War, and Women* (Scottdale, Penn.: Herald, 1983), pp. 117-18.

and that much in it contradicts Christ, and it also reckons that Christ is the norm for the whole of the Scriptures. So there are three authorities or norms (the First Testament, the New Testament and Christ), all in tension with each other. We surely cannot say that the Scriptures are divine in origin and authoritative in character and also say (for instance) that Moses and Joshua were mistaken in what they told Israel Yhwh said. The declaration would become internally coherent if we remove the statements about the divine origin and authoritative character of the First Testament and the New Testament, and leave Christ as the single authoritative norm, perhaps reckoning that "Jesus rejected the basic legal principle from the Torah that it was right to demand an eye for an eye and a tooth for a tooth, . . . thus placing his own personal authority above that of Moses."[99] This would produce a coherent statement, but it would still be a problematic one, because it introduces an incoherence into Jesus himself. Statements such as "I came not to abolish but to fulfill" and "Scripture cannot be broken" imply that he treats the First Testament as a norm rather than exalting himself above Moses.[100] He does not suggest that the appropriate response to recognizing diversity in Scripture is that "the Gospels in their direct witness to Jesus Christ are to be taken as final authority."[101]

The tension between the scriptural norms can be rather convenient. It means we can choose the stance we like and call that scriptural. James Brenneman has invited the church to face the necessary nature of this process. Isaiah 2:2-4 speaks of swords being made into plowshares; Joel 3:9-12 [4:9-12] speaks of the opposite. Rather than trying to see how both could be right within a larger framework, he sees readers having to decide which prophet is true and which is false. The community reading the Prophets has "canonical autonomy" in this connection. There is a "priority of the interpretative community over the text and its reader(s)."[102] This principle once more means we recognize no canon outside ourselves. Richard B. Hays similarly comments that Romans 13 and Revelation 13 "are *not* two complementary expressions of a single New Testament understanding of the state; rather, they represent radically different assessments of the relation of the Christian community to the empire." We must "choose between" these texts (or reject both).[103]

---

[99]Ronald J. Sider, *Christ and Violence* (Scottdale, Penn.: Herald Press, 1979), p. 26.

[100]There are other problems about Sider's statement concerning "an eye for an eye"; see §4.4 "Managing Redress."

[101]So Swartley, *Slavery, Sabbath, War, and Women*, p. 23.

[102]James Brenneman, *Canons in Conflict* (New York/Oxford: Oxford University Press, 1997), pp. viii, 140.

[103]Richard B. Hays, "Scripture-shaped Community," *Int* 44 (1990): 42-55, see pp. 46-47. I think there is actually less tension between the two texts than he implies; see §5.2 "The Superpower."

Rather, "the community must be prepared to accept creative tension as a permanent feature of its life."[104] Its understanding and the process of its decision-making can thus avoid some oversimplification.

Thinking Christologically

Jesus emphasizes challenges such as love of enemies, forgiveness and peacemaking, but talks less about these than he does about people being punished and sent to hell, and he indulges in more stirring up of conflict than in peacemaking. He thus parallels rather than resolves tensions that run through the First Testament. This suggests that the problem in the statement above goes back to its nonnegotiable starting point. Mennonites are called to witness to peace and to push the church to take seriously the radical nature of Christ's expectations. Like prophets, they have turned that into their norm. It is an oversimplification to say that Christ is their norm; they focus (not wrongly) only on some aspects of what Christ was about, but then narrow down Christ and the New Testament, and downgrade the First Testament in light of their narrow focus.

Other Christians downgrade the First Testament in order to exalt Jesus, as if we would not need Jesus if the First Testament told us all we need to know. Yet Jesus did not come to tell us things. His people were not in need of revelation. They had a perfectly good revelation. The problem lay in getting people to live by it. The promise of Jeremiah 31:33, Ezekiel 11:20, 36:27 was not of a new Torah but of the writing of the existent Torah in people's hearts.[105] Jesus came to do something about that, to see if becoming incarnate and dying for them and rising from the dead and pouring out the Spirit of God would make a difference.

In terms of his teaching about life with God, life in community and life as a self, Jesus did little more than express in sharp terms what he found in the First Testament. Insofar as he added to it, like any other prophet, what he was doing was building on it; the construction metaphor is less misleading than the evolution metaphor. The First Testament is the first story of the building; the New Testament is the superstructure. It is no wonder that Christians get into trouble because they try to live in a second story that has no first story. Assuming that the Torah belongs to a rather early stage of revelation encourages the church not to take to heart its admittedly basic exhortations. But the life of the church is often characterized by weaknesses such as worship of

---

[104]Joseph Blenkinsopp, *Prophecy and Canon* (Notre Dame, Ind.: University of Notre Dame, 1977), p. 94. Hauerwas infers that Scripture therefore is not infallible ("Moral Authority of Scripture," p. 362). This seems to me not to follow.

[105]Cf. Walter C. Kaiser, "Response to Wayne G. Strickland," in *Five Views on Law and Gospel*, ed. Wayne G. Strickland (Grand Rapids: Zondervan, 1996), pp. 302-8; see p. 304.

images, attaching Yhwh's name to things that are empty, a 24/7 attitude to work and activity, abuse, adultery, fraud and an attachment to "stuff" (let alone killing other Christians), and has not progressed beyond the Decalogue in its literal and primitive form, which names what we do not name and constitutes a serious challenge about behavior to the church.

Almost every line in the blessings that Jesus declares in Matthew 5:3-10 takes up phrases from the First Testament. Jesus does something with them that produces a whole greater than these parts, yet it is one that fits with the dynamic of its spirituality. The First Testament never says in so many words "love your enemies," but it gives people instructions that are tantamount to that (notably, Lev 19:17-18). It never says in so many words "forgive people their trespasses," but it gives vivid portrayals of people doing that (notably, Esau and Joseph). Jesus thus offers hermeneutical pointers that can enable people to see key issues in the First Testament that they might miss, such as love of enemies, forgiveness and peacemaking. He does not bring significantly new teaching, or does so only like any prophet.

Working Christologically involves recognizing that our ethical problem is so deep that Christ had to come to die for us, working with the critical principle he suggests, learning from the way he sometimes articulates more clearly the "how things were at the Beginning" element implied by the First Testament, and not narrowing him down to a focus on the commitments we ourselves are called to emphasize.

4.2 Marriage

Marriage is a relationship of lifelong mutual commitment between a man and woman whereby they take on a shared, egalitarian vocation in connection with subduing the earth and serving the ground, and enjoy a romantic and sexual relationship. In all its aspects it is compromised by human waywardness, and there are a number of ways of falling short of God's vision for it. The First Testament emphasizes the need to safeguard the exclusiveness of the sexual relationship and to protect the woman when the relationship goes wrong.

"Husbands" and "Wives"

The First Testament suggests a number of complementary understandings of marriage, and discussing its idea of marriage is complex, partly for semantic reasons. In English we have a number of words such as *engagement* and *marriage*, *husband* and *wife* that have seemed to cover the categories we need, and we easily assume that when English biblical translations use such words, they have the same meaning as they have in our culture (for instance, in the modern West). But we are also aware that our own culture changes, so that, for instance, it might once have seemed uncontroversial that marriage involves a man and a woman, whereas in the West at the beginning of the twenty-first century it suddenly became a question whether two women or two men might constitute a marriage. Further, the word *partner* has come to be used for a form of relationship that is not quite the same as marriage but neither is it a casual relationship. It is hardly surprising that the meaning of related terms is very different in the First Testament and no doubt varies within First Testament times and in different circles within Israel.[106]

The way Hebrew uses words that might seem equivalent to English ones is thus a sign and symbol of this difficulty. The words translated "husband" and "wife" are nearly always the regular words for "man" and "woman." So Elimelech is Naomi's *ʾîš* and Elkanah is Hannah's *ʾîš* (Ruth 1:3, 5; 1 Sam 1:8, 22, 23). Sarai is Abraham's *ʾiššâ* (Gen 11:29, 31) and Naomi is Elimelech's *ʾiššâ* (Ruth 1:1-2). This is not because Hebrew lacks more specific words. It has two words to identify a husband as his wife's owner and master. Uriah is Bathsheba's *baʿal* as well as her *ʾîš* (2 Sam 11:26); Abraham is Sarah's *ʾādôn* (Gen 18:12), and she is his *bĕʿûlâ* (Gen 20:3). Hebrew also has the word *pilegeš*, usually translated "concubine." Bilhah is both Jacob's *ʾiššâ* and his *pilegeš* (Gen 35:22; 37:2), as Keturah seems to have been in relation to Abraham (Gen 25:1, 6; 1 Chron 1:32). It seems likely that *pilegeš* was also Hagar's status, though she is only described as given to Abraham as *ʾiššâ* (Gen 16:3). *Concubine* is itself a complicated word in English. The *Concise Oxford Dictionary* first defines it in accordance with its etymology as meaning "a woman who cohabits with a man, not being his wife," but then adds as an alternative meaning "secondary wife." Readers often infer that the relationship between Abraham and Hagar was immoral in the sense that their sexual encounter took place in an irregular way because she was not his wife, but more likely she had a status like that of someone such as Bilhah or Zilpah (Gen 30:1-13); the relationship between her and Abraham was a regular one within the conventions of the culture. In Israel, at least, the term *secondary wife* perhaps need not imply that a man had a primary wife (the *pilegeš* in Judg 19–20 looks like her husband's only wife); it simply means she did not have a primary wife's status. We do not know what form her secondary status took; perhaps it involved her children's inheritance rights or related to her family's inability to provide her with a dowry.[107]

---

[106]For instance, as time goes on the plural expression *fathers' house* comes to be more prominent than *kin group*, but we are not sure how to relate the two: see H. G. M. Williamson, "The Family in Persian Period Judah," in *Symbiosis, Symbolism, and the Power of the Past*, ed. W. G. Dever and S. Gitin (Winona Lake, Ind.: Eisenbrauns, 2003), pp. 445-53; see p. 447.

[107]Cf. Carolyn Pressler, "The 'Biblical View' of Marriage," in *Engaging the Bible in a Gendered World*, K. D. Sakenfeld Festschrift, ed. Linda Day and Carolyn Pressler (Louisville/Lon-

So a Hebrew speaker referring to a man's partner has to choose between *'iššâ, bě'ûlâ* and *pilegeš*, all of which overlap with "wife," but none of which is synonymous with "wife." And referring to a woman's partner involves choosing between *'îš, ba'al* and *'ādôn*, all of which overlap with "husband," but none of which is synonymous with "husband." Sometimes, at least, choosing one word rather than another will make a significant point. The First Testament's general avoidance of the mastery and ownership words suggests an avoidance of the idea that a husband is a wife's owner or master and that she is his subordinate or possession. Indeed, Hosea implies that the Israelite ideal is that a woman would call her husband *'îšî*, not *ba'lî*, "my man" not "my master" (Hos 2:16 [MT 18]).[108]

Getting Married

Hebrew also has no word for "marriage," though it has a word for "wedding" (*hătunnâ*; Song 3:11), which is etymologically related to words for "in-laws." Not having a word for "marriage" is not an indication that Israelites did not recognize the idea, as the absence of formal laws governing marriage does not indicate that it was not a recognized social institution.[109] It may seem uneconomic not to have words for ideas that people do recognize, but this is a common feature of language.

Neither are there biblical prescriptions for what is involved in getting married. From Genesis 2:24 we might infer that it involves a man leaving his parents and uniting sexually with a woman ("cleaves") so that they "become one flesh." The last term is not another reference to the sexual act in itself but a way of saying that the two people become one family; your own "flesh" ("your own flesh and blood," we can say in English) is your own family (e.g., Gen 29:14; 37:27; Lev 18:6; 2 Sam 5:2). Genesis does not speak of marriage as a covenant, as it does not speak of the original relationship between God and humanity as covenantal, but marriage is a covenant elsewhere (Mal 2:14;[110] cf. Ezek 16:8; Prov 2:17), as it is described in many Christian marriage services. The term is appropriate because a covenantal relationship is one that people enter into by choice; it is not a natural relationship. There is no covenant between parents and children or children and parents; they live in mutual obli-

---

don: Westminster John Knox, 2006), pp. 200-11; see p. 202.

[108]Cf. Hans Walter Wolff, *Anthropology of the Old Testament* (London: SCM Press/Philadelphia: Fortress, 1974), p. 167. But Allen Guenther suggests that being a *bě'ûlâ* is a position of honor as the mistress of a household ("A Typology of Israelite Marriage," *JSOT* 28 [2005]: 387-407; see pp. 403-4).

[109]Bernard S. Jackson, *Wisdom-Laws* (Oxford/New York: Oxford University Press, 2006), pp 380-81.

[110]See Gordon Paul Hugenberger, *Marriage as a Covenant*, VTSup 52 (Leiden/New York: Brill, 1994), esp. pp. 27-47.

gation and commitment because they are one flesh by nature. Marriage involves an extraordinary act whereby two people of separate flesh agree to become one flesh. One might have thought that the bond between a man and his parents was so strong that he would live with them forever, but the much earlier bond between man and woman symbolized in her being made from a part of him means he abandons that relationship to stick with his woman.

If Genesis 2:24 does describe what is involved in getting married, it turns out to imply no wedding, no formal or socially recognized ceremony, no rite of passage. This opens up the possibility of some liberation for modern Western couples and probably for ancient Israelites who had great wedding celebrations. (One of my sons and his wife recently explained to us that the reason they lived together before their marriage—not something my wife and I found easy at the time—was not that they were not ready to make a lifelong commitment, as is often said about people living together, but that getting married is such a hassle.) But for ordinary people there might often be no such thing as a wedding ceremony or a wedding service, any more than they needed a wedding license. Marriages would be "common law" marriages,[111] but they generally took place within village communities, which would give them social sanction and stability that are lacking in Western societies— hence (in part) our need to shore them up with licenses.

Marriage normally involved a "two-stage procedure: . . . first a betrothal, accompanied by (at least the promise of) *mohar* [a marriage gift]; later the marriage itself, signified by the wife's move from her father's house to that of her husband, consummation, and, very often, a feast."[112] Thus many passages speak of the man "taking" a wife (*lāqaḥ*; e.g., Gen 4:19; 11:29; 25:1; 26:34; 28:1-2, 6) or "taking someone as an *ʾiššâ*" (e.g., Gen 25:20) or of someone else "taking" a wife for him (e.g., Gen 24). Hebrew also lacks a dedicated verb meaning "marry," and in modern translations the word for "take" is the verb most often translated thus. For a woman the common expressions are "be given to" or "become a man's" or "become the woman of" (e.g., Gen 38:14; Num 36).

Genesis 2:24 describes the man leaving his parents, though this is exactly what a man did not do; it was the woman who did so. Perhaps the very fact that a man stays with his family when he marries makes it important that he leaves them in an emotional sense or changes the order of his loyalties.[113] Whereas one of a man's primary duties was to honor his parents, Genesis

---

[111]Cf. Jon L. Berquist, *Controlling Corporeality* (New Brunswick/London: Rutgers University Press, 2002), p. 61.

[112]Jackson, *Wisdom-Laws*, p. 372.

[113]Cf. Gordon J. Wenham, "Family in the Pentateuch," in *Family in the Bible*, ed. Richard S. Hess and M. Daniel Carroll R. (Grand Rapids: Baker, 2003), pp. 17-31; see p. 18; *Story as Torah*, p. 32.

2:24 scandalously requires him to abandon them (*ʿāzab*) so that his woman becomes his first loyalty.[114] While some aspects of family in the First Testament contrast with Western culture, this latter notion contrasts with attitudes in some Asian cultures that make it hard for a man thus to change loyalties.[115]

Both the word *take* in connection with people acting on behalf of the man's family and the phrase *be given* point to the fact that marriage was not a decision of the couple alone but of their families, though it would be an exaggeration to say the couple had no say in the matter. When Isaac and Rebekah married, Rebekah seems to have more opportunity to say no than Isaac; "one would be hard pressed to find a woman in greater contrast to her suitor," who lets his father make all his decisions for him.[116] With Jacob and Rachel, Jacob takes the initiative, though matters work out rather different from his intention, and Laban "gives" both Leah and Rachel to Jacob without (as far as we know) asking their opinion. With Ruth and Boaz, Ruth takes an interesting initiative. Stories such as those of David and Michal suggest the possibility that the more important you are, the less freedom you are likely to have about your marriage. But whatever the involvement of the couple, marriage involved relationships between families. While people cannot marry within their own household, they can marry someone either within or outside their kin group; the former might be more usual or acceptable.

A Shared Vocation

Genesis 1–2 provides the background to the First Testament's assumption that there are what we would call husbands and wives, people who may be designated "her man," "his woman," who come together in a socially recognized union of two people in a new permanent relationship whose context is the proper one for sexual activity and the birth and upbringing of children. In Genesis 1, together they make up the image of God in the world, exercise authority over the world on God's behalf and have the task of subduing the earth. Genesis 2 pictures the woman made after the man and in light of the man's need, but this no more implies that she is subordinate to him than does the fact that in Genesis 1 the human beings are made after the animals and in light of what needs to be done for them. The second story complements the first in the way it spells out the similarity of woman and man. They are so similar, it is as if one is cloned from the other. He is *ʾîš*, she is *ʾiššâ*, as if it is *ʾîš*

---

[114]Cf. Samuel Terrien, *Till the Heart Sings* (Philadelphia: Fortress, 1985), pp. 14-15.
[115]Cf. Michael Schluter, "Family," in *Jubilee Manifesto*, ed. Michael Schluter and John Ashcroft (Leicester, U.K.: Inter-Varsity Press, 2005), pp. 154-74; see p. 161.
[116]Danna Nolan Fewell and David M. Gunn, *Gender, Power, and Promise* (Nashville: Abingdon, 1993), p. 72.

with a feminine ending (historically the words likely come from different roots, but the First Testament ignores or is unaware of this in playing with their similarity).

As there is no suggestion in Genesis 1–2 that men have authority over women, or husbands over wives, so there is no suggestion of the idea that wives are their husbands' property. She is "his woman/wife"; but his parents are "his father and mother," and he is "her man/husband" (e.g., Gen 2:24; 3:6). Neither is there much evidence elsewhere in the First Testament for the idea that wives are their husbands' property, while there is much evidence for the opposite.[117] A man is indeed bidden not to covet someone else's wife along- side his being bidden not to covet other items of property, and a married couple do belong to one another; in English we speak of "my wife" or "my husband."[118] We give ourselves to someone in marriage and we acknowledge that we no longer belong to ourselves and cannot give ourselves to someone else. We have noted that the First Testament makes very little use of terms that might suggest ownership such as *ba'al* and *bĕ'ûlâ*. In contrast to the asser- tion "it is certain that Israelite marriage in OT times was marriage by purchase,"[119] the First Testament nowhere speaks of buying or selling a wife as the usual practice. Laban's daughters do accuse him of in effect doing that (Gen 31:14-16), which shows it was not normal and accepted practice, and Boaz's acquiring of Ruth (*qānâ*; Ruth 4:8-10) is not regular purchase. Exodus 22:16-17 [MT 15-16] alone refers to a regular marriage payment, but the context is somewhat odd, and in Genesis 34:12 and 1 Samuel 18:25 the circumstances are exceptional. Jacob does pay Laban seven years' work per wife (Gen 29:15- 30). If money was involved in a marriage, it is no more self-evident that this signifies purchase than when people spend huge amounts in connection with a Western wedding.[120] One would not infer a property theory of marriage

---

[117]See, e.g., Grace Emmerson, "Women in Ancient Israel," in *The World of Ancient Israel*, ed. R. E. Clements (Cambridge/New York: Cambridge University Press, 1989), pp. 371-94; see pp. 382-83; Christopher J. H. Wright, *God's People in God's Land* (Grand Rapids: Eerdmans/ Exeter , U.K.: Paternoster, 1990), pp. 183-221.

[118]Deborah L. Ellens argues that in such texts in Deuteronomy a woman's sexuality is her husband's property, which is a narrower point (*Women in the Sex Texts of Leviticus and Deuteronomy*, LHBOTS 458 [London/New York: Continuum, 2008]).

[119]Hans Jochen Boecker, *Law and the Administration of Justice in the Old Testament and Ancient East* (Minneapolis: Augsburg/London: SPCK, 1980), p. 108. Contrast Roland de Vaux, *Ancient Israel* (London: Darton, Longman & Todd/New York: McGraw-Hill, 1961), p. 27. In the Middle East generally, something more like marriage by purchase may have been more common among propertied classes (cf. the discussion in Gerda Lerner, *The Creation of Patriarchy* [New York/Oxford: Oxford University Press, 1986], pp. 106-12, and her refer- ences).

[120]Thus *HALOT*'s translation of *mōhar* as "bride-money" is better than BDB's more specific "purchase-price."

from the question that still regularly features in marriage services, "Who gives this woman to be married to this man," with the associated action of passing on her hand to the groom, and we should be similarly hesitant about such an interpretation of Israel's language that could be read that way.

Gender Roles

Men and women are thus involved in a relationship of authority, yet it is not an authority they exercise over each other but one they exercise together over the world. Genesis 1–2 assumes an equality of status between them, in their relationship with each other and in their life in the world. They share in responsibilities and rights. In the terms of Genesis 2, the task is to serve the garden; the man and his woman are partners on the farm, though on average he will spend more time doing unskilled work in the fields, and she will spend more time doing skilled work closer to the home.[121] Their oneness is a oneness in activity, the everyday activity of each day. The First Testament would look quizzically at the idea that a couple spend most of their day doing quite unrelated things, whether he was at work and she was at home or they were both at work but in two different worlds. Both play indispensable and honorable, related and complementary, roles in the economy of life.

Not withstanding Genesis 3:16, the stories of married couples in the First Testament do not give the impression that husbands simply exercised authority over wives. When Abraham is scared he appeals to Sarah, rather than giving her orders (Gen 12:13), and she takes several initiatives in connection with Hagar; arguably Abraham is rather too cooperative in this connection (Gen 16; 21). Neither Rebekah nor Rachel behaves very subserviently to her husband, and we do not get the impression that this is odd, while Zipporah's decisive action in relation to Moses (like those of the women in Exodus 1–2) is crucial to the exodus story's not derailing. Indeed, "Zipporah's swift and

---

[121]Cf. Richard Lowery, *Sabbath and Jubilee* (St Louis: Chalice, 2000), pp. 10-11. See also Carol Meyers, "Women and the Domestic Economy of Early Israel," in *Women in the Hebrew Bible*, ed. Alice Bach (New York/London: Routledge, 1999), pp. 33-43; Meyers, "Material Remains and Social Relations," in *Symbiosis, Symbolism, and the Power of the Past*, ed. William G. Dever and Seymour Gitin (Winona Lake, Ind.: Eisenbrauns, 2003), pp. 425-44; Meyers, "Procreation, Production, and Protection," in *Community, Identity, and Ideology*, ed. Charles E. Carter and Carol L. Meyers (Winona Lake, Ind.: Eisenbrauns, 1996), pp. 489-514; Meyers, " 'Women of the Neighborhood' (Ruth 4.17)," in Irmtraud Fischer, "The Book of Ruth," in *Ruth and Esther*, ed. Athalya Brenner, FCB 2/3 (Sheffield, U.K.: Sheffield Academic Press, 1999), pp. 110-27; more generally, Meyers, *Discovering Eve* (New York/Oxford: Oxford University Press, 1988); Athalya Brenner, ed., *A Feminist Companion to Genesis* (Sheffield, U.K.: Sheffield Academic Press, 1993); Erhard S. Gerstenberger and Wolfgang Schrage, *Woman and Man* (Nashville: Abingdon, 1981), pp. 66-72; and on the background of theory, Roland Boer, "Women First?" *JSOT* 30 (2005): 3-28.

powerful move to the center of the stage thus challenges the patriarchal presuppositions of heroism."[122]

For Western people, stories such as those of Ruth and David also raise questions about gender and gender roles. Israelite life likely presupposed some practically determined division of roles. Each morning the men made their way to the fields to ensure that the family had something to eat and wear next year while the women undertook tasks at home to ensure that the family had something to eat today and something to wear tomorrow. This would encourage bonding among the men and among the women. Military activity would encourage the former; whether or not it is generally true that "male bonding characteristically excludes and undervalues women,"[123] one can see it illustrated in the story of David. The observance of purity customs, pregnancy, birthing and nursing babies would encourage the latter.

In relating to female sexuality, much of Scripture is concerned with procreation, ritual purity and possession,[124] though none figure in the Song of Songs. In Ruth, "from the start of the story, women deconstruct their gender by differentiating their roles," taking roles that would be seen as male, and one might wonder whether this deconstruction of gender provided impetus for social change.[125] But there is no actual indication that this was so.[126] Something similar emerges from the story of Esther. Both Vashti and Esther decline to play the roles allocated to them in relation to the Persian king, but they are once-off characters. The Song of Songs, Ruth and Esther open up possibilities that might otherwise never occur to readers. One can see how the Song of Songs still does this. Women in the West may continue to expect a man to take responsibility for initiation in a relationship; the Song opens up another possibility.

Romance

In speaking of man and woman in Genesis 1–2, the focus does not lie on relationships, intimacy and sex for their own sake but because of their significance for procreation and thus for the fulfilling of God's purpose in the world.

---

[122]Ilana Pardes, *Countertraditions in the Bible* (Cambridge, Mass./London: Harvard University Press, 1992), p. 85.

[123]Exum, *Fragmented Women*, p. 53.

[124]T. Drorah Setel, "Prophets and Pornography," in *Feminist Interpretation of the Bible*, ed. Letty M. Russell (Philadelphia: Fortress, 1985), pp. 86-95; see p. 88; cf. Clines, *Interested Parties*, p. 114.

[125]Jon L. Berquist, "Role Dedifferentiation in the Book of Ruth," *JSOT* 57 (1993): 23-37; see pp. 35-36. See further Irmtraud Fischer, "The Book of Ruth," in *Ruth and Esther*, ed. Athalya Brenner, FCB 2/3 (Sheffield, U.K.: Sheffield Academic Press, 1999), pp. 24-49.

[126]On "the inspiration of the role differentiation in the book of Ruth for Taiwanese women," see Julie L. C. Chu, "Returning Home," *Semeia* 78 (1997): 47-53.

Genesis is not concerned about romance; neither is the First Testament in general, nor the New Testament (in contrast to other ancient literatures).[127] Part of the reason may be the practical one that a traditional society cannot take for granted the birth of children or their growing to adulthood any more than the growth of food to feed the family. Indeed, there are many women and men in the Western world who cannot conceive or beget children (and parents who cannot assume their children will grow to adulthood, and who have a hard time being able to feed their families in healthy fashion). Psalm 128 talks about these things in terms of Yhwh's blessing and thus invites us not to take them for granted. It "articulates a theology of blessing as it celebrates the daily realms of work and family as gifts of God" and thus resists "our persistent tendency to view the world purely in secular terms."[128] In the Western world it may not seem obvious why conception, children and the family should be related to the idea of "blessing";[129] this indicates a difference between our way of thinking and Israel's. Even stories such as those of Abraham, Sarah and Hagar, and of Lot's daughters, witness to this difference. The importance of questions about fertility makes it noteworthy that in the case of human beings sexual activity is constrained in a way that limits procreation.

In the West, where eros is the god we worship, it is fortuitous that the Bible does not begin with romantic love, "the mad hunger for someone you don't know very well."[130] But fortunately for romantics, at least Jacob is one, though it gets him into trouble (Gen 29:18-30), and the Song of Songs is directly concerned with that mad hunger.[131] Here there is no reference to procreation and in these poems uniquely in the Bible human love is celebrated for its own sake.[132] Conversely it is good that it is also not the Scriptures' only treatment

---

[127]Cf. Berquist, *Controlling Corporeality*, pp. 51-52, referring to Michel Foucault, *The History of Sexuality*, 3 vols. (New York: Pantheon, 1978, 1985, 1986).

[128]J. Clinton McCann, "The Book of Psalms," *The New Interpreter's Bible* (Nashville: Abingdon, 1996) 4:639-1280; see p. 1201.

[129]Cf. Joseph L. Mangina, "Bearing Fruit," in *The Blackwell Companion to Christian Ethics*, ed. Stanley Hauerwas and Samuel Wells (Oxford/Malden, Mass.: Blackwell, 2004), pp. 468-480; see p. 468.

[130]Nick Hornby, *How to Be Good* (New York: Penguin Putnam, 2001), p. 200; cf. Deirdre N. McCloskey, *The Bourgeois Virtues* (Chicago/London: University of Chicago Press, 2006), p. 92.

[131]See further John Goldingay, "So What Might the Song of Songs Do to Them?" in *Reading From Right to Left*, David J. A. Clines Festschrift, ed. J. Cheryl Exum and H. G. M. Williamson, JSOTSup 373 (London/New York: Sheffield Academic Press, 2003), pp. 173-83, on which much of what follows is based; more generally Athalya Brenner, ed., *A Feminist Companion to the Song of Songs* (Sheffield, U.K.: Sheffield Academic Press, 1993); Athalya Brenner and Carole R. Fontaine, ed., *The Song of Songs*, FCB 2/6 (Sheffield, U.K.: Sheffield Academic Press, 2000); and on the Song of Songs as a "countertradition," Pardes, *Countertraditions in the Bible*, pp. 118-43.

[132]Cf. André LaCoque, "The Shulamite," in *Thinking Biblically*, ed. André LaCoque and Paul

of relationships between men and women, because it would surely then be merely escapist, fantasy literature.[133]

The poems do imply that the love relationship they celebrate belongs in the context of marriage. The one occurrence of a Hebrew word for "wedding" comes here, at the climax of a portrayal of a wedding procession (Song 3:6-11). In the context I take this to be an imaginative, poetic, hyperbolic portrayal relating to an ordinary couple; the groom is not literally Solomon, but groom and bride are like a king and queen for this glorious occasion. Either way, the poem implies an actual marriage taking place for this couple at some time. It coheres with this that Song 4:8–5:1 goes on to describe the woman as a "bride" (the word comes six times). The Song's poetic nature makes it impossible to know whether in real time the couple are in the midst of getting married (that is, these are wedding songs) or have just got married, or are looking forward to marriage, or married some time ago but are still rejoicing in this with the enthusiasm of young lovers. Indeed, it is an open question whether all the poems relate to the same (real or imaginary) couple. But the relationship presupposed by the song is an exclusive mutual commitment of the kind that one makes in marriage. The plea to make me like the seal on your heart (Song 8:6-7) has the same implication. This is no passing fancy that might cool down tomorrow and be succeeded by another relationship. This is the one.

Yet the poems make so little reference to marriage that it has been possible to maintain that it is not in fact within their purview. Marriage, is after all, a many-sided relationship of which romance is but one facet; indeed, in most cultures it has been a rather minor facet.[134] For much of the Torah the focus of interest is the procreation of children and their being brought up in a clearly defined marital-family context. For other parts of the Torah, the concern with marriage relates to questions about property, and over history generally this has often been the case. For Proverbs 7, whose language is in other respects strikingly similar to that of the Song, the concern is with adultery.[135] In Proverbs 31:10-31, the key thing about the ideal wife is that she can manage the house; romance and sex do not come into it. For kings such as Saul, David and Solomon, and would-be kings, marriage is about politics, political power and prestige.

Ricoeur (Chicago/London: University of Chicago Press, 1998), pp. 235-63; see pp. 238-39, against Brevard Childs, *Introduction to the Old Testament as Scripture* (Philadelphia: Fortress/London: SCM, 1979), p. 575. LaCoque later adds (p. 247) that this does not make the poems nontheological.

[133]Cf. Clines, *Interested Parties*, pp. 115-17

[134]See Stephanie Coontz, *Marriage, a History: From Obedience to Intimacy or How Love Conquered Marriage* (New York: Viking, 2005).

[135]Cf. Brevard S. Childs's comments in *Biblical Theology in Crisis* (Philadelphia: Westminster, 1970), pp. 191-94.

The significance of the Song is that it neglects questions about children, politics and property to focus on the enthusiasm of two lovers for each other.[136] The First Testament does not thereby imply that this is the central or sole significance of marriage, and this is a significant perspective for Western cultures because it contrasts with what our culture is inclined to tell us; thus when a couple find the romance has gone out of their marriage, they may think that its whole point has gone and may feel free to contract out of it and look for that with someone else, not taking account of the fact that sex and romance is but one facet of marriage.

But it is one facet. From the first line with its shocking beginning, "May he kiss me with the kisses of his mouth" (Song 1:2), the Song encourages people to rejoice in the physical pleasure of sex. It rejoices in smell, taste and sight, especially at every detail of the appearance of the beloved, at the physical beauty. His love makes her feel faint (Song 2:5; 5:8). Just a look can be overwhelming (Song 6:5; the verb is *rāhab* hiphil, linked with the name of the powerful mythic figure Rahab).[137] For both of them, love is expected to be intoxicating; it makes them giddy (Song 5:1). Her love reaches right into his heart and takes it away (Song 4:9): the man here uses a piel verb formed from the word for "heart," which might mean "you deeply moved my heart" (cf. English "you heartened me," though that does not have the right implication here) or might mean "you de-heartened me."[138] That would fit with a lover's feeling of having a hole inside, as if the heart has been removed. It is the only occurrence of the piel (did the man invent the word?).

The Power of Love

Groom and bride are just an ordinary couple (Song 1:5–2:3). She is either tanned through working in the fields or is dark-skinned (or both); she is a crocus of the kind that abounds in the Sharon plain, a wild lily, with no confidence in her own appearance. Yet she is beautiful, especially to him, like a wild lily among brambles, like the finest mare among the creatures pulling the Pharaoh's chariots (see also Song 4:1-7). Conversely, he is no giant redwood, but an apricot tree. At the same time, to her he is tall enough for her to sit in his shadow, and she can eat his fruit. He is like a gazelle on the mountains, as magnificent on their wedding day as Solomon (Song 3:6-11). To anyone else there is nothing special about him; but to her . . . (Song 5:9-16). She may even get her friends to wonder if they can rival her for him (Song 6:1-3).

---

[136]Cf. Roland E. Murphy, *The Song of Songs* (Minneapolis: Fortress, 1990), pp. 97-99.
[137]Not the Rahab of Josh 2, whose name is spelled differently.
[138]That is, the verb would be a piel privative.

There is an awesome power about their love.

> Make me like the seal on your heart,
>   like the seal on your arm.
> Because love is powerful, like death;
>   passion is intense, like Sheol.
> Its flashes are fiery ones,
>   Yah's flame.
> Mighty waters cannot quench love,
>   rivers do not sweep it off.
> If someone were to give all the wealth of his house for love,
>   people would totally disdain it. (Song 8:6-7)

These evocative lines are full of allusiveness, though their thrust is clear enough. First, the woman urges the man to make her into something that is closely attached to him. The seal, with which one confirmed ownership or identity, hung on a person's chest or was attached to their arm or hand. They would never let it go. Because of the force and fierceness of her love for him, which makes her so keen to have her commitment to him reciprocated, she wants the man to be attached to her like that.[139] The kind of love she feels—real love, she would call it—is as powerful and intense, as fierce and tough and unstoppable as death itself, the one reality whose grasp no one can finally evade. It is like a forest fire that no one can put out, or like the fiery arrows that a besieging army shoots into a city to set it on fire so that the inhabitants cannot put it out, or like the flaming arrows Yhwh shoots that no one can put out (e.g. Ps 18:8, 12-14 [MT 9, 13-15]; 38:2 [MT 3]; 120:4).[140] The water in all the oceans and rivers in the world or the underworld could not quench it. It is not susceptible to control, and thus money cannot buy it. A person cannot decide to stop loving someone, and neither can they decide to start doing so because they are paid enough. Perhaps we are to reckon that the person who would try to buy it is someone overwhelmed by love, but the tragedy of love is then that there is no way of forcing another person to reciprocate.

The Song's comments do deconstruct a little. The presupposition of the appeal in Song 8:6-7 is that the man can decide to make a commitment of love to

---

[139]In English the reference to the heart would itself suggest love, but in Hebrew this is not so; there is no particular connection between love and the heart. The exception that proves the rule is that when love and heart come together, a word such as *nepeš* ("soul") is added to heart: e.g., Deut. 6:5. Indeed, in the Song it is the *nepeš* with which the woman loves (Song 1:7; 3:1-4), not the heart. If "on your heart" means more than "on your chest," where the seal rests, it suggests attitude, priorities and commitment.

[140]But whereas the Ben Naphtali text has *šalhebet-yāh*, "flame of Yah," the Ben Asher text has *šalhebetyâ*, "its flame" (see BHS). Further, the Ben Napthali reading may be an instance of the use of the name of God as a superlative: so the EVV, though contrast Murphy, *Song of Songs*, p. 190; Richard S. Hess, *Song of Songs* (Grand Rapids: Baker, 2005), p. 233.

the woman. In some sense love is under our control. The same assumption underlies the woman's exhortation to her friends, "Why stir, why stir up love, before it so wishes?" (Song 8:4; cf. 2:7; 3:5). It is possible to stir up love or to hold it down.

The Ambiguity of Love

Yet in the Song the couple's relationship is characterized by longing (Song 1:7). They yearn to get away from everyone else (Song 2:8-14). In dreams the woman seeks her man and thinks she will never find him (Song 3:1-4), or in her sleepy state she cannot get to the door, and by the time she has got there, he is gone (Song 5:2-8). While there is no prohibition in this garden and no tension with the animal world, only encouragement to partake of its delights (Song 5:1),[141] the couple do not live in a world of their own, unaffected by their community. The woman is recurrently aware of the young women of Jerusalem, her peers or friends (Song 2:7; 3:5; 8:4). She is aware of the lookouts who might be friendly or might not (Song 3:3; 5:7). She is aware of pressure from her brothers who are suspicious of her relationship and want to "protect" her (Song 1:6; 8:8-10). A couple should not be surprised if their relationship meets with a divided response from their family or community. There is a vulnerability about it, like the vulnerability of a vineyard to foxes; it is subject to attack (Song 2:15). The man speaks of the woman metaphorically as his sister, as do Egyptian love poems,[142] and near the end of the poems she comments that she wishes she were his sister, so that she could greet him with open affection in the street without causing a scandal (Song 8:1).

"My love is mine and I am his" (Song 2:16). The English expression "my love" nicely corresponds to *dôdî*, which could denote "my beloved" (so EVV) or "my lover" (so commentators).[143] "I am my love's and my love is mine," she later says (Song 6:3), reversing the formulation in a way that nicely mirrors the reciprocal nature of the formula itself. "I am my love's and his desire is for me," she then says with further variation (Song 7:10 [MT 11]). The description of love in the Song of Songs is "at once exquisitely naive and profound."[144] "It speaks from lover to lover with whispers of intimacy, shouts of ecstasy, and silences of consummation."[145] In many respects it is not so different from the Egyptian love poems, though it does involve a man and a woman addressing

---

[141]Phyllis Trible, *God and the Rhetoric of Sexuality* (Philadelphia: Fortress, 1978), p. 151-52.

[142]See Tremper Longman, *Song of Songs,* NICOT (Grand Rapids/Cambridge: Eerdmans, 2001), p. 51.

[143]Murphy, *Song of Songs,* p. 138; Longman, *Song of Songs,* p. 118; Hess, *Song of Songs,* p. 86.

[144]Murphy, *Song of Songs,* p. 70.

[145]Trible, *God and the Rhetoric of Sexuality,* p. 144.

each other; the Egyptian poems are soliloquies.[146] Its egalitarian nature is expressed in the way the poems work. She does not have to wait for him to take the initiative; he does not have to feel that he has to do so.

Yet there is some ambiguity about that "desire" *(tĕšûqâ)*. The word comes on two other occasions in the First Testament. In Genesis 4:7 it is certainly negative; it denotes a wrong form of desire. In Genesis 3:16 it may also be negative, though the context is more ambiguous. Perhaps, poignantly, the woman's desire for her man is there a positive one,[147] to which he responds with an assertion of power. If so, the Song's vision is of that negative assertion of authority being replaced by a responsive desire on his part. The mutuality lost through disobedience to God is recovered.[148] But in Song 7:10 [MT 11], as in Genesis 4:7, the desire can be read negatively.[149] On this understanding, the mutuality of "my love is mine and I am his" disappears in this last occurrence of the formula. The Song then recognizes the truth that the relationship between a man and a woman is still played out east of Eden.[150] Indeed, in the First Testament love may seem lethal; its stories are inclined to link love and death.[151]

In philosophical discussion, erotic love has often been seen as an ethical negative or as something whose energy needs to be channeled or educated into something higher and less ambiguous; it is so affected by partiality and neediness, and it links with anger and hatred, shame and disgust, and can never totally escape these.[152] Perhaps Qohelet's gloomy and enigmatic comments about women (Eccles 7:23-29) connect with this. "I find more bitter than death the woman who is a trap," he says, and declares that he has not found one woman among a thousand.[153] He will go on to encourage husbands to enjoy life with the wife they love, which suggests this cannot be a simple generalization about all women. Perhaps it means he has not found the woman he can love and that he reckons he never will, or he is not describing all women as traps but declaring that the one who *is* a trap is a terrifying busi-

---

[146]Cf. Murphy, *Song of Songs*, pp. 47-48.

[147]Susan A. Brayford notes that this positive view of a woman's sexual desire (not confined to this passage with its uncertainty) then contrasts with the negative view that appears in other cultures ("To Shame or Not to Shame," *Semeia* 87 [1999]: 163-76).

[148]So Trible, *God and the Rhetoric of Sexuality*, p. 160.

[149]Cf. Francis Landy, "The Song of Songs and the Garden of Eden," *JBL* 98 (1979): 513-28; see pp. 524-25.

[150]But Richard M. Davidson argues that the love relationship in the Song does imply a "return to Eden" (*Flame of Yahweh* [Peabody, Mass.: Hendrickson, 2007], pp. 543-632).

[151]See Mieke Bal, *Lethal Love* (Bloomington: Indiana University Press, 1987).

[152]Cf. Martha Nussbaum, *Upheavals of Thought* (Cambridge/New York: Cambridge University Press, 2001), p. 461-63, 713.

[153]The TNIV has him saying he has not found an upright woman among a thousand, but the text itself is more allusive.

ness. Either way it is a comment on male experience that reflects how the Song of Songs does not come true for many men and many women, and it corresponds to the way Proverbs speaks. Nevertheless, Qohelet does encourage his reader to "enjoy [rāʾâ] life with the woman whom you love all the days of your empty life which he has give you under the sun" (Eccles 9:9). Postmodern work that it is, it knows that one cannot by means of philosophy find meaning through having the big questions about life answered, and turns to *la folie à deux* as the solution, rather than to other forms of folly.

Sex Demythologized

It has been suggested that the Song of Songs (or at least individual poems in earlier usage) related to sexual unions at the sanctuary; the suggestion is related to understandings of "fertility cults" and "cultic prostitution," though it is questionable whether either of the latter phrases provides appropriate models for anything that did happen in sanctuaries.[154] A related suggestion is that the poems once referred to the marriage of a god and goddess. Looked at in light of such understandings, a striking feature is that the Song contains no religious language at all except for that metaphor "Yah's flame" (if we do read the line that way). The poems thus dissociate sex from religion and from God.

Now a traditional society, in particular First Testament Israel, would not reckon people could live their sex lives without taking religious considerations into account—without taking Torah into account. (Even if the Song contained no indications of working with a marital framework, its inclusion in the Scriptures would have that implication.) They could not live on the dualistic principle that our souls and bodies are wholly separate realms, so that what we do with our souls and what we do with our bodies need not relate. God's command claims the whole person "and in so doing it is the decisive sanctification of physical sexuality and the sex relationship." It sanctifies us by including our sexuality within our humanity, and challenging us even in our bodily nature and therefore in our sexual lives to be true people: "to be a body but not only a body," to be also the spirit-impelled soul of our body and to be in spirit-impelled bodily relationship with this other person in his or her totality. Indeed, there is a certain naturalness or even

---

[154]See, e.g., Eugene J. Fisher, "Cultic Prostitution in the Ancient Near East," *Biblical Theology Bulletin* 6 (1976): 225-36; Jeffrey H. Tigay, *Deuteronomy*, JPS Torah Commentary (Philadelphia: Jewish Publication Society, 1998), pp. 480-81; and especially Christine Stark, *"Kultprostitution" im Alten Testament* (Vandenhoeck: Göttingen, 2006). Tikva Frymer-Kensky describes the idea of a sex cult in Israel or Canaan as "the product of ancient and modern sexual fantasies" (*In the Wake of the Goddesses* [New York: Free Press, 1989], p. 199). Cf. K. L. Noll, *Canaan and Israel in Antiquity* (London/New York: Sheffield Academic Press, 2001), pp. 259-61.

inevitability about that. There is no such thing as a simple physical union apart from the other aspects of our being as people.[155]

But the Song of Songs does point to distinguishing the realms of sex and God, as do a number of regulations in the Torah.[156] That is important in a context where the gods were also involved in sex, and important in a Western context where sex is God, for Christians as much as anyone else.

There is a subtle relationship between the stance that dissociates sex from God and the insistence that Israelites should not marry people who worship other deities. There is nothing defiling about people from other nations in themselves, and the Torah does not ban intermarriage as such.

Admittedly, there is some ambiguity about Genesis's stance on this question. On one hand, it is generally more open to outsiders and their faith than subsequent books. Yet Isaac and Jacob get their wives from the old country and not from the Canaanites (Gen 24; 29). The context refers only to the ethnic consideration; indeed, Abraham's extended family would not be Yhwh worshipers. Yet Abraham trusts Yhwh to provide from there (Gen 24:7-8) and Yhwh does. The detail of the story would then reassure them that they could trust God to provide against all the odds. Jacob finds Rachel by a similarly marvelous process, even if there is then a slip between cup and lip. But readers would likely understand Genesis 24 in light of the antipathy to Canaanites that is religiously based (e.g., Deut 7:3-4).

Conversely, the First Testament has no problem with a Moabite being an ancestor of David, because she has become a worshiper of Yhwh. But the involvement of foreigners with other deities would defile the people of Israel and the land of Israel; it would bring adherence to other gods into the heart of Israel's life, into marriages, households and communities. It is on this basis that Deuteronomy 7:3-4 bans marriage with the previous inhabitants of Canaan. It would be a different matter when, like Ruth and Rahab, they come to acknowledge Yhwh.[157] When the peoples around are threatening to overwhelm Judah, the stance in Ezra and Nehemiah may look tougher, and in light of modern study of ethnicity and multiculturalism Ezra may seem "bigoted"; indeed, perhaps the people he rejected were Judeans who had not gone into exile.[158] But Ezra's principle may be no different. People "have not separated themselves from the peoples of the lands with their abhorrent practices like those of the Canaanites" (Ezra 9:1). Marrying outside the faith compro-

---

[155]Karl Barth, *Church Dogmatics* (Edinburgh: T & T Clark, 1969), III/4:132, 134.

[156]See §6.2 "Maintaining and Losing Purity."

[157]Cf. the discussion in, for example, Hennie J. Marsman, *Women in Ugarit and Israel,* OTS 49 (Leiden/Boston: Brill, 2003), pp. 61-68.

[158]E.g., Daniel L. Smith-Christopher, "Between Ezra and Isaiah," in *Ethnicity and the Bible,* ed. Mark G. Brett (Leiden/New York: Brill, 1996), pp. 117-42, see pp. 126, 129.

mises the commitment of a household; it involves *ma'al* (Ezra 9:2, 4). The point is also implicit in Psalm 45 if it presupposes a king who is marrying a foreign princess, as kings such as Solomon often did. "Put out of mind your people and your father's household" (Ps 45:10 [11]), it bids, urging her to follow Ruth's example, as Solomon's and Ahab's wives notoriously did not.

Desire and Rule

Whether or not the Song pictures the relationship between a man and woman as spoiled, Genesis certainly does so. The person designed to be a helper becomes a hindrance. Yhwh had left her one step removed from hearing about how she and Adam were to conduct themselves in the garden, which perhaps leaves her more vulnerable to a suspicious interpretation of Yhwh's words such as the one a weird creature offers, and her husband does no better in heeding Yhwh's words even though he had heard Yhwh firsthand. No one comes well out of the story. It leads to recrimination, and has results in the relationship that will affect everyone who will follow.

That is the background to Yhwh's saying to Eve, "Your desire will be for your man; he will rule over you" (Gen 3:16). The meaning of *desire* is not the only ambiguity here. Each clause is preceded by *wĕ*, but it is not clear in each case whether it means "and" or "but." If the woman's "desire" is negative and suggests lust, the second *wĕ* will mean "and"; the spoiling of the relationship lies in the fact that " 'To love and to cherish' becomes 'To desire and to dominate.' "[159] But if the desire suggests a proper sexual longing, the declaration becomes grievous, as she has this longing for him, but his relationship with her is described as "rule." This might denote sexual domination, the forcing of sexual attention, though in that case one might have expected a more forceful verb. *Ruling* sounds more like headship, the idea that the husband makes the decisions. On either understanding of the first noun, then, hierarchy of relationship replaces the egalitarian one that was the creation design. Human disobedience introduces patriarchy into the world.

Is Yhwh simply predicting this spoiling or intending it? Yhwh does not say "I will make this happen" (contrast the immediately preceding declaration of intent about the pain of motherhood); we have noted that the First Testament never tells wives to obey their husbands or even to honor them. Yet in the context of such declarations of intent, this is a consequence of sin that Yhwh deems quite appropriate. But it hardly means humanity simply has to accept it. At least, we do not assume that we simply have to sit down under the declarations of intent about motherhood and decline to try to

---

[159]Derek Kidner, *Genesis* (London: Inter-Varsity Press/Downers Grove, Ill.: InterVarsity Christian Fellowship, 1967), p. 71.

make motherhood less painful. The statement does indicate that the relationship between husbands and wives is going to be fraught with tension and that a battle will be involved if it is to be the equal-terms relationship it was designed to be.

Regulations that follow in the Torah make allowance for the reality of brokenness in this relationship. These both work with the fact of patriarchy and seek to put some constraints on it by working against some of its more outrageous expressions.[160] The regulation about annulling vows (Num 30) starts from the assumption that a man (a father or husband) has some right to control the vows a woman makes; as the head of the household, he has to make its budget work. But if he does want to avoid the household having to bear the cost of the vow, he has to say so sooner rather than later. A rule for dealing with the accusation that a woman was not a virgin when she married (Deut 22:13-21) offers protection both to wives and to husbands; a wife is protected from frivolous accusation, a husband from deceit about his bride's sexual status and from finding himself with a child that is not his own. Admittedly the punishment for whoever is guilty seems excessive (the woman is to be stoned), and the procedure for establishing the truth seems unrealistic (and conversely to work in the woman's favor, since it would be easy for the girl's parents to fix the evidence of her virginity). But this suggests that as is often the case, these are not rules whose point is that they should be literally implemented; they were not. They make statements, propagate values and suggest parameters for working out questions of compensation.

Faithfulness

The First Testament urges men and women to be faithful to their wives and husbands. Proverbs 5:15-20 puts the positive point most evocatively. It starts from a decision of the will. Cisterns and wells are vital sources of life and refreshment; a well with fresh water is great, but many wells dry up in the summer and a cistern that has collected rain water is a vital back up. These provide an image for your relationship with your wife: she is the fountain for you to drink from with full satisfaction. Indeed, her water is more like wine that makes you reel and stagger like someone intoxicated. Proverbs 5 implicitly makes a promise: if you will relate to her with such an expectation, this will be the result.

It thus urges a man to reckon that faithfulness is not a burden but can be the way to fulfillment. The first promise it attaches to faithfulness is that the hoped-for fruit will result: the man's relationship with his wife will issue in their filling the streets with their progeny, fulfilling the ideal and practical

---

[160]See further §4.2 "Protecting Women in a Patriarchal Culture."

need to have a large family.[161] Thus will his wife be blessed. And that will be part of the reason for his rejoicing in his young wife.[162] But it will not be the entirety of the reason, Proverbs goes on. He will enjoy her appearance, like that of a hind or doe; loving someone and rejoicing in them makes them beautiful and makes you appreciate them. He will enjoy her love and her graciousness;[163] being loved and rejoiced-in makes you loving and gracious. He will enjoy their sexual relationship; being loved and rejoiced-in makes you more enthusiastic about that. He will keep being knocked over by her. The context suggests it is not merely the physical relationship that does this, but also not merely her love and graciousness toward him, and not merely her physical attractiveness, and not merely her capacity to bear children, but all of these and thus the totality of the relationship and what she is to him. So don't even think of looking elsewhere.

Whereas the Song of Songs may presuppose a marriage that is a love match, Proverbs may presuppose an arranged marriage, designed as much to facilitate relationships in the community and encourage its growth as for the benefit of the couple. Isaac and Rebekah had a marriage initiated by his father (she agreed to it, but before meeting Isaac), and Isaac loved Rebekah (Gen 24:67). But in what sense did he do so? Was he making a commitment, or was he besotted? Their subsequent relationship does not give the impression of a romantic relationship. On the other hand, Jacob does seem besotted with Rachel, though this began as a love match that then needed to be negotiated (Gen 29:16-20). The marriage of Elkanah and Hannah was probably arranged, and those of David and Michal and then Michal and Paltiel certainly were, but Elkanah loved Hannah, and Michal loved David, in that fuller sense, and it looks as if Paltiel loved Michal too, showing that life could get as complicated in Israel as it can in the West (1 Sam 1:5; 18:28; 2 Sam 3:16). Couples in traditional societies testify to the way an arranged marriage can become a love marriage. In Western marriage the starry-eyed couple starting a new family "is being left alone on hard and unforgiving terrain. Only the strong or lucky will survive." Israelite marriage had more chance of realizing the ideal of Christian marriage, which makes sense only on the assumption that it "is not a whole

---

[161]So I understand v. 16, with JPSV; for the verb, cf. Zech 1:17, also the niphal in Gen 10:18 (BDB has two roots *pûṣ*, but contrast *HALOT*). Other EVV take v. 16 to refer to his spreading his sexual favors around the community, or to his wife's doing so because of his neglect, and therefore turn the line into an unmarked question. But there is no hint that it is that.

[162]The EVV have "the wife of your youth," but in such construct phrases the second noun commonly functions adjectivally; for this expression, cf. Is 54:6 as well as Mal 2:15.

[163]The NRSV has "lovely" and "graceful" rather than "loving" and "gracious," but *'ahăḇîm* means "loving," and in that context *ḥēn* likely suggests "gracious" in the sense of accepting and caring.

communion of two, but a particular kind of grace-filled friendship within the fellowship of the Church."[164]

Pressures on Faithfulness

Proverbs 1–9 is the section of Scripture that gives most sustained attention to sexual faithfulness. This may reflect its background in a context when the Second Temple community is surrounded by other peoples and under various kinds of pressure from them, and a context where within God's people old certainties had gone (as Qohelet suggests) and old social structures no longer obtained. A positive aspect to the new ways of thinking this leads to is its picture of insight embodied as a woman (Prov 8:22-31). Further, Proverbs 31:10-31 (which pairs with chapters 1–9 as a frame round the book) pictures a woman exercising a many-sided responsibility, not simply following a man. "She is Wisdom incarnated within the household, the familial embodiment of Wisdom" and also "the economic engine of her household. . . . Yet domestic as it is, the valiant woman's domicile is not a gated household, shut off from the outer world. Her door is flung open on behalf of the community as much as her lips are parted wide to deliver wisdom and covenantal teaching," *tôrat-ḥesed* (Prov 31:26).[165]

Proverbs 1–9 does discuss marital faithfulness only from a man's angle. If that reflects realities of the social context, this likely does not merely suggest that social pressures no longer made it hard for women to be unfaithful, still less that they are by nature less inclined to unfaithfulness than men; indeed, the very need for exhortation on this subject presupposes that there were women who did not feel inhibited by marital vows. But Proverbs 1–9 as a whole often reads like a textbook for a theological school (Michael V. Fox calls it a series of "lectures"),[166] so its gendered-ness may link with the likelihood that there were no women in theological school in those days. In a twenty-first-century Western context, at least, at every point the sexual politics will need to be seen both ways.

Proverbs starts from the fact that married men in Israel, like married men in the church, do get into sexual relationships with other women. There is a thrill about falling in love with someone when your first love has grown cold, or an excitement about an affair (cf. Prov 5:20; 9:17). It also presupposes that some married women have affairs. Here they are presented as people who are somehow outsiders. This might mean that they are people from outside the

---

[164]David Matzko McCarthy, "Becoming One Flesh," in *The Blackwell Companion to Christian Ethics*, pp. 276-88; see pp. 276, 277.

[165]William P. Brown, *The Ethos of the Cosmos: The Genesis of Moral Imagination in the Bible* (Grand Rapids/Cambridge: Eerdmans, 1999), pp. 307-8.

[166]Michael V. Fox, *Proverbs 1–9*, AB (New York: Doubleday, 2000), p. 45.

community, like the women mentioned in Ezra-Nehemiah. But the traditional Western idea of "the other woman" similarly presents such a person as an outsider, as does the idea of the "loose woman," and Proverbs may simply be concerned about the woman who is on the loose, without family ties, perhaps because her own marriage has broken down, even if she is still living at home because she has nowhere else to go (cf. Prov 7).[167]

As a Wisdom book, Proverbs' response to that fact is not so much to say that having an affair is wrong, though it assumes this, but to declare that it is really stupid; this is the point it keeps attempting to drive home. To put it positively, "True eros can be found only with Wisdom."[168] Whether a person has an affair because of falling in love with someone else or because of the thrill of the experience, it will end in pain and loss, and ruin their life. Not least because of the relationship of household to land, the integrity of an Israelite marriage was integral to the integrity of the household, the kin group, the community and the people as a whole; unfaithfulness therefore did imperil a person's entire life (see Prov 6:24-35). Further, in traditional and modern societies, adultery can so inflame the party that has been betrayed that it can lead to the actual death of the adulterers, and Proverbs 5:23 and 9:18 may presuppose the same dynamic. A number of First Testament stories illustrate another aspect of the tragedy of extramarital sex, the way love can turn to hate or generate conflict between the families of the lovers (Gen 34; 39; 2 Sam 13).

When people have an affair, they may well tell themselves this love is a gift from God. If it is love, it cannot be wrong, can it? Oh yes, it can, Proverbs shouts. Having set an encouragement to an enjoyable marital sexual relationship in the context of warnings about adultery in Proverbs 5:15-20, it highlights the horrific nature of adultery by juxtaposing it with the wonder of sexual relationships that do not betray a marriage. It marvels at the wonder of "the way of a man with a girl" (Prov 30:19)[169] and then comments on the way of an adulteress "who eats and wipes her mouth, and says 'I have not done wrong' " (Prov 30:20).

Faithfulness, Yhwh and the Community

Proverbs' way of making the point of principle, as opposed to the pragmatic

---

[167]Cf. L. A. Snijders, "The Meaning of zār in the Old Testament," OTS 10 (1954): 1-154; see pp. 88-104; Wright, God's People in God's Land, pp. 93-97; Claudia V. Camp, "What's So Strange About the Strange Woman?" in The Bible and the Politics of Exegesis, N. K. Gottwald Festschrift, ed. David Jobling et al. (Cleveland: Pilgrim Press, 1991), pp. 17-31.

[168]Brown, Ethos of the Cosmos, p. 291.

[169]Roland E. Murphy suggests seeing the Song of Songs as an "expansion" of this phrase (Wisdom Literature [Grand Rapids: Eerdmans, 1981], p. 104).

one, is to add that having an affair cannot be consistent with reverence for Yhwh. Its argument is thus religious rather than moral. The ban on adultery in the Decalogue works in the same way. It is because Yhwh is the God who brought you out of Egypt that you do not commit adultery (Ex 20:14); here too it is part of reverence or obedience toward Yhwh. Adultery is a sin against God (Gen 20:6), as well as against a woman's husband; indeed, in Israel as elsewhere it can be the "great evil" or "great sin" (Gen 39:9; cf. 20:9). It is an act that defiles a person and thus makes it impossible to appear before Yhwh, makes them liable to be cut off from the people and endangers the entire people's relationship with God (Lev 18:20, 24-30). When prophets too upbraid men and women for adultery, they do so in Yhwh's name (Jer 5:7-9; Hos 4:14), and the upbraiding in Job 24:15-17 either urges or promises that Yhwh will do something about it. If a man's act takes place in circumstances that make it not quite count as regular adultery and he thus evades the threat of death (Lev 19:20-22), he must nevertheless not merely compensate the man for whom the woman in question is destined but bring an offering to make restitution to Yhwh, so as to make expiation and find pardon. Adultery thus appears and is seen as a sin against God in all the biblical genres.[170]

Hosea 4:10-12 suggest another take on this question. People "will eat but they will not be full, they will be immoral [*zānâ*] but not multiply, because they have abandoned Yhwh to practice immorality; wine and new wine take the understanding. . . . A spirit of immorality has led them astray; they have been immoral and abandoned their God." A number of aspects of the passage are unclear, but it does seem to bring together sex outside marriage, indulgence in food and drink, and abandonment of Yhwh. "Confusing physical intimacy with true intimacy is tantamount to apostasy" or apostasy leads to that confusion.[171]

Like Proverbs, elsewhere the Torah has its own framework and reasons for handling the question of adultery. It is concerned for the affect of adultery on the community. Thus, while the prophets' condemnation of adultery is capable of application to all sexual relationships in which one of the partners is married, and the Decalogue's prohibition of adultery is capable of application to both men and women, other individual regulations in the Torah are concerned with sex between a single or married man and a woman who is either married or engaged (Lev 18:20; 20:10; Deut 22:22-27). They are not so con-

---

[170]Cf. Lipka, *Sexual Transgression in the Hebrew Bible*, p. 43 (and see pp. 42-168); also Anthony Phillips, *Essays on Biblical Law*, JSOTSup 344 (London/New York: Sheffield Academic Press, 2002), pp. 74-95.

[171]Mayer I. Gruber, "Marital Fidelity and Intimacy," in *A Feminist Companion to the Latter Prophets*, ed. Athalya Brenner (Sheffield, U.K.: Sheffield Academic Press, 1995), pp. 169-79; see p. 175.

cerned with sex between a married man and an unattached single woman, or between single people, though there are regulations that cover these acts from different angles. Deuteronomy 22:13-21 presupposes that a man would expect his bride to be a virgin and reckons that when a single girl has sex she has done *nĕbālâ*, something outrageous, something that "seriously threatens the social order."[172] Similar implications emerge from the story of Shechem and Dinah, if this involved seduction but consensual sex rather than rape.[173] It too is an act of *nĕbālâ*, the kind of thing that is not done (Gen 34:7). The same is true of Amnon's rape of Tamar (2 Sam 13:12), though Tamar's story also makes clear that Amnon has done wrong against Tamar as well as against the community and against God. She is abased, shamed and desolated.[174]

The Torah may simply be working with an aspect of the double standard that has often affected attitudes to sex and thus be making regulations that in particular recognize male hardness of heart. There is little suggestion that adultery is a property offense, as if a husband owns his wife and another man is stealing something that belongs to him (though Lev 19:20 does look at things this way),[175] and if that were so, one would not expect the penalty to be death. Neither is there any suggestion that adultery is wrong because it constitutes unfaithfulness to the intimate relationship of a married couple; that is in line with its not seeing this as the heart of marriage. More likely, it sees adultery as an attack on the family. Societies and families often reckon it is important to know who is a child's biological father, and the birth to a married woman of a child whose paternity is uncertain can throw it into a turmoil that is both emotional and practical. Who accepts responsibility for this child? Does it have a right to share in the family's property? Avoiding sex with a married woman prevents such questions arising.[176]

In encouraging faithfulness Proverbs combines carrot and stick, encouragement and prohibition. Having waxed lyrical about the potential of a lov-

---

[172]Carolyn Pressler, *The View of Women Found in the Deuteronomic Family Laws*, BZAW 216 (Berlin/New York: de Gruyter, 1993), p. 30. On theories as to why virginity should seem important, see Tikva Frymer-Kensky, "Virginity in the Bible," in *Gender and Law in the Hebrew Bible and the Ancient Near East*, ed. Victor H. Matthews et al., JSOTSup 262 (Sheffield, U.K.: Sheffield Academic Press, 1998), pp. 79-96.

[173]See, e.g., Lipka, *Sexual Transgression in the Hebrew Bible*, pp. 184-99.

[174]See Phyllis Trible, *Texts of Terror* (Philadelphia: Fortress, 1984), pp. 37-63.

[175]Wright, *God's People in God's Land*, pp. 203-5. It is the only passage from the Torah that Countryman quotes in support of the view that adultery is primarily a property offense, though he later points to Job 31:9-10 and to the juxtaposition in the Decalogue of adultery and theft and of coveting a wife and a house (*Dirt, Greed, and Sex*, pp. 35-37, 148-49, 157).

[176]One expression for the prohibition of adultery might literally be rendered "into your neighbor's wife you shall not put your emission of seed" (Lev 18:20; cf. *HALOT*, p. 1488). Baruch A. Levine calls it a "formula for impregnation" (*Leviticus* [Philadelphia: Jewish Publication Society, 1989], p. 122).

ing relationship with one's wife, Proverbs 5:21-23 goes on to remind young men more prosaically that our entire lives are visible to Yhwh and that we will pay the price for our waywardness and folly, which is indeed the emphasis of this chapter (see Prov 5:1-14) and of Proverbs 1–9 as a whole. "Proverbs 7 may be read as a voice subversive of 'patriarchy,' understood here in terms of one of its aspects, the double standard."[177]

Safeguarding Faithfulness

Proverbs points to some guidelines for safeguarding against unfaithfulness, beyond the positive exhortation to develop your enthusiasm for your wife. One is owning the problem's existence. The chapters bring it out in the open rather than letting it be an issue one does not talk about. They are apparently written for the education of potential leaders in the community, and whereas people are often surprised at the "fall" of leaders in state or church, Proverbs implies that for various reasons leaders are especially inclined to have affairs, and it owns that fact in particular. It urges men to keep their head, to be wise, rather than being led by some other part of their anatomy. It also urges them to keep watch over their emotions, to keep watch over their heart or mind, because this is "the source of life" (Prov 4:23). The heart will imply the mind; it is a characteristic assumption of Proverbs that we need to think straight. When we are inclined to fall in love with someone inappropriate (indeed, perhaps with someone appropriate), then this is a moment to make sure of keeping our thinking cool. But the heart stands more broadly for the inner wellsprings, "the basic orientation of a person, embracing desires, emotions, and attitude."[178] That could link with the emphasis on a person's relating to God that has an unexpected place in the midst of Proverbs 1–9 with its emphasis on sexual faithfulness, at Proverbs 3:5-12.

For people in Western society there is another aspect of the significance of the inner wellsprings. We live in a radically consumerized society: "We have come to see and conduct not just the bartering of bread and soap but the whole of our lives in the ways of the market."[179] That is true about church, ministry, medicine—and relationships such as marriage, in which we "invest" expecting to see a return as our needs are met. If they are not, we will naturally withdraw our investment and make it somewhere else. Life is about choice, and if this relationship does not meet my needs, I choose another. We

---

[177]Alice Ogden Bellis, "The Gender and Motives of the Wisdom Teacher in Proverbs 7," in *Wisdom and Psalms*, ed. Athalya Brenner and Carole R. Fontaine, FCB 2/2 (Sheffield, U.K.: Sheffield Academic Press, 1998), pp. 79-91; see p. 85.

[178]Roland E. Murphy, *Proverbs*, WBC (Nashville: Nelson, 1998), p. 28.

[179]Rodney Clapp, *Families at the Crossroads* (Downers Grove, Ill./Leicester, U.K.: InterVarsity Press, 1993), p. 57.

have given up on the notion that marriage, as well as being covenantal as opposed to natural, is covenantal as opposed to contractual.[180] Admittedly this
is a difference that works only in English and not in Hebrew, where *bĕrît* is the
word for a contract or treaty as well as for a covenant. And as there is a contractual element to Western marriage, which is a legal arrangement, there are
analogous aspects to Middle-Eastern marriage, of which the marriage gift is
one.[181] But Proverbs 2:17, Ezekiel 16:8 and Malachi 2:14 more likely see marriage in light of the covenantal relationship between Yhwh and Israel than in
contractual terms; like that relationship, it involves an unqualified mutual
commitment, in sickness or health, for better for worse, till death us do part.
If that is the way we decide to see the marriage commitment in the wellsprings of our heart, we are more likely to stick to it faithfully. We would need
to be wary of taking the metaphorical marriage between Yhwh and Israel as
a guide to the way human marriages worked; Ezekiel's account of the way
Yhwh has treated his "wives" does not correspond to his apparent attitude to
his own wife.[182] But in other respects, if marriage became an image for Yhwh's
relationship with Israel, by a feedback process marriage might be expected to
reflect that relationship. For instance, Yhwh is committed for life to Israel and
is prepared to put up with whatever Israel does.

Alongside Proverbs' advice to men not to let their sexual attention wander,
its main piece of advice distinctively given to women is not to nag. Perhaps
these two are connected. Nagging might be a response to feeling neglected,
in which case it is unlikely to make the situation better; or it might be a cause
of being neglected. Either way, delighting in or giving space to or going easy
on one's husband are tougher, but Proverbs reckons they pay better.

The practice of circumcision also relates to questions about sexual faithfulness. Like sacrifices and festivals, circumcision is a sign with a number of
significances. It becomes a sign of membership of the covenant people (Gen
17). It is a more inclusive sign than this might seem to imply; it applies to Ishmael as well as Isaac and to servants born in the house or bought from a foreigner. That fits the fact that it is a widespread, though not universal, human
practice. It is also a less inclusive sign than this implies, insofar as mercifully
it applies only to males. In Genesis 17 it is an aspect of the re-solemnizing of
Yhwh's covenant with Abraham, which was first sealed with Abraham in
connection with the promise of the land in Genesis 15:18. Here the covenant
focuses on Abraham's becoming the ancestor of many offspring. In that con-

---

[180]Cf. Clapp, *Families at the Crossroads*, p. 118.

[181]On the basis of a comparison with Middle-Eastern documents David Instone-Brewer
simply declares that "marriage is a contract" (*Divorce and Remarriage in the Bible* [Grand
Rapids/Cambridge: Eerdmans, 2002], p. 1).

[182]See Marsman, *Women in Ugarit and Israel*, pp. 115-19.

nection, circumcision suggests the cutting down to size or disciplining or surrendering to Yhwh of the part of his body that will be the means of begetting progeny. It is hardly a coincidence that the sign of the covenant is applied to this part rather than (for instance) the ear, whose symbolism would also be apposite (Jer 6:10).[183] One thing circumcision represents is "a controlling of sexuality."[184] Genesis has already made clear that male sexuality needs such discipline; the sign of the covenant underlines the fact, and succeeding stories involving circumcision will emphasize it further. "Circumcision was for the ancient Israelites a symbol of male submission,"[185] to other men (Gen 34), to a woman (Ex 4), to God (Ex 4).[186]

Protecting Women in a Patriarchal Culture

Adultery is common, and so is suspecting one's partner of adultery. Numbers 5:11-31 provides a rite for when a husband suspects his wife; if he is right, this would bring pollution to her and thus to the community (v. 29). In a first-order sense, adultery is no more polluting than any other sexual act, but here the notion of pollution is being extended from the metaphysical to the interpersonal and moral sphere (as in passages such as Lev 18:24-30; Deut 24:4; Ezek 22:11).[187] There is no correlative rite for when she suspects him, but groundless suspicion on her part would not be as threatening to him as groundless suspicion on his part could be to her. Whether or not it is more common for husbands to suspect wives or wives to suspect husbands, perhaps (like the repeated stories in Genesis about husbands passing off their wives as their sisters) the regulation reflects men's fear of women's sexuality, and specifically their ambiguous feelings about their wives' sexuality.[188] But perhaps a common context in which the suspicion became urgent would be a conception in which for some reason the husband reckoned he had not been involved; the account of the consequences if she is guilty would fit with this.

---

[183]See Howard Eilberg-Schwartz, *The Savage in Judaism* (Bloomington: Indiana University Press, 1990), pp. 141-76, though he emphasizes "fertility, descent, and gender" (p. 141) rather than discipline.

[184]Berquist, *Controlling Corporeality*, p. 37.

[185]Howard Eilberg-Schwartz, *God's Phallus* (Boston: Beacon, 1994), p. 161.

[186]On Ex 4:24-26 see Athena Gorospe, *Narrative and Identity* (Leiden/Boston: Brill, 2007), esp. pp. 123-40, and her references.

[187]Cf. Baruch A. Levine, *Numbers 1–20*, AB (New York: Doubleday, 1993), pp. 207-8.

[188]See Alice Bach, "Good to the Last Drop," in *The New Literary Criticism and the Hebrew Bible*, ed. J. Cheryl Exum and David J. A. Clines, JSOTSup 143 (Sheffield, U.K.: Sheffield Academic Press, 1993), pp. 26-54; and on those stories in Genesis, J. Cheryl Exum, "Who's Afraid of 'The Endangered Ancestress'?" in the same volume, pp. 91-113. These essays also appear (with others on Num 5:11-31 in Bach, *Women in the Hebrew Bible*, pp. 141-56, 461-522. Exum's essay also appears in her *Fragmented Women*, JSOTSup 163 [Sheffield, U.K.: Sheffield Academic Press; Valley Forge, Penn.: Trinity, 1993], pp. 148-69), where she make the same comment on the Samson story (p. 62).

The rite itself involves the woman in shaming as if she is already reckoned guilty, but it does protect her from her husband's arbitrary violence or from divorce on the basis of mere suspicion. She has to drink a mixture of water and earth from the sanctuary floor, and the priest prays that if she is guilty, terrible bodily consequences may follow; they may denote her ceasing to be able to have children or losing a child she has conceived. If she remains healthy or keeps her baby, that will be a sign that her husband's jealousy was undeserved. Alongside the disincentive for her husband to make frivolous accusations of adultery as a basis for getting rid of her cheaply, the rite provides a disincentive for her to deny adultery and risk these consequences if she is actually guilty.

This passage and others such as Deuteronomy 22:22-30 [MT 22:22–23:1]; 24:1-4; 25:5-10 thus work with patriarchy but constrain it.[189] A man cannot get away with adultery knowing that only the woman will be punished. He cannot get away with seducing or raping a woman who is engaged or is single. He cannot take over his father's (former) wife. He cannot divorce his wife for some reason and let her become someone else's wife, and then decide to have her back when the second man divorces her or dies; the woman is thus protected from becoming "a kind of marital football,"[190] and her new husband is protected from her former husband's taking renewed interest in her.[191] A man cannot play fast and loose with his widowed sister-in-law who has no son and thus no heir to the household's land; she has the right to lean on him either to do his duty by her or properly to forgo his obligation and right (it might be in his interests to let his brother's land be unclaimed, so that he would eventually have a share in it or inherit all of it, without bothering with his sister-in-law) and leave her free to marry someone else. Such regulations start from the assumption that women have little or no independent status as owners of land and thus capacity to live an independent life, but they also make patriarchy deconstruct.

Divorce

We have noted that Jesus takes Genesis 1–2 to raise questions about the propriety of divorce.[192] There is no regulation in the Torah to govern divorce itself, as there is none to govern marriage; this regulation simply presupposes

---

[189]Cf. §4.2 "Desire and Rule"; and Dennis T. Olson, *Deuteronomy and the Death of Moses* (Minneapolis: Fortress, 1994), pp. 102-3.

[190]Christopher Wright, *Deuteronomy* (Peabody, Mass.: Hendrickson/Carlisle, U.K.: Paternoster, 1996), p. 255.

[191]At least, these would be effects of the regulation; we do not know what was its intention or rationale. See the discussion in, e.g., J. G. McConville, *Deuteronomy* (Leicester,U.K./Downers Grove, Ill.: InterVarsity Press, 2002), pp. 358-60.

[192]See §4.1 "Thinking Critically."

divorce. It is usually said that in Israel wives could not initiate a divorce,[193] but this seems to be an argument from silence within the First Testament; elsewhere in the Middle East and in the Second Temple Jewish community at Elephantine women could do so.[194] Deuteronomy also assumes the practice of documenting the divorce and assumes a divorced woman's right to remarry,[195] but forbids a man to remarry someone he has divorced. Jesus comments that Moses wrote this command because of people's hardness of hearts and that things were not like this from the beginning of creation, and goes on to quote Genesis 1:27 and Genesis 2:24. "Therefore, what God joined together, a human being is not to separate."

In contrast with Deuteronomy 24:1-4 and other passages that presuppose divorce (Lev 22:13; Num 30:9 [MT 10]), Malachi 2:10-16 overtly condemns it. Admittedly the text is tricky in various respects. It begins by speaking of people profaning the covenant of their ancestors. The expression is allusive and perhaps has several implications. People have broken their covenant with one another and with Yhwh in undertaking marriages with women who acknowledge different gods. And by divorcing their wives they have broken their marriage covenant.[196] It makes more coherent sense of the passage as a whole if they have divorced their Judean wives in order to undertake these other marriages. Perhaps their wives were unable to have children; by means of their new marriages the men were concerned to maintain their hold on their land and their position in Judah. This would add point to the prayer that follows, which refers to Yhwh's cutting them off from the tents of Jacob (especially in JPSV's version, which takes it explicitly to speak of their not having descendants), and to the reference to Yhwh's seeking "godly offspring."

Malachi goes on to offer further reason for the exhortation that no one should "break faith" with his wife. The EVV agree in translating it something like "For I hate divorce (Yhwh, the God of Israel, says) and covering one's clothes with violence," though the Hebrew is allusive.[197] An alternative is "For

---

[193]See, e.g., Emmerson, "Women in Ancient Israel," pp. 385-86.

[194]See J. Andrew Dearman, "Marriage in the Old Testament," in *Biblical Ethics and Homosexuality*, ed. Robert L. Brawley (Louisville: Westminster John Knox, 1996), pp. 53-67; see p. 67.

[195]Instone-Brewer notes that this regulation is unique to the Pentateuch over against other Middle-Eastern sources (*Divorce and Remarriage in the Bible*, pp. 20-33).

[196]The fact that Yhwh is witness to the abandoned marriage suggests that Malachi cannot be referring to people "divorcing" Yhwh; it is hard enough to imagine that Yhwh is the bride to the marriage, let alone the witness to it as well.

[197]There is no "I" before the participle "hate," though such pronominal subjects are occasionally omitted (see GKC 116s). Further "divorce" is *šallaḥ*, which looks like an imperative or an infinitive construct but which EVV likely take as a hapax noun. Likewise "covering" is *kissâ*, which looks like a third-person qatal, and the phrase it introduces (literally, "he covered violence over his clothes") is an unfamiliar idiom.

he has hated, divorced (Yhwh says), covered his clothes with violence."[198] Possibly the text has suffered in transmission because of arguments about the propriety of divorce within the Jewish community.[199] But the general point is clear, and Malachi is nearer to affirming the ideal implicit in Genesis 1–2 than to sympathizing with the allowance for human hard-heartedness in Deuteronomy 24:1-4.[200] Yet one should not absolutize his statement. If the background is the intermarriages reported in Ezra-Nehemiah, he might nevertheless sympathize with Ezra's leaning on people to divorce their foreign wives. He is concerned for Judean men to keep faith with their Judean wives in the context of their covenant relationship with them and with Yhwh. In other words, he speaks as a prophet rather than a scribe or legislator, as does Jesus.[201]

(I once knew a man who loved a divorced woman but would not marry her because of what Jesus said about divorce and remarriage. It is a very rare thing for someone to do something they do not wish to do just because Jesus said it. Every other Christian I know disapproves of divorce in principle but not in practice.)

Prostitution and Polygamy

Prostitute is another word for which Hebrew has no equivalent; both Hebrew words translated "prostitute" have rather broader meaning. The common word is *zōnâ* from the verb *zānâ*, meaning to act in a sexually immoral way. The less common word is *qādēš* with the feminine *qĕdēšâ* from the verb *qādēš*, meaning to be holy. It is usually assumed that this word technically refers to a hierodule, a person who engages in some form of sexual activity in a religious context (for instance, as an enacted prayer for fertility), but we have noted that the evidence for this is very allusive.[202]

Jon L. Berquist simply declares that in the First Testament "prostitution is denied" in the sense of not accepted,[203] noting Leviticus 19:29 and Deuteronomy 23:17, though it is of course recognized as a reality. In contrast, Gail Corrigan Streete simply declares that men "are permitted intercourse . . . uncon-

---

[198]This requires the repointing of *šallaḥ* to *šillaḥ*. See the discussion in John J. Collins, "Marriage, Divorce, and Family in Second Temple Judaism," in Leo G. Perdue et al., *Families in Ancient Israel* (Louisville: Westminster John Knox, 1997), pp. 104-62, see pp. 122-27.

[199]Cf. the comments in Andrew E. Hill, *Malachi,* AB (New York: Doubleday, 1998), pp. 221-59.

[200]Instone-Brewer argues that hating divorce means hating the marital unfaithfulness that leads to divorce, hating conduct that leads to divorce (*Divorce and Remarriage in the Bible,* pp. 54-58), but this seems forced.

[201]See A. E. Harvey, "Genesis versus Deuteronomy," in *The Gospels and the Scriptures of Israel,* ed. Craig A. Evans and W. Richard Stegner (Sheffield, U.K.: Sheffield Academic Press, 1994), pp. 55-65.

[202]See §4.2 "Sex Demythologized."

[203]Berquist, *Controlling Corporeality,* p. 97.

ditionally with prostitutes."[204] Joshua 2 does tell with relish and without criticism the story of Rahab, her "conversion," her facilitating of the Israelite attack on Jericho and her inclusion into the community. On the other hand, the story of Judah and Tamar (Gen 38) portrays Tamar's recourse to prostitution as the desperate act of a desperate (Canaanite?) woman, not simply a regular career option. Further, while the story recognizes that prostitution meets a need for a man on his own (Judah's wife has died), it also sets Judah's action over against the single Joseph's resisting the blandishments of Potiphar's wife (Gen 39), the more excellent way. In 1 Corinthians 6:12-20 Paul, like Jesus, refers back to Genesis 2:24 and suggests that it is also significant in this connection. It is not just a proper marital sexual union that makes two people one flesh. That happens with any sexual union, such as that with a prostitute. Christian freedom does not mean we can do what we like with our bodies, because what we do with our bodies we are doing with our selves. And we cannot become one flesh with a prostitute.

One can imagine a similar conversation about polygamy to the one Jesus and the Pharisees have about divorce, though the dynamics of the Torah's treatment are slightly different. Again there is no law that prescribes for it, though there are regulations that circumscribe it, such as Deuteronomy 21:15-17, which "perceives multiple wives as potential threats . . . to social stability."[205] But there is no condemnation of polygamy like the condemnation of divorce in Malachi 2:10-16, and Genesis and other books record many examples without making explicit adverse comment.

Most references to polygamy presuppose that a man's first wife could not have children or that multiplying wives is a sign of status or a means of developing relationships and alliances with other families or peoples, all of which are often true in traditional societies.[206] Polygamy is thus analogous to divorce in Western culture in being exceptional rather than the regular thing, however much it happened. Polygamy does mean no woman need remain single, no marriage need remain childless and no man need look outside his household for sexual expression if things do not "work" with his first wife; we may not care for this way of approaching those questions, but we can hardly reckon that our Christian cultures handle them so much better.[207]

Yet the way Genesis 1–2 speaks of "male and female" and certainly the

---

[204]Gail Corrigan Streete, *The Strange Woman* (Louisville: Westminster John Knox, 1997), p. 43.

[205]Pressler, *View of Women Found in the Deuteronomic Family Laws*, p. 17.

[206]Indeed, the last can be seen as the point (from the family's viewpoint) about marriage itself: see the comments in Naomi A. Sternberg, *Kinship and Marriage in Genesis* (Minneapolis: Fortress, 1993), pp. 6-9.

[207]Wolff, *Anthropology of the Old Testament*, p. 169.

way it describes Adam and Eve and their becoming one flesh suggests a monogamous relationship, and this is presupposed by many references to husbands and wives in the First Testament. And its descriptions of polygamous relationships can be read as deliberately drawing attention to the trouble they involve. Further, the regulations concerning sexual relationships in Leviticus 18 start from the fact that polygamy opens up the prospect of complications in sexual relationships in the family. So Moses' regulations that presuppose polygamy, and the practice of it in Genesis and elsewhere, again make allowance for human hardness of heart.[208]

The First Testament recognizes that people may be called to remain single (Jer 16:2) or may not have the possibility of marriage or at least of parenthood (Is 56:3-5), and that both can be positions of fulfillment or fruitfulness,[209] though "there is no such thing as a self-contained and self-sufficient male life or female life";[210] the single still share in the male-femaleness of the human community. But the First Testament has very little to say about this question and implicitly approaches it rather by seeking to locate everyone in a marital relationship. The New Testament has more by way of vision for a single life,[211] though it also sows seeds that bear fruit in the negative assessment of marriage, sex and children in the Patristic period.

Same-sex Unions

One can imagine a parallel conversation about same-sex relationships to those about divorce and polygamy, though the dynamics of the Torah's references are again not identical. Whereas the Torah allows for divorce and polygamy, Leviticus 18:22 and Leviticus 20:13 explicitly disallow homosexual acts.[212] Yet it also disallows many other practices (such as sex with a woman during her period) on the basis of a concern with purity and taboo, and in general such prohibitions are withdrawn in Christ. It has been argued that the Levitical ban on homosexual acts also ceases to apply once Christ has made all things clean.[213] But the context of these regulations in Leviticus implies that they are not simply concerned with purity and taboo. Leviticus

---

[208]David Daube notes rabbinic opinion to this effect ("Concessions to Sinfulness in Jewish Law," *Journal of Jewish Studies* 10 [1959]: 1-13; see p. 6).

[209]Cf. Barth, *Church Dogmatics*, III/4:142.

[210]Barth, *Church Dogmatics*, III/4:163.

[211]See, e.g., Clapp, *Families at the Crossroads*, pp. 89-113.

[212]The only other explicit First Testament references to homosexual acts come in Gen 19 and Judg 19, but these refer to casual and promiscuous homosexual sex, if not homosexual rape, so that the description of them as evil *(ra')* cannot simply be transferred to same-sex marriage. Ilona N. Rashkow groups homosexuality with incest, adultery and prostitution as the four "abominations" (*Taboo or not Taboo* [Minneapolis: Fortress, 2000], pp. 19-32).

[213]Cf. Countryman, *Dirt, Greed, and Sex*, pp. 244-45.

20:13 comes in the context of a ban on sex with a married woman or with other members of the household, and on marrying a woman and her mother, the concern apparently being with safeguarding the integrity and stability of the family. Leviticus 18:22 comes in the context of a ban on sex with your neighbor's wife or with an animal (which is called "confusion"), as well as on "sacrifices to Molek" and on sex with a menstruating woman; all (it says) are the kind of abhorrent practices that were the reason for throwing out the nations that inhabited Canaan before the Israelites. Homosexual practice and sex with animals, as well as sacrificing children, are referred to in ancient sources, but there is disagreement over whether the First Testament's ban on all homosexual acts is distinctive in its culture, as is becoming the case in Western culture.[214]

If we again consider how things were "at the beginning of creation," then Genesis 1–2 note that "God made them male and female" (Mk 10:6) and envisage sexual relationships only between a man and a woman. It seems likely that the Torah's ban on homosexual acts is based not just in rules about cleanness and taboo but on the purpose of creation. The major focus of Genesis 1–2 does lie on the link between sex and procreation, and on their basis alone it could be argued that once humanity has fulfilled the commission to fill the earth, there is no longer need to confine sex to heterosexual relationships. Yet the significance of sexual differentiation in Scripture and in human experience is broader than this. It is the elemental human differentiation, which marriage (and heterosexual relationships in general) declines to be overwhelmed by. "Homosexual practice cannot honor the creation of human life in the essential differentiation of male and female." It implies a "denial that the human being is good as God's creature in the polarity of being male and female." [215] For Paul in Romans 1:18-32 "the scriptures (notably Gen 2:18-25, Lev 18:22, and Lev 20:13) and creation itself establish heterosexual union as

---

[214]So, e.g., Gordon J. Wenham, "The Old Testament Attitude to Homosexuality," *ExpT* 102 (1990-91): 359-63. Donald J. Wold, *Out of Order* (Grand Rapids: Baker, 1998), pp. 43-61, concludes that "the categorical position of the Bible against homosexuality was apparently not assumed in Mesopotamia, Anatolia, or Egypt" but that we lack any evidence for Canaan (pp. 59, 60). See Martti Nissinen, *Homoeroticism in the Biblical World* (Minneapolis: Fortress, 1998); Phyllis A. Bird, "The Bible in Christian Ethical Deliberation concerning Homosexuality," in *Homosexuality, Science, and the "Plain Sense" of Scripture*, ed. David L. Balch (Grand Rapids: Eerdmans, 2000), pp. 142-76.

[215]Ulrich W. Mauser, "Creation and Human Sexuality in the New Testament," in *Biblical Ethics and Homosexuality*, ed. Robert L. Brawley (Louisville: Westminster John Knox, 1996), pp. 3-15; see p. 13. See further Christopher C. Roberts, *Creation and Covenant: The Significance of Sexual Difference in the Moral Theology of Marriage* (New York/London: T & T Clark, 2007). But elsewhere in *Biblical Ethics and Homosexuality* ("Textual Orientation," pp. 17-34; see pp. 26-27), Choon-Leong Seow disputes the appeal to Gen 1–2 in this connection.

the divine norm of creation."[216] On the other hand, Victor Paul Furnish argues that awareness that heterosexual relationships are typical of humanity no more excludes homosexual relationships than it excludes celibacy.[217] Frederick J. Gaiser asks whether Isaiah 56:1-8 provides a precedent for "overturning" an aspect of Torah in the way that Jesus also did.[218] One problem with this question is that this would seem to involve overturning the description of the way things were "at the beginning of creation" according to Genesis 1–2, not merely the way they are in the regulations that make allowance for our "hardness of hearts." [219]

Different Ways of Falling Short

Same-sex marriage parallels divorce/second marriage and polygamy in the way it falls short of the ideal that emerges from Genesis 1–2, that monogamous lifelong heterosexual marriage is the context for sexual activity. All fall short of that ideal at some point, and all might thus be reckoned to have parallel theological and moral status. If it is the case that many people are drawn by nature to other people of the same sex, this would not make a difference to that argument, any more than the fact that many people are drawn to have more than one partner of the opposite sex or drawn to have sex when they are not married. Indeed, the disciples were appalled by the demand Jesus placed in connection with divorce ("if we can't get divorced, it's better not to get married"!); "Jesus' words were, then, experienced as a provocation, an unwelcome revelation." But what we think is achievable "is not the measure with which human sexuality is discovered as God's creation."[220]

But it does become questionable why (for instance) the church in the West has taken a tough stance with regard to polygamy, and during the second half of the twentieth century came to take an easier stance with regard to divorce and remarriage, but to take a tougher stance with regard to homosexual activity. It seems likely that this is because churches are more aware of the many members or potential members who are divorced, that this accompanies an attitude of homophobia and a culturally imperialist attitude to polygamy,

---

[216]Charles H. Cosgrove, *Appealing to Scripture in Moral Debate* (Grand Rapids/Cambridge: Eerdmans, 2002), p. 39. See further Robert A. J. Gagnon, *The Bible and Homosexual Practice* (Nashville: Abingdon, 2001) for a systematic study of the biblical material that maintains this position.

[217]Victor Paul Furnish, "The Bible and Homosexuality," in *Homosexuality and the Church*, ed. Jeffrey S. Siker (Louisville: Westminster John Knox, 1994), pp. 18-35; see p. 23.

[218]Frederick J. Gaiser, "A New Word on Homosexuality?" *Word and World* 14 (1994): 280-93; see p. 288.

[219]As, indeed, Gaiser's earlier "Homosexuality and the Old Testament," *Word and World* 10 (1990): 161-64; see pp. 161-62, implies.

[220]Mauser, "Creation and Human Sexuality in the New Testament," p. 5.

and that both homosexuality and polygamy raise deep, unacknowledged and unresolved questions about order and taboo in the spirits of Christians.[221] In other contemporary contexts, people read Scripture through cultural lenses in which polygamy, brother-in-law marriage, and the despising and marginalizing of childless women are present reality, as they are in Deuteronomy.[222] Similar questions about differences in standards that reflect cultural contexts are then raised by the different stances that some African churches take to polygamy and homosexuality respectively. It would be more consistent to take a similar stance to all three ways of falling short of God's vision for sex and marriage. Judith Plaskow, while recognizing that Genesis 1 implies that heterosexual relationships are the norm, asks whether Genesis 3:16 suggests that "compulsory heterosexuality . . . appears under the sign and judgment of sinfulness."[223] Homosexuality is often seen simply as wickedness to berate. Could we rather see it in the context of the pain of human experience in the world under that sign?

4.3 Family

In Israel the household and the kin group provide the structures for life as a whole, including work, worship, teaching, discipline, generosity, hospitality and care for the stranger. Where people get into economic difficulties, the kin group has responsibility for helping the household to get through these. Its importance in these connections also means that the community needs ways of safeguarding its stability when it also becomes a place of conflict and oppression, particularly in connection with sex.

Definitions

Like marriage, and for overlapping reasons, family is a tricky subject to discuss. We might be inclined to assume we know what it is, but even if we do, it signifies something very different in Israel from what it signifies in Western society. Difficulties over terminology are again symbolic and confusing. The two key Hebrew terms are *mišpāḥâ* and *bayit* or *bêt ʾāb*, but they are used in varying ways in the First Testament, and both have been translated "extended family."[224] Insofar as they relate to each other, I refer to them as "kin group"

---

[221]Cf. Walter Brueggemann, *Theology of the Old Testament* (Minneapolis: Fortress, 1997), pp. 194-96.

[222]See Musimbi R. A. Kanyoro, "Biblical Hermeneutics," *RevExp* 94 (1996-97): 363-78.

[223]Judith Plaskow, *The Coming of Lilith* (Boston: Beacon, 2005), p. 202.

[224]Indeed, in the same volume: see Baruch A. Levine, "The Clan-Based Economy of Biblical Israel," in *Symbiosis, Symbolism, and the Power of the Past*, ed. W. G. Dever and S. Gitin (Winona Lake, Ind.: Eisenbrauns, 2003), pp. 445-53; see p. 447; H. G. M. Williamson, "The Family in Persian Period Judah," reporting the consensus view, pp. 469-85; see p. 472. Williamson himself later (p. 474) describes the household as an enlarged version of what

and "household." A kin group is a group of households tracing back their interrelationship to a common grandfather or great grandfather or ancestor; a group of kin groups then forms one of the twelve clans that comprise the people Israel. A kin group is the means whereby Israel looks after the long-term interests of the land and of the households that occupy it. A household (a cross between a nuclear family and an extended family) is the means whereby people's whole life is structured and organized, an arrangement for managing worship, teaching, work and property. In that connection it has direct responsibility for the land.[225] A household is not confined to people who are kin; it includes people such as servants and resident aliens (the English word *family* itself etymologically denotes a household of servants or *famili*).[226]

In Western thinking, when there is a married couple there is a household, because newly married couples commonly live on their own, though we might be more hesitant to refer to a married couple as a family. In the First Testament, it takes two generations to make a household. The term *bêt 'āb* (literally, a father's household) reflects the fact that marriage does not mean a man leaving his family; he stays in his father's household and his wife joins him there. They become one flesh in the sense that they come to belong to the same family, but they do not yet become a new family. As an adult with a staff of more than ten servants, Gideon is still part of his father's household; only at the end of his story is he described as going to his own household (Judg 6–8). Only when the father dies do a couple and their children become an independent household (perhaps not even then, depending on whether and how brothers divide the estate).

The problems of family in the Western world would not be solved if we simply tried to go back to the First Testament's pattern (though making home the basis of work would be a neat way of solving the problems on Los Angeles freeways). As in our own culture, in any case, there was not just one pattern, and the First Testament certainly does not imply that Israel got family right. (Every year as I teach Pentateuch I encounter students both horrified and encouraged by the dysfunctional nature of family life among Israel's heroes.) But travel broadens the mind. It enables us to look at our-

---

modern parlance calls a nuclear family, while S. Bendor sees a household as comprising several nuclear families (*The Social Structure of Ancient Israel* [Jerusalem: Simor, 1996]). See further Niels Peter Lemche, *Early Israel*, VTSup 37 (Leiden: Brill, 1985), pp. 245-59; Karel van der Toorn, *Family Religion in Babylonia, Syria and Israel* (Leiden/New York: Brill, 1996), pp. 194-205.

[225]On this social structure and the complexity of the nomenclature associated with it, see classically Gottwald, *The Tribes of Yahweh*, pp. 235-341, with Lemche's critique, *Early Israel*, pp. 245-74.

[226]Cf. Barth, *Church Dogmatics*, III/4:241.

selves with new eyes. It gives us another paradigm to think against, and a paradigm with particular weight for us because it comes from the Scriptures.[227] And Israel's model(s) do look as if (at least in theory) they managed some issues better than ours do.

The Household

A full-grown household might comprise a father and mother (who might be middle-aged by Western standards), their adult sons and their wives (perhaps in their twenties), and their children. These are the three generations of Exodus 20:5; if the household also includes aged grandparents, this comes to the four generations of that passage and implies the presence of other middle-aged couples, their adult sons and wives, and their children. Beyond the people who are family in this linear sense, the household may include widow(s) and orphan(s) from within the household or from the broader kin group, and servant(s) and employee(s) and resident alien(s) and a priest or Levite. (Almost) everyone in the community thus belongs in a household; conversely, while the core of the household is a group of people who are kin, normally a household is not confined to kin. A household will likely need to occupy several actual houses, and archaeological investigation of Israelite villages suggests that houses were built in clusters, though also that in some periods or in some areas, homesteads were located on the household's land.[228] One house might be big enough for something like a Western nuclear family, essentially comprising parents, two or three or four young offspring, and perhaps one or two of those persons who belong to the household in the broader sense. (Women might bear many more children than just suggested, but infant mortality was very high; in addition, exceptionally a man might have more than one wife and thus might have more children.)

Households of the size just envisaged, comprising several subgroups, are a practical unit in that they would make farming and domestic life more viable than it would be for a nuclear family on its own. But the stories of Abraham and Sarah, Isaac and Rebekah, and Jacob and his wives portray such households experiencing considerable conflict, like Western families. Brothers (Gen 4:9 implies) are supposed to look after each other, but there are pressures on them not to do so. Proverbs 6:16-19 sees the incitement of quarrels among brothers as the worst of a series of seven rather vicious wrongs; even if it sees it as only just as bad as those other wrongs, this still indicates that there was a problem here worth generating an aphorism about. Occupying

---

[227]See §1.2 "The Significance of Narrative" and §4.1 "Thinking Paradigmatically."

[228]Cf. Ferdinand E. Deist, *The Material Culture of the Bible* (Sheffield, U.K.: Sheffield Academic Press, 2000), p. 146; also Lawrence E. Stager, "The Archaeology of the Family in Ancient Israel," *Bulletin of the American Schools of Oriental Research* 260 (1985): 1-35.

several houses might help people cope with such conflict. Something like the nuclear family thus gave a degree of refuge from something like the extended family and vice versa.

Becoming a household was the first couple's implicit destiny from Eve's creation, but the point becomes explicit only with sadness when, before the first offspring have even been born, God speaks of the spoiling of the first household's life and relationships: "I will make very great your pain in pregnancy; in pain you will bear children" (Gen 3:16). Genesis does not here use the language for physical pain in giving birth (contrast passages such as Is 13:8; 26:17, which utilize the verb *ḥûl*). It is thus hardly suggesting that without human sin, giving birth might not have been painful physiologically (and it is difficult to see how that could ever have been so, given the nature of a woman's anatomy and physiology). It speaks first of the pain associated with pregnancy. This might suggest the pain of infertility and of the actions women take to make it possible for their husbands to have children, which the stories in Genesis illustrate. In the context of the words that follow about "desire" and "ruling," it might suggest the pain of the sexual relationship between a woman and her husband. In the context of Yhwh's subsequent words to Adam, which use the same word for pain (*yiṣṣābôn*) to refer to the pain or toil of Adam's work, it might suggest the hard work involved in pregnancy and birthing; women will bear many children, and that is hard work.[229] A little further on the verbs "get pregnant" and "bear" come in Genesis 4:1 as Eve gives birth to Cain, while subsequently "be in pain" describes Yhwh's feelings about human wrongdoing (Gen 6:6); in Genesis 4:1-8, too, the pain of motherhood is not just physical but emotional, the pain involved in watching your first son kill your second son.

Children

In the meantime, however, the inauguration of the first household is an occasion of joy. Eve's first baby is called Cain (*qayin*); she exclaims, "I have acquired [*qānâ*] a man with Yhwh" (Gen 4:1). She then has another child, Abel (*hebel*), but wisely refrains from pointing out that this name means "breath," the word that recurs in Qohelet to describe everything as a mere puff of wind. Presumably the name meant something else to Adam and Eve when they gave it to their second son, or perhaps like many English names (such as "John") people commonly used it without awareness of its etymology; it was just a name. The two boys grow and take complementary roles in making the household work; Abel looks after the animals, Cain the crops. The household

---

[229]Cf. Carol L. Meyers, "Gender Roles and Genesis 3: 16 Revisited," in *The Word of the Lord Shall Go Forth,* D. N. Freedman Festschrift, ed. Carol L. Meyers and M. O'Connor (Winona Lake, Ind.: Eisenbrauns, 1983), pp. 337-54 = *A Feminist Companion to Genesis,* pp. 118-41.

looks a functional Western family, with its two adults and two children. But two sons may quarrel, and eventually God comes between them, and the household ricochets from being raw material for a TV advertisement to being the epitome of dysfunction, with the parents standing back inactive like Adam while Eve was having her seminar with the serpent. Henceforth the household will be both the locus of the fulfillment of Yhwh's purpose and the locus of friction and disaster (see Noah's household, Terah's, Abraham's, Isaac's and Jacob's).[230]

In turn Cain starts a family, a household of his own because he has left home for different reasons than those implied by Genesis 2:24. Left with an empty nest and a lot of work, Adam and Eve bravely start again, and their son Seth has his own son Enosh, at last giving their household those regulation three generations. "Then people began to call in Yhwh's name" (Gen 4:26), to worship Yhwh or make their appeal to Yhwh for their needs or speak of Yhwh to other people. A relationship with Yhwh was a feature of this new household, perhaps a feature missing since Eve called in Yhwh's name when Cain was born, or since the two sons brought their offerings.

From the beginning, then, a marriage was designed to generate a household, initially to make it possible to fill the earth and serve the garden, then to make it possible to fulfill Yhwh's purpose to make Abraham a great nation such as will attract the world to Yhwh.

Not every marriage produced children. Sometimes women could not conceive, and presumably sometimes men were infertile. (Presumably Israelites noticed when a man's wife did not conceive and he took a second wife and she also did not conceive, and no doubt they worked out where the problem must lie, but perhaps they did not talk about that in public, and neither does the First Testament.) Sometimes having children implies an unjustified hopefulness for the future (Jer 16:1-4). Sometimes a determination to have children makes people go to desperate lengths that raise more questions than they answer (Gen 16; 19:30-38). In our own world, couples also may sometimes avoid having children because they have little hope for the future of the world, or think we have fulfilled the divine commission to fill the world, or like being on their own, or want to focus on other things, or cannot face the demands it will place on them. "Anthropologically, one of the greatest risks that human beings can undertake is the founding of a family," because the stakes and the potential for disappointment are so high.[231] Being willing to have children is an act of hope, not least of hope in

---

[230]Though the latter two may be seen as ultimately "stories of family reconciliations" (Wenham, *Story as Torah*, p. 37).

[231]Brigitte Berger and Peter L. Berger, *The War over the Family* (Garden City, N.Y.: Doubleday, 1983), p. 134.

ourselves; it implies "that we have something to pass on." By having children we contribute to a people.[232] One could say that it started this way, not least for someone like Eve.

God does not make it an invariable consequence of being married (that is, some people cannot have children), so we might not have to regard it as a categorical obligation, though a couple who avoid doing so would have to think hard about the reasons. Karl Barth asserts the "fact" that Genesis 1:28 was an unconditional command but ceases to be so after Christ (Who says this is a fact?), but also notes that avoiding having children means refusing "an offer of divine goodness, . . . a renunciation of the widening and enriching of married fellowship" made possible by the act of love.[233] Having an abortion would involve an overlapping set of theological questions; abortion was well-known in the ancient world,[234] so the fact that this possibility is not raised in the First Testament (even to be forbidden) suggests it was not thinkable in Israel.

A Whole Life Arrangement

Genesis 1–2 thus emphasizes the significance of children to the relationship between men and women. The reason there are human beings with this sexual differentiation is that this makes it possible for them to fill the earth. It is no good Adam being on his own (Gen 2 does not say he is lonely); Eve will be a help to him, by sharing in looking after the garden and enabling him to beget children who will do this.[235] In Genesis sex was created for the sake of procreation. In the Church of England Book of Common Prayer, marriage is ordained for the procreation of children, for sexual outlet for people who do not have the gift of continence and "for the mutual society, help, and comfort, that the one ought to have of the other." Genesis agrees that children come first, looks at sex a little more positively than the Book of Common Prayer (which is influenced by 1 Cor 7), but is rather less romantic about the friendship aspect to marriage. We have seen that, fortunately for romantics, the Song of Songs offers an understanding of men and women that values sex and relationships much more highly.[236]

---

[232]Stanley Hauerwas, *A Community of Character* (Notre Dame, Ind./London: University of Notre Dame, 1981), pp. 165, 172.

[233]Barth, *Church Dogmatics*, III/4:268, 269-70.

[234]See, e.g., Marten Stol, *Birth in Babylonia and the Bible* (Groningen: Styx, 2000), pp. 41-42; R. D. Biggs, "Conception, Contraception, and Abortion in Ancient Mesopotamia," in *Wisdom, Gods and Literature*, W. G. Lambert Festschrift, ed. A. R. George and I. L. Finkel (Winona Lake: Eisenbrauns, 2000), pp. 1-13.

[235]Cf. David J. A. Clines, *What Does Eve Do to Help?* JSOTSup 94 (Sheffield, U.K.: Sheffield Academic Press, 1990), pp. 25-48.

[236]See §4.2 "The Power of Love."

In traditional societies the household is "their basic functional unit."[237] It is close to being "a totalizing unit" whose members "would not only live together, socialize together, and worship together, but . . . would also work together, farm together, make tools and clothes together, and be dependent upon each other for their very survival."[238] The household is responsible for the entirety of its members' day-to-day life. It is the means of ensuring there is a place to shelter and sleep, and food to eat. To that end it looks after its plot of land, making sure it gets plowed and sown, crops get harvested, offerings get made, and grain gets stored for the next year. It negotiates marriages with people from other households, seeks redress when blood has been shed and exercises internal discipline over sexual conduct and other matters. The head of the household is also responsible for the protection of its members (Judg 6:30-31; 2 Sam 14:7). "The Israelite family was a community which shared life, dwelling place and belief to an extent and with an intensity that we in our atomized little remnant families can no longer imagine."[239] Given that it is not as natural to fathers to be involved in fathering as it is to mothers to be involved in mothering, the assumption of the "father-involved" family is significant.[240] The family's importance makes it not so surprising that Yhwh did not see to the preservation of the "Book of Yhwh's Wars" (Num 21:14) but that much of the First Testament comprises stories about families.[241]

The household's stability is key to the welfare of its members. When regulations in Deuteronomy put some constraints on patriarchy and thus work in favor of women, the reason they do so may be their concern for the household's stability. For its sake they affirm the hierarchical structure of the male-headed household,[242] though also for the sake of the stability of the household they limit the power of its head (e.g., Deut 21:15-17).[243] If the head of the household once had absolute power over it (Gen 31; 38),[244] Deuteronomy terminates

---

[237]David C. Hopkins, *The Highlands of Canaan* (Sheffield, U.K./Decatur, Ga.: Almond, 1985), p. 252.

[238]Berquist, *Controlling Corporeality*, p. 70.

[239]Gerstenberger, *Theologies in the Old Testament*, p. 25.

[240]Cf. John W. Miller, *Biblical Faith and Fathering* (Mahwah, N.J.: Paulist, 1989).

[241]Cf. David E. and Diana R. Garland, *Flawed Families in the Bible* (Grand Rapids: Brazos, 2007), p. 11.

[242]Esther Fuchs argues trenchantly that the biblical narratives are designed to serve a patriarchal agenda (*Sexual Politics in the Biblical Narrative*, JSOTSup 310 [Sheffield, U.K.: Sheffield Academic Press, 2000]).

[243]See Pressler, *View of Women Found in the Deuteronomic Family Laws*, e.g., pp. 1, 15-20, 93, 95-102. But Cheryl B. Anderson questions whether they really work in favor of women at all; subordinating women is a form of violence against women (*Women, Ideology, and Violence*, JSOTSup 394 [New York/London: T & T Clark, 2004], p. 101).

[244]Cf. Keith W. Whitelam, *The Just King*, JSOTSup 12 (Sheffield, U.K.: JSOT, 1979), pp. 40-41; but he notes that the evidence is very thin. Further, neither Gen 31 nor Gen 38 relates the actions of someone who is regarded as exactly a model head of a household.

it by making sexual conduct, murder and even filial disrespect matters of community concern.[245] In contrast, the household regulations in the New Testament epistles increase the authority of the master of the household. Not only are his children to obey him; so must his wife and his slaves (see, e.g., Col 3:18–4:1). Here the likely background is the desire to avoid giving the impression that the gospel was socially disruptive.[246]

A Worshiping Arrangement

As a totalizing unit the household is people's chief locus of worship and instruction.[247] It is in the context of the household that male babies and servants are circumcised and thus become part of the covenant community (Gen 17). Their circumcision affirms the covenant Yhwh made with Abraham and his household, both free and servant, both adults and children, both men and women (even though the latter are not circumcised),[248] both members of Abraham's physical family and foreigners. It declares the priority of Yhwh's promise and the possibility of living by it. Pesah reinforces this by relating how Yhwh brought the people out of Egypt in fulfillment of the promise, and Pesah is celebrated in the context of the household (Ex 12), again along with servants and resident aliens who have been circumcised and thus become members of the covenant community. The pilgrimage festivals of Shavuot and Sukkot too are celebrated in the company of sons and daughters, male and female servants, resident aliens, orphans, widows, and Levites (Deut 16:9-15). The household brings the offerings, tithes and firstlings to eat and rejoice before Yhwh (Deut 12:12, 18; 14:22-26; 15:19-20). It will be the household that is the natural context of prayer.[249] Calling in Yhwh's name (Gen 4:26) and teaching children to do so is a key feature of a household's life.

The household's celebrations are thus the context in which Israel tells the story of Yhwh's dealings with it. Moses imagines Israelite children at Pesah asking, "What is this service of yours?" and bids their father answer, "It is the Pesah sacrifice of Yhwh's, because he passed over the Israelites' households in

---

[245]Sivan, *Between Woman, Man and God*, pp. 15-16.

[246]See, e.g., James D. G. Dunn, "The Household Rules in the New Testament," in *The Family in Theological Perspective*, ed. Stephen C. Barton (Edinburgh: T & T Clark, 1996), pp. 43-63.

[247]On the actual practice of family religion as further indicated by archeological finds, see, e.g., Patrick D. Miller, *The Religion of Ancient Israel* (Louisville: Westminster John Knox/London: SPCK, 2000), pp. 62-76; van der Toorn, *From Her Cradle to Her Grave*, pp. 37-47; Stager, "The Archaeology of the Family in Ancient Israel."

[248]But on the gender significance of circumcision, see Lawrence A. Hoffman, *Covenant of Blood* (Chicago/London: University of Chicago Press, 1996).

[249]See Erhard S. Gerstenberger, *Der bittende Mensch* (Neukirchen: Neukirchener, 1980), pp. 153-60, 168-69; also Rainer Albertz, *Persönliche Frömmigkeit und offizielle Religion* (Stuttgart: Calwer, 1978), pp. 165-98.

Egypt when he hit the Egyptians, but rescued our households" (Ex 12:26-27). At the end of the week of eating flat bread, whether they ask or not, he is to point out that this is "because this is what Yhwh did for me when I left Egypt" (Ex 13:8). When they ask about giving the firstborn to Yhwh, he is to explain, "with strength of hand Yhwh enabled us to leave Egypt, the household of serfs, and when Pharaoh was too stubborn to let us go, Yhwh slew every first-born in the land of Egypt" (Ex 13:14-15). Joshua 4 assumes there will be some natural context when children will ask their parents the significance of twelve stones set up near Gilgal, and this will give parents opportunity to tell them how Israel as a whole crossed the Jordan on dry ground.[250] Quite generally, when Israelite children ask why Israel has all the requirements from Yhwh that it has on its life, the answer is, they emerge from the way Yhwh rescued us from Egypt and gave us the land (Deut 6:20-25).

The children ask about the regulations Yhwh gave *you*. Arguably Moses sidesteps the tricky question this raises, and encourages the parents to do so: they are to reply, *we* were serfs and Yhwh freed *us*, so now *we* must submit ourselves to these regulations. By implication the children are embraced by that, whether they like it or not. "Not with our ancestors/parents did Yhwh seal this covenant but with us, us here" (Deut 5:3). At the same time the Torah recognizes that people have to make their response and may decline to do so, as Israel's subsequent history makes clear.

It is a commonplace of postmodern thinking that our identity is story-shaped and is developed through our telling of our story. That is true of us as individuals, but it involves our story being part of a bigger story. Who we are as individuals is formed through our relationship with the story of our community, or rather communities.[251] Being human involves being a certain kind of person, someone characterized by a profile of virtues, but Scripture thinks of this in more than purely individual terms. And what we are as individuals depends for better or worse on the community in which we are nurtured. We are shaped first of all by the family community in which we live, work, learn and worship. And "the root of Jewish faith is . . . not a comprehension of ab-stract principles but an *inner attachment to sacred events*; to believe is to remem-ber, not merely to accept the truth of a set of dogmas."[252] The household cel-ebrations are the context in which the community's story is told, dramatized and sacramentally expressed, and thus shapes who people are; family life is the chief countercultural educational agent.

---

[250]See *OTT* 1:494.

[251]A classic early statement of what has become this commonplace is George W. Stroup, *The Promise of Narrative Theology* (Atlanta: Knox, 1981).

[252]Heschel, *God in Search of Man*, p. 213.

A Learning Arrangement

If many cultures have reckoned that "the chief means of moral education is the telling of stories,"[253] the First Testament's distinctive take on this assumption is that the stories concern God's acts more than human acts. This fits the view that "the moral life does not consist just in making one right decision after another; it is the progressive attempt to widen and clarify our vision of reality." It is "a way of attending to the world. It is learning 'to see' the world under the mode of the divine."[254] Telling the story in the context of the family plays a key role. But the implications of the stories do need spelling out. "The picture is that of a family continually in lively conversation about the meaning of their experience with God and God's expectations of them."[255] The Torah belongs to Israel as a whole; it is its naḥălâ and môrāšâ, like the land (Deut 33:4; Ps 119:111). On that basis the prophets can lambaste the people as a whole for abandoning it. And the family is the place where people are to receive their most systematic instruction in it.[256]

Parents thus have the task of teaching their children about Yhwh and Yhwh's expectations (Deut 6:7; cf. Deut 11:18-21), speaking of them at home and away, when going to bed and when getting up—in other words, all the time. Deuteronomy's regulations are to be repeated,[257] talked about and written on the doorposts of the house (Deut 6:7-9), literally or metaphorically. The household is to know what the regulations say. Parents are to make known to their children and their grandchildren, who with them comprise those three generations that make up a household, the things they saw at Horeb (Deut 4:9-10) so all three generations revere Yhwh (Deut 6:2). Conversely, parents are to be aware that if they make images (which could only happen if they put out of mind what they saw at Horeb), Yhwh will make terrible consequences abound for the children and the third generation, and even the fourth generation that comes about when

---

[253]Alasdair MacIntyre, *After Virtue*, 2nd ed. (Notre Dame, Ind.: University of Notre Dame Press, 1984), p. 114; cf. Paul Nelson, *Narrative and Morality* (University Park, Penn./London: Pennsylvania State University Press, 1987), for a critical discussion.

[254]Stanley Hauerwas, *Vision and Virtue* (Notre Dame, Ind.: Fides, 1974), pp. 44, 45-46, summarizing Iris Murdoch, "Against Dryness," in *Revisions*, ed. Stanley Hauerwas and Alasdair MacIntyre (Notre Dame, Ind./London: University of Notre Dame Press, 1983), pp. 43-50; cf. Nelson, *Narrative and Morality*, p. 119.

[255]Patrick D. Miller, *Deuteronomy* (Louisville: John Knox, 1990), p. 109. On Deuteronomy's stress on the home as a place for learning, see Edesio Sánchez, "Family in the Non-narrative Sections of the Pentateuch," in *Family in the Bible*, ed. Richard S. Hess and M. Daniel Carroll R. (Grand Rapids: Baker, 2003), pp. 32-58. And on the question whether the Bible is a suitable book for children to read, see Francis Landy, "Do We Want Our Children to Read This Book?" *Semeia* 77 (1997): 157-76.

[256]Cf. Moshe Greenberg, *Studies in the Bible and Jewish Thought* (Philadelphia: Jewish Publication Society, 1995), pp. 11-18.

[257]I take šānan piel here as a byform of šānâ (see *HALOT*) rather than a form from šānan "sharpen" (see BDB).

parents live long enough to see their great grandchildren (Deut 5:9). In a literal sense the questioners in Deuteronomy 6:20-25 might be small children, as they are in the Pesah service, but in Deuteronomy this teaching process stands for the passing on of Yhwh's truth from one generation to the next.

Adult children honor their parents even more profoundly than small children do by basing their life on the story of the exodus and on the obligations Yhwh laid on its beneficiaries. To honor one's parents thus means "to give them their due importance as teachers and counselors." That links with the promise that follows; "the parents convey to the children that knowledge and wisdom without the observance of which the dwelling of the people and therefore of these children in the land would be pointless and could have no permanence," and the children heed it. Proverbs can then be read as "a large-scale commentary on the fifth commandment."[258]

Thus Proverbs can take as the model for the relationship of teacher and student the relationship of parents and children (e.g., Prov 1:8, 10, 15); mentioning mother as well as father supports the idea that its references to parents teaching children have literal and not just metaphorical significance.[259] But Proverbs' more characteristic reference to father as the teacher further emphasizes the distinctive Israelite stress on the "father-involved" family.[260] So the grandfather-father-son relationship is key to the transmission of insight (Prov 4:3). And when that works, grandchildren are the glory of old men and parents are the glory of children (Prov 17:6). Proverbs begins by declaring that its teaching is for people who are already insightful and discerning, not only for the young and unformed (Prov 1:2-6); that is even more obviously true of the way Job and Qohelet encourage people to think through issues that occupy people more as they grow older.[261] The Wisdom tradition believes in lifelong learning.[262]

A Working Arrangement

Marriage and family are ways of making the practicalities of life work. We have noted that whereas the modern Western world stresses the relational and sexual aspect to marriage, marriage has usually been a way of arranging work matters and property matters; the notion of separate checkbooks and

---

[258]Barth, *Church Dogmatics,* III/4:244, 249.

[259]Cf. Tremper Longman, "Family in the Wisdom Literature," in *Family in the Bible,* ed. Richard S. Hess and M. Daniel Carroll R. (Grand Rapids: Baker, 2003), pp. 80-99; see p. 84.

[260]Cf. Miller, *Biblical Faith and Fathering,* pp. 79-85.

[261]I cannot resist repeating the saying that Solomon wrote the Song of Songs with the enthusiasm of youth, Proverbs with the wisdom of maturity, and Qohelet with the disillusion of old age (apparently based on *Song of Songs Rabbah* 1:1, §10).

[262]On the wisdom of the aged, see Rachel Z. Dulin, *A Crown of Glory: A Biblical View of Aging* (Mahwah, N.J.: Paulist, 1988), pp. 70-77.

separate work would seem strange to an Israelite. Genesis 1–2 fits with this. Humanity is created to subdue the earth and to serve the garden, and this is a major function of the household. It is a big enough unit to be able to undertake the tasks involved in making the farm work; its including servants, resident aliens and other employees links with that. This working aspect to the family is reflected in the Decalogue's requirement that the head of the household should free everyone to rest on the sabbath (Ex 20:8-11). This specifically includes servants, animals and resident aliens. All belong to the family, the working entity.

The Western assumption is that work and home are two separate worlds.[263] The nuclear family may spend leisure time together but it gives the most significant part of each day to activity unique to the individual family member in the company of a different grouping of people. Home and family are then a refuge from the toughness of the public world and the world of (paid) work (not to say school). Traditionally (that is, as we look back on the middle of the twentieth century), the Western family focused on children and the home is the wife's special domain. The relationships of the (nuclear) family make possible a meaningful human experience that compensates for the stresses and conflicts of the world of work. Toward the end of the twentieth century we might have seen that in terms of urbanization not only separating the world of work from that of home but perceiving the latter as the world of women and the former as that of men, and attributing greater value status to the former. This put men and women into bondage, though it was women who noticed their bondage and campaigned to be able to join the men in theirs. It was no answer to suggest that women should consider themselves lucky to be able to focus on a realm that brought fewer heart attacks, because that realm had little status and a small role when work and education had been taken from it.

In a traditional society such as Israel's it is in the context of the life and the work of the household that individuals find their significance, not least because it is the working unit. What the family does counts in a broad life-and-death way. No doubt this could be oppressive; if the work of the day generates conflict, there is no refuge from it. But women do have scope for responsibility and achievement in this connection. Whereas Euripides has one of Heracles' daughters commenting, "For a woman silence and discretion are best, and staying inside quietly at home,"[264] Proverbs 31:10-31 deconstructs the distinction between the public and the private sphere, declining to confine the

---

[263]See, e.g., Robert N. Bellah and others, *Habits of the Heart,* revised ed. (Berkeley/London: UCLA Press, 1996), pp. 85-112.

[264]*Heraclidae* 476, as translated in Exum, *Fragmented Women,* p. 42.

woman to the latter.[265] Charles Taylor contrasts the emphasis in Aristotelian ethics on contemplation and one's action as a citizen, the higher life of which ordinary life, family life, was merely the background, with the sense that ordinary life, family life, is the very center of the good life. Full human life is defined in terms of labor and production and of marriage and family life.[266] The First Testament affirms the latter.

Work as a Commodity

The point about work is not merely that it should be creative or fulfilling for the individual but that it is a way of serving the earth and serving other people.[267] Family is then the context in which human beings fulfill that creation commission and thus can be themselves, because work is integral to being human. In this sense the subjective aspect to work (what it means for workers) is as important as the objective aspect (the work done). Work is not "a special kind of 'merchandise,' or . . . an impersonal 'force' needed for production." Human work is not "solely an instrument of production" with capital "the basis, efficient factor and purpose of production"; that would be to deny "the principle of the priority of labour over capital." It would be to treat things as more important than people, and in this sense to be materialist.[268]

The change in understandings of labor is highlighted in John Paul II's encyclical *Centesimus annus*, marking the centenary of Leo XIII's encyclical *Rerum novarum*, a turning point in Roman Catholic social thought. That encyclical of 1891 had noted the radical changes that had come about in economics and society.

> A new form of *property* had appeared—capital; and a *new form of labour*—labour for wages, characterized by high rates of production which lacked due regard for sex, age or family situation, and were determined solely by efficiency, with a view to increasing profits.
>
> In this way labour became a commodity to be freely bought and sold on the market, its price determined by the law of supply and demand, without taking into account the bare minimum required for the support of the individual and his family. Moreover, the worker was not even sure of being able to sell "his own commodity", continually threatened as he was by unemployment, which,

---

[265]See Claudia V. Camp, *Wisdom and the Feminine in the Book of Proverbs* (Sheffield, U.K./ Decatur, Ga.: Almond, 1985).

[266]Charles Taylor, *Sources of the Self* (Cambridge, Mass.: Harvard University Press, 1989), pp. 13, 211-12.

[267]Stanley Hauerwas, *In Good Company* (Notre Dame, Ind./London: University of Notre Dame Press, 1997), p. 129, reflecting on the papal encyclical *Centesimus annus* <www.vatican.va/edocs/ENG0214/_INDEX.HTM>.

[268]Cf. John Paul II's encyclical *Laborem exercens* <www.vatican.va/edocs/ENG0217/_INDEX. HTM>, §§7, 8, 12. The last quotation is italicized.

in the absence of any kind of social security, meant the specter of death by starvation.[269]

Leo III himself noted that "it is neither just nor human so to grind men down with excessive labour as to stupefy their minds and wear out their bodies," and John Paul II added that things could hardly be said to have improved a century later.[270]

Children are part of the family work force, part of the household's resources. People would thus think about children in a very different way from that of Western society, which developed the notion of children's individuality and rights and of personal relationships with them ("the idea of childhood is one of the great inventions of the Renaissance").[271] The importance of children as resources may lie behind the assumption that Yhwh can make up for Job's loss of his first ten children by giving him ten more.[272] If a child gets injured before birth, the person responsible has to pay compensation to its father (Ex 21:22-25).[273] If a family gets into economic difficulty, the head of the household can sell the labor of his child, so that a boy can work for another household on their farm, and a girl can work in another house in anticipation of marriage within that household (Ex 21:7-11). Of course such practices were open to abuse, which the First Testament critiques (Lev 19:29; 2 Kings 4:1-7; Neh 5:1-5; Amos 2:6-7).

An Economic Arrangement

Many of the regulations in the Torah deal with the economic questions raised by marriage and family, as happens with Western marriage when couples decide whether to have joint checkbooks and credit cards, and joint ownership of property, how to allocate their assets to their dependents when they die, and what they will do with assets if the marriage breaks down.

The economic value of a wife means that a prospective husband may be expected to make a substantial gift to her father in recognition of the resource he is receiving. She will share with him in the work of the household and bear the children who will eventually add to the family labor force. But reference to such a marriage gift comes only three times, all in somewhat odd contexts (Gen 34:12; Ex 22:16-17 [MT 15-16]; 1 Sam 18:25),[274] and we do not know whether it seemed more like a payment or indemnity, or more like a bridal shower or

---

[269]*Centesimus annus* §4 <www.vatican.va/edocs/ENG0214/_INDEX.HTM>.
[270]*Centesimus annus* §§7, 8.
[271]Neil Postman, *Conscientious Objections* (New York: Knopf, 1988), p. 148, as quoted by James Francis, "Children and Childhood in the New Testament," in *The Family in Theological Perspective*, ed. Stephen C. Barton (Edinburgh: T & T Clark, 1996), pp. 65-85; see p. 66.
[272]Cf. Countryman's comments, *Dirt, Greed, and Sex*, pp. 149-50.
[273]If this is the passage's meaning; but see §4.4 "Managing Redress."
[274]See further §4.2 "A Shared Vocation."

a wedding gift list at a department store. It parallels these in being part of the social convention for establishing a marriage by the giving of goods. As well as receiving a marriage payment, the bride's family may send her off with a dowry, which could include servants and land as well as items such as jewelry, and comprises her share in the family inheritance. This will add to the sealing of the relationship between the families and to the resource she brings, and thus to the sealing of the marriage. At the same time her dowry remains in a sense hers, so that it gives her a measure of potential independence of her new family if she ever needs it. As long as she is married, her husband shares in its usefulness, but if she is widowed or divorced, it becomes her livelihood.[275]

Exodus 22:16-17 [MT 15-16] starts from the fact that if someone seduces a girl, he has made it less likely that someone else will want to marry her, so either the seducer must do so or he must compensate her father. We need not infer that the girl has no say in what happens.[276] Stories such as those of Isaac and Rebekah suggest that she could have a say, and this would then be one of the considerations that determined marriage or compensation, but the regulation in itself is not designed to handle those questions but to cover the economic considerations. The equivalent regulation in Deuteronomy 22:28-29 refers more explicitly to rape rather than seduction. It puts more pressure on the potential rapist (particularly the one for whom money is no object), and in a way thus offers the girl more protection than she would have if she simply becomes unmarriageable and threatened by either prostitution or destitution.[277] It requires the man both to pay compensation and to marry her, and in addition specifies that he could never divorce her; again presumably the girl and her father would have the right to decline the marriage. Likewise, a man who tries to divorce his wife fraudulently on the grounds that she was not a virgin has to pay compensation to her father as well as accepting a flogging (Deut 22:13-21).

Suppose a man had sold his daughter as a servant to another man on the understanding that she would in due course become his wife or his son's wife, or be redeemed and freed, or be pledged to another man as if she were her master's daughter. Then suppose another man has sex with her. That might well mean that neither the master nor his son nor the third man want to marry her. If she is not pledged to someone, the other man would have to marry her or pay her father the marriage payment (Ex 22:16-17 [MT 15-16]). If she is pledged to someone and thus is in effect married (Lev 19:20-22), the text

---

[275]Cf. Raymond Westbrook, *Property and the Family in Biblical Law,* JSOTSup 113 (Sheffield, U.K.: Sheffield Academic Press, 1991), pp. 142-64.

[276]Cf. 4.2 "Getting Married."

[277]Cf. Wright, *Old Testament Ethics for the People of God,* p. 332.

may again refer to some form of compensation, but it uses a word that comes only here, and translations differ.[278] But because she has not been redeemed or freed, in keeping with other Middle-Eastern laws neither the man nor the girl is to be put to death, perhaps because her status means their act is less of a threat to family life; she is in a half-way position between singleness and marriage, servanthood and freedom.

A Structure for Generosity and Hospitality

Centesimus annus declares that, "to overcome today's widespread individualistic mentality, what is required is *a concrete commitment to solidarity and charity*, beginning in the family."[279] Israel's understanding of the household is its key to care for widows, orphans, resident aliens and the poor in Israel,[280] and thereby to protecting widows and orphans from abuse (Ex 22:22-24 [MT 21-23]). It is thus the agent of hospitality (which does not imply a meal or an overnight bed but an ongoing life commitment). Admittedly, the exhortations and regulations concerning other forms of provision for the needy, such as gleaning, suggest that not all such people belonged to a household, and the position of Naomi and Ruth in Bethlehem looks rather different, as the practice of gleaning implied there looks rather different from that implied by the Torah.[281]

For Bildad, the essence of sin is for landed people to ignore the needs of people without land, whose position means they are poorer than oneself. If you have land to live on, you have a moral obligation to be generous to people who for some reason are not in that position, and to lend to them without imposing egregious conditions on the loan. If there are people lacking water and bread, it is your task to give and not withhold. If there are widows and orphans no longer within the family orbit of a landowner, your task is to give to them; Bildad speculates that Job has failed here (Job 22:6-9). Bildad thus understands wrongdoing in terms of omission rather than commission. It is not what we do but what we fail to do that makes us sinners. It is specifically the way we leave people in our community without the wherewithal for life. Isaiah 58:6-7 likewise critiques people for failing to share food, shelter and

---

[278]Hebrew etymology would suggest that the word, *biqqāret*, means "inquiry" (NRSV, DCH), but it is not clear why that should be mentioned. "Punishment" (TNIV, BDB) assumes that this is what the inquiry led to. "Indemnity" (JPSV, cf. HALOT) is based on a link with Akkadian *baqru*; it fits the context, but Jacob Milgrom (*Leviticus 17–22* [AB/New York: Doubleday, 2000], p. 1668) disputes the Akkadian argument.

[279]Centesimus annus §49.

[280]Cf. Leo G. Perdue, "The Israelite and Early Jewish Family," in Leo G. Perdue et al., *Families in Ancient Israel* (Louisville: Westminster John Knox, 1997), pp. 163-222; see pp. 171-72, 192-203.

[281]Cf. Deist, *Material Culture of the Bible*, p. 146.

clothing with other people who are flesh and blood like them. Job entirely agrees with Bildad, wishing only to sharpen the point, to wonder at the fact that God does nothing about it, to deny being guilty of such conduct and (backing up that denial) to call for calamity to fall on such wrongdoers (Job 24:1-25). His defensive review of his life includes the claim that he has not failed to share food and clothing with widow and orphan, and hospitality with the homeless and traveler (Job 31).

In passing, Genesis 18 tells us about an occasion when three men stand hovering by Abraham's tent where he is sitting at midday; Abraham instinctively gives them rest and refreshment, rather lavishly. Incidentally, too, Genesis 19 tells us about the way two of the three arrive at Sodom where Lot is sitting in the plaza at evening; Lot also instinctively gives them rest and refreshment, though the story then ricochets into horror. Even if he knows the men of Sodom will refuse his two daughters (it is the strangers they want to humiliate and rape), it illustrates how hopelessly Lot has been dragged down by his association with them. There is no indication that Lot is doing the right thing in light of a cultural commitment to hospitality that means he can hardly surrender his guests to the men of Sodom.[282] As is the case with Abraham's descent to Egypt, one decision has led to another, and a decision that seemed wisdom has become folly.

Family Discipline

You are to "honor your father and your mother, so that your days may be long on the ground that Yhwh your God is giving you" (Ex 20:12). "You are each one to revere his mother and his father" (Lev 19:3). Children are to do the opposite to striking or belittling their parents (Ex 21:15, 17; Lev 20:9). *Striking* does not refer to a casual slap (cf. Ex 21:12); the verb often implies killing (e.g., Ex 12:29; Lev 24:21), and "belittling" implies more than a casual insult, something like repudiation.[283] A concern for the proper honor of parents also underlies the expectation that sons should be responsive to their parents rather than being resistant and rebellious in relation to their exhortations to live sober and restrained lives (Deut 21:18-21).[284] The Decalogue reference to living long might imply encouraging a culture in which children care for their parents as they grow older, which will work in their own favor in due course (cf. Prov 19:26; 23:22-25; 28:24; 30:17).[285] Yet "honoring" and "revering" hardly focus on "car-

---

[282]Contrast the stance of commentators; cf. Rashkow, *Taboo or not Taboo*, pp. 104-6.

[283]Cf. Herbert C. Brichto, *The Problem of "Curse" in the Hebrew Bible*, rev. ed. (Philadelphia: Society of Biblical Literature, 1968), pp. 132-35.

[284]So Anselm C. Hagedorn, "Guarding the Parents' Honour," *JSOT* 88 (2000): 101-21. See also Elizabeth Bellefontaine, "Deuteronomy 21:18-21," *JSOT* 13 (1979): 13-31.

[285]On this, see J. Gordon Harris, *Biblical Perspectives on Aging* (Philadelphia: Fortress, 1987).

ing for,"[286] and the requirement to involve the elders and the whole community in the case of a wayward son (the son will be an adult) also implies that both the moral integrity and the stability of the household are important to the community.[287] This requirement does protect children from excessive punishment by their parents as well as protecting parents if family affairs get beyond them when they are doing their best to exercise discipline. Likewise, relating the promise about "living long" to the children in particular involves hypothesizing an ellipse, and on a more straightforward reading the promise links the long life of the whole community with the integrity of its households. The various regulations prescribing the death penalty for failing to honor one's parents have the same implication. The integrity of the household is key to the nation's integrity and its relationship with God; regulations relating to children and parents are "safeguards of the *national* well-being."[288] It is a mark of the society's collapse when sons, daughters and daughters-in-law dishonor or rise against fathers, mothers and mothers-in-law (Mic 7:6).

Part of Yhwh's purpose in "recognizing" Abraham is "so that he may command his children and his household after him to keep Yhwh's way by the faithful exercise of authority [*ṣĕdāqâ ûmišpāṭ]*" (Gen 18:19). Conversely, children are expected to walk in the ways of their parents, if those are good ways (1 Sam 8:3, 5). The head of the household is responsible for its discipline; he may pay a price if he does not exercise it effectively (1 Sam 2:22-34). That responsibility is explicit with regard to the observing of the sabbath, and implicit with regard to matters to do with debt servitude. One can imagine that he oversees arrangements for marriage, divorce, adoption and other aspects of what might be called family law, though there are no regulations in the Torah covering the regular process of these events, and that it would be his responsibility to deal with adultery on the part of one of his sons. Thus (negatively) the story in 2 Samuel 13 implicitly reports David's failure in not taking action when Amnon rapes Tamar. "A sensible son—the discipline of his father; the scoffer—he did not listen to rebuke" (Prov 13:1). It is in that context that physical discipline belongs (Prov 13:24); Proverbs' exhortation to the physical chastisement of children has been assumed to apply to small children, but its educational context in Proverbs suggests it rather relates to teenagers or young adults.

---

[286]Karel van der Toorn suggests that mother comes before father in Lev 19:3 because the verse refers to the obedience of small children to their mother, with whom they have most contact (*From Her Cradle to Her Grave* [Sheffield, U.K.: Sheffield Academic Press, 1994], pp. 27-28).

[287]Cf. Timothy M. Willis, *The Elders of the City* (Atlanta: Society of Biblical Literature, 2001), pp. 163-85.

[288]Wright, *God's People in God's Land*, p. 78.

The story of Noah and his sons provides a case study (Gen 9:20-27). Noah gets into a mess. He gets drunk, but perhaps had no reason to realize that this would be the consequence of his drinking grape juice that had been around for a while. No one has tried this before; things happen. The unexpected stumbling block put before Noah becomes an unexpected stumbling block put before his youngest son. He further compromises his father's honor rather than seeking to protect it; his brothers have the advantage of age and are better advised. Noah's eventual reaction is perhaps as bad as Ham's as he lays a curse on the boy. He will become the most menial servant to his own brothers. It foreshadows the only other concrete human curse in the First Testament, when Joshua curses some descendants of Ham to become servants in the sanctuary, consigned to chopping wood and fetching water for it (Josh 9:23). Meanwhile, Yhwh reclaims the right to curse and warns about human cursing (Gen 12:3). The First Testament tells no further comparable concrete stories of what dishonoring and honoring parents look like, yet perhaps the story nevertheless warns parents and children of the horrific consequences that can follow from parental misfortune, filial disdain and parental reaction. Or perhaps it warns parents and children that these things happen; deal with it.

Of course children may have to dissociate themselves from their parents (Ezek 20:18). Something has to happen when the head of the household ignores a regulation: for instance, by having sex with someone within it other than his wife or attempting to avoid treating his eldest son as his eldest (Deut 21:15-17). The regulation concerning brother-in-law marriage indicates that a woman could take such a matter to the elders (Deut 25:5-10);[289] perhaps this could happen over other matters if questions cannot be resolved within the household. Does Isaac have to let his father sacrifice him? Does a "dutiful daughter" have to let her father sacrifice her?[290] (I take it that Genesis 22 implies approval of the first but that Judges 11 implies disapproval of the second.)

Family and Church

The New Testament's attitude to the family moves in more than one direction in relation to the First Testament. The literal family becomes much less important. Even when one has allowed for the hyperbole in Jesus' declaration that being a disciple requires people to hate their family, the declaration implies a radical change in natural priorities. The church becomes the "household of faith," "the household of God" (Gal 6:10; 1 Pet 4:17). Whereas the First Testament household was the local embodiment of the people of God, now these

---

[289]The presupposition is thus that this arrangement is one that a widow will desire but the man in question may not; see Dvora E. Weisberg, "The Widow of Our Discontent," *JSOT* 28 (2004): 403-29. Cf. Gen 38.

[290]See Exum, *Fragmented Women*, p. 18.

two are separated. For the earliest Christians, "from baptism onwards, one's basic family consisted of one's fellow-Christians."[291] The First Testament, then, encourages us to a high view of the family; the New Testament bids us not overestimate its importance.

The first group of people who believed in the risen Jesus lived by expectations like those in the Torah, as the owners of property or land sold it and shared the proceeds with needy people within their groups (Acts 2:43-47; 4:32-37), but they soon found that this generated problems as well as solving them (Acts 5:1-11; 6:1). Christian faith did not involve living in community, as Israelite faith did, and when the first Christians sought to live in accordance with family-like assumptions, this led to conflict. They gave up the whole-life vision for family and community expressed in the First Testament. Nevertheless, given the New Testament's relativizing of the importance of the family and the collapse of the family in the West, this might be a model the church in the West needs to consider. The church might become the body that fulfills the vocation of the family for its members and thus draws the world toward a better way. This more "ecclesiocentric" approach to poverty[292] "provides the world with the means to know the substance of the good society."[293]

Insofar as the church declines to do that, it may be unlikely that Christians will be able instead by political means to fulfill aims fitting in with Scripture that it does want to affirm. John Howard Yoder tells a chilling story about attempts to end racially segregated housing in Evanston. Christian leaders were discussing how to lean on the city council in this connection until someone pointed out that most of the realtors and the sellers of houses were members of the churches. But preachers could not expect the members of their congregations to undertake open marketing unless they were compelled by the law. "Legislative implementation is only meaningful when it extrapolates or extends a commitment on the part of the Christian community which has already demonstrated the fruitfulness of that commitment." It follows that "the foremost political action of God is the calling and creation of his covenant people."[294]

---

[291]N. T. Wright, *The New Testament and the People of God* (London: SPCK/Minneapolis: Fortress, 1992), p. 190.

[292]See Ashley Woodiwiss, "Christian Economic Justice and the Impasse in Political Theory," in *Toward a Just and Caring Society*, ed. David P. Gushee (Grand Rapids: Baker, 1999), pp. 112-43; see pp. 141-43, following John Milbank, *Theology and Social Theory* (Oxford: Blackwell, 1990/Cambridge, Mass.: Blackwell, 1991).

[293]Stanley Hauerwas, *In Good Company* (Notre Dame, Ind./London: University of Notre Dame Press, 1995), p. 126

[294]John Howard Yoder, *For the Nations* (Grand Rapids/Cambridge: Eerdmans, 1997), pp. 188-89.

Kin Group and Land

Like many cultures and revolutionary movements over the centuries,[295] Israel assumes that you cannot own land. It is the starting point in part two of Jean-Jacques Rousseau's *Discourse on the Origin of Inequality*,[296] with its eventual polemic against the entire notion of property as the key cause of troubles between human beings. Other Middle-Eastern peoples also did not accept the principle of absolute ownership of land, which would make it possible to buy and sell it like any other commodity, but they then tended to focus control (and effectively ownership) of land in the monarchy. The jubilee regulation works against that, especially by its declaration that the land belongs to Yhwh.[297] The Torah seeks to make it impossible for the land to belong to the state or to the wealthy, though it does not succeed.

Yhwh's allocating the land to Israel to care for and live off makes Israelites like sharecroppers in relation to Yhwh. And in various ways the Torah requires them to express some recognition that the land belongs to Yhwh. That includes the offering of firstfruits and tithes, and the observance of a sabbath year; just as they are to work for only six days and keep off the seventh because it belongs to Yhwh, so they are to sow and harvest for only six years and keep off the seventh (Ex 23:10-11). Literally, they are to "let go" of the land, let it drop or sag or collapse *(šāmaṭ)*. The regulation may presuppose that all Israel observes the same sabbath year, though it does not make that specific. Nor does Leviticus 25:2-7, which neatly replaces *šāmaṭ* by a similar word with broader resonances: Israel must let the land stop or cease or observe a sabbath *(šabat)*. Translations speak of "rest," but the word denotes simply "cessation." The idea of rest for the land is suggestive for our attitude to getting the most out of land, but there is no indication in the Torah that the sabbath year is to benefit the land; Israelites anyway likely allowed their land to lie fallow more frequently than once every seven years.[298] The sabbath year is for Yhwh; 2 Chronicles 36:21 takes up that assumption in referring to the way the sabbath year had never been observed.

Exodus 23:10-11 does refer to the sabbath year opening up the possibility that the needy may eat from the land in this year (from what grows naturally, including vines and olives) and that wild animals may do so. It thereby

---

[295]See Tim Gorringe, *A Theology of the Built Environment* (Cambridge/New York: Cambridge University Press, 2002), pp. 65-72.

[296]Jean Jacques Rousseau, *Discourse on the Origin of Inequality* (Indianapolis: Hackett, 1992), p. 44.

[297]Cf. Jeffrey A. Fager, *Land Tenure and the Biblical Jubilee*, JSOTSup 155 (Sheffield, U.K.: Sheffield Academic Press, 1993), e.g., pp. 25-26, 86, 116-18; and the title of Norman C. Habel's study *The Land Is Mine* (Minneapolis: Fortress, 1995).

[298]On fallowing and related practices, see Hopkins, *Highlands of Canaan*, pp. 191-210.

links a religious instinct to a practice that could benefit the needy. Like the weekly sabbath, the sabbath year thus has more than one rationale, and the First Testament's way of thinking about land has implications for ecological ethics, but it does not work these out.[299] Its concern is both more down to earth and more religious. It is perhaps more surprising that the First Testament has little to say about the ethics of farming beyond one or two sayings on care for animals.[300]

The land is not just given to Israel as a whole but allocated to each of the twelve clans "for their kin groups" as their "possession" (e.g., Josh 13:24-31).[301] In Deuteronomy 33 and in Joshua, "the idea of possession of the whole land by the whole people is held to be expressed by the possession of the parts by the parts."[302] Joshua 13–19 describes this allocation in what might seem tedious detail, but it is this fact that generated property rights in Israel.[303] The kin group itself seems not then directly to control the land, unless some of it is community land, pasturage used by everyone, but distributes it to its households as their particular plot or "allocation." So the head of the household can speak of the land Yhwh has given *us*, but then give thanks for produce of the soil Yhwh has given *me* (Deut 26:9-10).

The clan's ongoing concern will be to ensure that its area of land stays among its households. Numbers 26:52-56 suggests that the allocation to the clans and the kin groups was made by lot but also in light of their size. Josephus assumes this took into account the value of different tracts of land—where one could plant grain and other crops, where one could grow olive trees and grape vines, and where it would be best to pasture flocks—though the First Testament does not say this.[304]

Household and Land

Land is central to a household's concerns because it is central to life. The reason land is a pivotal theme in the First Testament is not that land in itself is important. Land is important because food is important. The point about land is its being "the support- and supply system for the sustenance of human life."[305] If you have land, you can live; if you do not, you cannot, at least not

---

[299]See the comments in §4.1 "Thinking Exegetically."

[300]But see §6.3 "Relating to Animals."

[301]On the various "biblical land ideologies," see Habel, *Land Is Mine.*

[302]J. G. McConville, *God and Earthly Power,* LHBOTS 454 (New York/London: T & T Clark, 2006), pp. 115-16.

[303]Wright, *Old Testament Ethics for the People of God,* p. 89.

[304]Josephus *Antiquities* 5.1.21 [5.76-79]; cf. Shmuel Ahituv, "Land and Justice," in *Justice and Righteousness,* Benjamin Uffenheimer Festschrift, ed. Henning Graf Reventlow and Yair Hoffman, JSOTSup 137 (Sheffield, U.K.: Sheffield Academic Press, 1992), pp. 11-28.

[305]Cf. Rolf P. Knierim, *The Task of Old Testament Theology* (Grand Rapids/Cambridge: Eerd-

with any security. It is not by chance that land features in Yhwh's original promise to Abraham, and that this goes back to the way Genesis 1–2 speaks of the land (the *ʾereṣ* and the garden). "The man's primal vocation" is agricultural; "his very identity is bound up with the ground." Thus the Yahwist "cultivates an ethos from the ground up."[306]

When the head of a household dies, his sons may continue to live and work the plot of land as one unit, as is presupposed by the brother-in-law regulation (Deut 25:5-10). In enthusing about brothers living as one, Psalm 133 hints that they may find it hard to continue to do this. They may then opt to divide the household's land and property, so that each of them with their wife and children become separate households within the same *mišpāḥâ*, or together become a new *mišpāḥâ* (the daughters will likely have already married into new households). Indeed, a son may choose to leave his father's household and set up a separate one before his father dies, though he will not have a right to his share of the land at that point. Abraham leaves his father's household (Gen 12:1) with his wife, his adopted son and the people they had acquired in Haran to go to Canaan. They themselves count as a household (Gen 14:14; 15:2-3), though this household still sees itself as part of that one kin group, with other households (e.g., Gen 24:38-41), and it treats the kin group as the natural place to look for a husband or wife (Gen 24; 28–29). Generally, a person who flits from his home (literally, "his place") is like a bird that flits from its nest (Prov 27:8); there is hardly a verse in the Scriptures that contrasts more sharply with Western attitudes.

Women can inherit the household's land if their parents have no sons (Num 27:1-11). Other Middle-Eastern peoples allowed women to inherit;[307] but the societies that took this more egalitarian stance were more urbanized ones, not clan-based and land-based societies. Even in Numbers 27 the daughters receive the right to inherit only in order eventually to pass on the inheritance to their sons. The fundamental concern is with the kin group and clan and its land.[308] In that connection the Torah later makes a compromise over the women's rights, in order to keep the land in the clan; Zelophahad's daughters must marry within one of the clan's kin groups (Num 36). This would in any case be usual and would actually gives them more "choice" than women might usually have in marrying within their own kin group. The first new regulation (Num 27) recognizes their individual interests, though also their father's

mans, 1995), p. 234.

[306]Brown, *Ethos of the Cosmos*, pp. 220, 224.

[307]Zafrira Ben-Barak, "Inheritance by Daughters in the Ancient Near East," *Journal of Semitic Studies* 25 (1980): 22-34.

[308]Cf. Jacob Milgrom, *Numbers*, JPS Torah Commentary (Philadelphia: Jewish Publication Society, 1989), p. 482.

and their household's. The second (Num 36) recognizes the interests of the clan as a whole.[309]

The practice of brother-in-law marriage (Deut 25:5-10) offers another route to the same end. If a widow with no son marries someone else within the household and then has a son, the son counts as her husband's, his name is maintained over the relevant plot of land, and this keeps it in the household; it does not come to belong elsewhere through her marrying someone from another household.[310] Thus it would contribute to the viability of the household, to its having land to live by. The broader instinct to hold onto the land that one had received from one's ancestors (1 Kings 21:3) would have the same effect.

By Deuteronomy's rule Zelophahad's brother would marry his widow and beget a son who would count as Zelophahad's. Deuteronomy 25:5-10 does grudgingly recognize the brother's right to refuse to do this; it could be costly in one way or another. Further, a person such as Zelophahad might well be a widower or might have no brother. The story of Ruth likewise recognizes that the widow might be too old to have children, but it also tells of yet another way of achieving the same end. Her daughter-in-law stands in for her as potential mother of an heir, and Boaz undertakes the role of Elimelech's near relative when the nearest relative declines to do so. Their child thus becomes Naomi's and he maintains Ruth's first husband's name on his land and thereby maintains that household in existence. Pending that event, Naomi does seem at least to be in ultimate control of the land that had belonged to Elimelech and then to her sons, even if Elimelech and Naomi had already ceded it to someone else before the famine drove them to Moab. And this suggests we should not assume the economic vulnerability of a widow in regular circumstances.[311] The story also illustrates the difference between the legal position of widows (which can be poor) and their social status (which can be high).[312]

The Restorer

Suppose a household gets into economic difficulty. Perhaps its stretch of land is poor or poorly irrigated, or its members are not very good at farming, or lazy, or ill, or there is a drought, or its animals get sick or die, or an epidemic or fire destroys the crop. It may then fail to harvest enough grain

---

[309]Cf. Baruch A. Levine, *Numbers 21–36,* AB (New York: Doubleday, 2000), pp. 355-60.

[310]See, e.g., Westbrook, *Property and the Family in Biblical Law,* pp. 69-89. Sternberg in her *Kinship and Marriage in Genesis* sees the concern with marriage and kinship in Genesis as relating to inheritance of property and land.

[311]See Frank S. Frick, "Widows in the Hebrew Bible," in *A Feminist Companion to Exodus to Deuteronomy,* ed. Athalya Brenner (Sheffield, U.K.: Sheffield Academic Press, 1994), pp. 139-51.

[312]Cf. Deist, *Material Culture of the Bible,* pp. 263-65.

for the coming year and not have resources from previous years to take it through a bad year. Such hazards of farming in an area such as the hills of Judah and Ephraim can be exacerbated by political events. When Israel asked for stronger central government, Samuel warned them of the tax burden such government would bring them (1 Sam 8:10-17); the warning corresponds to the way things work out as David and Solomon develop a strong central administration. When Ephraim and Judah come under the control of the superpowers Assyria, Babylon and then Persia, this increases the tax burden on people (cf. Neh 5:1-13). The range of possible causes of calamity explains why poverty in the community is really inevitable (Deut 15:11; Mt 26:11).[313]

Strategies for dealing with poverty can vary, not least over whether one focuses on generating wealth or on equalizing wealth distribution. The First Testament implicitly questions whether these are alternatives. "You are not to hate your brother" (Lev 19:17); like love, hatred is not a mere emotion or attitude, but a practice. But the brothers of a poor man do hate him (Prov 19:7). Their heart sinks as they think about bailing him out, when they may be under pressure themselves. But it would be in the family's own interests to restore land that came to be leased to outsiders and to restore members who got into economic difficulty. In this situation, moral obligation rests specifically on his nearest relative, his "restorer" (*gōʾēl*, EVV "redeemer"; see Lev 25). If a householder would have to lease some of the family land in return for some grain, this restoring might mean paying off the debt so that the land stays within the kin group but is at least under the control of someone within it, or the land might be immediately restored to its household. The restorer is then to let his brother live with him as a brother and work like an employee, not like someone with the status of a debt servant, until the jubilee comes or until he has paid off the debt by his work. If the impoverished man has to sell himself to a resident alien as a debt servant, a member of his household or kin group ought to restore him so that he rather works for someone within the family.

In expounding its concern with people who become alienated from their land and developing its own vision, Leviticus 25 makes a link with Israel's awareness that Yhwh was the one who brought them out of Egypt and gave

---

[313]Cf. Judith Lingenfelter, "Why Do We Argue About How to Help the Poor?" *Missiology* 26 (1998): 155-66, building on the work of Michael Thompson, Richard Ellis and Aaron Wildavsky, *Culture Theory* (Boulder, Colo.: Westview, 1990). She notes that we cannot simply say that God is on the side of the poor, though that may be so when people's trouble is caused by the oppression of others; cf. Rodd, *Glimpses of a Strange Land*, pp. 161-84. On the vulnerability and hazards of farming in Canaan, see, e.g., Frank S. Frick, "Ecology, Agriculture and Patterns of Settlement," in *The World of Ancient Israel*, ed. R. E. Clements (Cambridge/New York: Cambridge University Press, 1989), pp. 67-93.

them the land (cf. Lev 25:38). It also links with the vision of the prophets and suggests how prophetic principle could be expressed as practical policy. It comes at the end of the "Holiness Teaching" beginning in Leviticus 19, a God-inspired dream of new foundations for Israel's life as a people and a new style of life for Israel, if God should give the people a chance to avoid exile or give them another chance after exile (see Lev 26). We might see Leviticus 19 and Leviticus 25 as framing this dream, with a wide-ranging program for personal ethics in Leviticus 19 in the form of an exposition of an ethos of neighborly life, and a program for social ethics in Leviticus 25 in the form of the establishment of some equality between rich and poor through the sabbath ordinance.[314]

Such a near relative is also responsible to act as restorer by taking redress on behalf of a member when blood has been shed. The kin group thus constitutes a general support structure for the household, a "protective association" of households.[315] One might reckon that it was as Lot's restorer that Abraham set off with his posse to rescue Lot when taken captive by the confederate kings (Gen 14). That vision of how things should work is thrown into relief by a consideration of how things could be in practice, illustrated by the story in Ruth. Perhaps because everyone is affected by famine and people cannot help one another, Elimelech is so helpless to provide for his household that they move to Moab, though the subsequent story in Ruth also illustrates the way the kin group could care for its weak.[316]

Keeping the Land in the Family

Suppose a household has no one to act as restorer; perhaps the resources of the other households in the kin group are stretched, or perhaps no one is willing to take the action required (perhaps they know why it has got into such trouble). And suppose a household from another kin group is prepared to support it and by doing so gains control of the household's land; the household thus leases its land to this other party and become sharecroppers on their own land. Over a period of time households could in effect lose their land permanently; they could never find a way of paying their debts and regaining it if no one from their kin group took action on their behalf. Middle-Eastern kings therefore sometimes (particularly on accession) declared the cancellation of debts so that debt serfs were freed and land reverted to the

---

[314]So Otto, *Theologische Ethik des Alten Testaments*, pp. 243-56.

[315]So Gottwald, *Tribes of Yahweh*, pp. 257-67. He then takes the genealogical linkage between the households as a fiction to express the kin group's unity. Contrast Bendor, *Social Structure of Ancient Israel*, pp. 82-86.

[316]Katherine Doob Sakenfeld entitles her study of Ruth and Naomi "Economic Survival and Family Values" (*Just Wives?* [Louisville/London: Westminster John Knox, 2003], p. 27).

household that owned it.[317] Possibly Zedekiah's edict described in Jeremiah 34:8-22 is an example of a Judean king doing the same thing. Jeremiah makes a link with the sabbath year regulation, which had evidently not been implemented, though Zedekiah's action was a once-off event and not part of a regular practice. Indeed, people perhaps went beyond what that regulation required, since they released *all* their servants. It may have been a purely selfish gesture, if siege conditions made it cost more to feed servants than people gained through having them. Or it may have been a gesture of obedience to see if it would lead Yhwh to bring about the relieving of the siege.

Either way, the release was short-lived. Perhaps Zedekiah's action was unpopular with the middle-class people who had made loans or enjoyed the free labor of the servants who would be released, and perhaps the king yielded to their pressure. The servants were soon back in their servitude. People "have turned back and profaned my name" in going back on the covenant sealed before Yhwh and subjugating these people as their servants again. "You have not obeyed me by proclaiming release to your kinfolk and neighbors" (Jer 34:16, 17). Yhwh's expectation is that they treat other people as members of the family and members of the community, but instead they treat them as possessions to be disposed of and reappropriated as it suits their bank balance, in the manner of employers laying off workers and then reemploying them with lower wages. In making the mistake of appearing before Yhwh to seal a commitment to put this right and then going back on that, they had also further profaned Yhwh's name by behaving as if they could solemnly invoke Yhwh and then break their word.

The jubilee would be a more systematic version of such an occasional practice. In Leviticus 25, the sabbath year is thus to be complemented by a jubilee year, once every forty-nine years; it is described in Scripture only here. (It is also mentioned briefly in Leviticus 27:16-25 and Numbers 36:4.) "Jubilee" comes from the Hebrew word for the blowing of a horn (*yôbēl*), the signal that this year was starting (Lev 25:9-10). The jubilee involved "proclaiming release" (*dĕrôr*), the expression in Jeremiah 34 for what was supposed to happen in the seventh year (cf. also Ezek 46:17; it is not clear whether Ezekiel is referring to sabbath or jubilee). Recognizing that sometimes people are driven to lease land outside their kin group, the regulation stipulates that this must not be allowed to continue indefinitely. It offers an alternative approach to the same issues as Exodus 21–23 and Deuteronomy 15 but focuses more on the preservation of the household and its land than on the individual, who is

---

[317]See, e.g., Westbrook, *Property and the Family in Biblical Law*, pp. 44-50; Jacob Milgrom, *Leviticus 23–27*, AB (New York: Doubleday, 2001), pp. 2167-69; Moshe Weinfeld, *Social Justice in Ancient Israel and in the Ancient Near East* (Philadelphia: Fortress, 1995).

unlikely to be helped much by a release that happens every forty-nine years.[318] In this situation the land is the household's collateral; it pays the loan in full, by working on it over the years until the jubilee, when its land returns to its control. In working out how much he is prepared to loan, presumably the lender will take into account the number of years until the jubilee (cf. Lev 25:16). But presumably a lender and debtor could negotiate for a shorter period. What the jubilee did was make sure land did not permanently fall out of a household's control.[319] In the jubilee year the allocation of the land among the kin groups was to go back to square one.

Leviticus recognizes that human selfishness means people would resist the jubilee principle. They would be tempted to try to make a profit out of other people's need. Not coveting your neighbor's house might refer to not having your eye on the land that his household occupies (cf. Is 5:8; Mic 2:1-2).[320] The jubilee regulations constitute the fullest exposition of the Tenth Commandment.[321] They are an expression of *mišpāṭ* (and of *ṣĕdāqâ*) even though this expression does not occur.[322] People would not want to lend money if they were not going to be able to make their profit, and they would try to get around the regulations. Leviticus 25 thus remind them to keep God in mind, to "revere God."

The Jubilee Vision

As there is no reference to Israel observing the sabbath year (with 2 Chron 36:21 implying they did not), so there is no indication that the jubilee year was ever implemented.[323] As with other provisions in the Torah that did not find implementation in Israel's life, this may indicate not that people were being disobedient but that they knew this was a vision rather than a policy. While the Torah includes regulations that look designed for quasi-legal literal implementation, other material looks more like concrete embodiments of a style of life. We would miss the point if we took them legally; we might fulfill the law's letter but not its visionary demand. Seeing the jubilee regulation in this way helps us handle the fact that as a "law" it would have its disadvantages:

---

[318]Cf. Tigay, *Deuteronomy*, p. 467.

[319]Cf. E. Calvin Beisner, *Prosperity and Poverty* (Westchester, Ill.: Crossway, 1988), pp. 62-65; Wright, *God's People in God's Land*, pp. 119-28, 176-80.

[320]So Marvin V. Chaney, " 'You Shall Not Covet Your Neighbor's House,' " *Pacific Theological Review* 15/2 (1982): 3-13.

[321]Walter Brueggemann, *Old Testament Theology: Essays on Structure, Theme, and Text* (Minneapolis: Fortress, 1992), p. 128.

[322]Mignon R. Jacobs, "Parameters of Justice," *Ex auditu* 22 (2006): 133-57; see p. 133.

[323]On this question, see, e.g., Robert Gnuse, "Jubilee Legislation in Leviticus," *Biblical Theology Bulletin* 15 (1985): 43-48. For the treatment of jubilee here, see John Goldingay, "Jubilee Tithe," *Transformation* 19 (2002): 198-205.

for instance, it could end up penalizing the hard-working and rewarding the lazy. Further, while the jubilee regulation tries to think through the practical outworking of the vision, takes account of the perspective of lender as well as borrower and recognizes that the value of the "lease" on land will diminish as the jubilee draws near, one cannot see how some of its requirements could be implemented. "Whether it was practiced or not, however, there the provision sits in the text, the culminating assertion of the God of Sinai (who is the God of the Exodus, who intends a very different regimen of social wealth and social power)."[324]

The problems the jubilee vision was designed to handle appear in Nehemiah 5:1-13. Moses' teaching about lending was being ignored in the context of pressures issuing from the failure of harvests and the demands of taxation made by a foreign government. Those have forced people to borrow money against the surety of their land, their children's freedom and their own freedom. Even if they regain their freedom in the seventh year, they are unlikely to be able to regain self-sufficiency as a household if they have lost their land. They will never be able to escape the poverty trap. Nehemiah insists that the well-off return property and land, and cease foreclosing (or charging interest) on loans. There is no reference to the jubilee, but it is a jubilee-vision that Nehemiah implements.

There were other occasions in scriptural times when people took the jubilee vision and applied it in fresh ways in their context.[325] In Isaiah 61:1-3 the speaker testifies to having been called by God "to proclaim release to captives." This is the one other place where that word *release* comes in the First Testament. The captives are the people of Judah, oppressed and depressed as a result of the devastation of Jerusalem and the decimation of its population. The whole people and the whole land are in a position like that of individuals who have become impoverished through bad harvests and have lost their land or freedom, and the chapter applies the "release" image to them. Second, the Qumran Melchizedek prophecy (11QMelchizedek) explicitly puts together Leviticus 25, Deuteronomy 15, Isaiah 61 and other passages and promises that in the last days (which the Qumran community believed were imminent) people will be released from their sins. Third, Luke 4 tells of Jesus following the Qumran prophecy in declaring that the last days have arrived; he is bringing about another embodiment of the ministry described in Isaiah 61. The context of his ministry suggests that the "release" of which he speaks is release from illness, demonic oppression and guilt.

---

[324]Brueggemann, *Theology of the Old Testament*, p. 190; the first two clauses are italicized.

[325]On the texts noted here and other instances of jubilee thinking in a broader sense see John S. Bergsma, *The Jubilee from Leviticus to Qumran*, VTSup 115 (Leiden/Boston: Brill, 2005).

The image of a special occasion when release is proclaimed is thus capable of being applied to different contexts when believers of vision see people in bondage and see this is God's moment for their release.[326] The Jubilee 2000 movement perceived the new millennium as another such moment. It saw that jubilee was not essentially eschatological or "spiritual" or Christological. The indebtedness of Two-thirds World countries puts them into another form of bondage, different from that in Leviticus, Nehemiah, Isaiah, 11QMelchizedek and Luke. The visionaries who gave birth to the Jubilee 2000 idea invited people to hear God calling us to see here another way the image of "release" can be realized in the world. The question of applying the jubilee vision outside the people of God would not arise for Israel, but it would arise in the context of the relationship of rich nations and poor nations. The jubilee once again puts some things back to square one rather than leaving people permanently oppressed by debts from which they can never recover. It gives people a new start.[327]

A Place of Conflict, Oppression, New Starts and Forgiveness

The story of Adam and Eve's family starts with jealousy and conflict between their adult sons, and with murder (Gen 4:1-16). The story of Isaac and Rebekah's family starts with rivalry and conflict between their sons in the womb, and goes on to deceit and intended murder; it also involves conflict between father and mother (Gen 25:19-28; 27:1-45). The story of Jacob's family starts with love and hatred and goes on to intended murder and actual selling into servitude; it also involves grief for the deceived father (Gen 37). Among Jacob's first four sons, Reuben has sex with one of his father's secondary wives, Simeon and Levi antagonize their father by slaughtering the men of Shechem, and Judah fails his daughter-in-law, unwittingly has sex with her, and is exposed by her. Psychoanalytic and anthropological insight suggests that conflict is built into the relationships of fathers and sons and the relationships of brothers.[328]

By no means do all these stories have Hollywood endings, but neither do they have us leaving the movie theater totally depressed.[329] While the cry of Abel's blood is not quenched and the story is allusive in its account of Cain,

---

[326]For examples over the centuries since the New Testament, see Hans Ucko, ed., *The Jubilee Challenge* (Geneva: World Council of Churches, 1997).

[327]But David Jobling critiques Jubilee 2000's too consensual hermeneutic of Lev 25 ("Daniel Patte's 'Tripolar Model' for Critical Biblical Studies," in *Reading Communities Reading Scripture*, Daniel Patte Festschrift, ed. Gary A. Phillips and Nicole Wilkinson Duran [Harrisburg, Penn.: Trinity, 2002], pp. 147-57). Cf. also Norman K. Gottwald's questions in "The Biblical Jubilee: In Whose Interests?" in *The Jubilee Challenge*, ed. Hans Ucko (Geneva: World Counicl of Churches, 1997), pp. 33-40.

[328]Cf. Devora Steinmetz, *From Father to Son* (Louisville: Westminster John Knox, 1991).

[329]See further §6.1 "Peaceableness and Forgiveness."

Adam and Eve do get a new start. Esau and Jacob find reconciliation and appear together for the last time burying their father. There is some ongoing ambiguity about the way Joseph relates to his brothers, which rather suggests he has not forgotten the way they treated him even though he says God has made him forget all his suffering and all his father's household, in making him fruitful in the land of his weakness (Gen 41:51-52). But his brothers come to beg his forgiveness, and he bids them not be afraid. He is not God. Does he mean redress is God's business? More explicitly, he takes into account the way God has worked through the brothers' action in keeping the family alive. The reality of his acceptance of them is expressed in the way he commits himself to providing for them (Gen 50:19-21).

Moses' relationship with his marital family is somewhat ambiguous. He was apparently content to settle down with Jethro, but when Yhwh summoned him to get back to Egypt to begin the process that will deliver Israel from Egypt, Yhwh makes no mention of his family and initially Moses seems to assume that he will leave Zipporah and their sons behind (Ex 4:18). But then he actually takes them. For Moses, "family concerns and vocation seem to be kept apart. . . . They remain compartmentalized in his thinking"[330] He only half-recognizes that his commitment to his adopted family and his yielding to his vocation stand in tension. Whether the object of Yhwh's attack is then Moses or his son, the attack constitutes a wake-up call. The uncircumcised state of Moses' son says something about the ambiguity of his family's relationship with Yhwh. The whole family is threatened by Yhwh's attack, but the person who takes the needed decisive action is Moses' Midianite wife. The family became one in its identity as she "charted her family's future"; "the involvement of Zipporah and her son in Moses' divine call shows the importance of the family in vocational and life choices."[331]

In Judges, as the stories develop and the scene becomes bleaker, the family becomes increasingly a locus of conflict and oppression. Abimelech kills seventy brothers. Jephthah is prepared to make his daughter into a sacrifice to Yhwh. A man surrenders his wife to gang rape and death. And the other clans determine to take action against their Benjaminite "brothers" (Judg 20:13), to great slaughter on both sides, the virtual elimination of the Benjaminite "brothers" and then a horrifying aftermath.[332] Second Chronicles 28:8, 11 likewise expresses disdain at the Ephraimites capturing 200,000 of their "brothers."

---

[330]Gorospe, *Narrative and Identity*, pp. 185, 186.

[331]Gorospe, *Narrative and Identity*, pp. 308, 309.

[332]See, e.g., Trible, *Texts of Terror*; Koala Jones-Warsaw, "Toward a Womanist Hermeneutic," in *A Feminist Companion to Judges*, ed. Athalya Brenner (Sheffield, U.K.: Sheffield Academic Press, 1993), pp. 172-86; Lapsley, *Whispering the Word*, pp. 35-67.

Constraints on Sexual Relationships in the Household

The Torah assumes that sexual activity is not merely private, "between consenting adults"; it has societal implications.[333] Many of Yhwh's expectations with regard to sexuality focus on the integrity and stability of the family.[334] As well as forbidding a man to "expose the nakedness of" another man's wife (that is, have sex with her), it forbids sex and therefore marriage with anyone within the household, such as one's mother, sister, step-sister, daughter-in-law or step-daughter, or with one's wife's sister during one's wife's lifetime (Lev 18:6-18). Although some of these prohibitions would presuppose that the woman's first husband (for instance, the man's father or son) had already died or that the couple in question had divorced, the forbidden sexual activity still involves "sexual bids for power" that are reckoned to be socially disruptive, "dangerous for the accepted social order and therefore morally and ideologically deviant."[335] The brother-in-law marriage requirement (Deut 25:5-10) may be an exception to these regulations, on the basis of its sharing their concern for the stability of the household. It might also be seen as an expression of the tenth commandment, hindering a man from declining to undertake his obligation through covetousness because he stands to lose, as Onan and the man who refuses to marry Ruth apparently recognize (Gen 38:9; Ruth 4).[336]

We have noted that the Torah implies disapproval of extramarital relations between single people and of prostitution, but does not make an issue of these, even though they were presumably more common than sex with one's mother-in-law. The regulations in Leviticus 18 perhaps presuppose that incest was prevalent in Israel, as it is in modern Western societies, and seek to outlaw it. It is surprising that sexual relationships between father and daughter are not mentioned, though they would be covered by the opening general ban on a man having a sexual relationship with "the flesh of his flesh," which applies more directly to his daughter, mother and sister than to the other relationships that are listed.[337] But Middle-Eastern laws

---

[333]See Tikva Frymer-Kensky, "Law and Philosophy: The Case of Sex in the Bible," *Semeia* 45 (1989): 89-102.

[334]Cf. Gerstenberger, *Theologies in the Old Testament*, pp. 69-71.

[335]Athalya Brenner, "On Incest," in *A Feminist Companion to Exodus to Deuteronomy*, ed. Athalya Brenner (Sheffield, U.K.: Sheffield Academic Press, 1994), pp. 113-38; see p. 134. Cf. Madeline Gay McClenney-Sadler, *Recovering the Daughter's Nakedness*, LHBOTS 476 (New York/London: T & T Clark, 2007).

[336]So Michael D. Matlock, "Obeying the First Part of the Tenth Commandment," *JSOT* 31 (2007): 295-310; cf. Tigay, *Deuteronomy*, pp. 232-33.

[337]Cf. Susan Rattray, "Marriage Rules, Kinship Terms and Family Structure in the Bible," in *Society of Biblical Literature 1987 Seminar Papers*, SBLSP 26 (Atlanta: Scholars, 1987): 537-44; see p. 542. The mother is explicitly mentioned in v. 7, but the word order ("your father's nakedness, yes your mother's nakedness, you shall not expose") suggests that the reason is to make the point that sex with her is banned also because it is "tantamount to having

often fail to state things that can be taken for granted.[338]

The framework to these regulations (Lev 18:1-5, 24-30) implies that they require people to behave differently from the Egyptians and the Canaanites, the people's former masters and the land's former occupants. Marriages involving some of these unions were indeed familiar in Egypt, but they were also familiar among Israel's forebears and in Israel in David's day, and we do not have evidence that all were practiced in Egypt or Canaan or that Egyptians and Canaanites in general undertook such unions or that these were distinctively immoral societies.[339] Perhaps the framework's point is that in a more general sense Israel needs to distance itself from the societies on either side of where it is in its history at this point, at Sinai, or perhaps it takes up hints in Genesis that when the ancestors indulged in many of these relationships, they did so under the influence of Egyptians and Canaanites.[340]

These practices would make Israel taboo (Lev 18:24-30). The notion of taboo is a metaphysical one rather than a moral one,[341] but the power of the notion of taboo makes it a useful adjunct to moral thinking. Forbidden sexual relationships make people taboo, and on a large scale that would make the land where they live taboo. That may make it necessary for the land to escape its taboo, which it does by vomiting out its inhabitants. The land of Canaan did that to the Canaanites; it will do it in turn to the Israelites if they take on the same behavior patterns. (Leviticus 26 subsequently speaks of this happening through Yhwh's direct action and through the action of enemies, as the Torah also describes the process whereby the Canaanites lost the land.)

For the Sake of the Household, the Women and the Man

In Leviticus 18:6 the reason for the prohibition on sex and marriage within the household is that these women are a man's "own flesh," literally "the flesh of your flesh" (but the text uses two different words for flesh, šĕʾēr and bāśār), "your closest flesh." The inclusion of, for instance, one's daughter-in-law shows that the concern is not about relationships with blood relatives but with people who already live together. Unions between half-siblings are also forbidden, while unions between cousins are allowed; the concern is not with eugenics. Passing down the land through families encouraged marriage within the kin group, to keep the land within the broader family (again, com-

---

sex with one's father" (Milgrom, *Leviticus 17–22*, p. 1537). Likewise the sister is explicitly mentioned in v. 9 in order to make clear that the ban applies to half-sisters.

[338]Cf. David Daube, *The Deed and the Doer* (West Conshohocken, Penn.: Templeton Foundation, 2008), pp. 16-17.

[339]See §4.2 "Same-sex Unions."

[340]Cf. Calum M. Carmichael, *The Spirit of Biblical Law* (Athens/London: University of Georgia Press, 1996), pp. 62-82.

[341]On taboo, see §6.2-4.

pare the story of Ruth). The regulations against incest safeguarded against that issuing in marriages within the household.[342] Coming to belong to the same household means people become the same flesh and blood, as close as people born within the same household. They become "one flesh" (Gen 2:24). A girl becomes not merely a daughter-in-law but a daughter.

As a whole, in different ways these rules serve the interests of the man, the women and the family as a whole. Whether or not it was their intent, they would "protect the Israelites, especially women, against what they perceived as the great vices of the era." Single women, divorced women and widows cannot be taken over sexually by another member of the family, especially its head; they can marry outside the family or stay single within the family.[343] Heroes such as Abraham, Jacob, Judah and Reuben were involved in unions forbidden here; this would make it especially important to establish that Yhwh forbad them. For girls, one act of sexual indulgence because she loves a boy can mean lasting sorrow and shame, whether she aborts the baby or has it and keeps it or has it and gives it away. So there is a case for protecting them.[344] The difficulty of a girl's resisting the advances of her father strengthens that case.

At the same time the first two rules (Lev 18:7-8) express a concern for the honor of the father.[345] Further, the account of the sanctions on illicit sex in Leviticus 20:9-21 begins with the penalty for belittling a parent, which points to the regulations' concern with safeguarding the household.[346] A father who honors the household and thus respects these bounds for sexual activity avoids destabilizing family relationships and safeguards the household, like people who honor their parents.

The link between sexual activity and the stability of the family (and thus of the broader structure of society) is also one key element in the background when the prophets use the imagery of sex and marriage in speaking of Yhwh and Israel. Their strategy is to play on male fantasies and fears of women's sexuality, and in that connection they appeal to cultural stereotypes about women. They do not take up the way husbands and wives were supposed to be or even the way they actually were, but the way they might be in the fantasies playing inside the heads of the prophets' male hearers. Communicating

---

[342]Cf. Levine, *Leviticus*, p. 254.

[343]Jacob Milgrom, *Leviticus* (Minneapolis: Fortress, 1994), p. 193 and pp. 195-96, comparing Jonathan R. Zeskind, "The Missing Daughter in Leviticus xviii," *VT* 46 (1996): pp. 125-30.

[344]Caitlin Flanagan, "Sex and the Teenage Girl," *New York Times*, January 13, 2008, p. WK 13.

[345]Plaskow, *Coming of Lilith*, p. 168.

[346]Indeed, Jonathan P. Burnside argues that vv. 9-16 are a spelling out of the nature of honoring one's parents ("Strange Flesh," *JSOT* 30 [2006]: 387-420).

in this way raises questions for readers who see the potential of this talk to validate the downgrading of women and violence toward them;[347] this is their strategy for getting their hearers to see themselves the way Yhwh sees them. On the other hand, when the First Testament's family patterns look instructive and make us feel wistful, usually we cannot simply imitate them; we need to formulate analogous "structures of grace," structures for implementing compassion.[348]

Foreigners and Migrants

There are millions of stateless people in the world.[349] Most lack access to resources, redress for abuses, schooling, health care, property ownership or a place to call home. Within the United States there are several million undocumented aliens. In most nations the main body of its people has a sense of really belonging, but a minority knows it does not fully belong. So it was with Israel. Such people may have come to the country as traders and may be well-off; Leviticus 25:47-49 refers to such foreigners being able to take on Israelites who needed to become servants because of debt. But they may have come because of famine or other economic reasons, like Elimelech and Naomi, or because they were fleeing servitude, like Hagar, or because of displacement through war, like people who fled to neighboring countries before or after the fall of Ephraim or Judah. Among the prophets, Jeremiah and Ezekiel especially refer to migrants (e.g., Jer 7:6; Ezek 22:7, 29), reflecting the social chaos brought about by the Assyrian and Babylonian invasions.

In the First Testament, migrants in any of these circumstances might be foreigners, but they might be Israelites who went to live in another clan's area (cf. 2 Chron 30:25).[350] Individuals may become de facto resident aliens because they have had to give up their land through debt (Lev 25:35) or for some other reason (cf. Judg 19:16; 2 Sam 4:3; 2 Chron 15:9; Jer 43:5). Levites had to reside as aliens wherever they could (Judg 17:7-9). It is the privilege and delight of Israelites to sojourn like resident aliens in Yhwh's house (Ps 15:1; 61:4 [MT 5]); and it is Moab's privilege to seek refuge as resident aliens on Zion too (Is 16:4). Indeed in the world we are all resident aliens and sojourners, people whose lives on earth pass like a shadow (Ps 39:12 [MT 13]; 119:19; 1 Chron 29:15). That sense might resonate concretely in the Second Temple community, back in the

---

[347]See, e.g., Renita J. Weems, *Battered Love* (Minneapolis: Fortress, 1995), pp. 41-42, 130.

[348]John Rogerson, "The Family and Structures of Grace in the Old Testament," in *The Family in Theological Perspective*, ed. Stephen C. Barton (Edinburgh: T & T Clark, 1996), pp. 25-42; see p. 41.

[349]The *New York Times* of April 8, 2007, reported a figure of fifteen million.

[350]For this emphasis, see Christoph Bultmann, *Der Fremde im antiken Juda* (Göttingen: Vandenhoeck, 1992).

land but living like serfs there (Neh 9:36-37). (Even more extraordinarily, Yhwh can be like a mere passing alien in the land: Jeremiah 14:8.)

Migrants are subject to and protected by the same laws and regulations as Israelites (e.g., Lev 24:22; Num 35:15). They can bring offerings and make expiatory sacrifices (Num 15:14-16, 27-29) and can take part in Pesah, but they must be circumcised in order to do so (Ex 12:48-49; cf. Num 9:14). They then become "like" natives of the land, though they do not seem to *become* natives.[351] They do not have to be circumcised to share in Shavuot and Sukkot, which were not so centrally festivals celebrating Yhwh's acts in delivering Israel.[352] Nor are they forbidden to eat animals that have died a natural death (Deut 14:21). The logic is likely that such an animal has not had its blood drained (cf. Deut 12:16, 23; 15:23). Like other rules about what can be eaten, this rule is concerned not with hygiene or health but with religion: it relates to Israel's being a people holy to Yhwh. The markers of Israelite distinctiveness do not apply to resident aliens and foreigners, so they can eat such animals. On the other hand, there is a difference between resident aliens and other foreigners. Israelites are to *give* the animal to the former, whereas they may *sell* it to the latter.[353] Resident aliens are people who have become part of the community because need has driven them here. Foreigners are temporary residents such as merchants or diplomats who do not need charity.[354] One might compare the position of many migrants and aliens in the United States, who include tenured professors of Old Testament who have taxation but no representation.

Caring for the Migrant

So "the alien is a *virtual* native, alike but different."[355] Uriah is still "the Hittite," Obed-edom is still "the Gittite," but "the alien can become an Israelite to all intents and purposes," benefiting from the same privileges and subject to the same obligations, on the basis of having gone through the same experience as Israel itself did.[356] Like full Israelites they may not offer their children to Molek (Lev 20:2). And if they act high-handedly and thus revile Yhwh, vio-

---

[351]Milgrom presses the point that a *gēr* never becomes in the full sense an Israelite: see *Leviticus 17–22*, pp. 1493-1501.

[352]Christiana Van Houten, *The Alien in Israelite Law*, JSOTSup 107 (Sheffield, U.K.: Sheffield Academic Press 1991), pp. 87-91.

[353]Van Houten, *Alien in Israelite Law*, p. 80-83.

[354]Cf. Patrick D. Miller, "Israel as Host to Strangers," in *Israelite Religion and Biblical Theology*, JSOTSup 267 (Sheffield, U.K.: Sheffield Academic Press, 2000), pp. 548-71; see pp. 549-53.

[355]Brown, *Ethos of the Cosmos*, p. 115.

[356]J. G. McConville, "'Fellow Citizens,'" in *Reading the Law*, J. G. Wenham Festschrift, ed. J. G. McConville and Karl Möller, LHBOTS 461 (New York/London: T & T Clark, 2007), pp. 10-32; see p. 23.

lating Yhwh's teaching, they will be cut off from Yhwh's people, the same as natives; which implies that there is a sense in which they belong to this people (Num 15:30-31).[357] Ezekiel 47:22-23 pushes the logic of that further in its vision for aliens being "like" natives in a new sense: if they have had children (which implies they really are permanent settlers) they will be able to possess land within the area of the clan where they live, in the same way as natives. It is a revolutionary new idea, like the vision in Isaiah 14:1; 56:7.

Pending such a revolution, however, resident aliens do not possess land on which to grow food to eat, so they are always vulnerable. Their vulnerability is increased by their having no kin group, no one to stand by them or stand for them (no *gōʾēl*). They live in this community; they are not just passing through. But they were not born here and are not sure they will die here. In practice they may be in the same position as the poor, though they are in a different position in the sense that they are not people who once had land but have become impoverished and lost it.[358] They are marginal to the society and belong more with widows and orphans in being vulnerable.

Israel started off as aliens in Canaan, then became aliens in Egypt. Only with their establishment in a dominant position in Canaan did they become people with land. They then become a people with resident aliens in their midst, who can work only as employees of someone who does have land, or in state service (for instance, Uriah was a member of David's army and Ebed-Melech was on the king's staff, while 1 Chron 22:2 refers to the temple laborers as resident aliens), or as traders in goods such as spices or precious stones (the standard Hebrew word for a trader is the word for a Canaanite), or in providing other services (for instance, Rahab perhaps continued as an innkeeper).

People who simply worked as employees were particularly vulnerable, and therefore the society was expected to care for them. While concern for the poor, the widow and the orphan is a regular feature of Middle-Eastern law, concern for the migrant is distinctive to Israel.[359] If Israelites care for the migrant, it will be an expression of their mind being circumcised, in light of Yhwh's character and of their own experience in Egypt (Deut 10:16-19). Such care for migrants is the first quality mentioned after their self-circumcision, as if to recognize that giving care for migrants does not come naturally. It might be aided by the reminder that Israelites in general should continue to view themselves as migrants and sojourners with Yhwh, because the land actually belongs to Yhwh (Lev 25:23). The Rechabites modeled that attitude

---

[357]See further van Houten, *Alien in Israelite Law*, pp. 138-57.

[358]Cf. van Houten, *Alien in Israelite Law*, p. 95, noting that Leviticus thus treats the alien with the poor, while Deuteronomy distinguishes them; she refers to an unpublished paper by Norbert Lohfink.

[359]So Milgrom, *Leviticus*, p. 225.

for the people as a whole (Jer 35:7). They are not to wrong migrants but to treat them as members of the community and care for them (Lev 19:33-34). The appeal to the fact that they know what it is like to be a migrant backs up the command not to wrong or oppress a migrant (Ex 22:21 [MT 20]; 23:9); it is the most prominent piece of argument that Exodus 21–23 offers for observing its injunctions. The repetition perhaps links with the fact that the context of the second injunction suggests it refers to fair treatment in the courts.[360] To underline the point, Israelites are not to reject an Egyptian (that is, one who wants to live in Israel), because they had been resident aliens in his land (Deut 23:7 [MT 8]). Someone who oppresses a migrant has forgotten or has never understood the nature of their own story and thus their own identity, and certainly cannot tell anyone else about it.[361]

4.4 Community

Although the First Testament literature was doubtless produced in the city and reflects city life, Israel was "an agrarian society,"[362] and for the vast majority of Israelites their community was the village where they had their homes as they worked the farmland surrounding it. But both for village and city, the First Testament is concerned to maintain a "good neighborhood"; the commandments aim at "securing the common good."[363] Scripture has an "intense vocation of community formation."[364] One reason this matters is that as well as being shaped by our family, we are formed by the broader community in which we live, work, learn and worship, which shapes our attitudes, beliefs and values,[365] as is true of a community such as Southern California where Christians and others often do not think community is a reality but are deeply shaped by their cultural community.[366]

In the First Testament the community needs to be one where people live in

---

[360]See van Houten, *Alien in Israelite Law*, p. 55.

[361]Cf. Brad J. Kallenberg, "Positioning MacIntyre Within Christian Ethics," in *Virtues and Practices in the Christian Tradition*, ed. Nancey Murphy et al. (Harrisburg, Penn.: Trinity, 1997), pp. 45-81; see p. 61, summarizing the work of Stanley Hauerwas.

[362]Hopkins, *Highlands of Canaan*, p. 15. Cf. Douglas A. Knight, "Village Law and the Book of the Covenant," in *"A Wise and Discerning Mind,"* Burke O. Long Festschrift, ed. Saul M. Olyan and Robert C. Culley (Providence, R.I.: Brown University Press, 2000), pp. 163-79; see p. 163.

[363]Cf. Patrick D. Miller, *The Way of the Lord* (Grand Rapids/Cambridge: Eerdmans, 2007), pp. 51-67, 145-53.

[364]Bruce C. Birch and Larry L. Rasmussen, *Bible and Ethics in the Christian Life*, rev. ed. (Minneapolis: Augsburg Press, 1989), p. 34.

[365]Cf. Stanley J. Grenz, "Ecclesiology," in *The Cambridge Companion to Postmodern Theology*, ed. Kevin J. Vanhoozer (Cambridge/New York: Cambridge University Press, 2003), pp. 252-68; see p. 255.

[366]Cf. Rodd, *Glimpses of a Strange Land*, p. 274.

proper relationships with one another, support one another when they get into difficulties, handle property questions, resolve conflicts and deal with wrongdoing in their midst.

The Village

As it takes several related households to comprise a kin group, so it might take several related kin groups to make up a village—though conversely a large kin group might live in several villages, or a kin group might be identical with a village. Indeed, the word *mišpāḥâ* can be used loosely to refer to a village itself. (It can also refer to a clan and even to a nation, as in Genesis 12:3.) So kin groups could come to be identified with a geographical location where their land was, and conversely geographical locations could be known by the name of the kin group that lived there. Bethlehem, Kiriat-jearim and Tekoa are the names of the heads of kin groups as well as the names of places (1 Chron 2:50-54; 4:5). A *mišpāḥâ* might thus be more a socio-economic than a kinship unit, or might be a socioeconomic unit that agrees to assume kinship ties.[367]

In the centuries before the monarchy and after the exile, the village's heyday, the average Israelite village might comprise fifty to two hundred people.[368] It would be the means of achieving tasks requiring resources beyond those of the household (and possibly kin group), such as ensuring water supply and irrigation, constructing terraces for fruit trees and maintaining the threshing floor.[369] The other members of the village are one's "neighbors" (*rēʿîm*), fellows or fellow citizens; the rarer word *ʿămîtîm* makes a nice link with *ʿam* ("people" in the sense of nation). The Torah can also speak of them as "brothers," even though they are not members of the same household or kin group. (Deuteronomy 22:2 alludes to a brother you do not know.) Anyone in the Israelite community is a brother or sister; the entire people is a family writ large. (This usage is often not apparent from NRSV or TNIV when they paraphrase in order to be gender-inclusive.)[370] All four words (*rēʿîm, ʿămîtîm, ʿam, ʾāḥ*), come together in Leviticus 19:15-18.

Household and kin group have "natural," that is traditional and accepted, ways of structuring themselves, with the senior male in the household as its

---

[367]Cf. Pamela Barmash, *Homicide in the Biblical World* (Cambridge/New York: Cambridge University Press, 2005), pp. 26-27.

[368]See Carol Meyers, "The Family in Early Israel," in Leo G. Perdue et al., *Families in Ancient Israel* (Louisville: Westminster John Knox, 1997), pp. 1-47; see p. 12; also Stager, "The Archaeology of the Family in Ancient Israel."

[369]See Hopkins, *Highlands of Canaan*.

[370]See further Walter Houston, "'You Shall Open Your Hand to Your Needy Brother,'" in *The Bible in Ethics*, ed. John W. Rogerson et al, JSOTSup 207 (Sheffield, U.K.: Sheffield Academic Press, 1995), pp. 296-314.

head. This means there is no danger of anarchy in the family; the land will get farmed and the family will have something to eat. The village or town has an analogous and related structure; its elders, the heads of households meeting together (a "squirearchy")[371] exercise governance within it and responsibility for it. This provides another reason for the importance of safeguarding the position of the heads of the household.[372] This conservative understanding of structure in the community is presupposed by Job's reflection on his past in Job 29 (cf. Job 31). Some people have more power, status and resources than others, and have a paternalistic role in relation to them. This is underlined by Job's dismissive description of the homeless social outcasts who have come to look down on him, which reverses the previous arrangement whereby he would have looked down on them (Job 30:1-8). Job, and implicitly the book, accepts the way society is and works within it. Job and his servants were equally made by God in their mother's womb, but this does not make him question an arrangement whereby he is master and other members of his household are servants (Job 31:13-15).[373] Positively, it means the community is "a society of hierarchies of status, but also of reciprocal obligation" whose societal ideal involves needy people getting looked after as the haves share with the have-nots.[374]

We know from archaeological finds and from the First Testament's references to *bāmôt*, the so-called "high places," that local communities or groups of local communities were a focus for worship, and one can see that people might feel the need for a place of worship that was shared with more people than the immediate family but did not involve pilgrimage to a central sanctuary some days' journey away. A number of narratives refer quite positively to celebrations at such sanctuaries (e.g., 1 Sam 9; 16; 20:6). But the First Testament offers little by way of direct positive evaluation of these or instruction for them; the worship it directly endorses is that of the family and the whole people.

Neighborliness

The word *neighbor* comes in densest concentration in Exodus 20–22. Indeed,

> the dominant impression one gets from the Book of the Covenant about what it means to be a man in its society is that as a man one is not essentially an individual, a self-determining moral agent, but rather a member of a band of "neigh-

---

[371]Oliver O'Donovan, *The Desire of the Nations* (Cambridge/New York: Cambridge University Press, 1996), p. 59.

[372]Phyllis A. Bird notes that the victims of poverty and oppression are regularly spoken of as male, even though women must also have suffered from poverty and oppression (*Missing Persons and Mistaken Identities* [Minneapolis: Fortress, 1997], pp. 67-78).

[373]Clines makes the point trenchantly in *Interested Parties*, pp. 122-44, esp. pp. 125-28.

[374]Mark Hamilton, "Job 29–31 and Traditional Authority," *JSOT* 32 (2007): 69-89; see p. 74.

bours," . . . something like a band of brothers, but without the implication of kinship. . . . There is barely a whiff of social hierarchy here.[375]

Neighbors include rich and poor, thieves and bribe-givers, feckless and irresponsible, unneighborly neighbors, but they are still neighbors. They are expected to look out for each other, maintaining a fair system for solving problems and resolving conflicts.

Psalm 144:12-15 expresses a longing that the whole community should have enough—indeed plenty—and that none should cry out in distress, and Psalm 112 suggests the dynamic whereby this comes about. Its foundation is commitment to Yhwh; in relation to other people, the good life involves doing right by other people in the community, which expresses itself in graciousness and compassion. People who live this good life then find that they enjoy a good life, as Jesus will also assume (Mt 5:5; 6:33; cf. 2 Cor 9:9-11). They see their children flourish and see themselves having regard. They enjoy wealth. Its blessing then lies in what it enables them to do for other people. The morally good life and the good life we enjoy turn out to overlap: graciousness and compassion are a blessing to the givers as well as to the receivers. Sharing possessions is "the mandate and symbol of faith": a clenched hand "manifests and makes real our closure against God and the world," while an open hand "reveals and makes actual our availability to God and the world."[376] Thus Psalm 41 declares a blessing on people who care about the powerless, feeble and insignificant rather than despising them. The poor are to be enabled to keep their self-respect, the guilty are not to be punished to excess and thereby belittled or degraded (Deut 25:1-3), and the aged are to be accorded esteem and honor (Lev 19:32). Conversely, there are things that are "not done" or are "abominations" in our community, and could mean we lose our proper place in it.[377] Honor and shame are thus influential buttresses for ethical concerns. People do the right thing and are honored; they do the wrong thing and are objects of opprobrium.[378]

Living properly with one's neighbors involves respect (Prov 11:12; 14:21), sexual faithfulness (Lev 18:20), fairness (Lev 19:15-16) and honesty (Ex 20:16; Lev 6:1-5 [MT 5:20-24]; 19:11, 13; Deut 19:14; 23:24-25 [MT 25-26]; Prov 3:27-29; 11:9). This can include confrontation (Lev 19:17), but no taking of personal redress (Lev 19:18). There is to be no belittling of the deaf or tripping up the

---

[375]David J. A. Clines, "Being a Man in the Book of the Covenant," in *Reading the Law*, J. G. Wenham Festschrift, ed. J. G. McConville and Karl Möller, LHBOTS 461 (London/New York: Continuum, 2007), pp. 3-9; see p. 4; and see what follows there for the lines that follow here.

[376]Johnson, *Sharing Possessions*, pp. 79, 109.

[377]On the idea of what "is not done," see Rodd, *Glimpses of a Strange Land*, pp. 44-47.

[378]See further §6.1 "Independence and Honor," "Honor and Shame."

blind (Lev 19:14). In fact, there is to be love: "You are to care for your neighbor as yourself; I am Yhwh" (Lev 19:18; cf. Prov 17:17). The exhortation to care for someone else "as yourself" is not concerned incidentally to encourage self-care, to get us to care about ourselves; the Torah knows that we naturally do so, even if in practice our self-love is counterproductive and more like self-hatred in its effect.[379] If anything, it makes our instinctive concern for ourselves a model for our concern for other people.

All this spells out what it means to treat fellow members of the community as if they are members of the same family (Lev 25:14). This logic appears most systematically in Deuteronomy, where the members of the local community are regularly portrayed as brothers: while the people indebted to a person are neighbors, they are brothers, as are people whose animals stray or get into trouble or even people being punished (Deut 1:16; 15:1-12; 22:1-4; 23:19-20 [MT 21-22]; 24:14; 25:3). Even Edomites are to be treated as brothers, though they cannot yet be admitted to the community (Deut 2:2-8; 23:7-8 [8-9]). This requirement is illustrated by Jesus' story about the Samaritan who went out of his way to help a Jew who had been mugged; caring about one's neighbor does not observe ethnic or religious boundaries.

The Psalter's vision is for a community that rejoices with the joyful and weeps with the weepers (Ps 34:3 [MT 4]; 35:13-14). It is through the exercise of such reciprocal obligation that people find the significance, sense of worth and affirmation that modern cultures associate with the workplace.[380] The story of Elisha and a woman in Shunem opens a delightful window on an Israelite community at its best. When Elisha wonders whether he can mediate with the authorities in some way for this woman who has cared for him, she tells him that "I live in the midst of my people" (2 Kings 4:13). Her community provides her with the protection she needs. (She does not refer to the focus of grief in her life, which it transpires Elisha could do something about.) Care for one's neighbor is further illustrated by Boaz as he goes well beyond the Torah's minimal requirements when Ruth comes to glean, in response to the way Ruth has gone well beyond the Torah's expectations (which did not bind her) in her commitment to Naomi.

Friendship

Etymologically, *rēaʿ* suggests that your "neighbor" is your friend, someone you associate with and spend time with (*rāʿâ*). While the family is vital, relationships with people outside the family are vital in their own way. Whereas

---

[379]See, e.g., Karl Barth, *Church Dogmatics* (Edinburgh: T & T Clark, 1970), I/2:387-88, 450-53; Milgrom, *Leviticus 17–22*, pp. 1655-56.

[380]Cf. Carol A. Newsom, "The Book of Job," *The New Interpreter's Bible* (Nashville: Abingdon, 1996), 4:317-637; see p. 541.

Western society stresses individual initiative and responsibility, Proverbs emphasizes the importance of talking things through with other people; "arrogance only issues in strife, but there is insight with people who take counsel" (Prov 13:10; 15:22). It knows that our friends shape us. "Someone who walks with the sensible becomes sensible, while the companion of fools suffers harm" (Prov 13:20). This saying involves a nice paronomasia, as "companion" is another word from *rāʿâ*, while "suffers harm" comes from *rāʿaʿ*, and underlines the inner link between this second, unwise form of companionship and its results.

The paronomasia in Proverbs 13:20 may reappear in Proverbs 18:24, resulting in some ambiguity in the first colon, but the sense is clear enough: "there is a friend who sticks closer than a brother." Friend is here *ʾōhēb*, someone who cares about you, and *sticks* is the verb describing a man in relation to a woman in Genesis 2:24. I take Proverbs 18:24 to disambiguate Proverbs 17:17, "A friend cares at all times, but [as] a brother he is born for adversity." Whereas in isolation the second colon could imply that "blood is thicker than water,"[381] that seems to contradict the first colon, which says that a friend (here *rēaʿ*) cares (*ʾāhēb* again) at all times, not just in the good times. So it makes better sense to take the friend and the brother to be the same person; a friend is like a brother. The second colon then heightens the first. A friend or brother cares about you at all times, but is especially important in the bad times. Thus "Do not abandon your friend and your father's friend, do not go to your brother's house in the time when disaster comes to you; a neighbor nearby is better than a brother far away" (Prov 27:10). Here the friend and the brother are different people, and the saying envisages a disaster happening when you live far away from your family. At this point as at many, Proverbs will be assuming an urban setting, in which people are more likely to live away from their kin group. On such occasions friendship is very important.

The two great First Testament friendships are Naomi and Ruth and David and Jonathan, though neither is straightforward. While Ruth loved Naomi, the women of Bethlehem recognized that arguably she did so more as a member of Naomi's family than as a friend (Ruth 4:15). But the death of their menfolk in effect dissolved the family relationship between them; it was then the natural thing for Ruth to go back to her original family, so her decision to commit herself to Naomi involved a free act of allegiance a little like that of friendship. When David killed Goliath, "Jonathan's spirit bound itself to David's spirit, and Jonathan loved David as himself" (1 Sam 18:1; the word *nepeš* recurs for "spirit" and "self," and the second phrase is similar to Leviticus

---

[381]Murphy, *Proverbs*, p. 131.

19:18, though *nepeš* does not appear there). "Jonathan and David sealed a covenant because he loved him as himself." The phrase nicely captures the reality and the limits of the relationship's mutuality. The two of them made a commitment, but "sealing a covenant" can be rather a business arrangement. Whereas JPSV has them "making a pact," TNIV and NRSV only have Jonathan making a covenant with David, and Jonathan's expressing his commitment with gifts to David symbolizes the way he will always be the giver in the relationship.

The story of Job illustrates the importance of friendship, though mostly in a negative way. Job is overwhelmed by his terrible affliction, and understandably his wife is also too overwhelmed to be of significant positive use to him. His friends come (actually from some distance, reversing the above logic) to grieve with him and comfort him, to wail and tear their robes and overwhelm themselves with dirt. They sit with him speechless for seven days. In light of the terrible cost when they open their mouths, it might initially seem that their silence is the best comfort they offer. But one wonders whether a week's pure silence counts as comfort, and whether their overwhelmed grief is too painful a mirror of Job's own, and whether it is this that tips him over the edge (Job 3:1).

Yet it seems to be their words rather than their silence that provoke the comment that "My brothers—they have betrayed, like a wadi." They are like a river whose streams flow in the winter but let you down in the summer, when you need them, or flow near their source in the snow-covered mountains but run out in the desert, where you need them (Job 6:15-20). Calling his friends his "brothers" fits with the comments in the Torah and Proverbs, but his experience also paints on a vast canvas a picture that recurs in the Psalms, where people who suffer can have their pain exacerbated rather than relieved by the response of their community (e.g., Ps 42:3, 9-10 [MT 4, 10-11]; 43:1-2). There is something grievously wrong and terrifying when the person who is attacking and taunting me is someone I know, someone with whom I enjoyed fellowship and shared in worship, but who has now "violated his covenant" (Ps 55:12-14, 20 [13-15, 21]).

"You see terrifying calamity and you are afraid," Job adds (Job 6:21). Their desperate attempts to persuade Job to look at his calamity in their way have their origin in their own fear. Perhaps they are afraid his suffering is contagious. Underneath that fear may be the awareness that granting Job's claim that his suffering is unjustified would imperil a key element in their worldview. This would be a frightening thing to let happen; friendship does not extend that far. As his brothers he could have asked them for help in getting him out of a financial hole, but he has done nothing like that. He wants them to tell him where he has gone wrong, but he knows that their rebukes are misguided. They are so self-centered in their ministry to him that, far from lending him money, they would be happy to barter over him, like Joseph's brothers.

Mutual Support

There are proper limits to friendship; you do not have to be stupid. "The person devoid of sense pledges his hand, standing surety for his friend" (Prov 17:18; cf. 6:1-5). As is the case with households in relation to the impoverishment of another household, you may otherwise simply join him in poverty, which will do neither of you any good. At another extreme, the quest for wealth easily excludes friendship; an ambitious person with no family and no friends has no time to acquire friends, but actually friendship has all sorts of practical advantages, in the form of mutual support, not least when we are under pressure (Eccles 4:7-12). The friendship of Ruth and Naomi enables them to find their way in a patriarchal world[382] and the friendship of Jonathan helps to save David's life.

Who are the poor? There are several different basic ways of understanding their position. Poverty can apply to a whole community: it then means being so short of food, clothing and shelter that you cannot really survive at all. Or individuals within a community may be in that position. Or some individuals within a society may be able to survive but lack aspects of life that most people in the community have. They eat, but unhealthily; they have clothes, but these are the castoffs of others; they have shelter, but live many people to a room; they have access to an ER, but otherwise lack health care. Hebrew speaks of the poor *(dal)* who are on the one hand needy *(ʾebyôn)* and on the other weak *(ʿānî)*.[383] In Israel the pressures of land and climate would always make life precarious; the demands of the monarchy and then of imperial taxation would increase that precariousness, and the situation would be worse when fellow Israelites took advantage of the ease with which precariousness became actual straits, especially for ordinary farming families and communities.

"One of the major issues facing any society is how to meet responsibly the needs of vulnerable individuals or groups."[384] The Torah expects a family to treat its resources as its means of being generous and supportive of its neigh-

---

[382]Cf. Trible, *God and the Rhetoric of Sexuality*, pp. 166-99.

[383]On the terms, see William R. Domeris, *Touching the Heart of God*, LHBOTS 466 (New York/London: T & T Clark, 2007), pp. 9-26; Domeris starts from Job 24. Cf. Conrad Boerma, *The Rich, the Poor—and the Bible* (Philadelphia: Westminster, 1979) = *Rich Man, Poor Man—and the Bible* (London: SCM Press, 1979), pp. 7-8; he also notes Job 24 (pp. 24-25).

[384]Michael Schluter, "Welfare," in *Jubilee Manifesto*, ed. Michael Schluter and John Ashcroft (Leicester, U.K.: Inter-Varsity Press, 2005), pp. 175-95; see p. 175.

bors. Conversely, when a household gets into economic difficulties, it will seek to borrow from another that has been more fortunate or more hardworking or more forward-thinking or more intelligent, so that it can have food to eat or seed to sow for the coming year. And when faithful people do well in life, that means they are in a position to give and to lend, and thus to be a blessing (Ps 37:26), which is what the First Testament encourages people to be willing to do.

One might have imagined that these faithful people would be expected to give, not just to lend (not to say to develop programs to solve the problems of the needy). But charity to meet people's needs may not treat them as part of *us*; it may rather deepen their alienation from us, "contrary to the relational vision of the biblical vision."[385] While Israelites are expected to be generous in giving to individuals who are intrinsically without resources, they are not expected simply to give away their resources to another household. A loan, as an act of support not a means of making money, helps a needy household get back on its feet and avoids bankrupting the lenders or imperiling their position; for instance, what they lend would be their reserve for when they are in trouble.

Jesus encouraged lending as an expression of love (Lk 6:27-36). The early church did try an alternative approach, but this did not work.[386] Jesus with his reference to lending puts the focus back on the same sort of community relationships that Leviticus 19 speaks of.

> These sayings of Jesus . . . call people in local village communities to take economic responsibility for each other in their desperate circumstances. Those addressed may have little or nothing themselves. But they are called upon to share what they have willingly with others in the community, even with their enemies or those who hate them. They are not to seek damages from a formal insult. They are even to render up the pledge for a loan that the unmerciful creditor has no right to take. (Do they thus avoid being taken into the court and taking each other into court, as Jesus admonishes in the related sayings in Luke 12:57-59/Matt 5:24-26?) The message seems to be: take responsibility for helping each other willingly, even your enemies, in the local village community.[387]

Rules about Lending

When Psalm 15 asks, "Who may sojourn in God's tent?" (that is, stay in God's presence), its answer includes the expectation that one would not lend money at interest. Ezekiel speaks in similar terms in listing obligations that people

---

[385]Wright, *Deuteronomy*, p. 192.

[386]See §4.3 "Family and Church."

[387]Richard A. Horsley, "Ethics and Exegesis: 'Love Your Enemies' and the Doctrine of Non-Violence" *Journal of the American Academy of Religion* 54 (1986): 3-31, see pp. 22-23.

should fulfill if they wish God to treat them as righteous (Ezek 18:8, 13, 17). He implies people were not fulfilling these obligations, and he later makes explicit that the well-to-do in Jerusalem have committed many of the wrongs he lists, including this one (Ezek 22:12). The Psalms and the prophets will be aware of the way people in urban contexts as well as rural ones get into difficulties and need such help.

Whereas it is the prophets' job to protest, identify root problems, challenge people about their values and lay out a utopian vision, it is the scribes' job to develop practical proposals to deal with issues and see how we might take a step or two in the right direction.[388] This is thus what the Torah does, and a number of its rules regulate the practice of lending.[389] First, Exodus 22:25 [MT 24] tells people not to behave like lenders *(nōšĕʾīm)* when they lend *(lāwâ)* money to people. It looks as if *lāwâ* refers to lending in general, the way an ordinary person might lend something to a friend, while *nāšāʾ/nāšâ* refers to something more formal, the kind of loan that might be expected to involve interest. The passage goes on to forbid Israelites to charge interest on loans. It may be "the only law which can be regarded as unique to Israel within the ancient Middle East."[390] Older English translations understand the words for "interest" to refer to "usury" (excessive interest), but Leviticus 25:36 and Deuteronomy 23:19 [MT 20] suggest that people must not impose any form of interest on any form of loan, in money or in kind. Not charging interest will play a key role in making it possible for the household in question to avoid sliding deeper and deeper into debt. When members of the community help a neighbor by leasing land when he is in difficulty; they are to do that in an honest way (Lev 25:14-17).

A system for lending and debt collection opens up the possibility of the local "economic" system working. Circumstances of one kind or another could mean that some families or villages would have surplus labor and others a labor shortage, or that through no fault of their own some families would be in trouble with their harvest when others succeeded, and some villages be in trouble when others succeeded. "Mutual cooperation and networks of exchange" could make it possible to cope with such eventualities.[391]

---

[388]Cf. Gustafson, "Varieties of Moral Discourse," pp. 50-55. As contemporary examples, he instances racism and poverty.

[389]For what follows, see Goldingay, "Jubilee Tithe."

[390]Rodd, *Glimpses of a Strange Land*, p. 151. But David L. Baker notes a similar contrast over the loss of things that were borrowed, and we have noted that the rules about care for migrants are also reckoned to be distinctive ("Safekeeping, Borrowing, and Rental," *JSOT* 31 [2006]: 27-42).

[391]See David C. Hopkins, "Life on the Land," in *Community, Identity, and Ideology*, ed. Charles E. Carter and Carol L. Meyers (Winona Lake, Ind.: Eisenbrauns, 1996), pp. 471-88; see p. 483.

In any group, its regulations or its leaders' exhortations may tell us nothing about how life was. As there is no reference in the First Testament to people keeping the sabbath year or the jubilee year, so there is no reference to people lending without interest, and many passages imply that people did lend at interest. Further, while the background of the rules about lending is agricultural, they are formulated generally enough to apply also when equivalent problems arise in an urban context, for merchants or trades people.[392] But well-to-do people who live in the city (though they presumably own land in the country) could become even wealthier by lending to people in trouble there, as well as to farmers who get into difficulties (e.g., Amos 2:6-8).[393] And it can seem that Yhwh does nothing about such practices. Job gives a moving poetic description of the way people cheat others and drive them into poverty, cold and wet, hungry and thirsty, scavenging and dispirited. Its punch line is that "God does not issue a charge" (Job 24:12). There are alternative translations, but all presuppose that God does nothing about the affliction of the poor. Ironically,[394] however, "one who increases his wealth by interest or charges, gathers it for someone who is gracious to the poor" (Prov 28:8). Whether the critique relates to different ways of charging for loans to the needy or relates to loans in kind and monetary loans, such lenders are charging for them instead of simply lending what they have, but whereas they think this is the way to make money, the saying declares that it backfires and ends up benefiting the victims. The lenders will not see the profit themselves. Habakkuk 2:6-7 warns or promises that this also works in international relations: a major power that behaves like a creditor accumulating pledges from weaker and poorer countries will in due course become the victim of its debtors. The tables will be turned. In contrast, things go well for the person who deals generously and lends freely (Ps 112:5). Perhaps this is the way God's alleged "preferential option for the poor" works.

My People, Your Brother

Exodus 22:25 [MT 24] requires lenders not to levy interest on "poor members of my people." The reference to the poor makes clear that the text does not refer to commercial loans. If successful Israelite farmers borrowed to enlarge their flocks or herds, the First Testament is not referring to such loans but to ones designed to help people in time of difficulty. The further motivation that

---

[392]Knight, "Village Law and the Book of the Covenant," emphasizes the extent to which even Ex 20:22–23:19 reflects urban concerns.

[393]See Bernhard Lang, "The Social Organization of Peasant Poverty in Biblical Israel," *JSOT* 24 (1982): 47-63.

[394]Cf. Timothy J. Sandoval, *The Discourse of Wealth and Poverty in the Book of Proverbs* (Leiden/Boston: Brill, 2006), pp. 197-200.

these are "my people" again implies that lenders should be careful how they treat borrowers. The requirement of caring for your neighbor offers no exemption if your neighbor is your enemy, and the Torah specifically requires you to help your enemy, which implies you cannot even hold back from lending because the needy person is your enemy. In reaffirming the Torah's expectation, Jesus urges his followers to lend to whoever asks for a loan (Mt 5:42) and makes explicit that this applies even to enemies, even if you do not expect to gain anything from the act (Lk 6:34-35). Fourth Maccabees, a Jewish work from about the same period, which some Christians came to treat as near canonical, claims that when people start conforming their lives to the Torah, even if they are by nature greedy they start lending to the needy without charging interest (4 Macc 2:8).

Leviticus 25:35-37 adds to the motivation by referring to the poor person as "your brother" (cf. Deut 15:7) and by urging the obligation to "revere God," and it includes reference to lending food, which makes more explicit the kind of predicament that the texts are concerned to prescribe for. It also presupposes further ways in which people may support a household in trouble. It speaks of letting your brother live with you as a resident alien, implying that he has had to forfeit the household's land. This might have been an aspect of the terms of the original loan. Alternatively, it might imply that the land was collateral for the loan and that the household has not been able to get on well enough to pay back the loan; the lender has therefore foreclosed on the loan and taken over management of the household's land. Either way, the household is now working like sharecroppers on its land, so that its labor will pay off the loan. If its own laziness or incompetence had contributed to its plight, management by another household might open up the possibility of turning it round. But the lender is bidden still to treat the borrower as a brother, who is not to be treated oppressively or shamefully.

There are other ways of "behaving like a lender" even if one keeps the regulation prohibiting lending at interest. Lenders are not to take as pledges necessities of life such as an ox or ass, or a garment, or a millstone—or a baby (Deut 24:6, 17; Job 22:6; 24:3, 9). They may not go into a man's house to seize his pledge, and may not sleep in it (Deut 24:10-13). One oppressive lender is a man who insists on taking away a widow's children (so that they can work for him) because of the household's debt (2 Kings 4:1).

In an ideal world, harvests would not fail. Indeed, Deuteronomy 15:3-6 declares that there will be no needy people in Israel if the nation lives in obedience to Yhwh. Of course it knows this will not happen. In a slightly less than ideal world, when some people end up in danger of starvation through crop failure, other people are freely to share their resources with them. Instead of coveting (Ex 20:17) there is to be generosity in lending and in remission of debts (Deut 15:1-11; compare the realism of Prov 14:20; 19:4). Israelites are thus not to be calculating in lending or giving to needy members of the Israelite family. It is a particular context in which they are to see their fellow Israelites as their brothers and sisters. The family had responsibility to support someone when they got into difficulty; Deuteronomy extends this to the nation. "You are to open your hand wide to your kin, to your afflicted person and to your needy person on your land" (Deut 15:11). The result will be that there are indeed no needy among the people.[395] This responsibility lies within the community, with the family. Other Middle-Eastern peoples emphasize the responsibility of the king in this connection. In Deuteronomy the release of people from debt "is no longer dependent on a benign ruler for its accomplishment"; neither can the family escape responsibility for it. More specifically, "the laws of Deuteronomy aim their rhetorical weaponry at those who have the power to effect change," the people who have power, the heads of households.[396]

The seeds of a successful credit-based income generation program have been described as putting people first; working with the poor instead of for the poor; combining the discipline of market forces, individual self-interest, and peer group acclaim, support and discipline; and rejecting modernization as the primary goal of development.[397] This analysis has substantial overlap with the implications of the First Testament's prescription.

Individual, Family, Community, State

In an agricultural context the recipients of loans will have to hope to grow more than they need during the coming year in order to pay back the loan, or to begin paying it back. Having to provide some sort of surety might be an incentive. And it is possible that their experience was a fluke and that they will succeed. But it is also possible that they will not and will get stuck in a cycle of shortfall and debt. Deuteronomy 15:1-11 thus prescribes a "letting go" (šĕmiṭṭâ) once every seven years. The background of this requirement is that the every seven years people had to "let go" of the land (šāmaṭ; Ex 23:11) in the sense of letting it lie fallow. Deuteronomy extends that to a letting go in connection with debts (Neh 10:31 [MT 32] makes a commitment

---

[395]Cf. Norbert F. Lohfink, "Poverty in the Laws of the Ancient Near East and of the Bible," *Theological Studies* 52 (1991): 34-50; see pp. 43-47; Martin J. Oosthuizen, "The Deuteronomic Code as a Resource for Christian Ethics," *Journal of Theology for Southern Africa* 96 (1996): 44-58; see pp. 53-55.

[396]Jeffries M. Hamilton, *Social Justice and Deuteronomy*, SBLDS 136 (Atlanta: Scholars, 1992), pp. 71, 137.

[397]Joe Remenyi and Bill Taylor, "Credit-Based Income Generation for the Poor," in *Christianity and Economics: The Oxford Declaration and Beyond,* ed. Herbert Schlossberg et al. (Grand Rapids: Eerdmans, 1994), pp. 46-56; see p. 51.

to this using different words), though it is not specific what is being let go. It might again be the land, which the household had had to pledge or forfeit in connection with receiving a loan, or the debt itself, or the people who were working off the debt; perhaps it makes little difference.[398]

It is not clear whether this means that debts are to be suspended so that people get a grace period or whether they are written off so that people get a whole new start.[399] Either way, an implication is that potential lenders must be wary of unwillingness to make a loan when the seventh year is imminent and they are quite likely not to get their payment, at least for that year. In the way they look at the needy, their eyes and their attitude of heart and mind need to be right, and therefore what they do with their hands (whether they are open or shut) needs to be right (Deut 15:7-10).[400]

It can seem that the family on one hand and free enterprise capitalism on the other are mutually supportive aspects of "the American way."[401] The First Testament suggests that there is a tension between these two, though it has a different understanding of family than the one recently assumed in the West. In addition, much depends on what one means by capitalism: economist Deirdre N. McCloskey means by capitalism "merely private property and free labor without central planning regulated by the rule of law and by an ethical consensus."[402] The modern world works with a tension between socialist and capitalist paradigms. In the extreme version of this tension, either the state looks after everything or all responsibility rests on the individual and on voluntary agencies.[403] The First Testament suggests a third way, in which more responsibility and power rest with the local community, the kin group and the household, than with the state or the individual.[404] Its approach thus

---

[398]See the discussion in, e.g., McConville, *Deuteronomy*, pp. 254-60.

[399]See, e.g., Wright, *God's People in God's Land*, pp. 147-48, 167-73; Houston, "'You Shall Open Your Hand to Your Needy Brother," pp. 303-4.

[400]Cf. Patrick D. Miller, *Deuteronomy* (Louisville: John Knox, 1990), p. 136.

[401]Cf. Clapp, *Families at the Crossroads*, p. 11.

[402]McCloskey, *The Bourgeois Virtues*, p. 14. In a caustic review, Eugene McCarraher comments that the freedom of labor consists only in a freedom to choose your master (*Books and Culture* 13/6 [2007]: 37-41 [p. 39]).

[403]Cf. the discussion in Stephen Mott and Ronald J. Sider, "Economic Justice: A Biblical Paradigm," in *Toward a Just and Caring Society*, ed. David P. Gushee (Grand Rapids: Baker, 1999), pp. 15-45; see pp. 25-26.

[404]Cf. Jeremy Ive's comments on "Relationships in the Christian Tradition" in *Jubilee Manifesto*, ed. Michael Schluter and John Ashcroft (Leicester, U.K.: Inter-Varsity Press, 2005), pp. 50-66; see pp. 60-65, in which he contrasts Thomas Hobbes's emphasis on the state and Jean Jacques Rousseau's emphasis on the individual with Reformed thinking about covenant and about the working of politics in Johannes Althusius which eventually issued in the work of Abraham Kuyper (e.g., *Christianity and the Class Struggle* [Grand Rapids: Piet Hein, 1950], pp. 57-58). The state has no authority over the family (cf. Kuyper, *Lectures on Calvinism* [Grand Rapids: Eerdmans, 1961], p. 91).

makes for a contrast with "the political illusion," the idea that the state is the proper (or even a possible) entity through which to achieve things that matter.[405] The First Testament's assumptions thus contrast with those of "liberal political theory" in which "society is composed of only two entities, the state and individual citizens" and where it is not inherent in human experience for us as adults to belong to a household or kin group, or we can decide what family means for us.[406] John Howard Yoder notes that the World Council of Churches has always paid lip service to the centrality of the local congregation in the creating of a new social life, but in practice has always assumed that what counts is the muscle and influence of power groups and leadership groups within the total social order.[407]

Loci of Responsibility

In the First Testament, "where there is no solidarity, Israel loses its *raison d'être* as God's people."[408] The state's key responsibility is simply the propagating of values and vision, by validating the collections of exhortations and policies that appear in Exodus-Deuteronomy. The Torah manifests an "aversion to the concentration of power."[409]

> A centralised system of taxation on income, wealth or expenditure was unnecessary due to the limited nature of the apparatus of central government. Instead, the criminal justice system and military were structured in such a way that did not require a police force, prisons or a standing army. Tithes of 10 per cent on income were directed to local poverty relief, the support of the local priests and Levites, or to religious celebrations (although the number of tithes in any one year remains uncertain).[410] The limited role of the state apparatus also reduced the potential for arbitrary confiscation—an all too familiar feature of monarchies at the time (1 Samuel 8).[411]

Conversely, the state's actual key failure lay in making it harder for the local community, the kin group and the household to look after its members, because in practice city and state draw resources to themselves through corruption, accumulation of land and state building projects, as Samuel warned. This process reduces the significance of democracy in the sense of an arrange-

---

[405]See Jacques Ellul, *The Political Illusion* (New York: Random House, 1972).

[406]Jon D. Levenson, *Resurrection and the Restoration of Israel* (New Haven, Conn./London: Yale University Press, 2006), p. 113.

[407]John Howard Yoder, *The Royal Priesthood* (Grand Rapids: Eerdmans, 1994), p. 96.

[408]Boerma, *The Rich, the Poor—and the Bible*, p. 67.

[409]Moshe Greenberg, "Biblical Attitudes Towards Power," in *Religion and Law*, ed. Edwin B. Firmage et al. (Winona Lake, Ind.: Eisenbrauns, 1990), pp. 101-12; see p. 109.

[410]Lev 27:30; Deut 14:28.

[411]Paul Mills, "The Divine Economy," *Cambridge Papers* 9 (2000) <www.jubilee-centre.org/document.php?id=30&topicID=3>.

ment that gives people the opportunity to elect their government every few years. It points rather to a form of democracy where the people (the *dēmos*) themselves rule *(krateō)* and are responsible for the covenant commitment to God that all must make. This might ameliorate the situation in which the Western nation that most forcefully advocates democracy is also the one with the biggest gap between rich and poor.

If "the church in its first and living sense means the local assembly, God's convocation in a particular time and place," something that can actually "gather" (Mt 18:20),[412] this follows that pattern. In discussing the family base of life and religion, Erhard S. Gerstenberger suggests that European and especially German theology and biblical scholarship have been oriented on the state, the mainstream church and society as a whole, and U.S. theology and exegesis focus more on individuals and their individual relationship with God, while Latin American theology came to ask more about families and local communities and their interpersonal relationships.[413] Again, the last seems to fit best with the First Testament.

Another way of articulating the question is to suggest that liberals and conservatives agree that getting out of poverty is the business of individuals, either with or without government help. But "this ideological world [shared by liberals and conservatives] is a world without families" and other groups.[414] (It is odd that conservatives argue for less government involvement in issues to do with poverty and more in issues to do with personal morality, while liberals argue for the opposite.)[415]

Respect for Property

While you cannot (in the strict sense) own land, the Torah presupposes that you can own houses, clothes and animals, and it seeks to protect ownership of these. The first two presuppositions might suggest that you can own what you make, but this would not cover the last. Rather, the property the Torah shows a concern for is the property that makes it possible for you to stay alive.

"You are not to see your brother's ox or sheep straying and ignore them"; you must take them back or look after them until you discover their owner.

---

[412]Luke Timothy Johnson, *Decision Making in the Church* (Philadelphia: Fortress, 1983), p. 24.

[413]Gerstenberger, *Theologies in the Old Testament*, pp. 89-90.

[414]Robert N Bellah, "Community Properly Understood," *The Responsive Community* 6/1 (1995-1996): 49-54; see p. 51; cf. Stephen V. Monsma, "Poverty, Civil Society and the Public Policy Impasse," in *Toward a Just and Caring Society*, ed. David P. Gushee (Grand Rapids: Baker, 1999), pp. 46-71; see p. 60.

[415]James Halteman, "The Market System, the Poor, and Economic Theory," in *Toward a Just and Caring Society*, ed. David P. Gushee (Grand Rapids: Baker, 1999), pp. 72-111; see p. 101.

The same applies to a donkey or a garment. And if a donkey or ox collapses under its burden, you must help your brother get it back on its feet (Deut 22:1-4). You can neither keep yourself to yourself and mind your own business nor reckon that finders keepers. Once more, the "brother" is simply a fellow member of the community, but you are to relate to him as you would to a member of your own household, even if your brother is your enemy (Ex 23:4-5). Caring for your neighbor, even if he is your enemy, means caring about the property he needs in order to live.

It links with this that Israelites are not to reap to the edges of the field or collect the gleanings of the harvest or pick the vineyard bare or collect the fruit that falls, but to leave all this for the weak and the alien (Lev 19:9-10; 23:22; Deut 24:19-22). As the right to property serves the right to life on the part of other people in the community, so does the limitation on the right to property. Deuteronomy 23:24-25 [MT 25-26] allows for the sustenance of travelers in an analogous way.

On the other hand, "you are not to steal" (Ex 20:15 [MT 13]).[416] Is the command designed to protect the poor or the well-off, the people with much that might tempt others, or the people with little whose theft might imperil their lives? We do not know the social milieu in which the command arose, so we cannot clarify its significance by considering that, but we can look at more specific commands that relate to the general one and may spell out its implications or point to the practices of which it is a distillation.[417] These cover compensation for stealing an animal or a garment, or negligently causing the death or loss of an animal or the stripping of a field or vineyard or setting fire to someone's grain (Ex 21:33–22:15 [MT 14]). This suggests that here too the property the Torah is concerned for is that which provides the family with the necessities for life such as its ox, donkey, sheep, grain, vineyard and clothing. The requirement that you must not move your neighbor's boundary marker (Deut 19:14) fits with this. The longstanding allocations of land were designed to ensure everyone has land and therefore can grow something to eat, so that moving boundary marks is associated with the oppression of the weak and needy (cf. Prov 23:10-11; Job 24:2-4; and the critique of Hos 5:10). In other words, you must not steal someone's land.

In that connection, "you are not to deal falsely or deceitfully one with another" nor "to swear falsely by my name" nor "to defraud" or "rob"; a concrete example is that "the wages of a laborer are not to remain with you until morning" (Lev 19:11-13). Restitution for theft can be stringent (fivefold for an ox, fourfold for a sheep) and includes the possibility of being sold into servitude if one

---

[416]There is no basis in the text for limiting this to stealing persons—that is, kidnapping.
[417]Cf. Robert Gnuse, *You Shall Not Steal* (Maryknoll, N.Y.: Orbis, 1985), p. ix.

cannot pay, though these penalties are less stringent than those of contemporary peoples, who might require thirtyfold compensation or death. There is no death penalty for theft as there is for breaking other commands in the Decalogue, though the ban on theft was important enough to be included in the Decalogue; it also requires a restitution offering to Yhwh. And the penalties are severe enough to act as a deterrent, to protect everyone in the community.

More radically, "you are not to want your neighbor's household. You are not to want your neighbor's woman or his male or female servant or his ox or his ass or anything that belongs to your neighbor" (Ex 20:17 [MT 14]). The expansiveness of the command may suggest awareness that it concerns a problem that needs emphasis. Wanting spoils the way people live together. Spelling the point out in terms of members of the household makes clear that in the summary opening clause *bayit* refers to the household, the people and animals, rather than to a physical structure; the First Testament is not very interested in the house as physical structure until it becomes grossly luxurified (and vain).[418] In contrast, in Deuteronomy 5:21 [MT 18] the order is woman, house, field, male or female servant, ox, ass, which leaves *bayit* more open in meaning. Deuteronomy also replaces the verb *ḥāmad* ("want") on its second occurrence by *ʾāwâ*, but the difference seems purely rhetorical (NRSV moves from "covet" to "desire").[419] Neither verb indicates an attitude or feeling that is inherently wrong; God can be the subject of both these verbs. The problem lies in the object the desire is attached to, and then in the actions to which it can lead.[420] These will include the actions proscribed in the preceding commands concerning honoring one's parents (because they teach one restraint: see Deut 21:18-21), murder, adultery and deceitful witness. It is in keeping with the Torah that Jesus affirms that anger and lust are as bad as murder and adultery (Mt 5:21-30).[421]

Resisting Market Forces

In an urban world the main source of income is employment and the main economic unit is the individual, but in a traditional society the main source of

---

[418]Cf. Gorringe, *Theology of the Built Environment*, pp. 86-87. But see also the comments in §4.3 "Keeping the Land in the Family."

[419]Against, e.g., Eduard Nielsen, *The Ten Commandments in New Perspective* (London: SCM Press/Naperville: Allenson, 1968), p. 43.

[420]On these alternatives as the focus of the command, see Alexander Rofé, "The Tenth Commandment," in *The Ten Commandments in History and Tradition,* ed. Ben-Zion Segal (Jerusalem: Magnes, 1990), pp. 45-65; Marvin L. Chaney, "'Coveting Your Neighbor's House' in Social Context," in *The Ten Commandments,* ed. William P. Brown (Louisville/London: Westminster John Knox, 2004), pp. 302-17.

[421]On the parallels between Jesus' teaching and that of Judaism in his day (and before and after), see David Flusser, *Jesus,* rev. ed. (Jerusalem: Magnes, 1997; 3rd ed., 2001), pp. 81-103.

income is land and the main economic unit is the household working the land and living off it. In light of the First Testament the notion that most people are employed by someone else rather than working within the context of the family is a weird one. Perhaps there is a connection between the two resonances of the word *work* in colloquial speech, "gainful employment" and "toil and drudgery";[422] neither connotation attaches to the word in the First Testament. If we ask how our practices might be reformed in light of the First Testament, then one step would be to give workers a share in the management and control of their work. This would again imply finding a third way between the capitalist and the collectivist (communist).[423]

But the household does not farm cash crops (if it makes a little surplus each year, this is available for lending, bartering and saving), and the biblical regulations concerning the land are "concerned less with the efficient use of a commercial asset than with protecting the rights of the family to the source of their economic survival."[424] The Torah's regulations severely impede the accumulation of economic power by their requirements concerning ownership of land, weekly sabbath, sabbath year, jubilee, tithes and the ban on lending at interest.

For centuries, "economics was understood as a sub discipline of ethics. In the nineteenth century this connection was severed, with disastrous consequences for both people and planet."[425] Now "nothing in our society is taught more effectively than the doctrine of the market," from which God is excluded, and the church works within its logic, but actually God is an economist,[426] and in laying down regulations such as those for the sabbath year "God intervenes in the economy to save life."[427] It is these constraints that prevent the accumulation of real property, "the basis of economic power," and must mean a "dampening of economic enterprise and growth" as "money cannot be used to make money."[428] The Western world came to make scientific progress, economic growth and technical advance the ultimate social goods, with everything subordinated to these; they are *"their own justification."* But this practice looks like our worship of a false god.[429] "If economics

---

[422]Miroslav Volf, *Work in the Spirit* (New York/Oxford: Oxford University Press, 1991), p. 9; his subsequent, chiefly New Testament-based, reflection on work in light of pneumatology and eschatology could be complemented by First Testament-based reflection.

[423]Cf. John Paul II, *Laborem exercens* §14.

[424]Westbrook, *Property and the Family in Biblical Law*, p. 11.

[425]Gorringe, *Theology of the Built Environment*, p. ix.

[426]M. Douglas Meeks, *God the Economist* (Minneapolis: Fortress, 1989), p. 37. Cf. Roelf Haan, *The Economics of Honour* (Geneva: World Council of Churches, 1988).

[427]Pablo Richard, "Now Is the Time to Proclaim the Biblical Jubilee," in *God's Economy*, ed. Ross Kinsler and Gloria Kinsler (Maryknoll, N.Y.: Orbis, 2005), pp. 43-58; see p. 45.

[428]Greenberg, "Biblical Attitudes Towards Power," p. 107.

[429]Bob Goudzwaard, *Capitalism and Progress* (Grand Rapids: Eerdmans, 1979), pp. 191, 152;

are to be judged by the service they provide for the flowering of the family, it might well be that we must challenge the tendency of the modern corporation to make efficiency the criterion of good business."[430] "Money must be allowed to die."[431]

"The sabbatical principle" of Deuteronomy 15 in particular "is a protest against the allegedly insuperable power of market forces," which may produce growth but also

> drive some people into deeper spirals of debt, dependence, and bondage. To apply sabbatical principles in such a world means to struggle for realistic and effective mechanisms that say "No" to the assumption that this is how it has to be; mechanisms that provide a breathing space ("rest") for recovery; mechanisms that restore the poor and empower them for meaningful belonging and participation in the community.[432]

"In the Bible, the right to property is subordinated to responsibility for the weak members of society, and furthermore, to their right to the means of production."[433]

The Community and Outsiders

That sabbatical principle and the expectations about loans apply only within the Israelite family and not to foreigners (Deut 15:3; 23:20 [MT 21]). Family members are not merely *the* poor and needy but *your* poor and needy. Paul's exhortation to do good especially to fellow members of the household of faith (Gal 6:10) fits with this. But the reason for foreigners taking out loans would be different. By definition they would not be people working family land who have got into difficulty but, for instance, merchants or tradespeople, who might want to take out something more like commercial loans;[434] the text refers to the "foreigner" (*nokrî*), not the "resident alien" (*gēr*), the immigrant

---

cf. Nicholas Wolterstorff, *Until Justice and Peace Embrace* (Grand Rapids: Eerdmans, 1983), pp. 59-60, 64.

[430]Hauerwas, *In Good Company*, p. 129, reflecting on the papal encyclicals *Rerum novarum, Laborem exercens*, and *Centesimus annus* <www.vatican.va/holy_father/john_paul_ii/encyclicals/index.htm>.

[431]Geiko Müller-Fahrenholz, "The Jubilee: Time Ceilings for the Growth of Money," in *The Jubilee Challenge*, ed. Hans Ucko (Geneva: World Counicl of Churches, 1997), pp. 104-11; see p. 108.

[432]Wright, *Deuteronomy*, pp. 195-96. Cf. Kinsler and Kinsler, *Biblical Jubilee and the Struggle for Life.*

[433]Boerma, *The Rich, the Poor—and the Bible*, p. 43. The sentence is italicized.

[434]Cf. Walther Zimmerli, *Old Testament Theology in Outline* (Atlanta: Knox/Edinburgh: T & T Clark, 1978), p. 137. Though Edward Neufeld suggests that the basic principle here is thus that one does not charge interest to members of one's family or community and therefore would not do so when an Israelite wants a loan for more "commercial" reasons ("The Prohibitions Against Loans at Interest in Ancient Hebrew Laws," *HUCA* 26 [1955]: 355-412).

who might get into difficulty to whom Israel was expected to show compassion. Indeed, the exemption of loans to foreigners might be a largely theoretical one; the issue would hardly ever arise, and permitting loans at interest to non-Israelites is a way of underlying the prohibition on loans at interest to nearly all the people that anyone would be asked to make a loan to. In other words, Deuteronomy's "caustic ethnic exclusiveness" or "separatism" was "largely polemical" and "more rhetorical than actual. Deuteronomy's ethnic concern was much more the establishing of a sense of ethnic kinship among Israelites and Judeans than it was the excluding of foreigners from participation within the community," as is indicated by its willingness to include foreigners who wanted to be fully part of the community.[435] Deuteronomy is then typical of First Testament thinking as a whole.

The permission to charge interest to foreigners was influential in encouraging Jewish people to be involved in the commercial world.[436] And if we look at the First Testament purely legally, it could also justify Western nations making loans to Two-thirds World countries on a commercial basis, if we view people outside our communities or nations as aliens rather than treating them like members of the family and needy. But we could choose to see other nations as our brothers and sisters, and apply to them the First Testament's perception of lending as a way to show compassion on the needy rather than a way to make money.[437] We could treat them as more like needy resident aliens than wealthy foreigners. The haves would thus share with the have-nots by lending and make that a means of being a blessing. We could also choose to follow the First Testament principle of giving priority to such an attitude over the question how good or bad the relationships are between lender and borrower. While the believing communities might be expected to think about such questions in this way in light of what we know about God's care for the whole world, the success of the Jubilee 2000 movement outside the church suggests that ordinary unbelievers often rise to a challenge of this kind, whereas the United States with its large and influential Christian community has been more resistant to it. And Michael Schluter comments that "Northern Europe and the US have now experienced four centuries of a financial system in which the Old Testament's re-

---

[435]Kenton L. Sparks, *Ethnicity and Identity in Ancient Israel* (Winona Lake, Ind.: Eisenbrauns, 1998), p. 283.

[436]See the discussion in Susan L. Buckley, *Teachings on Usury in Judaism, Christianity and Islam* (Lewiston, N.Y./Lampeter, Wales: Edwin Mellen, 2000).

[437]Jerome in fact notes that Ezek 18:8 does not limit refraining from charging interest to one's brothers (*Commentariorum in Ezechielem prophetam libri quatuordecim* [Patrologia Latina 25], column 176); over subsequent centuries Christian attitudes varied (see Benjamin N. Nelson, *The Idea of Usury*, 2nd ed. [Chicago/London: University of Chicago Press, 1969]).

lational precepts have been largely ignored," producing a system that "tends to exaggerate the economic cycle; is inherently unstable; . . . concentrates economic power in large companies; and acts to entrench inequalities of wealth within and between countries."[438]

Caring and Intolerance

So lending is a key way that neighbors are supposed to care for each other (Lev 19:18). In practice they sometimes speak emptiness to one another, saying things that have no corresponding truth. They speak smooth words but are double-minded. They talk neighborly, honorably and positively but seem to intend one thing and to have one attitude, but actually have another attitude and intend something else (Ps 12:2 [3]). The community (or elements within it) is often characterized as wicked, recalcitrant, godless, mischievous, greedy, murderous, thieving, adulterous, oppressive, arrogant, scoffing, trusting in worldly resources, deceitful and foolishly self-deceived (e.g., Ps 1; 5; 35; 36; 50; 52; 55). In a sense the wicked do not really belong to this community; the real Israel is the community of the faithful (Ps 1:5), the people who live up to the definition. Widow, alien and orphan comprise the people of Yhwh (Ps 94:5-6). But one has to deal with the community as it is, knowing conflict within as well as without, and a place where power can lie with the perjurers, the haves and the taunting, who stand over against the righteous, the godly, the committed, the covenant-keeping and the torah-delighting, who are powerless, fearful, fleeing, vengeful, vulnerable, groaning, with God's promise all they have to trust in.[439]

It is proper to be enraged at the faithless and to have nothing to do with them, and to be a friend or associate *(ḥābēr)* only of people who revere Yhwh and live by Yhwh's standards (Ps 119:53, 63); these are the people whose company we seek out and want to identify with. If people hate Yhwh, we have no business loving them in the sense of identifying with them and joining in their projects, as a prophet pointed out to Jehoshaphat when he made a marriage alliance with Ahab and thus got drawn into an attack on the Syrians that almost cost him his life and did bring the death of Ahab (2 Chron 19:2). "A person who covers an offense is one who seeks love, but someone who repeats a thing alienates a friend" (Prov 17:9). The EVV take this repeating *(śānē bĕ)* to denote going on about the offense or telling others about it instead of covering it, but the only other time the phrase occurs (Prov 26:11) it refers

---

[438]Michael Schluter, "Finance," in *Jubilee Manifesto*, ed. Michael Schluter and John Ashcroft (Leicester, U.K.: Inter-Varsity Press, 2005), pp. 196-215; see p. 212.

[439]Cf. John Goldingay, "Images of Israel: The People of God in the Writings," in *Studies in Old Testament Theology*, David Hubbard Festschrift, ed. Robert L. Hubbard et al. (Dallas: Word, 1992), pp. 205-21; see pp. 209-10.

to repeating a stupid act, and this connotation makes sense here. The subject of the second colon is the offender of the first colon, who fails to respond to forbearance by changing. The offended person wanted to encourage or maintain a friendship, but there are limits to patience, and friendship depends on mutual commitment, on reaching out and receiving a response. After all, "the person who loves offenses loves strife" (Prov 17:19).

Israelites are still expected to care for their neighbors even when they have given them reason to hate them, get their own back on them and hold grudges against them (Lev 19:15-18).[440] They are forbidden to neglect their neighbors by actions such as not rescuing an animal or refusing to make a loan, even if their neighbors are the sort of people who alienate their friends by their repeated hostility. But they are encouraged to tell Yhwh what they think about such people. The Psalms also remind us of the significance in this connection of questions about power. It is not the job of the powerful to tell the oppressed to love their oppressors. And they are not expected to let people simply get away with things. In Psalm 7:3-4 [4-5] a suppliant denies that there has been "meanness in my hand" yet goes on to recognize that to have "dealt calamity to my friend but released my watchful foe without reason" would be shameful. The EVV have "plundered" my watchful foe, but elsewhere the verb means "release" (cf. Ps 6:4 [5]). The EVV seem to be offended at the psalm's idea that releasing a wrongdoer would not be the "Christian" thing to do (nor the "Jewish" thing, to judge from JPSV). But the person who is welcome to spend time with Yhwh is one who despises people who deserve to be despised (that is, wrongdoers), honors people who revere Yhwh and implements a commitment to seeing that wrongdoers get punishment rather than going back on it (Ps 15:1, 4).

Resolving Conflict

Like the exhortations in Leviticus 19:15-18 about attitudes to other people, the regulations in Exodus 21–23 presuppose that the community experiences tensions and conflicts, and lay out examples of how to deal with them.[441] The ideal arrangement will be that the people concerned resolve them. One can imagine that if they are members of the same family, the head of the household would be responsible for seeing this happens. One of David's major failures lies here, in connection with Amnon's rape of Tamar. Of course locating responsibility at the household level does not guarantee fairness or success; heads of households have their prejudices, their blind spots and their limitations. When matters cannot be settled by intra-household negotiation, they might become the local

---

[440]See further §6.1.

[441]They are the starting point for Eckhart Otto's study in his *Theologische Ethik des Alten Testaments*, pp. 24-31.

community's business and thus the elders' business, as is presupposed by the regulation concerning a rebellious son (Deut 21:18-21).

If the people are members of different households, again the ideal arrangement will presumably be for the two households to resolve it, perhaps with the heads of the households negotiating the matter on their behalf. But it will be easy for personal feelings then to get out of hand, and in these circumstances too the community will need to be involved in resolving matters. Whereas the regular process of marriage and divorce was apparently a family matter not regulated by the Torah, the Torah does cover aspects of marriage and divorce that involve relationships beyond the family and become topics of dispute (e.g., Deut 22:13-29; 24:1-4). One can imagine that such matters would involve the elders; Ruth 4 gives a neat picture of the "wonderfully unbureaucratic" nature of their work, and an illustration of the way it involved managing questions in a way that prevents conflict. In a broader sense "it is all in the family" still.[442] The elders would presumably be involved in resolving conflicts over questions such as boundary disputes (Deut 19:14), property disputes (Ex 22:7-15 [MT 6-14]) and the loss brought about by injury (Lev 24:19-21).[443] Perhaps people might protest to the elders if farmers did not allocate the triennial tithe to the needy or someone tried to charge interest on a loan or a master failed to apply the six-year rule to a debt servant; Job's recollection in Job 29:12-17 implies as much. "A right of way, rights to a well, a theft of someone else's cattle, an assault which had a serious sequel, a death by violence, a claim to an inheritance":[444] these will have been the sort of questions that the gathering of the elders handled.

One concern of the administration of justice (as we would call it) in Israel is thus the protection of harmony and the resolution of disharmony in the community, and "covenant community" is "the Yahwistic alternative to conflict."[445] In Western thinking responsibility for administering justice lies with the city, the county or the state, not with the local community. Whereas more urbanized Middle-Eastern societies made matters such as the adjudication of homicide a state affair,[446] in Israel neither the king nor the state initi-

---

[442]Gerstenberger, *Theologies in the Old Testament*, p. 99.

[443]Naomi Sternberg suggests that transferring authority from the family to the elders was designed to transfer power to the state ("The Deuteronomic Law Code and the Politics of State Centralization," in *The Bible and the Politics of Exegesis*, N. K. Gottwald Festschrift, ed. David Jobling et al. [Cleveland: Pilgrim Press, 1991], pp. 161-70). There might be both gains and losses for women in this move. But the elders surely represent the local community more than the state.

[444]Ludwig Köhler, *Hebrew Man* (Nashville: Abingdon, 1956), p. 141.

[445]Paul D. Hanson, "Conflict in Ancient Israel and its Resolution," in *Understanding the Word*, B. W. Anderson Festschrift, ed. James T. Butler et al., JSOTSup 37 (Sheffield, U.K.: JSOT, 1985), pp. 185-205; see p. 188.

[446]Barmash, *Homicide in the Biblical World*, p. 45.

ates action to resolve conflict or bring about justice. There are no state punishments, state-imposed and state-collected fines, or imprisonment. The ordering of responsibility for justice is reversed, as is the case with economic questions.[447] The state's involvement is then to support the local community. It does this by approving and making known the collections of rules that we have in the Torah, not as a code that the elders are expected literally to apply but as a resource for their deliberation. It sets up the structure of havens for homicides to aid the elders in ensuring that homicide is investigated and that redress is then exacted where that is proper (Num 35:9-28; Deut 19:1-13; Josh 20). And it offers the facility of a higher authority that individuals can approach if they reckon the local community is handling a case in the wrong way (cf. 2 Sam 14:1-11), or that the elders themselves can refer to if they cannot resolve a case.

Managing Redress

One reason we have law is that people often do not turn the other cheek to their attackers, and if Yhwh leaves things as they are in Leviticus 19:17-18 with their expectation that people will turn the other cheek, then once people abandon that vocation, the rule of the jungle will apply and the result will be to increase rather than reduce conflict in the community. It will risk personal revenge, vendetta and lynching, as an offended person seeks to hurt the offender back, only more so. The first recorded wounding leads to seventy-sevenfold redress: "I have killed a man for wounding me" (Gen 4:23-24). The law therefore provides some principles that do not assume that people will be willing simply to forgive their attackers. In effect the Torah says, if people are not up to loving their enemy and want some redress, then here are some principles for administering it.

Exodus 21:22-25 describes a situation in which a fight between two men has led to injury to a pregnant woman, who has either miscarried or gone into premature labor; it is not clear which the text refers to.[448] It declares that the wrongdoer "shall definitely make amends [EVV 'fine' is misleading, as the payment does not go to the state] as the woman's husband sets for him and/but he shall give according to the arbitrators/assessments"; the precise meaning of the last word is also uncertain,[449] but it denotes some balancing of what the husband presses for and what people who are not involved reckon is fair. One can here imagine the elders being concerned with justice in the sense of

---

[447]Cf. 4.4 "Individual, Family, Community, State."

[448]See, e.g., Bernard S. Jackson, *Essays in Jewish and Comparative Legal History* (Leiden: Brill, 1975), pp. 75-107.

[449]See *NIDOTTE* 5:466-67.

regulating competing claims with fairness in order to achieve this.[450] Offended parties need to have a sense that justice has been done for them, but satisfying offended parties at the cost of unfairness to offenders will not achieve it.

Exodus 21:22-25 goes on to prescribe that if further injury has been caused, presumably to mother or baby (again the details are unclear), the wrongdoer "shall give life for life, eye for eye, tooth for tooth, hand for hand, foot for foot, burn for burn, would for wound, bruise for bruise" (cf. Lev 24:19-20; Deut 19:16-21). The "eye for eye" rule spells out a principle for decision making that constrains people's Lamech-like instincts in a number of ways. First, it set limits to it, forbidding people taking redress that goes far beyond the wrong. The redress must fit the offense. The rule "was the kind of formula which helped to regulate private vengeance throughout much of Western history."[451]

"Life for life, eye for eye, tooth for tooth" is rather a poetic formulation, which suggests it is no more a law in a Western sense than many other "laws" that are more like paradigms or exhortations or ethical statements or theological formulations, like Jesus' instruction about cutting off your hand. There is thus no necessary reason for interpreting "eye for eye" literally, and there are no reports of anyone in the First Testament doing so; the nearest is the Judahites' treatment of Adonibezek (Judg 1:6-7), and even that is described more as an instance of poetic justice. Making compensation to a person one has wronged by means of a monetary payment has commonly been the practice in traditional societies, and it is the assumption in the Mishnah and the Talmud; they do not assume that the rule implies physical retaliation.[452] When Jesus refers to "eye for eye" but omits reference to "life for life," this may link with the assumption that "eye for eye, tooth for tooth" refers to monetary compensation, whereas "life for life" was understood literally.[453] But he may

---

[450]Cf. Christopher D. Marshall, *Beyond Retribution* (Grand Rapids/Cambridge: Eerdmans, 2001), p. 28; he is concerned to urge that justice is more than this, but it does include this. See also Willis, *Elders of the City*, e.g., pp. 307-8.

[451]So Howard Zehr, *Changing Lenses*, 3rd ed. (Scottdale, Penn.: Herald, 2005), p. 102 (he actually says "formulae"). See further William Ian Miller, *Eye for an Eye* (Cambridge/New York: Cambridge University Press, 2006).

[452]See *b. Baba Kamma* 83b-84a and, e.g., Isaac Kalimi, "Targumic and Midrashic Exegesis in Contradiction to the *Peshat* of the Biblical Text," in Isaac Kalimi and Peter J. Haas, *Biblical Interpretation in Judaism and Christianity*, LHBOTS 439 (New York/London: T & T Clark, 2007), pp. 13-32; see pp. 13-18; Bernard S. Jackson, "The Original Oral Law," in *Jewish Ways of Reading the Bible*, ed. George J. Brooke (Oxford/New York: Oxford University Press, 2000), pp. 3-19; see pp. 11-16; David Daube, *Appeasement or Resistance* (Berkeley/London: UCLA Press, 1987), pp. 19-23.

[453]See the discussion in James F. Davis, *Lex Talionis in Early Judaism and the Exhortation of Jesus in Matthew 5.38-42* (New York/London: T & T Clark, 2005), pp. 55-100.

be reflecting the particular formulation in Leviticus 24:20 (as opposed to Ex 21:24 and Deut 19:21), where "life for life" is separated from the other formulas.[454] If the regulation implies that a person was entitled to press for the physical punishment, this might act as a deterrent to a master who might injure a servant[455] or to other people for whom monetary compensation would be no problem. A flat physical compensation system such as is encapsulated in this principle could thus protect servants and other poor people.[456] In Deuteronomy 19:15-21 it might refer to the mutilation of a corpse after a person's execution (cf. Deut 21:22; Josh 10:26; 1 Sam 31:8-10; 2 Sam 4:12; 21:1-14).[457]

We have noted that Ronald J. Sider described the demanding of an eye for an eye as a basic legal principle from the Torah, which Jesus rejected.[458] It is not a basic legal principle from the Torah. It does not refer to what it is right to demand but about how punishment is to be framed or limited.[459] And Jesus elsewhere accepts the principle it states: for instance, he says that people who do not forgive will not be forgiven (Mt 6:15).

Making Restitution

A second significance of the prescription in Exodus 21:22-25 is that it does put the emphasis on the offender making restitution to the offended person rather than on the offended person's getting revenge. Human justice seeks to mirror God's justice, which "redeems, reconciles, and restores."[460] As well as making decisions fairly, it requires restitution that will restore the victim and contribute to reconciliation. "Western civilization began as an unhappy compromise between the Biblical standard of *restitution* and a Greco-Roman and pagan criminology which . . . leaned heavily towards *punishment.*"[461] The importance of restitution is the significance of monetary penalties being not fines paid to the state, as if it were the entity chiefly offended, but compensation made to the victim. This is illustrated by the rules on theft in Exodus 22:2-3 and Leviticus 6:1-5 [MT 5:20-24].[462] Again, whereas there is no actual punishment for hurting someone in a way that confines them to bed for a while but from which they recover reasonably fully, the person who

---

[454]So Carmichael, *Spirit of Biblical Law*, p. 125.

[455]So Crüsemann, *Torah*, p. 159.

[456]Cf. ibid., p. 163; Tikva Frymer-Kensky, "Tit for Tat," *Biblical Archaeologist* 43 (1980): 230-34; she emphasizes the Middle-Eastern background of the principle.

[457]So Calum M. Carmichael, *The Spirit of Biblical Law* (Athens/London: University of Georgia, 1996), pp. 105-7.

[458]Sider, *Christ and Violence*, p. 26; see §4.1 "Thinking Communally."

[459]As John H. Yoder recognizes in *The Original Revolution* (Scottdale, Penn.: Herald Press, 1971), p. 49.

[460]Marshall, *Beyond Retribution*, pp. 35-95, 97.

[461]Rushdoony, *Institutes of Biblical Law*, p. 515.

[462]Cf. Crüsemann, *Torah*, pp. 168-69.

did the hurt must pay for the other's treatment and make compensation for the work he has been unable to do (Ex 21:18-19). In connection with restitution as with redress, one aspect of the significance of a regulation such as Exodus 22:22-25 is again is to set limits on what is imposed on people. The regulation may be simply permissive, "he may give."[463] It might then imply that the person who was wronged can negotiate compensation appropriate to the hurt.

Reframing redress as restitution rather than revenge also has significance for the offender. Proverbs notes that love covers all offenses (Prov 10:12) yet also that parents discipline the children they love, and Yhwh does the same (Prov 3:11-12). Taking up the latter passage, Hebrews 12:4-11 comments that when God or parent to fail to exercise discipline, this is a gesture of neglect not of love. In the First Testament God's punishment is commonly designed to be restorative, to draw people to change their way of life (e.g., Amos 4:6-11). Likewise some human punishment is designed to be disciplinary, as *mûsār* and *tôkaḥat*. It is difficult to be sure when these words denote verbal chastisement and correction and when they signify physical punishment, but some passages require the latter (e.g., Prov 22:15; 29:15; and Prov 3:11-12 as understood in Heb 12:5-11). The discipline of having to make restitution means the offender might come to see things from the angle of the person who was wronged. The punishment can also act as a deterrent to other people (Deut 17:12-13; cf. 1 Tim 5:20).

In 2007, Los Angeles newspapers carried reports of an assault on Cardinal Roger Mahoney involving his being punched, knocked to the ground and kicked; he did not report the assault to the police, but later spoke of it in an address. Let us suppose he had the right not to seek to prosecute his attacker. How should the law itself deal with such wrongdoing? My turning the other cheek when I am attacked might drive my attacker to repentance, but it might simply encourage my attacker, and I might then not even be doing my attacker a favor. Although it might be hoped that nonviolence would constrain or even halt the spread of violence, a woman who had dealt with many battered women comments that Jesus' injunction to turn the other cheek "has killed more women than any of us here would dare to count."[464] While it is my vocation to turn the other cheek, it is the law's vocation to discipline my attacker, not only for my sake nor only to deter other people but for the attacker's sake.

---

[463]See, e.g., Bernard S. Jackson, "Talion and Purity," in *Reading Leviticus*, ed. John F. A. Sawyer, JSOTSup 227 (Sheffield, U.K.: Sheffield Academic Press, 1996), pp. 107-23; see p. 109.
[464]Gary A. Phillips and Danna Nolan Fewell, "Ethics, Bible, Reading As If," *Semeia* 77 (1997): 1-21; see p. 1.

Community Integrity

God sometimes simply forgives people, and sometimes disciplines them; but not all God's punishments have that disciplinary aim. When Adam and Eve do wrong, Yhwh throws them out of Eden so that they may not eat of the life tree. This is not for their sake. Rather, if a couple who were resistant to God were to eat from the tree and live forever, this would permanently skew the world. There would be something warped about the whole of reality. (It is the metaphysical issue raised by the movie *Dogma*.) The broader necessity for God to punish people who insist on living their own way has a similar rationale. Jesus' comments about judgment and the possible impossibility of forgiveness (Mt 6:15; 7:1-2) imply that the kingdom of heaven would be skewed by the presence of people who hold onto grudges and judge others. Jesus thus forbids people to operate by a principle of redress or retribution in regard to the wrong others do to them, but assumes that God operates by a principle of redress or retribution on behalf of the people who are sinned against. His exhortation and warning about forgiveness thus fits the Torah and also corresponds to Ecclesiasticus 27:30–28:7, which recognizes that anger is an abomination and that taking vengeance will lead to the Lord doing the same to us; "forgive your neighbor's injustice, and then when you pray your sins will be forgiven."[465]

Both Testaments, then, forbid people to take redress, but reckon that God does so, and also expect the community to do this so that its own life keeps its integrity. So a congregation is to treat someone who wrongs another and is unrepentant as a pagan or tax collector (Mt 18:17) and to expel the wicked from its midst (1 Cor 5:13). Analogously, the life of the Israelite community is deformed by the presence of people who think it is okay to kill other people, steal their animals, seduce their wives and young girls, or deride Yhwh. Unless such people repent and throw themselves on Yhwh's mercy, the community cannot simply let them carry on that way. Taking action against them protects its own life. As well as safeguarding its harmony, controlling redress and encouraging restitution, it defends its own integrity. Wrongdoing throws it out of kilter. Taking action against wrongdoers restores the balance in the community and in the world; it reverses the wrong. It purges evil from it. It indicates its disowning of certain deeds and its affirmation of the boundaries of acceptable behavior.[466]

So there is a sense in which every wrong is committed against the people as a whole and that every wrong is a crime, and every wrong imperils the relationship between Israel and Yhwh. If someone wrongs someone else and

---

[465]Cf. David Flusser, *Jesus*, 3rd ed. (Jerusalem: Magnes, 2001), pp. 84-85.
[466]Marshall, *Beyond Retribution*, p. 112.

steals something, this is also an offense against Yhwh (*mā'al*) because it happens in the community where Yhwh dwells. It requires the person to confess what happened and as well as make restoration to the victim, also to offer a sacrifice in respect of the offense done to Yhwh (Lev 6:1-7 [MT 5:20-26]; Num 5:5-8). If the offender does not deal with the matter, the local community acts on the whole people's behalf in taking up such issues; the elders will be responsible for removing offenses from the community, and punishment is designed to effect this.

The punishment for many wrongs is to be cut off from among one's people. Some of these wrongs are ones no one might ever know about (e.g., Lev 7:20-21), and sometimes it is explicit that God cuts the person off (e.g., Lev 17:10), so it is unlikely that the phrase refers to a punishment applied by the community, such as expulsion or execution. Rather the phrase declares that God will certainly punish the person. In the case of an unsolved murder, the elders of the nearest city have to accept responsibility on the community's behalf and take appropriate action (Deut 21:1-9).[467]

Execution

Exodus-Deuteronomy does declare that execution is the punishment for a substantial number of offenses: for murder or culpable responsibility for someone else's death (Ex 21:12, 29; Lev 24:17, 21; Num 35:16-21, 31), hitting or cursing a parent (Ex 21:15, 17; Lev 20:9), kidnapping (Ex 21:16; Deut 24:7), giving any of one's offspring to Molek (Lev 20:3), adultery and certain other forbidden sexual acts (Ex 22:19 [MT 18]; Lev 20:10-16; Deut 22:20-22), belittling Yhwh (Lev 24:13-16), coming near the wilderness dwelling if you are not an Aaronide (Num 1:51; 3:10, 38; 18:7), sabbath breaking (Ex 31:14-15; 35:2; Num 15:35), encouraging people to serve other gods (Deut 13; 17:2-7), resisting a court decision (Deut 17:12), and incorrigible waywardness or rebelliousness (Deut 21:18-21). Many of the acts are offenses against the Decalogue, though there is no execution for theft (contrast the Laws of Hammurabi 6-11, 21-22, 25).[468] All are acts that imperil the community from the inside and therefore require action.[469] The sanction will also act as a deterrent with regard to fundamental community norms (cf. Deut 13:11 [12]).[470] When someone is to be executed by stoning for serving other deities, the whole community is involved in the investigation of the matter, and then in the execution itself; it is "a form of execution without an executioner."[471] The witnesses throw the first

---

[467]Cf. Willis, *Elders of the City*, pp. 145-62.

[468]See *ANET*, pp. 166-67.

[469]Cf. Louis Stulman, "Encroachment in Deuteronomy," *JBL* 109 (1990): 613-32.

[470]Cf. Otto, *Theologische Ethik des Alten Testaments*, pp. 32-47.

[471]Tikva Frymer-Kensky, "Pollution, Purification, and Purgation in Biblical Israel," in *The*

stone; then the main stoning involves the whole community (Deut 17:7). Thus the whole community identifies with the repudiation of the wrongdoing in question. It is a formalized expression of community outrage.

Yet it is hard to find examples of the community implementing these regulations. Although the First Testament refers to many acts of adultery (including David's), it never refers to an adulterer or adulteress being executed. The nearest it comes to that is Genesis 38:24-26 (though both parties are widowed) where the threat of execution is never implemented and fulfills a rhetorical function, establishing the hypocrisy of the one demanding it (Jn 8:1-11 will repeat this).[472] Likewise, when people give false testimony (1 Kings 21), commit murder (2 Sam 11–12) or break the sabbath (Neh 13:15-21), they are not executed.

It seems that the threat of execution is more like a declaration of how strongly Yhwh disapproves of such acts and how firmly Israel is to disavow them, or of the punishment that Yhwh may personally bring about. "Legal codes, in their details, are symbolic attempts to work out in concrete behavioral terms the implications of deeply held values and principles" about matters such as life and death.[473] But they are not designed for implementation by a court. This would fit with Yhwh's telling the first human beings that the penalty for eating of the knowledge tree will be death, but not exacting this punishment, with Jesus' reference to execution for belittling a parent (Mk 7:10) and with Paul's failure to refer to the execution of homosexuals (Rom 1:27). The Talmud likewise notes the comment of a sage that the execution of a rebellious son had never happened and never would; it is designed so that "one may profit from the gruesome warning."[474]

Perhaps execution is a possible but maximum penalty; in Cain's and David's cases, for instance, Yhwh is free to require a lesser punishment (with David, signifying so via a prophet). Possibly an offended party had the right to demand the execution of an adulterer, but it was usual if not invariable for the offended party to exercise the right to receive some other compensation for the wrong, a ransom for the man's life (cf. Prov 6:20-35).[475] When people

---

Word of the Lord Shall Go Forth, D. N. Freedman Festschrift, ed. Carol L. Meyers and M. O'Connor (Winona Lake, Ind.: Eisenbrauns, 1983), pp. 399-414; see p. 406.

[472]The actual deaths of Jesus and of Stephen can also be seen as executions, though Jesus' execution is determined by the Roman authorities and Stephen's death might rather be seen as a lynching.

[473]Peter J. Haas, "'Die He Shall Surely Die,'" *Semeia* 45 (1989): 67-87; see p. 84. Cf. §1.2 "The Need for Instruction" and §4.1 "Thinking Exegetically" above.

[474]*B. Sanhedrin* 71a; cf. Sheldon H. Blank, "The Hebrew Scriptures as a Source for Moral Guidance," in *Scripture in the Jewish and Christian Traditions*, ed. Frederick E. Greenspahn (Nashville: Abingdon, 1982), pp. 169-82; see p. 171.

[475]Cf. Lipka, *Sexual Transgression in the Hebrew Bible*, pp. 1-41.

who serve other gods are killed, it is by the action of a prophet such as Elijah or a king such as Jehu outside a legal framework. Such execution is not capital punishment in the sense of a legal penalty imposed by a court but a prophetic act undertaken in Yhwh's name and on behalf of the community for the sake of its cleansing.

Capital punishment might seem to ignore the Decalogue's own declaration, which now appears in translations as "you shall not murder" but in the KJV read "thou shalt not kill" (Ex 20:13; Deut 5:17).[476] The verb is *rāṣaḥ*; the more common verbs for "kill" are *mût* and *hārag*. But *rāṣaḥ* does most often refer to homicide, deliberate or accidental. While it can denote legal action by a blood restorer[477] or a court (Num 35:26-30) or an animal's killing someone (Prov 22:13), it seems forced to see it as pointing to a prohibition on any killing, including war and execution.[478] But it might be wise to play safe and not go in for either kind of killing.

Yhwh and Murder

When Cain kills Abel, the first "sin," Yhwh recognizes that Abel's blood is crying out from the ground; Genesis 4:10 uses the plural of the word for "blood," which often suggests "violently spilled blood." Yet Yhwh responds to the cry not by spilling Cain's blood, as if another death solves the problem caused by the first, but by banishing Cain. Indeed, Cain will be protected from death, and anyone who kills him will suffer sevenfold punishment (a formula that also indicates that this killer will not be executed but will be punished in a variety of different ways). Soon, however, Lamech is also involved in killing (Gen 4:23), and violence spreads until the earth is full of it (Gen 6:11, 13). When David has Uriah killed but then acknowledges his wrongdoing, Nathan says, "Yhwh has caused your sin to pass away [*ʿābar* hiphil]; you will not die" (2 Sam 12:13). It is not clear that Yhwh has "forgiven" David (NLT) or "remitted" his sin (JPSV). Yhwh will require a terrible price for it in the short term, and the story implies that the unraveling of David's family (with its acts of illicit sex and violence that recall David's) follows from these events. But Yhwh does not require his execution. In turn, David does not require

---

[476]See Wilma Ann Bailey, *"You Shall Not Kill" or "You Shall Not Murder"?* (Collegeville: Liturgical, 2005).

[477]In light of its prominence in passages such as Num 35, Brevard S. Childs sees it as originally referring to the kind of slaying that requires the response of a blood restorer (*Exodus* [London: SCM Press, 1974] = *The Book of Exodus* [Philadelphia: Westminster, 1974], pp. 419-21), while Mark E. Biddle suggests that it referred to the "vigilante justice" undertaken by the blood restorer (*Deuteronomy* [Macon, Ga.: Smith & Helwys, 2003], p. 113). But it came to have broader significance.

[478]See, e.g., Peter C. Craigie, *The Problem of War in the Old Testament* (Grand Rapids: Eerdmans, 1978), pp. 55-63.

Absalom's execution for the murder of Amnon.

In restarting the human race after the flood, God lays down explicit declarations concerning this violence, though they are elliptically expressed.

> I will seek out your blood, which belongs to your lives. From every animal I will seek it out, and from a human being. And from a human being, from an individual his fellow, I will seek out the life of a human being. The person who sheds the blood of a human being, by/for[479] the human being his blood shall be shed, because in the image of God he made the human being. (Gen 9:5-6)

While Yhwh may be here commissioning human beings to punish other human beings by executing them, Yhwh may be referring not to execution but to a cycle of violence. Jacob then echoes Yhwh's expectation (Gen 34:25-30), as David's story does, and Yhwh's statement compares with Jesus' warning that all who take the sword will perish by the sword (Mt 26:52). This fits with the declaration of Yhwh's personal intention to seek out the murderer's life. Yhwh is not merely predicting the consequence of murder but affirming it, because it unwittingly affirms the enormity involved in murder, the attack on God's image. Murderers will pay for their deed with their life, but this can come about in more than one way, and Yhwh is not laying down a law for capital punishment for murder.

Whereas in the West we have specialized personnel acting on behalf of the state to deal with offenses such as murder, in Israel this was in the first instance the duty of the victim's family, in the person of the blood restorer.[480] But responsibility for seeing that injustice is not done in this connection rests with the community as a whole, not least through the provision of havens for people accused of murder. Given that a person who kills someone by accident may be in danger of lynching, the homicide can take refuge there while the elders investigate the matter (Ex 21:12-14; Deut 19:1-13). The state thus functions to limit the power of families to go in for lynching or vendettas.[481] (This temptation is not limited to families: there have been cases in Britain where people have been summarily arrested and imprisoned, but fortunately not executed, because of popular indignation at terrible crimes and pressure on

---

[479]"For" would be a more usual meaning for *b*. But for the meaning "by," see Num 36:2; Deut 33:29; Is 45:17 (see *DCH*, though it also allows that other possibility), and this fits the context.

[480]Barmash, *Homicide in the Biblical World*, p. 26. On the notion of the blood restorer or blood vengeance, see Hendrick G. L. Peels, *The Vengeance of God*, OTS 31 (Leiden/New York: Brill, 1995).

[481]Cf. Levine, *Numbers 21–36*, p. 566; Baruch Halpern, "Jerusalem and the Linages of the Seventh Century BCE," in *Law and Ideology in Monarchic Israel*, ed. Baruch Halpern and Deborah W. Hobson, JSOTSup 124 (Sheffield, U.K.: Sheffield Academic Press, 1991), pp. 11-107; see pp. 16-17.

the police to produce people who could be punished.)[482] A person found guilty of murder is then handed over to the blood restorer. But murder is the concern of the whole community, and the blood restorer fulfills his task on behalf of the clan and the community and not just of the grieving family (cf. Deut 19:11-13). The blood-restorer system deals with the pollution brought by murder and also functions as "a legal mechanism that both assures the redress of wrongs and controls the violence to a level tolerable in the community."[483]

A Series of Interests

The logic of execution is that the murderer's blood expiates for the blood that otherwise defiles the land (Num 35:31-34) or thus "burns up," consumes, that blood (Deut 19:13). This consideration would exclude ransom (Lev 24:17-21). The same necessity to "burn up the evil" from the community and thus utterly remove it applies to the offenses of serving other gods and giving false testimony; "your eye must not show pity" (Deut 13:1-10 [MT 2-11]; 17:7; 19:19-21). Literal implementation is necessary if the punishment is to act as a deterrent to the rest of the community (Deut 13:11 [MT 12]; 19:20; 21:21). The requirement that an ox goring someone to death ("the most celebrated animal in legal history")[484] is likewise to be executed (Ex 21:28-32) also issues from the fact that execution is not a punishment but a cleansing of the land. The whole community is involved in stoning the animal, but the manner of execution avoids contagion through touching something that is taboo because it has killed.[485] When the murderer cannot be identified, the death of a heifer makes up for the lack (Deut 21:1-9). One death has made up for another; "the circle has been closed; what the slayer took away has been restored and replenished."[486] Where the homicide was totally accidental, the fact that the homicide stays in the safe haven until the high priest's death (Num 35:32) suggests it is this death that closes the circle.[487]

There is something paradoxical about this way of thinking, because another death threatens defilement as well as removing it: someone who has been executed can be impaled, but they must be buried before nightfall, as their body is an insult to God or is belittled by God, and defiles the land (Deut

---

[482]Cf. Wright, *Deuteronomy*, p. 223.

[483]Barmash, *Homicide in the Biblical World*, p. 23.

[484]Jackson, *Wisdom-Laws*, p. 256.

[485]The rationale is thus not that the animal is held responsible for the deed. See Bernard S. Jackson, *Essays in Jewish and Comparative Legal History* (Leiden: Brill, 1975), pp. 108-21.

[486]Levine, *Numbers 21–36*, p. 563. Paradoxically, the regulation does not refer to the actual spilling of the heifer's blood, perhaps because this would look too much like a sacrifice made away from the sanctuary.

[487]Cf. Milgrom, *Numbers*, p. 510.

21:22-23). So does shedding more blood really solve the problem caused by the first killing? (If the high priest's natural death had expiatory significance,[488] it did not simply perpetuate the shedding of blood.)

The regulations concerning homicide in fact mediate between a series of interests. On behalf of the victim, the victim's family may reckon that the principle of redress is the vital one. The community will also be aware of the rights of the homicide and the awfulness of taking another life. It will be aware both that murder stains the land and the community, and that executing an innocent person would stain the land with blood rather than remove a stain. It needs to make sure there is adequate evidence of guilt; no ransom can then be insisted on. If the killing was accidental, the accused is protected from the desires of the family, though this may mean staying in the safe haven (Num 35:30-32). If the accused is guilty of causing death by negligence, ransom may be possible (Ex 21:30-32); it would be a form of compensation to the bereaved family. In connection with actual murder, other Middle-Eastern laws allow both for redress in the form of execution or mutilation and for ransom if the victim's family is willing, and different regulations and narratives in the First Testament give varying impressions regarding execution and ransom (see, e.g., Ex 21:12-14, 30-32; 2 Sam 21:1-9).[489] Possibly death is the maximum penalty, in light of which the level of ransom might be set.[490] The story of the woman from Tekoa presupposes that David was not wrong in failing to require Absalom's execution (but is Yhwh implicitly behind the strange circumstances of his death?). She implicitly accepts the principle of executing a murderer but argues that there are other moral principles that can override it. In her case and his, these are principles related to the preservation and upholding of the family (2 Sam 14).[491]

In 1881 a Sioux called Crow Dog killed another Sioux called Spotted Tail over several personal and public matters. Through the application of traditional Sioux law, the families settled the matter, bringing about reconciliation between them and restoration of harmony within the tribe, by Crow Dog's family paying restitution to the victim's relatives in the form of cash, eight horses and a blanket. Believing the Sioux punishment too light for murder, federal agents arrested Crow Dog and charged him with murder, and he was sentenced to death, but this was overturned on the basis that federal courts had no jurisdiction over crimes committed by one Indian against another. Congress later closed this loophole to prevent such resolution of serious

---

[488]Cf Greenberg, *Studies in the Bible and Jewish Thought*, p. 48.

[489]See, e.g., Phillips, *Essays on Biblical Law*, pp. 49-73; Raymond Westbrook, *Studies in Biblical and Cuneiform Law* (Paris: Gabalda, 1988), p. 46.

[490]Westbrook, *Studies in Biblical and Cuneiform Law*, p. 78.

[491]Cf. Barton, *Understanding Old Testament Ethics*, pp. 5-6.

crimes.[492] Attitudes to murder among traditional cultures such the Native American and the ancient Israelite differ in their entire framework of thinking from those among Western peoples and thus provide resources to aid Western cultures to think about the question in fresh ways.[493]

The Administration of Justice

The process of justice, as well as the actual laws, needs to be just. The members of the community themselves have to exercise their responsibility if the elders are to be able to do their work properly in this connection. This requires that the witnesses tell the truth when a matter comes before them (Ex 23:1-3, 6-8). "You are not to testify [lit., "respond"] against your neighbor as a deceitful witness" (Ex 20:16). People are not to pass on false evidence or conspire with a guilty person to pervert justice or take a bribe or side with the majority because they are the majority (or, as JPSV translates, side with the powerful because they are the powerful). Nor must they side with the poor because they are the poor; truth is everything (Lev 19:15-16). But neither must people pervert the justice due to the needy.

The Torah seeks to safeguard against mistaken conviction: two or three witnesses are required if a person is to be put to death for worshiping another god, or, indeed, in connection with any alleged wrongdoing (Deut 17:6; 19:15). "In the areas of evidence, judgment, and sentencing the Mosaic law functions more restrictedly than the American judicial system. Fewer people would be convicted under the Mosaic code than under the penal codes of any of our fifty states."[494] Where someone does tell lies in giving testimony, they are to be given the punishment they were seeking for the other person, without pity: life for life, eye for eye, tooth for tooth, hand for hand, foot for foot (Deut 19:16-21). While in other contexts this requirement may limit punishment, here it is designed to further fair administration of justice by threatening severe punishment for perjury, though it again need not imply that people were actually to be maimed, and it might still presuppose that compensation can replace the maiming, at least for noncapital offenses (Num 35:31).

In practice the machinery of justice may nevertheless tend to work against the ordinary person. Forfeiture of land will mean forfeiture of one's place among the elders, so that the administration of justice can come into

---

[492]See Sidney L. Harring, *Crow Dog's Case* (Cambridge/New York: Cambridge University Press, 2002).

[493]See Christopher Townsend, "An Eye for an Eye," *Cambridge Papers,* March 1997 < www. jubilee-centre.org/document.php?id=16>.

[494]David Llewellyn, "Restoring the Death Penalty," in *Capital Punishment Study Guide,* ed. L. Kehler et al. (Winnipeg: MCC Victim Offenders Ministries, 1980), p. 41, as quoted in Marshall, *Beyond Retribution,* p. 207.

the hands of the wealthy who are then in a position to use the court to enhance their position further.[495] Kings came to be responsible for justice in Israel as elsewhere in the Middle East. But "kings of flesh and blood cannot always be relied on." On the other hand, a distinguishing feature of the biblical texts over against Middle-Eastern laws is that "the Bible . . . contains the voice of dissent as much, if not more, than that of the establishment." In the Middle-Eastern law codes the kings praise themselves for making sure that the law is fair, while the First Testament criticizes the kings for not doing so.[496]

The Torah recognizes that in some cases there may not be enough evidence to decide a matter. Exodus 22:7-15 [MT 6-14]) prescribes that where a question of theft is one person's word against another, they bring the matter before God to decide, or a person swears innocence before God over the matter, and that will decide it; this might imply having recourse to a local sanctuary. Like divorce, in an ideal world oaths would be unnecessary and would not need rules to cover them, as is reflected in Jesus' ban on oaths (Mt 5:33-37). But in the world in which we live, people lie, and taking an oath before God provides a disincentive to doing so. Thus Solomon prays that Yhwh may get involved when one person has wronged another but this leads to a dispute and to the taking of oaths, and may vindicate the innocent person and bring on the head of the guilty person the consequences of their act (1 Kings 8:31-32).

Methods of resolving conflicts that work in the village may work less well in an urban context where life and relationships are more complicated. At the same time the city's structures may help people from the country. Deuteronomy 17:8-13 adds the provision that where a case is too hard to decide locally, people are to go to "the place Yhwh your God will choose" and take the matter to the priests and the ruler/governor/judge (šôpēṭ) there (cf. Deut 19:16-21); their decision is then final. Second Chronicles 19:5-11 describes Jehoshaphat appointing in Judean cities such authorities (šôpĕṭîm) and also some Levites, priests and family heads for this role. Priests are not elsewhere involved in judicial processes, but Deuteronomy 17:8-13 follows a regulation about people guilty of serving other gods, which may suggest it is in matters of legitimate and illegitimate religious practice that the priests are the deciders; the Chronicles passage could have the same implication. Jehoshaphat's action also bears correlation with that of Moses in appointing leaders (śārîm, Ex 18:21; Deut 1:15) or heads (rāšîm, Ex 18:25; Deut 1:13) or authorities (šôpĕṭîm, Deut 1:16) who would make decisions for people (šāpaṭ,

---

[495]Cf. Wright, *Old Testament Ethics for the People of God*, pp. 303-4.
[496]Westbrook, *Studies in Biblical and Cuneiform Law*, pp. 29, 134-35.

Ex 18:22; Deut 1:16), and all this suggests that such a decision-making structure is one that worked in the city, where the complexities of life and relationships make decision making by the elders of the households or kin groups impractical.

A Relational Social Order

The First Testament makes clear that we should not romanticize Israelite community, any more than the community life of other traditional societies. "The *Gemeinschaft* of olden times was defective. The murder rate in villages in the thirteenth century, to take the English case, was higher than comparable places now. . . . The imagined extended family of 'traditional' life never existed." For example, "The Russian *mir* [rural commune] was neither ancient nor egalitarian, but a figment of the German Romantic imagination. Vietnamese peasants did not live in tranquil, closed corporate communities."[497] Yet in light of the place of lawyers in U.S. life, it is ironic that "the Puritans of the Massachusetts Bay Colony were fearful of the tendencies of English society towards a lawyer-order, and they began by banning a professional, paid lawyer-class. Every man had an obligation to know the law by means of the Bible." The jury system developed on the basis of this conviction.[498] The vision of the community taking responsibility for justice seems worth holding onto.

Following on Tanzania's formation as an independent country in 1964, President Julius Nyerere attempted to turn the new nation's society (back) into something that was systematically village-based, on the basis of the concept of *ujamaa*, "extended family" or "kinship" as an economic system,[499] though the imposition of this structure involved collectivization and strong state control. The project failed, partly through external political and economic factors. But Bill McKibben argues[500] that the time has now come when the developed world has to turn away from the massive to a more localized, communitarian, small-scale world; the *New York Times* review of McKibben's book bore the headline "Be My Neighbor."[501] He argues that it is unrealistic

---

[497]McCloskey, *Bourgeois Virtues*, p. 141; she gives references for the evidence.

[498]Rousas John Rushdoony, *The Institutes of Biblical Law* ([Nutley, N.J.]: Presbyterian & Reformed, 1973), p. 517.

[499]See Julius K. Nyerere, *Freedom and Socialism = Uhuru na Ujamaa* (London/New York: Oxford University Press, 1970).

[500]See Bill McKibben, *Deep Economy: The Wealth of Communities and the Durable Future* (New York: Times Books, 2007). In *The Comforting Whirlwind* (Grand Rapids: Eerdmans, 1994), pp. 8-32, McKibben compares the orthodoxy that economic growth is a good thing with the orthodoxies of Job's friends; it does not survive examination in light of the facts of life.

[501]Lance Morrow, "Be My Neighbor," *New York Times Sunday Book Review*, April 22, 2007, p. 9.

to reckon that we can continue extending the good life of the high-end sub-urb and thus inviting the whole world to seek to emulate it. We could and need to move toward an intelligent, socially responsible, nonideological lo-calism, with communities producing more of their own food, energy and cul-ture. That would adjust down our material expectations, but not make us less happy. Kent A. Van Til likewise notes how there is no necessary link between more free exchange and more well-being.[502] We need once again to "depend on those around us for something real." The Jubilee Centre in Cambridge, U.K., argues that our vision for the future in this connection needs to be guided by the Bible's paradigm of a "relational social order."[503]

4.5 Servanthood

In First Testament thinking, servanthood or slavery functions especially as an aspect of the life of family and community; it is simply for convenience that I separate out the discussion. The First Testament ideal is that the family is the structure for work and that servanthood is all humanity's vocation. The notion that some people become other people's servants in a long-term or one-way fashion is thus an odd one, but it provides ways of dealing with some problems that arise in the real-life world, and it can work in a satisfactory fashion for servants and masters. Such servanthood is very different from slavery as modern readers understand it, but it is open to abuse, and it re-quires safeguards.

Slavery

Western readers instinctively assume that they know what "slavery" is and that the moral judgments it deserves are obvious, and they naturally interpret the information the First Testament gives us on "slavery" in light of that as-sumption. But this process of interpretation actually involves considerable con-necting of dots, such as is already involved in the process of translating texts into English; inevitably readers understand the texts in light of the way trans-lators have already connected the dots. But this makes poor sense of many of them, partly because "slavery" works out in different ways in different contexts.

The *Concise Oxford Dictionary* defines a slave as "a person who is the legal property of another or others and is bound to absolute obedience, human chattel." A slave has no rights and slave owners may assume they are free to do with the slave as they wish and to require of the slave whatever they wish. To put it more sharply, "slavery is the permanent, violent domination of na-

---

[502]Kent A. Van Til, *Less Than Two Dollars a Day* (Grand Rapids: Eerdmans, 2007), pp. 40-47.
[503]John Ashcroft and Michael Schluter, "A New Framework for the Social Order," in *Jubilee Manifesto*, ed. Michael Schluter and John Ashcroft (Leicester, U.K.: Inter-Varsity Press, 2005), pp. 17-33; see p. 19.

tally alienated and generally dishonored persons."[504] Such slavery was a reality in the Roman world, is accepted in the New Testament and is the institution that shapes the modern understanding of the word *slavery* through the existence of the enforced ownership and violent submission of African Americans to white slave owners.[505] But it is doubtful whether it ever appears in the First Testament or elsewhere in the Middle East.[506] According to M. I. Finley, "there have been only five genuine slave societies, two of them in antiquity, classical Greece and classical Italy"; the other three are the United States, the Caribbean and Brazil.[507] Slavery is a Western phenomenon.

Different from slavery is serfdom, when for some reason a person is bound to work on the land for a master and has no way out of doing that. When the land changes ownership, the serfs go with it, but a serf is not a chattel without rights. A variant on serfdom, or a subset of it, is debt bondage, when a person is bound to work for someone else in order to pay off debts to him or her.[508] Forms of these types of servitude do appear in Israel, as they do among other Middle-Eastern peoples, alongside permanent chattel slavery on a smaller scale and without the assumptions built into the European notion. The Torah's particular concern is to regulate these (especially debt bondage) and to limit their baneful effect. Other Middle-Eastern law codes did the same thing.[509]

Understanding the First Testament's approach to the issue is again further complicated by the way the relevant Hebrew words work. The word routinely translated "slave" is ʿ*ebed* (ʾ*āmâ* and *šipḥâ* are the female equivalents).[510] This

[504]Orlando Patterson, *Slavery and Social Death* (Cambridge, Mass./London: Harvard University Press, 1982), p. 13; cf. Allen Dwight Callahan et al., "The Slavery of New Testament Studies," in *Slavery in Text and Interpretation,* ed. Allen Dwight Callahan et al., *Semeia* 83-84 (Atlanta: Society of Biblical Literature, 1998), pp. 1-15; see p. 1; also Richard A. Horsley, "The Slave Systems of Classical Antiquity and Their Reluctant Recognition by Modern Scholars," *Semeia* 83-84 (Atlanta: Society of Biblical Literature, 1998), pp. 19-66.

[505]On the use of Scripture in connection with the nineteenth-century debate about slavery, see Swartley, *Slavery, Sabbath, War, and Women,* pp. 31-64.

[506]Cf., e.g., Muhammad A. Dandamaev, *Slavery in Babylonia* (DeKalb, Ill.: Northern Illinois University Press, 1984); Marvin A. Powell, ed., *Labor in the Ancient Near East* (New Haven, Conn.: American Oriental Society, 1987); Dexter E. Callender, "Servants of God(s) and Servants of Kings in Israel and the Ancient Near East," *Semeia* 83-84 (1998): 67-82.

[507]M. I. Finley, *Ancient Slavery and Modern Ideology* (New York: Viking, 1980), p. 11.

[508]For this threefold characterization, see G. E. M. de Ste. Croix, "Slavery and Other Forms of Unfree Labour," in *Slavery and Other Forms of Unfree Labour,* ed. Léonie J. Archer (London: Routledge, 1988), pp. 19-32; see pp. 21-23.

[509]The matter of substance and the problem about language is thus not only an issue with regard to Israel, but with regard to other ancient Middle-Eastern cultures as well as other parts of the world; see I. J. Gelb, "Definition and Discussion of Slavery and Serfdom," *UF* 11 (1979): 283-97; I. M. Diakonoff, "Slave-Labour vs. Non-Slave Labour," in *Labor in the Ancient Near East,* (New Haven, Conn.: American Oriental Society, 1987), pp. 1-3.

[510]It is common to reckon that an ʾ*āmâ* can be married (to her master or to another servant)

is the word for a serf and for a bondman, but also for a servant who is not actually bound to a master, for a servant of the king who would be a high-ranking state official, and for a servant of God such as the king himself. The word simply "denotes a subordinate."[511] Given the fact that the word never refers to slavery as commonly understood in English, "slave" is a question-able translation for ʿebed. Whereas European languages, including New Tes-tament Greek, have separate words for "slave" and "servant," and have needed them, Hebrew has only the one word ʿebed, and this reflects the fact that its cultural context and framework of thinking is different; it does not need a word for slave because it is not acquainted with slaves. The term cor-relative to ʿebed is not "owner," baʿal, but "master," ʾādôn: passages where both words come particularly frequently include Genesis 24, 44; Exodus 21; 1 Samuel 25; 2 Samuel 14; 19; 1 Kings 1; 2 Kings 5.[512]

To avoid the misleading connotations of "slave," I revert to KJV's translation of ʿebed as "servant."[513] The word marks the difference between people who have power and authority and give orders, and people who do what they are told. God or king or master decides what shall be done; servants do it.

Working for Someone Else

A master certainly has the right to give orders to an ʿebed, but the chapters just listed and other parts of the First Testament make clear that he does not have absolute rights over an ʿebed. An ʿebed is someone who works for an ʾādôn and within that framework does what the ʾādôn requires. The relation-ship between them is more like that of boss and worker than that of slave owner and slave, no doubt with all the variety that can attach to the former. It can be an oppressive relationship; hence the need to regulate it. But there is nothing inherently lowly or undignified about being an ʿebed; being the ʿebed of someone important carries dignity with it. It is an honorable term. In the Western world, freedom is an ultimate value. This is not so in Israel, where the issue is whom you are serving (as Bob Dylan put it, you "gotta serve somebody"),[514] and much of your significance comes from here.

---

while a šipḥâ is an unmarried girl who serves the mistress of the house. In light of Zim-babwean practice, Dora R. Mbuwayesango suggests that she is specifically a woman who is not a man's wife but one through whom he might legitimately have children; Hagar is a šipḥâ ("Childlessness and Woman-to-Woman Relationships in an African Patriarchal Society," *Semeia* 78 [1997]: 27-36 [p. 30]). But it does not seem that such distinctions can always be maintained; cf. *HALOT* on šipḥâ; also the discussion in Marsman, *Women in Ugarit and Israel*, pp. 447-49.

[511]J. Pedersen, *Israel: Its Life and Culture I-II* (London: Oxford University Press, 1954), p. 44.

[512]baʿal is used of the owners of animals; we have noted that it can refer to a husband but that the First Testament does not usually utilize it in this connection.

[513]The KJV does also occasionally translate "bondman" or "manservant."

[514]The title of a song on the album *Slow Train Coming*.

The First Testament's use of ʿ*ebed* for human relationships reflects the fact that not everyone is their own boss; some people work for someone else, as most people do in the Western world. Its discussion of ʿ*ăbōdâ* is then comparable to our discussion of employment, except that in the First Testament working in the family business is the norm and working for someone else is odd. So-called slaves were "largely residential, domestic workers. . . . They complemented, but were not a substitute for, the labour of free members of the household. . . . Such slavery could be said to be little different *experientially* from many kinds of paid employment in a cash economy." [515]

Indeed, "worker" might be another reasonable translation of ʿ*ebed*. Three Hebrew nouns are commonly translated "work." One is *mĕlāʾkâ*, the word for God's work in creation and the work involved in building the wilderness dwelling or the walls of Jerusalem (Gen 2:2-3; Ex 35–36; Neh 4). It suggests activity that issues in the making of something. Another is *maʿăśeh*, which likewise suggests what people "do" and especially what they "make" (ʿ*ăśâ*; Ex 23:12, 24; 26:1, 31). The third is ʿ*ăbōdâ*, which suggests the object or person for whom someone works. The words ʿ*ābad*, ʿ*ăbōdâ* and ʿ*ebed* (serve, service/ servitude, servant/serf) are thus relational or social terms, pointing to the worker's relationship to the boss rather than to the activity of the work or the end result. "Work" is BDB's first meaning for ʿ*ābad*, which is the verb Laban and Jacob use to describe Jacob "working for" Laban over the years (Gen 29:15-30). Even God can be involved in ʿ*ăbōdâ* (Is 28:21), at least ironically. It can suggest hard work (e.g., Num 4:47), though when it has negative implications it may be qualified by other words to indicate that (e.g., Ex 1:14).

In the realm of work, why should there be some people who are masters and others who are servants, some people who give orders and others who obey them? When "work" starts in Genesis 1, it is first of all God's activity, and then by implication humanity's activity as God commissions humanity to continue the work God has initiated but not completed. The first creation story portrays men and women made in God's image to rule the world on God's behalf. By implication all human beings are servants of God, and there is no suggestion that they are designed to be under each other's mastery. Explicit "service" starts in the second story, where humanity is created to "serve" the ground (Gen 2:5, 15). Human beings are created to be workers and servants, but there is no talk of them working for or serving each other. There are no kings and subjects, no leaders and led, and no masters or servants. No doubt there is a sense in which all people were designed to be one another's servants, though that point is not made, but there is no headship or servitude attaching to some people but not others. Humanity as a whole has the respon-

---

[515]Wright, *Old Testament Ethics for the People of God*, p. 333.

sibility of both mastering the earth and serving it.

This vision survives in part in the First Testament's ideal in which each family in Israel has its own plot of land and works out its own destiny there. It farms its land self-sufficiently—indeed, with a little surplus so that it can be generous toward the needy, trade for things it cannot grow and lay something aside for the future. It serves Yhwh and it serves the ground; it does not serve human bosses. After all, the servant and the employee long for the end of the day and look forward to their wages (Job 7:2). Thus the First Testament's dream is that everyone should sit under their own vine and fig tree (1 Kings 4:25 [MT 5:5]; Mic 4:4; cf. 2 Kings 18:31; Zech 3:10). In other words, everyone is his own master. The description does not have the individualistic implications that it would have in an urbanized society, though it does have patriarchal ones. It will assume the household has a master who sits in the midst of his household under the vine and fig tree. But it does imply this household has the resources to decide its own destiny. The master of the house is his own boss. The First Testament has a different ideal from that assumed in the Western world, where we take for granted that everyone should have employment; the First Testament's ideal corresponds more closely to the implications of Genesis 1–6.

Whereas from the Beginning It Was Not So, It Became So

But at the beginning, Adam and Eve let the serpent master them rather than mastering it. Eve offers to lead Adam astray and Adam accepts. Both are soon then unsuccessfully hiding from Yhwh, and Adam is unsuccessfully blaming Eve and Eve is unsuccessfully blaming the serpent. The human failure to subdue the created world issues in a divine curse that turns "work" or "service" into "labor" or "toil" (*'iṣṣābôn*) and produces a situation whereby one person "rules" over another (Gen 3:16-19; cf. Gen 5:29). Lordship of one human being over another comes about only as a result of human disobedience to God. Serving the earth becomes tougher because people are doing it outside God's park, away from its water supply (Gen 3:23). When Adam and Eve's son takes on the task of serving the ground, his sin causes that service to become even harder (Gen 4:2, 12). Human life "is built up every day from work, from work it derives its specific dignity, but at the same time work contains the unceasing measure of human toil and suffering, and also of the harm and injustice which penetrate deeply into social life within individual nations and on the international level."[516] The contrast of thistle, thorn and brier over against garden or park corresponds to the tough realities of agricultural life in the hill country of Canaan.[517]

---

[516]John Paul II, *Laborem exercens* §1.
[517]Deist, *Material Culture of the Bible*, pp. 147, 156-57.

Henceforth the First Testament takes for granted a state of affairs in which there are bosses or masters and workers or servants. The first explicit reference to some people being required to "serve" others comes after the sin of Ham. Noah's three sons form the fountainhead of a new humanity comprising one household, but that sin will have its poisonous fruit in the way Ham's son Canaan will end up as the "the servant of servants," the most servile servant, the lowest ʿ*ebed*, to his brothers (Gen 9:25-27). It is a terrible curse that servitude will come to be part of this family's life, that it will be servitude of such an abject kind and that it is indeed one of the first features of human life that Genesis portrays within this new humanity. The two forms of service that God designed (Gen 1–2), service of God and of the earth, give way to a form of service that goes right against God's design. It is particularly odd and grievous that family relationships should be characterized by some people being subjected to a servant relationship with others. Ideally brothers and sisters, parents and children, uncles and aunts and nieces and nephews, rejoice to serve each other, but the family is not designed to be a place where some people are always the servants, others always the masters.

The first actual servants in Genesis appear as part of Abraham's household (Gen 12:16). Tellingly, they are mentioned not only in the same breath as animals but in the midst of them: "sheep, oxen, male donkeys, male and female servants [ʿ*ăbādîm* and *šĕpāḥōt*], female donkeys, and camels." Notwithstanding the absence of *baʿal* language, the notion of ownership is thus not inappropriate to the relation of masters and servants. The servants are part of Abraham's wealth and a sign of his blessing (cf. Gen 20:14; 30:43). But it is just as well he has them, and not just for his own sake (Gen 14:15).

Subsequently, Deuteronomy addresses the kind of person who could be expected to have male and female servants, as could his neighbor (Deut 5:14, 21 [MT 18]; 12:12, 18; 16:11, 14). Gideon has a substantial number of them (Judg 6:27). In the idyllic story of Ruth, Boaz is not merely running a family farm (actually the story is rather quiet about his family, as it needs to be to make its plot work) but utilizing a labor force of reapers, his "boys" (Ruth 2:9, 15, 21); the term is often used for people who could be referred to more technically as servants. Job had a very large body of servants (Job 1:3). Ziba, who had been Saul's servant and becomes Mephibosheth's, himself had sons and servants who would become Mephibosheth's servants and would farm the land he inherited from Saul and who are all Ziba's *môšāb*, people residing with him (2 Sam 9:9-13). Elisha talks about Gehazi buying male and female servants (2 Kings 5:26). The Second Temple congregation listed in Ezra 2 came to 42,360 plus their 7,337 male and female servants (and 200 singers), which offers an insight into the proportion of servants to the community as a whole at this moment.

Servants may be subject to transfer from one master to another, with no implication that they have any choice in the matter (e.g., Gen 20:14). But there is no implication that being a servant implies being subject to every whim of your master, as if he had the right to do with you whatever he wished. If a master knocks out a servant's eye or tooth, he or she goes free (Ex 21:26-27). If a master so ill-treats a servant that he or she dies, "he" is to be "punished" (NRSV, TNIV) or "avenged" (JPSV) (Ex 21:20-21).[518] Elsewhere the penalty for killing someone would be death, and it seems this would also be the case in connection with a servant. All this is the more striking given that the servant in question may well be a foreigner.[519]

Permanent Servants

But the idea of Israelites having Israelite servants is also odd. Israelites are Yhwh's servants, as a result of Yhwh's bringing them out from Egypt (Lev 25:42). Yhwh does not speak of having "freed" them (freedom is not a value); Yhwh rather transferred them from one service to another. They are therefore not in a position to sell themselves as servants to another master, as foreigners can (Lev 25:44-46).[520] The situation with people is the same as with land. Both belong to Yhwh. They therefore cannot belong to someone else, except on a temporary basis. They can be leased, but not sold. They cannot become your *naḥălâ* or *'ăḥuzzâ* or *yĕruššâ*, your permanent property such that you could pass on to your children.[521]

We may guess that a common reason Israelites became servants was that they lost their land through the Assyrian conquest or through the encroach-

---

[518]It is not clear whether the "he" is the servant or the master, though even in the former case, "avenge" is somewhat misleading since that word is inclined to suggest personal vindictiveness, whereas *nāqam* suggests "legitimate, righteous, even necessary enactment of justice by a legitimate authority" (Peels, *Vengeance of God*, p. 265).

[519]That is, in light of Ex 21:2-6 it seems likely that the text refers to a "Hebrew" servant, which probably means he is a foreigner (see on "Foreign Servants" later) and might also explain why the text does not simply say that the master is to be executed. Although its use of *nāqam* might suggest the servant's family exacting retribution (so, e.g., J. P. M. van der Ploeg, "Slavery in the Old Testament," in *Congress Volume: Uppsala 1971*, VTSup 22 [Leiden: Brill, 1972]: 72-87; see p. 79), a foreigner would be unlikely to have family present to do so. Perhaps that is the point; in the absence of family to exact redress, the regulation implies either that the community must see to it (so, e.g., Peels, *Vengeance of God*, pp. 69-76), or that Yhwh will do so (cf. Gen 4:15).

[520]Lev 25:39-51 sometimes uses the verb *qānâ*, which can refer to acquisition by purchase, but need not do so (see Gen 4:1; 14:19); it sometimes uses the verb *mākar*, which more commonly denotes selling. I have assumed that in passages such as Lev 25:39 and Deut 15:12 the niphal of *mākar* should be rendered reflexively ("sell himself") rather than passively; EVV vary.

[521]On the importance of this idea in Lev 17–26, see Jan Joosten, *People and Land in the Holiness Code*, VTSup 67 (Leiden/New York: Brill, 1996), pp. 93-136.

ment of other peoples on nominally Israelite land, or through crop failure and debt that eventually led to their ceding it to someone else and working in the manner of sharecroppers on what had once been their land. *Servant* is then an economic term as well as a social or relational one, somewhat like *serf*. It refers to someone who works for a landholder, perhaps someone who has been able to take over the land of people whose farm has failed. Such a farm would be able to absorb extra labor, as Boaz could, and "servants" would find a place there.

We do not know whether such servants had any form of freedom to decide to leave their service—whether they were more like employees than serfs. But even if they were legally free to leave their work, as pure debt servants were not, for practical purposes that may be a distinction without a difference. Like many employees in the modern world, although legally free, a servant may have nowhere else to go and no alternative but to stay, however badly their master (or employer) treats them. Their advantage is that as servants they are part of the master's household; they get fed, sheltered and looked after like members of the family. Possibly they also get some sort of wage. Leviticus 25:49 allows for the possibility that a person who sells himself into servitude to a resident alien might prosper to such an extent that he can restore himself, which might imply that he has saved up his wages. If Deuteronomy 15:18 argues that a servant costs only half as much as an employee (cf. JPSV, TNIV), it might seem unlikely that a servant could earn enough for that, but the passage may argue only that a servant costs only the same as an employee (cf. NRSV).[522] Perhaps this possibility of self-restoration is merely a theoretical provision, or perhaps it allows for the servant prospering in some other way: for instance, receiving an inheritance or marrying well, like the Egyptian servant who married the daughter of Sheshan, a descendant of Caleb, who had no sons (1 Chron 2:34-35).

But perhaps many people would be reasonably happy to settle for being long-term or lifelong servants. Servants do count as part of the family, so that God's covenant with Abraham applies to servants born in the household (that is, the children of servants such as the man who plays a prominent role in Gen 24) and to servants bought from a foreigner (Gen 17:12-13, 23-27). Such people join in Pesah (Ex 12:44). The master is to make sure that male and female servants have the opportunity to share with the family in the rest of the sabbath (precisely because he knows what it can be like to be a servant, in Egypt) and in the rejoicing and feasting of Israel's worship and festivals at the sanctuary (Deut 5:12-15; 12:12, 18; 16:11, 14); they cannot be made to work when he is not. The situation of servants could be secure and reasonably comfortable, and one can even imagine people who started off as debt servants vol-

---

[522]See Mayes, *Deuteronomy*, p. 253.

unteering to become permanent servants because they love their master and his household, and it is good for them to be with their master (Deut 15:12-18).

The Advantages of Servanthood

A servant who accepted a wife from his master (someone who was presumably already a long-term servant) would have to realize that this implied staying a servant for life; he cannot simply walk out with her and any children who have been born (Ex 21:4-6). This regulation may thus work at least as much in favor of the master as of the servant. It would mean that in practice any marriage between servants would lead to permanent servitude; indeed, masters could thus use male servants to breed permanent servants for them.[523] Yet the wording of Deuteronomy 15:12-18 points away from a purely cynical understanding of the possibility of becoming a servant for life. And it underlines the oddness of the fact that Western people are so offended by Middle-Eastern servitude when our practice of imprisonment as well as of employment seems much more dehumanizing compared at least with the theory of servitude, whereby a person "was still free to enjoy his own marital and family life, remained within the community, sharing its seasons and festivals, and was engaged in normal, useful work alongside the rest of the community."[524] In *East of Eden*, John Steinbeck pictures a Chinese man who had studied at the University of California giving an account of why he was content to be a servant.

> I don't know where being a servant came into disrepute. It is the refuge of a philosopher, the food of the lazy, and, properly carried out, it is a position of power, even of love. . . . A good servant has absolute security, not because of his master's kindness, but because of habit and indolence. . . . My master will defend me, protect me. You have to work and worry. I work less and worry less.[525]

I was once a boss (I ran a seminary); I sleep better now that I am just a servant.

In the First Testament, too, a relationship of mutual respect and trust can develop between servant and master, as is illustrated by the story of the servant commissioned to find a wife for Isaac (Gen 24). Prophets such as Elijah and Elisha have servants who are their "right-hand men." To reverse the analogy in Psalm 123, as a suppliant's eyes look to Yhwh for a demonstration of grace, so the eyes of servants look to the hand of their master and

---

[523]Bernard S. Jackson, "Biblical Laws of Slavery," in *Slavery and Other Forms of Unfree Labour*, Léonie J. Archer (London: Routledge, 1988), pp. 86-101; see pp. 93-94; cf. Crüsemann, *The Torah*, p. 156.
[524]Cf. Wright, *Old Testament Ethics for the People of God*, p. 310.
[525]John Steinbeck, *East of Eden* (New York: Penguin, 2002), pp. 163-64.

mistress.[526] Even a foreigner can do well as a servant, like the aforementioned Egyptian servant who married the daughter of Sheshan. It is even possible for a servant with insight to rule over a son who lives shamefully and to gain a share in the family property with the brothers (Prov 17:2), though Proverbs implies that in an ideal world servants will stay in their place (Prov 19:10; 30:22; cf. Eccles 10:7).

Although there is some condescension involved in referring to servants as "boys," the stories of such servants illustrate the good relations that can obtain between masters and boys. Boaz greets his reapers, whom Ruth can call his boys, "Yhwh be with you," and they respond, "Yhwh bless you!" (Ruth 2:5-6, 21; the foreman of the reapers is also simply called Boaz's boy). Saul takes one of his father's boys when he goes to look for the lost donkeys, and the boy shows more knowledge and initiative in finding the solution to the problem, provides a quarter at the crucial moment and sits next to Saul at a banquet (1 Sam 9).

Job half-recognizes that on the basis of an understanding of creation, one might infer that having servants is odd: "Did I reject the case of my servant or my maidservant when they had an issue with me? . . . Did not the one who made me in the belly make him, form us in the womb together?" (Job 31:13, 15). It is often argued that this is a "revolutionary" view,[527] but it is not difficult to imagine the Abraham of Genesis 24 taking this stance. The contrast is not between differences in attitude at different periods in Israel's history but between the life of Israel at its best and the boundary marks set up by the Torah to deal with difficult or potentially oppressive situations.

Debt Servants

The Torah then takes a similar stance to servanthood as it does to the breakdown of marriage. It does not simply ban it in Israel; this would not work. It seeks to make sure it does not get out of hand. In Leviticus 25:35-46 there are two stages to what may happen when an Israelite is in trouble. First, a fellow Israelite (his "brother") may make a loan to him. But if he becomes chronically unable to support himself and his family, in effect all he can do is sell his labor and become his neighbor's "servant," in the way we sell our labor in the Western employment system, except that he gets paid in advance. He is then rather like a resident alien, a laborer on his own or on someone else's land. If he does thus sell himself to someone else (hire himself out, we might say), "you must not make him serve you with the servitude of a servant." The fol-

---

[526]I do not think I formulated this point, but I do not know where I read it.

[527]E.g., Georg Fohrer, "The Righteous Man in Job 31," in *Essays in Old Testament Ethics*, J. P. Hyatt Memorial, ed. James L. Crenshaw and John T. Willis (New York: Ktav, 1974), pp. 1-22; see p. 15.

lowing verses suggest this means not simply making him a permanent servant but having him stay with the household as or like a resident employee.
Over a period of time he can then work himself out of debt and servitude and
regain control of his farm. "The Israelite can, therefore, never become a slave;
if he is reduced to indebtedness, his status is that of a *śākîr*, a wage-earning
day laborer."[528]

Leviticus does not mention any limitation to the time he may have this status
shorter than the jubilee period. This contrasts with the limiting of servitude to
six years in Exodus 21:2-6 and Deuteronomy 15 (where vv. 1-11 concern remission of debts every seven years for the whole community, while vv. 12-18 concern the release of a servant after six years of his particular service).[529] But there
is no reference to Israel ever observing the sabbath-year freeing of debt servants,
any more than other sabbath year or jubilee regulations. The nearest to an exception (significantly) is the story in Jeremiah 34 about it *not* happening.[530]

Leviticus adds that a servant's master must not rule over him with harshness (*perek*; Lev 25:43, 46, 53), which suggests physical violence or "backbreak-
ing labor."[531] It is the term for the way the Egyptians treated the Israelites (Ex
1:13-14); the only other passage where the word comes is the critique of Israel's
leaders in Ezekiel 34:4. Deuteronomy 15:12-18 makes explicit that the regulation about release applies to women as well as men. Exodus 21:2-6 did not
cover the possibility of a woman having to become a debt servant (only of a
man having to give up his daughter), but this became no mere theoretical possibility; it would presumably be the next recourse of the widow in 2 Kings
4:1-7, after she had given up her children. Deuteronomy 15:12-18 also adds that
at the end of the six-year period the master is to set up the servant well with
animals, grain and fruit, so that he can establish himself again as a free man.
As well as being "the last safety net in the social welfare system,"[532] servitude
also thus opens up the possibility of a fresh start. The seventh year is "a time
of grace in order to begin anew."[533] Three ethical assumptions may underlie
the law: that servitude is better than poverty, that membership of a family

---

[528]Milgrom, *Leviticus 23–27*, p. 2217.

[529]Tigay, *Deuteronomy*, p. 468.

[530]John Andrew Dearman argues that prophets such as Amos and Micah rejected debt servitude in principle (see *Property Rights in the Eighth-Century Prophets*, SBLDS 106 [Atlanta:
Society of Biblical Literature, 1988], pp. 18-57). Whereas the Torah seeks to balance the
interests of poor debtors and wealthy creditors, the prophets simply take the side of the
former.

[531]So Rashi; cf. Baruch A. Levine, *Leviticus*, JPS Torah Commentary (Philadelphia: Jewish
Publication Society, 1989), p. 179.

[532]Georg Braulik, *The Theology of Deuteronomy* (North Richmond Hills, Tex.: BIBAL, 1994),
p. 140.

[533]Harold Reimer, "A Time of Grace in Order to Begin Anew," in *God's Economy*, ed. Ross
Kinsler and Gloria Kinsler (Maryknoll, N.Y.: Orbis, 2005), pp. 71-88.

may be more important than individual freedom and that individuals matter and should be given opportunity to "escape poverty while maintaining dignity and worth."[534]

Such servitude compares with the indentured service that enabled many European and some African people to earn their passage to America in the sixteenth and seventeenth centuries, before imposed slavery began. Here people freely sold their labor to someone for a certain number of years. The difference in this First Testament situation is that effectively they have no option. Servitude is a means of paying off a debt they take on as a result of their impoverishment, or a means of paying for the redeeming of that debt by someone else. It implies a man can no longer sit under his own vine and fig tree, but its limitation to six years retains the vision that he can return to that. "As a mechanism for dealing with debt it compares favourably with, for example, Victorian debtor prisons."[535]

Compromising over Servitude

Before the head of a household hires himself out as a servant, he will do that with his children (cf. 2 Kings 4:1-7; Neh 5:1-5); hiring himself out means abandoning them, whereas if he hires them out, he may be able to find a way back to survival for the whole family. Indeed, Exodus 21:2-11 implies that most servants were children or young people, as has often been the case.[536] The *Los Angeles Times* of March 19, 2006, describes how between fall 2005 and spring 2006, after a long drought in Kenya, Soitanae Ole Kyologo watched helplessly as forty-eight of his fifty cattle dropped dead. He had no way to feed his family. In desperation he arranged to marry his daughters, aged eight and nine, to another man for three cows each, plus some blankets and cash. This is against the law, but according to child advocates there had been a perceptible increase in the number of underage marriages since cattle started dying. Part of the background to the regulation about girls sold as servants (Ex 21:7-11) may be similar, though it may be less desperate. A family too poor to raise a dowry might provide for a girl's future by letting her become a servant in another family that will then be committed to ensuring her security.[537] A girl's servitude presupposes she will marry the master and will cease to be a servant when that happens. The regulation gives her minimal protection

---

[534]Timothy John Turnham, "Male and Female Slaves in the Sabbath Year Laws of Exodus 21:1-11," in *Society of Biblical Literature 1987 Seminar Papers*, SBLSP 26 (Atlanta: Scholars, 1987): 545-49; see p. 549.

[535]John Ashcroft, "The Biblical Agenda," in *Jubilee Manifesto*, ed. Michael Schluter and John Ashcroft (Leicester, U.K.: Inter-Varsity Press, 2005), pp. 82-101; see p. 100.

[536]Crüsemann, *Torah*, p. 156.

[537]Cf. Allen Guenther, "A Typology of Israelite Marriage," *JSOT* 28 (2005): 387-407; see p. 389.

from sexual abuse (cf. Amos 2:7),[538] protecting her if the marriage never takes place or if the master also marries another wife. He cannot simply sell her to another family but must let her be redeemed by her own family or (presumably at the end of the six-year period) simply set her free.

The possibility that many or most servants were young people may link with the comment in Proverbs that "with words a servant is not disciplined" (Prov 29:19); Proverbs is taking the same stance in relation to servants as it does to other young people. But no doubt it would be more tempting to overdo punishment than is the case with one's own teenage children, as the regulations in Exodus 21:20-21 presuppose.

In the real world, free lending to the needy of the kind the Torah and Jesus prescribe does not happen very much in Christian countries or Christian churches, and perhaps it did not happen very much in ancient Israel. It is once again typical of the Torah's instructions that they start from how things work out in the real world. They focus on the practicalities of the compromise between the interests of the impoverished and the interests of the people who might help them. So they allow servitude, even on the part of wives and children, because this can be in the interests of both the impoverished and the master. The impoverished find a way of surviving and perhaps a new start; the master gets cheap labor. The limitation on the time people can be made to serve means that a person who is doing well cannot make someone serve him for a lifetime in return for helping the servant avoid starvation. Hammurabi's Code allowed only a three-year period of servitude, which might seem better, though not if one allows that a thirty-year mortgage has advantages over a ten-year mortgage; allowing servitude for six years and not a mere three might increase the incentive to take on a servant. Six years is a compromise between the two interests.

By its nature servanthood involved compromise. Stephen L. Carter notes that Thomas Jefferson and Abraham Lincoln both compromised over the abolition of actual slavery. Writing as an African American and presumably the descendant of slaves, he does not mean this as a criticism. Both presidents were moving toward the goal of abolishing slavery, but were prepared to make compromises in order to keep moving toward that goal. By compromising on slavery, Lincoln was able to preserve the Union and move toward abolition. If he had not compromised on slavery and had given up the Union, he would also have lost the possibility of abolition. "A compromise can possess integrity" if it does "move you toward your goal rather than away from it," move you toward what you know is good and right. Pope John Paul, Carter notes, makes a similar comment on the appropriateness of

---

[538]Crüsemann, *Torah*, pp. 157-58.

pro-life politicians supporting legislation that limits abortions but does not ban them. "Integrity will at times require that we take what we can get."[539] Or as Barack Obama put it (paraphrasing Reinhold Niebuhr), "we have to make these efforts knowing they are hard, and not swinging from naïve idealism to bitter realism."[540]

It is striking that Exodus 21–23 begins with detailed regulations not merely about servitude but about the freeing of servants. The chapters are an odd collection, which by no means cover Israel's life in comprehensive fashion. John Rogerson suggests that "the purpose of the selection was to make a theological statement about the character of God and of the divine requirements for Israelite society" and that in this connection "the release of slaves is put first . . . because it is not God's will that there should be slaves in Israel."[541]

Foreign Servants

A variety of circumstances could turn a person from working on their family's land into being someone else's servant, working on his land. This happens to Jacob, for instance, because he needs to leave home and go to a foreign country. Deuteronomy 28:68 imagines Israelites at their wits' end seeking to sell themselves into permanent servanthood to foreigners. Servanthood might be the result of wrongdoing (cf. Gen 43:18). Joseph was sold as a servant (Ps 105:17), and kidnapping and selling people as servants, often in a foreign country, was common enough in the Middle East; it is forbidden in Exodus 21:16 and Deuteronomy 24:7. This is likely part of the background to the rule that when servants escape from their master, you should let them reside with you rather than turning them in (Deut 23:15-16 [MT 16-17]), though no questions are asked about why they escaped. Perhaps they were ill-treated, like Hagar (Gen 16);[542] Yhwh does not apply to her any rule about letting fugitive servants go free, but that does mean that she keeps her place in the family of promise. The regulation about not turning in a fugitive servant might discourage ill-treatment of servants.[543] Or perhaps they just wanted to get out of their servanthood. This might be true of Shimei's two servants who escaped, whom Shimei went to reclaim (1 Kings 2:39-40). The rule about colluding with people escaping servitude perhaps means the Torah's entire acceptance of "slavery" deconstructs.[544]

---

[539]Stephen L. Carter, *Integrity* (New York: HarperCollins, 1997), pp. 46, 47.

[540]Barack Obama, quoted by David Brooks, "Obama, Gospel and Verse," *New York Times*, April 26, 2007, p. A23.

[541]Rogerson, *Theory and Practice in Old Testament Ethics*, p. 26.

[542]See Phyllis Trible, *Texts of Terror* (Philadelphia: Fortress, 1984), pp. 9-35.

[543]Cf. Crüsemann, *Torah*, p. 233.

[544]David J. A. Clines, "Ethics as Deconstruction," in *The Bible in Ethics*, ed. John W. Rogerson et al, JSOTSup 207 (Sheffield, U.K.: Sheffield Academic Press, 1995), pp. 77-106; see pp.

As was the case for people leaving Israel and ending up as servants, personal or economic pressures might be reasons why foreigners ended up as servants in Israel. Leviticus 25:6 refers to śĕkîrîm ("paid" workers, employees), and tôšābîm ("residents," presumably resident aliens) as well as ʿăbādîm and ʾāmôt.[545] "Employees" and "residents" cannot take part in Pesah, not having been circumcised (Ex 12:45); the implication is that the terms refer to foreigners, and the expression may be a hendiadys for foreign employees who do not expect to stay permanently.[546] The sabbath rules in Exodus 20:10 and Exodus 23:12 refer on one hand to "your male or female servant" and "the son of a maidservant" (a servant born in the household) and on the other to "the resident alien," a foreign servant. Leviticus 22:10-11 discusses whether a priest's servant may eat of the holy offerings of which the priest eats. Is such a person more like a member of the priest's family (who can so eat) or more like an outsider? The answer is that whereas a resident employee who has not become a permanent member of the community may not eat of the holy offerings, a person whom the priest has acquired with money may do so like people born in the priest's house. The implication will be that he has been circumcised, as Genesis 17:12-13 required. He counts as a member of the family.

The regulation in Exodus 21:2-6 speaks of someone acquiring or buying "a Hebrew servant." Ironically in light of the word's later usage, the word translated "Hebrew," ʿibrî, is of broader application than the word Israelite. Similar words in other languages, such as ḫabiru, apparently designate people who stand outside the regular Middle-Eastern state structures, outside the citizenry, and may well be foreigners from the perspective of the speaker. So the person referred to here may not be an Israelite.[547] The regulation's significance then is that it prohibits their permanent inescapable servitude; they too are bondservants, who must be freed after six years of service. It thereby extends the Torah's protection to foreign servants, though it also safeguards the interests of their masters and thus does so without being unrealistic. On the other hand, Deuteronomy 15:12-18 speaks of such Hebrews as "brothers," which implies that here they are Israelites, possibly Israelites of a lower social class, perhaps people who have totally lost their land, possibly because they have moved from the area of another clan; in effect, "Hebrew servants" are resident aliens who have had to become bond-

---

77-81.

[545]On the relationship between gēr and tôšāb, see van Houten, *Alien in Israelite Law*, pp. 124-31.

[546]So Milgrom, *Leviticus 23–27*, pp. 2161, 2221-22, though he understands the expression to mean employees who are resident with the householder (as opposed to day laborers) and who might be Israelites or foreigners.

[547]See the discussion in *HALOT;* but contrast Phillips, *Essays on Biblical Law*, pp. 96-110.

servants.[548] In either case, then, the Hebrew servants would have no land to return to on gaining their freedom, and this would add to the motivation to seek permanent servant status.

Leviticus 25:44-46 makes explicit that Israelites may indeed "acquire" (*qānâ*, perhaps "buy") permanent, foreign servants from foreign peoples or from resident aliens and their families, so that they become "property" (*ʾăhuzzâ*) which they "come to own" (*nāḥal* hitpael) in such a way as to be able to pass it on to their children, for them to "enter into possession of" (*yāraš*) as "permanent property" (*ʾăhuzzâ leʿôlām*). The difference between the meaning of these various words is not clear, but all can also be used of land, which one does not absolutely own. Exodus 21:20-21 may likewise refer to a servant as the master's property (literally, his money).[549] This is mentioned as the basis for not punishing the master if the servant recovers from his master's ill-treatment; it rather suggests that the master has responsibility to ensure that the servant does recover (cf. Ex 21:18-19).[550] Monetary or property language is thus sometimes used, though even the passage about the ill-treatment of a servant shows he has rights. So does a woman captured in war; she cannot be sold (Deut 21:10-14). She is not a chattel.[551]

Serfs

Foreigners were routinely captured in war; indeed a desire to expand the labor force can be a reason for making war.[552] Some would then become servants under the king, others the servants of individual Israelites. Isaiah 14:2 promises the Israelites that they will have their former captors as menservants and maidservants: one should hardly press this promise too literally, but it does imply a background in a practice. Goliath presupposes that the losing side in the fight between him and an Israelite champion would become the servants of the winning side, though in the event the Philistines run and get killed (1 Sam 17:9, 51-52). Death is often the fate of the actual fighters in a war; the captives will then be the women, girls and children, and Deuteron-

---

[548]Frank Anthony Spina discusses the relationship of these two designations in "Israelies as *gērîm*, 'Sojourners,' in Social and Historical Context," in *The Word of the Lord Shall Go Forth*, D. N. Freedman Festschrift, ed. Carol L. Meyers and M. O'Connor (Winona Lake, Ind.: Eisenbrauns, 1983), pp. 321-35; see pp. 330-32.

[549]But Westbrook argues for the translation "it [the redress] is his money": the debt for which the servant served is cancelled as redress (*Studies in Biblical and Cuneiform Law*, pp. 99-100).

[550]On Ex 21:20-21, see Gregory Chirichigno, *Debt-Slavery in Israel and the Ancient Near East*, JSOTSup 141 (Sheffield, U.K.: Sheffield Academic Press, 1993), pp. 155-77.

[551]Pressler, *View of Women Found in the Deuteronomic Family Laws*, p. 15; cf. also p. 91.

[552]Cf. Victor H. Matthews, "The Anthropology of Slavery in the Covenant Code," in *Theory and Method in Biblical and Cuneiform Law*, ed. Bernard M. Levinson, JSOTSup 181 (Sheffield, U.K.: Sheffield Academic Press, 1994), pp. 119-35; see pp. 121-22.

omy lays down some safeguards for women captives (Deut 20:14; 21:10-14; cf. Judg 5:30). Second Kings 5 describes how the Syrians captured an Israelite girl who became an attendant for the Syrian general's wife; when he contracted skin disease, the girl cared enough for him to offer her mistress advice on where he could get his disease cured. When Syria and Ephraim subsequently defeated Judah, Ephraim took 200,000 Judeans captive, but they were then forbidden by a Samarian prophet to make them servants and told rather to send them back home (2 Chron 28:8-15).

As a result of the work of Joseph, in the context of the famine, the Egyptian government was in a position to turn everyone in Egypt into state "serfs" (Gen 47:19, 25 JPSV), which the Israelites did not think would mean being unreasonably treated (Ex 5:15-16), though when Israelites speak of Egypt as "a household of serfs" (Ex 13:3, 14; 20:2), they perhaps have their oppression in mind. Passages such as 1 Kings 9:21 refer to a permanent serfdom that cannot be escaped except by flight. For their building projects, David and Solomon made the survivors of the indigenous peoples of the land into a labor force (2 Sam 20:24; 1 Kings 9:20-21). The expression mas-ʿōbēd seems literally to denote a "serving gang" (cf. Deut 20:11; Josh 16:10; 17:13). Translations have expressions such as "forced labor," which give a misleading impression if they imply people in chains overseen by men with whips. It need not imply they are made to work excessively hard or are ill-treated; they are simply not free to give up this work. Solomon also conscripted Israelite labor in connection with building the temple, but apparently this does not count as making them into serfs, perhaps because it was temporary (1 Kings 5:13 [MT 27]; 9:22). "Solomon's servants" (e.g., 1 Kings 9:27) were likely war captives, but the context suggests they were not merely unskilled laborers. Their position as state serfs ironically parallels that of Israelites in Egypt. On the other hand, Samuel's warnings about the ways of kings (1 Sam 8:11-17), which would lose their rhetorical force for people reading the book if they do not correspond to how things came to be, include the observation that kings will conscript people to serve in their administration, work their farms, make weapons for their army and provide for their palace. This (in combination with the taxes that Samuel's warning also describes) would also have the effect of making it increasingly difficult to look after the land from which laborers were thus taken, and thus drive families into debt and into servitude.

Some war captives would become Yhwh's servants, in recognition of the fact that Yhwh made the victory possible (Num 31:32-47). This may be the origin of the nětînîm, etymologically people "given [to Yhwh]," who work as assistants to the Levites and appear alongside the descendants of Solomon's servants (Ezra 2:43-58; 8:20). In effect this was also the role of the Gibeonites who tricked the Israelites into taking them on as servants rather than killing them and who became "hewers of wood and drawers of water" for the sanctuary (Josh 9). In Ezekiel 44:6-9 Yhwh bans the involvement of uncircumcised foreigners in the work of the sanctuary, though this would still allow the involvement of foreigners who had become full members of the community.

When Leviticus 25:46 bids Israelites not to rule harshly over one another because they belong to the same family, this could be read as implying that they can treat foreign servants thus, but that would more likely miss the point, given the significance of the same expression to describe the Egyptians' treatment of Israelites (Ex 1:13-14). Leviticus has in mind what Israelites must not do to Israelites, not what they may do to foreigners. And whereas in other respects this passage does draw contrasts between servitude of Israelites and servitude of foreigners, it pointedly does not extend this to the way Israelites may treat foreigners by saying "you may treat them with harshness." Other comments on the treatment of servants do not suggest that the requirements apply only to Israelites.

Slavery in the New Testament

In the New Testament the word *slavery* is more appropriate than it is in the First Testament. Roman slavery is something more like the possession of another person as property for life in such a way that they become subject to the master's absolute power. It is not the same as the slavery that European slave-traders facilitated and Americans accepted, but it is more like that than First Testament servitude is.

Jesus never said anything about slavery. He neither indicated that he accepted it nor that he disapproved of it. Likewise the rest of the New Testament never indicates that it disapproves of slavery. There is thus a contrast with the attitude of the Essenes, according to Philo, who repudiated slavery.[553] The New Testament does declare that in Christ there is neither slave nor free, but also that in Christ there is neither male nor female and neither Jew nor Greek (Gal 3:28). Its point with regard to the latter two categories is not to abolish them; nor does it point toward their eventual abolition. Its aim is to assert that we all come to be children of God on the same basis, though faith in Christ. Elsewhere, the New Testament can be reckoned to undergird slavery. Colossians 3:22–4:1 tells slaves to obey their masters in every way; masters are bidden to be fair in their treatment of slaves, but not to free them in accordance with the Torah. Slaves are to be submissive and give satisfaction in every respect (Tit 2:9-10), to regard their masters as worthy of all honor

---

[553]See Philo *Every Good Man Is Free* 12 [79]. Accounts of the Essenes vary; but even if Philo is wrong, or not all Essenes took the attitude he describes, his discussion indicates that a Jew of New Testament times could envisage repudiation of slavery in a way that the New Testament does not.

and not to take advantage if their masters are believers (1 Tim 6:1-2), and to accept their masters' authority whether they are kind or harsh (1 Peter 2:18). None of these letters contains any exhortation to slave owners.[554]

Margaret Davies thus comments on a contrast between the First Testament and the New Testament. The former has two approaches to social ethics. It legislates for the social order, attempting to place limits on the oppression of the weak by the powerful. It also places moral obligations before people, attempting to get them to be generous and considerate to the needy. In contrast, the New Testament writings "provide nothing like the breadth of vision in social affairs to be found in the Jewish scriptures."[555] They encourage charity but have no vision for empowering the needy to support themselves or for encouraging justice in society. "A comparison with Deuteronomy and Leviticus shows that the New Testament represents an impoverishment of traditions, an impoverishment which allowed gross injustice to flourish in Christian countries through the centuries."[556] Richard A. Allbee makes the point by suggesting that if there is a difference between the First Testament and the New Testament, it is that the former makes love a matter of regulation for the life of the community while the latter lets it be simply a matter of interpersonal relationships.[557]

Theologically, one might express it in terms of the New Testament letters being written in a way that makes allowance for the hardness of Christian hearts. Western history supports the implication that they were harder than Israelite hearts.[558] Even at the end of the twentieth century a state senator could claim the Bible's support for slavery, "attempting to draw on the cultural authority of the Bible to promote his regressive political position,"[559] as people do to promote warmaking.

---

[554]For varied understandings of Paul and slavery, see the articles in *Semeia* 83-84 (1998). The interpretation of Paul's instruction regarding Philemon, in particular, is a matter of debate. S. Scott Bartchy notes ways in which the New Testament subverts slavery: see "Slavery: New Testament" in *The Anchor Bible Dictionary*, ed. David Noel Freedman and others (New York: Doubleday, 1992), 6:65-73.

[555]"Work and Slavery in the New Testament," *The Bible in Ethics*, ed. John W. Rogerson et al, JSOTSup 207 (Sheffield, U.K.: Sheffield Academic Press, 1995), pp. 315-47; see p. 321.

[556]Ibid., p. 347.

[557]Richard A. Allbee, "Assymetrical Continuity of Love and Law between the Old and New Testaments," *JSOT* 31 (2006): 147-66.

[558]But John Howard Yoder offers a positive interpretation in *The Politics of Jesus*, rev. ed. (Grand Rapids: Eerdmans/Carlisle, U.K.: Paternoster, 1994), pp. 163-92.

[559]Jennifer A. Glancy, "House Readings and Field Readings," in *Biblical Studies/Cultural Studies*, ed. J. Cheryl Exum and Stephen D. Moore, JSOTSup 266 (Sheffield, U.K.: Sheffield Academic Press, 1998), pp. 460-77; see p. 476.

5

CITY AND NATION

The First Testament is more obviously concerned with questions about political and social life than is the New Testament.[1] But "what light can we get on the troubles of the great capitalistic republic of the West from men who tended sheep in Judea or meddled in the petty politics of the Semitic tribes?"[2] Quite a lot, actually, though seeing this light may take sharp vision. "We are left with the logically perplexing but morally empowering paradox that the Bible is both grossly irrelevant in direct application to current economic problems and incredibly relevant in vision and principle for grasping opportunities and obligations to make the whole earth and its bounty serve the welfare of the whole human family."[3]

5.1 City

As there would be logic in thinking about the family before thinking about marriage, so there would be logic in thinking about the nation and state before thinking about the city. In Israel it is the nation's, and even more the state's, existence that encourages and necessitates the development of the city as a means of administration (that is, taxation) and defense; this links with the city's having a "drive towards collective power."[4] But there is also logic in moving from the village to the city and then to the nation and state, and again I follow Genesis in doing so. City and village live in codependence. The city is a place where economic disparity becomes much more marked than it is in the village, so it becomes the context for thinking about questions concerning wealth and poverty. Related to this, it is a place where honesty and fairness are imperiled and the community needs systems for safeguarding them.

---

[1]Kornelis H. Miskotte, *When the Gods Are Silent* (London: Collins/New York: Harper, 1967), p. 271.

[2]Walter Rauschenbusch, *Christianity and the Social Crisis* (Louisville: Westminster John Knox, 1991), p. 1; cf. J. David Pleins, *The Social Visions of the Hebrew Bible* (Louisville: Westminster John Knox, 2001), p. vii.

[3]Norman K. Gottwald, *The Hebrew Bible in Its Social World and in Ours* (Atlanta: Scholars Press, 1993), p. 364.

[4]William P. Brown, *The Ethos of the Cosmos: The Genesis of Moral Imagination in the Bible* (Grand Rapids/Cambridge: Eerdmans, 1999), p. 171 (commenting on the city in Gen 4–11).

City and Village

Whereas an Israelite village might be the home of between fifty and two hundred people who serve the land around it, a city is larger and the land is not everyone's focus. Some people in the city would farm the area around, like villagers but commuting further, perhaps for several hours a day like people in Southern California, and at about the same speed sitting on their asses.[5] Boaz and his farmhands going out from the city to the fields and sleeping there during harvest time (Ruth 2–3) illustrate the pattern. Boaz's alter ego will be the woman running her household in Proverbs 31, a woman who is something like the kind of person Naomi might have been if only circumstances had been different. So some city dwellers will be laborers who have lost their land but are able to make life work as farmhands. Others will be tradespeople, merchants, priests and Levites, members of the state administration, and members of the royal family.[6]

As usual, we have to be careful about terms.[7] In Hebrew a village, a local residential community focused on the land, can itself be called an ʿîr, usually translated "city." And of course the scale of both village and city is quite different from those of our urbanized world. A more illuminating linguistic antithesis is that between the fortified city, ʿîr mibṣār, and the open village, kōper pĕrāzî (e.g., 1 Sam 6:18; villages or hamlets can also be referred to as settlements or homesteads, ḥăṣērîm). This antithesis indicates that one importance of the city is that its walls, watchtowers and gates make it a place that can offer security. Genesis 4:13-17 and Genesis 11:4 perhaps imply the assumption that this is the reason for the city's development, so that its origin is analogous to that of the monarchy; its ambiguous theological and ethical evaluation is also analogous.[8] In Genesis 11:1-9 there is "one people," and they want to build a city to "make a name for ourselves, lest we scatter over the face of

---

[5]Frank S. Frick reckons that Israelite farmers might spend up to four hours per day commuting between their home and their land (*The City in Ancient Israel* [Missoula, Mont.: Scholars Press, 1977], p. 95).

[6]On the city, see further Frick, *City in Ancient Israel*; Don C. Benjamin, *Deuteronomy and City Life* (Lanham, Md./London: University Press of America, 1983); Edward Neufeld, "The Emergence of a Royal-Urban Society in Ancient Israel," *HUCA* 31 (1960): 31-53; Volkmar Fritz, *The City in Ancient Israel* (Sheffield, U.K.: Sheffield Academic Press, 1995); and more broadly, Paula M. McNutt, *Reconstructing the Society of Ancient Israel* (Louisville: Westminster John Knox/London: SPCK, 1999).

[7]See trenchantly Michael Patrick O'Connor, "The Biblical Notion of the City," in *Constructions of Space II*, ed. Jon L. Berquist and Claudia V. Camp, LHBOTS 490 (New York/London: T & T Clark, 2008), pp. 18-39.

[8]See Jacques Ellul, *The Meaning of the City* (Grand Rapids: Eerdmans, 1970), pp. 1-9; and *OTT* 2:535-37. For the association of these in negative evaluation, see also Nicolae Roddy, "Landscape of Shadows," in *Cities through the Looking Glass*, ed. Rami Arav (Winona Lake, Ind.: Eisenbrauns, 2008), pp. 11-21.

the earth." In response to this empire-building instinct, Yhwh's instinct is to fulfill their fears and scatter them; the story has been repeated in the history of many empires and superpowers. Yhwh's further response is to promise to make Abraham a great nation and make his name so great it will be used in prayers for blessing (Gen 12:1-3). The city continues to be the basis for human confidence, and it is critiqued for that.[9] In Genesis it starts off as a way of finding a security different from the one Yhwh devises, and in Israel's heyday David establishes a capital city as part of making Israel into a proper nation. Yhwh then retrospectively chooses Zion and thus harnesses it to the divine purpose. "The history of the city" is "divided into two by Jesus Christ";[10] but his Father had already divided it into two.

City and village could have lived in a positive and constructive codependence.[11] A well-defended city would be a refuge for country people in time of war. Perhaps this is one significance of referring to the villages in the area of a city as its daughters (e.g., Neh 11:25-36); the mother city protects its daughters. But the metaphor also hints at the subordination of village to city and obscures the dependence of the city on the village (no village, no food) unless one keeps in mind that mothers are dependent on daughters. Many walled cities contained public buildings, a sign of the cost of the city to people who farm, and ironically, for many of its inhabitants the city came to be a place of danger, as it is today.[12] The polemics of the eighth-century prophets presuppose that as big cities develop as centers of government and administration, rich and powerful people there gain control of much of the land but do not directly farm it themselves. As anticipated by Samuel, the king also gains control of much of the land, in accordance with the Canaanite pattern. We do not know how far the relationship of city and country involved mutual dependence and complementarity (as perhaps implied by Deut 28:3), how far exploitation and an oppressive codependence;[13] there were certainly elements of each.

City and Family

Within the First Testament as a whole most of the explicit talk about life in the

---

[9]Cf. Frick, *City in Ancient Israel*, pp. 223-24

[10]Ellul, *Meaning of the City*, p. 173.

[11]Tim Gorringe compares the relationship of country towns (as opposed to big cities) to countryside in Britain or the United States (*A Theology of the Built Environment* [Cambridge/New York: Cambridge University Press, 2002], p. 115)

[12]Cf. John D. Mason, "The Good City," in *Toward a Just and Caring Society,* ed. David P. Gushee (Grand Rapids: Baker, 1999), pp. 340-95; see p. 344; Lester L. Grabbe, "Introduction and Overview," in *"Every City Shall Be Forsaken,"* ed. Lester L. Grabbe and Robert D. Haak, JSOTSup 330 (Sheffield, U.K.: Sheffield Academic Press, 2001), pp. 15-34; see pp. 30-33.

[13]See, e.g., Leslie J. Hoppe, *There Shall Be No Poor Among You* (Nashville: Abingdon, 2004), pp. 10-12.

city comes in the Prophets and the Wisdom books. Here the city raises two main ethical issues: wealth and poverty, and honesty. Linking these observations suggests that a major problem in the city is the capacity of the elders or other city government to use their position to their own advantage, as local politicians more concerned about their own prosperity than about their people and willing to use dishonesty to further their prosperity.[14]

Even in the country, settled life would implicitly compromise the significance of kinship structures for Israelites. The village community is a geographical entity, not a kinship one, as is reflected in the ambiguity of the relationship between kin group and village (are the two the same or does a village comprise several kin groups, or does one kin group occupy several villages?). But life and work in the city more radically undermine Israel's household-kin group structure. In origin or in theory, a city will be made up of kin groups, like a large village (Jonathan's ruse in 1 Sam 20:8-29 involves the claim that David's *kin group* was having a feast in his *city*). City life need not overwhelm that natural human family structure.[15] But many people who live in the city are not involved with the land, and for them the household-kin group structure will have less practical significance than it does in the country. Many will be involved in specialized trades, which also distances them from the land.

The Torah's vision is that all the families in Israel should be at least economically viable, and hopefully prosperous. There will not be poor families and rich families (cf. Deut 15:4). As John Calvin puts it, the best way to preserve people's freedom was to maintain a situation of rough equality between people so that there are neither very rich nor very poor in the community, and people cannot get into a position whereby they can oppress people poorer than them.[16] Israel's family-based structure can then embrace people such as widows and orphans who lack resources, and when a family falls below the line of viability, a stronger one is expected to help it find its way back. But such traditional family structures of life and work do not fit the pattern of urban life. People who live in the city include wealthy people who live off the produce of land they have been able to take over, which is worked by employees or servants on their behalf, both foreigners and Israelites who had lost their land. And they include an underclass that has a hard time making ends meet. City life encourages social stratification rather than the relatively egalitarian arrangement of the household-kin group structure.

---

[14]See further §7.1.

[15]Cf. S. Bendor, *The Social Structure of Ancient Israel* (Jerusalem: Simor, 1996), pp. 98-107.

[16]John Calvin, *Commentaries on the Four Last Books of Moses* (Grand Rapids: Eerdmans, 1950) 3:154, but reflecting the translation quoted in Stephen Mott and Ronald J. Sider, "Economic Justice: A Biblical Paradigm," in *Toward a Just and Caring Society*, ed. David P. Gushee (Grand Rapids: Baker, 1999), pp. 15-45; see p. 23.

The city offers new opportunity for gaining wealth, both relatively legitimate and relatively illegitimate. People who do well can more easily hold onto their wealth, use it for their own benefit and increase it. People who wish to take advantage of the weak (for instance, by lending at interest and driving people into servitude) can more easily do that. Thus the process of urbanization is not inherently wrong, but it issues in an arrangement that facilitates wrong.[17] The link between urbanization and the development of state structures for administration and the collection of taxes (whether undertaken in a relatively just or a relatively self-indulgent fashion) exacerbates this, as do the demands of tribute from imperial powers, beginning as Assyria took an interest in Ephraim and Judah and continuing through to the end of First Testament times.

Economic Disparity

A life focused on farming and shepherding did not make it impossible to become wealthy or chronically impoverished. Even in Saul's day, before the urban developments encouraged by David and Solomon's monarchy, there are many people in distress and in debt, and there are farming magnates such as Nabal who have been able to accumulate huge herds (1 Sam 22:2; 25:2).[18] Yet to judge from the housing, people living in villages had similar standards of living, and the same is true in some urban contexts. But the development of cities sees much more diversity, with some houses being much larger and more impressively constructed than others, as archaeological work again shows. Amos testifies to some being better appointed as well as better built (Amos 3:15; 5:11; 6:4). The development of cities was linked with the monarchy, as it needed regional administrative centers,[19] and in these cities the buildings occupied by officials were particularly fine, and the cities would be better fortified.[20]

In propagating its ideals for Israelite life the Torah mostly focuses explicitly or implicitly on the life that most Israelites live, which continues to be in the country. Only rarely does it raise questions distinctive to the city (e.g., Lev 25:29-31, an inset on a special question about the city in a chapter that as a whole has a country focus). By implication, even there it wants to see the social structures of village life still working. "It is first and foremost the Deuter-

---

[17]On the possible processes and mechanisms involved, see Walter J. Houston, *Contending for Justice,* LHBOTS 428 (New York/London: T & T Clark, 2006), pp. 18-51.

[18]Cf. Willy Schottroff, "The Prophet Amos," in *God of the Lowly,* ed. Willy Schottroff and Wolfgang Stegemann (Maryknoll, N.Y.: Orbis, 1984), pp. 27-46; see p. 37.

[19]Cf. G. W. Ahlström, *Royal Administration and National Religion in Ancient Palestine* (Leiden: Brill, 1982), pp. 1-43.

[20]Cf. Ferdinand E. Deist, *The Material Culture of the Bible* (Sheffield, U.K.: Sheffield Academic Press, 2000), pp. 195-209.

onomy which shows us the importance of the city. . . . We may call it a municipal law. . . . It is the town it reckons with as the responsible factor, thus increasing the authority of the elders of the city."[21] Strands in the Torah that do belong to an urban context reaffirm and rework the expectations associated with those old social structures, rather than making new proposals. And for the sake of everyone in the city (the needy, the administration, the faithless, the faithful), Israel is to inscribe the regulations in the Torah on the city gates (Deut 6:9). Deuteronomy addresses the whole community, and the whole community has a role in seeing that the Torah gets implemented or has an interest in knowing how they are due to be treated. But the Torah says virtually nothing about wealth, perhaps partly because this is not a topic about which a community makes rules and regulations.

As it is the Prophets and the Wisdom books that most discuss the issues raised by city life, so it is they that most discuss wealth as a moral issue. The difference points to a different way of seeing society and a different social context. "The man who disappears into the city becomes merchandise."[22] Given that it is easier to become wealthy in the city, it is not surprising that these works, which implicitly or explicitly reflect the life of the city, take wealth as a major topic. In another contrast with the Torah, they presuppose a situation more like that in a Western nation, where there are wealthy people and poor people, though the main body of the populace is located in between these categories. The similarity with Western experience links with this phenomenon's connection with the nature of urban life.

Proverbs does not imply that the mere existence of economic disparity between different people is an evil. "The Old Testament does not present equality of wealth as an ideal."[23] Its emphasis lies on the wealthy being generous and the faithless stopping being faithless. "The social ideal they [the prophets] project is that of a benevolently hierarchical society,"[24] indeed a benevolently patriarchal society. The male heads of households have the power to decide how the household's wealth is used; allusions to the faithful and the faithless in the Torah, the Prophets (e.g., Ezek 18), Proverbs and Job commonly refer to men.

---

[21]J. Pedersen, *Israel: Its Life and Culture I-II* (London: Oxford University Press, 1954), p. 35.

[22]Ellul, *Meaning of the City*, p. 55.

[23]Cyril S. Rodd, *Glimpses of a Strange Land* (London: T & T Clark, 2001), p. 181. On pp. 161-84 Rodd usefully surveys the material on poverty in the First Testament and (acerbically) the scholarship on the question. See further the discussion between Richard J. Coggins, "The Old Testament and the Poor," *ExpT* 99 (1987-88): 11-14; Sue Gillingham, "The Poor in the Psalms," *ExpT* 100 (1988-89): 15-19; J. Emmette Weir, "The Poor Are Powerless," *ExpT* 100 (1989-90): 13-15; R. Norman Whybray, "Poverty, Wealth, and Point of View in Proverbs," *ExpT* 100 (1988-89): 332-36; Mark Sneed, "The Class Culture of Proverbs," *SJOT* 10 (1996): 296-308; and now Timothy J. Sandoval, *The Discourse of Wealth and Poverty in the Book of Proverbs* (Leiden/Boston: Brill, 2006).

[24]Houston, *Contending for Justice*, p. 100.

The issue throughout is: how am I to conduct my relationships with my dependents justly, that is, in a way embracing an understanding of myself as a member of a community, of my dependents as human beings like myself and equally members of my community, and of God as the one who exhibits, commands and enforces compassion, concern for the needs of human beings, and integrity?[25]

Job gains much of its power from this background assumption. The reason Job's experience raises questions is that as an extraordinarily rich and thus powerful person in the community, Job has used his wealth and power responsibly, for the benefit of the needy. The story presupposes the importance of such *ṣĕdāqâ* on the part of the individuals with wealth and power in the community, a matter of personal commitment in the context of a community ethos, alongside the concrete regulations about the community's treatment of needy people such as appear in Deuteronomy 15 or Leviticus 25.[26]

Wealth and Poverty

From the outset (Prov 1:10-19) Proverbs "intimates the ambivalent status of material wealth . . . as a good, but not an ultimate good." Wealth is attractive, but "not so valuable as to justify its acquisition by any or unjust means." Yet wealth points to all that is desirable.[27] Proverbs' view of wealth is complex rather than merely ambiguous.[28] It is typically realistic about wealth: "The wealth of the rich is their fortified city; the poverty of the poor is their ruin" (Prov 10:15). There are things you can do with wealth. You can placate someone who is angry or buy yourself success or open the way to the presence of important people (Prov 21:14; 17:8; 18:16). Gifts at Christmas, at weddings and at showers have a relational and a transactional role. They signify something of the way we see a relationship and develop it. We are embarrassed at giving or receiving when it is not reciprocal or when the value of the gifts does not balance. A gift at the right moment may compensate for an offense we have caused. In a traditional society, too, the giving of gifts is part of how life works; it need not imply what we would call bribery. On the other hand, the person with the resources to offer gifts may overestimate their power, and it would be nice to think that gifts to influence the course of justice will not be accepted.

The converse of the power of wealth is the weakness of poverty. "All the relatives of a poor person reject him, how much more do his friends avoid him" (Prov 19:7; cf. Prov 14:20; 19:4). "The poor person utters pleas for grace,

---

[25]Ibid., p. 117.
[26]Ibid., pp. 126-33.
[27]Sandoval, *Discourse of Wealth and Poverty in the Book of Proverbs*, pp. 72-73, 74, 83.
[28]Ibid., p. 205. Cf. Jacques Ellul, *Money and Power* (Downers Grove, Ill.: InterVarsity Press, 1984), with the foreword by David W. Gill, p. 8.

but the rich person gives tough answers" (Prov 18:23). He has considerable opportunity to do so: "Many people entreat a noble, and everyone is a friend of a giver of gifts" (Prov 19:6). The advantages of wealth suggest that Proverbs 10:15 would naturally constitute an encouragement to seek wealth and avoid poverty, and the book reckons that poverty often issues from laziness (e.g., Prov 10:4; 19:15). The sluggard is one of its antiheroes (e.g., Prov 6:6-11). If you till your land, you have something to eat; if you do not look after your vineyard, you get no grapes (Prov 12:11; 20:4, 13; 24:30-33). But elsewhere in the First Testament, "poverty is a scandalous condition inimical to human dignity and therefore contrary to the will of God. . . . It is not caused by fate; it is caused by the actions of those whom the prophet condemns" (e.g., Is 10:1-2; Amos 2:6-7).[29] Either way, "poverty results from decisions people make. Poverty does not just happen; it occurs because people make it happen"—either the people who end up poor themselves, or (more often in terms of what the Scriptures say) other people who treat them oppressively.[30]

The aphorism about the advantages of wealth and the vulnerability of poverty (Prov 10:15) might imply an encouragement to the wealthy to take account of the needs of the poor. Certainly this is explicit elsewhere. "The person who gives to someone poor will lack nothing, but one who shuts his eyes will be much cursed" (Prov 28:27). While it is all right to rejoice when the wicked have received their proper reward (e.g., Prov 1:26), "the person who mocks the poor insults his maker; the person who rejoices at calamity will not go free" (Prov 17:5; cf. Prov 14:31). It can falsely imply that people deserved what happened, which excuses one from helping them. In keeping with the First Testament's commitment to the poor, the hungry and the grieving, and its declaration that calamity will come to the powerful and wealthy, Jesus declares blessings on the former and woe on the latter (Lk 6:20-26).

Insight and Folly in the City

While wealth is a fortification, "the way of Yhwh is a fortification for people of integrity, but a ruin for wrongdoers" (Prov 10:29). For Job to have trusted in his wealth would have been as much a denial of God as worshiping the sun or the moon (Job 31:24-28). It would also have been foolish.

> Yhwh's name is a fortified tower;
>> the faithful person runs into it and is secure
> The rich person's wealth is his fortified city;
>> like a secure wall, in his imagination. (Prov 18:10-11)

---

[29]Gustavo Gutiérrez, *A Theology of Liberation* (Maryknoll, N.Y.: Orbis, 1973/London: SCM Press, 1974), pp. 291, 292.

[30]Leslie J. Hoppe, *There Shall Be No Poor Among You* (Nashville: Abingdon, 2004), p. 171.

Given that the first saying does not always work, one might wonder whether the juxtaposition of the two sayings invites the reflection that the rich person is wise to keep one eye on his wealth as well as one on Yhwh. But the last word confronts that. There is nothing imaginary about the protection of Yhwh's name, but there is about the protection of wealth.

Wisdom thinking is likely an urban phenomenon. "The city produces, and singularly so, in the intellectual life. Nowhere else do ideas evolve so rapidly."[31] Proverbs is admittedly not simply an urban document. Developing over centuries, its material sometimes suggests the life and teaching of the family, sometimes the life of the city and the teaching of the court college, and sometimes the issues that concern the theological school. Its attitude to wealth and poverty reflects all three. Its commendation of concern for the poor fits the first, its stance on wealth suggests the city, while its concern to reassure people that life does work out in a fair and logical way suggests students in theological school, who always fret about theodicy.

Having described how things will be when Yhwh implements a proper order in the society, Isaiah paints a contrasting portrayal of how they are now (Is 32:6-8). Folly, wrongdoing, irreligion, inhumanity, deceit and shame come together in a frightful brew. The same act is an embodiment of all these; the same person is a stupid, evil, irreligious, inhuman, lying scoundrel.

The implication of Isaiah's words is not quite that this is the characteristic nature of life in Jerusalem or that the leadership and the "nobility" in general are involved in this wicked folly (though this might be true), but that the government fails to take action to see that people are protected from such scoundrels. These are people who know how to use the system so as to ensure that they have plenty of food and drink for themselves by taking advantage of ordinary people who get into misfortune. In theory the system has built-in safeguards against that, designed to protect ordinary people, and the vocation of noble people is to take a stand against such misuse of the system. In the context Isaiah may refer to taking the stand in the literal, legal sense, to oppose misuse of the legal system. If they fail to do that, clever people can usually find their way round the constraints of the system, and the government is doing nothing to stop them.

Actually, they ought to be scared, because they ought to consider who they are. They are indeed fools, because (for instance) in the end they are not acting in their own interests; truth will catch up with them, and they will end up ashamed. There really is such a thing as moral evil, and causing or allowing needy people to remain hungry and thirsty is not merely, for instance, one of those regrettable features of life that result from the fact that everyone has

---

[31]Ellul, *Meaning of the City*, p. 151.

accept responsibility for their own destiny. And the folly is compounded and the evil-doing is complicated by God's involvement in these matters, which means, for instance, that the scoundrels make their legal statements before God and are thus involved in lying before God and not merely before a human court.

The able people in the city are wise to be people of insight.

Where There Is Love

The ordinary person may feel jealous of the wealthy who have an honored place in the community and receive everyone's attention, but this does put pressure on them. There are always people seeking to get them to use their power or wealth for their advantage. "Wealth is a ransom for a person's life, but the poor does not hear a threat," or does not listen to one (Prov 13:8). There is a strange sense in which wealth issues in vulnerability, whereas poverty means you have nothing to lose to people's intimidation. In Western nations people can have power and resources, and thus have a full experience of the good life, yet often not feel that their life is a feast; as China develops, its people have been going through the same experience. In contrast, "all the days of a weak person are bad, but a good attitude is a feast continually" (Prov 15:15). If you belong to the element in the community that lacks power and resources and has only just enough to get by, then you never experience the good life you see portrayed on television, yet this does not stop you enjoying a feast, because everything depends on attitude of heart. Festivity issues from within, not from without. "With reverence for Yhwh, a little is good, better than great wealth and turmoil with it" (Prov 15:16). The saying does not claim that wealth always brings turmoil, but that there is a fair chance of this. Nor is it quite commending poverty, and it speaks of people who have "a little," which implies having just enough rather than being perpetually hungry. But we are always tempted to reckon that enough is not enough: "Sheol and Abaddon cannot be satisfied, and the eyes of a human being cannot be satisfied" (Prov 27:20).

So more brings disadvantages, while a little in the context of a relationship with Yhwh brings no trouble. A third saying in this sequence links with that. "When love is there, a meal of vegetables is good, better than a fattened ox when there is hate with it" (Prov 15:17). Alongside reverence for Yhwh are good relationships with one's nearest and dearest rather than ones characterized by hostility or resentment (which "turmoil," *mĕhûmâ*, can denote). "When peace is there, a dry crust is good" (that is, even if you lack olive oil to dip it in),[32] "better than a house full of contentious sacrifices" (Prov 17:1). A fattened

---

[32]See Raymond C. Van Leeuwen, "The Book of Proverbs," *The New Interpreter's Bible* (Nash-

ox perhaps implies a great family celebration, but such occasions, like Thanksgiving or Christmas, can become the times when family resentments and quarrels find powerful expression. The good life, even when combined with religious observance, cannot make up for being a dysfunctional family or community, whereas family or community happiness can make up for a simple life, even make it rich.

The dynamics need not work out that way. "A man who is poor but extorts from the impoverished—driving rain and there is no food" (Prov 28:3). The EVV rework the opening noun to turn the extortioner into a ruler,[33] but the more striking MT statement fits better with the striking image in the second colon. Oppression can divide the oppressed against each other. One poor person might be driven to get a job exacting taxes and thus being the means of oppressing other poor people, or a debtor might act oppressively in relation to his own creditor, as in Jesus' story (Mt 18:23-35). Such people become like heavy rain at harvest that ruins crops instead of making them grow.

There is another sense in which wealth and turmoil may go together. Creating wealth itself involves toil—not merely hard work, but hard work that feels laborious. "What do people get for all the toil and mental striving with which they toil under the sun? Because all their days are suffering and their work is a vexation. Even at night their minds do not rest. This too is emptiness" (Eccles 2:22-23). And what is the point of putting in all that effort to get wealthy when it leaves you on your own with no time to enjoy yourself (Eccles 4:7-8)? When you can never have enough, partly because the more you have, the more people want a share (Eccles 5:10-12 [MT 9-11])?

The Vulnerability of Wealth

So "do not toil to get rich; in your discernment, hold back. Do you let your eyes flit on it—it is gone, because it really does make wings for itself, flits into the heavens like an eagle" (Prov 23:4-5). The saying neatly reuses its key verb: you let your eyes "fly" on wealth but you find that wealth itself "flies" off (cf. Prov 28:22; Eccles 5:14 [MT 13]).

And even if it does not flit, you will. Accumulating wealth does no lasting good, because you cannot take it with you when you die, and who knows how your heir will look after it? Even if he is a wise person, he is not someone who has toiled for it, as you did, so what was the point of all that toil (Eccles 2:18-21; cf. 5:14-16; 6:1-9)? So it is foolish to fret at the way people get wealthy (maybe by shady means), because wealth cannot buy long life (Ps 49). Being able to afford healthy food and a good health plan may buy you extra years,

---

ville: Abingdon, 1997) 5:17-264; see p. 166.

[33]For instance, reading *rōš* instead of *rāš*.

but you are still subject to God's deciding when your time comes. People do not live by bread alone but by every word that issues from Yhwh's mouth (cf. Deut 8:3); that is, God makes the decision about whether we live or die, and God does not accept bribes. That applies to the rich and the poor, the wise and the stupid, people of status and people with none. People can deny the reality of death and fool themselves that they will live forever, but in this respect we are the same as animals—we die.

"A trustworthy person abounds in blessings, but one eager to get rich will not go free" (Prov 28:20). Trustworthy people may abound in the blessings or fruitfulness they bring or in those they receive. In contrast, people eager to get rich and therefore willing to cut corners or ignore the needs of the poor neither give blessings nor receive them. They will find their get-rich-quick schemes are their downfall. As an economics professor put it, an economy grows in "ethical soil."[34]

"Rich people are wise in their own eyes"; they draw the natural inference that their earning such wealth is evidence of their wisdom. "But poor people who have discernment can search them out" (Prov 28:11): they can see into them, understand them where they cannot understand themselves, see through them. The people who think they are wiser than average, and certainly wiser than those who lack the insight to gain wealth, are actually less so. Indeed, by implication, they are also less wealthy than (some) poor people, because in lacking wisdom and discernment they lack the more valuable asset that these poor people have.

Proverbs' material on wealth makes clear its intrinsic systematic contradictoriness. It knows that contrasting statements need to be made on its subject. It thus anticipates the questions expounded more extensively in Job and Qohelet.[35] Righteousness leads to wealth, except when it does not. Further, Proverbs recognizes, though it does not emphasize, that "faithful people will do well" is not reversible as "people who do well are faithful."[36] Often the rich in Proverbs are the faithless. Qohelet is more systematic in questioning whether faithful people do well and faithless people do badly; to Qohelet, experience seems more "ethically neutral"[37] or at least ethically ambiguous.

The distinctiveness of its warnings about laziness generating poverty makes this aspect of Proverbs worth attending to rather than ignoring, even

---

[34]Deirdre N. McCloskey, *The Bourgeois Virtues* (Chicago/London: University of Chicago Press, 2006), p. xiii.

[35]Cf. Raymond C. Van Leeuwen, "Wealth and Proverbs," *Hebrew Studies* 33 (1992), pp. 25-36.

[36]Cf. Tomáš Frydrych, *Living Under the Sun*, VTSup 90 (Leiden/Boston: Brill, 2002), pp. 39-40.

[37]Ibid., p. 44.

as we set it in the context of the complementary perspectives of the Torah, which simply stresses generosity and passes no judgment, and of Job[38] and the Prophets, who stress the oppression of the powerful and make no comment on people's possible responsibility for their poverty.[39] Indeed, the prophets refer to the poor rather less frequently than their reputation for siding with the poor would make one expect; "it is only the wisdom writings which show any concern for the poor as *poor.*"[40] There is a scholarly tradition of reading Proverbs' attitude to the poor pejoratively. The reading requires considerable inference and depends on speculative theories about the book's social context. (Is the reading designed to make us wealthy Western scholars feel less guilty?) A readerly approach rather than a speculative sociocritical one suggests we acknowledge the way its aphorisms can thus be used to bolster the position of wealthy people such as us.

Inclusiveness

Wealth makes it possible to have a really great time. And the First Testament likes the idea of people having a really great time. It enthuses over festivals where people enjoy and eat their fill of all the good things God has given them (e.g., Deut 26:11, 12). It is less enthusiastic about the idea of some people having a great time while others are excluded. James W. McClendon's second image for sin is "rupture"; it frustrates one of the aims of creation, that "human beings are made for company with one another, and together made for fellowship with God."[41] It is a sign of social and moral breakdown within society when it is characterized by self-indulgence on the part of some people that is only possible on the basis of their improving their own position at the expense of others, accumulating land and ignoring the needs of the less well-off. Their prosperity is built on their treatment of other people. There is a link between their being champion drinkers and their accepting bribes to treat the faithless as faithful and thus deprive the faithful themselves of their vindication (Is 5:22-23).

Generally the main object of the prophets' invective is the men who take the lead in business and politics, but occasionally they turn to the women, implying the assumption that women and men share responsibility for what is wrong in the society. In a patriarchal society the men's business is to lead

---

[38]Cf. Pleins, *Social Visions of the Hebrew Bible*, pp. 500-6; he speaks of "the centrality of poverty in the Book of Job" (p. 504).

[39]Pleins notes that "the prophets stood in opposition to the wise"; but it is then noteworthy that they do not critique the attitude of the wise to the poor. They critique their reliance on human planning and decision-making that excludes Yhwh, which Proverbs also critiques (*The Social Visions of the Hebrew Bible*, p. 456).

[40]Rodd, *Glimpses of a Strange Land*, pp. 170, 273.

[41]James W. McClendon, *Systematic Theology: Doctrine* (Nashville: Abingdon, 1994), p. 132.

and the women's to look nice at dinner parties, and in Judah the women
take their vocation seriously. They look as impressive as the men do. They
will be put down in a way equivalent to the men (Is 3:16–4:1). Amos 4:1 confronts the leading women of Samaria in connection with their self-indulgence. Its address of them as "cows of Bashan" may come across cruder than
Amos's actual words would (we might say they were "fat cats").[42] Bashan,
the modern Golan Heights, is an area of fine pasturage; cattle that lived
there lived well. The women in Samaria are able to live well-fed lives in the
manner of those cattle, but they are able to do so because they are implicated in the oppressive crushing of the needy poor for which their husbands
are more directly responsible but which makes their fine lifestyle possible.
They "exploit the poor" and "crush the needy." "Exploit" (ʿāšaq) suggests a
particular form of oppression, oppression of an economic kind whereby
people with power use their power to build up their own resources from
those of people without power and thus increase the economic disadvantage of such people, the kind of semi-legal or not obviously illegal oppressive action that takes advantage of people's vulnerability and gullibility to
rob them of what belongs to them by right. It denotes practices such as holding back wages (Deut 24:14-15) and lending money on interest (Ezek 22:12) as
well as dishonest trading practices (Hos 12:7 [MT 8]). Whereas one can rob
the rich, one cannot ʿāšaq the rich. The verbs *exploit* and *crush* thus complement each other. The first is the means of reaching the end stated by the
second. And it is by associating themselves with their husbands' exploiting
of the needy poor that the women of Samaria are able to live like fat cats.
There is some irony about their peremptory ordering about of their husbands, their lords (ʾādôn—a very unusual term for "husband"),[43] as they
"say to their lords, 'Bring something so we can drink!' "

Micah 7:1-2 laments the situation in the land. It is as empty as an orchard
at the end of the harvest, a particularly efficient harvest; but what it is empty
of is committed and upright people. "All of them lie in wait to shed blood; one
person hunts his brother with a net/with annihilation."[44] The subsequent
words make clear that the passage is not talking about common criminals but
about leaders, people in authority and important people (haśśar, haśśōpēṭ,
haggādôl), who are good at doing what is bad, at taking decisions in accordance with what they can make out of it (Mic 7:3).[45] "The best of them is like a
brier, the most upright worse than a thorn hedge" (Mic 7:4)—not a fruit tree
producing something that could please one's appetite but a bramble bush that

---

[42]I owe this suggestion to Jennifer Bashaw in a seminar.
[43]See §4.2 " 'Husbands' and 'Wives.' "
[44]The context would allow either understanding of ḥērem.
[45]The details of the translation are uncertain, but this much is clear.

only hurts. So (like a character in a spy movie or a film noir) the prophet warns his hearers not to trust anyone—neighbor, friend, lover: "The members of the household are a person's enemies" (Mic 7:5-6).

Is this Yhwh's own warning and lament? It is easy to imagine Yhwh grieving over the moral state of the city, looking round for just one person among the leadership who could rejoice God's heart, and finding none. But the next line (Mic 7:7) begins "but I will look to Yhwh," so Yhwh is not the one doing the grieving. This "I" initially sounds like the prophet speaking in the manner of Jeremiah when he is bidden by Yhwh to search the city for one honorable person and is unable to find one (Jer 5:5). But that next line continues, "I will wait for my God who delivers," and goes on to urge, "Do not rejoice over me, my enemy. If I have fallen, I shall get up; if I sit in darkness, Yhwh is my light" (Mic 7:7-8). *Enemy* is feminine, and it seems that here city speaks to city. Reading Micah 7:1-6 in association with Micah 7:7-10 suggests the lament is the city's own. The personified city grieves over what it has become, like a mother grieving over the behavior of her children

"People who mock inflame a town, but wise people turn away anger" (Prov 29:8). "When the faithful exult, there is great glory" (Prov 28:12). Apparently the faithful are exulting because they are in power, and that means the people as a whole gain glory or are glorying in who the people in power are. "But when the faithless arise, people are hunted down," the saying continues. Having faithless people in power is bad news for the society as a whole, because they will use their position to benefit themselves and to hound people—for instance, to appropriate their possessions. To restate the point, "when the faithless arise, people hide themselves," keep a low profile, "but when they perish, the faithful increase" (Prov 28:28). "When the faithful increase, the people rejoice, but when the faithless rule, the people groan" (Prov 29:2).

Awareness of Yhwh

Isaiah indicts people who spend the whole day drinking and making music and thus "do not pay attention to what Yhwh is doing" (Is 5:12). Given that a traditional society does not separate sacred and secular, this drinking and music-making would likely belong to a religious festival (cf. 1 Sam 1:3, 9, 14), particularly before the Deuteronomic reform (which made "nonreligious festivals" more feasible). That would give more point to the accusation of failing to pay attention to what Yhwh was doing, failing to acknowledge Yhwh (Is 5:12-13). When the festival happens in the city, it becomes a place for teaching (Neh 8). They were missing the point of the occasion even while they were enjoying drink and music, like Christians missing the point of worship while they are enjoying the music and the opportunity to express their feelings. They do not look up from their immediate concern with their own needs and experience to the bigger picture of God's activity in relationship to the world and to them, and to acknowledge what God is doing. They are ignoring the solemn warnings in their worship, reinforced by prophets such as Isaiah, about Yhwh's intentions regarding their future. While Isaiah often criticizes people with money or power, this critique applies to "my people," to the whole community (Is 5:13-14). Festivity, drink and music can be means whereby ordinary people, especially poor people, seek to dull their sensibilities, as well as means whereby well-to-do people indulge themselves. Lemuel's mother somewhat dourly and ironically urges him as king to keep away from alcohol but to leave it to the hapless and the people in bitter distress: "Let them drink and forget their poverty and not remember their hardship any more" (Prov 31:6-7). Yet the well-to-do obviously have special scope for such self-indulgence.

Isaiah later indicts parallel indulgence in Samaria, the city that constitutes a majestic garland crowning the fertile land surrounding it, where people also parade their own garlands at their lavish official banquets: "Oh, the majestic garland of the drunks of Ephraim and the wilting flower of its glorious beauty, that which is on the head of people bloated with rich food, overcome by wine" (Is 28:1). These sumptuous banquets earn envious reports even on the Jerusalem chat shows, but actually there is something sad about their decadence, as about all decadence. The symbol of this is the way the flowers on their wreaths wilt, and thus come to deny what they initially symbolize. They end up suggesting death rather than majesty. The political context implied by the setting in Isaiah adds a further nuance. These are the last days of Ephraim. The Assyrians will shortly take Samaria and transport its people. These drunks are fiddling while Rome burns, anticipating Belshazzar's great final banquet (Dan 5).

As far as we know, Isaiah did not go north to address Ephraim or send his message there but uttered this declaration in Judah, like his other prophecies, and it could thus function as an encouragement to Judah about Ephraim's fate—perhaps ideologically so. But in the context it rather recalls the declarations about other peoples (and about Judah itself) in Amos 1–2 that lead into an indictment of Ephraim and add force to it. Here, conversely, Isaiah goes on to indict Judah for sins like those of Ephraim. A people that affirms the indictment of Ephraim has condemned itself. Its political situation has been similar to Ephraim's, except that it has been able to choose whether to be vulnerable to or reliant on Assyria, on the Ephraimite-Syrian coalition itself, or on Egypt. Its religious leaders, like Ephraim's, are also the worse for drink and nauseatingly dissolute (Is 28:7-8). They fail to face the real issues that confront the city.

Encouraging People to Keep Their Land or Appropriating It

The theory about mutual care in the community is that people who are doing all right at a particular time support people who are not; in a few years time the situation may be reversed. Proverbs' vision about wealth would mean the wealthy join in that dynamic. In practice the temptation is to use other people's need as a means of making money, as can happen with a nation's health insurance industry. The First Testament narrative gives the impression that in premonarchic times, there was not much servitude of the kind described in Exodus 21. It was the changed conditions of the monarchy that led to it.[46] The household is key to relationships with Yhwh and with the land, and therefore in both respects to the well-being of the nation. But developments brought about by the monarchy undercut the household and thus fatally imperiled the whole structure.[47] By compromising the viability of the household, the growth of the city compromised the structures for caring for the poor as well as increasing their numbers.[48]

If people could not own land, they could not sell it, but they needed ways of being able to use it as an asset—almost the only thing they possessed—as collateral in times of trouble. That was what made it possible for the well-off to accumulate land, to become de facto owners of vast tracts, a development apparently built into the transition from a subsistence to a market economy.[49] In effect they own the whole land, Isaiah declares hyperbolically, "people who join house to house, who unite field to field, until there is no room and you are settled alone in the midst of the land" (Is 5:8). Possibly they were ignoring Israelite theory about land ownership and behaving as if land could be bought and sold.[50] But they hardly needed to do so; they could make the regulations in the Torah work their way.[51]

Ahab had a distinctive way of doing that. Micah 6:16 comments on the way the city it addresses has observed all Omri's laws and all Ahab's habits. The city may be Samaria, whose life was directly shaped by the policies of Omri

---

[46]Cf. Frank Crüsemann, *The Torah* (Minneapolis: Fortress/Edinburgh: T & T Clark, 1996), pp. 152-53.

[47]Christopher J. H. Wright, *God's People in God's Land* (Grand Rapids: Eerdmans/Exeter : Paternoster, 1990), pp. 104-9.

[48]Cf. Leo G. Perdue, "The Israelite and Early Jewish Family," in Leo G. Perdue et al., *Families in Ancient Israel* (Louisville: Westminster John Knox, 1997), pp. 163-222; see pp. 209-12; he associates this especially with the growth of the power of the state and thus with the monarchy.

[49]So D. N. Premnath, "Latifundialization and Isaiah 5:8-10," *JSOT* 40 (1988): 49-60; see p. 49.

[50]Cf. the discussion in John Andrew Dearman, *Property Rights in the Eighth-Century Prophets,* SBLDS 106 (Atlanta: Society of Biblical Literature, 1988), pp. 62-77.

[51]Cf. on the passage Eryl W. Davies, *Prophecy and Ethics,* JSOTSup 16 (Sheffield, U.K.: JSOT, 1981), pp. 65-89, esp. p. 69.

and Ahab; Hosea and Amos speak in similar terms to Micah's about the city's economic practices (Hos 12:7-8 [MT 8-9]; Amos 8:4-6). But the city may be Jerusalem, which is more commonly Micah's own focus. The idea then is that Jerusalem has come to be infected with the same plague as Samaria.[52] Jerusalemites would therefore be unwise to react with contempt and horror to its fate without reflecting on their own situation. The context suggests Micah has in mind the two kings' economic and social policies (epitomized by the story of Ahab, Jezebel and Naboth's vineyard) more than their religious policies, though these were interwoven.[53] They have had the effect of creating a landless underclass,[54] just what the Israelite system was designed to make impossible.

It is possible that the "extortion" of the prophets includes the central administration's imposing of taxes and annexing of land in order to do its job, as it saw it (e.g. Mic 2:1-2); this would be in keeping with aspects of Samuel's warnings (1 Sam 8:10-18). But there are no passages that must be read that way, and many that imply that the problem is powerful people's instinct to increase their own wealth. "In most cases the desire for greater wealth is the chief reason for oppression."[55]

Appropriation extends beyond individual landowners. "The rulers of Judah have become like people moving a boundary" (Hos 5:10). The context is the convolutions of relationship between Assyria, Syria, Ephraim and Judah in the eighth century, which have apparently included some Judean appropriation of Ephraimite land; the boundary with Ephraim lay only a few miles north of Jerusalem. It is a national equivalent to an individual defrauding someone else of land by shifting the boundary markers between their holdings. Indeed, the boundaries between clan holdings were more directly divinely established than the boundaries between the allocations of kin groups and households, which could be renegotiated. On this larger scale, too, one clan or nation has no right to appropriate land from another. The principle of family morality applies to national morality. Judah has ignored it, and opened itself to terrible divine fury (Hos 5:10).

Supporting the Weak and Needy, or Taking Advantage of Them

Amos remonstrates with Israel concerning the selling of people into servitude: "They have sold faithful people for silver, needy people for the sake of

---

[52]The MT speaks of "the contempt of my people," which rather suggests Samaria is the city and Judah is horrified; LXX has "peoples," which makes it easier to see Micah as addressing Jerusalem.

[53]See Leslie C. Allen, *The Books of Joel, Obadiah, Jonah and Micah* (London: Hodder/Grand Rapids: Eerdmans, 1976), pp. 381-82.

[54]Cf. M. Daniel Carroll R., "Family in the Prophetic Literature," in *Family in the Bible*, ed. Richard S. Hess and Carroll (Grand Rapids: Baker, 2003), pp. 100-22; see p. 113.

[55]Elsa Tamez, *Bible of the Oppressed* (Maryknoll, N.Y.: Orbis, 1982), p. 32.

some shoes" (Amos 2:6). These were people who were faithful and needy—not faithful and wealthy (in which case they would need no mercy) nor faith-less and wealthy (in which case they would need no mercy) nor faithless and needy (in which case they might deserve no mercy).[56] Such considerations did not enter into what happened when their harvest failed and they got into debt. Money and land were all that mattered. The allusion to a pair of shoes may refer to transactions involved in taking possession of a piece of land (e.g., Deut 25:9-10; Ruth 4:7-8) or may suggest the debt was trivial (just the value of a pair of shoes) and thus heighten the magnitude of the wrongdoing.

Amos goes on to berate the way "a man and his father go to a girl, so as to profane my holy name" (Amos 2:7). We are unclear about aspects of the prac-tices that Amos condemns. It is usually assumed that the first part refers to having sex (though the verb is *hālak* rather than *bô*ʾ).[57] But we do not know whether this is a religious rite or whether the girl is a prostitute or a servant girl of whom two men are taking advantage or a girl whom a man has sex with and who might be on the way to marrying her, and whom her prospec-tive father-in-law will then not leave alone. But it is clear that the girl is the victim of these two men as the faithful, needy, poor and weak were the vic-tims in the preceding lines and will be again in the next line. And this treat-ment of a young girl means Yhwh's holy name is profaned.

"On garments taken as pledges they stretch out by every altar; wine from people being fined they drink in the house of their God" (Amos 2:8). This further critique makes it more likely that the profaning of Yhwh's name in-volves a religious rite. Once again, money is all that counts, and people are bringing into Yhwh's house the profits of the tough stance they take to the faithful needy. They come for a festive sacrificial meal and make themselves comfortable lying on garments taken in pledge—so what are the debtors ly-ing on or in, given that their coat is also their blanket (cf. Ex 22:25-27 [MT 24-26])? The wealthy indulge themselves at these festivities on the compensation they have been paid. Perhaps the implication is that they need not have ex-tracted this or that the compensation was excessive.

Yhwh later compares Ms. Jerusalem unfavorably with her sister Ms. So-dom (Ezek 16:49-51). She and her "daughters," the settlements around her, "had prestige, plenty of food, and secure prosperity, but they did not support the weak and needy." "I saw it," Yhwh adds, in words that recall the story that goes on to relate Sodom's sexual impropriety, but it is the combination of prosperity and self-indulgence that appalls Yhwh. The EVV import value judg-

---

[56]Nor is the point that they were "innocent" (so, e.g., Hans Walter Wolff, *Joel and Amos* [Philadelphia: Fortress, 1977], p. 133).

[57]Thus Hans M. Barstad sees her as the host at a religious meal (*The Religious Polemics of Amos,* VTSup 34 [Leiden: Brill, 1984], pp. 11-36).

ments into the description of Sodom's flourishing, as if the words meant arrogance, too much food and complacent ease, but the words do not require such connotations and make life too easy for readers. There is nothing inherently wrong with prestige, plenty of food and security—these are God's good gifts. But they put a temptation before people who receive them. They can tempt people into self-centeredness. The test of whether they have done so is the community's behavior toward the weak and needy. "They were on high, and they committed abomination before me." Their abomination lies in their attitude as well-off people to less well-off people.

Honesty

The city is a place of trade. There, it will be important that people have "true balances, true weights, a true bushel, and a true gallon" and not falsify measures of length, weight and capacity (Lev 19:35-36). They are to use the same weights and measures for all transactions, not using large and small ones according to which will work in their favor (Deut 25:13-16).

In practice the city is a place of dishonesty and thieving, so that its sanctuary becomes a place where thieves can hide out (Jer 7:9-11; cf. Hos 4:2; Zech 5:3-4: these prophets belong to three different centuries). Thus "Yhwh's voice calls to the city" (Mic 6:9). Yhwh has seen there the faithless house with its faithless storehouses, built up by faithless scales, a bag of false weights and by the accursed short *ephah* whereby people receive (say) three-quarters of a bushel of grain instead of the bushel they paid for (was it cursed by the human beings who were cheated or by Yhwh?). The city's wealthy people are such because they are "full of lawlessness" (*ḥāmās*, which often means violence, but can also have this more general meaning). The population as a whole is also dishonest (Mic 6:10-12).[58] As in our own society there were few safeguards against business swindles, and dishonesty at the level of the well-to-do was matched by dishonesty among ordinary people.

For the merchants of Samaria, their own profit is the key good. Amos 8:4-6 describes them as people who trample on the needy or pant after them, who put a stop to the weak people in the land. It is an odd expression, but it opens up a paronomasia when Amos goes on to picture them asking, "When will the new moon be over so that we can sell grain, the sabbath stop be over so that we can offer wheat for sale, reduce the ephah and increase the shekel[59] and bend false scales, buy the poor for silver and the needy for the sake of some shoes, and sell the sweepings of the wheat?"

The all-consuming profit-oriented spirit underlying business practice not

---

[58]I paraphrase the passage; other details of it are uncertain.
[59]That is, give people low weight and charge them too much.

only ignores any concern with the rights and needs of other people in the community and specifically needy people, and not only ignores principles of honesty and integrity in business dealing. It makes business people unable to stop. Every month begins with a holiday, and that is a real nuisance because it means a day when one cannot do business. Every week ends with a holiday, an even bigger nuisance. Business people do not want to be distracted from the real purpose of life by sitting under their vine and fig tree with their family, doing nothing. Nor do they want there to be days such as these that belong distinctively to God and that stand as a reminder that life is not all about activity. The sabbath was a day Yhwh set aside and sanctified. It especially belonged to Yhwh. Israel was therefore to keep off it. But people were inclined to treat it just like any other day, working on the sabbath as they did on other days. They profaned (*ḥālal* piel) or ignored Yhwh's sabbath instead of sanctifying them (Ezek 20:12-13, 16, 20-21, 24; 22:8, 26; 23:38). They made it ordinary. Jeremiah similarly exhorts the people not to work on the sabbath and specifically not to carry burdens on the sabbath, in order to keep it holy (Jer 17:19-27); the concrete requirement may suggest a ban on trade (cf. Neh 13:15-22).

In Amos the context may also suggest that allowing observance of sabbath and new moon benefits the needy and poor, who need their day off as people who work hard for employers. Employed people such as the poor and needy are not people who work their own land, or at least work for themselves, who have more fulfilling and perhaps less wearisome work lives and can decide for themselves to take such days off.

The focus of that indictment in Amos 8:4-6 still lies on the fact that the paramount importance of turning a profit means it is fine to swindle other people. The opening line makes the point nicely by its reuse of the verb *šāʾap/šûp* ("trample on/ pant after"; cf. Amos 2:7). There is some confusion between these two verbs, and this makes it possible to make a point by utilizing their two unrelated basic meanings.[60] Merchants trample on the needy because they yearn so strongly for their assets. The paronomasia is reinforced by the reappearance of this feature in the parallel colon, where *šābat* (hiphil "to cause to cease") anticipates the subsequent reference to the sabbath (*šabbāt*).[61] The business community hates the day when everything stops; that prevents it bringing the lives of the needy to a stop. The paronomasia underlines an implication of the indictment, that there is an inbuilt link between a concern to turn a profit and a susceptibility to exploit needy people and trade dishonestly. The business community cannot wait for the new moon and sab-

---

[60]See *HALOT*.

[61]In the translation above I thus added the word "stop" in the second line, to try to bring out the point.

bath to be over, not merely so that it can resume trade but so that it can resume dishonest trade—because if making a profit is the paramount good, it immediately follows that this rules out honesty as well as holy days or holidays. It is a very challenging task to combine a concern about profitable business-dealing with devotion to God, humanness and honesty, as both capitalist and socialist systems show in contrasting ways. But corruption has the most devastating affect on a society. In the Two-thirds World it is a decisive factor in holding back the development of well-being. In the West it is a decisive factor in the ongoing collapse of the society.

In the early twentieth century, journalist Lincoln Steffens investigated the state of local politics in a number of cities and found that everywhere it was the businessmen who were the sources of corruption, with businessmen and politicians collaborating. Business needed separating from politics, he argued, because business is fundamentally and centrally about making a profit, and it is stupid to expect businesspeople to look after any interests apart from their own.[62]

Enforcing Justice

The nearest the First Testament has to alternative structural proposals for dealing with a situation in which poverty can develop in an urban society is its emphasis on the responsibility of the king for seeing that needy people get treated with ṣĕdāqâ (e.g., Ps 72). The mechanisms that generated the problem (urbanization and the centralization of power in capitals such as Jerusalem and Samaria and in other big cities that are major state administrative centers) must become the mechanisms that deal with the problem. David, Solomon and Josiah are kings who see that authority is exercised with faithfulness (2 Sam 8:15; 1 Kings 10:9; Jer 22:15), though they are the (partial) exception rather than the rule (cf. Jer 22:13-19). The king's exercising this responsibility is also the implication of the bidding in Deuteronomy 17:14-20. This does not seem to imply that kings take proactive measures to ensure the needs of the poor are met in Jerusalem or Samaria, let alone in Lachish or Beersheba; central government did not concern itself with internal affairs in the different parts of the realm. The expectations of kings do not provide a basis for arguing that central government should be involved in social welfare programs.[63] It did mean that when cases were brought to the king, he was to adjudicate them or see that they were adjudicated in a way that took note of the rights of

---

[62]See Lincoln Steffens, *The Shame of the Cities* (New York: Hill and Wang, 1957); cf. Adam Cohen, "Editorial Observer," *The New York Times*, April 11, 2004, p. WK 10.

[63]An argument that recurs in Gushee, ed., *Toward a Just and Caring Society*. (I do not imply that government should not be so involved, only that exegetically this is a bad argument.)

the needy, and that the same standards would be applied by his administration elsewhere; compare the account of Jehoshaphat appointing "judges" in all the fortified cities (2 Chron 19:4-7).

Here, the administration of justice is *the* task of government.[64] As the city is the location of violent wrongdoing, so it must be the location of the forceful putting down of wrongdoing, in the first instance not for the sake of punishing the sinner but for the sake of rescuing the sinned against. Such violent action is an aspect of faithfulness in the community. Yhwh expects the people of Jerusalem, and specifically its leaders, to exercise authority on behalf of the orphan and defend the cause of the widow (Is 1:10, 17) and thus avoid their abuse (Ex 22:22-24 [MT 21-23]). What sort of action does that involve? The prayer in Psalm 72:4 moves from exercising authority on behalf of the weak to rescuing the needy to crushing their oppressors. The sequence is significant. First there is the exercise of authority, which might imply simply the taking of decisions by a court. But that is useless unless it leads to action to rescue the needy. That in turn has to look in the face the possible necessity to take violent action against their oppressors.

As Job looks back over his life before it collapsed, he can recall how respected he was in the community because of the role he played among the elders gathered at the gate, where he was respected for his leadership, but specifically used his power to see that the weak got justice (Job 29:12-17). The role Job accepted becomes the role of the king (Ps 72), but it starts off as the role of the elders in his city as a group, and thus of Job as one of them. It involves taking responsibility for the vulnerable in society who are subject to the oppression of the powerful. This means taking their cry seriously. The elders exercise this responsibility in a judicial context as they sit taking counsel, and Job claims to have done this not merely for people who count but for people whom he would not have acknowledged or recognized as important (or in connection with causes he did not recognize—that is, even when he doubted if there was anything in them).[65] This did not merely mean passing resolutions. Becoming eyes and feet for the vulnerable again means being prepared to take forceful action to implement decisions, not to punish wrongdoers but to rescue their victims. Job had been prepared to do that, breaking teeth if necessary to rescue the oppressed. The language is metaphorical; the needy person is *like* prey in the mouth of a beast. But the literal action would require a willingness to be violent. Perhaps Job did not personally take this action, but he would have to be party to someone doing so. The faithful exer-

---

[64]Nicholas Wolterstorff, *Until Justice and Peace Embrace* (Grand Rapids: Eerdmans, 1983), p. 63, referring to Herman Dooyeweerd, *Roots of Western Culture* (Toronto: Wedge, 1979).

[65]Cf. KJV; the expression surely does not merely refer to the person he did not *know* (so EVV).

cise of authority can involve it. A father's job is to take such forceful action on behalf of the members of his household; Job has treated these members of the community as like his own children in this way.

Social Justice

Such mutual support and protection of the weak is central to what Israel understands by *mišpāṭ ûṣĕdāqâ*, the phrase commonly translated "justice and righteousness," but which Moshe Weinfeld declares to be the Hebrew equivalent of "social justice."[66]

The notion of social justice is a hazy one. It resembles words such as community, intimacy, and relational, warm words whose meaning may seem self-evident and which we assume are obviously biblical categories, when actually they are rather undefined and culture relative. The phrase *social justice* seems to have been devised in the nineteenth century by Luigi Taparelli in the context of the Roman Catholic Church's developing awareness of a need to think through issues raised by the industrial revolution and by the revolutions of 1848.[67] Taparelli went back to Aquinas in order to consider these questions in a "natural law" framework so as to reestablish a link between law and ethics. "Social justice" then implies the idea of a "just society," one in which different individuals and groups in society get a "fair share" of its benefits. But Christians disagree about what constitutes a just society and how we achieve it (for instance, how far by governmental intervention to effect income redistribution and how far by market forces and the encouragement of philanthropy). Roman Catholic concern for social justice has made a point of seeking to avoid simply "baptizing" a rightist or leftist view and of asking what might be a distinctively Christian view, and contributing to this question would be an important point about asking how the First Testament looks at such issues. But the meaning of the phrase *social justice* has become opaque over the years as it has become a buzz expression.

Middle-Eastern social documents typically emphasize the importance of society being administered in a way that protects people such as orphans and widows who have no powerful male to protect their interests. They prohibit high interest on loans to needy people, establish standard values for weights

---

[66]He suggests that the hendiadys *mišpāṭ ûṣĕdāqâ* is Israel's most common equivalent to the concept of social justice (" 'Justice and Righteousness'—צדקה וּ מׁשׁפּט—The Expression and its Meaning," in *Justice and Righteousness*, Benjamin Uffenheimer Festschrift, ed. Henning Graf Reventlow and Yair Hoffman, JSOTSup 137 [Sheffield, U.K.: Sheffield Academic Press, 1992], pp. 228-46; see p. 228). I would rather say it suggests a way of reframing the concept of social justice.

[67]See Thomas C. Behr, "Luigi Taparelli D'Azeglio, S.J. (1793—1862) and the Development of Scholastic Natural-Law Thought As a Science of Society and Politics," *The Journal of Markets and Morality* 6 (2003): 99-116.

and measures, grant legal rights to slaves, regulate debt servitude and other problems caused by loans, establish levels of compensation for damaging someone else's property or theft, and regulate property rights, inheritance rights, and day laborers' wages.[68] As is the case with the Torah, it is misleading to call these documents "laws"; it is not always clear where they are laying down regulations for courts to administer or stating policies the king would implement or commending practices the populace would be urged to live by. "In the ancient Near East the rich were brought up to care for the poor." It is just a simple point about what it means to be human. But "the social reality often seems to have been quite different."[69]

There is substantial overlap between these concerns and those of the Torah, the Prophets and the Wisdom books, and between the way the two sets of literature approach the issues in question. Both assume it is appropriate to make compromises between ideals and human "hardness of heart";[70] both compromise between the interests of the rich and powerful and the needs of the poor and weak. The First Testament provides a new rationale and new vision for caring for the poor, one that is more community based. Absent from the First Testament are the class assumptions that appear in Middle-Eastern documents; present are concerns for the immigrant and the stress on the sabbath, the ban on lending at interest within the community, and more sympathy for the position of debt servants.

> The key to understanding the biblical model is that the production and sale of goods is almost entirely left to the unfettered operation of market forces, while the laws governing the use of labour, the allocation of land and the role of finance are tightly drawn so as to ensure a minimum level of income and wealth for all. . . . The two recurring themes overarching this fundamental insight are that the rough equality of wealth, income and opportunity are encouraged without the need for a large centralised state (in the form of a monarchy); and that the interests of "finance" are made subservient to those of interpersonal relationships.[71]

The Faithful Exercise of Authority

Mišpāṭ ûṣĕdāqâ is a less hazy notion than "social justice." It is the community's elders who are responsible for seeing that *mišpāṭ ûṣĕdāqâ* is a reality in the

---

[68]See, e.g., *ANET*; cf. the summaries in Léon Epzstein, *Social Justice in the Ancient Near East and the People of the Bible* (London: SCM Press; Valley Forge, Penn.: Trinity Press International, 1986), pp. 3-42.

[69]Norbert F. Lohfink, *Option for the Poor* (Berkeley, Calif.: BIBAL, 1987), pp. 17, 29.

[70]See §4.1 "Thinking Critically."

[71]Paul Mills, "The Divine Economy," *Cambridge Papers* 9 (2000) <www.jubilee-centre.org/document.php?id=30&topicID=3>.

community's life. The first of the two words refers to the making of a decision, the exercise of authority. The second refers to the way the decision is made and the authority exercised: namely, so as to do right by the people in one's community. The concept is actually closer to faithfulness than to justice or righteousness. The two words thus complement each other. *Mišpāṭ* means being in a position to call the shots; *ṣedeq* means what is right.[72] (The Ugaritic *Keret* story talks about *ṣdq* and *mšr*, which is equivalent).[73] The elders need to be committed to *mišpāṭ* as well as *ṣĕdāqâ*; their faithfulness needs to be a matter of action not just a value they affirm. They need to be committed to *ṣĕdāqâ* as well as *mišpāṭ*; their authority needs to be exercised in a faithful way, not a wicked way. It is in this sense that there is no tension between love and justice, in God or in human beings. Both are concerned with taking action for people that will do the best thing for people. Indeed, Leo Adler translates *ṣĕdāqâ* "love" and comments that it is precisely the opposite of *iustitia*, "justice."[74] While Weinfeld does declare that doing *mišpāṭ ûṣĕdāqâ* "implies maintaining social justice in the society, so that equality and freedom prevail,"[75] he soon adds that it is "associated with *mercy and loving-kindness* or . . . with the context of ameliorating the situation of the destitute . . . by the elimination of exploitation and oppression"[76] (see, e.g., Jer 22:3; Ezek 45:9).

"Few themes are more central to any discussion of social ethics than justice."[77] It is therefore ironic that the notions of justice and of social justice are unfocused ones. And where people have focused their understanding of them, the result is likely not to correspond to a way of thinking that appears in the either Testament. For instance, E. Calvin Beisner argues that showing partiality to the poor is wrong because it is not in keeping with justice, which by its nature is impartial.[78] David Miller sees understandings of justice as characteristically involving equal treatment of people in allocating resources or treating people in accordance with their deserts or respecting each person's rights.[79] Stephen Mott and Ronald J. Sider list five important types of justice (procedural, commutative, distributive, retributive and restorative)

---

[72]James P. M. Walsh, *The Mighty From Their Thrones* (Philadelphia: Fortress, 1987), pp. 2-7.

[73]Surely not different, as Epzstein argues (*Social Justice in the Ancient Near East and the People of the Bible*, p. 46); contrast Moshe Weinfeld, *Social Justice in Ancient Israel and in the Ancient Near East* (Philadelphia: Fortress, 1995), pp. 25-26.

[74]Leo Adler, *The Biblical View of Man* (Jerusalem/New York: Urim, 2007), p. 37.

[75]So Weinfeld, *Social Justice in Ancient Israel and in the Ancient Near East*, p. 5.

[76]Ibid., p. 7.

[77]Wright, *Old Testament Ethics for the People of God*, p. 253.

[78]E. Calvin Beisner, *Prosperity and Poverty* (Wheaton, Ill.: Crossway, 1988), p. 52 (ironically, in the context Beisner notes that the First Testament notion of "justice" does not imply equality).

[79]David Miller, introduction to *Pluralism, Justice, and Equality*, ed. David Miller and Michael Walzer(Oxford/New York: Oxford University Press, 1995), pp. 1-16; see p. 1.

and in defining them use the word *fair* with regard to each of them.[80] Both the words *justice* and *righteousness*, and *fairness*, in fact skew the First Testament's way of thinking. Understandings of justice are characteristically rationalist, self-interested, individualistic, abstract, ahistorical, secular and focused on consumption of goods.[81] *Righteousness* is about personal uprightness; the First Testament does believe in that, but *ṣĕdāqâ* is not its word for it. Elsewhere, indeed, Beisner warns about obscuring the distinction between justice and grace;[82] the notion of *ṣĕdāqâ* does exactly that. *Justice* is about treating everyone the same way and about establishing guilt and then punishing, whereas the focus of *ṣĕdāqâ* lies on making things right,[83] for both people who have been treated wrongly and for people who have got into trouble through their own actions. It works within the context of a relationship.[84] That concern with making things right got overwhelmed in the context of Greco-Roman thinking, and "an eye for an eye" and other aspects of biblical "justice" came to be understood in that framework.[85]

Fairness in the Legal System

If it is the vocation of people in power to exercise their authority in a faithful way, to live by *mišpāṭ* and *ṣĕdāqâ*, then the exercise of authority is something precious for ordinary people, something to savor. But the people in power in the community can turn the exercise of authority into something that leaves a bad taste in the mouth. They "turn authority into wormwood and bring faithfulness to the ground" (Amos 5:7). Instead of exalting faithfulness in the way they exercise authority, they have demoted it and trampled it into the dirt—indeed, turned it into poison (Amos 6:12). "Oppressors have power and mastery because they belong to the governing class or are allied with it."[86]

Thus money also rules in connection with the way the legal system works. Putting people into servitude for debt was not in itself illegal; the ruthless were simply living by the letter of the law. But it might involve perverting justice (as Amos 2:6 may in fact imply when it speaks of selling faithful people for silver). There were certainly other occasions when people

---

[80]Stephen Mott and Ronald J. Sider, "Economic Justice: A Biblical Paradigm," p. 17.

[81]Cf. Ted Grimsrud, "Healing Justice," in *Peace and Justice Shall Embrace,* Millard Lind Festschrift, ed. Ted Grimsrud and Loren L. Johns (Telford, Penn.: Pandora, 1999), pp. 64-85; see p. 65.

[82]E. Calvin Beisner, "Justice and Poverty," in *Christianity and Economics,* ed. Herbert Schlossberg et al. (Grand Rapids: Eerdmans, 1994), pp. 57-80; see p. 73.

[83]Cf. Enrique Nardoni, *Rise Up, O Judge* (Peabody, Mass.: Hendrickson, 2004).

[84]Cf. Epzstein, *Social Justice in the Ancient Near East and the People of the Bible,* pp. 47-48.

[85]Cf. Howard Zehr, *Changing Lenses,* 3rd ed. (Scottdale, Penn.: Herald Press, 2005), pp. 153-55. On the relationship of retribution and justice, see Susan Jacoby, *Wild Justice* (New York: Harper, 1983).

[86]Tamez, *Bible of the Oppressed,* p. 33.

perverted the law to make it work their way. They could "trample the head of poor people into the dirt on the ground" quite legally, but they also "divert the way of the weak" (Amos 2:7). That implies action that evades the workings of the law. Someone's "way" can be their legal rights (cf. Is 40:27; also Prov 17:23 with ʾōraḥ rather than derek); these are being diverted. The law is being derailed in order to reduce poor and weak people to near death (dirt on the ground), to nothing.

The prophets thus "regard the judicial establishment as an opportunity to make money and cut the poor off from access to justice."[87] There are analogies with modern societies in which the law is a means of making money, like health care. They have done that specifically in the way they manipulate the legal system. The wealthy people and the ordinary people alike appear at the city gate at the assembly of the elders to resolve disputes, but the wealthy have ways of ensuring that poor people get a raw deal there. The wealthy know it is frequently not in their interest to have disputes resolved in a way that takes all the facts into account or makes compromises, and they hate it when someone wants to sort matters out in that way. It is much better for them if they can simply appeal to their standing in the community and insist that the court applies the letter of the law to the case (Amos 5:10-11). When they are themselves sitting as members of the court, they naturally sympathize with their own peers when disputes come before them. Nor are they beyond taking a bribe in order to "exclude" needy people at the gate—that is, to see that they lose their case (Amos 5:12).

Yhwh summons people in Ashdod (MT) or Assyria (LXX) and Egypt to come and look at what is happening in Samaria: "They do not know how to do right (Yhwh's oracle), the people who treasure outrage and violence in their strongholds" (Amos 3:10). Literally these people are treasuring up fine pottery, ivory paneling and quality furniture, but these beautiful things are the fruit of outrage and violence (both words suggest violence), so that in effect this is what these fine possessions represent. "Like a basket that is full of birds" after the hunter has caught them, "so their houses are full of deceit"—that is, of the gains that have come from their deceitful behavior. This is the way they "have become great and rich. . . . They have not made a proper decision for the orphan, in order that they [themselves] may prosper" by taking advantage of the orphan's vulnerability, "or given judgment for the needy" (Jer 5:27-28).

While there is wrong that comes about by accident, and there are occasions when people do much better than others because they work harder, there are occasions when these things involve deliberate deceit and fraud or involve

---

[87]Crüsemann, Torah, p. 163. See further Dearman, Property Rights in the Eighth-Century Prophets.

people knowing how to make the legal system work to their advantage. Such people spend the evenings when they cannot be doing business thinking out how to swindle other people of their land once morning comes (Mic 2:1). They might do that by the kind of scheme that robbed Naboth of his land (1 Kings 21)—Micah is thus not necessarily concerned about the oppression of the poor but about the oppression of ordinary people. Or they might do it in quite legal ways, planning to make loans to people that they will never be able to repay, so that the lenders will be able to foreclose on their security, their homes and land. Thus people who are in short-term need are turned into the long-term poor. The fraudulent "want" things, fields, houses, lands (the verb is *ḥāmad*, the verb in the Decalogue; see Ex 20:17) and are determined to get them (Mic 2:2). They are like those people waiting impatiently for the sabbath to come to an end so they can restart swindling people (Amos 8:5).[88]

Protecting Innocent Blood

Deceit is a theme that runs through the First Testament's understanding of Israel's worship, its relationship with God, its external politics and its internal relationships. It is a prominent aspect of faithlessness or sin. Words that deceive are a key means whereby people manifest their faithlessness toward the needy. Proverbs 30:11-14 analyzes a quartet of wrongs in such a way as to come to a climax with such deceit, condemning people who belittle their parents, who delude themselves about their moral state, who stand superior in relation to other people, and "whose teeth are swords, whose jaws are knives, for consuming the weak from the land/earth, the needy from among humanity." The last is even worse than those other wrongs. Such deceit is even more vicious when it is exercised by the administration and the legal system.

The vocation of the legal system is to protect the innocent. But when Isaiah expounds Yhwh's distaste for the people's worship, it is because "their hands are full of blood" (Is 1:15). There are several ways this might come about. Ordinary members of the community might be involved in violent assault on one another, perhaps because someone had offended their neighbor or because they had robbed them or because of sexual improprieties, and Isaiah specifically points to neglect of people such as the oppressed, orphans and widows (Is 1:17). But he also refers to community leaders manipulating the procedures of law so that people are found guilty of wrongs they have not committed, which might cost them their lives and again so that the rights of widows and orphans are bypassed (Is 1:23).[89]

"On your coattails is found the life blood of the innocent poor" (Jer 2:34).

---

[88]Hans Walter Wolff, *Micah* (Minneapolis: Augsburg Press, 1990), p. 77.
[89]On the passage, see Davies, *Prophecy and Ethics*, pp. 90-112.

When Jeremiah speaks of people killing prophets (Jer 2:30), no doubt he meant that literally, and it is a charge that they would have granted, like people killing each other in the name of religion during the Reformation; they would simply have said they were quite justified and quoted chapter and verse from the Torah to prove it. But when he speaks of their killing the poor, more likely people would not have recognized the charge. Usually the poor die because ordinary people do not help them and rather make the most of their own more privileged position, as happens in relations between the Western world and the Two-thirds World.

Likewise Ezekiel moves from talking about the people's religious abominations to talking about the accumulation of wealth through violence (Ezek 7:11, 23). "Is it too slight for the household of Judah to do the abominations they have done here, that they have filled the country with violence and further angered me?" (Ezek 8:17). For "violence" JPSV has "lawlessness"; the word is again *ḥāmās*, which suggests both violation of law and violence towards other people, these being two sides of a coin. When people abandon the rule of law, this frees them to indulge in more violence; when they act with violence, they flout the law. On the other hand, paradoxically people can use the rule of law to indulge in violence—for instance, in depriving people of their freedom or land. Indeed, when God lets executioners loose in the city, it is because "the country is full of bloodshed" (Ezek 9:9).[90] When he comes to criticize the leadership, in between Yhwh's splendor moving from the temple's inner threshold to the east gate and its moving away from the city to the east, it is because of the people they have slain in the city (Ezek 11:1-12). Jerusalem is both defiled by its pillars and culpable for the blood shed in it, the entire leadership being involved in this bloodshed (Ezek 22:4). Indeed, the violence itself defiles the city (Ezek 22:2-3). The violence is expressed or extends into other practices in the city. "Father and mother are slighted in you.[91] The alien is taken advantage of in your midst. Orphan and widow are maltreated in you" (Ezek 22:7). False accusation and bribery facilitate it, charging interest on loans and other shrewd business practices take further advantage of the vulnerability of poorer members of the community, and in all this they "have put me out of mind (my Lord Yhwh's oracle)" (Ezek 22:12). In effect that makes the leadership "like a roaring lion tearing prey," except that in their case they "have devoured lives"; in the course of defrauding people of their wealth they have made many widows (Ezek 22:25). "Secure city," "faithful

---

[90]See P. J. Harland, "A Land Full of Violence," in *New Heaven and New Earth*, Anthony Gelston Festschrift, ed. P. J. Harland and C. T. R. Hayward, VTSup 77 (Leiden/Boston: Brill, 1999), pp. 113-27.

[91]The succeeding clauses make it clear that Ezekiel here refers to the vulnerable, so these will be elderly parents whom their family does not look after.

city" and "holy city" (Is 1:21, 26; 48:2) has become bloody city, like Nineveh (Nah 3:1). And the victims' blood lies there in the city crying out for God to act in retribution on the wrongdoers and thus put things right (Ezek 24:7-8). "The city is the place where man is all-powerful, where he establishes his own justice, opposed to God's will. . . . The city is intimately connected with murder; she is warlike and bloody."[92]

To Hananiah the act of oppression that matters is Babylon's oppression of Judah, which surely cannot be Yhwh's will. To Jeremiah the oppression that matters is that of the ruling class within Judah over ordinary people.[93]

5.2 Nation

The First Testament has a clear profile of character virtues for Israel as a nation. It is called to maintain its distinctiveness over against other nations, and in doing so to manifest trust in Yhwh, insight, compassion and honesty. That will form a key part of the way it fulfills the vocation that the church will come to share, to be a visible human society that embodies something of the nature of the kingdom of God and promises that this kingdom will become a reality,[94] though in the West our narcissism means "the cultural odds are too much stacked against the formation of genuine Christian community."[95]

Nationhood and Nationalism

Genesis 1–11 suggests that the existence of a many nations in their diversity is as much part of God's blessing the world as the existence of couples and families; it is perhaps more clearly a blessing than the existence of the city, which is rather ambiguous in its origins. But Genesis 1–11 tells of the rebellion and downfall of the world of nations as it tells of the rebellion and downfall of the first couple and the first family. As the first couple were condemned to disharmony, so were the nations. As the first couple were thrown out of the garden lest they eat of the tree of life in their wayward state, so the nations were scattered lest they fulfill their purpose to build a tower that would reach the heavens. But there is then no suggestion in Genesis 12:1-3 that Abraham and his family are being taken out of the world of the nations[96] any more than they are taken out of the world of family and marriage. Abraham is not called

---

[92]Ellul, *Meaning of the City*, p. 93.

[93]Henri Mottu, "Jeremiah vs. Hananiah," in *The Bible and Liberation*, ed. Norman K. Gottwald (Maryknoll, N.Y.: Orbis, 1983), pp. 235-51, see p. 244.

[94]Cf. Karl Barth, *Church Dogmatics* (Edinburgh: T & T Clark, 1967), IV/2:719-26; cf. John Howard Yoder, *The Royal Priesthood* (Grand Rapids: Eerdmans, 1994), pp. 106-8.

[95]Marva J. Dawn, *Reaching Out Without Dumbing Down* (Grand Rapids: Eerdmans, 1995), pp. 105, 131.

[96]Against John Goldingay, *Theological Diversity and the Authority of the Old Testament* (Grand Rapids: Eerdmans, 1987/Carlisle, U.K.: Paternoster, 1995), p. 61.

out of Babel (and Ur is the place his father leaves). Abraham does leave his home country, but he also leaves his father's household, so leaving implies no negative judgment. And his destiny is to be a great nation.

As is the case with the family, speaking of the nation is complicated by the fact that the assumptions and terms of the modern world differ from those of the premodern world. Maximally, a nation is a people that has a common land, sense of ethnicity, sense of identity, culture, language, religion and commitment. But these features form a set of Wittgensteinian family resemblances; it is possible to lack some of the characteristics and still be a nation (one can ask how many do different modern nations possess). So Deuteronomy, for instance, in seeing Israel as destined and summoned to live the life of a nation, understands this as involving (among other things) secure possession of its land, faithfulness and good order in its common life, and commitment to Yhwh in everyday life and worship. The nation of Israel shares an ancestry, a story, a land, a set of relational values and commitments that it is supposed to embody, and a set of religious and cultural practices that it is also supposed to observe and that articulate and propagate the ancestry, the story, and the values. All of that could give it a sense of identity over against other nations.

Yet people who end up living outside the land do not thereby cease to be part of Israel. People who live in the land but cannot trace their ancestry to Jacob can still become part of Israel if they make a commitment to Israel's values and practices. Conversely, people who disaffirm the values or the practices imperil their place in the nation, and people who will not accept these values or practices cannot be fully part of it; it would be on this basis, not for ethnic reasons, that marrying a non-Israelite would be opposed.

In light of the way ethnic and cultural identity can become so important and can generate such conflict, we might reckon we should forgo distinctives and focus on the universal (the Enlightenment assumption) or aim at mutual appreciation and pluralism (one postmodern option) or abjure the corporate and focus on the individual (another postmodern option).[97] The First Testament's attitude excludes the last. It presupposes that there are indeed universal values and that Yhwh is involved in the story of all nations. It also presupposes that Yhwh is pursuing a vitally important project through Israel, yet this does not necessitate Israel's refusing other cultures and nations their place, though it excludes letting itself be overwhelmed by them.

Further, nothing of what makes Israel Israel implies that it can be nationalistic in the sense of seeing itself as superior to other nations.[98] In a radio ad-

---

[97]Cf. Miroslav Volf, *Exclusion and Embrace* (Abingdon: Nashville, 1996), p. 20.

[98]Cf. J. G. McConville's comments, *God and Earthly Power*, LHBOTS 454 (New York/London: T & T Clark, 2006), pp. 82-85. But "nationalism is a contested concept" (Mark Brett, "Nationalism and the Hebrew Bible," in *The Bible in Ethics*, ed. John W. Rogerson et al.,

dress during the 1991 Gulf War, in keeping with claims that have been made in the past, President George H. W. Bush described the United States as "the finest, most loving nation on Earth," compelled to make war by a vision of "the triumph of the moral order,"[99] while in his resignation speech in 2007 Prime Minister Tony Blair described Britain as "the greatest nation on earth."[100] A brief Internet search indicates that this claim has also been made for Australia and Canada. In contrast, Deuteronomy reminds Israel that it is not a morally impressive nation; it is small and annoying, not noteworthy for its faithfulness or integrity but consistently stubborn, defiant and faithless (Deut 9:1-24). While Deuteronomy also comments on the waywardness of the Canaanites, it does that rather more briefly.

Exclusiveness

Whereas the First Testament thus gives no encouragement to Israel to think it is superior, it does urge it to see that it is different and needs to stay that way. Outside Genesis the First Testament rarely works with an attitude of "ecumenical bonhomie."[101] In Second Temple Palestine there are descendants of Judeans who had not gone into exile, of Judeans who had gone into exile in Babylon and had now returned, of Ephraimites who had remained there after the Assyrian conquest, and of foreign settlers brought there by the Assyrians. And outside the land there are Judean communities in Babylonia, Persia, Egypt and nearer countries such as Ammon, and the descendants of Ephraimites exiled by the Assyrians.[102] All these groups might see themselves at least as part of Israel, religiously or theologically; all might be inclined to excommunicate many of the others (see Ezek 11:15-21; 33:23-29; Ezra; Nehemiah).[103]

In the first direct comments on Israel's relationship with the peoples it will live among, in Exodus 23:27-33, 33:1-3 and 34:11-16, Yhwh promises to throw out the Canaanites from their land (*gāraš* qal or piel). There is no talk here of the Canaanites being annihilated, by Yhwh or by Israel, nor even of their being thrown out immediately, though it is assumed that eventually Israel will come to possess the whole land, and Yhwh's declarations of intent correspond

---

JSOTSup 207 [Sheffield, U.K.: Sheffield Academic Press, 1995], pp. 136-63; see p. 140).

[99]George H. W. Bush, "Radio Address to the Nation on the National Day of Prayer," *American Presidency Project*, February 2, 1991 <www.presidency.ucsb.edu/ws/index.php?pid=19270>, quoted by Stanley Hauerwas, *In Good Company*, p. 54.

[100]Alan Cowell, "Blair Says He Will Leave Office in June," *New York Times*, May 11, 2007, p. A3.

[101]Gordon J. Wenham's phrase in "The Religion of the Patriarchs," in *Essays on the Patriarchal Narratives*, ed. A. R. Millard and D. J. Wiseman (Leicester, U.K.: Inter-Varsity Press, 1980), pp. 157-88; see p. 184.

[102]Cf. Sara Japhet, *From the Rivers of Babylon to the Highlands of Judah* (Winona Lake, Ind.: Eisenbrauns, 2006), pp. 96-116; see pp. 97-100.

[103]See *OTT* 1:740-51.

to what happened over time. The emphasis lies not so much on physically removing them as on separation from them, removing the possibility of close relationships with them (*gāraš* qal usually refers to divorce), and on destroying their forms of worship.[104] Israel's story over the centuries coheres with this emphasis, in negative fashion. As the Former and Latter Prophets portray matters, actually Israel rather consistently assimilates to the religious and social practice of the local peoples among whom it lives, as Christians do.

Deuteronomy 23:1-8 [MT 2-9]) subsequently lays down instructions concerning who may not be admitted to Yhwh's *qāhāl* (assembly). This includes any Ammonite or Moabite (a distant relative, but belonging to a people that had acted with enmity to Israel), for ten generations (in effect, forever). It includes any Edomite (who is a "brother") or Egyptian (in whose land Israelites had lived as aliens), for three generations; we do not know the basis for the distinction in terms of years. Subsequent parts of the First Testament implicitly assume that Ammon, Moab, Edom and Egypt implies all foreign peoples (see 1 Kings 11:1-2; Lam 1:10; Ezra; Nehemiah).[105] What is the implication of not being admitted to the *qāhāl*? Such people would be able to live as resident aliens in Israel, would be protected by the regulations concerning aliens and would be able to take part in the festivals; Deuteronomy 16 is specific that they can take part in Shavuot and Sukkot. Possibly the *qāhāl* is here the political assembly rather than the worshiping congregation; this might fit the reference to not seeking their *shalom*, which could imply treaty relationships. Yet that distinction is a rather Western one; if the assembly were allocating land or deciding to make war, it would be doing so in Yhwh's name and presence. Other passages assume that foreigners who become worshipers of Yhwh become fully part of Israel, even though they continue to be aware of their ethnic background. Ruth continues to be "the Moabite" and Ebed-Melech "the Sudanese." Such a person thus "contests the tendency to model state citizenship in terms of kin relations" or ethnicity[106] in the way that "the *gēr* . . . is accepted and integrated into the rules of the daily life of the community" but "is still different."[107] So perhaps Deuteronomy 23:1-8 [MT 2-9] refers to people who do not want to become quasi-Israelites (which for the men would imply circumcision).

Israel is also not to admit anyone castrated or genitally mutilated. It is not clear whether this implies only eunuchs or also people accidentally wounded,

---

[104]Crüsemann, *Torah*, p. 127.

[105]Cf. Tigay, *Deuteronomy*, pp. 478-79.

[106]Bonnie Honnig, "Ruth, the Model Emigrée," in *Ruth and Esther*, ed. Athalya Brenner, FCB 2/3 (Sheffield, U.K.: Sheffield Academic Press, 1999), pp. 50-74; see p. 74.

[107]Rolf Rendtorff, "The *Gēr* in the Priestly Laws of the Pentateuch," in *Ethnicity and the Bible*, ed. Mark G. Brett (Leiden/New York: Brill, 1996), pp. 77-87; see p. 81.

nor is the reason for this action stated. It can hardly be merely their being disabled and incomplete, since other disabilities or lacks do not have this consequence. It might imply revulsion at the act of mutilation or rejection of a pagan practice or a desire to affirm life or a conviction that people should in principle be capable of playing a part in generating the future Israel. For ten generations the *qāhāl* is also not to admit a *mamzēr*, which might mean anyone born of a prohibited union, though even if that is right, we do not know what kind of prohibited union it refers to (e.g., incest or adultery or intermarriage).

Vocation

Exclusiveness goes along with vocation, as is the case with all talk of election in Scripture. As a nation Israel has a role in relation to other nations, though it would be misleading to call it a mission. Throughout, the First Testament recognizes that Yhwh is concerned for the nations. From the beginning Yhwh intends to fulfill the creation plan to bring blessing to them and intends to use Abraham's people to that end (Gen 12:1-3). But this does not require Abraham's people to do anything apart from going where Yhwh says and letting Yhwh bless it so that the nations pray to be blessed as it is blessed. In keeping with this intention and pattern, Israel has a priestly relationship with Yhwh (Ex 19:5-6). This does not mean it has a priestly responsibility to the world. It means it becomes a microcosm of Yhwh's rule in the world and of a nation's close relationship with Yhwh. It is designed be a working model of what Yhwh intends for all the nations.

Israel was thus designed to be an alternative community.[108] It arose in a context where empires such as Egypt ruled over areas such as Canaan and appropriated a significant proportion of their resources without giving commensurate benefits, where the Canaanite city states did the same to surrounding areas, and where kings and other powerful people in the cities did the same to the city-states themselves. By the design embodied in the beginnings of its life in Canaan and expressed in the Torah, it then embodied a social revolution that reasserted the autonomy of a decentralized community in which power was diffused, "carrying on their life so as to do for themselves what states claimed to do for them" and thus free from paying taxes, rent or interest on loans when they were in need.[109] The nature of this social revolution indicates one reason why a modern nation such as Britain or the United

---

[108]See, e.g., Bruce C. Birch, *Let Justice Roll Down* (Louisville: Westminster John Knox, 1991), pp. 172-73.

[109]Gottwald, *Hebrew Bible in Its Social World and in Ours*, p. xxvi. To describe this social structure, Gottwald here abandons the expression "egalitarian" used in *The Tribes of Yahweh* (Maryknoll, N.Y.: Orbis, 1979/London: SCM Press, 1980).

States can hardly see itself as a "new Israel."[110]

It is in keeping with this intention and pattern that Isaiah 42:6-7 declares, "I called you in faithfulness and hold you by your hand, I guard you and make you into a covenant for people, into a light for nations, by opening blind eyes, by bringing out captive from dungeon, people who live in darkness from prison." Israel was designed to be a covenant for people by embodying what it is like to be in a covenant relationship with Yhwh. That would make it a light for nations, the means of opening their blind eyes. Their eyes cannot see because they are sitting in the dark of a dungeon; Israel will be the means of bringing them out of their dungeon. The irony is that in the exile Israel itself is sitting in a dungeon of blindness, so it cannot be the means of this revelation coming to the nations. But Yhwh intends to restore Israel and make it possible for it to fulfill that role (cf. Is 49:6). Even then this does not exactly mean that Israel has a mission to fulfill. All it has to do is open its own eyes, and then be prepared to explain how it is that things have turned out the way they have.

Israel's destiny to be a great nation and a means of bringing blessing to other nations carries no implication that it is to impose the blessing of its own way of seeing things on other nations. It is not called to force its values on other peoples but simply to embody them. Still less is there any suggestion that it is destined to rule over other nations, though its king was destined to do so. Apart from the few decades during David and Solomon's time when it dominated its immediate region, Israel never became an imperial power. There is some irony in postcolonial readings of the First Testament when they imply that Israel is an imperial power like Britain or the United States. The First Testament narrative as a whole "is framed by landlessness and dispossession. We are not reading a text written by conquerors, but by losers."[111]

Trust on the Journey

We have noted that there was nothing about Israel in itself that made it special or deserving of Yhwh's choice of it. It was that choice of it that made it special. Yhwh provides no rationale, or rather Yhwh thinks in terms of a rationale lying in what Yhwh will do with Israel, not in what Israel already is. Its very existence, and also its existence in the land, issue from Yhwh's choice and action. With inexorable logic it follows that Israel should make trust in Yhwh key to its life as a nation.[112] The difficulty of that challenge emerges at the beginning of its story.

---

[110]Gottwald, *Hebrew Bible in its Social World and Ours*, pp. 307-23.

[111]Tim Gorringe, *A Theology of the Built Environment* (Cambridge/New York: Cambridge University Press, 2002), p. 60.

[112]See §2.3; this section spells out the implications for the nation.

Like some Christian spirituality the First Testament assumes that individuals are on a life journey, though it focuses on the way everyone is challenged to walk rather than a way distinctive to each person.[113] Further, in the First Testament the people of God is also on the way corporately, on a way of obedience to Yhwh. "Be careful to do as Yhwh your God commanded you; do not turn off right or left. In all the way that Yhwh your God commanded you, you are to walk" (Deut 5:32-33 [MT 29-30]). Deuteronomy expounds this image most systematically. "At each point, the people of God face a decision," a challenge "to respond to the love of Yahweh shown to them by loving him in return," that is, by "obedience to his revealed word."[114]

When the First Testament does speak of a distinctive or unique journey, it also applies this image not to the individual but to the nation. At the beginning Israel was summoned to undertake a journey that it did not wish to take. In Exodus 1 it stands a third of the way between the declaring of God's promises and their fulfillment: it has experienced an extraordinary increase that has turned it into a people big enough to represent a threat to the Pharaoh, but it is living in the wrong country (the promise of a land has not been fulfilled) and under the wrong conditions (it is hardly an embodiment of blessing that would draw the world). But Moses has almost as much difficulty persuading it to begin a journey toward the promised land as he had persuading the Pharaoh to let it do so.

Subsequently, Moses recalls urging Israel at Kadesh-barnea to go up and take possession of the land "as Yhwh said to you"; they were not to be afraid or dismayed. They suggested sending spies to reconnoiter the land, and the spies brought back a positive report of it (Deut 1:20-25). Moses' memory makes for an interesting contrast with Numbers 13–14, where the reconnoiter is Yhwh's idea and most of the spies bring back a negative report. But the people's response implies that the negative aspect had indeed been present in the small print of the spies' report; the people refused to go up because they were convinced they would get wiped out. Despite the fact that they had been experiencing Yhwh's guidance and provision in the "great and terrible wilderness" through which Yhwh had been "carrying" them as a man carries his child, they did not trust Yhwh (Deut 1:30-33). Yhwh's angry reaction caused them to do what Yhwh and Moses earlier proposed, but Yhwh was not now with them, so they were defeated.

When the next generation reaches the edge of the promised land, it first

---

[113]See §2.1 "Following Yhwh."

[114]J. G. Millar, "Living at the Place of Decision," in *Time and Place in Deuteronomy* by J. G. McConville and J. G. Millar, JSOTSup 179 (Sheffield, U.K.: Sheffield Academic Press, 1994), pp. 15-88; see p. 88; cf. J. Gary Millar, *Now Choose Life* (Leicester, U.K.: Inter-Varsity Press, 1998/Grand Rapids: Eerdmans, 1999), pp. 67-98.

defeats and annihilates the peoples immediately east of the Jordan. Reuben, Gad and half of Manasseh are to settle there, but first, they must help the other clans take the land west of the Jordan (Deut 2:24–3:20). Deuteronomy implicitly locates its audience in a situation in which they have begun to occupy the land, but the major task lies ahead. They need to commit themselves afresh to Yhwh's expectations as they contemplate crossing the Jordan. They need to look back and look forward. They have taken a long time to get to this point because of their resistance to Yhwh, but this does not mean they will not get to the land. If anything, it proves the opposite; it proves Yhwh is committed to getting them there whatever happens. It further presupposes that the different clans within the nation are to be committed to one another. No clans can rest while others are not at rest (cf. Josh 1:12-15).

Trust and Politics

Israel's subsequent experience in the land made trust seem a hazardous basis for political policy, and in Israel's mind a major reason for having centralized government was so that it could fight for its freedom under human leadership rather than rely directly on Yhwh's leadership (1 Sam 8). Yet this did not alter the fact that it lived in an insecure world. "Earth changes . . . mountains fall down . . . waters foam"; more literally, nations rage and kingdoms fall (Ps 46:2-3, 6 [MT 3-4, 7]). Everything can seem in danger of collapse. Little Israel cannot pretend to take charge of its destiny in this context. All it can do is trust Yhwh. "God is for us refuge and strength, help in trouble, readily available. Therefore we are not afraid" (Ps 46:1-2 [MT 2-3]).

To speak of God as refuge is doubly metaphorical. An individual in danger from a flood could literally take refuge on a rock or in a cave. Such an individual could metaphorically take refuge in Yhwh. A little nation in danger cannot go somewhere to escape from a threat. All it can do is wait. Fortunately Yhwh is not only refuge (something to which people go) but help (something or someone that comes to people), and help readily available—more literally "very findable"; Israel can call out for Yhwh and Yhwh will come.

Metaphorical floods threaten to overwhelm; but there is a metaphorical river whose streams gladden God's city. More literally, "Yhwh Armies is with us, Jacob's God is Israel's haven" (Ps 46:7, 11 [MT 8, 12]). Therefore the nations' raging will get them nowhere. Yhwh stops them fighting and destroys their weapons. This is not so much because Yhwh has peace-loving instincts as because they are in effect pretending to be God. Thus Yhwh bids them, "Stop, and acknowledge that I am God. I will be high among the nations, I will be high in the earth" (Ps 46:10 [MT 11]). Israel can feel secure because it benefits from and shelters behind Yhwh's insistence that the nations acknowledge who is God.

Israel has to decide to live by that. As Isaiah classically put it, "If you do not stand firm in faith, you will not stand firm at all" (Is 7:6-9).[115] Syria had leaned on Ephraim to join it in resisting Assyrian rule, and the two intend to force Judah to join them. When this was reported to King Ahaz, "his heart and his people's heart shook as the trees of the forest shake before the wind" (Is 7:2). Humanly speaking, this was not unreasonable. But Yhwh sent Isaiah to tell Ahaz, "Be careful. Calm down. Don't be afraid. Your heart must not fail because of these two smoking stubs of firebrands, at the raging fury of Rezin and Syria and the son of Remaliah," who are planning to attack and take Jerusalem and put their puppet in Ahaz's place (Is 7:4-6). This plan will fail.

After all, Syria has only Damascus and Ephraim has only Samaria. These are impressive cities, but they have no promise of Yhwh attaching to them. Yhwh's commitment to Jerusalem makes it "Secure Town" or "True Town" (*qiryâ ne'ĕmānâ*), a place where Yhwh's decisive faithfulness is at work (Is 1:21). And even though it fails to live up to that name and description, it is still destined to be the place where the nations will come to listen to Yhwh, not to attack it (Is 2:2-4). Yhwh is committed to defending and delivering it (Is 31:5). That is why trust or faith is a key principle for Judean politics.

There is another theological consideration, Yhwh's commitment to David and his line as well as to Jerusalem. The story in Isaiah 7 begins by referring to Ahaz as "David's household." Being heir to Yhwh's promises to David is the basis on which Ahaz is expected to build his political policies, the basis for confidence in Yhwh's support against other kings. After all, Damascus as the capital of Syria has only Rezin, and Samaria as the capital of Ephraim has only Pekah, to whom Isaiah dismissively refers only by the name of his father Remaliah. The implication is not that Isaiah has better intelligence on the power of Syria and Ephraim. It is that Isaiah knows that no promise of Yhwh attaches to them. That is why they are only smoking stubs of firebrands.

Signs to Encourage Trust

Behind and in front of those commitments to Jerusalem and to David is the fact that Yhwh has "plans" for Middle-Eastern history (Is 14:24-27). In the long term these plans clash with the Syro-Ephraimite "plans" to bring trouble to Judah (Is 7:5). So people who make "plans" for Judah's destiny are going to find they get nowhere (Is 8:10). While Yhwh is also "planning" trouble for Judah (Is 5:19), that involves using Assyria, whom Syria and Ephraim want to resist. Yhwh also has a "plan" to put Assyria down, and intends to do it in Judah (Is 14:24-27).

---

[115]The NRSV seeks thus to represent Isaiah's paronomasia, which uses two forms of the verb *'āman*.

It is hard to live in politics on that basis. Isaiah therefore offers Ahaz a sign. With magnificent theological correctness Ahaz declines on the basis that this would involve testing Yhwh, and we all know that is wrong (e.g., Deut 6:16). Along with the motif of trust, the notion of testing Yhwh goes back to the beginning of the nation, though in a paradoxical way. In light of the people's behavior between Egypt and Moab, Moses warns Israel in future not to test Yhwh as they had at "Testing" (Deut 6:16; cf. Ex 17:1-7). Isaiah knows that Ahaz dare not risk asking for a sign, because he would then have to live by it, so he gives Ahaz a sign anyway. By the time a girl has got pregnant and had her baby, it will have been proved that "God-is-with-us," which is what she will therefore call her baby (Is 7:14). We do not know whether Isaiah has a particular girl in mind, though if he refers to a wife of Ahaz, the sign would have particular point as encouraging trust in Yhwh's promise to David's line. God will have been shown to be "with" Judah or "with" David's household (that is, God will have been shown to be active on their behalf), in fulfillment of another version of Yhwh's commitment to people and king (e.g., 1 Kings 1:37; 11:38; Ps 46:7, 11 [MT 8, 12]). The pressure from Syria and Ephraim will be gone; indeed, within a handful of years (again, the details are unclear) the countries of the two peoples will themselves have been devastated (Is 7:15-16).[116]

So far so wonderful. But it will do Ahaz no good, because terrible trouble will still come on Ahaz (presumably because of the refusal to trust that has dominated the passage), not at the hands of Syria and Ephraim but at the hands of Assyria itself, whom Ahaz will be inclined to trust instead (Is 7:17).

The promised birth of a baby is not the last sign to make this point. Isaiah writes a message on a large tablet, easy to read and perhaps functioning a little like a billboard (Is 8:1). He gets the date of the writing witnessed. The message says, "pillage hurries, looting speeds." Then Ms. Isaiah gets pregnant and he gives their son this phrase as his name. In itself it is enigmatic, like "Leftovers-are-to-return" (Is 7:3); Yhwh explains that it refers to the looting of Damascus and Samaria. Again, that is good news insofar as it means the putting down of these peoples who are pressuring Ahaz. But the witnessing implies that the event designed to bring deliverance will again do Ahaz no real good because he will not have believed the prophet. Judah ignores "the river whose streams gladden God's city" (Ps 46:4 [MT 5]). The unprepossessing stream that flows from the Gihon spring symbolizes Yhwh's provision for the city. But Ahaz's Judah has refused this provision. It will therefore

---

[116]Mt 1:23 uses Is 7:14 to illumine the significance of Jesus. The Spirit-inspired "fulfillment" or "filling out" of the promise in this new context does not need to have any connection beyond the verbal with the promise's Spirit-inspired original meaning, and it does not have any such connection.

experience a much more terrifying river. "This people has spurned the waters of Shiloah, flowing gently . . . and therefore my Lord is bringing up against them the waters of The River, strong and mighty," the Euphrates, which stands for "the king of Assyria and all his splendor." It will overwhelm Judah like a flash flood until "it reaches neck high" (Is 8:6-8). The hearers are to imagine themselves overwhelmed by such a flood and all but drowning.

"It is not easy to be a king of Israel or Judah. I have great sympathy for King Ahaz."[117] The idea of trust in God stands in tension with an aspect of the fundamental instinct of any nation. But it is urged to trust. A whole series of stories in 2 Chronicles 13–17; 20 portray trust as key to political and military success. There is a mistaken form of trust in crises (1 Sam 4:1-11) but also a right kind (1 Sam 7:7-11).

Refuges True and False

Yhwh later bids Isaiah dramatize the humiliated exile of the people of Egypt and Sudan as they are defeated by Assyria, so that in Judah "people will be dismayed and confounded because of Sudan their hope and Egypt their boast" (*mabbāṭ, tip'eret*; Is 20:5). These are the peoples Judah "looks to" (the first noun comes from the verb *nābaṭ* hiphil) for an alliance against Assyria, instead of looking to Yhwh (contrast, e.g., Ps 34:5 [MT 6]). They have become Judah's boast, replacing Zion or the temple or Yhwh (see, e.g., Ps 89:17 [MT 18]; 96:6).

The subsequent story of Hezekiah and the Assyrian king Sennacherib contains an "unparalleled concentration" of *bāṭaḥ* ("trust, rely on") and related words.[118] An earlier Assyrian king, Shalmanezer, had captured Samaria and transported the Ephraimites, and Sennacherib himself had then taken all the Judean cities apart from Jerusalem and exacted heavy tribute from Hezekiah. But Hezekiah resisted surrendering his capital. Sennacherib asks:

> What is this trust with which you have trusted? . . . On whom have you trusted that you have rebelled against me? Now, you have trusted on this broken reed of a staff. . . . Such is Pharaoh, the king of Egypt, to all who trust in him. But if you say to me, "It is in Yhwh our God that we have trusted," is he not the one whose houses and altars Hezekiah did away with?

Sennacherib's aides segue into addressing Hezekiah's aides and his people. "Hezekiah must not make you trust in Yhwh. . . . Did any of the gods of the nations save his land from the hand of the king of Assyria?" When Sennacherib is compelled to break off his siege, he reasserts his message to Heze-

---

[117]Jonathan Magonet, *Bible Lives* (London: SCM Press, 1992), p. 118.

[118]Moshe Greenberg, *Studies in the Bible and Jewish Thought* (Philadelphia: Jewish Publication Society, 1995), p. 66.

kiah, "Your God in whom you are trusting must not deceive you in saying that Jerusalem will not be given into the hand of the king of Assyria" (Is 36:4-18; 37:10).

The account of Hezekiah's response to this assault on his attitude of trust earns him the tribute, "it was in Yhwh the God of Israel that he trusted" (2 Kings 18:5). Isaiah himself is implicitly more equivocal, implying that Hezekiah himself was more equivocal. In Isaiah 28:11-19 his message is, "This is the place to settle; settle the weary, this is the place of repose." Yhwh has established that principle as the foundation for Zion's life; "the person who trusts will not make haste; and I will make authority the line, faithfulness the plummet."[119] But Isaiah accuses Judah of saying they "have sealed a covenant with death, . . . had a vision[120] with Sheol," which will mean that "the sweeping scourge, when it passes through, will not come to us, because we have made deception our refuge, we have hidden in falsehood."

In the literal sense they said nothing of the sort. They thought they were finding a real refuge, a real hiding place from the storm about to break over the Levant. The language may refer to Judah's political policy of entering into treaty relationships with other peoples in order to buttress its military position, or to its having recourse to other deities who could guarantee its future (such recognition of other deities might be involved in the solemnizing of treaties). Either way, in effect Isaiah accuses them of blasphemy. They have no right to be using words like *covenant* and *vision* in this way, or words like *refuge* and *hiding place* (for which see, e.g., Ps 91:1-2). And what they think is the way to preserve life is actually the way to Sheol. What they think is the way to turn away the sweeping Assyrian scourge is incapable of doing so. They are taking refuge or finding a place to hide in empty and powerless political and religious entities, entities that promise what they cannot deliver. The political entities have no power over against Assyria when Assyria has Yhwh behind it, and the religious entities have no reality, period.

Isaiah's words also raise a sharper possibility. While the Psalms sometimes speak of Yhwh in person as the people's refuge and hiding place, they also speak of Zion and the temple in those terms (e.g., Ps 27:4-6). But Judah is inclined to treat Zion and the temple as absolutely guaranteed places of safety. Surely Yhwh will never let Zion be overwhelmed. Thus even Zion and the temple can become falsehood and deception, in the absence of an attitude of steadfast trust in Yhwh.

---

[119]The details of the lines are unclear, but in the context I take the first line of v. 17 to continue to describe the principles on which Yhwh builds Zion, the line and plummet being the tools of a builder (so with regard to rebuilding after the exile, e.g., Jer 31:39; Zech 1:16; 4:10), not the tools of a destroyer (as in 2 Kings 21:13).

[120]The EVV translate "pact," but see BDB.

Judah has to make a choice between covenant with the Holy One and covenant with death.[121] Indeed, it has made a choice.

Theopolitics

Prophets such as Isaiah and Jeremiah believe in "theopolitics," in the determination of politics (particularly foreign affairs) by reference to the will of God.[122] Isaiah 30:1-3 takes up again the motif of the nation behaving as if it is free to formulate plans to safeguard its own destiny when Yhwh is the person who expects to exercise that responsibility. Yhwh speaks about them "sealing an agreement," literally "pouring an offering," with some irony if one may assume that it refers to the formal ceremony whereby parties made a commitment to a treaty, because presumably Judah makes its offering to Yhwh. Yet the agreement that it guarantees does not come "from my spirit." It is one that flouts Yhwh's authority. There is more irony, indeed horror, in the further unfolding of the reproach. The people look for strength with Pharaoh and take refuge in Egypt's shade. "Strength" *(mā ʿôz)*, "seek refuge" *(ḥāsâ)* and "shade" *(ṣēl)* are words that describe the role Yhwh is committed to playing in relation to Israel (e.g., Is 25:4; Ps 27:1-4 [MT 2-5]; 91:1-4). So the people are piling up one shortcoming or failure on another. They are asking Pharaoh to play the role that Yhwh is supposed to fulfill for them. The same issue emerges in the subsequent comment that they "have trusted in oppression and someone devious, and leaned on him" (Is 30:12). The devious oppressor is Pharaoh, but trust and lean *(bāṭaḥ, šā ʿan* niphal) are verbs that deserve Yhwh as their object (e.g., Is 10:20; 26:3-4; 37:10; 50:10). They are treating as a refuge *(maḥseh)* and hiding in *(sātar)* something that will prove deceptive (cf. Is 28:15).

"The Lord Yhwh, Israel's holy one, has said this: In returning and settling you will find deliverance; in quietness and in trust will be your strength" (Is 30:15). Prophets often urge Israel to return to Yhwh instead of having recourse to other deities, and Isaiah may refer to returning to Yhwh from having recourse to other political resources of deliverance—political ones rather than religious ones. Or he may refer to returning to a policy of settling and trusting. The end result will be the same. Understandably, Judah thinks that strength and deliverance depend on taking responsibility for its destiny and on taking sensible political action. Isaiah says it lies elsewhere, in an irrespon-

---

[121]Paul D. Hanson, "Covenant and Politics," in *Constituting the Community*, S. Dean McBride Festschrift, ed. John T. Strong and Steven S. Tuell (Winona Lake, Ind.: Eisenbrauns, 2005), pp. 205-33; see 228.

[122]Cf. Yair Hoffman, "Reflections on the Relationship between Theopolitics, Prophecy and Historiography," in *Politics and Theopolitics in the Bible and Postbiblical Literature*, ed. Henning Graf Reventlow et al., JSOTSup 171 (Sheffield, U.K.: Sheffield Academic Press, 1994), pp. 85-99; see pp. 85-86; on p. 89 he notes Martin Buber's reference to "theopolitics" in *The Prophetic Faith* (New York: Harper, 1960), p. 135.

sibly relaxed trust in Yhwh that things will turn out all right.

Isaiah 31:1-3 makes the same point in yet different words. Here Judah sends ambassadors to Egypt because it sees Egypt as its help or helper (*'ezrâ, 'ôzēr*); but that is the role Yhwh is supposed to play (e.g., Ps 22:19 [MT 20]; 27:9; 30:10 [MT 11]; 54:4 [MT 6]). It relies on and trusts its military hardware, its chariots and steeds[123] (the verbs are again *šāʿan* niphal, *bāṭaḥ*). It does not regard Yhwh *(šāʿâ)*—the word looks similar to "rely on" but it means not so much "look to" as "respect." People do not take seriously the fact that Yhwh is Israel's awe-inspiring "holy one." They have recourse to *(dāraš)* other human resources rather than Yhwh, in the same way as in other contexts they have recourse to other deities (contrast, e.g., Ps 34:4, 10 [MT 5, 11]; 77:2 [MT 3]; 105:4).

Trust in God is the key to Judean politics. Presumably it is also fundamental to the politics of the church. If it does not stand firm in faith, it may not stand firm at all. Is every government expected to make trust in God the key to politics? God is not committed to Washington or London as God was (and might still be) to Jerusalem, nor to these cities' leaders as God was to David, nor does God have plans for them in the same sense. On the other hand, God does expect nations to behave in moral ways, and they might at least need to face the question whether choosing to intervene in a foreign country should become a question that involves moral courage and not just military calculation and economic interest.

The Fruitfulness of Trust

The experience of the nation in this connection is the experience of the individual writ large (or vice versa?). Jeremiah 17:5-8 takes up conventional teaching (also expressed in Ps 1) and speaks of the curse that rests on someone who trusts in human beings, who thus makes flesh their strength and lets their heart turn away from Yhwh; this curse contrasts with the blessing that rests on someone who trusts in Yhwh. The curse means withering like a bush in the desert; the blessing means flourishing even when the heat is on. One might imagine Yhwh encouraging Jeremiah to apply such teaching to his own life or encouraging the exiles to apply it to their lives.[124] In the context it is more likely a comment on Judah's political policies. A century after Isaiah's day, Judah's besetting temptation is still to assume that alliances with other nations are the key to its political destiny, whereas Jeremiah takes the view that Judah's attitude to Yhwh is the key. He is taking the same stance as Isaiah, though the context gives a different slant to his comment. In Isaiah's day Judah seems

---

[123]Or riders; the word can mean either.
[124]So respectively William L. Holladay, *Jeremiah 1* (Philadelphia: Fortress, 1986), p. 489-93; Terence E. Fretheim, *Jeremiah* (Macon, Ga.: Smith & Helwys, 2002), p. 257.

rarely to have needed rebuking for religious practices such as making images or worshiping other deities. The problem was that its orthodox adherence to Yhwh and its political policy-making (and its community life) happened in separate compartments. In Jeremiah's day the situation is complicated by the fact that Judah is involved in worship that the prophet disapproves as well as in questionable political and social life. Its heart has more comprehensively turned away from Yhwh. It thinks that trust in political alliances and adherence to other deities is the key to a secure future. Jeremiah reminds it of the principles of Wisdom piety and implies that these apply to national life as well as personal life. Its present trust and adherence render the nation like one of the spiky plants or feeble trees that are the only kind that can survive in the desert. Things are quite different when people really make Yhwh their trust. Jeremiah highlights the radicalism of this trust by the way he repeats the point: he speaks of "the person who trusts in Yhwh, whose object of trust is Yhwh." That makes such a person like a well-irrigated tree that produces foliage and fruit through the height of summer or through a drought. Being interpreted: far from being destroyed by the international political crises, Judah will come through them triumphantly, flourishing as a nation.

Jeremiah follows that with a related warning about the total crookedness of the human heart, which makes it impossible to be really sure you ever know another human being's heart. This impossibility does not apply to Yhwh's knowing; Yhwh can probe the heart, test the inward being, in order to deal with a person in accordance with their ways (Jer 17:9-10). Jeremiah thus continues to speak in terms that would elsewhere be a comment on human nature in general but here suggest a comment on seventh-century Judah. Officially Judah claims adherence to Yhwh, both in its religion and in its politics. But what is the government's actual stance? It is notoriously difficult for ordinary people (such as prophets) to know what the government is doing; governments have ways of concealing that. An Assistant Secretary of Defense, Arthur Sylvester, once declared, "It is a constant in history that the government has the right to lie to save itself," and added, "Information is an instrument of power."[125] Presidents claim "executive privilege" in order to protect themselves. "L'état: c'est moi." But Yhwh knows what really goes on. And Yhwh will deal with the nation in accordance with that knowledge.

Confidence True and False

There is a mirror image of such refusal to trust Yhwh. As the prophets often see it, Israel has every reason to be fearful about the future, but it is often

---

[125]Arthur Sylvester, quoted by Jacques Ellul, *The Political Illusion* (New York: Random House, 1972), p. 72. I believe the statement was made in the aftermath of the Bay of Pigs invasion of Cuba in 1961.

confident about its position in the world, confident about its power and security, confident about its capacity to solve its problems and confident about
the future.

Amos is offended by the lifestyle of the administration (Amos 6:1-7). Their
houses are filled with lovely furniture, they eat well, they drink well, they
dress well, they entertain themselves, and there is something inherently offensive about this. Perhaps that is clearer to a man from the country, as Western ways that seem unobjectionable to us can seem offensive to people from
the Two-thirds World until they become their own ambition. Further, there
are uncomfortable parallels between their nation's festive banquets and the
worship occasions Amos has previously condemned, with their fine food and
music (Amos 5:21-23). These banquets do not even make a pretense at honoring Yhwh in more than a formal sense. No doubt grace was said. But while
Samaria was the capital and perhaps these were state banquets that were
looked on with awe by "the household of Israel," the First Testament does not
refer to there being a national sanctuary in the city, so any honoring of Yhwh
might be perfunctory.[126]

Yet this is not Amos's main concern. Rather he laments the way people are
"relaxing in Zion" and "living confident on Mount Samaria" (Amos 6:1). The
leadership is fiddling while Rome burns. The reference to Zion either catches
people's attention by starting from the people in the other kingdom or points
something out to later southern hearers of Amos's words: either way, the
problem in Samaria is not peculiar to it. The issue in both capitals is not
merely the leaders' self-indulgence or slighting of Yhwh but their doing so in
a relaxed and confident way that implies they have nothing to worry about.
Like a superpower unwilling to learn the lessons of history, they are incapable of learning lessons from the calamities that have overcome other peoples
(Amos 6:2). Indeed, their little local military achievements have convinced
them that they are invincible (Amos 6:13). They push out of their thinking and
talking the "evil day" (that is, Yhwh's day!—cf. Amos 5:18-20), the day when
calamity might and will come, and they thereby bring near the "reign of violence" in their midst (Amos 6:3).

In the context that sounds not so much an accusation that they base their
own lives on violence (though elsewhere Amos makes clear that this is his
assessment) but a warning that they are unwittingly hastening the day when
a violent invader will sweep through their streets and through the dinner
parties where they are "lying on ivory couches, sprawled on their sofas, eat-

---

[126]Cf. Jörg Jeremias, *The Book of Amos* (Louisville: Westminster John Knox, 1998), pp. 110-14;
though for the view that there would have been a sanctuary there, see, e.g., G. I. Davies,
Hosea (London: MarshallPickering/Grand Rapids: Eerdmans, 1992), pp. 195-96.

ing lambs from the flock, calves from the midst of the stall, . . . singing to the sound of the lute, like David, devising musical instruments for themselves, . . . drinking bowls of wine and rubbing themselves with the finest oils" (Amos 6:4-6). They will again experience the oppression they once experienced in Egypt and are thus forbidden to indulge in (Amos 6:14; cf. Ex 3:9; 23:9). There was nothing wrong with banquets in themselves; the Torah encourages them. But Amos knows the ruin of Joseph is coming and feels sick at the prospect, whereas people are too busy enjoying themselves to share this feeling in the pit of their stomachs that might make them want to do something about it (Amos 6:6). "Not to be preoccupied with the ruin of Israel, and not to sense the present or have an intuition of the future, is the most serious charge that can be directed against politicians."[127] Instead they are going to find themselves in an honored position at the front of a procession leading to exile. Eventually Babylon will experience the interruption of a jubilant and exultant state banquet by a word from Yhwh, and then the fall of a kingship (Dan 5), but Israel will experience it first.

Yhwh elsewhere makes that point to the people of Jerusalem, declaring the intention to attend to people who are too settled and relaxed (Zeph 1:12). They live there in the city convinced they are secure, settled like wine maturing, but they will find their rest rudely disturbed. They do not believe that Yhwh is active in their life as a people: "Yhwh does not do good nor does he do bad." Their words anticipate a challenge that Isaiah 41:23 issues to other deities: do good or bad, do anything to provide evidence that you have the power to act. There are people in Jerusalem who see Yhwh as failing that challenge. It is not so much that they do not believe in Yhwh as that they do not see Yhwh as involved in their life, either to bring blessing or to bring disaster. Perhaps they believe they are in control of their destiny; perhaps they believe that other deities are in such control. It is wiser to have reservations about how the future may turn out. It does not rest on the people themselves.

Politics, Religion and Unreality

There is an overlap between people's religious allegiance and their political policies; the twenty-first century began with a political and military conflict between the Muslim world and the Christian world. Some of the religious practices condemned by the Prophets are (among other things) practices that enable Israel to identify with Assyria, Egypt or Babylon. Ahaz "sacrificed to the gods of Damascus who had defeated him, and said, 'Because the gods of the kings of Syria were helping them, I will sacrifice to them so that they may

---

[127]So Julius Wellhausen according to J. Alberto Soggin, *The Prophet Amos* (London: SCM Press, 1987), p. 105 (without a reference).

help me' " (2 Chron 28:23). Yhwh has attacked Ephraim and Judah like a maggot or like a cancer or like a lion, and they have the perverse but sad stupidity to think they can find healing for their wounds by sending to the king of Assyria: "But this man cannot heal you or cure your sore" (Hos 5:12-14).

Jeremiah condemns the same politics a century later (Jer 2:14-25). Yhwh is the one who reckons to "lead you on the way" (in fact, Yhwh is your shepherd), and they are supposed to follow. Going to Egypt or Assyria involves abandoning Yhwh, and it does not work. By a "natural" process, Judah's wrongdoing will itself punish or discipline them. Their very turning away will rebuke them. Jeremiah speaks both of their having recourse to Egypt and Assyria and of their having recourse to the Masters, and the two forms of turning from Yhwh are related; they are parallel expressions of a refusal to revere Yhwh or serve Yhwh. As is the case with their theology, in turning to other political resources no doubt Judah did not see itself as turning away from Yhwh. But it involves abandoning Yhwh, and that leads to a bitter end. Doing what is bad has bad results—the double meaning of *ra‘* (Jer 2:19)[128] is telling. Judah will be put to shame by its turning to other nations as it will be put to shame by its turning to other deities (Jer 2:26, 36).

In a parallel way the horrific allegory about Israel's unfaithfulness in Ezekiel 16 first talks of Jerusalem's worship of other gods, then moves to talk of unfaithfulness involving other nations, Egypt, Assyria and Babylon. Israel's unfaithfulness was both religious and political. Ezekiel's subsequent allegory about Oholah and Oholibah (= Samaria and Jerusalem) then makes the point that recourse to other nations does not work (Ezek 23). Assyria and Babylon, the "lovers" to whom the sisters were attracted, turned against them. Superpowers such as Assyria and Babylon support smaller powers such as Ephraim or Judah only because it is in their interests. Their stance is wholly cynical. They are using them for their own ends. When it suits them, they cast them off. Yet that will be Yhwh's own means of rebuking the two countries for turning to the superpowers for the support they were supposed to find in Yhwh.

Yhwh looks for reality and abhors unreality or falsehood *(šeqer)*.[129] In Jeremiah's day there is an unreality about Judah's turning to Yhwh, a contrast between its formal turning and its inner attitude where people are still attached to other deities (Jer 3:10). There is an unreality about their swearing in Yhwh's name; their oath does not correspond to their action (Jer 5:2; 7:9).

In general, indeed, they speak unreality rather than reality (Jer 9:3, 5 [MT 2,

---

[128]If the first occurrence, like the second, refers to trouble rather then wrongdoing (cf. JPSV), the point still emerges from the double usage of the word in the broader context (see Jer 2:3, 13, 19, 27, 28, 33).

[129]See Thomas W. Overholt, *The Threat of Falsehood* (London: SCM Press, 1970).

4]). There is an unreality about how people relate to one another. "They have bent their tongue; their bow is falsehood. They have not been strong in the land for truth but have advanced from evil to evil and do not acknowledge me." No one can even afford to trust their neighbors or members of their family; everyone cheats and lies in order to gain. "They have taught their tongue to speak unreality" (Jer 9:3-5 [MT 2-4]). Ironically, that is so even though there is also an unreality about the deities to which Israel turns. The deliverance Israel thinks it can find from the hills with their sanctuaries for the Master is illusory (Jer 3:23). Images likewise are not real—there is no breath in them (Jer 10:14; 51:17). The people are trusting in unrealities (Jer 13:25). It is odd for Israel not to recognize this when the nations themselves are destined to do so (Jer 16:19-20).

The prophets prophesy by an unreality (Jer 5:31; 20:6) even when they prophesy by Yhwh's name (Jer 29:9), and they prophesy unreality (Jer 23:25, 26; 27:10, 14, 16; 29:21, 23)—for instance, unreal dreams (Jer 23:32). They live by an unreality (Jer 23:14). They practice unreality—that is, either they share in the falsehood of the people's life (if we read in light of what precedes) or they lay a prospect before people that does not correspond to how things will be (if we read in light of what follows) (Jer 6:13; also Jer 8:10). The visions they share are false—they do not come from Yhwh and they do not correspond to reality (Jer 14:14). They cause people to trust in something false (Jer 28:15; 29:31). In trusting in the fact that Yhwh's palace stands in their midst, they are trusting in an unreality, because Yhwh is not necessarily committed to living there (Jer 7:4, 8). The result of their prophecy is unreality (Jer 27:15).[130]

Insight

Judah's recourse to false refuges and its failure of trust make it "a household of evildoers" (Is 31:1-2). Yet Isaiah's main point here is that its policies are not merely wrong but ludicrous. It is using its "insight" to devise "wise" policies such as seeking an alliance with Egypt to ward off trouble from elsewhere, and thus relying on Egypt with its chariots and steeds because of their numbers and strength. That is just so stupid. Has Judah really not considered the fact that Yhwh has a certain amount of insight and skill in policy-making? Has it forgotten Yhwh's proven capacity as a troublemaker? A marker of folly is the incapacity to see when one is acting against one's own interests. Judah is characterized by a strange stupidity that makes it unable to see the obvious facts about itself, about its desolation and devastation (Is 1:5-8).

---

[130]Jeremiah also declares that the deceptive pen of the scholars has acted to bring about deception (Jer 8:8). The saying does not fit the pattern of the other occurrences of *šeqer* (which usually refer to the prophets or the people as a whole) and we do not know what it refers to, though it is a saying to scare the pants off an Old Testament scholar.

Do the Judeans not believe Yhwh could do that again (Is 31:2-3)? Have they forgotten the warnings Yhwh has issued, or do they think Yhwh might go back on those words? Are they not aware of the difference between human beings and God at the level of strength and power? Have they not thought about the fact that for all their strength, horses are flesh and not spirit? To say they are flesh is not to say they are sinful; *bāśār* does not carry the connotations of Pauline *sarx*. It is simply to say they are merely physical, bodily. For all their impressive strength, they are in a different league from God, who is spirit—which stands for a dynamism, vitality and vigor of a wholly other order. Yhwh only has to put out a hand and these superficially dynamic helpers will fall over, along with the people who hired them. They will all come to an end.

A nation depends on insight if it is to make its way toward its destiny. But this nation is extraordinarily slow to learn a lesson from its experience. And it can be hard to face facts. Hosea 7:9-15 describes how foreigners have consumed Ephraim's resources; the foreigners may be the Syrians with whom Ephraim allied against Assyria, and the Assyrians who imposed tribute and invaded Ephraim for its recalcitrance. Ephraim has not faced all this. It is like a man who has gone gray under the pressure of life but hides from that fact. This once impressive and powerful nation has been humbled before its own eyes, but this has not driven it to turn to Yhwh as the one who could solve its problems. Its people have as much sense as the simple young person that Proverbs desperately tries to knock some sense into. They are like pigeons, creatures of small brain, cooing in different directions, flitting between submission to Assyria and conspiratorial alliance with Egypt, but really having no idea how to shape a wise national policy. They will find Yhwh has a way with small-brained birds.

The tragedy is that there is someone who could buy them out of their enslavement, but they do not believe this, and they say so, at least in their hearts. If they turn to Yhwh at all, they do so only in pretense. Instead of appealing to Yhwh they just lie there wailing about the political trouble they are in, or they do cry out to Yhwh when they lie there wailing, following the example of their ancestors ("cry out," *zāʿaq*, in Hos 7:14 is the verb in Ex 2:23; Judg 3:9, 15), but this appeal does not come from their heart. It does not reflect real commitment.[131] "They cry out to me, 'My God we acknowledge you,' " Yhwh subsequently comments (Hos 8:2), but they are deceiving themselves or trying to deceive Yhwh. They plan evil against Yhwh, the one who trained them up to make them the strong power they once were but no longer are, plan to make more alliances that deny the mutual commitment of God and people

---

[131]Cf. Hans Walter Wolff, *Hosea* (Philadelphia: Fortress, 1974), p. 128.

(Hos 7:15). In effect, in the very act of negotiating an alliance with the Egyptians, their tongues curse Yhwh. In bemoaning their actions Yhwh takes up the language of the Psalms, speaking like someone who is the victim of conspiracy and cursing. Perhaps they have indeed used this language to Yhwh in their prayers or in their secret thoughts. Whether that is so or not, it is this language that Yhwh uses to characterize their treatment of their God, reversing the regular direction of that language. So "Israel has rejected what is good" (Hos 8:3), turned its back on what is best for it, abandoned the way that leads to blessing.

Self-deception

Likewise the reason terrible disaster is coming on Judah is that "my people are stupid, they have not acknowledged me. They are foolish children, they are not sensible. They are clever at doing what is bad but they do not know how to do what is good" (Jer 4:22). Jeremiah's words nuance the notion of wisdom and stupidity. These involve practical insight; the people cannot see what is best for them. They involve moral insight; the people do not know how to do what is right. They involve relational insight; the people do not see that they need to submit to Yhwh. All three forms of insight point in the same direction. The people are not put in a difficult position, as if some considerations pointed one way and other considerations another. The people are triply senseless. They say, "Trouble will not come upon us. We will not see sword or hunger"—the two perils that invasion and a siege of Jerusalem would mean (Jer 5:12).

"Listen to this, will you, stupid people, senseless, who have eyes but do not look, ears but do not listen. Will you not revere me (Yhwh's oracle)? Will you not writhe before me?" (Jer 5:21-22). The people are stupid, but willfully so, and it is thus their own responsibility. They have eyes and ears, but they do not use them. Yhwh's questions may then express astonishment, but more likely they express determination. In light of Yhwh's last verb, perhaps *yārē'* here denotes "fear" and not "revere." Their stupidity lies in not acknowledging the facts about Yhwh and about Yhwh's frightening power. Either they should be more awed by Yhwh or they should trust Yhwh rather than the lesser deities they have recourse to. How extraordinary that they fail to revere Yhwh as the one who makes sure the rains fall at the time they need them to make the crops grow (Jer 5:24).

There are several levels of pathos about Israel's position (Jer 50:6-7). They are lost sheep, and in principle being lost is not the sheep's fault. In their capacity as sheep they are dependent on shepherds to lead them in the right way, and their shepherds have failed them. The mountains and hills are not only the place where sheep find their proper pasturage but the place where its leadership (e.g., priests and prophets) encourage Israel to indulge in pagan rites (e.g., Jer 3:23). But the people cannot evade responsibility by appealing to their bad leadership. They themselves decided to forget their fold, the place they came from, the place where they lived with Yhwh, a place of safety, and thus found themselves vulnerable to the animals of the wild—that is, to foreign peoples. These peoples can argue that they are not guilty for taking advantage of sheep that have been so stupid as to abandon their true pasture, people who knew that their ancestors had proved Yhwh to be the hope they could rely on.

For Isaiah, again, they are "people who say, 'He can speed, he can hasten his deed, so that we can see it. The plan of Israel's holy one can hurry to come about so that we can acknowledge it" (Is 5:18-19). Perhaps Judeans actually expressed such challenges to Yhwh to act, in their hearts or in their actual conversations. Yet when Isaiah puts skeptical words on his people's lips elsewhere, they indicate the implications of their attitudes rather than their actual words (Is 28:15; 29:15; 30:10-11; cf. Zeph 1:12).[132] That would fit with the declaration that they do not pay attention to what Yhwh is doing (Is 5:12). Either way, they know Isaiah talks about Yhwh having negative intentions for them, and they do not believe him. They will believe it only when they see it. They do not disbelieve in Yhwh's involvement in their life. They rather believe that Yhwh is a God of love and cannot imagine Yhwh would intend suffering for them. The people of God are those who believe in God and trust God. They know God is committed to them. They trust in God's love for them. But such trust can involve self-deception and be another aspect of their sin.

Mouth and Mind

If Isaiah 5:18-19 relates the people's actual words, they would mean them as expressions of skepticism about Isaiah, not about Yhwh. They cannot believe Yhwh will cause them to suffer. They will only believe Isaiah when he is proved right by events. So what they are doing is pretending that the future will be good (Is 5:20-21). It will be characterized by light and it will be sweet to the taste. They will not face the fact that actually it looks bad, dark (cf. Amos 5:18). It will taste bitter. And these are people who are supposed to be the wise and discerning—in other words, Isaiah is speaking to the community's leaders. They think they have the insight to formulate policy for Israel's life, but in reality they completely lack insight.

Isaiah has another way of expressing the nation's attitude to the future, by referring to the attitude of heart and mind that the nation takes to Yhwh.

---

[132]Cf. above on "Refuges True and False."

Christians draw the antithesis between acceptable and unacceptable worship by asking whether worship comes from the heart. Isaiah 29:13-16 asks and answers that question in a way that sounds similar, but its antithesis is actually different. It refers to the way people draw near to Yhwh with their mouth and honor Yhwh with their lips. The trouble is they keep their hearts far away from Yhwh; "their reverence for me was a human command, learned." The heart stands for the thinking, attitude and motivation of the person; it may include reference to the emotions, though that is not the main point about reference to the heart, and reference to the heart is not the main way of referring to the emotions.

"The prophets' ethical challenge" requires "re-visioning worship."[133] Isaiah grants that Judah's worship is theologically entirely correct. It is an astonishing compliment, in light of what prophets usually have to say, but there were indeed times when this was so (for instance, during Hezekiah's reign). There was no mention of the Master in this liturgy. But Hezekiah's reign saw another problem. The question was whether reverence for Yhwh influenced political policies, whether people *lived* by faith. In worship they declared that Yhwh was king of kings and lord of lords, but they did not believe this in their hearts, as their political policies indicated. In their hearts people trusted the insight of their policymakers. They think they are people of discernment, and they shape the policies of the nation in light of that. In doing so they ignore Yhwh and fool themselves that they can hide their plans from Yhwh (or at least they behave as if they think they can do that). They behave as if they have discernment but Yhwh has none.

Once again Isaiah brings out the implications of people's attitudes and speaks of these as if they are people's conscious attitudes when they are actually only implicit. Judah's policymakers took part in the worship of the temple and declared their faith in Yhwh as lord of lords, and in their conscious minds meant every word. They perhaps then reckoned that the policies they went about formulating in the royal court, next to the temple, constituted their taking proper responsibility before Yhwh for their people's destiny. Isaiah sees them as venturing deep into the dark away from Yhwh. They make their plans in the realm of death and think they will get away with that (Is 29:14-15).

They are unconsciously turning things upside down (Is 29:16), behaving as if the relationship between themselves and Yhwh is the opposite of what it is, as if they are in charge of shaping Judah's political destiny. They are behaving like fools who say in their hearts that there is no God. More explicitly, they are behaving as if their views on Judah's political policies make sense and Yhwh's

---

[133]Carol J. Dempsey, *Hope Amid the Ruins: The Ethics of Israel's Prophets* (St Louis: Chalice, 2000), p. 107.

do not. So Yhwh will act in such a way as to demonstrate the folly of trust in them.[134]

Lowliness

Pride means a majesty that can express itself in self-confidence and self-assertiveness rather than submission to God and to other people. Isaiah comments on the loftiness in the way Judah looks about (Is 2:11; 5:15). It does so with a kind of justified pride. Yet that exaltedness in its gaze (lit. "eyes") compromises the facts about who has the really majestic gaze, who is entitled to look about with true *kābôd*. "Their tongue and their deeds are against Yhwh, rebelling against his majestic gaze" (Is 3:8). "The regard of their face [or their regard of other people's face] witnesses against them" (Is 3:9). The way they look at people issues in not treating people equally (cf. Deut 1:17; 16:19). There is a link between how they look at themselves in their impressiveness, how they look at other people in light of how impressive they are and how they thereby compromise the majesty of Yhwh. But "Yhwh Armies has a day against everything exalted and high, against everything lofty, and it will drop down" (Is 2:12). That includes impressive things such as Lebanese cedars, Bashan oaks, high mountains, tall towers, fortified walls, Tarshish ships: all of these. "Human loftiness will bow, the exaltedness of people will drop down; Yhwh alone will tower on that day" (Is 2:17).

English translations' use of words such as *pride* and *haughtiness* in this passage is not exactly wrong, but it obscures the passage's dynamic. Isaiah's problem is human exaltedness or achievement, which makes the people of God able to be self-sufficient or gives them resources to create self-sufficiency. The problem with their attitude is not pride in the sense of self-congratulation and an expectation that others will acknowledge them, but a sense of having the means to control their destiny. Their capacity to access the resources of east and west, accumulate military hardware, manufacture inspiring religious artifacts, construct imposing buildings and design outstanding trading craft makes them more and more impressive as human beings. It makes them look and feel like gods, and thus constitute a challenge to God. An awareness of their importance and exaltedness tempts a people to do their own thing and ignore what Yhwh says. It makes them unconcerned for Yhwh's splendor (Jer 13:9-10, 15-17). When calamity came on Ephraim, it responded with "loftiness and magnitude of spirit," challenged to stand tall and build better than it had before (Is 9:9-10). "Israel put its maker out of mind and built palaces (and Judah has built many fortified cities)" (Hos 8:14). But that was their further undoing.

---

[134]See further M. Daniel Carroll R., "Impulses Toward Peace in a Country at War," in *War in the Bible and Terrorism in the Twenty-First Century*, ed. Richard S. Hess and Elmer A. Martens (Winona Lake, Ind.: Eisenbrauns, 2008), pp. 59-78.

David had known what he was doing when he made Jerusalem his capital. Although it stands lower than the mountains around, it stands on a spur of a mountain chain that makes it virtually unassailable on three sides. But that could make its occupants overconfident, as the Jebusites perhaps were (cf. 2 Sam 5:6) and as the Judeans became. Yhwh therefore declares, "Now: I am against you who sit over the valley, rock over the plain." They say, "Who can come down against us? Who can get into our refuges?" Actually, there is one who can. "I will light a fire in its forest and it will consume all that is around it" (Jer 21:13-14). The physical strength of the city will give no protection when it is not matched by a moral strength. Yhwh will have no more trouble burning its "forest," its magnificent cedar palaces, than in setting light to a forest in the dryness of summer.

When Yhwh indicts Judah for allowing itself to be influenced by foreign ways of discovering what the future holds, from the east and the west, there is likely a connection with the indictment that follows, that its country has huge hordes of silver and gold, of horses and chariots (Is 2:6-7). Judah is flourishing economically and internationally, imperiling its relationship with Yhwh by its assimilation to religious and political resources from abroad. Horses and chariots are the Hummers of the ancient world, sometimes luxury items enjoyed by a small number of well-to-do people, in particular of the royal court, but more intrinsically the latest in military hardware. Judah's multiplying of them is a sign of its wealth, prestige, sophistication and reliance on such resources rather than on Yhwh. Wealth gives access to political and military resources that distance the nation from Yhwh.

It is natural for a superpower to base its foreign policy on its trading and economic interests, and Assyria did this, but Yhwh will put it down for that (e.g., Is 10:5-19). It needs a higher ideal for its politics, one that recognizes its role as God's agent.

The Politics of Compassion

Israel's attitude to other nations is thus to involve a form of distancing. When Yhwh is seeking to wean Israel from reliance on them or fear of them, this often involves reminding Israel of the calamity that is coming to these nations. There is good practical reason neither to fear them nor to rely on them. Yet interwoven with these reminders are declarations that imply a stance something like compassion toward them. Told that calamity is imminent, Assyria turns to Yhwh and turns away from its violence, and to Jonah's chagrin, the compassionate God relents of the intention to send the calamity (Jon 3:9–4:2). Yhwh expects that compassion to be reflected in human politics.

The actual word *compassion* occurs in connection with Babylon in its relationship with Israel, not as the attitude Babylon actually took but as the attitude that it ought to have taken. Again this involves a certain paradox. Baby-lon was Yhwh's means of bringing calamity to Israel. Yet Babylon fulfilled this role all unawares. As far as it was concerned, what it was doing was building and maintaining an empire. "I was angry with my people, I pro-faned my possession, and gave them into your power. You did not show them compassion; on an elder you weighted your yoke heavily" (Is 47:6). The mes-sage addresses Babylon personified as a woman. The First Testament assumes that men also show compassion (cf. Ps 103:13), but the word *(raḥămîm)* is the plural of the word for the womb, so if Babylon can be personified as a woman, compassion is an attribute that might have been expected of it. Yet its treat-ment of Israel showed none. Even an imperial power is expected to have com-passion as part of its nature and activity.[135] The day before I write, representa-tives of Two-thirds World countries pulled out of talks about trade with countries such as the United States and Britain, which (they argued) were not open to changing the terms of trade so as to stop putting Two-thirds World countries at such a disadvantage and thus further reducing the possibility that their peoples might (for instance) have enough to eat.

The same expectation of compassion applies to Israel in its attitude to peo-ples on the receiving end of Yhwh's harshness. Unlike Babylon, Israel is not the means of punishing other nations, but also unlike Babylon it has every reason to be relieved when the nations get their comeuppance. But it is ex-pected to care about them.

The motif recurs through the poems about the nations in Isaiah 13–23. It is understated at the beginning. Isaiah 13:1–14:23 laments Babylon's own downfall and indirectly thereby rejoices in the collapse of Israel's oppressor and overlord; yet the lament form semi-invites the listener to see the suffer-ing and grief of this from Babylon's angle. After bidding Philistia not to re-joice when it gets a temporary respite from Assyrian aggression, and thereby warning Judah not to think about joining Philistia in rebelling against As-syria, Isaiah 14:28-32 closes with a message for the Philistine envoys, who are perhaps in Jerusalem to invite Judah into such an alliance: "Yhwh: he established Zion, and in it his weak people will find shelter." It sounds more than merely a message that says "we are okay"; it implicitly invites Philistia to join Judah in finding refuge in Yhwh. "Zion exists for a purpose, namely, to serve as a refuge for the needy. . . . That is the litmus test for Zion's suc-cessful mission among the nations."[136] The point is more explicit in the po-ems about Moab in Isaiah 15–16. Moab was involved in that rebellion, so the

---

[135]See Walter Brueggemann, *A Social Reading of the Old Testament* (Minneapolis: Fortress, 1994), pp. 111-33.
[136]Pleins, *Social Visions of the Hebrew Bible*, p. 232.

poems again warn Judah not to join in, and again do so by lamenting Moab's coming devastation. But at their center they urge Moab to seek refuge in Zion and to look to the Davidic king for protection. "Compassion to war refugees is the concrete form of Israel's role in the international arena."[137] In Isaiah 17–18 there is more talk of nations turning to Yhwh. This motif then comes to a climax in the poems about Egypt in Isaiah 19, which envisage Egyptians swearing allegiance to Yhwh, crying out to Yhwh in distress and knowing Yhwh delivering and healing them, and joining the Assyrians in worshiping Yhwh. The poems close with the vision of Israel as a blessing in the midst of the earth as it stands between Egypt and Assyria, and is one with them in being Yhwh's people.

Jesus once rebuked the disciples for wanting to call down fire in the manner of Elijah in order to burn up people who rejected him; "the Son of Man did not come to destroy people's lives but to save them" (Lk 9:52-56).[138] George B. Caird comments, "Elijah was typical of the whole Old Testament, which knew no other way of dealing with the enemies of Israel than to call down God's curse upon them."[139] This is a weird observation in a number of ways (especially from the pen of such a great exegete, who came from the same city as I did and went to the same high school and whose lectures influenced me profoundly as an undergraduate). Israel must not fall into the trap of trusting other nations as resources, but neither must it fall into the trap of thinking that Yhwh is interested only in Israel or that it can despise them. It is invited into compassion for them and anticipation of their coming to worship Yhwh. Alongside and standing in tension with the will to exclude is the will to embrace.[140] Jesus' expectation that the disciples will love their enemies fits with this attitude; he also manifests both the will to exclude and the will to embrace. The New Testament three times reports him exhorting the disciples to love their enemies (Mt 5:44; Lk 6:27, 35); it also notes that caring for your enemies is a First Testament bidding (Rom 12:20). Three times too it reports Jesus referring to the promise that the Messiah's enemies will be put under his feet (Mt 22:44; Mk 12:36; Lk 20:43; cf. also Lk 19:27), and four times it refers to this promise as applying to Jesus' enemies (Acts 2:35; 1 Cor 15:25; Heb 1:13; 10:13).[141]

---

[137]Ibid., p. 233.

[138]The actual words quoted do not appear in some manuscripts, though they also come elsewhere in the Gospels.

[139]George B. Caird, *The Gospel of St Luke* (Harmondsworth, U.K./Baltimore, Md.: Penguin, 1963), p. 140; cf. John Ferguson, *The Politics of Love* (Cambridge: James Clarke, 1970?), p. 22.

[140]See Volf, *Exclusion and Embrace*.

[141]See further §6.1 "Caring for One's Enemies."

Honesty in Politics

Beginning in Hosea 11:12 [MT 12:1], Yhwh utters a great protest about Ephraim's deceit in the realm of politics. On one hand, Ephraim seals a covenant with Assyria. In a political context one would usually translate the noun *běrît* as treaty rather than covenant, but that might cause us to underinterpret Hosea's point. After all, Israel has sealed a covenant with Yhwh, and one of the terms of that covenant is that Israel is not free to enter unilaterally into covenant relationships with other powers. Sealing a covenant with Assyria is an act of unfaithfulness to its existent covenant commitment. There is then a further point and another level of deception. Ephraim is also transporting olive oil to Egypt, which suggests keeping up the payments on another relationship, or sealing one.[142] Ephraim is not only presuming to run its own political life instead of deferring to Yhwh, and thus being unfaithful to Yhwh. There is this other way in which its political relationships are characterized by deceit. "They multiply lying" (Hos 12:1 [MT 2]). Truly, Yhwh is "surrounded" by deceit. Once again they think they are being wise, but they are actually playing with fire or (in Hosea's own imagery) playing in the wind that will drive them away. Instead of sheltering from it, especially from the gale-force wind that comes off the desert, they are encouraging it, trying to make it at home, trying to attract it, because they think it will help them. As if! But the wind is a destroyer. Their deceit means they are actually courting ruin.

The behavior of Israel is anticipatorily mirrored in the life of Jacob (Hos 12:3 [4]). Hosea does not focus on the act of deception whereby he robbed his brother of his birthright, but on events that preceded and followed it, on the causes and consequences of his deception. The deception issued from the desire to push his brother out of the way (*ʿāqab*). That itself hints at deception (*ʿoqbâ*). And it led God in due course to confront him and try to put him down, but Jacob's instinct for self-preservation or self-advancement meant he kept fighting even with God or God's representative (*śārâ*).[143] Hosea encapsulates the consistency of Jacob's character that runs through his life and change of name. He is a grabber and deceiver from the beginning and a contender to the end, Jacob from the beginning and Israel to the end.[144]

---

[142]So Dennis J. McCarthy, "Hosea xii 2," *VT* 14 (1964): 215-21.

[143]"He contended with *ʾĕlōhîm*"; that might refer to God, but Hosea goes on to refer to an aide, suggesting that it denotes a heavenly being representing God. The ambiguity corresponds to the way Gen 32 tells the story.

[144]Of course when his parents named him "Jacob" they did not consciously designate him "Grabber" or "Deceiver" but one whom "[God] Protects," from *HALOT*'s *ʿāqab* II. But *ʿāqab* II does not otherwise occur in Hebrew, and it was fortunate or unfortunate that in Hebrew *ʿāqab* I generates words for the heel and for reaching after someone from behind and for deception. Similarly, in itself "Israel" does not mean "He contends with God" but "God contends" or "God rules." See, e.g., *TDOT* and *HALOT*.

Not only did Jacob contend with the heavenly figure; he overcame him. Oddly, however, it is at that point that Jacob weeps and pleads for grace: "He ruled over an aide[145] and prevailed; he wept and pleaded for grace with him" (Hos 12:4 [MT 5]).[146] In Genesis's words, he refuses to let the aide go unless he blesses Jacob. The victory in itself is hollow unless it takes Jacob forward with regard to the question that has haunted him throughout his life, the question of the blessing. It is a further oddity that Hosea then also refers to Yhwh's finding Jacob and speaking with him at Bethel (Hos 12:4 [MT 5]). In Genesis Yhwh's first appearing at Bethel (Gen 28:10-22) preceded the fight at the Jabbok (Gen 32:22-32), though a second appearing at Bethel comes later (Gen 35:9-15), and Hosea may have known the stories in a different order from the one in Genesis. Further, Hosea again leaves the logic unstated, though the point may be the divine generosity implied by Jacob's plea for grace. More than once (the verbs are yiqtol), either side of the fight at the Jabbok, Yhwh took the initiative in seeking Jacob out and speaking with him.

Commitment in Political Decision-making

How does all this affect the hearers? They have to see themselves in Jacob. But they also may and must see their God in Jacob's God. "There [at Bethel] he would speak with *us*," Hosea says as he explicitly reads Jacob's descendants back into the story. They may allow this with enthusiasm because Jacob's God was one who acted in grace with this recalcitrant grabber, deceiver and contender. They must thus return "through" their God (Hos 12:6 [MT 7]), with Yhwh's help: return to the land, like Jacob, but also return to Yhwh? For they must also take this God seriously as "Yhwh, God of Armies." The grace and the power make it both possible and necessary to return to the land and/or to return to this God.

Such returning needs to issue in the manifestation of *ḥesed, mišpāṭ*, and an attitude of waiting for Yhwh (Hos 12:6 [MT 7]). This interesting trinity invites comparison with Micah's trinity of *mišpāṭ, ḥesed* and diffidence or modesty or reserve or a refusal to be self-confident (Mic 6:8),[147] as well as Hosea's own pairing of *ḥesed* and acknowledgment of God (Hos 6:6). There needs to be a commitment of people to God and one another (*ḥesed*), an exercise of authority that expresses this (*mišpāṭ*) and an attitude of waiting for Yhwh to act that contrasts with the instinct to take initiatives in relation to political resources

---

[145]The EVV render the verb *wayyāśar* as if it also comes from *śārâ* "contend," but it is pointed like a form from *śārar* "rule," making a paronomasia with the earlier verb.

[146]The oddness generates the suggestion that one should translate the colon "God (the aide) ruled over him and prevailed" (cf. NEB) or emend it to provide some such meaning. This smoothes the argument, though the logic is little affected.

[147]Cf. §2.3 "Trust and Waiting"; also §6.1 "Goodness and Reserve."

such as Assyria or Egypt or the religious resources of the Masters. Ephraim must wait "continually," not fitfully as it is inclined (cf. Hos 6:4). And all this must be done with honesty rather than deception. Otherwise the argument that Yhwh has with them will issue in terrible trouble.

That sets agenda for Ephraim. Dishonest trading characterizes the nation's internal life, but it also provides a figure for its foreign policy; it is the way the nation as a whole has come to manage its affairs. Hosea points the finger at "a trader with false balances in his hand" (Hos 12:7 [MT 8]). The Ephraimites will have nodded; they will all have disapproved of traders with false scales, when they were their victims. And they will have liked the fact that the Hebrew word for "trader" is "Canaanite" (apparently because the Canaanites were a trading people). But Hosea then catches his audience out, because the trader is Ephraim itself, which has shown itself in another way no different from the Canaanites. "Ephraim has said, 'Yes, I have become rich, I have found strength for myself' " (Hos 12:8 [MT 9]). By implication it has become rich through fraud. It has indeed shown itself a worthy son of Jacob, who had behaved with falsehood (Gen 27:35, the same word as here) and had contended with God when he had reached the "strength" of manhood; Hosea repeats the earlier word. And its "finding" strength rather contrasts with Yhwh's "finding" Jacob in grace. Ephraim knows how to look after itself without having recourse to God, which was at least a folly Jacob did not fall for.

Ephraim acknowledges ʾwn (wealth) but not ʿwn (guilt), Hosea goes on to say (Hos 12:8 [MT 9]). By his collocation of the two similar words Hosea hints that wealth and guilt are closer together than Ephraim admits. Again all this leads into a declaration regarding who Yhwh is, which Ephraim needs to take more seriously: "I am Yhwh your God from the land of Egypt" (Hos 12:9 [MT 10]). It is formally a different declaration, though it has similar implications regarding Yhwh's being a God of grace and power. Both were involved in being the God who brought people out of Egypt, and both have been involved in being Israel's God since (the expression could refer to either of these). In not throwing themselves on God in any way, they lay themselves open to action that undoes Yhwh's work over the centuries. "I will again make you live in tents as in the days of the appointed festival," Yhwh warns (Hos 12:9 [MT 10]). They are used to living in makeshift shelters once a year for a festival that commemorates the exodus, but one can imagine that they prefer the proper homes and warm beds where they enjoy the fruits of their dishonesty for the rest of the year. They will find themselves losing them.

Accepting the Position of Underling

Israel's regular position in the world is as the underling of a superpower, Egypt, Assyria, Babylon, Persia, or Greece, and later Rome. The superpower is sometimes an oppressor whom Yhwh promises to defeat and dethrone, sometimes Yhwh's agent in punishing Israel, sometimes a means of Yhwh's positive purpose being achieved, though whatever role it is fulfilling, it does so mostly unconsciously. The First Testament does not treat this situation of subservience as normal in the sense of natural; as Jesus notes, Yhwh's intention was that from Zion Israel's priest-king should rule the nations rather than vice versa (Ps 110; Mk 12:35-37). Yet neither do the prophets ever tell Israel to attempt to fight against the occupying power or assert independence from it. Indeed, they condemn the idea of plotting rebellion against Assyria or Babylon, and declare that Yhwh is the one who overthrows the superpower, without involving Israel in the process. Yhwh is the warrior.[148] Israel's vocation is to settle down, live with the situation until Yhwh changes it, call on Yhwh to do that and pray for its overlords (Jer 29:7). It does not have to do anything to bring about the imperial powers' downfall or to bring about peace in the world, but simply watch Yhwh do these things as it lives its life as a nation filled with Yhwh's blessing that draws the nations to it. Psalm 133 exclaims, "How good, how lovely is kinfolk living as one," underlines the point with a couple of slightly enigmatic similes, then closes with the explanation that on Zion "Yhwh commanded the blessing, life for evermore." Kinfolk living together in harmony is a means of blessing being released; it is also the blessing itself. How great it would be if the people of God lived together in harmony and worshiped together in harmony. That is the blessing and the means of being a blessing.

The hints of exceptions to the rule about a submissive attitude to the superpower do little more than prove the rule. As a nation, Israel begins its life as the underling of the major regional power; its midwives and the family of Moses do not assume that they owe the state obedience or truth-telling (Ex 1:8–2:10). To get Israel out of Egypt there was no need for Yhwh to engineer a confrontation with the Pharaoh, but Yhwh did engineer one and thereby hint at that aspect of Israel's vocation, specifically its leadership's vocation, to critique and confront the superpower,[149] but the way Moses does this is by passing on messages and performing tricks. Subsequently, Israel's priest-king does wield his staff over the nations in Psalm 110, but Yhwh seems to do the actual fighting. The suffering of Yhwh's servant in Isaiah 40–55 may issue from the imperial authorities' action and be a reaction to the servant's passing on Yhwh's messages to it; if so, that is the most active thing Israel does in relation to Babylon. Israel's commission there is

---

[148]Cf. Millard C. Lind, "The Concept of Political Power in Ancient Israel," *ASTI* 7 (1970): 4-24; *Yahweh Is a Warrior* (Scottdale, Penn.: Herald, 1980).

[149]Cf. Walter Brueggemann, *Hope Within History* (Atlanta: Knox, 1987), pp. 10-16.

indeed to pass on a message, to point out what Yhwh has done and is doing, to be witnesses (see Is 43:10, 12; 44:8). As Jews who have seen what God did in Jesus, the Jesus community then takes up Israel's task of being witnesses to what God has done (Acts 1:8).

The New Testament's view of the relationship of God, superpower and people of God follows the First Testament's. If Jesus rejects the Sadducean way (doing the realistic best that could be done), the Zealot way (revolutionary violence), the Essene way (withdrawal into the desert) and the Pharisaic way (being separate within regular society) in favor of creating a new society characterized by abnegation of power and practicing forgiveness,[150] then (not surprisingly) he thereby reasserts the First Testament's stance in relation to the superpower. Although his talk of loving enemies in Matthew 5:43-44 takes as its starting point a command about one's attitude to fellow members of one's own local community, the broader context in Matthew 5:41 makes reference to the kind of compulsion the Roman occupying forces might impose, and the allusion to rescue from enemies in Luke 1:71, 74 also suggests the imperial forces. So Jesus may include them when he tells his disciples to love their enemies, as the pacifist church of succeeding centuries assumed. But love for one's enemies does not rule out expecting God to rescue us from them.

Dietrich Bonhoeffer suggests that in issuing his command Jesus "released his community of disciples from the political forum of the people of Israel"; while affirming the old covenant, he signified that God was now to relate in a new way to Israel and have Israel relate in a new way to its enemies: "As a result, there will be no more wars of faith. God promised that we would gain victory over our enemies precisely by loving them."[151] But there was nothing so new about Jesus' command. Israel had never fought wars of faith or wars of any other kind against its overlords, and had always been expected to submit itself to them and even to pray for them. Jesus does not offer guidance on how Christians should run an empire, though fortunately the First Testament has already done so.

The Nation's Sovereignty

The juxtaposition of Romans 12:17-21 and Romans 13:1-7 has similar implications. In the first passage Paul urges the congregation to live in peace with its enemies and not seek redress from them, noting that this has the backing of

---

[150]So Yoder, *For the Nations*, pp. 169-79. But it is not clear that "the question for Jesus' followers was whether to make war on the Romans" (Glen H. Stassen and David P. Gushee, *Kingdom Ethics* [Downers Grove, Ill.: InterVarsity Press, 2003], p. 155). As is the case for Jesus' followers today, the immediately pressing questions about enmity are surely more local.

[151]Dietrich Bonhoeffer, *Discipleship* (Minneapolis: Fortress, 2001), p. 138.

the First Testament. He refers to Proverbs 25:21-22 not Leviticus 19:18, but his exhortation fits the local community context there and in Matthew 5:43-44. His exhortation to peacemaking (Rom 14:19) likewise concerns the life of the congregation; other similar exhortation have a broader concern with relationships in the local community (Heb 12:14; Jas 3:18). In Romans 13:1-7 Paul then urges the congregation to submit to the governing authorities, in keeping with the First Testament's attitude to the superpowers of its day. There is a sense in which the Christians are to resist them,[152] though only by standing firm in faith rather than being overwhelmed by them. Nowhere does the New Testament encourage people to take any political initiatives in relation to the governing authorities. Rome's position as God's servant in Paul's day is the same as Babylon's position as God's servant in Jeremiah's day, and the church's acceptance of the superpower's authority rather than rebelling against it follows Israel's acceptance of Babylon's authority.[153]

For only a short period in First Testament times was Israel an independent nation, controlling its own destiny. When it had kings, they were mostly subservient to an imperial power. Half way through the time from Moses to Jesus, Israel lost its monarchy and thus lost that veneer of independence. Throughout the rest of First Testament times (except for a century following the Maccabean deliverance), it was effectively a colony under the government of an occupying power. To complicate matters, the end of monarchy and statehood coincided with a development whereby the nation became divided into people living in Judah and people spread around the surrounding countries. From then on, the Jewish people as such was no longer a political entity. Jews were scattered around the world, the citizens of many states. The church built on this pattern as the diffusion of Jewish communities around the world became the base for the spread of the church around the world, and the means of this. It is important for Paul both that he is a son of Abraham and that he is a Roman citizen.

Yet neither Testament accepts Israel's colonial status as a situation to last forever. Yhwh's exhortation to "seek the well-being of the city where I have exiled you" (Jer 29:7) does not imply "the acceptance of a non-sovereign, nonterritorial self-definition."[154] Yhwh goes on to promise to bring the Judeans back to Jerusalem. Exile is not to be their ongoing destiny. In his exposition of this passage, Yoder pointedly stops his quotation immediately before this promise; it is only on this basis that he is able to argue that the way of disper-

---

[152]Vernard Eller, *King Jesus' Manual of Arms for the 'Armless* (Nashville: Abingdon, 1973), p. 195.

[153]See John Howard Yoder, *The Politics of Jesus,* 2nd ed. (Grand Rapids: Eerdmans/Carlisle, U.K.: Paternoster, 1994), pp. 193-214.

[154]So Yoder, *Royal Priesthood,* p. 133.

sion is now the norm for Israel.[155] On the eve of Jesus' birth, the Holy Spirit inspires Zechariah to see John the Baptist as heralding a time when God will deliver Israel from its enemies (Lk 1:71, 74); Mary's song (Lk 1:51-55) has similar implications. Jesus' disciples then wonder whether his resurrection might be the moment when he will restore *hē basileia* to Israel.[156] Although Jesus says they cannot know *when* this will happen, he does not question *that* it will happen; they are just to get on with that vocation to be witnesses (Acts 1:6-8). The First Testament basis for such expectations lies in the promises Yhwh makes through the prophets. The prophets (particularly Isaiah) look forward to Israel's political restoration, to the nations coming to recognize Yhwh, and to the termination of war, and see all these as interrelated; Jesus implies the same assumption. Zechariah and Jesus do not spiritualize such promises. They do not imply that Jesus' coming ratifies the way the Jewish people has become something more like a faith community than a nation.

The Superpower

The visions in Daniel with their sequences of empires imply the assumption that the domination of nations by a sequence of empires is an ongoing feature of world history that will be brought to an end only by an act of God. These visions also make explicit a point implicit in First Testament history as a whole, that there is no relationship between the history of the world and its superpowers and the fulfillment of God's ultimate purpose in the world. The superpower is not part of the creation order. Creation envisaged no such exercise of authority; this came about only through humanity's rebellion against God. The superpower is both an expression of rebellion against God and a means God uses to restrain rebellion. The histories of the nations "are not God's history. They are not the way God would have his kingdom present in the world." The true history of the world "is not carried by the nation state. . . . This history is the history of godlessness." Our task is not to think that by taking the helm of international history we can contribute to bringing in God's kingdom, but to witness to the fact that a superpower will never do that.[157] Paradoxically, one of the ways Daniel and his friends do so is by involving themselves in the history of the superpower, but by doing this in a way that shows how in itself it is not God's history. Daniel and his friends, and Mordecai and Esther, have to work out what it means to "render to Cae-

---

[155]John H. Yoder, "Exodus and Exile," *Cross Currents* 23 (1973): 297-309; see pp. 305-6. It is astounding that Yoder on these pages accuses other people of "arbitrary selectivity" in their interpretation.

[156]Dominion over the world? self-government? monarchy? The ambiguity parallels that attaching to *mamlākâ, mamlākût* and *malkût;* see the introduction to §5.3.

[157]Stanley Hauerwas, *Against the Nations* (Minneapolis: Winston, 1985), pp. 195, 196, 197.

sar and to render to God"—when they can work with Caesar and when they cannot. People such as Joseph, Ezra and Nehemiah (and Paul) also do so by making the superpower the unwitting agent of Yhwh in furthering the divine purpose even while it is actually concerned for itself.

Both Testaments implicitly recognize that if governing authorities are to achieve anything, their first task is to stay in power; "the principal characteristic of government is the right of life and death." By God's will and as God's servant it bears the sword (Rom 13:4; 1 Pet 2:14), to execute justice, to defend the state against its enemies and to thwart rebellion.[158] But the affirmation this gives the state should not be overestimated.[159] The fact that unbeknown to themselves, wicked empires such as Assyria, Babylon and Rome are Yhwh's servants does not imply a positive view of their moral status. As time went on, the church came to work out its attitude to the empire only on the basis of a particular interpretation of Romans 13, "on the basis of a kind of monism,"[160] rather ignoring the different perspective of Revelation 13. Nowadays, for other Christians the danger is the opposite monism. But in any case, Romans 13 is perhaps not really so different in its understanding of the empires from Revelation 13.[161]

Early in the twenty-first century, the writer and most readers of this volume could be tempted to rejoice in the idea that people should settle down, accept the superpower's authority and love their enemies, because that means accepting our authority and loving us, and most people who oppose war and advocate nonviolence belong to an imperial power that maintains its position by violence. Nonviolence is the bright idea of the colonialist bourgeoisie when under pressure from the people it has exploited,[162] and "the proponents of the interpretations emphasizing radical love" on the basis of Matthew 5:44 are "in most cases Christian Euro-American exegetes."[163] In other words, the past few pages have ideological implications.

Fortunately, there are ways of subverting our possibly ideological interpretation of Scripture. One is that encouraging people to accept the superpower's authority as God's servant offers only short-term comfort. As Britain

---

[158]Kuyper, *Lectures on Calvinism*, p. 93.

[159]Oliver O'Donovan begins his *The Ways of Judgment* (Grand Rapids/Cambridge: Eerdmans, 2003; pp. 3-4) by noting that the state's authority is limited to the task of government (he also notes that this contrasts with the role of the state in First Testament Israel, though I take this to be because he is talking about the equivalent of the empire, not the equivalent of Israel itself).

[160]Ellul, *Violence*, p. 2.

[161]Cf. Dale Aukerman, *Darkening Valley* (New York: Seabury Press, 1981), pp. 92-99.

[162]Frantz Fanon, *The Wretched of the Earth* (New York: Grove, 1966), pp. 48-49.

[163]Daniel Patte, *Ethics of Biblical Interpretation* (Louisville: Westminster John Knox, 1995), p. 53.

and Russia have already found, no superpower lasts. Another is that if a superpower wishes to be an exception to this rule, Yhwh has expectations that it had better fulfill. Superpowers are challenged to acknowledge Yhwh, and not be oppressive (Egypt), nor deify themselves (Assyria), nor fail in compassion (Babylon). Further, the final downfall of Greek power in Jerusalem in the 160s in partial fulfillment of Yhwh's promises in Daniel 7–12 did involve action on part of the people of Judah that Yhwh blessed and used. When smaller powers pull down a superpower from its position, they likely do so as Yhwh's agents. Yhwh's putting down the Seleucids suggests a warning for the equivalents of the Seleucids in the Western world. Conversely, if a superpower were to decide on the countries where it would intervene on the basis of its own interests or of what seemed feasible, not on the basis of what was morally right, it might not be surprising if it experienced terrible reversals.

5.3 Kingdom

As the First Testament tells the story, in Egypt, at Sinai, and in crossing the Jordan (Ex 33:13; Deut 26:5; Josh 3:17), and thus before its arrival in the land, Israel is both an ʿam and a gôy, both a people and a nation. It is both an entity that sees itself as ethnically one, a huge family, and also a political entity whose members are aware of belonging together. As such it is set over against other political entities, even if it does not have a set and organized political structure and ongoing form of centralized government.

A state is an entity that has such a form and authority structure and capacity to control.[164] Whereas in Deuteronomy a king is only an "if" (Deut 17:14-20), eventually Israel does want to submit itself to a central government and thereby give itself a sense of identity with other peoples.[165] Thus with Saul, David and Solomon it becomes for a while a mamlākâ, mamlākût and malkût, a kingdom. This notion of "kingdom" (e.g., 2 Chron 11:17; 14:5 [4]; 17:5) is a subset of the idea of "state" and is as near as Hebrew gets to a word for state.[166] For only a few decades was Israel a monarchical state; it soon split into politically separate kingdoms, and even they lasted for a relatively short period within First Testament times. There was thus little correlation between the state structure and the reality of Israel, as there is little correlation between the separate denominations that we call "churches" and the Church. The two

---

[164]On the question of defining a state in connection with Israel, see Margreet Steiner, "Propaganda in Jerusalem: State Formation in Iron Age Judah," in *Israel in Transition*, ed. Lester L. Grabbe, LHBOTS 491 (New York/London: T & T Clark, 2008), pp. 193-202.

[165]On the underlying factors in such a development, see Frank S. Frick, *The Formation of the State in Ancient Israel* (Sheffield, U.K./Decatur, Ga.: Almond, 1985).

[166]But these words, mamlākâ, mamlākût and malkût, commonly denote "kingship" or "reign."

kingdoms could be mutually independent yet could still be seen by the prophets as one Israel, either now or destined to be so in the future.[167]

A Means of Discipline

In the West we are shaped by our family and local community, but perhaps more by the broader community, our cultural community and national community. In Israel, without the same means of travel and communication, the nation and the broader culture have less opportunity to affect the local community, the family and the individual. The Torah can describe the way the whole people once stood before Yhwh and was addressed by Yhwh, but settling in the land diffuses the community. Insofar as the Torah implies a vision for bringing home to clans, villages and families the ethos expected of the nation, this vision is centripetal rather than centrifugal, through the people's gathering each year for the major festivals when Israel retells how Yhwh brought it into being, makes links between this and the people's ongoing agricultural life, and works out the implications for worship and local community life.

In reality, settling in the land leads to the situation of moral, religious and social collapse described in Judges, when "there was no king in Israel" (Judg 21:25). Judges thus implies that the nation needed to become a state because the lack of firm central government meant everyone was doing what was right in their own eyes. Likewise, part of the logic of the people's desire for a king is that Samuel's sons and prospective successors do not walk in his ways but twist *mišpāṭ* (1 Sam 8:1-5).[168] If a constitution is "the means of bringing the government of a state under law,"[169] the teaching in the Torah is indeed Israel's constitution, and it does bring the king under law; the vocation of the state and the king itself is to bring the nation under that law. "Without sin there would have been neither magistrate nor state-order. . . . Every rule and ordinance and law would drop away." But given the fact of sin, they are necessary.[170] And then "all law is a form of warfare" that refuses to make peace with evil.[171]

How is the state to bring the nation under the Torah? How would it go about stopping someone like Micah stealing silver from his mother and mak-

---

[167]W. D. Davies, *The Gospel and the Land* (Berkeley/London: University of California Press, 1974), pp. 109-10.

[168]The passage is a neat indication of the fact that *mišpāṭ* in itself does not mean "justice" in the sense of something that actually *is* just; it refers to the process of decision-making.

[169]Julian Rivers, "Government," in *Jubilee Manifesto*, ed. Michael Schluter and John Ashcroft (Leicester, U.K.: Inter-Varsity Press, 2005), pp. 138-53; see p. 140.

[170]Abraham Kuyper, *Lectures on Calvinism* (Grand Rapids: Eerdmans, 1961), p. 80.

[171]Rousas John Rushdoony, *The Institutes of Biblical Law* ([Nutley, N.J.]: Presbyterian & Reformed, 1973), p. 93.

ing an image, the context of the first comment on Israel's having no king (Judg 17)? How would it go about stopping people like the Danites reckoning it was a good idea to steal this image, the context of the second such comment (Judg 18)? How would it go about stopping people like the Benjaminites behaving toward the Levite's wife in the horrific way they do, the context of the third (Judg 19)? How would it go about stopping the rest of the clans dealing with Benjamin the way they do and then stopping them coping with the consequences, the context of the last such comment (Judg 20–21)? Judges does not say, and the way the story continues to unfold does not clarify the point. Indeed, it makes it deconstruct. It is not obvious that Saul, David, Solomon or their immediate successors make much difference to the situation in Israel. Later Judean kings such as Jehoshaphat are portrayed as attempting to do so in sending out teams to teach the Torah (2 Chron 17:7-9), but such ventures are feasible within the reduced confines of Judah in a way they would not be in relation to Israel as a whole or in relation to Ephraim.

"There are many autonomous spheres of social activity . . . such as sexuality, marriage, home and family, labor, art, science, education, philosophy, religion" that, "though involved in the fall and to a degree affected by it . . . exist before and apart from civil government. . . . Only government appears to be a distinct sphere coming into existence subsequent to and as a result of the primitive fall of man."[172] But precisely its intrinsic link with human sin makes it counterintuitive to declare that "as the force for the maintenance of order and peace among men, government should police the 'spheres,' "[173] and Israel does not seem to have drawn that inference. If anything, the spheres need to police the government. Governments are, after all, more directly under the sway of powers subordinate to Yhwh that are inclined to fail to work by Yhwh's priorities (e.g., Ps 82), of what the New Testament similarly calls principalities and powers. Personal weakness and political power add to that pressure.

> The biblical story of the fortunes and misfortunes of King David's dynasty seems to have trouble keeping its agenda straight: if we thought it was preoccupied by the serious business of political and military history, . . . the narrative is interrupted by disturbing sex scenes. . . . Israel is threatened from without and from within and within the very midst are acts of adultery, rape, and incest. . . . Politics and sexuality are so deeply and complexly integrated as to be one.[174]

---

[172]Robert Duncan Culver, *Toward a Biblical View of Civil Government* (Chicago: Moody Press, 1974), p. 283.

[173]Ibid., p. 283. Earlier (p. 68) Culver declares that the basis for civil government lies in "man's constitution by creation," which seems in contradiction to that, though the context perhaps suggests only that the capacity for exercising power over one's fellows was there.

[174]Regina M. Schwartz, "Adultery in the House of David," *Semeia* 54 (1990): 35-55; see pp. 45-46.

Going astray with other women and going astray with other deities are not so separable. The Solomon story will offer another riff on such awarenesses, as the subjection of people to conscripted labor accompanies marriages to the devotees of other deities.[175]

The Failure of the State

Thus the trouble is that "the more power grows, the more values disintegrate," so that there is a tension between the state's vocation and its necessary way of operating. Any political order based on values is "an infinitely fragile thing, a rather astonishing human achievement, and one that had to be maintained by will-power, sacrifice, and constant renewal."[176] But power works against all that, and thus against the achievement of the moral goals of being a state. The power of the state is therefore a frightening fact. In defining state, Max Weber, taking up a comment of Leo Trotsky, declared that "a state is a human community that (successfully) claims the *monopoly of the legitimate use of physical force* within a given territory . . . a relation supported by means of legitimate (i.e., considered to be legitimate) violence." If there were no violence, there would need to be no state.[177] If an absolute ethic says "do not resist evil with force," for the politician the reverse holds, "you must resist evil with force."[178]

Having strong central government did not work to achieve its alleged moral goals, or worked in only the most limited way. While subsequent parts of the First Testament tell no stories as horrific as the ones in Judges, on the whole they portray a people characterized more by the absence of the faithful exercise of authority (*mišpāṭ ûṣĕdāqâ*) than by its presence, and they indicate that this disorder by its nature regularly issued from the action of the monarchy and the rest of the officials of state, who have responsibility for the exercise of authority. This is not surprising; in Judges, moral and social disorder characterized the leadership at least as much as the ordinary people. It is usually the case that leaders in church and state are no more upright or mature than their people. The difference is that leaders are in a position to do more harm; they have power and authority.

As Samuel points out, central government invariably imposes terrible burdens on communities and families (1 Sam 8:11-17). Their sons and daughters, their servants and their animals will serve in the army, on the king's land,

---

[175]This comment emerges from the fact that David Jobling's "'Forced Labor'" follows Schwartz's paper (*Semeia* 54 [1990]: 57-76), though he does not make the point.

[176]Jacques Ellul, *The Political Illusion* (New York: Random House, 1972), p. 81 (where the words are italicized) and p. 89.

[177]Max Weber, *Politics as Vocation* (Philadelphia: Fortress, 1965), p. 2; German original 1919.

[178]Cf. Ibid., p. 46.

and in his palace, instead of on the family's land and in its house. And how will the king get that land? He will seize it from you, perhaps using the same methods that other powerful and well-resourced people use. He will impose taxes on you to support his administration and to meet the cost of keeping other kings off his back (e.g., 2 Kings 15:19-20). And you will end up his serfs, as you were once Pharaoh's serfs in Egypt, and you will cry out to Yhwh, as you once did in Egypt. The story of Joseph anticipates the point. There, the state provides, even for people in Canaan, but also enslaves. Joseph buys up all the grain then sells it (Gen 41), and finally makes people give up their land and become state serfs (Gen 47).

In theory the monarchic state could be the means whereby Yhwh governs Israel. But the civil sphere tends to take over the religious sphere. One might see Amos's challenge to Amaziah and his master (Amos 7:10-17) as concerning whether they see Ephraim as an independent state or a people belonging and subservient to Yhwh.[179]

A Means of Coordination and Control

Governmentally, the Canaanites, whose life and history is the background to the life and history of Israel in the land, are not a single entity but a collection of city-states ruled by kings. It is from a city such as Megiddo or Beth-shean that its king and his administration rule the area around, in the manner described in 1 Samuel 8:11-17. As First Testament usage hints, the Canaanites are not a definable ethnic or political entity. *Canaan* is a geographical term, covering Syria-Palestine as a whole, and the Canaanites are the various groups who live there.[180] Politically, in the thirteenth century the area is under Egyptian control and thus subject to Egyptian taxation.[181] Egyptian governors ruled the cities that in turn controlled the farming people in the surrounding country, though Egyptian control apparently collapsed in the twelfth century, the period that sees significant development in the mountains where the First Testament locates Israel. Were it not for the biblical story that tells of the Israelites arriving from outside, one might assume that this area was settled from the Canaanite plains.[182]

Israel's lack of a city focus means it differs from Canaan (and Philistia) in

---

[179]Cf. Patrick D. Miller, "The Prophetic Critique of Kings," in *Israelite Religion and Biblical Theology*, JSOTSup 267 (Sheffield, U.K.: Sheffield Academic Press, 2000), pp. 526-47; see p. 531.

[180]On this, and for what follows, see K. L. Noll, *Canaan and Israel in Antiquity* (London/New York: Sheffield Academic Press, 2001).

[181]Cf. 5.2 "Vocation."

[182]Though see further Amihai Mazar, "The Israelite Settlement," in *The Quest for the Historical Israel* by Israel Finkelstein and Amihai Mazar (Atlanta: Society of Biblical Literature, 2007), pp. 85-98.

its form of nationhood and government, but both peoples are more like federations than unified states. Indeed, if we press etymology, a federation is exactly what Israel was; *foedus* means "covenant," and the Israelite clans are supposed to live in covenant with one another. In this sense it is artificial to polarize "Canaanite" and "Israelite" too sharply. Often the First Testament does not see the Canaanites as more wayward religiously or more oppressive socially than many other peoples, including Israel in many periods. At the same time, "the Canaanites" can designate the inhabitants of the land as people whose religion had distinctively degenerate features, such as a willingness to sacrifice a child, and who oppose Israel's covenant vision of how things should be and affirm exploitative and oppressive ways of organizing society.[183] One might thus see "the Canaanites" as an ideological term, a little like "the Russians" or "the Soviets" or "the Germans" or "the Nazis" or "the Muslims" or "the Americans" or "the Europeans." It is not so much a title as a slur.

Over against the structure of the Canaanites, then, Israel differs for the first centuries of its existence in having no cities, kings or system of administration. Joshua and Judges express directly and indirectly, in positive and negative ways, the importance of the clans sticking together or coming together for mutual support in crises, but there is no structure to make that happen. Joshua describes how the whole people are involved in occupying the land and in reaffirming covenant commitment to Yhwh; it also almost begins and almost ends with narratives of some anxiety about whether the clans that settle east of the Jordan will continue really to see themselves as one with the western clans (Josh 1:12-18; 22:1-34).

Judges maintains the theory that its story is about Israel as a whole while also acknowledging that the events it relates concern particular clans or groups of clans, and Deborah's song both rejoices in the multiclan involvement in the conflict with Jabin and chunters about the clans that did not take part (Judg 5:13-18). As Judges tells the story, after Joshua's death the clan federation has no federal government at all; there is no central authority that can compellingly summon or organize the nation into doing anything. Indeed, there is little clan government (what we might see as the equivalent of state government in the United States). Power is radically diffused and located chiefly in local communities, kin groups and households. The elders of these local communities succeed Joshua (Josh 24:31) and are key to the administration of justice and to control of the land, which would

---

[183]Cf. Walter Brueggemann, *The Covenanted Self* (Minneapolis: Fortress, 1999), pp. 27-28, comparing Niels Peter Lemche, *The Canaanites and Their Land*, JSOTSup 110 (Sheffield, U.K.: Sheffield Academic Press, 1991), who shows how hard it is to identify Canaan or the Canaanites historically.

be by far the most important factor in making life work. This control thus did not lie with a king, ordinary people being his sharecroppers; if there is anyone in a position like the king in Israel, it is the divine King, who indeed asserts ownership of the land.

It is commonly maintained that economic and social factors would have been at least as important as external pressures in turning Israel into a state with a central government.[184] The state as such is an agency of coordination and an agent of control; it may be seen in functionalist terms or in conflict terms, or both perspectives may be needed.[185] The people of Israel as a whole wanted to become a monarchy, but Samuel gave them that warning that kings would soon be making demands on them not just coordinating their energies. When Rehoboam tries to rule by force and does nothing to win his people's allegiance, he meets with resistance that all but destroys his monarchy. Whereas Israel's problem before the monarchy, when power was diffused in Israel, was a lack of coordination, its problem once it had kings was an excess of centralized power.

"Defense"

In 1 Samuel 8 the people go on to argue that they need a king so that when subjected to external pressure they can fight for their freedom under human leadership rather than rely directly on Yhwh's leadership. The arrival of the Philistines in Canaan brings a crisis of this kind both to Canaan and to Israel. Historically, it was the Philistines as much as the Israelites who brought about the demise of Canaanite domination in the land. In Samuel's time the Israelites had won a telling victory over the Philistines that confirmed their control of the hill country, but it left the Philistines in control of the plains. And the people wonder what will happen after Samuel's death. The prospect of this event makes them urge the appointment of a king who will "govern us and go out at our head and fight our battles" (1 Sam 8:20). Notwithstanding the affront implied by the people's request for a king, that is also the logic when Yhwh designates Saul as king in connection with recognizing Israel's need for a deliverer (1 Sam 9:15-16; cf. 1 Sam 10:1). Saul soon proves himself in this connection (1 Sam 11), and it is the context of his further achievements and of his downfall (1 Sam 13–15). It is then as a warrior that David commends himself (1 Sam 17).

The point about having a central government can thus be expressed in one word, the euphemism *defense*. A major reason why states exist is so that the

---

[184]E.g., Rodney R. Hutton, *Charisma and Authority in Israelite Society* (Minneapolis: Fortress, 1994), pp. 77-78, and his references.

[185]For a more multifaceted account, see Norman K. Gottwald, *The Politics of Ancient Israel* (Louisville: Westminster John Knox, 2001), pp. 7-10, 113-20.

people who belong to them can maintain themselves and assert themselves over against other states.[186] War is the means whereby they do so. Israel's recognition that in order to fight its battles it needs to become a state with a central government correctly reflects the fact that war is of the essence of statehood. While "all war is unjust and all force to be condemned . . . this is a matter for the moralist or the individual; the state cannot possibly judge in this fashion. It would simply condemn itself to disappear and be replaced by another state that would show less compunction to use force."[187] States exist in order to maintain, defend and extend themselves in relation to other states. The use of force and violence externally as well as internally is inherent to their nature and purpose.[188] It is idle to ask whether a state may or may not defend itself; to deny this would be to say it cannot be a state. The bishops meeting at the Council of Arles in 314, convened by Constantine (!), recognized that forbidding the state the right to go to war was to condemn the state to extinction.[189] The First Testament simply assumes this.

Even before Israel is a state, the First Testament simply accepts that as a nation Israel is involved in war. This goes with the territory, one might say. On the way from Egypt to Canaan (for instance) it fights back when Amalek attacks, avoids fighting when Edom attacks, and defeats and "devotes" the people of Arad when they attack (Ex 17:8-16; Num 20:14-21; 21:1-3).[190] On this journey there is no occasion when Israel opens up hostilities against another people, and there is some attempt to avoid conflict, but there is no inclination to lie down and die rather then fight when provoked. The stance to Edom (and to Sihon and Og), with the desire to avoid conflict and live at peace, rather contrasts with David's later attitude. The practice of devoting defeated peoples is one Israel devises; Numbers 21:1-3 is the first reference to it, and one that compares with the Moabite theology and practice expressed in the victory stele referring to King Mesha's practice of *ḥērem* on Israel in honor of Chemosh.[191] But Yhwh accepts Israel's proposal. War continues to be a feature of Israel's life throughout its story; there is no development or evolution toward a different stance. In the Persian period Nehemiah leads the Judeans in taking up the sword so as to be prepared to defend themselves against people

---

[186]See the discussion in Victor H. Matthews and Don C. Benjamin, *Social World of Ancient Israel 1250–587 BCE* (Peabody, Mass.: Hendrickson, 1993), pp. 55-75; they also note broader factors that would drive Israel toward centralized statehood.

[187]Ellul, *Political Illusion*, p. 77.

[188]Cf. Emil Brunner, *The Divine Imperative* (London: Lutterworth, 1937/Philadelphia: Westminster, 1947), pp. 469-70.

[189]Ellul, *Violence*, p. 5.

[190]On "devotion," *ḥērem*, see §2.5 "The Offering of Human Beings."

[191]*ANET*, pp. 320-21; cf. Susan Niditch, *War in the Hebrew Bible* (New York/Oxford: Oxford University Press, 1993), pp. 31-37.

who try to stop them rebuilding the city walls (though they do not have to use them) and Chronicles retells with relish stories about great Judean battles.

You do not have to be a nation or a state in order to make war, as Genesis 14 shows. But it sure helps. And the bigger the state, the bigger the war, as we see today. So if we want to end war, we should end states. No war, no states; no states, no war. Readers are put back into the position of the people in 1 Samuel 8, asked whether as a people or nation they really want to be a state or whether it would be better to live by trust[192] and when this does not work, let themselves be conquered.

Constitutional Order

Once Israel has a centralized government rather than being merely an unorganized collection of clans among whom power is diffused, prophets from time to time commission a coup d'état, but in general its prophets and thinkers prefer order to revolution. "Luxury does not befit a fool; how much less that a servant rule over princes" (Prov 19:10; cf. Eccles 10:5-7, 16-17). A servant becoming a king turns order upside down, like a secondary wife or servant girl replacing the wife who has been mistress of the house (cf. Deut 21:15-17; 1 Sam 1; and the family tensions in Genesis), or a fool being full of food when he ought to be paying the penalty for his folly; it makes the earth tremble (Prov 30:21-23).[193]

That is likely part of the background to the polemic in Hosea 6:11b–7:2, which leads into critique of Ephraim in connection with one of its coups. Yhwh has chastised and hurt, but also restored and healed Ephraim,[194] but instead of taking that as a stimulus to reflection on its wrongdoing and on Yhwh's grace, it treats it as another opportunity to indulge in wrongdoing. Ephraim's waywardness thus "reveals itself" or comes to the surface. While disaster is one experience that causes people to reveal who they are by their reaction, blessing also does so. When things go well, this gives people opportunity to forget the wickedness of the past that led to the trouble they got into or rather to resume that wickedness, and they thus take no account of the fact that Yhwh does not put their wickedness out of mind. "Their misdeeds are all around them" (Hos 7:2). It is as if they are a coat or a wall or an army or a flood that surrounds them. Yhwh looks at them, but can only see the deeds. They cannot get out from them, their deeds are like sol-

---

[192]See §5.2.

[193]See Raymond C. Van Leeuwen, "Proverbs 30:21-23 and the Biblical World Upside Down," *JBL* 105 (1986), pp. 599-610.

[194]The EVV take the line to refer to a hypothetical restoration, but the expression (preposition plus infinitive) is a regular way to refer to an actual event. See, e.g., Wolff, *Hosea*, pp. 106, 123.

diers attacking them or floodwaters threatening to drown them. And these deeds are not just ones from the past that continue to stand before Yhwh but deeds that people continue to do blatantly, "in your face" in relation to Yhwh (Hos 7:2). Thus in a sense Yhwh does not have to keep their wrongdoing in mind; they keep reminding Yhwh of it. (Yhwh speaks elsewhere of not keeping our wickedness in mind—see, e.g., Isaiah 43:25; Jeremiah 31:34— but perhaps there has to be some reciprocity about that dynamic; the assurance that Yhwh will act thus is an incentive to turn, but if we decline to turn, Yhwh may decline to put out of mind.)

The deceit that epitomizes this wrongdoing may express itself in many ways. Here Hosea goes on to describe one of the many occasions in Ephraim when conspirators assassinated the king, then concludes, "They devour their leaders. All their kings have fallen; there is no one among them calling on me" (Hos 7:7). The people failing to call on Yhwh might be Ephraim as a whole, who no more respond to disaster than to healing by calling on Yhwh. But perhaps they are the conspirators. To judge from his condemnation of Jehu (Hos 1:4), Hosea would likely reckon that murdering a king was wrong in itself, perhaps because all murder is wrong. Certainly his account of the coup (Hos 7:3-7) suggests distaste for such deceit and treachery, and he might assume that a coup imperils order in the community in a way that is rarely worth the risk. First Kings 19 and 2 Kings 9–10 show that Yhwh's attitude to Jehu was more complicated than we would realize from Hosea. Jehu is Yhwh's means of bringing about the downfall of Ahab's line. Yhwh can affirm revolution as well as order. And in the context of the decades during which violence keeps begetting violence in ninth-century Ephraim, Elisha moves between a peace-loving, communitarian praxis and a violent one.[195]

Hosea's explicit critique takes up the assumption that the key to solving the nation's problems is bringing about a change of government. Hosea thinks the key is calling on Yhwh. It is natural both for revolutionaries and for people in democracies to think as Ephraim does, as if a change of government will improve things; thus over shorter or longer periods Britain switches between Conservative and Labour, the United States between Democrats and Republicans. It is grievous for the people of God to think like that.

Hosea 8:4 goes on to bring together two aspects of the people's faithlessness, the political and the religious: "These people have appointed kings, but not with my will; they have appointed rulers, but I did not acknowledge them. With their silver and gold they have made images for themselves—so that it[196] might be destroyed." The wrong in both may lie in the fact that the people

---

[195]Cf. Hannelis Schulte, "The End of the Omride Dynasty," *Semeia* 66 (1994): 133-48.
[196]Apparently the precious metal.

are deciding what happens. Certainly Yhwh objects to the people deciding who rules them (so much for democracy in the sense of people electing their government). The two expressions imply more than merely seeking Yhwh's confirmation of plans they formulate. Their royal appointments are more literally "not from me"; they ought to issue from divine initiative and do not. The people appointed as rulers are not people Yhwh "acknowledged" in the way Yhwh acknowledged Jeremiah when he was still in the womb (Jer 1:5); again, the expression indicates that Yhwh is not talking about responding to human choices but about taking an initiative. Appointing kings and rulers is like appointing prophets. It is not something that can be done on human initiative. It would not be surprising if Yhwh also objects to the idea that people make up their own mind about how to represent God. The problem with images (*ʿăṣabbîm*) is similarly that they are things that are "shaped" (*ʿāṣab*), by human beings. Such an image is "from Israel" (not "from Yhwh"); "an artisan made it—it is not a god" (Hos 8:6). But these things that people shape are also things that will cause them pain (the other root *ʿāṣab* means hurt or pain). Hosea will soon go on to note the way they have built lots of altars, but these are merely altars for sin, and that is at least partly because their enthusiasm for making altars contrasts with their treating as alien the teaching that Yhwh is enthusiastic about (Hos 8:11-12).

They will find themselves destroyed by "the burden of kings and rulers" (Hos 8:10). The leaders who bear responsibility for these policies will fall: "Their rulers will fall by the sword because of the cursing of their tongues; this is their jabbering in the land of Egypt" (Hos 7:16).

The War Between the States

We have considered one category of relationship between Israel and other nations or states, that whereby it is the underling of a superpower.[197] Another category involves Israel's interrelationship with neighboring states of more comparable power such as Philistia, Moab and Syria in the monarchic period, or Ammon, Samaria and Ashdod in the Persian period. It is a feature of history that such peoples bump up against each other, commonly out of a desire to take over land or resources. War then involves solving such conflicts by violence rather than, for instance, by discussion in a context of law.

There are many theories about the causes of war, economic, psychological, anthropological and sociological. The First Testament simply recognizes war as a reality of human life. Israel lives with the reality of tensions between nations and the way one people group lords it over another. It no doubt assumes that there were no wars in Eden, but it makes no explicit link

---

[197]See §5.2

between the original human rebellion against God and the emergence of war, like the link it makes with the other sad human realities that appear in Genesis 3:14-19. It does see the tensions between the nations as going back to the misty beginnings of their history, when God set the world going again after almost destroying it (Gen 9:18-27). Noah's discovery of the pleasure and the pain of viticulture is followed by his personal discovery of the pain of parenthood—pain in the way his son treats him and pain expressed in his reaction. Typically, the narrative is hardly designed simply to convey a straightforward moral lesson ("Don't get drunk," "Don't dishonor your parents"). It rather goes on to own the disjointedness of the human community in which one group lords it over another in ways that may reflect the unwisdom of some and the way others respond in contempt and in retaliation. The First Testament treats that as a fact of life, like breakdowns of relationship between friends or family members.

Subsequently in the First Testament, war is not one thing.[198] There are liberative wars, defensive wars, aggressive wars and punitive wars. There are organized wars undertaken by organized states, feuds, raids, and acts of retaliation undertaken by groups, and conflicts that are more like the one or more like the other. Both Israel and its enemies use the ordinary methods for making war, including deceit as well as extraordinary bravery, and Yhwh uses both. War is simply a reality of human life in which Yhwh sometimes takes part and makes work in relatively godly and moral ways or to godly and moral ends. So in Judges, Kings and Chronicles, when the people turn their back on Yhwh, Yhwh repeatedly uses other peoples as a means of punishing Israel. Sometimes Yhwh does the fighting and Israel watches, sometimes Israel fights successfully and there is no mention of Yhwh's involvement, sometimes Yhwh commissions Israel to make war, sometimes Israel makes war and Yhwh joins in. Yhwh thus regards war as less alien than sex, which Yhwh has nothing to do with. Notwithstanding the First Testament's insistence on dissociating Yhwh from death as from sex, it does not dissociate Yhwh from action that brings death. God is much involved in violence in the First Testament. It has been argued that monotheism is inherently inclined to violence,[199] but it is not clear that this can be supported either by historical or logical arguments;[200] in Israel's world polytheistic peoples do not seem to be

---

[198]See *OTT* 1:474-85; Niditch summarizes studies concerning the interrelationship between war and social organization and the sense in which war can mean many different things in different social contexts (*War in the Hebrew Bible*, pp. 13-20).

[199]See, e.g., Regina M. Schwartz, *The Curse of Cain* (Chicago/London: University of Chicago Press, 1997).

[200]Erhard S. Gerstenberger suggests that monotheism more likely encourages "the greatest possible openness to the justified claims of equality of all people" (*Yahweh the Patriarch* [Minneapolis: Fortress, 1996], p. 110). See also Miroslav Volf, "Christianity and Violence,"

less violent than Israel, and over the centuries the Israelite-Jewish people has been victim of violence more often than exponent of violence, though the same is not true of the church.

The Function of Scripture

The First Testament thus does not critique peoples for going to war, nor does it imply any rules for when a nation should make war; it seems to accept that nations make war to defend themselves, to defend others, to enlarge their territory or power, and to take redress on others, and it makes little judgment on questions about war's propriety. Amos does see the acts condemned in Amos 1:3–2:3 as something like war crimes, and it would fit with Amos then to view 9/11 as a horrendous crime rather than an act of war, and to respond to it in that light, within a framework of (international) law.[201] Translations of Amos have the word *transgression* to describe these acts, though *pešaʿ* is more strictly an act of rebellion; thus it is Yhwh who will act against the rebels. Yet the action is such that presupposes human mediation (e.g., Amos 1:4-5), though there is no suggestion that it is Israel's business to be Yhwh's agents in this respect. Yhwh uses the empires or other nations to achieve that. In other words, Amos could suggest a First Testament equivalent to the idea of seeing action designed to protect innocent third parties and maintain order between nations as "just policing" (rather than "just war").[202]

In arguing thus, however, we would work with the advantages and disadvantages of treating Scripture as a resource for supporting stances that we wish to take on other grounds, rather than a resource for reshaping our thinking.[203] It is often argued that rejection of war and a commitment to nonviolence in some sense goes back to Scripture, though the "in some sense" is difficult to spell out. M. I. Finley wrote of the "teleological fallacy," which

> consists in assuming the existence from the beginning of time . . . of the writer's values . . . and then examining all earlier thought and practice as if they were, or ought to have been, on the road to this realization; as if [writers] in other periods were asking the same questions and facing the same problems as those of the modern historian and his world.[204]

It is common to argue that our convictions about, for instance, the aboli-

---

in *War in the Bible and Terrorism in the Twenty-First Century*, ed. Richard S. Hess and Elmer A. Martens (Winona Lake, Ind.: Eisenbrauns, 2008), pp. 1-17; see pp. 7-9.

[201]See, e.g., Duane K. Friesen, "Naming What Happened and How We Respond," *Peace Office Newsletter* 32/2 (2002): 7; cf. Gerald W. Schlabach, "Warfare vs. Policing," in *Just Policing, Not War*, ed. Gerald W. Schlabach (Collegeville, Minn.: Liturgical, 2007), p. 78.

[202]On this, see, e.g., Schlabach, ed., *Just Policing, Not War*.

[203]See the comments on "isms" in §1.1 "Ethics and Spirituality."

[204]M. I. Finley, *Ancient Slavery and Modern Ideology* (New York: Viking, 1980), p. 17.

tion of slavery or the equality of women work out the implications of declarations such as Galatians 3:28; these implications are "latent" in the text.[205] This applies to studies that find "the roots of pacifism in the Old Testament."[206] It also applies in connection with the New Testament. But of the three Christian stances to war that Roland H. Bainton identifies, pacifism, crusade and just war theory,[207] none has a distinctively scriptural or Christian origin; all are of pagan background. Whereas crusade is the one with the clearest basis in Scripture, and arguments for pacifism and just war involve considerable inference from Scripture, the latter are the ones that appeal to Christians.

On the other hand, neither should one overestimate the influence of Scripture in causing people to make war. While Christians in Europe and in the United States have justified war against Muslims and Native Americans, for instance, by appeal to the Pentateuch, it hardly follows that "the particular violence of the Hebrew Scriptures has inspired violence."[208] The Crusaders and the *Conquistadores* made some appeal to Deuteronomy and to the stories in Joshua, and also quoted the Gospels ("compel them to come in"), but these texts were hardly the basis for their actions. Rather, with war-making as with pacifism "texts tended to become mirror images of the readers who assumed into their textual readings their own values as explicit modes and strategies for their reading processes."[209] The Crusaders' and the *Conquistadores'* theological rationale for their actions lay elsewhere, and there were arguments among the Spaniards about the applicability of these texts and about the applicability of other texts, such as ones expressing concern for the poor.[210]

Contexts and interests do have a huge influence on the way people read Scripture. Michael Walzer notes that Augustine originally opposed action like that in Exodus 32:25-29, but in different circumstances justified state per-

---

[205]William C. Spohn, *What Are They Saying about Scripture and Ethics?* rev. ed. (Mahwah, N.J.: Paulist Press, 1995), p. 7.

[206]The subtitle of Jacob J. Enz, *The Christian and Warfare* (Scottdale, Penn.: Herald, 1972); cf. T. R. Hobbs, *A Time for War* (Wilmington: Glazier, 1989), pp. 210-14.

[207]Roland H. Bainton, *Christian Attitudes Toward War and Peace* (Nashville: Abingdon, 1960); cf. Robert G. Clouse, ed., *War: Four Christian Views*, rev. ed. (Downers Grove, Ill.: InterVarsity Press, 1991); the fourth here is non-resistance.

[208]Niditch, *War in the Hebrew Bible*, p. 2. Cf. John J. Collins, "The Zeal of Phinehas," *JBL* 122 (2003): 3-21.

[209]Robert Carroll, "Poststructural Approaches, New Historicism and Postmodernism, in *The Cambridge Companion to Biblical Interpretation,* ed. J. Barton (Cambridge/New York: Cambridge University Press, 1999), pp. 50-66; see p. 50, quoted by Robert Setio, "A Text of War in the Context of War," in *Sense and Sensitivity,* Robert Carroll Memorial, ed. Alastair G. Hunter and Philip R. Davies, JSOTSup 348 (London/New York: Sheffield Academic Press, 2002), pp. 289-301; see p. 300.

[210]See, e.g., Kenneth R. Chase and Alan Jacobs, ed., *Must Christianity Be Violent?* (Grand Rapids: Brazos, 2003), esp. pp. 23-49; Luis N. Rivera, *A Violent Evangelism* (Louisville: Westminster John Knox, 1992), esp. pp. 235-71.

secution of heretics, that Thomas Aquinas saw that action as one in which God was involved but not one that there was grounds for repeating, and that Calvin saw it as a basis for the saints taking such action.[211] It is doubtful if the dynamic of any of the wars of, say, the past six centuries involved peace-inclined peoples suddenly realizing that the Scriptures encouraged war and therefore deciding to start one, or even feeling free to fight a war they would otherwise have hesitated to fight.

When War Became a "Problem"

In the premodern world and in the West until the Enlightenment, "most people . . . took warfare for granted as an utterly unavoidable part of the social order. . . . The Enlightenment, however, popularized the notion that war was a barbaric relic of mankind's infancy, an anachronism that should soon vanish from the Earth."[212] Both the First Testament and the New Testament work with the pre-Enlightenment assumption as far as this age is concerned, accepting war as a reality while also implying that it had no place at the Beginning and declaring that it will have no place at the End. Thus the First Testament does not concern itself with seeking to terminate war, but does promise that Yhwh will do so. Indeed, it looks more overtly or more frequently to the future ending of war than it does to the end of those other sad human realities that Genesis sees as issuing from human rebellion. It is striking that through the book of Amos Yhwh is nine times "the God of Armies" but in its closing vision of peace this title disappears (it reappears in Lxx).[213] As with the fall of the superpowers, this is not an ending Israel is to bring about, but one Yhwh will definitely bring about. In the meantime neither Testament rejoices in war, though neither do they lose sleep over it. It is just one of those things, like death, taxes, patriarchy, servitude and the distinction between clean and taboo. Deal with it.

In the modern Western world, as children of the Enlightenment non-Christians and Christians came to agonize about war as they did not previously. War then became a "problem," which it is not in the First Testament or in the New Testament,[214] nor in biblical study until recent decades.[215] One

---

[211]Michael Walzer, "Exodus 32 and the Theory of Holy War," *Harvard Theological Review* 61 (1968): 1-14; cf. *Exodus and Revolution* (New York: Basic, 1985), pp. 62-64.

[212]David A. Bell, "Apocalypse No," *Los Angeles Times*, January 28, 2007, p. M6.

[213]M. Daniel Carroll R. infers that the book might seem therefore to deconstruct itself ("Reflecting on War and Utopia in the Book of Amos," in *The Bible in Human Society*, John Rogerson Festschrift, ed. M. Daniel Carroll R. et al., JSOTSup 200 [Sheffield, U.K.: Sheffield Academic Press, 1995], pp. 105-21; see p. 119); but more plausibly it points to the difference between "now" and "then."

[214]Cf. Peter C. Craigie, *The Problem of War in the Old Testament* (Grand Rapids: Eerdmans, 1978), pp. 12-13; Hobbs, *Time for War*, pp. 16-17.

[215]Niditch notes that even classic works on Old Testament ethics from the early twentieth century "show little interest in war" (*War in the Hebrew Bible*, p. 6). The same is true of

reason for Western unease is that war usually involves people being killed without direct connection to whether they individually "deserve" that (for instance, they may not have been involved in the state's decision to go to war). This especially bothers people in the West because we have come especially to emphasize the individual and the right of the individual to fair treatment. In the twentieth century, agonizing about war increased, especially among Christians in the United States. One might guess at a number of reasons. In the first part of the century the horrific nature of events in the 1914 to 1918 war stimulated agonizing.[216] In the aftermath of the 1939 to 1945 war, the development of atomic and nuclear weapons further did so. Perhaps modern war is as different from First Testament war as modern slavery is different from First Testament "slavery." In this context the way the First Testament talks about war became a "problem," like the way it talks about "slavery." As happens with other areas of life such as marriage and the family, we then work with the assumption that our framework for looking at the question is the natural one and is self-evidently correct, and read Scripture in light of it. Yet when we find we have problems with Scripture's approach to a question, this may well mean it has important things to say to us.

One might guess that a reason why some U.S. Christians emphasize peacemaking is that their nation has war deeply engrained in its history and is the world's main war-maker. "Americans love to fight, traditionally. All real Americans love the sting and clash of battle."[217] This makes some Christians feel bad; our unease with war in the First Testament reflects unresolved issues in our spirits. Further, many U.S. Christians believe their nation should play an aggressive war-making role in the world. If war is to be reduced in the world, it will be important for our church to face its own affirmation of such instincts and thus help the nation to do so and to rethink its understanding of its place in the world. This does not mean never making war; there may well be occasions when war is the lesser evil. It does point to another reason why we should be very hesitant about going it alone. An inherently belligerent nation should not trust its own judgment.

A Means of Yhwh's Ruling the World

As a rationale for the monarchy, harnessing the nation's forces so it can defend itself against other nations works no better than other rationales. Under its kings, Israel, Judah and Ephraim lose wars as disastrously as they

---

John Murray's *Principles of Conduct* (Grand Rapids: Eerdmans/London: Tyndale, 1957).

[216]But for the horror of the Civil War, see Drew Gilpin Faust, *This Republic of Suffering* (New York: Knopf, 2008).

[217]There are various versions of this line from General George S. Patton; I quote it from D. A. Lande, *I Was with Patton* (St. Paul: MBI, 2002), p. 113.

win them, and they still generally live in subservience to other powers. That is so alongside the paradox that in yielding to Israel's desire for a king, Yhwh adds a further significance to the monarchy: it is a means of Yhwh exercising authority over other nations. "Rulers," Oliver O'Donovan comments, "overcome by Christ's victory, exist provisionally and on sufferance for specific purposes."[218] That was already their status in First Testament times, in light of creation, which gives them no place and arguably leaves no room for them, and also in light of Yhwh's action in Israel (see Ex 15:1-18). But Yhwh makes the institution that was not part of the original divine purpose into the means of executing it (see especially Ps 2). Instead of Israel's monarchy mimicking that of the nations, the nations' monarchy is subjected to Israel's. Already in Israel rulers "have to confront a society which witnesses to the Kingdom under which they stand and before which they must disappear." [219] "Society and rulers have different destinies: the former is to be transformed, shaped in conformity to God's purpose; the latter are to disappear, renouncing their sovereignty in the face of his." In a sense they have no alternative; their subjects have already withdrawn their recognition from their rulers. [220]

Unfortunately the notion of Yhwh's ruling the nations by means of the king (or otherwise, for that matter) also remained an aspiration rather than a reality. The First Testament leaves us to infer why that is so. Psalm 72 offers pointers to the answer as it sets before the Israelite king the nature of the rule that will make it possible for this king to rule the nations on Yhwh's behalf (there is a neat irony about the reference to Solomon in its heading, whatever the nature of the link with Solomon that this note implies). Instead, the Israelite state turns itself into something between a magnified version of a Canaanite state and a major regional power such as Egypt.[221] To keep it in being, a temple of Yhwh in its capital becomes an adjunct to the monarchy. War plays an inevitable role in its reaching that position and also plays a role in its keeping itself in being in succeeding centuries. In effect, Psalm 2 suggests that Yhwh would turn Israel into an imperial power by means of which to rule the world. But as it grew toward being an imperial power, it turned out to have the same moral weaknesses as any other imperial power, and under Rehoboam's auspices fell to earth as quickly as it rose.

It would require some extraordinary activity on Yhwh's part for things to turn out otherwise. We have seen that the state is an inherently ambiguous

---

[218]Oliver O'Donovan, *The Desire of Nations* (Cambridge/New York: Cambridge University Press, 1996), p. 231.

[219]Ibid.

[220]Ibid., p. 193.

[221]Cf. Deist, *Material Culture of the Hebrew Bible*, p. 281.

entity. The family, the local community and the nation are not so. They are wayward in practice, but they are not wayward by their intrinsic nature; in the Garden of Eden one can imagine them being faithful entities. The state comes into existence only because there is waywardness in the world, as an attempt to restrain that waywardness, and it is itself an embodiment of faithlessness in its calling to exercise the authority that belongs to God. It is "a God-given order of sinful reality." The very fact that leads to its introduction, Israel's need or desire for strong human leadership, is the need that makes it into an inherently imperfect institution, one that has to work by force even in the very course of being God's servant. "The fundamental character of the state is not right but might."[222]

The great prophetic promises of Jerusalem's restoration (e.g., Is 60–62) envisage the nations submitting themselves to Jerusalem but set this submission in a religious context not a political one. The promises concern Jerusalem's role as the city where the temple is. There is no state and no king ruling the nations in their picture. When the prophets do speak of a future king, they focus on his role as shepherd of Israel. By its nature the notion of Messiah is also an inherently ambiguous one, because it links inextricably with the notion of the state. The First Testament thus sometimes affirms it and sometimes ignores or sidesteps it (the only role Is 60–62 give to an anointed person is preaching, in Is 61:1). This faces Jesus with a dilemma: is it more misleading to agree to being described as the Messiah or to reject it? His compromise is implicitly to accept it but to bid his disciples not to tell people he is the Messiah and to take other models from the First Testament as their clues for understanding him (Mk 8:27-31).

Kingdoms After Christ

Jesus does comment on the blessedness of peacemakers (Mt 5:9), and once again his commendation takes up First Testament attitudes, such as the exhortation to seek peace (Ps 34:14 [15]) and the promises for people of peace (Ps 37:37). It also corresponds to insights expressed by other Jews of his day. Gamaliel's grandfather, Hillel, for instance, urges, "Be of the disciples of Aaron, loving peace and pursuing peace"; Gamaliel's own son Simeon adds, "By three things is the world sustained: by truth, by judgement, and by peace," and in support of his statement quotes Zechariah 8:16 (*m. Abot* 1.12 and 18). Neither the First Testament nor the Jewish writings infer from their love of peace that one could not be involved in war if war came. Neither does Jesus indicate that he drew this inference; like slavery, it is not an issue he discusses. It is thus ironic when a pacifist suggests that people who hold to other

---

[222]Brunner, *Divine Imperative*, pp. 444, 446.

positions use arguments from silence.[223] The fact that Jesus bids people to love their enemies and be peacemakers does not establish what he would say about a situation in which his disciples found themselves citizens of a state that was making war on another state or was the victim of an attack from another state or had had people kidnapped by another state (Gen 14). The New Testament does not include war-making in its list of activities that are incompatible with Christian profession, nor does it give any indication of hesitation about the profession of soldier. In preparation for the Lord's coming, soldiers are told to be good soldiers; they are not told to give up their profession (Lk 3:14). Jesus has nothing but commendation for the spirituality of the centurion in Matthew 8:5-13, and Acts 10 takes a similar stance in relation to the devout centurion Cornelius. If Jesus were a pacifist or proto-pacifist, one might have thought he would view being a soldier or centurion as a little like being a prostitute or adulterer, but to such men the New Testament does not say "Neither do I condemn you; go and sin no more," but the equivalent of "don't overcharge your clients." The mixedness in attitudes within the Scriptures continues in the post-New Testament church.[224]

Individual soldiers and the Roman occupying forces appear from time to time in the New Testament, reminding us that life in Palestine, at least, was what it was because of Roman conquest of the area. The New Testament needed an attitude to life under a superpower, and it takes the same one that the First Testament took. It does not need an attitude to war between states. It expects such wars to continue; it does not offer disciples instruction about what to do if they are drafted. It does imply the assumption the First Testament implies, that statehood and the interrelationship of states, like empire, has no ultimate significance; God's ultimate purpose does not come to fulfillment via states. "Politics is part of that which has been overcome, and its continuance is as a residual hangover."[225]

Perhaps one reason the New Testament does not handle issues such as involvement in war that will recur in history, is that it has no vision of history continuing. "Originally, Christianity was not supposed to have a history because the Messiah had come. There wasn't even supposed to be such a thing as Christianity." When Jesus did not come again, the church became the tem-

---

[223]So Myron S. Augsburger, "Christian Pacifism," in *War: Four Christian Views*, ed. Robert G. Clouse, rev. ed. (Downers Grove, Ill.: InterVarsity Press, 1991), pp. 81-97; p. 84. With further irony, two pages previously Augsburger lays out no less than eight presuppositions (concerning matters such as hermeneutics and eschatology) that he describes as the "basis for my position."

[224]See David G. Hunter, "A Decade of Research on Early Christians and Military Service," *Religious Studies Review* 18 (1992): 87-94.

[225]Bartholomew, "Introduction," p. 35, summarizing the thinking of Oliver O'Donovan. He makes this a contrast over against the First Testament; I see it as a similarity.

porary shelter until he did "(Plan B)."[226] God's own rule of the world had arrived with Christ's coming, and questions about the relationships of the nations or the morality of slavery or the appropriateness of a more egalitarian approach to marriage had lost their significance. "Whereas the reality of war belongs to the Old Testament's perception of ongoing human history, for the New Testament this history is no longer an essential issue. . . . The end of history is already determined by the eschatological presence of Jesus Christ and the eschatological existence of his church." In light of that, "the affairs of this world, including its wars, had become irrelevant." But given that human history has now continued for another two millennia, "the Old Testament's full attention to war . . . is primary for any theological agenda."[227] The demoting of the significance of states, history and war had already happened in the First Testament, as much on the basis of a theology of how things were from the Beginning as a theology of how things will be at the End. But in thinking through this agenda, both sorts of theology make it appropriate to take a stance that is profoundly skeptical about the value, values and ultimate importance of the state.

A more historical way to put the point would involve noting a difference between the two sets of Scriptures. The Scriptures of the First Testament come not merely from the decisive moment of the exodus and immediately succeeding decades, when Yhwh definitively asserted kingship in the world (Ex 15:1-18),[228] but from succeeding centuries when Israel experienced and was compelled to reflect on the ambiguity of the relationship between that reign and the realities of history. The Scriptures of the New Testament come simply from the decisive moment of the Christ event and immediately succeeding decades when God had again definitively asserted kingship, and not from succeeding centuries when the church experienced and was compelled to reflect on the ambiguity of the relationship between that reign and the realities of history.

Church and State

The United States continually broods over the relationship between church and state, and Christians often seek to correlate that with New Testament thinking, which is then contrasted with First Testament thinking. (This brooding is one of the markers of the United States being a postcolonial

---

[226]John D. Caputo, *What Would Jesus Deconstruct?* (Grand Rapids: Baker, 2007), p. 60.

[227]Rolf P. Knierim, "On the Subject of War in the Old Testament and Biblical Theology," in *Reading the Hebrew Bible for a New Millennium,* ed. Wonil Kim et al. (Harrisburg, Penn.: Trinity Press International, 2000), 1:73-88; see pp. 87, 88. Compare the quotation from Miskotte in the introduction to this chapter.

[228]I do not imply that Ex 15:1-18 was composed then, though it may have been.

culture at the same time as a superpower; the former finds expression in its ongoing preoccupation with both using and abjuring European categories.) The European countries indeed once modeled themselves on monarchic Israel, which was in the interest of their monarchs. There are two kingdoms, Luther declared, "the temporal, which governs with the sword and is visible; and the spiritual, which governs solely with grace and with the forgiveness of sins." Israel is a mixture, half way between these.[229] But Europe long ago abandoned that model, which was just as well, because it does not work, and it works even less well for a superpower, which has to see itself as more like Egypt, Babylon or Rome than Israel. It has been suggested that "both Jesus and Moses rejected the state for an alternative vision, and their rejection of the state is central to biblical faith. Joseph and Daniel, however, held high state office, though they rejected the wisdom by which the state is operated."[230] But neither Moses nor Jesus rejected the state. Both rejected—in the sense of refusing to acknowledge the authority of—the empire. But Western Christians cannot see their relationship with their own state as like Israel's relationship with the empire, though Christians under the domination of a superpower might do so.

There can be nothing in the First Testament about the relationship of church and state as there can be nothing about organ donors, because no one had thought of the idea. Indeed, "the Old Testament had no concept of the state" in the sense of an institution relating to the civil sphere separate from the religious sphere.[231] Neither does the idea of separating church and state correspond to any aspect of New Testament thinking. In "render to Caesar," "Caesar" is not the state but the empire, the occupying power. The kingdom of Judah is still both the religious and political entity of which people such as Jesus were citizens. The Christian church and Christians individually in the United States or Britain are not in a position analogous to that of first-century churches in relation to the Roman state, because they are themselves citizens of a past or present superpower. Further, because their countries are democracies, they share in responsibility for its actions. They cannot dissociate themselves from it, unless they burn their passports or citizenship documents and adopt a position like that of Neturei Karta, the "guardians of the city," who live in Jerusalem but do not recognize the state of Israel.

The idea of the separation of church and state came about in the Enlighten-

---

[229]Martin Luther, "How Christians Should Regard Moses," in *Word and Sacrament* 1, Luther's Works 35 (Philadelphia: Muhlenburg, 1960), pp. 161-74, see p. 164.

[230]Millard C. Lind, "Law in the Old Testament," in *The Bible and Law,* ed. Willard M. Swartley (Eckhart, Ind.: Institute of Mennonite Studies, 1982), pp. 9-41; see p. 32.

[231]Brevard S. Childs, *Old Testament Theology in a Canonical Context* (London: SCM Press, 1985/Philadelphia: Fortress, 1986), p. 178.

ment and was formulated in the context of the French and U.S. revolutions in the eighteenth century. Except in the United States and one or two European or European-influenced countries, church and state or religion and state have never been separated.[232] The idea of separating church and state is foreign to Scripture. This need not mean it is antiscriptural; it might mean only that it is an idea that no one ever thought in terms of. But as an essentially Enlightenment idea, it is rather suspicious.

A nearer model for confronting the state is not Moses before Pharaoh or Jesus before Pilate but the prophets before the kings. Prophets and kings still do not correspond to church and state; prophets are members of the state and kings are leaders of the people of God. But prophets do confront the state. One irony here is that Israel's leader (Moses) starts off as the agent of confrontation, while the kings, who are in some sense Moses' successors, become the recipients of this confrontation. We might well see the church as having a prophetic role in relation to the state, but the church would have to become prophetic in its life. Neturei Karta belong to the larger Jewish group the Haredim, the people who tremble (at Yhwh's word; Is 66:2, 5). Their aim is to embody that in their lives.

But the Roman Christians would surely have included citizens, and Romans 12–13 urges love of enemies in relation to Rome.

Rules of Engagement

Whereas the New Testament has nothing much to tell us about being a state or being citizens of a state, the First Testament suggests two perspectives, which would be its equivalents to just-war thinking and to pacifism, alongside its working with the idea of crusade.

By anticipation Deuteronomy 20–24 sets constraints around Israel's war making, which one could relate to just-war thinking. We do not know the chapters' historical background. (Deuteronomy has been dated in every period of First Testament history and there is no prospect that the question will ever be resolved.) But in terms of the story from Deuteronomy to Kings, it does suggest a perspective within which to consider the (mostly or entirely) aggressive wars that David fights against Philistia, Edom, Moab, Ammon and Syria in 2 Samuel 8–11, in the course of his carving out a small empire. Deuteronomy 20 lays down some rules for such war that involve marked contrasts with the presuppositions of David's story and of wars in later periods.

First, making war is the people's business, not the government's or the army's. It is "you" who set out for war (Deut 20:1), the same "you" that Moses

---

[232]Cf. N. T. Wright's opening comments in "Paul and Caesar" in *A Royal Priesthood? The Use of the Bible Ethically and Politically,* ed. Craig Bartholomew et al. (Grand Rapids: Zondervan/Carlisle, U.K.: Paternoster, 2002), pp. 173-93; see p. 173.

regularly addresses (here it is singular). The companies (literally, "thousands"; e.g., Num 1:16; 31:4-14; 1 Sam 17:18; 22:7)[233] by which it is organized are the same as the kin groups, a subset of the clan, as the alternation of the two words shows (e.g., Judg 6:15; 1 Sam 10:19), or rather the company comprises all the adult males within the kin group. In other words, the army is the (males among the) people as a whole. Perhaps the implication is that a kin group's obligation to fight wars that Yhwh determines follows from its acceptance of the privilege of living on a particular tract of land that belongs to Yhwh.[234] Officials that the people themselves appoint in turn appoint the people's military commanders (Deut 20:9).[235]

Before a battle the priest addresses the army and bids it take no account of differences in the size of the two forces; it is not to be afraid if the other side is much bigger and better-equipped (Deut 20:1-4). The reason is that Yhwh is with you. The instruction undermines any arms race, any argument for spending more and more on the military budget at the expense of education, health care and care of the elderly. "The whole spirit of this chapter is actually *anti*militaristic."[236] The priests' involvement in this bidding matches other aspects of priestly involvement in warfare (e.g., Num 31–32). Numbers 27:15-23 is particularly significant. Joshua, as Moses' successor in his capacity as commander-in-chief, is to "stand before Eliezar the priest, who will ask on his behalf for the decision of the Urim before Yhwh;[237] at his word they will go out [to battle] and at his word they will come in, he and all Israel with him, all the community." Just war reckons that the state has responsibility for making war and that the government decides when to do so, but here "evaluation of and participation in war are responsibilities of the sanctuary, not of the state."[238]

In keeping with the priest's exhortation, the officials (not the commanders) send some people home (Deut 20:5-9). They might come to quite a number. They include people who have built a new house and not dedicated it, planted a vineyard and not harvested it, or arranged a marriage but not entered into it; their death in battle would mean they seemed to be accursed (Deut 28:30). Another regulation prescribes that a newly wedded man should not have to undertake military service (Deut 24:5). "His household" (his family) takes

---

[233]Bendor suggests that these are also the "thousands" of passage such as Ex 34:7 (see *Social Structure of Ancient Israel*, p. 94).

[234]Cf. Wright, *God's People in God's Land*, pp. 72-76.

[235]Cf. Crüsemann, *Torah*, p. 244, with TNIV's translation rather than NRSV or JPSV.

[236]Christopher Wright, *Deuteronomy* (Peabody, Mass.: Hendrickson/[Carlisle, U.K.]: Paternoster, 1996), p. 228.

[237]See further §7.3 "A Ministry of Supervision and a Ministry of Music."

[238]Cf. Thomas B. Dozeman, "The Book of Numbers," in *The New Interpreter's Bible* 2:1-268 (Nashville: Abingdon, 1998), p. 257.

priority over war. The officials also dismiss anyone who is afraid.

In approaching a town, the army is to invite it to make peace, though admittedly this amounts to surrendering peacefully (compare the English expression "come quietly");[239] its people then become a conscript labor force.[240] If it declines, the army devotes the city's men (that is, its army) but keeps the women and property as spoil. This applies only to towns outside Canaan; in the case of Canaanite towns, everyone must be devoted (Deut 20:10-18). There is a nice ambiguity here. Does "this" mean the opportunity to surrender or simply the way Israel is to treat cities that do not surrender? Israel evidently did treat many Canaanite communities in the first way, insofar as Canaanites appear as a labor force in the subsequent story (1 Kings 9:20-21).[241]

In besieging the town the army must not fell fruit trees (Deut 20:19-20). Succeeding chapters add that the army is to keep the camp pure from nocturnal emissions and clean from excrement (Deut 23:9-14). If a man fancies one of the women in the captured town, he can take her home and let her put off her captive's garb, then mourn her parents for a month; after that he can marry her, unless he has changed his mind about wanting to do that, in which case he must free her (Deut 21:10-14). He cannot either rape her or sell her or enslave her.

These regulations place wonderful constraints on the exercise of war. The army officers are subordinate to the priests, who declare that practical military considerations are irrelevant to fighting battle. They are also subordinate to the community's administrative officials, who tell the army that personal circumstances override commitment to war. Limits are placed on the fighting; in effect, civilians are protected. The army is to be kind to fruit trees. Women are protected from rape and from arbitrary change of mind by the soldiers. The regulations would be the despair of the commander-in-chief of an army, presumably the king,[242] like the requirements of the Geneva Convention.

The Rechabites as a Model

Pacifism, the notion of people refusing to take part in war on the basis that war is wrong, does not appear in either Testament, any more than the notion

---

[239]Cf. D. J. Wiseman, "'Is It Peace?'" *VT* 32 (1982): 311-26; see p. 320. Tigay emphasizes the sense in which *šālôm* and the related verb can indicate surrender (*Deuteronomy*, pp. 188-89 and the note).

[240]On the implications of this phrase, see §4.5 "Serfs."

[241]See the discussion in Mark E. Biddle, *Deuteronomy* (Macon, Ga.: Smith & Helwys, 2003), pp. 316-17; he refers to Ramban (Nachmanides), *Commentary on the Torah: Deuteronomy* (New York: Shilo, 1976), pp. 238-39.

[242]Cf. Alexander Rofé, "The Laws of Warfare in the Book of Deuteronomy," *JSOT* 32 (1985): 23-44; see p. 32.

of a state not taking part in war. It is one of the isms (e.g., feminism, vegetarianism, teetotalism) that are able to find material in Scripture to buttress its emphasis, but this is what they are then doing—utilizing material that works within a different framework; the isms themselves do not appear there.[243] Given the assumption that war has no place at the Beginning and will have no place at the End, the idea that people who believe in God should behave now in light of the Beginning and the End is one that fits with strands of biblical thinking. It is not an inference that Jesus drew; no one ever asked him about his attitude to war as the Pharisees asked him about divorce. One can imagine this might have been his reply, though at least as likely he would have turned the question back on the questioners in some way so as to push his own agenda.

Stanley Hauerwas has argued that it is important that some Christians are vegetarians as it is important that some are pacifists, as a reminder to the church and to the world that God's creation is not meant to be at war with itself.[244] (One might argue that it is also important that some identify with the other isms, for analogous reasons.) In the First Testament the Rechabites[245] provide a model for such remembrancers. They were in fact teetotalers, though apparently not feminists or vegetarians, and certainly not pacifists: Jonadab, a son or descendant of Rechab as the original head of their household, was an enthusiastic and active participant in Jehu's violent revolution and in his slaughter of worshipers of the Master (2 Kings 10). He then laid on the household the charge to abstain from wine as an aspect of holding back from settled life and civilization in general. They were not to build houses, sow fields, plant vineyards or own such things; they were to live in tents. Perhaps Jonadab made a link between Canaanite-style worship of the Master, the settled and civilized Canaanite style of life, and the degenerate nature of the Canaanite style of life and worship. It would provide a basis for Christians withdrawing from California instead of rushing to move here like everyone else. Jonadab's stance might also link with the conviction sometimes expressed in the First Testament that Israel was more faithful to Yhwh before settling down in Canaan (cf. Jer 2:2).

The Rechabites always kept Jonadab's charge. There is no direct indication that Yhwh called them to it, yet Jeremiah declares Yhwh's blessing on them for doing so. (Apparently he does not see their taking shelter in Jerusalem during Nebuchadnezzar's invasion as compromising it; it is another indication of the First Testament nonlegalistic stance to matters such as vows.) In

---

[243]Again see §1.1 "Ethics and Spirituality."
[244]Hauerwas, *In Good Company*, pp. 196-97.
[245]See, e.g., Frick, *City in Ancient Israel*, pp. 211-17.

the context of Jeremiah 35 this declaration has a rhetorical function; the Rechabites appear only because they model a faithfulness to their charge that contrasts with the rest of Judah's ignoring of Yhwh's charge. Yet the declaration is real, and implies that Yhwh approves their stance, even though it was Jonadab's own idea rather than Yhwh's, and even though it contrasts with the stance Yhwh expected of the rest of the people. Their stance modeled something. They functioned as remembrancers.

Pacifists have such a relationship with the rest of the community. In a context in which nations such as the United States and Britain go to war, it is a plausible idea that God calls some people to refuse to be part of that. They remind us that war is unnatural, does not belong to the Beginning or the End, and they make us unable to rest easily with the compromises involved in living in the now and accepting nationhood, the compromises involved in not burning our passports. James McClendon identifies three ways of understanding our relationship with the world: the church's calling is to interact with the world (H. R. Niebuhr), to be a model to the world (Karl Barth) or to interpret the world (Stanley Hauerwas).[246] Rechabites and pacifists do all three.

A Pacifist State

There are many issues on which both First Testament and New Testament suggest a variety of possible stances, and whether to make war is one of them. This means we have to make a choice.[247] Sometimes Yhwh chooses to act in mercy, sometimes according to people's deserve. Sometimes Jesus is available to heal people, sometimes he gets away from them. Sometimes he speaks harshly, sometimes kindly. Sometimes God forgives, sometimes God does not. To act or speak one way at a given moment is not to rule out the possibility of acting the other way on another occasion. But the actions of Yhwh and the actions of Jesus are not random, and our decisions are context-dependent. It is quite possible to maintain that our day is one in which we should all refuse to make war without it being necessary to claim that Jesus would always have taken this stance or that he thereby questions the stance that Joshua took.

The question a Christian pacifist poses may be not "should nations make war" but "should Christians fight? Does the Bible allow or forbid Christians to participate in their nations' wars?"[248] Behind that question is one concerning

---

[246]See James McClendon, *Systematic Theology: Ethics* (Nashville: Abingdon, 1986), pp. 230-32.

[247]Albert Curry Winn, *Ain't Gonna Study War No More* (Louisville: Westminster John Knox, 1993).

[248]Willard M. Swartley, *Slavery, Sabbath, War, and Women* (Scottdale, Penn.: Herald, 1983), p. 96.

the relationship between Yhwh and the state. Rechabites and pacifists set themselves over against the state in parallel radical ways and fulfill their vocation in doing so. In Britain the chief minority party in parliament is termed "Her/His Majesty's Loyal Opposition." (The concept of "loyal opposition" is also sometimes used in the United States.) By scrutinizing and looking for holes in every proposal that Her/His Majesty's Government presents to parliament, the party that opposes that government is being loyal to the monarch. Pacifists fulfill an analogous role. And sometimes the opposition party wins a change to government proposals. Perhaps U.S. or British pacifists could persuade their government to become pacifist, or at least nonaligned or neutral, like Switzerland. Although "the New Testament writers articulate the ethics of discipleship, not the ethics of public policy,"[249] if people should not fight, then that truth applies to the nation, not just to private individuals. Perhaps U.S. or British pacifists could start by persuading Christians to decline to fight wars; that would mean they had persuaded a majority of the country, and in the United States it would have the effect of turning the nation from the great warmaker into the great peacemaker. We could at least start by agreeing to take up the stance of the pre-Constantinian church and affirm the Mennonite Central Committee's Modest Proposal for Peace (without its tongue in its cheek), "Let the Christians of the world agree that they will not kill each other."[250] It would indicate that our oneness in the body of Christ counts for more than our membership of our nation, whereas present Western practice indicates the opposite. (The 2008 conflict between Russia and Georgia caused consternation among Orthodox Christians in the two countries because it opened up the possibility of their fighting each other, which had never previously been a prospect.) Accepting this imperative would have made a significant difference to casualty rates in the twentieth century.

As its preamble with its reference to two "nations" and "peoples" indicates (Gen 25:23), the story of Jacob and Esau speaks to the hostile relationship of Israel and Edom, which surfaces throughout First Testament times. It offers an implicit critique of Jacob as well as Esau. It wonders at Esau's willingness to be reconciled with his brother and poignantly portrays Jacob's incapacity to imagine this possibility. And it portrays the two brothers finally living separately but peacefully.[251]

---

[249]Christopher D. Marshall, *Beyond Retribution* (Grand Rapids/Cambridge: Eerdmans, 2001), p. 9.

[250]See, e.g., L. Gregory Jones, "Secret of Nyamirambo," *The Christian Century* 122/25 (2005): 45; cf. Volf's comment that "in situations of conflict Christians often find themselves accomplices in war, rather than agents of peace" (*Exclusion and Embrace*, p. 54).

[251]Cf. Frank Crüsemann, "Dominion, Guilt, and Reconciliation" *Semeia* 66 (1994): 67-77; see pp. 71-72.

But What About the Canaanites?

While Israel's relationship with the superpower of its day raises one set of questions and its relationship with neighboring states raises other questions, a further set is raised by the special case of its relationship with the Canaanites. Whereas the exodus was once a favored starting point for a positive understanding of Yhwh and Israel, now its essential connection with the displacement of the Canaanites makes it a rather ambiguous event.[252] Exodus and Joshua have become colonizing and imperializing texts;[253] Deuteronomy and Joshua have become texts of terror.[254] And when people think about Old Testament ethics, often the first thing that comes to mind is the slaughter of the Canaanites, which evokes the modern expression "ethnic cleansing," though for a variety of reasons the fate of the Canaanites is about as illuminating a starting point for understanding First Testament ethics as Genesis 22 would be for an understanding of the family.[255] The introduction of the phrase "ethnic cleansing" reflects how the question behind the question concerning whether God really told Israel to slaughter the Canaanites is whether someone today might claim that God gave them a similar command.[256]

Yhwh's original commands concerning the Canaanites in Exodus 20–34 did not speak of "devoting" them (*ḥāram* hiphil)[257] but simply of avoiding intermarriage with them and destroying their places of worship.[258] Only in Yhwh's restatement of all this in Deuteronomy 7:2 and Deuteronomy 20:17 does Yhwh add a command to devote them; strictly, it is Moses' command rather than Yhwh's, but that is true of Deuteronomy in general and hardly provides a get-out.

There are further parallels with Genesis 22. In neither case did the commission to kill get implemented. Joshua and subsequent books make clear that Israel did not systematically devote the Canaanites. Genesis 22 involves

---

[252]See Robert Allan Warrior, "Canaanites, Cowboys, and Indians," *Christianity and Crisis* 49 (1989-1990): 261-65 and often anthologized; more systematically, Michael Prior, *The Bible and Colonialism* (Sheffield, U.K.: Sheffield Academic Press, 1997); from the Palestinian angle, Naim S. Ateek, *Justice, and Only Justice* (Maryknoll, N.Y.: Orbis, 1989).

[253]See Musa W. Dube, *Postcolonial Feminist Interpretation of the Bible* (St. Louis: Chalice, 2000), pp. 57-80.

[254]Gorringe, *Theology of the Built Environment*, p. 60, following Norman C. Habel, *The Land Is Mine* (Minneapolis: Fortress, 1995).

[255]Though John W. Miller hints that this might not be such a bad place, since it indicates that "sacrificing a child was not the will of heaven. Within the culture of the time this was a momentous breakthrough. It still is." Thus Gen 22 is "a charter of children's rights" (*Biblical Faith and Fathering* [Mahwah, N.J.: Paulist Press, 1989], pp. 155, 159).

[256]Cf. Norman K. Gottwald, "Theological Education as a Theory-Praxis Loop," in *The Bible in Ethics*, ed. John W. Rogerson et al., JSOTSup 207 (Sheffield, U.K.: Sheffield Academic Press, 1995), pp. 106-18; see p. 115.

[257]See §2.5 "The Offering of Human Beings."

[258]See §5.2 "Exclusiveness."

a commission that Yhwh withdraws, and the narrative ends up as (among other things) an account of why Israelites do not sacrifice their children. We may suspect that Yhwh never intended Abraham to go through with the sacrifice; Yhwh wanted to know whether he would do so. Deuteronomy 7 involves a partly analogous commission to devote the Canaanites that Israel did not fulfill, and ends up as (among other things) an explanation of why Israel got into a mess in its relationships with the Canaanites. Deuteronomy 7 in fact parallels many other rules in the Torah, not least ones that prescribe execution, in that as far as we can tell, Israel never went in for execution on anything like the scale that one might expect from the Torah.[259] Deuteronomy 13:12-18 [13-19] also commissions Israel to devote any Israelite town that worships other gods, and heroes such as Elijah and Josiah do kill priests and prophets who sacrifice to other gods (1 Kings 18:40; 2 Kings 23:20), as does Jehu (2 Kings 10),[260] but as far as we know, Israel never went in for devoting towns that worshiped other gods (which was more or less every town in Israel).

What the Command Meant . . .

When Yhwh threatens to put Israel itself to *ḥerem* and then acknowledges having done so (Is 43:28; Jer 25:9), the language involves monumental hyperbole. While Joshua does speak of Israel devoting certain towns and peoples, even these accounts can give a misleading impression. When a city is in danger of falling, people do not simply wait there to be killed; they get out.[261] "At the voice of horseman and archer, the whole city flees. They go into the thickets and climb among the rocks. The whole city is abandoned; there is not a man living in them" (Jer 4:29). The flight of the people of Beeroth (2 Sam 4:3) may be an example;[262] and in the 580s, this is what happened in Jerusalem (see, e.g., Jer 43:5-6). That might be one reason why peoples that have been annihilated have no trouble reappearing later in the story; after Judah puts Jerusalem to the sword, its occupants are still living there "to this day" (Judg 1:8, 21). Only people who do not get out, such as the city's defenders, get killed.

Whereas Joshua and Judges comment a number of times on Israel's failure to dispossess the Canaanites of their land (e.g., Josh 13:13; 16:10; 17:13; Judg

---

[259]See §4.4 "Execution," "Yhwh and Murder," "A Series of Interests."

[260]We have noted that the First Testament as a whole is ambivalent about him (see §5.3 "Constitutional Order").

[261]David Merling, *The Book of Joshua* (Berrien Springs, Mich.: Andrews University Press, 1997), pp. 188-96. On the relatively small number of deaths implied by Joshua, see pp. 106-211.

[262]Jacob Milgrom, *Leviticus 23–27*, AB (New York: Doubleday, 2001), p. 2419.

1:19-33), they never comment on Israel's failure to devote them. Their only negative comment in connection with devoting things concerns Achan's appropriation of some stuff (Josh 7). The contrast with the narratives concerning Amalek (Ex 17:8-16; 1 Sam 15) highlights the lack of critique in the narratives concerning the nonannihilation of the Canaanites. In other words, the First Testament does not tell the story in such a way as to imply that Yhwh intended a literal implementation of the Deuteronomic command concerning annihilating the Canaanites, which Israel did not obey.

What this suggests is that Israel knew how to read the Torah. It knew it was not to assume a literalistic understanding of the Deuteronomic command to devote the Canaanites. Moses did not mean the instruction, and Joshua did not feel bound by it; or rather, Moses absolutely meant it, but also meant it not to be taken literally. Literally, Israel was to dispossess the Canaanites and destroy their forms of religion and have nothing to do with them; metaphorically or hyperbolically, it was to give them over to Yhwh.[263] Israel knew that the Torah comprises theology, religion and ethics in the form of regulations, and not merely laws for implementing. The commission to devote the Canaanites is chiefly an expression of how radically Israel must avoid being influenced by Canaanite religion, or how radically it should have avoided it.

In reading Deuteronomy, Israel would be helped by the fact that Deuteronomy 7 is part of the preaching about attitudes in Deuteronomy 5–11, not part of the practical instructions in Deuteronomy 12–26, as the directives about matters such as breaking down altars in Exodus 34:11-16 were. When Deuteronomy comes to practical instructions, what it bids Israel do is again to destroy the Canaanite worship sites, including their altars, pillars and images (Deut 12:2-3). They are not to ask about how the Canaanites worshiped their gods and do likewise, because their forms of worship (such as offering up their children) are loathsome or abhorrent (Deut 12:30-31). Within Deuteronomy 12–26, Deuteronomy 20:17 does mention ḥērem, and Joshua makes clear that the Israelites did indeed devote some people in cities they conquered, but the place of such devoting is much smaller than is often assumed.

Does the regulation concerning devoting things really become unobjectionable if it was never literally meant? If Israelites were then ever in a position to apply it, is it not likely they would do so?[264] Actually there were occasions when they could have done so, but they did not. Even Deuteronomy 20:17 refers only to the former occupants of Canaan, and the practice Deuteronomy commissions is not one that later Israel followed any more than Joshua

---

[263]Cf. R. W. L. Moberly, "Toward an Interpretation of the Shema," in *Theological Exegesis*, B. S. Childs Festschrift, ed. Christopher Seitz and Kathryn Greene-McCreight (Grand Rapids/ Cambridge: Eerdmans, 1999), pp. 124-44; see pp. 133-37.
[264]So Niditch, *War in the Hebrew Bible*, p. 74.

did in relation to those peoples. Saul does not seek to devote the Philistines, and David does not seek to devote the surrounding peoples whom he conquered. Neither Ephraim nor Judah took on Assyria, Babylon, Persia or the local equivalents of the Canaanites in the Second Temple period. Neither Deuteronomy nor Joshua sets a pattern it invites later Israel to follow, or that later Israel does follow.[265]

We do not know when Deuteronomy was composed, but the First Testament suggests four contexts against which to read it. Its literary context place it on the eve of the people's crossing into the land, and we have seen that Joshua and Judges imply people did not take literally its talk of annihilating the Canaanites. Second Kings 22–23 suggests we read it against the background of the time of Josiah, where "the radicalization of the tradition of separation from the Canaanites . . . is part of the way of preventing Israel's own impending destruction."[266] The context suggested by Deuteronomy-Kings as a whole, the context of the exile, is one where that is no longer an open question; Israel's failure to fulfill Moses' command concerning ḥērem explains why Israel has become its victim. The fourth context is the story in Ezra-Nehemiah, whose reforms again suggest links with Deuteronomy. Here too there is no indication that Judah was inclined to a literal understanding of the command concerning ḥērem, but it knew that the command placed serious obligations upon it.

. . . and What Joshua Did

At the beginning of Joshua, Yhwh commands Joshua to take the people across the Jordan to enter into possession of the land (there is no mention of killing anyone) and to follow Moses' teaching in doing so. Joshua's spies then get entangled with Rahab and end up sparing her and her household in contravention of the literalistic meaning of that teaching (as Israel subsequently spares the Hivites of Gibeon).[267] Yet Joshua 2–6 gives no hint of disapproving of this as an act of disobedience, rather than assuming Yhwh might view it with enthusiasm in light of Rahab's powerful testimony. Indeed, perhaps the Rahab story is *the* paradigmatic story in Joshua. Israel welcomes this foreigner into the community on the basis of her acknowledging Yhwh. "The story as a whole calls into question the validity of the assumption that sacrificial war-

---

[265]Cf. Lawson G. Stone, "Ethical and Apologetic Tendencies in the Redaction of the Book of Joshua," *CBQ* 53 (1991): 25-36. It is a huge exaggeration to describe Joshua as "a thinly disguised Josiah" (Lori L. Rowlett, *Joshua and the Rhetoric of Violence*, JSOTSup 226 [Sheffield, U.K.: Sheffield Academic Press, 1996], p. 181); see Richard S. Hess, "War in the Hebrew Bible," *War in the Bible and Terrorism in the Twenty-First Century*, ed. Richard S. Hess and Elmer A. Martens (Winona Lake, Ind.: Eisenbrauns, 2008), pp. 19-32; see pp. 27-29.
[266]Crüsemann, *Torah*, p. 130.
[267]McConville, *God and Earthly Power*, pp. 103-5

fare against the outsider is the preferred way of shaping the boundaries of the new covenant community."[268]

Or perhaps the stories of Rahab and of the city of Jericho itself are the twin paradigmatic stories, expressive of the choice put before peoples by Yhwh and by Israel. Near Jericho a warrior appears to Joshua and asks whether he is on the side of Israel or its adversaries (Josh 5:13-15). "Neither," the warrior replies; "I am the commander-in-chief of Yhwh's army." The action against Jericho will not be Joshua's action and will not be open to being prevented by Joshua's adversaries. Yhwh has put down the empire of Egypt and now intends to put down the city-states of Canaan. Moses did nothing in relation to the first except deliver messages and perform tricks. Similarly, all Israel does at the initial, archetypal victory over Jericho is process round the city and shout, then devote its population and their valuables to Yhwh, and place a curse on it; the First Testament makes clear the cost involved in someone evading the obligation to devote the plunder to Yhwh and in ignoring the curse (Josh 7; 1 Kings 16:34). On the other hand, the subsequent victory over Ai eventually requires a serious fighting force and a stratagem; it is through these that Yhwh guides Israel so as to give the city into its power (Josh 8).

The narrative does note that Israel got itself deceived into sparing the Gibeonites through not consulting Yhwh, though it also notes that Israel then kept its commitment to Gibeon and defended it from the attacks of five "Amorite" kings (Josh 10). Indeed, most of Joshua's battles here and in the north (Josh 11) are defensive. Joshua rarely initiates conflicts. This links with the fact that Joshua's wars are not waged against Israel's enemies. There is no history of animosity between these peoples and Israel. They are simply peoples God wants action taken against because of their waywardness. So Joshua would not be in tension with Jesus' words about loving enemies and forgiving people. There are no references to Joshua and company not loving their enemies or not being prepared to forgive people who wronged them. Turning local peoples into a work force, as happened to the Gibeonites, seems to be Israel's more regular way of treating them, though in the first instance they simply live cheek by jowl with them (e.g., Josh 16:10; 17:12-13; Judg 1:27-35).

Joshua's extraordinary victory over Jabin of Hazor (Josh 11), which closes the story of Israel's entry into the land, is far more miraculous than the one at Jericho.[269] Jabin takes the field against Joshua with an enormous, well-equipped army. Yhwh declares, "Do not be afraid of them, because tomorrow at this time I am giving all of them slain before Israel." There is no reference

---

[268]Gordon H. Matties, "Can Girard Help Us to Read Joshua?" in *Violence Renounced,* ed. Willard M. Swartley (Telford, Penn.: Pandora, 2000), pp. 85-102; see p. 91.

[269]On what follows, see Brueggemann, *Social Reading of the OT,* pp. 285-318.

to Israel itself killing anyone, as there was not in Yhwh's instructions at Jericho, but nor is it explicit who is to do the slaying. What is explicit is Israel's commission to hamstring the horses and burn the chariots. These are the military hardware that symbolizes the technologically advanced Canaanite state and gives it an edge over other peoples and a capacity to oppress them, though it turns out to be useless when Yhwh gets involved in a conflict; the First Testament is thus elsewhere rather dismissive of horses and chariots when Israel comes to trust in them. Once again the scene and the commission are redolent of the scene and the divine action at the Red Sea a generation or two previously. They also make for a suggestive collocation with those first instructions in Exodus 20–34; Israel is to destroy and thus distance itself from the Canaanites' forms of worship and their forms of warfare. Joshua fulfills Yhwh's commission, though also devotes all the population of the city in accordance with Moses' charge to him (so Josh 11:12-15, to ignore some tensions in the relationship of what Joshua precisely did to what Moses precisely said), as he had bidden the Israelites to devote the people of Jericho.

The Implications

The First Testament portrays the Israelite settlement in Canaan as actually not so different in its violence or slaughter from other conflicts in Israel's or other peoples' histories. It was a unilateral act of aggression that involved killing people and appropriating their land like that of European settlers invading America, Africa, Australasia or Asia from the fifteenth century onward. Nor, of course, were those invasions a new feature of human history. It is at least plausible that the Native Americans who were displaced by European settlers had themselves displaced its previous inhabitants. Certainly conflicts between Native American groups were not merely a result of the European invasion. Joshua thus raises ethical questions, but ones not very different from others involved in looking at Israel as a state.

I am not sure that "the narrative criticizes by exposing the terror of the original act of violence."[270] The narrative does not show any particular awareness of that terror. Its stance in relation to events rather parallels its stance in relation to events that we find comparably dismaying, such as the offering of Isaac, the Levites' slaughter of their kin, the death of Nadab and Abihu and the man collecting wood on the sabbath, and Uzzah who reaches out to steady the covenant chest when it threatens to fall, along with Jesus' cursing of the fig tree and his rejection of the Canaanite woman (!), and the death of Ananias and Sapphira. All seem shocking and enigmatic to modern Western readers, but most of them, at least, are related in a way that does not suggest they

---

[270]Matties, "Can Girard Help Us to Read Joshua?" p. 92, summarizing Girard.

are expected to arouse horror. Perhaps the narrative relates such events as belonging to another time, a time we are fortunate not to belong to.

The book of Amos begins by critiquing surrounding peoples for actions that are essentially similar to those of Joshua and the Israelites, but then refers positively to the way Yhwh "destroyed the Amorites before them" when bringing them up "to take possession of the Amorites" (Amos 1:3–2:10). Amos discretely does not mention that it was the Israelites who did the actual destroying, though presumably he assumes this. He apparently assumes that there are acts of war that are all right and ones that are not. The *ḥērem* does not evoke a crusader or "holy war" mentality. Indeed, it involves acting as God does: it is an act of creation, bringing order out of chaos and making the promised land a place of order.[271]

This puts the Canaanites in the company of Egypt, Assyria, Babylon and later of Ephraim and Judah themselves. Egypt, Assyria and Babylon are punished for their ruthless and pretentious conduct as superpowers. Ephraim and Judah are punished and dispossessed for their particular rebellion against Yhwh's special revelation to them. God acts against all these peoples by means of war, getting Assyria, Babylon and Persia (among others) to embark on wars against each other and against Israel. Indeed, Israel was the victim of such treatment much more often than its agent. Yhwh can summon an enemy to make war against Zion (Jer 4:6) and describe a great army as "people made holy for me" (Is 13:3).

"Wars of Yhwh" rather than "holy war" is the First Testament's own actual expression in this connection (e.g., Num 21:14). That phrase has several implications. Human history, politics and international relations do not proceed entirely under their own steam, with Yhwh simply leaving the world to its own devices; Yhwh is involved in the world. Yhwh sometimes acts in supranatural ways but usually works via human beings. Yhwh makes war using earthly powers as the means of getting things done, though usually these wars are ones that nations were intending to make for their own reasons, not because they were seeking to pursue a moral end or because they had a sense of being called by God. Yhwh uses human wars in this way to two ends, to bring down powers that ought to be brought down and to raise up peoples that Yhwh wishes to raise up. The idea does not presuppose that Yhwh is involved in all human history, politics and international relations in the way just described. Not every war undertaken by any nation is undertaken as part of Yhwh's direct will, and not every war brings down powers that deserve it

---

[271]Milgrom, *Leviticus 23–27*, p. 2417, again following Stern, *The Biblical Herem*, who bases his theory on a study of the Moabite Mesha inscription, the only clear Middle-Eastern occurrence of *ḥērem*.

or elevates peoples Yhwh wishes to elevate. It takes a prophet to know whether and how a particular war fits into Yhwh's purpose.

The Moral Question

The First Testament shows an awareness that giving Canaan to Israel raises an ethical question. Yhwh cannot simply act in Israel's favor and in the disfavor of another people. Yhwh needs to do the right thing by the Canaanites as well as by the Israelites. The First Testament is less courageous than Paul, who is prepared for God to decide unilaterally who should be the objects of mercy and compassion and who should not (Rom 9:15-21).

The First Testament's rationale is that the Canaanites are a faithless and wayward people. Yhwh makes this point in explaining to Abraham that there must be considerable delay before his descendants can come to possess the land Yhwh has promised him, "because the waywardness [ʿāwōn] of the Amorites is not yet full" (Gen 15:16). They must be treated fairly, and there is no basis at the moment for dispossessing them. They can be thrown out of the land only when there is a moral basis for doing so. In effect, Deuteronomy 9:4-5 argues that their moment has now come. It is because of their faithlessness [rešaʿ] that they are being thrown out. While there is no great ṣĕdāqâ about Israel, there is definite rešaʿ about the Canaanites.

Wherein lies their banefulness? Norman Gottwald's thesis was that Israel's distinctiveness over against the Canaanites lay in the egalitarian nature of its society, and while this attractive theory involves considerable inference, it is a plausible view that what George Mendenhall called the "paganization of Israel" in its social structure from David onward involved assimilation to the indigenous culture of the land. While the Canaanites in Joshua's day were under Egyptian domination, like Israel under Assyria and Babylon later, they were also themselves stratified societies under the domination of large landowners, with a king at the top of this pyramid—again like Israel later. It is over against such societies that the Torah sets out a vision of Israel as an alternative community.[272]

The First Testament itself stresses the Canaanites' religious depravity more explicitly than their social inequality. From David onward, Israelite kings took the Canaanites as a model for their religion as well as their politics. In light of this, Deuteronomy retrospectively commissions Israel as agents of Yhwh's destruction of Canaan, its culture and its religion (and its politics). While the reason for Yhwh's taking decisive action against the Canaanites is thus similar to that for taking action against Egypt, Assyria, Babylon and in due course Ephraim and Judah themselves, that they were serious wrongdo-

---

[272]Cf. §5.2 "Vocation."

ers, an extra reason applied to the Canaanites is their distinctive potential to exercise an egregious influence on Israel. It may be that their waywardness was no greater than that of other societies and that Yhwh was no more involved in their downfall than in that of others, but there was this particular reason for Yhwh to be concerned about their waywardness and involved in their downfall. Their religion was natural and their social structure was simply realistic; hence the fact that Israel eventually adopted both and that most "Christian" nations have done so.[273]

Yhwh's assessment puts the Canaanites in the same position as the Amalekites, the other victims of divinely commanded *ḥērem* in the First Testament. Deuteronomy 25:17-19 makes explicit the wrongdoing in Amalek's godless action in attacking the struggling Israelites (Ex 17:8-16). Its memory is to be blotted out, in light of its attack on people when they were vulnerable; but behind that is the fact that Amalek did not revere God. Like Amos, Deuteronomy sees the nations as responsible to God for their behavior, reckons there are certain sorts of behavior that every nation should know is wrong, and presupposes that God cannot be assumed simply to tolerate wrongdoing but may act in judgment on it.

Perhaps this is one reason why Western Christians do not like the story of Yhwh using Israel to put down the Canaanites. If there is anything in the Gottwald-Mendenhall thesis, it would provide good reason for Western countries to dislike the story of the dispossession of the Canaanites. We are more in the position of the Canaanites than in that of the Israelites.

The Theological Question

The dispossession of the Canaanites raises theological questions as well as moral ones. Israel undertakes this invasion because Yhwh commissions it. Once again, the story parallels Genesis 22. There Abraham goes to the verge of a supremely unethical act on the basis of God having told him to undertake it. Were the Israelites fooling themselves or seeking to fool someone else, like European settlers in the Americas and elsewhere? Their argument was then ideological. They were rationalizing their own aggression against the Canaanites. Maybe they thought they had heard Yhwh, but actually they had not. Is their claim in principle a feasible one in light of the rest of the Scriptures?

Underlying the suspicion that the Israelites were fooling themselves is another objection. Surely God does not act that way. Surely God does not punish whole nations. It would not be fair. It would mean so many "innocent people" getting punished. While a literalistic reading of Deuteronomy and Joshua likely makes this seem a much bigger issue than historically it was, a less lit-

---

[273]Cf. Gottwald, *Hebrew Bible in Its Social World and in Ours*, pp. 50-54.

eralistic reading does not mean it ceases to be an issue. It is not one peculiar to this particular theological and ethical question. It is a fact of experience recognized by both Testaments that the members of a nation are bound together in their destiny, for good and for ill, like the members of a family. The First Testament has little of the modern instinct to distinguish between combatants and noncombatants, recognizing that these are battles between peoples not between professional armies.

To say Yhwh cannot be engaged when calamity comes to nations implies that the interrelationships of the nations have no ethical or theological meaning, which the First Testament would see as a more worrying view. The story of Israel and the Canaanites reminds individualistic cultures that we are indeed bound up with one another. In Britain or the United States, the faithful suffer with the faithless and the faithless benefit with the faithful. "The United States may attack Cuba or not attack her. The academically preferable possibility of confronting with hostile measures only those sympathizing with the regime simply does not exist." Yhwh has to live with the same dilemma, which might explain much divine inaction (cf. Gen 18:22-32).[274]

Or perhaps it cannot be the case that God acts in such a way because "one fundamental aspect of the holiness and perfection of God is that He loves His enemies."[275] God's love would exclude doing that kind of thing to the Canaanites. A presupposition of Yhwh's being prepared to harness human war-making and violence is indeed that Yhwh is prepared to be violent, even if violence is self-perpetuating, reciprocal, undifferentiated, ineffective and debasing.[276] So the First Testament assumes God acts violently in putting down superpowers such as Egypt, Assyria and Babylon.

The New Testament also affirms frequently how Jesus is prepared to act violently as well as being concerned to bring peace and forgiveness. He whips the moneychangers in the temple (Jn 2:13-16). He curses a fig tree and it withers (Mt 21:19). The Son of Man will send his angels to weed out of his kingdom people who do evil and to throw them into the blazing furnace, where there will be weeping and gnashing of teeth (Mt 13:41-42). As king he will send into the eternal fire nations who did not give food, drink and clothing to his brothers and sisters (Mt 25:41). The man who goes to a distant country to be crowned king orders the death of the "enemies" who did not want him as king (Lk 19:27). At Nazareth Jesus speaks of his ministry as the year of the Lord's favor (Lk 4:19), and at this point he omits the colon in Isaiah 61:2 about this being the day of redress, but the implementing of Yhwh's will and the putting down

---

[274]David Daube, *The Deed and the Doer* (West Conshohocken, Penn.: Templeton Foundation, 2008), p. 180.

[275]Ronald J. Sider, *Christ and Violence* (Scottdale, Penn.: Herald, 1979), p. 28.

[276]Ellul, *Violence*, pp. 93-108.

of Israel's overlords are two sides of a coin, as the parallelism in Isaiah 61:2 implies, and he later declares that the siege of Jerusalem will bring "days of punishment . . . to fulfill all that is written" (Lk 21:22). The plural and the reference to the punishment of Jerusalem make his precise words closer to Hosea 9:7, but the talk of punishment and the closing phrase about fulfilling *all* warns against inferring that Jesus only talks about comfort. There is rather less in the Gospels about peace than there is about punishment. Jesus does not see his love for the world as incompatible with sending people to hell; the revolutionary nature of Jesus' teaching over against the First Testament is that the punishment he envisages for his enemies is much worse.

There is a tough side to God and to Jesus as well as a merciful side. That is again bad news for major power such as Britain and the United States, but good news for many peoples, as Mary's song assumes (Lk 1:51-55).

Once-for-all Events . . .

There is a more concrete aspect to the theological significance of Israel's occupation of Canaan. This event plays a uniquely foundational role in the fulfilling of Yhwh's purpose for the world. One aspect of blessing Abraham and his descendants is to give them this land, and that Yhwh's blessing is the means of bringing blessing to the nations (Gen 12:1-3). Israel's taking over Canaan is a once-off aspect of Yhwh's way of bringing blessing to the world as a whole. It is a once-off, once-for-all event for theological reasons, not accidental ones or ethical ones, a stage in the fulfillment of God's creation purpose. Humanity was commissioned to subdue the earth/land, and Israel is doing so. The Canaanite federation, like the Egyptian superpower, is put down as a stage in achieving Yhwh's purpose in the world. "Joshua is . . . a victory over Chaos, affirming Yahweh's rule in the world and his resolve to liberate from tyrannical power."[277]

As is the case in connection with war in general, it is only in the context of modernity that Christians have had a problem with God's commissioning Israel to dispossess the Canaanites. Notwithstanding their commendations of peacemaking, neither Jesus nor the Second Testament writers give any indication that they see anything problematic about Joshua's wars. While Jesus does not mention Joshua, the saintly Stephen in his address to the Sanhedrin in Acts 7, when he is about to die with a prayer for his killers' forgiveness on his lips, comments without critique on the way Joshua and the Israelites "dispossessed the nations that God drove out before our ancestors" (Acts 7:45). It was a stage in God's purpose to restore the world, which aimed at the deliverance of people like the Canaanites but entailed (as happened with one of Je-

---

[277]McConville, *God and Earthly Power*, p. 101; see also pp. 100-3.

sus' disciples) as its negative side disaster for people who are resistant to it. Likewise Paul, who notes that Christ died for us when we were enemies and commends love as the fulfilling of the Torah (Rom 5:10; 13:8), in Acts notes without negative comment how God destroyed seven nations in Canaan before giving their land to Israel (Acts 13:19). And Hebrews 11:32-38 commends the example of Israelite warriors who "through faith conquered kingdoms, . . . became mighty in war, put foreign armies to flight."

The revisionist understandings of Israel's story in Acts and Hebrews, made in light of Christ's coming, would have made it entirely possible to reframe the story in Joshua, but the New Testament does not do so. It accepts the First Testament approach to these events. Did the New Testament writers not understand the implications of Jesus' words about loving enemies, whereas we now do? More likely we are making Jesus an advocate for a case he did not make. Given Yhwh's vision for a universal peace (e.g., Is 2:4), as Israel stands on the edge of the promised land is it the case that military conquest "is part of the fractured reality within which God and God's people work"?[278] Maybe so, but there is no indication that either Testament sees it thus.

Often the scriptural story relates events that happened once and for all (*hapax* or *ephapax*). Christ died to sin "once for all" (Rom 6:10); he suffered for sins "once" (1 Pet 3:18); he offered himself "once for all" (Heb 7:27; Hebrews especially spells out the fact and the importance of the once-for-all nature of this event). It is a common human experience that some event is of great importance precisely because of its once-for-all nature. It is relevant because it does not need to happen again, not because it does happen again. On July 4 the United States enjoys a great celebration of its independence that is hugely important to it because that independence does not have to be won again. It happened once for all. The Juneteenth celebration of the abolition of slavery is hugely important because that event means African Americans never have to fight for their emancipation again. It happened once for all.

. . . Not Precedents to Be Followed

Christian unease with the story of Israel and the Canaanites links with a common Christian assumption that everything in the scriptural story sets a pattern to be imitated; it is something that might be expected to happen again.[279] That assumption seems to make it easier to relate the Scriptures to ourselves. Perhaps the problem links with our fondness for the idea of the "authority" of Scripture. Authority is apt to suggest the right to tell us what to

---

[278]Dennis T. Olson, *Deuteronomy and the Death of Moses* (Minneapolis: Fortress, 1994), p. 93.
[279]The energy of Jeremy Young's book *The Violence of God and the War on Terror* (London: Darton, Longman & Todd, 2007/New York: Seabury Press, 2008) emanates from the conviction that the biblical accounts of violent events encourage or validate human violence.

do, so ascribing scriptural authority to Joshua is apt to suggest that it tells us what to do. But biblical narrative tells us what God has done and what people have done; its relationship to what we should do may be very indirect. The way Scripture sometimes helps us find God's mind is by providing us with various ways of looking at an issue (for instance, by telling us various sorts of stories) so that we can imagine working with them or can dream of others. That might mean discovering what we should do, but the main point about the Scriptures hardly lies there. Scripture is not merely a revelation concerning what are the right things for human beings to do and the wrong ones for them to avoid; to a great extent, people know that. Scripture is a revelation concerning what God has been doing in events, which can help us see what God might be doing now in events and align ourselves with it.[280] "We will understand the Christological significance of these events only if we suspend the moral question which we immediately wish to put to them. The Christian reading of the Old Testament has been constantly baffled by a failure to understand this."[281]

Israel's dispossessing the Canaanites appears in Scripture not because it is a model for what might happen again but because it is not. It happened once for all. Because the event had foundational significance, Yhwh's commission to Israel to attack the Canaanites was not a model for subsequent Israelite military practice; it was no more a model or precedent than Abraham's offering of Isaac was a model for subsequent Israelite fatherhood. "The military conquest of Canaan was a once-for-all, time-bound event consigned to the past in the plan of God. God never told the Israelites later in their history to embark on another holy war."[282] And Israel managed to tell these stories without being turned into people who were always making war. For them, *ḥērem* belonged to the past. Jews have always been among the least war-making peoples in the world (whereas Christians have been much more inclined to making war). In this case war was not simply "politics by other means," as Carl von Clausewitz put it. It was a religious act by a religious community. It was designed to serve Yhwh and Yhwh's ends; this links with the way Israel could be its victim as easily as its beneficiary.[283] The fact that the First Testa-

---

[280]Cf. James M. Gustafson, "The Place of Scripture in Christian Ethics," *Int* 24 (1970): 430-55; see p. 439.

[281]Oliver O'Donovan, *Resurrection and Moral Order* (Leicester, U.K.: Inter-Varsity Press/ Grand Rapids: Eerdmans, 1986), pp. 157-58; cf. Craig Bartholomew, "Introduction," in *A Royal Priesthood? The Use of the Bible Ethically and Politically,* ed. Bartholomew et al. (Grand Rapids: Zondervan/Carlisle, U.K.: Paternoster, 2002), p. 24; though O'Donovan draws different theological inferences.

[282]Olson, *Deuteronomy and the Death of Moses,* p. 93. Cf. Charles Sherlock, *The God Who Fights* (Lewiston, N.Y./Lampeter, Wales: Edward Mellen, 1993), pp. 97-104.

[283]Susan Brooks Thistlethwaite, "'You May Enjoy the Spoil of Your Enemies,'" *Semeia* 61

ment itself uses this understanding against Israel much more often than in its favor may give credence to the one occasion when it uses it in Israel's favor.

In both Testaments God usually takes the punitive action, as happened at the Red Sea, though God does make use of the imperial instincts of imperial powers. But instead of personally throwing the Canaanites out of the land, Yhwh commissions Israel to do so. This commission (along with that regarding the Amalekites) is unparalleled. A link with God's original commission to humanity to subdue the earth may offer some insight on why God involves Israel in the defeat of the Canaanites rather than taking direct action.

Perhaps Yhwh involves Israel also because that will be an expression of its own commitment. Israel needs to disavow the religious and sociopolitical stances of the Canaanite city-states. Yhwh's requirement is then a little like the expectation that the witnesses and the whole community should be involved in stoning someone convicted of worshiping other gods (Deut 17:2-5), or like that extraordinary commission of Abraham to offer up Isaac as a means of testing him (Gen 22:1). Yhwh's bidding Israel to take action against Canaan tests its commitment to Yhwh and its abjuring of Canaan's worship and politics.

(1993): 59-75; p. 61, 68. The translation of *On War* that I have (Ware, U.K.: Wordsworth, 2000), p. 22, has "a mere continuation of policy by other means."

PART THREE

LIVING WITH OURSELVES

When we have given appropriate attention to life in relation to God and to life as members of communities, we can come to consider our individual selves. Because we are thinking about *our* life in relation to God and in relation to our communities, there is some overlap in our consideration of these questions, but they imply a difference in the angle of our approach. In considering living with ourselves, in chapter six we look at the individual in general, then in chapter seven at leaders in particular.

6

SPIRITUALITY AND CHARACTER

Spirituality can have many different meanings, but in some way it suggests a stress on a realm or experience or reality not confined to the material or this-worldly or empirical. While a sensitivity to spirituality may make people look outward to the way they relate to the world and to other people, it is a realm they are aware of by looking inside themselves. In that respect our Western notion of spirituality reflects "our modern sense of the self" which is "related to, one might say constituted by, a certain sense . . . of inwardness."[1] This finds expression in our emphasis on reflection, silence, retreat, quiet times, meditation, centering and journaling.

There is none of this in the First Testament or the New Testament, where the sense of self (if people have such a thing) is relentlessly constituted by a sense of outwardness, external expression, noise and activity.[2] Within a scriptural framework this entire volume on "Israel's Life" concerns the realm of the spiritual, which embraces the way we relate to God, the way we relate to other people and the way we relate to ourselves. The sons and daughters of God are the people who are led by the spirit of God to walk in God's ways (Rom 8:14).

In speaking of "spirituality" as an aspect of "living with ourselves," then, I am using the word in accordance with its resonance in a contemporary Western context. Modern and postmodern people cannot help belonging to their culture, and God meets us where we are, with our need for withdrawal, silence and journaling if we have that need. At the same time, if our sense of self is thus culturally shaped, we can only gain from the broadening that the Scriptures offer us.

---

[1]Charles Taylor, *Sources of the Self* (Cambridge, Mass.: Harvard University Press, 1989), p. 111.

[2]See David J. A. Clines's comments on Gregory the Great's interpretation of Job, *Interested Parties*, JSOTSup 205 (Sheffield, U.K.: Sheffield Academic Press, 1995), pp. 149-50, which also show how the focus on inwardness goes back at least to the medieval period. One evidence of the point is that First Testament texts that are quoted to encourage quiet meditation work only on the basis of having alien meanings attributed to them (the "still small voice" in 1 Kings 19:12 tends to disappear in modern translations, and the "be still" of Ps 46:10 [MT 11] is a demand to stop fighting, to "desist" [JPSV]).

6.1 Godlikeness

Ethics involves the study of right and wrong, of what counts as ethical and unethical action. We have thus been considering ethics, too, through much of part one and part two of this volume. But behind the ethical act is the ethical person, and the nature of the person and his or her values play a decisive role in determining how that person sees ethical questions and makes ethical decisions.[3] Indeed it has been simply asserted that " 'ethics' is the system of the virtues"[4] and that "character is the chief architect of our decisions and actions" and "community is the chief architect of character."[5] These assertions overstate their point, given that the way we think about God and the world and about the aim or purpose of human life, and the way we understand ourselves, have a key effect on our decisions; herein lies one significance of First Testament narratives with their stress on plot at least as much as on character.[6] Thus Paul Ricoeur distinguishes between ethics, which concerns "the *aim* of an accomplished life," and morality, which concerns "the articulation of this aim in *norms*." In principle ethics (understood in this sense) comes first, but it has to pass through the sieve of the norm, yet the norm has to refer back to the aim when it leads to impasses in practice.[7]

But the person I am and the values I consciously or unconsciously affirm will indeed have a very significant effect on the decisions I take about life. And I am called to be a person of similar character to Yhwh: committed, compassionate, patient, peaceable, forgiving, caring for my enemies, faithful, passionate, angry, disgusted. I am called to be a person of goodness and integrity, independent of the faithless and honored by the faithful community.

The Character of Yhwh and the Character of Israel

Outside Christian faith the four traditional cardinal virtues are courage, justice, temperance and wisdom.[8] Philo added godliness and kindness (right at-

---

[3] See John Barton, "Virtue in the Bible," in his *Understanding Old Testament Ethics* (Louisville/London: Westminster John Knox, 2003), pp. 65-74.

[4] Deirdre N. McCloskey, *The Bourgeois Virtues* (Chicago/London: University of Chicago Press, 2006), p. 64. She goes on to refer to Alasdair MacIntyre, *After Virtue*, 2nd ed. (Notre Dame, Ind.: University of Notre Dame Press, 1984).

[5] Bruce C. Birch and Larry L. Rasmussen, *Bible and Ethics in the Christian Life*, rev. ed. (Minneapolis: Augsburg Press, 1989), p. 81; both statements are italicized. Cf. Stephen E. Fowl and L. Gregory Jones, *Reading in Communion* (London: SPCK/Grand Rapids: Eerdmans, 1991).

[6] See §1.2 "The Significance of Narrative" and the introduction to chap. 2; in critique of "virtue ethics," see Harry Bunting, "Ethics and the Perfect Moral Law," *Tyndale Bulletin* 51 (2000): 235-60.

[7] Paul Ricoeur, *Oneself as Another* (Chicago/London: University of Chicago Press, 1992), p. 170.

[8] See, e.g., Cicero *Concerning Duties* bk. 1.

titudes to God and to other people).[9] Paul emphasized what became the three cardinal Christian virtues, faith, hope and love (1 Cor 13), which with those four "pagan" qualities comprise a neat seven virtues. The woman in Proverbs 31:10-31 is a particularly powerful embodiment of them.[10] In the contemporary Western world the cardinal values might be freedom, independence, choice, equality, prosperity and security.[11] *Habits of the Heart* identified key U.S. values as success, freedom and justice.[12] How would the First Testament see virtues and values?

Israel is to walk in Yhwh's ways; but Yhwh's ways reflect who Yhwh is.[13] The life the First Testament wants people to live is not merely a matter of specific acts, the offering of right forms of worship and the making of right decisions. It is indeed concerned about the character that finds expression in the worship and the acts, and about a vision of what counts as good. These interact with each other.

The Torah makes clear what kind of person Yhwh is:

> God compassionate and gracious, long-tempered and big in commitment and trustworthiness, extending commitment to thousands, carrying wrongdoing, rebellion, and failure, but certainly not acquitting, attending to the wrongdoing of parents on children and grandchildren, on those of the third and fourth [generation]. (Ex 34:6-7)

Occasionally, the Torah makes explicit that these characteristics of Yhwh are also to be characteristics of the community that names Yhwh's name; it is another way of saying that Israel is to be holy like Yhwh. But reference to these traits is much more characteristic of the Psalms, the Wisdom books and the Prophets. Here too they can be ascribed to Yhwh, but they also describe what human beings are supposed to be.[14] Compassion *(raḥămîm)* is the attitude of parents to their children, who are the children of a mother's womb *(reḥem;* e.g., 1 Kings 3:26; Ps 103:13); it is an attitude Yhwh looks for within the community (Zech 7:9) and even looks for (and fails to find) in a superpower like Babylon (Is 47:6), and in a farmer's attitude toward his animals (Prov 12:10). Graciousness is a quality of a good person; it is characteristically expressed in generosity (Ps 112:5; cf. Ps 37:21, 26; Prov 14:31; 19:17; 28:8). Long-

---

[9]See Philo *The Special Laws* 4.132-238, and *The Virtues* 1-174.

[10]Cf. Ellen F. Davis, "Preserving Virtue," in *Character and Scripture,* ed. William F. Brown (Grand Rapids/Cambridge: Eerdmans, 2002), pp. 183-201; see pp. 195-96.

[11]John Ashcroft, "The Relational Dynamic," in *Jubilee Manifesto,* ed. Michael Schluter and John Ashcroft (Leicester, U.K.: Inter-Varsity Press, 2005), pp. 105-21; see pp. 116-21.

[12]Robert N. Bellah et al., *Habits of the Heart,* rev. ed. (Berkeley/London: UCLA Press, 1996), pp. 22-26.

[13]Cf. §2.1 "Walking Yhwh's Way."

[14] See, e.g., José Porfirio Miranda, *Marx and the Bible* (Maryknoll, N.Y.: Orbis, 1974/London: SCM Press, 1977).

temperedness is a sign of wisdom and a key to peace, and is better than power or prestige (Prov 14:29; 15:18; 16:32; Eccles 7:8). Commitment (*ḥesed*) and trustworthiness are qualities Yhwh looks for in the life of Israel in the land, and Yhwh indicts the people when they are missing (Hos 4:1; Zech 7:9); commitment is one of Yhwh's key expectations (Hos 6:6; Mic 6:8), while a person who acts in relation to other people in trustworthy fashion is a person who will live (Ezek 18:8-9; cf. Zech 8:16). Those qualities also imply a willingness to carry other people's wrongdoing, rebellion and failure by seeking to bring them back to Yhwh, without acquitting them of their wrongdoing as if it did not matter. The Prophets embody the two sides to that stance; Jeremiah and Ezekiel pay the price for the ministry they exercise in seeking to bring people back to God without ever compromising on the insistence that the people come back and thus find acquittal.

Goodness and Reserve

Micah 6:8 offers a neat summary of goodness.[15]

> He has told you, mortal, what is good,
>   what Yhwh is seeking from you:
> Nothing but exercising judgment,
>   being dedicated to commitment,
>   and walking diffidently with your God.

The pairing of judgment and commitment, *mišpāṭ* and *ḥesed*, reappears in Hosea 12:6 [MT 7], but it also recalls the more characteristic First Testament pairing of *mišpāṭ* and *ṣĕdāqâ*. As the latter pairing suggests the exercise of authority in a way that does right by people, so this pairing suggests the exercise of authority in a way that expresses commitment to people. Either version then implies being Godlike, because it is when Yhwh is acting in *mišpāṭ* and *ṣĕdāqâ* or in *mišpāṭ* and *ḥesed* that Yhwh is most Godlike; they are the very expressions of Yhwh's holiness (Is 5:16). They are also thus the very expressions of Yhwh's goodness. Ultimately, Yhwh is the only holy one, and also the only good one (Mk 10:18).

In the context Micah 6:3-5 recalls how in its worship Israelites were regularly reminded of what Yhwh was like and of how Yhwh had acted for them, which provided the models for the way they were expected to relate to the needy, with *mišpāṭ* and *ḥesed*. We could likewise summarize much of that divine self-description in Exodus 34:6-7 as declaring that Yhwh is characterized

---

[15]See M. Daniel Carroll R., " 'He Has Told You What Is Good,' " in *Character Ethics and the Old Testament*, ed. M. Daniel Carroll R. and Jacqueline E. Lapsley (Louisville/London: Westminster John Knox, 2007), pp. 103-18 (though Carroll focuses on "the good" elsewhere in Micah).

by the two virtues of faith and love; thus faith and love are the appropriate responses to Yhwh, and faith and love toward other people are also appropriate responses to that same reality.[16] But Micah's final prescription then turns that upside down, insofar as it implies our recognizing that we are *not* God. We do indeed respond to Yhwh's exercise of *mišpāṭ* and *ḥesed* by exercising *mišpāṭ* and *ḥesed* ourselves; but in the act of doing so, we respond to Yhwh's awesome holiness by walking reservedly or diffidently or modestly in Yhwh's company.[17]

On one hand, then, humanity is made in God's image, and there are virtues that constitute Godlikeness. But humanity is also made somewhat lower than God (Ps 8:5), flesh not spirit (Is 31:3), and there are virtues associated with the fact that we are definitely not Godlike, but are Godward. As well as walking *with* Yhwh, people may walk about *before* Yhwh.

Enoch walked about with God (Gen 5:22, 24), and it was with God that Noah walked about (Gen 6:9; the word order puts the emphasis thus). Genesis has just told us that Noah was a person of faithfulness and integrity that contrasted with the characteristics of his generation, and his walking about with God rather than with his contemporaries explains this. It is the way one becomes someone who shares Yhwh's traits. The hitpael verb suggests not a single movement from A to B but the ongoing, crisscrossing movement of life. It is the word for touring the whole of the land in Genesis 13:17 and Joshua 18:4, 8, for Yhwh's walking about among Israel in Leviticus 26:12 and 2 Samuel 7:6-7, and for Yhwh's afternoon stroll in Genesis 3:8. Perhaps the implication is that Adam and Eve were naturally avoiding joining in Yhwh's walk, but Enoch and Noah did not avoid it.[18] Noah is thus an example of a faithful man who walks about (that is, lives his life) with integrity (Prov 20:7—three words related to the words in Gen 6:9). If you walk about *with* Yhwh, you catch the faithfulness and the integrity of the one whose company you keep.

But as well as walking about *with* Yhwh, people need to walk about *before* Yhwh. Abraham was so bidden, and he claims to have done so (Gen 17:1; 24:40; cf. Gen 48:15). Eli's priestly family had been destined to do that (1 Sam 2:30). Hezekiah sees himself as having walked about before Yhwh with steadfastness and with a whole heart (2 Kings 20:3). Walking about before Yhwh in the light of life, walking about where Yhwh's light shines on people and gives them fullness of life, would be the result of Yhwh's act of deliverance (Ps 56:13 [MT 14]; 116:9). Whereas walking about *with* Yhwh can mean catching Yhwh's characteristics, walking about *before* Yhwh implies knowing Yhwh is watch-

---

[16]Cf. Luke T. Johnson, *Sharing Possessions* (Philadelphia: Fortress, 1981/London: SCM Press, 1986), p. 107.

[17]See §2.2 "Diffidence."

[18]Cf. Deryck Sheriffs, *The Friendship of the Lord* (Carlisle, U.K.: Paternoster, 1996), p. 33.

ing us, which is both a blessing (because Yhwh's gaze means Yhwh's provision) and a constraint (because it inhibits us from wrongdoing; though that too is a blessing).

Commitment and Love

In the Septuagint *hesed* usually appears as *eleos*, pity, and thus in the Vulgate as *misericordia* and in the KJV as "mercy," but this misses the heart of the word's meaning. The NRSV usually has "steadfast love" or "loyalty," the TNIV "kindness" or "love," sometimes qualified by a word such as "unfailing." The word suggests a practice of generosity or good will or beneficence that is extraordinary because it takes place either when there is no particular prior relationship between people and thus no obligation, or when there is a prior relationship but there is some reason why *hesed* could not be expected (for instance, because the other person has let you down). The nearest English word is *commitment*. It is the Hebrew equivalent of *agapē* in the New Testament, the love that "can be thought of as a commitment of the will to the true good of another."[19] A *ḥāsîd* is someone who does more than the law requires. It is the opposite of falsehood (*šeqer*; Gen 21:23). Indeed, a *ḥāsîd* not only avoids deceiving a fellow human being (Lev 25:17); "he will not even deceive himself." "Socrates taught us that a life without thinking is not worth living. . . . The Bible taught us that life without commitment is not worth living."[20] "The tendency of formulated law is to help establish a traditional order of life. Love is more flexible and can bring new solutions to new situations."[21]

Abraham appeals to *hesed* with some chutzpah when he leans on Sarah to say she is his sister and is by implication unattached, and thereby to risk being taken into a king's harem (Gen 20:13). It is on the basis of their relationship that he can ask for this astonishing act of commitment. Rahab appeals to the way she has shown *hesed* to the Israelite spies as she urges them to show *hesed* to her and her family when the Israelites take Jericho (Josh 2:12-14). The word appears in the company of *ḥēn* (grace; Gen 19:19) and of *ʾĕmet* (steadfastness, truthfulness; Gen 32:10 [MT 11]; 47:29; Josh 2:14; 2 Sam 2:6), and occasionally of reference to a covenant (Gen 21:22-32; Deut 7:9, 12). It is expressed in rescuing someone from death or protecting them (Gen 19:19; Josh 2:12-14; 1 Sam 20:8, 14), in being economical with the truth to protect someone (Gen 20:13), in caring about a widow on her own and a man on his own (Ruth 3:10), and in giving someone proper burial (2 Sam 2:5-6). The promise for the future of Jerusalem is that "a throne will be established with commitment, and one will sit on

---

[19]McCloskey, *Bourgeois Virtues*, p. 91.
[20]Abraham Heschel, *God in Search of Man* (New York: Farrar, 1986), pp. 11, 216.
[21]Wolfhart Pannenberg, *Systematic Theology*, 3 vols. (Grand Rapids: Eerdmans/Edinburgh: T & T Clark, 1991, 1994, 1998), 3:76.

it with truthfulness in the tent of David, one who exercises authority and who seeks the exercise of authority and speeds up faithfulness" (Is 16:5).

Being human involves both being an individual and being part of communities to which we are committed. It is a matter of both the corporate and the individual. We are responsible for making our own individual decisions and in some contexts for standing apart from the community, but more often for keeping a commitment to the community even though it goes against our preferences. Some contexts require a renewed emphasis on the importance of individual awareness and responsibility, such as the situation where people are inclined to overemphasize the way the children's teeth are set on edge by the grapes the parents ate (Ezek 18). Some contexts require a renewed emphasis on the importance of corporate awareness and commitment to the community.

In the past, European and U.S. culture held individual and community together, but in the late twentieth century the individual came to dominate. A communitarian context emphasizes thinking in terms of "we," an obligation to accept and abide by the decisions of the group, a focus on its success and achievement, a respect for its other members, an evaluation of one's work on the basis of the way it contributes to the group, and a concern to preserve honor and respect within it. An individualistic context emphasizes thinking in terms of "I," independence over against group decisions, a focus on individual success and achievement, self-respect, an evaluation of one's work on the basis of what it means to oneself and a concern to preserve one's own values.[22] *Habits of the Heart* argues that the presumed right to individual fulfillment means other people have no ultimate claims on us; "individualism lies at the very core of American culture." [23] Our only ultimate obligation is to our own well-being.[24] But the divorce of the individual from the community has generated "the empty self."[25] A first fruit of God's liberation of people is that we are "drawn out of solitariness into fellowship,"[26] drawn into commitment.

---

[22]See, e.g., Bruce J. Malina, *The New Testament World*, rev. ed. (Louisville: Westminster John Knox, 1993), pp. 63-89; cf. K. C. Hanson, "Sin, Purification, and Group Process," in *Problems in Biblical Theology*, Rolf Knierim Festschrift, ed. Henry T. C. Sun et al. (Grand Rapids/Cambridge: Eerdmans, 1997), pp. 167-91; see pp. 167-74.

[23]Bellah et al., *Habits of the Heart*, p. 142. They go on to note the ambiguity of the notion of individualism; see also pp. viii-xi, xxii-xxviii.

[24]See further Lewis B. Smedes' discussion of "The Making and Keeping of Commitments" in *Seeking Understanding: The Stob Lectures, 1986–1998* (Grand Rapids/Cambridge: Eerdmans, 2001), pp. 1-42.

[25]Philip Cushman, *Constructing the Self, Constructing America* (Cambridge, Mass.: Perseus, 1995), p. 6.

[26]Karl Barth, *Church Dogmatics* (Edinburgh: T & T Clark, 1962), IV/3, ii:664.

Compassion and Patience

Compassion links naturally with commitment (Ps 103:4; Jer 16:5; Zech 7:9). Like commitment, compassion is an act of the will, but it is also more intrinsically an emotion. It suggests a feeling of pain at another person's actual or potential grievous misfortune.

"Emotions shape the landscape of our mental and social lives." They do not let that landscape just sit inert; they bring about geological upheavals. They do not just empower decisions taken on purely rational grounds. For better or for worse, they "are part and parcel of the system of ethical reasoning."[27] And compassion is "the emotion most frequently viewed with approval in the tradition [of Western philosophical debate about emotion]"; it is also "central to several Asian cultural traditions" as well as having a significance within the framework of evolutionary biology.[28] In Aristotle's analysis it involves the conviction that the person did not deserve their misfortune, and the presupposition that in some sense we can identify with this person as someone like us or someone who matters to us.[29] Neither seems to be required in the First Testament.

Compassion is the first characteristic Yhwh claims in the self-description at Sinai (Ex 34:6). The story of Yhwh's involvement with Israel then shows us what compassion and Yhwh's other qualities look like, and stimulates our imagination regarding what it might look like in us. In this respect more than most, the First Testament expects us to be Godlike.

The first human being who shows compassion is Joseph, in fulfillment of his father's prayerful hope (Gen 43:14, 30); the description points to the physiological basis of compassion ("his bowels did yearn," KJV translates). The next human being to feel compassion is a mother concerned for her son in danger (1 Kings 3:26), appropriately because of that fact that *raḥamîm* is the plural for the word for the womb. While it is the instinctive feeling of a mother, it is also natural to a father (Ps 103:13). We have noted that even military victors are expected to show compassion toward their victims, though this expectation is inclined to be unmet (Is 47:6; Jer 6:23; Amos 1:11)[30] and thus a situation may require divine intervention (1 Kings 8:50; Ps 106:46).

Compassion contrasts with mercy, which involves leniency but need not imply emotion. When Nathan tells his story about a ruthless sheepholder, in falling into his trap David sees the man's offense (and his own) as lying in the fact that he had no pity or would not spare (*ḥāmal*); he was "sparing" (the

---

[27]Martha C. Nussbaum, *Upheavals of Thought: The Intelligence of Emotions* (Cambridge/New York: Cambridge University Press, 2001), p. 1.

[28]So ibid., pp. 299, 301.

[29]So ibid., pp. 306-22. Nussbaum adds that compassion involves wonder.

[30]See §5.2 "The Politics of Compassion."

same verb) about his own large flock but not about the poor man (2 Sam 12:1-6). Jonah 4 draws attention to a contrast between Yhwh's pity for Nineveh (*ḥûs*) that leads to Nineveh's being spared, and Jonah's anger at this attitude on Yhwh's part.

Yhwh's self-description (Ex 34:6-7) suggests related attitudes to wrongdoing that human beings are expected to imitate. Yhwh is long-tempered, and for human beings, "a long-tempered person—much insight, but a hasty spirit raises stupidity" (Prov 14:29). The aphorism is allusive, but the drift is clear; being short-tempered either manifests stupidity or issues in stupidity. "An angry man stirs up strife, but a long-tempered person calms a quarrel" (Prov 15:18). "It is better to be a long-tempered person than a warrior, better to rule over one's spirit than to take a city" (Prov 16:32). Conversely, "someone who is big in fury bears a punishment" (Prov 19:19). "A person without control over his spirit is an open city [*or* a breached city], without walls" (Prov 25:28). "Cease from anger, give up fury, do not be wrathful only to do evil" (Ps 37:8). "It is better to be patient in spirit [literally, "long in spirit"] than majestic in spirit" (Eccles 7:8). In Esther, anger plays a key role in the portrayal of the stupid king and his stupid servant (Esther 1:12; 3:5; 5:9).

Peaceableness and Forgiveness

Exodus 34:6-7 goes on to note that Yhwh carries waywardness, rebellion and shortcoming, and Genesis narrates examples of people doing that and thus encouraging peaceableness. Esau becomes understandably enraged at Jacob's cheating him of his rights as the firstborn son and plans to kill him (Gen 27:41). Jacob therefore flees, but in due course returns, assuming Esau will still be full of resentment, and bringing gifts designed to pacify him (Gen 32:21). He finds Esau actually running to welcome him back like the prodigal father (Gen 33). In Exodus 34:6-7, carrying waywardness issues from grace as well as from compassion, and Esau's carrying Jacob's waywardness is similar. "The only thing that can be truly forgiven is the unforgivable" because only then is it gratuitous.[31] In practice we often make forgiveness conditional, for instance, on a person's repentance, but that looks like a transaction; forgiveness is an act of grace. Joseph too has every right to be full of resentment at the way his brothers had treated him, and there is some ambiguity about whether he is subsequently testing them in a reasonable way or disciplining them (as Gen 42–43 might imply) or playing with them to get his own back (as Gen 44 might imply). Only in Genesis 45 does it become clear, or perhaps only at that stage does Joseph himself decide which stance to take, and the end of

---

[31]John D. Caputo, *What Would Jesus Deconstruct?* (Grand Rapids: Baker, 2007), p. 60, summarizing Jacques Derrida, *On Cosmopolitanism and Forgiveness* (New York/London: Routledge, 1997).

the story is not reprisal but confession, forgiveness and reconciliation (Gen 50:15-21). Having suffered one way, he suffers another; for "forgiveness itself is a form of suffering" because it involves giving up the right to justice.[32]

Abraham has already acted in peaceable fashion when his company and Lot's cannot get along because there is not enough pasturage for both. He takes the initiative that involves letting Lot choose the land he wants; Abraham will have what Lot does not want (Gen 13:5-18). While there is no explicit conciliatory ending to his Egyptian adventure (Gen 12:10-20), his quarrels with Abimelech do eventually come to an end with a covenant (Gen 20:1-18; 21:22-32). Jacob assumes that his sons' clever plan for slaughtering the men of Shechem is no way to behave (Gen 34), though he is perhaps most concerned for the backlash.

Saul takes a similar stance to that of Esau and Joseph, though he does so as a king who can pardon a wrongdoer rather than as an ordinary Israelite forgiving another. When he was designated king, "some scoundrels [běnê běliyya'al] said, 'How can this man deliver us?' They scorned him and brought him no tribute" (1 Sam 10:27). Whereas they might seem to have every reason for their skepticism, his subsequent action on behalf of Jabesh-Gilead proved them wrong, and the people as a whole urge their death: they had been refusing to acknowledge Yhwh's word. "But Saul said, 'No one will be put to death this day, because today Yhwh has brought about deliverance in Israel' " (1 Sam 11:13). The day of Yhwh's deliverance is a day of grace and mercy, and it is appropriate to extend that grace and mercy to these scoundrels.[33]

Such stories illustrate the way "the intelligence of a person lengthens their temper"; further, the passage of time then makes forgiveness possible, and as a result, "their attractiveness lies in passing over a rebellion" (Prov 19:11). "Hatred stirs up strife, but love covers over all acts of rebellion" (Prov 10:12). It is proverbs and narratives such as these that provide the First Testament's explicit and implicit models for conflict resolution as the theo-poetics of the impossible expresses itself in "the madness of forgiveness, generosity, mercy, and hospitality."[34]

Caring for One's Enemies

"You are not to hate your brother in your thinking. You are to rebuke your fellow citizen; do not carry sin because of him. Do not exact redress and do

---

[32]Miroslav Volf, *Exclusion and Embrace* (Nashville: Abingdon, 1996), p. 125; he refers to comments of Dietrich Bonhoeffer (see *Discipleship* [Minneapolis: Fortress, 2001], p. 88).

[33]Cf. Rolf P. Knierim, "On the View of Reality and Public Human Ethos in the Bible," in *Reading the Bible for a New Millennium,* ed. Wonil Kim et al. (Harrisburg, Penn.: Trinity Press International, 2000), 2:42-57; see pp. 47-48.

[34]Caputo, *What Would Jesus Deconstruct?* p. 88.

not hold onto things with members of your people. Care for your neighbor as yourself" (Lev 19:17-18). The context makes clear that the "neighbor" you are to care for includes "your enemy"; indeed, people would hardly require an exhortation to care for their neighbor when this person was their friend. The verbs for "hate" and "love/care for" commonly refer not merely to feelings but to attitudes that express themselves in negative or positive action; the participle "one who hates" is the word for an "enemy." And like the Decalogue the exhortations have the word for "not" that is used with statements rather than with commands, which paradoxically strengthens the command; they might all be read as definitions of who "you" are, rather than merely exhortations. And four times they are buttressed by the declaration, "I am Yhwh."

Caring for a neighbor who behaves as an enemy expresses itself in turning the other cheek to an attacker (Is 50:6; Lam 3:30)[35] and in kindness that may win the enemy to remorse and a change of heart (Prov 25:21-22).[36] In Leviticus 19, caring for your neighbor comes at the end of a sequence of exhortations about relationships, dealing with dishonesty, fraud, abuse, partiality and hostility. Most are thus negative exhortations, and the closing positive exhortation to care for your neighbor summarizes the positive corollary of refraining from such attitudes and acts. Among our brothers, neighbors, fellow citizens and members of our people, whoever are the people who are close to us and do wrong to us, our vocation is to rebuke and care, not to hate and take redress. We might even infer that rebuking is an expression of caring.

Jesus speaks of the possibility of setting "your neighbor" over against "your enemy," though we do not know of any Jewish groups that actually inferred that it was okay to hate your enemy.[37] Many other commands in the Torah make clear the assumption that your neighbor would indeed usually be the person you might be at enmity with (e.g., Deut 27:17, 24); an Akkadian "Counsel of Wisdom" urges, "Unto your opponent do no evil; your evildoer recompense with good."[38] Jesus' bidding to his disciples to love their enemies

---

[35]Glen H. Stassen and David P. Gushee note that Jesus' exhortation about turning the other cheek takes up the actual words of Is 50:4-9 (*Kingdom Ethics* [Downers Grove, Ill.: InterVarsity Press, 2003], p. 139).

[36]And Yhwh "will reward you," the EVV have. But the verb (*šālēm* piel) is related to the word *shalom*: pursuing the way of *shalom* issues in experience of *shalom*.

[37]Richard A. Burridge comments that "John does not give any license to the natural reaction to hate one's enemies, in the vituperative manner of the Qumran material (see, e.g., *Hymns* 14; *Manual of Discipline* 9. 15-22)" (*Imitating Jesus* [Grand Rapids: Eerdmans, 2007], p. 329); see also the discussion in W. D. Davies, *The Setting of the Sermon on the Mount* (Atlanta: Scholars Press, 1989), pp. 245-48. But these passages focus on repudiating God's enemies, not on the community's enemies, and they do not seem more vituperative than parts of the New Testament (e.g., 2 Thess 1:5-9).

[38]*ANET*, p. 426; cf. Walther Eichrodt, *Theology of the Old Testament* (London: SCM Press/

(Mt 5:43-44) thus makes explicit something the Torah itself requires, and he speaks like other Jewish teachers of his day,[39] as he does elsewhere in Matthew 5. He too will likely be referring to relationships within the community, as when Paul quotes Proverbs 25:21-22 (Rom 12:20-21). And the idea that members of the Christian community should love one another could have made a revolutionary difference to church history. In Matthew's context the command could also refer to the hostility of people outside the Christian community, neighbors who might persecute believers or members of one's own family (cf. Mt 10:34-36).

When a person harms someone else, then, what is to happen? Exacting redress (nāqam), taking retribution on a personal basis, is forbidden to human beings and must be left to Yhwh. Proverbs 25:21-22 exhorts people to give their enemies something to eat and drink when they are hungry and thirsty, "because you are heaping coals on their head, and Yhwh—he will recompense you." An enemy may be overcome by a demonstration of generosity and concern, and be won to remorse. "The pain of contrition purifies and recreates; it is the birth pangs of a new brotherhood."[40] One can see this working out in the cases of Esau when he seems no longer to hold a grudge against his brother for stealing his blessing, and of Joseph when he likewise seems no longer to hold a grudge against his brothers for selling him into servitude; both see their brothers brought to remorse. Beyond this, Proverbs promises that Yhwh will be pleased with you and will reward you. Forgoing seeking recompense, you will be given it.

Genesis does not actually say that Esau forgives Jacob; it rather portrays the one who was formerly planning to kill Jacob now embracing him (Gen 33:4). Joseph's brothers ask for his forgiveness, though he does not explicitly grant it; he rather notes that God has dealt with his brothers' evil deed and transformed it into something else, and promises to provide for them (Gen 50:15-21). Perhaps "Joseph has a role to play, but it is not to forgive."[41] That is God's business. But Joseph's action, like Esau's, shows he has given up any desire for vengeance. While these stories would also speak to relationships between Israel and Edom and among the Israelite clans as well as to relationships within families, this hardly means they do not speak to interpersonal, intracommunity relationships. The Pharaoh likewise asks for Moses' forgiveness and asks Moses to

---

Philadelphia: Westminster, 1961), 1:95.

[39]Cf. E. P. Sanders, *Judaism* (London: SCM Press/Philadelphia: Trinity Press International, 1992), pp. 234-35; William Klassen, *Love of Enemies* (Philadelphia: Fortress, 1984), pp. 43-71.

[40]William McKane, *Proverbs* (London: SCM Press/Philadelphia: Westminster, 1970), p. 592; cf. Murphy, *Proverbs*, p. 193.

[41]Patrick D. Miller, "Divine Command and Beyond," in *The Ten Commandments*, ed. William P. Brown (Louisville/London: Westminster John Knox, 2004), pp. 12-29; see p. 29.

forgive him and pray for him; the text does not say that Moses forgave but it does say that he prayed (Ex 10:17-18). Laban and Jacob resolve their differences and enter into a mutual covenant to remain on friendly terms, though the reader worries that neither knows about Rachel's deception of the two of them, which surely stands as an ongoing complication of the relationship (Gen 31).

Faithfulness and Passion

The first person whom Scripture commends is Noah, and he is commended because he is *ṣaddîq*, "faithful." In general the world is characterized by corruption and violence; Noah is a person of faithfulness and integrity (Gen 6:9). Perhaps these form a double antithesis. Faithfulness is the opposite of violence; integrity is the opposite of corruption. The adjective *ṣaddîq* is a general purpose word for a good man (see also Gen 7:1), and if there is a cardinal virtue in the First Testament, *ṣědāqâ* is it. Elsewhere, it stands over against general words for wickedness (Gen 18:23-28; Ps 1; 37; Prov 10–12). This fits with the fact that in Yhwh's case Isaiah can see it as a manifestation of Yhwh's holiness, Yhwh's distinctive deity (Is 5:16).

Hosea's use of *ṣědāqâ* in a similar context to Micah's *ḥesed* reflects how the two are related. This time the Septuagint renders by *dikaiosynē* (righteousness), the Vulgate by *iustitia* (justice) and English translations usually by "righteousness," but the problem in these equivalents surfaces when modern translations elsewhere also render by words such as deliverance, salvation, victory and triumph (e.g., Judg 5:11; Is 46:12-13). Closer to the heart of the idea of *ṣědāqâ* is the idea of doing the right thing, and specifically doing the right thing by people with whom one is in relationship. The word suggests active faithfulness.

Such faithfulness stands over against gaining wealth by fraud (Prov 10:2), treachery (Prov 11:6), lies (Is 28:17) and the cry *(ṣě ῾āqâ)* of peoples whose blood has been made to flow (Is 5:7). It suggests the commitment of the powerful to using their power on behalf of the needy and powerless rather than turning such people into their victims (e.g., Jer 22:2-3, 15-17). It suggests a stance toward Yhwh and towards one's neighbor (Ezek 18; 33). Freedom or liberation "is no end in itself; it is the beginning of [a] process that is to be followed by the life of the liberated themselves in justice."[42]

After the conclusion of the glorious promises that dominate Isaiah 40–55, the next chapter opens with a bidding to "guard authority and act with faithfulness, because my deliverance is about to come, my faithfulness to appear" (Is 56:1). The logic is neatly allusive. The reminder about *mišpāṭ* and *ṣědāqâ* recalls the eighth-century prophets and implies that the ball lies in the commu-

---

[42]Knierim, "On the View of Reality and Public Human Ethos in the Bible," p. 47.

nity's court to make the crucial decisions about its life that will decide its future. But the subordinate clause rather recalls Isaiah 40–55 in the way it restores ṣĕdāqâ to being Yhwh's business, and affirms that it is Yhwh's act of deliverance and thus Yhwh's ṣĕdāqâ that will decide the community's future. The "because" that links these two clauses only underlines the tension between them. What is the nature of their relationship? It is not simply that the community's stance is the decisive factor in whether it experiences Yhwh's faithfulness expressed in deliverance. But neither is it that the community will get delivered whether or not it cares about mišpāṭ and ṣĕdāqâ. The logic of the relationship matches that presupposed by Paul in passages such as Romans 6. Yhwh's faithfulness in deliverance is not conditional on human response, but it must inspire human response. To try to reexpress the relationship in tighter terms is to turn it into a contractual relationship rather than a personal one. In a relationship of friendship or love, neither party has the decisive word independently of the other. It is an ongoing story of initiative and response by both sides.

This will involve the affective as well as the conative. I rejoice in Yhwh's teaching, and "my eyes have run down streams of water because people have not kept your teaching" (Ps 119:136). Someone who cries a river because of seeing people ignore Yhwh's teaching can hardly be personally ignoring it. Similarly, "my passion has destroyed me, because my foes have ignored your words (Ps 119:139). "Passion" (qin'â) can imply jealousy or anger, but it refers more generally to depth and intensity of emotions, emotions that can consume a person. We might wish to get them under control, but we may not be able to; they burn like fire (Cant 8:6). "The cruelty of fury and the flood of anger: but who can stand before passion?" (Prov 27:4). Here the suppliant acknowledges the interwoven causes of those intense emotions. They relate to being under attack, but also to the way those attacks mean people are ignoring Yhwh's expectations of people, so that the passion is also felt for God's sake (Ps 69:9 [MT 10]; cf. Jn 2:17). The reference to such passion signals the psalmist's not being someone who ignores Yhwh's words. Passion energizes faithfulness.

Anger and Disgust

In Yhwh, tagging along behind compassion, grace, patience, commitment, steadfastness and a willingness to carry waywardness, come an insistence on not acquitting and a determination to let the consequences of waywardness run on through the family. Yhwh's self-description does not clarify how these two sets of inclinations interrelate except by implying that the first set has priority. The first comes more naturally, but Yhwh is capable of implementing the second.[43]

---

[43]See *OTT* 2:156-70.

In humanity these two sets of inclinations and obligations are again combined, though both are themselves affected by human sinfulness. Sometimes we are compassionate and long-tempered when we ought to be severe. David is the great embodiment of this weakness in his relationships with his sons Amnon and Absalom, which lead to the unraveling of his monarchy. David gets angry about Amnon's rape of Tamar, but does nothing about it because he loves Amnon (2 Sam 13:21).[44] The opposite of love is not anger but indifference, and anger may be an expression of love.[45] Urging people to be slow to anger itself implies that eventually anger may be appropriate, as Yhwh's example also shows. In Western culture we find it hard to grant that. A research library lists almost four thousand titles on love, but only forty-one on hate, suggesting that "denial plays a role in this silence about hate."[46]

In Saul's case, getting angry is a fruit of the Spirit. It is when Yhwh's spirit comes on him in power that his anger bursts into flame and he takes action on behalf of the people of Jabesh (1 Sam 11:6). Micah similarly describes himself as filled with a vehement energy that comes from Yhwh's spirit, in denouncing wrongdoing in Judah (Mic 3:8).[47] We speak of the sufferings of Job. "Why don't we also speak of 'the anger of Job'? For most of his words have a tone of vehement complaint, reproach, aggression. Assailed by attack, he insists on confrontation."[48] Psalm 119:53 speaks of the way "rage" like that of a fire or a storm "has gripped me because of the faithless, people who abandon your teaching." Once again, to say this is to indicate a claim to be seriously committed against the stance of such people. "I hate them," declares Psalm 139:19-24. I take commitment so seriously. Anger needs to be not merely a feeling but a commitment that leads to action, as it is in Yhwh. To put it yet another way, "I have seen betrayers and loathed them, people who did not keep your statement" (Ps 119:158; cf. v. 163). Seeing, and seeing the profit that these people's actions led to, could lead to joining them, but instead it led to this more proper reaction of loathing and disgust *(qût)* which again implies that we would not dream of going that way ourselves; this verb too comes in Psalm 139:21. Such "disgust" follows Yhwh's example (Ps 95:10); it is a form of Godlikeness. Augustine comments on Psalm 139:19-24 that while we are commanded to love our enemies, we are not commanded to love God's enemies.[49]

---

[44]Though the reference to his love for Amnon does not come in MT (see NRSV mg).

[45]Alastair V. Campbell, *The Gospel of Anger* (London: SPCK, 1986), p. 30.

[46]David Augsburger, *Hate-Work* (Louisville/London: Westminster John Knox, 2004), p. vii.

[47]Cf. Carroll, "'He Has Told You What Is Good,'" p. 107.

[48]Lytta Basset, *Holy Anger* (Grand Rapids/Cambridge: Eerdmans, 2007), pp. 11-12.

[49]Augustine *Expositions on the Book of Psalms,* Nicene and Post-Nicene Fathers 1.8 (Edinburgh: Clark/Grand Rapids: Eerdmans, 1989), p. 640.

Human sinfulness means we can be sinfully angry as well as sinfully merciful. That is true of Saul, whose anger becomes a liability (1 Sam 20:30). It is true in a different sense of David; when he hears Nathan's fictitious story about a sheep farmer, he gets very angry and declares that there should be appropriate severe action (2 Sam 12:5-6). "Loose-tongued people inflame a town, but the wise turn away anger" (Prov 29:8). "A hot-tempered person rebels much" (Prov 29:22). "The weak-minded choose to hate. . . . It's the least painful thing to do."[50] People used to be urged to control their anger; now they are advised to let it out. Neither piece of advice can be generalized. Repression may be unhealthy; expression may be self-perpetuating.[51]

Integrity

Yhwh is characterized by integrity, and integrity is another way human beings are called to be Godlike. The EVV often translate *tāmîm* "blameless," but this is misleading. The word is not negative. It does not denote the absence of something (blame) but the presence of something (uprightness). More literally it suggests being complete or whole in the sense of steadfastly committed to what is right. Psalm 18:23-32 [MT 24-33] is noteworthy: "I have been *tāmîm* with him [Yhwh] and have kept myself from waywardness. . . . With the person who is *tāmîm* you show yourself *tāmîm*. . . . God—his way is *tāmîm*. . . . The God who has girded me with strength and made my way *tāmîm*. . . ." It is the first quality Psalm 15 lays down to describe the person who wants to spend time in Yhwh's company. Integrity or wholeness is commonly a prescription for an animal to be offered to Yhwh, but lovers think their beloveds are *tām* (Song 5:2; 6:9). As a moral quality, it is a description of the lives of Noah and Job (Gen 6:9; Job 1:1) and a prescription for Abraham's life (Gen 17:1).

It is thus an aspect of the commitment God expects of us and assumes it is possible for us to offer. This stance parallels that in Philippians 3:6, 12-14 and the exhortations in the Sermon on the Mount rather than that in Romans 7. Yhwh expects our lives to be fundamentally oriented to what is right, though without setting up unrealistic expectations about their being sinless and therefore blameless. When people come to spend time in Yhwh's company, they may come with an offering that recognizes shortcomings they need to own. They are not blameless, but if they are fundamentally committed, they can still come. But if there is something wrong with the central orientation of their lives, they have to change that. Instead of being a whole person, a person of integrity and commitment, it is possible to be a divided person (Ps 119:113), one who will not make up his or her mind whether or not to live by Yhwh's

---

[50]See Yiyun Li, "A Man Like Him," *New Yorker,* May 12, 2008, pp. 104-11; see p. 107.
[51]Campbell, *Gospel of Anger,* pp. 27-31.

commands and promises, whether to follow Yhwh or the Master (1 Kings 18:21; cf. Josh 24:15; Mt 6:24). Such people have to make up their minds before coming into Yhwh's presence.

"Yhwh my God, if I have done this, if there has been meanness in my hands, . . . may an enemy pursue me and overtake me" (Ps 7:5 [MT 6]). A number of psalms presuppose that the suppliant has been falsely accused of some wrongdoing. One can imagine a person on trial before the elders in the village, or before the city authorities as happens in the Naboth story (1 Kings 21), while 1 Kings 8:31-32 has a person swearing before Yhwh in the temple that they have not committed some offense. A psalm such as this might be used in such a context. As usual, the psalm is not implying a claim to sinlessness, but to innocence of this wrongdoing. It also recognizes that we have to be open to God's scrutiny in this connection; it goes on to note that "the faithful God probes minds and hearts" (literally, hearts and kidneys). God can discover whether we had been plotting to do wrong to someone, whether we had been behind a wrong thing that happened. Integrity is a matter of the mind and heart as well as the action.

Psalm 119:14 speaks similarly of joy: "In the way of your declarations I have rejoiced as over all wealth." Once more, feelings have a decisive influence on behavior. A feature of First Testament spirituality is joy in the fact that Yhwh has told us what to do and joy in doing it. Yhwh's commands are not a burden to us. We joy in them because they are Yhwh's and because they prescribe what is best for us. Nevertheless, it is quite something to declare that they give us as much joy as having all the wealth in the world, or to declare "I exult over your statement like someone who finds much plunder" (Ps 119:162). "In your laws I will delight," Psalm 119:16 adds, though again recognizing the need to go on, "I will not ignore your words"; that expression is perhaps a litotes, indicating "I will give my whole mind to them as well as rejoicing in them with enthusiasm." They then taste so fine, they slide down my throat like honey (Ps 119:103). Indeed, I find wonders there (Ps 119:129). There are wonders in Israel's story, but there are also wonders in Yhwh's teaching about our lives. It is wondrous that we are not left ignorant of Yhwh's teaching, the key to good fortune, honor and life. If we sometimes do not see this teaching as wonderful, as unlocking our lives rather than closing them down, we need Yhwh to open our eyes to the facts (Ps 119:18).

Wholeness

Integrity is a matter of the heart as well as action. The converse is also true. It needs to be a matter of the outer life as well as the heart. In Psalm 15 it keeps company with faithfulness and truthfulness, and it is spelled out as involving neighborly speech, giving honor and shame to the right people, and handling money with generosity and honesty. The outward life is as important as the inner attitude. It is not the case that the heart is "the only thing that counts in life,"[52] any more in the First Testament than in the New Testament. If the whole person is an integrated person, integrity is acted out as well as characterizing the inner being. In that respect, the Gentile Abimelech (Gen 20:5-6) seems more integrated than Abraham, who is sometimes presented as a model of piety but has also been seen as comic character, trickster, character in a tragedy, savage parent and unworthy husband.[53]

Psalm 119 begins with a comment on the good fortune of people who are *tamîm* in their way of life, then describes them as people "who walk in Yhwh's teaching, . . . who observe his declarations, who have recourse to him with all their heart." The two lines hold together integrity of outward life (it is a matter of the way you walk) and the inner attitude that characterizes you. Psalm 119:13 does the same, in different dynamic: "in my heart I have treasured your statement so that I may not fall short in relation to you." The heart is the wellspring of life and of obedience. If Yhwh's teaching has reached deep into my heart and I then treasure it there, it can shape my thinking and decision-making. I know I need my heart to be of integrity in connection with Yhwh's laws, but this is also necessary "so that I may not be shamed," in the sense that the inner integrity will issue in outer integrity and thus in honor (Ps 119:80).

In keeping with this, Psalm 119:5 expresses the desire, "O that my ways may be firm in keeping your laws." The talk of ways, firmness and keeping again indicates that outward life counts, while the passion indicated by the form of a wish indicates that inner attitude matters too. The verse also reflects the need for the interior argument instanced by Psalms 42–43. The inner passion energizes the outward action, makes the outward action more likely to be maintained. Not the beginning of something, "but the continuing unto the end until it be thoroughly finished yields the true glory."[54]

The word *wholeness* is historically related to the word *holiness*, as German *heil* ("whole/intact/healed") is related to *heilig* ("holy/sacred"). That raises the question whether there is a link between the realities as well as the words. It would be unwise to infer this from the etymology or the history of the words' development, which is never in itself a guide to the meaning of words. (The

---

[52]Against T. C. Vriezen, *An Outline of Old Testament Theology* (Oxford: Blackwell, 1962), p. 329 (2nd ed., Oxford: Blackwell/Newton, Mass.: Branford, 1970, p. 391).

[53]See Mary E. Mills, *Biblical Morality* (Aldershot, U.K./Burlington, Vt.: Ashgate, 2001), pp. 32-46.

[54]So Francis Drake before a battle, as quoted in Julian S. Corbett, *Drake and the Tudor Navy*, 2 vols. (London: Longmans, 1898), 2:100, who gives a reference to the British Calendar of State Papers: Domestic, cci. 33.

English word *nice* is related to a Middle English word meaning "stupid/wanton" and a Middle French word meaning "silly/simple," and all go back to Latin *nescius*, which means "ignorant"). The question is, does the way people use words suggest a link that reflects the historical connections? The answer for *holy* and *whole* is that there is no link between the words in usage, except for people with a theological interest who become aware of this piece of linguistic history and suggest it points to something significant, the idea that you need to be a person of moral integrity (holy) if you are to be a whole (healthy, integrated) person, or that you need to be a whole person if you are to be a holy person. Both might be true (or might not), but the history of words would illustrate the point rather than be evidence for it.

Independence and Honor

To be compassionate when others are tough, committed when others are conformist, angry when others are tolerant involves a willingness to be different. The reason why Israel has prophets is to tell it things that are the opposite of its inclinations. It does not need prophets to reassure it that God approves of its instincts. Exercising authority with commitment and walking diffidently in Yhwh's company do not come naturally. It is more usual to exercise authority in order to benefit ourselves and to want to make a difference and leave a legacy. Goodness means not being concerned for ourselves or our achievements or our legacy. That means standing out from the crowd.

The Psalter opens by declaring a blessing on people who "have not walked by the plans of the faithless or stood in the path of failures or sat in the seat of mockers" (Ps 1:1). The psalm knows that life involves action, and it involves standing firm in the path we decide to take. If there is a linear sequence in its opening statements, their implication is that action and consistency can then take us into a position of power, give us a seat in the body that makes decisions for the community. We come to be part of the group that makes plans for the community's future. (What shall we do about developing downtown, about traffic congestion and commuting time, about skid row?) But such decisions are often taken by groups who are as concerned for themselves as for the community, by faithless people, people who fail to take right priorities into account, who regretfully write off the idea that questions about faithfulness and pressures on the family need to influence the community's plans. Look after the bottom line, and the trickle-down effect will benefit everyone. The psalm declares a blessing on people who refuse to think that way, and who refuse to walk that way.

In another sense the First Testament does not expect people to stand out. When the community is functioning properly, it honors right living and shames waywardness, and the First Testament assumes we rightly value and take pride in such honor. So wisdom, gracefulness, faithfulness, commitment and even lowliness of spirit lead to a person's finding honor and being able to hold onto it (Prov 3:35; 11:16; 21:21; 29:23). Conversely, people who rejoice in or plan for the undeserved downfall of others or who trust in resources other than Yhwh or indulge in false forms of worship should and do find shame instead of honor (2 Chron 30:15; Ps 35:26; 40:14-15 [MT 15-16]; 109:29; Is 41:11; 45:16). As a person of uprightness, integrity, wealth and seniority in the community, Job had been a person of honor. In recalling the time when he had this honor (Job 29), he emphasizes both his recognition and his taking action on behalf of the vulnerable and against the abuser. "His honour, which is renewed daily, consists in being able to give."[55] But now he has lost his honor and come to be shamed (Job 19:1-9; 29:7-11, 20-25; 30:1-10; cf. Ps 69:19 [MT 20]). Conversely, David starts as an insignificant person, even someone belittled, and becomes a person of honor (which means Jonathan moves in the opposite direction), then finds his honor imperiled or compromised in various ways.[56] A person in that position has to try to hold on to the conviction that in due course Yhwh will vindicate and bring to honor (Ps 73:24; Is 50:6-9).

As I recognize and live by Yhwh's commands, I have honor rather than shame in the community, an aspect of the good fortune obedience brings (Ps 119:6). Obedience generates prosperity and thus honor; disobedience generates trouble and thus shame. At least that is how things should work, though pleas such as "Take away from me taunt and shame, because I have observed your declarations" (Ps 119:22; cf. 31) indicate they do not always do so. Sometimes people think we are stupid for walking Yhwh's way. Sometimes walking Yhwh's way leads to trouble rather than blessing. The psalm thus urges Yhwh to make things work out as the theory says.

The replacement of honor by shame sometimes threatens Israel itself or actually happens to Israel (Ps 44:9, 13-16 [MT 10, 14-17]; Is 30:1-5; 42:17). The one prayer in Psalm 123 is for Yhwh to be gracious, and the one reason is "because we have become so full of shame." The community is simply an object of scorn to the secure or complacent and to the impressive and majestic, such as big powers like Assyria in Hezekiah's day or smaller powers like neighboring Persian provinces in Nehemiah's day. If Yhwh abandons it, Yhwh thereby shames it.[57]

Communities can thus use the ascription of honor or shame as a means of

---

[55]J. Pedersen, *Israel: Its Life and Culture I-II* (London: Oxford University Press, 1954), p. 214.

[56]See Gary Stansell, "Honor and Shame in the David Narratives," *Semeia* 68 (1994): 55-79.

[57]Cf. Lyn M. Bechtel, "The Perception of Shame within the Divine-Human Relationship," in *Uncovering Ancient Stones*, H. N. Richardson Festschrift, ed. Lewis M. Hopfe (Winona Lake, Ind.: Eisenbrauns, 1994), pp. 79-92; see pp. 82-84.

leaning on their members to abide by the community's ideals.[58] People gain much of their sense of self from their honored place in the community. This is the case in a broader sense in Western society where our friends or gang or scholarly guild give us our sense of self. The guild of Old Testament scholars, for instance, honors certain theories and methods and shames others, and within it different groups shame and honor certain theories and methods. Deuteronomy honors certain patterns of behavior and shames others, such as the avoidance of brother-in-law marriage (Deut 25:5-10).[59] It is vital to keep our recognition with the rest of our community. In urban societies we do not have a village community that gives or withholds honor to us, but we do have our communities—our circle of friends, our gang, our guild. Few people can live on in the same way if they become shamed before their community, and being discredited in the eyes of other groups, other gangs, other guilds, imperils our very sense of life. Losing our place in the community, having honor replaced by shame, means we no longer know who we are; in effect, it means we cease to exist. Honor means having a proper sense of one's own dignity and worth; shame means lacking these. "In the experience of shame, one's whole being seems diminished or lessened."[60]

Honor and Shame

In the First Testament the idea of having a totally independent mind or keeping to oneself or seeking and valuing solitariness or insisting on making up one's mind about what one wants to do independently of other people is alien and might seem pathological. On the other hand, Esther "acts behind the mask of 'feminine shame'"; the book implies that "powerless women—and Jews—can invoke power as long as they maintain required appearances."[61] Old Testament scholars do something similar.

But one should not exaggerate the importance of honor and shame or universalize certain ways of understanding them.[62] In the first-century Mediter-

---

[58]See Lyn M. Bechtel, "Shame as a Sanction of Social Control in Biblical Israel," *JSOT* 49 (1991): 47-76. She notes the wide range of Hebrew terms for shame, which rather contrasts with its limited vocabulary for speaking of guilt (pp. 54-55).

[59]See David Daube, "The Culture of Deuteronomy," *Orita* 3 (1969): 27-52.

[60]Bernard Williams, *Shame and Necessity* (Berkeley/London: University of California Press, 1993), p. 89; he is discussing the notion of shame in Homer and in Greek tragedy.

[61]Lillian R. Klein, "Honor and Shame in Esther," in *A Feminist Companion to Esther, Judith and Susanna*, ed. Athalya Brenner (Sheffield, U.K.: Sheffield Academic Press, 1995), pp. 149-75; see p. 175.

[62]And one should be wary of the binary pairing of these terms, which became fashionable in biblical studies. "Honour/shame does not emerge as a useful binary pairing for the purposes of examining human interactions in biblical literature" (Johanna Stiebert, *The Construction of Shame in the Hebrew Bible*, JSOTSup 346 [London/New York: Sheffield Academic Press, 2002], p. 166).

ranean world, for instance, male honor includes an emphasis on sexual aggressiveness and precedence, while women are expected to be submissive to authority, deferential, diffident, passive and restrained.[63] Many stories in Genesis undermine such assumptions. While the realm of sexual behavior is often safeguarded by considerations of honor and shame, the Song of Songs ignores this framework.[64] The Book of the Covenant with its stress on neighborliness ignores questions of mutual honor and shame.[65]

Conversely, shame does not essentially relate to moral questions. If my crops fail or I get incurably ill or I lose a battle, I am shamed, perhaps because in other people's eyes it implies I had done wrong and am being punished, but perhaps because it implies I trusted in the wrong God. When something happens that threatens our sense of honor it is natural to pray, "May I not be shamed, may my enemies not exult over me, yes, may none of those who look to you be shamed, may those who are unfaithful without reason be shamed" (Ps 25:2-3). And further, "The people who look for you must not be shamed because of me. . . . The people who seek help from you must not be dishonored because of me" (Ps 69:6 [MT 7]). The suppliant is someone such as a king or governor or priest with whom other people in the community are identified; the leader's shame is the whole community's reviling. And "it is passion for your house that has destroyed me; the reviling of people who revile you has fallen on me" (Ps 69:9 [MT 10]). One can think of someone campaigning for proper worship of Yhwh in the temple when other people practiced worship by means of images or worshiped other deities as well as Yhwh. Psalm 70 goes on to urge that attackers should be shamed but that the people who seek help from Yhwh should rejoice in Yhwh. Psalm 71 likewise sets salvation, rescue and deliverance over against shame, reviling and dishonor. Either the suppliant must be shamed or the attackers must be, though we have noted that it is possible for shame then to issue in restoration.[66]

Shame in the First Testament (and the New Testament) as we have so far considered it has different connotations to those attached to it in psychology. There it suggests a deep and generalized inner sense of unacceptability and worthlessness, though this sense is no doubt one that has internalized community and family convictions. Guilt is then a feeling of having done wrong in a particular matter rather than a state of responsibility for a wrong deed

---

[63]So Malina, New Testament World, p. 52.

[64]See Diane Bergant, "'My Beloved Is Mine and I Am His,'" Semeia 68 (1994): 23-40; see pp. 36-37.

[65]See David J. Clines, "Being a Man in the Book of the Covenant," in Reading the Law, J. G. Wenham Festschrift, ed. J. G. McConville and Karl Möller, LHBOTS 461 (London/New York: Continuum, 2007), pp. 3-9; see pp. 7-8.

[66]See §3.3 "Mercy and Punishment."

(whether one acknowledges this or not). But shame in the First Testament does also affect people's view of themselves and the way they stand before Yhwh. Ezra prostrates himself before Yhwh and declares, "my God, I am humiliated and ashamed to raise my face to you, my God, because our wayward acts—they multiplied, above our head, and our guilt—it grew to the heavens" (Ezra 9:6). Ezra's prayer also indicates how honor and shame pass from one generation to the next; he shares in the shame that comes from the actions of Israel over the centuries. Yhwh's very graciousness in restoring the people will make people feel such consuming shame (Ezek 36:31-32), though that need not be permanent (Is 54:4).

But a sense of defilement and inner shame indeed are elemental human awarenesses.[67] That leads into a consideration of holiness and purity, though the First Testament's framework for thinking about these has a broader background and content.

6.2 Holiness and Purity

"The problem to my professors was how to be good. In my ears the question rang: How to be holy."[68] That is a good biblical question. In the First Testament holiness links concretely with food, time, death and sex. These may be key areas of life in all cultures; they are certainly so in the modern West. But in connection with these, the First Testament talks about holiness in very different ways from anything Western people are used to, and any illumination we gain from it will come by a hermeneutical process involving an act of imagination.[69] The issues raised by talk of holiness again concern more than morality. The First Testament's talk of and provision regarding holiness and purity indeed link with that elemental human awareness of defilement and inner shame[70] and also relate to the distinctiveness of the people of God over against the rest of the world. Both these make it illuminating. I am called to be holy and to be pure, and thus to live in light of the order of creation. The First Testament expects this to be embodied in my life, so that it contributes to the achievement of God's missional purpose.

Distinctiveness

In the New Testament, holiness is both a descriptive metaphysical, theological category and a prescriptive religious and behavioral one. The church *is* a holy

---

[67]Cf. Walter Brueggemann,, *Theology of the Old Testament* (Minneapolis: Fortress, 1997), p. 194; see Paul Ricoeur, *The Symbolism of Evil* (Boston: Beacon, 1995), pp. 25-46.

[68]Abraham Joshua Heschel, *Moral Grandeur and Spiritual Audacity* (New York: Farrar, Straus, Giroux, 1996), p. 129.

[69]See §4.1 "Thinking Hermeneutically."

[70]See §6.1 "Honor and Shame."

people and people who belong to Christ *are* holy (e.g., Col 3:12; Heb 3:1; 1 Pet 2:9), set apart from the rest of the world as people who belong to God in a distinctive sense. At the same time they are challenged to *be* holy, to *live* holy lives, lives characterized by uprightness and resistance to evil desires that will then contrast with those of people who do not name the name of Christ (e.g., Tit 1:8; 1 Pet 1:14-22). This New Testament usage follows that in the First Testament, where "holiness" signifies both Israel's status or position and its obligation or vocation. Israel *is* "a people holy to Yhwh" (e.g., Deut 7:6); at the same time, "you *are to be* holy because I, Yhwh your God, am holy" (e.g., Lev 19:2).

When Yhwh is described as "holy," the Masoretes give it the full spelling *qādôš*, whereas when Israel is so described, they give it the short spelling *qādōš*.[71] Israel's holiness is not fully like Yhwh's. But for Yhwh and for Israel, key to the idea of holiness is distinctiveness or separation, and the holiness to which Israel has to be committed is that distinctiveness. Its separation does not mean it has to avoid contact with other peoples; there is nothing defiling about such contact. But Israel belongs to God and it must behave in light of that. This belonging to God has moral implications, but the First Testament does not use "holiness" language to make the point, as the New Testament does. It rather keeps "holiness" language for use in that other connection. Holiness denotes belonging to God. Thus the language of holiness first occurs in Scripture to refer to God making the sabbath holy (Gen 2:1-3), to a prostitute as a "holy woman" (Gen 38:21-22), and to Moses standing on holy ground (Ex 3:5). In each case words from the root *qādaš* signify being separate and distinct and associated with the supernatural realm, but they do not have moral connotations. Hebrew usage compares with that of cognate words in Akkadian and Ugaritic.[72] The Canaanite gods were holy, but they do not look very moral. The opposite of holy is then not sinful but common, ordinary or everyday (Lev 10:10). English translations use words such as *profane*, *pollute* and *defile* for words from the root *ḥalal*, but these give a misleadingly pejorative impression. There is nothing necessarily wrong with being nonholy, common, ordinary, everyday.

But if something *is* holy, it must *be* holy. Yhwh made the sabbath, the line of Aaron, the sanctuary, its offerings and its accoutrements holy (e.g., Ex 20:11; 29:33; 30:29, 32). They simply are holy, and human action neither brings that about nor has the power to undo it. Yet it is Israel's responsibility then to make the sabbath holy (Ex 20:8), to make Yhwh's house holy (2 Chron 29:5, 17), to let holy things be holy to them (Ex 30:36-37), and it is the priests' responsibility

---

[71]Cf. Jacob Milgrom, *Leviticus 17–22*, AB (New York: Doubleday, 2000), p. 1607.
[72]See, e.g., Baruch A. Levine, "The Language of Holiness," in *Backgrounds for the Bible*, ed. Michael Patrick O'Connor and David Noel Freedman (Winona Lake, Ind.: Eisenbrauns, 1987), pp. 241-55; see pp. 242-43.

to make themselves holy (e.g., Ex 19:22). Yhwh made Israel holy to Yhwh (e.g., Deut 7:6; 14:2, 21; 26:19), but Israel then must *be* holy (Ex 22:31 [MT 30]; Lev 11:44); before appearing at Sinai, Yhwh tells Moses to make Israel holy (Ex 19:10, 14).

Indeed, "you are to make yourselves holy and become holy, because I Yhwh am your God, and you are to keep my laws and do them; I Yhwh am making you holy" (Lev 20:7-8). The combination of the hitpael verb, the verb *hāyâ* plus the adjective, and the piel, makes several points. It is the Israelites' task to make themselves holy and become holy, as it will be the task of people who believe in Jesus when this possibility is extended to them (1 Pet 1:15-16). Until that time it is impossible for anyone apart from an Israelite to be holy, but it is possible for all Israelites to be that. Holiness is not limited to priests; it is a democratic notion.[73]

Yet Yhwh brings this about. How do these two relate? Yhwh makes the Israelites holy by giving them laws to obey, and the Israelites make themselves holy and become holy by obeying these laws. There is indeed a sense in which they simply *are* a holy nation, because Yhwh separated them from other peoples, yet also a sense in which they have to *become* that. But it is not so difficult to become holy by obeying Yhwh. To stay with the themes of Leviticus 19, it simply requires action such as not sacrificing your children to Molek, not consulting mediums, not belittling your parents, not committing adultery and not marrying your sister. It is not that complicated. This could set an attractive prospect before ordinary people. You do not need to be born in the right clan to be holy; you do not need to be rich, clever, powerful or even religiously inclined or monumentally self-disciplined in order to count to Yhwh. You just have to be holy in these down-to-earth ways. You then count as Yhwh's holy people.[74]

The Pure and the Taboo

Alongside the distinction between holy and common is the distinction between pure and taboo (*ṭāhôr* and *ṭāmēʾ*; see again Lev 10:10). The two Testaments' use of language about purity overlaps with their use of language about holiness. Paul speaks of people abounding in love, insight and righteousness, and thus being pure and blameless for the day of Christ (Phil 1:9-11). Purity involves being free from sin; it is an image for a moral state. Similarly, "evil intentions are an abomination to Yhwh, but gracious words are pure" (Prov 15:26). Proverbs 30:12 speaks of "a generation that is pure in its own eyes but it is not washed of its filth."

---

[73]Cf. Jacob Milgrom, *Leviticus* (Minneapolis: Fortress, 2004), p. 249.
[74]Cf. ibid., p. 248.

But in the First Testament, once again this language does not usually refer to moral purity. When English translations have words such as *pure* denoting moral propriety, usually the text is using words signifying innocence or physical cleanness (e.g., Job 15:14; 25:4, *zākâ*; Ps 24:4, *bar*). When the First Testament talks about things being *ṭāhôr*, the focus lies elsewhere. As the opposite of "holy" is not "sinful" but "ordinary, everyday," so the opposite of *ṭāhôr* is not "sinful" but *ṭāmēʾ*. The EVV usually translate *ṭāmēʾ* "impure" or "unclean," but these words give the impression that being *ṭāmēʾ* is something to do with hygiene if not to do with morality. But only some taboo things are unhygienic and only some unhygienic things are taboo, and the New Testament's abandoning the purity-taboo scheme would be odd if it mainly concerned hygiene. Further, as negative words *impure* and *unclean* suggest the absence of a quality, whereas *ṭāmēʾ* is a positive word.

Using a foreign word such as *taboo* carries its own disadvantages,[75] and in connection with the First Testament it does not carry the connotation of avoiding danger,[76] but it is a less misleading word than *impure* or *unclean*. In the First Testament taboo involves the fact that there are things of a nonmoral kind that have something mysterious or off-limits about them that makes them incompatible with who Yhwh is and thus with who Israel is. No single explanation accounts for every instance of the categorizing of things as taboo. There are several symbolisms involved in the purity-taboo system, overlapping in what they point to in realms such as food, time, death and sex. Different aspects of the purity-taboo system then underlie different prohibitions and provisions in the Torah, and a particular prohibition or provision may express more than one of these aspects. So there are varying ways in which the rules about purity and taboo express truth about Yhwh and thus truth about living a human life, and make it possible to embody these.

The distinction between pure and taboo first appears in Genesis 7–8 in connection with distinguishing among animals. The story assumes that its readers would be familiar with the idea, and also implies that it is not a distinction introduced at Sinai but one going back to creation. But the notion of taboo is most systematically expounded in Leviticus 11 in connection with animals that are pure, and thus can be eaten, and ones that are taboo, and thus cannot be eaten. Again, no single explanation of the distinction works for everything. But one explanation trades on the close links between Leviticus 11 and Genesis 1, which emphasizes the orderly nature of the world God

---

[75]Walter Burkert, *Homo Necans* (Berkeley/London: University of California Press, 1983), p. xxi. My friend Philip Jenson has therefore urged me to give up the word, but I have been unwise enough to ignore him.

[76]See the study of the word's background and definition in Franz Steiner, *Taboo* (London: Cohen & West, 1956).

created. There, everything is in its place and all living creatures inhabit their proper sphere: water, air or land. All belong to distinguishable species; most of the occurrences of the word *species* or *kind (mîn)* come in Genesis 1 and Leviticus 11 (the others come in similar contexts in Gen 6–7; Deut 14; Ezek 47:10). Leviticus 11 and Deuteronomy 14 then presuppose that most animals have means of moving that are appropriate to their sphere. Fish have fins and scales for swimming; birds have two wings to fly, but also two legs to walk; land animals have four legs and divided hoofs.[77]

Keeping Things in Order

It is thus fine for Israelites to eat creatures that belong to "proper" species and inhabit their "proper" sphere, but not creatures that seem to cross species or spheres and thus confuse these (such as sea creatures that lack fins and scales, or insects that walk like animals, or animals that do not both have proper divided hoofs and chew the cud). There is a sense in which such creatures are not whole; purity and taboo link with wholeness.[78] (The most common use of the word *ṭāhôr* in other connections than distinguishing between pure and taboo is to refer to pure gold, gold unmixed with anything alien, in passages such as Exodus 25.) The things the people of God are to eat are to reflect the order that God introduced into creation. They are called to embody the nature of God's ordering of creation in their life, and thus to be different from other peoples, who do not do that: see Leviticus 20:22-26, which has in common with Genesis 1 a distinctive repetition of the verb *separate* (*bādal* hiphil; cf. also Lev 10:10; 11:47). It is simply "for you" as Israelites that some animals are taboo (Lev 11).[79] Not eating them is part of Israel's holiness, its distinctiveness; other peoples may eat them.

This approach does not explain all aspects of the distinctions Israel is called to make, and considerations such as hygiene, everyday custom, religious practice, practicality and association with foreigners and their worship (all of which could rule out the pig) likely contributed to the development of the taxonomy. But the principle of making distinctions is one that creation and Israel's life have in common.[80] Indeed, the fact that Israel is called to live

---

[77]The classic study is Mary Douglas's *Purity and Danger* (London: Routledge/New York: Praeger, 1966), also *Implicit Meanings* (London/Boston: Routledge, 1975), pp. 249-318, though her thesis has been critiqued, refined and developed by her and by others (see, e.g., Walter Houston, *Purity and Monotheism*, JSOTSup 140 [Sheffield, U.K.: Sheffield Academic Press, 1993], pp. 93-123; Jonathan Klawans, *Impurity and Sin in Ancient Judaism* [New York: Oxford University Press, 2000], pp. 7-19).

[78]Cf. John E. Hartley, *Leviticus*, WBC (Dallas: Word, 1992), p. lx.

[79]Cf. Mary Douglas, *Leviticus as Literature* (Oxford/New York: Oxford University Press, 1999), p. 137.

[80]Jon D. Levenson, *Creation and the Persistence of Evil* (Princeton, N.J./Chichester: Princeton University Press, 1994), p. 119.

by distinctions written into creation could also suggest that other peoples might be expected to perceive something of what living before God involves. This coheres with the First Testament assumption that other peoples know what God requires of them and are guilty for ignoring it (e.g., Amos 1:3–2:3). There is such a thing as natural law,[81] a created order[82] of which created humanity has some awareness.

Yhwh is a whole being, creation is a whole place and the sanctuary is to reflect this. So only a person who is whole can offer sacrifices and only animals that are whole can be sacrificed (Lev 21:16-23; 22:21-25).[83] Priests with certain physical shortcomings can share in the holiest of sacrifices, but they are "not to make my holy places into common places, because I, Yhwh, am making them holy" by my presence. The parallel with creation clarifies that the need for priests to be physically whole does not imply there is anything "wrong" with disability. Animals that do not fit into the broad categorization of species, and in this sense are flawed, are still part of the good creation, and being taboo does not mean being disgusting. But in these connections the creatures become symbols, and the human body is also a theological symbol. Sacrifice is "a form of philosophy by enactment,"[84] and bodily integrity is a symbol of theological and moral integrity. The classification of creation in terms of pure and taboo is "a sermon on God's pattern of the universe" to which the distinction between fertility and covenant is key.[85]

Living in Light of Creation

Purity is thus expressed not by withdrawal from the world but by the way we live in the world.[86] Observing the rules about pure and taboo animals provides Israel with a way of fitting in the world as God created it, in its properly structured way. It follows from God's original purpose in creation that God's deliverance of Israel aimed to free people to live the lives they were intended to live at the beginning, the regular, cyclic life of relaxation, festivity and worship structured by the year, the season, and the week. The regulations in the Torah work out in detail how Israel is to live its created life. And in this con-

---

[81]Cf. Rodd, *Glimpses of a Strange Land*, pp. 52-64, following the work of John Barton: see *Ethics and the Old Testament* (London: SCM Press/Harrisburg, Penn.: Trinity Press International, 1998), pp. 58-76; *Understanding Old Testament Ethics*, pp. 32-44, 77-144.

[82]As Oliver O'Donovan prefers to call it: see *Resurrection and Moral Order* (Leicester, U.K.: Inter-Varsity Press/Grand Rapids: Eerdmans, 1986), pp. 31-52, 85-86.

[83]So Douglas, *Leviticus as Literature*, pp. 45-46.

[84]Ibid., p. 68.

[85]Ibid., p. 174.

[86]Cf. J. H. Hertz, *The Pentateuch and Haftorahs: Leviticus* (London/New York: Oxford University Press, 1951), pp. 190-91; cf. Gordon J. Wenham, *The Book of Leviticus* (Grand Rapids: Eerdmans, 1979), p. 265.

nection "the Torah regards limitations on man's appetite as fundamental to a proper way of life."[87] Here, food and sex have something in common. We may not do as we like with regard to either. Israel's diet reflected and reinforced its theology and its ethic.[88]

A similar implication regarding Israel's embodying of God's creation work in its life follows from God's working for six days and then stopping. Not only do we follow God's example but we live specifically in light of the way God created the world (Ex 20:8-11). People (and animals) are to keep off the sabbath because Yhwh claimed this time each week to commemorate the completing of the work of creation. Implicitly, a creation theology underlies other commands, concerning the way parents and children relate, the way human beings treat other human beings who were created to image God, the way marriage images God's faithfulness and the way we respect the property (land, animals, produce) with which God in creation provided humanity. Israel's life reflects the way God created the world. God's creative work even produces the means whereby business is conducted fairly: "A right balance and scales are Yhwh's: all the stones in the bag are his making" (Prov 16:11). Proper human conduct corresponds to the way God created things.

The principle of living by the structured and ordered nature of the created world illumines other regulations in the Torah. One should not mix things that are made separate. So one should not interbreed animals or yoke together different animals or mix crops in a field or combine materials such as wool and cotton in clothes or let different sexes wear each other's clothes or let humans have sex with animals (Lev 19:19; Deut 22:5, 9-11; 27:21). Deuteronomy thus shows its own "concern for the integrity of all forms of life and the preservation of the distinctions of the created order,"[89] "a concern for the order and structure of things, the recognition of difference and sameness, and a desire to maintain things as God has created them."[90] Creation involved God making distinctions, between light and darkness, the waters above and the waters below, day from night (Gen 1:4, 6-7, 14, 18). Mixing things implies a return to *tōhû wābōhû*.[91] A hallmark of the holiness of the people of God is a reverence for and a participation in the order of the cosmos.[92]

Mixtures were allowed, indeed commissioned, in the curtains of the sanctuary and the high priest's ephod (e.g., Ex 28:6), and were present in associa-

---

[87]Jeffrey H. Tigay, *Deuteronomy*, JPS Torah Commentary (Philadelphia: Jewish Publication Society, 1998), p. 137.
[88]See further §6.4.
[89]A. D. H. Mayes, *Deuteronomy* (London: Oliphants, 1979), p. 306.
[90]Patrick D. Miller, *Deuteronomy* (Louisville: John Knox, 1990), p. 162.
[91]Cf. C. Houtman, "Another Look at Forbidden Mixtures," *VT* 34 (1984): 226-28.
[92]Cf. Mark E. Biddle, *Deuteronomy* (Macon, Ga.: Smith & Helwys, 2003), p. 347.

tion with Yhwh in heaven in the person of the cherubim; these were hybrid creatures, most explicitly in Ezekiel 1.[93] And paradoxically, as reminders of Yhwh's commands ordinary Israelites are to make fringes with blue cords on the corners of their garments (Num 15:37-41), which would be rather splendid decorations of the kind that a significant person might wear; they would likely imply that the garment combines wool yarn with linen. Normally that was forbidden to laypeople (compare the juxtaposition in Deut 22:9-12); in other words, it is a holy mixture. Thus these fringes or tassels mean that ordinary Israelites are dressed a little like priests, as is befitting people who are called a priestly kingdom and a holy nation, and are all called to be holy.[94]

Maintaining and Losing Purity

Purity and taboo apply to aspects of people's lives that fit well or badly with who Yhwh is. Sex is an example of the latter. If you have had sex, you have been involved in something that is the antithesis of who Yhwh is, as one to whom sexual activity is alien (as it is not to the being of other gods). So the First Testament reckons we must dissociate sex from God; at least, that is the effect of its attitudes.[95] We must keep what is taboo away from the holy (Lev 22:1-3). When about to appear at Sinai, Yhwh tells Moses to make Israel holy and get them to wash their clothes; Moses implicitly infers that this sanctifying involves abstaining from sex and thus avoiding getting bodily fluids on their clothes (Ex 19:10, 14-15).[96] When the people are about to cross the Jordan and experience Yhwh act, Joshua similarly instructs them to make themselves holy (Josh 3:5). When they are about to meet for Yhwh to identify who has appropriated taboo objects from Jericho, Joshua is to make them holy by bidding them make themselves holy (Josh 7:13).

Although there is nothing sinful about sex (in the right circumstances) because purity is not an intrinsically moral category, purity does also attach

---

[93]Milgrom, *Leviticus*, p. 236.

[94]Cf. Jacob Milgrom, *Numbers*, JPS Torah Commentary (Philadelphia: Jewish Publication Society, 1989), pp. 410-14.

[95]If rather Deborah Ellens is right that sex is taboo not because sex must be dissociated from God but because all genital flow, even regular genital flow, makes you taboo: see "Menstrual Impurity and Innovation in Leviticus 15," in *Holy Woman Holy Blood*, ed. Kristin De Troyer et al. (Harrisburg, Penn./London: Continuum, 2003), pp. 29-43; see p. 41; cf. Deborah Ellens, *Women in the Sex Texts of Leviticus and Deuteronomy*, LHBOTS 458 (London/New York: Continuum, 2008), pp. 47-72

[96]If the taboo concerns bodily fluids, there is no implication that there is something taboo about women as women that makes it impossible for them to be present when Yhwh appears, though Judith Plaskow comments that Moses' actual formulation ("Do not go near a woman") addresses the community at this vital moment only as men, which for a feminist makes this as disturbing a verse as any in the Torah (quite a statement!) (*Standing Again at Sinai* [San Francisco: Harper, 1990], p. 25).

to proper moral and religious behavior, as holiness issues in proper moral and religious behavior. More specifically, taboo attaches to immoral and ir-religious behavior. If you are immoral, you are also taboo; "pollution is not identical with morality and involves a mystical surplus that cannot be reduced to it."[97] For instance, Leviticus 18 closes its list of prohibitions on different forms of sexual and family relationships with a comment on the way they make people taboo and the way they constitute waywardness. Following the traditional gods of the land made the Israelites themselves taboo, and their presence thus brought a taboo on the land, which was a catastrophe (Jer 2:7, 23). In general, Judah's waywardness, failure and rebellion carry taboo and mean the people need purification (Jer 33:8; cf. Ezek 14:11). It is not that they are then metaphorically taboo; they are literally taboo.[98] In the sense that they cannot go into God's presence in that condition, being immoral also stands in too great tension with who Yhwh is. Purity is a metaphysical state. As purity means not carrying taint such as the taint of sex that makes it impossible to draw near to Yhwh because it clashes with who Yhwh is, so it also means not carrying taint such as the taint of faithlessness to Yhwh or to other people, which also makes it impossible to draw near to Yhwh because it clashes with who Yhwh is. Thus restoration from wrongdoing needs to include the removal of taint so that I may associate with Yhwh. "Purify me from my fault. . . . Unfault me with hyssop so that I may be pure. . . . Create for me a pure heart" (Ps 51:2, 7, 10 [MT 4, 9, 12]).

Purity, Ethics and Wrongdoing

A traditional understanding of the purity rules reverses the relationship between taboo and morality, reckoning that it is not the case that immorality carries taboo implications but rather that taboo carries moral implications. Thus not consuming blood and avoiding eating animals that kill for food teaches us to have reverence for life. Not tearing food from living animals teaches us to avoid inflicting unnecessary pain. Not eating from food that has not been tithed or shared with the needy teaches us to acknowledge the one who provides our sustenance and to act justly. This argument is given a new twist by René Girard, who notes that once blood gets spilled, more blood gets spilled. Violence is contagious. Declaring blood taboo has the potential to delay or even halt the potential of a frightening escalation of violence.[99] And it might link with the fact that the created world is also characterized by vio-

---

[97]Judith Plaskow, *The Coming of Lilith* (Boston: Beacon, 2005), p. 168.

[98]Cf. Jonathan Klawans, "The Impurity of Immorality in Ancient Judaism," *JJS* 48 (1997): 1-16; see pp. 1-6; cf. Klawans, *Impurity and Sin in Ancient Judaism*.

[99]Cf. the argument of René Girard, *Violence and the Sacred* (Baltimore/London: Johns Hopkins, 1989), pp. 28-34.

lence, as some animals kill other animals for food. In Genesis 1, alongside the fact that God gives to the animal and the human world plants and fruit as food, God commissions humanity to tame the world, which implies controlling its violence. But instead humanity joins in the violence. The pure-taboo distinction and the shortcoming it implies about the created world would only have become an issue once humanity had started eating animals.

The affliction that made Miriam taboo was a punishment for wrongdoing (Num 12), and this is so with some other such afflictions in Scripture (2 Kings 5:19-27; 2 Chron 26:16-20). Both Testaments agree with the usual view that illness may well have such a meaning. But both Testaments safeguard against the assumption that this is always so. The purity regulations themselves point in both directions. Their connection with events or phenomena such as motherhood, menstruation and mold points away from any necessary link with wrongdoing. Rather, their significance is that they draw attention to the need to safeguard facts such as Yhwh's being the God of life. On the other hand, when skin disease disappears, the person has to offer a reparation offering as well as a whole offering, grain offering and purification offering. That invites the inference that the person had done wrong in relation to God in some way. It might be that Yhwh had afflicted them with the disease in the manner of Miriam or Uzziah; a person with skin disease would at least be wise to ask the question whether there is wrongdoing they need to acknowledge as well as taboo they need to observe. Alternatively, it might be that the disease had involved them in subsequent wrongdoing; they might, for instance, have let themselves be in contact with the sanctuary or with something else that was holy, or with someone who would go into the sanctuary or be in contact with something holy (for instance, by eating holy food) (cf. Lev 15:31). It is to safeguard against this that people with skin disease live separately and warn people not to have contact with them (Lev 13:45-46; cf. Num 12:14-15).

Instead of denying that sickness can result from wrongdoing, the purity rules enabled people to live with the premise but deny the conclusion that this is generally or always so.

> Unlike the plagues sent against the people of Israel for murmuring in the Book of Numbers, in Leviticus leprosy and blemishes are not punishments. You cannot look at an afflicted person and speculate: "Tut, tut, which sin brought it on him?" Under this doctrine, misfortunes do not betray a sinner. Accusing is thwarted.[100]

Afflicted people can accept the quarantine that comes with their illness,

---

[100]Mary Douglas, "Sacred Contagion," in *Reading Leviticus*, ed. John F. A. Sawyer, JSOTSup 227 (Sheffield, U.K.: Sheffield Academic Press, 1996), pp. 86-106; see p. 97.

and priests have the authority to declare that a person is clear of it and can come back into the community. Illness is just one of those things, not a sign of sinfulness. Only refusal to undertake the prescribed steps turns a person into a sinner. Thus sin can issue from taboo status, but sin does not cause taboo status in this connection. At the same time the multiplying of the offerings reassured the afflicted person that they really were restored to their relationship with Yhwh and with the community.

Keeping Distinctive Over Against the World

Israel's holiness lies in distinctively belonging to Yhwh. Distinguishing holy and ordinary, and also pure and taboo, then contributes to its manifesting its distinctiveness over against other peoples. Whereas some inference is involved in the theory that the purity-taboo scheme relates to the order of creation, both the First Testament and the New Testament are explicit that the regulations concerning creatures that may or may not be eaten are designed to make Israel distinctive and separate. God has made a distinction between Israel and other peoples, and between creatures that Israel is to treat as taboo and ones it may treat as pure (Lev 20:24-26; cf. Lev 11:45-47). It is an aspect of Israel's being a holy people. Israel's observance of these distinctions is an expression of its accepting its position as a people that God has distinguished from the rest of the world. That was partly to ensure that it did not come to behave like other peoples in ways that were religiously or morally reprehensible. As well as working with distinctions written into creation, not mixing cotton and wool symbolized the need to keep separate things and people that are different. The instructions themselves emphasize the importance of making distinctions, of keeping things separate. And it is the priests' vocation to help Israel make the distinctions between pure and taboo, and avoid the latter (Lev 10:10-11), so that it can fulfill its vocation to be a distinctive, holy people, who draw attention to Yhwh.

Simply having random distinctive rules about what one eats would have this effect. Some paradox is involved here. Israel's particular set of regulations is distinctive, but most peoples have some customs concerning what one does and does not eat, often ones that puzzle or appall other peoples. The British call the French "frogs," the French call the British "les rost bifs." Yet the animals Yhwh allowed and forbade to Israelites were not so different from those eaten or not eaten elsewhere in the region.[101] Further, both Testaments also make clear that the rationale concerning which animals may be eaten, that it expresses Israel's distinctiveness, does not apply to other aspects of order and taboo. The taboo on consuming blood applies to other peoples as

---

[101]Houston, *Purity and Monotheism*, pp. 124-217.

well as Israel. Some regulations avoid practices associated with other religions: as the children of Yhwh, Israelites are not to gash themselves or shave the front of their heads for the dead, because they are a people holy for Yhwh, chosen from among the peoples of the world as a special treasure (Deut 14:1-2). But that would not explain many of the practices, and this particular regulation also links with a feature of First Testament theology, its attitude to death and the dead.[102]

Similarly, one aspect of the rationale underlying the food rules and some other regulations is that things that are separate should be kept separate, which links with this particular significance of the scheme. Israel is not to get mixed in with other peoples in such a way as to lose its identity as the people of Yhwh. There is no ban on marrying a person of another race, nor does Ezra require the dissolution of marriages on the basis of their being of mixed race. Being of non-Israelite origin is not a disqualification for membership of the community in any period. The question is, what God do you serve?[103] The reason for not marrying a Canaanite is that this will turn you away from following Yhwh and lead to your serving other deities (Deut 7:3-4). A Canaanite who has made a commitment to Yhwh is a different matter. Worshipers of Yhwh and worshipers of the Master are like chalk and cheese; they should not be mixed. The purity-taboo scheme embodies this principle. God turns the taxonomy of the animal world into a teaching tool for Israel. It corresponds to the way God wants Israel to see itself in relation to the world.

> I am Yhwh your God who made you distinct from the peoples. You shall distinguish between pure and taboo animals and between pure and taboo birds and not make yourselves abhorrent [*šāqaṣ* piel] with animals or birds or anything with which the ground swarms, which I have made distinct for you as taboo. You shall be holy to me, because I Yhwh am holy and have made you distinct from the peoples to be mine. (Lev 20:24-26)

Holiness implies separation and thus separating. Yhwh has distinguished Israel from other peoples, and Israel must therefore distinguish pure animals and birds from taboo ones, and thereby keep Yhwh's name holy rather than making it ordinary (Lev 22:1-2, 31-33).

So there is indeed nothing wrong with other peoples eating the camel or the pig, but for Israel they are taboo. It is in this sense that they are an abomination (*tô'ēbâ*, Deut 14:3). Whatever Israelites felt about them, they are to treat them as abhorrent because eating them would mean abandoning their vocation to be a people set apart or made distinct by Yhwh. *Abomination* is an ac-

---

[102]See §6.3.

[103]See, e.g., Hyam Maccoby, "Holiness and Purity," in *Reading Leviticus*, ed. John F. A. Sawyer, JSOTSup 227 (Sheffield, U.K.: Sheffield Academic Press, 1996), pp. 153-70.

tion term that means Israel is to keep rigorously away from eating these creatures.[104] Either side of Deuteronomy's characterization of taboo creatures as *tôʿēbâ* are declarations that Israel is "a people holy to Yhwh your God"; the first declaration continues, "you Yhwh chose to be for him a specially treasured people, from all the peoples that are on the earth" (Deut 14:2, 21). Thus God's missional purpose lay behind the purity system. It was designed to keep Israel distinctive in a way that the world could see. It is then in this same connection that the system is abolished (Acts 10). After Jesus' death, resurrection and commission to take the gospel to the world, there are no purity rules.[105] Yhwh's concern to reach the nations will now work itself out in a different way.

Holiness, Purity and Faithfulness

Yhwh's holiness is Yhwh's distinctiveness. It consists in a decisive commitment to faithfulness, which distinguishes Yhwh from human beings and from other deities. Israel's holiness involves Israel's distinctiveness, and it also consists in a decisive commitment to faithfulness. Like purity, this holiness does not imply withdrawal from the world; indeed, it can be expressed only in the world.

In the First Testament, the holiness-purity system and the priorities of *ṣĕdāqâ* were mutually reinforcing. In principle, abolishing the first does not imperil the second, but in practice it may do so; it makes everything rest on the moral perceptiveness and decision-making of the individual.[106]

> Judaism inherits from the development of custom and thought in pre-biblical and biblical times a law of animal kinds that summarizes in itself a great richness of symbolic themes. It stands for the order and peace of a civil society over against the disorder and violence of the wild; for the just and traditional ordering of society against anarchy; for the purity of the sanctuary against the permanent threat of pollution; for the holiness of the people of God as his devoted ones; for their protection against pressures from without, and their separation from all that would threaten their dedication to their one God; for the possibility, not confined to Israel alone, of living in peace with God's creatures and in

---

[104]Douglas, *Leviticus as Literature*, pp. 167-69. But Thomas Kazen argues that both purity rules and moral rules may have a background in a sense of disgust ("Dirt and Disgust," in *Perspectives on Purity and Purification in the Bible*, ed. Baruch J. Schwartz et al., LHBOTS 474 (New York/London: T & T Clark, 2008), pp. 43-64; cf. his *Jesus and Purity* Halakhah (Stockholm: Almqvist & Wiksell, 2002), pp. 200-62.

[105]Cf. L. William Countryman, *Dirt, Greed, and Sex* (Philadelphia: Fortress, 1988), esp. pp. 138-43; though I have noted in §4.2 "Same-sex Unions" that this does not carry all the implications that he suggests.

[106]Cf. Houston, *Purity and Monotheism*, p. 268; Howard Eilberg-Schwartz, *The Savage in Judaism* (Bloomington: Indiana University Press, 1990), pp. 195-206.

the experience of his presence. It does not merely symbolize these; by the constant practice of the rules it actually inculcates them.

When early Christianity abandoned the law of forbidden food it rejected, to all appearance, all those good things. What did it get in return?[107]

It did gain the capacity to reach out to the world cross-culturally. But what it lost was significant. Sometimes Orthodox and Catholic forms of Christian faith have regained elements of what was lost, in practices such as fasting on Friday. In Protestant faith there were once some slightly comparable practices such as wearing special clothes for church, observance of Sunday as a sabbath and avoiding certain forms of leisure activity, but those have now largely died in the West, so there are no formal markers of Christian commitment. Perhaps it is no coincidence that there are also few markers in terms of ṣĕdāqâ. Christians' practice with regard to wealth, work, sex, family and war is not very different from that of other people. "To the extent that the lifestyles of modern Christians are largely indistinguishable from those characteristic of the surrounding culture, the call to visible holiness—separateness—must be reiterated."[108]

These dynamics underline the importance of the missional-church movement's emphasis on Christian practices, or they suggest a nuancing of it so as to include symbolic practices as well as ones that directly embody ṣĕdāqâ, so that we enable Christians "not merely to believe their faith but to grasp it in vivid and concrete ways, not merely to make moral decisions in its light but to live it, without having to think about it, in the minute particulars of their lives."[109] The church needs practices that bind it, in the manner of traditional Roman Catholicism and Judaism. Its being needs to be embodied.[110] Alasdair MacIntyre has emphasized the notion of practices in connection with Christian identity and ethics. A "practice" is a "coherent and complex form of socially established cooperative human activity through which goods internal to that activity are realized in the course of trying to achieve those standards of excellence which are appropriate to, and partially definitive of, that form of activity."[111] The Torah offers a rich account of the practice that was to characterize Israel. Its regulations neatly combine expression of identity and of ethical commitments, for instance in encouraging respect for the order of God's creation.

Such practices indeed fulfill a missional function. In the West they do so

---

[107]Houston, *Purity and Monotheism*, p. 258.
[108]Biddle, *Deuteronomy*, p. 247.
[109]Houston, *Purity and Monotheism*, p. 282.
[110]Cf. Stanley Hauerwas, *In Good Company* (Notre Dame, Ind./London: University of Notre Dame Press, 1997), pp. 24-25, 31.
[111]See MacIntyre, *After Virtue*, p. 187.

by raising questions, by making people ask whether there might be more to life than meets the eye. In traditional cultures with their emphasis on ritual and the way it shapes people's lives and religion, Christian faith might enable the gospel to get home by working with ritual rather then reckoning that the gospel has no place for it.[112]

Purification

Moses' inference in Exodus 19:14-15[113] recognizes that taboo can affect things that come into contact with the object to which it attaches. Yhwh and death are antithetical. (Again there is a contrast with other gods, who can be involved in death in varying ways.) A corpse is therefore taboo, and its taboo nature affects the person who touches it. A person who thus becomes taboo and then goes into the sanctuary risks the sanctuary being affected and becoming taboo, and because of the antithesis between Yhwh and death risks Yhwh's refusing to be there, or by juxtaposing death and Yhwh risks an explosion. So priests are to "separate the Israelites from their taboo, so that they may not die through their taboo, in bringing taboo on my dwelling that is among them" (Lev 15:31).[114] Leaving a corpse exposed in the land would likewise bring a taboo on the land, which could be catastrophic (Deut 21:22-23).

Purity is important to the individual, the community, the sanctuary and the land; defilement can have catastrophic effects for any of these, in that it can cause Yhwh to withdraw from the entity in question. As is the case with sin or dirt in human relationships, it might be possible to ignore a small amount of defilement, but repeated acts of defilement have a cumulative effect. So it is important to undo defilement, to purify things as you go along, as it is important to undo the effects of sin or to remove dirt. Otherwise, Yhwh might cut off the individual (they might be struck down by Yhwh or die before their time or not have children through whom they would continue to belong to the people, or be struck down by illness and unable to go to the sanctuary). Or Yhwh might abandon the people or punish the land by making it unfruitful (in which case it might then vomit out the people who caused this) or leave the sanctuary and withdraw its protection from attack. If the priests fail to teach and work with the pure-taboo distinctions, the sanctuary and the land lose their purity and the people lose their raison d'être.

So a person needs to become free of any taboo that comes to attach to them. That may require an offering (e.g., Lev 12) or it may be dealt with by ceremo-

---

[112]Cf. Gerald A. Klingbeil, *Bridging the Gap* (Winona Lake, Ind.: Eisenbrauns, 2007), pp. 239-40.

[113]See the earlier "Maintaining and Losing Purity."

[114]The verb *nāzar* hiphil, translated "separate" is used in an odd way, but its precise meaning does not affect the point here.

nial washing (e.g., Lev 11:24-40), but with the ordinary taboos of everyday life, all that is required is time for their effect simply to wear off, as can be the case with the effect of things that human beings do to one another. For the people and the land, too, time is a factor in their purification; after some decades Yhwh can face having the people back and the land can face having them back.[115] But as some taboos can have catastrophic effects on relationships or situations, so acts such as murder, kidnap and enslavement, serving other deities, and adultery are profoundly defiling. They too can make Yhwh withdraw from the individual, the community, the sanctuary or the land, with those same consequences. The profundity of the defilement issuing from such acts means there can be no rite of purification for a person who has undertaken them. As with other wrongdoings, all one can do is throw oneself on Yhwh's mercy in the hope that Yhwh may remove the wrongdoing and remove the taboo. Yhwh can purify people (Ezek 36:25; 37:23). In the absence of such turning to Yhwh that will lead to Yhwh dealing with the wrongdoing, the community's task will be to burn up the evil or the blood from its midst (e.g., Deut 13:5 [MT 6]; 17:7; 19:13; 24:7).

6.3 Relating to Life and Death

Living in light of creation implies living in harmony with creation. This has implications for what and how I eat; it makes killing and eating created things look odd. It has implications for the way I think about life and death, and the way I think about dying.

Serving God's World

The present context of the developed and developing world makes it important to reflect on our relationship with the world as well as with God, the community and ourselves. A famous parlor game involves identifying the eleventh commandment (for instance, "You shall not get found out"). To expand the Decalogue so as to relate scriptural perspectives to our current context, rather than assuming that they are a timeless and seamless whole, we might suggest "You shall not spoil the earth." Within the First Testament our relationship with the world is not as prominent as those other relationships, but it is more

---

[115]Cf. Tikva Frymer-Kensky, "Pollution, Purification, and Purgation in Biblical Israel," in *The Word of the Lord Shall Go Forth*, D. N. Freedman Festschrift, ed. Carol L. Meyers and M. O'Connor (Winona Lake, Ind.: Eisenbrauns, 1983), pp. 399-414; see pp. 411-13; the preceding paragraphs have profited from this paper. Regina M. Schwartz emphasizes the link between purity, land, monotheism, monogamy and endogamy, but this seems to give too narrow or tight an account of the First Testament's concerns in this connection (and the First Testament does not show much explicit interest in monogamy, or in monotheism as opposed to mono-Yahwism) (*The Curse of Cain* [Chicago/London: University of Chicago Press, 1997], pp. 62-76).

prominent than we have noticed, and the twenty-first-century context does bring to our attention aspects of the First Testament that we might miss. As feminism opened up the possibility of the "retrieval" of liberating egalitarian aspects of the Scriptures, earth-centered readings make possible the retrieval of ways the scriptural text affirms the earth's own value and rights.[116]

The object of creation was not that people should live in relationship with God or with each other, or just be themselves. Humanity was commissioned to be fruitful, multiply, fill the earth and thus subdue it *(kābaš)* and rule over its creatures *(rādâ)* (Gen 1:28). It does not follow that we are therefore invited to "use" it "to create wealth"[117] or that God puts at our disposal "all the resources that the earth (and indirectly the visible world) contains and which, through the conscious activity of man, can be discovered and used for his ends."[118] Indeed, that inference is reckoned implausible by the subsequent creation story in which Adam is formed to "serve" the garden on God's behalf (ʿābad; Gen 2:15). Rather than the land serving us, we serve the land; ǎdāmâ comes before ʾereṣ and has prior claim.[119]

If "ethical imperatives derive their force solely from the relationship between *man-as-he-is-in-his-untutored-self* and *man-as-he-would-be-if-he-realized-his-telos*"[120] and "the Enlightenment project" had to fail because it abandoned the idea that there was an answer to the question "What is human life for?"[121] then this is Genesis's answer to that question. It is a very different sort of an-

---

[116]See, e.g., Norman C. Habel, ed., *Readings from the Perspective of Earth,* and *The Earth Story in the Psalms and Prophets* (Sheffield, U.K.: Sheffield Academic Press/Cleveland: Pilgrim, 2000; 2001); Habel and Shirley Wurst, ed., *The Earth Story in Genesis,* and *The Earth Story in Wisdom Traditions* (Sheffield, U.K.: Sheffield Academic Press/Cleveland: Pilgrim, 2001). Habel notes (*Readings,* pp. 25-37) that this earth-centered reading, like feminist reading, is concerned to retrieve not only material that interpreters have suppressed but also material that the Scriptures themselves have left unexpressed.

[117]Against Stephen Mott and Ronald J. Sider, "Economic Justice: A Biblical Paradigm," in *Toward a Just and Caring Society,* ed. David P. Gushee (Grand Rapids: Baker, 1999), pp. 15-45; see p. 18.

[118]From the encyclical of John Paul II, *Laborem exercens* (Hales Corners, Wis.: Priests of the Sacred Heart, 1981), §4 <www.vatican.va/holy_father/john_paul_ii/encyclicals/documents/hf_jp-ii_enc_14091981_laborem-exercens_en.html>. Stanley Hauerwas is more swingingly critical of the encyclical and its proof-texting in *In Good Company,* pp. 109-24, partly because Gen 1–2 does not fit Hauerwas's theology too well.

[119]Tim Gorringe, *A Theology of the Built Environment* (Cambridge/New York: Cambridge University Press, 2002), p. 59.

[120]Brad J. Kallenberg, "Positioning MacIntyre within Christian Ethics," in *Virtues and Practices in the Christian Tradition,* ed. Nancey Murphy et al. (Harrisburg, Penn.: Trinity Press International, 1997), pp. 45-81; see pp. 62-63, summarizing implications of MacIntyre's *After Virtue.*

[121]Cf. Brad J. Kallenberg, "The Master Argument of MacIntyre's *After Virtue,*" in *Virtues and Practices in the Christian Tradition,* ed. Nancey Murphy et al. (Harrisburg, Penn.: Trinity Press International, 1997), pp. 7-29; see p. 11.

swer from the one that emerges from the Aristotelian tradition in terms of
virtue, rationality and blessing.[122] It is not the First Testament's last statement
about our relationship to the world. Humanity is to wonder at creation (e.g.,
Ps 104), to respect its independence (Job 38) and to be depressed by it (Eccles
1).[123] But its opening expectation is that we are to buttress and indeed extend
the order God has written into the world in creating it. Life involves living in
accordance with the way God created the world and fulfilling our role there.

Our eating is one way we do that. The First Testament assumes that eating,
like sex, needs some regulation.[124] The instructions in Leviticus and Deuteronomy build on implications of Genesis. Both Genesis 1 and Genesis 2 suggest that God's creation intention was that we would live in accordance with
creation by not eating other things that have the breath of life in them. God
gave humanity and the animals everything that grows as their food (Gen
1:29-30); God told Adam that he could freely eat of all the trees in the orchard,
bar one (Gen 2:16-17). Human beings were to rule over the animals, but this
did not mean they could eat them. Indeed, one major effect of subduing them
and ruling them would be to cause them not to eat each other.

Killing for Food

Outside the Garden all this changed. Immediately, human beings were offering animals as well as vegetables to God, and therefore they were killing
them, and also killing each other. Soon, "the earth was full of violence," and
that was the reason God decided to put an end to "all flesh," human and animal (Gen 6:11-13), or nearly put an end to it, and then start again. But the ideal
relationship between humanity and the animate world cannot now be realized. "A dreadful fear of you" will rest on the animal world, and humanity
will be free to eat animal flesh (Gen 9:2-3). The first declaration follows from
the second. At creation, humanity's commission to subdue the earth was not
a reason for fear. Humanity's ruling over the animate creation is something
the latter could welcome, as in due course the nations will be quite happy to
come to Zion to have Yhwh make decisions between them (Is 2:2-4). Humanity is the creation's parallel safeguard against itself, making it possible for
nature to live in harmony. The animate world thus had no reason to fear its
exercise of authority. But at the new creation after the destruction, things are
different;[125] human beings can eat animals.

Practicality would limit the extent to which human beings would kill animals to eat them; they could not afford to do so very often. Further, while

---

[122]See Kallenberg, "The Master Argument of MacIntyre's *After Virtue*, pp. 17-19.
[123]See further Habel and Wurst, ed., *Earth Story in Wisdom Traditions.*
[124]Cf. 6.2 "Keeping Things in Order," "Living in Light of Creation."
[125]See further *OTT* 1, chaps. 1-2.

realistically acknowledging that the original commission must be changed given the violent instincts of human beings as well as those of animals, God still set constraints for humanity. Humanity may eat meat; but "flesh with its life, its blood, you may not eat" (Gen 9:4). Subsequently, the Torah further limits meat eating for Israel. There are only a few animals that people can eat, and one of the distinctions between creatures that may or may not be eaten is that the latter tend to be carnivores (which preserves a vestige of the creation concern). The ban on consuming their blood would concern fellowship offerings, which laypeople shared in eating; the question of eating meat from which blood had not been drained would not arise with other sacrifices. Further, in Jewish practice the slaughter of an animal involves cutting its throat and thus letting it die as painlessly as possible, and this practice may be implied by the First Testament word for sacrificial slaughter, *šāḥaṭ* (e.g., Lev 1:5, 11).[126] The animal has to be killed in a humane way. All this severely circumscribes killing and implicitly encourages reverence for life.[127] The dietary restrictions placed on Israel aimed "to allow man to satiate his lust for animal flesh—and yet not be dehumanized in the process."[128]

Leviticus 17:3-9 further requires that when people kill an animal, they bring it before Yhwh to present as an offering. It is not clear whether this presupposes that killing an animal for an ordinary celebration would be permissible away from the sanctuary (as Deuteronomy allows) or whether it presupposes that there would be a number of sanctuaries (as was often the case in Israel) or whether it presupposes a community within reach of the one sanctuary (like the wilderness community or the early postexilic community around Jerusalem) or whether it would apply only to areas within reasonable reach of the sanctuary or whether it refers only to killing animals in connection with fellowship offerings. The fact that some understandings of the rationale would be impractical hardly means they are wrong. This would again reflect the way regulations in the Torah can be teaching, theological ethics or liturgical theology, rather than direct prescriptions for behavior. One reason for the regulation is to ensure people are not offering the animal to a goat

---

[126]So Jacob Milgrom, *Leviticus 1–16*, AB (New York: Doubleday, 1991), pp. 713-18.

[127]Cf. Jacob Milgrom, "Ethics and Ritual," in *Religion and Law,* ed. Edwin B. Firmage et al. (Winona Lake, Ind.: Eisenbrauns, 1990), pp. 159-91; see pp. 189-91. It seems to require more inference to reckon that the move to eating animals is a positive one (so Edwin Firmage, "The Biblical Dietary Laws and the Concept of Holiness," in *Studies in the Pentateuch,* ed. J. A. Emerton, VTSup 41 [Leiden/New York: Brill, 1990], pp. 177-208; see pp. 196-97; cf. Bernard F. Batto, "Creation Theology in Genesis," in *Creation in the Biblical Traditions,* ed. Richard J. Clifford and John J. Collins [Washington, D.C.: Catholic Biblical Association, 1992], pp. 16-38; see pp. 20-22).

[128]Jacob Milgrom, "The Biblical Diet Laws as an Ethical System," *Int* 17 (1963): 288-301; see p. 288.

demon; perhaps this form of forbidden worship gets special mention to counter the possibility that Leviticus 16 encourages people in that direction. But before coming to this rationale, Yhwh declares that people who fail to bring the animal before Yhwh in that way have blood attributed to them. They have shed blood. The expression usually refers to killing human beings, though Yhwh does not require that the person be treated as a murderer and thus liable to execution. But the expression stops only a little short of that, and Yhwh does declare that the person "will be cut off from among his people."[129] There is thus a contrast between the "high visibility" of blood in Israelite ritual and the strong prohibition on consuming blood; further, both contrast with the "lack of blood-consciousness in the Mesopotamian temple ritual."[130]

Sanctifying the Meal

The seriousness with which Leviticus takes killing an animal recalls the way Genesis 9:4-6 associates abstaining from blood with the requiring of a reckoning in connection with spilling human blood. God breathed life into animals as God breathed life into human beings. Killing them is an assault on that act of God and needs to be faced up to and expiated.[131] It involves usurping God's right to be the person who gives life and takes away life. While coming to accept the human instinct to kill animals in order to eat them, God devised ways for people to put right the offense this caused. So when they kill an animal, they do not consume its blood, which symbolizes its life; instead they offer it to God to make expiation for what they have done so that they do not forfeit their lives as a consequence of killing another being.[132] The offering of the animal's blood takes the place of their blood or implies a recognition that the animal's life belongs to God. Offering the animal to God is humanity's way of associating God with the eating of meat and with the violence involved in doing so. God's accepting the institution of sacrifice, along with the requirement that we drain its blood, is God's way of accepting and affirming this arrangement. "When taken up into the ritual frame, violence (bloodshed) in the form of killing the victim is 'sanctified.' " Further, the communal na-

---

[129]See §6.2 "Purification."

[130]Klingbeil, *Bridging the Gap*, p. 233, referring to Tzvi Abusch, "Blood in Israel and in Mesopotamia," in *Emanuel*, E. Tov Festschrift, ed. Shalom M. Paul et al., VTSup 94 (Leiden/Boston: Brill, 2003), pp. 675-84, who in turn refers to the work of A. Leo Oppenheim: see *Ancient Mesopotamia*, rev. ed. (Chicago/London: University of Chicago Press, 1977), p. 192.

[131]So Milgrom, e.g., *Leviticus 17–22*, p. 1474; cf. William W. Hallo, "The Origins of the Sacrificial Cult," in *Ancient Israelite Religion*, F. M. Cross Festschrift, ed. Patrick D. Miller et al. (Philadelphia: Fortress, 1987), pp. 3-13; see p. 5; Miller, *The Religion of Ancient Israel* (Louisville: Westminster John Knox/London: SPCK, 2000), p. 125.

[132]On "expiation," see §2.5 "The Reparation Offering."

ture of this rite means that "the blood that had the potential to destroy relationships (Gen. 9:4-6) has become instead the mechanism to promote those same communal ties through atonement."[133]

Leviticus 17:10-16 further expounds the logic of that. "The life of the flesh is in the blood." The point is a commonsense one.[134] When blood flows out from human beings or animals, their life flows out. They die. The sacrificial system therefore gives a key place to blood. Sacrifices require the death of animals, and the rituals involving blood make clear that the event has involved a death and that this death is being appealed to. Hence the fact that "I myself have given it [the blood] to you on the altar to make expiation for your lives, because the blood, as life [*or* with life], makes expiation." In turn, in light of the huge significance of blood in connection with sacrificial events (which are often meals), Yhwh again declares that people should abstain from consuming blood.

The question of letting its blood flow does not arise if people eat an animal that has died of natural causes or has been killed by another animal; then they are simply to wash and recognize that they remain taboo for that day, perhaps in recognition of their not being able to do anything about the blood. But they did not kill the animal, and therefore they have no need to offer expiation for this act or to offer a ransom. Leviticus 22:8 prohibits priests from eating such creatures; Deuteronomy 14:21 prohibits it to the entire people, because Israel is holy to Yhwh, but allows it to aliens and foreigners. The killing of wild animals, which would not be offered as sacrifices, involves letting their blood pour onto the ground and covering it with earth, perhaps so that it does not cry out to God as Abel's blood did, perhaps as an act of reverence toward that life. Deuteronomy 12 provides for alternative ways of fulfilling the same principles.

A Christian assembly in Jerusalem met to discuss what Torah-based obligations should be expected of Gentiles who come to believe in Jesus, and agreed that Gentiles should be encouraged to refrain from what has been sacrificed to idols, from blood, from what is strangled, and from *porneia* (Acts 15:29). The first three of these expectations correspond with Leviticus 17; the meeting's assumption will be that these are expectations going back to the Noah covenant that are thus binding on Gentiles. Paul (who took part in the

---

[133]Richard D. Nelson, *Raising up a Faithful Priest* (Louisville: Westminster John Knox, 1993), p. 66.

[134]Well, subject to William K. Gilders's comment on how little we really know about what the authors of Leviticus actually believed about blood and its cultic roles ("Blood as Purificant in Priestly Torah," in *Perspectives on Purity and Purification in the Bible*, ed. Baruch J. Schwartz et al., LHBOTS 474 [New York/London: T & T Clark, 2008], pp. 77-83; see p. 83).

meeting) recognized the force in the argument that there was no harm in eating meat that had been sacrificed to idols; after all, they do not exist. But this is a rather high-flown argument, not one that the First Testament would use (as it demotes other gods rather than denying their existence) and not one even Paul is inclined to follow (see 1 Cor 8; 10).

The food regulations thus encourage reverence for life as well as respect for the order of creation, and once again raise questions about the identity of Western Christian lifestyle with that of the surrounding culture and reiterate the call to visible holiness.

Relating to Animals

The First Testament shows no concern for animals equivalent to our "modern urban sentimental feelings towards them."[135] But there are other respects in which it presupposes that we still cannot do what we like with creation. Human beings exercise authority over animals, and subject to certain constraints treat them as their servants (Ex 21:28–22:15 [MT 14]). Yet "the faithful person acknowledges the needs/feelings/person (nepeš) of his animal, but the compassion of the faithless is cruel" (Prov 12:10). One reason why an animal's owner should not work on the sabbath is so that the family's animals may have their day of rest (Ex 20:10; 23:12). One function of the sabbath year is to give the wild animals chance to eat (Ex 23:11). You are not to muzzle an ox while it is threshing (Deut 25:4). When you see your enemy's animal lost or struggling, you are to help him or it (Ex 23:4-5).

And you are not to cook a baby goat in its mother's milk (Ex 23:19; 34:26; Deut 14:21). Looking for rationales for this ban involves considering principles implied by other regulations. Cooking the animal in milk is a good way to cook it, to give the meal flavor, but a family will not possess a huge number of goats, and the milk is quite likely to be its mother's.[136] Making the means of life (a mother's milk) into the means of death is a shockingly inhumane act. That might also underlie the ban on capturing a mother bird and her offspring (Deut 22:6-7) and the more general requirement about not slaughtering animals with their offspring, along with the requirement that a newborn animal stay with its mother for a week before being acceptable as an offering (Lev 22:27-28), and the expectation of humane slaughter previously noted. It might be questioned whether there is anything very humane about merely regulating the way the goat is cooked or postponing the moment when a newborn animal meets its fate. (It is said that human mothers are well-advised to give up a child for adoption when they are born, not to

---

[135]Rodd, Glimpses of a Strange Land, p. 218; see further pp. 207-33.
[136]Cf. Tigay, Deuteronomy, pp. 140-41.

wait); but this is perhaps too rational and hard-headed.

Further, Israel sees itself and its world "in the mirror of nature."[137] The animal world is one of Israel's root metaphors. Yhwh is a shepherd; Israel is a flock (not a herd of pigs). Israelites are sheep; their attackers are wild beasts. Relations within the animal world help it understand and communicate relations within the human world. The metaphor presupposes a linkage between the natural world and the human world, which also has behavioral implications. Israel is to treat the natural world in ways analogous to the way it treats the human world: for instance, nature and animals take sabbaths. As well as benefiting the animals, this buttresses the human rules, which are "part of nature," part of the way the world is created. More solemnly for the animal world, its particular closeness to the human world makes it possible for animals to substitute for humans in offerings. Indeed, domestic animals belong to the human community. With humanity, animals observe the sabbath, owe their firstborn to Yhwh but may have them redeemed, may pay the ultimate penalty for killing someone, and need to be treated with reverence when they are killed for food.[138] The practices involved in making it possible for us to eat meat in the Western world are unspeakably horrible. They are much less horrible in a traditional society, and linking an animal's death with worship gives it meaning and dignity.[139] Sacrificial animals join Israel in being singled out for the inexpressible honor of being consecrated to God. "This paradigm turns the covenant animals into vassals in relation to the people of Israel, as are the people of Israel the vassals of God."[140]

Israelites are to be concerned for trees too. They are not to destroy fruit trees in the course of war (Deut 20:19-20), though they may destroy other trees. "The regulations remind the reader of the interface of the natural and the human; the welfare of both are inseparable."[141] No doubt plant liberation will come in due course, and we shall simply eat minerals, which would be a way to survive.

Eating and Fasting

Eating or drinking is mentioned on average more than once per page of the

---

[137]Eilberg-Schwartz, *The Savage in Judaism*, p. 115; and the chap. this introduces, for what follows here.

[138]See Houston, *Purity and Monotheism*, pp. 184-88.

[139]Jean-Louis Durand, "Greek Animals," in *The Cuisine of Sacrifice among the Greeks*, ed. Marcel Detienne and Jean-Pierre Vernant et al. (Chicago/London: University of Chicago Press, 1989), pp. 87-118; see pp. 87-88; cf. Douglas, *Leviticus as Literature*, p. 67.

[140]Douglas, *Leviticus as Literature*, p. 149.

[141]Miller, *Deuteronomy*, p. 171.

NRSV.[142] It is an elemental human activity. It is fundamental to our individual human life; eating together is fundamental to family and society, and to a community's relationship with God. Food can be seen as one of the dozen most prominent features of "the good life" as the First Testament sees it.[143] Given the impossibility of understanding the big picture of what the world or life are about, or of knowing how the future may turn out, or of evading death, or of being able to end oppression in the world, the best thing is to find enjoyment in those elemental activities of eating bread and drinking wine that are God's gift to us (Eccles 2:24; 3:13; 5:18 [MT 17]; 8:15; 9:7). Whereas Israel's worship and spirituality made a point of dissociating Yhwh from other elemental human experiences such as sex and death, it required people to eat and be festive before Yhwh, and risked speaking in terms of "our God's food" even while knowing that Yhwh did not actually eat. Perhaps the sacrificial, sacramental meal reflected the sacramental nature of every meal or perhaps it implied a distinction over against the nonholy nature of everyday eating,[144] or perhaps we may read it both ways.

The First Testament also takes for granted that people sometimes refrain from eating. "Fasting ranks among customs and manners" and is thus as a rule not the subject of legal prescriptions.[145] While referring to it from time to time (e.g., Joel; Neh 1:4), the First Testament does not make an issue of it or explain its rationale. If anything, its concern is that this outward expression of self-denial should not become a way of avoiding the forms of self-denial that really count (Is 58).

Fasting appears most commonly as an expression of grief in mourning or contrition or other such circumstances (e.g., 1 Sam 31:13; 2 Sam 1:12; Zech 7:1-7; 8:18-19) and as the accompaniment of seeking God's help or guidance (e.g., Ex 34:28; 1 Sam 7:6; 14:24; 28:20; 2 Chron 20:3; Ezra 8:21-23; Esther 4:16; Ps 35:13-14; Jer 14:11-12) or both (Judg 20:26; 2 Sam 12:16; 1 Kings 21:9; Jer 36:9; Joel 2:12; Jon 3:5-9; Neh 1:4). Distress or depression commonly puts people off their food (1 Sam 1:7; 20:34; 1 Kings 21:4,) and grief naturally does that. Fasting is then a marker of identifying with the bereaved. The Expiation Day is an occasion when people "afflict themselves" (e.g., Lev 16:29) and refrain from work, and they will also have refrained from food; other passages make explicit that one "afflicts oneself with fasting" (Ps 35:13; cf. Ezra 8:21; and the parallelism in Is 58:3-5). David does so in connection with finding the covenant chest or pro-

---

[142]Cf. Rolf P. Knierim, *The Task of Old Testament Theology* (Grand Rapids/Cambridge: Eerdmans, 1995), p. 229.
[143]So R. Norman Whybray, *The Good Life in the Old Testament* (New York/London: T & T Clark, 2002), p. 6. The others are security, land, power, long life, wealth, family, justice, laws, wisdom, pleasure and trust in God.
[144]Knierim, *Task of Old Testament Theology*, p. 230.
[145]H. A. Brongers, "Fasting in Israel," *OTS* 20 (1977): 1-21; see p. 2.

viding a permanent home for it; his affliction may refer to his vowing the expenditure of resources or his refusing relaxation or sleep (Ps 132:1-5; compare the woman's vow of self-affliction in Num 30:13 [MT 14]).

Hearing of the *maʿal* in which the Jerusalem community is involved, Ezra afflicts himself by tearing his clothes, his hair and his beard, and sitting desolate all day (Ezra 9:3-5). He later apparently maintains his fast through the evening and overnight, in contrast to the usual custom of maintaining one's fast only through the daylight hours.

Safeguarding the Distinction between Life and Death

There are broader senses in which the purity-taboo system is "preoccupied" with matters of life and death.[146] It expresses reverence and awe in relation to life and safeguards or affirms the distinction between life and death. These belong apart. The distinction is one of those mysteries of nature to which humanity reacts with awe.

Yet there is an odd facet to the relationship between life and death. In theory these are absolute opposites, yet they easily get confused. There is room for debate about when life begins, and it can be difficult to be sure when life ends; people may look dead but still be alive. In the Western world this is a factor involved in debates over abortion and about life-support machines. The Torah's regulations about bodily emissions suggest a related concern. An odd thing about menstruation is that it involves blood and thus looks like a sign of death, but it is actually a sign that a woman could conceive new life. There is something odd, mysterious and worrying about it, appropriate qualities to make it a taboo. It makes a woman *dāwâ*, which could mean "ill" or "faint" or "weak." It is her *niddâ* (Lev 12; 15): the word has been translated by words such as "filthiness" or "abomination," but KJV's "separation" seems all that is required. The emission of semen too suggests the begetting of new life, and it is appropriate to keep separate a life-giving material (semen) and a death-suggestive material (blood) by not having people have sex while the woman is menstruating. And as menstruation signifies that the means to life will actually be "wasted," will die, so this commonly happens to semen.

Perhaps there is another implication in making menstruation a cause of taboo. Menstruation has connotations of both sex and violence and their interconnection. "Sexuality leads to quarrels, jealous rages, mortal combats. It is a permanent source of disorder even within the most harmonious of communities."[147] We would like to hide from the link of sex and blood; menstruation brings it to our attention.

---

[146]Emanuel Feldman, *Biblical and Post-Biblical Defilement and Mourning: Law as Theology* (New York: Yeshiva University Press, 1977), p. 13.

[147]Girard, *Violence and the Sacred*, p. 35.

Menstruation and the emission of semen thus require washing and some time to elapse before the person goes to the sanctuary, a week for menstruation (the sort of time it could usually last) and a day for the emission of semen. They do not require an offering to make expiation for their taboo; there is nothing abnormal or objectionable about them that requires such action, as there is with irregular discharges that constitute departures from the regular norm (see Lev 15).[148] This contrasts with the recurrent assumption in the history of interpretation that menstruation and its "uncleanness" link with women's distinctive sinfulness and constitutes "the curse" that issues from "the curse of Eve," which issued from her sin. Many cultures have imposed quarantine or other restrictions on menstruating women—that is, the men in these cultures have done so, out of some fear of the phenomenon. The occasional metaphorical reference to *niddâ* in the First Testament (e.g., Ezra 9:11) may reflect a similar feeling on the part of Israelite men. But in the First Testament's own teaching, menstruation and other taboo states do not count as "abominations," like other taboos such as forbidden foods, sexual unions, forms of worship and unethical practices. Nor do they involve quarantine. They simply mean that the person may not have contact with anything sacred by, for instance, partaking of a sacrifice or going to the sanctuary (cf. Lev 12:4). In some cases taboo status can be communicated to someone else, so other people who have touched the taboo person also cannot have contact with anything sacred, and priests therefore have to be on their guard about such contact; contravening this principle is a serious offense. But that is so with all taboos.

Giving birth also conveys taboo, doubly so if the mother bears a daughter; all being well, she will herself be giving birth in due course (Lev 12). The longer taboo does not imply some sort of inferiority; taboo does not do this. (In rabbinic Judaism, touching the Scriptures themselves makes a person taboo.) It may reflect an awareness of the danger involved in birthing and of infant mortality. A mother is doubly close to death, her own and her child's. Giving birth involves considerable flowing of blood: it brings new life, but also the threat of death.[149] "Begetting and birth are the nexus points at which life and death are coupled," points at which "there appears to be a departure or a transfer of vital force."[150] At the end of the taboo period following childbirth, a woman does make a whole offering and a purification offering, and thus

---

[148]Cf. Kathleen O'Grady, "The Semantics of Taboo," in *Holy Woman Holy Blood*, ed. Kristin De Troyer et al. (Harrisburg, Penn./London: Continuum, 2003), pp. 1-28; see p. 5.

[149]Baruch A. Levine, *Leviticus*, JPS Torah Commentary (Philadelphia: Jewish Publication Society, 1989), p. 249.

[150]Rachel Adler, "Tumah and Taharah," in *The Jewish Woman*, ed. E. Koltun (New York: Schocken, 1976), pp. 63-71, as quoted by Milgrom, *Leviticus 1–16*, p. 768.

makes expiation and becomes pure. It is often explicit that coming to the end of a taboo also involves bathing, and this may be assumed where it is not explicit (for instance, in the case of menstruation and birthing).[151]

Jon L. Berquist suggests that the rules about taboo in connection with bodily emissions are so demanding that they would make life impossible.[152] He may exaggerate their demands; sexual intercourse did mean being taboo till next evening, but that did not mean avoiding human contact, only refraining from going into the sanctuary. But he may be right that we should no more be literalistic about the implementing of these regulations than about others. Once again, they are as much a form of teaching as a set of regulations to be implemented.

Yhwh and Death

In addition to safeguarding the distinction between life and death, and related to that, the purity system preserves the distance of Yhwh from death. The First Testament manifests no difficulty about being in contact with death, as is involved for instance in burying someone. But purity and taboo do apply to aspects of people's lives that fit well or badly with who Yhwh is, and thus particular taboos relate to death. If you have been in contact with a corpse, you have been in contact with something that is the antithesis of who Yhwh is as "the living God"; perhaps the system is aware of a contrast over against Canaanite gods who could die or were closely involved with death. Further, many cultures reckon that there is contagion about death and about some illnesses, physical and mental. We may be hesitant about wearing a dead person's clothes and may quarantine or avoid people who are physically or mentally sick. The First Testament works with such assumptions but provides for the routinizing of contagion and for ways of dealing with it.

So while contact with a corpse is not wrong, it does incur a taboo. Here too as there is nothing sinful about being common/everyday rather than holy, so there is nothing sinful about being mysterious or worrying or off-limits, about being taboo rather than pure. But things that are taboo cannot be brought into association with God. You need to be free of your taboo if you are to go to the sanctuary, a place of life, the dwelling of "the living God."[153] You cannot go straight from death to worship. The stain of death needs to be removed from people if God is to have anything to do with them. Sacrifice does that because it presents something that gives up life

---

[151]Cf. Milgrom, *Leviticus 1–16*, p. 919.

[152]Jon L. Berquist, *Controlling Corporeality* (New Brunswick, N.J./London: Rutgers University Press, 2002), p. 42.

[153]See Philip P. Jenson, *Graded Holiness*, JSOTSup 106 (Sheffield, U.K.: Sheffield Academic Press, 1992), pp. 111-14.

and accepts death, and thus changes places with the person who has given up life and been affected by death.

This likely underlies the taboo arising from certain skin conditions (Lev 13:1-46). As the TNIV and NRSV note, the reference is not to leprosy but to some skin diseases, but the regulations are not concerned with treating an illness but with handling the consequent taboo. People who have this affliction look as if they are wasting away, falling apart, dying; so they are taboo. When Miriam is stricken with skin disease, Aaron cries out, "may she not be like someone dead, someone who comes out from their mother's womb with half their flesh eaten away" (Num 12:12). So people so afflicted are to behave like mourners (Lev 13:45), and when they are restored, the symbolism of the event cries out "life": it involves a living bird, living water and life blood (Lev 14:1-9). Their restoration means a transition from death to life.[154] Similar phenomena in cloth or in buildings points in the same direction, though where this cannot be remedied, the cloth or the building have to be destroyed (Lev 13:47-59; 14:33-53). The repeated law about not cooking a baby goat in its mother's milk may presuppose the same symbolism; the means of life is becoming the means of death.[155]

The ritual involving the ash from the remains of a red heifer (Num 19) underlines the importance of dealing with the taboo of death, which affects anyone who has contact with someone who has died or has been in their home, and also affects the furnishings of the home, the open vessels there and the clothes of a person who becomes taboo. The ash is mixed with water, which is kept in order to be used whenever it is needed as a kind of alternative form of purification offering (Num 19:9). But possibly "the hidden agenda of Numbers 19 is the cult of the dead," and perhaps this is so with other provisions relating to the link of death and taboo. People want to stay in contact with their loved ones when they have died. Concern with the barrier of death is a perennial and natural human concern. People want to know what has happened to their loved ones, to make contact with them, to honor them or to ask their advice or their prayers. In traditional societies religious rites in connection with death or with one's dead relatives involve practices such as sacrifices on behalf of dead people in the hope of ensuring that they reach a pleasant afterlife or that these dead people will exercise their influence or power positively rather than negatively in connection with the living.[156] Over against the human instinct to want to be in touch with the realm of the dead, the First Testament places a barrier between this life and the continuing sad

---

[154]Cf. Milgrom, *Leviticus 1–16*, p. 889.

[155]So Philo *The Virtues* 142-44.

[156]Baruch A. Levine, *Numbers 1–20*, AB (New York: Doubleday, 1993), p. 472. See §2.5 "Offerings and Death."

life of Sheol. Making offerings in connection with the dead reflects resistance to recognizing this barrier.

A number of observances forbidden in the Torah relate to death. People are not to cut their hair and gash themselves for a (dead) person, as signs of mourning (Lev 19:27-28; Deut 14:1). Prophets often critique these practices, which were evidently prevalent in Israel (e.g., Is 3:24; 22:12; Jer 16:6; 41:5; Ezek 7:18) and among other peoples (e.g., Is 15:2; Jer 47:3, 5; 48:37). Gashing occurs in connection with the prophets in 1 Kings 18:28, whose action may link with mourning the death of the Master;[157] this link would fill out the nature of the rite as forbidden because of its link with another religion.

Mortality and the Ages of Humanity

In Psalm 71 a suppliant apparently stands in mid-life and looks over life as a whole. The word *always* or *continually* (*tāmîd*) comes more often in this psalm than in any other passage: the psalm asks that we may "always" be able to come to Yhwh for protection so that Yhwh will "always" be our hope and "always" be our praise. It looks back on a life upheld by God from before birth and then from youth. It has been a life of always experiencing Yhwh's faithfulness, doing so recurrently: that is, Yhwh is always responding with faithfulness as we face the problems and crises of life (the word *faithfulness* also comes more in this psalm than any other passage in the First Testament). So the suppliant stands between youth and old age. Will that faithfulness continue into old age when strength fails? The attacks of enemies even now, when the suppliant still has strength, make that question the sharper. The suppliant seeks to motivate Yhwh by pointing out how continuing faithfulness will make possible a continuing proclaiming of Yhwh's acts, even to the next generation. It is the way the suppliant will "make a difference" and "leave a legacy."

"Yhwh, make me acknowledge my end—the number of my days, what they are; I want to acknowledge how passing I am" (Ps 39:4 [MT 5]). The EVV have "make me *know*," but the suppliant seems to be well aware of how short life is or how short this particular life may be. The issue is whether we come to terms with the fact that our lives are going to come to an end. (I live in a culture that likes to reckon that death is voluntary.) It is a human instinct to attempt to get control of our death, and the more control of its life a culture or an individual has gained, the more it will expect to be able to win control here. People with resources will certainly expect to be able to do so, and not without reason in the sense that resources enable you, for instance, to buy good food and health care and a corps of bodyguards. But Psalm 49:7 [MT 8]

---

[157]See, e.g., Mayes, *Deuteronomy*, p. 239.

comments that actually wealth "cannot at all redeem a person, give God his ransom." You can never have enough for that redemption price. Look the facts in the face, Psalm 49 goes on. The insightful die as surely as the stupid. They leave their resources to other people even though they thought they would live in their extensive homes forever. (They will find that actually their grave is their home forever, as the LXX reads this line.) Money can no more buy life than buy love.

We are not here for ever. We are transients not residents in life. We are in the position of Abraham and Sarah in Canaan, or Elkanah and Naomi in Moab, or the refugees in Israel whom the Torah bids Israel to treat generously because they have no inheritance there, no secure place. "You have made my days handbreadths; my span is as nothing before you" (Ps 39:5 [MT 6]). A handbreadth is a measure one would use in connection with something very small. Our lives are only a few inches long. "Yes, every human being, standing firm, is altogether breath; yes, a man goes about in the shadow" (Ps 39:5-6 [MT 6-7]). Even when standing firm, or apparently so, a person is no more substantial than a breath. Every week or two one hears about someone in their thirties who has just lost the battle with cancer or dropped dead of a pulmonary embolism. The psalm may refer to our living our lives in the shadow of death, or may refer to our living our lives as a shadow; there is no substance to them and they soon disappear. The next line fits that: "It is for a breath that people hustle; he heaps things up, but does not know who gathers them." We are quite evanescent. As Ecclesiastes never tires of pointing out, we can put huge energy into accumulating stuff, but not have chance to enjoy it. It is not merely the fact of death but its arbitrariness that gets him; it makes all human effort empty and it makes him (or it makes his alter ego) hate life and hate the effort he puts into it and give himself to despair (yāʾaš piel; Eccles 2:17-20).

Being Mindful of Death

So "I am a sojourner with you, a transient like my ancestors" (Ps 39:12 [MT 13]). But the "with you" changes the entire perspective of the confession. Sojourners and transients live "with" a family and thus have protection and provision. They will never be permanent possessors of the land, and human beings will not live forever; but they have provision and protection while they are there, and so does a human being. There is a link between "we with God" and "God with us." The "we with God" is "enclosed" in the "God with us." It *is* biblical faith, biblical love and biblical hope. Faith, hope and love are in us, but they do not have their origin in us. They have their origin in their object, basis and content, in the God who inspires them.[158]

---

[158]See Karl Barth, *Church Dogmatics* (Edinburgh: T & T Clark, 1961), IV/1:15.

The suppliant has already drawn the inference that given our vulnerability and transience, "what do I look to, my Lord?—my hope is in you" (Ps 39:7 [MT 8]). The context does not suggest that the suppliant expects Yhwh to grant the gift of eternal life; rather Yhwh is the one who makes possible full enjoyment of this life. The psalm asks for Yhwh to look away in the sense of ceasing to pay attention to the suppliant's wrongdoing, "so that I may smile before I go, and there is nothing of me" (Ps 39:13 [MT 14]). Life is short, but this does not make it worthless. Life is worth living for as long as we have it. It is as we live our lives in the awareness that we are on our way to death that we are able to live them to the full, savoring every precious limited moment. Death is the end of everyone, and the living take that to heart; the heart of the wise is in the house of mourning (Eccles 7:1-4). Even in youth we are wise to remember that we are on our way to death, in order to be able to enjoy life sensibly (Eccles 11:9–12:7). "Death is the beginning of life in Qohelet."[159]

> Death is the touchstone of our attitude to life. People who are afraid of death are afraid of life. It is impossible not to be afraid of life with all its complexity and dangers if one is afraid of death. This means that to solve the problem of death is not a luxury. If we are afraid of death we will never be prepared to take ultimate risks; we will spend our life in a cowardly, careful and timid manner. It is only if we can face death, make sense of it, determine its place and our place in regard to it, that we will be able to live in a fearless way and to the fullness of our ability. Too often we wait until the end of our life to face death, whereas we would have lived quite differently if only we had faced death at the outset.
>
> Most of the time we live as though we were writing a draft for the life which we will live later. We live, not in a definitive way, but provisionally, as though preparing for the day when we really will begin to live. We are like people who write a rough draft with the intention of making a fair copy later. But the final version never gets written. Death comes before we have had the time or even generated the desire to make a definitive formulation.
>
> The injunction "be mindful of death" is not a call to live with a sense of terror in the constant awareness that death is to overtake us. It means rather: "Be aware of the fact that what you are saying now, doing now, hearing, enduring or receiving now may be the last event or experience of your present life." In which case it must be a crowning, not a defeat; a summit, not a trough. If only we realized whenever confronted with a person that this might be the last moment either of his life or of ours, we would be much more intense, much more attentive to the words we speak and the things we do.
>
> Only awareness of death will give life this immediacy and depth, will bring

---

[159]Mark K. George, "Death as the Beginning of Life in the Book of Ecclesiastes," in *Strange Fire,* ed. Tod Linafelt (Sheffield, U.K.: Sheffield Academic Press/New York: New York University Press, 2000), pp. 280-93; see p. 282; cf. *OTT* 2:636, and pp. 631-44 generally.

life to life, will make it so intense that its totality is summed up in the present moment. All life is at every moment an ultimate act.[160]

Mourning and Hope

Israelites do not show fear of death in itself; while they rail against violent death, unjust death and death before its time, they accept death at the end of a full life. This does not mean they do not mourn or grieve; "on the whole, the mourning rites of biblical Israel are strikingly parallel to those of the ancient Near East."[161] Abraham laments Sarah, weeps for her and negotiates for her a burial place in the land (Gen 23). Joseph laments and mourns Jacob (Gen 50:10). All Israel weeps for Aaron (Num 20:29) and for Moses (Deut 34:8). David and his men tear their clothes and lament and weep and fast for Saul and Jonathan and the Israelite army (2 Sam 1:11-12). Job tears his clothes and shaves his head on hearing of the death of his staff and children (Job 1:20). And then the time for mourning comes to an end, and Yhwh moves Israel on (Deut 34:8-9). Perhaps this is part of the significance of the behavior of David that puzzles his servants, when he fasts as he prays for his son but gives up fasting as soon as the child dies (2 Sam 12:15-24).

In Deuteronomy, Moses' death comes at the end of the book, but as a theme Moses' death (and death in general) recurs through it. In Deuteronomy 12–28, "the language of 'death' and 'dying' saturates these laws," but then "Moses' death outside the land of promise is a central metaphor for the reality of human finitude at both an individual and a corporate level" and "a reminder that the full experience of the promised land would always in some way be beyond their grasp. Moses' demise is a metaphor for the necessary and inevitable losses and limits of human life and power before God."[162]

Such an understanding of Moses' death suggests a broader point about the significance of death and the hope of resurrection. Looking forward to resurrection is a matter of looking forward to the consummation of God's purpose for Israel and thus for the church. When we stop thinking in terms of the immortality of the soul and start thinking in terms of the resurrection of the body, we still skew our understanding if we focus merely on our bodily resurrection as individuals. This is not to say that the resurrection of individuals

---

[160]Metropolitan Anthony of Sourozh (Anthony Bloom), "Preparation for Death," in *Seasons of the Spirit,* ed. George Every et al. (London: SPCK, 1984), p. 42; reprinted from *Sobornost* 1/2 (1979).

[161]Xuan Huong Thi Pham, *Mourning in the Ancient Near East and the Hebrew Bible,* JSOTSup 302 (Sheffield, U.K.: Sheffield Academic Press, 1999), p. 27.

[162]Dennis T. Olson, *Deuteronomy and the Death of Moses* (Minneapolis: Fortress, 1994), pp. 17, 19.

will not happen. It is to say that "without the restoration of the people Israel, a flesh-and-blood people, God's promises to them remained unfulfilled, and the world remained unredeemed. . . . When the programmatic question is defined as 'Will I have life after death?' the discussion has already gotten off on the wrong foot."[163] In this connection, once more, the First Testament understands and experiences the relationship between individual and community differently from modernity. Jacob "went down to Egypt and sojourned there small in number, but became a great, strong, and populous nation" (Deut 26:5). Jacob is "embedded in, indeed, indistinguishable from, his family."[164] It links with this that both Jacob and Joseph want their remains taken from Egypt to Canaan (Gen 47:30; 50:25). Their identity survives their death. God keeps promises to them by keeping promises to their family and people.[165] "The primary concern of the Jew is not to merit an honorable seat in the Garden of Eden but, rather, that he assure the continued existence of the people Israel."[166]

6.4 Relating to Time and Stuff

As holiness relates to places, people and acts, so it relates to time; indeed time (specifically, the seventh day in the week) is the first reality to which the First Testament relates holiness. The seventh day sets the other six into a context and helps people get them into perspective. It is a stopping day, a resting day and a day that marks God's people out. It is also a day that relativizes the importance of acquiring stuff and encourages the First Testament virtue of contentment. Tithing as a practice that relates to stuff corresponds to the practice of sabbath in relation to time; it both presupposes and fosters that virtue.

Holiness and Time

"Time in the modern world seems to be in short supply."[167] We might link this with the view that sees God as outside time, which problematizes time as an aspect of sinful human life. Time becomes secularized. This could not happen in Israel because Yhwh was closely involved with time on the macro scale (creation, promise, exodus, occupation of the land, monarchy, fall of

---

[163]Jon D. Levenson, *Resurrection and the Restoration of Israel* (New Haven, Conn./London: Yale University Press, 2006), p. x. See further Kevin J. Madigan and Jon D. Levenson, *Resurrection* (New Haven, Conn./London: Yale University Press, 2008).

[164]Levenson, *Resurrection and the Restoration of Israel*, p. 29.

[165]Ibid., pp. 108-22.

[166]Heschel, *Moral Grandeur and Spiritual Audacity*, p. 65.

[167]Michael S. Northcott, "Being Silent," in *The Blackwell Companion to Christian Ethics*, ed. Stanley Hauerwas and Samuel Wells (Oxford/Malden, Mass.: Blackwell, 2004), pp. 414-26; see p. 414.

the kingdoms, exile, restoration, the coming Day), on the micro scale (day, week, month, year, seven years, forty-nine years), and in connection with human lives (birth, maturity, senescence, death). "Modernity arises from the idea that the future is empty, up for grabs, and that collectively human beings make their own future and even the future of the planet."[168] The baptized version of this idea is that we are responsible to bring in or further God's kingdom. Israel assumed that God's reign depends on what God did at the Beginning and at the exodus, and on what God will do at the restoration and at the End. Every year its festivals reminded it that it lived in this theologico-temporal context. They made Beginning and End present realities. This means Israel has all the time in the world.[169] Sabbath gives weekly testimony to the fact that God could stop work, having ordered all things well,[170] and it links with the fact that in the land Israel enters into God's rest. Because God has completed that work, human beings can afford to take time for feasting, hospitality, the nurture of children and care for the sick and disabled.[171]

As holiness relates to places (such as sanctuaries and places where Yhwh has appeared), to people (such as priests) and to acts (such as sacrifices and sacraments), so it relates to time. Yhwh makes claims with regard to time as well as to place, people and acts.[172] Indeed, arguably the Bible is more concerned with time than with space, and "Judaism is a *religion of time* aiming at *the sanctification of time*."[173] The day of Yhwh is more important than the house of Yhwh. The temple was David's idea; the sabbath was God's. The first thing God made holy was time; the holiness of the sabbath preceded the holiness of anything, and the Decalogue mentions only holy time, not holy place.[174]

So the First Testament is very concerned about time, like the modern Western world, but it has a quite different way of looking at time.

> The importance of time is not its speed in reaching a goal, but its rhythm in relationship with objects in creation. Thus time highlights interrelationships in creation. . . . The ideal rhythm of time is woven into the pattern of creation, including day and night (Gen 1:3-5), sabbath (Gen 2:1-3), and months and years (Gen 1:14-19). These rhythms are not obstacles to be overcome by humans. On

---

[168]Ibid., p. 415, referring to William Schweiker, "Time as Moral Space," in *The End of the World and the Ends of God,* ed. Michael Welker and John C. Polkinghorne (Harrisburg, Penn.: Trinity Press International, 2000), p. 129.

[169]Cf. Northcott, "Being Silent," p. 418.

[170]Ibid., p. 420.

[171]Ibid., p. 420.

[172]Cf. Thomas B. Dozeman, "The Book of Numbers," in *The New Interpreter's Bible* 2:1-268 (Nashville: Abingdon, 1998), p. 229.

[173]Abraham Joshua Heschel, *The Sabbath* (New York: Farrar, 1984), pp. 6, 8.

[174]Cf. ibid., p. 79.

the contrary, human life is enriched when it corresponds to the temporal patterns of creation.

Achieving holiness involves conforming to the rhythm of creation.[175]

The moments of transition in time are then the moments of worship: the transition from night to day and day to night, from one week to the next, and from one month to the next, and the significant moments in the year in spring, summer and fall. At each of these moments "work is replaced by worship."[176]

The church's calendar largely ignores creation. The Liturgy of the Hours did so, and although morning and evening offices parallel the morning and evening sacrifices, they do not take place at dawn and twilight, and in any case they have largely been abandoned. Compline also suggests an instructive comparison and contrast as it replaces a creation-related rite by a personal or family-related rite that marks when we go to bed and does not relate to creation. The church's calendar ignores the months and replaces the sabbath by Sunday as a commemoration of Jesus' resurrection, disregarding the pattern of creation.[177] The First Testament and later Jewish faith harnessed the natural sequence of Massot, Pentecost and Sukkot to the commemoration of Yhwh's acts in delivering Israel, and in origin the Christological sequence of Advent, Christmas, Lent, Easter and Pentecost in part did that (for instance, Christmas took over a natural mid-winter festival). But for the most part the Christological sequence ignores creation. Ironically, in practice the natural sequence of New Year, Valentine's Day, Mother's Day, Father's Day and Harvest (not to say Halloween) means at least as much to Christian people as the Christological sequence, and even Easter and Christmas function as much as natural and family festivals as Christological festivals, or more so. Perhaps Israelites too were more aware of the significance of Massot, Pentecost and Sukkot in connection with the cycle of nature than in connection with the events of deliverance with which they came to be linked.

The Six Working Days

Humanity has a paradoxical relationship with the world and with work, and work arouses conflicting emotions in people. In the twenty-first century whole cultures are workaholic. Individuals' entire sense of being and counting comes from their work; innumerable people work at several part-time jobs simply to pay the rent and eat (not to say study at seminary).

---

[175]Dozeman, "Numbers," pp. 234-35.

[176]Ibid., p. 235.

[177]On the debate over whether the sabbath command still holds (and whether it is legitimate to see Sunday as the sabbath), see the illuminating study of Willard M. Swartley, *Slavery, Sabbath, War, and Women* (Scottdale, Penn.: Herald, 1983), pp. 65-95.

God commissioned human beings to subdue the world but also to serve the garden.[178] Psalm 8 marvels that "you made them rule over the work of your hands, you put all things under their feet"—domestic animals, creatures of the wild, birds, fish and other sea creatures (Ps 8:6-8 [MT 7-9]). Whatever this rule was designed to involve, it has not come about. No wonder creation groans for its redemption (Rom 8:22). But the psalm does not imply that we have lost the opportunity to fulfill Yhwh's vision or that it has an eschatological perspective or that it depends on the Messiah's coming. (When Hebrews 2:6-8 uses the psalm, it is using it to help us understand the significance of Jesus, not helping us understand the psalm itself.) The psalm looks with wonder at Yhwh's majesty, then continues to look with wonder at the commission Yhwh gave humanity. It invites us to take up with hope the commission Yhwh gave us at creation, reckoning that Yhwh still intends it to be fulfilled. Very obviously, at the least it commissions us to take a lead in not despoiling the earth, which Christian nations have been especially good at. As a fruit of God's liberation, "borne as with eagles' wings above the abyss" we are "delivered from indecision and set in action," because we know that all we have to do is undertake "the most immediate act of obedience," the immediate small next step.[179]

To put it another way (Gen 2), God's making the world was like a king's planting a farm or park or orchard, into which God put humanity to "serve" the ground and to "serve" and "look after" the estate, but also with the freedom to live off its fruit. Once again, humanity has authority over the animals (Adam names them), though it does not occur to Adam or Eve to eat them. But one of God's creatures and the fruit of a tree are their downfall. Noah is likewise overcome by the fruit of another tree (Gen 9:20-21). Genesis does not tell us whether anyone had warned him that the fruit of this tree could have such unfortunate consequences.

The working days and the stopping days are mutually interpreting; we understand each in relation to the other. During the first week, they had a linear relationship; first the working days, then the stopping day. That linear order might suggest the reflection that we do not rest in order to work, but work in order to rest.[180] The intended end state of the Israelites' liberation from Egypt was not freedom but rest.[181] While "the world was brought into being in the six days of creation, yet its survival depends upon the holiness of the seventh

---

[178]See §6.3 "Serving God's World."

[179]Barth, *Church Dogmatics* IV/3, ii:669, 670.

[180]Heschel, *Sabbath*, p. 14.

[181]Nicholas Wolterstorff, *Until Justice and Peace Embrace* (Grand Rapids: Eerdmans, 1983), p. 53.

day."[182] For subsequent humanity, the six days and the seventh have a dialectical relationship. Against the background of work we understand rest, and against the background of rest we understand work. It is against the background of the ordinary that we understand the holy, and against the background of the holy that we understand the ordinary. The practice of sabbath makes a difference to the other six days, not least because it makes us look at the world as God's and as good, and not, for instance, as to be treated as a mere impersonal thing, and it makes us think about and reevaluate work. This is not to downgrade the importance of work. Proverbs commends hard work and reckons it pays (e.g., Prov 10:4; 14:23; 19:15, 24). But "the Sabbath commandment demands the faith in God which brings about the renunciation of man, his renunciation of himself, of all that he thinks and wills and effects and achieves." It thus makes us free from ourselves and free for ourselves, in being absolved from the care of our work. It also makes us free for God, free to listen to God.[183]

Our work ultimately gets us nowhere (Eccles 1:2-11). Taken too seriously, it becomes toil (*'āmāl*) and it involves too much thinking things out and planning and striving (*ra'yôn*), and agonizing by night as well as by day (Eccles 2:22-23), and it generates the pointless ambition to achieve more or get more than someone else (Eccles 4:4). It is "achievement without production,"[184] or production without achievement. But if we do not have too high expectations of its effectiveness, we can start enjoying it (Eccles 2:24; 3:13, 22). This would make it especially appropriate to reckon that we work in order to rest rather than the other way around; and willingness to stop work for a day would be a sign that we do not take it too seriously. While the slothful starve, there is no need to go to the other extreme; it is better to have enough and relax than to strive after plenty (Eccles 4:5-6).

The Stopping Day

The sabbath is the one portion of time that Yhwh declares to be holy; indeed it is the only element within creation that Yhwh declares to be holy. It is the day Yhwh "stopped" (rather than "rested"; *šābat*) (Gen 2:2). It is "a sabbath of sabbath-ness,"[185] a total sabbath, a holy occasion, a sabbath for Yhwh, in all your settlements (Lev 23:3): not just in the sanctuary, and not just in the life of individuals. It is "the feast of creation." [186] To honor the sabbath is "to be in tune

---

[182]Heschel, *Sabbath*, p. 76.

[183]Barth, *Church Dogmatics* III/4:59, 60.

[184]Antonius H. J. Gunneweg and Walter Schmithals, *Achievement* (Nashville: Abingdon, 1981), p. 32.

[185]We do not know the precise significance of *šabbātôn*, but it certainly intensifies *šabbat*.

[186]Jürgen Moltmann, *God in Creation* (London: SCM Press/San Francisco: Harper, 1985), pp. 276-96.

with a God-intended temporal framework of creation. . . . Israel, in mirroring God's way of being on this day, sets aside one day when they attend not to their own responsibilities and freedoms . . . but to God's ordering of life."[187]

Because God has made the sabbath holy (Gen 2:3), therefore you must (Ex 20:8; Deut 5:12). It is meaningful for humanity, and meaningful for God.[188] Thus observing the sabbath is a basic obligation for Israel. "In sabbath is lodged the locus of ethical order."[189] That is so even in connection with work for Yhwh, as is emphasized at the close of the instructions for constructing the wilderness dwelling and at the opening of the account of their fulfillment (Ex 31:12-17; 35:1-3). Its infringement will not pay (Ex 16:27-29) and is very risky (Num 15:32-36). The sabbath command is the longest section in the Ten Words, partly because it seeks to eliminate possible loopholes in its requirement. Not only must the head of the house stop work; he may not ensure that work continues by having it done by other people, or even by an animal.[190] Perhaps there was some contentiousness about its observance, which may also be reflected in the variety of the First Testament's rationales for observing it.[191]

The basic one is that the sabbath belongs to Yhwh, like tithes or firstlings and first fruits or the holy place in the sanctuary. The seventh day is "a sabbath to Yhwh your God" (Ex 20:10; Deut 5:14). Israelites are therefore to remember (that is, be mindful of and therefore observe) the sabbath by keeping it holy (Ex 20:8) and treating it as belonging to God; it is off-limits. It is not merely a sabbath for you, for you to benefit from. It is for Yhwh. The way this expresses itself is that people are free to work for six days (the yiqtol verb is closer to giving permission than issuing a command) but are then to come to a total stop and not to do any work.

The first version of the Decalogue makes the link with creation. God worked for six days and then "rested," and therefore blessed the seventh day and made it holy. The meaning of "resting" (nûah) is likely not so different from that of "stopping":[192] it does not so much mean a positive enjoyment of relaxation as simply a kind of settling down or halting, as when Noah's ark rested on a mountain or the feet of the priests rested in the Jordan (Gen 8:4; Josh 3:13). The sabbath is a day when people are to stop doing things and stand still in recognition of the fact that this is the day Yhwh stopped doing things and stood still.

---

[187]Terence E. Fretheim, *God and World in the Old Testament* (Nashville: Abingdon, 2005), pp. 61, 64.

[188]Heschel, *Sabbath*, p. 53.

[189]William P. Brown, *The Ethos of the Cosmos: The Genesis of Moral Imagination in the Bible* (Grand Rapids/Cambridge: Eerdmans, 1999), p. 121.

[190]Cf. John I. Durham, *Exodus*, WBC (Waco, Tex.: Word, 1987), p. 289.

[191]Cf. §4.1 "Thinking Hermeneutically."

[192]Cf. Gnana Robinson, "The Idea of Rest in the Old Testament and the Search for the Basic Character of Sabbath," *ZAW* 92 (1980): 32-42.

The notion of blessing a day is a puzzling one. Blessing normally signifies either making someone or something fruitful or praising someone or something. Perhaps God makes the sabbath fruitful in the sense of making the person who observes it fruitful, though this risks a utilitarian attitude to the sabbath that stands in tension with its nonutilitarian point. Perhaps "by blessing the final day of creation, Yahweh assigns an ongoing, creative function to the sabbath."[193] Perhaps blessing the sabbath means making it a blessing.[194] Or perhaps God blesses in the sense of praises the sabbath because of enjoying what it brought, the sense of a task completed that it signified.[195]

> Israel has given the nations two archetypal images of liberation: the exodus and the sabbath. The exodus from slavery into the land of liberty is the symbol of external freedom; it is efficacious, operative. The sabbath is the symbol of inner liberty; it is rest and quietude. . . . They are the necessary complements of one another.[196]

Sabbath Rest

While Genesis 2:1-3 and the first sabbath command (Ex 20:8-11) do not seem to talk about the sabbath as a day of restfulness, the second sabbath command (Ex 23:12) requires householders to cease from work so that their animals may rest and that their servants may draw breath and find refreshment: it thus repeats *šābat* and *nûaḥ* but adds *nāpaš* (niphal). The animals thereby come into the enjoyment of God's rest and the servants likewise find refreshment as God did (so the third sabbath command, Ex 31:16-17).[197] The sabbath gives people freedom from their bosses and freedom from themselves. "God's rest on the seventh day thus becomes a holy commission for Israel equal to the 'great commission' of Genesis 1:28. Work and rest, rule and release find a constructive equilibrium in Israel's vocation, as they have in God's creation of the cosmos."[198]

The fourth sabbath command (Ex 34:21) refers to plowing and harvest, and thus suggests the natural idea that the original ban on work on the sabbath concerned the work of the farm. Exodus 35:3 adds lighting a fire, which might relate to the work of a craftsman (such as the construction of the wilderness dwelling will require) or to cooking. Later passages presume a reformulation

---

[193]Brown, *Ethos of the Cosmos*, p. 121.

[194]Moltmann, *God in Creation*, p. 281-83.

[195]On this meaning of *bārak*, see §1.2 "Honor."

[196]Moltmann, *God in Creation*, p. 287.

[197]The only other occurrence of *nāpaš* is 2 Sam 16:14, where David and his company stop to draw breath when on the run from Absalom.

[198]Brown, *Ethos of the Cosmos*, p. 87. (Brown brings together Gen 1:28 and Ex 31:17 partly on the basis that both belong to P).

and extension of that in terms of carrying loads, and buying and selling (Neh 13:15-22; Jer 17:19-27; Amos 8:5). The ban on cooking in Exodus 16:23 may relate only to the manna, and the punishment for collecting wood may also be situational (Num 15:32-36).

Like the version in Exodus 20, the Deuteronomic version of the Decalogue emphasizes that as householders rest *(nûaḥ)*, they are to also to make that possible for their households, which includes their servants. But it also adds yet another argument. They are to bear in mind that they and their people were servants in Egypt and Yhwh brought them out from there (Deut 5:12-15). It is not merely that servants and others may enjoy rest, but that looking at their servants resting on the sabbath reminds masters of what they were and of what Yhwh did for them. Whereas in Exodus 20 the object of "bearing in mind" is the sabbath itself, here it is that experience and that act, so that the sabbath serves the Deuteronomic concern for bearing in mind Yhwh's act of deliverance. Sabbath is an occasion for the exercise of faithfulness in the community as opposed to oppressing people.

There were special offerings on the sabbath (Num 28:9-10), and it was the kind of day when it might seem natural to consult a prophet (2 Kings 4:23), but it is not particularly a worship occasion, and in general "the priestly instructions for keeping the sabbath were not elaborate."[199] Proper observance of the sabbath will make proper worship possible, but sabbath and worship are not closely related. If people observe the sabbath by not working, Yhwh will ensure that the regular round of worship continues, but that regular round involves everyday events, festival occasions and occasional events; it does not focus on the sabbath. Sabbath is about the home, the household and hospitality.

Sabbath as a Marker

A particular belief or practice can be an indicator of whether the people of God stands or falls.[200] In terms of practices, for different reasons, in different contexts and for different groups, these beliefs or practices have included abstinence from alcohol or refusal to fight or opposition to abortion or opposition to/support for gay relationships. In Exodus the sabbath starts off life as one command among ten, and not at the top of the list, though it is empha-

[199]John G. Gammie, *Holiness in Israel* (Minneapolis: Fortress, 1989), p. 22. Niels-Erk A. Andreasen maximizes the worship aspect (*The Old Testament Sabbath*, SBLDS 7 [Missoula, Mont.: Society of Biblical Literature, 1972], pp. 141-50).

[200]*Articulus stantis et cedentis ecclesiae.* The phrase seems first to appear in the writings of Balthasar Meisner, who attributes it to Martin Luther as a description of the doctrine of justification by faith (so Arthur Carl Piepkorn, *The Sacred Scriptures and the Lutheran Confessions* [Mansfield, Conn.: CEC, 2007], p. 260).

sized in various ways. By the time we reach some of the Prophets, it has climbed near the top. When Israel was living cheek by jowl with the Canaanites, it would already be a marker that made the whole structure of their life different. For the Canaanites the new moon and the full moon were the key regular occasions. For Israel, the new moon had some significance but not the full moon, and the sabbath was far more important than either.

It gained even more significance in this connection during and after the exile. Isaiah 56:2 promises good fortune for the person who keeps the sabbath rather than treating it as just an ordinary day, as the community's neighbors did. This is counterintuitive. Not to trade on the sabbath seriously reduces opportunity to succeed in business. The prophet does not promise that people will do so well on the other six days that they will not lose out, in the manner of the Israelites in the wilderness who found enough manna on Friday to last two days. The exhortation does not even promise that people will do well enough, even if not as well as the most successful foreigners who are free to trade on the sabbath. It does promise, specifically to eunuchs and foreigners who accept this discipline, the joy of making their mark within the people of God and of participating in the worship of the temple (Is 56:3-8). Thus "Sabbath, identity and universalism go together after the return from exile."[201] There are more important, more worthwhile, and more joyful things in life than doing well; or rather doing well can profitably be redefined as having a different form of recognition of who they are.

In Amos's day there were people who hated the sabbath because it made them give up making a profit for a day—and, moreover, give up swindling people (Amos 8:4-5). In contrast, Isaiah 58:13-14 promises blessing for people who view the sabbath as something lovely or delightful or luxurious (ʿōneg). They do not pursue their own affairs on the sabbath but treat it as "my holy day." We are normally masters of our time, free to decide how to use it. "The Israelite is duty-bound, however, once every seven days to assert by word and deed that God is the master of time." Every seventh day Israelites renounce their autonomy and affirm God's dominion over them.[202]

For Jewish people living in contexts where they are outnumbered or otherwise under threat, the sabbath has indeed been an indicator whether the people of God stands or falls. If people are willing to keep the sabbath they will likely stay loyal to their faith and do the right thing in other ways. If they are not, they will likely yield in other ways. Or rather, if they fail to keep the sabbath, it becomes irrelevant what right or wrong they do in other respects.

---

[201]The title of an article by Bernard Gosse, *JSOT* 29 (2005): 359-70.
[202]Matitiahu Tsevat, *The Meaning of the Book of Job and Other Biblical Studies* (New York: Ktav, 1980), p. 48.

Keeping the sabbath is *the* marker of commitment to right and avoidance of wrong.

The whole of time is not the same and does not belong to us in the same way. In the Western world, the sabbath has also risen to great importance within God's commands. Observing the sabbath repudiates the 24/7 attitude. We have become aware of the frantic nature of our lives and know that sabbath confronts this and offers hope to us.[203] We know that as in Amos, a major hindrance to keeping sabbath is the felt need to make money and that we need to affirm that we need not work seven days because otherwise we will not have enough (Ex 16).

Contentment

There is thus a link between sabbath and wealth. Wealth is a monumentally attractive thing. The First Testament gives incidental testimony to this by comparing the value of wisdom with that of wealth (e.g., Job 28:18; Prov 16:16); this affirms its value as well as relativizing it.[204] "The connection between being a Christian [or an Israelite] and the way we own and use things" is "one of the knottiest questions imaginable."[205] Our possessions live close to who we ourselves are. Fear of a prosperity gospel leads Christians to downplay any link between godliness and material blessing, but the way the Scriptures speak means "there is really no option but to think that God's blessing is tied (but not limited) to material goods." The question then is whether we "hold our possessions in a way that bears witness to God's character," the character of the one who gives.[206]

After a command about the sabbath closes the more directly God-ward part of the Decalogue, a command about desire closes the more people-ward part. "You will not desire your neighbor's house. You will not desire your neighbor's wife or his servant or his maid or his ox or his donkey or anything that belongs to your neighbor" (Ex 20:17). Alternatively, "Nor will you desire your neighbor's wife. Nor will you long for your neighbor's house or his land, or his servant or his maid, his ox or his donkey, or anything that belongs to your neighbor" (Deut 5:21). It has been questioned whether *ḥāmad* actually refers to mere "desire" or rather to an intention to appropriate, but the main basis for this questioning lies in the conviction that the Decalogue simply

---

[203]Norman Wirzba, *Living the Sabbath* (Grand Rapids: Brazos, 2006).

[204]See Timothy J. Sandoval, *The Discourse of Wealth and Poverty in the Book of Proverbs* (Leiden/Boston: Brill, 2006), pp. 71-113.

[205]Johnson, *Sharing Possessions*, p. 1.

[206]Stephen Fowl, "Being Blessed," in *The Blackwell Companion to Christian Ethics*, ed. Stanley Hauerwas and Samuel Wells (Oxford/Malden, Mass.: Blackwell, 2004), pp. 455-67; see pp. 456, 466.

could not be concerned with desire.[207] One could almost see the Deutero-nomic version of the command with its adding of reference to longing (*ʾāwâ* piel) as designed to forestall that questioning. The command is concerned with desire. But of course desire does lead to action: "Do not give me poverty or riches, let me devour my appointed bread, so that I may not be full and renounce, and say 'Who is Yhwh,' or so that I may become poor and steal, and dishonor the name of my God" (Prov 30:8-9). Proverbs also emphasizes con-tentment in its "better than" sayings (e.g., Prov 15:16; 28:6). Qohelet's reason for agreeing is more down-to-earth. If you are a person like a king and can fulfill all your desires, you will find they yield only a huge emptiness (Eccles 2:1-11). People who love money cannot have enough money or are not satisfied with money or find that burdens come with it or lose what they work so hard to gain (Eccles 5:11-17 [MT 10-16]).

In itself desire or longing is a morally neutral instinct. God gave the first human beings trees with desirable fruit that becomes a metaphor for sexual desire or delight; God gave Israel a desirable land, and God's decisions about what we should do are desirable (Gen 2:9; Ps 19:10 [MT 11]; 106:24; Song 2:3). God feels desire (e.g., Ps 68:16 [MT 17]).[208] God likewise feels longings (Ps 132:13-14), and human longings may be fine (e.g., Ps 10:17; Is 26:8-9). The ques-tion is whether your desire or longing gets attached to things it is all right to desire or things that it is not (cf. Gen 3:6; also Prov 6:25; 21:25-26; Mic 2:2). De-sire thus parallels the related instinct of jealousy. A man or woman is prop-erly jealous of their spouse's commitment, and Yhwh is jealous of Israel's commitment. We are properly jealous for Yhwh's own sake. Yet Psalm 73:2-3 speaks of almost tumbling from the right path through being jealous of how well faithless people were doing in life. Their lives work out so well (in the short term, the suppliant eventually reaffirms), so it is tempting to worship their gods or adopt their (im)moral principles. Jealousy thus has the capacity to rot the bones (Prov 14:30). Given that *qinʾâ* can refer to passion more generally,[209] that aphorism may have passion in mind and not specifically jealousy; but Psalm 73:21-22 goes on to indicate that in any case, jealousy does rot the mind, generating bitterness, hurt, stupidity and aggressiveness to-ward God.

Genesis 13–14 notes the ambiguity of stuff. It starts from the enrichment of Abraham and Lot, which is what leads to there being a problem between them. Before we read of the trouble that issues from Sodom's faithlessness, we read of the way Lot's enrichment leads to his being captured; the four

---

[207]See Jackson, *Essays in Jewish and Comparative Legal History*, pp. 203-11.
[208]TNIV has "chose," but it is the same verb as in the commandment (cf. NRSV).
[209]See §6.1 "Faithfulness and Passion."

kings take the stuff from Sodom and Gomorrah, and they take Lot. And Abraham goes to recapture (1) Sodom and Gomorrah's stuff, (2) Lot and his stuff, and (3) the women and the rest of the people (Gen 14:11-12, 16). The king of Sodom is willing for Abraham to keep the stuff, but Abraham refuses to be enriched by the king. And Yhwh apparently responds by promising Abraham much stuff; Yhwh also promises that Israel will eventually leave Egypt with much stuff, as Abraham had (Gen 15:1, 14; cf. Gen 13:1-2). It will in due course become rather clearer that Lot had thought things through on the wrong basis when choosing land that was well-watered but was near Sodom, whose inhabitants were evil people, sinners against Yhwh (Gen 13:13). Moses later urges parallel considerations to the Israelites on the edge of the land (Deut 8:11-20). They will eat their fill there, build fine houses and multiply herds, flocks, and other wealth, but a number of dangers then threaten. They may ignore Yhwh in the sense of taking no notice of Yhwh's expectations of them. They may think they themselves are responsible for their achievements, as if it were not Yhwh who brought them there against all odds. They may start serving other gods; in the context, the implication would be that they seek other gods' help in connection with making sure they have enough stuff.

Making a "transition from the forcible domination of things to the free territory of man and the human" is another fruit of God's liberation of people; it is then only people that we care about, not things, not "machinery and gadgets."[210] Temperance is one of the four classic virtues.

Wanting

As the Decalogue ends by proscribing covetousness, Psalm 119:36 sets up a contrast between covetousness or "gain" and the heart's being inclined to Yhwh's declarations about how to live life. Leadership requires the sort of people who are not set on gain for themselves, which their position will enable them to pursue by dishonest means (e.g., Ex 18:21; Jer 6:13). The Decalogue's stance strikes at the heart of Western economies, whose functioning depends on covetousness, the habit of going shopping, the desire to acquire "stuff," the attitude the West has propagated elsewhere in encouraging globalization. In the West, dominated by commercialism, the indicator of being the church lies in refusal to go shopping.

> Shortly after World War II, a retailing analyst named Victor Lebow spoke all too prophetically. "Our enormously productive economy," he said, "demands that we make *consumption our way of life; that we convert the buying and selling of goods into rituals, that we seek our spiritual satisfaction,* our ego satisfaction, in consump-

---

[210]Barth, *Church Dogmatics* IV/3, ii:666, 667.

tion." What Lebow hoped for has come to pass.[211]

Rodney Clapp adds that this affects not only the way we live but (perhaps more insidiously) the way we think. The metaphor of the market (investment, choice) shapes the way we speak of family, marriage, friendship and church.[212] As a Christian economist, even Deirdre N. McCloskey, who wants to debunk the idea that capitalism is wrong and other such progressive notions, also wants to debunk Lebow. "It is not economic prudence to 'keep us all at work' by spending on luxuries and working, working, working."[213] And a reviewer of her work notes that all this soul- and body-destroying process produces is "a mountain of shabby, meretricious crap."[214]

"The empty self," which is "committed to the values of self-liberation through consumption . . . is the perfect complement to an economy that must stave off economic stagnation by arranging for the continual purchase of surplus goods."[215] The pursuit of the good is replaced by the pursuit of goods.[216] The division between rich and poor means that the poor are inferior and second-rate, and do not count, but arguably the rich are worse off. "Many passages in the Bible insist that the rich need to be concerned about themselves, for example about the soul that they are in danger of losing."[217] And even if I do not renounce Yhwh or steal, I may just end up poor: preoccupation with enjoyment, and specifically with wine and makeup, issues in poverty (Prov 21:17; 23:20-21). A person of integrity uses wealth in appropriate ways (lending it to people in difficulty) and gains it in appropriate ways (not by receiving bribes) (Ps 15:5). The First Testament is not big on frugality or self-denial in themselves, though it implies an approach to such questions while coming at them from another angle. It emphasizes indulgence in the context of generosity and hospitality, which imply self-denial and frugality; what one shares with others one is denying oneself. Psalm 112 combines observations about where wealth properly comes from and where it goes to. It issues from revering and obeying Yhwh. It issues in graciousness and compassion: "He spreads about, he gives to the poor; his faithfulness stands forever."

---

[211]Rodney Clapp, *Families at the Crossroads* (Downers Grove, Ill./Leicester, U.K.: InterVarsity Press, 1993), p. 57. For the quotation he refers to Alan Durning, "How Much Is Enough," *Utne Reader* July-August 1991, p. 73. The emphasis is Clapp's.

[212]See §4.2 "Safeguarding Faithfulness."

[213]McCloskey, *Bourgeois Virtues*, p. 460

[214]Eugene McCarraher, in *Books and Culture* 13/6 (2007): 37-41; see p. 39.

[215]Cushman, *Constructing the Self, Constructing America*, p. 6.

[216]Ibid., p. 68; see further pp. 73-90.

[217]Conrad Boerma, *The Rich, the Poor—and the Bible* (Philadelphia: Westminster, 1979) = *Rich Man, Poor Man—and the Bible* (London: SCM Press, 1979), p. 77.

Tithing as an Intuition

In substance, talk about tithing links with talk about stuff, while the Bible's actual way of speaking about tithing instructively parallels its references to sabbath. From Genesis to Malachi and on into the New Testament, tithing is a norm, but its significance is understood in a number of different ways. The practice hardly changes, but its aim and meaning are worked out anew in different contexts and connections. The implication would be that tithing remains a norm today, but that we may need to discern afresh what God wants to do through tithing.[218]

Tithing starts in Genesis 14 (translations vary over whether they use the word *tithe* or the word *tenth* for ma'ăśēr). Abram has gone off on that risky expedition to fight with forces that have taken Lot as a prisoner of war. He has returned not only with Lot but also with much plunder. Some of Abram's allies come to see him on his return, and one of them is the king of Salem, Melchizedek, who is also "priest of God Most High." He blesses Abram, and Abram gives him a tenth of his plunder. Genesis has not reported any specific divine instruction about tithing; like sacrifice in Genesis 4 and the leaving of the ground fallow in the sabbath year, tithing is not a special revelation from God but a human instinct or a part of general revelation.[219] Special revelation comes in due course in the way God harnesses these natural human instincts and instructs people to express them. Abram knows that tithing is a human thing to do, as faithfulness, love, justice, worship and prayer are human things to do. People are made that way. He can assume that this king of Salem understands this too. When God gives you something, you recognize where it came from by giving some of it back to God.

Tithing next appears in the story of Jacob (Gen 28:10-22). Jacob is on his way out of the land of promise, on the run from the brother whom he has swindled of his rights as firstborn. Yhwh appears to him and promises to keep him safe and bring him back to the land, and in response Jacob promises to tithe whatever Yhwh gives him. In light of the calculating nature of Jacob, "grabber" by name as well as by personality, it is tempting to read his commitment cynically: "if you are going to look after me and give me food and clothing and bring me back here in prosperity and peace, then you can be my God, and I will give you a tenth of all that you give me." Tithing can be a means of indulging in our instinct to calculate, a means of being selfish.

Yhwh's own first instructions about tithing (Lev 27:30-33) constitute a caveat about trying to evade the challenge of tithing. Tithing applies to produce

---

[218]For what follows, see John Goldingay, "Jubilee Tithe," *Transformation* 19 (2002): 198-205.
[219]On the Middle-Eastern background to tithing, see H. Jagersma, "The Tithes in the Old Testament," *OTS* 21 (1981): 116-28.

and to animals, and the way you tithe animals is by giving up every tenth animal that passes under the shepherd's staff. What happens if your best sheep happens to be the tenth? Can you substitute a less flourishing sheep for that one? No substitutions are allowed.

What happens to tithes? Numbers 18:21-32 gives one answer. Tithing is a means of seeing that the ministry is supported. Tithes go to the clan of Levi, whose task is to look after the services at the sanctuary. They have no land to work, so the tithe of the rest of the clans' work and land goes to them. "Underlying all the ancient Near Eastern sources dealing with the tithe is the notion of a tax that is indispensable for the maintenance of the temple and its personnel."[220]

Deuteronomy also affirms that tithes go to the Levites (Deut 12:1-19) but adds a special provision for every third year (Deut 14:22-29; 26:12-13). The calendar is thus divided into seven-year periods in which there are two "regular" years, a "third" year, two more "regular" years, another "third" year, then the sabbath year, after which the cycle starts again. In the "third" year, the tithes are to benefit not only Levites but also immigrants, orphans and widows, who are in the same position as Levites in having no land from which to gain their livelihood. (What are these needy groups supposed to do for the two intervening years? The way questions such as this arise with a number of the policies set forth in the Torah, not least the jubilee regulations, may show that these are once again more like God-given dreams than God-given policies. People have to work out how to realize the dream.)

The offerers themselves share in eating tithes (Deut 12:17-19; 14:22-29). In doing so they give concrete expression to their recognition that Yhwh owns the land and that it is Yhwh who has given them its produce. Eating it before Yhwh, they are enjoying the land as Yhwh intended. At the same time, they are subordinating themselves to Yhwh by going to the place Yhwh designates and by giving generously to their fellows, the Levites and the needy. They are embodying an awareness of the link between obedience and blessing. Indeed, "in bringing the tithe the offerers are actually enjoying the benefits which Yahweh had set before them."[221]

Reworking Tithing

Joshua-Kings refers only once to tithes, with some solemnity. If you insist on having kings, Samuel warns, you will pay for it, literally (1 Sam 8:15-17). Like the word for "offering," the word for tithe or tenth can have both a secular

---

[220]Jacob Milgrom, *Leviticus 23–27*, AB (New York: Doubleday, 2001), p. 2425.
[221]J. G. McConville, *Law and Theology in Deuteronomy*, JSOTSup 33 (Sheffield, U.K.: JSOT, 1984), p. 84.

and a religious meaning; it can denote a tax.[222] Kings will take a tithe of your grain and vines and sheep for their staff. Perhaps Samuel means they will appropriate the tithes that are due to the ministry and to the needy, or perhaps he means they will add a second tithe to the first, to pay for the cost of having a monarchic state. Either way it is an indication that tithing can be a means of the leadership oppressing ordinary people.

Unsurprisingly, there are indications in the First Testament that people often failed to tithe (e.g., Neh 13:10-12), but there is also a reminder that the practice of tithing can be a substitute for real commitment. Amos 4:4 implies that people were faithful in tithing as they were faithful in worship, but their giving was not matched by a commitment to faithfulness within the community. Some believers lived in fine homes, had good incomes and enjoyed a cultured life, but they thus benefited from the fact that the way society worked made other believers much more poorly off (e.g. Amos 5:11-13; 6:4-6). The well-off could afford to tithe and still be well-off, and thus their tithing had become one of the ways they avoided God's lordship of their lives.

Like Amos, Malachi also faults the people's tithing practice. Heavy with irony, Malachi 3:6-12 refers first to the consistency of Yhwh's relationship with Israel over the centuries. Perhaps Yhwh implies that people have been accusing Yhwh of failing to keep consistent faithfulness; they are not convinced that Yhwh has been relating to them in love, and they cannot see Yhwh acting with the decisive authority that is supposed to be a divine characteristic (Mal 1:2; 2:17). I have not changed in the way I relate to you, Yhwh declares. The very fact that you continue in existence is an indication of that. Israel has not come to an end, despite a consistency in its character that both compares and contrasts with Yhwh's. For generations (since the exile? since before the exile? since the beginnings of the people's history?) they have been consistent in ignoring Yhwh's expectations of them. Specifically, they have failed to bring their tithes and contributions. (The second word may refer to the "tithe of the tithe" that the tithe-recipients themselves offered.)[223] Their practice fits with what we know or infer about other areas of Yhwh's expectations. Sabbath years were not observed (cf. 2 Chron 36:21), debtors were not released after their six years of service (see Jer 34) and we have no record of the jubilee year ever being observed. No doubt people often experienced hardship as crops failed or the kings raised punitive taxes (and had more efficient means of collecting them than Yhwh employed), and it was hard to surrender so much to the temple.

Like Haggai and Zechariah, Malachi assumes that the worship of the sanc-

---

[222]Cf. Gary A. Anderson, *Sacrifices and Offerings in Ancient Israel* (Atlanta: Scholars Press, 1987), p. 81.
[223]See, e.g., Andrew E. Hill, *Malachi*, AB (New York: Doubleday, 1998), p. 306.

tuary matters. None of these prophets were priests, but all assume that expressing a relationship with Yhwh through the priestly system is an important aspect of the community's relationship with God. Failures in relationships with other members of the community earn Yhwh's disfavor, and failures in attitudes to Yhwh do the same.

Like Haggai in his talk about hardship and the building of the temple, Malachi reverses the cause-effect link between hardship and failure to tithe. The latter causes the former, not vice versa. In failing to tithe, people have been "cheating" Yhwh (*qābaʿ*). The rare verb uses the same root letters as the name Jacob (*ʿāqab*), the ancestor whom Yhwh mentions here, and thus generates a paronomasia with the root behind the name. Even the swindler Jacob was honorable in paying tithes and offerings; at least, he promises to offer them (Gen 28:22), though we hear nothing of his doing so. But this people's cheating means there is no food in Yhwh's house, which is not a direct deprivation for Yhwh but is a failure that makes the whole life, ministry and worship of the temple unviable. Even Jacob knew that paying tithes made sense; if God promises to give him so much, it is wise to pay a tithe back to hold God to that commitment.

Like Haggai, Malachi promises that keeping a commitment to the temple will make other things work out; withholding this commitment is actually short-sighted. Yhwh's making things work out is not merely an other-worldly, eschatological or spiritual matter. It relates to ordinary life. When Yhwh is involved, this becomes extraordinary life. The challenge to "test" (*bāḥan*) Yhwh is another irony. Testing God is usually an offense, it is the kind of thing that the "arrogant" do (Mal 3:15) or of course the doubting (Ps 95:9; also using *nāsâ*, Ps 106:14; Deut 6:16). "Go on, then, test me, if that is the kind of people you are" says Yhwh.

The process whereby the First Testament always assumes that people will tithe but keeps changing the way it sees the purpose of tithes invites the church to continue to tithe but to ask again what to do with tithes. There is no basis for saying that tithes must be paid to the church. Indeed, instead of using tithes to pay pastors and keep church buildings ambient, we might use them to offer nourishment, education, basic health care and health education for people in the Two-thirds World.

6.5 Insight

Much First Testament thinking about spirituality and character is expressed in the Wisdom books. Indeed, the word *ḥokmâ*, usually translated "wisdom," has been described as "coextensive" with our word "spirituality."[224] It denotes

---

[224]Knierim, *Task of Old Testament Theology*, p. 283.

the application of heart and mind, under the influence of the spirit, to living life in accordance with the way the world is and for the sake of what is good, in reverence for Yhwh and acknowledgment of Yhwh. This issues in discernment regarding how life works and mindfulness regarding what Yhwh has done and what Yhwh expects of us, but also in recognition of life's ambiguities and courage in facing doubt and questions.

The Wisdom of Human Experience

Wisdom thinking makes systematic use of the commonsense assumption that we learn from experience (or are wise to do so). We note how life works and live by what we learn. Wisdom thinking itself does that reflectively and systematically. It puts the emphasis "on the empirical evidence of Wisdom's effectiveness, on her earthiness and her full involvement in worldly affairs" as wisdom shapes the policies of nations and the lives of human beings in a way that can be "empirically verified."[225] "The wisdom practised in Israel was the response of a Yahwism confronted with specific experiences of the world. In its wisdom Israel created an intellectual sphere in which it could discuss the multiplicity of trivial, daily occurrences and also basic theological principles."[226] The fact that Wisdom is anchored in life and experience suggests that it would be a natural resource for women's spirituality insofar as "feminist spirituality is always anchored in life, that is, human experience, including women's experience."[227]

The aphorisms in Proverbs can give the appearance of being a collection of unrelated individual observations, yet Proverbs also hints that they are a whole. One pointer (though not one that claims too much) is that many are arranged so as to link with one another verbally or substantially. Another is the characterization of Wisdom as a person (Prov 8:22-31),[228] which goes beyond the personification of commitment or truthfulness elsewhere (e.g., Ps 89:14 [MT 15]) which affirms that God is personally committed and faithful; it implies the conviction that there is a unity and coherence about reality. Proverbs majors on the nature of this order, though it also recognizes paradox and questions; Job and Ecclesiastes major on the questioning of that order, though they do so in a longing or quest for its refinement.[229] Linking

---

[225]William McKane, *Proverbs* (London: SCM Press/Philadelphia: Westminster, 1970), p. 343.

[226]Gerhard von Rad, *Wisdom in Israel* (London: SCM Press/Nashville: Abingdon, 1972), p. 307.

[227]Silvia Schroer, "Wise and Counselling Women in Ancient Israel," in *A Feminist Companion to Wisdom Literature*, ed. Athalya Brenner (Sheffield, U.K.: Sheffield Academic Press, 1995), pp. 67-84; see p. 81.

[228]Cf. Michael V. Fox, *Proverbs 1–9*, AB (New York: Doubleday, 2000), p. 293.

[229]Rodney R. Hutton, *Charisma and Authority in Israelite Society* (Minneapolis: Fortress, 1994), pp. 190, 191.

personified wisdom with God then suggests how urgently God in person presses people to live by wisdom, to live in light of how things are. Our human quest to discover order corresponds to and even responds to God's promise that there is order.

Insight comes from reflection on experience. But our personal experience would be a narrow base on which to build our lives. In a therapeutic culture, such as the one that often prevails in the West, we do not question "the underlying ideology of self-contained individualism or the valuing of 'inner' feelings or the unquestioned assumption that health is produced by experiencing and expressing those feelings."[230] But by limiting ourselves to our present experience and assumptions, we condemn ourselves to a very limited ideology. "Those who cannot remember the past are condemned to repeat it,"[231] and for much of our "memory" of the past we are dependent on other people. The wisdom of the family and the community, past as well as present, and the wisdom of Israel, passes on to us what other people have learned, so that we do not need forever to reinvent the wheel.

Wisdom Passed On

In this connection Job's four interlocutors "are not straw men, set up just to be knocked down by Job's arguments. On the contrary, they represent the best thinking available at the time within the intellectual tradition of the sages."[232] That is true from the beginning of Eliphaz's argument, even though he buttresses it with the declaration that the message came to him in a vision at night, a spiritual experience when he found himself being asked questions about whether human beings can be in the right before God or more faithful than God (Job 4:12-17). Having made his affirmation (that trouble comes only to wrongdoers and that God's discipline is to be welcomed), he concludes his first address by bidding Job, "Now: we have investigated this—so it is; listen to it—you yourself, acknowledge it for yourself" (Job 5:27). Does Eliphaz mean he has investigated the question empirically? He implies at least that his view is open to such testing ("Think. . . . I have seen . . ." [Job 4:7-8]). Confronted by Job's declarations based on his experience, Eliphaz protests that it is ridiculous for Job to behave as if he is the first ever human being, one whose own wisdom goes back to the beginning of the human race; on the contrary, Eliphaz also affirms, his own teaching and that of his friends is based on wisdom passed down over the generations (Job 15:7-10, 17-18).

---

[230]Cushman, *Constructing the Self, Constructing America*, p. 2.

[231]George Santayana, *Reason in Common Sense*, vol. 1 of The Life of Reason (New York: Collier, 1962), p. 184.

[232]Joseph Blenkinsopp, *Sage, Priest, Prophet* (Louisville: Westminster John Knox, 1995), p. 52.

In principle he is right that it is at least risky to pit one's individual present experience against the corporate wisdom of the human race that has accumulated over the generations, as if one was the first person ever to try to think through a problem or to have a particular experience. C. S. Lewis suggested that every time one reads a new book one should re-read an old book to compensate for it.[233] Such a view especially confronts modern attitudes, where we behave as if we indeed reckon that nothing that was thought or said in the past is worth considering now. It also confronts the young adult's natural assumption (to be articulated by Elihu) that older people know nothing worth knowing. So Eliphaz puts together what he has heard (what the tradition teaches) and what he has seen (the way it has been proved in his experience, or the way it has been reaffirmed in the kind of visionary experience he refers to in Job 4:12-16).

If Eliphaz reckons to have tested his views empirically, one must comment that he must have turned his eye away from much contrary evidence. If he means his teaching has special authority because it came as a heavenly revelation in response to his seeking God, then Job and Ecclesiastes would agree that this argument also falls if his teaching fails to survive empirical testing. If he means he has investigated the accepted wisdom on the subject, and this is its conclusion, so much the worse for the accepted wisdom, Job and Ecclesiastes would agree.

But how can the accepted wisdom be wrong? Perhaps because everything depends on *whose* experience has been allowed to contribute to the tradition's formation.[234] That formation reflects questions about power. As the Psalms make clear, "innocent sufferers" become demonized and marginalized; their experience does not contribute to the tradition to which Bildad appeals (Job 8:8-10). But it does contribute to the form of the tradition that eventually appears in the Scriptures, which include the protest psalms and Job and Ecclesiastes. In appealing to the teaching that has been passed on through the generations, Bildad may have in mind the idea that this teaching goes back to primeval generations, but if so, the First Testament's own story subverts him. Its opening pages tell Cain and Abel's story, which conflicts with Bildad's claim that this teaching has always emphasized that God punishes the faithless and protects the innocent.

Inspired Wisdom

The trouble with Job, the friends reckon, is that he sets too much store by his

---

[233]See his introduction to Athanasius of Alexandria, *On the Incarnation* (Crestwood, N.Y.: St. Vladimir's Seminary, 1996), pp. 3-10; see pp. 3-4.

[234]Cf. Carol A. Newsom, "The Book of Job," *The New Interpreter's Bible* (Nashville: Abingdon, 1996), 4:317-637; see p. 405.

individual experience. The trouble with his friends, Job reckons, is that they do not set enough store by it in their emphasis on what doctrine says. "Yes, I could talk like you if you were in my place" (Job 16:4-5). I could pontificate about how life works. "If you were in my place." It makes all the difference. A major difference between Proverbs and Ecclesiastes, too, is that the latter refuses to be bound by the teaching of the tradition. What one can observe "under the sun" is what counts. Ecclesiastes is radically empirical.[235]

On the other hand, Elihu expostulates, age is no guarantee of insight. The test is a posteriori not a priori: is there insight in the content of the teaching? To Elihu it is self-evident that there is not much in the addresses of Eliphaz, Bildad and Zophar, and Yhwh will eventually agree (Job 42:7-8). Actually, Elihu believes, "it is the spirit in a person, the breath of the Almighty, that gives them understanding," and Elihu is compelled by the spirit inside him. He speaks as one whom the spirit of God made, one to whom the breath of the Almighty gives life (Job 32:8, 18; 33:4). So strong is this inner compulsion, Elihu declares, that there is no way he could hold in his thoughts; he would explode. And that is as well, because holding in his thoughts would involve a deference to Job's three friends that amounted to regard for human beings merely because of who they are; and God would punish that (Job 32:19-22).

Elihu may be expressing one of two different convictions; it makes sense to reckon that the unclarity over which one he intends is significant. He could be implying that the source of understanding is the "ordinary" human insight implanted in humanity through our creation. We are created in God's image, and God's breath is breathed into us; that is the source of our insight. Or he could be referring to a special activity of the spirit of God breathing insight into human beings on particular occasions. In the cases of Solomon and Daniel, wisdom is a divine gift not a human achievement (e.g., 1 Kings 3; Dan 1:17), and Proverbs 2:6-11 generalizes the point.[236]

Either way, Elihu implies the rather Western conviction that the test of whether we have something to say is the strength of feeling that lies inside us. We feel deeply moved. That proves it. It is a common human experience to sense that we did not ourselves generate an insight we have—it "came to me."

The point is embodied in references to dreams and visions, which appear (perhaps surprisingly) quite prominently in connection with Wisdom thinking. Thus the First Testament's first wise man (Gen 41:33, 39) is a dreamer and a dream interpreter (Gen 37; 40–41). Solomon, the great embodiment and

---

[235]Cf. Michael V. Fox, *A Time to Tear Down and a Time to Build Up* (Grand Rapids/Cambridge: Eerdmans, 1999), pp. 75-77; Tomáš Frydrych, *Living Under the Sun*, VTSup 110 (Leiden/Boston: Brill, 2002), pp. 71-72.

[236]The same is true of practical skills, also called *ḥokmâ*, in, e.g., Ex 28:3; 31:3, 6.

patron of wisdom, experiences Yhwh appearing to him in a dream, in which he then asks for the gift of wisdom. "Solomon awoke: and it had been a dream" (1 Kings 3:15). In Western thinking that would mean "it was only a dream." In First Testament thinking its being a dream means it really came from God and would come true, as it then does. Elihu makes the same appeal (Job 33:15).

Clarity and Ambiguity

The expression of wisdom in Proverbs comes in the form of *měšālîm*. The conventional translation "proverbs" is unsatisfactory, but there is no English word that corresponds better to the word's significance.[237] While quite a number of the *měšālîm* are proverbs, straightforward, punchy, practical aphorisms summing up an insight about life, much of Proverbs is not. To begin with, Proverbs 1–9 comprises homilies of ten verses or more, not aphorisms, though their content is often less down-to-earth than at first seems to be the case. They speak about wisdom, sexual faithfulness and religious faithfulness, and do so rather ambiguously and allusively, and in the process speak lyrically about God's work of creation. Further, the aphorisms that dominate the rest of the book sometimes sum up an insight in a transparent way, but sometimes stimulate thought rather than making thought unnecessary: "The heart knows its own bitterness, and in its joy no one outside can share"; or "even in laughter the heart may suffer, and pain is the end of joy"[238] (Prov 14:10, 13). Elsewhere in the First Testament *māšāl* can refer to discourses such as Balaam's or Ezekiel's (e.g., Num 23:7; Ezek 20:49 [MT 21:5]) that by their nature are figurative and puzzling; the EVV use words such as *oracle* and *allegory*.

So the wisdom of Proverbs is not as straightforward as the word *proverb* suggests. Indeed, the opening statement of the book's purpose hints at this, as the sayings exist "for understanding a proverb and a mystery, the words of the wise and their enigmas" (Prov 1:6). Even if we start from the fact that *māšāl* can denote a straightforward aphorism, the neat structure of this line points up the nonstraightforward aspect to wisdom. Both cola begin with harmless-looking references to ordinary sayings (proverbs and the words of the wise) but go on to point up the way the book deals in mysteries and enigmas (*mělîṣâ, ḥîdâ*). For *mělîṣâ*, DCH offers translations such as "figure," "allusive saying" and "trope." For *ḥîdâ*, it suggests "riddle," "obscure saying" and "problem." This fact is itself a parable of the way First Testament wisdom recognizes the ambiguity and complexity of life. In Israelite Wisdom "there is no attempt to achieve a theoretical, self-contained picture of the world" or of

---

[237]On the meaning of *māšāl*, see, e.g., McKane, *Proverbs*, pp. 22-33.
[238]In Mt this last colon is even more enigmatic: lit., "its end joy pain."

human nature, "but, rather, a notable caution with regard to comprehensive attempts at explanations; in contrast to this, there is an unfinished and unfinishable dialogue about man and world."[239]

The opening of Proverbs thus sets up the expectation that its teaching will be of practical use but also that it will want to help people face the enigmatic side to life. It combines straightforward teaching with reflection that recognizes mystery and depth, as do the Torah and the Prophets. That opening declaration leads into its explicitly setting its practical advice in the context of attitudes to Yhwh: "The beginning/first principle of knowledge is reverence for Yhwh" (Prov 1:7). While that statement appears elsewhere in different formulations, its location here after the comment about mystery and enigma is suggestive. It points to the awareness that becomes explicit in different ways in Ecclesiastes and Job, that wisdom recognizes limits to our understanding and bows in submission and trust before God in connection with our grasp of the big questions to which we would like to know the answers but do not.[240]

Thus Proverbs can urge people to "acquire" wisdom and discernment (Prov 4:5, 7), yet Job 28 can declare that the source of wisdom and understanding is quite hidden from humanity (Job 28:20-27). This is an appropriate reflection at the end of the fruitless debates between Job and his friends, which have shown that no one in the debate actually knows the principles on which God relates to someone like Job. One implication of this clash is that there is a form of wisdom and discernment that can be acquired, but another form that God has declared off-limits.

Faith and Doubt

The Scriptures' ambiguity can amount to contradiction.

> Do not answer stupid people in accordance with their foolishness,
> lest you too become like them.
> Answer stupid people in accordance with their foolishness,
> lest they be wise in their own eyes. (Prov 26:4-5)

This pair of sayings appears in the Talmud's discussion of contradictions in Scripture, which are said to have led to the sages' attempts to "hide" Ezekiel and Ecclesiastes as well as Proverbs. The term (*gānaz*, from which comes the word for a storeroom for old scrolls, *gĕnîzâ*) will refer to attempts to render them effectively de-canonical, like Luther's stance in relation to James, rather than implying that the community is still discussing whether they should

---

[239]Von Rad, *Wisdom in Israel*, p. 318.
[240]Philip Jenson suggests to me that the relative prominence of dreams and visions in Wisdom is a sign of Wisdom's acknowledging its limits.

become canonical. The Talmud's own stance is to seek to reconcile differences within the books or between them and the Torah; in this case it argues that the first proverb relates to matters of learning, the second to general matters.[241] But the sayings themselves refer to no boundaries of that kind and more likely their juxtaposition makes explicit a feature that recurs in Proverbs and elsewhere. There are few rules for life that always work. Both sayings express wisdom. Insight involves the discernment to see when to apply the first saying, when to apply the second.

Wisdom may be no use to people, if they lack that discernment. "Legs hang down from someone lame, and so does a proverb in the mouth of stupid people" (Prov 26:7). (The saying is clear enough, though hurtful to the handicapped; my wife's legs hang down useless like that. But much of Scripture is hurtful to someone—to women or the blind or the deaf. In inspiring Scripture, God was willing to risk that in order to get a point home to people in general.) Furthermore, "A brier comes into the hand of a drunk, and so does a proverb in the mouth of stupid people" (Prov 26:9). This saying is more allusive. Perhaps the brier is in the drunk's hand as a weapon, and Scripture on the lips of a stupid person can do much harm, as church history clearly shows. Or perhaps the brier is in the drunk's hand because he has fallen against it or grabbed hold of it and it has hurt him, and Scripture on the lips of a stupid person can likewise do them much harm.

The *nābāl* says "God is not here" and behaves accordingly (Ps 14:1). He says it not merely with his lips but in his heart. The statement sums up his deepest convictions, the well-spring that drives his life. It does not imply a denial that God exists; this strange view has not been within the purview of most societies. Rather, he believes God sticks to heaven. As far as earth is concerned, God can be discounted. It is the attitude the Rabshakeh expressed to Hezekiah (2 Kings 18:29-30). While the *nābāl* is a fool, the opposite of someone who shows insight, he is also a scoundrel, someone who makes a point of acting in a corrupt way rather than a good way and avoids seeking help from God (Ps 14:2). He assumes he can and must fix things himself and that in doing so he can safely leave moral considerations out of account.

The scoundrel and the psalmist are both clear that insight and morals go together. The scoundrel has one set of theological convictions (God is in heaven and is not involved here) and moral convictions (we can do what we like and we must take responsibility for our destiny). The psalmist has a different set of theological convictions (God is in heaven and is also involved here) and moral convictions (we do what is good and we seek help from God; the only "plan" we have is to make God our refuge).

---

[241]*b. Shabbat* 30b.

In the Western world it does not work like that; many atheists are moral, and many believers do not think God is at work in the world and do think they need to fix things. In the First Testament, too, believers often question whether God is at work in the world, though they do so more openly than Western believers. Indeed, protest, questioning and doubt feature more prominently in the First Testament than they do in the surrounding cultures and religions.[242]

The Freedom to Question and Face Facts

Job and his friends trade accusations that each other's words are mere *rûaḥ*, mere wind, no more substantial than breath (Job 6:26; 15:2; 16:3). In response to the first such comment, Bildad begins his address to Job by asking, "How long will you say such things, with the words of your mouth a powerful wind?" (Job 8:2). For all their windy quality, he recognizes that they have been very powerful. Indeed, describing them as a "powerful" wind *(kabbîr)* takes us back to the "great" wind that destroyed Job's son's house (Job 1:19). They have the destructiveness of powerful waters (Is 17:12; 28:2). They are destructive, because they threaten to bring down the edifice comprising the teaching of Israel's sages with the authority that attaches to something handed down and proved by generation after generation of people since the earliest times who have experienced God at work in their lives (Job 8:8-10). Bildad goes on to affirm how at the center of this teaching is the conviction that God makes decisions about people's lives in a faithful way, protecting the innocent and upright and putting down the faithless. Job's claim that God has undeservedly attacked him subverts that edifice. Indeed, as Bildad shrewdly expresses it, it undermines not merely the particular convictions of the sages, but the central conviction of mainstream First Testament faith that God is characterized by an exercise of authority in doing right by people, by *mišpāṭ* and *ṣedeq* (Job 8:3).

The conclusion to Ecclesiastes (Eccles 12:9-14) is expressed in the third person, suggesting it was written by someone other than "Qohelet" himself—though scholars have been known to refer to themselves in the third person. It begins by describing him as a *ḥākām*, a man of wisdom and insight, who "taught the people knowledge. He listened to, investigated and arranged many sayings. He sought to find pleasing words, and what was written was upright and words of truth."

But the general cast of these words of truth is very different from that of the ones in Proverbs. Qohelet's blurb writer thus adds that the words of peo-

---

[242]Robert Davidson, *The Courage to Doubt* (London: SCM Press, 1983/Philadelphia: Trinity Press International, 1989), p. 209.

ple like him are like goads. They pierce painfully into the thinking of the person who hears them and make this person say ouch, but because they express truth they are able to spur the person on. They are also like nails or pegs—perhaps another way of expressing their painfulness (if you are the wood into which they are driven), but perhaps an assurance that one can safely hang one's life on them. That would link with the further reassurance that they were given by one shepherd, which the JPSV and TNIV's margin assume denotes Yhwh as Israel's unique Shepherd. This human teaching is of divine origin.

"Beyond these," the blurb comments, "beware," and adds the seminarian's favorite half-verse, "there is no end to the making of many books, and much study is a wearying of the flesh." In the context the comment concerns not the writing and reading of books in general but the particular role and effect of a book like Ecclesiastes. One such book in the Scriptures is a gift from God, but if the Scriptures were full of books like Ecclesiastes, we would be in trouble. To safeguard the point further the blurb adds that when all is said and done, what counts is revering God, keeping his commands in the awareness that "God brings every deed to account, including every hidden thing, whether good or bad." It is one of the convictions that Qohelet himself finds uncomfortably evidenceless. "The whole of life at best is mystifying and enigmatic."[243] There is no point putting huge effort into trying to get the big picture, to solve the ultimate philosophical questions. It just makes you sad and angry (Eccles 1:12-17; 2:12-17).

Job asks questions because of the grim nature of what has happened to him in particular. Qohelet gives no indication that anything grim has happened to him, nor are his gloomy observations an indication that he is clinically depressed. He is simply appalled because of what he sees in the world (that is doubtless true of the author of the book of Job, but within the book, the questions arise from this individual's own experience). He speaks as a qōhelet, a member of the qāhāl; he (or she, as the word is feminine) is usually reckoned to be a representative of it, a teacher or preacher. But what he does is ask questions about its faith, questions to which he does not have the answers. This is not what preachers or teachers are supposed to do. They are supposed to offer people the reassurances that they allegedly want to hear, the kind of reassurances that Job's friends offer. Qohelet declines to fulfill people's expectations. He asks questions and leaves them floating in the air. Or he asks questions and leaves us with uncomfortable answers (Eccles 1:3-11).

[243]Brueggemann,, *Theology of the Old Testament*, p. 395.

Reflection

In terms of a possible First Testament perspective on virtues, Proverbs might suggest "prudence" in the form of purposefulness *(mĕzimmâ)* or discernment *(bînâ)* or shrewdness *('ormâ)*.[244] It is not only a concern in Proverbs. The collection of Hosea's prophecies comes to a close with a rhetorical question asking whether anyone is discerning enough to reflect on all we have read in this book and to acknowledge its truth (Hos 14:9 [MT 8]). After all, it goes on to suggest, there are some clear lessons emerging from a consideration of the book. First, Yhwh is a sure guide to right paths. The people who have preserved Hosea's message have recognized in them a description of those right paths. It then comments that the faithful walk in them, which may seem like a tautology, but the final colon, "while rebels fall on them," suggests it is not. The antithesis to "walking" is not "deviating" but "falling." People who follow the path that Yhwh indicates to be the right one find it is safe and secure. It leads somewhere. They walk tall in it. One might have expected this last colon to declare that rebels walk on a different path and thus fall. Instead, it declares that the path that is a way to life for the faithful is for rebels like one riddled with potholes that make them fall over.

The answer to the question "Who is discerning so as to reflect on these things, who is reflective so as to acknowledge them?" might be "No one." No one is discerning enough to understand this book, a reflection that commentators have echoed.[245] No one is discerning enough to see how its promises can come true. No one is submissive enough to acknowledge the truth of its account of life with Yhwh, by living by it. But the line that follows puts a question mark by such a gloomy inference. The faithful do walk in them.

The sensible person will thus keep reflecting on this teaching of Hosea's. As Israel's wisdom teaching itself keeps implying, to those who have will more thus be given. The wise are people whose wisdom makes them open to growing in wisdom. The stupid are people not open to reflection who thus shrink. But there is something else. It might be possible to reflect but then do nothing. Discernment needs to generate reflection; reflection needs to proceed to acknowledgment, a recognition that affects life.

"It was not with our ancestors/parents that Yhwh sealed this covenant but with us ourselves here today, all of us, alive" (Deut 5:2-3). The sentence sets up the contrast sharply, as scriptural rhetoric sometimes does when it means "Not so much this as that" or "not only this but that" (e.g., Hos 6:6). Further, *'ăbōtênû* can be read in several ways. Yhwh did not seal the cove-

---

[244]Davis, "Preserving Virtue," pp. 183-201.
[245]Cf. G. I. Davies, *Hosea* (London: MarshallPickering/Grand Rapids: Eerdmans, 1992), pp. 310-11.

nant just with Israel's ancestors, Abraham, Isaac and Jacob, but with their descendants. Yhwh did not seal the covenant just with the parents of the generation on the edge of the land but with that generation itself, the people who did not die in the wilderness but who are still now alive. Yhwh did not seal the covenant just with the first generations of Israel (either the exodus generation or the generation that entered the land) but with the succeeding generations, people in David's or Josiah's or Ezra's day. The covenant permanently bound Yhwh to Israel. It is as if the generation about to enter the land or the generation that hears Deuteronomy read was actually present when Yhwh sealed the covenant in Genesis 15 or Genesis 17 or Exodus 34. "Face to face Yhwh spoke with you on the mountain from the midst of the fire," Moses goes on (Deut 5:4), pushing the rhetoric to its limits and beyond. It is as if the generation about to enter the land was there at Sinai, but the entire logic of their being the people about to enter the land depends on the fact that they were not there at Sinai, otherwise they would be dead. Yet the fact that Yhwh reconfirmed and resealed the covenant with *Israel* at Sinai means that in effect they were there.

The logic reappears in Deuteronomy 6:20-25. Parents are to explain to their children the meaning of the commitments they accept, and they will do so by describing what Yhwh had done "before our eyes." By definition, the generation that speaks was not alive to see these events. But through hearing the story, it is as if they were there. Thus for the children to whom they speak, they model the possibility of having been in effect there.

Mindfulness

Yhwh's commands are the key to understanding (Ps 119:98-100, 104). "Christian meditation is not transcendental meditation. It is meditation on an object."[246] Such meditation or mindfulness or active remembering is key to First Testament spirituality. Memory is the way we make sense of things, the way the community of faith orders the world.[247] Remembering and forgetting are not acts that are out of our control; the Hebrew words suggest being mindful and putting out of mind.

What are the Israelites supposed to remember? They are not to forget the things they saw (Deut 4:9). This might refer to the things they saw at Sinai, such as the blazing flame and the dark cloud that suggested but hid Yhwh's presence and pointed to the fact that Yhwh could not be imaged. Or it might refer to the things they saw at Baal-peor, when Yhwh wiped people out for

---

[246]Jürgen Moltmann, *The Spirit of Life* (Minneapolis: Fortress, 1992), p. 203.
[247]Mary Katharine Deeley, "Memory and Theology," in *Reading the Hebrew Bible for a New Millennium,* ed. Wonil Kim et al. (Harrisburg, Penn.: Trinity Press International, 2000) 1:108-20; see p. 108.

following Baal (Deut 4:3, 11). Certainly they are urged at length to remember and not to forget (it is the only occasion when Moses combines these words) the long story of their defiance of Yhwh from the time they left Egypt, at Sinai and through the wilderness, which means that their being given the land does not reflect their deserve but the faithlessness of its current occupants (Deut 9:4-7). They are to remember their wrongdoing, even though Yhwh forgets it. They are to remember what Yhwh did to Miriam as a chastisement (Deut 24:9).

They are to remember the way along which Yhwh led them through the wilderness in which Yhwh humbled them to test them (ʿānâ piel, nāsâ piel; JPSV "test you by hardship") to discover whether they would live in obedience (and always provided for them) (Deut 8:2). They are to remember that Yhwh trains or disciplines them (yāsar) as parents do their children (Deut 8:5). The JPSV and NRSV go on, "therefore keep the commandments," implying that this discipline would be a response to disobedience, but the "therefore" represents a mere w ("and"), and the TNIV more plausibly takes the discipline to refer to what Yhwh has been doing with them in giving them a tough time in the wilderness to train them in this reliance, and not merely to chastise them for their failure. It is not that disobedience issues in discipline but that discipline issues in obedience. They are not to forget the covenant that Yhwh sealed with them that forbad the making of any divine image (Deut 4:23). They are to remember what Yhwh did to the Pharaoh, so as to be encouraged to believe Yhwh can deal with future foes (Deut 7:18). They are to remember what Amalek did in attacking the weary and thus showing no reverence for God, and be agents of Yhwh's punishment of them (Deut 25:17-19).

They are to remember that they were servants in Egypt, and therefore be encouraged to be merciful to their own servants and let them observe the sabbath and take part in festivals, to release them with generous provision when they have completed their period of service, and also to be fair and considerate to the vulnerable (Deut 5:15; 15:15; 16:12; 24:18, 22). When they have cities, land and food, they are not to forget Yhwh as the one who brought them out of the household of servants—not, interestingly, as the one who gave them these gifts (Deut 6:10-13); land can be "the enemy of memory. . . . Guaranteed security dulls the memory."[248] They are not to forget Yhwh and serve other gods; Yhwh must be the object of their reverence and service, and the one by whom they swear, rather than other deities (Deut 8:19-20).

---

[248]Walter Brueggemann, *The Land* (Philadelphia: Fortress, 1977/London: SPCK, 1978), p. 54; cf. J. G. McConville, *Law and Theology in Deuteronomy*, JSOTSup 33 (Sheffield, U.K.: JSOT, 1984), p. 85.

They are to come to acknowledge that they do not live by bread alone but on the basis of what Yhwh says (Deut 8:3). The statement is another allusive one. It could remind them that they live because of their obedience to what Yhwh says, or because living depends on Yhwh's promises and/or on Yhwh's decision and that merely having bread does not guarantee it, or because Yhwh's word can mysteriously keep them alive even if they have no bread, or because Yhwh's word can commission other forms of food than regular bread, such as the manna, or because it is quite possible to live on simple things such as manna if that is what Yhwh decrees.

They are to worship Yhwh their God for what they receive (Deut 8:10). They are not to forget Yhwh and give up their obedience when they are doing well in the land; they are to remember that it is Yhwh who gives them the power to get wealth, not their own capacity to do so; they are not to let their minds get lofty (Deut 8:11-18). They are to retell their story as a people (Deut 26:5-9), and on their arrival in the land they are to set up there stones inscribed with the words of Moses' teaching, and to proclaim them in the people's hearing (Deut 27:1-14). They are to proclaim them before the whole people at Sukkot every seventh year and to put a copy beside the covenant chest, "as a witness against you" (Deut 31:10-13, 26).

As an aid to such mindfulness, Israelites are to make fringes on the corners of their garments as reminders of Yhwh's commands (Num 15:37-41). The commemorations of the exodus will serve as a sign on people's hands and a reminder or a headband on their foreheads (Ex 13:9, 16). Yhwh's commands are to be put on people's minds and hearts, bound as a sign on their hands, serving as a headband on their foreheads, and inscribed on their doors and city gates (Deut 11:18-20; cf. Deut 6:9). In isolation one might reckon that these expressions are figurative in Exodus 13 and Deuteronomy 11 but literal in Deuteronomy 6. Literally or metaphorically, people thereby remind themselves who they are (the exodus people) and what obligations they accept. Yet one cannot see one's own headband; it is more visible to other people. And the house door and the city gate also speak to other families and other communities about the nature of one's commitment. There is a place for the private (Mt 6:1-18) and a place for the publicly visible (Mt 5:14-16).

6.6 Speech

Spirituality involves careful attention to speech—to what we speak and what we listen to. Words are powerful things. They can be both life-giving and death-dealing. We are often wise to be sparing with them. Paradoxically, however, reproving and painful words can be means to life. Much depends on the relationship of which they are part, which also affects the First Testament's attitude to when we owe people the truth.

Life-giving Words

"The mouth of the faithful talks insight, their tongue speaks with authority; their God's teaching is in their heart, their feet do not waver" (Ps 37:30-31). Mouth and tongue stand between heart and feet. Ideally speech combines insight and authority; it does so if Yhwh's teaching is written into the mind. A mark of commitment to Yhwh's teaching and expectations is to talk about them: "With my lips I have proclaimed all the decisions of your mouth" (Ps 119:13). Of course there is such a thing as lip service, and proclaiming what God has laid down that we should do does not in itself prove anything. But in more healthy contexts, taking things on our lips means they become part of us; when other people have heard us say these things, it becomes shameful to do something other than what we have said. We "murmur" Yhwh's orders or laws or teaching or word (Ps 119:15, 23, 48, 78, 148); *śîaḥ* suggests strong feelings outwardly expressed.[249] In Psalm 119:97-100, the context indicates that the murmuring relates to the way this teaching endows wisdom others do not have, so that we murmur about the "wonders" of it. Murmuring to oneself or to other people or to Yhwh about it is a mark of commitment to it. "The yawning chasm that separates the wise from the foolish is reflected by their verbal performance. . . . Authentic discourse . . . reflects the unity of beauty and truth."[250] Speech can be death-dealing, and when it involves reproof and correction can be painful even when it is designed to be constructive, but it is designed to be life-giving, a means of blessing.

"There is joy for a person in a response from someone's mouth, and a word at the right moment—how good it is!" (Prov 15:23). When people ignore us, taking no notice of our questions, contributions to a discussion, pleas or ideas, we feel hurt. Conversely, when we have said nothing but need someone to reach out to us with an idea or an encouragement—"how good it is!" "Gracious words—a honeycomb, sweet to the taste and healing for the body" (Prov 16:24). The proverb invites us to imagine the sweetness of the honey being savored on the lips, sliding down the throat and spreading its healing power around the body as a whole. The EVV have "sweet to the soul"; in connection with the image of eating, "taste" makes sense for *nepeš*,[251] though the translation "soul" does bring out how pervasive is the effect of gracious words. They refresh the whole person.

The mouth can speak truth, wisdom and reverence for God, and thus bring life to the individuals it addresses, to the community and to its owner. It can also speak deception, stupidity and godlessness, and thus be destructive of

---

[249]Cf. the comments on *hāgâ* in §2.1 "Delighting in Yhwh."
[250]Brown, *Ethos of the Cosmos*, p. 303.
[251]Cf. BDB, p. 660.

other people, the community and oneself (Prov 10:18-21). "A soft response turns away fury, but a painful word arouses anger" (Prov 15:1). Oddly, while we may be inclined sometimes to speak toughly, we do not like being on the receiving end of tough talk. Perhaps one background factor is the ambiguity in the expression "painful word." The pain is that caused to the word's recipient, but the phrase could also refer to the pain felt by the speaker; painful words often issue out of pain and then cause more pain.[252]

A parallel ambiguity attaches to the verbless declaration, "the healing/ gentleness [marpē'] of the tongue—a tree of life, but crookedness in it—a crushing in the spirit" (Prov 15:4). Crookedness in the tongue can generate crushing in the spirit of the person to whom one speaks, but also in the spirit of the one who speaks; and it can reflect already existent crushing in the spirit of the speaker.[253] The meaning of marpē' seems sometimes to link more with rāpâ ("heal"), sometimes more with rāpā' (sink, relax).[254] Sometimes both meanings make sense, and readers may have been expected to infer both rather than assuming that there were two different words. Here, one's first insight is that the tongue can be a means of healing and thus of life. The aphorism makes a point that is the converse of the earlier observation about a harsh word arousing anger (Prov 15:1). While speech can injure people and injure relationships, it can also heal them. Its effect can be like that of the healing balm that comes from some trees. But the second colon with its reference to crookedness makes one reconsider another aspect of the meaning of the first, since crookedness of speech arguably makes for a better parallel with gentleness or restraint. Exercised with gentleness or restraint rather than crookedness, the tongue brings healing and thus life rather than crushing someone's spirit. That may even be the case when the tongue says something tough, if it says it with gentleness. It is unlikely that the proverb implies that such crookedness merely crushes the inner person. If the "spirit" here were the nepeš, we might reckon it denoted the person as a whole, but it is actually rûaḥ, which points more to the person's energy and dynamism.

Death-dealing Words

So speech is both life-giving and death-dealing, and not only to other people. "The mouth of the faithful is a fountain of life," while "the mouth of a fool is imminent ruin" (Prov 10:11, 14). The mouth has extraordinary significance. "Those who guard their mouths guard their lives; those who open their mouths wide—it is ruin for them" (Prov 13:3).

"The person who goes about as a slanderer/informer/trader [rākîl] reveals

---

[252]Cf. Van Leeuwen, "Book of Proverbs," p. 148.
[253]Cf. Davis, Proverbs, Ecclesiastes, and the Song of Songs, p. 98.
[254]See HALOT.

secrets; do not associate with anyone who has a big mouth" (Prov 20:19). We do not know the precise connotation of *rākîl*, but the idea is clear enough. There are people whose inclinations or lives take them from one place and one person to another, and who pick up information and dispense it as they go. They thus become attractive sources of information, but there is a price to pay; your own secrets will be the subject of their conversation tomorrow.

The people who are welcomed to spend time with Yhwh are those who "have not gone about talking." But this means not merely avoiding being a gossip or loudmouth but avoiding being ones who have "caused calamity for their fellows or taken up abuse against their neighbors" (Ps 15:1-3). For a person's throat can be an open tomb, waiting to devour others, and that because their tongue is slippery and there is no truth in their mouth (Ps 5:9 [MT 10]). Such people speak untruths that are plausible enough to get believed and dangerous enough to bring death. Their words are smooth but empty, not so much empty trivialities and harmless flatteries but statements that are big on plausibility and ostensible friendliness but lacking in substance; "by a double mind they speak" (Ps 12:2 [MT 3]). They seem and purport to think and intend one thing but actually think and intend something very different. Their words are thus the expression of an abandonment of commitment and truth in the community. And they are "big words." Psalm 12 goes on to explain this by commenting on that strange power of words: "With our tongue will we prevail." Words can be a means of great achievement. But in this case it is violent and destructive achievement. "Our lips will be our blade" (Ps 12:4 [MT 5]). They can cut people down as effectively as a sword.

In relating the words that report these empty but dangerous words, in its own words Psalm 12 expresses a rather direct urging of Yhwh. It opens in a distinctly straight way, "Do deliver, Yhwh," mincing no words and wasting time on no polite preliminaries. The words with which victims groan in protest would look or sound much feebler than those of their attackers. "Yhwh must cut down all smooth lips": all the victims do is make declarations about what Yhwh must do. These are only the words of the weak, and all they are is groans. Yet actually they turn out to be powerful because they attract Yhwh's attention.

Indeed, they provoke a third form of speech, Yhwh's own words, which take the form of a declaration of determination to arise in order to deliver: "Because of the devastation of the weak, because of the groaning of the needy, now I will arise" (Ps 12:5 [MT 6]). One might have thought that the trigger would have been the closing words of the plotters that the suppliant has reported, "Who will be our lord [*ʾādôn*]?" That might have been enough to provoke the real Lord to respond. But actually it is those feeble groans that do so. The response takes the form of a kind of sworn testimony as Yhwh solemnly avers that action will indeed come.[255] And when Yhwh speaks, there is no doubt that action will come. Yhwh's words are pure in the sense that they have survived a rigorous quality-testing in the heavenly cabinet, with the adversary looking carefully for flaws in them.

Blessing Words

Words of blessing are life-giving words.[256] "Yhwh's blessing to you; we bless you in Yhwh's name": so in the regular course of events people can address one another (Ps 129:8). They may also bless one another without actually using the word *bless*, as happens in Ruth (see Ruth 1:8-9; 2:4, 12; 4:11-12, 14, as well as 2:19-20; 3:10).[257] Blessing someone is a way of praying for them or is related to praying for them. Prayer in the sense of pleading arises from a situation of illness, oppression or loss, and it seeks deliverance, seeks for things to be put right. Blessing arises from a situation of reasonable normality. There are no problems to be solved, unless they are the ones that will arise from the imminent death of a father (who is often the agent of blessing), and even this occasion of blessing promises the opening of a way into the future.

In Deuteronomy 33 Moses blesses the people; in 1 Chronicles 16:2 David does so; in Numbers 6:24-26 Yhwh prescribes the way the priest is to bless the people.[258] In Psalm 20 the people bless the king (cf. Ps 72:15). In blessing, leader and people thus live in a relationship of codependence. In themselves, the people's words might imply that they are simply expressing their desire for Yhwh to bless the king, but his eventual reaction in the psalm implies that it is more than that: "Now I know that Yhwh is delivering his anointed," he responds. He knows there is power and effectiveness in his people's blessing. Yhwh will see it comes true. The psalm eventually closes with a prayer for Yhwh to deliver the king, but this follows up the declaration of blessing addressed to the king that dominates the psalm, a declaration of confidence in what Yhwh will do, a promise of what Yhwh will do, and an affirmation of what Yhwh will do, like Eli's words to Hannah in 1 Samuel 1:17. The blessing apparently does not make prayer redundant. Perhaps the opposite is the case: given the declaration of blessing, prayer can be more confident. In a sense it is easy for the people to assume the authority to declare this blessing. They know the nature of Yhwh's commitment to the king, and so does he. But this commitment still needs claiming, especially in a situation of pressure. Pro-

---

[255]I take *yāpîaḥ* as from *pûaḥ* II "witness" rather than *pûaḥ* I "breathe" (see *HALOT*).

[256]See especially Claus Westermann, *Blessing in the Bible and the Life of the Church* (Philadelphia: Fortress, 1978).

[257]Miller calls Ruth and Num 6:24-26 the two great blessing texts (*They Cried to the Lord*, pp. 290-98).

[258]See §7.3 "A Ministry of Blessing."

claiming it strengthens both him and them, both objectively and subjectively.

The various aspects of the people's blessing are likely all facets of the one declaration, that Yhwh will deliver the king. They want Yhwh to respond to him when he prays in time of trouble, for instance when he is battling invading enemies. They thus want Yhwh to send him help from Zion to wherever he is fighting (the help might equally be seen as coming from Yhwh's heavenly dwelling; the psalm later puts it that way). They thus want Yhwh to accept his offerings, the offerings that would accompany such prayers for help. They want Yhwh to prosper the battle plans he makes. And as a result of all that, they want to be in a position themselves to celebrate his deliverance. The last line comes close to making explicit their personal interest in Yhwh doing what they describe. They are blessing the king; but they are thus expressing their hopes for themselves. Neatly, blessing rebounds on itself, or rather, Yhwh makes that happen: "I will bless people who bless you" (Gen 12:3).

As with intercession the initiative with regard to blessing may come from the human being who blesses, or from the God who blesses. In the first case, "blessing you" means calling on God to bless you; that is, the person says, "May you be blessed/you are blessed before or by Yhwh." The blessing itself comes from God; when the human being blesses, this means uttering such a prayer.[259] Thus "Melchizedek blessed him [Abram], saying 'Blessed be Abram of God Most High'" (Gen 14:19). Rebekah's family bless her, saying "May you become thousands upon thousands" (Gen 24:60). Isaac blesses Jacob and prays similarly (Gen 28:1-4). When priests bless the people, they say, "Yhwh bless you and keep you, Yhwh shine his face on you and be gracious to you, Yhwh turn his face to you and grant you *shalom*" (Num 6:22-26). Eli in effect blesses Hannah when he says, "Go in peace, and the God of Israel—he will give [or may he give] what you asked" (1 Sam 1:17). "Eli would bless Elkanah and his wife, saying 'May Yhwh grant you offspring by this woman'" (1 Sam 2:20). When Solomon blesses the people, he prays for Yhwh to be with them, to incline them to obey Yhwh and to keep noting his prayer (1 Kings 8:55-61).[260] When the priests bless the people after Hezekiah's Pesah, "their voice was heard and their plea came to his holy abode, to the heavens" (2 Chron 30:27).

Performative Words

In some contexts blessing may mean nothing more than greeting (e.g., 1 Sam

---

[259]See Jeffrey H. Tigay, *Deuteronomy*, JPS Torah Commentary (Philadelphia: Jewish Publication Society, 1998), p. 226, following Moshe Greenberg, *Biblical Prose Prayer* (Berkeley/London: University of California Press, 1983), pp. 30-36.

[260]The nature of the blessing in 1 Kings 8:14 is harder to see; perhaps the statement anticipates vv. 55-61.

25:14), as is the case in English, yet other contexts make clear that blessing can be a powerful and effective form of speech. Blessing is thus related to prayer. Its presupposition again parallels that of intercession, in effect that God has delegated to a member of the cabinet the freedom and responsibility to act on the cabinet's and on God's behalf. Balaam's comment is illuminating: "I received [a command] to bless; when he blesses, I cannot reverse it" (Num 23:20). Balaam blesses Israel and declares that it will flourish, but he does so in light of a commission from God, which makes blessing a kind of performative speech that proclaims that something is going to happen, and thereby makes it happen. It presupposes that the person blessing has the authority and power to utter such a word effectively. God has such authority and power by virtue of being God; human beings have it if God grants it.

Like intercession, the commission or power to bless rests especially with people in particular positions. Yhwh commissions Levi, and specifically the priestly line, "to bless in his name" (Deut 10:8; 21:5; 1 Chron 23:13); Numbers 6:22-27 gives the text for this blessing. Pharaoh assumes that Moses can bless him, as he assumes that Moses can intercede for him (Ex 12:32), and Moses blesses the people as a whole before his death, as he prayed for them in crises during his life. Joshua blesses individuals and clans (Josh 14:13; 22:6-7). All twelve clans stand on Mount Gerizim and Mount Ebal for the Levites to bless (and curse) the people (Deut 27:11-13; Josh 8:33). David blesses the people (2 Sam 6:18). Fathers can bless their children, not only by bestowing position and possessions on them (see Gen 27) but by making pronouncements regarding their destiny (see Gen 48; 49). A father blesses his household (2 Sam 6:20; 1 Chron 16:43). A seer such as Balaam can bless.

As with intercession, ordinary people can also bless. By sundown a creditor must return a cloak taken in pledge from a needy person; the debtor will then bless the creditor, for whom this will count before Yhwh as an act of faithfulness (as a result of the blessing as well as of the deed?) (Deut 24:10-13). The relationship between blessing and prayer is suggested by the juxtaposed warning that if a person abuses a worker, the worker will "call to Yhwh against you" and it will count as a sin (Deut 24:14-15). Blessing thus by no means moves only down from people higher in the social hierarchy, but also upward (1 Kings 1:47). The people of Judah bless those who volunteer to move to Jerusalem (Neh 11:2). People may say to others, "Yhwh's blessing on you! We bless you in Yhwh's name!" (Ps 129:8); to say "in Yhwh's name" is to presuppose that Yhwh has given the speakers the power to bless.

Cursing is a parallel form of performative speech that also proclaims that something is going to happen and thereby makes it happen (e.g., Gen 9:25; Num 22–24; Judg 5:23; 2 Sam 16:5-14; 2 Kings 2:24; Neh 13:25). "One who gives to the poor—no lack; but one who shuts his eyes—much cursing" (Prov 28:27).

Like the power to bless, the power to curse may thus come with someone's position or may also reside in ordinary people, though there is little indication that it was simply an open possibility or commission for humanity, parallel to blessing. Further, it works on a moral basis, so that speaking about the power of cursing is not to say it operates by some power of its own, independently of Yhwh or of right and wrong. "Like a sparrow in flitting, like a swallow in flying, so is a curse without reason, which does not come about" (Prov 26:2). Yhwh can protect from the will to curse; a human curse cannot overwhelm a divine commitment to bless (Num 22:12). Parallel to the instances of praying for one's enemies is Job's claim: "If I would rejoice at my enemy's misfortune, exulted because trouble found him. . . . I have not given my mouth to sin by asking for his life with a curse" (Job 31:29-30). The exception that proves the rule is the self-curse of Deuteronomy 27:13-26 involved in the people's saying "Amen" to the Levitical curses that are potentials rather than applying to specific people.

Sparing Words

It is through speech that we express our wisdom and convey wisdom to other people, and also express our stupidity and encourage folly in others (Prov 15:2). There is thus something to be said for silence. "People with much knowledge are sparing with their words, people of insight are cool-spirited," or "People who are sparing with their words are ones who have much knowledge, people who are cool-spirited are people of insight" (Prov 17:27). Although the expression "cool-spirited" comes only here, its meaning is clear enough. It denotes keeping one's cool instead of being hot-tempered; this suggests that the first line has in mind not merely the general temptation to talk a lot, even about subjects one knows about, but the specific temptation to blow one's top over a subject that one feels strongly about. Conversely, the next line adds, fools who keep their mouths shut may be taken for persons of insight (Prov 17:28).

"You have seen a man hasty in his words; there is more hope for a fool than for him" (Prov 29:20). Indeed, more generally "the person who hurries misses the way" (Prov 19:2). The more profound reason for silence is that we learn by listening, not by talking. "Fools do not delight in insight but only in their mind disclosing itself" (Prov 18:2). The speech of fools brings trouble to them: strife, blows, ruin, entrapment (Prov 18:6-7). "Answering someone before listening—that is stupidity and shame" (Prov 18:13). "People who guard their mouth and their tongue guard their life from calamity" (Prov 21:23).

Admittedly books such as Job and the Psalms rejoice in loquaciousness. On one hand Zophar begins his first address by commenting on the large number of Job's words. The phrase recurs from Proverbs 10:19, which observes that "with a large number of words, offense is not lacking."[261] Zophar goes on to describe Job as "a man of lips," a speechifier, characterized by "empty talk" (*bad*). He pretends to have lots to say about God's ways, as if anyone could understand them (Job 11:1-9). Ironically, of course, Zophar uses quite a few words to make his point, though not as many as his friend Eliphaz, the first loquacious speaker in this book (see Job 3–4). Job returns the compliment in urging Zophar and his friends, in keeping with Proverbs 17:28, "If only you would keep totally quiet, so that this would be your wisdom" (Job 13:5), though he wants this so that they will listen to him speak (at length) (Job 13:6; cf. Job 13:13, 17). But "sufferers attract fixers the way roadkills attract vultures."[262]

It can be when one is discomforted by someone's words that there seem to be too many of them. The context in Proverbs suggests it has in mind words addressed to other people. One should perhaps also be wary about how much one says about God (what fool would write books about this?). Perhaps the Psalms imply that speaking at length *to* God is wiser than speaking at length *about* God, though Qohelet also comments that addressing "a large number of words" to God can be unwise (Eccles 5:3 [MT 2]), and personally never addresses any. Neither is Qohelet addressed by God, unlike Job.[263]

There are other reasons to be sparing with one's words. "Through being long-tempered a commander can be won over, and a gentle tongue can break someone's strength" (Prov 25:15). It would be odd to think of someone being long-tempered with the one who rules over them and wanting to break their strength (lit., "bones"). Is the commander the leader of an enemy force with whom one is negotiating? Or is this an aphorism for the king about how to handle his own commander? What is clear is that keeping cool and speaking cool can achieve what a show of force cannot achieve. Again, "the good sense of a person makes them slow to get angry and their glory lies in passing over an offense" (Prov 19:11; cf. Prov 20:3). "An even temper is an aspect of a disciplined person; it amounts to a toughness of intellectual and temperamental make-up which enables one to remain calm and unflurried even when subject to intense pressure or provocation," and to shrug off an insult.[264] Paradoxically, "one gains glory by giving up a common means of protecting it—argument."[265]

In a modern culture whatever here applies to speech applies to writing. In

---

[261]Cf. Newsom, "Book of Job," p. 419.

[262]Eugene H. Peterson, *The Message* (Colorado Springs: NavPress, 2002), p. 840.

[263]W. Lee Humphreys, *The Tragic Vision and the Hebrew Tradition* (Philadelphia: Fortress, 1985), pp. 131-32.

[264]McKane, *Proverbs*, p. 530.

[265]Clifford, *Proverbs*, p. 177.

e-mails we express our wisdom and convey wisdom to others, and express our stupidity and engender folly.

Reproving Words

Yet over against the importance of gentleness and restraint in speech is the importance of reproof, argument and chiding *(tôkaḥat)*, for reproof can generate not only wisdom (Prov 15:5) but also (consequently) life: "the person who spurns reproof dies" (Prov 15:10). So "teach me, and I myself will be silent; help me see how I have gone wrong" (Job 6:24). Indeed, "someone wise rebuking a listening ear" is "a gold ring or an ornament of gold" or "gold apricots in silver settings," though it needs to be "a word spoken at the right moment/ in the right way" (Prov 25:11-12). It does require wisdom to know how to rebuke at the right moment or in the right way (the word *ʾōzen* comes only here, but cognates suggest some such meaning). But if we can manage to speak thus and gain a hearing, it is as precious and impressive as beautiful and valuable jewelry.

John Howard Yoder sets two lines from Proverbs 27:5-6 as the epigraph to his discussion of "Binding and Loosing":[266] "Open reproof is good, better than hidden love; the wounds of someone who loves are trustworthy; the kisses of an enemy are earnest/profuse." They thus lead into a quotation of Matthew 18:15-20. But in each line the second colon is not very clear. Perhaps hidden love is love that hides from being confrontational.[267] "Hidden love" would then involve an ellipse; further, the saying does not say that the reprover is one who loves. More likely the point is that open confrontation does us more good (whether the reprover is friend or foe) than being secretly appreciated by someone. In the last colon, the two translations reflect the meaning of the two possible roots *ʿātar*, though both involve some inference. But the positive point is clear: reproof is good (whoever gives it, actually), and even though it hurts, it needs to be trusted when it comes from someone who loves, while we need not to be deceived by the niceness of an enemy. Thus "iron sharpens iron, and an individual sharpens the face of his friend" (Prov 27:17). The saying may have implications for the broader way friendship develops us, but the general context and the imagery suggest it will refer especially to the challenges and rebukes friends give each other, whatever the implications of the enigmatic reference to the "face."[268]

So the tongue can be a tree of life when it is rebuking as well as when it is

---

[266]Reprinted from John Howard Yoder, *The Royal Priesthood* (Grand Rapids: Eerdmans, 1994) in *Virtues and Practices in the Christian Tradition*, pp. 132-60; see p. 133, with the chapter heading "Practicing the Rule of Christ."

[267]See, e.g., McKane, *Proverbs*, p. 610.

[268]Cf. Van Leeuwen, "Book of Proverbs," p. 232.

being gentle. We therefore decline to pay attention to it at our peril. The self-assured *(lēṣîm)* are people who know what to do, speak but do not listen, do not like rebuke, do not open themselves to it, and therefore do not go to the wise because that is what they will get from them (Prov 15:12). Even hitting such people gets nowhere, though it may have an effect on the naive (Prov 19:25; cf. Prov 21:11). The self-assured and other stupid people (in the context, these are people who mock at the judicial process and seek to subvert it) are destined to receive physical punishment for their mockery (Prov 19:28-29), but it is just that, punishment expressing society's disapproval and affirming its values, not correction that hopes to reform the offender.

"A man much reproved, one who keeps his neck firm, will suddenly break, beyond healing" (Prov 29:1). Perhaps all those rebukes generate the firmness with which the person stands their ground, fulfilling the warning in passages such as Isaiah 6:9-10; criticism and threats have the opposite effect to that intended. Or perhaps the firmness is what causes the reproofs to be repeated. Either way, the first colon describes a constant pattern with which the second colon's sudden punctiliar event contrasts, but also links. Sometimes the very strength of a muscle or a building is what makes it vulnerable to sudden stress, and the calamity that follows may be the greater. Stiffening the neck leads to breaking it, without the prospect of repairing it; that is the nature of a broken neck.

"A person who reproves someone will in the end find more favor than someone with a flattering tongue" (Prov 28:23). "In the end," in the long run; in the short term someone may well be angry at our reproof. Conversely, "people who flatter their friends spread a net for their feet" (Prov 29:5). They may spread a net for their own feet or for their friends, and they may do the latter intentionally (that is, they are plotting to lead them astray) or unintentionally (they may lead them astray by well-meant flattery). Ezekiel 3:18 warns that someone who fails to warn others risks being held responsible for their blood. "Our seemingly spiritually based respect for the freedom of the other can be subject to the curse of God." To decline to admonish is to decline to recognize our shared human need.[269]

"Reproof" often stands in parallelism with "correction" *(mûsār;* e.g., Prov 15:5, 32). In other contexts *correction* implies action that chastises,[270] but here the parallelism suggests correction by rebuke rather than by action (cf. Prov 19:27, where "correction" is paralleled by "knowledgeable words"). Eliphaz reminds Job that he has often "corrected" people (the EVV oddly translate

---

[269]Dietrich Bonhoeffer, *Life Together/Prayerbook of the Bible* (Minneapolis: Fortress, 1996), p. 104.

[270]Cf. §4.4 "Making Restitution."

yāsar "instructed"); we know he is about to receive some of his own medicine. But thereby he reckons he has "strengthened failing hands" (Job 4:3), emboldened other people to stand firm in their integrity when they were tempted to falter. That is the aim of correction. On the other hand, we should not water down *mûsār* so that it merely means discipline in a broad sense.[271] It suggests the painful side to learning. And when Eliphaz speaks of God's reproof and correction, he presumably means the chastising action that Job has experienced, and the way he goes on to speak of God's injuring and wounding confirms that (Job 5:17-18).

Painful Words, True Words

As reproof, speech is a great way to hurt people. "How long will you torment my spirit, crush me with words?" Job asks. "As comforters, Eliphaz, Bildad and Zophar leave a lot to be desired."[272] Their reproof is the means of shaming him and of exalting themselves in relation to him (Job 19:1-5). Of course this was not their (conscious) intention. They were sincerely seeking to win him back to a right relationship with God, to get him to reaffirm the true view about God's character and God's relationship with us, the view he would once have affirmed. But that involves ignoring the facts about him and thus tormenting him with a view of God that does not work and a hurtful view of himself. It involves inventing facts about him, or at least (so far) about his children. If their charges were true, their shaming would be appropriate, but in reality their shaming of him is undeserved. It also has the effect of exalting themselves in relation to him. It makes them morally superior and it also reassures them that their view of God is right.

Zophar will similarly begin the next of the friends' addresses, "My disquieting thoughts—they make me respond, yes, because of my inward agitation; I hear correction that humiliates me, and my insightful spirit makes me answer" (Job 20:2-3). It is not difficult to see why Zophar is so disquieted and agitated. Job is questioning something fundamental to the very framework of Zophar's worldview. Job's correction indeed threatens to humiliate him, especially insofar as Zophar presents himself as a teacher. Job undermines his teaching and thus undermines him as a teacher. So he must reaffirm that he is a person of insight, though there is some irony in the fact that all this merely leads him to reaffirm yet again on the basis of the tradition (Job 20:4) the inevitable fate of the wicked, which Eliphaz and Bildad have described at great length without facing the tension with the facts provided by Job's experience

Three sayings about correction in Proverbs 15:31-33 abound in paradox.

---

[271]So, e.g., von Rad, *Wisdom in Israel*, p. 53.
[272]Oliver Leaman, *Evil and Suffering in Jewish Philosophy* (Cambridge/New York: Cambridge University Press, 1995), p. 23.

"The ear that listens to life-giving correction lodges among the wise." Correction is indeed a painful experience. It seems negative; no one likes being told they are doing wrong. Yet it is actually life-giving (literally, "correction of life"). "A stable self is achieved in large part by accepting correction from others who see us differently," the principle underlying the practice of spiritual direction.[273]

Proverbs goes on, "people who spurn correction reject themselves, but people who listen to reproof gain understanding." Suppose we want to grow as persons, to gain understanding in heart or mind (*lēb*), to love and accept ourselves rather than hate and reject ourselves (*śānē'*), as Western attitudes often encourage us to do. We will then respond positively when put right by someone else, rather than spurning such correction.

Then, "reverence for Yhwh—correction that gives wisdom, and before honor—weakness." The third saying takes up the familiar connection between wisdom and reverence for Yhwh and adds this emphasis on correction. Perhaps it suggests that Yhwh is the ultimate source of correction and discipline (the correction and discipline that engenders wisdom), so that reverence for Yhwh involves submitting to this correction. The second colon is even more striking, giving special respect to "weakness." The EVV translate *'ŏnāwâ* "humility," but that English word rather implies an attitude of modesty on the part of someone who may actually be, for instance, gifted or powerful. Here as usual the word denotes actual powerlessness. Reverence for Yhwh turns upside down understandings of power. To put the links another way, "a consequence of weakness is reverence for Yhwh, wealth, honor, and life" (Prov 22:4).

Words belong in the context of true relationships. Jonah's words about revering Yhwh as the one who made the sea and the dry land clash with his actions.[274] He flees to the sea to escape God's commission, and when Yhwh causes a terrible storm at sea, sleeps while the pagan sailors pray. The rest of his story continues to expound this tension. In contrast, the midwives in Exodus 1:15-21 revere God and therefore disobey the king, then lie about the consequences; and God blesses them. Moses' sister is not very straightforward in the way she manipulates Pharaoh's daughter into hiring his mother as his nurse, and God blesses her shrewdness. Moses and Aaron's words to the Pharaoh in Exodus 5:1-4 do not look very true, as the Pharaoh spots (Ex 5:9); the same applies to many of their subsequent statements to the Pharaoh. Rahab lies to save the Israelite spies, Jael lies to kill Sisera, Michal lies to save David, David lies to get bread and to save himself, and Jeremiah lies to save himself

---

[273]Davis, *Proverbs, Ecclesiastes, and the Song of Songs*, p. 99.
[274]Samuel Balentine, *Prayer in the Hebrew Bible* (Minneapolis: Fortress, 1993), pp. 71-80.

(Josh 2; Judg 4; 1 Sam 19; 21; Jer 38:24-28).[275] Truthfulness is important because and insofar as it respects and builds up the community, and lying is wrong because and insofar as it is "contrary to community."[276]

6.7 Suffering

Suffering appears in a chapter on "Spirituality and Character" because the First Testament does not seek to explain suffering but to help people live with it. Suffering issues from our vulnerability to life and death and other people. It can then be a challenge to be met or an argument to be engaged in or a spur to penitence or a vocation to be accepted. The question it raises is whether we can hold onto God and hold onto hope.

Starting Points

Suffering involves the imposition on someone of serious pain or loss or short-fall in relation to what seems to make for full human life, particularly as we see other people experiencing life. It thus gives the person a sense of serious deprivation. It is something that happens to you; you are not in control. In the First Testament, Erhard S. Gerstenberger and Wolfgang Schrage analyze suffering in terms of loss (of property, persons, honor), illness, violence (in family and clan, through structures such as the monarchy, in war), fear, and failure.[277]

In Western Christianity suffering is *the* problem, as it often is for Jews.[278] In the First Testament and in the New Testament this is not so. Western Christians speak of it as a key question that inhibits people coming to believe in God, though my suspicion is that this is a projection of the extent to which it tempts us to give up on God. In the First Testament *the* questions are ones such as whether and how people are going to worship Yhwh, whether they are going to trust Yhwh and obey Yhwh, how they are going to relate to one another as families, as communities and as a nation. But suffering is *a* problem there. Handling the question why bad things happen to good people, and how you react when they do, has a place in First Testament spirituality, though the question's profile differs from the one it manifests in Western spirituality. The First Testament focuses more on why Yhwh allows bad people to thrive

---

[275]See Tikva Frymer-Kensky, *In the Wake of the Goddesses* (New York: Free Press, 1989), pp. 136-40. On the limits to telling the truth, see further Dietrich Bonhoeffer, *Ethics* (New York: Simon & Schuster, 1995), pp. 358-67.

[276]Martin A. Klopfenstein, *Die Lüge nach dem Alten Testament* (Zürich: Gotthelf, 1964), p. 353; cf. Preuss, *Old Testament Theology* 2:195. See further Rousas John Rushdoony, *The Institutes of Biblical Law* ([Nutley, N.J.]: Presbyterian & Reformed, 1973), pp. 542-49.

[277]Erhard S. Gerstenberger and Wolfgang Schrage, *Suffering* (Nashville: Abingdon, 1980), pp. 22-102.

[278]See Harold S. Kushner, *When Bad Things Happen to Good People* (New York: Schocken, 1981).

and why Yhwh allows them to oppress good people. Notwithstanding shorter life-expectancy and natural disasters, it focuses less on the fact that life or the world in general can be unfair. And insofar as it raises that question, it does so within the context of a relationship with God. It does not ask, Why does God allow bad things to happen to people? It asks, Why have you allowed this bad thing to happen to me? And it does not intend the question very literalistically. It is not a question that looks for answers but one that looks for action. What is a question on the surface is under the surface an appeal or exhortation, Make it stop.

Yet even that appeal is probably not meant very literalistically, because Israelites knew that God often did not do so. This points to another antithesis. In Western Christianity suffering is something that needs to be explained; "the problem of suffering" is a problem of understanding. For Israel, suffering "did not have to be 'explained.' Rather, what was required was the means to go on even if the evil could not be 'explained.' "[279] Israel shares the assumption that comes from other contexts where life is hard, that suffering "is not something you eliminate, but rather something with which you must learn to live."[280] And thus "Why?" is transformed into "What for?" in the sense of what purpose can this experience fulfill.[281]

The First Testament offers resources for understanding and for living with suffering. The plural "resources" is a more important plural than most. Suffering is the paradigm case of an issue on which we have no comprehensive perspective and for which there is no integrated approach. The First Testament implicitly recognizes that what we have is a number of partial, unrelated insights and a number of strategies that are worth trying. Suffering may be a challenge, a test, a chastisement, a discipline or a vocation; or none of those "explanations" may work. It may simply be an unintelligible enigma. This is not to rule out the possibility that God may have a comprehensive understanding of it, only to deny that God has shared one with us (cf. Eccles 3:11). Job demonstrates that theodicy is a pointless exercise because we do not have access to God's wisdom on the matter.[282] His book is an exercise in antitheodicy. Antitheodic statements do not "justify, explain, ascribe positive meaning, account for, resolve, understand, accept, or theologically rectify the presence of evil in human affairs." Rather "they express anger, hurt, confu-

---

[279]Stanley Hauerwas, *Naming the Silences* (Grand Rapids: Eerdmans, 1990/Edinburgh: T & T Clark, 1993), p. 49 (he is actually speaking of 'the early Christians").

[280]Stanley Hauerwas, *Suffering Presence* (Notre Dame, Ind.: University of Notre Dame Press, 1986/Edinburgh: T & T Clark, 1988), p. 24.

[281]Cf. Gershom M. H. Ratheiser, Mitzvoth *Ethics and the Jewish Bible*, LHBOTS 460 (New York/London: T & T Clark, 2007), pp. 258-59.

[282]Cf. Andrew E. Steinmann, "The Structure and Message of the Book of Job," *VT* 46 (1996): 85-100; see p. 95.

sion" and "do not try to silence suffering people."[283] In effect, God makes this point to Job in Job 38–39. Indeed, the nature of the book of Job as a whole illustrates the point about partial insights and possible strategies. It is for this reason that the book deconstructs, which is not to say it is incoherent.[284] Taking up Mikhail Bakhtin's understanding of Job as a polyphonic text, one that expresses truth "dialogically,"[285] Carol A. Newsom comments that "the proper response to such a book . . . is to inject oneself into the conversation, but with the awareness that the final word can never be spoken."[286]

Meeting a Challenge

The First Testament's initial perspective is implicitly that facing suffering is part of the challenge of being human that emerges from God's not having created the world a place that was finished. It is a place that is ordered and good, indeed very good, but a place that requires subduing by humanity. Further, one of the creatures Yhwh made suggests that the human beings should ignore the one constraint Yhwh placed on them. So the first human beings face challenges and temptations from the beginning. Taming the world and resisting the serpent are tough tasks.

Testing is integral to human experience. The first two concrete stories the Bible tells (Gen 3–4) concern testing. Adam and Eve are tested by the requirement that they forgo the fruit of a tree that will grant them wisdom, the capacity to distinguish between good and bad. Cain is tested by Yhwh's having regard for Abel and not for him. Whatever made Yhwh not pay regard to him, the issue that concerns Genesis consists of how he handles what follows: it is now that sin is at his door, lying there, like the serpent lurking about looking for a chance to tempt Eve. "We only gain autonomy by our willingness to make suffering our own through its incorporation into our moral projects."[287]

Through the journey to Canaan Yhwh humbled (*ʿānâ* piel) and disciplined (*yāsar* piel) and thus tested Israel (*nāsâ* piel). The object was to find out what was in Israel's heart, whether it would stay obedient, and to lead it to acknowledge that one does not live by bread only but on what Yhwh says (Deut

---

[283]Zachary Braiterman *(God) After Auschwitz* (Princeton, N.J./Chichester, U.K.: Princeton University Press, 1998), p. 37.

[284]See David J. A. Clines, *What Does Eve Do to Help?* JSOTSup 94 (Sheffield, U.K.: Sheffield Academic Press, 1990), pp. 106-23.

[285]Mikhail Bakhtin, *Problems of Dostoevsky's Poetics* (Minneapolis/London: University of Minnesota Press, 1984), esp. 280; also *The Dialogic Imagination* (Austin: University of Texas Press, 1981).

[286]Carol A. Newsom, *The Book of Job* (New York/Oxford: Oxford University Press, 2003), pp. 21, 30.

[287]Hauerwas, *Suffering Presence*, pp. 33-34.

8:2-6). Conversely, having life easy makes it tempting to put Yhwh out of mind and give up one's obedience (Deut 8:7-18); one has to make sure one worships Yhwh for these good things.[288] Moses does not say that *shalom* is thus also a test, but this is an implication. It can mean our heart grows lofty and we behave as if we brought about our own *shalom*.

Suffering as a test is where the story of Job starts. Yhwh is proud of the incomparably committed and upright Job, but a member of Yhwh's court who is called the Adversary (not "Satan"),[289] and apparently is responsible for making sure that no one gets away with anything they should not get away with, raises the question whether Job is like this only because of what he gets out of it. What if his life were not so blessed? Therefore the blessings are taken away, and so is nearly everything else.

On Mondays, Wednesdays and Fridays I assume this tells us something that is in some sense actually (if analogically) true about affairs in heaven; on Tuesdays, Thursdays and Saturdays I assume Job 1–2 is part of the stage-setting for the main part of the book and is parallel to the details in Jesus' parables or the tricky imagery in Revelation in being not something to base doctrine on where it is not paralleled elsewhere in Scripture (on Sunday I go to church). On any understanding, the chapters introduce the way suffering tests, whether this is divinely determined or satanically instigated or "just one of those things." It brings out whether we will maintain our integrity or revile God and die (Job 2:9);[290] in the context of suffering, a central issue in Job is "a struggle to maintain integrity and faith."[291] Suffering brings out whether we will try to maintain silence or turn our back on God rather than batter on God's chest (Job 3–27). It brings out whether we can live with ignorance or insist on being the center of the universe, and whether we think we could run it better than God (Job 38–41). It brings out whether we will make our home on the ash heap forever or eventually determine that enough is enough (Job 42:6).[292] It brings out whether we will agree to the dubious theology of our advisers or insist on telling the truth about God (Job 42:8).

Psalm 119:75 declares, "I have acknowledged, Yhwh, that your decisions are faithful," that they lead to blessing; but it then adds, "in truthfulness you have made me weak." When we cannot see why Yhwh has made us undergo reversals, on the basis of proving in the past that Yhwh's decisions are faithful we know that somehow these do not compromise Yhwh's truthfulness. Per-

---

[288]See further §6.5 "Mindfulness."

[289]See *OTT* 2:54-55.

[290]See §2.2 "Honor."

[291]Steinmann, "Structure and Message of the Book of Job," p. 89.

[292]Literally, Job says "I despise and repent over dust and ashes." It is hard to justify the standard translation "I despise *myself* and repent *in* dust and ashes."

haps they instance how the significance of reversals lies not in what caused them but in the purpose they serve. The psalm has just declared, "it was good for me that I was made weak so that I might learn your laws" (Ps 119:71). Being made weak issues in openness to Yhwh's teaching.

Arguing with One's Self

From time to time, psalms issue exhortations to the soul or self to be silent for God (Ps 62:5 [MT 6]) or to rest (Ps 116:7) or to praise Yhwh (Ps 146:1), but it is in the context of suffering that Psalms 42–43 present us most systematically with a suppliant's internal argument. "Why are you cast down, my soul, and tumultuous within me? Wait for God, because I will yet confess him for the deliverance that comes from his face" (Ps 42:5 [MT 6]); the argument then repeats (Ps 42:11 [MT 12]; 43:5) with variations, of which the most significant is that the last colon becomes "confess him, the deliverance of my face, my God."[293] Like Psalm 22, these two psalms insist on facing two sets of facts. (Psalm 22 also implies an internal argument, though it is explicitly a prayer laying two sets of facts before Yhwh.) Here the facts concern present and future. On one hand, there is the trouble that prevents the suppliant from coming to the sanctuary, the trouble Yhwh has brought about ("all your breakers and your waves have passed over me"), and the attacks and taunts of other people. "Where is your God," people keep saying, and the suppliant keeps hearing them; no doubt the problem is not only that *they* are saying this but that the suppliant's heart is echoing their words. There is a tumult in the suppliant's spirit that contrasts unhappily with the tumult of a festival. And on the other hand, there is the extraordinary certainty of eventual freedom to come into Yhwh's presence: I shall join that "tumult keeping festival," "Yhwh will command his commitment," "I will confess you with the lyre."

It is obvious where the first set of facts comes from; it reflects concrete experience. It is not so obvious where the second set comes from. But the conviction is there. The internal argument presupposes that Yhwh *will* "send out your light and your truthfulness; they themselves can lead me, they can bring me to your holy mountain, to your dwelling." The only question is when. The puzzle is the tension between what the suppliant knows will be and what is now. The challenge is to live with the tension between present and future realities. That is what is involved in "waiting." Waiting makes the future present in the suppliant's spirit (cf. Heb 11:1).[294] Reference to being "mindful" that the time will come when it is again possible to be in Yhwh's presence involves

---

[293]The repetition of the argument indicates that in some sense Ps 43 belongs with Ps 42, though we do not know whether the two psalms were originally one and have been divided or whether Ps 43 was composed to expand on Ps 42.

[294]Or (for British readers), waiting takes the access out of wanting.

using the verb *zākar*, usually translated "remember."[295] In Hebrew it is possible to "remember" the future in the sense of being mindful of it as just as certain a reality as the past.

While prayer involves a conversation with God, and God may use a priest or a prophet to answer the questions we bring to God, the psalm presupposes that we can also take some initiatives ourselves in not only asking questions but answering them. It also presupposes that God listens to the argument we have with ourselves, which (in this psalm at least) we are having before the God who is also the psalm's addressee.

Even in conversation with God a divine response will not necessarily terminate the argument, at least until the response in words becomes a response in deeds. In a conversation with ourselves, that is more naturally so. The self-exhortation in Psalm 42:5 [MT 6] is followed by further expressions of pain. The hoped-for "sound" of the worshiping crowd contrasts with the present "sound" of crashing waters. The prospect of "passing" through the sanctuary contrasts with the present fact that these waters are "passing" over me. The suppliant's mindfulness toward that worship contrasts with Yhwh's declining to be mindful toward the would-be worshiper.

The self-exhortation in Psalm 42:11 [MT 12] is likewise not the end. Psalm 43 does imply progress; it speaks as though the battle is won. Yet the self-exhortation then recurs in Psalm 43:5; actual deliverance has not yet come. If the suppliant is sure of answer in the stage-one sense, stage two still lies in the future;[296] waiting continues.

The argument may not even cease when the suffering is over. In a thanksgiving psalm a worshiper issues the bidding, "Turn, my spirit, to your complete rest, because Yhwh—he has dealt with you," and then (addressing God) goes on, "because you have pulled away my life from death, my eye from tears, my foot from being pushed down; I shall walk about before Yhwh in the lands of the living" (Ps 116:7-9). In the aftermath of the experience of suffering and deliverance, and a fortiori in the context of ongoing life in which we walk before Yhwh, walking the way that Yhwh watches over, we remind ourselves of what Yhwh has done and argue ourselves into resting on the basis of this. Feelings can afford to catch up with the fact of deliverance, the second colon affirms.

Being Driven to Turn

"Before I became weak I was going astray, but now I have kept your statement" (Ps 119:67). The suppliant in Psalm 119 usually claims a life of integrity,

---

[295]See §6.5 "Mindfulness."
[296]See §3.3 "Decision and Action."

but typically does not pretend that this implies sinless perfection. We all stray and none of us can therefore claim not to deserve Yhwh's chastisement. Suffering is sometimes deserved by the people who experience it. The only thing wrong with this regular human assumption is that people universalize it, as Job's friends do. But there are indeed times when suppliants stand under Yhwh's wrath not inexplicably (as in Ps 6) but explicably: "there is no soundness in my flesh because of your rage; there is no well-being in my bones because of my failure" (Ps 38:3 [MT 4]). Communal lament and penitential prayer are thus rival reactions to suffering. Perhaps lament gave way to penitence, or perhaps they stood head to head.[297] Where penitence is the appropriate reaction to suffering, another fruit of God's liberation of us is that we no longer have "to exist in the dialectic of the moral and the immoral, but may now exist in that of forgiveness and gratitude." All our acts of obedience are fallible and sinful, but this is okay because they are "done on the basis of the forgiveness" that has come to us.[298]

The First Testament suggests three ways in which sin and suffering may link, specific or short-term, general or longer-term, and universal or very long term. The last appears only in the connection between Adam and Eve's sin and our experience of toil and pain. Genesis does not make explicit that this includes our experience of illness; I am not clear that I should see my wife's multiple sclerosis as resulting from Adam and Eve's sin. Genesis is more explicit concerning a link between Adam and Eve's act and the widespread human sense that work becomes toil and the widespread experience of marital and family tension and breakdown.

Ezra 9 illustrates the other two forms of link. It sees a connection between the community's low state in Ezra's day and its sinfulness over the centuries, and another connection with the particular scandal of the community's acceptance of marriages between Judeans, who served Yhwh, and other people, who did not. The prophets likewise commonly take famine, drought and other disasters as chastisements designed to drive Israel to self-examination and turning to Yhwh.

Elihu shares their perspective. He is angry at Job because he insists on being in the right over against God, but he is also angry with Job's friends because they have merely scolded Job and not said anything constructive or pointed him to any way forward (Job 32:1-5). He agrees with them that Job is in the wrong, but he has a more caring view of God than they do. He has the pastoral heart of someone who knows Yhwh is a God of love. He knows God

---

[297]See Dalit Rom-Shiloni, "Socio-Ideological *Setting* or *Settings* for Penitential Prayers?" in *Seeking the Favor of God*, ed. Mark J. Boda et al. (Atlanta: Society of Biblical Literature, 2006), 1:51-68, and other essays in this volume. See the introduction to §3.6.
[298]Barth, *Church Dogmatics* IV/3, ii:670, 671.

would want to win Job back to the commitment he professes but must have actually abandoned. So he tries to get Job to see why God sends such chastisement to people. It is not merely punitive but designed to get them to change their ways, suppress their self-assertion and thus save them from a worse fate. God "opens their ear to correction [*mûsār* again] and says they are to turn from wickedness," in order to deliver them from distress into a broad place (Job 36:10, 16). Suffering can set us back on the right path.

Elihu's critique could seem to apply to the prophets. They commonly lambaste Israel without offering them a way out, and can thus be read as declaring inevitable judgment; only rarely do they explicitly urge people to "turn" or repent. But from time to time they make clear that this is the object of Yhwh's action; it is chastisement or discipline or correction designed to get Israel to turn and thus avoid a worse fate. But Elihu is right that Job's friends give little sign that they have this pastoral aim; they are more concerned to keep their theological perspective intact. And Elihu is right that the troubles God sends can be designed to make people turn from wrong religious or moral ways, and turn back to right ways and back to God. But ironically, he is just as wrong as the friends about the relevance of his convictions to Job. He thus illustrates the pastoral danger of his pastoral insight. But the danger of his insight should not issue in a refusal to recognize that it sometimes applies.

At the Mercy of Life and Death

As a result of Adam and Eve's act of disobedience, Adam's efforts to produce food will now be hard and frustrating. And subsequently the First Testament incorporates many stories about people coping with shortage of food and shortage of water. Famine is the first thing that happens to Abraham and his family after their arrival in the land, and the experience recurs for Isaac, for Jacob and later for Elimelech and his family (Gen 12:10; 26:1; 42:1-5; Ruth 1:1-2). In the wilderness on a number of occasions the Israelites likewise are threatened by lack of water (e.g., Ex 15:22-23; Num 20:2). Whether this issues from the challenges built into the way God created the world or from the original human sin, it is (often) not the result of the sin of the people who have the experience. When people lack food in Genesis and Ruth, they seem to assume this is "just one of those things" rather than, for instance, chastisement for wrongdoing, and the heads of households assume they have to take responsible action to see their families have something to eat. In contrast, when people lack water in Exodus and Numbers they assume they have been let down by Moses or Yhwh rather than that they are being chastised for wrongdoing. But in both contexts the results are not very happy.

Israelites are also more accepting of illness, mortality, death and bereavement than Westerners. "In good times, enjoy the good times; in bad times see that this as well as the other does God bring about" (Eccles 7:14). Not many of the psalms fret about these experiences, and Job does so only because of the monumental disjunction between his extraordinary commitment to Yhwh and his extraordinary experience of illness and loss. Naomi does the same when she urges, "Do not call me Naomi [Delight], call me Mara [Bitterness], because Yhwh has made my life very bitter. I was full when I went and bitter when Yhwh brought me back. Why call me Naomi when Yhwh has afflicted me, Shadday has brought trouble to me?" (Ruth 1:20-21). Israelites hope to live through a normal lifespan but accept that death then brings life to a satisfactory end as one goes to join one's ancestors. What they chafe about is death that comes before its time. It is in this connection that the First Testament focuses on illness, attack and bereavement. It is in this connection that the main significance of sickness in Scripture is as "a forerunner and messenger of death" and "an element and sign of the power of chaos and nothingness."[299]

It is appropriate that this power overtakes faithless people before it otherwise would and that then "death shepherds them" (Ps 49:14 [MT 15]); they find that they have joined its flock. Death, not Yhwh, is their shepherd. People who rely on Yhwh rather than on their wealth have a different experience. They too will eventually die, but they do not share the assumption of the wealthy that they can buy a long life for themselves and perhaps buy an early death for people they want to get out of the way. "God will redeem my life from the power of Sheol, for he will take me" (Ps 49:15 [MT 16]). The statement of faith is too broad for us to reckon it refers to a "taking" like Enoch's or Elijah's (Gen 5:24; 2 Kings 2). Like other passages it rather refers to a "taking" or rescuing from trouble (cf. Ps 18:16 [MT 17]), in the way that sometimes people such as Elisha and his servant in 2 Kings 6 or the three young men in Daniel 3 experience marvelous rescues from their oppressors. Death does not wait till the end to reach out for people. They may find themselves in its grip when they are still alive. "Death's ropes encompassed me, Belial's torrents overwhelmed me, Sheol's ropes encircled me, death's snares confronted me" (Ps 18:4-5 [MT 5-6]). But Yhwh rescues.

Yhwh's capacity to rescue means there is no need to be afraid when someone gets rich (Ps 49:16 [MT 17]). We may envy the rich, but we may also fear them. Wealth means power; lack of resources means powerlessness. The wealthy can cause life-threatening trouble for ordinary people; they can get away with things. The psalmist may also hint at a less down-to-earth fear, that the power of wealth imperils the understanding we would like to have about the basis of human life. It does not do so, says the psalm. People who

---

[299]Barth, *Church Dogmatics*, III/4:366, 368.

trust in Yhwh find Yhwh can rescue them, and people who trust in their resources find these cannot rescue them.

At the Hands of People

Not only are Israelites less preoccupied by suffering than Westerners; they
are thus preoccupied by different forms of suffering. "The Old Testament
speaks less about natural human suffering than of the pain that humans receive from other humans."[300] When Hannah cannot have children, is consumed by weeping and is "bitter" in spirit like Naomi, it is not just because of
her inbuilt woman's sense of nonfulfillment but because of the way her co-
wife treats her (1 Sam 1:10). The Psalms especially fret over suffering that
takes the form of the unfair and unjustified attacks of other people, which
bring shame and either the threat of death or an aggravation of some experience such as illness that threatens death. "Suffering never develops only in
the individual. . . . Others are involved also, as the ones who cause it, as on-
lookers, or as friends."[301]

That too goes back to near the Beginning. Before declaring that food is going to be hard to grow, Yhwh declares that human relationships are now to be
causes of suffering. Eve's relationship with her children and her husband are
going to involve pain. Her second son is murdered by her first son because
God likes the second's sacrifice more than his big brother's, so that his blood
cries out from the ground. His story leads into much more suffering for the
victims of violence, which becomes pervasive in human life (Gen 4:23; 6:11),
and to pain for God (Gen 6:6). Noah, the exception to the rule about violence,
finds aspects of the patterns of Genesis 3–6 repeated in his own experience
and wills servitude for some of his descendants (Gen 9:20-27).

The first individual spectacularly oppressed through being a servant is
Hagar, who suffers on account of her gender and her race as well as her
class.[302] While she names God "God of my seeing" and her son's name testifies to the fact that "God listens" (Gen 16:13, 15), subsequently she seems to
have forgotten both those truths; all she can do is sit and wait for her son to
die. Yet if she has forgotten that God listens, God has not done so. God listens
to Ishmael's cry, living up to his name, and provides for Ishmael and his
mother. Hagar's hopelessness does not mean she is hopeless. The second individual spectacularly oppressed through being a servant is Joseph. Ironically, he is then the unintentional means of the Israelites becoming corporately oppressed in Egypt as "a household of servants."

It is to be expected that being a servant of Yhwh brings trouble. People

---

[300]Cf. Preuss, *Old Testament Theology*, 2:141.

[301]Gerstenberger and Schrage, *Suffering*, p. 13.

[302]Phyllis Trible, *Texts of Terror* (Philadelphia: Fortress, 1984), pp. 9-35.

generally cannot handle the witness of Yhwh's servants. Whereas the First Testament is inclined to portray affliction by outsiders (Assyria, Babylon, Persia) as quite justified, in connection with undeserved affliction, it puts the emphasis on the affliction that comes from insiders. It is the people of God itself that cannot bear what Yhwh's servants say, and therefore attacks them. The same is true in the New Testament, where most talk of persecution concerns the way some members of the Jewish people (people who not believe in Jesus) treat other members of the Jewish people (people who do). Likewise, persecution within the subsequent life of the church commonly involves some members afflicting other members.

Further, "suffering makes the other a stranger and our first reaction is to be repelled."[303] We do not want to experience the pain of others. If suffering people work hard at getting well, we may be willing to be with them, but if they do not or if their suffering continues, the experience results in alienation from their friends. So if we want to keep our friends, we have to deny our pain and deal with it on our own.[304] "It is the burden of those who care for the suffering to know how to teach the suffering that they are not thereby excluded from the human community."[305]

Westerners like to think that our decisions as individuals decide our destinies as individuals, and the First Testament allows for this as an aspect of the truth (see Ps 1). But Abraham's questioning of Yhwh in Genesis 18:23-32 recognizes that our destinies as individuals are bound up with our communities, for good and ill. If I had not been born in the 1940s with the potential the postwar situation in Britain opened up for children from working-class backgrounds, I would not be sitting on my patio in Pasadena writing this book now. Conversely, there are African American teenagers who would still be alive in Pasadena today if they had been born on another side of town.

Jeremiah has an aide called Baruch who writes down his prophecies at his dictation and reads them in the temple courts. This leads to his being summoned before Judean leaders, who take the scroll to read to the king, but warn Baruch to go into hiding with Jeremiah. The king burns the scroll and seeks to arrest them both, "but Yhwh hid them" (Jer 36:26). Jeremiah then dictates an enlarged version of the scroll. In the process, Yhwh gives him a message for Baruch: "You have said, 'Oh no, because Yhwh has added grief to my pain; I am weary with my groaning, and rest—I have not found any.' " Yhwh intends to let the city fall. "And you: should you look for great things for yourself? Do not look for them"; but in the midst of the disaster, Baruch

---

[303]Hauerwas, *Suffering Presence*, p. 25.
[304]Cf. ibid., pp. 77-78.
[305]Ibid., p. 26.

will not lose his life wherever he may go (Jer 45:1-5). And like Jeremiah, he survives the fall of Jerusalem, but like Jeremiah, he gets taken off against his will to Egypt (Jer 43:1-7). But the promise thus comes true. In between these events, when King Zedekiah gives leave to Judean leaders to do as they wish with Jeremiah and they put him in a cistern where he would die of hunger, Ebed-Melech the Sudanese, one of the king's staff, intervenes to get him rescued (Jer 38:1-13). Yhwh subsequently bids Jeremiah promise Ebed-Melech that on the day of Jerusalem's fall he would be preserved from death, "because you have trusted in me" (Jer 39:15-18). But the comments of Jeremiah and Ezekiel imply that many faithful people died in the siege and fall of Jerusalem (and being carted off to Egypt was not exactly the future Jeremiah had in mind), while the people who survived and were taken off into exile, or who survived and remained in Judah, look no better than the people who died. The faithful sometimes suffer because they are caught up in the destiny of the faithless.

In the Form of Weakness

The people of God typically live as the weak (ʿǎnāwîm/ʿǎnayyîm—I take these as alternative forms with the same meaning), as people without power or influence or status. In theory, being weak need not mean being ill-treated, oppressed or cheated out of their rights, but in practice that is what happens (EVV often translate the words "afflicted"). These are commonly the people who get wrongfully killed, or live in danger of that, but whose cry Yhwh heeds and whose defenselessness Yhwh graciously sees (Ps 9:12-13 [MT 13-14]; 10:17). The weak are also the needy (ʾebyônîm; the words come in parallelism at Ps 9:18 [MT 19]; 12:5 [MT 6]; 37:14), people without resources. They are the "broken" (Ps 9:9 [MT 10]; 10:10, 18). The EVV call them the "oppressed," which they are, but that word is a little abstract. Although this group of words is mostly used figuratively, its concrete background manifests itself in terms that refer to dust, to the pounding of the ocean on the seashore and to physical crushing. The oppressed are people who have been beaten down, shattered, crushed.

Psalm 37 sets the weak over against the faithless and thus implies that the weak are also the faithful; indeed, explicitly they are the "upright" (Ps 37:11, 14). This need not be so; there is a significant correlation between weakness and faithlessness as well as one between weakness and faithfulness, and in each case the correlation can work either way. It cannot be assumed that the weak will be faithful or the faithful weak, any more than that the weak will be faithless or the faithless weak. Thus in itself there is nothing affirming about being designated as "weak." The word does not imply "meek," as the Aramaic equivalent can. The LXX translates it thus in Psalm 37, and Matthew

5:5 thus probably has this implication when Jesus quotes the line (and having the psalm and Jesus talking about meekness rather than weakness would of course be an encouragement to the writer of this volume and to most readers of it, because we do not belong to the weak and needy, but we might aspire to belonging to the meek). The psalm's promise is that the weakness of the faithful will not last forever; "they will take possession of the land" (not "the earth," an unnecessary luxury) and thus have the wherewithal to grow what they need. The promise is not that they earn or even qualify for possession of the land but that God's commitment to the weak over against the powerful will bring this about. God's promise emerges from God.

The A to Z of spirituality in Psalm 34 (it is an alphabetical psalm) is a spirituality of weakness, the testimony of one weak person talking to other weak people about how one rejoices in weakness (Ps 34:2, 6 [MT 3, 7]). It speaks of the experience of terror, trouble and inner crushing. It makes the paradoxical declaration that the faithful, the holy ones, the servants of Yhwh, go through many "bad experiences," yet that Yhwh "guards all their bones; not one of them is broken." The link between the two is the challenge to pay attention to what Yhwh has done for other people and let that drive us to call out to Yhwh ourselves. It makes no promise of a trouble-free life, but it does assume that our lives are lived with an alternation between trouble and deliverance. The key to the alternation is that we keep revering Yhwh as the one who delivers and thus keep turning to Yhwh as the one who delivers, rather than accepting that we simply live with trouble, or living in denial, or thinking we can solve our own problems. The Psalter also makes clear that this does not always work; we often cry out that Yhwh has abandoned us. But it does not therefore abandon the vision expressed in Psalm 34.

"If you really listen to the voice of Yhwh your God, do what is upright in his eyes, heed his commands and keep all his laws, I will not bring on you any disease that I brought on Egypt, because I am Yhwh your healer" (Ex 15:26). Likewise the individual who is the kind of person who refuses to share the attitude and the life of the faithless and instead loves Yhwh's teaching, talks about it and lives by it will become like a tree planted by a good water supply, which stays green and fruitful; in comparable fashion, such people will make everything they do thrive (Ps 1). And they do; except when they do not. The psalm's promises and their shortcoming are paralleled by those of Jesus. "Seek first the reign and his righteousness, and all these things [food, drink, clothing] will also be provided for you" (Mt 6:33). And they are; except when they are not. Yet Psalm 1 is the context in which the Psalms' protests and prayers are set, as Jesus' promises are the context in which Christian experience is set. They remind us not to let the experience of suffering make us think that the relationship between right living and blessing is random.

Accepting a Vocation

The story of Job implies another insight about suffering that is about as dangerous as those of the prologue or the three friends or Elihu or Job himself or Yhwh. It is that suffering is a vocation through which a ministry can be fulfilled. The figure of Job has "enabled people to speak truthfully about their destiny without compromising their faith in the biblical God."[306] Countless people have been taken on in their relationship with God through reading the story of Job, not to say that of his household staff, his children and his wife. I imagine talking to them in heaven and asking them what they make of the unfair way their lives turned out, a question that is more pressing for those who simply lost their lives than it is for Job. (The book leaves us less certain about the position of his wife, whether or not she is the mother of the ten more children whom he begets in the last chapter.) I imagine them saying, "Yes, it seemed unfair, especially through those long, boring centuries in Sheol, for much of which we had no idea that resurrection was eventually going to come. But when Jesus came and told us about that, and now that we experience it, this made it easier. And now we know how significant our story has been for people and how it has helped them to live with their suffering and with God, we are okay about it. Admittedly talk of 'accepting a vocation' is Pickwickian; when the hurricane swept through, it did not ask whether we wanted to accept this vocation, any more than God did when he summoned Moses or Jeremiah or when he bowled Paul over. But we did have to decide whether to affirm it as opposed to going kicking and screaming and forever 'rage against the dying of the light.'[307] And now, at least, we can affirm it."

Something similar is true about Yhwh's servant in Isaiah 52:13–53:12.[308] This servant found himself experiencing an extreme form of the suffering and humiliation that Judah as a whole experienced in the exile. It was evidently an extreme form because the Judean people (it is hard to tell whether they are in Jerusalem or in Babylon), who were themselves in an afflicted state, apparently see it is as worse than their own experience. They were inclined to take the view that Job's friends took and assume he deserved it. Marked suffering suggested marked sin. But there was something about this assessment that made things not add up. This servant just accepted the trouble that came. He did not rail or chafe or complain at what happened to him. And people knew that if they tried to be specific about the wrongdoing he

---

[306]Richard L. Rubinstein, "Job and Auschwitz," in *Strange Fire*, ed. Tod Linafelt (Sheffield, U.K.: Sheffield Academic Press/New York: New York University Press, 2000), pp. 233-52; see p. 233.

[307]From Dylan Thomas's poem "Do Not Go Gentle into That Good Night," Poets.org <www.poets.org/viewmedia.php/prmMID/15377>.

[308]See further §7.7.

was supposed to be guilty of, they could not do so. All this eventually made them realize that their assessment of him must have been wrong. He was rather less of a wrongdoer than they, not rather more. So why was he suffering? He was sharing in their suffering when he did not deserve to, sharing with them the suffering they deserved. And he was doing that as part of his ministry, like a prophet such as Jeremiah. Yes, God was requiring that he suffer, not as a consequence of his wrongdoing, but actually as a consequence of theirs. It was a price he had to pay for exercising a ministry to them.

They came to see there was something else. He was suffering in a way he did not deserve. Like Job's servants and children, that meant he had to make up his mind what stance to take to his suffering. "Suffering combines a peculiar passivity with a sense of agency."[309] In one sense Yhwh's servant had no choice about whether to accept his suffering. In another sense he did have to make a decision about it. He could decide to make it his vocation, turn a liability into an asset. Suppose he took his acceptance of his suffering as something he could offer God. He ministered to a people who needed something to offer God. They were in terrible debt to God for the way they had behaved, for the slight they had offered God over centuries and over decades. How could they make up for that? What could they offer? They had nothing. But this servant had something, this suffering that he had accepted. Suppose he offered that to God on their behalf? Perhaps God could accept that, and perhaps the people could let him be their representative in making that offering, and perhaps this could do something to effect reconciliation between these two parties. Perhaps that was even God's own intention?

Accepting suffering as a vocation can achieve things in connection with other people's understanding of themselves and with their relationship with God and with God's relationship with them. It is something that then makes it possible for the sufferer to say, "Yes, it was terrible, but it was okay."

Holding onto God

In the context of his inexplicable suffering, Job "believes now in justice in spite of believing in God, and he believes in God in spite of believing in justice," but he holds onto the conviction that they can be brought together.[310] Yet for him, of course, merely pondering this question is not what preoccupies him. A further fruit of God's liberation of people is "a liberation from anxiety to prayer," to prayer that resembles the cry of "a child on the dark street running to meet its father as he returns home in the evening: . . . not to particu-

---

[309]Hauerwas, *Suffering Presence*, p. 28.

[310]Martin Buber, *The Prophetic Faith* (New York: Harper, 1960), p. 192; cf. Steven Kepnes, "Job and Post-Holocaust Theodicy," in *Strange Fire*, ed. Tod Linafelt (Sheffield, U.K.: Sheffield Academic Press/New York: New York University Press, 2000), pp. 252-66; see p. 261.

larly pious fervent or beautiful prayer . . . but simply to prayer."[311] " 'Theodicy' is what relatively healthy people think about in the face of suffering; *lament* is what sufferers must do—it is the voice of theodicy in life." But "there is something shameful when people of faith first become intimately involved with suffering when it comes to them, and when the first lament we utter is our own."[312] Most of our study of prayer in chapter three is thus significant for the question of spirituality and suffering.

While Psalms 42–43 illustrate one way prayers can articulate the debate involved in theodicy, Psalm 27 illustrates another. "For you my heart said, 'Inquire of my face'" (Ps 27:8). The suppliant senses an inner voice urging, "Go and talk to Yhwh about it," but apparently the inner voice can be viewed as Yhwh's, as it says "inquire of *my* face." Psalm 27:14 subsequently reports another inner voice that is apparently distinguishable from Yhwh's: "Look to Yhwh; be strong; may your heart take courage; yes, wait for Yhwh." This well illustrates the paradoxical nature of human workings. The exhortation implies that the suppliant is not trusting Yhwh; yet the fact that the suppliant is uttering it implies that the suppliant is trusting Yhwh. The nature of Psalm 27 easily lends itself to such an argument, as it combines statements of trust that recall Yhwh's acts in the past (in the manner of a thanksgiving) with pleas presupposing urgent need in the present. While the direct aim of thanksgiving or testimony is to honor Yhwh and build up other people's faith, its indirect affect is to build up the faith of the testifier. It makes it possible to pray more confidently. In prayer we speak to ourselves as well as to God, reminding ourselves of occasions when God has reached out to deliver in answer to our prayers and thus building up our confidence in the present crisis.

Psalm 35 is a sustained plea from someone under attack, for Yhwh to protect and fight on the suppliant's behalf. It contains no hint that the suppliant will be engaged in either self-defense or attack. Yhwh must bring about the fall and shaming of these attackers. The suppliant is full of fear and rage, and does not think to ask Yhwh to take away these emotions. Both can be appropriate responses to attack. The psalm does not imply that fear and rage should lead to action (as happened in the aftermath of 9/11). It does imply that fear and rage energize prayer, so that it would be a shame if the suppliant was not overwhelmed by fear and rage. They are designed by God, part of the way we are made, created to issue in this fruit. Our sinfulness means we can let our capacity for mercy receive inappropriate expression by letting people get away with things they should not get away with, but we do not therefore seek to avoid ever being merciful; we have to learn

---

[311]Barth, *Church Dogmatics*, IV/3, ii:671, 673. See further chap. 3 of this volume.
[312]James T. Butler, "Impossible Questions and Faithful Responses" (unpublished paper).

to discern moments for mercy and moments for toughness. Likewise our sinfulness means we can let fear and rage express themselves in inappropriate forms, such as self-defense or revenge or preemptive attack, but this too does not mean we should avoid expressing them at all. The psalm models how to channel them into prayer.

What the Psalms especially fret about in this connection is not so much the experience of suffering itself but the questions it raises about how Yhwh is relating with the suppliants, on what basis that relationship works. This is also and especially true about Job. While his loss, bereavement and illness are the experiences that provoke Job's confrontation of Yhwh, they open up these broader questions about the nature and basis of Yhwh's relationship with him.[313] "The true sorrow in all his sorrows, and therefore the primary subjects of his complaints," lies in his knowledge that in what has happened to him "he has to do with God, and his no less profound ignorance how far he has to do with God."[314] "This relationship with God, then, is the true grief of Job and the real subject of his complaint. . . . It could be argued that the problem which Job sets up in his Book is not so much about the rationale for the suffering of the innocent, but is rather about our relationship with God."[315]

Holding onto Hope

At a strategic point half way through the Psalter, Psalm 73 describes the way someone was tempted to turn aside from the way of faithfulness to Yhwh because faithless people do so well in life. They live without any moral commitment, brazenly scheme against other people and confidently discount the idea that God takes any notice of what happens on earth, yet they enjoy good health and prestige, and live carefree and prosperous lives. They do not share in the burdens and afflictions that affect other people. In contrast, the suppliant is rewarded for an inwardly and outwardly pure life by continuous oppression from people, and is tempted to reckon that maintaining a moral commitment is pointless and that life is unintelligible. In the context of unintelligible suffering, psalms usually concern themselves with Yhwh's removing the suffering, but Psalm 73 focuses on the unintelligibility. If I could only understand what is going on and how God is involved in the world . . .

But that sense of bewilderment is now past. The change came about as "I went to God's sanctuary, where I considered their end." The psalm does not indicate how going to God's sanctuary had that effect, but in some way it meant a reentry into an alternative world, into the real world. In a variety of

---

[313]Cf. Henry McKeating, "The Central Issue of the Book of Job," *ExpT* 82 (1970-1971): 244-47.
[314]Karl Barth, *Church Dogmatics*, IV/3, I:401.
[315]Leaman, *Evil and Suffering in Jewish Philosophy*, p. 13. Cf. R. Norman Whybray, *Wisdom* (Aldershot, U.K./Burlington, Vt.: Ashgate, 2005), p. 199.

ways the sanctuary affirms that things are other than what they seem; it does so when worship takes place, but also even when it does not. In the world outside, it does not look as if Yhwh is king, but in worship we affirm Yhwh is king. In the world outside, it looks as if the faithless do well, but the sanctuary brings home that Yhwh does act to protect the faithful and put down the faithless. Going to the sanctuary encourages a person to "consider their end," to be reminded of the truth about such people. In the world outside, it looks as if Assyria and Babylon, Samaria and Ammon do well, but going to the sanctuary reminds of Yhwh's commitment to Israel. (The psalm begins "Yes, God is good to Israel," which implies such a comparison and suggests a speaker such as Nehemiah; the NRSV changes it to "God is good to the upright," which gives the psalm an intra-community focus and one that corresponds better to modern concerns.) Going to the sanctuary rebuilds the suppliant's confidence that this will happen. It rescues the suppliant from the bitterness, hurt and stupidity that threatened to overwhelm. Yhwh will put the oppressors down, and Yhwh will "take me to honor," restore my position in the community.

The suppliant's change of attitude does not issue from coming to focus on an inner awareness of God's presence and an inner relationship with God, which then becomes more important than the outward circumstances. Nor is the suppliant's confidence an eschatological one, a conviction about being taken to heaven that means a deliverance from hostile outward circumstances. The First Testament does not go in for eschatological resolution of the question of theodicy (except perhaps in Dan 12). Like Job, the psalm reaffirms its conviction that Yhwh is involved in the present in the whole of life, not merely in the realm of the spirit or in heaven. That renewed confidence means that in the meantime, until the moment of reversal comes, the suppliant is able to affirm that being with Yhwh is enough. It has been enough in the past: "I have always been with you; you have held my right hand." The testimony indicates a renewed recognition either of the way Yhwh has been faithful in past times of crisis and has delivered the suppliant, or of the fact that Yhwh has been present and protecting in this present crisis; for all the grimness of what has happened, the suppliant is still standing. Either way, it has been enough in the past and it will be enough in the future. "Although my flesh and my heart have come to an end, God is the crag of my heart and my allocation, forever." The suppliant has had Yhwh as refuge, and is now confident again that the moment will come when it is possible to "speak out about all your acts," the acts that will have put down the faithless and restored the faithful. As is the case in many psalms, the suppliant is in a different place at the end from the beginning, not because the situation has changed but through having a different relationship with the situation. The suppliant has a new attitude. In other psalms this issues from an awareness of a new fact, that Yhwh has heard a prayer and responded to it. In this psalm it issues from a renewed awareness of an old fact.

Many psalms on either side of Psalm 73 recognize that things do not always work out the way the suppliant expects, as Job's experience is not replicated in the lives of many. Psalm 73 encourages suppliants to hold onto hope.

6.8 Transformation

What is it that makes a person or a community change into something more like what Yhwh looks for? It requires Yhwh to teach us and us to be committed to Yhwh's teaching. And it requires imagination and action.

Yhwh's Teaching

In the process of transformation, what is the relationship between divine grace and human willpower?

Psalm 143:7-10 pleads for divine guidance in one's religious and moral life. When Christians think and pray about divine guidance, we are inclined to relate this to life decisions about who to marry or what job to apply for. When the New Testament speaks of being led by the Spirit, it has in mind the Spirit's moral leading, being led in God's ways, and in this respect it follows the pattern of psalms such as Psalm 119 and Psalm 143. We may think we know what is right and that our problem lies in doing what we know is right, and we seek God's help for that. The Psalms know we are only too capable of deceiving ourselves about what to do in our moral and religious lives, and we need God to break through our self-deception and enable us to see how to walk and what is acceptable to God. Here I am, surrounded by enemies, so "show me your way, Yhwh, lead me on a level path" (Ps 27:11). When we are surrounded by enemies, it is easy to rationalize about what is the right way. We need God to show us. We pray, "Make me acknowledge your ways, Yhwh, teach me your paths, guide me on the way in your truthfulness" (Ps 25:4-5): that is, let me see you acting in a way that reflects who you are, so that I come to make that the basis of the way I act.

Sometimes we do know what is right, but that is not all we need. We ask, "teach me, Yhwh, the way of your laws, so that I may observe it to the utmost; enable me to understand, so that I may observe your teaching and keep it with all my heart" (Ps 119:33-34). This does not imply we do not know or understand the content of Yhwh's expectations, which are straightforward enough. But we need Yhwh to write them on our hearts and into our attitudes, to open our eyes to their wonders and broaden our minds so we embrace them (Ps 119:18, 32); after all, many people do not think it is wonderful to be expected to worship Yhwh alone, or to do so without using an image, or to observe the sabbath. So we go on to ask, "Direct me in the pathway of your commands, because I take pleasure in it," which sounds like a request for guidance that presupposes that our heart is in the right place. But we go on, "Incline my heart to your declarations and not to gain; make my eyes pass on from seeing emptiness—in your way make me live" (Ps 119:35-37). This again implies recognizing that something needs to happen to our spirits if we are to be inspired to walk the right way. I need to incline my heart to Yhwh's instructions, but I need Yhwh to incline my heart to those instructions. My commitment is a necessary but not a sufficient prerequisite to my living by Yhwh's teaching.

Thus Psalm 141:3-4 asks Yhwh to "set a watch at my mouth, keep guard at the door of my lips." The context indicates that it does not refer to the ease with which unwise or unkind or defensive words escape from our mouths, though no doubt one might pray the prayer in this connection. It goes on, "Do not turn my heart to something evil, to having dealings in faithlessness with people who do harm." The words about which the First Testament is often concerned are words of deceit and plotting. The suppliant knows it could be tempting to speak these kinds of words and asks Yhwh to "set a watch at my mouth" in that connection. Not making my heart turn to something evil would be another aspect of the divine action the suppliant needed in that connection. We need Yhwh to be the kind of friend or superior who stiffens our resolve, and thus our words and our action, by the way they argue with us, not urging us to decide, say and do the wrong thing, but urging us to decide, say and do the right thing. That will mean (the psalm goes on) resisting the lure of the pleasures that come from associating with people who take the opposite stance.

So there is a subtle relationship between God's grace and our commitment. I must be committed to walking in God's way, yet I appeal for God's help in order to be able to do so.

My Commitment

So I ask Yhwh, "incline my heart to your declarations and not to gain," but I also affirm, "I inclined my heart to do your laws, forever, to the utmost" (Ps 119:36, 112). The contrast suggests that we are divided people; one aspect of our being is tempted to avoid Yhwh's way, another really wants to walk in it (cf. Rom 7). While my commitment is a necessary but not a sufficient prerequisite to my living by Yhwh's teaching, Yhwh's commitment is also a necessary but not a sufficient prerequisite to my living by Yhwh's teaching. I have to make my commitment. "Everything is in the hands of heaven except the fear of heaven, as it is said, 'And now, Israel, what doth the Lord thy God require of thee, but to fear . . .' " (Deut 10:12).[316]

I pray, "Teach me, Yhwh, the way of your laws, so that I may observe it to the utmost" (Ps 119:33). The psalmist knows what Yhwh's laws say; being taught their way means being taught to do what they say. I need Yhwh to teach me; yet I have to do the obeying, the walking. Yhwh points out the way to me, points out its advantages and encourages me to walk in it, but I have to do the walking. Both Testaments reckon that God's will has been made know to us with great clarity (e.g., Deut 30:11, 14; Mic 6:8; cf. Mk 10:17-19). Yet they also reckon we have to "seek and inquire after" God's will (cf. Rom 12:2; Phil 1:10).[317]

"I run in the way of your commands, because you broaden my mind" (Ps 119:32); the image of running—not merely walking, the usual verb—suggests enthusiasm and personal commitment. Proverbs 1:16 and Proverbs 6:18 associate running with the enthusiasm of people's wrongdoing; the psalm associates it with doing right. But the reason I have this enthusiasm and commitment is that Yhwh broadens my mind. That image has different implications from the ones that obtain in English. Broadening is an image for deliverance, but the idea here is that my mind is broad enough to embrace all that Yhwh says (in English, that might seem to imply narrow-mindedness). The ideal is not to be constricted by what I already think but to be open to new horizons, and Yhwh is the key to that broadening. To put it another way, "Make my eyes pass on from seeing emptiness; in your way make me live" (Ps 119:37). The things that look broadening are actually so narrow, they are empty. The way that looks constricting and the way to death is actually the way to life. That is so because "your command is very broad" (Ps 119:96). It covers many eventualities. All the guidance we need is there.

So I am responsible for my way; yet I need Yhwh to enable me to walk it. Remove crooked speech from you, remove your feet from evil, Proverbs 4:24, 27, urges. "Remove the way of falsehood from me; grace me with your teaching," Psalm 119:29-30 nevertheless asks, and then goes on, "I have chosen the way of truthfulness; I have set my mind on your decisions." In the First Testament choosing is usually Yhwh's business, so the psalm is making a strong affirmation of our human responsibility, alongside its strong affirmation of the need for Yhwh to make that choosing possible; the reference to grace underlines the point. Yhwh's teaching is a gift of grace that opens up the possibility of obedience. (There is certainly no tension here

---

[316]*B. Berakot* 33b; cf. Saadya Gaon, *The Book of Beliefs and Opinions* (New Haven, Conn.: Yale University Press/London: Oxford University Press, 1948), p. 189; Michael Walzer, *Exodus and Revolution* (New York: Basic Books, 1985), p. 81.

[317]Brevard S. Childs, *Biblical Theology in Crisis* (Philadelphia: Westminster, 1970), pp. 126-27.

between grace and law.) The psalm keeps expressing a commitment to a life of integrity, but keeps recognizing that we can never simply assume we will not fall into a "way of falsehood" in relation to Yhwh or in relation to other people.

Our relationship to Yhwh is founded on Yhwh's grace and love, and when we appeal to Yhwh's promises, behind that we appeal to who Yhwh is. Yet our relationship with God is a personal one; it is, in fact, a relationship. So our appeal also presupposes that our attitude to Yhwh is right. Thus the Psalms commonly appeal to the fact of our obedience as a reason why Yhwh should answer our prayers. There is a paradoxical form of insecure security about this relationship with Yhwh, such as often obtains in relationships. I can be confident about it, but I cannot take it for granted.

Christians often query the appropriateness of the psalmists' confidence in claiming to be committed to Yhwh. The Psalms also recognize that keeping this commitment is not easy. The suppliant is committed to Yhwh, but is aware of needing Yhwh to be at work in relation to heart, mouth and action if today's commitment is to hold for tomorrow. Yhwh can exercise decisive influence over us for good or bad, as our family and friends do, only much more so. Our friends and family can dangle in front of us legitimate delights that could issue from right living, or forbidden delights that could issue from wrongdoing. Yhwh can do that more powerfully. That does not remove the possibility and necessity for our commitment, but it sure puts pressure on. We are well-advised to beseech Yhwh to influence us toward what is good by reminding us of its delights.

Imagination

Transformation depends on imagination. Isaiah 40–55 declares that Yhwh is acting right now to restore Israel to freedom and to restore Jerusalem to its proper state. But people cannot see Yhwh acting. If they are to give God's act the right response, they need imagination. Isaiah 52:7-10 urges Jerusalem to respond to Yhwh's act, by breaking out and resounding. The first verb is a complicated one; there may be two or three roots *pāṣaḥ* but it is striking that Greek *rhēgnymi* and English "break out" apply to speech, and it would not be surprising if the prophet or the hearers of this prophecy brought together the idea of breaking something open and of breaking out in speech. Sometimes speech compels itself from inside the person, breaks out of their inner being without their mind or will being the main conscious agent in making this happen. It is almost as if they rather resist it. Go on, let yourselves respond to this message, says the prophet. Let go. Don't let your conscious mind control it. The verb *rānan* (resound) likewise suggests a kind of noise, the noise that actually issues from the throat when someone breaks out.[318] The city is to put aside its fears and inhibitions and let itself break into such a cry.

On what basis can the wastes of Jerusalem break out? They do so on the basis of things they hear. They hear a messenger's voice announcing an act of deliverance that promises *shalom*, announcing that Yhwh is newly asserting kingly authority. They throw their arms round the messenger who has the dirty feet that are so welcome. They hear the city's own lookouts shouting, more loudly than they have ever shouted before, that behind the herald they can see the King. Lookouts and herald are not the only witnesses. Yhwh has been acting with such dynamic divine power that all the nations can also see. The fall of Babylon was a very public event.

Yet there is something strange about the way the prophet speaks about Yhwh reigning, comforting and restoring. They are qatal verbs, the form that describes a concrete, actual event, which is therefore usually an event that has actually taken place. But this complex of events has not yet taken place or is at best under way. The prophet gives the game away by pairing yiqtol verbs with the qatal verbs. The lookouts *have* raised their voice?—well, they *will* resound together, they *will* look at Yhwh's return. Yhwh *has* bared his holy arm before the eyes of all the nations?—well, all earth's farthest reaches *will* see our God's deliverance. None of these events has happened at the time the prophet speaks. They are certain because Yhwh's mind is set on them, and the campaigns of Cyrus provide evidence that this is so. But one need not read the events that way, and anyway Cyrus might suddenly die and the Persian campaign collapse or the Babylonians might get their act together or Persia's accession might do no more good to the Judeans than Babylon's accession. The proclamation depends on a leap of faith in the message that has come to the prophet, on the basis of its fitting with what the prophet knows of Yhwh, of the moral and theological necessity that Yhwh so act one day, and of particular statements by earlier prophets. It is this that makes possible a move from wondering whether Yhwh is behind Cyrus to conviction that issues in such declarations.

To draw the hearers into the same conviction, the prophet appeals to their imagination. Imagine hearing the voice of a messenger and then the follow-up voice of a lookout. Imagine that the messenger is testifying to something that has actually happened and the lookouts can actually see the king returning at the head of a victorious army. The city's people, and the exiles who overhear the prophet speak to Jerusalem in this way, can see and hear nothing. The prophet is the nearest they have to messenger and lookout, one reporting what they have said and seen, but that issues from the

---

[318]See §2.7 "Sound and Movement."

prophet's own inspired imagination. The city is urged to begin resounding on the basis of sharing the prophet's flight of imagination. Its tumultuous roar does not respond to things it has yet seen but to things it knows it will see. It resembles the roar of a soccer crowd when it knows the team is about to come through the tunnel into the arena. The roar anticipates the event but is based on knowledge that it is coming. Living before God involves the imagination of faith.[319]

"Imagination remains at the core of moral reflection. Moral imagination generates the world of what ought to be, thereby making moral living possible." It does not exactly make the world; objectively, the world exists. But subjectively it makes the world for us. It also makes moral living possible through driving us out of our own world into the world of others. (Of course, we also need reflection, which "provides the direction, indeed the criterion for the constructive use of imagination.")[320]

Waking Up, Getting Out

As the fall of Babylon approaches, Yhwh urges Jerusalem to "wake yourself, get up" (Is 52:1-2). It has been lying prostrate under the influence of a cup of poison (Is 51:17-23), and it cannot bring about its own release from Babylonian control or fetch its own people back. Nor can the people simply decide to come back; restoring the city and delivering the exiles is Yhwh's task. Yet it is not accomplished without city and exiles laying hold of their deliverance. The city lies comatose and feeble, disheveled and fettered, profaned by foreign feet and stained by Israelite faithlessness. But because Yhwh is in the midst of delivering it from Babylonian domination, it can start laying hold of its deliverance now. Decades will pass before Judeans build its walls and construct new houses out of that lovely Jerusalem stone, but the sleeping giant can start waking up now and start asserting itself, start clearing the rubble out of its streets and out of the temple ruins against the moment when the altar will be reestablished and the festivals be newly celebrated.

Even more than that, there is a change of attitude that needs to come about. Instead of being cast down and helpless, it needs to see that it has life and strength. Even if it is outwardly desolate and bleak, it needs to see itself as beautiful and free. Even if foreign and Israelite feet and hands have defiled it, it needs to see that it *is* the holy city and that its defilement now lies in the past—or it needs to be taking steps to make sure that it lies in the past. The guarantee of what Yhwh intends to do is a basis for a change of attitude and life now.

---

[319]Cf. Stanley Hauerwas's chapter "On Keeping Theological Ethics Imaginative," in *Against the Nations* (Minneapolis: Winston, 1985), pp. 51-59.
[320]Brown, *Ethos of the Cosmos*, pp. 20-22.

The point is summed up by the variation between the forms of the Masoretic Text at the end of Isaiah 52:2. One form of the text declares that the guards are loosing the chains that bind the prisoners to the prison wall before they make a run for it; it uses a qatal verb, suggesting a real, actual event, not just a possible event or the idea of an event. In effect, the release has happened; that is the fact that needs to shape people's understanding of their situation, their present and their future. But the other form of the text bids them loose the chains themselves. The guards have gone but they threw down the keys before they left. Either way, there is no need for the captive, the city, just to sit there. There is a bidding for the exiles with parallel implications (Is 52:11-12). They cannot actually leave Babylon yet, but the moment when they will do so is round the corner, and they need to ready for it. They can start packing their bags or tying up their business affairs.

More importantly, they too need to change their mindset. In their minds they need to leave Babylon now. Their leaving relates directly to that waking of Jerusalem. They leave in order to take back there the surviving effects from the temple, the objects that Nebuchadnezzar's army did not simply destroy, which will symbolize the continuity between the First Temple and the Second. These exiles' job is to return these. It is no use their enjoying freedom in Babylon after the Persians' arrival. Once emigration is allowed, they need to be lining up round the block to get visas, because they have a vocation to fulfill.

To that end they need to make sure they preserve their purity. It will be no use their taking back the influence of Babylon and its images when Yhwh is promising that Gentile profaneness and Israelite pollution will no more defile the city. The city they will be leaving is full of potential to pollute Yhwh's people. They need to be starting now to make sure they keep separate from that pollution. Like the city of Jerusalem, they too have a promise from Yhwh to be inspired by and to act in light of. When their ancestors left Egypt they did so in haste, fleeing from Pharaoh and his army. The exodus from Babylon will be a more relaxed affair. They will not need to compromise over possible pollution (there will be plenty of time to search out possible "leaven") because Yhwh will be protecting them against any threats in front or behind.

The exhortations to city and exiles are both implicit promises. They are a way of saying that the time is imminent when the city does sit in state instead of lying in a stupor, a time when the exiles are free to emigrate instead of being compelled to live in this polluting land. But the promise does thus imply a change of attitude now, and perhaps a change of behavior now, to prepare for the action that will soon be needed.

"Don't look back," Yhwh's aides urged Lot (Gen 19:17). Many, perhaps most

Judeans, did not leave Babylon to return to Jerusalem. But even they need to leave Babylon in their minds. The continuing faithful existence of a Judean community in dispersion has depended on their doing that. Lot's wife does look back, perhaps imagining the potential sons-in-law they have had to abandon, and becomes frozen in her gaze. And thus she and Lot between them take their daughters to a grim fate that reflects the way they have all been shaped by living near Sodom.

Conversion and a New Rule of Life

How do we become Godlike? In Psalm 95 Yhwh speaks of loathing the wilderness generation and declaring they would not enter the land. Why did Yhwh not rather work at their growing out of waywardness into responsiveness? Actually that is exactly what Yhwh is doing in the psalm. It is possible to think of God bringing about a miraculous change in people by reforming their inner being and changing them into responsive people (or perhaps it is not), but it would not be surprising if God refrained from doing that with people as it would involve short-circuiting the process of getting people to take responsibility for themselves.

Parents passionately want their children to grow into people who identify with their own values, but they cannot manipulate this into happening or force it, because manipulation or force cannot produce that end. So they try various other ways of making it happen. They model these values for themselves. They tell their children what these values are. They encourage their children with the blessings that will follow from adhering to them and warn them about the consequences that will follow from ignoring them. They make their children the objects of their love, because love shapes character. They put their children through tough experiences because tough experiences shape character. They give them scope to make their own decisions so that they have opportunity to work with those values. And then they sit back and hope nervously that all this will work, high on expectancy but sometimes experiencing disappointment.

God does all these things in relation to Israel. The Scriptures are the embodiment of God's doing so. They tell Israel the story of God's involvement with it, because that helps them discover their identity. They tell Israel what God expects of them. They promise Israel what will issue from heeding this and warn what will issue from ignoring it. God makes Israel the object of love and takes Israel through tough experiences of the kind that can shape its character. And then God sits back and hopes nervously that all this will work, high on expectancy but sometimes experiencing disappointment; what Yhwh hoped and thought they would do, they do not do (see, for instance, Is 5:7; Jer 3:19-20).

In the terms of this model, our transformation involves our growing from childhood to adulthood. But there are limitations to the model. "The Christian [and the Israelite] moral life is finally not one of 'development,' " because that does not suggest radical transformation, "but of conversion."[321] The First Testament does not believe in moral growth but in conversion.[322] People need to turn right round *now* (Ezek 18).

---

[321]Stanley Hauerwas, *A Community of Character* (Notre Dame, Ind./London: University of Notre Dame Press, 1981), p. 130.
[322]Barton, *Understanding Old Testament Ethics*, p. 68.

7

LEADERS AND SERVANTS

The First Testament speaks much about people who lead Israel (so we might have considered them in part two) and who serve Yhwh by doing so (so we might have considered them in part one). But a key issue their stories and their testimonies raise is who they are in themselves and what their life and activity means to them and costs them. This gives me a pretext for setting a consideration of them in part three and thereby making the three parts of this volume balance nicely. It also enables me to give them the extended treatment they deserve (because they are an important theme in the First Testament) but also, by coming to them last, to suggest their relative unimportance (because leadership is such an immoderate preoccupation in Western thinking).

7.1 Servants and Leaders

In the First Testament, leaders of Israel are servants of Yhwh. Of course, all Israel are Yhwh's servants, and having some human beings in authority over others is a weird notion. It is a condescension to human sinfulness. Further, leaders tend to be at least as sinful as those they lead, and leadership is commonly a form of oppression. The notion that leaders must be subordinate to Torah has the potential to safeguard against the temptations of power, though this potential is not much realized.

A Theology of Servant-Leadership

Leadership is not a category the First Testament or the New Testament works with. This is not proven by the mere fact that the Scriptures lack words that cover the range of the English words *leader* or *leadership*. Sometimes cultures have concepts for which their languages do not have words. More significant is the fact that the Scriptures do have an expression for the range of people that Western thinking refers to as leaders. That expression is "servants of Yhwh." This reframes the category in significant ways.

It does not focus on turning them into "servant leaders" in the sense that this expression has in modern Western thinking, where the (alleged) object of the service is people, though there is one notable occasion when the First Testament speaks of leaders as their people's servants. When people campaign for a reduction in the burden Solomon's policies imposed on them, the elders advise Rehoboam, "If you become a servant to this people today and serve them, and answer them by speaking kind words to them, they will become servants to you always" (1 Kings 12:7). King and people become each other's servants. But generally in reframing the position of leaders, the First Testament puts in the forefront their being servants of Yhwh. This removes questions about their ability, their "leadership potential." It implicitly revolutionizes questions about identifying leaders and training leaders. It reduces the gap between these persons and their people, because both are servants of Yhwh; we have already made extensive use of the expression "servanthood" in connection with Israel as a whole.[1]

There is a more paradoxical aspect to the category of "servants." Human beings were designed to be servants of the land and servants of one another, but the idea that some are regularly in a position of servanthood to some other people in a one-way fashion was not part of creation's design. It came about through human sin.[2] Related questions are raised by the idea that some people might be servants of Yhwh in a sense in which others are not, and more clearly by the idea that some people have authority over others. Humanity was designed to be a democracy in the etymological sense of the word, which means that "the people govern,"[3] not merely that they elect their government. As Bob Dylan put it in "Gates of Eden" on the album *Bringing It All Back Home*, "There are no kings inside the Gates of Eden." In Genesis 1:26-28 all humanity is created to have authority, not over one another but over the earth. In Genesis 2:15 the first human being is created to serve not other human beings but the ground. But humanity accepts the authority of a creature rather than exercising authority over it and as a consequence finds authority being exercised by one creature over another (Gen 3:1-6, 16). We see leadership then flourishing in the lives of people such as Cain, the first murderer and city-builder, Lamech, the first polygamist and multiple avenger, and Nimrod, the first warrior and king (Gen 4:17, 19, 23-24; 10:9-10). There is very little sign of "leadership" having positive connotations in Genesis. Most of the good guys (Noah, Abraham, Isaac, Jacob) do not lead anyone, and the result of Joseph's leadership is to turn everyone in Egypt, including his own family, into state serfs (Gen 47:13-26).

Paradoxically, "good" leadership becomes necessary because "bad" leadership precedes it. It was not only in Israel and in the period of the judges that people did what was right in their own eyes because there were no kings

---

[1] See chaps. 2 and 3.
[2] See §4.5 "Working for Someone Else" and "Whereas from the Beginning It Was Not So, It Became So."
[3] John Howard Yoder, *The Priestly Kingdom* (Notre Dame, Ind.: University of Notre Dame Press, 1984), p. 151; cf. §4.4 "Loci of Responsibility."

(Judg 21:25). "With rebellion in the land, its rulers are many, but with a discerning person who is knowledgeable, order persists" (Prov 28:2). Although the second colon is allusive, the general point is clear: order is better than a coup, not least because coups tend to multiply oppression rather than freedom (as their supporters may hope).

Good and Bad Leadership

The First Testament manifests "an attitude toward power torn between ideal and reality."[4] In human society as the Torah envisages it, power is diffused. Parents are responsible for the education and discipline of their children; elders decide on matters of dispute in the local community; priests have key roles in worship and teaching. Further, individuals are not confined to one role. A prophet such as Ezekiel could be a priest, a priest such as Ezra could be a theologian and thus by implication a scholar (cf. Ezra 7:25), personified Insight can speak like a prophet (e.g., Prov 1:20-33), and a scholar such as Daniel can confront a king like a prophet (Dan 4:27 [MT 24]).

The First Testament describes a number of recurrent forms of leadership, which all have strengths and weaknesses.[5] Kings can exercise an authority that harnesses the resources of the nation so that it can take on its enemies and develop its own economic and cultural life, but doing so encourages the development of a class system that makes some people well off and others less so than they would have been. Priests can safeguard, mediate and encourage the people's relationship with God and God's with them, but they can encourage a relationship that is more religious form than experiential reality. Prophets can be the means of God's breaking into the system, the nation's religious life and its politics with a word that the institution cannot generate, but they can also simply be another way of reinforcing the system, the religious life and the politics. Experts (EVV "wise") can mediate pragmatic empirical wisdom and ensure that the insight that has developed over the generations does not get lost, but they can end up wooden like Job's friends or proponents of practical atheism like the people Isaiah attacks. Likewise, kings, priests and prophets can and do lead their people into forms of worship that do not honor Yhwh.

Ironically and grievously, kings and other leaders are just as much affected by sin as the people they lead, perhaps more so because they have opportunity to sin in more spectacular ways, and especially if they want to be leaders, because that is a sign of something wrong. The instructions for purification

---

[4]Moshe Greenberg, *Studies in the Bible and Jewish Thought* (Philadelphia: Jewish Publication Society, 1995), p. 60.
[5]Cf. Walter Brueggemann, *Theology of the Old Testament* (Minneapolis: Fortress, 1997), pp. 697-703.

offerings prescribe the action that needs to be taken when the priest incurs guilt and brings guilt on the people and when the "leader" *(nāśîʾ)* does so, as well as when the community as a whole or some individual does so by their own action (Lev 4). The offenses of leaders have disastrous consequences for their people. If the pastor preaches an incomplete or slanted version of the gospel, the congregation suffers.

Sinfulness is characteristic both of "charismatic" leadership, the kind that people exercise because of their leadership ability, and of "institutional" leadership, such as kingship or priesthood, the kind legitimated and constrained by law or tradition.[6] Indeed, one might treat the theme of leadership as a subset of the theme of sin. Leadership exists only because of sin, and the First Testament offers "critique after critique to unseat each of it own authorized institutions (judgeship, priesthood, monarchy, prophecy)."[7] Whatever form of leadership one can think of, it goes wrong: kings, officials, priests and prophets are mentioned together because this is what they have in common (Jer 2:26; 4:9; 8:1; 32:32; cf. Zeph 3:4). Esther is, among other things, an exposition of "The Politics of Folly."[8] Qohelet says, Don't ever be surprised when leadership is a means of oppression rather than service. Leadership is simply a chain of corruption, a legalized protection racket designed to benefit people in power (Eccles 5:8-9 [MT 7-8]). "Government even in its best state is but a necessary evil, in its worst state an intolerable one."[9]

It is thus a particularly significant insight of First Testament theology that the idea of leadership needs to be replaced by the idea of servanthood. Moses is not a leader but a servant, and not a servant of the people but a servant of God.[10] Leadership then appears as the subject of promise. "The concept of the leader" is "a kind of secular imitation of the concept of the election of Jesus Christ." He is the locus of grace, freedom, responsibility and power. This represents an inversion of what Christ was as servant.[11] In contrast, the Western church emphasizes leadership and empowerment. Those of us who are servants do not wish to stay that way, and people who care for those without power assume they should not stay that way.[12] The New Testament congrega-

---

[6]The typology is Max Weber's. See his *The Theory of Social and Economic Organization* (New York: Free Press/London: Collier-Macmillan, 1969), p. 328.

[7]Regina M. Schwartz, *The Curse of Cain* (Chicago/London: University of Chicago Press, 1997), p. 9.

[8]J. David Pleins, *The Social Visions of the Hebrew Bible* (Louisville: Westminster John Knox, 2001), p. 191.

[9]Thomas Paine, *Common Sense and Other Political Writings* (Indianapolis: Bobbs-Merrill, 1953), p. 4.

[10]See *OTT* 1:425-37.

[11]Karl Barth, *Church Dogmatics* (Edinburgh: T & T Clark, 1967), II/2:311.

[12]John Howard Yoder, *For the Nations* (Grand Rapids/Cambridge: Eerdmans, 1997), p. 47.

tion has been described as a community of conversation guided by agents of direction (prophets), agents of memory (scribes or narrators), agents of linguistic self-consciousness (teachers) and agents of order and due process (overseers, elders, shepherds).[13] It would not be difficult to adapt this statement so that it became a description of Israel. But Western Christian communities are guided by managers.

Community, Leadership and Torah

Deuteronomy emphasizes that Israel has a wayward spirit. It is from Deuteronomy that Jesus gets his phrase about the people being tough-minded, which explains the way its provisions contrast with the way things were at the Beginning (Mk 10:5). One way it works with people's waywardness is in assuming that society depends on authority structures.[14] The distinctive collocation of material regarding governors, officials, priests, kings, Levites and prophets in Deuteronomy 16:18–18:22 suggests a focus on that. Yet Deuteronomy also puts the society in charge over the authority structures, not vice versa. It both centralizes and democratizes some of the exercise of authority by requiring the entire community to appoint local rulers and officials, obliging local communities to consult the priests and the ruler at the central sanctuary, and banning their recourse to people such as mediums. But it also leaves much of the process of decision-making in the setting of local communities, places moral constraints around the exercise of authority, places specific constraints on the monarchy, refuses priests and Levites the possession of land and makes them dependent on the community, and warns people not to trust prophets just because they are prophets but to accept responsibility for discerning whether the word they have spoken actually came from Yhwh. And it leaves all these loci of authority in tension with each other. "Deuteronomy thus moves beyond what ethicist Paul Lehmann describes as the false opposition between hierarchy and equality to a model of 'reciprocal responsibility' involving both those who hold authority and those who are led."[15]

The authority of the Torah is then of key importance in this connection. The Torah is to rule the people's lives, the leadership's task is to work to this

---

[13]Yoder, *Priestly Kingdom*, pp. 28-34.

[14]Cf. Mark E. Biddle, *Deuteronomy* (Macon, Ga.: Smith & Helwys, 2003), p. 296.

[15]Dennis T. Olson, *Deuteronomy and the Death of Moses* (Minneapolis: Fortress, 1994), pp. 78-79, referring to Paul Lehmann, "The Commandments and the Common Life," *Int* 34 (1980): 341-55, and to Louis Stulman, "Encroachment in Deuteronomy," *JBL* 109 (1990): 613-32, who adds that Deuteronomy also puts constraints round the power of the head of the family and gives more authority to the elders (see pp. 628-30). See also Norbert Lohfink, *Great Themes from the Old Testament* (Chicago: Franciscan, 1981/Edinburgh: T & T Clark, 1982), pp. 55-75 = Duane L. Christiansen, ed., *A Song of Power and the Power of Song* (Winona Lake, Ind.: Eisenbrauns, 1993), pp. 336-52.

end, and the people's responsibility is to hold the leadership to the same judgment. "Deut 16:18–18:22 is radical in its opposition to ANE modes of administration that emphasize the role of the king." Instead it gives power to the people and to Torah.[16]

Josephus calls Deuteronomy Israel's "polity" or "constitution."[17] The distinctiveness of this "social charter" lies in "its concern to empower a broad constituency of the community" as it addresses "all Israel," "both as a corporate entity and as a collectivity of individual selves."[18] Indeed, one might see the Torah as a whole in this way; Yhwh demands that the covenant requirements in Exodus 21–23 be set before the entire people and that in the "divinely ordained polity" the society that is envisaged "lacks a strong, prestigious focus of power."[19] The requirement regarding the reading and teaching of the Torah to the entire people also has the effect of preventing the accumulation of power through control of information. It puts responsibility on the people as a whole for implementing the Torah in its life, and (whether or not it intends to do so) frees people to critique human authorities: subjects to critique their rulers; laypeople their priests, Levites and prophets; children their parents; and the poor the rich.[20] The requirement contrasts with the practice in some evangelical churches of not reading Scripture and leaving the power to interpret Scripture in the control of the pastor.

Conflict

Conflict between leaders is a regular part of Israel's life, as it is a regular part of the church's life.

Miriam and Aaron attack Moses for marrying a Sudanese wife and combine that with questioning whether Yhwh speaks only through Moses (Num 12:1-3). That leads Yhwh to assert the unique significance of Moses. He is not merely a prophet, with whom Yhwh speaks in visions and dreams, but a supremely trustworthy person with whom Yhwh speaks mouth to mouth

---

[16]Peter T. Vogt, *Deuteronomic Theology and the Significance of* Torah (Winona Lake, Ind.: Eisenbrauns, 2006), pp. 224, 225.

[17]E.g., Josephus *Antiquities* 4.8.2 [4.184]. See J. Gordon McConville's emphasis on Deuteronomy's significance for political theology, not least in its implicit critique of David-Zion theology, in "Law and Monarchy in the Old Testament," in *A Royal Priesthood? The Use of the Bible Ethically and Politically,* ed. Craig Bartholomew et al. (Grand Rapids: Zondervan/ Carlisle, U.K.: Paternoster, 2002), pp. 69-88.

[18]S. Dean McBride, "Polity of the Covenant People," *Int* 41 (1987): 229-44; see pp. 237, 243, = *A Song of Power and the Power of Song,* pp. 62-77; see pp. 70, 77.

[19]Moshe Greenberg, "Biblical Attitudes Towards Power," in *Religion and Law,* ed. Edwin B. Firmage et al. (Winona Lake, Ind.: Eisenbrauns, 1990), pp. 101-12; see pp. 105. Greenberg also comments on the way the Torah attempts to prevent the accumulation of economic power (see §4.4 "Loci of Responsibility").

[20]Cf. Greenberg, "Biblical Attitudes Towards Power," pp. 107-9.

and plainly rather than in enigmatic words. As a servant who is a member of Yhwh's household, Moses is like one of the later prophets who stand in Yhwh's court and take part in its deliberations, but even among such, Moses has a unique status. The statement points to the permanent authority of the word of Moses (enshrined in the Torah) over the visions and words of prophets and the teaching of priests. Miriam (as prophet and as the leader in the conflict?) is punished by being temporarily afflicted with a skin disease, which would require her to remove herself momentarily from the community; which leads Aaron to turn to Moses on her behalf, and Moses to cry out to Yhwh on her behalf.

The Levite Korah, with Dathan, Abiram and On, Reubenites, and 250 other Israelite leaders arise against Moses and Aaron and accuse them of elevating themselves over the congregation as a whole (Num 16). Moses treats this as especially a complaint on the part of Korah and other Levites over against Aaron; they want to share in the priesthood. He also summons Dathan and Abiram, but they refuse to come, though in replying make clear that for their part their complaint concerns Moses' own leadership and specifically his action in punishing people. That issues in the death of the complainants and in further conflict involving the people as a whole, which leads Moses to bid Aaron make expiation for them, though 14,700 die, and leads Yhwh to give a sign to confirm the position of Aaron. The people then come to recognize the need that leads to the clan of Levi being in its special position (Num 17:12-13 [MT 27-28]); if anyone in the community can casually go into Yhwh's dwelling, that is bound to have horrific consequences. The troublesome and unimaginable story does recognize that Yhwh must resolve such disputes, not the leaders themselves. And while Korah, Dathan and Abiram may be wrong about Moses and Aaron, the problem they identify is real. Eventually Moses and Aaron almost prove them right (Num 20:1-13).

So these stories undergird the position of both Moses and Aaron. The Torah's sole paragraph about kings (Deut 17:14-20) emphasizes the importance of kings submitting themselves to Moses' Torah (cf. Ps 89:30-32 [MT 31-33]; 132:12). Indeed, having a copy of the Torah made for him so that he can study it every day is the one positive task Deuteronomy enjoins upon the king; his role is thus "simply to be the model Israelite."[21] Joshua's leadership operates on that basis. When Moses asks Yhwh to appoint someone over the community for the time after he himself dies, to lead them in and out like a shepherd, and Yhwh designates Joshua as a man who has spirit in him and bids Moses give him some of his honor or majesty or status (*hôd*) so that the whole com-

---

[21]Hans Walter Wolff, *Anthropology of the Old Testament* (London: SCM Press/Philadelphia: Fortress, 1974), pp. 197-98.

munity may pay heed to him, Yhwh adds that he is to stand before Eleazar the priest, who will ask for the decision of the Urim before Yhwh for him (Num 27:15-23).[22] It is on the basis of such guidance that he will lead the flock in and out. Yhwh's instructions to Joshua (Josh 1:1-9) then reexpress this in the terms that apply to the king in Deuteronomy 17:14-20. His leadership operates in the context of Yhwh's promise to give his people the land, and therefore he is to be confident about that, but the further key to his success is to make sure he exercises his leadership on the basis of the teaching Moses enjoined on him (that is, Deuteronomy). "This book of teaching is not to leave your lips, but you are to recite it day and night," so as to make sure of this. In this respect Joshua is to live like a king (or vice versa) but also to live like an ordinary Israelite (Ps 1:2) (or vice versa). If that can be taken for granted, then the people's subservience to its leadership can be affirmed (Josh 1:16-18). The other end of Joshua's time as leader is marked by a challenge to serve Yhwh and abandon other deities, and by writing laws into a book in the manner of Moses (Josh 24:1-28).

For the kings Psalm 72 spells out the implications, and 1 Kings 9–11 urges them on Solomon and then critiques him for not accepting this subordination. The basis for the critique of David in 2 Samuel 11–12 is strikingly less specific; "despising Yhwh's word" suggests reference to a prophetic word, perhaps that in 2 Samuel 7, though the phrase does significantly parallel Numbers 15:31. Joshua-Kings then comprises "an assessment of the demise of Israel and Judah . . . in which Hezekiah and Josiah are pitched as reformist heroes. . . . A focus on the institution of kingship drives the entire work."[23] It implies the expectation that the monarchy will be reestablished, but it also implies that it must observe the constraints of exclusive trust in Yhwh and devotion to Yhwh in subservience to the prophets, and that both must be subordinate to Moses.

Impressiveness

Human leaders look impressive, but Psalm 146 warns about being misled: "Do not rely on leaders, on a human being, with whom there is no deliverance; his breath goes, he returns to his ground, on that day his deliberations have perished." Of course you may have no alternative. Or perhaps you have. "The good fortune of the people who have the God of Jacob as their help, whose expectation is in Yhwh their God." They can trust in this Yhwh, the creator, the one who keeps faith, exercises authority for the oppressed, gives food to the hungry, frees prisoners, opens the eyes of the blind, lifts up the

---

[22]See further §7.3 "A Ministry of Supervision and a Ministry of Music."
[23]Pleins, *Social Visions of the Hebrew Bible*, p. 99.

bowed down, watches over strangers, relieves orphan and widow, subverts the way of the faithless—and who will reign forever. How foolish to rely on human rulers, whether Israelite kings, imperial powers, Judean governors or the leaders of other local peoples. They are but human. They are vulnerable. They die, and their projects and plans die with them. They cannot do those things that Yhwh does.

Leaders experience pressures that other people do not. They consequently call on the God who is in their midst in urgent ways and find God's answers, and they are able to demolish the attacks on them. They then come back to the community to tell it about this and thus encourage it (e.g., Ps 118). They prove Yhwh's commitment, and their story encourages the community to live confident of Yhwh's commitment. It is tempting for people to trust in their leaders or for them to trust in the support of other powerful people, but their testimony shows the wisdom of rather taking refuge in God.[24] It is tempting to assume that the humanly impressive wins the day, but the humanly unimpressive is what often does so, because God's presence and activity turn all other odds upside down. So leaders and community join in celebrating the day when God has acted, in processing, making offerings, rejoicing, lifting God high and making this experience the basis for urging God to complete the work of which this is part.

The natural rule is to choose the strong to lead, but Yhwh chooses the weak, people whom one would not naturally choose (Abel, Jacob, Joseph, Moses, Saul, David). There is no one on earth more weak (ʿānāw) than Moses (Num 12:3). Admittedly, people such as Joseph, Saul and David are good-looking guys, yet they are also people with manifest character weaknesses such as ambition, fear, indecisiveness and sexual indiscipline, and generally these weaknesses become more rather than less problematic as time goes by. Further, the way these leaders are expected to exercise their leadership goes against the natural rule (for instance, when Gideon reduces his army to three hundred).[25] Yet, paradoxically, God's way of doing things such as freeing prisoners and watching over strangers does often involve using people who are willing or want or have the instinct to be involved in politics or leadership, who may do it as God's servants and agents (Moses, David) or may not.[26]

Further, "Eminence before ruin, exaltation of spirit before a fall; better to be lowly in spirit with the weak than to share spoils with the eminent" (Prov 16:18-19). The traditional rendering of the first aphorism is "Pride goes before a fall," but the aphorism is more equivocal and thought-provoking. "Emi-

---

[24]Cf. James L. Mays, *Preaching and Teaching the Psalms* (Louisville: Westminster John Knox, 2006), p. 148.

[25]Martin Buber, *On the Bible* (New York: Schocken 1982), pp. 141-42.

[26]E. Hill, *Prayer, Praise and Politics* (London: Sheed & Ward, 1973), pp. 70-73

nence" *(gā'ôn)* is not usually a negative idea, and the aphorism makes the more worrying, more realistic and less moralistic point that people in a position of importance and power often find themselves thrown from it, and not merely because their attitude to their position has gone wrong. Likewise the "weak" (*'ăniyyîm* K, *'ănāwîm* Q) are people who are powerless and resourceless. Weakness may encourage humility or it may not, but these adjectives too have no inherent moral connotations. It is the qualification "exaltation *of spirit*" that introduces the moral idea. It might then carry back its connotations into the first, but the rhetorical delay ("in spirit" is the last word in the line) encourages a more subtle reading. Important people can fall from their position when there is nothing wrong with their attitude, but ordinariness removes one factor that generates calamity. Being among the rich and powerful means you are always in danger of that fall. It is better to be an average person with enough to get by but nowhere to fall and nothing to be anxious about. If you get ambitious to join the rich and powerful and thus surrender your contentment, that qualification "lowly *in spirit*," introducing the moral idea, encourages you not to be so stupid. "Before ruin a person's heart is high, and weakness goes before honor" (Prov 18:12). Exaltation of heart might imply pride and weakness might imply humility, but the saying also suggests a more phenomenological point. What goes up comes down; what is now down may soon be on high. Who knows? Thus "better to be long-tempered than a warrior, to be a person with self-control than one who takes a city" (Prov 16:32).

Qualifications for Servanthood

Moses (and Miriam and Aaron) come from a distinguished community of servants of Yhwh (Ex 1–2). There are the two midwives who revere Yhwh and therefore deceive the king and let Israelite baby boys live. There are Moses' mother and sister who also deceive the king's daughter and keep him alive. Moses starts off as a rather fumbling servant of his people but then proves a more successful servant of some Midianite girls.

But none of that involves a commission from a master. When a commission comes, Moses tries hard to evade it, but as Jeremiah will find, when Yhwh's mind is made up, there is no resisting (Ex 3–4). There is no indication in the account that Moses has the personal gifts or spiritual qualities to make a leader. Fortunately this does not matter, because he does not have to undertake what we would think of as a leadership role. All that is required of Moses and Aaron is to keep acting as Yhwh commands. That does not exactly involve them in doing anything. They are bidden to give commands to the Pharaoh to get him to release the people from his servitude so that they can serve Yhwh, to issue threats to him and to be the means of doing extraordinary signs before him, so that he and the rest of the world acknowledge that Yhwh is God. And their efforts are a complete failure in the sense that the Pharaoh never finally does what Yhwh bids until Yhwh brings about a terrible act of destruction.

They are also failures in their relationship with their own people. They have a hard time keeping the Israelites focused on leaving Egypt and a hard time keeping them focused on getting to the promised land. The most important thing Moses does is plead with Yhwh not to treat them as they deserve (Num 11:2). But he also gets angry with his task and protests to Yhwh at the burden Yhwh places on him in having to look after this people with their complaints (Num 11:10-15). This leads Yhwh to withdraw some of the spirit that was on Moses and put it on seventy of the elders who can share the burden of the people with him, which causes them to "behave like prophets," presumably something like speaking in tongues, for a while (Num 11:16-25). Moses is not troubled by reports of spiritual goings on outside his supervision; he would be happy for all Yhwh's people to be prophets, for Yhwh's spirit to be on them all (Num 11:26-30).

When Yhwh determines to destroy the people with an epidemic and dispossess them because they do not think they can overcome the Canaanites, and to make of Moses a much more numerous nation, Moses argues Yhwh out of this intention by means of a reminder of the divine nature that Yhwh had revealed at Sinai, as one characterized by long-temperedness and commitment in carrying waywardness and rebellion (Num 14). At the same time Moses has to confront the Israelites when they decide to march on Canaan, having seen they were wrong earlier, but finds them less amenable to reason than Yhwh is. They also complain at Moses personally. When they lack bread and water and have come to loathe the food they do have, they attack Yhwh and Moses for bringing them out from Egypt to die in the wilderness (Num 21:4-5). Then, when Yhwh sends poisonous snakes against them, they beg Moses to plead with Yhwh for them, and he does so, and Yhwh responds. Moses and Aaron's eventual failure is that "you did not trust in me in making me holy in the eyes of the Israelites" (Num 20:12). For Deuteronomy one implicit significance of the fact that Moses must die east of the Jordan is that Israel will enter the land under another leader (Deut 3:22-28) and with the vast restatement of Yhwh's instructions that Moses will now give ("So now, Israel, listen").[27] Moses is not indispensable. Which is what he argued at the beginning.

The success of leaders is regularly interwoven with their failure, as is the case with Moses and David. Indeed, the Bible is inclined to a "glorification

---

[27]Cf. Biddle, *Deuteronomy*, pp. 73-74.

of failure" which culminates in the line of the prophets, who are nearly all failures.[28]

Trust for the Challenges of Leadership

Leaders often have a hard time trusting Yhwh when they face the challenge of leadership. Deborah knows Yhwh intends to use Barak to rescue Israel from Jabin, king of Hazor. "If you go with me, I will go, but if you will not go with me, I will not go" (Judg 4:8). One sympathizes, though Deborah's response is roughly "Okay, you wimp." Barak wins the victory, but the glory goes to Deborah and Jael.

Gideon's tale is also a comic one, or a tragicomedy. Yhwh's aide appears to him and says, "Yhwh is with you, mighty warrior" (Judg 6:12). Gideon has problems with both halves of this greeting. If Yhwh is with us, why are we in such a mess? And how can I be a mighty warrior, being the youngest member of a household in the lowliest clan in Manasseh? The latter objection is quite reasonable if one leaves Yhwh out of account. But Yhwh enjoys using feeble and unfashionable people like little brother Othniel, left-handed or handicapped Ehud, Shamgar with his Canaanite name, wimpy Barak and disbelieving Gideon. "Give me a sign that you are the one speaking with me" (Judg 6:17). So Yhwh does, and Gideon cannot get out of doing what Yhwh says and pulling down the family altar to the Master in the village. He does it when no one is looking, but he is found out all the same.

There was just one thing required of Gideon to make him count among the good guys. It was not whether he *really trusted* in Yhwh; evidently he did not. It was rather whether he really trusted *in Yhwh*. What matters is not whether someone trusts or doubts, but who they do put their trust and doubt in. From the beginning, when the aide declared that Yhwh was with him, Gideon's reaction was not "Actually we are servants of the Master, not Yhwh." His reaction presupposed a commitment to Yhwh rather than the Master; the question was, is Yhwh really committed to us. Yhwh has no problem with thinness of trust as long as it is located in the right place. The thinness of trust that makes Gideon ask for a sign and then, when he has received one, makes him act by night is no problem to Yhwh. What counts is his willingness to act on the basis of his thin trust. Gideon's father also comes good in this context. It was he who had maintained an altar to the Master, and had given his son the suspicious name Jerub-Baal, which was open to reinterpretation (Judg 6:32) but surely implied a commitment to Baal, the Master. Yet when his fellow villagers want to execute Gideon for his action, Joash's reaction is to urge people to let the Master do his own dirty work. "If he is a god, let him contend for

---

[28]Buber, *On the Bible*, p. 143.

himself." It rather looks as if Joash has been brought back to trust in Yhwh, or at least that he is open to moving in that direction. Even the thinness of Gideon's trust that wants two more signs before he takes any more action is no problem to Yhwh (Judg 6:35-40). Choosing people of deeper faith would enable Yhwh to economize on signs, but perhaps Yhwh has to make the most of the talent available.

Yhwh subsequently managed to reverse all these dynamics (Judg 7). Gideon had too big an army. It would look as if it is the size of an army that is the crucial factor that determines success or failure. Without a murmur Gideon let his army be cut down by more than 99 percent. Then Yhwh gave him another free sign, and when he heard about it, "he bowed down" and summoned his three hundred to attack, because "Yhwh has given the Midianite camp into your hands" (Judg 7:15). The wimp has turned into a mighty warrior.

Signs are an ambiguous business. Yhwh offers a sign to another leader who is understandably scared stiff of the political and military pressures he faces (Is 7:11). Cleverly, he declines to test Yhwh; he gets a sign anyway, but it will do him no good.[29] On the other hand, Ahaz's successor asks Yhwh for a sign that the same prophet's promise of healing will come true, and Yhwh grants an extraordinary one (Is 38:7-8, 22). Similarly, when Yhwh reaffirms the implausible promise about giving Abraham a land, Abraham asks how he can be sure that this will happen, and Yhwh in effect gives him a sign, a very down-to-earth one involving an implicit self-curse: may I be cut up like these animals if I do not keep my promise (Gen 15:7-21). It is worth a leader taking the risk of telling Yhwh that we need a sign if we are to believe. We may get a rebuke; but we may get a sign.

Power Corrupts?

Leaders are supposed to lead, and they are in trouble when they do not or when they lead the wrong way. In the First Testament their vocation is to lead people in their relationship with God, and failure means failure in this respect. But having gifts of leadership or being put into a position of leadership through birth or being elected to leadership does not depend on being more committed to God than other people. Nor does it carry with it any resources that lead to greater such commitment. Indeed, it brings with it various pressures that drive a person in the opposite direction. In the church it is hard for power not to corrupt people, and so it was in Israel.

Micah summons Israel's "heads" and "rulers" (qāṣîn) to listen, and asks them a rhetorical question (what else is he in a position to do?). "Should you not acknowledge how to exercise authority, you who are against good and for

---

[29]See further §5.2 "Signs to Encourage Trust."

evil?" (Mic 3:1). The EVV have the community's leaders not "knowing" how to lead, but more likely *da'at* has its common implication of acknowledging and committing oneself. As leaders they have a responsibility to be concerned for what is right. Should they not both know how to exercise authority and also acknowledge how to do so and commit themselves to this *(da'at 'et hammišpāṭ)?* Authority is supposed to be exercised in a way that promotes good rather than evil (cf. Amos 5:15), but leaders characteristically promote evil rather than good because they are concerned for what is best for themselves (cf. Is 5:20). Micah goes on to a horrified and horrific description of these leaders butchering their people, anticipating Ezekiel's condemnation of shepherds who feed off the sheep instead of feeding them (Ezek 34:1-10). And these sheep are the "household" or family to which the leaders belong; it is as if they were abusing their own children. "What is now happening in Jerusalem is an unheard-of economic cannibalism practiced by the heads and leaders."[30] For Micah, they are "my people." Are they not "my people" for these leaders? One can imagine the people are crying out to their leaders, whose vocation was to be concerned for their welfare not to attack it, and crying out to Yhwh, who one hopes responds to them; Micah comments that eventually their leaders are going to cry out to Yhwh, but Yhwh "will hide his face from them," will not respond to their cry (Mic 3:4).

Micah goes on to restate the point to these leaders, doubling the reference to the position of the people they are oppressing as their "household" (Mic 3:9-12). He complements the earlier rhetorical question with a statement: they make the exercise of authority into an abomination.[31] Their exercise of authority makes it into the kind of thing that any decent Israelite would reject as incompatible with faith in Yhwh. "They twist everything that is straight": it is another fresh and vivid way of saying they are against good and for evil. They are people who are responsible for developing the city, which in Micah's day saw unprecedented expansion, but they are doing so by means of bloodshed and oppression (cf. Jer 22:13-17). With the usual irony, that might mean repeating the kind of ill treatment Egypt had once imposed on Israel, forcing men to work on arduous and dangerous construction projects (such as the Siloam tunnel?). Or it might mean financing the building of well-appointed houses for themselves by acquiring other people's land and thus their means of life. Micah makes explicit that this can involve not merely making the law work to their advantage but perverting its working by accepting bribes to get people to make the "right" decision. Leaders can usually be bought (cf. Is

---

[30]Hans Walter Wolff, *Micah* (Minneapolis: Augsburg Press, 1990), p. 100.
[31]EVV understand the piel of *tā'ab* to mean "regard as an abomination," but "make into an abomination" (cf. Ezek 16:25) better fits the parallelism in this context.

1:23). Nor are they the only people for whom money talks; the same is true of priests and prophets.

False Confidence

Yet at the same time they rely on Yhwh (Mic 3:11), which is what Israel is supposed to do. All the First Testament's other references to relying on Yhwh are positive, while its negative references to reliance denote relying on the wrong thing (e.g., Is 10:20). These leaders reassure themselves that Yhwh is in the midst and that therefore things will be okay. Micah does not say whether they are right or wrong in that double conviction. Other prophets affirm it (e.g., Jer 14:9; Hos 11:9). Zephaniah 3 refers three times to Yhwh's being in the midst but is more ambiguous about whether that is a threatening reality or a reassuring one. In the midst of the city are officials like lions and wolves night and morning, prophets who are reckless and faithless in their encouragement of this, and priests who fail to give the instruction on distinguishing between holy and everyday that is their responsibility. Their behavior contrasts with the nature and behavior of Yhwh, "the faithful one in its midst" (Zeph 3:5). In the midst of the city the leadership is a frightening presence, whereas Yhwh's presence there is an encouraging one. Night and morning the leadership feed off the people; morning and evening Yhwh acts with authority and faithfulness. Perhaps Zephaniah refers to the faithful way Yhwh maintains the sequence of morning and evening.[32] Yhwh's faithfulness is an encouragement to the people; it means the day of reckoning for the leadership must come. The city's prophets cannot be relied on; Yhwh can. Its priests give decisions that cannot be trusted; Yhwh's can. Yhwh's presence in the midst of the city will turn out to be a solemn reality for them. In Amos 5:17 Yhwh's presence is unambiguously threatening. Relying on Yhwh through being confident that Yhwh is in the midst has made people's offense greater. This leads to the saying of Micah's that everyone remembered, about the city being turned into a total ruin, a field for plowing, and the temple mount being turned into nothing more than an impressive example of a Canaanite sanctuary (Mic 3:12; cf. Jer 26:17-19).

Much later, Ezekiel has a vision of twenty-five leaders whom God describes as "the men who think up wrongdoing and formulate bad policy in this city, who say 'No building houses in the near future: this is the pot and we are the meat' " (Ezek 11:2-3). The leaders do not see themselves as thinking up wrongdoing. They see themselves as the good meat in the pot (the good figs, to use the image in Jer 24). The future of Yhwh's work lies with them. The aim of

---

[32]See Jimmy J. M. Roberts, *Nahum, Habakkuk, and Zephaniah* (Louisville: Westminster John Knox, 1991), p. 214.

their meeting is perhaps to formulate wise political policies for the city. They are half way between the fall of Jerusalem in 597 and that in 587, but they do not know this. They see themselves as leaders of a community recovering from the fall in 597, and they are planning for a better future. Or (on gloomier days) they see themselves as leaders of a community that may indeed face another Babylonian invasion and that needs to prepare wisely for that. They do not think they are formulating bad policy. When they see themselves able to take over the houses of people who have been carried off into exile (people such as Ezekiel and his community) and therefore not needing to build their own, they are only following an example within Scripture (Deut 6:10-11). One of the most frightening problems of leadership is self-deception. There is always another way of looking at the situation.

There are moral reasons why their way cannot be right. Yhwh addresses them as "household of Israel." This is the entity of which they are leaders. The phrase again underlines the scandal in what follows. "You have slain many in this city. You have filled its streets with the slain" (Ezek 11:5-6). We do not know whether Ezekiel refers to religious persecution (for instance, the killing of prophets as collaborators), to the political policies that led to the earlier fall of Jerusalem and thus brought death to many people, to lawless gang violence as the structures of society collapse, or to the use of legal means to deprive people of their land and thus ultimately of their lives. Ezekiel later compares them to "wolves tearing prey, in shedding blood, in destroying lives, for the sake of acquiring wealth" (Ezek 22:27).

Far from being safe in this "pot," they will end up as dead as the people for whose deaths they are responsible (Ezek 11:7-11). Nebuchadnezzar will indeed slay the king's sons in (or on the run from) this city. Within Ezekiel's vision, at least, one of the leaders immediately drops dead.

Irresponsible Shepherding

"Shepherd" is a standard image for leadership in the Middle East. Shepherds were responsible for making sure their flocks had water and food and were protected from other animals, and to that end they exercised firm authority over them. Shepherding is not a "pastoral" image; "shepherds with their flocks" can be an expression for invading kings with their armies (Jer 6:3; cf. Jer 12:10; 25:34-37; 51:23). Shepherding was a tough outdoor job involving hard and dangerous work, but giving one the opportunity to make a little on the side (for instance, by sheep stealing). It is not a frequent image for the ministry of priests or prophets; the king of a Middle-Eastern people was commonly described as its shepherd, but the First Testament uses the word in the plural, not as a term for the king in particular but for leaders in general.

"The shepherds rebelled against me" (Jer 2:8): here the term may cover both religious and political leaders. Identifying with Jerusalem, Jeremiah laments the city's (imminent) destruction and the scattering of its population, "because the shepherds have been stupid and have not had recourse to Yhwh. Thus they have not acted sensibly,[33] and all their flock has scattered" (Jer 10:21). Therefore "the wind will shepherd your shepherds." Or is it "will feed on your shepherds" or "will shepherd your partners" (so LXX)?[34] Jeremiah has already said "for all your lovers have been crushed," and he now goes on, "and your lovers will go into exile" (Jer 22:20, 22). "My people have been lost sheep," led astray by their shepherds and paying the price for it as they wander on the mountains with no resting place (Jer 50:6-7). "Hey, shepherds, destroying and scattering the flock I pasture. . . . You have scattered my flock and driven them away and not attended to them. Now: I am attending to you" (Jer 23:1-2). Yhwh will also personally shepherd the flock (Jer 23:3; 31:10). But in addition, "I will set up shepherds over them, and they will shepherd them. They will not be afraid any more, or dismayed, and none will be missing"[35] (Jer 23:4). "I will give you shepherds of my choice[36] and they will shepherd you with knowledge and discernment" (Jer 3:15); that is what shepherds require.

Ezekiel 34 develops the shepherd image most systematically. The shepherds have been feeding themselves instead of feeding the sheep. It is the inbuilt temptation of leadership, particularly in systems that require people to volunteer for or seek leadership, such as democratic states and churches. People end up as leaders because they want to be leaders. They are fulfilling themselves. It is almost impossible to imagine that they will lead in an unselfish way. So pastors and politicians commonly live better than their congregation or community, receive a better salary, eat better food, enjoy better health care and look forward to a better pension. Instead of feeding the sheep, they feed off them.

Yhwh has several pieces of good news for the flock. Most basically, Yhwh will take responsibility for shepherding the flock. In the First Testament God intended to be the people's king, and in the New Testament Christ intended to be the people's shepherd. The idea that Israel should have a human king emerged from its own desire, as did the idea that a Christian congregation should have a human shepherd. Perhaps these developments were inevitable,

---

[33]The EVV translate "prosper," but this more common meaning of *śākal* (hiphil) makes better sense in the context (cf. Vg).

[34]There are two verbs *rāʿâ*, one meaning "shepherd" or "graze," the other meaning "associate with/be a friend of."

[35]The verb is again *pāqad* (though now niphal), the verb translated "attend to" two verses previously.

[36]Lit. "according to my heart."

but they have significant down sides, and Yhwh intends to give the other system another chance by sacking the shepherds and assuming direct responsibility for the sheep for a while. Yhwh will seek out the sheep where they are scattered as a result of the neglect of their shepherds and bring them back to pasture on the mountains of Israel and by their watercourses. The self-serving of the shepherds will be replaced by the faithfulness of Yhwh.

One of the vocations they have neglected is that of keeping discipline among the sheep and goats. It is said that one of the reasons why churches have inadequate pastors is that they only have laypeople to choose from. The sheep share the selfishness of the shepherds. So one task Yhwh will take on is the disciplining of the flock so that they eat and drink in a way that does not spoil the pasturage and the water for other members, and so that the members who are already fat and strong do not use their strength to push out the ones who are thin and weak. The kings were supposed to prevent some people having opportunity to become wealthy at the expense of others who lose the possibility of living securely with a confidence about where next year's meals are coming from, but they have failed to do so. Yhwh will take action to ensure this.

There is some irony about the fact that subsequently Zechariah 10:2-5 has to rework these promises again, when once more the people are wandering like sheep without a shepherd.

Elders

Any First Testament community would be expected to have a group of elders, who were literally the senior members of the community, probably the heads of families, many of them people whom we would call middle-aged.[37] The elders were the community's guardians, not least when they gathered at the city gate to make decisions and solve community disputes, like a court. In Jerusalem there is an analogous group of senior members of the nation as a whole. The First Testament has various terms to describe the people in such a position; no doubt names and roles changed over the centuries. For the nation as a whole, while prophets share visions and priests offer teaching, elders shape policy (Ezek 7:26); this threefold division corresponds to that between priests, prophets and experts (Jer 18:18). Where there is no king and court, the elders are the main leadership group. It is they whom Joel begins by addressing (Joel 1:2, cf. Joel 1:14; 2:16).

Exodus 18:12 presupposes the existence of a group of elders, who join in a sacrificial meal with Moses, Aaron and Jethro. In Exodus 18:13-27 the judge-or king-like Moses is sitting all day making decisions *(šāpaṭ)* for the people,

---

[37]See §4.4; and Hanoch Reviv, *The Elders in Ancient Israel* (Jerusalem: Magnes, 1989).

and his father-in-law advises him to appoint a body of "heads" or "leaders" (śarîm) to do this (cf. 1 Sam 8:12). In Numbers 11, for parallel reasons Yhwh bids Moses select seventy of the elders to share the burden of carrying the people, and Yhwh puts on them some of the spirit that was on Moses, some of Yhwh's own spirit (Num 11:25, 29). Neither story indicates that they function by working out how to apply Moses' teaching to the people; Exodus 18:20 implies that Moses should teach them, and they should then be in a position to determine most questions for themselves. When the elders offer Rehoboam good advice about being a servant to his people (1 Kings 12:6), its basis looks more like common sense or "wisdom." Perhaps this fits the fact that in Numbers 11:16-30 their appointment is marked by extraordinary (temporary) spiritual manifestations. That event conveys the gift of wisdom. Jethro advises Moses to choose people to make decisions who are capable, trustworthy, people who revere God and repudiate concern for monetary gain (Ex 18:21). Moses' later recollection is of getting the people to choose them but specifying that they should be wise, discerning and well-known (or experienced) (yĕduʿîm; Deut 1:13). He recalls commissioning these leaders (śōpĕṭîm) to listen to people, to make decisions (śāpaṭ) in a faithful fashion with impartiality between Israelites and aliens, ordinary people and important people alike; they are not to be intimidated by anyone, because the decision belongs to God (Deut 1:16-17).

Deuteronomy 16:18 requires Israel to appoint governors/authorities/judges (śōpĕṭîm) and administrators (śōṭĕrîm) in all its cities to make decisions (mišpaṭ) for the people with faithfulness (ṣedeq). These are hardly the elders by another name; elders do not require such appointment. Rather they are a form of local government appointed from the center.[38] Elsewhere, "officials" (śārîm) occupy the place of elders, in association with the kings in running affairs of state (e.g., Is 32:1; Jer 1:18; 17:25). Perhaps a city might have both elders who had that position in the community as the heads of households and officials who looked after the king's interests in connection with matters such as collecting taxes. Second Chronicles 19:5-7 in fact describes Jehoshaphat as appointing authorities/governors/judges. Taking up the exhortation in Exodus 23:6-8, Deuteronomy 16:19-20 goes on to declare that they are not to twist or slant their decisions by showing partiality or accepting bribes, and Jehoshaphat repeats the point (cf. Ps 15:5; 26:10). They are to commit themselves to total faithfulness (ṣedeq ṣedeq): "faithfulness, faithfulness you are to pursue."

It would indeed be people in such a position who would have opportunity to take a bribe, on which Deuteronomy 27:25 declares a curse. In Job 15:34-35, Eliphaz declares the conviction that in the end bribes will not pay, and Isaiah

---

[38]See, e.g., A. D. H. Mayes, *Deuteronomy* (London: Oliphants, 1979), p. 264.

33:15-16 promises rewards to people who refuse bribes. Proverbs 17:8, 23 and 21:14 note that bribes often do work. It is not thereby approving of them or encouraging them; indeed, it notes that the faithless offer bribes to pervert the process of decision-making *(mišpāṭ)*. Proverbs simply notes how things are in life, because wise people need to take account of the facts. Bribery was common in the culture, as it is in the modern world (1 Sam 8:3; Is 1:23; 5:23; Mic 3:11). Proverbs' comment about perverting the process of decision-making exactly corresponds to the exhortation in Exodus 23:6-8. In accepting bribes, you have ignored me, Ezekiel 22:12 comments. After all, Yhwh is one who does not take bribes (Deut 10:17; 2 Chron 19:7).[39]

Leadership in Corruption

The need for such exhortations reflects the fact that the elders' leadership is like everyone else's. In Isaiah 3:13-15, instead of exercising their responsibility as a community court, they are the subject of a greater court's deliberations. Instead of protecting the vineyard, they have pillaged it. They too have made their leadership the opportunity for doing well for themselves. Instead of protecting the rights of the weak they have themselves pillaged the weak. The elders and leaders would be familiar with the teaching that prohibits the crushing of the weak (see Prov 22:22-23) especially if the elders are the experts whose teaching is collected in Proverbs. In Isaiah 3:13-15 that teaching has been recast into the form of a judicial accusation, accompanied by the even more vivid accusation that they have ground the people as if they were grain trapped between two millstones.[40] And they are taking the risk of doing that to "my people," the vineyard. One can hardly suggest that the weak are identified with "my people"; the elders and leaders also belong to "his people," and the weak of other nations do not belong to my people (though this is not to say Yhwh could not care about them, as a passage such as Ps 82 makes clear). But the weak of Israel *do* belong to my people. The elders and leaders have been unwise to mess with them.

One key way the elders did that was by the way they managed legal processes (Is 10:1-2). There is a form of robbery that involves breaking into people's houses and stealing things, but Isaiah is concerned about a form of robbery that uses the law rather than flouting the law. Western agricultural policies are formulated so as to protect their peoples and work against the possibility that people in the Two-thirds World should be able to compete and

---

[39]Michael Goldberg links this with the fact that that Israel brought its tithes and offerings to Yhwh *after* the harvest as an expression of gratitude; it did not try to bribe Yhwh earlier in the year to ensure a good harvest ("The Story of the Moral," *Int* 38 [1984]: 15-25).

[40]Bernhard Duhm, *Das Buch Jesaia*, rev. ed. (Göttingen: Vandenhoeck, 1902), p. 26; cf. Hans Wildberger, *Isaiah 1–12* (Minneapolis: Fortress, 1991), p. 143.

thereby improve their own standard of living. Our local newspaper reports that our city authorities grant exemptions to laws about advertising and about occupying the sidewalk to businesses in a richer part of town but prosecute businesses in a poorer part of town for the same actions. In Israel, too, people in power could use legal processes to deprive vulnerable people such as widows and orphans of their land. They are again taking the risk of messing with members of "my people." They will find it gets them nowhere, because on the day of calamity the wealth they have accumulated will offer them no protection (Is 10:3-4).

In Jerusalem the elders are involved in unorthodox worship at least as much as anyone else (Ezek 8:11-12). No wonder the capacity to shape policy will desert them (Ezek 7:26). That will be the least of their problems (Ezek 9:6). In Babylon the elders sit before Ezekiel (Ezek 8:1), apparently wanting to discover what he has to say, but to what end or in what context? They come to consult Yhwh through him, but they are worshiping other gods as well as Yhwh or are worshiping Yhwh with aids such as columns and images that they believe are proper but Yhwh does not, and Yhwh is not open to being consulted by such people (Ezek 14:1-8). They will get an answer, though not of the kind they look for. Their block of stone that they see as an aid to worship is a block of stone that will actually cause them to fall to their death. When they come again "to inquire of Yhwh" and sit before Ezekiel to see if Yhwh will speak to them through him (Ezek 20:2), his only response is an indictment. Ezekiel goes on at length about the wrongdoing of their ancestors, but does this on the basis of the fact that they are carrying on in the same ways. "And shall I be available to be consulted by you, household of Israel?" (Ezek 20:31).

Psalm 101 provides a leader with a declaration of allegiance to affirm. The Church of England *Book of Common Prayer* prescribes its use at the anniversary of a king's accession. It begins by declaring the intention to praise "commitment and authority" (that is, the exercise of authority in a way that expresses commitment to Yhwh or to the community) and to expound on the nature of integrity, the way that is whole (*derek tāmîm*). The adjective suggests the wholeness of that commitment. It is not compromised. There is no divided heart here. Can we believe such a declaration by a leader? It goes on to declare the intention to "go about with integrity of heart within my house": in other words, this integrity will characterize the leader's behavior when no one is looking, in the privacy of home, and it will indeed characterize the heart, the inner being, the wellspring of outward life. Specifically, the psalm goes on, there will be no secret recourse to other deities, no secret collusion with people of deceit, no private recognition of wrongdoing. All this heightens the stakes. Is this simply the boldness of someone who is willing to be flagrantly untruthful? Yet the fact that this person makes this statement to Yhwh heightens the stakes in another sense. The leader would have to be a very convinced atheist to look Yhwh in the eye and make such statements knowing them to be false. Even David broke down before Yhwh. And out in the world the leader will implement that allegiance. There will be zero tolerance for people who plot against their neighbors out of their greed to defraud them; conversely, the policy will be to support people of integrity.

The Christian nations, in the West and in Africa, are especially troubled by corruption in the highest levels of government and in the world of business. In the democratic world, rulers are people who wanted power, and many of them are in church on Sundays. The psalm invites them to look God in the face and declare that they have exercised their leadership with commitment and integrity along lines the psalm describes.

The Price the People Pays

"All their officials are rebels"; all their *śārîm* are *sōrĕrîm* (Hos 9:15). Ordinary individuals are rebels, but the rebelliousness of leaders is a much more disastrous fact. It multiplies itself, as the faithfulness of leaders might if there were such a thing. "Your leaders lead you astray, they confuse the course of your paths" (Is 3:12). Yhwh is therefore taking away from Judah all its regular forms of leadership and leaving it in the charge of women and young people (Is 3:1-12). They might do the job better, yet their removal is a sign of judgment for a people that assumes proper leadership belongs in the hands of older men or that wrongful leadership is better than anarchy. Such leaders must be deposed. The people's leadership is a means of oppression, but its removal will mean more oppression, so its removal means calamity.

Hosea 5:1 bids the household of Israel, but also specifically priests and royal household, to listen, "because authority belongs to you." The indictment that follows applies to the whole people, but priests and royal family are specified. The people as a whole are guilty for their wrongdoing, but priests are the people who allow and facilitate, and perhaps take initiative, in the observances that constitute unfaithfulness to Yhwh. Further, the activities at the sanctuary stand under royal patronage (cf. Amos 7:10-17). The king cannot wash his hands of what goes on in the sanctuaries. Authority *(mišpāṭ)* belongs to him.[41]

In Isaiah's day, when Yhwh sent a "word" that brought destruction to city and forest, the people pulled themselves together like U.S. citizens after 9/11 and determined to replace the buildings with better ones. So Yhwh aroused enemies to the east and to the west against them. They still did not turn to

---

[41]If one should translate "the judgment is yours" in the sense that the judgment will fall on you (cf. NRSV, TNIV), this presupposes the same point.

Yhwh. Isaiah's earlier language recurs (Is 9:14-17 [MT 13-16]). "So Yhwh cut off from Israel head and tail, frond and reed, in one day"; Isaiah explains, "elder and dignitary, that is the head; prophet, teacher of falsehood, that is the tail." It is they who have been destroyed, on the basis of their having been people who led the community astray, so that "its led [that is, the people led by these leaders] have become ones who are confused."[42] The young men, the orphans and the widows are implicated in the society's corruption and pigheadedness as a result of the way their leaders mislead, and they are paying the price. The earlier threat (Is 3:1-12) is here an actuality. Terribly, while it is an act of deliverance for the people as a whole (who wishes to be led by misleaders?) it is simultaneously another calamity (who wishes to be led by nobody?)

The entire people has been led radically astray, so that it is characterized by corruption, wickedness and pigheadedness.[43] Its having been so led does not exempt it from calamity. People are expected to resist leadership that leads astray or they are finding that this is a consequence of being bound together in the web of life, for better and for worse. The leadership has been cut off and the people left leaderless, and Yhwh did not have mercy on the needy in taking this action.[44] The priests, experts, shepherds and prophets have misled, but the people are responsible for following. They liked the way they were misled (Jer 2:8; 5:30-31).

Experts

Alongside priest and prophet in Jeremiah 18:18 appears the *ḥākām*, conventionally "wise [man]." There is no very satisfactory translation of the word. The *ḥăkāmîm* are sages, intellectuals, philosophers, academics, writers, theologians, thinkers, scholars and teachers. It is usually assumed that their reflection and teaching lie behind and are expressed in the "Wisdom" books, where even the aphorisms about ordinary life are expressed as sayings comprising parallel bicola that suggest they have a literary rather than a popular origin.[45] We might see them as Israel's practical theologians.[46] But they are also the guardians and communicators of a tradition of learning that can guide people in the administration. They work on the basis of reason, experience and tradition, though this will also involve faith and commitment to the Torah. In the present context we are concerned with their role as "scribes" or court

---

[42]The other verb *bālaʿ* "devour" would also provide appropriate meaning here.

[43]*ḥānēp, mēraʿ, nĕbālâ.*

[44]On possible historical backgrounds, see, e.g., Hans Wildberger, *Isaiah 1–12,* p. 236; Joseph Blenkinsopp, *Isaiah 1–39,* AB (New York: Doubleday, 2000), p. 219. The lack of historical reference facilitates our looking at the pattern in the passage as a whole.

[45]Cf. Joseph Blenkinsopp, *Sage, Priest, Prophet* (Louisville: Westminster John Knox, 1995), p. 41.

[46]Brueggemann, *Theology of the Old Testament,* p. 685.

counselors. I refer to them as "experts" because in Western culture this covers several significances of *ḥākām*. They have special knowledge, this knowledge has practical application, they have a reputation as people who can be resources for decision makers, and they work behind the scenes in rather faceless fashion so that we do not know so much of precisely who they were or how they worked.

The time of Hezekiah gives us a glimpse of their activity, as they appear in connection with him and his period in Isaiah as well as in Proverbs. The stories in Daniel give us another. Daniel and his friends were people who had been trained in Jerusalem in the expertise they would need for work in the court and in politics there; Nebuchadnezzar enrolls them in the Babylonian graduate school, which he assumes to be somewhat superior, but finds that it has nothing to teach them (Dan 1:4, 17, 20), and they prove invaluable to his administration.

"Wisdom in Israel needs to be understood as a serious way in which responsible, reasonable knowledge of the world and passionate trust in God are held together."[47] Thus the introduction to Proverbs accumulates expressions to signify the pragmatic value of its insight, but then comes to declare that "the beginning [or first principle] of knowledge is reverence for Yhwh," the kind of acknowledgment that issues in submission and obedience (Prov 1:1-7). Indeed, a colon in the middle of this introduction suggests a nuancing of that definition; it slips in reference to "faithfulness in the exercise of authority, and integrity." Israel's responsible knowledge of the world includes those qualities.

Therein lies the dilemma or the besetting temptation of the experts. It was tempting in Israel as it is in the modern West to let expertise be value neutral; it concerns itself only with what works. Many of the aphorisms in Proverbs do that; taken in isolation from their context they imply no religious or ethical commitment. The experts are tempted to leave questions of value to other people, such as priests and prophets. It is for this reason that Isaiah, in particular, attacks them and declares that the expertise of the experts will fail (Is 29:14).[48] The experts counsel the administration to make its decisions on a sensible, pragmatic basis. Isaiah knows that this is not only wrong and not only a betrayal of their own vocation (to hold together practical knowledge of the world and trust in Yhwh) but also a policy that will fail.

---

[47]Walter Brueggemann, *The Creative Word* (Philadelphia: Fortress, 1982), p. 68. In this book Brueggemann takes Jer 18:18 as key to understanding the background to the First Testament as a whole.

[48]See William McKane, *Prophets and Wise Men* (London: SCM Press/Naperville, Ill.: Allenson, 1965).

7.2 Kings

The period when Israel had kings is relatively short, but the First Testament pays considerable attention to it. For Christians the fact that kingship provided an image for Jesus as "Messiah" heightens the false impression that monarchy was Israel's "normal" state. More than any other form of leadership, it illustrates the way people whose vocation is to exercise authority in faithfulness are regularly people who oppress Israel.

The Tension and the Permission

Within the Torah visions of Yhwh's blessing for the people include a leader of Judah who holds the scepter over the people as a whole (Gen 49:10) and will wield the scepter over the nations (Num 24:17).[49] The First Testament's vision for kingship is also vividly expressed in Psalms such as Psalm 2, 45, 72, and 110, where Israel's kingship is the means whereby Yhwh wills to govern the world as a whole and implement compassion and faithfulness within Israel itself; Yhwh is committed to the kings to that end. Chronicles (in a time when there are no kings) also enthuses over the Davidic monarchy. Its kings sit on Yhwh's throne reigning over Israel on Yhwh's behalf; Yhwh's kingdom lies in their power and will always do so (e.g., 1 Chron 17:13-14; 28:5; 29:23; 2 Chron 9:8; 13:5, 8). David is important for Israel's sake rather than vice versa (1 Chron 14:2).

Yet being both a theocracy, a kingdom over which Yhwh reigns, and a monarchy, a kingdom over which a human ruler reigns, stand in some tension. Further, even more than other forms of leadership, kingship is in tension with the First Testament understanding of humanity as well as its understanding of Yhwh. Among other Middle-Eastern peoples the king imaged God in the world and thus ruled over the world, and this theology undergirded the king's position, but in the First Testament, humanity, male and female, is made in God's image and put in control of the world (Gen 1:26-28; Ps 8:3-8 [MT 4-9]). The same point is implicit in the "democratizing" of the Davidic idea in Isaiah 40–55.[50]

In practice Israel's monarchy never became Yhwh's means of governing the world nor of implementing compassion and faithfulness in Israel, and

---

[49]Cf. Walther Eichrodt, *Theology of the Old Testament* (London: SCM Press/Philadelphia: Westminster, 1961), 1:473-74. He starts from a conviction about the early date of these passages; I prefer to avoid that kind of argument.

[50]Cf. Rainer Albertz, *A History of Israelite Religion in the Old Testament Period*, 2 vols. (London: SCM Press/Louisville: Westminster John Knox, 1994), 2:425; and on ambiguity of attitude after the exile, see Paul L. Redditt, "The King in Haggai-Zechariah 1–8 and the Book of the Twelve," in *Tradition in Transition*, ed. Mark J. Boda and Michael H. Floyd, LHBOTS 475 (New York/London: T & T Clark 2008), pp. 56-82.

this was in keeping with uneases about kingship that Yhwh expressed in connection with its introduction. The account of "the first attempt at establishing the monarchy in Israel" (Judg 9:8-15) "exposes the monarchy to resounding laughter,"[51] while the account of its actual establishment is explicit in its disquiet and foreboding (see 1 Sam 8). It involves dismissing Yhwh as king. And it will bring a huge cost, because central government appropriates huge resources to itself, partly for the execution of projects the people desire, but much of it to give the government a good life. In the people's mind the monarchy was "intended primarily to ensure a united military leadership in defensive warfare," but it became a "decisive factor" in shaping Israel's economic structures.[52] Someone has to pay for the splendid life of the court, the administration of the state and the professional army, and provide the labor for the king's projects. It would be surprising if the story of Ahaz and Naboth is the only one that could be told about royal appropriation of land that had once been allocated to the kin groups.

Samuel-Kings thus accepts the monarchy while warning of the consequences of centralized power. Samuel makes the point most dialectically in his farewell address (1 Sam 11), which reaffirms that the people did something very wrong in asking for a king yet affirms that it is nevertheless still open to them to revere and serve Yhwh with all their heart. Deuteronomy also accepts it, while putting constraints around it. Israel may set a king over it, but he must be someone chosen by Yhwh, an Israelite, someone "from among your brothers"; he must not accumulate horses, wives and possessions, and must keep reading this teaching of Moses in Deuteronomy so as to live by it and not exalt himself over the brothers from whose midst he was appointed.[53] There is some contrast between these conditions and the actual exercise of kingship on the part of a king such as Solomon (1 Kings 3–11). Indeed, "the conditions laid down for a king are so constrictive as to make the institution virtually unrecognizable in terms of ancient Near Eastern expectations."[54]

Divine Kingship and Human Kingship

Like all leadership, which theoretically exists for the sake of those it leads, kingship comes to be important in its own right. Psalms and Chronicles wit-

---

[51]Wolff, *Anthropology of the Old Testament*, p. 193; see further pp. 192-98.

[52]Willy Schottroff, "The Prophet Amos," in *God of the Lowly*, ed. Willy Schottroff and W. Stegemann (Maryknoll, N.Y.: Orbis, 1984), pp. 27-46; see p. 38; cf. Pleins, *Social Visions of the Hebrew Bible*, p. 254.

[53]See further §7.1 "Conflict."

[54]J. G. McConville, "Time, Place and the Deuteronomic Altar Law," in *Time and Place in Deuteronomy*, ed. J. G. McConville and J. G. Millar, JSOTSup 179 (Sheffield, U.K.: Sheffield Academic Press, 1994), pp. 89-139; see p. 108.

ness to a growing gap between people and king, and a shrinking gap between king and God (Ps 45:6 [MT 7]). In theory worship of the one true God relativizes all other powers. "But what happens if one earthly norm becomes excluded from the relativization of all that is mundane?"[55] Nevertheless the First Testament as a whole keeps emphasizing both a positive view of the monarchy and a negative one, though First Testament scholarship has identified with the latter rather than accepting this ambiguity.[56]

The confrontation between Amos and the Bethel priest Amaziah (Amos 7:10-17) raises the question of the relationship of divine and human kingship in a different way. Amos has spoken of sanctuaries being devastated and of Yhwh falling on the household of Jeroboam with the sword. Amaziah takes a report to his king, but speaks of Jeroboam's dying by the sword and Israel being exiled. The common element in Amos's words and Amaziah's report is the fall of Jeroboam as king. It is as if that is the key issue.

The situation involves a replay of events in Egypt centuries previously, not only in the oppression of the people but in the way this leads to a confrontation between two kings. Human kings are people who oppress their subjects; Yhwh as King is someone who from time to time stands up to them. In the context of international politics the king of Ephraim is a smaller fish than the king of Egypt, but in the context of God's purpose a king in Israel is much more significant than a king in Egypt. Both pretend to an authority over Israel that they do not really have, but there is more enormity about an Israelite king doing so. "Amos has said this," says Amaziah, using similar language to that which Amos would use about his own words, except that Amos would say "Yhwh has said this," speaking as the divine King's aide. Amaziah is not prepared to think of Amos's words as Yhwh's words; at least, he is not prepared to refer to them thus. He knows who is king, and Amos is "conspiring" against the "real" king (conspiring with whom?—with Yhwh?). The verb and its linked noun (*qāšar, qešer*) are ones most often used in Samuel-Kings for conspiring against the kings of Ephraim and Judah, and to suggest that Amos is so conspiring would be a plausible theory. A prophet had commissioned Jeroboam's great-grandfather to instigate a coup against the then king, and Ephraim's history is full of such events. Amaziah is not so wrong. The temple in Bethel is "the sanctuary of the king," "the house of the kingdom/king-

---

[55]Paul D. Hanson, *The People Called* (New York: Harper, 1986), p. 122. See further John Goldingay, "Images of Israel: The People of God in the Writings," in *Studies in Old Testament Theology*, David Hubbard Festschrift, ed. Robert L. Hubbard et al. (Dallas: Word, 1992), pp. 205-21.

[56]See J. M. Roberts, "In Defense of the Monarchy," in *Ancient Israelite Religion*, F. M. Cross Festschrift, ed. Patrick D. Miller et al. (Philadelphia: Fortress, 1987), pp. 377-96; see p. 377; contrast the survey in Antonius H. J. Gunneweg and Walter Schmithals, *Authority* (Nashville: Abingdon, 1982), pp. 31-48, 54-108.

ship." "In the name of the state, the priest forbids Amos from speaking at the state sanctuary, and thus in actuality tries to forbid God from speaking and acting with regard to his own people."[57] Amos is a threat to the household of Jeroboam and the land cannot endure his words. They will take its people off into exile. But Amaziah's actions contribute to the bringing about of those two events rather than to their avoidance.

In theory there is no conflict between the two kings,[58] but that is only theory.[59]

Faithfulness in Exercising Authority

Psalm 72 offers "a vision of the kingdom of God"[60] in the hand of David's successors. It is a prayer, but a cunning composition, full of irony as well as promise, of deference as well as implicit challenge. After the invocation of God, it begins with the desire that the king may be able to exercise authority, the power to make decisions *(mišpāṭ)*. This might seem an odd prayer. Exercising authority is what the king does. Thus his anger means death, so don't antagonize him, and his favor means life; it is as welcome as a rain cloud in spring (Prov 16:14-15). Yet he can never take his position for granted; he is always vulnerable to a coup. Indeed, Psalm 72 actually asks that the king may be able to exercise *God's* authority. It might thus seem to advertise itself as a distinctly subservient and ideological composition.[61] But its talk of God giving him "decisions" (plural) may already subvert that implication, because it recalls the *mišpāṭîm* in Exodus-Deuteronomy, and the *mišpāṭ* Samuel puts into writing (1 Sam 10:25). So does the reminder that the people in question is "your [Yhwh's] people," not merely "his people." The king will be unwise to ill-treat Yhwh's people. The opening lines' parallelism is more explicitly subversive, because alongside the freedom to exercise authority they set the exercise of faithfulness. The psalm thus begins with classic prophetic concerns, the exercise of authority in a way that expresses faithfulness to God and faithfulness to the people.

"Commitment and truthfulness protect a king, and he sustains his throne by commitment" (Prov 20:28). It is in this way that the king encourages stabil-

---

[57]Jörg Jeremias, *The Book of Amos* (Louisville: Westminster John Knox, 1998), p. 140.

[58]Sigmund Mowinckel, *He That Cometh* (Nashville: Abingdon/Oxford: Blackwell, 1956), pp. 171-72.

[59]Cf. Brueggemann, *Theology of the Old Testament*, pp. 603-4.

[60]Patrick D. Miller, "Power, Justice, and Peace: An Exegesis of Psalm 72," *Faith and Mission* 4/1 (1986): 65-70; see p. 65.

[61]Walter J. Houston speaks of "Psalm 72 and the Ideology of Royal Justice," though he recognizes the way the psalm subverts ideology (*Contending for Justice*, LHBOTS 428 [London/New York: T & T Clark, 2006], p. 138; see also "The King's Preferential Option for the Poor," *BibInt* 7 [1999]: 341-67).

ity. These virtues are like royal bodyguards, with a power of their own to sustain the proper order of society. Elsewhere Yhwh is asked to appoint such bodyguards (Ps 61:7 [MT 8]), which personify aspects of Yhwh's own character (e.g., Ps 43:3; 89:24 [MT 25]). Here the qualities exist in their own right, or more likely (if we read the first colon in light of the second) personify aspects of the king's character.

> There is divination on the lips of the king;
>> in exercising authority his mouth does not betray.
> Authentic scales and balances belong to Yhwh;
>> all the weights in the bag are his work.
> Acting unfaithfully is an abomination to kings,
>> because the throne stands firm through faithfulness.
> Faithful lips are a king's delight,
>> and he gives himself to someone who speaks uprightly. (Prov 16:10-13)

If only! The single saying that does not refer to the king implicitly sets the comments about the king's power into a moral context. The word *mišpāṭ* (translated "exercising authority" and "authentic") recurs in the first two sayings and points to the tension between them. In a literal and legal sense the king set the standard for weights (cf. 2 Sam 14:26).[62] The implication of verse 11 is that the king has a broader responsibility before God for honest dealings in the community. That fits the observation in Judges 17:6 and Judges 21:25 that before there were kings people did what they liked and moral and social chaos ensued; "the monarchy was not only the upholder, but also the creator of law and order in Israel."[63] But "the king's rage is like a lion's growl; his favor is like dew on grass" (Prov 19:12; cf. Prov 20:2). He can act to punish evil and encourage good or to put down faithful people and encourage the faithless, or he can act without principle either way.

Fight the Good Fight

Saul's charismatic gift as king was the capacity to take decisive action in making war (see 1 Sam 11).[64] David had no need of such special endowment, since God could look into his heart and see that by nature he had the heart of a warrior as well as the heart of someone committed to Yhwh's cause, the kind of qualities he showed when he insisted on taking on Goliath (1 Sam 17). On their wedding day subsequent kings were reminded of their obligations as kings (perhaps the king's wedding would take place at an annual celebration

---

[62]Cf. Raymond C. Van Leeuwen, "The Book of Proverbs," *The New Interpreter's Bible* (Nashville: Abingdon, 1997), 5:17-264; see p. 160.

[63]J. Pedersen, *Israel III-IV* (London: Oxford University Press, 1953), p. 33.

[64]See Tryggve N. D. Mettinger, *King and Messiah* (Lund: Gleerup, 1976), pp. 233-53.

of his accession), and in particular of the responsibility to fight for truthfulness and faithfulness that issued from being king (Ps 45:1-7 [MT 2-8]). In keeping with the people's own rationale for having a king, to have someone to fight its battles, Psalm 45 sees fighting as key to kingship, just as the position of commander-in-chief of the armed forces is key to a U.S. President's role. Fighting the good fight is the way to use the glory and majesty attaching to their position. It is in this connection that the king wields his staff. But Psalm 45 sees the significance of his fighting in a different way from 1 Samuel 8:20, or sets its concern in a broader framework. The king's vocation is not to fight for his country but to fight for a truthful purpose and a faithful cause. It is a vocation Saul initially fulfilled. As the king makes that his priority, he and other people will see awesome deeds done. That expression would point to God's deeds. God engages in the king's battling for the cause of truthfulness and faithfulness. It is the king who fights; they are the awesome deeds of his right hand. But God works with him and through him. His victories reflect the fact that he sits on God's throne, ruling Israel on God's behalf and destined to rule the world on God's behalf.

Fighting for faithfulness and attacking unfaithfulness is the framework in which Psalm 45 sets its vision of his spectacular victory over his enemies. Its encouragement to militarism is open to ideological appropriation, the ancient equivalent to providing moral justification for a war that is really designed to safeguard the oil supply. And sometimes national leaders fail to act for the cause of truthfulness because they do not see this as serving their national interests. Why should they take the risk? Sometimes they act for their national interests rather than because of a concern for what is right, even if they veil their motivation with moral considerations. By providing this overt moral rationale for the king's policies, the psalm provides a basis for the king's evaluation and critique. And when it promises that the king will retain the throne and not be deposed by some external opponent or through an internal coup, it implicitly links this promise to the fact that his commitment to uprightness, truthfulness and faithfulness is not mere theory but practice, and that the king's warrior activity has this rationale, not mere self- or national aggrandizement. It issues from God's lasting commitment to David, but that itself also presupposed this commitment to faithfulness and integrity in action. That is why God has anointed this king beyond the leaders of other peoples (or rather than other potential leaders within his own people), or why God will stand by that anointing. "A king who makes decisions truthfully for the poor—his throne stands firm forever" (Prov 29:14).

Unfortunately the Saul who did not wish to be king and by nature showed no activist gifting came to be someone who became quite happy to make (bad) decisions and quite attached to being king. It is the usual way.

Action on Behalf of the Weak

To make its opening point more definite, Psalm 72 adds that the king is thus to exercise authority for the weak among the people, delivering the needy by crushing the robber (Ps 72:4). As well as exercising his authority to protect ordinary people (EVV commonly use words such as "judge"), the king is called to exercises force and violence, not to put down popular movements but to put down the wealthy and powerful with whom government is usually allied (cf. Is 11:4). His exercise of authority in the cause of faithfulness is thus to imitate God's. Crushing the people who oppress the weak by extortion will ensure that the faithful flourish in the land, rather than being put down, driven into poverty or tempted to join the exactors because it pays (Ps 72:6-7).

"The king sits on the throne of judgment and winnows every evil person with his eyes" (Prov 20:8). He is the final court of appeal, and his decision is thus final. He *is* the Supreme Court. His task is then to winnow wheat from chaff, good from bad, like Solomon with the two women (1 Kings 3:16-28). He does that with his eyes, the means of his knowledge of what goes on, but also the embodiment of his majesty and power to act (cf. Prov 15:3; 22:12). "A wise king winnows out the faithless and drives the wheel over them" (Prov 20:26). Here the saying first nuances the identity of the subject; it is the wise king who acts thus. Then it nuances the notion of winnowing: before scattering the chaff/faithless, the farmer may begin the process of separating wheat from chaff by driving his thresher over the wheat.

Psalm 72 goes on to pray for or promise the king's rule over and recognition by the world. The basis for that is his having pity on the weak, poor and needy, and his acting to deliver and restore them from viciousness and violence (Ps 72:12-14). As their restorer (gōʾēl) the king acts as if he were the next of kin who is morally responsible to take action on behalf of members of his family when they are in need; the king is invited to see his relationship with people in family terms. This action starts within his own people; it is the action the first part of the psalm spoke of. But a king with such priorities will be an inestimable blessing to any people he rules. Perhaps the psalm implies a natural or moral order about the cosmos that generates a link between caring for the weak and finding oneself in a position of authority. Or perhaps it implies that the nations will be drawn to acknowledge a ruler who manifests these qualities. Either way, the king really gains through being in a position of power over such an empire, but the peoples of the empire also gain when such a king is their emperor. He does more than rule; he exercises domination (rādâ; Ps 72:8; cf. Ps 110:2). He takes forceful action against lawless violence as well as against his and Yhwh's enemies (insofar as these are not the same thing as lawless violence). Once again, this middle section of the psalm thus puts the deliverance of the weak and needy at the heart of what it means to exercise authority. The psalm's last line tightens the screw. The king so acts because the blood of the needy is valuable in his eyes. Leaders of nations have to take economics seriously; in modern nations it is often their first priority. This prayer turns regular economic priorities upside down. It is the blood of the needy that has economic value.

"The monarchy, denounced, by and large, for its actual practice, could be rescued as a critical ideal by putting it at the service of one of Israel's original political aims: God's liberating justice for the oppressed."[65] There were signs that David could do that, but he could not be faithful and decisive in private as well as in public, and this rebounded on his leadership, and even his religious commitment was mixed up with political calculation (2 Sam 6).

Insight

All this constitutes a challenge to the king, but it has promises attached to it. It will mean that the land prospers (Ps 72:3). The prayer does not say that God will make this happen (though it no doubt assumes that) but again implies a moral cause-and-effect nexus built into reality. When the cosmos is in proper order, with power used to protect the weak against the strong, this proper order also operates in other spheres—for instance, making nature work the way it should. Thus the king is like abundant rain falling. His faithful action generates flourishing in nature as naturally as rain does.

A second promise is that the king's policies will lead to people revering Yhwh (Ps 72:5). Needy and oppressor will do so in different ways and for different reasons, but both will recognize the king's faithful exercise of authority as coming from Yhwh and will bow before Yhwh in response. The psalm later returns to a prayer that looks rather ideological, in speaking of world dominion and world tribute for the king (Ps 72:8-11). One background is Yhwh's purpose to rule the world from Jerusalem. The king sits on Yhwh's throne there, ruling on Yhwh's behalf, as Psalm 2 makes more explicit. The prayer that he may enjoy tribute from the whole world still looks worrying. Perhaps it may be set in the context of the assumption expressed elsewhere (e.g., Is 60) that this tribute goes not merely into royal coffers and the accumulation of a more substantial harem but into temple coffers for the sustaining of the worship of the God of all the world.

Psalm 72:15-17 goes on to ask that the king may flourish and live long so that he becomes a standard for prayers for blessing, like Abraham, and asks that people may in turn pray for him and bless him. If he is that kind of king,

---

[65]Richard Bauckham, *The Bible in Politics* (London: SPCK/Louisville: Westminster John Knox, 1989), p. 49.

they will be glad to do so. Every time a king heard this psalm used in the temple, it might provoke mixed feelings. He found substantial affirmation and promise, but also worrying challenge. It as evidently subverts his position as buttresses it.

The king needs insight if he is to fulfill such a psalm's expectations. Proverbs 25:2-7 spells that out. First, he needs to know what is going on. He needs to know what is happening on the international scene in order to look after the nation's affairs, to know what is going on in his own nation if he is not to be the victim of a coup, to know his people's needs and attitudes, to be able to discover the truth about questions of justice. God can afford to be elusive; the king has to be involved. Yet there is a converse. The king needs to know all this and to formulate policies with regard to it all, and no one else (maybe not even his closest advisers) will ever know all he knows and thinks. He searches out, but he is never searched out. He stands in isolation. No wonder a wise man like Gideon or Saul refuses to be drafted or hides among the baggage.

Second, for all that, the king must pay attention to the people who surround him. His first obligation is to see that his kingdom is characterized by faithfulness (ṣĕdāqâ), and to that end it is fundamental that his cabinet comprises people so characterized. The threats to his throne may come from people nearest to it, so for the sake of his own position he needs to ensure that faithless people are removed, as a smith sees dross is removed to allow something creative to emerge. "A ruler who listens to lies—all his officials are faithless" (Prov 29:12). His openness to lies will rebound on him. He has encouraged faithlessness that can be used against him.

Third, his power is something those who get near to him always need to remember. It is tempting to want to become part of the power structure, but such desires easily backfire. Like the president in the White House, the king has the power.

Insight is Solomon's charismatic gift as king (1 Kings 3; 2 Chron 1). Unfortunately, Solomon could be wise only on a narrow front. The depiction of him as the patron of wisdom carries with it a monumental irony. The behavior of his successors underlines the point as his son Rehoboam ignores wise advice while Jeroboam "takes advice" and on its basis sets up special sanctuaries at Dan and Bethel (1 Kings 12:6-11, 28). Ahab's subsequent marriage to Jezebel (1 Kings 16) illustrates the same "wisdom" that Solomon had shown in his marriages.

A King Who Uses His Position So He Can Live Well

Leaders regularly use their position to enable them to live better than their people. King Lemuel's mother draws her son's attention to the temptation to make it the opportunity to indulge in wine, women and perhaps song. She sardonically suggests that alcohol is for those who need something to enable them to forget the hardships of their lives, not those who need a clear head to enable them to focus on relieving the needs of such people: "Open your mouth for the dumb, to make decisions for all the wretched, open your mouth, exercise authority with faithfulness, decide for the weak and needy" (Prov 31:8-9). The dumb are people who have no one to speak for them, whose voice is not heard. The king's job is not only to hear it but to articulate it.

In a systematic indictment toward the end of the story of the monarchy, Jeremiah lambasts the kings of his lifetime. There is Jehoiakim who will pay for his life with an ignominious and unlamented death, because he "builds his house on nonfaithfulness, his penthouse on misjudgment" as he forces people to work on the building for nothing. It is a fine house, "paneled with cedar, painted with vermilion." But is a fine house what makes a king? (Jer 22:13-15a). The king has that special commitment to *mišpāṭ uṣĕdāqâ*, the making of decisions in a way that pursues faithfulness in the community. Jehoiakim has given into the temptation of leadership memorably announced in Samuel's warning about the very nature of monarchy (1 Sam 8:11-18), though by no means confined to that particular form of leadership; we see it in presidents of states and companies. Possessing power makes it possible to exercise power in a way that furthers one's own interests, and one of the ways we do that is in making sure our own lives are more comfortable. We have ways of rationalizing this process. The king can reckon that the splendor of his monarchy appropriately symbolizes the splendor of his state and even the splendor of his God. Building a fine palace necessitates that some way or other the center draws to itself resources that otherwise would have enabled ordinary people to live more livable lives. The pastor having a good benefits package ensures he can focus on the ministry without worrying about his family's health care.

Jeremiah's words about profiteering, shedding innocent blood, extortion and tyranny imply not merely this Marxian point but also that the king requires people to work on his project as a conscripted unpaid or lowly paid labor force. The same would be true of the other monumental building projects that are a recurrent feature of Israel's story. Jeremiah looks at royal splendor in a different way (Jer 22:15b-17). It is not competing in cedar that makes a king. Real splendor lies in the implementation of *mišpāṭ uṣĕdāqâ*. Those were the priorities of Jehoiakim's father, the great Josiah. He lived his life as king ("he ate and drank") in such a way as to observe *mišpāṭ uṣĕdāqâ*. Further, he applied himself to defending the position of the lowly and needy, ordinary people who got into difficulties and were then at the mercy of the ancient equivalent of the loan shark. Instead of taking advantage of them in such a way as also to be able to claim to be doing them a service (I will give you money for your land) he actually did seek to support them. "Is this not to acknowledge me?" Yhwh asks. Jehoiakim is the kind of person who gains wealth fraudulently, but he will have to abandon it, and the policies by which he has operated will be discredited (Jer 17:11). Whereas the human king thus faces mid-life loss and eventual exposure for his stupidity, the divine King sits in glory on a throne that was established from the beginning, and this King will continue to be Israel's hope in the future. People who abandon Yhwh and Yhwh's ways will come to shame (Jer 17:12-13).

Nehemiah claims to have exercised his governorship in a way Jeremiah would have approved (Neh 5:14-19). One might take a suspicious stance in relation to his making this claim, but it is still significant that he recognizes this is a claim it would be important to make.

A King Who Never Has a Chance, and One Who Can Never Make Up His Mind

Jehoiakim's teenage son Jehoiachin succeeded him. He "did what was wrong in Yhwh's eyes," in his three-month reign doing nothing to reverse his father's policies (2 Kings 24:9). Presumably he was only a puppet for the administration that continued from his father's time, and Kings' routine evaluative comment is as much a comment on the administration as on him. He bears the evaluation because he *is* the king; that goes with the territory. It is thus pointed that Jeremiah's description of his deposition makes no reference to his having deserved it. Yet during those three months of his reign, and thus certainly before this "boy-king"[66] can have had much chance to take any initiatives in Jerusalem, Yhwh swears a fearsome solemn oath about him, to fling him, his mother and his offspring out of the land, never to return (Jer 22:24-30). Jehoiachin personally has done nothing to deserve his fate. Calamity comes to him because he is his father's son, his mother's son and the puppet of his administration. It is not a judgment on him but a judgment on the Davidic line. When the prophecy describes him as childless, its point is not that he will literally beget no children but that none of his sons will succeed him. Historically they indeed do not, though the prophecy's point is something more far-reaching. Yhwh has had it with the Davidic line. The declaration about Jehoiachin leads into a comment about shepherds and Yhwh's action against them (Jer 23:1-4). In isolation this would refer to the country's leadership broadly, but in the context it constitutes Yhwh's general comment on the Davidic monarchy. Yhwh intends to take back the task of shepherding from the people to whom it was delegated, though to do so only temporarily, pending the establishment of a better group of shepherds; this does not ex-

---

[66]William L. Holladay, *Jeremiah 1* (Philadelphia: Fortress, 1986), p. 606.

clude the eventual reestablishment of the Davidic line (Jer 23:5; cf. Ezek 34).

The story of Jehoiachin's successor, Zedekiah, has a different profile. He sometimes consults Jeremiah and asks him to intercede with Yhwh, yet does so via intermediaries, or in person but secretly (Jer 21:1-2, 37:3, 17). Along with the people, he makes a covenant that they will all free their Israelite bondservants in keeping with principles that emerge from the exodus, but does not hold the people to this commitment (Jer 34). He sometimes confines Jeremiah (Jer 32:2-3) but sometimes protects him when his staff are more inclined to be tough (Jer 37:11-21). Yet he asks why Jeremiah declares that the city is going to fall (Jer 32:3-5), a question to which it does not take a rocket scientist to give several answers (and to which Jeremiah gives none). He never stands up to his staff enough to escape the judgment that he did not listen to Yhwh's word through Jeremiah (e.g., Jer 37:2). When they declare that Jeremiah should be put to death, he responds, "Well, he is in your hands. The king cannot do anything against you" (Jer 38:5), though he then responds to a challenge from an African who urges him to rescue Jeremiah. He asks Jeremiah for advice but cannot take it because he lives in fear of his own people (Jer 38:19). He is a small man incapable of responding to the gigantic demands of the position he is put in. This is a common experience with a nation's leadership, and another sign that Yhwh will need to give Israel a different kind of king, one who is prepared to take the apparent risk of living by Yhwh's word and standing up to political pressures.

An Arrangement That Gets People Nowhere

Hosea had wistfully hoped that people would eventually see the point: "We have no king, because we do not revere Yhwh, and the king—what would he do for us?" (Hos 10:3). Hosea anticipates a time when Ephraim's monarchy has been terminated, presumably by Assyria's imposing direct rule, and when people will therefore acknowledge the truth about the situation and about the monarchy. This hardly constitutes their recognizing that monarchy is in principle in conflict with revering Yhwh. Rather they acknowledge that the fall of their monarchic state came about because of their not revering Yhwh. That being the key factor in their destiny, having a king again would in itself get them nowhere. As is the case with comments on the unacceptability of sacrifice, from such a comment about the monarchy one cannot infer an attitude to monarchy in principle. The issue people have to face is monarchy in practice.

The passage goes on, "They utter words, swearing empty oaths, sealing a covenant. But the exercise of authority spreads like a toxin on the furrows of the field" (Hos 10:4). Is this Hosea's comment or does it continue the imagined words of the people? In the first case, it may take further Hosea's critique of the process whereby Ephraim appoints its kings. Their recurrent coups involve them in making decisions for themselves rather than following Yhwh's directions and in breaking oaths of loyalty and covenants between king and people (cf. Hos 7:3-7). Alternatively (necessarily, if these are the people's words), the comment raise questions about the way the kings exercise responsibility for honorable government. The implicit critique of government is not the one made in Psalm 72, relating to the nation's communal life. It concerns the honor of its relations with other peoples. They negotiate and swear oaths to conclude treaties, but do so in a way that ignores their obligations to Yhwh, or they renege on their word.

Either way, the exercise of authority *(mišpāṭ)* is poisonous, and the poison spreads wide. It affects the whole of the nation's internal life, not just its internal politics or its external relationships. Either people and government behave honestly on all fronts, or they can be trusted on none. Once it seems acceptable to deceive in one direction, it will seem acceptable in others. Once one group deceives, another will follow their example. The process is indeed toxic.

> Whenever the monarchy was confronted by any problem it would always fail to rise to the occasion, and grasp at false expediencies. . . . Instead of becoming the leaders who would guide the nation to an ever deeper understanding of God's will in the changing political situation the kings entangle both themselves and the people in the sin of brutal and self-seeking power politics, knowing no maxim but that of worldly self-aggrandizement by any and every means, and so coming rapidly to disaster. There can be no sympathy for this totally corrupted institution.[67]

Ephraim is ruined. Its help lay in Yhwh, but it would not look there. "Now where is your king so that he can deliver you, in all your cities your leaders, of whom you said, 'Give me a king and officials'?" (Hos 13:9-10). Israel thought that having kings was the solution to its problems, but the vagaries of its experience have proved it wrong. When Shalmanezer removed Hoshea from the throne and laid siege to Samaria (2 Kings 17:4-5), that brought Ephraim's history to an end. There were no human resources for this leaderless community. Yhwh was always the only one who was any help to it, and the nation has turned away from that resource in the conviction that it needs some more visible help or deliverer. The statement about Yhwh being its sole help is equivalent to the original objection to kings; Yhwh was supposed to be Israel's king. Yhwh had then given kings to Israel as much as an expression of anger as anything else (Hos 13:11). Here Hosea generalizes the point and applies it to the dethroning of kings as well as to their enthroning.

---

[67]Eichrodt, *Theology of the Old Testament*, 1:450.

Burdensome Princes

Ezekiel often refers to the king of Judah as *nāśîʾ* (prince, leader) rather than *melek* (e.g., Ezek 12:10, 12). One advantage of this word is its similarity to the word *maśśāʾ*, which refers both to the burden the king and other people carry as they flee from the city, the burden he was to the community, the burden of the prophet's message, and the burden that king and people are to the prophet. Ezekiel most often uses the term *king* to refer to the head of a great power such as Babylon, Egypt or Tyre. In speaking of Israel's future ruler, too, he most often uses the term *nāśîʾ*. He also uses that word to refer to the leaders of other nations and to the present leaders of Judah, often in the plural (Ezek 21:12 [MT 17]; 22:6; 45:8, 9). The traditional translation "prince" suggests someone who is not a king, president or head of state; he does not have ultimate power. By describing the coming David only as a prince, a second-in-command (e.g., Ezek 34:24; 37:25), he draws attention to the fact that Yhwh is Israel's king. The failure of kingship might make one yearn for the kind of leadership Israel had in the old days, when Yhwh was Israel's king. But this arrangement was not exactly a success; everybody did what was right in their own eyes then. Even then the people did have leaders, and they were not unqualified successes (think of Abimelech, Jephthah or Samson). Cutting down the king so that he is simply a prince might be another way of squaring the leadership circle.

While the promises about the coming David as shepherd and king suggest a wide-eyed idealism, the term *nāśîʾ* and the regulations for the prince complement that with a hardheaded realism. The prince will have his own allocation of land in the new Jerusalem, which puts him in a special position. But the object is that "my princes shall no more afflict my people but give the land to the household of Israel, to their clans. The sovereign Yhwh has said this: 'Enough of your violence and forcefulness, princes of Israel. Exercise authority with faithfulness. Give up your evictions of my people' " (Ezek 45:8-9). The king is allocated land; therefore he should keep off other people's (Ezek 46:18). Because of poverty or an offer they cannot refuse, people might again feel the pressure to sell their land, and that would enable the prince to find ways of accumulating land, as the earlier kings did. This regulation forestalls that.

The principle that princes are not to burden people is taken further in the regulations for the people's offerings. These first make the princes responsible for standardization of weights and measures, an equivalent to making sure that companies cannot swindle investors, which further implies that the princes' priority is protecting the people rather than benefiting from them. They then prescribe quite "moderate" contributions from the people,[68] which

---

[68]Walther Eichrodt, *Ezekiel* (London: SCM Press/Philadelphia: Westminster, 1970), p. 572.

the prince apparently receives only in order to pass them on to the temple officials. The idea of a taxation system is thus ratified, but turned into a means whereby the people support their worship, and the involvement of the prince would have the capacity to hinder the priesthood (to which Ezekiel belonged) from making this a means of their "feeding off the sheep." The regulations protect the people, and also emphasize the prince's obligations in providing for sacrifices.

The book of Ezekiel locates this vision at a time when there was at least one and quite likely two ex-kings of Judah living in the Babylonian community. People who expected the community eventually to return to Judah may only have been unsure how to decide which would be the one who would reign. The situation they were familiar with was one in which the temple was an adjunct to the state (compare Amaziah's comment about the Bethel temple in Amos 7:10-17). Ezekiel sets boundaries round the monarchy so that it can resume neither its habit of living off the people nor its habit of influencing what went on in the sanctuary. The prince has certain privileges (e.g., Ezek 44:1-3; 46:1-18), but they are circumscribed. He has no priestly role like that exercised by Melchizedek and other Middle-Eastern kings, and by Solomon (e.g., 1 Kings 8:22).

7.3 Ministers

Protestant interpretation of the First Testament has often taken a negative attitude to priesthood[69] and a positive attitude to prophets. This links with a positive attitude to community rather than institution, to charisma rather than office.[70] The First Testament recognizes that ambiguity attaches to both priests and prophets, as to monarchy. Positively, priests and Levites have a ministry of worship, supervision, music, blessing and teaching. But they commonly lead Israel in worship by means of images and in other ways conduct their ministry as if Yhwh were just like the Master.

History and Theology

There were no priests or deacons in Genesis. Anyone can pray or offer sacrifice, though the head of the family would usually take the lead. When places

---

[69]See, e.g., Blenkinsopp, *Sage, Priest, Prophet*, pp. 66-67; Lester L. Grabbe, *Priests, Prophets, Diviners, Sages* (Valley Forge, Penn.: Trinity Press International, 1995), pp. 1, 41. There is an interesting treatment of prophets and priests in T. C. Vriezen, *An Outline of Old Testament Theology* (Oxford: Blackwell, 1962), pp. 256-69 (2nd ed. [Oxford: Blackwell/Newton, Mass.: Branford, 1970], pp. 230-42); in different ways in the two editions Vriezen both asserts that it is the prophets that really count, yet also acknowledges the vital importance of the priests in a way that really contradicts this.

[70]Cf. the discussion in Rodney R. Hutton, *Charisma and Authority in Israelite Society* (Minneapolis: Fortress, 1994).

of worship are simply altars without associated sanctuaries, anyone may make offerings there. When sanctuaries come into being there naturally also come into being groups of people to look after them. Yet although Yhwh takes the initiative in setting up a priesthood and does not express hesitations about it such as apply to kingship, having priests stands in some tension with Israel's being a priestly kingdom in which all serve. The arrangement again parallels that in Christian faith, where the New Testament sees the Jewish-Gentile church, a renewed version of Israel, as itself a priesthood (1 Pet 2:9) and leaves no room for an arrangement whereby one man rules a congregation, but the church subsequently invents the position of senior pastor.

Priests appear out of the blue in Exodus 19:22. Perhaps the story is told in a way that corresponds to the subsequent arrangement, with priests playing the role that would make sense in light of later practice. There is some variety in the First Testament about who can be priests, about the relationship between the role of the priests and the role of the clan of Levi as a whole, and about the role of nonpriestly Levites in different periods.[71] There are a number of lists of the responsibilities of the whole clan of Levi or of the Aaronic line as priests or of the nonpriestly Levites (e.g., Deut 10:8; 21:5; 33:8-10; 1 Chron 23:13). These lists vary, in light of differences in theory or practice in different periods; I will not draw attention to these differences except where they open up theological questions. We do not know the answers to many of the historical questions about the priesthood. As is often the case with First Testament study, there are too few dots and too large gaps for us to trace the history that these data reflect. The Torah's narrative account of priesthood does not aim to offer a historical presentation; "the canonical presentation suggests the conclusion that the actual history of priesthood bears little relation to its theological understanding."[72]

Leadership in state and in church sometimes works by families and sometimes works independently of families. Britain has a hereditary monarchy and one partly hereditary house of government, but most power lies with a house that is wholly elected, while in the Church of England there are relatively few examples of priests whose sons or daughters become priests. The United States has elected presidents, governors and houses, but one or two dynasties with a sequence of members of the family in the White House, in governor's residences and in the houses, and many more pastors whose children follow them into the pastorate than is the case in Britain. In Israel, Judah

---

[71]See, e.g., Menahem Haran, *Temples and Temple-Service in Ancient Israel* (Winona Lake, Ind.: Eisenbrauns, 1985), pp. 58-111; Richard D. Nelson, *Raising up a Faithful Priest* (Louisville: Westminster John Knox, 1993), pp. 1-15.

[72]Jo Bailey Wells, *God's Holy People,* JSOTSup 305 (Sheffield, U.K.: Sheffield Academic Press, 2000), p. 101.

had a hereditary monarchy, but Ephraim was inclined to change dynasties. Priesthood mostly worked by families, prophecy did not.

Oddly enough, both the hereditary principle and the "occasional" principle make the same theological statement. Both affirm Yhwh's sovereignty. Yhwh's choice of Levi does so; there is no way someone can decide to be a priest or decide not to be. Yhwh can choose Saul, then choose David from a different family, then make a commitment to David's line from henceforth. Both forms of action express Yhwh's sovereignty. Both exclude a person campaigning to be leader.

Parallel questions arise concerning gender. In the United States, Britain and Israel, most kings, presidents, prime ministers and members of government, and most pastors are men. In Israel, priests were men, but prophets could be women. In confining membership of the Twelve to men, Jesus was perhaps working with contemporary social convention, but this does not explain Yhwh's confining the priesthood to men, since other Middle-Eastern peoples did have women priests. Perhaps a key consideration was the relationship among other peoples between having priestesses and having goddesses; eliminating goddesses perhaps encouraged the eliminating of priestesses and vice versa.[73]

Ordained Ministry

The clan of Levi is to stand before Yhwh to attend on or minister to Yhwh (šārat; Deut 10:8; 21:5). The verb overlaps in meaning with the more common ʿābad "serve," but it is more inclined to suggest particular concrete acts and often underlines the subordinate nature of the service, though this does not imply that such ministry is anything less than a great honor.

The expression for ordination is literally "filling the hand." Akkadian uses analogous expressions for the inauguration of a king as well as of a priest, the object placed into the king's hand being a scepter, a sign of authority. The expression is a metaphor for authorization, "a symbolic act that transfers authority from one person to another."[74] Given the solemn and awe-inspiring nature of a priest's responsibility, it is appropriate that a solemn "rite of passage" takes a person from being a layman with its privileges, constraints and obligations to being a priest with its privileges, constraints and obligations

---

[73]Cf. the discussion in Hennie J. Marsman, *Women in Ugarit and Israel*, OTS 49 (Leiden/ Boston: Brill, 2003), pp. 486-547; also Mary Hayter, *The New Eve in Christ* (London: SPCK, 1987), pp. 7-79.

[74]Baruch A. Levine, *Numbers 1–20*, AB (New York: Doubleday, 1993), p. 155; cf. Jacob Milgrom, *Leviticus 1–16*, AB (New York: Doubleday, 1991), p. 539. It is less likely that the idiomatic expression refers to their being provided with sustenance (though of course they were); cf. *TDOT*, 8:301-6.

(Lev 8–9).[75] It takes seven days to ordain the priests because it is such a significant transition; the priests being ordained stay at the entrance of the meeting tent for that time. It compares with the seven days of birth, marriage and mourning (Gen 17:12; 29:27; 50:10).[76] The priest wears special clothes, as we do for moments of transition such as marriage. People who encroach on the realm of the holy risk their lives, and priests do so habitually in moving between the realm of death and the realm of life; daubing them with blood (Lev 8:23-24) protects them in this connection.[77] While smearing oil can have a cosmetic or therapeutic purpose (e.g., Ps 104:15), it can also have a ceremonial significance in marking a transition from one position to a more elevated one. In Israel such "anointing" is mainly used in connection with kings and priests; it is once applied to a prophet (1 Kings 19:16), though in rather distinctive circumstances.[78] It makes someone holy (Lev 8:12), moving him from ordinary status to the divine sphere; thus when a king has been anointed, it would be sacrilegious to attack him (e.g., 1 Sam 24:7-8).

The ordination of Levites (Num 8) involves a parallel but naturally less elaborate rite.[79] The Levites are taken from among the Israelites and set apart from them in place of the firstborn of the people whom Yhwh would otherwise claim. They are cleansed, have expiatory offerings made for them and are offered to Yhwh: they are brought near Yhwh; the people lay hands on them, perhaps as a sign of identification with them; they are presented (literally, "elevated") before Yhwh; and they are given to Yhwh.

Priests offer sacrifices on behalf of the community and of individuals (Deut 33:10; cf. 1 Sam 2:28), and they are supported through the people's tithes, offerings and sacrifices.[80] When someone brings a purification offering or a restitution offering, the priests eat part of it (Lev 6:24 [MT 17]–7:7); the implication seems to be that they eat it on Yhwh's behalf as part of making the rite effective, and thus share with Yhwh in seeing that expiation gets made (Lev 10:17 makes this more explicit).[81] The rite thus requires action on the wrongdoer's part, but also requires the involvement of a priest who can act visibly and sacramentally toward the wrongdoer as well as toward God.[82] Hosea sardonically comments that thus "it is off my people's purification offerings [or

---

[75]See Philip P. Jenson, *Graded Holiness*, JSOTSup 106 (Sheffield, U.K.: Sheffield Academic Press, 1992), pp. 130-32.

[76]Milgrom, *Leviticus 1–16*, p. 538.

[77]See Frank H. Gorman, *The Ideology of Ritual*, JSOTSup 91 (Sheffield, U.K.: Sheffield Academic Press, 1990), pp. 131-35.

[78]On the metaphorical anointing in Is 61:1 (cf. Ps 105:15?), see §7.5 "Herald."

[79]See Jenson, *Graded Holiness*, pp. 119-21.

[80]See further Hutton, *Charisma and Authority in Israelite Society*, pp. 145-51.

[81]Roy Gane, *Cult and Character* (Winona Lake, Ind.: Eisenbrauns, 2005), pp. 91-105.

[82]Cf. Walter Brueggemann, *Finally Comes the Poet* (Minneapolis: Fortress, 1989), pp. 23-33.

off my people's sin] that they feed, and to their waywardness they lift up their desire" (Hos 4:8). The more people come short of Yhwh's expectations, the better the priests and their families eat.

Managing a Relationship

But sacrificing comes last in the account of Levi's role in Deuteronomy 33:8-10. It is not the priests' most characteristic or central raison d'être, which one might describe as "maintaining the order of life in the community"; in that connection "priestly responsibility for ritual purity and proper order served to keep the community from the threats of impurity and disorder."[83] Ordination makes the priests holy, removing them from the realm of the everyday and making them free to operate in the realm of the sacred. They have the important task of instructing the community on Yhwh's expectations, which safeguard it from imperiling its relationship with God and causing Yhwh to withdraw from it. They thus play a key role in maintaining its order and keeping it in relationship with Yhwh. The Levites share in that role; they are also part of the buffer between the people and Yhwh's holiness. They are human beings, who can thus represent their people, but they are designated and sanctified by God, so they can mediate between people and God.

The people and its camp are inevitably affected by taboos brought about by factors such as contact with death and sinful behavior, both of which would make entering Yhwh's presence impractical and dangerous because it might cause Yhwh to withdraw. Priests help people dispose of taboo and mediate between the everyday and the holy. One of the Levites' tasks as gatekeepers is to make sure people do not risk offending Yhwh by coming in a taboo state or coming too close to areas of the sanctuary that especially speak of Yhwh's transcendent holiness. The version of the story of Uzzah and the covenant chest in 1 Chronicles 13-15 links with that point.

This does not mean that Yhwh is not involved with the people or that they cannot approach Yhwh. Originally, anyone could talk with Yhwh at the Meeting Tent (Ex 33:7). Even after the priestly and levitical arrangement is introduced, the Psalms and the stories of people such as Hannah continue to assume that ordinary people can go into Yhwh's presence, know they are in Yhwh's presence and be in conversation with Yhwh. The priests' mediating function does not mean they relate to God in the people's place. People do not simply show up, deposit their sacrificial animals and then wait outside while the priest offers them. The arrangement is more like one whereby the king's attendants conduct people into his presence; it involves "a partnership of trust

---

[83]Patrick D. Miller, *The Religion of Ancient Israel* (Louisville: Westminster John Knox/London: SPCK, 2000), p. 162.

between the priest and the layman"[84] (or laywoman). The priesthood of Levi is set within the context of the priesthood of Israel as a whole; it serves it rather than replacing it.[85] But it is necessary to affirm and safeguard the holiness as well as the accessibility of Yhwh, and the priestly system focuses more distinctively on that. Yhwh's relationship with the people needs some management, both on a regular and an occasional basis. Yhwh is God; Israel is not. The sanctuary is holy; the camp is not.

With the termination of the monarchy, the high priest comes to be *the* leader of the community, and within the First Testament there are hints of his coming to have that significance or at least of his capacity to have it. But in general he is simply the head priest, and the roles of sanctuary leadership and political leadership are kept separate.

A Ministry of Supervision and a Ministry of Music

Numbers 3–4 first details the role of Levi in the context of the need to care for the wilderness sanctuary on its journey to Canaan. In the temple the Levites then act as wardens, gatekeepers, sacristans, caretakers and deacons, looking after the sacred vessels, supplies, storerooms, temple tax, treasury and tithes, keeping guard over the sanctuary, and protecting its purity (e.g., 1 Chron 23; 26). In addition, they are musicians, fulfilling part of the function of prophets, such as Miriam and Deborah for whom praise is a prophetic activity, as in 1 Samuel 10:5 (see 1 Chron 25; also 2 Chron 34:30, where the Levites replace the prophets of 2 Kings 23:2).[86] The fact that leading music in worship is primarily a matter of providing a rhythm would mean music leaders would not need the kind of musical gifts presupposed by the Western tradition. The Levites and priests also function as officers, magistrates, administrators and civil servants (Deut 17:8-13; 1 Chron 26:29-32; 2 Chron 19:4-11). Below them are the assistants, the *nĕtînîm*, people "given" by David to serve the Levites (Ezra 8:20). Their role looks similar to that of the Gibeonite "servants" who cut wood and fetch water for the sanctuary (Josh 9:22-27).

In contrast to Assyrian and Babylonian priests, Israel's priests "performed neither incantation, exorcism, divination, nor healing."[87] Priests and Levites do mediate Yhwh's guidance and decisions to people by means of the Urim and Thummim (Deut 33:8), contained in the ephod worn by the priest (Ex 28:15-30), the breast piece of decision (compare the reference to the ephod in 1 Sam 2:28; also 1 Sam 23:6-12). These are perhaps objects such as a pair of stones with something signifying yes on one side and no on the other (1 Sam 14:36-

---

[84]Cf. Milgrom, *Leviticus 1–16*, p. 56, and pp. 52-57 generally.
[85]Wells, *God's Holy People*, p. 128.
[86]See Blenkinsopp, *Sage, Priest, Prophet*, pp. 94-98, esp. p. 97.
[87]Milgrom, *Leviticus 1–16*, p. 52.

42).[88] They do not always give an answer (1 Sam 28:6); perhaps an answer requires both stones to come out with the same side showing. But certain apparent instances of the use of something like Urim and Thummim (e.g., 1 Sam 23:1-6; 30:7-8; 2 Sam 5:17-25) imply more than merely a yes-no response. An answer can thus involve something more like a prophetic word from a priest. Eli the priest declares that Yhwh accepts Hannah's prayer and declares Yhwh's *shalom* to her (1 Sam 1:17). Prophets declare that Yhwh does or does not accept the people's prayer, and they promise *shalom* to people or deny it. Priests declare that a sacrifice was properly offered and thus valid.

The roles of priest and prophet could therefore be hard to distinguish.[89] Both declare Yhwh's word; both teach. Like priests, prophets commonly function at sanctuaries; Samuel can be consulted there (1 Sam 9). They are thus resources for people who need guidance from God or need prayer, and they gain their livelihood through this work; Saul and his boy assume they must be able to give Samuel something in connection with seeking his help (1 Sam 9). It is strange and disturbing when Yhwh does not answer Saul by dreams or by Urim or by prophets (1 Sam 28:6). People come to inquire of both priests and prophets concerning fasts related to mourning for Jerusalem (Zech 7:3). There are Levitical families that prophesy to the accompaniment of music (1 Chron 25:1-5; cf. 2 Chron 20:14 for an instance), and the names of these same Levitical families appear in the headings to psalms, suggesting that these psalms issue from that ministry. (But when priests and prophets are mentioned together, it is usually because both are subject to critique: e.g., Jer 5:31; Lam 4:13).

A Ministry of Blessing

Like prophets, priests facilitate the relationship between Yhwh and the people in both directions. They bless in Yhwh's name (Num 6:22-27; cf. Deut 21:5), and when they do so, Yhwh commissions them three times to utter the divine name over the people: "Yhwh bless you. . . . Yhwh shine his face to you. . . . Yhwh raise his face to you." Thus, Yhwh adds, "they are to put my name on the Israelites, and I will bless them." Yhwh blesses the people, but the priest does also. Yhwh chooses to work via the priest, who receives the power to speak performative words, words that effect what they refer to. But Yhwh so acts via the priest, and the priest mediates this blessing by putting Yhwh's name on the people, because the name expresses and brings Yhwh's being and nature, and thus Yhwh's presence and activity.

Yhwh can look back to a time when the priesthood fulfilled its ministry in

---

[88]Though the point depends here on the longer LXX text, followed by NRSV and TNIV.
[89]Cf. Walther Zimmerli, *Old Testament Theology in Outline* (Atlanta: Knox/Edinburgh: T & T Clark, 1978), p. 96.

proper fashion. Yhwh made a permanent *shalom* covenant with Levi (Mal 2:5-6). This goes back to the decisive action of Aaron's grandson when Israel was drawn into the worship of its neighbors' deities and into intermarriage with them, drawing down Yhwh's wrath (Num 25:10-13). It was a sign that Levi would indeed stand in awe of Yhwh's name even when other elements among the clans did not.

The priesthood of Malachi's day fails to live up to its origins. They have corrupted or spoiled their covenant. They have not yet destroyed it, for Yhwh still wants it to stand, but they have definitely disfigured it. They collude with the people in letting them think it is fine to offer animals that are blind, lame, sick or stolen, thereby actually defiling Yhwh's altar—indeed, defiling Yhwh. They are thus involved in showing contempt for Yhwh's name. If they treated a human governor thus, they would get no acceptance! And acceptance is priests' business. So Malachi urges the priests, "entreat Yhwh so that he may show grace to us" (Mal 1:9). Praying for the people was the priests' vocation; every time they offered a sacrifice, they did so. But it looks as if the challenge is ironic, because the priests' behavior makes it unlikely that Yhwh will take any notice of them, especially as their intercessions accompanied those sacrifices of maimed or stolen animals. Indeed, he adds an opposite wish, that they should lock the doors of the sanctuary so that they might not be making offerings that have no point, because Yhwh will not accept them.

The priests have thus undermined the basis for the people's prayers in colluding with them in making unacceptable offerings. But this is not the only way they will make the people lose out. Worse than that, "I will send the curse against you and curse your blessings" (Mal 2:2). "The" curse is presumably that attached to the regulations in the Torah concerning proper life with Yhwh (e.g., Deut 28:20, where "the curse" comes). But further, whereas it was the priests' privilege to declare and thus transmit Yhwh's blessing to the people, Yhwh will turn that arrangement upside down. Blessing does not work *ex opere operato*, as if it were a kind of magic. The priests will declare blessings, but this will not work, because they will be overridden by Yhwh's intention. Indeed, by a kind of poetic justice, Yhwh will turn the blessings themselves inside out. When a priest declares a blessing, it will have the effect of a curse.

It is only fair if the priests also pay a price in their own person. "Now: I am dismissing your seed for you and spreading dung on your faces, the dung of your festal sacrifices" (Mal 2:3). Yhwh is rebuking and dismissing not only the ministry of the present generation but that of their sons who are due to continue it. Instead of being kept distanced from the unpleasant parts of the animals offered in sacrifice, the contents of their internal organs, the priests are defiled by them. Further, "I myself am making you despised and humili-

ated by the whole people because you do not regard my ways or show favor
through your teaching" (Mal 2:9). Their calling is to regard Yhwh and be the
means of Yhwh showing favor to them—literally, the means of Yhwh's face
being lifted up in relation to them, or of Yhwh's lifting their face, as they lift
their face toward the people (cf. Mal 1:8-9; Num 6:26). But they have failed to
do either. By not regarding Yhwh's ways they fail to show their own or Yhwh's
favor to the people.[90]

Yet all is not lost. As usual when Yhwh threatens trouble, the idea is that
the threat should not be implemented. Yhwh's threats are set in the midst of a
charge to start honoring Yhwh's name instead of dishonoring it, because
Yhwh still wants the covenant with Levi to stay in being (Mal 2:4). They can
be a means of blessing again.

A Ministry of Teaching

Priests teach Israel Yhwh's decisions or rules for life and Yhwh's teaching
(Deut 33:10; Jer 18:18). As they are responsible for enabling people to come
near to Yhwh, as opposed to approaching Yhwh on the people's behalf, so
they are responsible for enabling people to get to know Yhwh's teaching, as
opposed to keeping it to themselves as "esoteric doctrine."[91] It is necessary for
the whole people to be holy, so they need to know what holiness involves. It
would be on the basis of this expertise that the priests were also in a position
to decide on disputes between people (Deut 21:5; cf. Deut 17:8-13).[92] In Leviticus 10:10-11 their teaching especially relates to matters concerning purity (cf.
Deut 24:8; Ezek 44:23; Hag 2:11-13). In teaching people about the nature of
faithfulness to Yhwh and the unacceptability and danger of turning away
from such acknowledgment of Yhwh, a priest functions as Yhwh's aide
(mal'āk), like Yhwh's supernatural aides (the "angels") and like prophets such
as Malachi, "my aide" (Mal 2:7).

There will be some questions that the Torah as it exists in their day answer, and some where the priests themselves have to determine the right
judgment. Perhaps the Torah itself came into being partly through this process. Much of the teaching in Exodus, Leviticus and Deuteronomy will then
be both the resource and the deposit of the priests' teaching ministry. In a
later period, at least, this priestly teaching also involves something more sys-

---

[90]The EVV take the last phrase to have an unfavorable sense as referring to lifting the face
in the sense of showing partiality. But there is no other reference to this in the context,
the grammar works easier if we take this as something they should have done, parallel to
having regard to Yhwh's ways, and this fits the other occurrences of the expression noted.
Cf. Andrew E. Hill, *Malachi*, AB (New York: Doubleday, 1998), pp. 217-8.

[91]Milgrom, *Leviticus 1–16*, p. 53.

[92]See Jeffrey H. Tigay, *Deuteronomy*, JPS Torah Commentary (Philadelphia: Jewish Publication Society, 1998), pp. 164-65.

tematic. Chronicles has Jehoshaphat sending a road show of officials, Levites and priests around Judah instructing people from the scroll of Yhwh's teaching (2 Chron 17:7-9).

It is to the end of seeing that Moses' teaching is implemented in Judah that Ezra comes from Babylon to Jerusalem (Ezra 7:6, 10), and as priest and theologian for a whole morning he reads to the people from the scroll of Moses' teaching, with the Levites clarifying its meaning and implications for them (Neh 8). The action agreed to regarding intermarriage is action according to the Torah (Ezra 10:3), yet it involves an act of interpretation; the local peoples have to be evaluated as equivalent to the nations Israel was forbidden to marry (e.g., Deut 7:1-4). Nehemiah 13:1-3 (cf. Deut 23:1-9) follows a similar procedure, also presupposed by Ezra 6:18 (since a division of priests and Levites into sections is unmentioned in the Torah).[93]

But it was often the case that the priests failed in their teaching role. They "have done violence to my teaching" (*ḥāmas*), encouraged people to ignore key distinctions and thus attacked Yhwh's teaching and pushed it out of the way (Ezek 22:26; cf. Zeph 3:4). They have "disregarded my sabbaths" (Ezek 22:26). The distinctive expression suggests they not merely shared in the general profaning of the sabbath in their everyday lives but were also not teaching people properly about the sabbath or not implementing the distinctive sabbath observances in the temple (see, for instance, Ezek 45:17; 46:1-5). The other Levites were also implicated in Israel's wandering away from Yhwh; indeed, they were more guilty, because they had facilitated this worship. They "ministered to them before their pillars, and became for the household of Israel a punishing stumbling block" (Ezek 44:12). Israel's very spiritual leaders tripped them up spiritually. Instead of having true teaching in their mouths and thus turning many people from waywardness, they have made many people fall through their teaching (Mal 2:8).

Acknowledging Yhwh

When Amaziah the priest at Bethel confronts Amos, he receives a terrible warning about his personal fate and that of his family as well as about Ephraim's (Amos 7:16-17). These catastrophes need not have been decided on. They are consequences of his attempt to assert authority over Amos, even if in an equivocal way. Although he simply reports Amos's words to Jeroboam and urges Amos to flee instead of having him arrested, he gets no remission for that. The key question is the action he takes in regard to the message, not the possibly more equivocal inner attitude. Amaziah has sealed his own, his

---

[93]Cf. Sara Japhet, *From the Rivers of Babylon to the Highlands of Judah* (Winona Lake, Ind.: Eisenbrauns, 2006), pp. 137-51.

family's and (because of his position) his people's fate.

The failure of priests thus has terrible consequences for their people as well as for themselves. Hosea, too, confronts "a priest," in Hosea 4:4-10. This may be an individual, perhaps the senior priest, as when the man of God confronted Eli (1 Sam 2:27-36) or Amos confronted Amaziah. Or the individual may stand for the priesthood as a whole. Either way, the unspecific nature of his words make them able to confront any priest, particularly any leading priest. Indeed, it is not always clear where Hosea is talking about the priesthood and where he is talking about the people, and it is not clear whether he is saying that the fate of the priests will be the same as that of the people or vice versa. This actually underlines the fact that the life and destiny of both are interwoven. (Hosea 5:1-7 will imply the same point.)

He declares that the people are ruined through failing to acknowledge Yhwh.[94] But behind that failure is a failure of the priests who were supposed to lead them in this acknowledgment. Yhwh points the finger with emphasis: "*You* have rejected acknowledgment."[95] They have acknowledged other gods alongside Yhwh, made offerings to them and helped people seek guidance from them. They are involved in a religious equivalent of promiscuity. Indeed, they have "devoted themselves" to it. With some irony, the verb is *šāmar*, the regular word for "keeping" or "observing" the covenant or the statutes, or for the Levites "keeping" their charge. They have "put your God's teaching [*tôrâ*] out of mind." The context (Hos 4:1-2) has referred to murder, theft and adultery, almost as if quoting from the Decalogue. Hosea 8:12 refers to written *tôrâ* that Yhwh gave the people, for which the priests would be responsible (cf. Deut 31:9-13; 33:10).[96] The period was one of flourishing religious life, but that very passage referring to the gift of written *tôrâ* also makes clear that the multiplying of sanctuaries and priestly activity does not mean a flourishing of true religion (cf. Hos 8:11). The more the priesthood has flourished, the more spectacularly it has failed. Perhaps there is a causal link here. Numbers can seem to be important: numbers of people taking part in worship, numbers of people on the staffs of sanctuaries. But numbers then become an end in themselves. The bigger the staff, the more giving from the congregation is needed to sustain it and the more the staff has to scratch where the congregation itches.

So they have failed to acknowledge Yhwh in their own lives and in the way they exercise their ministry on people's behalf, and in encouraging the acknowledgment of Yhwh in their teaching ministry. Even that is not all. They

---

[94]See §2.1 "Acknowledging Yhwh."
[95]The "you" is expressed even though the verb form is explicitly second-person.
[96]Cf. Hans Walter Wolff, *Hosea* (Philadelphia: Fortress, 1974), p. 79.

then profit from encouraging the people not to acknowledge Yhwh, simply by virtue of the fact that they gain their livelihood from their ministry. It is through sharing in the offerings that they have something to eat, but these offerings are the means of acknowledging the Master (e.g., Hos 2:8, 13 [MT 10, 15]) rather than Yhwh.

Perhaps they do not see themselves as having abandoned Yhwh. They may have thought of Yhwh as if Yhwh were like the Master. Or they have set their recognition of Yhwh in the context of recognition of other deities. Different deities have different roles and concerns just as different human beings have different roles and concerns. But Yhwh does not see it that way. Yhwh claims to be the only God worth calling God, and setting Yhwh alongside other deities is not to acknowledge who Yhwh truly is. It is in effect to abandon Yhwh.

The priests will pay a price (Hos 4:6-10). If they do not acknowledge Yhwh, Yhwh will not acknowledge them but will reject them as priests. They will be demoted from the honor of their priestly position. And because they have put Yhwh out of mind, Yhwh will put their children out of mind, no longer recognize a priesthood that issues from this line. Priests and people will not exactly starve but they will not really have enough; the gods from whom they seek their provision will not provide for them. They will chase after these other gods in the conviction that they can make them multiply as a people, but these gods will not be able to do that. Or they will be involved in sexual rites designed to encourage fertility, but these rites will not work. Such consequences thus constitute both deliberate punitive action on Yhwh's part, a personal response to a personal rejection and the natural outworking of people's own acts.

A Self-imposed Confusion

Whereas the priests' responsibility is to keep the people in order, they are susceptible to being led astray by their people. Aaron set a fine example (Ex 32:1-6). An even trickier aspect of their position is that once Israel has a monarchy, they serve by the king's appointment (e.g., 1 Kings 2:35). The main sanctuaries, at least, are the king's sanctuaries (Amos 7:13) and the priests are "his priests" (2 Kings 10:19). In theory priests are independent of the king; priesthood is based on descent and is not subject to governmental appointment. In this sense state and religion are separate.[97] But in practice kings have ways of co-opting priesthood by direct appointment or indirect influence. Priests are also capable of going astray by their own initiative, as Nadab and

---

[97]Ze'ev W. Falk, "Religion and State in Ancient Israel," in *Politics and Theopolitics in the Bible and Postbiblical Literature*, ed. Henning Graf Reventlow et al., JSOTSup 171 (Sheffield, U.K.: Sheffield Academic Press, 1994), pp. 49-54; see pp. 49-50.

Abihu's story shows (Lev 10). Eli's sons do so for the usual ordinary human reasons, sex and money, or at least the possibility of keeping body and soul together (1 Sam 2:12-17, 22-25; cf. Jer 6:13; Mic 3:11).

After lamenting decadence in Ephraim and warning of its judgment, Isaiah declares that priest and prophet go astray because of drinking (Is 28:7-8). They naturally participate in community banquets, both because they are part of the nation's leadership and because these events would take place on religious occasions such as Pesah or Sukkot (compare Eli's accusation about drunkenness at Sukkot [1 Sam 1:13]). Perhaps it is not surprising if they sometimes get drawn into an excess of indulgence, like other members of the community, as pastors often share the weaknesses of their congregations. Isaiah also sees their personal confusion through drink as a figure (if not a cause) of their professional confusion. They go astray in the words they say to people as prophets and priests, as well as wandering about unable to walk a straight line. Priests err in the advice they give people when they bring them questions about behavior or religious practice or in the way they resolve disputes. Prophets err in the responses they give people about personal issues in their lives and the interpretation of their own visions or other people's. Isaiah puts us on the track of this second critique by using verbs such as stumble and wander astray (šāgâ, tā'â), which more commonly refer to moral and religious straying than to literal straying. He also implies the point in the words that follow, though they are difficult to interpret:

> Whom could he instruct in knowledge,
>   to whom could he explain a message?
> People weaned from milk,
>   taken from the breast?
> For ṣaw lāṣaw ṣaw lāṣaw
>   qaw lāqāw qaw lāqāw,
>   a little here, a little there. (Is 28:9-10)

Either Isaiah is ridiculing the average prophet or priest, or prophets and priests are ridiculing him. Either way it is because the other party's message seems trivial and insulting to anyone's intelligence. Priests and prophets might be ridiculing Isaiah because of the apparently simplistic nature of his message about trusting Yhwh and doing nothing, instead of taking responsibility for your destiny. They might also be picking up one of his own leitmotifs: only a little time, only a little group of survivors (Is 10:25; 16:4; 24:6; 29:17).[98] Isaiah might be ridiculing the average prophet or priest by referring to the questions raised by their drunken lifestyle, to the incoherent nature

---

[98]Admittedly the word here is zě'êr, there miz'ār, but these do comprise all the occurrences of the Hebrew root in the First Testament, apart from Job 36:2.

of their drunken words or to their ululating or speaking in tongues. Either way, they are confused and leading others astray as well as going astray themselves.

In keeping with the First Testament's warnings about calamity coming on ministers, Jesus warns spiritual leaders about how they "use religion and their knowledge of the law to assert themselves, their pious reputations, and their financial interests."[99]

The Consecrated Ones

Modern translations transliterate the noun *nāzîr* "Nazirite," but the word is a common noun for someone who becomes consecrated or set apart to Yhwh (cf. LXX, Vg), perhaps for a period of time (so in Num 6:1-21), perhaps for life (so in Samson's case). Hannah commits Samuel to lifelong consecration to Yhwh and to never having his hair cut, though she does not use the word *nāzîr*. Samson is to be a consecrated person because of being someone through whom Yhwh intends to deliver Israel. The commitment involves restricting oneself in certain areas of life:[100] abstinence from alcohol, refraining from cutting one's hair and avoiding contact with corpses. The point about the last is the usual one that there should not be contact between death and the living God. The point about not cutting the hair perhaps links with the ban on cutting one's hair in connection with mourning rites (e.g., Deut 14:1); that is, it represents an abstaining from other cultures' religious observances. In the Samson story the hair is a symbol of his strength, but perhaps only because it is a sign of his dedication (see also Judg 5:2), though in other cultures hair is a sign of life and vitality.[101] Abstinence from alcohol would mean not taking part in community festivities. Amos 2:11-12 indicates that "forcing Nazirites to drink wine disqualifies them from doing whatever it was they were supposed to do. Would that we knew what it was!"[102]

7.4 Prophets, Central and Marginal

Defining prophets is problematic. They can be seen as social critics (Amos), political critics (Isaiah), moral critics (Jeremiah) and religious critics (Ezekiel). They have been understood as seers foretelling the future, social reformers, charismatics, visionaries, ecstatics, poets, theologians, preachers of repentance, mediators, politicians. It is doubtful whether one under-

---

[99]Allen Verhey, *The Great Reversal: Ethics and the New Testament* (Grand Rapids: Eerdmans, 1984), p. 15.

[100]Cf. Levine, *Numbers 1–20*, p. 219.

[101]See, e.g., Jacob Milgrom, *Numbers*, JPS Torah Commentary (Philadelphia: Jewish Publication Society, 1989), pp. 356-57.

[102]Levine, *Numbers 1–20*, p. 230.

standing fits all, unless it is somewhat vacuous. A Wittgensteinian set of "family resemblances" offers a more plausible approach. A prophet shares God's nightmares and dreams, speaks like a poet and behaves like an actor, is not afraid to be offensive, confronts the confident with rebuke and the downcast with hope, mostly speaks to the people of God, is independent of the institutional pressures of church and state, is a scary person mediating the activity of a scary God, intercedes with boldness and praises with freedom, ministers in a way that reflects his or her personality and time, is likely to fail.[103] No prophet manifests all these characteristics; a person might be called a prophet if manifesting most of them. "Each society in which prophets are read and pondered has tended to inject its own value structures and models when speaking about Israel's prophets."[104] All four prophets just named—Amos, Isaiah, Jeremiah, Ezekiel—declare what Yhwh is going to do in the future; none are reformers; none are individuals working on their own if they can help it. Their task is to confront people and king with the demands and the resources of Israel's true faith, which people and king are commonly inclined to ignore. Like kings and ministers, prophets commonly go astray and fail to reflect Israel's true faith in their proclamation and in their lives. They need to watch for divine aides and pay attention to donkeys (Num 22:22-35).

Voice of the Tradition

Prophets share with priests responsibility for teaching the people about Yhwh's expectations and offering people guidance when they have a question that needs resolving. Their teaching alongside that of priests likely contributed to the Torah as we know it (especially in Deuteronomy). It is an oversimplification (on both sides) to suggest that prophets address the powerful, while the New Testament addresses the powerless.[105] They do address leading groups such as elders, priests, other prophets and people who have accumulated land and thus wealth. They also confront ordinary people and the community as a whole.[106] Ignoring them leads to calamity overcoming the people (2 Kings 17:10; Ezra 9:10-12; Dan 9:6, 10).

    They do not always bring bad news. Sometimes they confront the despair-

---

[103]Cf. John Goldingay, *Prophecy Today* (Cambridge: Grove, 2003).

[104]David L. Petersen, "Introduction," in *Prophecy in Israel*, ed. David L. Petersen (Philadelphia: Fortress/London: SPCK, 1987), pp. 1-21; see p. 1. Cf. Gene M. Tucker, "The Role of Prophets and the Role of the Church," in *Prophecy in Israel*, pp. 159-74.

[105]H. Richard Niebuhr, "Introduction to Biblical Ethics," in *Christian Ethics*, ed. Waldo Beach and H. Richard Niebuhr, 2nd ed. (New York: Ronald, 1973), pp. 10-45; see p. 34.

[106]Cf. Patrick D. Miller, "The World and Message of the Prophets" and "The Prophetic Critique of Kings," in *Israelite Religion and Biblical Theology*, JSOTSup 267 (Sheffield, U.K.: Sheffield Academic Press, 2000), pp. 508-25, 526-47.

ing community by bringing unbelievable good news. Then,

> the hope-filled language of prophecy . . . is the language of amazement. It is a language that engages the community in new discernments and celebrations just when it had nearly given up and had nothing to celebrate. The language of amazement is against the despair just as the language of grief is against the numbness. . . . There is no more subversive or prophetic idiom than the practice of doxology which sets us before the reality of God.[107]

Whether they bring confrontational bad news or confrontational good news, they exist in order to say something old that should be familiar. "Do you not know? Do you not hear? Has it not been told you from the beginning. . . . Have you not come to know? Did you not hear? Yhwh is God of old, creator of the ends of the earth" (Is 40:21, 28). How ought they to know and where ought they to have heard? There is a range of possibilities. Reference to Yhwh's nature as creator may suggest the Psalms. When Amos critiques the war practices of surrounding nations, he appeals to standards of right and wrong that he assumes all civilized people acknowledge. When Hosea and Jeremiah refer to Israel's wrongdoing, they suggest awareness of the basic covenant requirements known to us in the Torah.

Prophets also share with priests an involvement with institutional loci of government and religion, royal court and sanctuary. Gad and Nathan function as consultants to David as king, and Nathan at least is subject to the temptation to be the king's yes-man (2 Sam 7:3), while 1 Kings 22 presupposes quite a vast corps of prophetic consultants available to Ahab. To use a sociological model, we can distinguish between central and peripheral prophets,[108] people located at and identified with court and sanctuary who support the social and political order, and people not so identified who work to change things. Prophets such as Elijah and Amos would come in the latter category. Yet Gad did not start off as a royal prophet; he was identified with David when Saul was king and David was on the run (1 Sam 22:1-5). Nathan is capable of listening to Yhwh, confronting and challenging David (2 Sam 7; 12). Ahab's corps includes someone who invariably prophesies trouble for him (1 Kings 22:8). The Psalms, texts generated by and used in the worship of the temple, incorporate prophetic-style confrontations (e.g., Ps 50; 95). The accounts and records of prophecy are present in the Scriptures because the mainstream, official community (for in-

---

[107]Walter Brueggemann, *The Prophetic Imagination* (Philadelphia: Fortress, 1978/London: SCM Press, 1992), p. 69.

[108]See especially Robert R. Wilson, *Prophecy and Society in Ancient Israel* (Philadelphia: Fortress, 1980); David L. Petersen, *The Roles of Israel's Prophets*, JSOTSup (Sheffield, U.K.: JSOT, 1981); building on I. M. Lewis, *Ecstatic Religion* (Harmondsworth, U.K./Baltimore: Penguin, 1971).

stance, in the temple) came to accept them; if they started off as peripheral, they were adopted into the mainstream. Nor can it ever be assumed that prophets who are quite separate from the state will not be led astray, as Jonah and Jeremiah illustrate. "Yhwh cautioned me not to walk in the path of this people" in the way they talk about conspiracy, Isaiah says, perhaps referring to the conspiracy to replace Ahaz. Nor are Isaiah and his associates (Yhwh speaks in the plural) to be awed by what awes the people, perhaps the threat from Ephraim and Syria. They are to keep their awe for Yhwh (Is 8:11-13).

Prophets and Kings

"The interplay of 'charismatic' and 'institutional' dynamics is therefore much more subtle than is often assumed by those who line up 'cultic prophets' against 'free prophets' or 'central prophets' against 'peripheral prophets.'"[109] Prophets exist in order to say something new and different, or provide divine guidance when there arises a whole new question such as the introduction of kingship or the building of a temple and the making of arrangements for its worship (1 Sam 8; 2 Sam 7; 2 Chron 29:25). But if "the task of prophetic ministry is to nurture, nourish and evoke a consciousness and perception alternative to the consciousness and perception of the dominant culture around us,"[110] that can be done from the inside of the institution as well as from the outside. For the individual, however, there is a difference between a private person who finds himself or herself driven to prophesy, and a court or sanctuary prophet who finds himself or herself driven to take a more radical stance over against state or sanctuary.[111]

Moses can be called a prophet (Deut 34:10), as can Miriam (Ex 15:20), Deborah (Judg 4:4) and Samuel (1 Sam 3:20). As directly summoned to their task, prophets continue the sequence begun by the two "servants of Yhwh," Moses and Joshua (e.g., Deut 34:5; Josh 24:29), and the "deliverers" or "leaders" (conventionally "judges") in the book of Judges (e.g., Judg 3:9, 10), most of whom are of "socially marginal origin"; they are Canaanites or outlaws or sons of dubious unions.[112] The difference between Isaiah and Jeremiah over against Moses and Joshua is that Israel now has settled orders of leadership. In this context, prophets are "dissidents,"[113] designed to be "a destabilizing

---

[109]Hutton, *Charisma and Authority in Israelite Society*, pp. 105-37; cf. Petersen, *Roles of Israel's Prophets*, esp. pp. 9-15.

[110]Brueggemann, *Prophetic Imagination*, p. 13.

[111]Cf. Norman K. Gottwald's discussion in *The Hebrew Bible in Its Social World and in Ours* (Atlanta: Scholars Press, 1993), pp. 111-17.

[112]Blenkinsopp, *Sage, Priest, Prophet*, p. 130.

[113]Ibid., p. 2.

presence."[114] "In the prophet . . . the sovereign freedom of YHWH expresses itself."[115]

> He is like God in the suddenness, the surprisingness of the encounter he initiates. . . . He utters grace and judgment with an authority that goes as far as functional self-identification with God. He suffers with God, who is despised and rejected. . . . He suffers because of God and his incomprehensible decrees, and yet he shares and accepts the knowledge of God's future. He shares the impartiality of YHWH. . . . He reflects the freedom of the Word. . . . And, remarkably, in all this he is only the exponent of that which the people . . . could or must be and will be [cf. Num 11:29; Joel 2:28 (MT 3:1)].[116]

The task of many prophets is to mediate the will of the divine King to and concerning the human king (e.g., 1 Sam 10; 15; 1 Kings 11:29-39), to proclaim Yhwh's expectations regarding him, and to announce what Yhwh intends to do (1 Kings 22; Amos 5:18-20). In Israel as elsewhere in the Middle East, prophets are thus adjuncts to the king. In the First Testament narrative, prophecy did not start that way (there are prophets before and after there are kings), but it comes to be that way. One might reckon that the king co-opts prophecy and makes it serve the royal agenda, as he co-opts priesthood. If so, this works only in the short run. Prophets are soon confronting kings, as Nathan learns to and as prophets such as Elijah, Micaiah and Elisha do. Even Balaam works for hire, but knows he must say only the words Yhwh puts in his mouth (e.g., Num 22:8, 18, 35, 38). In 2 Kings 19–20, in a crisis Hezekiah sends a deputation to consult Isaiah and receives a reassuring response, but subsequently Isaiah takes the initiative with a gloomier one; in 2 Chronicles 32 Hezekiah and Isaiah pray together about the crisis. King Josiah sends Hilkiah the priest to inquire of Yhwh when they find the teaching scroll, and Hilkiah leads a deputation to consult the prophetess Huldah, even though one might have thought that the scroll's implications were somewhat clear (2 Kings 23; 2 Chron 34).

One way or another, "prophets and kings belong together"[117] in a codependent relationship with built-in tension; prophets and kings often have reason to fear each other. Ahab has reason to fear Elijah because he claims to possess authority over the rain and thus over whether Ahab's people have anything to eat, whereas Ahab attributes this authority to the Master and his prophets and priests. Elijah has reason to fear Ahab, or at least his wife, who has killed many prophets and intends to treat Elijah the same way. Ahab has reason to

---

[114]Walter Brueggemann, *A Social Reading of the Old Testament* (Minneapolis: Fortress, 1994), p. 223.
[115]Kornelis H. Miskotte, *When the Gods Are Silent* (London: Collins/New York: Harper, 1967), p. 289.
[116]Ibid., pp. 290-91.
[117]Miller, *Israelite Religion and Biblical Theology*, p. 526.

fear Elijah because Yhwh commissions him to instigate a coup and to tell Ahab that he will die a violent death. Micaiah has reason to fear Ahab, who has him put in prison, and Ahab has reason to fear Micaiah, who predicts his demise in battle. The Syrian king has reason to fear Elisha, who can pass on his battle plans to the Ephraimite king. Elisha has reason to fear the Syrian king, who is not pleased.

A Specific Divine Initiative

The clan of Levi and the household of David were put in their position by Yhwh's choice, but once Yhwh has taken that action and entered into covenant relationship with them, it establishes their position as Yhwh's servants permanently or until Yhwh takes the further deliberate action of removing them from it. Other leaders, such as the elders, occupy their position by virtue of their place in society (for instance, they are the heads of households). It is different with a prophet such as Amos.

When Amaziah reports to Jeroboam that Amos is "conspiring" against the king in the very midst of the household of Israel, it would be easier to laugh off this southerner's mouthing off about the king if he had stayed in Judah. "The country cannot endure (kûl hiphil) his words" (Amos 7:10). The verb is a telling one. Its two other occurrences with this meaning refer to the world not being able to endure Yhwh's fury or to endure Yhwh's day when it comes on them (Jer 10:10; Joel 2:11). While Amaziah may mean merely that the country cannot tolerate Amos's words, his expression more likely suggests that these words will destroy the country. In whatever sense he meant it, he is right, perhaps more right than he knew. His words draw attention to the power of a prophet's words. Yet his reaction is not to bid the king to heed Amos's words but to seek to silence them so that the events they announce may not happen. He urges Amos to get back to Judah and earn his living by prophesying there, not here in Bethel, a royal sanctuary, a national house of worship.

Amos famously, though not entirely clearly, responds, "Whereas I was not a prophet and not the son of a prophet but a cattleman and tender of sycamore figs, Yhwh took me from following the flock, and Yhwh said to me, 'Go and prophesy to my people Israel' " (Amos 7:14-15). It is not clear whether Amos is denying being a prophet now (perhaps because in Amos's day "prophet" suggests someone who earns a living by functioning at the sanctuary) or whether he is simply pointing out that he became a prophet through Yhwh's initiative. Either way, it was not because prophecy ran in the family (as is properly the case with kingship and priesthood) or because he had been to prophetic seminary with the other "sons of the prophets." He is prophesying at Bethel because Yhwh took him and told him to do so. He was plucked from his previous occupation to speak for Yhwh and is therefore someone Amaziah cannot trifle with. He is not open to being ordered around (or even given friendly advice) by the likes of Amaziah or by his king. He acts under a higher authority.

Amos and Amaziah have different perspectives on the sanctuary's significance. Amaziah feels called to protect it in one way, Amos in another. Amaziah does not want Amos to rock the boat; Amos reckons that the boat is heading for the rocks anyway. "The issue of leadership is not, as it is often assumed to be, one of effectiveness or other skills, but *perspective*, how one sees and is oriented."[118] "The first responsibility of a leader is to define reality."[119] Something happens to prophets that makes them aware of facts that everyone ought to be aware of.

The story in Amos 7:10-17 is not the only one concerning a Judean prophet sent to Bethel by Yhwh. If the Amos story is scary in its implications for the Bethel administration, 1 Kings 13 is also scary for the prophet, who discovers the hard way that a specific divine initiative makes categorical demands on him as well as on those to whom he is sent.[120]

Deuteronomy's teaching about prophecy (Deut 18:15-22) follows on its stern warning about seeking guidance from the dead or by other spiritual means (Deut 18:9-14). Such practices "owe their prominence to the universal human desire to learn the future and in some way control it, especially in times of illness and war. The Torah does not deprecate this desire but insists that it be pursued only by means chosen by God, particularly prophecy."[121] Those practices that other peoples utilize commonly involve turning to spiritual resources other than Yhwh. The First Testament puts a ban on divination, the use of technique to discover what is happening or what is going to happen. It does not imply that such techniques cannot work. They are banned because Israel is to seek such revelation from Yhwh. Even the use of Urim is a means of doing that. Israel has no collection of signs and omens that enable people to work out the meaning of events or to discover what is likely to happen without referring the question to Yhwh. And prophecy is the symbol of the fact that it is in Yhwh's court to decide when such revelation is to be given.[122]

Indeed, Deuteronomy reverses the initiative involved in receiving revelations. Seeking guidance by these means puts the seekers in control; they are the ones who make the move. Moses' description of prophecy puts Yhwh in

---

[118]Cf. Patrick D. Miller, "Toward a Theology of Leadership," in Miller, *Israelite Religion and Biblical Theology*, pp. 658-66; see p. 666.

[119]Max De Pree, *Leadership Is an Art* (New York: Dell, 1990), p. 11.

[120]See *OTT* 1:673.

[121]Tigay, *Deuteronomy*, pp. 173-74.

[122]Cf. Yehezkel Kaufmann, *The Religion of Israel* (Chicago: University of Chicago Press, 1960/ London: George Allen, 1961), pp. 42-53, 87-101.

control; Yhwh takes the initiative, even though it is also a response to the people's fear of being directly confronted by Yhwh. Notwithstanding Moses' distinctiveness, Yhwh promises, "I will raise up a prophet for them from the midst of their brothers, like you, and I will put my words in his mouth, and I will speak to them all that I command him" (Deut 18:18). The promise is fulfilled in a sequence of individuals such as Deborah, Elijah, Isaiah, Jeremiah, Huldah and Ezekiel, as is the warning about the consequences of not heeding such a prophet.

An Invariable Divine Initiative

When you see two people walking together, it (usually) means they arranged to meet, doesn't it? When a lion roars, it usually means it has caught something, doesn't it? When a bird is caught in a trap, it means someone set the trap, doesn't it? When a trap snaps shut, it means there is something in it, doesn't it? When the lookout blows a horn on the city walls, it means people become afraid on the assumption that attackers are near, doesn't it? The questions began with something harmless, but they have become more and more sinister. Further, when disaster comes on a city, that implies Yhwh is acting, doesn't it? (In isolation, that could refer to Yhwh acting in response to the disaster, but the context suggests reference to Yhwh causing it.)

The irrelevant-looking rhetorical questions in Amos 3:3-6 first establish that things in life are connected. One thing links with another. It is a pattern about life. The questions then come to a climax with the declaration about the link between disaster and Yhwh, a much more contentious one. Elsewhere the First Testament makes very clear that Yhwh purposefully causes some disasters that come to some cities, though it does not suggest that Yhwh is behind every disaster that comes to every city. On the other hand, the Psalms imply that when Israelites experience a calamity, they assume that in some sense Yhwh is responsible for it. By implication they assume nothing happens in the world without at least Yhwh's permission. The question is not whether Yhwh causes or allows calamities, but why Yhwh is doing so and whether Yhwh will act to reverse them.

Elsewhere Amos, like other prophets, indicates that Israel has experienced calamities that Yhwh intentionally brought about (Amos 4:6-11), in keeping with the warnings in Leviticus 26 and Deuteronomy 28. Yes, Yhwh has brought all manner of disaster on cities in Ephraim in people's recent experience. "Does disaster come on a city and Yhwh has not acted?" (Amos 3:6). Amos has slid from talk in terms of Yhwh's responsibility for everything to talk in terms of these actual disasters. Placing that question at the end of the sequence, Amos seeks to convey the implication that a positive answer to the earlier questions implies a positive answer to this one. It is not merely a rhetorical trick but an invitation to a decision. "Only connect."[123] Everything is connected. Our individual experiences are part of one world, God's world. There is nothing that lacks linkage and meaning. The nature of these links varies, and in my summary of Amos's questions I have expressed them more equivocally than Amos did. People do meet accidentally and then go for a walk. Disasters do come that Yhwh has not brought about (except in that general sense just referred to). So the rhetorical question about disaster is an invitation to insight.

It leads into the first actual statement in Amos 3:3-8.[124] When Yhwh does so act (ʿāśâ recurs, again preceded by the negative lōʾ, though the verb is now yiqtol), Yhwh's plan (sôd) is revealed to a prophet. Once more that might be a statement relating to Ephraim's present situation. Amos has declared that its repeated rebellions will mean trouble of the kind described in Amos 4:6-11. Presumably Amos has his own ministry in mind, and this section offers a defense of its plausibility. The troubles that have been coming to Ephraim have all been announced through Amos and other prophets.

"A lion has roared—who will not be afraid? The Lord Yhwh has spoken— who will not prophesy?" (Amos 3:8). The roaring of the lion is not merely an illustration of linkage. Yhwh, after all, *is* a lion (Amos 1:2); the link between lion and prey is more worrisome than we might think if we forget to read it in light of that line at the beginning of the book. Yhwh equals lion; city equals prey. We may infer likewise that bird equals city and trap equals disaster Yhwh has brought on it. But a city being afraid is then not merely an illustration of something else. The city is a real city such as Samaria, a lion has roared at it, and the prophet is the city's lookout warning of the danger that confronts it. Fear is appropriate. And a prophet is not someone taking up the role because it seems a nice idea or because of having been trained or because of having a gift of insight, but because of having heard Yhwh speak. What then can he do but prophesy?

Guides Keeping Israel on the Right Road, Lookouts with Eyes Open

Yhwh follows the promise about raising up a prophet with a warning that not every prophet is someone raised up by Yhwh (Deut 18:20-22). Prophets may speak in Yhwh's name oracles that Yhwh has not given them; one test is whether their words come true. They may speak words in the name of other deities, in which case their words clearly did not come from Yhwh, even if they do come true. Whereas we might assume that prophets are by definition people who faithfully serve Yhwh and serve their people, the first extensive discussion of prophecy in the First Testament concerns prophets' capacity to

---

[123]The epigraph to E. M. Forster, *Howard's End* (New York: Penguin, 2000).

[124]Whether or not it is an additional comment to Amos's own words: see, e.g., J. Alberto Soggin, *The Prophet Amos* (London: SCM Press, 1987), p. 58.

draw people after other deities and offer signs and portents to back up their proposals (Deut 13:1-5 [MT 2-6]).

Prophets such as Micah and Jeremiah imply that most prophets lead Israel astray. One would like to think of the prophets as people who help keep Israel on the straight and narrow and going in the right direction, and who point out when it has wandered astray and is going round in circles like someone who has had too much to drink. Actually they propagate this wandering and collude with it ("Have another little drink" [e.g., Mic 3:5-8]). They "bite with their teeth," which sounds like a reference to their having food to bite on and thus to the fact that they earn their living through their work as prophets; in Jerusalem "its priests teach for a fee, its prophets divine for money" (Mic 3:11). In theory that need not mean they led people astray; people such as Gad and Nathan seem to have been on the king's payroll. But it is hard to bite the hand that feeds you, and you are more likely to tell the people who pay your salary what they want to hear. You are likely to proclaim *shalom*, to be encouraging, to tell such people that things are going to be fine, whether or not there are grounds for promising this, whereas you may be prepared to be hostile to people who will not make any contribution toward your livelihood when you ask them (Mic 3:5). How can you serve Yhwh and serve people if they do not keep their pledges?

Prophets are thus telling people who are doing well that they will continue to do well and telling people who are not doing well that things will only get worse. They will therefore lose their capacity to be prophets (Mic 3:6-7). They will no longer be able to see or discern. Although they are false prophets, this does not mean they are pretending to believe they have words from God or a vision from God. They believe they do. But they will find that even these words and visions that lead people astray no longer come. They will know there is no longer any response from God, instead of thinking they have a response from God.

Micah is a different matter. He knows he has the strength and authority to speak to Israel, even though he has to speak in a much harder way, to talk to Israel about its rebellious failure to walk Yhwh's way (Mic 3:8). The other prophets will have claimed the moving of Yhwh's spirit as the basis for their prophesying. It is perhaps for this reason that the real prophets often avoid doing so. Micah then makes this claim polemically and ironically. "You know the prophets talk about being impelled by Yhwh's spirit? Well, I will tell you the kind of thing someone does when truly impelled by that spirit. Such a prophet talks loudly and forcefully about the disobedience and shortcomings of Israel, not about *shalom*."[125] Poignant indignation at the prophets leading "my people" astray has to be accompanied by this confrontation.

---

[125]"With Yhwh's spirit" fits clumsily into the sentence in Mic 3:8 and may be a gloss identifying Yhwh's spirit as the source of Micah's strength.

A community always needs lookouts, people who warn them of danger, as guard dogs warn of wild animals coming to attack a flock. *Lookout* is a term especially applied to Ezekiel (Ezek 3:17-21; 33:1-9), but applicable to prophets in general. The trouble is that the lookouts are blind and the dogs have lost their bark (Is 56:9-12), damaging disabilities for their task. The flock is therefore in mortal danger. The prophet goes on to refer to them as the shepherds of the flock, which may broaden out the identity of the addressees; they are the leaders of the community. They have no insight. They are blind, partly because they are blind drunk, but they are also blind to the realities of the future that advances on their people. They believe everything will be fine, when actually it will be calamitous. Communities have to trust their shepherds/lookouts/leaders but simultaneously to keep an eye on them to make sure the lookouts are keeping their eye open for them. There is always a serious danger that the leaders are stupid and will end up taking the opportunity for ceaseless self-indulgence that their position gives them; in this prophet's day that is true of every one of them without exception. Communities always need to take this fact seriously.

The prevalence of deceptive prophecy makes its elimination an appropriate aspect of Yhwh's promise of the community's cleansing after the exile (Zech 13:1-2). It is often said that prophecy did die out after the exile, though this seems to be an argument from silence, and it would be an odd way for Yhwh to fail to fulfill a promise to the prophet who speaks in Isaiah 59:21:

> And I—this is my covenant with them (Yhwh has said). My spirit that is on you and my words that I have put in your mouth will not depart from your mouth and from the mouth of your offspring and from the mouth of their offspring (Yhwh has said) from now and forever.

Passing the Moral Test

There is little moral emphasis in prophecy before the eighth century; the focus of prophets such as Elijah and Elisha lies elsewhere. This changes with the "morality prophets."[126] By Jeremiah's day this is implicitly key to understanding the difference between the message of a prophet such as Jeremiah or Ezekiel and that of the many other prophets in Judah and Babylon.

Jeremiah begins from the prophets' own immoral lives (Jer 23:9-15), comparing them unfavorably with the Samarian prophets who prophesied by the Master and thus led the people astray. The verb *(tāʿâ)* again suggests making them wander about helplessly as if they do not know where they are or where home is, like lost sheep or like drunks. Prophesying by the Master meant the prophets led their people into a religious wasteland where they too wandered

---

[126]Petersen, *Roles of Israel's Prophets*, pp. 63-69.

lost. So how could the Judean prophets be worse? Here, Jeremiah's stress lies on matters of morality and social life. He begins by accusing them of sexual unfaithfulness, a plausible charge as this is commonly a problem with people in leadership, in religious matters or in political life. He goes on to accuse them of living by a lie, which could imply serving the Master but in this context (given that he is contrasting them with the Samarian prophets) more likely implies that they were involved in deception and fraud.[127] That would fit with the ensuing accusation that they strengthen the hands of wrongdoers, so that people do not turn from wrongdoing. From the Jerusalem prophets "perversion" thus spread through the whole land. There is some indication of an etymological link between perversion (ḥănuppâ) and wandering or going astray, and forms of these roots come close together here (as they do in Is 32:6). Jeremiah thus describes the prophets and priests as ḥānēp and also declares that their way leads into darkness. The word suggests a distortion of proper, straight, orders of existence.[128] More concretely, such perversion or distortion often manifests itself in deception and other such antisocial conduct,[129] and that is the more specific context here.

The positive potential of prophetic leadership is huge, but so is its negative potential. Sexual unfaithfulness or deception and fraud on the part of an ordinary person are wicked, but on the part of prophets or priests they have devastating implications. Elihu is wise enough to know that a ḥānēp must be kept from ruling, and puts in parallelism with that word a reference to people who ensnare the people (Job 34:30). The people have to accept some responsibility here. They should not listen to these prophets whose words make the people empty, as Jeremiah puts it in what may be a piece of linguistic creativity (hābal hiphil appears only here [Jer 23:16]). The people are strangely inclined to abandon Yhwh and go after hebel (Jer 2:5), gods that have no substance. That is a direction the prophets are themselves taking people, instead of witnessing to the God who has substance. They are turning the people into what they worshiped. As a result of these prophets' ministry, their people end up as disgusting as Sodom and Gomorrah, and will be treated like them. But their blood is on the hands of their prophets.

> The visible gives access to the invisible; the moral gives critical purchase on the spiritual. Claims to speak for God can be meaningfully tested both in terms of the moral character, disposition and behaviour of the speaker and in terms of the moral and theological content of the message.[130]

---

[127]On šeqer, see §5.2, "Politics, Religion and Unreality."

[128]Cf. TLOT, 1:447-48.

[129]Cf. TDOT, 5:38-39.

[130]R. W. L. Moberly, Prophecy and Discernment (Cambridge/New York: Cambridge University Press, 2006), p. 225.

A Word from Outside the Self?

Those other prophets speak just like Jeremiah or Ezekiel, saying "Yhwh has said this" and "listen to Yhwh's word" and "Yhwh's oracle" (Jer 28:11; Ezek 13:2, 6). They want to build up the community. They speak in a way that coheres with earlier prophecy. They share their visions of the future with the community, and because the visions concern the future, the community cannot immediately tell whether these or the visions of Jeremiah and Ezekiel are right. Hananiah promises the protection and deliverance of Jerusalem in the same way as Isaiah; "he has very aptly been called a caricature of Isaiah. . . . He parrots Isaiah."[131] He might claim that Josiah's reform meant people could expect Yhwh to protect the community, in fulfillment of promises in the Torah. But such prophets prophesy out of their own imagination, more literally "out of their heart" (Ezek 13:2; cf. Jer 14:14; 23:16). Their prophecy comes from the innermost center of their own being, but that is all. It does not come "from Yhwh's mouth" (Jer 23:16). They use their own tongues and say Yhwh speaks (Jer 23:31). But when this is really so, Yhwh manipulates the tongue (cf. Jer 1:9); not with these prophets. They share their dreams with the community, but their content shows that these too are simply their own dreams (Jer 23:27-32). Dreams can be means of Yhwh's giving someone a revelation (e.g., Joel 2:28 [MT 3:1]), but it is even more possible for them to be simply wish fulfillment and means of making people put Yhwh's name out of mind. Indeed, in effect this is the dreamers' unconscious intention (Jer 23:27). So by all means let the prophets share their dreams, but let there be no confusing of these with Yhwh's word any more than you want to confuse straw with wheat (Jer 23:28).

They are "stupid prophets," *hannĕbî'îm hannĕbālîm* (Ezek 13:3). There is only one letter's difference between being a prophet like Ezekiel and being stupid like Nabal. Such stupidity does not mean having a low IQ but willfully confining yourself to your own limited insight and thus laying yourself open to disaster. "They follow their spirit," which is arguably what a prophet such as Elijah did, but they show it is quite possible to speak things that reflect deep conviction and sincere spirituality but for this to come simply from the self and not from God. And thus "they have not seen" (Ezek 13:3); their following their own spirits has deprived them of insight.[132] Yhwh did not send them, command them or speak to them (Jer 14:14; 23:21, 32; Ezek 13:6). They sent themselves. They have not stood in attendance in Yhwh's royal cabinet

---

[131]Buber, *On the Bible*, p. 168.

[132]Commentators usually take the odd expression *ûlĕbiltî rā'û* to indicate that they had not seen anything before speaking, but *lĕbiltî* usually means "lest" (cf. v. 22) and it fits the context to take the clause to refer to the result of their listening to their own hearts and spirits.

and taken part in the discussions of what was happening on earth and what should be done about it, so that they were in a position to share this information (Jer 23:18-22). They were not among the aides sent from this cabinet to act or speak on the King's behalf.

The prophets think Yhwh is near, and talk that way (Jer 12:2; 23:23). They are quite confident about their understanding of Yhwh's relationship with the people. But Yhwh is also far off, and that in two senses. Although always on their lips, Yhwh is far from their hearts. They are not consciously duplicitous, saying something different from what they think, promising *shalom* when they know Yhwh intends calamity. Alas, their inner thinking matches their words. That is why Yhwh is far from their hearts. They are misguided in the way they think.

Then there is the other sense in which they think Yhwh is near. They say Yhwh is near the people; that can of course be an entirely proper assurance to give them (e.g., Deut 4:7; Ps 119:151). But Yhwh can also be far off, especially when people's wrongdoing drives Yhwh away (e.g., Ps 10:1; Prov 15:29). The prophets narrow down the theological truth about Yhwh. They affirm the immediately encouraging truths and sideline the less comfortable ones. They are reckless or extravagant *(pāḥaz)* and faithless or treacherous (Zeph 3:4). They speak with confidence and generosity words that come from their own hearts and minds, and they thus let down the people who look to them for God's word.

There are also women who prophesy (they are not actually called "prophets"), operating more in the sphere of the home, more like fortunetellers, offering people guidance and gaining financially as they share in the offerings associated with seeking God's guidance (Ezek 13:17-23). They also "prophesy from their heart." They too minister in Yhwh's name, but use the techniques of traditional religion to gain guidance and protect people from trouble and from demonic forces, and end up with results that do not come from Yhwh. They have thus "profaned me among my people." Further, diviners can be quite misleading, telling a sick person that they will recover and they do not, or saying they will die and they do not. These prophets' declarations also issue from their own hearts and from the use of their techniques, and the proof of that is that their promises and warnings have no religious and moral rationale and are again bound to give false promises of life and false warnings of trouble. They have "saddened the heart of the faithful with lies when I was not hurting them, and encouraged the faithless not to turn from their wrong way, to gain life." They are like hunters trapping animals and bringing about their deaths without endangering their own lives; at least, so they think. But "I will rescue my people from your hand, and you will acknowledge that I am Yhwh." Whereas never be-

fore in Ezekiel has Yhwh referred to Israel as my people, the term comes
seven times in this chapter, suggesting Yhwh's particular grief when spiritual leaders lead Yhwh's people astray.

Avoiding False Promises

The prophets surely ought to be interested in rebuilding the community's
walls so that it takes the right side and stands firm in the battle that is coming, the battle that Yhwh's Day will bring. But instead they are more like jackals scrabbling about among the ruined walls (Ezek 13:4). Their sincerity is
shown in the way "they wait for the confirming of their word" (Ezek 13:6).
They offer people a picture of a better future, but their picture is "empty vision" and their message "deceptive prognostication" (Ezek 13:7; cf. Ezek 22:28;
Jer 14:14). It has no corresponding reality in heaven and thus will have no corresponding reality on earth. It is like the prognostication of a diviner, and it
is bound not to come true. These prophets are "prophesying lies" and doing
that in Yhwh's name, with Yhwh's authority, associating Yhwh with *šeqer* (Jer
14:14; cf. Jer 23:25-26, 32). They talk about a coming *shalom*, community well-
being in the broadest sense, when there is no *shalom*. Or they talk about *shalom*
in the sense of peace, when the reality will be invasion and destruction. They
talk about "peace you can trust" *(šĕlôm ʾĕmet)*. Thus "they have treated the
wound of my people as if it were slight." They have offered the patient false
reassurances when she needed to face up to a serious medical problem (Jer
6:14; 8:11; 14:12-13). They offer soothing prognostications (Ezek 12:24) but have
thus led Yhwh's people astray (Jer 23:32), led them off the right road into
trackless, waterless wilderness where they will die. The people are inclined to
reckon that the future will turn out all right and the prophets encourage them
in that disastrous misconception. They are like contractors putting a coat of
plaster on a mud wall and encouraging the impression that it will stand firm
like a proper stone wall when actually it is bound to collapse on its builders
when the wind blows. And God is going to make the wind blow (Ezek 13:10).

Anyone who has stood in the heavenly cabinet knows that the attitudes
that were being expressed there were very tough. The talk was all about
wrath and tempest and anger, and about giving these free expression until
Yhwh "has effected and implemented the intentions in his mind" (Jer 23:19-
20). As Jeremiah goes on to put it, Yhwh's word is like fire and a jackhammer
(Jer 23:29). Indeed, he points out to Hananiah, this is the regular nature of
prophecy.

> The prophets who came before you and me, from ancient times, prophesied of
> war, famine and epidemic against mighty countries and great kingdoms. The
> prophet who prophesies of *shalom*—when the prophet's word comes about, it
> can be acknowledged that Yhwh sent that prophet. (Jer 28:8-9)

Yhwh's word can be more like rain that encourages growth (e.g., Is 40:6-8). But the point about prophecy is to confront the thinking of the people of God, and the people of God often needs shaking out of a sense that it is okay. That is certainly so in Jeremiah's day. Yhwh is set on destruction rather than building (Jer 1:10). How could it be otherwise, given the conduct of the people? "If they had stood in my council, they would have proclaimed my words to my people and turned them from their wrong way, from their wrong acts" (Jer 23:22). Their not having stood in Yhwh's council will be one reason why they are reduced to stealing prophetic messages from one another (Jer 23:30).

Jeremiah had earlier put it more ironically and perhaps more chillingly. Yhwh had said that sword and famine would consume them; the other prophets had said this would not happen. Therefore sword and famine will consume these prophets, and consume the people to whom they prophesy. Precisely the promise that there will be no sword and famine will be the lie that brings sword and famine on them (Jer 14:11-16). Hananiah's breaking Jeremiah's wooden yoke imposes on the people an iron yoke in its place (Jer 28:12-14). They could have accepted Nebuchadnezzar's authority and carried on life in their own land, but by rejecting that, they are subjecting themselves to a much tougher version of that authority when Nebuchadnezzar devastates the city and exiles its population.

Beware the Fate of Prophets

A terrible fate therefore awaits Hananiah (Jer 28:15-17). Yhwh did not send him, and he has made people trust in falsehood. He has the city's blood on his hands. He has not merely encouraged Judah to revolt against Babylon but "spoken rebellion against Yhwh." The penalty for that is death (Deut 13:5 [MT 6]). The community had been inclined to apply that principle to Jeremiah, though it never did, but it did apply it to Uriah (Jer 26). The community will not apply it to Hananiah, because it is not convinced that he is a false prophet like Jeremiah. So, Jeremiah declares, Yhwh will do so. And Hananiah dies. The story does not tell us that Jeremiah was right that Yhwh was going to see to Hananiah's death or that Yhwh brought about his death or how Hananiah died or that this happened in fulfillment of Jeremiah's or Yhwh's word. It carries implications about those questions, but its nonexplicitness preserves the reality of the situation as the community experiences prophecy. It always has to decide how to respond to prophecies and to events, and to take responsibility for its destiny in light of the questions the story leaves open.

A grim fate also awaits Pashhur, a priest and overseer of the temple, but also someone whom Jeremiah could describe as "prophesying," by/in/with lies (Jer 20:6). When Pashhur "hit" Jeremiah and confined him, this "hitting" is likely not just an act of assault or a judicial act such as having Jeremiah flogged. Both the hitting and the confinement will have been a sign-act of the kind that prophets undertook, like Hananiah's, a symbolic implementation of Yhwh's punishment of Jeremiah for being a false prophet. As he does to Hananiah later, Jeremiah responds by turning the tables, though not with another sign-act but with a verbal message. Grimly, such a prophet takes with him to his fate not only himself and his household but all his "friends" (fellow priests? fellow prophets?) to whom he prophesied. There will be people who go into exile and may look forward to returning. Pashhur is not among them.

Ezekiel makes the point more generally and perhaps even more chillingly: the prophets "will not be in the assembly of my people, they will not enroll on the list of the household of Israel, they will not come to the soil of Israel" (Ezek 13:9). There will be a return from exile and a new community in the land, but they will not be in it. Yhwh's hand will be stretched out to them as it has been stretched out to Ezekiel, but to a negative rather than a positive end (Ezek 13:9; cf. Ezek 2:9). "The prophets will become wind; the word is not in them" (Jer 5:13). They will blow away. "Am I a God nearby," Yhwh says, "and not a God far away?" (Jer 23:23). Yhwh's being far away might become a strange form of reassurance. It implies Yhwh does not bother with us. We are safe. But Jeremiah goes on to affirm that Yhwh is not that far away. Indeed, there is no place that far away. There is nowhere for prophets or their people to hide from Yhwh (Jer 23:24; cf. Ps 139:1-12; Amos 9:1-4).

There is another way to look at the activity of prophets in Babylon (see Ezek 14:1-11). Yhwh declares that the people's addiction to forms of religion that amount to abominations means they have no right to consult Yhwh by means of a prophet. A person who does try to consult Yhwh will receive a direct answer, and this will not be a pleasant experience. Yet there are prophets in Babylon apart from Ezekiel from whom people do get answers. The people speak of them as prophets Yhwh has established (Jer 29:15). Jeremiah is even more severe about them than about the prophets in Jerusalem. He contradicts their message about *shalom* for the people who had not been taken into exile with a declaration about war, starvation and epidemic for the Davidic king, the people (*'am*) in Jerusalem, and their kin, as people who took no notice of earlier prophets (Jer 29:16-19). He likewise declares a terrible sentence on named prophets in Babylon who prophesy lies and engage in affairs, and on another named prophet who had encouraged priests in Jerusalem to silence Jeremiah for telling the Babylonian community that their exile would last many years (Jer 29:20-32).

Such prophets are deceived. Who deceived them? Ezekiel's previous implicit answer was that they are self-deceived. His alternative answer is that Yhwh deceived them. These are people involved in willful deceit of their people or in outrageous forms of worship or both, and their pretending to respond to people when Yhwh has determined to stay silent or to respond in deed rather than word adds to their culpability. Paradoxically, Yhwh will work via their self-deception in such a way as to claim responsibility for it. Yhwh's relationship with them will be a little like that with Pharaoh, who stiffened his own resolve but was (all unbeknown to himself) responding to an initiative of Yhwh in acting to stiffen his resolve. And because this involvement of Yhwh's does not mean they cease to be responsible for their resistance to Yhwh in pretending to speak in Yhwh's name, they will pay the ultimate penalty.

7.5 True Prophets

Kingship is a human initiative of which Yhwh can wrest control. Prophecy is more like a divine initiative of which humanity can wrest control. When Yhwh is in control of prophecy, what does it look like?

Claimed and Consecrated

A prophet is indeed someone of whom Yhwh determined to take control, whom Yhwh determines to turn into a servant. Jeremiah's testimony expresses the paradoxical nature of the relationship between Yhwh's determination and Jeremiah's person. Yhwh formed Jeremiah in the womb, but it was Jeremiah who came out from the womb. Yhwh had "acknowledged" Jeremiah there (*yāda'*), which implies something more like a foreknowledge and recognition of who Jeremiah would be than a foreordaining of this. Jeremiah is in a similar position to Abraham and Moses, to whom the same verb is applied (Gen 18:19; Ex 33:12, 17). But Yhwh had also consecrated him there. This is a striking verb. Prophets were not holy people, like priests, though Jeremiah came from a priestly family. The firstborn son of a family was holy; perhaps Jeremiah was his parents' first son, and Yhwh is claiming his life on that basis.

When Jeremiah objects to Yhwh's commission on account of his age and lack of eloquence, Yhwh's response is not to assure him that he has potential Yhwh has foreseen but to declare that Yhwh's sovereignty must and can overrule these objections. He must obey, and Yhwh will put the words in his mouth. Jeremiah is being summoned into Yhwh's service in the manner of a king's servant (e.g., Jer 25:4). The king exercises absolute authority over his servants. He says go, and they go. He tells them what to say, and they say it. Jeremiah is to act thus. The master's power is then committed to the servant's protection. This may not be merely out of concern for the servant. The master's own reputation is tied up with his servant. To attack the servant is to attack the master.

Thus the master expects total commitment from the servant, threatens devastating consequences if that is not forthcoming, but also offers total commitment if it is (Jer 1:17-19). In light of the pressure people put on him, Jeremiah will be tempted to give up and think he can get out of the discomfort of the confrontational ministry Yhwh imposes on him and get back into his regular place in the community. He needs then to know that this is not an option. Yhwh will not allow him to regain his accepted place in the community in this way. That is the threat. But he is also given the encouragement that Yhwh will enable him to stand resolutely firm before everyone. They will find him as hard to break as a city would be if it had iron pillars and bronze walls (no such thing exists). Such God-given strength will mean the whole country can attack him but they will not overcome him. "I [am/will be] with you," Yhwh says. Therein lies the strength of iron or bronze that will make the "city" unconquerable because it will not run out of the resources that will enable it to withstand.

Jeremiah's awareness that he lacks the qualifications for being a prophet is irrelevant to Yhwh. There is nothing special about being one through whom Yhwh speaks. It is not a sign of deep commitment or spirituality or insight. Once, there was a "word that came to Jeremiah from Yhwh after Nebuzaradan the captain of the guards had set him free" (Jer 40:1). We then look in vain for a regular word from Yhwh. What we find is a word from Nebuzaradan about Yhwh's having warned Jerusalem about coming disaster and having now brought it about because of the people's wrongdoing. He declares that Jeremiah himself is now free to go to Babylon under a witness protection program (he had, after all, been a good friend of Babylon in advocating surrender to Babylon) to live wherever he likes in the land. Yhwh speaks through the foreign official, and leaves it to Jeremiah to decide what he now does.

Moses, likewise, is simply someone who managed to escape the infanticide that perhaps took leaders with more potential, who tried to kill someone without being seen, failed and then ran for his life, who also thought his own identity mattered in relation to fulfilling Yhwh's commission, who did not know who to say Yhwh was, who doubted whether people would believe him and whether he could speak well enough, who totally resisted being drafted by Yhwh and thus infuriated Yhwh, who had not circumcised his son (but he did defend some shepherd girls and did know how to have the right awed response to the presence of God) (Ex 1–4). All Moses has to do is deliver Yhwh's message to the people and to Pharaoh, and deliver Yhwh's signs. No gifts of leadership are required. The only requirement is willingness to serve Yhwh and courage to say what Yhwh says, but even if you were to profess the lack of these, the signs are that this would make no difference to Yhwh.

Embodying Israel's Vocation

Prophets are subordinate to Yhwh; they are also subordinate to Yhwh's purpose with the community. Isaiah 49:1-6 records the testimony of a prophet who initially speaks in similar terms as Jeremiah about Yhwh's summons from the womb, has also wrestled with Israel's recalcitrance, but also speaks of Yhwh's calling in a new way. Yhwh's more specific words to him, "You are my servant," likewise recall the description of Isaiah ben Amoz (Is 20:3); elsewhere Elijah (for instance) is "Yhwh's servant," as is Jonah (2 Kings 9:36; 14:25). But Yhwh's next ascription is extraordinary. In some sense this prophet *is* Israel. That causes pause and makes us reconsider those preceding descriptions of the prophet. In previous chapters of Isaiah it has been Israel that was shaped from the womb (e.g., Is 44:2, 24), Israel that has been Yhwh's servant (most recently, Is 48:20) and Israel (among others) that has been summoned by Yhwh (Is 41:9). But we have also discovered that there is no way Israel is up to the role of servant at the moment (e.g., 42:18-25). Yhwh is now calling the prophet to fulfill Israel's role. Through the prophet Yhwh will manifest splendor, another aspect of Israel's destiny (Is 44:23). The prophet is someone whose whole life work ("summoned from the womb") is to embody what it means to be Israel and thus to be the means of displaying God's splendor in the way the entire community was supposed to do but cannot do because of its resistance to its Master. This becomes the prophet's task, though the prophet may fulfill it through a ministry to the community that enables it to become what it was called to be. For the community is still the entity with the status and vocation of servant; the interim servant must not fall into the trap of thinking to take it away.

Yhwh more or less makes that explicit in talking about the servant's task. First, the prophet talks about turning Jacob to Yhwh and stopping Israel withdrawing, or gathering Israel to Yhwh.[133] All three expressions have similar implications. They presuppose the reality that caused the exile and still seems to be true, that Israel has turned away from Yhwh and needs to be turned back, that Israel has withdrawn from Yhwh and needs to be brought back. It is not the prophet's task to rubber stamp its turning away from Yhwh and take up the task of being servant in its place, in a latter-day equivalent to the move Moses would not cooperate with at Sinai. It is the prophet's task to bring the people back, not to take their place. Perhaps that is one reason why it involves a sword and an arrow. The prophet's stance in relation to the people needs to be a confrontational one, or at least to include a confrontational aspect (as it has), like that of a prophet such as Isaiah ben Amoz.

---

[133]K has *l'* ("not"), Q *lô* (to him). They then link with two different meanings for *'āsap*, which can mean either "gather and bring together" or "gather and take away" (see BDB).

The prophet's task can also be described in terms of "raising Jacob's clans" and "turning Israel's shoots." If we look at the first expression in isolation it would point to the rebuilding of the community in a broader sense; referring to Israel's "shoots" also draws attention to the community's state as mere leftovers, shoots growing from a felled tree. This prophet's task relates to the community's renewing in that broader sense. Yhwh intends to see it flourish and to restore Jerusalem itself. On the other hand, mention of "turning" those shoots takes up that verb that refers to turning the community back to Yhwh.

Either way, Yhwh's point is that for this servant, raising Jacob's clans and turning Israel's shoots is too small a task. This is a doubly ironic remark. The book of Isaiah as a whole, and the rest of the First Testament, might suggest that both restoring the community in a general sense and restoring its relationship to God are somewhat monumental tasks. And this prophet-servant has just acknowledged how daunting the task looks. It is wearying, it drains energy, and it seems to lead nowhere. It is to such a disillusioned servant that Yhwh says, "All right then, I have a bigger task for you." The bigger task is to be a light to the nations, to be Yhwh's deliverance to earth's end. How is the prophet to do that? Proclaiming that Babylon is to fall and that Israel is to be restored has that effect. The proclaiming of such events and their then happening can draw the world to acknowledge that Yhwh is God and thereby to find deliverance. Again, the prophet's light-bringing servant ministry does not sideline the community as if God had cast it off, but puts it in the spotlight where in God's purpose it belongs.

Student

A prophet has to stay in school in order to fulfill such a ministry. The further prophetic testimony in Isaiah 50:4-9 is often referred to as a "servant song," and the following verses do implicitly identify the speaker as Yhwh's servant, but the testimony itself is not a song and it speaks in other terms. The speaker is a student, one who speaks of having "a students' tongue." The previous occurrence of the word *limmûd* came in a commission to "seal the teaching among my students" (Is 8:16). If those are the words of Isaiah ben Amoz, we can see the prophet who speaks among the exiles two centuries later as one of the students of that prophet; Isaiah 40–55 does suggest a ministry inspired by Isaiah ben Amoz as well as Jeremiah, which might be one reason for this prophet's anonymity. But one can as easily read Isaiah 8:16 as Yhwh's words (Isaiah's declaration of intent to wait for Yhwh in Isaiah 8:17 is then Isaiah's response to them). This prophet is then one of Yhwh's students.

The student's task is to sustain the weary. It is a pastoral task. The weary are the exiles in Babylon, perhaps weary of life in a foreign land, weary of being cast off by Yhwh, weary of praying and getting no answer (on their self-perception, though Yhwh's perception is rather different). They need to be helped to keep going, not, for instance simply to assimilate to their surroundings and become Babylonians like anyone else. Many of them had Babylonian names and had learned Babylonian trades. Daniel portrays people trained in Babylonian learning and having to decide whether to eat Babylonian food and join in Babylonian worship. Yes, they need sustaining. The means of the prophet's sustaining is rather feeble. It is "a word." The nature of that word or message we may infer from the deposit of the student's ministry. It is a word about Yhwh's intentions for coming events, about who Yhwh is and about who they are. It is sometimes a directly comforting word, sometimes a confrontational one. Either way it is intended to be sustaining, to keep them going.

To the end of having a students' tongue, Second Isaiah also needs a students' ear. Second Isaiah is indeed a student of Isaiah ben Amoz, someone who declares the new implications of the key theological fact in Isaiah's theology, that Yhwh is the holy one. The understanding of a prophet's relationship with God expressed in Isaiah 49–50 indicates that Second Isaiah is also a student of Jeremiah. The prophet knows how to learn from what Yhwh has said in the past (to learn from Scripture, we might say). But being mentored by a pair of dead guys is a rather Pickwickian concept. Being a student implies a relationship with a teacher you can hear speaking to you now, at least online. Second Isaiah is talking about that kind of student-teacher relationship. It is as well that this prophet also has Yhwh as mentor.

How does one move between learning from those earlier prophets to knowing what to say now, in a context that requires a message consistent with what came before but recognizing that the situation has moved on? Each morning Yhwh wakes this prophet with some insight on this question. (We may allow for a little hyperbole; the point is that Yhwh's relationship with this prophet is analogous to that of a teacher to a pupil whom the teacher mentors on a daily basis.) It is the person who has a students' ear who can then exercise a students' tongue. Yhwh not only wakes the ear (to speak metonymically) and speaks into the ear but opens the ear to make sure the message gets home to the person. Successful communication requires a sender, a message and a receiver. All are there.

One might have thought that being a student was a harmless occupation, harmless to the students and harmless to other people. When Yhwh is the mentor, matters turn out differently. Yhwh's teaching seems a threat to people; these may be Babylonians or other Judeans. When God speaks, it can seem a threat to the people of God and also to the world. That arouses a desire to silence the person through whom the teaching comes. Perhaps this student had worked that out before it happened, or perhaps it came as a surprise to find that bringing good news met with opposition in both quarters. Perhaps the student was immersed enough in Jeremiah not to be surprised, or perhaps it was people's hostility that directed the student's attention to Jeremiah and made Yhwh's student a student of Jeremiah as well as of Isaiah ben Amoz. Either way, accepting people's attacks and shaming was a corollary of being a student. Like Jeremiah, this student had to be identified with Yhwh as mentor as well as with Israel as the people that was itself designed to be a student cohort. The challenge to a student then is not to fall into the same rebelliousness as the world and the people of God. This student is able to do that because of knowing some facts about Yhwh. "The Lord Yhwh will help me." People who accuse the student of not really being mentored by Yhwh, of being opposed to Yhwh's purpose rather than identified with it, will find they cannot carry their case. The teacher will vindicate the student, demonstrating by events that the student's account of the teacher's words is the right one.

Herald

At the center of the visions of a new Jerusalem in Isaiah 60–62 (and of Is 56–66 as a whole) comes yet another testimony, in Isaiah 61:1-3. "The spirit of my Lord Yhwh is on me, because Yhwh has anointed me," it begins. This prophet's self-understanding is thus expressed in terms that echo a number of earlier passages in Isaiah: the sending of Isaiah ben Amoz, the coming of Yhwh's spirit on the shoot from Jesse's stump, the presence of Yhwh's spirit on Yhwh's servant, the sending of Yhwh's servant, the anointing of Cyrus, the sending with the spirit of Yhwh, the anointing of Yhwh's servant,[134] the promise of Yhwh's spirit being on you (Is 6:8; 11:1-2; 42:1, 19; 45:1; 52:14; 59:21). In Christian thinking, anointing with the Holy Spirit has become a single idea, but that is a result of this passage's influence; elsewhere "anointing" and "the spirit of Yhwh" are separate ideas. The coming of Yhwh's spirit on someone is an act of Yhwh that cannot be made to happen, an act whereby someone is enabled to do things that would otherwise be impossible. Anointing with oil is a human act (though done in Yhwh's name) designed to consecrate, designate and authorize someone for a role. Thus prophets were not anointed; being made a prophet is an unmediated divine act.[135] The links with previous passages in Isaiah imply a claim to be a fulfillment of Yhwh's promise about a king to implement the vision about kingship, to be commissioned like Cyrus to bring people liberation, to be a fulfillment of Yhwh's promise about anointing a servant, and to be given the servant's role of binding up the broken rather than dismissing them in their brokenness.

---

[134] On Is 52:14, see §7.7 "Eventually Triumphant."
[135] See §7.3 "Ordained Ministry."

After that, the description of the role of the anointed might seem to descend to bathos. The speaker is not a king but a reporter, someone sent with news. The word usually implies good news, as it does here (justifying LXX's verb *euangelisasthai*), though it need not do so (e.g., 1 Sam 4:17). The verb suggests further links with earlier parts of Isaiah, where news-bringing was an important motif (see Is 40:9; 41:27; 52:7). The herald's identity is not clear there; it is the message that counts. What is clear is that one would not expect a king to be a herald, given that kings employ heralds, though it would not be beyond a creative prophet to recast the king's significance in such terms (Is 55:3-5 has turned David into a witness). In Isaiah 61:1-3 the speaker is commissioned like a king and like a prophet, but given the task of a reporter that belongs to neither. The task is not to take action to implement *mišpāṭ ûṣĕdāqâ*, like the king in Isaiah 11, or to confront people over their failings, like the prophet in Isaiah 48 (and this prophet elsewhere in Isaiah 56–66). It is to transmit a piece of news that can minister to people who are weak and broken; the task relates to the vocation of both king and prophet. The people as a whole are weak and broken at heart, in a way reflected in Ezra-Nehemiah ("heartbroken" gives the wrong impression; the idea is that their brokenness affects both body and spirit and reaches down into their inner beings). But good news has the capacity to change them.[136]

The news concerns the proclamation of release and liberty for captives and prisoners. That idea of release for captives mixes metaphors. Release (*dĕrôr*) is for bondservants (e.g., Jer 34), and in the exile the people had been like serfs, but they were more literally captives and prisoners. Back in the land they are still rather like that, like serfs as a community (e.g., Neh 9:36), and in addition they are making bondservants of one another (Neh 5). In proclaiming release the herald indeed acts like a king (Jer 34:8), but in Israel this proclamation is not intrinsically a king's task but that of the community as a whole (Lev 25:10; Jer 34:17; cf. Deut 15:1, though there the proclamation concerns *šĕmiṭṭâ*, "remission," rather than *dĕrôr*). In a nonmonarchic context a priest or a leader such as Nehemiah might proclaim release or remission.

Here the subject is not the proclaiming of a regular release (or rather, an irregular one, since as far as we know Israel never did proclaim a release, as Jer 34 reflects). Release is an image for the restoration Yhwh is bringing about for the whole community. Yhwh is therefore the king who is proclaiming release, and the herald is Yhwh's mouthpiece. (Perhaps the herald's anointing, indeed, is that of a priest whose task might include this proclaiming.)

---

[136]In Is 58:7 the weak are a group within the community, as was the case in preexilic prophecy, but in (e.g.) Is 41:17; 49:13; 51:21; 54:11 the weak are the community as a whole. This understanding better fits Is 61:1-9 (against Joseph Blenkinsopp, who dissociates vv. 3b-7 from vv. 1-3a [*Isaiah 56–66*, AB (New York: Doubleday, 2003), pp. 223-26]).

Worshiper

Yhwh is declaring that this is a year in which Yhwh's pleasure or will is going to be implemented. The EVV render this as a year of Yhwh's favor, but this misses the point (the word is *rāṣôn*, not *ḥēn*). The LXX was nearer in describing this as a year acceptable to Yhwh (cf. Lk 4:19).[137] At present the nations are implementing their own will in the people's life (e.g., Neh 9:37). Yhwh is going to put that right. In the terms of the heralding of news in Isaiah 52:7-10, Yhwh intends to start reigning again. Yhwh's reign or pleasure will mean favor for Israel, but that is not the main point. It is that Yhwh is exercising sovereignty. But the day of Yhwh's pleasure is the day when Israel's overlords are put down and punished.[138] The news of what Yhwh has done in declaring that a release is on its way, and the proclamation of that release, has the power to bind up the people who are broken inside and outside. It has the power to comfort mourners and inspire them to clean off their signs of grief and put on garments and makeup appropriate to a festive celebration.

In this context the true prophet's job is to proclaim that news. The message is one Hananiah had proclaimed a century previously, but it had then been untrue. Hananiah too had repeated what Isaiah had said, because the situation of threat seemed the same, "but the situation was *not* the same. . . . Hananiah did not know that there was such a thing as a different historical juncture."[139] A true prophet is someone who knows what time it is. "The authentic prophet must be able to distinguish whether a historical hour stands under the wrath or the love of God."[140] Hananiah's message is an idea whose time has now come.

After some further description of the nature of that release and restoration, the "I" of the herald returns (Is 61:10-11), but the herald has now become a worshiper, changing positions and personally responding to the news.

It would not be surprising if a royal herald wore special garments that speak of the one the herald represents. This herald wears "deliverance garments," garments that match the message and themselves proclaim the deliverance people are about to experience and the *ṣĕdāqâ* this deliverance expresses. Indeed, they guarantee or initiate that deliverance, as Jeremiah's breaking a pot guaranteed and initiated the disaster that this message re-

---

[137]Even more oddly, there the EVV also render *eniauton kuriou dekton* "a year of the Lord's favor."

[138]On Jesus' partial quotation of Is 61:2 in Lk 4:17, see §5.3 "The Theological Question."

[139]Buber, *On the Bible*, p. 168.

[140]Eva Osswald, *Falsche Prophetie im Alten Testament* (Tübingen: Mohr, 1962), p. 22; cf. Martin Buber, *The Prophetic Faith* (New York: Harper, 1960), p. 178; also James L. Crenshaw, *Prophetic Conflict*, BZAW 124 (Berlin/New York: de Gruyter, 1971), pp. 53-54; James A. Sanders, *From Sacred Story to Sacred Text* (Philadelphia: Fortress, 1987), p. 84.

verses. The herald looks down at these clothes and feels like a groom or bride dressed up for his or her great occasion. The message cannot but overcome its very herald, who can only burst out in joy. It is joy in God rather than in being a herald or in the wonder of what this means for the recipients of the news. That implicitly invites the audience into the same celebration.

For either party the celebration is anticipatory, as usual. The herald wears deliverance garments in order to proclaim and initiate the deliverance itself. They proclaim that it will indeed be true that Yhwh makes an act of *ṣĕdāqâ* spring forth before the world in a way that brings praise to Yhwh's name. It is as sure as the fact that fruit grows from the soil each year. So the herald can begin rejoicing now and thereby draw the city into rejoicing. The rejoicing is for Yhwh's sake, but telling us about the rejoicing is for the community's sake. Actually it is another way of heralding news.

Strange Shepherd

A prophet who functions in the temple is involved in a pastoral ministry, like that of a priest, to people who come to bring their questions and their suffering to Yhwh. Prophets were also healers; we could say that healing was an aspect of their pastoral role. Elisha offers Naaman some tough love, a way to find healing, and some pastoral guidance (2 Kings 5). Hosea, who spends much of his time confronting and warning and some of it telling his story, also spends some of it exhorting: "Come, let us turn to Yhwh, for he has torn us, but he will heal us; he has hit us, but he will bandage us" (Hos 6:1). Indeed, this is not really an exhortation, in that it is not in the imperative but in the cohortative. Hosea identifies himself with the people as a whole; he wants to turn to Yhwh with them.

In Zechariah 11:4-17 Yhwh speaks to the prophet as a shepherd (so here it is a prophet who is the shepherd, not a king). The account of this conversation with God is disturbing and obscure in detail, though not in the general picture. Yhwh bids the prophet tend the sheep, the people in the community. But they are sheep destined for slaughter, the kind over whose sale their owner will rub his hands. Nor will they earn any pity from their (other) shepherds; this was the destiny of sheep, after all. These shepherds presumably stand for other leaders of the community (prophets, priests, government). The prophet sees the sheep as the victims of their shepherds, yet does not, for instance, undertake better shepherding for them or promise them that Yhwh will do so or will commission better shepherds (contrast, e.g., Ezek 34). Yhwh commissions this shepherd to join with the other shepherds.

The imagery is different from Isaiah 6, but the implications are similar. There the prophet has a vision of Yhwh exalted as the holy one and volunteers to accept a mission as Yhwh' messenger. It transpires that the commission involves making people deaf and blind so that they do not turn to Yhwh and find deliverance. As a result they will find themselves the victims of terrifying, total devastation. Here the shepherd is similarly sent to fatten sheep for killing. So he sets about tending the sheep with the aid of two staffs, presumably staffs of the kind a shepherd would use, one called Delightfulness, the other called Binders. He gets rid of three other shepherds (presumably bad shepherds like the pitiless ones he mentioned earlier, but we do not know what this refers to) yet then runs out of patience with the flock, and they come to hate him. So he declares that he intends to abandon them to their fate. He breaks the Delightfulness staff "so as to annul my covenant that I had sealed with all the peoples, and it was annulled that day. The sheep merchants[141] who were watching me acknowledged that this was the word of Yhwh."

I take the first staff to refer to the delightfulness of the land in its flourishing and the people's prosperity (e.g., Gen 49:15; Job 36:11), and the covenant with the peoples to refer to the "covenant of the people" in Isaiah 42:6 and Isaiah 49:8, the phrase making more explicit that the covenant applies to other peoples and not just to Israel. It was in restoring Israel and making it flourish again that Yhwh would advertise to the peoples the possibilities inherent in a relationship with Yhwh. But Second Isaiah worked in a context when that was hope rather than reality, and this prophet sees the situation not to have moved on at all. Therefore the flourishing and its witness to the world are cancelled.

Then he breaks the second staff, "so as to annul the brotherhood between Judah and Israel." Here too Zechariah is taking up exilic promises; Ezekiel 37:15-28 also proclaims that the two peoples will become one again. It will be as if two sticks are indissolubly joined as one. Zechariah's picture reverses the symbolism. One stick is broken into two.[142]

As if that is not enough, Yhwh goes on in effect to recommission the prophet as a parody of a good shepherd. He is to take up the equipment of a foolish shepherd and model the work of a shepherd Yhwh will send who is the opposite of the good shepherd pictured in Ezekiel 34 and the very embodiment of the shepherds Yhwh there condemns. He will be a shepherd who will *not* attend to the lost or seek the young or heal the injured, and will feed on the sheep instead of feeding them. But a poetic footnote adds that the worthless shepherd will get his reward.

All this may relate mainly to the prophet's own day, but may picture Yhwh's relationship with Israel over the centuries with this shepherd standing for the sequence of prophets and his present ministry being the exemplar that

---

[141]Presupposing *kĕnaʿăniyyê* for MT *kēn ʿăniyyê* , "the weak among [the sheep]," with BHS.
[142]Cf. Paul D. Hanson, *The Dawn of Apocalyptic* (Philadelphia: Fortress, 1985), pp. 343-45.

his contemporaries have to come to terms with.[143] It is a solemn near-end to the story of prophecy in the First Testament.

Argumentative

With Habakkuk, Yhwh engages in argument—admittedly an argument initiated by the prophet, which is (to judge from the order of the book) apparently the process that makes him into a prophet. Habakkuk begins by challenging Yhwh in the manner of the Psalms, protesting at the strife, violence and disorder of the community's life, unconstrained by the exercise of authority based on proper teaching, and conversely making such teaching and exercise of authority impossible. Indeed, we may assume that the usual rule obtains that the people who exercise authority in the community are themselves heavily involved in the wrongdoing, in fraud and violence. Community life is totally broken down. There is no indication that Habakkuk is especially the victim of the wrongdoing he describes; he is not lamenting his own suffering. He is offended at the monstrous situation he confronts in the community, at which Yhwh seems not to be so offended. No matter how loud he shouts about it, Yhwh will neither listen nor do anything. It would be logical to reckon that the "teaching" is that of the "teaching scroll" discovered in Josiah's reign. Habakkuk is then referring its actual failure to make a significant difference to Judah's life—and suggesting that God bears responsibility for this? After all, the scroll spoke of sanctions in connection with ignoring it, but Yhwh is turning a blind eye.

Yhwh does respond, speaking in the imperative plural so that this reply to Habakkuk takes the form of an address to the people as a whole (Hab 1:5-11). They are invited to raise their heads and look at what is happening on the international scene. This is not to imply that we can date the oracle on the basis of what we know of the rise of Babylon; Habakkuk might be speaking thus when Babylon is only a speck on the horizon, or speaking some years later and inviting people to reflect on the way events have unfolded. Yhwh goes on at some length in describing Babylon's willfulness, power, confidence, self-aggrandizement, military might, skill, determination, plundering and enslaving. Again, we need not infer Habakkuk is relying on reports from the front or on special revelations from Yhwh. One superpower is much the same as another and is described as such. The bad news or good news (according to how you look at it) is that this new superpower is heading Judah's way. That will sort Judah out.

This response does not satisfy Habakkuk. Indeed it scandalizes him, and

---

[143]Cf. Ben C. Ollenburger, "The Book of Zechariah," *The New Interpreter's Bible* (Nashville: Abingdon, 1996), 7:733-840; see pp. 823-24.

he does not hesitate to say so. Yhwh has given hostages to fortune in noting that the Babylonians seize homes that do not belong to them, make up their own rules for the conduct of relationships and worship themselves, their power, and their glory. How can they be Yhwh's agents? (Hab 1:12-15). Habakkuk reminds Yhwh of three characteristics of the divine being and activity.

First, Yhwh is the God who "of old" personally defeated evil (e.g., Is 51:9) and will do so again "in days to come," exercising authority and arbitrating between peoples (e.g., Is 2:4). Further, Yhwh is not a here-today-gone-tomorrow dying-and-rising God like some others whom Habakkuk could name. So what is Yhwh doing now, proposing to act via Babylon as if lacking the life to act in person? Habakkuk makes no mention of the fact that this practice on Yhwh's part has been long accepted by prophets such as Isaiah and Habakkuk's contemporary Jeremiah, though Isaiah, at least, hints at an awareness of the issue in promising that Assyria will get its comeuppance for its own wickedness (Is 10:5-27).

Second, Yhwh is someone who declines to contemplate one people doing wrong by another without doing something about it, so what is Yhwh doing in regard to such wrongdoing? Habakkuk picks up the language he used about Yhwh's making him contemplate wrongdoing. Yhwh is either calmly watching Israel do wrong and staying silent (if Habakkuk is repeating the earlier protest) or calmly watching Babylon act just as wrongfully, except on a vaster scale.

Third, Yhwh has made humanity as helpless as the fish in the sea or the creeping things on the ground. Their helplessness is no problem as long as no one is trying to take advantage of it, but now Babylon is doing exactly that, like a fisherman catching fish on Lake Galilee and returning home rejoicing. And Yhwh lets that happen. What is Yhwh doing?

Patient

Habakkuk intends to wait on Yhwh for a reply (Hab 2:1). The declaration offers further insight on the way the relationship between prophet and Yhwh worked.[144] A prophet could confront Yhwh quite argumentatively, but (like Job) could not control when a word from Yhwh came. Sometimes Jeremiah does not know what to say. After Hananiah broke the yoke off his neck to signify Yhwh's deliverance of Judah, contrary to Jeremiah's message, Jeremiah just "went on his way." He had nothing to say at the time. Only afterward (we do not know how long afterward) did he know what to say, when Yhwh's word came to him (Jer 28:11-12). When Judeans ask for advice on what to do

---

[144]If actually we have a literary construction here, that may even strengthen the point, because it still indicates how an author would think of the way this relationship worked.

after Gedaliah's assassination, Jeremiah has to wait ten days before he knows what to say (Jer 42:7). Even though he then says the same thing he has been saying for years (submit to Babylon and things will work out), he knows he has to know Yhwh has spoken to him afresh each time he speaks.

Habakkuk, too, could not will a response from Yhwh, nor think up a response and assume it was Yhwh's. Prophecy and theological reflection are two different things. He has to wait. But he commits himself to a waiting that will not give up until there is a response, like the waiting of the metaphorical lookouts on Jerusalem's walls who keep urging Yhwh to reestablish Jerusalem (Is 62:6-7).

And there is such a response, though initially it might seem doubly unsatisfying, like that to Job. Yhwh bids Habakkuk write down a vision that will come true at a future time (Hab 2:2-3). It might seem unsatisfying because it fails to address Habakkuk's point, which is that the Babylonians are even more corrupt than Judah, and can therefore hardly be allowed to function as Judah's judge and jailor. And it might seem unsatisfying because far from promising immediate action, it gives notice that there will be no action for a while. While putting the vision into writing could make it available (for instance, by posting the tablets in a public place such as the temple courtyards), the usual reason for writing down a prophecy is to preserve it in fixed form against the day when it comes true, and that fits with the fact that Yhwh intends to act in a while, but not now. The response does assert that there will be action, but it does not indicate what kind.

Its declaration is to be unequivocal, plain, easily read. There is no obscurity about it. Is Yhwh speaking to the fact that often prophecy is expressed in symbols and images? Only rarely is it concrete in a way that means it can be held accountable. Yhwh here promises something unequivocal. Even if it does not promise action this month or this year, it promises action, and when its time comes, it will not fail. We might compare its point with the feelings a couple have about the coming birth of their baby. Pregnancy takes time, but the baby's time will definitely come. And thus "the faithful person will live by its truthfulness" (Hab 2:4),[145] will live in the meantime strengthened and enabled by the fact that God is going to fulfill this promise.

Prophecy is often obscure but immediate. This prophecy is clear but distant. What is its content? Yhwh goes on to describe the fate of the willful person, who has greedily "gathered for himself all the nations" (Hab 2:5, 16, 20). In the context it is clear enough who is the unnamed wrongdoer. Baby-

---

[145]The EVV have "his" rather than "its" (cf. Rom 1:17), but this fits less well in the context, though Habakkuk would agree with Paul's point. We do not know the meaning of the first colon in Hab 2:4.

lon is the superpower that has taken over all the nations in Habakkuk's world. Perhaps it saw itself as leading the nations beneficently into a united future with all the advantages of centralized government and common policies throughout their world. Yhwh sees it as guilty of wrongs against humanity and against the land or earth, against cities and their inhabitants, against forests and their wild creatures. It has acquired gains to the ultimate detriment of its own house. It has tried to set itself so high that it can never be pulled down (the impressive buildings of Babylon did reach into the sky), but ironically this very effort will be its downfall. The stones and beams in the buildings' walls will cry out against the bloodshed at whose cost they were built, like blood crying out from the ground on which it had been shed (Gen 4:10). Unwittingly Babylon has formulated policies that will bring it shame, not the splendor it seeks. It has made other people drink poison (that is, it has defeated and decimated them) and has thus exposed their helplessness and shamed them, but it will find itself having to drink its own medicine. It has trusted in images it has made for itself, but it will find they let it down. It will long to discover what to do now, but will find that (unlike Yhwh before whom Habakkuk stood waiting for a word) these images cannot speak. All it can do is stand in silence before Yhwh in the holy palace in the heavens (Hab 2:6-20).

Interruptive

The conversation is not over. Habakkuk speaks once more. Indeed, Habakkuk might seem to be interrupting God, whose words would continue satisfactorily from Habakkuk 2:20 to Habakkuk 3:3 if they were allowed to do so. It is particularly ironic that Habakkuk thus interrupts Yhwh just after Yhwh calls for silence. But Habakkuk gets away with it, perhaps partly because this time his interruption amounts to an amen to Yhwh's word.[146] Habakkuk has listened to what Yhwh has to say and now stands in awe at the deed Yhwh intends to undertake, rather than disputing it (Hab 3:2).[147] He has moved from dispute to submission, like Job. Yet he does not simply yield to silence (any more than Job does?).

He is not keen on the idea that Yhwh's action might have to wait a long time (it will actually wait nearly a century). He wants to see action "in the

---

[146]Cf. Elizabeth R. Achtemeier, *Nahum–Malachi* (Louisville: Westminster John Knox, 1986), p. 54.

[147]Out of the context one would refer the *šĕmaʿ* to the account of Yhwh's deeds in the past, but this seems irrelevant in the context, and the usage here compares with that of *šĕmûʿâ* elsewhere (e.g., Obad 1). Likewise the context (Hab 1:5) suggests that Yhwh's *pōʿal* is not Yhwh's past activity or Yhwh's activity in general but the coming deed Yhwh has announced.

midst of the years," in the meantime, "in the here and now."[148] He wants to
see the message brought to life, turned into reality and acknowledged as
Yhwh's act. "In the turmoil may you be mindful of compassion" (Hab 3:2).
This colon is usually reckoned to begin with a reference to Yhwh's wrath, but
rōgez is not a usual word for wrath. It and related words more often suggest
turmoil or tumult, which fits the context. The turmoil is the world's turmoil
as people are experiencing it "in the midst of the years." So Habakkuk is
pleading for Yhwh not to leave the world in its turmoil. He wants Yhwh to act
in compassion. That further buttresses the plea for Yhwh to act now. There is
no indication that Habakkuk is concerned for Judah alone, as is often the case
when prophets speak of Yhwh acting in compassion. Yhwh's message has
spoken of the way the nations as a whole sit under the oppression of the superpower, and Habakkuk pleads for compassion for them all.

Habakkuk has engaged Yhwh in a dialogue reminiscent of Abraham's
(Gen 18:23-33), but with implications for the nations that are almost the opposite to those of Abraham's. Now he reports a vision of Yhwh coming to act
in the manner Yhwh did in the past (Hab 3:3-15), a vision that constitutes
Yhwh's last word in this dialogue. Habakkuk recalls how more than once in
the past Israel had known Yhwh to journey to Canaan from the southern wilderness, the mysterious, marginal realm where Yhwh's original home on
earth was located (see Deut 33; Judg 5). Psalm 68 prays for Yhwh to do that
again, and Hab 3 pictures Yhwh doing so. As Yhwh had thus gone before Israel to defeat the Canaanites and then come to defeat Jabin, so Yhwh will act
again to put "the nations" (that is, the empire) in their place and deliver Judah. At Yhwh's behest will be epidemic and plague, the agents Yhwh had
used in putting the Egyptian empire in its place. The Canaanites thought of
these frightening, unstoppable forces as deities. Israel knows there is no real
deity apart from Yhwh and that these terrifying forces are under Yhwh's control, like the Destroyer at the exodus (Ex 12:23) and the aide who "destroys"
Israel by means of an epidemic in David's day (2 Sam 24:15-16). They are negative equivalents to agents such as the commitment or steadfastness that also
serve Yhwh (e.g., Ps 23:6; 43:3). They are aspects of Yhwh's own person (it is
also Yhwh who strikes the Egyptians and Yhwh who manifests commitment
and steadfastness to people), yet they can be distinguished from Yhwh as
semi-hypostasized realities. Such an act will manifest the kind of power and
splendor that will reverberate through the cosmos. Yhwh's majesty and
praiseworthiness will be reflected in the heavens by the clouds that simultaneously reveal and obscure Yhwh's coming, and in the lightning that illumines the sky against this somber backcloth and points to the intervention of

---

[148]J. H. Eaton, *Obadiah, Nahum, Habakkuk, Zephaniah* (London: SCM Press, 1961), p. 110.

this fiery warrior deity to sort out affairs on earth in the way Habakkuk has urged. It will raise the question whether behind the empire's assertiveness is the assertiveness of cosmic powers of disorder, the Rivers and the Sea. The superpower is the current embodiment of these powers, and Yhwh's acts will be assertions of ferocious power against these realities.

Responsive

Habakkuk tells us of his response, or rather his responses (Hab 3:16). It would again be an exaggeration to say that at last the questioning, indignant prophet is silenced. He keeps talking, but his talk has a different tone. The vision of Yhwh's coming has not silenced him, but it has alarmed him. The world is in a turmoil; Habakkuk is now consumed by a turmoil of his own at the prospect of what Yhwh intends to do to resolve the world's turmoil. He expects that situation to continue.[149] But he comes near to silence in declaring his commitment to "settling down" (*nûaḥ*) in the midst of both turmoils while he awaits the act that corresponds to the vision, as Yhwh had urged (Hab 2:3).

Further, he declares the intention to rejoice exultingly in Yhwh "when the fig does not bud and there is no produce on the vine, the olive crop has failed and the fields do not produce food, the sheep have been cut off from the fold and there are no cattle in the pens" (Hab 3:17-18). Present experience is along these lines. That might issue from Babylonian invasion, or in the context the images might be a metaphor for adversity, or perhaps Habakkuk imagines things getting worse as natural disaster adds to military invasion, so that he is portraying a possible "worst-case scenario."[150] Whether adversity takes the form of imperial oppression or natural disaster, the prophet has become convinced that they are not the end of the story. Yhwh will bring him and his people out the other side of these troubles (Hab 3:19). A time of exultation and rejoicing will come. Habakkuk is not envisaging an eschatological deliverance in the sense of a far-off event that he will not see, but a deliverance that he will experience. Indeed, he implies, he intends to begin that exulting and rejoicing now; the verbs are cohortative.

On the usual dating of the prophet, the fall of Babylon in 539 did not happen within Habakkuk's lifetime, but it happened. A prophet has to live with Yhwh's decisions about when a vision finds fulfillment. Perhaps one consideration that helps him do so is the very fact that (like most prophecies) this vision is not a wholly novel one. It constitutes a reassertion of Yhwh's known pattern of activity. Its failure to refer to Babylon by name is a symbol of that.

---

[149]The verbs move to yiqtol for the middle line. I hesitate to take this as merely a rhetorical variation from the qatal forms in the first line with the EVV.

[150]Jimmy J. M. Roberts, *Nahum, Habakkuk, and Zephaniah* (Louisville: Westminster John Knox, 1991), p. 157.

The pattern it speaks of has obtained before, not least in Babylon's own defeat of Assyria, within Habakkuk's lifetime. Whether he himself sees its next embodiment is not so important. It will need to be repeated again and again over coming millennia.

7.6 Poets, Visionaries, Actors

"The proper instrument of prophetic activity is the spoken and, as time goes by, to a greater and greater extent the written word."[151] Prophets relate what they have seen and heard. It is not exactly testimony, since instead of being delivered in court, their witness involves them declaring what they hear in Yhwh's court to people who do not have access to it. The trouble is that these people are constitutionally unwilling to listen to them. So prophets search with burning urgency for a way of getting through to them. Seeking to do so, they speak metaphorically, obliquely, provocatively, subtly, indelicately, visually, familiarly, realistically and grippingly. And seeking to do so, they not merely speak but act and let their message be embodied in their personal experience and lives.

Metaphorically

There is a more profound reason than people's willful stupidity for prophets' casting around with burning urgency for a way of communicating with them. Even if people wanted to listen, what prophets must seek to convey is deep and mysterious. As preachers need to be "poets that speak against a prose world,"[152] so "what a prophet has to say can never be said in prose."[153] Poetry is the natural discourse of prophets. One reason is that they want to speak about Yhwh, and while there are one or two literal statements that can be made about Yhwh (Yhwh is holy), most interesting and compelling statements about Yhwh involve imagery: Yhwh is a shepherd, Yhwh is a lion, Israel is a vine, the relationship between Yhwh and Israel is like a marriage. While there are clear-cut and straightforward truths about everyday matters that can be expressed in straightforward ways, there are meaningful and momentous truths to which regular language is inadequate, and that applies to most truths about God and us. Symbols are what then make communication possible.

The prophets who have books named after them manifest considerable rhetorical skill. They are capable of speaking in pithy one-liners and in sus-

---

[151]Eichrodt, *Theology of the Old Testament*, 1:342. Eichrodt italicizes the first six words.

[152]Walter Brueggemann, *Finally Comes the Poet* (Minneapolis: Fortress, 1989), p. 3; he italicizes the words.

[153]Hans Urs von Balthasar, *The Glory of the Lord* (New York: Crossroad, 1982), p. 43; cf. Brueggemann, *Finally Comes the Poet*, p. 4.

tained, lengthy, complex compositions. They speak not in the doggerel verse of Proverbs but in the sophisticated poetry of Job. They make skilled use of irony, rhetorical questions and other devices. They show themselves aware of Israel's own traditions, of contemporary international affairs and of contemporary political issues in Judah and Ephraim. They evidently belong to "a socially and economically superior, *literate* stratum of the population." But the fact that they more often critique people called "prophets" than see themselves as prophets (see, e.g., Mic 3:5-8) makes them also more like "dissident intellectuals" than prophets. "No other ancient Near Eastern society that we know of developed a comparable tradition of dissident intellectualism and social criticism."[154]

Recognizing that making things as clear and explicit as possible is not the only key to communication, Yhwh bids Ezekiel to "propound an allegory, read a poem *(ḥûd hîdâ ûmĕšōl māšāl)* to the household of Israel" (Ezek 17:1-2). Sometimes Yhwh tells things straight in the hope that this will achieve communication, but sometimes not, in the hope that this will achieve communication. Communication is not merely a matter of expounding truths as clearly as possible. There are none as blind as those who won't see, and one gets nowhere by making things perfectly clear to people who are unwilling to see. So Yhwh communicates in other ways. Joel begins (Joel 1:2-20) by urging people to listen, then asks a question, then issues a rhetorical exhortation, then describes something the audience knows well though perhaps does so hyperbolically, then issues a metaphorical exhortation to an imaginary audience, then describes the situation again but does it both more metaphorically and more concretely, then issues a series of exhortations to people to do something that they were surely doing already, then speaks more theologically about the significance of the events, then puts the suffering of people and animals into the kind of a prayer that the people might utter, then puts it into the kind of prayer that an individual might utter.

Obliquely

Isaiah begins, "Listen, heavens, attend, earth, for Yhwh has spoken: 'I reared children and brought them up, but they—they rebelled against me' " (Is 1:2). Isaiah is addressing the Israelites, Yhwh's children, but does so indirectly. It is their rebelliousness that makes this necessary. Indeed, the very existence of prophecy in the form(s) in which it appears in people such as Isaiah presupposes that people are not minded to take any notice of Yhwh and that a prophet is someone who battles for attention. Seeking to manipulate people into listening by addressing someone else is one way of trying to get atten-

---

[154]Blenkinsopp, *Sage, Priest, Prophet*, pp. 141, 144, 154.

tion. Prophets often address other nations (or their gods), but the real audience is Israel itself. Yhwh is seeking to get through to Israel regarding its attitude to other nations or their gods. The great master of such indirect address is Second Isaiah, in whose work we keep needing to bear in mind the distinction between the audience on the stage (where the prophet addresses the nations or their gods) and the audience in the house (the Judean community). The prophet knows it is hard to get through to the people of God but also trusts it is not impossible and knows it is not enough simply to rely on God to bring home the significance of a straightforward message. For similar reasons prophets sometimes speak in enigmatic ways. Jeremiah is to tell people, "Every pitcher is to be filled with wine" (Jer 13:12). It is a puzzlingly pointless declaration. It seeks to win the attention of people and make them think, in the manner of a parable.

Prophets use their imagination, and they appeal to the imagination of their hearers. Even when they describe some event in apparently straightforward terms, we have to be wary of understanding it prosaically. Yhwh declares that the king of Assyria

> will not come into this city; he will not shoot an arrow there. He will not draw near to it with a shield; he will not throw up a ramp against it. The way that he came, he will return; into this city he will not come (Yhwh's oracle). I will protect this city and deliver it for my sake and for the sake of David my servant. (Is 37:33-35)

Indeed, Sennacherib did not enter Jerusalem. Yhwh did protect it and deliver it. But Sennacherib did besiege the city and set up siege ramps against it. Perhaps Yhwh had a change of mind about how near to let Sennacherib get, or perhaps the concrete pictures were never meant as literal prophecies about the details of the way Yhwh would deliver the city.

Isaiah also gives a concrete picture of Babylon's fall and its consequences (Is 13:19-22), as does Jeremiah, in greater detail (Jer 50). But the actual fall of Babylon does not correspond to their picture. The language of these prophecies recycles the language of Yhwh's warnings against Israel. Their point is to signify that Babylon's destruction will correspond to Israel's.[155] Isaiah 46:1-2 offers another description: "Bel has knelt down, Nebo is bending over, their images have come to belong to animals and cattle; the things you carry are loaded as a burden on a weary animal. They bent over and knelt down all at once; they cannot free the burden, but have themselves gone into captivity." This sounds like a description of an event that is taking place, but it is given before the event. The event has taken place in Yhwh's intention but has not yet

---

[155]Terence E. Fretheim, *Jeremiah* (Macon, Ga.: Smith & Helwys, 2002), p. 623.

happened in Babylon itself. And when it does so, to judge from the account given by the victor (there is no account within the First Testament) it will look very different. This is a picture painted by a divinely inspired imagination, designed to encourage and challenge Judeans for whom the event is still future but who need to start living in light of its certainty. The images in the portrayal reflect what actually happens when Middle-Eastern peoples bring their gods into a city when siege is threatened, when these images are taken off by a city's captors or when each year the community carries them about in procession. Familiarity with such events generates a portrayal that will communicate with the Judean (or for that matter Babylonian) people. It does not generate a literal picture of what will happen.

Provocatively

"Come to Bethel," Yhwh invites the Israelites: "and rebel" (Amos 4:4). The irony is designed to jolt people into seeing the significance of their worship.

There were prophets who said they were sent with Yhwh's word, just like Jeremiah or Ezekiel, but who colluded with people whose worship offended Yhwh. When such people sought Yhwh's guidance, these prophets offered such guidance. So were they sent from Yhwh, as they said? Well, says Ezekiel, it is not that Yhwh will decline to respond to such seekers. "I will make answer to them myself," Yhwh says, by setting my face against them and making them a portentous sign to people and destroying them from among Israel. Ezekiel does not say what exactly this will involve. His focus lies somewhere else. His interest lies in what we are to make of it when prophets do respond to such a person. Were such prophets sent by Yhwh? Indeed they were, said Ezekiel: Yhwh had seduced them into such a ministry, and Yhwh would also destroy them from among Israel (Ezek 14:6-11). Does he really mean Yhwh seduces such prophets? Perhaps his declarations do witness to a very strong understanding of Yhwh's sovereignty, like Micaiah's in attributing false prophecy to Yhwh (1 Kings 22). But in both passages one needs to note the rhetorical context. Micaiah is trying to bring the king to his senses; Ezekiel is trying to get through to a group of scandalously willful elders, who will even come to seek guidance from Yhwh when they are also involved in or identified with forms of worship that Yhwh regards as abominations. We do not know that these elders were involved in human sacrifice. Ezekiel wants to shock by identifying their forms of worship with such forms and by suggesting how far Yhwh would go in punishing them.

Something similar may be true about Ezekiel's comments elsewhere on the sacrificing of children to Yhwh, part of mainstream Israelite worship from time to time to which the books of Kings refer with horror. Ezekiel has Yhwh saying, "I myself gave them statutes that were not good and decisions by which they would not live, and defiled them by their gifts in their delivering up every first issue of the womb so that I might devastate them, so that they might acknowledge that I am Yhwh"; the "delivering up" is a delivering up to fire (Ezek 20:25-26, 31). No doubt the people who practiced such forms of sacrifice saw them as God-given, like Yhwh's one-time instruction to Abraham to sacrifice Isaac. Ezekiel affirms that they are right. Yhwh prescribed these sacrifices as an act of punishment. After all, Yhwh had given them regulations whereby people could live and had given them Yhwh's sabbaths as a sign of sanctifying them, and they had rejected these (Ezek 20:11-13, 21, 24). So Yhwh punished them by giving them these other statutes and decisions, means of offering gifts that were defiling rather than sanctifying.

Yhwh also declares that the people will never be allowed simply to give themselves to serving wood and stone, like other peoples; rather Yhwh will insist on reigning over them and will fetch them from the countries where they have gone to stay and bring them back to Israel (Ezek 20:32-37). Yet Yhwh then bids them, "But you, household of Israel—the Lord Yhwh has said this: 'Each of you, go and serve your pillars, but afterward, if you are not listening to me . . . And my holy name you shall no more profane with your gifts and your pillars.' "[156] The bidding makes it sound as if Yhwh is releasing Israel, abandoning it to worship as it wishes, but the subsequent threat in the dramatically incomplete "if" clause and the declaration that follows make as clear as do the preceding words that Yhwh is doing no such thing. Saying "Do go and serve your pillars" is a way of saying "Don't even think about it."

Subtly

Israel is Yhwh's vineyard; it is a familiar image, but Isaiah makes it the subject of a puzzling song. "Let me sing for my friend my love song about his vineyard" (Is 5:1). There are several levels of subtlety about the prophecy. Isaiah speaks like the best man at a wedding who is evidently a gifted singer-songwriter and has written a song for the groom to express his love for his bride. It transpires that the love song is about a vineyard, which is not so puzzling; such imagery is common in love songs (see the Song of Songs). But the song worryingly uses the short second cola typical of sad songs rather than joyful ones, and soon it explicitly turns into a blues, an indictment of the vineyard/bride rather than a celebration of her. We can imagine the wedding guests becoming very embarrassed. Indeed, the song reads more like the indictment at divorce proceedings: "What more was there to do for my vineyard that I did not do in it? When I expected it to produce grapes, why has it produced

---

[156]There is uncertainty about the translation of the words that follow and thus about how far the irony extends.

wild grapes? (Is 5:2). In asking these questions the songwriter draws the audience into the song's drama. Asking questions always draws the hearers into the message and attempts to overcome any inclination on their part to stay distant from the prophet's words.

Isaiah's audience would be quite able to work out that this is not a song about an upcoming marriage or an ordinary failed marriage. The imagery would be familiar to them, and once it becomes clear that there is more to this song than meets the ear, they would have little difficulty interpreting the allegory. The groom/vinedresser is Yhwh, the bride/vineyard is Israel. But the song dramatically holds back from making its interpretation explicit until it has drawn a terrifying portrayal of the vinedresser/husband/deity's destruction of the vineyard. Isaiah thus deals with Israel as Nathan deals with David (2 Sam 12:1-15), though not quite as subtly because of using that familiar imagery that the audience would be able to interpret. But if the rhetoric does its work in seducing the audience, it will have drawn a response from it and thus drawn it into condemning itself. The power of a love song first wins an audience; combined with that, the dismaying ferocity of its volte-face has the capacity to draw the audience to look at itself in a new way. If the audience answers the questions properly, it will have found itself guilty.

There is further subtlety about the prophet's eventual equivalent to Nathan's "You are the man." "The household of Israel is the vineyard of Yhwh Armies, the person in Judah is the plantation he enjoyed tending. He expected leadership *(mišpāṭ)*, but there—a bloodbath *(mišpāḥ)*; [he expected] faithfulness *(ṣĕdāqâ)*, but there—an outcry *(ṣĕʿāqâ)*." The punch line to the "song" first makes explicit the key to the allegory. Then it underlines the poignant and extraordinary nature of the sequence of events by its two observations on Yhwh's involvement in them. First, Yhwh really is like a man in love with his bride. Yhwh has not merely been a hard-working farmer but has loved gardening the way a true gardener does. Yhwh is emotionally involved in growing vines. Second, as a gardener Yhwh had expectations, and these were disappointed. Perhaps the idea that Yhwh could have been mistaken in expectations would be as scandalous to Israelites as it may be to us. Both these ideas about Yhwh form a further means of seeking to get through to Isaiah's audience. The paronomasia adds to the effect. There is a terrible contrast between faithfulness in the community and the cry of outraged suffering that comes from people who have their lives destroyed by other people in the community, but the words for these two realities sound almost identical. Likewise there is a terrible contrast between the proper exercise of authority in the community and the pouring out of people's blood there, but the words for these two realities are also almost identical. Actually they are not. As far as we can tell, Isaiah invents the word *mišpāḥ* so that he can make his point.

Ezekiel also reworks this image in another sinister fashion. Never mind about the fruit of the vine: What about the wood? The communication's subtlety lies partly in the way Yhwh makes the point. As Isaiah announces the attention to sing a song, Ezekiel begins with a riddle: "How is vine wood better than any other wood?" Proceeding in this way again draws the hearers into the process of communication, and this before they know whether they can afford to be drawn in. They have to think out the implications of the prophet's declarations before knowing what the cost of this will be. "In no way," is the answer. It is useless, unlike that of the olive. You cannot make bowls or coat pegs of it. All you can do is use it for fuel—burn it up (Ezek 15). That is worrying if you *are* the vine.

It is characteristic of the prophets, the Psalms and the other poetic books to make use of paronomasia, repetition, irony, metonymy and metaphor. Such literary devices presuppose a sense that there is a unity of reality, grounded in God. Things that do not look as if they connect actually do so. One God lies behind them. The First Testament can presuppose connection and relationship even where things look unconnected or conflicted and can assume there is meaning and coherence even where things look meaningless and fragmented.

Indelicately

As Isaiah reworks the vine image in sinister fashion, Jeremiah reworks the marriage image in the same way (Jer 2–3), and Ezekiel does this even more sinisterly (see Ezek 16). His allegory is also the parade instance of Ezekiel's showing himself the master of bad taste (oddly, perhaps, for a priest), with its portrait of the baby girl wallowing in blood, then lying naked Lolita-like in puberty, which becomes a lewdly detailed account of her subsequent promiscuity and a faithlessness that involves her paying for sex rather than charging for it.

Yhwh will use any means to communicate, and bad taste is certainly among them. Yhwh uses Ezekiel's Gothic imagination again in inspiring a complex allegory about an eagle, a cedar, a vine, another eagle and an uprooting (Ezek 17). All these are familiar images, but they turn out to refer to different entities from those one might have expected. It might be hard for the audience to resist the temptation to try to work out what the story means, though they are destined to fail, like the readers of a detective story failing to draw the right inferences from the clues they are given. Once again Ezekiel's audience is thus drawn into the poem, and once again, when they discover what it means, it will be too late for them to withdraw unscathed. Either they will have been manipulated into facing facts or they will have been pushed deeper into resistance to Yhwh.

Death is no joke. In our culture the funeral may be the one occasion where formality still obtains. I am not sure whether my sons will accede to my wish to have "Bat Out of Hell" played at mine. In the First Testament a death is the one occasion when we find David expressing his feelings, even if someone in his court ghostwrote his dirge (2 Sam 1:17-27). On a later occasion Israelites heard a solemn prophet uttering a funeral dirge. "She has fallen, she will not rise again," he laments (Amos 5:2). "Maiden Israel" eventually turns out to be the subject of the verb. The people who overhear the dirge ask who has died and discover that they have. Yhwh likewise bids Ezekiel, "You, lead a dirge for the leaders of Israel" (Ezek 19:1). Ezekiel intones an allegory about a mother who watches one of her sons be dragged off to Egypt and another be dragged off to Babylon. Perhaps the allegory refers to Hamutal, birth mother of Jehoahaz and Zedekiah; perhaps it also refers to Jerusalem as the mother of such sons. Either way it has frightening implications because it talks as if the fate of Zedekiah and Ms. Jerusalem is as fixed as that of the presumably long-dead Jehoahaz and Hamutal. The devastating and heartless picture constitutes another attempt to get the city, the leadership and the exiles to see sense.

There is a place in Moab called Madmen, which would offer temptation to someone writing in English. In Hebrew it could be linked to a word for silence or one for wailing, and Jeremiah makes a pun on its name in this connection (Jer 48:2). Fortunately or unfortunately *madmēnâ* is also Hebrew for a cesspit, and Isaiah thus puns on the town's name in a different way, promising that "the Moabites will be threshed in their place like straw being threshed in a cesspit."[157] Indeed, the prophet seems to have invented a new word for "straw" (*matbēn*, replacing the usual *teben*) to provide another paronomasia. The prophet goes on, "and they will spread their hands in the midst of it to swim as swimmers spread their hands to swim, but he will humble their majesty" (Is 25:10-11). Moabites swimming in a cesspit? Commentators routinely critique or defend or apologize for the image, but ultimately there is nothing more violent here than appears in many other passages. What is noteworthy is the bad taste, by Western standards, and perhaps by Middle-Eastern ones. Yhwh inspires prophets to speak in the manner of late-night cable TV, not public service television.

Visually

Yhwh's aides need to make Yhwh's intentions as clear, as unambiguous and as compelling as possible, and they thus need to use all means to bring home the significance of their message. They therefore do not confine themselves to

---

[157]There is also a place near Jerusalem called Madmenah (Is 10:31).

words. They speak of visions, and they dramatize their message, often embodying it in themselves in various senses.

The opening chapter of Isaiah is "the vision of Isaiah son of Amoz that he
saw concerning Judah and Jerusalem in the time of Uzziah, Jotham, Ahaz and
Hezekiah," though it is also "the word that Isaiah son of Amoz saw concerning Judah and Jerusalem" (Is 1:1; 2:1).[158] The verb *saw* recurs in the first and
greatest of the poems in Isaiah about other nations, "the Babylon poem that
Isaiah son of Amoz saw" (Is 13:1). In general Isaiah is more aural than visual,
and less visual than Jeremiah and Ezekiel, and one should not press the language. Although he appeals to the imagination, "listen" is more his imperative than "look." It is the *sound* of an army mustering that he draws attention
to (Is 13:4). Yet precisely for this reason, his using the language of sight is
noteworthy.

It is characteristic of prophets to appeal to their own visionary experiences
and to communicate by relating them. "What are you looking at, Jeremiah?"
The answer is, "a branch of almond," the "waking tree" whose name suggests
that "I am wakeful over my word to fulfill it." Later the reply is, "a heated pot
. . . with its top facing away from the north"—perhaps this implies that it is
boiling over in a southerly direction, suggesting the trouble about to boil over
upon Judah (Jer 1:11, 13). Jeremiah may be literally looking at a tree and a
cooking pot or may be seeing them in his mind's eye, though even if the latter
is the case, the vision picks up everyday experiences he does have and turns
them into pictures of what Yhwh is doing. Everyday reality has a mysterious
capacity to be the means of Yhwh's unveiling events of epoch-making significance, because both belong to one reality and one Yhwh. Even if Jeremiah
is literally looking at a tree or cooking pot, the vision requires that an insight
should come to the inner eye, which the outward reality triggers. For Jeremiah's audience too, even if they are also thus looking literally, the prophecy
requires the involvement of their imagination and their insight.

"Take this cup of wine (wrath)[159] from my hand and make all the nations
to whom I am sending you drink it," Yhwh bids Jeremiah. "So I took the cup
from Yhwh's hand and made all the nations to whom Yhwh sent me drink it"
(Jer 25:15, 17). Jeremiah reports this as if it were a straightforward this-worldly
event, and in a sense it does represent a definite concrete experience. Yet here
it is clearer that the entire event takes place in Jeremiah's mind's eye. While
we might imagine the vision beginning from an international diplomatic
banquet in Jerusalem at which the host bids a server to pass a cup of wine

---

[158]I argue that Is 1:1 and 2:1 are the introduction and conclusion to Is 1 in "Isaiah i 1; ii 1,"
   VT 48 (1998): 326-32.
[159]The construction is ungrammatical—hence this way of representing the sentence.
   "Wrath" interprets the word "wine."

round the assembled guests, it is enough to suppose that it starts from the more regular experience of the passing round of a cup at a regular meal. In any case, the communicative effect of the prophecy depends on people *hearing* the prophecy but then *imagining* the scene Jeremiah has described.

Ezekiel starts his ministry with the heavens opening so that he sees a vision (Ezek 1:1). Then he is taken off to Jerusalem to witness the offensive worship of the temple and in light of that to watch the city's punishment fall (Ezek 8–11). Here the visual leads into the verbal rather than vice versa, as Isaiah 6 suggests is true of Isaiah. His initial vision expresses Yhwh's message but also constitutes the experience that sets him going on his ministry and provides part of the grounds for people's needing to pay attention to him. Yhwh does not grant people visionary experiences just so they can see God or in response to their seeking such experiences or as a means of their enjoying fellowship with Yhwh, but to prepare them to be sent to do something and to provide the content of a message or the evidence that they have been so sent.

Like their words, the prophets' visions do more than illustrate something that is to happen. The almond waking to life and the pot boiling over (Jer 1:11-16) are not mere illustrations but events taking place in symbol before the eyes of the prophet and then of the prophet's audience. There is a quasi-sacramental relationship between the waking tree and Yhwh's waking, and between the overflowing pot and the approach of hordes from the north. The occurrence of the visionary event is a sign that the event itself is occurring.

Familiarly

Yhwh bids Jeremiah get to the potter's workshop, where he watches as a piece of clay will not form right and the potter reworks it. Yhwh enables him to see that this provides an image for what Yhwh is doing with his people (Jer 18:1-6). Human actions and familiar experiences can be a means of seeing how God acts, though this comes about through an interaction between God's speaking and human experience. The insight did not come without the human experience, but neither did it come without the divine word that both initiates the visit and reveals the significance of what went on. Further, there is not a mere simple one-to-one relationship between the experience and the word Yhwh builds on it. They relate to each other like the circles in a Venn diagram. There is rich potential and suggestiveness in the experience and thus some complexity about the insights that can emerge from it. Yhwh's word takes the significance of the experience in two or three directions. Judah is like the clay in Yhwh's hand; by implication, so are other peoples; so is the calamity Yhwh is shaping (Jer 18:6, 7-10, 11). Yet Yhwh's word is semi-independent of the experience; not everything in Yhwh's word issues from the experience. The potter's work links only partially with that talk of the dynamic relationship between Yhwh's threats and promises, the responses of their recipients, and Yhwh's relenting (Jer 18:7-12).

After Ezekiel, the most systematic visionary is Zechariah, and Zechariah's visions are less inclined to be disguised sermons; their imagery is fresh, like Amos's. Precisely for that reason, they need interpreting, and a distinctive feature of Zechariah's visions is the systematic involvement of a heavenly aide bringing Yhwh's word in the context of the visions and explaining their significance (see Zech 1:8–6:8). Yhwh also speaks direct to Zechariah as to other prophets (e.g., Zech 6:9-15), so it is not the case that Yhwh has become distanced from the prophet. But in the visions an aide explains the vision rather than Yhwh. This contrasts with visions in Amos and Ezekiel in which Yhwh in person dialogues with the prophet (e.g., Amos 7:1-9; Ezek 37:1-14). Matters are more ambiguous in Ezekiel's grand vision of goings on in Jerusalem (Ezek 8–11) which involves a humanlike figure who might be God or might not—the ambiguity or fluidity recalls that of the identity of the figures who sometimes appear in Genesis and Judges. God's appearing guarantees the divine origin of the revelation. The appearing of a figure one step removed from being God recognizes the metaphysical problematic involved in God's appearing in person, famously declared to Moses (Ex 33:12-23).

Zechariah's visions begin from realities of everyday life—the horses and chariots of the Persian information system, horns and smiths, a builder with a measuring line, a trial scene, a lamp stand and two olive trees, a scroll, and a basket. For prophet and people these become transparent to non-everyday realities. The everyday is capable of revealing the extraordinary if God chooses to make it do so. The horses and chariots become part of the information system whose report stimulates action in the heavenly court and of implementing its decisions. Horns and smiths become the agents of Israel's affliction and the agents whereby those nations will have their power trimmed. The man with the measuring line becomes someone who risks limiting the dimensions of Jerusalem. The trial scene becomes one taking place in heaven and issuing in the restoring of a defiled high priest. The lamp stand and the olive trees become Yhwh's way of shining into the community and providing for it. The scroll becomes a flying imprecation effective all over the world. The basket is stuffed with faithlessness to Yhwh and taken off to Babylon where it belongs.

Zechariah's visions are thus not preoccupied by everyday concrete practicalities—there are no equivalents to the architectural measurements for the temple in Ezekiel. But neither does Zechariah have visions of God, like the same Ezekiel. His visions stand somewhere between these. The scenes take place on earth, but they are otherworldly in their imagery and reference. "Zechariah's visions comprise the doing of theology."[160]

Realistically, Grippingly

Isaiah senses a winter storm swirling up from the south, as terrifying as a whirlwind. He hears from God some initial explanation in terms of treachery and destruction (Is 21:1-10). The agents are Elam and Media, so the victim might be Babylon as it was earlier, but for the moment we are left to inference. Even if Isaiah makes that inference, his reaction is a paralyzing anxiety and panic. Is he simply identifying with the horror of what is coming for the unsuspecting Babylonians, eating and drinking unaware that tomorrow they die? Or is he embodying Judah's possibly distraught reaction to the fall of its ally against Assyria? Or is the distress of Babylon good news for Judeans in exile, about to be liberated?

A decent thriller film has the audience shrinking back in their seats in apprehension. When Jeremiah sees and hears (in his spirit) Jerusalem's attackers advancing from the north, he reacts as if seeing and hearing the real thing, because he is so seeing and hearing. His insides writhe, his heart thuds, his bones tremble, he stumbles about like a drunk, he cannot keep silence (Jer 4:19; 23:9). He is about once more to describe frightful wrongdoing in Judah, but it is not this that crushes him. It is Yhwh's word that does that. He is overcome by the horror of Yhwh's response to the country's wrongdoing, with the consequent desolation of this land that issues from Yhwh's curse (Jer 23:10). This withering of the land is presumably a reality (cf. Jer 14:1-6). On this occasion it is not the content of his vision that horrifies Jeremiah. Perhaps his horror reflects more an awareness that this "natural disaster" is an expression of Yhwh's wrath, issuing from the failure of Judah's own prophetic and priestly leaders, which means it is only the beginning of further trouble that must fall on these prophets and priests in particular (Jer 23:11-15).

Similarly the dissolution of the cosmos (a figure for the dissolution of Judah) happens before his eyes:

> I looked at the earth—and there, a formless waste:
> to the heavens—and their light was gone.
> I looked at the mountains—and there, they were quaking;
> all the hills were trembling.
> I looked—and there, no humans beings were left;
> all the birds in the heavens had fled.

---

[160]David L. Petersen, *Haggai and Zechariah 1–8* (Philadelphia: Westminster, 1984/London: SCM Press, 1985), pp. 113, 115.

> I looked—and there, the garden land was desert
>   and all its cities had been pulled down,
>   before Yhwh, before his angry burning. (Jer 4:23-26)

Telling the people of his reaction is part of Jeremiah's seeking to get them to share his sense that calamity really is coming, and therefore to react in the appropriate way now.

> Flee for refuge, Benjaminites,
>   from the midst of Jerusalem!
> Blow the horn in Tekoa,
>   raise a signal in Bet-hakkerem. . . .

> For Yhwh Armies has said this:
> "Cut down her trees,
>   cast a ramp against Jerusalem." (Jer 6:1, 6)

Perhaps his fellow Benjaminites have already fled south to the safety of the big city (cf. Jer 4:5-6); now there is not even any safety there, nor further south, so real is the invasion threatening Judah.

Dramatically

The prophets' signs also seek to communicate the fact that calamity really is coming and to provoke a response. Actions can reinforce words and can also implement words. Baptism and the giving of a ring in marriage do the latter as well as the former. For a while Isaiah went around in garments made of coarse cloth rather than, for instance, linen (Is 20); this would suggest poverty or grief (cf. Is 3:24; 15:3; 22:12). Then he took those off and went around wearing (virtually?) nothing, like someone who has lost everything and is being taken off into exile. Both acts embody the fate coming to Egypt, Sudan and also Judah; in the second sign the depiction of the peoples' fate is taken up another notch.[161] Both bring home the reality of what will happen and guarantee or begin to implement it, because they emerge from the will of the God who is bringing about the thing signified as well as the sign.

Yhwh bids Jeremiah undertake sign acts involving linen underclothes, a pitcher and a yoke (Jer 13; 19; 28). The only witness of the sign act with the underclothes is Jeremiah himself; it might reinforce his conviction about his message. But Yhwh instructs Jeremiah to tell the people what Yhwh had said to him in connection with the sign act (Jer 13:12a).[162] So the report of a sign act can also function for the people, who reenact the event in their mind's eye, in

---

[161]Cf. Hans Wildberger, *Isaiah 13–27* (Minneapolis: Fortress, 1997), p. 294.
[162]Verse 12a belongs with what precedes; MT thus places its section break after v. 12a. Cf. Holladay, *Jeremiah 1*, p. 394.

the way the sign act functions for all who hear of it through the written account of the event.

In contrast, Jeremiah is to take some of the elders and senior priests as witnesses when he breaks a pitcher in the Valley of Hinnom. The symbolic act relates to the "real" act Yhwh is doing: "You are to break the pitcher before the eyes of the people who go with you and say to them, 'Yhwh Armies has said this: So will I break this people and this city, as one breaks a potter's vessel, which cannot ever be mended' " (Jer 19:10-11). The location is telling. It is where people offered their most offensive act of worship (cf. Jer 7:31). So wrongdoing, punishment and the sign act that implements the punishment for the wrongdoing all come together. Yet the story never records Jeremiah actually implementing Yhwh's commission. A reference to his return from the valley to speak in the temple court implies he did so, but the omission of reference to the event again puts the emphasis on the significance of the sign act for people who read about it, who vastly outnumber the people who witnessed it.

During the reign of Zedekiah, Yhwh bids Jeremiah make himself a yoke with its straps and bars, and put it on as if he were an ox (Jer 27:2). In itself that does not imply punishment or even discomfort; an ox's yoke is not inherently uncomfortable. It does imply submission and hard work. The yoke symbolizes the Levantine peoples' destiny to be in submission to Nebuchadnezzar, like oxen to a farmer. And it signifies that they *will* be in such submission. Putting the yoke on Jeremiah begins to put into effect the yoking of the peoples. The sign act might have another implication. The yoke also resembles the restraint put on a prisoner of war. So it might offer a choice to the people. Either accept one form of Nebuchadnezzar's yoke or you will wear the other.

Other prophets such as Hananiah know how such sign acts work. Hananiah declares that Yhwh is breaking the king of Babylon's yoke on Judah,[163] and thus takes the yoke off Jeremiah's neck and breaks it, declaring that within two years Yhwh will break Nebuchadnezzar's yoke from the neck of all the nations (Jer 28:2, 10-11).

Personally

The prophets' signs often involve their own beings, and do so in demanding ways. Yhwh eventually bids Jeremiah undertake a hopeful sign act not unlike Hananiah's. On one of the darkest days when the city is about to fall and its people are about to be taken into exile, Yhwh bids him exercise his obligation and right to redeem a stretch of family land from his cousin. Only a fool

---

[163]In Jer 28:2 Hananiah uses the qatal, which I take to be performative (cf. JPSV), then uses the yiqtol in Jer 28:4.

would invest in real estate at this moment in history. But it is a sign. "For Yhwh Armies, the God of Israel, has said this: 'Houses, fields and vineyards will again be bought in this country'" (Jer 32:15). The sign is performed before witnesses, with the real estate documents sealed so that others in the future may also have the evidence that Yhwh had been involved and so that when such purchases are indeed renewed, people may know this is not mere chance. It is not the result of the vagaries of history but the fulfillment of a declaration of intent by Yhwh.

Jeremiah never marries or has children, because the terrible disaster that threatens Jerusalem makes this no place to bring children into the world (Jer 16:1-4). He gives up going to wakes and celebrations, because of Yhwh's withdrawal of šālôm, of ḥesed and of raḥămîm from the people (Jer 16:5-9). This frightening withdrawal makes it inappropriate to join in wakes because people's individual loss is of trivial significance in light of the coming disaster, when death will be so pervasive that there will be no one to bury or grieve. It makes it equally inappropriate to join in celebrations because there will soon be nothing to celebrate. Refraining from marriage will not merely be a symbolic decision but an inevitability.

The first occasion when Ezekiel fulfills his calling as a lookout involves (paradoxically) shutting himself up at home (Ezek 3:22-27). Indeed, he ties himself up there, and Yhwh stops him speaking except when Yhwh opens his mouth to deliver a message. Being confined and tied up might suggest the constraints of the siege coming to Jerusalem (cf. Ezek 4:8). It might suggest his response to his people's turning their backs on his message; he withdraws from regular contact with them. It might suggest Yhwh's own withdrawing from them. Both God and prophet will only break silence in order to berate and warn. Only the arrival of news that Jerusalem has fallen will be the occasion for release (Ezek 33). Symbol has become reality, word has become event and warning can now yield to promise, or rather one scene in a symbolic drama can be succeeded by another.

Ezekiel goes on symbolically to dramatize more directly the coming siege itself, the years of wrongdoing that make it inevitable, and the years of exile that must follow (Ezek 4:1-5:4; 12:1-7). He lies on his side for 390 days and for 40 days to represent those years—perhaps symbolically, in a way that did not involve dramatic time being the same as real time.[164] He sustains himself on the food and drink of someone enduring siege or exile, narrowly escaping the defilement bound up with exile. He burns a third of his hair, scatters a third outside a representation of the city, scatters the final third even further, yet

---

[164]We are not sure of the precise reference of the 390 years, though in some way they refer to Israel's long past history of unfaithfulness and consequent chastisement.

holds back a few of the last third, and then destroys some of those. He acts out the night flight of a refugee from the city with the minimum of possessions, avoiding one last look at the land because of the pain of leaving it. Yhwh tells him, "I hereby make you a portent for the household of Israel" (Ezek 12:6), an embodiment of the threat that hangs inexorably over Jerusalem and thus over the future of the people already in exile.

The possibility that such dramatic actions may get through when bare words fail is again implicit in Yhwh's commission to Ezekiel to dramatize the Jerusalemites' coming refugee flight from the city, which is based on their not having eyes to see or ears to hear (Ezek 12:2-3). Perhaps drama reaches different eyes or opens up smeared eyes. At least the drama is effective in making people ask what it was about: what was Ezekiel doing? (Ezek 12:9). But these dramatic actions too have that further significance. If Judah does not turn in response to them, the signs become the implementing of what they signify.

Experientially

Human experiences become the means whereby Yhwh communicates with a (prospective) prophet and through the prophet with other people. Yhwh tells Hosea to go and marry "a woman of *zĕnûmîm* (Hos 1:2). The EVV have "a woman of whoredom," but that gives the wrong impression. While sex for money and adultery would be instances of *zĕnûmîm* or *zĕnût*, the words denote any behavior that does not observe society's standards for sexual conduct. Gomer might be a prostitute; Yhwh subsequently describes the land as unfaithful to its husband and receiving payment for it (Hos 2). She might be a woman reckoned to be an easy lay. She might be someone who had once been the victim of date rape, but whom the whole village knows not to be a virgin, and who might therefore be virtually unmarriable. In Israel, if there were people involved in sexual acts in the course of worship (for instance, acts designed as acted prayers for fertility), a prophet might also term this *zĕnût*. Any forms of sexual conduct outside of marriage could provide an image for Israel's relationship with Yhwh as illicit or promiscuous: "Go, get yourself an immoral woman and immoral children, because the land is totally immoral in its relationship with Yhwh" (Hos 1:2).

Yhwh communicates not only through Hosea and Gomer's experience. Their first child carries the name "Jezreel" in connection with the bloody deeds done in the Ephraimite royal city of Jezreel some decades previously (2 Kings 9–10). Naming the child Jezreel signifies the implementing of Yhwh's intent to destroy the Ephraimite monarchy. Arguably much tougher are the names Yhwh gave to their next two children, "Not-compassioned" and "Not-my-people." Yhwh will not merely act against the Ephraimite monarchy but will no longer care about the people as a whole or "carry" them (that is, forgive them). The people has continued in existence because Yhwh did have compassion on them and has been willing to carry their wrongdoing, like a parent putting up with their offspring's infuriating behavior. But eventually the parent may decide it is necessary to take a stand; this moment has arrived for Yhwh. The other name has even tougher implications: "You are not my people and I am not there for you." This (un)naming terminates the mutual relationship between Yhwh and Ephraim.

As well as being hard for palace and people, giving children such names is hard for the parents and children, though the names do not refer to the children themselves but to the land. We should be wary of taking too literally the idea of giving the children symbolic names. Yhwh makes Isaiah and his sons "portentous signs in Israel" (*ʾôt ûmôpēt*), embodiments by their deeds and names of Yhwh's imminent intention to act in devastating ways (Is 8:18; 20:3). But was "Plunder-hastens-looting-speeds" (Is 8:3) the name Mr. and Ms. Isaiah used when they called their son in for dinner? Would "The-mighty-God-is-a-wonderful-counselor-the-eternal-father-is-a-ruler-bringing-well-being" (Is 9:6 [MT 5]) be the name whereby his subjects addressed their king? When Moses asks for God's name, he is told that it is "I-will-be-what-I-will-be," or something like that (Ex 3:14), but this is not the way people address God. The point lies in the event of the naming (and its subsequent reporting in Hosea's book). We may imagine Hosea declaiming each name at the community celebration of the child's birth, when the child is given its name (cf. Lk 1:59-66). It works like Jeremiah's breaking a pot. The sign proclaims the reality to which it refers, and because God commissioned it, sets under way the event itself.

Nevertheless the naming is a sign of the way Yhwh assumes the right to use people in the divine purpose, adults and children. For Yhwh the rights of the individual are not the ultimate priority. Yhwh is concerned to communicate with Israel and is prepared to use individuals such as Hosea, Gomer and their children to that end, even if this makes things hard for them. There are bigger "goods" than their rights as individuals, as is also reflected in the story of a leader such as Moses, a king such as Saul or a prophet such as Jeremiah. Perhaps Yhwh takes the view that being drawn into the divine purpose is a privilege that outweighs the cost. Perhaps that was true for Hosea, who is required to forgo the possibility of a regular marriage and family experience. Perhaps there is a converse truth for Gomer. An immoral woman could not expect to be treated as a regular woman, and like Job's family she may subsequently be glad that she was sucked from obscurity (and shame?) into a place in Yhwh's purpose. But the Scriptures do not feel obliged to tell us what she, her children and her husband made of their destiny. This point that so interests us does not concern them. They have bigger issues to focus on, which they invite us to share. What went on between these people and God is between them and God, though (to judge from the Psalms) we are free to protest to God about it and tell God it looks objectionable; but then we have to leave it to God.[165]

Bodily

When Yhwh commissions Ezekiel by the Chebar Canal, this involves the physical as well as the visual and the verbal. "Yhwh's hand came on him there" (Ezek 1:3; cf. Ezek 3:22; 8:1; 37:1; 40:1; Is 8:11). In isolation we might take this as a conventional metaphor, but other contexts suggest it indicates a strong bodily awareness of Yhwh's presence and activity geared to Ezekiel in particular. He feels their impact in his own person (Ezek 3:14; 33:22). Even in connection with a vision, talk of Yhwh's hand "falling" on him (Ezek 8:1) implies a bodily experience, as does the sense of being grasped by the hair and then transported elsewhere (Ezek 8:3; cf. Ezek 37:1; 40:1).

The result of seeing Yhwh is that Ezekiel physically prostrates himself before Yhwh. Not only does Yhwh then bid him stand but "a spirit came into me as he spoke to me, and stood me on my feet" (Ezek 2:2). At the end of his inaugural experience a spirit lifts him up and carries him to a gathering of the exiles, where he sits in a state of shock for a week (Ezek 3:12-15; cf. Ezek 3:24; 8:3; 11:1, 24a; 43:5). Standing him on his feet and carrying him about in the air are the only two activities credited to this "spirit." This does not suggest the activity of one of those many spirits that serve Yhwh (e.g., 1 Kings 22:21; 1 Chron 12:18 [MT 19]). It rather corresponds to the description of the spirit/wind/breath's activity in the vision of the dry bones (Ezek 37:1-11). "Vigor" or "courage" fits one kind of reference, "wind" the other,[166] but these are not ordinary liveliness and wind. They are extraordinary vigor that reflects God's liveliness and dynamic energy and overcomes natural lack of energy and life, and wind that does not merely carry someone about randomly like a hurricane but directly serves God's will. In this sense they involve the activity of "the spirit" (NRSV) or "the Spirit" (TNIV), though Ezekiel implicitly distinguishes it from the activity of "Yhwh's spirit" or "God's spirit" (Ezek 11:5, 24b; 37:1).

In between these physical experiences comes another. Yhwh shows Ezekiel a scroll and requires him to eat it; the experience is real enough to make him register a particular taste (Ezek 3:1-3). The people will find Yhwh's words sour, and in a sense they cannot be blamed. Ezekiel finds them tasting sweet, despite their toughness. The implication of this experience might seem to be

---

[165]See further §6.7 "Accepting a Vocation."
[166]Cf. Moshe Greenberg, *Ezekiel 1–20*, AB (Garden City, N.Y.: Doubleday, 1983), pp. 62, 70.

that Ezekiel directly receives from Yhwh the actual words he is to speak, yet this does not make them Yhwh's words in such a direct sense that Ezekiel himself cannot be discerned in them. Different prophets have different emphases and ways of articulating their message. Ezekiel's priestly background finds clear expression in his message. Perhaps we may push further the scroll image. Yhwh's message comes to Ezekiel in such a way that he makes it part of his own person. He assimilates it. He then expresses it himself. It finds expression through him.

Having one's being drawn into one's prophecy brings pain. Jeremiah identifies with his people in the terrible affliction that is coming to them and speaks of the agonized weeping he expects to experience (Jer 13:17). Micah envisages going round the community like someone in mourning, lamenting so loud he sounds more like a howling animal than a human being (Mic 1:8-9). He will go around barefoot and unclothed—not a sign of mourning but a dramatization of the consequences of defeat and of being taken as a humiliated captive into exile; here his behavior will resemble Isaiah's (Is 20). Micah does not want it to happen but knows it must. Perhaps his action will even make it happen. Or paradoxically, perhaps it will stop it happening, if it brings the people to their senses or causes Yhwh to have a change of mind anyway (see Jer 26:16-19).

Ezekiel stays at home to embody Yhwh's attitude to them. He lies on his side and thus in his body "carries the wrongdoing of the household of Israel" and then that of the household of Judah (Ezek 4:6). In other words, in symbol he bears Ephraim's punishment, reminding his audience of the years of going astray and consequent loss it went through, and then similarly bears Judah's punishment, reminding them of Judah's going astray and dramatizing the years of punishment that are now beginning. Ezekiel experiences them in his own body, with the possibility that somehow this may cause them to turn back to Yhwh and avoid experiencing them in their own bodies. He experiences the fear and dismay involved in the taking of Jerusalem and the desolating of the land (Ezek 12:17-20). He staggers, grieves and sighs as if he has gone through some heart-breaking bereavement (Ezek 21: 6-7 [MT 11-12]); it is as if Ezekiel goes through it in advance as a sign of its reality and certainty. Yhwh forewarns him that his own wife is going to die suddenly, but tells him he is not to mourn her, even though she is the delight of his eyes. The reason is that the people will not mourn when Yhwh profanes the sanctuary, even though it is their strength and pride, the delight of their eyes, and the heart's desire of the people in exile, and even though the city's fall means the death of the sons and daughters they left behind in Jerusalem. Indeed, it is *because* of these events that they will not mourn. The events will be so overwhelming that they will preclude alleviation by the regular mourning rites. The exiles will be too stunned. That is how Ezekiel is when his wife dies. He is thus a portent for them (Ezek 24:15-24). Once again, it is not the prophet alone but the prophet and his wife who are part of his ministry, because it is precisely the most precious of relationships like that of marriage that can speak most powerfully about the relationship between God and the people.

7.7 Victims

Being a prophet is no calling to seek. It can mean being put at risk, put under pressure, treated toughly, driven to prayer for redress, having no way out of your ministry, wishing you had never been born, feeling pain and grief, sharing your people's suffering. But it can mean being Yhwh's agent in bringing about their restoration and eventually being triumphant and vindicated.

Put at Risk

Yhwh's confronting Israel by means of these human aides can easily put them at risk, though at least Yhwh forewarns the unsuspecting Jeremiah (Jer 11:18-23). Huge demands are made of these people through whom God communicates. No one makes this clearer than Jeremiah, the man caught in the middle between Yhwh and Israel, caught "between forces totally out of phase with each other."[167]

"Yhwh said this: Go down to the house of the king of Judah and speak there this word. . . . For Yhwh said this about the house of the king of Judah: You are Gilead to me, or the summit of Lebanon;[168] I swear I will make you a desert, uninhabited cities." Jeremiah 22 goes on at some length like this about specific Judean kings, Shallum (Jehoahaz), Jehoiakim, Coniah (Jehoiachin); Jeremiah 23 adds a caustic oracle about the king whose name, Zedekiah, said something about Yhwh and Faithfulness that his life did not match. While the kings' disinformation and damage-limitation machine may have contributed significantly to the process whereby (in Jeremiah's perception, at least) the prophet was merely reduced to a laughingstock, it was no risk-free enterprise to stroll down to the palace to deliver such oracles in the ears of the king's staff and his court.

At the beginning of Jehoiakim's reign, Jeremiah declares that the temple is to be destroyed as the Shiloh temple was, and that the city is to be devastated in a way that will appall the whole world. The entire company gathered in the

---

[167]W. Lee Humphreys, *The Tragic Vision and the Hebrew Tradition* (Philadelphia: Fortress, 1985), p. 86, referring to Abraham Joshua Heschel, *The Prophets* (New York: Harper, 1962). But see also Daniel L. Smith-Christopher's comments on Ezekiel in *A Biblical Theology of Exile* (Minneapolis: Fortress, 2002), pp. 75-104.

[168]That is, they are veritable forests, so much splendid woodwork is there (cf. 1 Kings 7:2-5).

temple courts, with the priests and prophets, lays hold of him and declares he must die (Jer 26:8). Their point may not be simply that he is acting treasonably. They have some excuse for suggesting he is liable to execution as a false prophet (cf. Deut 18:20-22). As he observes himself on another occasion, he has for years been predicting a calamity that never comes. They therefore arraign him before the king's officials. Jeremiah responds to the implicit charge that he is a false prophet by declaring that he has spoken thus only because Yhwh commissioned him to do so; the Deuteronomic text does not apply to him. He further appeals to another Deuteronomic provision in warning them not to bring on themselves the guilt of executing a man undeservedly (Deut 19:10). The people therefore change sides and with the officials declare that he should not be executed. They are supported by some elders who remind them of the precedent of Micah. When he declared that Jerusalem was to be devastated, the king responded not by executing him but by seeking to make peace with Yhwh, who relented about the disaster Micah had announced (Jer 26:16-19). Jeremiah likewise escapes through the support of someone with influence at court; another prophet is not so fortunate and loses his life (Jer 26:20-24).

There would be further reasons why his prophesying put his life at risk. Perhaps it is a more extreme version of the destroying of his words that Jehoiakim attempted (Jer 36). Jeremiah speaks with the authority of Yhwh's aide and his words implement Yhwh's intent, so both destroying the words and killing the aide may be designed to ensure that the words do not find fulfillment and that the aide cannot utter any more dangerous words. At another level we know that the Judean leadership naturally saw Jeremiah as a subversive figure in Jerusalem. His critique of the temple and the leadership, and his talk of the Babylonian king as Yhwh's servant, could be expected to have a bad affect on morale in Jerusalem. It would be wise to silence him.

Put Under Pressure and Treated Toughly

All this puts unbearable pressure on Jeremiah. Indeed, he wishes he had never been born (Jer 15:10). His reference to his birth recalls his account of his commissioning as a prophet (Jer 1:4-10). It has issued in his being someone whose task is to engage in a running argument with Israel on Yhwh's behalf. Personally he has not engaged in the kind of transactions that issue in conflict between individuals such as matters involving money, but not surprisingly, his argumentativeness antagonizes everyone.

As usual, Yhwh's response (Jer 15:11-14) is not reassuring, though the verses are hard to interpret. Jeremiah then returns to his recollection of his commission (Jer 15:15-18). His spending his whole time denouncing the city, the country and its leadership understandably antagonizes everyone. But he did not go in for this role because he was by nature a negative person but because Yhwh commissioned him. And he was happy to accept Yhwh's charge (eventually; to judge from Jer 1:4-10, this is a slightly selective recollection of his commission). Yhwh's negative word became something with which he identified enthusiastically when Yhwh unilaterally declared ownership of his life, declared that he was to be Yhwh's servant. (The fact that the one imposing ownership was Yhwh, God of Armies would concentrate the mind.) It meant he let that threatening word be his pleasure and forwent more normal human pleasures such as enjoying the company of his peers and taking part in community festivity. Although he was not the kind of gloom-head people wanted around on such occasions, it is a terrible, almost unbearable deprivation to be cut off from the community like that. To make it worse, the people whose death he is threatening are naturally reversing the compliment. Yhwh commissioned him at the beginning, but Yhwh is now doing nothing about the imperiling of his life by his ministry. A servant needs his master's support and protection. Jeremiah needs Yhwh to act against his persecutors and not to be lenient to them and thus sacrifice his life. He looks to Yhwh for deliverance like a man looking to a water source in the wilderness, and finds that Yhwh is like a water source that turns out to be empty.

Again as usual Yhwh's response is as direct and confrontational as Jeremiah's challenge (Jer 15:19-21). "If you turn back, I will take you back; you will stand before me. If you produce something valuable rather than something worthless, you will be like my mouth." Yhwh does not go in for defense, explanation or apology. A prophetic relationship with Yhwh frees a servant to be direct in speaking with the master but once again also leaves a master free to be straight, plainspoken and unyielding in response. Like Job, Jeremiah has to accept his place in Yhwh's scheme of things. He can then have the honored place of being this master's servant. The master chef does not choose to explain to the busboy why the oven is turned up so high. If he does not like the heat, he must get out of the kitchen. If he is willing to get on with the job (Yhwh does not quite say he has to do it without complaining) then he can do so. It is all the same to Yhwh. Yhwh does not have to use Jeremiah. There are other ways of getting the job done. Everything depends on whether Jeremiah wishes to be associated with the project Yhwh is engaged in.

There is no explanation and no promise that the persecutors will be put down (though there are many promises with that implication elsewhere), but there is a promise of protection. Here Yhwh's words do offer some response to Jeremiah. In speaking of Yhwh's commission or "acknowledgment" of him and of his taking Yhwh's words in his mouth, Jeremiah picked up the terms of his commission. Implicitly Yhwh does the same in speaking of making him a fortified bronze wall to the people; the promise reuses the verb Yhwh used when saying "I will make you a prophet to the nations" (Jer 1:5). Yhwh does so again in speaking of his becoming (once more) Yhwh's mouthpiece, and more explicitly in the promise, "I will be with you . . . to rescue you (Yhwh's oracle)" (cf. Jer 1:8). Yhwh's toughness comes out in adding nothing to what has been said before, but Yhwh's mercy comes out in reaffirming what has been said before. Jeremiah could be forgiven for thinking his situation looked desperately perilous; Yhwh promises to stand by the declaration that was made before it looked that way.

Driven to Prayer for Terrible Action

Jeremiah still has to live with the situation. Following the example of psalms that assume that if something needs to be said once, it may need to be said twice or three times, Jeremiah takes up matters again (Jer 17:14-18). He asks for healing, which Yhwh has perhaps implicitly promised, and again for deliverance, which Yhwh has explicitly promised (cf. Jer 15:18, 20-21). People still doubt whether Yhwh will ever do what depressing prophets such as Jeremiah predict. He has not shrunk from the ministry Yhwh commissioned him for, but he again recalls that he had no personal desire to deliver a gloomy message and does not look forward to the day of calamity coming on Judah. The words he uttered were words Yhwh acknowledged (that is, determined); again he recalls a key verb from his commission. They came from before Yhwh's face; again, he takes up Yhwh's words (see Jer 15:19). Yhwh told him not to break before them (Jer 1:17); he feels as if Yhwh is breaking him. Yhwh promised to intervene on his behalf in his personal time of calamity (Jer 15:11); he needs Yhwh to keep that undertaking. Yhwh has promised that people like kings, leaders, priests and prophets will come to shame (e.g., Jer 2:26); it takes some faith to believe this will be their fate and not Jeremiah's. Yhwh has promised shattering upon shattering for Judah, and Jeremiah was himself then overwhelmed by the prospect (Jer 4:19-20), but now he needs to see that double shattering because it is either them or him.

Yhwh has nothing to say in response. Later, Jeremiah tries again (Jer 18:18-23)—later in the order of the book, though we do not know whether the material comes in chronological order. The ministry of priest, prophet and counselor are predicated on the assumption that the nation is following the right religious and political policies. Jeremiah's words sound the death knell for the people who are currently involved in these ministries, as well as amounting to treason. Priest, prophet and counselor therefore plan to let his words be the death of him rather than the death of them. Once more, no doubt they want to silence him in order to stop him having a negative effect on morale and undermining their ministry that seeks to encourage the people and build up morale, and once more their reference to not heeding his words suggests they also want to silence him to stop his words about calamity being effective and thus terminating their ministry when the calamity actually happens. Either way, they are paying him a weird compliment, though Jeremiah can hardly see it that way.

Jeremiah protests to Yhwh that his aim has been to do good to the people, not least by pleading with Yhwh not to act in wrath against them (e.g., Jer 4:10). Their response is to do ill to him.[169] The nature of his prayers therefore changes. He stops opposing Yhwh's intention to bring calamity on the people and accedes to it. Famine, slaughter, bereavement, panic: it will all be fine. Let their wrongdoing be remembered, not forgotten. The appearance of Jeremiah's prayers in his book suggests that even with hindsight neither Jeremiah nor his immediate community nor the subsequent Jewish and Christian communities saw any problem about his expressing himself in this way. Perhaps they recognized that in some ideal world a prophet would not feel and pray that way, or that in the actual world this prophet did feel and pray that way and that this was all right with Yhwh, or that asking Yhwh to take action involves a remarkable holding back from taking any action oneself. And further, talking about his prayers may be another device to try to get people to change, by scaring them with the possibility that Yhwh may answer them.

In the short term Yhwh keeps quiet about most of that. Yhwh does not rebuke Jeremiah, as happens on other occasions, nor compliment Jeremiah on his personal restraint when faced by attacks, nor directly declare the intention to accede to the prayer. Eventually Yhwh does what Jeremiah asks; indeed, Yhwh is already set on that course. Jeremiah is not asking for something Yhwh has not thought of doing. The prayer is a belated affirming of the intentions Yhwh has been long announcing (e.g., Jer 6:11-12; 14:7-12). Indeed, it is not purely centered on himself. People's attacks on Jeremiah are not personal to him but express their repudiation of Yhwh. It is here that their wrongdoing and sin lie. Jeremiah is urging Yhwh to trip them up and take action on them not merely for his sake but for Yhwh's, in accordance with the intentions Yhwh has already announced but is slow about implementing.

In the book of Jeremiah, his prayer is immediately followed by a commission from Yhwh and an aftermath that resonates with it. Yhwh bids him speak to some priests (among others) about the ill that is to come on Jerusalem, about people seeking their life, about slaughter there and about the frustrating of its strategy as people are killed by the sword (Jer 19). The words resonate with the words of the prayer. Yhwh's word confirms that Yhwh means to

---

[169]Holladay takes "Does ill make recompense for good?" as his opponents' words (*Jeremiah 1*, pp. 527-33). That would make the verbal expression of the point less sharp, but not affect the general point.

implement the intention Jeremiah has now acceded to. But it immediately results in one of these leading priests hitting Jeremiah and in Jeremiah's condemning him for his prophesying (Jer 20:1-6).

Having No Option

There follows one final reversion to protest (Jer 20:7-18). Once again Jeremiah
looks back to his commission, when Yhwh persuaded him into a task he did
not wish to undertake. He was no volunteer like Isaiah or like a Christian
believing he or she has a call to the ministry. He did not want the task Yhwh
required of him, but Yhwh overruled his unwillingness, like a man persisting
in courting a girl who several times says no. The image is a useful one for
understanding this process. Yhwh does not exactly force him; in theory he
could continue to resist Yhwh's plan. But in the end, how can you resist when
Yhwh will not take no for an answer? That would be okay, except that the
work Yhwh was commissioning him for never came to fruition. Perhaps he
implies Yhwh had thus not merely "enticed" him (NRSV) but "deceived" him
(TNIV).[170]

Yhwh's enticing or deceiving is uncomfortably similar to Yhwh's action
through the prophets who brought Ahab a false promise of victory (1 Kings
22:19-23), when Yhwh enticed prophets to bring a victory promise that was
designed to deceive. Jeremiah has understood Yhwh's relationship with the
other prophets of his day in a similar way (Jer 4:10). Here, that is how he sees
Yhwh's relationship with him personally in connection with his proclamation of calamity. Yhwh enticed him into making it, not just once but time and
again, but the calamity never comes. Yhwh has commissioned him to be a
false prophet. His prophecy's failure has turned him into a laughingstock.
Despite the horrifying nature of Yhwh's word with its message about terrible
calamity, he had consumed and internalized that word; it had become for him
a delight and the joy of his heart (Jer 15:16). Now because its horrifying message never comes true, it has become for him constant reproach and derision.
"It is embarrassing to be a prophet. . . . None of the prophets seems enamored
with being a prophet nor proud of his attainment." Indeed, "Jeremiah hated
his prophetic mission."[171]

"Go on, proclaim your 'Terror all around' message, Jeremiah. In fact, we
will join in the proclamation." Perhaps they are simply mocking him; perhaps these apparent "friends" are going through the motions of supporting
him in order to manipulate him into getting himself into deeper water. Either
way, ultimately they want to silence him, either, once again, because they

---

[170]On the translation of *pātâ*, see (e.g.) Fretheim, *Jeremiah*, pp. 290-91.
[171]Heschel, *Prophets*, pp. 20, 151.

recognize the danger that his prophetic word will find fulfillment or because his preaching is bad for morale; it amounts to treason.

Fortunately they have overreached themselves. They want to entice and prevail or to deceive, but we already know Yhwh controls this activity. This has now turned from being bad news to being encouragement, from working against Jeremiah to working for him. They want to exact their redress, but redress is Yhwh's business (cf. Jer 11:20; 46:10; 50:15, 28; 51:6, 11, 36); they are again encroaching on Yhwh's territory. Their overreaching parallels that of the Assyrians (see Is 36:18-20; 37:4), whose act must provoke Yhwh into a response. In Jeremiah it provokes an analogous reaction to Isaiah's, a declaration of confidence in Yhwh as the terrifying warrior who will see that his persecutors' action leads to their downfall, not his.

One point about this proclamation is again for it to falsify itself. Yhwh's preference is to get people to turn back, so it will be unnecessary to bring about the calamity, and issuing such warnings is one way Yhwh seeks to get people to turn. Further, Yhwh is notoriously long-tempered and is thus inclined to keep giving Judah one more chance, even though all they do is laugh at Yhwh's messenger. So Jeremiah's experience is quite explicable. But this does not make it a lot easier to put up with.

Jeremiah has tried giving up his task, but then finds himself subject to another compulsion, one located inside and not just outside. Speaking of it as a burning fire suggests he has internalized Yhwh's wrath. He has consumed Yhwh's words about a calamity to come (Jer 15:16) and cannot simply hold onto them. They demand expression. That in itself carries an implicit testimony to the truth of his word. If he were wrong and were a false prophet, then he would not be seething with divine wrath. Thus he knows that the one who is with him, as he had been promised from the beginning and subsequently repromised (Jer 1:8; 15:20), is Yhwh, the terrifying warrior, not an impotent one (contrast Jer 14:9).[172] It is therefore not so worrying to be confronted by terrifying persecutors (cf. Jer 15:21). His persecutors will stumble, not he. In the long term it will be the other prophets who will be discredited, not he.

Wishing He Had Never Been Born

So Jeremiah can give praise to Yhwh as the one who rescues the needy from the hand of the wicked (Jer 20:13). He is again taking up Yhwh's own words (see Jer 1:8; Jer 15:20-21). His talk of Yhwh's having actually done so may reflect a particular rescue, like his escape from Pashhur after one night under confinement, just related (Jer 20:1-6). Or it may parallel the way psalms speak

---

[172]Cf. Holladay, *Jeremiah 1*, p. 557.

as if a response to prayer has already come, and the way Jeremiah and other prophets speak of Yhwh's act of punishment or restoration as if it has already come, when they have come only within Yhwh's intent.

Either way, he is soon in the same place as before, only worse, wishing he had never been born and doing so more systematically than he had earlier (Jer 20:14-18). Once again, his talk of his birth recalls his account of his commission (Jer 1:4-10). If his terrible commission goes back to before he was born, it would be better if he had never been born. His words as a whole in Jeremiah 20:7-18 constitute a kind of parody of Psalm 22. That psalm keeps moving between outspoken and distraught protests about human persecution and divine abandonment, and trustful affirmations of Yhwh's involvement in the suppliant's life. In that dialogue, affirmation eventually wins a triumphant victory as the last third of the psalm praises Yhwh for responding to these protests. Jeremiah 20 involves an analogous dialogue between protest and affirmation, but protest wins the triumphant victory.

When his words come to an end the chapter closes with no response from Yhwh. It thus anticipates his story as the book goes on to tell it. There he goes through a series of experiences of mocking, assault and imprisonment. During a lull in the siege of Jerusalem he leaves the city in connection with some aspect of his inheritance there (the text is obscure) and gets arrested as a deserter, beaten and imprisoned, but he begs for the king's protection, and gets it (Jer 37:11-21). Yet then the king gives him over into the power of his staff, and Jeremiah ends up left to die in a disused water cistern until someone else leans on the king to reverse his stance once more (Jer 38). He is eventually forced to go off to Egypt with Judean refugees, who are still intent on walking the opposite way to whatever Yhwh directs. And that is the last we see of him (Jer 44).

In another sense it is by no means the last we see of him. Chapters 45, 46–51 and 52 all follow, and deny any too negative reading of his story. And in another sense he does receive a response to his lament in chapter 20, because chapter 21 follows. In the context of the siege of Jerusalem, King Zedekiah sends someone else called Pashhur and a priest called Zephaniah to see if there is a word from Yhwh, and Yhwh provides Jeremiah with a response. So God does not commiserate with Jeremiah, yet neither does God rebuke him, but sidesteps his lament and gets him to carry on with his ministry.[173] Indeed, God requires him to tell people to leave the city and surrender to the besieging Babylonians (Jer 21:9), which would certainly look like the advice of a traitor (cf. Jer 38:4).[174] The protests, the tough divine responses and the chal-

---

[173]Cf. Fretheim, *Jeremiah*, p. 297.
[174]Cf. Holladay, *Jeremiah 1*, p. 574.

lenge to get back to his vocation parallel those to Elijah in 1 Kings 19, where "the therapy for the burned-out prophet" lies in "the divine instruction to get back to work." It is effective.[175]

In the end, no, Yhwh did not deceive Jeremiah. But yes, Yhwh did prevail over him to draw him into a role that he had no desire to fulfill and that cost him physical suffering, emotional pain and social shame, and Yhwh responded to his protests just with an insistence that he carry on. No ravens feed Jeremiah as they fed Elijah; no angel stops the lion's mouth, as it did for Daniel.[176] Yhwh was ruthless in relating to Jeremiah.

Hurt

For all his being consumed by Yhwh's wrath, Jeremiah does not lose a sense of deep sadness at his people's waywardness and at the danger it has put itself in. Fundamental to a prophet is "a fellowship with the feelings of God, a *sympathy with the divine pathos.*"[177] Jeremiah embodies that most clearly. He is full of God's wrath; he also has to identify with God's attachment to Israel and "learn the grief of God in having to spoil what is intimately precious to Him."[178] Admittedly, it is not certain whether Jeremiah here speaks of Yhwh's grief; it is hard to tell whether Jeremiah is talking about Yhwh's sadness as well as his own.[179] But we do know from elsewhere that Yhwh feels grief over people's waywardness. The first emotion the First Testament attributes to Yhwh is grief, when Yhwh's heart was saddened at how the world turned out (*'āṣab* hitpael; Gen 6:5-6). Grief has been part of God's experience from near the beginning of things;[180] it was then part of God's experience with Israel from its beginning (Ps 78:40-41; Is 63:10).[181] Grief, like anger, is a reaction to loss and to being let down and abandoned. Jeremiah's grief will be a mirror of Yhwh's.

He feels a terrible sickness at the prospect of the trouble coming on city and country, and at the people's own bafflement at Yhwh's abandonment of them, yet recognizes that this comes as a result of having let the people's faithlessness provoke the divine anger (Jer 8:18-22). Jeremiah (and Yhwh) is like someone whose nearest and dearest has been grievously wounded. The people's question about Yhwh's presence and their comment about the har-

---

[175]Cf. Miller, "Toward a Theology of Leadership," p. 665.

[176]Gerhard von Rad, *Old Testament Theology*, 2 vols. (Edinburgh: Oliver & Boyd, 1962, 1965), 2:207.

[177]Heschel, *Prophets*, p. 31.

[178]Ibid., p. 149.

[179]Joseph M. Henderson argues that the pain is Jeremiah's, the wrath Yhwh's, though also assimilated by Jeremiah ("Who Weeps in Jeremiah viii 23 [ix 1]?" *VT* 52 [2002]: 191-206).

[180]Terence E. Fretheim, *The Suffering of God* (Philadelphia: Fortress, 1984), p. 112.

[181]See *OTT* 1:133-34.

vest both suggest that the city has not yet fallen, but it has undergone terrible distress. One might imagine it having experienced a long siege, but it would be prosaic to seek to move from the depiction of feelings to a literal context. The passage parallels Jeremiah's panic at the wasting at Jerusalem when he sees it in his mind's eye. The grief anticipates the trouble that lies ahead of the people; telling them of it once again attempts to get them to turn.

Like anyone else whose nearest and dearest has been grievously wounded, Jeremiah (and Yhwh) also feels their hurt. He hears a cry coming not just from Jerusalem itself, one that could be escaped by turning one's ears away. It is audible all over the country. It assails his ears from all quarters. Insofar as Yhwh feels a pain at what is happening, it is a self-imposed pain; Yhwh is having to hold back from acting in light of such realities.

When Yhwh asks, "Why did they provoke me with their images?" (Jer 8:19), the implication is not "Why did I let myself be provoked?"; the objective provocation made action necessary. Nor is the question an expression of puzzlement at the mystery of the people's perversity, like Yhwh's earlier "Why?" (Jer 8:5). The question is itself an expression of regret at the way they made action necessary. And necessary it became. But on Jeremiah's part, statements of grief surround the awareness of necessity and the divine wrath that he also shares. There is some poignancy and agonizing in the allusion to the people's question, "Is Yhwh not in Zion?" Yhwh is there, but is doing nothing. "Is her King not in her?" Only here in Jeremiah is Yhwh the people's King (cf. Zeph 3:15).[182] That description underlines the point. Kingship suggests a sovereignty in their destiny that works for flourishing and freedom. But Yhwh is not acting as their King. There is similar poignancy and agonizing over their lament that the months pass and they have not been delivered.[183] Yhwh is by nature deliverer but is not acting as such.

Mourning

The tension emerges further in the verses that follow (Jer 9:1-2 [MT 8:23–9:1]). Jeremiah speaks of two wishes; one seems to be his own, one Yhwh's.[184] One is to be able to grieve for "my dear people" on the scale appropriate to the magnitude of the disaster that is coming. The other is to be able to get away from "my people" because of the magnitude of their act of rejection. In their re-

---

[182]Yhwh is King in relation to the nations in Jer 10:7, 10; 46:18; 48:15; 51:57.

[183]We do not know exactly what this line refers to. It might suggest a siege that has lasted through the summer into the fall or might be quoting a proverb about a crisis that seems to go on forever.

[184]The Hebrew Bible appropriately links the first verse with what precedes as it concludes Jeremiah's expression of grief; the section division in Masoretic mss actually runs from 8:18–9:3 [MT 2]. The EVV neatly link it with what follows as the succeeding verse begins in the same way as the first.

course to other gods they have betrayed Yhwh like a man leaving his wife to go off with another woman, walking out on his wife to expend his energy on pleasing this other (cf., e.g., Jer 3:1, 20; 5:7, 11, 19). In response, Yhwh wishes to leave them, with the hurt anger that characterizes a woman in that position.

Jeremiah soon has Yhwh continuing, "Now: I am smelting them and testing them, because how am I to act in the presence of my dear people?" (Jer 9:7 [MT 6]). The verse is jerky, but it strikingly juxtaposes Yhwh's intention to act tough with the fact that the object of this action is "my dear people," literally, "my daughter-people," someone on whom Yhwh looks as a daughter.[185] Yhwh has already commissioned Jeremiah to smelt and assay the people, and Jeremiah 6:27-30 has reported the conclusions of this investigation, while here the more immediate context has made clear that the people are indeed "reject silver" (see Jer 9:2-6 [MT 1-5]), and in a moment Yhwh will speak of attending to them and gaining redress from them (Jer 9:9 [MT 8]). What is Yhwh then doing in determining personally to smelt and test them again?

Smelting and testing is unpleasant, but it is not in itself punishment. Is Yhwh again smelting and testing because of still hoping to be proved wrong? Does hope live eternal in the divine breast? How otherwise is Yhwh to act? The alternation continues as Yhwh speaks of punishment. Perhaps one sign of distaste for punishment is the way Yhwh speaks of it euphemistically. When the people are involved in recourse to other gods and in deceit and swindling in relation to one another, "should I not attend [*pāqad*] to such deeds? On a nation such as this should my soul not take its redress?" (Yhwh has already asked these questions in Jer 5:9, 29.) The EVV translate *pāqad* "punish," but it means "attend to"; it is a rather understated threat.

Jeremiah's reference to ointment from Gilead (Jer 8:22) had ironic significance (see Jer 46:11; 51:8-9). No doctor and no healing resin can heal a wound as serious as this one. The wound is fatal, and surveying the corpses of people who have died through famine in the city and by the sword outside it as a result of the way prophets and priests have fulfilled their ministries, Yhwh bids Jeremiah weep day and night for it (Jer 14:17-18). When calamity comes to Judah, many will lose their lives, but some will survive to be taken into exile. There "they will think about me among the nations where they have been taken captive, how I was broken with their immoral heart that turned away from me and with their immoral eyes that turned away to their pillars" (Ezek 6:9). In the words of the tough-minded Ezekiel, the description of Yhwh as broken (*šābar* niphal) by the people's unfaithfulness is especially remarkable.

---

[185]Emphasizing that this expression expresses the grief that belongs especially to Jeremiah rather than to Yhwh, Henderson assumes this instance results from textual corruption ("Who Weeps in Jeremiah viii 23 [ix 1]?" p. 195).

Yhwh's own experience is mirrored in the fate of the people's incense altars and pillars (Ezek 6:4, 6) and in the fate of Jerusalem, its prophet and its people (e.g., Jer 14:17; 23:9—the same verb), or vice versa. In Ezekiel, too, Yhwh's brokenness (Ezek 6) has to be set alongside Yhwh's anger (Ezek 5). Both are aspects of Yhwh's passion or pathos.[186] Behind the anger is Yhwh's brokenness, behind the brokenness is Yhwh's anger. Yhwh wills these events, but Yhwh also commissions women to lament over them (Jer 9:17-22 [MT 16-21]).

Eventually Triumphant

Isaiah 40–55 sets against the traditional figures of king, priest and prophet one whose role overlaps with each of theirs but whose person and role has a new profile. The designation "Yhwh's servant" goes back to Moses and applies to kings, prophets and foreign emperors, but the profile of this figure in Isaiah 40–55 is very distinctive. The First Testament's portrait of servanthood comes to its climax here, especially in Isaiah 52:13–53:12. Moses is among the figures in the background of the portrait, but it is the climax partly because the Israelite king is also in the background (a servant of Yhwh like David), and so is the priest (a servant of Yhwh like Aaron), and so is the prophet (a servant of Yhwh like Isaiah or Jeremiah).

The passage describes the experience of Yhwh's servant and the significance attaching to him, but it does not indicate who it refers to. It is a kind of promise or job description. While the nearby context also does not unequivocally identify the servant, it has described Israel as Yhwh's servant and also described the prophet thus. Their experience contributes to the portrait, and they are entitled (or warned) to find themselves in it. If there is an answer to the question who the passage refers to, it is the prophet who spoke in Isaiah 49:1-6 and Isaiah 50:4-9, but it is not essential to answer this question in order to perceive the passage's vision of service.

Christians traditionally see Jesus as *the* fulfillment of the servant vision, but the New Testament does not see the passage as a "prophecy" of which there is just that one "fulfillment," nor does it use the passage to prove Jesus is the Messiah. It sees Jesus as one fulfillment of this vision, but not the only one. It also applies the passage to the vocation of the church (e.g., 1 Pet 2:21-22). The passage indicates how servanthood can work, whoever the servant is. It can involve hurt and pain, but a hurt and pain that are productive for other people and are not the end of the story for the servant.

The First Testament encourages the expectation that a king should be a physically and intellectually impressive figure, tall, dark, handsome and in-

---

[186]For this word, see Heschel, *Prophets*, pp. 285-382; further, Jürgen Moltmann, *The Trinity and the Kingdom of God* (London: SCM Press, 1981) = *The Trinity and the Kingdom* (San Francisco: Harper, 1981), pp. 21-60, and his references.

sightful. Consider, for example, David (notwithstanding Yhwh's words about looking at the inner person), Absalom and the king of Tyre (1 Sam 16; 2 Sam 14; Ezek 28). This is a reasonable assumption, for God made body and mind, and one would expect God to bless the body and mind of one that God intends to use. Yhwh's servant will be an impressive figure, but for some while he belies such expectations (Is 52:13-15).

Initially the passage focuses on the recognition of his impressiveness, which then makes it possible to face the rest of the vision, though even the immediate reference to people's horror at the sight of him advertises where the vision is to go. Yhwh's servant will gain the majesty of a king who surpasses all other kings, even though going through appalling experiences on the way. He will have royal insight; the verb *(śākal)* is one that especially applies to the king. It combines the ideas of insight and success, and hints at the way the former is of key importance to the latter. The servant is a David-like figure in this respect (e.g., 1 Sam 18:5, 13, 30; and the promise about David's shoot in Jer 23:5). He will have super-royal majesty; he will rise and exalt himself and be very high. Some of that too recalls David, as the fulfillment of old and not so old promises (Num 24:7; 1 Sam 2:10; 2 Sam 22:49). More strikingly, it also recalls descriptions elsewhere in Isaiah of qualities or achievements that lead to people being put down; their majesty threatens to rival Yhwh's majesty (e.g., Is 2:12; 3:16). Indeed, the very words that describe the position of Yhwh's servant are words that can describe Yhwh's own position as one exalted on high (see especially Is 5:16; 6:1). Yhwh's servant shares in Yhwh's exaltation. That is not so surprising a declaration; a servant does share in the majesty of the master. The surprise in this picture lies in the appalling horror of the servant's journey to that exaltation.

Recognized by Nations and Kings and by Us

Describing the servant as of remarkable appearance continues to suggest he is a David-like figure (e.g., 1 Sam 16:18; 17:42), and describing him as anointed also fits with that aspect of the expectations of kingship, for the king was *the* anointed.[187] Alongside the declaration that the servant will share in Yhwh's exaltation is the affirmation that his anointed appearance and look are not merely the equal of David's or other kings' but their superior. Corresponding to that is the further assertion that kings will shut their mouths at him. He

---

[187]The EVV speak of the servant being "marred" or "disfigured," following LXX and Jerome in deriving the word *mišḥat* from *šāḥat* "spoil, ruin" (cf. BDB), but that would be the only occurrence of this noun. There is an established noun *mišḥâ* (of which this would be the construct) from *māšaḥ* "anoint," which usually refers to the anointing oil or to the anointed share (the share belonging to the anointed people, the priests). This makes better sense in the context.

will realize the vision for the anointed king that appears in Psalm 2:1-2.

Nations and kings appear together here as they do in the psalm, but here the nations are also the object of the servant's spattering,[188] which is more a priestly note than a royal one. It recalls the other context for thinking about anointing, for priests were also anointed, so in spattering nations this servant will be a more remarkable priest than any other as well as a more remarkable king than any other. It is not explicit what he spatters them with. It could be water or oil, but the account of covenant sealing at Sinai suggests it is more likely blood. Such spattering is not a means of cleansing or forgiveness, but a sign of being sealed into a covenant relationship with Yhwh (Ex 24:8). So Yhwh's servant is a means of the nations being sealed into such a relationship, a plan Second Isaiah has already referred to (Is 42:6; 49:8). Previously nations and kings have not heard of the possibility. It was Yhwh's intention from the beginning of creation, but only rare people who happen to have been in the right place at the right time have come to know of it, people such as Jethro and Balaam, Rahab and Ruth, Uriah and Naaman. Now nations and kings will know. Thus their submissive astonishment at the work of Yhwh's servant has more positive connotations for them than the submission of which Psalm 2 spoke.

The First Testament does not envisage there being a problem about God forgiving the world, as Christian thinking has often suggested, as if God's own holy nature forbad such an act. There *is* a problem about getting the world to come to acknowledge God and thus to find forgiveness. It is the exaltation of this servant who has suffered that will bring them to that acknowledgment. On the other hand, this passage (like Is 40–55 as a whole) does not put the emphasis on the blessing this will bring to nations and kings themselves, but on the way this acknowledgment contributes to the servant's exaltation. At the end of this servant poem the imagery will ricochet back to the form it has in Isaiah 52:13-15, and Yhwh will declare that because of his faithful work "I will give him a share among the many; he will share out the powerful as spoil" (Is 53:12). He will be like a king who has fought victoriously as Yhwh's general. Yhwh will thus enable him to enjoy the fruits of triumph, plundering the army he defeats. Yes, nations and kings will shut their mouths at him.

The vision offers encouragement to anyone called to be Yhwh's servant. Yhwh is committed to the exaltation and fruitfulness of the servant portrayed. It also offers encouragement to anyone unsure whether the world will ever

---

[188]The NRSV, JPSV "startle" presupposes that *yazzeh* comes not from the regular *nāzâ* but from a homonym otherwise unknown in Hebrew. This seems a hazardous and unnecessary hypothesis.

come to acknowledge Yhwh. This servant will draw the nations into a covenant commitment to Yhwh.

It will not only be the world that is astonished at the servant. "We" are also astonished (Is 53:1-6). The people of Yhwh always finds it difficult to accept the prophet's account of the way Yhwh works. It is the destiny of Yhwh's servants to have their people hesitate to believe that they are indeed Yhwh's servants. They do not behave like proper leaders. They are not forceful and dynamic. They do not impress the world. So how can they impress Israel or the church? "Who could have realized that we have a revelation of the power of God in this person?" After all, this is not someone who looks like a shoot from the stock of Jesse but one who reminds us of a shoot growing out of dry ground, thin and weedy. He does not have the majestic appearance of a proper leader like David. There is nothing to attract us to him. He is not an inspiring leader. He is not merely ordinary, but distinctively pathetic, like God in the movie *Dogma*. He is the kind of person you look away from. It has been suggested that the prophet is describing someone with a disfiguring skin disease; the prophecy is too allusive to come to that concrete conclusion, but this suggestion gives the right idea regarding the servant's appearance and people's consequent reaction.

Sharing Suffering

When we get ill, we may ask, What did I do to deserve this? When other people get ill, we may ask, What did they do to deserve that? When they fail to get healed, we may be tempted to reckon that they have not prayed with enough faith or tried the right course of treatment. The servant's contemporaries (like Job's friends) inferred from his ill fortune that he must indeed have done something to deserve it. Actually (they have eventually come to realize), he was suffering in order to help them in some way.

This does not need to imply suffering instead of them. The original audience of this prophecy, the Judeans in the sixth century, were suffering themselves. The servant did not suffer in their place. He suffered with them. He carried their weaknesses, took up their great suffering, shared in their experience of displacement and loss. If David helps us understand the exalted servant, Jeremiah helps us understand the suffering servant. He was attacked as a false prophet and treated as someone working against Yhwh's purpose rather than for it, and he shared in the displacement and loss of exile when he did not deserve it.

The servant has analogous experiences that people reckoned came because he was unfaithful to Yhwh, but that actually came because he was fulfilling his vocation from Yhwh by sharing in people's displacement and loss. Ironically, the people suffering because of their unfaithfulness were the other exiles, not him. He was suffering to identify with them not only in their loss but in the sin that had caused it. They had wandered away from Yhwh like sheep wandering away from their shepherd, turned to go their own way rather than walking with Yhwh and in Yhwh's way. His suffering came because he shared in that and also because of the treatment they meted out to him in return for the ministry he exercised as a result of Yhwh's calling. Yhwh thus let their wrongdoing fall on him.

But they have come to realize that "he was hurt because of our rebellions." The people of God who speak thus had to come to a radically new assessment of the significance of the servant's affliction. How did that come about? There was something uncanny about the way the servant handled his experience, something that did not fit their assumptions about him (Is 53:7-9). They assumed he was under God's deserved punishment for his wrongdoing, though he was refusing to acknowledge the real truth about what was going on. But the uncanny thing was the way he accepted the affliction that came to him rather than struggling against it. Here he perhaps goes beyond Jeremiah. Do people in this situation react to their punishment as he did? "He would not open his mouth," the vision twice notes, as if this were especially extraordinary. And it is. The correct First Testament reaction to suffering is to protest at it, as the examples of Jeremiah, Job and countless psalms show. But this servant would not open his mouth, and certainly was not guilty of doing wrong by means of his words.[189] What is going on here? Who is this person?

As the First Testament does not think there is a problem about God's forgiving the world's wrongdoing, nor does it think there is a problem about God's forgiving the people of God when they turn from that wrongdoing, as if doing that compromised God's holiness. The holiness of God is dominated by mercy (cf. Hos 11). The First Testament does see a problem in how the people of God can be prevailed on to turn back to Yhwh and be weaned from their rebelliousness and turned into a people that live in covenant. God's servant achieves that. He is someone who needs to expect to be attacked by the people of God and by the world, but through this extraordinary life with its acceptance of affliction and its triumphant vindication, the deep-seated obtuseness of God's people is at last overcome.

Yhwh's Agent

The point about sharing in the people's deserved experience of suffering and letting them afflict him, then, is similar to the point about Jeremiah's going

---

[189]The "because" in v. 9 is perhaps ironic—the EVV render *kî* "although," but it is questionable whether it ever means that.

through such trouble. It was to put things right between Judah and God, to encourage a healing of that relationship, to get Judah to turn back to Yhwh. The servant suffers to make things well for the people of God, to bring them *shalom*, to bring them healing (Is 53:5). The NRSV and TNIV have this happening because the servant is undergoing "punishment," but the word *(mûsār)* is a term for the disciplining of a child by a parent or that of a pupil by a teacher, designed to bring the person to change or grow.[190] It is not a term for judicial action designed to effect retribution for an offense. Isaiah 53 does not use a judicial framework for understanding the relationship between God and people. The servant is not punished for wrongdoing committed by others, an idea that would be abhorrent to the First Testament. By its nature guilt is not transferable. In any case, we have noted that Israel was itself punished for its wrongdoing by being taken off into exile (Is 40:2). The servant was not "punished" except in the sense of sharing the experience that constituted punishment for them.

They have born their punishment. But it has not changed them. They are no more inclined to commitment to Yhwh than they were before. How might they be changed? Perhaps they will be moved and comforted by his willingness to share their suffering, or perhaps they will be brought up short by his putting up with their affliction yet continuing to seek to reach them in Yhwh's name. Perhaps one or other of these will provide the moral breakthrough that enables them to see themselves and see Yhwh afresh, and respond to that new seeing. It is as if he is a pupil chastised by the teacher when it is the other pupils who need to learn something; through watching him accept that chastisement, they do learn it.

The (imaginary?) testimony that the vision relates declares that this has indeed happened. His silent acceptance of suffering with them and from them has driven them to move beyond antipathy and distaste. There was something more going on here than their initial easy judgment assumed. They realized that instead of seeing him as faithless (evidently under God's punishment) and seeing themselves as relatively faithful, they had to turn this assumption upside down. He was the faithful one. That meant they were the faithless. Some of their prophets had always been saying that, and this servant's acceptance of suffering with them and from them enabled them to see that those prophets were right.

And Yhwh was behind all that (Is 53:10-11a). After all, it is Yhwh who sends prophets and thus sends them into a ministry that involves suffering for the people they seek to reach. That is regularly the dynamic of prophecy. It is not the stated reason why prophets attempt to evade their vocation, but it would

---

[190]Cf. §4.4 "Making Restitution."

be a good reason. The community was not so wrong when it inferred that God struck this servant. Yes, "Yhwh let fall on him the wrongdoing of all of us" (Is 53:6). Yhwh required of him a ministry that was bound to mean people's opposition and attacks. "He determined the crushing of the one he weakened." But "Yhwh's determination will succeed by his hand." Thus when it is all over he will be able to see results from it. He will look at the way Yhwh's determination has been fulfilled, and will be filled with delight. The EVV's "satisfaction" rather understates the significance of *śābaʿ*; the JPSV has "enjoy it to the full."

In isolation, admittedly, that is a rather remote involvement of Yhwh in the process whereby the people find healing and restoration. But the community's opening comment was that there was a revelation of Yhwh's arm in these events. Yhwh did not merely initiate a course of action from the safe distance of the court in heaven. Yhwh was involved in person in what went on. Talk of Yhwh's arm suggests Yhwh acting in power and might. The prophet has just spoken of Yhwh's arm being bared (of Yhwh's sleeves being rolled up) in order to act against Babylon (Is 52:10). We might expect that the revelation of Yhwh's arm lay in the victorious vindication of the servant, but the community's words point in a different direction. They imply it would have been very difficult to recognize the act of Yhwh's arm, given where it was undertaken. Yhwh's arm is revealed in the activity of the servant in accepting suffering, not merely in the eventual triumph of the servant. Jeremiah again stands in the background. The way he spoke suggested Yhwh shared in his ministry. His pain was also Yhwh's pain. His rejection was Yhwh's rejection. When a prophet reached out to the people in Yhwh's name, this was Yhwh reaching out to them, and when the people refused to respond to the prophet, they were refusing to respond to Yhwh. Yhwh would thus be grieving over the cost Jeremiah paid for his ministry, but also experiencing the pain of personal rejection and paying the price for reaching out to them. That process is repeated when Yhwh's arm makes itself known in the ministry of this servant.

Faithfully Offering Reparation

There is another form of Yhwh's involvement, a paradoxical one in light of that activity of Yhwh's arm. The vision talks about the servant laying down a reparation offering (*ʾāšām* [Is 53:10]).[191] This coheres with the other priestly

---

[191]See §2.5 "The Reparation Offering." The second colon in v. 10 can be read in two ways. I take *napšô* as the subject of the verb *tāśîm* (which is not a regular word for "making" an offering), as the JPSV seems to presuppose. The NRSV and TNIV take it as the object and construe the verb as second person ("If you lay down his person as a restitution offering"). The "you" is presumably Yhwh (so explicitly TNIV). Theologically this under-

motifs in the vision (anointing, spattering). A reparation offering presupposes that people have acted in a way that causes offense. They have not treated someone as who they are, and they have thus taken away something of this person's proper honor. They therefore need to do something to make up for their offensive act. A reparation offering makes symbolic and substantial restitution for such wrongdoing and thus restores a relationship to what it was before. It recognizes responsibility and guilt, and seeks to make up for something that has been taken away.

How does the servant do that? What the servant offers Yhwh is his own life and in particular his suffering.

It is not absolutely clear whether the vision implies that the servant actually dies as a result of his ministry. Being cut off from the land of the living is a metaphor that would naturally suggest this, but it need not do so. He was allocated a burial place, but the passage does not say he occupied it. He exposed himself to death, but this might not mean he actually died. And while the talk of vindication, having children and living a long life could presuppose he died and Yhwh has brought him back to life, this is not mentioned. Fortunately, the resolution of this question does not affect the comment about making a reparation offering, because such an offering need not require a death (e.g., 1 Sam 6). The servant's life could offer such reparation, whether or not it has come to an end in death.

Either way, the statement presupposes possibilities inherent in the servant's experience of affliction. His faithful commitment to Yhwh in his ministry constitutes a stark contrast to the community's faithless abandonment of Yhwh. In this ministry he represents Yhwh to the people, embodying Yhwh's commitment to them and Yhwh's challenge to them. But he is like a prophet in that he also identifies with his people, offering the commitment to Yhwh it failed to offer. The possibility the vision raises is that his extraordinary commitment with its willingness to go to the death could make up for the people's shortfall of commitment. Quantitatively there was no comparison, of course, but reparation offerings need not work on the basis of offering equivalence, as the instructions in Leviticus 5 as well as 1 Samuel 6 show. The reparation is symbolic as well as substantial, and either may have prominence. The people's failure to honor Yhwh, to treat Yhwh as God, has put the world out of kilter. The servant's remarkable honoring of Yhwh might restore its balance.[192]

---

standing would suit me very well, but the trouble is that Yhwh is referred to in the third person in both cola on either side, so this understanding seems unlikely and not one we can build on theologically.

[192]Christian thinking has taken Is 53:10 as an exposition of substitutionary atonement, but actually a reparation offering was not an atoning sacrifice (it was not a sacrifice at all) and it did not involve substitution—as (e.g.) the story in 1 Sam 6 shows.

So when a servant of God silently accepts the attacks that come from the people of God and resists the temptation to respond with deceit or violence, that can be an offering to God made on behalf of the attackers, which God may accept as making up for the attackers' faithlessness.

One evidence that Yhwh has indeed accepted this self-offering will be the servant's restoration. Against all the odds, he will indeed see offspring and live a long life. His work will be fruitful in bringing into being the offspring Yhwh longs to see and longs to restore (e.g., Is 41:8; 43:5; 44:3; 48:19). The people will live and flourish rather than wither and die. They will see long days.

So the servant's ministry is one exercised in acknowledgment (of Yhwh), the kind of acknowledgment that again means the servant fulfills Israel's own vocation (Is 53:11b-12). They were a people who went into exile through lack of acknowledgment (of Yhwh, Is 5:13; there too *da'at* comes without qualifier). The servant gives Yhwh the kind of willing service that Yhwh deserves, and thus shows himself faithful to many.[193] He is faithful toward Yhwh and faithful toward them. Indeed, his obedience to Yhwh goes far beyond anything Yhwh asked of them, in his willingness to bear their wrongdoing. People in Jerusalem complained at the fact that they had to "bear the wrongdoings" of their ancestors (Lam 5:7); they suffered the consequences of their ancestors' wrongdoing. The servant bears the wrongdoing of these same people and their contemporaries in Babylon. They sinned; he experiences the consequences. That is how he shows himself faithful to them and to God. Whereas those Jerusalemites sometimes tried to get out of being identified with their ancestors' wrongdoing when maybe they needed to face up to facts, he let himself be numbered with the rebels when he was not one. He thus carried the failure of many. They themselves were carrying their failure, bearing their responsibility for it, living with the consequences of it. He joined them in this when there was no moral reason why he should do so. And all this put

---

[193]In the expression *yaṣdîq ṣaddîq*, as usual I translate words from the root *ṣdq* with words for faithfulness rather than justice. The verb is usually taken as a regular hiphil with *lārabbîm* as its object, "he will justify many." But the preposition is then odd, and I therefore take this as an internal hiphil, like the one in Is 52:13 ("act with insight"). The subsequent adjective spells this out, as in the expression "reign as king." See Bo Reicke, "The Knowledge of the Suffering Servant," in *Das ferne und nahe Wort*, L. Rost Festschrift, ed. F. Maass, BZAW 105 (Berlin: de Gruyter, 1967), pp. 186-92; see pp. 190-91. This understanding of the sentence also gets us out of the difficulty that it is hard to imagine the First Testament using talk of "justifying the many" when they are guilty as a way of describing how people are put right with God or hard to imagine readers understanding the text that way. One justifies the innocent and condemns the guilty, not vice versa (e.g., Ex 23:7; Deut 25:1). This does not mean that the First Testament cannot imagine Yhwh forgiving guilty people. The point is rather that it is hard to imagine it talking about this as *justifying* them.

him in a position to appeal for them as one identified with them, and to turn his experience into a reparation offering.

The First Testament does not lay before us a challenge to be leaders—it is disillusioned about leadership. It does lay before us such a vision of servant-hood.

CONCLUSION

These three volumes have sought to expound the nature of Israel's gospel, its faith and its life. As is the nature of a gospel, Israel's gospel is an account of what Yhwh has done in its life, which provides the framework for its self-understanding and also by its narrative nature provides it with a way of discussing tricky theological questions. Israel's faith builds on that narrative by articulating an understanding of the nature of Yhwh and the nature of Israel, the nature of the world and the nature of humanity. Israel's life involves living with Yhwh, living with one another and living with ourselves in light of the gospel and the faith. My hypothesis is that the threefold structure of this theology in terms of gospel, faith and life does reasonable justice to the Scriptures' own dynamic. (I do not imply that no other way of handling the questions could do so.) It also corresponds to some analyses of Christian theology's own vocation. Nicholas Lash sees theology's dynamic as set between the poles of narrative and metaphysic, but then adds that it also needs to be checked by praxis, in "patterns of action and suffering, praise and endurance."[1] David Ford speaks of "three basic categories through which human and Christian identity can be conceived," story, system and performance.[2] This third volume has been concerned with the "patterns" as they emerge from the First Testament, with the "performance" it requires.

In *Israel's Gospel*, the final chapter set Israel's story in the context of Jesus' story and vice versa, by considering the way the First Testament story continued in the New Testament. In *Israel's Faith*, at the end of each chapter on a theological theme I added some reflection on what extra perspectives the New Testament added. In *Israel's Life* I have woven more references to the New Testament throughout because the material seemed to point in that direction. I close by reflecting further on the way Christians interact with the First Testament, in light of the work as a whole.

---

[1]Nicholas Lash, "Ideology, Metaphor, and Analogy," in *Why Narrative?* ed. Stanley Hauerwas and L. Gregory Jones (Grand Rapids: Eerdmans, 1989), pp. 113-37; see p. 117.
[2]David Ford, "System, Story, Performance," in *Why Narrative?* ed. Stanley Hauerwas and L. Gregory Jones (Grand Rapids: Eerdmans, 1989); he emphasizes the priority of narrative and sometimes implies the order "story, system, performance" (e.g., p. 194).

Useful for Teaching

> All scripture is God-breathed and useful for teaching, for rebuke, for correction, for training in righteousness, so that the person who belongs to God may be equipped, thoroughly equipped for every good deed. (2 Tim 3:16-17)

While this declaration can be extended in its application so that it covers the New Testament, in itself it is referring to the First Testament. Yet from the worship and life of churches in the West, you would never have realized that they accepted this. They may or may not read bits of the First Testament in church, but their preachers are unlikely to preach from it and their people are unlikely to read it. My passion in these three volumes has been to expound its significance in a way that shows something of the truth of those two verses.

The First Testament is the opening part of the church's twofold Scriptures, and it would have been natural to attempt to write a biblical theology rather than an Old Testament theology; indeed, I do now hope to go on to do so (more briefly!). At least it is the case that writing an Old Testament theology is not as odd an enterprise as writing a New Testament theology, because from the beginning the New Testament was designed to be a supplement to the First Testament that took the First Testament for granted. It was not designed to be a balanced account of Christian faith. So the perspective of the New Testament in isolation from the First Testament is bound to be skewed. And this is reflected in the skewed nature of Christians' usual perspective on Christian faith, based as it is merely on a reading of the New Testament, and a selective one at that, and a reading heavily influenced by postbiblical tradition at that. So the passion to which I have referred compelled my focusing on the First Testament.

In Many Ways and Through a Son

> Having spoken in many separate ways of old to the ancestors through the prophets, God spoke in these final days to us through a Son. (Heb 1:1)

A number of misapprehensions concerning the First Testament have based themselves on the letter to the Hebrews. Like other parts of the New Testament, this letter utilizes the First Testament to provide illumination on the issues it needs to expound; it does not seek to do justice to the First Testament itself. And its opening lines have been misunderstood as an assertion that God's revelation in the First Testament was partial and incomplete, when they actually make a different point and one that is close to being the opposite. The contrast they draw is between a revelation that took scattergun form and a revelation that was embodied in one person. That is the difference between what God said through the prophets and through Christ. But (Hebrews implies) the content of what God said through the prophets and through

Christ is the same. There is consistency between God's speaking in the Scriptures, though there is also sequence and story.

It is no accident that both Testaments are dominated by the story whose significance I sought to expound in *Israel's Gospel*. It coheres with something about the content of their theology. But biblical study and Christian theology has a hard time working with this aspect of the Scriptures.

No book has aided me more in understanding the place of the Bible in church and academy in the West than Hans W. Frei's *The Eclipse of Biblical Narrative*.[3] In reading Scripture, Frei argues, people used to make two key assumptions about its narrative, and specifically about the truth of its narrative. It was true historically and true theologically. The narrative recounted things that actually happened, and its readers needed to see their lives in light of this narrative. In the eighteenth and nineteenth centuries these two assumptions and these two links collapsed.

On one hand, critical study established that there was a difference between the story the Scriptures told and the events to which the narrative refers. It then assumed it had to decide which of these it was interested in. But there was no contest. In the context of modernity, history was God. So critical study abandoned the study of the biblical text in its own right for the investigation of the events that lie behind it. And that became the focus of scholarly biblical study for much of two centuries. And one consequence is that scholarly study had virtually nothing for the preacher or the ordinary Christian who wants to live in light of 2 Timothy 3:16-17.

One can now see that Frei's own work was a sign of the "collapse of history"[4] and the resurrection of narrative, which underlay my first volume. This is not to go back on the discerning of a difference between story and history, but to reckon that God was involved in the crafting of the story as well as in the events in the history, and was involved in the crafting of the story even when it differed from the history. God likes history, but God also likes stories such as the parables and does not mind mixing them.[5] And generally it is the story, not the history, that preaches.

But with grievous irony, the postmodern context that made possible a renewed interest in narrative, or of which it was a sign, also made more radical the abandonment of the other link that Frei described. It was once the case that Christians assumed that the biblical story was true not only historically but theologically. It was the metanarrative in light of which we understand

---

[3]Hans W. Frei, *The Eclipse of Biblical Narrative* (New Haven, Conn./London: Yale University Press, 1974).

[4]Cf. Leo G. Perdue, *The Collapse of History* (Minneapolis: Fortress, 1994); *Reconstructing Old Testament Theology: After the Collapse of History* (Minneapolis: Fortress, 2005).

[5]See *OTT* 1:859-83.

our story. The second unraveling that Frei analyzed involved the abandonment of that assumption. Instead of evaluating their story by the scriptural story, people came to evaluate the scriptural story by their story.

In the eighteenth and nineteenth centuries a distinguishing mark of evangelical scholarship and faith was to resist both the developments Frei analyzed. Evangelicals insisted that the biblical narrative was wholly historical; this was the context of the development of concepts such as the infallibility of Scripture. There was no gap between narrative and history. Evangelicals also insisted that the scriptural story was theologically true; this was the context of the development of concepts such as the authority of Scripture.

Given the choice between either holding onto the narrative or giving up the conviction that the locus of revelation lay there and relocating it in the history that lies behind the narrative, they made the right decision. It is still appropriate to resist the assumptions of the Jesus Seminar. But standing on the shoulders of giants, we can now see that the choice was a false one. God was involved in the events of the biblical story and in the development of a narrative that was sufficiently factual but could incorporate nonfactual material. Both the investigation of the divinely engineered or divinely overseen events and the study of the divinely inspired or divinely overseen narrative are proper tasks, and we do not have to assimilate either the events and the narrative or the two forms of study.

Written for Us

> What does the Scripture say? "Abraham trusted in God, and it was reckoned to him as righteousness". . . . It was not written for him alone that "it was reckoned to him" but also for us. (Rom 4:3, 22-23)

With regard to the second issue, the irony is that many evangelicals have come unconsciously to share in modernity's assumptions about the relationship of Scripture's story and our story. Whereas once the principle was to understand our story in light of the scriptural story, now that order is reversed. Whereas once the principle was that the scriptural story is true and my experience needs to be interpreted in its light, now the principle is that my experience is true and the scriptural story needs to be interpreted (which often means "evaluated") in its light. Generally we do not feel free to do this by actually saying that the Bible is wrong. Rather people note that the Bible is located in its culture, with the inevitable result that it has limitations that emerge from this. But we deceive ourselves about the principle that makes it possible to perceive this: namely, our assumption that we are right. We do not ask questions about the way our thinking is distorted because of the culture we live in.[6] In such evangelical circles, authority lies in the contemporary church and its tradition, and in the individual believer, not in Scripture.

What would happen if we were to start giving the scriptural narrative its due? A number of aspects of its nature are worth noting in this connection. The first is that the Bible is about God. The chapter titles of *Israel's Gospel* seek to reflect that: they all have "God" as the first word. The First Testament reminds us that Christian faith is not about me but about God. And it reminds us that Christian faith is not about Jesus but about God, as Jesus himself kept emphasizing. The point about Jesus was to embody who God is, to show God's power and God's mercy, to embody God's willingness to pay the price for human sin, to restore Israel in its relationship to God, and to make it possible for the Gentile world to relate to God.

Those chapter titles then followed the word *God* with a verb. The First Testament is about acts of God.[7] Whereas it is possible for such an emphasis to give Christians the excuse to avoid being active in the world and leave everything to God, we are in more danger of the opposite mistake, of thinking that we are responsible to bring about the fulfillment of God's purpose, to bring about or at least to further the kingdom of God, to bring about social justice in the world. One would have thought that two Christian millennia might have suggested we are unlikely to achieve this. God is the key.

Further, those verbs were aorist verbs. Key to the achievement of God's purpose in the world is acts God undertook once and for all. That is integral to the notion of Christian faith being a gospel, a piece of news about something God has done. In the present volume I have noted the significance of that fact for aspects of our reflection on ethics.[8] In Romans, key to Paul's argument is the fact that Abraham came before Moses, that a relationship based on an act of trust came before the filling out of that relationship by obedience expressed in symbolic acts such as circumcision or substantial acts such as those the Torah goes on to detail.

At the same time this First Testament narrative is far longer than necessary in order merely to recount God's once-for-all acts, and one reason is that narrative makes it possible to discuss complex theological questions. Another feature of evangelicalism has been its attachment to the idea of a simple gospel, and the basic nature of that gospel is indeed straightforward. "Abraham trusted in God, and it was reckoned to him as righteousness." But many key questions about God and us are also mysterious. What is the relationship between God's grace and our obedience, God's love and God's anger, God's sovereignty and

---

[6]See §4.1.

[7]On issues raised by this now-unfashionable notion, see my *Approaches to Old Testament Interpretation,* 2nd ed. (Toronto: Clements, 2002), pp. 66-96, 191-97.

[8]See §5.3.

our responsibility? The First Testament narrative with its theological implications rescues us from an oversimplified faith and gives us ways of thinking about mysterious, complex, involved questions of this kind.

Not to Abolish but to Fulfill

> Do not think that I came to put down the Law and the Prophets. I did not come to put down but to fill out. (Mt 5:17)

Conventionally, Jesus "fulfilled" the Law and the Prophets. That English verb has a fairly clear and precise meaning. We fulfill our undertakings by doing what we say; we fulfill people's hopes or fears by doing what they long for or worry about. Jesus indeed fulfilled divine commitments and human hopes that are expressed in the Torah as well as in the Prophets. Yet this is not the point he goes on to elaborate in the context in Matthew 5, nor do the Gospels anywhere else give specific examples of his fulfilling the Torah in this sense. He does also fulfill the commands in the Torah (though he sometimes gets into trouble for sitting fast and loose to these), and in Matthew 5 he goes on to emphasize the importance of a detailed obedience to the Torah. Yet to understand this as constituting his "fulfilling" the Torah does involve stretching the meaning of the verb. But further, the verb translated "fulfill" *(plēroō)* does not have as precise a meaning as that English word; it is the ordinary word meaning "fill." Thus, when Jesus "fulfills" prophecies, commonly he does not merely do what the prophet encouraged people to expect; he "fills" the prophecies, fills them up or fills them out, overfills them. With regard to the Torah, too, it makes sense to think of him "filling" it, filling it up and filling it out, as much as fulfilling it. That would be a good description of what he goes on to do in Matthew 5.

He did not come to abolish, destroy or pull down the Torah. You would never have thought so from the way Christians relate to the Torah, and to the Prophets and the Writings. As we ignore them in connection with our theology, so we ignore them in connection with our lives. There they are, full of vision about marriage and family and community, about city and nation and state, and we ignore them. There they are, full of practical policy ideas about how to put flesh on the bones of their vision for these different realms, and we ignore them. Here we are, in a terrible mess about the way we organize marriage, family and local community, about the way we organize city life and national life, and we ignore them. It is not surprising that the secular world does so. It is grievous that the church does so.

God's vision was for Abraham and Sarah's family and offspring to become a blessing, an embodiment of what a nation looked like when it enjoyed God blessing and a stimulus to any nation to pray for that blessing for itself. It was designed to be a working model of what it meant to be a people. God was realistic about the fact that the people of God remained one characterized by hardness of heart, by stubborn attitudes, by closed minds, and made allowance for that, but God also held a vision before it and sought to win it to commitment, with the prospect of the blessing that would issue from following God. It was designed to be an alternative community. In practice the church is often simply an alternative version of the same old godless community, an embodiment of that community with nominal reference to God tacked on.

I sometimes get in trouble with students for underestimating the significance of the new teaching that Jesus brought, because I don't think Jesus brought much by way of new teaching. The reason is that Israel did not need new teaching. It had perfectly good teaching already. (Jeremiah had promised it a new covenant that involved the Torah being written into its attitudes; he did not promise it a new Torah.) What it needed was someone who could turn it into an embodiment of this teaching. It needed someone to do something, not to teach something. That was what Jesus came to do. But if readers of this present volume should join in my students' critique and reckon that Jesus expects higher standards of the church than the ones God expected of Israel, I do not mind that critique if the readers then set about leading the church so that it becomes an embodiment of those standards.

Be Filled with the Spirit

> Be filled with the Spirit, speaking to each other in psalms, hymns and spiritual songs, singing and making music in your heart to the Lord, giving thanks always for all people in the name of our Lord Jesus Christ to God the Father. (Eph 5:18-20)

> Through all prayer and petition, pray at all time in the Spirit. To this end be alert with all persistence and petition concerning all the saints, and for me, so that a message may be given to me as I open my mouth to make known with freedom the revelation of the gospel. (Eph 6:18-19)

While the center of *Israel's Life* has considered the way we live with other people, the first and last sections have considered how we live with ourselves and with God. In these areas too we ignore Scripture. Ephesians urges us toward a life of worship, prayer, thanksgiving and intercession. It does not tell us what that looks like. It does not need to do so, because the First Testament has already done so. Yet the church largely ignores the guidance the First Testament offers on the nature of worship, prayer and spirituality.

In the twenty-first century, what might be the structure of a life shaped by the First Testament? Here is a Decalogue. You can choose which you obey. But do some of them.

- Praise God at dusk and at dawn.
- Relax and sleep for the time in between.
- Grow things to eat.
- Tithe what you grow.
- Keep out of department stores and shopping malls (beware the Internet too).
- On Thursdays, pray laments for people who are suffering.
- On Fridays, think about the fact that you are going to die.
- On Saturdays, have a day's rest (you can tend your garden if it's not your regular work).
- On Sundays, talk with your friends or family about Scripture.
- Three times a year, hold a week-long holiday with your friends or family, and celebrate what God has done for us in nature and in delivering us.

Those are just regular, rule-of-life kinds of things. This volume is full of other things to do when occasion demands or invites.

BIBLIOGRAPHY

Achtemeier, Elizabeth R. *Nahum—Malachi*. Atlanta: Knox, 1986.

Ackroyd, Peter R. "The Vitality of the Word of God in the Old Testament." *ASTI* 1 (1962): 7-23.

Adamo, David Tuesday, ed. *Biblical Interpretation in African Perspective*. Lanham, Md./Oxford: University Press of America, 2006.

Adler, Leo. *The Biblical View of Man*. Jerusalem/New York: Urim, 2007.

Aejmelaeus, Anneli, *The Traditional Prayer in the Psalms*/Ludwig Schmidt, *Literarische Studien zur Josephgeschichte*. BZAW 167. Berlin/New York: de Gruyter, 1986.

Ahlström, G. W. *Royal Administration and National Religion in Ancient Palestine*. Leiden: Brill, 1982.

Allbee, Richard A. "Assymetrical Continuity of Love and Law between the Old and New Testaments." *JSOT* 31 (2006): 147-66.

Allen, Leslie C. *The Books of Joel, Obadiah, Jonah and Micah* (London: Hodder; Grand Rapids: Eerdmans, 1976.

———. "The First and Second Books of Chronicles." *The New Interpreter's Bible*, 3:297-659. Nashville: Abingdon, 1999.

———. *Psalms 101—150*. WBC. Rev. ed. Nashville: Nelson, 2002.

Alt, Albrecht. *Essays on Old Testament History and Religion*. Oxford: Blackwell, 1966.

Anderson, Cheryl B. *Women, Ideology, and Violence*. JSOTSup 394. New York/London: T & T Clark, 2004.

Anderson, Gary A. *Sacrifices and Offerings in Ancient Israel*. Atlanta: Scholars Press, 1988.

———. *A Time to Mourn, a Time to Dance*. University Park, Penn.: Pennsylvania State University Press, 1991.

Anderson, Gary A., and Saul M. Olyan, ed. *Priesthood and Cult in Ancient Israel*. JSOTSup 125. Sheffield, U.K.: Sheffield Academic Press, 1991.

Andreasen, Niels-Erik A. *The Old Testament Sabbath*. SBLDS 7. [Missoula, Mt.]: Society of Biblical Literature, 1972.

Arav, Rami, ed. *Cities Through the Looking Glass*. Winona Lake, Ind.: Eisenbrauns, 2008.

Archer, Léonie J., ed. *Slavery and Other Forms of Unfree Labour*. London: Routledge, 1988.

Ateek, Naim S. *Justice, and Only Justice*. Maryknoll, N.Y.: Orbis, 1989.

Athanasius of Alexandria. *On the Incarnation*. With an Introduction by C. S. Lewis. Crestwood, N.Y.: St. Vladimir's Seminary Press, 1996.

Augsburger, David W. *Hate-Work*. Louisville/London: Westminster John Knox, 2004.

Augustine of Hippo. *Expositions on the Book of Psalms*. Nicene and Post-Nicene Fathers 1.8. Edinburgh: T & T Clark; Grand Rapids: Eerdmans, 1989.

Aukerman, Dale. *Darkening Valley*. New York: Seabury Press, 1981.

Bach, Alice, ed. *Women in the Hebrew Bible*. New York/London: Routledge, 1999.

Bahnsen, Greg L. *No Other Standard: Theonomy and Its Critics*. Tyler, Tex.: Institute for Christian Economics, 1991.

———. *Theonomy in Christian Ethics*. 2nd ed. Phillipsburg, N.J.: Presbyterian & Reformed, 1984.

Bailey, Wilma Ann. *"You Shall Not Kill" or "You Shall Not Murder."* Collegeville, Minn.: Liturgical Press, 2005.

Bainton, Roland H. *Christian Attitudes toward War and Peace*. Nashville: Abingdon, 1960.

Baker, David L. "Safekeeping, Borrowing, and Rental." *JSOT* 31 (2006): 27-42.

Bakhtin, Mikhail M. *The Dialogic Imagination*. Austin: University of Texas Press, 1981.

———. *Problems of Dostoevsky's Poetics*. Minneapolis/London: University of Minnesota Press, 1984.

Bal, Mieke. *Lethal Love*. Bloomington: Indiana University Press, 1987.

Balch, David L., ed. *Homosexuality, Science, and the "Plain Sense" of Scripture*. Grand Rapids: Eerdmans, 2000.

Balentine, Samuel E. *Prayer in the Hebrew Bible*. Minneapolis: Fortress, 1993.

———. *The Torah's Vision of Worship*. Minneapolis: Fortress, 1999.

Ball, Edward, ed. *In Search of True Wisdom*. R. E. Clements Festschrift. JSOTSup 300. Sheffield, U.K.: Sheffield Academic Press, 1999.

Balthasar, Hans Urs von. *The Glory of the Lord*. New York: Crossroad, 1982.

Barker, William S., and W. Robert Godfrey, ed. *Theonomy: A Reformed Critique*. Grand Rapids: Zondervan, 1990.

Barmash, Pamela. *Homicide in the Biblical World*. Cambridge/New York: Cambridge University Press, 2005.

Barnhouse, Donald Grey. *His Own Received Him Not, But . . . .* New York/London: Revell, 1933.

Barrick, W. Boyd. *BMH as Body Language*. LHBOTS 477. New York/London: T & T Clark, 2008.

Barstad, Hans M. *The Religious Polemics of Amos*. VTSup 34. Leiden: Brill, 1984.

Barth, Karl. *The Christian Life*. Grand Rapids: Eerdmans, 1981.

———. *Church Dogmatics*. 13 vols. Edinburgh: T & T Clark, 1936-1969.

Bartholomew, Craig, et al., ed. *A Royal Priesthood? The Use of the Bible Ethically and Politically*. Grand Rapids: Zondervan; Carlisle, U.K.: Paternoster, 2002.

Barton, John. *Ethics and the Old Testament*. London: SCM; Harrisburg, Penn.: Trinity Press International, 1998.

————. *Joel and Obadiah*. Louisville/London: Westminster John Knox, 2001.

————. *Understanding Old Testament Ethics*. Louisville/London: Westminster John Knox, 2003.

————, ed. *The Cambridge Companion to Biblical Interpretation*. Cambridge/New York: Cambridge University Press, 1999.

Barton, Stephen C., ed. *The Family in Theological Perspective*. Edinburgh: T & T Clark, 1996.

Basset, Lytta. *Holy Anger*. Grand Rapids/Cambridge: Eerdmans, 2007.

Bauckham, Richard. *The Bible in Politics*. London: SPCK; Louisville: Westminster John Knox, 1989.

Bauer, Susan Wise. *The Art of the Public Grovel*. Princeton, N.J.: Princeton University Press, 2008.

Bauman, Zygmunt. *Postmodern Ethics*. Oxford/Cambridge, Mass.: Blackwell, 1993.

Bechtel, Carol M., ed. *Touching the Altar*. Grand Rapids/Cambridge: Eerdmans, 2008.

Bechtel, Lyn M. "Shame as a Sanction of Social Control in Biblical Israel." *JSOT* 49 (1991): 47-76.

Becking, Bob, and Eric Peels, ed. *Psalms and Prayers*. OTS 55. Leiden/Boston: Brill, 2007.

Behr, Thomas C. "Luigi Taparelli D'Azeglio, S.J. (1793—1862) and the Development of Scholastic Natural-Law Thought As a Science of Society and Politics." *The Journal of Markets and Morality* 6 (2003): 99-116.

Beisner, E. Calvin. *Prosperity and Poverty*. Westchester, Ill.: Crossway, 1988.

Bellah, Robert N. "Community Properly Understood." *The Responsive Community* 6/1 (1995-1996): 49-54.

Bellah, Robert N., et al. *Habits of the Heart*. Rev. ed. Berkeley/London: UCLA Press, 1996.

Bellefontaine, Elizabeth. "Deuteronomy 21:18-21." *JSOT* 13 (1979): 13-31.

Bellis, Allis Ogden, and Joel S. Kaminsky, ed. *Jews, Christians, and the Theology of the Hebrew Scriptures*. Atlanta: Society of Biblical Literature, 2000.

Ben-Barak, Zafrira. "Inheritance by Daughters in the Ancient Near East." *Journal of Semitic Studies* 25 (1980): 22-34.

Bendor, S. *The Social Structure of Ancient Israel*. Jerusalem: Simor, 1996.

Benjamin, Don C. *Deuteronomy and City Life*. Lanham, Md./London: University Press of America, 1983.

Bennett, Harold V. *Injustice Made Legal*. Grand Rapids/Cambridge: Eerdmans, 2002.

Bennett, John C. *Christian Ethics and Social Policy*. New York: Scribner's, 1946.

Bergant, Diane. "'My Beloved Is Mine and I Am His.'" *Semeia* 68 (1994): 23-40.

Berger, Brigitte, and Peter L. Berger. *The War over the Family*. Garden City, N.Y.: Doubleday, 1983.

Bergsma, John S. *The Jubilee from Leviticus to Qumran*. VTSup 115. Leiden/Boston: Brill, 2007.

Berquist, Jon L. *Controlling Corporeality*. New Brunswick/London: Rutgers University Press, 2002.

———. "Role Dedifferentiation in the Book of Ruth." *JSOT* 57 (1993): 23-37.

Berquist, Jon L., and Claudia V. Camp, ed. *Constructions of Space II*. LHBOTS 490. New York/London: T & T Clark, 2008.

Beyerlin, Walter. *Wider die Hybris des Geistes*. Stuttgart: KBH, 1982.

Biale, David. *Eros and the Jews*. New York: Basic Books, 1992.

Biddle, Mark E. *Deuteronomy*. Macon, Ga.: Smith & Helwys, 2003.

Billman, Kathleen D., and Daniel L. Migliore. *Rachel's Cry*. Cleveland: United Church Press, 1999.

Birch, Bruce C. *Let Justice Roll Down*. Louisville: Westminster John Knox, 1991.

Birch, Bruce C., and Larry L. Rasmussen. *Bible and Ethics in the Christian Life*. Rev. ed. Minneapolis: Augsburg Press, 1989.

Bird, Phyllis A. *Missing Persons and Mistaken Identities*. Minneapolis: Fortress, 1997.

Blank, Sheldon H. "The Hebrew Scriptures as a Source for Moral Guidance." In *Scripture in the Jewish and Christian Traditions*, pp. 169-82. Edited by Frederick E. Greenspahn. Nashville: Abingdon, 1982.

———. "Some Observations Concerning Biblical Prayer." *HUCA* 32 (1961): 75-90.

Blenkinsopp, Joseph. *Isaiah 1—39*. AB. New York: Doubleday, 2000.

———. *Isaiah 56—66*. AB. New York: Doubleday, 2003.

———. *Sage, Priest, Prophet*. Louisville: Westminster John Knox, 1995.

Bloch, Ernst. *The Principle of Hope*. 3 vols. Oxford: Blackwell; Cambridge, Mass.: MIT Press, 1986.

Blumenthal, David R. *Facing the Abusing God*. Louisville: Westminster John Knox, 1993.

Boda, Mark J. *Praying the Tradition*. BZAW 277. Berlin/New York: de Gruyter, 1999.

———. "The Priceless Gain of Penitence." *Horizons in Biblical Theology* 25 (2003): 51-75.

Boda, Mark J., et al., ed. *Seeking the Favor of God*. Vol. 1. Atlanta: Society of Biblical Literature, 2006.

Boda, Mark J., and Michael H. Floyd, ed. *Tradition in Transition*. LHBOTS 475. New York/London: T & T Clark 2008.

Boecker, Hans Jochen. *Law and the Administration of Justice in the Old Testament and Ancient East*. Minneapolis: Augsburg Press; London: SPCK, 1980.

Boer, Roland. "Women First?" *JSOT* 30 (2005): 3-28.

Boerma, Conrad. *The Rich, the Poor—and the Bible*. Philadelphia: Westminster, 1979. = *Rich Man, Poor Man—and the Bible*. London: SCM, 1979.

Bonhoeffer, Dietrich. *Discipleship*. Minneapolis: Fortress, 2001.

———. *Ethics*. New York: Simon & Schuster, 1995.

———. *Life Together/Prayerbook of the Bible*. Minneapolis: Fortress, 1996.

Booth, Wayne C. *The Company We Keep*. Berkeley/London: University of California Press, 1988.

Bourdillon, M. F. C., and Meyer Fortes, ed. *Sacrifice*. London/New York: Academic Press, 1980.

Boyce, Richard Nelson. *The Cry to God in the Old Testament*. SBLDS 103. Atlanta: Scholars Press, 1988.

Braiterman, Zachary. *(God) After Auschwitz*. Princeton, N.J./Chichester, U.K.: Princeton University Press, 1998.

Braulik, Georg. *The Theology of Deuteronomy*. North Richmond Hills, Tex.: BIBAL, 1994.

Brawley, Robert L., ed. *Biblical Ethics and Homosexuality*. Louisville: Westminster John Knox, 1996.

Brenneman, James. E. *Canons in Conflict*. New York/Oxford: Oxford University Press, 1997.

Brenner, Athalya, ed. *A Feminist Companion to Esther, Judith and Susanna*. Sheffield, U.K.: Sheffield Academic Press, 1995.

———. *A Feminist Companion to Exodus to Deuteronomy*. Sheffield, U.K.: Sheffield Academic Press, 1994.

———. *A Feminist Companion to Genesis*. Sheffield, U.K.: Sheffield Academic Press, 1993.

———. *A Feminist Companion to Judges*. Sheffield, U.K.: Sheffield Academic Press, 1993.

———. *A Feminist Companion to the Latter Prophets*. Sheffield, U.K.: Sheffield Academic Press, 1995.

———. *A Feminist Companion to the Song of Songs*. Sheffield, U.K.: Sheffield Academic Press, 1993.

———. *A Feminist Companion to Wisdom Literature*. Sheffield, U.K.: Sheffield Academic Press, 1995.

———. *Judges*. FCB 2/4. Sheffield, U.K.: Sheffield Academic Press, 1999.

———. *Ruth and Esther*. FCB 2/3. Sheffield, U.K.: Sheffield Academic Press, 1999.

Brenner, Athalya, and Carole R. Fontaine, ed. *The Song of Songs*. FCB 2/6. Sheffield, U.K.: Sheffield Academic Press, 2000.

———. *Wisdom and Psalms*. FCB 2/2. Sheffield, U.K.: Sheffield Academic Press, 1998.

Brett, Mark G., ed. *Ethnicity and the Bible*. Leiden/New York: Brill, 1996.

Brichto, Herbert C. *The Problem of "Curse" in the Hebrew Bible*. Rev. ed. Philadelphia: Society of Biblical Literature, 1968.

Brock, Brian. *Singing the Ethos of God*. Grand Rapids/Cambridge: Eerdmans, 2007.

Brongers, H. A. "Fasting in Israel." *OTS* 20 (1977): 1-21.

Brooke, George J., ed. *Jewish Ways of Reading the Bible*. Oxford/New York: Oxford University Press, 2000.

Brown, William P. *The Ethos of the Cosmos: The Genesis of Moral Imagination in the Bible*. Grand Rapids/Cambridge: Eerdmans, 1999.

———, ed. *Character and Scripture*. Grand Rapids/Cambridge: Eerdmans, 2002.

———. *The Ten Commandments*. Louisville/London: Westminster John Knox, 2004.

Brueggemann, Walter. *The Covenanted Self.* Minneapolis: Fortress, 1999.

——. *The Creative Word.* Philadelphia: Fortress, 1982.

——. *Finally Comes the Poet.* Minneapolis: Fortress, 1989.

——. *First and Second Samuel.* Louisville: Westminster John Knox, 1990.

——. *Hope Within History.* Atlanta: Knox, 1987.

——. *Interpretation and Obedience.* Minneapolis: Fortress, 1991.

——. *The Message of the Psalms.* Minneapolis: Augsburg Press, 1984.

——. *Old Testament Theology: Essays on Structure, Theme, and Text.* Minneapolis: Fortress, 1992.

——. *The Prophetic Imagination.* Philadelphia: Fortress, 1978; London: SCM, 1992.

——. *The Psalms and the Life of Faith.* Minneapolis: Fortress, 1995.

——. *A Social Reading of the Old Testament.* Minneapolis: Fortress, 1994.

——. *Theology of the Old Testament.* Minneapolis: Fortress, 1997.

——. *Worship in Ancient Israel.* Nashville: Abingdon, 2005.

Brunner, Emil. *The Divine Imperative.* London: Lutterworth, 1937; Philadelphia: Westminster, 1947.

Buber, Martin. *On the Bible.* New York: Schocken 1982.

——. *The Prophetic Faith.* New York: Harper, 1960.

——. *Two Types of Faith.* London: Routledge, 1951.

Buckley, Susan L. *Teachings on Usury in Judaism, Christianity and Islam.* Lewiston, N.Y.; Lampeter, Wales: Edwin Mellen, 2000.

Bultmann, Christoph. *Der Fremde im antiken Juda.* Göttingen: Vandenhoeck, 1992.

Bunting, Harry. "Ethics and the Perfect Moral Law." Tyndale Bulletin 51 (2000): 235-260.

Burkert, Walter. *Homo Necans.* Berkeley/London: University of California Press, 1983.

Burnett, Joel S., et al., ed. *Diachronic and Synchronic.* LHBOTS 488. New York/London: T & T Clark, 2008.

Burnside, Jonathan P. *The Signs of Sin.* JSOTSup 364. London/New York: Sheffield Academic Press, 2003.

——. "Strange Flesh." *JSOT* 30 (2006): 387-420.

Burridge, Richard A. *Imitating Jesus.* Grand Rapids: Eerdmans, 2007.

Butler, James T. "Impossible Questions and Faithful Responses." Unpublished paper.

Butler, James T., et al., ed. *Understanding the Word.* B. W. Anderson Festschrift. JSOTSup 37. Sheffield, U.K.: JSOT, 1985.

Cahill, Lisa Sowle. "The New Testament and Ethics." *Interpretation* 44 (1990): 383-95.

——. *Theological Bioethics.* Washington, D.C.: Georgetown University Press, 2005.

Caird, George B. *The Gospel of St Luke.* Harmondsworth, U.K./Baltimore, Md.: Penguin, 1963.

Callahan, Allen Dwight, et al., ed. *Slavery in Text and Interpretation.* Semeia 83-84 (1998).

Calvin, John. *Catechism of the Church of Geneva*. Center for Reformed Theology and Apologetics <www.reformed.org/documents/calvin/geneva_catachism/geneva_catachism.html>.

———. *Commentaries on the Four Last Books of Moses*. 4 vols. Grand Rapids: Eerdmans, 1950.

———. *Commentary on the Book of Psalms*. 5 vols. Grand Rapids: Eerdmans, 1948-1949.

———. *Institutes of the Christian Religion*. Philadelphia: Westminster/London: SCM, 1961.

Camp, Claudia V. *Wisdom and the Feminine in the Book of Proverbs*. Sheffield, U.K./Decatur, Ga.: Almond, 1985.

Campbell, Alastair V. *The Gospel of Anger*. London: SPCK, 1986.

Capps, Donald. *Biblical Approaches to Pastoral Counseling*. Philadelphia: Westminster, 1981.

Caputo, John D. *What Would Jesus Deconstruct?* Grand Rapids: Baker, 2007.

Carmichael, Calum M. *The Laws of Deuteronomy*. Ithaca, N.Y.: Cornell University Press, 1974.

———. *The Spirit of Biblical Law*. Athens/London: University of Georgia Press, 1996.

Carroll R., M. Daniel, and Jacqueline E. Lapsley, ed. *Character Ethics and the Old Testament*. Louisville/London: Westminster John Knox, 2007.

Carroll R., M. Daniel, et al., ed. *The Bible in Human Society*. John Rogerson Festschrift. JSOTSup 200. Sheffield, U.K.: Sheffield Academic Press, 1995.

Carter, Charles E., and Carol L. Meyers, ed. *Community, Identity, and Ideology: Social Science Approaches to the Hebrew Bible*. Winona Lake, Ind.: Eisenbrauns, 1996.

Carter, Stephen L. *Integrity*. New York: HarperCollins, 1997.

Chaney, Marvin L. "'You Shall Not Covet Your Neighbor's House.'" *Pacific Theological Review* 15/2 (1982): 3-13.

Charlesworth, James H., ed. *The Old Testament Pseudepigrapha*. 2 vols. Garden City, N.Y.: Doubleday, 1983.

Chase, Kenneth R., and Alan Jacobs, ed. *Must Christianity be Violent?* Grand Rapids: Brazos, 2003.

Chesterton, G. K. *What's Wrong with the World*. London: Cassell; New York: Dodd, Mead, 1910.

Childress, James F. "Scripture and Christian Ethics." *Interpretation* 34 (1980): 371-80.

Childs, Brevard S. *Biblical Theology in Crisis*. Philadelphia: Westminster, 1970.

———. *Biblical Theology of the Old and New Testaments*. London: SCM, 1992; Minneapolis: Fortress, 1993.

———. *Exodus*. London: SCM, 1974. = *The Book of Exodus*. Philadelphia: Westminster, 1974.

———. *Introduction to the Old Testament as Scripture*. Philadelphia: Fortress; London: SCM, 1979.

————. *Old Testament Theology in a Canonical Context*. London: SCM 1985; Philadelphia: Fortress, 1986.

Chirichigno, Gregory. *Debt-Slavery in Israel and the Ancient Near East*. JSOTSup 141. Sheffield, U.K.: Sheffield Academic Press, 1993.

Christiansen, Duane L., ed. *A Song of Power and the Power of Song*. Winona Lake, Ind.: Eisenbrauns, 1993.

Chu, Julie L. C. "Returning Home: The Inspiration of the Role Differentiation in the Book of Ruth for Taiwanese Women." *Semeia* 78 (1997): 47-53.

Clapp, Rodney. *Families at the Crossroads*. Downers Grove, Ill./Leicester, U.K.: InterVarsity Press, 1993.

Clements, R. E., ed. *The World of Ancient Israel*. Cambridge/New York: Cambridge University Press, 1989.

Clifford, Richard J., and John J. Collins, ed. *Creation in the Biblical Traditions*. Washington, D.C.: Catholic Biblical Association of America, 1992.

Clines, David J. A. *Interested Parties*. JSOTSup 205. Sheffield, U.K.: Sheffield Academic Press, 1995.

————. *Job 1–20*. WBC. (Dallas: Word, 1989).

————. *What Does Eve Do to Help?* JSOTSup 94. Sheffield, U.K.: Sheffield Academic Press, 1990.

Clouse, Robert G., ed. *War: Four Christian Views*. Rev. ed. Downers Grove, Ill.: InterVarsity Press, 1991.

Coats, George W., and Burke O. Long, ed. *Canon and Authority*. Philadelphia: Fortress, 1977.

Coggins, Richard J. "The Old Testament and the Poor." *ExpT* 99 (1987-1988): 11-14.

Collins, John J. "The Zeal of Phinehas." *JBL* 122 (2003): 3-21.

Collins, John J., and Robert A. Kugler, ed. *Religion in the Dead Sea Scrolls*. Grand Rapids: Eerdmans, 2000.

Cosgrove, Charles H. *Appealing to Scripture in Moral Debate*. Grand Rapids/Cambridge: Eerdmans, 2002.

Cothey, Antony. "Ethics and Holiness in the Theology of Leviticus." *JSOT* 30 (2005): 131-51.

Countryman, L. William. *Dirt, Greed, and Sex*. Philadelphia: Fortress, 1988.

Cover, Robert M. "*Nomos* and Narrative." *Harvard Law Review* 97/4 (1983): 4-68.

Craigie, Peter C. *The Problem of War in the Old Testament*. Grand Rapids: Eerdmans, 1978.

Crenshaw, James L. *Ecclesiastes*. Philadelphia: Westminster, 1987; London: SCM, 1988.

————. *Prophetic Conflict*. BZAW 124. Berlin/New York: de Gruyter, 1971.

Crenshaw, James L., and John T. Willis, ed. *Essays in Old Testament Ethics*. J. P. Hyatt Memorial. New York: Ktav, 1974.

Crüsemann, Frank. *The Torah*. Minneapolis: Fortress/Edinburgh: T & T Clark, 1996.

Culver, Robert Duncan. *Toward a Biblical View of Civil Government*. Chicago: Moody Press, 1974.

Cushman, Philip. *Constructing the Self, Constructing America*. Cambridge, Mass.: Perseus, 1995.

Dandamaev, Muhammad A. *Slavery in Babylonia*. DeKalb: Northern Illinois University Press, 1984.

Daube, David. *Appeasement or Resistance*. Berkeley/London: UCLA Press, 1987.

———. "Concessions to Sinfulness in Jewish Law." *JJS* 10 (1959): 1-13.

———. "The Culture of Deuteronomy." *Orita* 3 (1969): 27-52.

———. *The Deed and the Doer*. West Conshohocken, Penn.: Templeton Foundation, 2008.

Davidson, Robert. *The Courage to Doubt*. London: SCM, 1983; Philadelphia: Trinity Press International, 1989.

Davies, Eryl W. *Prophecy and Ethics*. JSOTSup 16. Sheffield, U.K.: JSOT, 1981.

———. "The Morally Dubious Passages in the Hebrew Bible." *Currents in Biblical Research* 3 (2005): 197-228.

Davies, G. I. *Hosea*. London: MarshallPickering; Grand Rapids: Eerdmans, 1992.

Davies, W. D. *The Gospel and the Land*. Berkeley/London: University of California, 1974.

———. *The Setting of the Sermon on the Mount*. Atlanta: Scholars Press, 1989.

Davis, Ellen F. *Getting Involved with God*. Cambridge, Mass.: Cowley, 2001.

———. *Scripture, Culture, and Agriculture*. Cambridge/New York: Cambridge University Press, 2008.

Davis, James F. *Lex Talionis in Early Judaism and the Exhortation of Jesus in Matthew 5.38-42*. New York/London: T & T Clark, 2005.

Dawn, Marva J. *Reaching Out without Dumbing Down*. Grand Rapids: Eerdmans, 1995.

Day, John. *Molech*. Cambridge/New York: Cambridge University Press, 1989.

Day, John N. "The Imprecatory Psalms and Christian Ethics." *Bibliotheca Sacra* 159 (2002): 166-86.

Day, Linda, and Carolyn Pressler, ed. *Engaging the Bible in a Gendered World*. K. D. Sakenfeld Festschrift. Louisville/London: Westminster John Knox, 2006.

Dearman, J. Andrew. "The Family in the Old Testament." *Interpretation* 52 (1998): 117-29.

———. *Property Rights in the Eighth-Century Prophets*. SBLDS 106. Atlanta: Society of Biblical Literature, 1988.

Deats, Paul, ed. *Toward a Discipline of Social Ethics*. W. G. Muelder Festschrift. Boston: Boston University Press, 1972.

Deist, Ferdinand E. *The Material Culture of the Bible*. Sheffield, U.K.: Sheffield Academic Press, 2000.

Dempsey, Carol J. *Hope amid the Ruins: The Ethics of Israel's Prophets*. St. Louis: Chalice, 2000.

De Pree, Max. *Leadership Is an Art*. New York: Dell, 1990.

Derrida, Jacques. "Force of Law." In *Deconstruction and the Possibility of Justice*, pp. 3-67. Edited by Drucilla Cornell et al. New York: Routledge, 1992.

———. *On Cosmopolitanism and Forgiveness*. New York/London: Routledge, 1997.

Detienne, Marcel, Jean-Pierre Vernant et al. *The Cuisine of Sacrifice among the Greeks.* Chicago/London: University of Chicago Press, 1989.

De Troyer, Kristin, et al., ed. *Holy Woman Holy Blood.* Harrisburg, Penn./London: Continuum, 2003.

Dever, William G., and Seymour Gitin, ed. *Symbiosis, Symbolism, and the Power of the Past.* Winona Lake, Ind.: Eisenbrauns, 2003.

Domeris, William R. *Touching the Heart of God.* LHBOTS 466. New York/London: T & T Clark, 2007.

Dooyeweerd, Herman. *Roots of Western Culture.* Toronto: Wedge,1979.

Douglas, Mary. *Purity and Danger.* London: Routledge/New York: Praeger, 1966.

———. *Implicit Meanings.* London/Boston: Routledge, 1975.

———. *Leviticus as Literature.* Oxford/New York: Oxford University Press, 1999.

Dozeman, Thomas B. "The Book of Numbers." *The New Interpreter's Bible* 2:1-268. Nashville: Abingdon, 1998.

Driver, S. R. "Propitiation." In *A Dictionary of the Bible* 4:128-32. Edited by James Hastings. Edinburgh: T & T Clark; New York: Scribner's, 1947.

Dube, Musa W. *Postcolonial Feminist Interpretation of the Bible.* St. Louis: Chalice, 2000.

Duhm, Bernhard. *Das Buch Jesaia.* Rev. ed. Göttingen: Vandenhoeck, 1902.

Dulin, Rachel Z. *A Crown of Glory: A Biblical View of Aging.* Mahwah, N.J.: Paulist Press, 1988.

Durnbaugh, Donald F., ed. *On Earth Peace.* Elgin, Ill.: Brethren, 1978.

Durham, John I. *Exodus.* WBC. Waco, Tex.: Word, 1987.

Eaton, J. H. *Obadiah, Nahum, Habakkuk, Zephaniah.* London: SCM, 1961.

Eichrodt, Walther. *Ezekiel.* London: SCM; Philadelphia: Westminster, 1970.

———. *Theology of the Old Testament.* 2 vols. London: SCM; Philadelphia: Westminster, 1961, 1967.

Eilberg-Schwartz, Howard. *God's Phallus.* Boston: Beacon, 1994.

———. *The Savage in Judaism.* Bloomington: Indiana University Press, 1990.

Ellens, Deborah L. *Women in the Sex Texts of Leviticus and Deuteronomy.* LHBOTS 458. London/New York: Continuum, 2008.

Eller, Vernard. *King Jesus' Manual of Arms for the 'Armless.* Nashville: Abingdon, 1973.

Ellington, Scott A. *Risking Truth.* Eugene, Ore.: Pickwick, 2008.

Ellul, Jacques. *The Meaning of the City.* Grand Rapids: Eerdmans, 1970.

———. *The Political Illusion.* New York: Random House, 1972.

———. *Violence.* New York: 1969; repr. Oxford: Mowbray, 1978.

Emerton, J. A. "New Light on Israelite Religion." *ZAW* 94 (1982): 2-20.

Enz, Jacob J. *The Christian and Warfare.* Scottdale, Penn.: Herald Press, 1972.

Epstein, Heidi. *Melting the Venusberg.* New York/London: Continuum, 2004.

Epzstein [for Epsztein], Léon. *Social Justice in the Ancient Near East and the People of the Bible.* London: SCM; Valley Forge, Penn.: Trinity Press International, 1986.

Exum, J. Cheryl. *Fragmented Women.* JSOTSup 163. Sheffield, U.K.: Sheffield Academic Press/Valley Forge, Penn.: Trinity Press International, 1993.

———. *Tragedy and Biblical Narrative*. Cambridge/New York: Cambridge University Press, 1992.

Exum, J. Cheryl, and David J. A. Clines, ed. *The New Literary Criticism and the Hebrew Bible*. JSOTSup 143. Sheffield, U.K.: Sheffield Academic Press, 1993.

Exum, J. Cheryl, and Stephen D. Moore, ed. *Biblical Studies/Cultural Studies*. JSOTSup 266. Sheffield, U.K.: Sheffield Academic Press, 1998.

Exum, J. Cheryl, and H. G. M. Williamson, ed. *Reading From Right to Left*. David J. A. Clines Festschrift. JSOTSup 373. London/New York: Sheffield Academic Press, 2003.

Fager, Jeffrey A. *Land Tenure and the Biblical Jubilee*. JSOTSup 155. Sheffield, U.K.: Sheffield Academic Press, 1993.

Falk, Ze'ev W. *Hebrew Law in Biblical Times*. 2nd ed., Winona Lake, Ind.: Eisenbrauns, 2001.

Faust, Drew Gilpin. *This Republic of Suffering*. New York: Knopf, 2008.

Felder, Cain Hope. *Troubling Biblical Waters*. Maryknoll, N.Y.: Orbis, 1994.

Feldman, Emanuel. *Biblical and Post-Biblical Defilement and Mourning: Law as Theology*. New York: Yeshiva University Press, 1977.

Ferguson, John. *The Politics of Love*. Cambridge: James Clarke, ?1970.

Fewell, Danna Nolan, and David M. Gunn. *Gender, Power, and Promise*. Nashville: Abingdon, 1993.

Finkelstein, Israel, and Amihai Mazar. *The Quest for the Historical Israel*. Atlanta: Society of Biblical Literature, 2007.

Finley, M. I. *Ancient Slavery and Modern Ideology*. New York: Viking, 1980.

Firmage, Edwin. "The Biblical Dietary Laws and the Concept of Holiness." In *Studies in the Pentateuch*, pp. 177-208. Edited by J. A. Emerton. VTSup 41. Leiden/New York: Brill, 1990.

Firmage, Edwin B., et al., ed. *Religion and Law*. Winona Lake, Ind.: Eisenbrauns, 1990.

Fitzpatrick-McKinley, Anne. *The Transformation of Torah from Scribal Advice to Law*. JSOTSup 287. Sheffield, U.K.: Sheffield Academic Press, 1999.

Flusser, David. *Jesus*. 3rd ed., Jerusalem: Magnes, 2001.

Ford, David F. "System, Story, Performance." *Anglican Theological Review* 67 (1985): 232-54. Reprinted in Hauerwas and Jones, *Why Narrative?* pp. 191-215.

Ford, David F., and Daniel W. Hardy. *Jubilate: Theology in Praise*. London: Darton, Longman & Todd, 1984. = *Praising and Knowing God*. Philadelphia: Westminster, 1985. Rev. ed. *Living in Praise*. Grand Rapids: Baker, 2005.

Foster, Robert L., and David M. Howard, ed. *"My Words Are Lovely."* LHBOTS 467. New York/London: T & T Clark, 2008.

Fowl, Stephen E., and L. Gregory Jones. *Reading in Communion*. London: SPCK; Grand Rapids: Eerdmans, 1991.

Fox, Michael V. *Proverbs 1–9*. AB. New York: Doubleday, 2000.

———. *A Time to Tear Down and a Time to Build Up*. Grand Rapids/Cambridge: Eerdmans, 1999.

Freedman, David Noel, et al., ed. *The Anchor Bible Dictionary*. 6 vols. New York: Doubleday, 1992.

Frei, Hans W. *The Eclipse of Biblical Narrative*. New Haven, Conn./London: Yale University Press, 1974.

Fretheim, Terence E. *God and World in the Old Testament*. Nashville: Abingdon, 2005.

———. *Jeremiah*. Macon, Ga.: Smith & Helwys, 2002.

———. *The Suffering of God*. Philadelphia: Fortress, 1984.

Frick, Frank S. *The City in Ancient Israel*. SBLDS 36. Missoula, Mt.: Scholars Press, 1977.

———. *The Formation of the State in Ancient Israel*. Sheffield, U.K./Decatur, Ga.: Almond, 1985.

Friesen, Duane K. "Naming What Happened and How We Respond." *Peace Office Newsletter* 32/2 (2002): 7.

Fritz, Volkmar. *The City in Ancient Israel*. Sheffield, U.K.: Sheffield Academic Press, 1995.

Frydrich, Tomáš. *Living Under the Sun*. VTSup 90. Leiden/Boston: Brill, 2002.

Frymer-Kensky, Tikva. *In the Wake of the Goddesses*. New York: Free Press, 1989.

———. "Law and Philosophy: The Case of Sex in the Bible," *Semeia* 45 (1989): 89-102.

———. "Tit for Tat." *Biblical Archaeologist* 43 (1980): 230-34.

Fuchs, Esther. *Sexual Politics in the Biblical Narrative*. JSOTSup 310. Sheffield, U.K.: Sheffield Academic Press, 2000.

Fuller, Daniel P. *Gospel and Law*. Grand Rapids: Eerdmans, 1980.

Gagnon, Robert A. J. *The Bible and Homosexual Practice*. Nashville: Abingdon, 2001.

Gaiser, Frederick J. "A New Word on Homosexuality?" *Word and World* 14 (1994): 280-93.

Gammie, John G. *Holiness in Israel*. Minneapolis: Fortress, 1989.

Gane, Roy. *Cult and Character*. Winona Lake, Ind.: Eisenbrauns, 2005.

Garland, David E., and Diana R. *Flawed Families in he Bible*. Grand Rapids: Brazos, 2007.

Gelb, I. J. "Definition and Discussion of Slavery and Serfdom." *UF* 11 (1979): 283-97.

Geoghegan, Jeffrey C. " 'Until This Day' and the Preexilic Redaction of the Deuteronomistic History." *JBL* 122 (2003): 201-27.

George, A. R., and I. L. Finkel, eds. *Wisdom, Gods and Literature*. W. G. Lambert Festschrift. Winona Lake, Ind.: Eisenbrauns, 2000.

Gerstenberger, Erhard S. *Der bittende Mensch*. Neukirchen: Neukirchener, 1980.

———. *Theologies in the Old Testament*. Edinburgh: T & T Clark; Minneapolis: Fortress, 2002.

———. *Yahweh the Patriarch*. Minneapolis: Fortress, 1996.

Gerstenberger, Erhard S. and Wolfgang Schrage. *Suffering*. Nashville: Abingdon, 1980.

———. *Woman and Man*. Nashville: Abingdon, 1981.

Gillingham, Sue. "The Poor in the Psalms." *ExpT* 100 (1988-89): 15-19.

Girard, René. *Violence and the Sacred*. Baltimore/London: Johns Hopkins, 1989.

Gnuse, Robert. "Jubilee Legislation in Leviticus." *Biblical Theology Bulletin* 15 (1985): 43-48.

———. *You Shall Not Steal*. Maryknoll, N.Y.: Orbis, 1985.

Goldberg, Michael. "The Story of the Moral." *Interpretation* 38 (1984): 15-25.

Goldingay, John. *Approaches to Old Testament Interpretation*. Rev. ed. Leicester, U.K./Downers Grove, Ill.: Inter-Varsity Press, 1990; reprinted Toronto: Clements, 2002.

———. *Daniel*. WBC. Dallas: Word, 1989.

———. "The Dynamic Cycle of Praise and Prayer in the Psalms." *JSOT* 20 (1981): 85-90.

———. "Images of Israel: The People of God in the Writings." In *Studies in Old Testament Theology*. David Hubbard Festschrift. pp. 205-21. Edited by Robert L. Hubbard et al. Dallas: Word, 1992.

———. *Isaiah*. Peabody, Mass.: Hendrickson/Carlisle, U.K.: Paternoster, 2001.

———. "Isaiah i l; ii 1." *VT* 48 (1998): 326–32.

———. "Jubilee Tithe." *Transformation* 19 (2002): 198-205.

———. *Old Testament Theology*. Volume 1: *Israel's Gospel*. Downers Grove, Ill.: Inter-Varsity Press, 2003; Carlisle, U.K.: Paternoster, 2006.

———. *Old Testament Theology*. Volume 2: *Israel's Faith*. Downers Grove, Ill.: Inter-Varsity Press; Carlisle, U.K.: Paternoster, 2006.

———. *The Message of Isaiah 40–55*. New York/London: T & T Clark, 2005.

———. *Models for Interpretation of Scripture*. Grand Rapids: Eerdmans; Carlisle, U.K.: Paternoster, 1995.

———. *Prophecy Today*. Cambridge: Grove, 2003.

———. *God's Prophet, God's Servant*. Rev. ed. Toronto: Clements, 2002.

———. *Psalms*. 3 vols. Grand Rapids: Baker, 2006, 2007, 2008.

———. *Theological Diversity and the Authority of the Old Testament*. Grand Rapids: Eerdmans, 1987; Carlisle, U.K.: Paternoster, 1995.

Goldingay, John, and David Payne. *Isaiah 40–55*. International Critical Commentary. New York/London: T & T Clark, 2006.

Gorman, Frank H. *The Ideology of Ritual*. JSOTSup 91. Sheffield, U.K.: Sheffield Academic Press, 1990.

Gorospe, Athena E. *Narrative and Identity*. Leiden/Boston: Brill, 2007.

Gorringe, Tim. *A Theology of the Built Environment*. Cambridge/New York: Cambridge University Press, 2002.

Gosse, Bernard. "Sabbath, Identity and Universalism Go Together After the Return from Exile." *JSOT* 29 (2005): 359-70.

Gottwald, Norman K. *The Hebrew Bible in Its Social World and in Ours*. Atlanta: Scholars Press, 1993.

———. *The Politics of Ancient Israel*. Louisville: Westminster John Knox, 2001.

———. "Recent Studies of the Social World of Premonarchic Israel." *Currents In Research: Biblical Studies* 1 (1993) 163-89.

———. *The Tribes of Yahweh*. Maryknoll, N.Y.: Orbis, 1979; London: SCM, 1980.

————, ed. *The Bible and Liberation*. Maryknoll, N.Y.: Orbis, 1983.

Gottwald, Norman K, and Richard A. Horsley, ed. *The Bible and Liberation*. Rev. ed. Maryknoll, N.Y.: Orbis; London: SPCK, 1993.

Goudzwaard, Bob. *Capitalism and Progress*. Grand Rapids: Eerdmans, 1979.

Gowan, Donald E. "Wealth and Poverty in the Old Testament." *Interpretation* 41 (1987): 341-53.

Grabbe, Lester L. *Leviticus*. Sheffield, U.K.: Sheffield Academic Press, 1993.

————. *Priests, Prophets, Diviners, Sages*. Valley Forge, Penn.: Trinity Press International, 1995.

————, ed. *Israel in Transition*. LHBOTS 491. New York/London: T & T Clark, 2008.

Grabbe, Lester L., and Robert D. Haak, ed. *"Every City Shall Be Forsaken."* JSOTSup 330. Sheffield, U.K.: Sheffield Academic Press, 2001.

Gray, George Buchanan. *Sacrifice in the Old Testament*. Oxford: Clarendon Press, 1925.

Green, Arthur, ed. *Jewish Spirituality*. 2 vols. New York: Crossroad, 1986-1987; London: Routledge, 1986-1988.

Greenberg, Moshe. *Biblical Prose Prayer*. Berkeley/London: University of California Press, 1983.

————. *Ezekiel 1—20*. AB. Garden City, N.Y.: Doubleday, 1983.

————. *Studies in the Bible and Jewish Thought*. Philadelphia: Jewish Publication Society, 1995.

Grimsrud, Ted, and Loren L. Johns, ed. *Peace and Justice Shall Embrace*. Millard Lind Festschrift. Telford, Penn.: Pandora, 1999.

Groves, Philip, ed. *The Anglican Communion and Homosexuality*. London: SPCK, 2008.

Guenther, Allen. "A Typology of Israelite Marriage." *JSOT* 28 (2005): 387-407.

Gunneweg, Antonius H. J., and Walter Schmithals. *Achievement*. Nashville: Abingdon, 1981.

————. *Authority*. Nashville: Abingdon, 1982.

Gunton, Colin E., ed. *The Cambridge Companion to Christian Doctrine*. Cambridge/New York: Cambridge University Press, 1997.

Gushee, David P., ed. *Toward a Just and Caring Society*. Grand Rapids: Baker, 1999.

Gustafson, James M. "The Place of Scripture in Christian Ethics." *Interpretation* 24 (1970): 430-55.

————. "Varieties of Moral Discourse." In *Seeking Understanding: The Stob Lectures, 1986–1998*, pp. 43-76. Grand Rapids/Cambridge: Eerdmans, 2001.

Gutiérrez, Gustavo. *A Theology of Liberation*. Maryknoll, N.Y.: Orbis, 1973; London: SCM, 1974.

Gutman, Joseph. "The 'Second Commandment' and the Image in Judaism." *HUCA* 32 (1961): 161-74.

Haan, Roelf. *The Economics of Honour*. Geneva: World Council of Churches, 1988.

Haas, Peter J. "'Die He Shall Surely Die.'" *Semeia* 45 (1989): 67-87.

Habel, Norman C. *The Land is Mine*. Minneapolis: Fortress, 1995.

————, ed. *Readings from the Perspective of Earth*. Sheffield, U.K.: Sheffield Academic Press; Cleveland: Pilgrim, 2000.

————. *The Earth Story in the Psalms and Prophets*. Sheffield, U.K.: Sheffield Academic Press; Cleveland: Pilgrim, 2001.

Habel, Norman C., and Shirley Wurst, ed. *The Earth Story in Genesis*. Sheffield, U.K.: Sheffield Academic Press/Cleveland: Pilgrim, 2001.

————. *The Earth Story in the Psalms and Prophets*. Sheffield, U.K.: Sheffield Academic Press; Cleveland: Pilgrim, 2001.

Hagedorn, Anselm C. "Guarding the Parents' Honour." *JSOT* 88 (2000): 101-21.

Halbe, Jörn. "Erwägungen zu Ursprung und Wesen des Massotfestes." *ZAW* 87 (1975): 324-46.

————. "Passa-Massot im deuteronomischen Festkalender." *ZAW* 87 (1975): 147-68.

Hallesby, Otto. *Prayer*. London: Inter-Varsity Fellowship, 1959.

Halpern, Baruch, and Deborah W. Hobson, ed. *Law and Ideology in Monarchic Israel*. JSOTSup 124. Sheffield, U.K.: Sheffield Academic Press, 1991.

Hamilton, Jeffries M. *Social Justice and Deuteronomy*. SBLDS 136. Atlanta: Scholars Press, 1992.

Hamilton, Mark. "Job 29–31 and Traditional Authority." *JSOT* 32 (2007): 69-89.

Hanson, Paul D. *The People Called*. New York: Harper, 1986.

Haran, Menahem. *Temples and Temple-Service in Ancient Israel*. Winona Lake, Ind.: Eisenbrauns, 1985.

Harrelson, Walter. *From Fertility Cult to Worship*. Garden City, N.Y.: Doubleday, 1970.

————. *The Ten Commandments and Human Rights*. Philadelphia: Fortress, 1980.

Harris, J. Gordon. *Biblical Perspectives on Aging*. Philadelphia: Fortress, 1987.

Hartley, John E. *Leviticus*. WBC. Dallas: Word, 1992.

Harvey, A. E. "Genesis versus Deuteronomy." In *The Gospels and the Scriptures of Israel*, pp. 55-65. Edited by Craig A. Evans and W. Richard Stegner. Sheffield, U.K.: Sheffield Academic Press, 1994.

Hauerwas, Stanley. *Against the Nations*. Minneapolis: Winston, 1985.

————. *A Better Hope*. Grand Rapids: Brazos, 2000.

————. *A Community of Character*. Notre Dame, Ind./London: University of Notre Dame Press, 1981.

————. *In Good Company*. Notre Dame, Ind./London: University of Notre Dame Press, 1997.

————. "The Moral Authority of Scripture." *Interpretation* 34 (1980): 356-70.

————. *Naming the Silences*. Grand Rapids: Eerdmans, 1990; Edinburgh: T & T Clark, 1993.

————. *Suffering Presence*. Notre Dame, Ind.: University of Notre Dame Press, 1986; Edinburgh: T & T Clark, 1988.

————. *Vision and Virtue*. Notre Dame, Ind.: Fides, 1974.

Hauerwas, Stanley, and L. Gregory Jones, ed. *Why Narrative?* Grand Rapids: Eerdmans, 1989.

Hauerwas, Stanley, and Samuel Wells, ed. *The Blackwell Companion to Christian*

Ethics. Oxford/Malden, Mass.: Blackwell, 2004.

Hauerwas, Stanley, with Richard Bondi and David B. Burrell. *Truthfulness and Tragedy*. Notre Dame, Ind.: University of Notre Dame Press, 1977.

Hays, Richard B. *Echoes of Scripture in the Letters of Paul*. New Haven, Conn./London: Yale University Press, 1989.

———. "Scripture-shaped Community." *Interpretation* 44 (1990): 42-55.

Hayter, Mary. *The New Eve in Christ*. London: SPCK, 1987.

The Heidelberg Catechism. Center for Reformed Theology and Apologetics <www .reformed.org/documents/index.html?mainframe=http://www.reformed. org/documents/heidelberg.html>.

Heider, George C. *The Cult of Molek*. JSOTSup 43. Sheffield, U.K.: JSOT, 1985.

Henderson, Joseph M. "Who Weeps in Jeremiah viii 23 [ix 1]?" *VT* 52 (2002): 191-206.

Herman, Judith L. *Trauma and Recovery*. New York: Basic, 1997.

Hertz, J. H. *The Pentateuch and Haftorahs: Leviticus*. London/New York: Oxford University Press, 1951.

Heschel, Abraham Joshua. *God in Search of Man*. New York: Farrar, Straus & Giroux, 1976.

———. *The Insecurity of Freedom*. New York: Farrar, Straus & Giroux, 1967.

———. *Moral Grandeur and Spiritual Audacity*. New York: Farrar, Straus & Giroux, 1996.

———. *The Prophets*. New York: HarperCollins, 2001.

———. *The Sabbath*. New York: Farrar, Straus & Giroux, 1984.

Hess, Richard S., and Elmer A. Martens, ed. *War in the Bible and Terrorism in the Twenty-First Century*. Winona Lake, Ind.: Eisenbrauns, 2008.

Hess, Richard S., and M. Daniel Carroll R., ed. *Family in the Bible*. Grand Rapids: Baker, 2003.

Hill, Andrew E. *Malachi*. AB. New York: Doubleday, 1998.

Hill, E. *Prayer, Praise and Politics*. London: Sheed & Ward, 1973.

Hobbs, T. R. *A Time for War*. Wilmington: Glazier, 1989.

Hoffman, Lawrence A. *Covenant of Blood*. Chicago/London: University of Chicago Press, 1996.

Holladay, William L. *Jeremiah*. 2 vols. Philadelphia: Fortress, 1986; Minneapolis: Fortress, 1989.

Hopfe, Lewis M., ed. *Uncovering Ancient Stones*. H. N. Richardson Festschrift. Winona Lake, Ind.: Eisenbrauns, 1994.

Hopkins, David C. *The Highlands of Canaan*. Sheffield, U.K./Decatur, Ga.: Almond, 1985.

Hoppe, Leslie J. *There Shall Be No Poor Among You*. Nashville: Abingdon, 2004.

Horsley, Richard A. "Ethics and Exegesis: 'Love Your Enemies' and the Doctrine of Non-Violence." *Journal of the American Academy of Religion* 54 (1986): 3-31.

———. "Paul and Slavery." *Semeia* 83-84 (1998): 153-200.

———. "The Slave Systems of Classical Antiquity and Their Reluctant Recognition by Modern Scholars." *Semeia* 83-84 (1998): 19-66.

Houston, Walter J. "The King's Preferential Option for the Poor." *BibInt* 7 (1999): 341-67.

———. *Purity and Monotheism.* JSOTSup 140. Sheffield, U.K.: Sheffield Academic Press, 1993.

———. *Contending for Justice.* LHBOTS 428. New York/London: T & T Clark, 2006.

Houtman, C. "Another Look at Forbidden Mixtures." *VT* 34 (1984): 226-28.

Hugenberger, Gordon Paul. *Marriage as a Covenant.* VTSup 52. Leiden/New York: Brill, 1994.

Humphreys, W. Lee. *The Tragic Vision and the Hebrew Tradition.* Philadelphia: Fortress, 1985.

Hunter, Alastair G., and Philip R. Davies, ed. *Sense and Sensitivity.* Robert Carroll Memorial. JSOTSup 348. London/New York: Sheffield Academic Press, 2002.

Hunter, David G. "A Decade of Research on Early Christians and Military Service." *Religious Studies Review* 18 (1992): 87-94.

Hutton, Rodney R. *Charisma and Authority in Israelite Society.* Minneapolis: Fortress, 1994.

Hyatt, J. Philip. *Commentary on Exodus.* London: Oliphants, 1971. = *Exodus.* Grand Rapids: Eerdmans, 1980.

Instone-Brewer, David. *Divorce and Remarriage in the Bible.* Grand Rapids/Cambridge: Eerdmans, 2002.

Jackson, Bernard S. "The Ceremonial and the Judicial." *JSOT* 30 (1984): 25-50.

———. *Essays in Jewish and Comparative Legal History.* Leiden: Brill, 1975.

———. *Wisdom-Laws.* Oxford/New York: Oxford University Press, 2006.

Jacobs, Alan. *Looking Before and After.* Grand Rapids/Cambridge: Eerdmans, 2008.

Jacobson, Rolf. "The Costly Loss of Praise." *Theology Today* 57 (2000): 1-9.

Jacoby, Susan. *Wild Justice.* New York: Harper, 1983.

Jagersma, H. "The Tithes in the Old Testament." *OTS* 21 (1981): 116-28.

Janowsky, Oscar I., ed. *The American Jew.* New York: Harper, 1942.

Janzen, David. *The Social Meanings of Sacrifice in the Hebrew Bible.* BZAW 344. Berlin/New York: de Gruyter, 2004.

Janzen, Waldemar. *Old Testament Ethics.* Louisville: Westminster John Knox, 1994.

Japhet, Sara. *From the Rivers of Babylon to the Highlands of Judah.* Winona Lake, Ind.: Eisenbrauns, 2006.

Jay, Nancy. *Throughout Your Generations Forever.* Chicago/London: University of Chicago Press, 1992.

Jenson, Philip P. *Graded Holiness.* JSOTSup 106. Sheffield, U.K.: Sheffield Academic Press, 1992.

Jeremias, Jörg. *The Book of Amos.* Louisville: Westminster John Knox, 1998.

Jerome [Eusebius Hieronymus]. *Commentariorum in Ezechielem prophetam libri quatuordecim.* Patrologia latina 25 (1845).

Jobling, David, et al., ed. *The Bible and the Politics of Exegesis.* N. K. Gottwald Festschrift. Cleveland: Pilgrim, 1991.

John Paul II. *Veritatis splendor.* The Vatican <www.vatican.va/edocs/ENG0222/_INDEX.HTM>.

Jones, L. Gregory. "Secret of Nyamirambo." *The Christian Century* 122/25 (2005): 45.

Johnson, Luke T. *Decision Making in the Church.* Philadelphia: Fortress, 1983.

―――. *Sharing Possessions.* Philadelphia: Fortress, 1981; London: SCM, 1986.

Jones, Serene. " 'Soul Anatomy': Calvin's Commentary on the Psalms." In *Psalms in Community*, pp. 265-84. Edited by Harold W. Attridge and Margot E. Fassler. Atlanta: Society of Biblical Literature, 2003.

Joosten, Jan. *People and Land in the Holiness Code.* VTSup 67. Leiden/New York: Brill, 1996.

Joyce, Paul. "Lamentations and the Grief Process." *BibInt* 1 (1993): 304-20.

Kaiser, Walter C. *Toward Old Testament Ethics.* Grand Rapids: Zondervan, 1983.

Kalimi, Isaac, and Peter J. Haas. *Biblical Interpretation in Judaism and Christianity.* LHBOTS 439. New York/London: T & T Clark, 2007.

Kanyoro, Musimbi R. A. "Biblical Hermeneutics." *RevExp* 94 (1996-1997): 363-78.

Kaufmann, Yehezkel. *The Religion of Israel.* Chicago: University of Chicago Press, 1960; London: George Allen, 1961.

Kazen, Thomas. *Jesus and Purity Halakhah.* Stockholm: Almqvist & Wiksell, 2002.

Keel, Othmar. *The Symbolism of the Biblical World.* New York: Seabury Press, 1978.

Kidner, Derek. *Genesis.* London: Tyndale Press/Downers Grove, Ill.: Inter-Varsity Press, 1967.

―――. *Psalms.* 2 vols. London/Downers Grove, Ill.: Inter-Varsity Press, 1973-1975.

Kim, Wonil, et al., ed. *Reading the Bible for a New Millennium.* 2 vols. Harrisburg, Penn.: Trinity Press International, 2000.

Kinsler, Ross, and Gloria Kinsler. *The Biblical Jubilee and the Struggle for Life.* Maryknoll, N.Y.: Orbis, 1999.

―――, ed. *God's Economy.* Maryknoll, N.Y.: Orbis, 2005.

Kirkpatrick, A. F. *The Book of Psalms.* Cambridge: Cambridge University Press, 1910.

Kiuchi, N. *The Purification offering in the Priestly Literature.* JSOTSup 56. Sheffield, U.K.: JSOT, 1987.

Klassen, William. *Love of Enemies.* Philadelphia: Fortress, 1984.

Klawans, Jonathan. *Impurity and Sin in Ancient Judaism.* New York: Oxford University Press, 2000.

―――. "The Impurity of Immorality in Ancient Judaism." *JJS* 48 (1997): 1-16.

Kleinig, John W. *The LORD's Song.* JSOTSup 156. Sheffield, U.K.: JSOT, 1993.

Klingbeil, Gerald A. *Bridging the Gap.* Winona Lake, Ind.: Eisenbrauns, 2007.

Klopfenstein, Martin A. *Die Lüge nach dem Alten Testament.* Zürich: Gotthelf, 1964.

Knierim, Rolf P. *The Task of Old Testament Theology.* Grand Rapids/Cambridge: Eerdmans, 1995.

Knight, Douglas A., ed. *Ethics and Politics in the Hebrew Bible. Semeia* 66 (1994).

Knohl, Israel. *The Divine Symphony: The Bible's Many Voices.* Philadelphia: Jewish Publication Society, 2003.

———. *The Sanctuary of Silence.* Minneapolis: Fortress, 1995.

Köhler, Ludwig. *Old Testament Theology.* Philadelphia: Westminster/London: Lutterworth, 1957.

Kratz, Reinhold G. "Die Gnade des tägliche Brots." *Zeitschrift für Theologie und Kirche* 89 (1992): 1-40.

Kraus, Hans-Joachim. *Psalms 1—59.* Minneapolis: Augsburg Press, 1988.

———. *Psalms 60—150.* Minneapolis: Augsburg Press, 1989

———. *Worship in Israel.* Oxford: Blackwell; Richmond: Knox, 1966.

Kuyper, Abraham. *Lectures on Calvinism.* Grand Rapids: Eerdmans, 1961.

LaCoque, André, and Paul Ricoeur. *Thinking Biblically.* Chicago/London: University of Chicago Press, 1998.

Lande, D. A. *I Was with Patton.* St. Paul: MBI, 2002.

Landy, Francis. "Do We Want Our Children to Read This Book?" *Semeia* 77 (1997): 157-76.

Lang, Bernhard. "The Social Organization of Peasant Poverty in Biblical Israel." *JSOT* 24 (1982): 47-63.

Lapsley, Jacqueline E. *Whispering the Word.* Louisville: Westminster John Knox, 2005.

Lash, Nicholas. "Ideology, Metaphor, and Analogy." In *Theology on the Way to Emmaus,* pp. 95-119. London: SCM, 1986. Reprinted in Hauerwas and Jones (ed.), *Why Narrative?* pp. 113-37.

Leaman, Oliver. *Evil and Suffering in Jewish Philosophy.* Cambridge/New York: Cambridge University Press, 1995.

Lehmann, Paul. "The Commandments and the Common Life." *Interpretation* 34 (1980): 341-55.

Lemche, Niels Peter. *The Canaanites and Their Land.* JSOTSup 110. Sheffield, U.K.: Sheffield Academic Press, 1991.

———. *Early Israel.* VTSup 37. Leiden: Brill, 1985.

Lerner, Gerda. *The Creation of Patriarchy.* New York/Oxford: Oxford University Press, 1986.

Levenson, Jon D. *Creation and the Persistence of Evil.* Princeton, N.J./Chichester, U.K.: Princeton University Press, 1994.

———. *The Death and Resurrection of the Beloved Son.* New Haven, Conn./London: Yale University Press, 1993.

———. *Resurrection and the Restoration of Israel.* New Haven, Conn./London: Yale University Press, 2006.

———. *Sinai and Zion.* Minneapolis: Winston, 1985.

———. "The Theologies of Commandment in Biblical Israel." *HTR* 73 (1980): 17-33.

Levine, Baruch A. *Leviticus.* JPS Torah Commentary. Philadelphia: Jewish Publication Society, 1989.

———. *Numbers 1–20.* AB. New York: Doubleday, 1993.

———. *Numbers 21–36*. AB. New York: Doubleday, 2000.

Levinson, Bernard M. *Deuteronomy and the Hermeneutics of Legal Innovation*. New York/Oxford: Oxford University Press, 1997.

———, ed. *Theory and Method in Biblical and Cuneiform Law*. JSOTSup 181. Sheffield, U.K.: Sheffield Academic Press, 1994.

Lewis, I. M. *Ecstatic Religion*. Harmondsworth, U.K./Baltimore, Md.: Penguin, 1971.

Li, Yiyun. "A Man Like Him." *New Yorker*. May 12, 2008, pp. 104-11.

Lightner, Robert P. "Theological Perspectives on Theonomy." *Bibliotheca Sacra* 143 (1986): 26-36, 134-45, 228-45.

Linafelt, Tod, ed. *Strange Fire*. Sheffield, U.K.: Sheffield Academic Press; New York: New York University Press, 2000.

Linafelt, Tod, and Timothy K. Beal, ed. *God in the Fray*. Walter Brueggemann Festschrift. Minneapolis: Fortress, 1998.

Lind, Millard C. "The Concept of Political Power in Ancient Israel." *ASTI* 7 (1970): 4-24.

———. *Yahweh Is a Warrior*. Scottdale, Penn.: Herald, 1980.

Lingenfelter, Judith. "Why Do We Argue About How to Help the Poor?" *Missiology* 26 (1998): 155-66.

Lohfink, Norbert. *Great Themes from the Old Testament*. Chicago: Franciscan, 1981; Edinburgh: T & T Clark, 1982.

———. *Option for the Poor*. Berkeley: BIBAL, 1987.

———. "Poverty in the Laws of the Ancient Near East and of the Bible." *Theological Studies* 52 (1991) 34-50.

Longenecker, Richard N. *New Testament Social Ethics for Today*. Grand Rapids: Eerdmans, 1984.

Lowery, Richard. *Sabbath and Jubilee*. St. Louis: Chalice, 2000.

Luther, Martin. "How Christians Should Regard Moses." In *Word and Sacrament* I, pp. 161-74. Luther's Works 35. Philadelphia: Muhlenburg, 1960.

———. *The Large Catechism*. The Book of Concord <www.bookofconcord.org/largecatechism.html>.

———. *Selected Psalms*. 3 vols. Luther's Works 12-14. St. Louis: Concordia, 1955, 1958, 1958.

MacIntyre, Alasdair. *After Virtue*. 2nd ed. Notre Dame, Ind.: University of Notre Dame Press, 1984.

Madigan, Kevin J., and Jon D. Levenson. *Resurrection*. New Haven, Conn./London: Yale University Press, 2008.

Magonet, Jonathan. *Bible Lives*. London: SCM, 1992.

Malina, Bruce J. *The New Testament World*. Rev. ed. Louisville: Westminster John Knox, 1993.

Marshall, Christopher D. *Beyond Retribution*. Grand Rapids/Cambridge: Eerdmans, 2001.

Marsman, Hennie J. *Women in Ugarit and Israel*. OTS 49. Leiden/Boston: Brill, 2003.

Matlock, Michael D. "Obeying the First Part of the Tenth Commandment." *JSOT* 31 (2007): 295-310.

Matthews, Victor H., and Don C. Benjamin, *Social World of Ancient Israel 1250–587 BCE*. Peabody, Mass.: Hendrickson, 1993.

Matthews, Victor H., et al., ed. *Gender and Law in the Hebrew Bible and the Ancient Near East*. JSOTSup 262. Sheffield, U.K.: Sheffield Academic Press, 1998.

Mayes, A. D. H. *Deuteronomy*. London: Oliphants, 1979.

Mays, James L. *Preaching and Teaching the Psalms*. Louisville: Westminster John Knox, 2006.

Mbuwayesango, Dora R. "Childlessness and Woman-to-Woman Relationships in an African Patriarchal Society." *Semeia* 78 (1997): 27-36.

McBride, S. Dean. "Polity of the Covenant People." *Interpretation* 41 (1987): 229-44.

McCann, J. Clinton. "The Book of Psalms." *The New Interpreter's Bible* 4:639-1280. Nashville: Abingdon, 1996.

McClendon, James W. *Systematic Theology*. 3 vols. Nashville: Abingdon, 1986 (2nd ed., 2002), 1994, 2000.

McClenney-Sadler, Madeline Gay. *Recovering the Daughter's Nakedness*. LHBOTS 476. New York/London: T & T Clark, 2007.

McCloskey, Deirdre N. *The Bourgeois Virtues*. Chicago/London: University of Chicago Press, 2006.

McConville, J. G. *Deuteronomy*. Leicester, U.K./Downers Grove, Ill.: Inter-Varsity Press, 2002.

———. *God and Earthly Power*. LHBOTS 454. New York/London: T & T Clark, 2006.

———. *Law and Theology in Deuteronomy*. JSOTSup 33. Sheffield, U.K.: JSOT, 1984.

McConville, J. G., and J. G. Millar. *Time and Place in Deuteronomy*. JSOTSup 179. Sheffield, U.K.: Sheffield Academic Press, 1994.

McConville, J. G., and Karl Möller, ed. *Reading the Law*. J. G. Wenham Festschrift. LHBOTS 461. New York/London: T & T Clark, 2007.

McKane, William. *Prophets and Wise Men*. London: SCM; Naperville, Ill.: Allenson, 1965.

McKeating, Henry. "The Central Issue of the Book of Job." *ExpT* 82 (1970-71): 244-47.

———. "Sanctions against Adultery in Ancient Israelite Society." JSOT 11 (1979): 57-72.

McKibben, Bill. *The Comforting Whirlwind*. Grand Rapids: Eerdmans, 1994.

McNutt, Paula M. *Reconstructing the Society of Ancient Israel*. Louisville: Westminster John Knox/London: SPCK, 1999.

Meeks, M. Douglas. *God the Economist*. Minneapolis: Fortress, 1989.

Merling, David. *The Book of Joshua*. Berrien Springs, Mich.: Andrews University Press, 1997.

Mettinger, Tryggve N. D. *King and Messiah*. Lund: Gleerup, 1976.

Metz, Johann Baptist, and Karl Rahner. *The Courage to Pray*. London: Burns & Oates, 1980.

Meyers, Carol L. *Discovering Eve*. New York/Oxford: Oxford University Press, 1988.

Meyers, Carol L., and M. O'Connor, ed. *The Word of the Lord Shall Go Forth*. D. N. Freedman Festschrift. Winona Lake, Ind.: Eisenbrauns, 1983.

Middlemas, Jill. *The Troubles of Templeless Judah*. Oxford/New York: Oxford University Press, 2005.

The Midrash on Psalms. 2 vols. New Haven, Conn.: Yale University Press, 1959.

Milazzo, G. Tom. *The Protest and the Silence*. Minneapolis: Fortress, 1992.

Milbank, John. *Theology and Social Theory*. Oxford: Blackwell, 1990; Cambridge, Mass.: Blackwell, 1991.

Miles, Jack. *God: A Biography*. New York/London: Simon & Schuster, 1995.

Milgrom, Jacob. "The Biblical Diet Laws as an Ethical System." *Interpretation* 17 (1963): 288-301.

———. *Cult and Conscience*. Leiden: Brill, 1976.

———. *Leviticus*. Minneapolis: Fortress, 2004.

———. *Leviticus 1–16*. AB. New York: Doubleday, 1991.

———. *Leviticus 17–22*. AB. New York: Doubleday, 2000.

———. *Leviticus 23–27*. AB. New York: Doubleday, 2001.

———. *Numbers*. JPS Torah Commentary. Philadelphia: Jewish Publication Society, 1989.

Millar, J. Gary. *Now Choose Life*. Leicester, U.K.: Inter-Varsity Press, 1998; Grand Rapids: Eerdmans, 1999.

Millard, A. R., and D. J. Wiseman, ed. *Essays on the Patriarchal Narratives*. Leices-ter, U.K.: Inter-Varsity Press, 1980; Winona Lake, Ind.: Eisenbrauns, 1983.

Miller, David, and Michael Walzer, ed. *Pluralism, Justice, and Equality*. Oxford/New York: Oxford University Press, 1995.

Miller, John W. *Biblical Faith and Fathering*. Mahwah, N.J.: Paulist Press, 1989.

Miller, Patrick D. *Deuteronomy*. Louisville: John Knox, 1990.

———. *Israelite Religion and Biblical Theology*. JSOTSup 267. Sheffield, U.K.: Sheffield Academic Press, 2000.

———. "Power, Justice, and Peace: An Exegesis of Psalm 72." *Faith and Mission* 4/1 (1986): 65-70.

———. *The Religion of Ancient Israel*. Louisville: Westminster John Knox; London: SPCK, 2000.

———. *The Way of the Lord*. Grand Rapids/Cambridge: Eerdmans, 2007.

———. *They Cried to the Lord*. Minneapolis: Fortress, 1994.

Miller, Patrick D., et al., ed. *Ancient Israelite Religion*. F. M. Cross Festschrift. Philadelphia: Fortress, 1987.

Miller, William Ian. *Eye for an Eye*. Cambridge/New York: Cambridge University Press, 2006.

Mills, Mary E. *Biblical Morality*. Aldershot, U.K./Burlington, Vt.: Ashgate, 2001.

Mills, Paul. "The Divine Economy." *Cambridge Papers* 9 (2000). <www.jubilee-centre.org/document.php?id=30&topicID=0>.

Miranda, José Porfirio. *Marx and the Bible*. Maryknoll, N.Y.: Orbis, 1974; London: SCM, 1977.

Miskotte, Kornelis H. *When the Gods Are Silent*. London: Collins/New York: Harper, 1967.

Mitchell, Christopher Wright. *The Meaning of* brk *"to Bless" in the Old Testament*. SBLDS 95. Atlanta: Scholars Press, 1987.

Moberly, R. W. L. *Prophecy and Discernment*. Cambridge/New York: Cambridge University Press, 2006.

Moltmann, Jürgen. *God in Creation*. London: SCM; San Francisco: Harper, 1985.

———. *The Spirit of Life*. London: SCM; Minneapolis: Fortress, 1992.

———. *Theology of Hope*. London: SCM; New York: Harper, 1967.

———. *The Trinity and the Kingdom of God*. London: SCM, 1981. = *The Trinity and the Kingdom*. San Francisco: Harper, 1981.

Moran, William L. "The Ancient Near Eastern Background of the Love of God in Deuteronomy." *Catholic Biblical Quarterly* 25 (1963): 77-87.

Morrow, William S. *Protest against God*. Sheffield, U.K.: Sheffield Phoenix, 2006.

Mosala, Itumeleng J. *Biblical Hermeneutics and Black Theology in South Africa*. Grand Rapids: Eerdmans, 1989.

Mowinckel, Sigmund. *He That Cometh*. Nashville: Abingdon; Oxford: Blackwell, 1956.

———. *Psalmenstudien*. 2 vols. Amsterdam: Schippers, 1961.

———. *The Psalms in Israel's Worship*. 2 vols. Oxford: Blackwell, 1962.

Muffs, Yochanan. *The Personhood of God*. Woodstock, Vt.: Jewish Lights, 2005.

Muggeridge, Malcolm. *Something Beautiful for God*. London: Collins/Fountain, 1977.

Murdoch, Iris. "Against Dryness." In *Revisions*, pp. 43-50. Edited by Stanley Hauerwas and Alasdair MacIntyre. Notre Dame, Ind./London: University of Notre Dame Press, 1983.

Murphy, Nancey, et al., ed. *Virtues and Practices in the Christian Tradition: Christian Ethics After MacIntyre*. Harrisburg, Penn.: Trinity Press International, 1997.

Murphy, Roland E. *Ecclesiastes*. WBC: Dallas: Word, 1992.

———. *The Song of Songs*. Minneapolis: Fortress, 1990.

———. *Wisdom Literature*. Grand Rapids: Eerdmans, 1981.

Murray, John. *Principles of Conduct*. Grand Rapids: Eerdmans; London: Tyndale, 1957.

Nardoni, Enrique. *Rise Up, O Judge*. Peabody, Mass.: Hendrickson, 2004.

Nelson, Benjamin D. *The Idea of Usury*. 2nd ed., Chicago/London: University of Chicago Press, 1969.

Nelson, Richard D. *Raising Up a Faithful Priest*. Louisville: Westminster John Knox, 1993.

Nelson, Paul. *Narrative and Morality*. University Park/London: Pennsylvania State University Press, 1987.

Neufeld, Edward. "The Emergence of a Royal-Urban Society in Ancient Israel." *HUCA* 31 (1960): 31-53.

———. "The Prohibitions against Loans at Interest in Ancient Hebrew Laws." *HUCA* 26 (1955): 355-412.

Newsom, Carol A. "The Book of Job." *The New Interpreter's Bible* 4:317-637. Nashville: Abingdon, 1996.

―――. *The Book of Job.* New York/Oxford: Oxford University Press, 2003.

Niditch, Susan. *War in the Old Testament.* New York/Oxford: Oxford University Press, 1993.

Niebuhr, H. Richard. "Introduction to Biblical Ethics." In *Christian Ethics,* pp. 10-45. Edited by Waldo Beach and H. Richard Niebuhr. 2nd ed., New York: Ronald, 1973.

Nielsen, Eduard. *The Ten Commandments in New Perspective.* SBT II/7. London: SCM; Naperville: Allenson, 1968.

Noll, K. L. *Canaan and Israel in Antiquity.* London/New York: Sheffield Academic Press, 2001.

North, Gary. *Victim's Rights.* Tyler, Tex.: Institute for Christian Economics, 1990.

―――, ed. *Theonomy: An Informed Response.* Tyler, Tex.: Institute for Christian Economics, 1991.

Nussbaum, Martha. *The Fragility of Goodness.* Cambridge/New York: Cambridge University Press, 1986.

―――. *Love's Knowledge.* New York/Oxford: Oxford University Press, 1990.

―――. *Upheavals of Thought.* Cambridge/New York: Cambridge University Press, 2001.

Nyerere, Julius K. *Freedom and Socialism: Uhuru na Ujamaa.* London/New York: Oxford University Press, 1970.

Nysse, Richard. "Moral Discourse on Economic Justice: Considerations from the Old Testament." *Word and World* 12 (1992): 337-44.

O'Connor, Michael Patrick, and David Noel Freedman, ed. *Backgrounds for the Bible.* Winona Lake, Ind.: Eisenbrauns, 1987.

O'Donovan, Oliver. *The Desire of the Nations.* Cambridge/New York: Cambridge University Press, 1996.

―――. *Resurrection and Moral Order.* Leicester, U.K.: Inter-Varsity Press; Grand Rapids: Eerdmans, 1986.

―――. *The Ways of Judgment.* Grand Rapids/Cambridge: Eerdmans, 2003.

Ogletree, Thomas W. *The Use of the Bible in Christian Ethics.* Philadelphia: Fortress, 1983; Oxford: Blackwell, 1984.

Ollenburger, Ben C. "The Book of Zechariah." *The New Interpreter's Bible* 7:733-840. Nashville: Abingdon, 1996.

Olson, Dennis T. *Deuteronomy and the Death of Moses.* Minneapolis: Fortress, 1994.

Olyan, Saul M., and Robert C. Culley, ed. *"A Wise and Discerning Mind."* Burke O. Long Festschrift. Providence, R.I.: Brown University Press, 2000.

Oosthuizen, Martin J. "The Deuteronomic Code as a Resource for Christian Ethics." Journal of Theology for Southern Africa 96 (1996): 44-58.

Oppenheim, A. Leo. *Ancient Mesopotamia.* Revised ed. Chicago/London: University of Chicago Press, 1977.

Osswald, Eva. *Falsche Prophetie im Alten Testament.* Tübingen: Mohr, 1962.

Otto, Eckhart. *Theologische Ethik des Alten Testaments.* Stuttgart: Kohlhammer, 1994.

Paine, Thomas. *Common Sense and Other Political Writings*. Indianapolis: Bobbs-Merrill, 1953.

Pardes, Ilana. *Countertraditions in the Bible*. Cambridge, Mass./London: Harvard University Press, 1992.

Park, Sejin. *Pentecost and Sinai*. LHBOTS 342. New York/London: T & T Clark, 2008.

Patrick, Dale. "Job's Address of God." *ZAW* 91 (1979): 268-82.

Patte, Daniel. *Ethics of Biblical Interpretation*. Louisville: Westminster John Knox, 1995.

Patterson, Orlando. *Slavery and Social Death*. Cambridge, Mass./London: Harvard University Press, 1982.

Pattison, George. "Violence, Kingship and Cultus." *ExpT* 102 (1990-1991): 135-40.

Paul, Shalom M. *Studies in the Book of the Covenant in the Light of Cuneiform and Biblical Law*. VTSup 18. Leiden: Brill, 1970.

Pedersen, J. *Israel: Its Life and Culture I-II*. London: Oxford University Press, 1954.

———. *Israel: Its Life and Culture III-IV*. London: Oxford University Press, 1953.

Peels, Hendrick G. L. *The Vengeance of God*. OTS 31. Leiden/New York: Brill, 1995.

Perdue, Leo G. *The Collapse of History*. Minneapolis: Fortress, 1994.

———. *Reconstructing Old Testament Theology: After the Collapse of History*. Minneapolis: Fortress, 2005.

Perdue, Leo G., et al. *Families in Ancient Israel*. Louisville: Westminster John Knox, 1997.

Petersen, David L. *Haggai and Zechariah 1—8*. Philadelphia: Westminster, 1984; London: SCM, 1985.

———. *The Roles of Israel's Prophets*. JSOTSup 17. Sheffield, U.K.: JSOT, 1981.

———, ed. *Prophecy in Israel*. Philadelphia: Fortress; London: SPCK, 1987.

Peterson, Eugene H. *The Message*. Colorado Springs: NavPress, 2002.

———. *Where Your Treasure Is*. Grand Rapids: Eerdmans, 1993.

Petrella, Ivan, ed. *Latin American Liberation Theology*. Maryknoll, N.Y.: Orbis, 2005.

Pham, Xuan Huong Thi. *Mourning in the Ancient Near East and the Hebrew Bible*. JSOTSup 302. Sheffield, U.K.: Sheffield Academic Press, 1999.

Phillips, Anthony. *Essays on Biblical Law*. JSOTSup 344. London/New York: Sheffield Academic Press, 2002.

Phillips, Gary A., and Danna Nolan Fewell. "Ethics, Bible, Reading As If." *Semeia* 77 (1997): 1-21.

Phillips, Gary A., and Nicole Wilkinson Duran, ed. *Reading Communities Reading Scripture*. Daniel Patte Festschrift. Harrisburg, Penn.: Trinity Press International, 2002.

Piepkorn, Arthur Carl. *The Sacred Scriptures and the Lutheran Confessions*. Mansfield, Conn.: CEC, 2007.

Plaskow, Judith. *The Coming of Lilith*. Boston: Beacon, 2005.

———. *Standing Again at Sinai*. San Francisco: Harper, 1990.

Pleins, J. David. "Poverty in the Social World of the Wise." *JSOT* 37 (1987): 61-78.

———. *The Social Visions of the Hebrew Bible*. Louisville: Westminster John Knox, 2001.

Powell, Marvin A., ed. *Labor in the Ancient Near East.* New Haven, Conn.: American Oriental Society, 1987.

Premnath, D. N. "Latifundialization and Isaiah 5:8-10." *JSOT* 40 (1988): 49-60.

Pressler, Carolyn. *The View of Women Found in the Deuteronomic Family Laws.* BZAW 216. Berlin/New York: de Gruyter, 1993.

Preuss, Horst Dietrich. *Old Testament Theology.* 2 vols. Louisville: Westminster John Knox; Edinburgh: T & T Clark, 1995 and 1996.

Prior, Michael. *The Bible and Colonialism.* Sheffield, U.K.: Sheffield Academic Press, 1997.

Rad, Gerhard von. *Old Testament Theology.* 2 vols. Edinburgh: Oliver & Boyd; New York: Harper, 1962 and 1965.

———. *Wisdom in Israel.* Nashville: Abingdon; London: SCM, 1972.

Rainey, Anson F. "The Order of Sacrifices in Old Testament Ritual Texts." *Biblica* 51 (1970): 485-98.

Rashkow, Ilona N. *Taboo or Not Taboo.* Minneapolis: Fortress, 2000.

Ratheiser, Gershom M. H. Mitzvoth *Ethics and the Jewish Bible.* LHBOTS 460. New York/London: T & T Clark, 2007.

Rattray, Susan. "Marriage Rules, Kinship Terms and Family Structures in the Bible." In *Society of Biblical Literature 1987 Seminar Papers,* pp. 537-44. SBLSP 26. Atlanta: Scholars Press, 1987.

Reicke, Bo. "The Knowledge of the Suffering Servant." In *Das ferne und nahe Wort.* L. Rost Festschrift, pp. 186-92. Edited by F. Maass. BZAW 105. Berlin: de Gruyter, 1967.

Reventlow, Henning Graf. *Gebet im Alten Testament.* Stuttgart: Kohlhammer, 1986.

Reventlow, Henning Graf, et al., ed. *Politics and Theopolitics in the Bible and Postbiblical Literature.* JSOTSup 171. Sheffield, U.K.: Sheffield Academic Press, 1994.

Reventlow, Henning Graf, and Yair Hoffman, ed. *Justice and Righteousness.* Benjamin Uffenheimer Festschrift. JSOTSup 137. Sheffield, U.K.: Sheffield Academic Press, 1992.

Reviv, Hanoch. *The Elders in Ancient Israel.* Jerusalem: Magnes, 1989.

Rice, Gene. "An Exposition of Psalm 103." *Journal of Religious Thought* 39 (1982-83): 55-61.

Ricoeur, Paul. *Oneself as Another.* Chicago/London: University of Chicago Press, 1992.

———. *The Symbolism of Evil.* Boston: Beacon, 1995.

———. *Time and Narrative.* 3 vols. Chicago/London: University of Chicago Press, 1984, 1985, 1988.

Roberts, Christopher C. *Creation and Covenant: The Significance of Sexual Difference in the Moral Theology of Marriage.* New York/London: T & T Clark, 2007.

Roberts, Jimmy J. M. *Nahum, Habakkuk, and Zephaniah.* Louisville: Westminster John Knox, 1991.

Robinson, Gnana. "The Idea of Rest in the Old Testament and the Search for the Basic Character of Sabbath." *ZAW* 92 (1980): 32-42.

Robinson, N. H. G. *The Groundwork of Christian Ethics*. London: Collins, 1971.

Rodd, Cyril S. *Glimpses of a Strange Land*. London: T & T Clark, 2001.

————. "On Applying a Sociological Theory to Biblical Studies." *JSOT* 19 (1981): 95-106.

Rofé, Alexander. "The Laws of Warfare in the Book of Deuteronomy." *JSOT* 32 (1985): 23-44.

Rogerson, John W. *Theory and Practice in Old Testament Ethics*. JSOTSup 405. New York/London: T & T Clark, 2004.

Rogerson, John W., et al., ed. *The Bible in Ethics*. JSOTSup 207. Sheffield, U.K.: Sheffield Academic Press, 1995.

Rousseau, Jean Jacques. *Discourse on the Origin of Inequality*. Indianapolis: Hackett, 1992.

Rowlett, Lori L. *Joshua and the Rhetoric of Violence*. JSOTSup 226. Sheffield, U.K.: Sheffield Academic Press, 1996.

Ruether, Rosemary Radford. "Feminism and Patriarchal Religion." *JSOT* 22 (1982): 54-66.

Rushdoony, Rousas John. *The Institutes of Biblical Law*. [Nutley, NJ]: Presbyterian & Reformed, 1973.

Russell, Letty M., ed. *Feminist Interpretation of the Bible*. Philadelphia: Fortress, 1985.

Saadya Gaon. *The Book of Beliefs and Opinions*. New Haven, Conn.: Yale University Press; London: Oxford University Press, 1948.

Sakenfeld, Katherine Doob. *Just Wives?* Louisville: Westminster John Knox, 2003.

Sanders, E. P. *Judaism*. London: SCM; Philadelphia: Trinity Press International, 1992.

Sanders, James A. *From Sacred Story to Sacred Text*. Philadelphia: Fortress, 1987.

Sandoval, Timothy J. *The Discourse of Wealth and Poverty in the Book of Proverbs*. Leiden/Boston: Brill, 2006.

Santayana, George. *Reason in Common Sense*. The Life of Reason, Vol. 1. New York: Collier, 1962.

Sawyer, John F. A., ed. *Reading Leviticus*. JSOTSup 227. Sheffield, U.K.: Sheffield Academic Press, 1996.

Schlabach, Gerald W., ed. *Just Policing, Not War*. Collegeville, Minn.: Liturgical Press, 2007.

Schlossberg, Herbert, et al., ed. *Christianity and Economics: The Oxford Declaration and Beyond*. Grand Rapids: Eerdmans, 1994.

Schluter, Michael, and John Ashcroft, ed. *Jubilee Manifesto*. Leicester, U.K.: Inter-Varsity Press, 2005.

Schluter, Michael, and Roy Clements. *Reactivating the Extended Family*. Cambridge: Jubilee Centre, 1986.

Schottroff, Willy, and Wolfgang Stegemann, ed. *God of the Lowly*. Maryknoll, N.Y.: Orbis, 1984.

Schwartz, Baruch J., et al., ed. *Perspectives on Purity and Purification in the Bible*. LHBOTS 474. New York/London: Colloquium, 2008.

Schwartz, Regina M. "Adultery in the House of David." *Semeia* 54 (1990): 35-55.

————. *The Curse of Cain*. Chicago/London: University of Chicago Press, 1997.

Scroggs, Robin. "The New Testament and Ethics." *Perspectives in Religious Studies* 11 (1984): 77-93.

Segal, Ben-Zion, ed. *The Ten Commandments in History and Tradition*. Jerusalem: Magnes, 1990.

Seitz, Christopher, and Kathryn Greene-McCreight, ed. *Theological Exegesis*. B. S. Childs Festschrift. Grand Rapids/Cambridge: Eerdmans, 1999.

Sheriffs, Deryck. *The Friendship of the Lord*. Carlisle, U.K.: Paternoster, 1996.

Sherlock, Charles. *The God Who Fights*. Lewiston, Mont./Lampeter, U.K.: Edward Mellen, 1993.

Shoemaker, H. Stephen. "Psalm 131." *RevExp* 85 (1988): 89-94.

Sider, Ronald J. *Christ and Violence*. Scottdale, Penn.: Herald Press, 1979.

Siker, Jeffrey S. *Scripture and Ethics*. New York/Oxford: Oxford University Press, 1997.

————, ed. *Homosexuality and the Church*. Louisville: Westminster John Knox, 1994.

Simkins, Ronald A., and Stephen L. Cook, ed. *The Social World of the Hebrew Bible*. *Semeia* 87 (1999).

Sivan, Hagith. *Between Woman, Man and God*. JSOTSup 401. New York/London: T & T Clark, 2004.

Smedes, Lewis B. "The Making and Keeping of Commitments." In *Seeking Understanding: The Stob Lectures, 1986–1998*, pp. 1-42. Grand Rapids/Cambridge: Eerdmans, 2001.

Smith-Christopher, Daniel L. *A Biblical Theology of Exile*. Minneapolis: Fortress, 2002.

Sneed, Mark R. "The Class Culture of Proverbs." *SJOT* 10 (1996): 296-308.

Snijders, L. A. "The Meaning of *zār* in the Old Testament." *OTS* 10 (1954): 1-154.

Soggin, J. Alberto. *The Prophet Amos*. London: SCM, 1987.

Sparks, Kenton L. *Ethnicity and Identity in Ancient Israel*. Winona Lake, Ind.: Eisenbrauns, 1998.

Speiser, E. A. "The Stem *pll* in Hebrew." *JBL* 82 (1963): 301-6.

Spiekermann, Hermann. "Lieben und Glauben." In *Meilenstein*. H. Donner Festschrift, pp. 266-75. Edited by Manfred Weippert and Stefan Timm. Wiesbaden: Harrassowitz, 1995.

Spohn, William C. *What Are They Saying About Scripture and Ethics?* Rev. ed. Mahwah, N.J.: Paulist Press, 1995.

Stager, Lawrence E. "The Archaeology of the Family in Ancient Israel." *Bulletin of the American Schools of Oriental Research* 260 (1985): 1-35.

Stahl, Nanette. *Law and Liminality in the Bible*. JSOTSup 202. Sheffield, U.K.: Sheffield Academic Press, 1995.

Stansell, Gary. "Honor and Shame in the David Narratives." *Semeia* 68 (1994): 55-79.

Stark, Christine. *"Kultprostitution" im Alten Testament*. Vandenhoeck: Göttingen, 2006.

Stassen, Glen H., and David P. Gushee. *Kingdom Ethics*. Downers Grove, Ill.: Inter-Varsity Press, 2003.

Steiner, Franz. *Taboo*. London: Cohen & West, 1956.

Steiner, George. *Real Presences*. London: Faber; Chicago: University of Chicago Press, 1989.

Steinbeck, John. *East of Eden*. New York: Penguin, 2002.

Steinmann, Andrew E. "The Structure and Message of the Book of Job." *VT* 46 (1996): 85-100.

Steinmetz, Devora. *From Father to Son*. Louisville: Westminster John Knox, 1991.

Stern, Philip D. *The Biblical Ḥerem*. Atlanta: Scholars Press, 1991.

Stiebert, Johanna. *The Construction of Shame in the Hebrew Bible*. JSOTSup 346. London/New York: Sheffield Academic Press, 2002.

Stol, Marten. *Birth in Babylonia and the Bible*. Groningen: Styx, 2000.

Stone, Lawson G. "Ethical and Apologetic Tendencies in the Redaction of the Book of Joshua." *CBQ* 53 (1991): 25-36.

Stout, Jeffrey. *Ethics after Babel*. Boston: Beacon, 1988.

Streete, Gail Corrigan. *The Strange Woman*. Louisville: Westminster John Knox, 1997.

Strickland, Wayne G., ed. *The Law, the Gospel, and the Modern Christian*. Grand Rapids: Zondervan, 1993. Reissued as *Five Views on Law and Gospel*. Grand Rapids: Zondervan, 1996.

Stroup, George W. *The Promise of Narrative Theology*. Atlanta: Knox, 1981.

Stulman, Louis. "Encroachment in Deuteronomy." *JBL* 109 (1990): 613-32.

Sun, Henry T. C., et al., eds. *Problems in Biblical Theology*. Rolf Knierim Festschrift. Grand Rapids/Cambrige: Eerdmans, 1997.

Swartley, Willard M. *Slavery, Sabbath, War, and Women*. Scottdale, Penn.: Herald Press, 1983.

Swartley, Willard M., ed. *The Bible and Law*. Eckhart, Ind.: Institute of Mennonite Studies, 1982.

———. *Violence Renounced*. Telford, Penn.: Pandora, 2000.

Tamez, Elsa. *Bible of the Oppressed*. Maryknoll, N.Y.: Orbis, 1982.

Taylor, Charles. *Sources of the Self*. Cambridge, Mass.: Harvard University Press, 1989.

Terrien, Samuel. *Till the Heart Sings*. Philadelphia: Fortress, 1985.

Thistlethwaite, Susan Brooks. " 'You May Enjoy the Spoil of Your Enemies.' " *Semeia* 61 (1993): 59-75.

Thomas Aquinas. *Summa theologica*. Christian Classics Ethereal Library <www.ccel.org/ccel/aquinas/summa.html>.

Tigay, Jeffrey H. *Deuteronomy*. JPS Torah Commentary. Philadelphia: Jewish Publication Society, 1998.

Toorn, Karel van der. *Family Religion in Babylonia, Syria and Israel*. Leiden/New York: Brill, 1996.

———. *From Her Cradle to Her Grave*. Sheffield, U.K.: Sheffield Academic Press, 1994.

Townsend, Christopher. "An Eye for an Eye." *Cambridge Papers* March 1997. <www .jubilee-centre.org/document.php?id=16>.

Trible, Phyllis. *God and the Rhetoric of Sexuality.* Philadelphia: Fortress, 1978.

———. *Texts of Terror.* Philadelphia: Fortress, 1984.

Tsevat, Matitiahu. *The Meaning of the Book of Job and Other Biblical Studies.* New York: Ktav, 1980.

Turnham, Timothy John. "Male and Female Slaves in the Sabbath Year Laws of Exodus 21:1-11." In *Society of Biblical Literature 1987 Seminar Papers*, pp. 545-49. SBLSP 26. Atlanta: Scholars Press, 1987.

Ucko, Hans, ed. *The Jubilee Challenge.* Geneva: World Council of Churches, 1997.

Van der Ploeg, J. P. M. "Slavery in the Old Testament." In *Congress Volume: Uppsala 1971*, pp. 72-87. VTSup 22. Leiden: Brill, 1972.

Vanhoozer, Kevin J., ed. *The Cambridge Companion to Postmodern Theology.* Cambridge/New York: Cambridge University Press, 2003.

Van Houten, Christiana. *The Alien in Israelite Law.* JSOTSup 107. Sheffield, U.K.: Sheffield Academic Press 1991.

Van Leeuwen, Raymond C. "The Book of Proverbs." *The New Interpreter's Bible*, 5:17-264. Nashville: Abingdon, 1997.

Van Seters, John. *The Life of Moses.* Kampen: Kok, 1994.

Van Til, Kent A. *Less Than Two Dollars a Day.* Grand Rapids: Eerdmans, 2007.

Vaux, Roland de. *Ancient Israel.* London: Darton, Longman & Todd; New York: McGraw-Hill, 1961.

Verhey, Allen. *The Great Reversal: Ethics and the New Testament.* Grand Rapids: Eerdmans, 1984.

Visotzky, Burton L. *The Genesis of Ethics.* New York: Three Rivers, 1996.

Vogt, Peter T. *Deuteronomic Theology and the Significance of Torah.* Winona Lake, Ind.: Eisenbrauns, 2006.

Volf, Miroslav. *Exclusion and Embrace.* Nashville: Abingdon, 1996.

———. *Work in the Spirit.* New York/Oxford: Oxford University Press, 1991.

Volz, Paul. *Das Neujahrsfest Jahwes.* Tübingen: Mohr, 1912.

Vriezen, T. C. *An Outline of Old Testament Theology.* Oxford: Blackwell, 1962. 2nd ed., Oxford: Blackwell/Newton, Mass.: Branford, 1970.

———. *The Religion of Ancient Israel.* London: Lutterworth; Philadelphia: Westminster, 1967.

Walsh, James P. M. *The Mighty from Their Thrones.* Philadelphia: Fortress, 1987.

Walzer, Michael. *Exodus and Revolution.* New York: Basic Books, 1985.

———. "Exodus 32 and the Theory of Holy War." *Harvard Theological Review* 61 (1968): 1-14.

Wambacq, B. N. "Les origines de la *Pesah* israélite." *Biblica* 57 (1976): 206-24, 301-26.

———. "Les *Maṣṣôt.*" *Biblica* 61 (1980): 31-54.

Warrior, Robert Allan. "Canaanites, Cowboys, and Indians." *Christianity and Crisis* 49 (1989-1990): 261-65.

Webb, William J. *Slaves, Women & Homosexuals.* Downers Grove, Ill.: InterVarsity Press, 2001.

Weber, Max. *Politics as Vocation*. Philadelphia: Fortress, 1965.

———. *The Theory of Social and Economic Organization*. New York: Free Press; London: Collier-Macmillan, 1969,

Webster, John. *Barth's Ethics of Reconciliation*. Cambridge/New York: Cambridge University Press, 1995.

———. ed. *The Cambridge Companion to Karl Barth*. Cambridge/New York: Cambridge University Press, 2000.

Weems, Renita J. *Battered Love*. Minneapolis: Fortress, 1995.

Weinfeld, Moshe. *Deuteronomy and the Deuteronomic School*. Oxford/New York: Oxford University Press, 1972.

———. *Social Justice in Ancient Israel and in the Ancient Near East*. Philadelphia: Fortress, 1995.

Weir, J. Emmette. "The Poor Are Powerless." *ExpT* 100 (1989-90): 13-15.

Weisberg, Dvora E. "The Widow of Our Discontent." *JSOT* 28 (2004): 403-29.

Weiser, Artur. *The Psalms*. London: SCM; Philadelphia: Westminster, 1962

Wells, Jo Bailey. *God's Holy People*. JSOTSup 305. Sheffield, U.K.: Sheffield Academic Press, 2000.

Wenham, Gordon J. *The Book of Leviticus*. Grand Rapids: Eerdmans, 1979.

———. "The Gap between Law and Ethics in the Bible." *JJS* 48 (1997): 17-29.

———. *Story as Torah*. Edinburgh: T & T Clark, 2000; Grand Rapids: Baker, 2004.

Werline, Rodney A. *Penitential Prayer in Second Temple Judaism*. Atlanta: Scholars Press, 1998.

Westbrook, Raymond. *Property and Family in Biblical Law*. JSOTSup 113. Sheffield, U.K.: Sheffield Academic Press, 1991.

———. *Studies in Biblical and Cuneiform Law*. Paris: Gabalda, 1988.

Westermann, Claus. *Blessing in the Bible and the Life of the Church*. Philadelphia: Fortress, 1978.

———. *The Living Psalms*. Grand Rapids: Eerdmans; Edinburgh: T & T Clark, 1989.

———. *The Praise of God in the Psalms*. Richmond: Knox, 1965. Enlarged ed., *Praise and Lament in the Psalms*. Atlanta: Knox, 1981.

Westermeyer, Paul. *Let Justice Sing*. Collegeville, Minn.: Liturgical Press, 1998.

Whitelam, Keith W. *The Just King*. JSOTSup 12. Sheffield, U.K.: JSOT, 1979.

Whybray, R. Norman. *The Good Life in the Old Testament*. New York/London: T & T Clark, 2002.

———. "Poverty, Wealth, and Point of View in Proverbs." *ExpT* 100 (1988-89): 332-36.

———. *Wisdom*. Aldershot, U.K./Burlington, Vt.: Ashgate, 2005.

Wildberger, Hans. *Isaiah 1—12*. Minneapolis: Fortress, 1991.

———. *Isaiah 13—27*. Minneapolis: Fortress, 1997.

———. *Isaiah 28—39*. Minneapolis: Fortress, 2002.

Wilkinson, Bruce. *The Prayer of Jabez*. Sisters, Ore.: Multnomah, 2000.

Williams, Bernard. *Shame and Necessity*. Berkeley/London: University of California, 1993.

Williamson, Hugh G. M., ed. *Understanding the History of Ancient Israel*. Oxford/New York: Oxford University Press, 2007.

Willis, Timothy M. *The Elders of the City*. Atlanta: Society of Biblical Literature, 2001.

Wilson, Robert R. *Prophecy and Society in Ancient Israel*. Philadelphia: Fortress, 1980.

Winn, Albert Curry. *Ain't Gonna Study War No More*. Louisville: Westminster John Knox, 1993.

Wiseman, D. J. " 'Is It Peace?' " *VT* 32 (1982): 311-26.

Witvliet, John D. *The Biblical Psalms in Christian Worship*. Grand Rapids/Cambridge: Eerdmans, 2007.

Wolff, Hans Walter. *Anthropology of the Old Testament*. London: SCM; Philadelphia: Fortress, 1974.

————. *Hosea*. Philadelphia: Fortress, 1974.

————. *Joel and Amos*. Philadelphia: Fortress, 1977.

————. *Micah*. Minneapolis: Augsburg Press, 1990.

Wolterstorff, Nicholas. *Until Justice and Peace Embrace*. Grand Rapids: Eerdmans, 1983.

Wright, Christopher. *Deuteronomy*. Peabody, Mass.: Hendrickson; Carlisle, U.K.: Paternoster, 1996.

————. *God's People in God's Land*. Grand Rapids: Eerdmans; Exeter: Paternoster, 1990.

————. *Living as the People of God*. Leicester, U.K.: Inter-Varsity Press, 1983. = *An Eye for an Eye*. Downers Grove: InterVarsity Press, 1983. Revised and expanded as *Old Testament Ethics for the People of God*. Downers Grove, Ill.; Leicester, U.K.: Inter-Varsity Press, 2004.

Wright, David F. "Calvin's Pentateuchal Criticism." *Calvin Theological Journal* 21 (1986): 33-50.

Wright, N. T. *The New Testament and the People of God*. London: SPCK; Minneapolis: Fortress, 1992.

Yoder, John H. "Exodus and Exile." *Cross Currents* 23 (1973): 297-309.

————. *For the Nations*. Grand Rapids/Cambridge: Eerdmans, 1997.

————. *The Original Revolution*. Scottdale, Penn.: Herald Press, 1971.

————. *The Politics of Jesus*. Rev. ed. Grand Rapids: Eerdmans; Carlisle, U.K.: Paternoster, 1994.

————. *The Priestly Kingdom*. Notre Dame, Ind.: University of Notre Dame Press, 1984.

————. *The Royal Priesthood*. Grand Rapids: Eerdmans, 1994.

Yoo, Yani. "*Han*-Laden Women." *Semeia* 78 (1997): 37-46.

Young, Jeremy. *The Violence of God and the War on Terror*. London: Darton, Longman & Todd, 2007; New York: Seabury Press, 2008.

Zehr, Howard. *Changing Lenses*. 3rd ed. Scottdale, Penn.: Herald, 2005.

Zenger, Erich. "'Dass alles Fleisch den Namen seiner Heiligung segne.'" *Biblische Zeitschrift* 41 (1997): 1-27.

Zeskind, Jonathan R. "The Missing Daughter in Leviticus xviii." *VT* 46 (1996): 125-30.

Zimmerli, Walther. *Old Testament Theology in Outline*. Atlanta: Knox; Edinburgh: T & T Clark, 1978.

———. *Man and His Hope in the Old Testament*. London: SCM; Naperville, Ill.: Allenson, 1971.

Author Index

Subject Index

Scripture Index